Current Studies of Diversity and Pattern in World Prehistory

Support and Sponsor

The Institute of Korean Prehistory publishes this book with a sponsor from the Kooklin Bank Co., Korea.

Current Studies of Diversity and Pattern in World Prehistory

Copyright © Institute of Korean Prehistory (IKP) 2025
25, Yongambuk-ro 120beon-gil, Sangdang-gu Cheongju, Chungbuk 28763, Korea
http://www.ikp.re.kr

All rights are reserved by IKP. Except as permitted under current legislation, no part of this work may be published, transmitted, recorded, or reproduced in any form, or by any means without the prior permission of the copyright owner.

Edited by   Chief editor Kidong BAE
            Co-editor Jong-yoon WOO and Ju-yong KIM

Printed in Korea by Hyean Publishing Co.
3, Wausan-ro 35-gil, Mapo-gu, Seoul, Korea
hyeanpub@daum.net

ISBN 978-89-8494-749-8 93910
₩ 100,000

Current Studies of Diversity and Pattern in World Prehistory

Chief editor Kidong BAE
Co-editor Jong-yoon WOO
Ju-yong KIM

Institute of Korean Prehistory

Prologue: Invitation to SUYANGGAE

Yung-jo LEE
President, Institute of Korean Prehistory (IKP)
Chairperson, Suyanggae International Symposium Executive Committee (SISEC)

1. Background of Suyanggae International Conference

My first encounter with Suyanggae felt nothing short of destined. When our team first arrived at the site, we were met with an unrelenting downpour—nearly 750 millimeters of rain soaked the landscape. Undeterred, we pressed on, exposed to the heavy rainfalls as we surveyed the area that would soon vanish beneath the rising waters. It was during this survey that we stumbled upon a remarkable find: an abundance of stone tools crafted from dark, glossy jade-like stones and layers of shale. The moment our weary team—exhausted after two grueling days in the rain—laid eyes on those artifacts is etched into my memory as one of the most exhilarating experiences of my career. This sense of destiny, combined with the sheer joy of discovery, carried us through four rigorous rounds of full-scale excavation. In the end, we documented a remarkable 1,250 square meters of archaeological remains before the site was permanently submerged. Fortunately, the national newspaper Chosun Ilbo recognized the importance of our discovery and published an article that raised public awareness. Their call to establish a "prehistoric education center" deeply resonated with me, and it became clear that sharing our findings at an international level would be the most meaningful way to realize this vision. That opportunity came in May 1989, when I was honored to represent Korea at the "World Summit Conference" organized by Professor R. BONNICHSEN of the University of Maine. It was there that I had the privilege of meeting Professor Xinzhi WU from China and Rector Nikolai DROZDOV from the USSR—an encounter that would open many new doors. These connections soon led to a series of invitations to prestigious international conferences: the "60th Anniversary of the Peking Man Excavation" in Beijing (October 1989), the Novosibirsk Conference in Russia (August 1990), the "200th Anniversary of the Opening of the Port of Sapporo" in Japan (June 1992), and the Vladivostok Conference in Russia (March 1994). At each gathering, I presented the discoveries and significance of the Suyanggae site, gradually helping it gain international recognition as a site of considerable academic value. These experiences also inspired us to host our own conference. In October 1996, we held the "20th Anniversary International Conference of the Durubong Excavation." It was after this event that I met Mr. Jae-Ho KIM, then President of the DanYang Cultural Center (Munhwawon). Our shared vision laid the foundation for what would become the Suyanggae International Symposium.

2. The Inaugural Symposium and Expanding Horizons: The 1st and 25th Symposia

The inaugural Suyanggae and Her Neighbors symposium, held from October 25 to 28, 1996, became a reality thanks entirely to the bold vision and generous dedication of Mr. Jae-Ho KIM. His leadership continued with the successful organization of the second symposium, which took place from September 20 to 30, 1999. The third installment was held in celebration of my respected mentor, Professor Jia Lanpo—an esteemed academician of the Chinese Academy of Sciences—on the occasion of his 90th birthday. This landmark event was co-organized with the Institute of Vertebrate Paleontology and Paleoanthropology (IVPP) of the Chinese Academy of Sciences. It was during this symposium that we officially adopted Suyanggae and Her Neighbors as the permanent title of the series. Supported by a grant from the Korea Research Foundation, the conference was recognized even by our Chinese colleagues for its significant academic contributions and for elevating the standing of Korean archaeology within the global research community. The 4th through 7th symposia, as well as the 10th, were hosted a total of six times by Danyang County under the dedicated leadership of Governor Geon-Pyo LEE. These events reflected not only the county's pride in its heritage but also its deep commitment to raising the scholarly stature of the Suyanggae site. Visiting scholars from around the world continue to commend Danyang as the proud home of Suyanggae, acknowledging its lasting contributions to the study of prehistory. In contrast, the 8th symposium was brought to life through the timely and heartfelt support of Professor Masao AMBIRU of Meiji University in Japan. A longtime participant of previous Suyanggae events, Professor AMBIRU deeply recognized the importance of the site in relation to Japan's Paleolithic heritage. He played a key—perhaps even fateful—role in co-hosting the conference and curating a special exhibition at the Meiji University Museum in May 2004. This exhibition featured artifacts from the Suyanggae site, including materials from Durubong and Gunang Cave, and offered a comprehensive look at my own research journey. It proved pivotal in introducing my work to a broader international audience and led to further collaborative invitations from institutions abroad. That event marked the first time an international conference was held alongside a special exhibition–an impactful precedent that bore significant fruit. One of Professor AMBIRU's students, now Professor Kaoru OTANI, later pursued graduate studies at Chungbuk National University and conducted research with our institute. She earned her doctorate from Meiji University and now serves as a vital link between Korean and Japanese Paleolithic scholarship. Her continued academic growth is highly anticipated, and I look forward to the important contributions she is sure to make in the years ahead. The 9th symposium marked the second occasion supported by my own research funding. It was held in conjunction with the 5th World Archaeological Congress (WAC-5) in Washington, D.C., where more than 120 symposia were hosted by scholars from around the globe. The Suyanggae session included a presentation on the excavation and radiocarbon dating of rice grains discovered at the Sorori site in Cheongju. This breakthrough received international acclaim when Archaeology, a leading American quarterly, named it the "Excavation of the Year." Dr. WHITEHEAD's subsequent article, World's Oldest Rice Found, brought the discovery into the global spotlight. It was later included in Archaeology: Theories, Methods, and Practice by C. RENFREW and P. BAHN (4th to 7th editions, 2004-2020), under the distinguished section titled "First Domestication: Rice." The 11th through 19th symposia were held in rotation through the enduring friendship and collaboration with Rector Nikolai DROZDOV of Krasnoyarsk State Pedagogical University (Russia), Director Lucyna DOMAŃSKA of the Institute of Archaeology at Lodz University (Poland), and Deputy Director Xing GAO of the Institute of Vertebrate Paleontology and Paleoanthropology (IVPP), Chinese Academy of Sciences. Professor Xing GAO notably hosted the Suyanggae Conference on four separate occasions. Thanks to their sincere cooperation and unwavering dedication, the Suyanggae International Symposium was able to continue growing and developing over the years, earning the deep respect and recognition of all those involved. The subsequent event, the 20th(1) in the series, was held in Haifa, Israel, in celebration of the 80th birthday of Professor A. RONEN. This gathering offered a rare and valuable opportunity to visit world-renowned archaeological sites. It was followed by the 21st, held for the second time in the United States at the University of Wyoming under the direction of Professor M. KORNFELD. A highlight of this event was the visit to the Hell Gap site, famous for its Paleoindian remains, where participants could examine the full stratigraphy and observe the development and transformation of projectile point technology. A particularly memorable moment was the presentation of a plaque of appreciation to Professor G.C. FRISON, the most senior and esteemed scholar in American Paleoindian archaeology, in recognition of his ongoing contributions to the field. Participants also had the opportunity to visit other major excavation sites, gaining a deeper appreciation for the labor and significance of fieldwork. Notably, the conference and its full scope were featured prominently on the front page of the Star Herald, a leading newspaper in the central United States. The 22nd Suyanggae International Symposium was held for the third time in Russia, in Sakhalinsk, thanks to the dedicated efforts of Professor A. VASILIEVSKY. This meeting offered participants the opportunity to study archaeological sites and artifacts from the Russian Far East alongside the remarkable experience of observing live salmon in their natural habitat. The following 23rd event, held in Malaysia, was organized through the efforts of Professor M. SAIDIN of University Sains Malaysia. It proved to be a significant event, shedding light on the formation of the Lenggong site–shaped by volcanic activity–and its relationship with handaxe industries. The 24th Suyanggae Symposium, held in Beijing in 2019, was organized and hosted by Professor X. GAO under the theme "Zhoukoudian and Suyanggae" to commemorate both the 90th anniversary of the discovery of the first Peking Man skull and the late Professor Abraham Ronen. Notably, the Suyanggae session was elevated to a global-scale symposium, consisting of three sessions that featured five keynote lectures, eight papers on Neighbours in Eurasia, and six papers on Suyanggae and Neighbours in Asia. A highlight of the event was a visit to the Zhoukoudian Peking Man Site Museum, which showcases fossils of *Homo erectus* estimated to be as old as 700,000 years. From 2020 to 2022, the global pandemic caused a temporary suspension of the Suyanggae Symposium. In 2022, the 25th Suyanggae Symposium was held at the Institute of Korean Prehistory to commemorate the 80th Birthday of Professor Yung-

Table 1 List of annual organizing and hosting country for the Suyanggae and Her Neighbours International Symposium

Abroad	No.	Duration	City / Country	Nations	Papers
	1	'96. 10. 25~28 (4)	Danyang / Korea	4	5
	2	'97. 9. 21~30 (10)	Danyang · Cheongju / Korea	4	14
●	3	'98. 11. 24~28 (5)	Beijing / China	3	19
	4	'99. 11. 7~13 (7)	Danyang · Cheongju / Korea	3	6
	5	'00. 12. 7~13 (7)	Danyang · Cheongju / Korea	3	9
	6	'01. 12. 9~15 (7)	Danyang · Cheongju / Korea	5	9
	7	'02. 7. 14~21 (8)	Danyang · Cheongju / Korea	7	17
●	8	'03. 6. 21~26 (6)	Washington DC / USA	4	9
●	9	'04. 5. 14~18 (5)	Tokyo / Japan	5	11
	10	'05. 11. 6~13 (8)	Danyang · Cheongju / Korea	7	16
●	11	'06. 9. 17~24 (8)	Łódź / Poland	8	16
●	12	'07. 8. 7~15 (9)	Krasnoyarsk · Kurtak / Russia	5	27
●	13	'08. 12. 5~10 (6)	Miyazaki / Japan	6	16
●	14	'09. 10. 19~23 (5)	Beijing / China	9	19
	15	'10. 5. 21~28 (8)	Danyang · Cheongju / Korea	8	19
●	16	'11. 8. 14~21 (8)	Yangyuan / China	13	30
●	17	'12. 7. 4~13 (10)	Krasnoyarsk · Kurtak / Russia	12	28
●	18	'13. 6. 25~7.1 (7)	Yinchuan / China	9	23
●	19	'14. 6. 22~7.1 (10)	Łódź / Poland	9	25
●	20-1	'15. 6. 21~28 (8)	Haifa / Israel	7	28
	20-2	'15. 11. 1~8 (8)	Danyang / Korea	10	27
●	21	'16. 7. 26~8.3 (9)	Wyoming State University / USA	11	27
●	22	'17. 7. 5~12 (8)	Sakhalin / Russia	9	32
●	23	'18. 7. 1~8 (8)	Penang / Malaysia	12	35
●	24	'19. 12. 1~8 (8)	Beijing / China	8	19
	25	'22. 9. 22 (1)	Cheongju / Korea	1	1

* Korean Domestic 10 times and Abroad 16 times. Total 188 days of the symposia
* Total 182 participating countries and 487 papers presented during the symposia

jo LEE. During Professor LEE's presentation on *Suyanggae Prehistory Studies and Its Internationalization*, a proposal was put forward to establish an editorial board dedicated to collecting and reviewing papers from the Suyanggae Symposia, and organizing them thematically for publication in an English-language volume.

3. Summary

In Summary it is a great joy to take a closer look at the Suyanggae Symposia through a visual overview to understand their scope and accomplishments better. As shown in the table, the Suyanggae International Symposium has been held ten times in Korea and sixteen times abroad—five times in China, twice in Japan, once in Malaysia, once in Israel, twice in Poland, three times in Russia, and twice in the United States—spanning three continents, eight countries, and fifteen cities. In total, the symposia have taken place over 188 days, with scholars from 182 countries presenting 487 papers. We plan to classify and compile these papers by topic and publish them in both print and e-book formats, with the goal of contributing further to the advancement of global scholarship. I want to express my heartfelt gratitude to the many SISEC members and the Suyanggae family, who have shared in this journey of friendship and academic collaboration across borders for more than 25 years.

Lastly, I extend my deepest gratitude and heartfelt admiration to Professor Kidong BAE, Chair of the Editorial Committee, who led the creation of this outstanding volume despite challenging circumstances. I also offer sincere praise and warm thanks to Vice Chairs Director Jong-yoon WOO and Dr. Ju-yong KIM, whose wholehearted dedication greatly contributed to this work.

I am equally grateful to the editorial board members—Professors Heon-jong LEE, Gi-kil LEE, and Hyeong-woo LEE—and President N. I. DROZDOV, Professor L. DOMAŃSKA, Professor Xing GAO and Prof. Masao AMBIRU for their valuable contributions and tireless efforts.

Dear Professor Lee Yung-jo

Nicolay Ivanovichi DROZDOV

Doctor of Historical Sciences, Professor,
Honored Scientist of the Russian Federation,
Honorary Doctor of Chungbuk National University and
Honorary Citizen of Danyang County, Republic of Korea

I

Please accept my heartfelt congratulations on the 60th anniversary of your distinguished scientific career in the study of the Paleolithic era, not only in the Republic of Korea but also across the world.

Your colleagues, students, and friends take immense pride in your legacy as a world-renowned scholar and an exceptional individual – kind, compassionate, and a dedicated advocate for archaeology. Your contributions as a researcher, organizer, and popularizer of archaeological science are truly remarkable. Among your many achievements, you have established four archaeological museums, with the Suyanggae Museum in Danyang standing out as the most renowned.

Your excavations and research at the Suyanggae Paleolithic site have earned you global recognition, making significant contributions to the field not only in Korea but also among Paleolithic archaeologists worldwide.

One of the most extraordinary discoveries at the Suyanggae site, particularly at Loc. 6, is the world's oldest tanged points. A particularly fascinating find is a 40,000-year-old polished river pebble of the roller type, marked with what appears to be a star map and counting signs. This unique artifact demands deeper scientific and interpretative analysis – not only by archaeologists but also through artificial intelligence.

Your groundbreaking research on the Early Late Paleolithic has been published in monographs and esteemed scientific journals across Russia, the USA, China, Poland, Japan, France, Malaysia, and beyond.

You also founded the Suyanggae and Neighbors international research symposium – first under the auspices of the prestigious Chungbuk National University and later through the Institute of Korean Prehistory, which you established. Under your leadership, the Suyanggae and Neighbors conferences have been successfully held in Krasnoyarsk, Novosibirsk, and several other countries.

In recognition of your invaluable collaboration with Krasnoyarsk State Pedagogical University, named after V.P. Astafiev, you were awarded the title of Honorary Doctor of Archaeology. As a distinguished representative of global science, you have frequently lectured on Korean archaeology, leaving an indelible mark on scholars and students alike.

Your warmth, wisdom, and unwavering support have earned you the affectionate nickname "Papa Lee" among your students – a testament to the deep respect and admiration they hold for you. This, I believe, is the highest praise one can receive for their dedication to education and mentorship.

Another lasting legacy of your career is the establishment of your own archaeological school. Over the years, you, along with your students, master's candidates, and doctoral researchers, have explored numerous Paleolithic sites in Korea. Many of your students have gone on to become esteemed scholars in the study of Korea's ancient history. Together, you have also created a remarkable archaeological museum at Chungbuk National University – an invaluable institution that serves as a landmark for both the university and the city.

It has been nearly 40 years since our first meeting at an international conference at the University of Maine in Orono (USA). Since then, we have been as close as brothers – one Korean, one Russian – united by our shared passion for archaeology and a lifelong friendship. Over the years, our bond has grown into a true family connection, and it brings me great joy that our children and grandchildren continue this cherished friendship.

Dear Professor Lee Yung-jo, I wish you good Siberian health, new discoveries, and many more years of scientific achievement.

With deepest respect, and from Russia with love

Congratulations

Lucyna DOMAŃSKA
Professor, University of Lodz, Poland

On behalf of the Institute of Archaeology at the University of Lodz, Poland. I am honored to extend my warmest congratulations to Professor Lee Yung-jo on the remarkable milestone of 60 years of academic excellence and the successful organization of 25 conferences in the prestigious Suyanggae and Her Neighbors series.

Professor Lee Yung-jo has dedicated his research and teaching career primarily to two esteemed Korean institutions – Yonsei University and Chungbuk National University. In addition, he has served as a Visiting Professor at several universities in the United States (University of Illinois, University of California) and in Russia (Krasnoyarsk State Pedagogical University). His outstanding contributions to scientific research and education have been widely recognized. Notably, he was awarded the title of Honorary Doctor of Archaeology by Krasnoyarsk State Pedagogical University in 2004, and in 2006, the Institute of Vertebrate Paleontology and Paleoanthropology, Chinese Academy of Sciences, honored him with the title of Honorary Doctor of Science.

Professor Lee has played a pivotal role in leading numerous scientific organizations and continues to do so as Honorary President of institutions such as the Asian Paleolithic Association, Goyang Gawaji Rice Museum, Korean Paleolithic Association, and Korean Museum Studies Association. In 2005, he became Director of the Institute of Korean Prehistory and later assumed the role of President, overseeing its research activities and initiatives.

Among his many contributions, his fieldwork at the Suyanggae sites holds particular significance. His research began under the Chungju Dam Submerged Area Research Group Program (1983–1985) and has continued through various subsequent scientific programs. Excavations at Suyanggae have yielded numerous Upper Paleolithic workshops, where blades, blade cores, and various flint tools were produced. These discoveries have significantly advanced our understanding of blade technology and its origins in Southeast Asia.

In 1996, Professor Lee Yung-jo founded the international conference series Suyanggae and Her Neighbors, creating a global platform for scholars to discuss Stone Age archaeology. Under the leadership of the Suyanggae International Symposium Executive Committee, which he chairs, these conferences have been hosted by leading scientific institutions in Asia, Europe, and the United States. The Institute of Archaeology at the University of Lodz had the privilege of organizing this esteemed conference in 2006 and 2014. Over the years, the Suyanggae and Her Neighbors series has become a key forum for global discussions on Paleolithic archaeology.

Professor Lee is the author of 10 books, 555 articles, and 45 field research reports, as well as the co-editor of 42 additional books. The majority of his works focus on Paleolithic archaeology, and his scholarly contributions have profoundly shaped our understanding of the earliest periods of human history. His research has provided new perspectives on the origins of Eurasian settlement, the development of blade technology in Southeast Asia, and the interactions between Paleolithic hunter-gatherer groups in Siberia, China, and Japan.

The Institute of Archaeology at the University of Lodz has enjoyed over 20 years of fruitful collaboration with Professor Lee Yung-jo. Our partnership has led to significant scientific advancements, and Professor Lee has become a trusted friend of our university. More broadly, he has played a key role in promoting Polish archaeology in international academic exchanges. In 2014, in recognition of his outstanding contributions, he was invited to join the distinguished group of scientists honored by the University of Lodz Senate as special friends of the university. The university leadership is deeply grateful for his unwavering support and commitment to strengthening our institution's connections with major research centers in the Far East. The Rector of the University of Lodz particularly acknowledges Professor Lee's invaluable role in promoting our university and fostering relationships with leading scholars in the region.

We look forward to continuing our collaboration, further expanding academic exchanges between archaeologists from Korea and Poland, and deepening our shared commitment to the advancement of Paleolithic research.

We extend our best wishes to Professor Lee Yung-jo for continued scientific success, groundbreaking discoveries, and many more years of scholarly excellence.

Congratulatory Remark

Masao AMBIRU

Professor Emeritus, Meiji University, Japan

The study of Korea's Paleolithic began with the excavation of the Seokjangri site in 1964. Since then, research on the Late Paleolithic period has evolved through three distinct phases, notably marked by the excavations at Suyanggae site Loc.I (1983–1985) and Suyanggae site Loc.VI (2013–2015). The excavation of Suyanggae Loc.I, along with the First International Academic Conference held in 1996, played a pivotal role in defining Sumbe-tsilgae (Tanged-point) and microlithic artifacts as key cultural markers of Korea's Late Paleolithic, which extended across East Asia. Furthermore, the excavation of Suyanggae Loc.VI provided crucial stratigraphic evidence capturing the transition from Sumbe-tsilgae culture to microlithic culture.

In this regard, the history of Late Paleolithic research in Korea can be categorized into three stages, defined by the excavations at Suyanggae Loc.I and Loc.6. These stages include: 1. The first stage – prior to the excavation of Loc.I, 2. The second stage – from the excavation of Loc. 1 to just before the excavation of Loc. 6, and 3. The third stage – after the excavation of Loc. 6. These can also be understood as the Discovery Stage, the Enlightenment Stage, and the Systematization Stage in the development of Korean Late Paleolithic research.

It was during the second stage, in 2005, that the Institute of Korean Prehistory was established. Chairman Lee Yung-jo, who had led the excavation of Suyanggae Loc.I two decades prior, later concluded the excavation of Suyanggae Loc.6 ten years after founding the institute. Now, in 2025, as we mark a decade since the excavation of Loc.6, we also celebrate the 20th anniversary of the Institute of Korean Prehistory. This milestone coincides with the 40th anniversary of the completion of the excavation at Suyanggae Loc.I, symbolizing a significant turning point that aligns with the founding of the institute.

The meticulous and forward-thinking research planning of Chairman Lee Yung-jo is evident in this chronological interplay between the excavations at Suyanggae and the establishment of the Institute of Korean Prehistory. At the same time, this milestone signals the dawn of a new era in the study of Korea's Late Paleolithic period.

On this remarkable occasion, I extend my heartfelt congratulations to the Institute of Korean Prehistory on its 20th anniversary and wish continued growth and success to all of its dedicated staff.

Reflection and Congratulations
Honoring Professor Lee Yung-jo on His 60-Year Legacy in Archaeology

Xing GAO
Professor, Institute of Vertebrate Paleontology and Paleoanthropology (IVPP), Chinese Academy of Sciences

It is with great joy and the deepest respect that I extend my warmest congratulations to Professor Lee Yung-jo on his remarkable 60-year journey in the field of archaeology. His extraordinary contributions to the advancement of prehistoric archaeological research, particularly in fostering academic exchange and collaboration between China and Korea, have left an indelible mark on the discipline.

Professor Lee's work has not only bridged historical gaps but has also established a lasting scholarly legacy, inspiring future generations to build upon the foundations laid by their predecessors. His unwavering dedication has promoted bilateral and multilateral academic cooperation, deepened research into Paleolithic archaeology in East Asia and beyond, and strengthened mutual trust and friendship among archaeologists across borders.

I was privileged to witness a historic milestone in this journey – the first visit of Professor Lee and other Korean scholars to China in October 1989. This significant event took place during the International Paleoanthropology Symposium in Fangshan, Beijing, commemorating the 60th anniversary of the discovery of the first Peking Man skull. At the time, diplomatic ties between China and South Korea had yet to be formalized, making the presence of the Korean delegation all the more remarkable. Their journey was not without challenges, requiring detours through Hong Kong and Japan to obtain the necessary visas. Despite these obstacles, their perseverance paved the way for 35 years of close scholarly exchange and collaboration between Chinese and Korean Paleolithic archaeologists.

Professor Lee played a central role in this academic partnership. As a student of Professor Sohn Pokee, he nurtured and mentored young scholars, including Kong Soo-jin and Cho Tae-sup, ensuring the continuation of cross-generational knowledge sharing. Thanks to the efforts of Professor Lee and esteemed colleagues such as Professor Bae Kidong, Chinese and Korean archaeologists began engaging in joint field studies at key sites, from Zhoukoudian and Nihewan in China to Suyanggae and Chongok-ni in Korea. These exchanges deepened scholarly understanding and fostered lasting professional and personal friendships between researchers.

One of Professor Lee's most enduring contributions was the establishment of the International Symposium on Suyanggae and Her Neighbors. Initially focused on the Suyanggae site in Korea, the symposium evolved into a global platform for Paleolithic research, expanding to China, Japan, Siberia, Israel, Poland, Malaysia, and the United States. Under his leadership, the symposium not only advanced academic discussions but also helped cultivate a truly international community of scholars.

I was fortunate to become part of this academic network, assisting in organizing key symposiums in China in 2011, 2013, and 2019. These gatherings provided invaluable opportunities for scholars to present groundbreaking research, engage in field investigations, and strengthen collaborative efforts. Through these events, Professor Lee's vision of an interconnected, globally engaged archaeological community became a reality.

Over the past 60 years, Professor Lee has excavated numerous significant prehistoric sites, made groundbreaking discoveries, published extensively, and played a pivotal role in the establishment of archaeological museums. His scholarly achievements have earned him the highest recognition and respect, both in Korea and internationally. While history will rightfully document his legacy, I take this moment to highlight his pioneering role in fostering international archaeological cooperation and shaping the next generation of scholars.

How far-reaching can one individual's influence be? How profoundly can one scholar shape the course of an entire field? Professor Lee Yung-jo has provided us with an extraordinary answer – setting a standard of excellence that few can match.

On this momentous occasion, my colleagues in China and I extend our sincerest congratulations and deepest admiration. We wish Professor Lee continued health, vitality, and success as he forges ahead in his academic journey, guiding and inspiring us all.

PREFACE

Editors-in-Chief **Kidong BAE**
co-editor **Jong-yoon WOO** and **Ju-yong KIM**

This book is a collection of papers on various topics of prehistoric archaeology worldwide, but it was created for a very special occasion. It consists of papers by a group of scholars called the 'Suyanggae Family'. The term 'Suyanggae' may be unfamiliar to archaeologists who do not work on the East Asian Paleolithic. Still, it is the name of a very early Late Paleolithic site in the central region of the Korean Peninsula. The most important reason for naming the society after the site is the proactive leadership of Lee, Yung-jo, Professor Emeritus of Chungbuk National University and President of the Institute of Korean Prehistoric, as an archaeologist, to make the value of the site he excavated widely known to the world.

In the name of Suyanggae, the name of the site, the conference has been held 25 times almost every year for the past 30 years in cities worldwide with well-known archaeological sites or active research. It was held in 25 cities in Eurasia and the Americas (including 6 cities in Korea), so it can be said that it contains the core contents of prehistoric archaeology that spans the Old and New Worlds. It is an international annual academic meeting of prehistoric archaeology that has never been held in this field of science. Through this conference, many discourses on the prehistoric cultures of the world were formed, and the participating scholars from each region, that we call 'the Suyanggae Family', were truly considered a community of archaeologists like 'a family'. This book is published to commemorate the 60 years of archaeological scholarship and the 80th birthday of Professor Emeritus Lee yung-jo, founder of this meeting, with the contribution of papers by members of the scholarly community called again 'the Suyanggae Family'. Although that birthday had already passed at the time of the publication, it was designated to commemorate the 25th anniversary of the Suyanggae International Symposium, which could not be held due to the pandemic.

The title of this book, *Current Studies of Diversity and Pattern in World Prehistory*, emphasizes the fact that it consists of papers on the results of prehistoric archaeological research conducted by Suyanggae families around the world. Of course, it does not show the entire prehistoric era evenly or distribute them in a balanced manner by region, but the title was chosen because it presents diverse prehistoric cultural phenomena from all over the world. I expect that it will be sufficiently understandable that it contains a lot of contents related to the 'Danyang Suyanggae Late Paleolithic site', which can be said to be the most outstanding achievement of Professor Emeritus Lee, Yong-jo's archaeological career, and the 'Cheongju Sorori site', which attracted international attention due to the discovery of very old rice grains. The two sites are the very reason for creating this book.

As can be seen from the examples of prehistoric culture in this volume, prehistoric culture may look simple and have many common elements in different regions, but also showed regional diversity. The grand pattern of the process of cultural evolution in many regions of the World, from the primitive forms of the stone tool culture in the early stage to the emergence of handaxes, and then, to the elaborate stone tools like blade tools around the time of the emergence of modern humans, is not very different. However, the timing of emergence of particular culture may differ, and there are also significant differences in technology and style. In some regions, some particular cultures are not observed in archaeological sites. Many monographs contain efforts to understand the current archaeological achievements of prehistoric culture. Profound questions, not only in prehistoric archaeology, but in whole fields of archaeological science, 'Why common?' and 'Why diverse' are always the prime themes to be pursued upon our rigorous attempts of pattern recognition. This book is expected to provide an example of regional diversity and an opportunity to understand the flow or pattern of culture that ran through prehistoric times temporally and regionally, and to initiate new discussions of diverse topics in prehistoric archaeology.

The 44 papers included are divided into seven groups, and the chapters are divided roughly according to chronological order: Chapter 1. Environment and Culture of the Early Paleolithic Age, Chapter 2. Late Paleolithic Culture of Siberia and the Far East, Chapter 3. Late Paleolithic Site of Suyanggae, Chapter 4. Culture of the Holocene Transition, Chapter 5. Sorori, Cheongju and Ancient Rice in East Asia, Chapter 6. Neolithic Age, and Chapter 7. Papers on Museums. Except for the papers on museums, all are about prehistoric times. Papers related to the Suyanggae and Sorori sites, which are Professor Lee, Yong-jo's most important archaeological achievements in prehistoric archaeology, are collected in Chapters 3 and 5, respectively, with relative order of the cultural evolution.

First, Chapter 1 presents papers related to stone tool making, including a new proposal to explain the handaxe making corresponding to Mode 2A under the name of Chongoknian (=Jeongoknian) after the name of the first site in East Asia as a new name for the handaxe making (Bae); cases of core-flaked stone tool making appearing before the Acheulian in China (Bie et al.); handaxe from the Bose site in southern China and the handaxe found at the An khe site in central Vietnam (Xie et al.); a stratigraphic comparison of the stone tool making at the Mansuri site in Cheongju, which is believed to be one of the oldest stone tool sites in the Korean Peninsula (Takehana et al.); and a comparative study of the stone tool making at the Mansuri site with the stone tool making at the Tautabel-Arago Cave in southern France (Takehana et al.). In addition, articles related to the evolutionary process to modern humans are included. This paper organizes the entire evolutionary process leading to the symbolic ability of modern humans into the order of emergence of human characteristics based on the principles of human evolution (Otte), the differences in cultural evolution between East Asia and western Eurasia based on the conservatism shown in stone tool making in China and the emergence process of regional modern humans through genetic exchange (Gao), and organizes the stratigraphy of remains found in the Middle to Late Pleistocene in the Sudan, North Africa to conclude that *Homo erectus* appeared in this region early with Acheulean stone tool making, and modern human appeared after MIS9 (Masojć). In addition, the animal fossils corresponding to the Early Pliocene discovered in the Jinyuan Cave in Dalian, Liaoning Peninsula, Northeast China, where the discovery of archaic *Homo sapiens* at the Jinniushan attracted worldwide attention in the early 1980s (Jin et al.) can be said to be a hint about the possibility of new data on hominin evolution along with the study of the Quaternary environment in the region.

Chapter 2 consists of papers related to the Late Paleolithic. There is a paper that discusses the view that the introduction of blade technology in the Korean Peninsula was around 35,000 years ago, the introduction and general chronology of lithic assemblages, and an attempt to explain the mixed appearance of pebble stone tools in the Late Paleolithic (Lee and Lee), a paper discussing the chronology and characteristics of the Late Paleolithic industries, which initially evolved from early core-flake stone tool making, from 50,000 to 20,000 years ago excavated from the Nosan-ri site in Cheongju(Yun et al.), and a paper that explains the distribution and geological background of the sites between MIS4 and MIS2 found over the past 20 years in the southwestern region of the Korean Peninsula, namely the Honam region, and the characteristics of lithic industries (Lee G.K.).

The study on the adaptation of hunter-gatherer groups to the changes in climate and ecosystem in the northern East Sea Rim (Sea of Japan) region before the warming of the Holocene climate(Sato) is very encouraging in terms of its methodology for explaining the adaptation process of prehistoric people through patterns of stone tool production. An approach to the subsistence strategies of prehistoric people from relics based on the typical geographic environment of Japan, lava flows and topographic conditions are also interesting (Kumai). The distribution of water resources at the distal end of the lava flow, the distribution of stone tool materials such as obsidian, and the prehistoric people's livelihood strategies within the ecosystem through the estimation of fauna and flora are discussed through the discovered relics. It is argued that the relics including stone industries found at several newly investigated sites in the Zhengzhou area of China will allow us to confirm the cultural development stages from the Middle Paleolithic to the Late Paleolithic, and again to the Neolithic Ages, and will also provide important clues for understanding the emergence and adaptation of modern humans in the region (Wang et al.). There is a report (Drozdov et al.) of Middle to Late Stone Age work found at several sites in the basin of the Abakan River, south of Matkechik, Siberia. Stone tools from cobblestones were collected from many localities along the slopes of the Abakan River. The stone discs with holes in the center, discovered in the graves of two Gravettian sites in Moravia, are argued examples of a culture that persisted for a long time particularly in northern Eurasia, based on presence of similar ones of different materials at sites of later period, even in iron age in Siberia and China (Svoboda).

In Chapter 3, papers on the Suyanggae site, a representative Late Paleolithic site in the Korean Peninsula and East Asia, are bound together. A paper on the geological formation process and stratigraphic chronology of the Suyanggae site(Kim et al.), explains that the site is located on the 2nd and the 3rd terraces, with the lower part of sediments consisting of fluvial layers deposited by the flow of a river, while the upper part consisting of sediments from hilly slopes. A paper that summarizes the chronology of stone tool production and cultural changes at the Suyanggae site (Otani et al.) is included. In this paper, the earliest culture at the Suyanggae site appears to be the early Late Paleolithic aspect, and is differentiated from the previous cultural stages in the Paleolithic Age in the Korean peninsula. This is considered as sound evidence of a significant cultural change in the early Late Paleolithic period. In the early cultural layer of the Suyanggae site Loc. 6, where the strata and stone industries remains are well preserved, large blade and tang points appeared at its early stage, but the size of blade gradually gets smaller toward later stages, and from the second cultural layer, we can see that micro-blade technology appeared. Next, Micro-blade technology of the Suyanggae site was claimed (Lee, S.W. et al.) to appear in 25,000 BP (35,000 BP?), while blade and tanged point appeared in earlier cultural layers. Analyzing the tanged points from the Suyanggae site Loc. 6 shows that they became smaller and more standardized over time (Kim et al.), which can be said to be a case that clearly shows the evolution of stone tools even during the Late Paleolithic. A research of use-wear patterns on tanged points (Akoshima et al.) confirmed multiple functions rather than being simply used as a spear tip through microscopic analysis at various levels of magnification. With a general observation of Paleolithic sites in the Danyang area where the Suyanggae site is located, micro-blade technology from the cultural layers at different localities was reviewed based on the process of preparation and disposal of cores (Lee). The hominin fossil from the Gunang Cave dated 30,000-40,000 BP with associated animal bones, along with the Sangsi Man, is believed to represent prehistoric people that flourished during the early Upper Paleolithic Age in the Danyang Area, while the Hungsu Jevenile in late Upper Paleolithic (Park and Lee)

Chapter 4 contains papers on regional cultural phenomena changing from the Late Paleolithic to the Neolithic or new adaptations during the transition from the late Pleistocene to the early Holocene. The bifacial pointed tool discovered at the Tingka site in Malaysia was 12,000 years old, and was claimed to have a unique craftsmanship different from the Hoabinhian Nhinh culture (Saidin). In island regions of Northeast Asia, such as Sakhalin and the Kuril Islands in Russia, new cultures such as of subsistence economy and rituals emerged during the transition to the Neolithic between 13,000 and 8,500 years ago, and the migration of residents during this period took place not simply due to environmental factors but also cultural decisions (Grischenko et al.). The argument of artifacts that are often not well preserved in archaeological sites, such as leather or fur clothes, could reflect cultural characteristics much better than stone tools that we commonly use to confirm cultural patterns or the dynamics of exchange (Grøn and Klokkernes) is a very suggestive paper for all archaeologists. During the period of the transition from the Mesolithic to the Neolithic in Poland, the climate warming, forests expansion, and on the other hand, sea-level rising caused people to move to the southern lowlands. In this process, while on the one hand, the Maglemose culture continued, but on the other hand, a new culture emerged (Domańska and Wąs). Long research of the Hell Gap site, a representative site of Paleoindian culture in North America, made significant progress in understanding the temporal changes of the Paleoindian culture that had been uncertain until lately through the analysis of overlapping stratigraphy(Kornfeld and Larson). It is also an important case of regional patterns in the most turbulent period of human cultural history. With a case study of the Federsee Lake site in southern Germany, the model of Ideal Free Distribution is recommended to understand patterns of site distribution in a certain environment by examining factors and their role in the process of decision making (Jochim).

Chapter 5 is a collection of papers on archaeological rice grains discovered in the Sorori site, Cheongju, in the central part of the Korean Peninsula, and rice grains in China. It is generally known that rice cultivation began in Southeast Asia in the early Holocene, but these papers claim that rice grains of a similar time period have been discovered in Northeast Asia. The Sorori rice grains are an intermediate stage between ancient and modern rice, and are 2,000 years earlier than those discovered in China (Kim K.J. et al.).

It is also claimed that rice grains may have spread through domestication from wild rice for various reasons during the Bölling-Allerode (B/A) warm period around 15,000 years ago(Kim J.Y. et al.). In the paper, the AMS age of the organic muddy layer of the Younger Fluvial Deposits of the Sorori site, where the rice seeds were collected from, was determined to be between 12,500 and 17,300 years ago, which is claimed to be the oldest age in the world. Evidence of rice found in China consists of 255 cases in various forms, and many of them have been found in the middle and lower reaches of the Yangtz River and the upper reaches of the Huai River. Based on dates of rice evidence between 14,000 and 3,500 BP, it is argued that rice was spread in China at least 10,000 years ago (Tang and Lee). The rice from the Yuchanyan site in 1993 is identified to fall between the category of *Oryza rufipogon* and *Indica*, but closer to the former through analysis of the length of the well-preserved rice grains, and is claimed the oldest type of rice in the world (Yuan).

Chapter 6 includes examples of Neolithic and later cultures from around the world during the Middle Holocene. Volhynian flint transported from as far away as Ukraine at the Wilkostowo site in the Polish Lowlands, a village site dated the 4th millennium BCE, is suggesting the possibility of long-distance trade for producing diverse stone tools including spearheads at the site (Domańska et al.). In Taiwan, the Neolithic culture begins around 6,000-5,500 BP, and shows a gradual development, and the hunter-gatherer groups being rapidly eliminated as a result of competition with food-producing immigrants in the adaptation process to diverse ecological environments. An evaluation of existing models to understand the process of adaptation to different ecological environments has been made (Yu). The paper (Kim and Bae) that attempts to estimate the time period of use of the Amsadong Neolithic village in the Han River basin in the Korean Peninsula on the pattern of the scale and cycle of the Han River floods presents a new genre of geo-archaeology of Neolithic settlement. The Ulju Bangudae petroglyphs in southeast of the Korean Peninsula is claimed to support the arguments of the Neolithic Age of the site based on presence of whale bones in Neolithic shell middens and other sites which may be quite likely to make a valid reason for whaling depicted on the engravings (Kang), while in the early study of the petroglyph by late Professor Kim Won-yong, it was claimed that forms of spearhead and of crossbow on engravings could be those of the Bronze or Iron Age. The types of stone and iron tools used to make engravings has been tried to determine by an analysis of silicon replicas of the lower engravings of the Shalabolino rock art in Siberia (Drozdov et al.). Various animal resources of sedentary people during the Ferro-Chalcolithic period in the RARH region of West Bengal, India, were depleted due to climate change and excessive hunting (Ghosh). Chapter 7 is dedicated to studies of several site-museums.

I, as the Chief of the editors, would like to express my deepest gratitude to the authors who willingly contributed to this book, and have patiently waited for its publication for a long time since their submissions. I would also like to acknowledge the generous consideration and effort of Director Woo, Jong-yoon and his staff, particularly the financial support of the Institute of Korean Prehistoric Culture, for the publication of this book. I sincerely hope that this book shall remain as a living testimony to the Suyanggae Annual International Symposium, which has continued under the passionate leadership of Professor Lee, Yong-jo for over a quarter of a century. An additional volume covers the histories of Prof. Lee's life-long contribution to archaeology and of the Suyanggae International Symposium.

CONTENTS

Current Studies of Diversity and Pattern in World Prehistory

005 **Prologue: Invitation to SUYANGGAE**
Yung-jo LEE

008 **Congratulations**
Dear Professor Lee Yung-jo _ *Nicolay Ivanovich DROZDOV*
Congratulations _ *Lucyna DOMAŃSKA*
Congratulatory Remark _ *Masao AMBIRU*
Reflection and Congratulations _ *Xing GAO*

012 **Preface**
Kidong BAE, Jong-yoon WOO and Ju-yong KIM

Chapter 1.
Environment and Culture of the Early Paleolithic Age

021 **Chongoknian; Korean Handaxes a new synthesis, and its implication for pattern of Paleolithic industries in East Asia**
Kidong BAE

033 **Before the Emergence of Acheulean : New Archaeological Evidence from Jinshuihe River Valley in the Hanzhong Basin, Central China**
Jingjing BIE, Wenting XIA, Shejiang WANG

041 **A comparative study of Bose and An Khe industries**
Guangmao XIE, Qiang LIN, Yan WU

052 **Statistical comparison of the lithic industries from the Far East and Caune de l'Arago in France; as the Central Point of Loc. 1, Mansuri Site in Korea**
Kazuharu TAKEHANA, Kazuto MATSUFUJI, Yung-jo LEE

067 **Chrono-typological studies of lithic industries from the Mansuri Paleolithic Site Locality 1 in Korea**
Kazuharu TAKEHANA, Yung-jo LEE, Kaoru OTANI

076 **The place of humankind in the biomechanical evolution of living organisms according to A. Leroi-Gourhan**
Marcel OTTE

087 **Archaeological studies on the origin of modern humans in China**
Xing GAO

097 **Chronological aspects concerning the Middle and Late Pleistocene hominin presence in Sudanese Nubia, NE Africa**
Mirosław MASOJĆ

104 **The first discovery of Plio-Pleistocene mammalian faunal sequence and suspected artifacts from Jinyuan Cave of Luotuo Hill, Dalian, Northeast China**
Changzhu JIN, Yuan WANG, Wenhui LIU

Chapter 2.
Late Paleolithic Culture of Siberia and the Far East

121 **The study of blade tool industry in Korea**
Heon-jong LEE, Sang-seok LEE

126 **The Lithic Assemblages and Chronology of Nosan-ri Paleolithic site, Cheongju, Korea**
Byeong-il YUN, Kaoru OTANI, Yung-jo LEE

131 **Growth and Status of Paleolithic Research in Southwestern Korea**
Gi-kil LEE

144 **Environmental fluctuation in the Northern Circum Japan Sea Area in the Upper Paleolithic and subsistence adaptation of prehistoric hunter-gatherers**
Hiroyuki SATO

152 **Geological requirement for the Paleolithic site in the volcanic area**
Hisao KUMAI

156 **New achievements of Paleolithic research in Zhengzhou and related issues**
Youping WANG, Wanfa GU, Yue FENG

161 **The Search for the Paleolithic in the Republic of Khakassia (Southern Siberia)**
N.I. DROZDOV, D.N. DROZDOV, V.I. MAKULOV

167 **Towards the roots of Eurasia : The Moravian stone discs**
Jiří SVOBODA

Chapter 3.
Late Paleolithic Site of Suyanggae

175 **Upper Paleolithic site-forming process and chronostratigraphy of the Suyanggae sites (Loc. 1, Loc. 3, Loc. 6), Danyang County, Korea**
Ju-yong KIM, Yung-jo LEE, Jong-yoon WOO, Ho-seong SUH, Seung-won LEE, Keun-chang OH

185 **Characteristics of the blade technology in the Korean Peninsula with a focus on CL 4 and CL 3 at Suyanggae 6 (SYG 6)**
Kaoru OTANI, Jong-yoon WOO, Yung-jo LEE

196 **The Emergence of Microblade culture at the Suyanggae site**
Seung-won LEE, Yung-jo LEE

204 **An analysis of end-scrapers by manufacturing technology in the Upper Paleolithic from the Suyanggae site, Loc. 6, in Danyang, Korea**
Eunjeong KIM, Seung-won LEE, Jong-yoon WOO, Yung-jo LEE

217 **On the use-wear analysis of tanged points from Loc. 1 and 6, Suyanggae site, Korea**
Kaoru AKOSHIMA, Hyewon HONG, Seung-won LEE, Jong-yoon WOO, Yung-jo LEE

238 **The Paleolithic survey in Danyang, South Korea : Focusing on the results and future tasks**
Jungchul LEE

252 **A review of the Late Pleistocene hominid fossil remains in the southern part of Korea**
Sun-joo PARK, Yung-jo LEE

Chapter 4.
Culture of the Holocene Transition

261 **Evidence of a pointed bifacial flake in Tool Workshop 12 ka at the Tingkayu site, Sabah, Malaysia**
Mokhtar SAIDIN

267 **Modeling the islanders' behavior in the insular world of the Far East during the Pleistocene/Holocene transition within the Terminal Paleolithic/Incipient Neolithic boundaries**
Vyacheslav A. GRISHCHENKO, Kimura HIDEAKI, Alexander A. VASILEVSKI

274 **A specter from the Lithic Stone Age to the Non-Lithic Fur and Bone Age**
Ole GRØN, Torunn KIOKKERNES

284 **The Mesolithic in Poland in light of field research of the Institute of Archaeology, University of Lodz**
Lucyna DOMAŃSKA, Marcin WĄS

292 **Hell Gap: Then and now**
Marcel KORNFELD, Mary Lou LARSON

303 **The IFD Model of Palaeolithic and Mesolithic Sites on the Federsee, Germany**
Michael JOCHIM

Chapter 5.
Sorori, Cheongju and Ancient Rice in East Asia

311 **Radiocarbon age of the Cheongju Sorori rice and its significance in understanding human environmental settings**
KyeongJa KIM, Yung-jo LEE, Ju-yong KIM

316 **Geomorphic background and pedo-sedimentary matrix formation of the Sorori Paleolithic site in Miho River, Korea**
Ju-yong KIM, Yung-jo LEE, Jong-yoon WOO, Keun-chang OH, Seung-won LEE

322 **Rice (*O. sativa*) remains excavated in China**
Shengxiang TANG, Yung-jo LEE

329 **Yuchanyan ancient rice and generation of rice agriculture of China**
Jiarong YUAN

Chapter 6.
Neolithic Age

343 **Wilkostowo 23/24: An example of the Neolithic chipped flint inventory from the Polish Lowlands**
Lucyna DOMAŃSKA, Seweryn RZEPECKI

351 **Can human behavioral ecology models contribute to understanding the Neolithization of Taiwan? Considering the Ideal Despotic Distribution and Allee Effects Model**
Pei-Lin YU

364 **Preliminary research on the formation and post-depositional processes in Amsa-dong Neolithic site, Seoul**
Kiryong KIM, Kidong BAE

371 **A reconsideration of the chronology of the Bangudae petroglyphs in prehistoric Korea**
Bong Won KANG

380 **Shalabolino's petroglyphs technique analysis : Experience of trace research**
N.I. DROZDOV, E.G. DEVLET, E.Y. GIRYA, V.I. MAKULOV

385 **Exploitation beyond subsistence of faunal resources at "RARH" (West Bengal, India) by new settlers during the Ferro-Chalcolithic period**
Manomay GHOSH

Chapter 7.
Papers on Museums

395 **The Suyanggae and Gawaji Rice Museums from the European Perspective of Public Archeology**
Marcel BARTCZAK, Lucyna DOMAŃSKA, Yung-jo LEE, Jong-yoon WOO

403 **A study on the interpretation and presentation of the prehistoric culture and ecological environment at the Suyanggae Prehistory Museum**
Jong-ho CHOE, Yung-jo LEE

408 **National museums and national identity in South Korea**
Yoon Ok Rosa PARK

417 **The construction process and significance of Jeongok Prehistory Museum**
Hanyong LEE

Appendix

424 • About the Contributors

431 • International Symposium: SUYANGGAE and Her Neighbours (1–25th)

462 • Suyanggae Academic Awards (2008–2022)

463 • SUYANGGAE International Symposium Executive Committee (SISEC)

464 • Institute of Korean Prehistory (IKP) Overview

466 • INDEX

471 • International Members of Editorial Committee

Chapter 1.
Environment and Culture of the Early Paleolithic Age

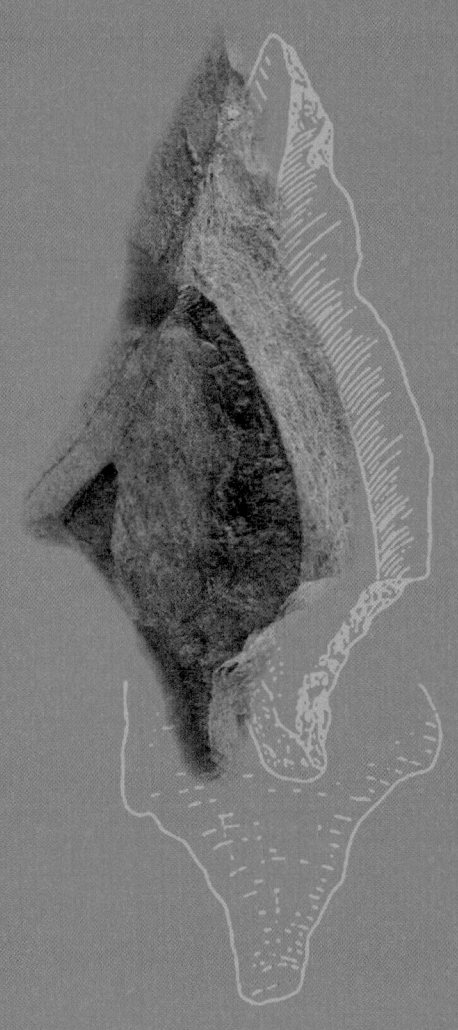

Chongoknian; Korean Handaxes a new synthesis, and its implication for pattern of Paleolithic industries in East Asia

Kidong BAE

Professor Emeritus, Hanyang University, Korea ; bkd5374@gmail.com

ABSTRACT

Handaxe industries found in the Hantan-Imjin River Basin (HIRB) have often been associated with the Acheulean stone tool industry. However, it has been often mentioned that most of handaxes in East Asia exhibit some differences in their degree of refinement, thinnness, and symmetry and extensiveness of retouch from Acheulean handaxes. Chongokni Site in the HIRB is the first site where Acheulean-typed handaxes, dated back to the late Middle Pleistocene, were identified in East Asia. Handaxes from the HIRB feature minimal shaping. Most of handaxes are often retouched partially or shows very limited secondary retouches on tips except ovate handaxes. A new term, "Chongoknian" represents handaxe industries of such characteristic in the Korean peninsula, and also one of the example of Mode 2A, a newly revised the Clark system of lithic evolution, stage of handaxe industries without any prepared flaking technique, while Mode 2B for the typical Acheulean handaxe industry. An important aspect in understanding variations of handaxe culture is that cultural diversity emerges as early humans adapt to their respective environments with variable strategies. A new paradigm shift in approaching cultural diversity on the basis of new synthesis of current archaeologcial data in East Asia will improve our understadning of hominin's adaptive behavior in particular environment. Further research will be necessary to delve deeper into this process.

국문초록

한탄-임진강 유역에서 발견된 주먹도끼공작은 흔히 아슐리안 주먹도끼공작으로 설명되는 경우가 많다. 그러나 일반적으로 동아시아 지역에서 발견되는 주먹도끼들은 정련도, 단면두께, 평면상의 대칭정도 그리고 가공의 강도에 있어서 아슐리안과는 큰 차이가 있다. 한탄-임진강 유역에 있는 전곡리 유적은 동아시아에서 최초로 중기 홍적세의 중후반부에 속하는 아슐리안형 주먹도끼가 발견된 바 있다. '전곡리안'은 한반도에서 발견되는 그러한 특성의 주먹도끼 공작을 지칭하는 용어로 제기되었다. 또한 클라크가 제시한 석기진화과정을 단계별로 구분한 시스템을 세분한 모드 2A의 지역적인 양상으로 분류하였는데 전형적인 아슐리안은 모드 2B로 구분되었다. 주먹도끼의 다양한 형태를 이해하기 위해서는 고인류가 각각의 살고 있는 환경에 적응하는 과정에서 선택적으로 작용하는 문화적인 다양성의 결과라는 점을 인식하여야 할 것이다. 이제는 서구적인 접근체계로서 '아슐리안' 또는 '아슐리안 형' 등의 석기분류 용어를 통한 석기문화 이해에서 벗어나서 동아시아 전반적인 구석기공작에 대한 종합적인 검토를 통해서 새로운 관점의 변화가 과거 특정환경 속에서 일어나는 고인류의 문화적인 선택에 의한 행위를 이해할 수 있도록 하여야 할 것이다. 이러한 새로운 시각에서 연구가 앞으로 진작되는 것이 필요하다.

Keywords : Hantan-Imjin River Basin (HIRB), Chongokni Site, Handaxes, Acheulean, Mode 2A, Mode 2B, Movius line, Levallois

1. Introduction

It is time to approach handaxe industries in East Asia from different perspectives. Many of the debates stemming from the East–West dichotomy of handaxe assemblages noted by Movius (1948) continue (Clark, 1998; Dennel, 2015; Norton et al., 2008; Schick, 1994; Yi and Clark, 1983). However, at present, it is well known that current data about handaxes in East Asia demonstrate that morphological differences between handaxes from various regions in the World may not be as profound as those originally proposed. Contemporary discussions are instead focused on differences from the western standard, the Acheulean, not on commonalities with variations of grand patterns of Paleolithic culture in the early part of Pleistocene.

Various typed handaxes were used in different environments in the World during the 2 million years (Shipton and Petraglia, 2010). Heavy-duty stone tools classified as handaxes undoubtedly served common functions and possessed certain fundamental technological characteristics. However, regional characteristics of handaxes also have significant implications for understanding human evolutionary processes in particular environments. Factors caused morphological variations have been the critical issue in handaxe archaeology. Although many hypotheses have been proposed (Bae, 1988; Hutterer, 1977; Lycett and Gowlett, 2008; Lycett and Norton, 2010), few have sufficiently explained geographical variations in handaxes. It would be more productive to develop a relevant methodology of understanding morphological patterns of handaxe industries and possible implications for human behavior and regional adaptation with a new perspectives.

East Asian handaxes are sometimes described to as 'Acheulean-typed', or 'Acheulean-like' (e.g., Hou et al., 2000; Li et al., 2014; Wang et al., 2013), while at the same time, have been described with different terminologies by regional archaeologists. It would be more appropriate to devise a single term for handaxe industries in East Asia given their relatively common cultural characteristics. Considering that the first Acheulean-typed handaxes were claimed (Kim and Jeong, 1978) and rich morphological diversity which comprises most of types, and relatively high frequency in the composition of the lithic industry, the handaxe industry of the Chongokni[1] site is the most typical and will undoubtedly solidify its cultural uniqueness (Bae, 2021). The name "Chongoknian," which represents the characteristics of the handaxes found at this site, shares commonalities with those from other handaxe sites in the Korean peninsula as well as those in the HIRB (Bae, 1994, 2017).

During the last several decades, handaxe industries have been found in many regions in China, including Luonan in Central China (Wang et al., 2012), Bose in southwestern China (Hou, 2014), and many localities in central China (Li et al., 2014). Current observations of handaxe industries not just in the Korean penisula but throughout East Asia indicate that the concept of "Chongoknian" could be extended geographically to represent the features of handaxe culture across this continental part of East Asia. In this article, patterns of handaxe industries in the HIRB will be explained with a focus on the Chongokni site.

2. Discovery of the Chongokni site and researches

Upon the astonishing discovery of handaxes, including cleavers which is not common in East Asia, at the Chongok archaeological site in 1978, systematic surface surveys had already commenced. Since 1979, a substantial number of excavations have been carried out. A series of archaeological excavations and other scientific research projects from 1979 to 1983 provided significant information about the handaxe industries, as well as the geological structure, of the site (Kim et al., 1983). Since the first campaign of the research, several rescue excavations were carried out in the zone of the National Historical Monument and also in the buffer zone surrounding the designated core area.

With rapid social development occurring in the Chongok area, an extensive survey, including pit-excavation of the entire zone, was carried out in 2,000 to collect stratigraphic data and determine the localities of stone artifact concentrations, which is essential for establishing a long-term plan for developing the preservation strategy of the site (Bae et al., 2001). The well-known of the excation locality, the E55S20 pit (**Fig. 1**), nicknamed the Chicken Cage pit, was excavated during the campaign. Horizontal beddings of aeolian sediment of about 5m was exposed above alluvial depsoit on the op of the Chongok basalt. Extensive scientific analysis of the sediment exposed in this pit yielded extremely valuable information about site formation processes and age of the site through international collaborations with Japanese team (Matzufuji ed., 2008) and also the French team (de Lumley et al., 2011). Analysis of the pit sediment has provided a basic framework for understanding environmental changes and the chronology of sedimentation at the locality. Matrix blocks of the sediment of the E55E20 pit are stored at the Chongok Prehistory Museum for future analysis. In the early 2000s, several large-scale salvage excavations were carried out by several different institutes at some localities and yielded a good number of handaxes, including well-fabricated cleavers. New attempts at age dating provided a range of ages from the late Middle Pleistocene and strengthened the

---

[1] Chongokni (全谷里) = Jeongokni

Fig. 1 Sediment at E55S20 Pit, Chongokni site

assertion of the presence of a Middle Pleistocene handaxe industry.

The discovery of Chongok prompted further investigations into the HIRB, leading to the continuous discovery and excavation of numerous Paleolithic sites. Numerous handaxe sites were found, particularly in the HIRB, to the west of the Chongokni site, and at the lower reach of the Han River basin. As of now, there are two designated National Historical Monuments in the HIRB: the Chongokni site and the Juwolli-Gawolli site. Over the last 50 years, our knowledge of Paleolithic culture, including handaxe culture, has been greatly improved owing to many archaeological and other scientific research projects and in spite of different views of the chronology of cultural layers.

3. Handaxes in the Hantan and Imjin River Basin (HIRB)

The region with the most concentrated presence of handaxes in the Korean Peninsula is the HIRB (Fig. 2). Handaxes have been discovered at various sites in the adjacent Kimpo and Paju areas, which are downstream from the confluence of the Imjin and Hantan Rivers (Fig. 3). Determining the chronological order of these findings is, however, complicate and a task for future research. A wide range of absolute age dates of sediments containing handaxe industries has been observed among archaeological sites and even within the same site, which might be the result of various factors, including different post-depositional processes and dating errors. Following the initial discovery at the Chongokni site, other sites along the Hantan and Imjin Rivers (Yi, 2011), including Jangsan-ri, Geumpari, Juwolli, Gawolli, Jangnamgyo Bridge, Wondang-ri, and Namgye-ri have yielded handaxes, from either archaeological excavations or surface surveys. The majority of handaxe artifacts have been recovered from areas downstream of the HIRB, to the east of the Chongokni site, while very few were found in upper reach of the Hantan River. This pattern of distribution of handaxes in the HIRB is thought to have been resulted from the difference of time of two basalt-bed formations at the two regions of the river basin on the basis of age dates of the two basalt flows, 0.5 MBP for the Chongok Basalt and 0.15 MBP for the Chatan Basalt (Nagaoka, 2006) (Fig. 4). Notably, at some sites, including Chongokni and other locations within the HIRB, a distinctive feature is the presence of cleavers and thick ovate handaxes. These handaxe types are uncommon in other regions of East Asia and could thus be considered a regional diversity. It might be premature, however, to conclude that such regional lithic assemblages directly signify cultural differences. While variations in stone tool compositions are evident, making a direct link to cultural differences among sites requires careful consideration of various factors, including environmental influences, technological capabilities, resource availability, and social practices. Analyzing these aspects in conjunction with the archaeological record can provide a more comprehensive understanding of the cultural implications behind these variations in stone tool assemblages.

Indeed, it is important to take into conisderation of geological formation process of sites for clear understanding of hominin's behavior at sites because archaeological contexts and composition of lithic artifacts often have been transformed seriously from the oroginals. The lack of standardized classification system can result in similar lithic artifacts being termed or classified differently. This highlights the need for a clear and consistent terminology and classification methods within the field of archaeological research. It is essential to account for these factors when interpreting and comparing findings from various sites and regions.

New findings of handaxes in East Asia have provided valuable insights that can help understand cultural evolution in general. The distribution of handaxe industries beyond the Chongokni site in Korea indicates that Chongokni handaxes are not exceptional in this region but are instead

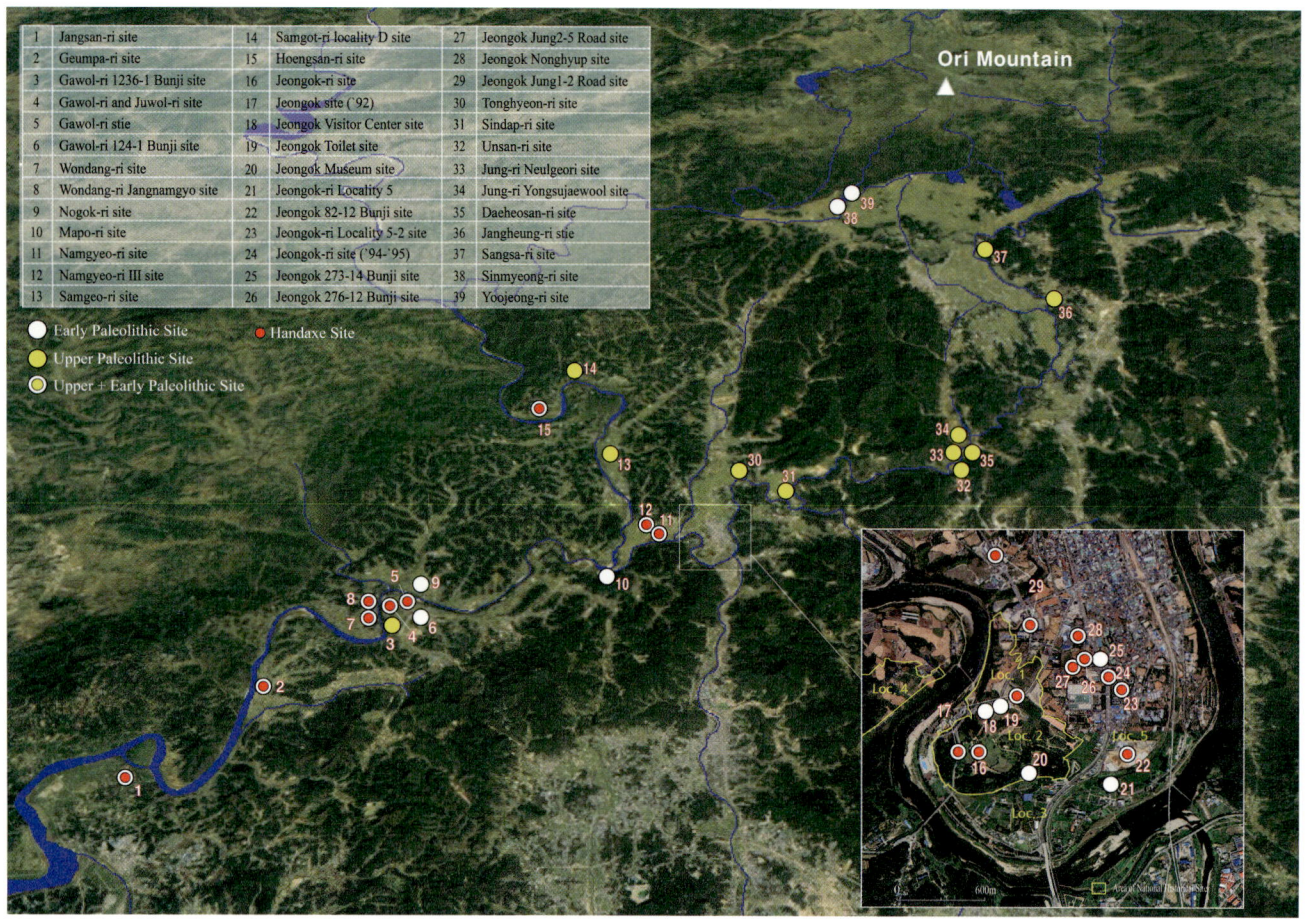

Fig. 2 Paleolithic Sites in the HIRB

Fig. 3 Distribution of Handaxe sites in Paju and Kimpo, Lower Han river basin

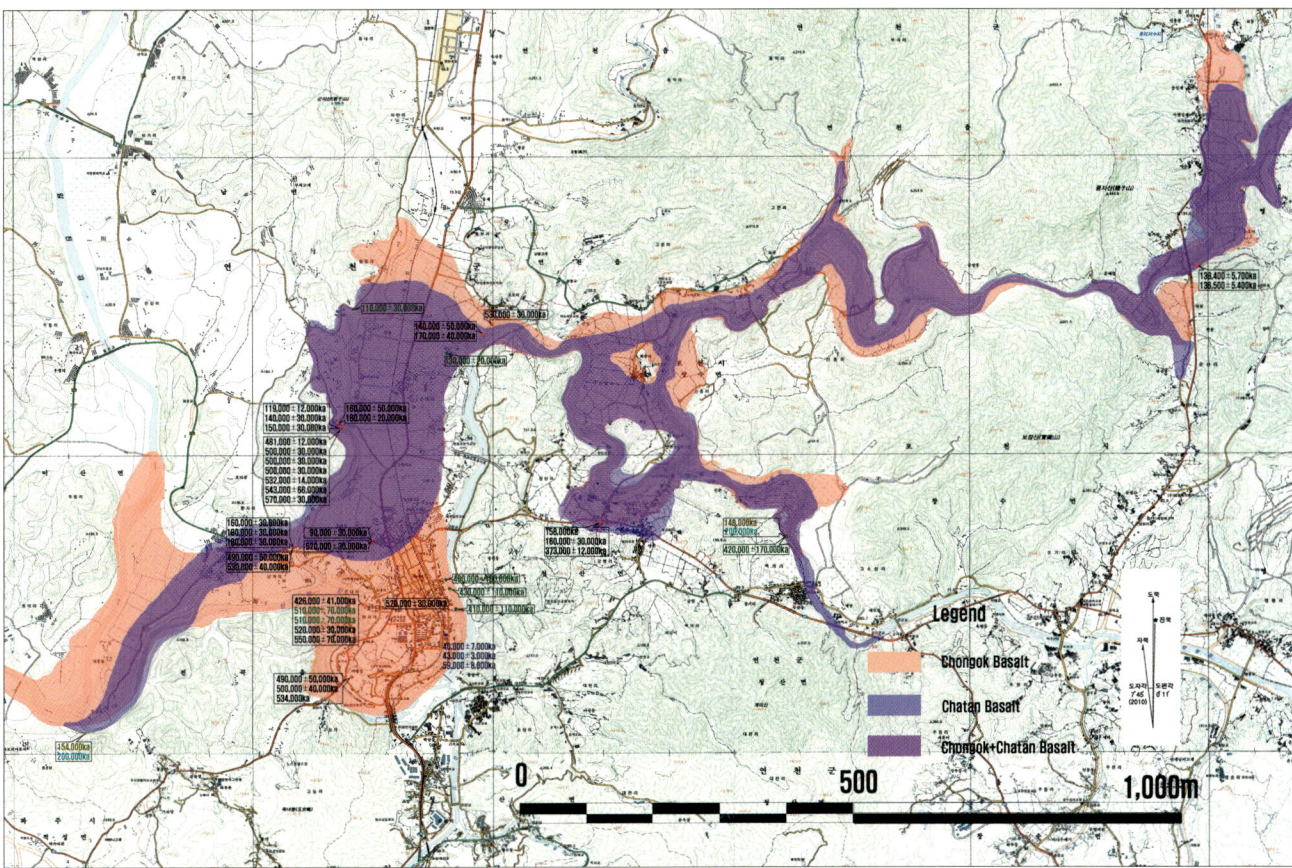

Fig. 4 Distribution Map of Chongok Basalt and Chatan Basalt and K-Ar Dates

part of a larger regional pattern of Paleolithic culture. It is reasonable to expect that the number of new handaxe sites will increase in the future. The perspective that geographical differentiation is solely based on the presence or absence of the most developed type of handaxes, as Movius theorized, can lead to a misunderstanding of the cultural dynamics of prehistoric humans. The approach should now shift toward understanding the geographical diversity of handaxes and the evolutionary significance of the patterns they exhibit in consideration of their regional paleoenvironmental context (Bae, 2021; Hou, 2014). As evidence for such endeavors, the handaxes found at Chongokni and other sites in the HIRB hold particular value, serving as both epoch-making material in the history of Paleolithic archaeology and a potential inspirational source for new explanations of geographical patterns of cultural evolution.

4. Handaxe Industry from sites in HIRB

4.1. Raw materials

With some exceptions, handaxes in the HIRB were predominantly made from river cobbles of quartzite or quartz vein. High-energy rivers flows deposit large, rounded cobbles on the channel bed, which are used as a good source of raw materials for stone tools. The cortex of cobbles is often observed in stone artifacts. At the Chongokni site, excavations have revealed large quartzite cobble stones with diameters ranging from 70 to 80cm that were likely transported to the location by groups of people as they are too heavy to be carried by a single person. Of course, it is very unusual, while smaller stones were likely also brought to the site from the ancient channel bed and used as raw materials for making stone tools. The presence of the large stones indicates a collaborative effort to collect and transport raw material, highlighting the cooperative nature of the process. In addition to these common stones, volcanic rocks like basalt or tuff were also used, but, due to their relatively weak properties, only occasionally so. Ultimately, it is likely that people primarily used stones that were readily available along local riverbanks, as they did not need to travel long distances to obtain them.

Quartzite and quartz vein are among the most frequently encountered lithic materials in the Korean Peninsula. Although they offer a high knapping potential and a strong edge, their toughness often leads to knapping difficulties, and internal flaws, such as joints or cracks, can cause unintended fractures during production. In the HIRB, well-shaped handaxes were often made of relatively homogeneous and fine-grained quartzite. Among quartz vein rocks, some include coarse particles and weaker rock

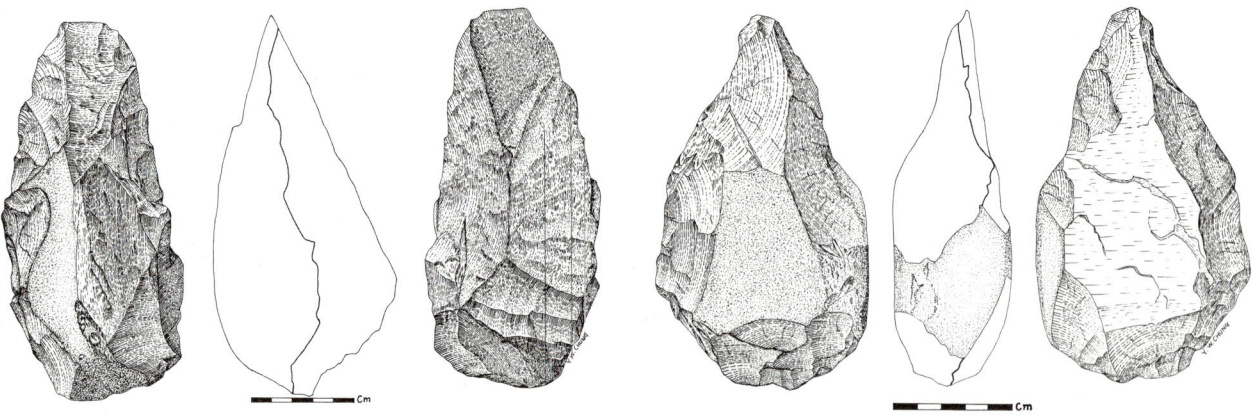

Fig. 5 Handaxe, Chongokni

Fig. 6 Handaxe, Chongokni

Fig. 7 Handaxe, Chongokni

Fig. 8 Cleaver, Chongokni

cohesion, making them unsuitable for detaching large flakes for primary form for handaxe making. Understanding knapping strategies requires the examination of the nature of raw lithic material, including its texture, toughness, and fracture patterns in order to understanding strategy of shaping final products.

4.2. Morphological classification: Form, working edge, and reduction strategy

Handaxes are classified based on various attributes; form of cutting edge, plan form, body section, etc. The first prioirty of criteia is the shape of the cutting edge. Depending on the shape of the cutting edge, the overall plan and the extent of finishing can vary, possibly based on the preferences of the maker. Handaxes in the HIRB are broadly categorized into four types based on the type of cutting edge and plan form. The first type, a similar category known as the "Ficron" in the West, features a narrow horizontal cutting edge, curved or linear, on the distal end, often called 'chiesel tip' (**Fig. 5**). The second type has a strong triangular sectioned pointed edge similar to a spearhead, often called 'pick' (**Fig. 6, 9**), The third type is ovate, shaping large part of or entire body with bifacial or partial bifacial retouches without any sharp edge (**Fig. 7, 10**). Finally, there are cleavers, which are retouched on sides leaving unretouched sharp horizontal cutting edge on distal end of large flake (**Fig. 8**). There are some variations in degree of retouches with a few typical ones. Among the four types, the pointed type is predominately present in assemblages. Additionally, in some examples, the core or cobble was crafted to make use of the naturally occurring pointed part of the raw material, without any modification. However, while handaxe with chiesel tip (Ficron-like type), triangular-pointed tip(pick) and cleavers have clear functions, some of the oval-shaped handaxes lack an identifiable cutting edge, making their function less apparent. Items falling within the oval-shaped category vary, from diamond-like shapes to real ovate. However, they typically have a rounded outline without a prominent tip, and many retain a thick body. These were likely intended for use as core tools for pounding, but their distinct differences in craftsmanship from polyhedrals and any other amorphous form of

Fig. 9 Handaxe, Chongokni **Fig. 10** Ovate handaxe, Chongokni **Fig. 11** Extra big handaxe, Chongokni

cores make a straightforward determination challenging. Some of the ovate-type handaxes excavated thus far from Chongokni were shaped by exceptionally deliberate retouches to make smooth peripheral line and symmetrical plan. It may be critical issue to consider a possiblity possibility that these handaxes may have had alternative, unknown functions in addition to chopping and pounding despite their axe-like appearance.

Handaxes from HIRB generally have a size corresponding to the length of a human palm. However, there are some exceptions in their size. Smaller stone tools that have the characteristic shape of handaxes with tip could have possibly served as toys for children. In contrast, very large and oversized handaxe-shaped lithic tools have been discovered at several localities in the HIRB (Fig. 11). It remains uncertain whether these artifacts were actually used as tools, or instead functioned as pounding stones, or were employed for some other purpose, or just well controlled cores. The fact that the sharp end of these tools was meticulously worked through continuous strikes suggests they were indeed used as a tool. While wielding such large handaxes with one hand would likely have been feasible only for individuals of large stature, it is plausible to speculate that they could have been used with both hands. Yet, the utility of such large tools might have been quite limited in scope.

Stone tools can undergo continuous transformations as they are used. The stone tools found at archaeological sites might have been crafted and used for their intended purpose until disposal at the sites. On the other hand, there are instances where stone tools underwent several stages of modification and were repeatedly used for different purposes until eventually being discarded. In this regard, various types of handaxes can be temporally correlated with other types, such as choppers, various types of handaxes and even polyhedral, indicating trans-morphological relationships through time. Moreover, individual types of handaxes may have been subject to different transformational stages and processes, which contrasts with other archaeological artifacts that remained in their completed forms before being discarded. This difference underscores a limitation of the formal typology employed by archaeologists as a means of cultural reconstruction. In this regard, handaxes reveal a lifetime of hidden histories, the unraveling of which remains a highly constrained endeavor. Handaxes excavated at the Chongokni site are no exception. Therefore, more attention should be paid to conjoined pieces and to the fabrication processes of heavy-duty tools, if any possibilities are observed.

4.3. Process of shaping handaxes

The production process of handaxes can be broadly categorized into two methods based on the characteristics of the core or primary form (the initial stone used for shaping). One approach involves using large flake, often obtained from sizable boulders, as the primary form for crafting handaxes. The other method involves using river pebbles or irregularly shaped stones as cores for shaping. In many cases, using large flakes as cores tends to result in the production of flatter handaxes. These larger primary forms are often obtained through the use of the block-on-block percussion technique, in which one large rock is struck against another to obtain sizable flakes. In this case, it is common to utilize the sharp edge of the flake, but often, due to the thinness of the core, shaping efforts are limited, resulting in many natural surfaces being retained on the handle or body of the handaxe. When using whole river cobbles or irregularly shaped rocks as cores, the inherent shape of the core is often preserved. This is likely due to a production strategy aimed at obtaining the desired edge by leveraging the natural form of the core.

The bifacial flaking technique, which leaves zigzagged edges on the sides of the handaxe, is sometimes used, but handaxes are more commonly created by applying unidirectional flakings at various points of the core. In this method, a thick body section is often maintained, resulting in handaxes with a strong, triangular, cross-sectioned edge on the distal end. Furthermore, numerous cases have been observed in which handaxes were crafted by shaping only the tip while leaving the thick body section intact. Additionally, some handaxes have been found that have chisel-like ends or rounded, elliptical edges; these have been classified as "pointed type." Another technique involves using a core made of flat, angular stones. The sides of the core are processed at a slightly sharp angle by performing unilateral flakings on both sides in opposite directions, resulting in the formation of an oval handaxe. In this case, the central cross-section of the stone tool becomes diamond-shaped, with flat natural surfaces partially remaining on both sides.

When viewed as a holistic process, tool production is generally aimed at selecting suitable raw materials and creating functional edges with minimal shaping. In the context of East Asian lithic technology, this approach is sometimes referred to as "expedient tool production technology," which may also be implicitly applicable to handaxe production (Bae, 2021; Lee, 2010). In other words, the approach signifies the most "labor-economic" process of handaxe production and can be deemed the most efficient method for crafting handaxes for their desired function.

4.4. Function of handaxes

Handaxes are versatile tools capable of performing various functions. In the context of European and African lithic technology, handaxes are sometimes classified as "large cutting tools." However, it is rare to find handaxes in the Korean Peninsula that possess long and sharp cutting edges. Instead, many possess strong triangular tips or short, straight edges on the distal end, making their specific function a significant topic in Paleolithic archaeology. It is speculated that these handaxes might have been used for various tasks requiring robust tools of a certain weight. Potential uses include digging in the ground to obtain plant roots, breaking branches, or even breaking the bones of large animals. However, none of these hypotheses can be conclusively proven through archaeological evidence. Indeed, it is clear that the presence of such strong and robust tips would have been necessary in the specific context of their subsistence environment. When a function of cutting was required, cleavers or commonly associated large flakes with long cleaving edge might have fulfilled this role.

5. Age of Handaxe at the Chongokni site

The presence of handaxes in the lower cultural layers of the Chongokni deposit, specifically immediately above the alluvial sandy sediment of flood plains, suggests that handaxes were used from the initial stages of the Chongok archaeological site after the basalt flow (Bae, 1988). While there have been debates about the stratigraphy of handaxe finds, evidence from excavations conducted in the early 1980s as well as recent excavations at Locality 5 to the east of the National Road 3, which reveal similar temporal stages of sediment layers, suggests that handaxes were already in use from the beginning of the sedimentation at the Chongokni site. In addition to previous attempts at optically stimulated luminescence (OSL) and Al/Be datings representing the Middle Pleistocene (summary in Bae, 2021; Lebatarta et al., 2018; Matsufuji, 2008), new OSL ages and cosmogenic ages, Al/Be ages, obtained from samples at Locality 5 have dated the lower cultural layer to older than 200,000 BP, approaching 250,000 BP (Kim et al., 2023; Lee et al., 2023). Thus, it is evident that handaxes were definitely being used by 'archaic' Homo in the HIRB at least 300,000 BP years or earlier, late Middle Pelistocene, considering rapid erosional process of basalt bed down to current level of river channel after formation of 0.5 MBP. This is the oldest age for handaxes in the Korean Peninsula discovered thus far. The duration of these handaxe industries in the HIRB is not yet clear, but it is not observable at sites to the east of Daehoesan-ri, Pocheon. No handaxes have been retrieved from excavations at many Upper Paleolithic sites in the upper reaches of the Hantan River basin (Seo, 2019). This absence suggests that handaxes were not in use as a major tool type before the beginning of the Late Paleolithic period. While a geographic association should be made between handaxes in the Korean Peninsula and China, a significant temporal gap exists between the two regions in terms of the emergence of handaxes and their duration of use. However, current dating of handaxes in the Bose Basin and Luonan area of China indicates that they were in use earlier than those from the Chongokni site and other sites in the Korean Peninsula. Therefore, conducting comparative studies on handaxe cultures in these regions to explain their variations and cultural evolution in East Asian archaeology is challenging. However, recent excavations in the Luonan Basin have revealed a cultural layer associated with handaxes dating back to approximately 250,000 years ago (Wang and Zhang, 2023). The handaxes from this period are notably sophisticated and include examples similar to those found in Western Acheulean cultures. This suggests a high level of tool-making sophistication during this period in the region. These new dating measurements could become crucial for better understanding the development of handaxes in the East Asian region from handaxes in early sites in China.

6. Chongoknian, Mode 2-A in Clark's system of stone tool evolution

Graham Clark (1977) categorized the technological progression of global stone tool industries into five modes. He referred to the earliest stage of stone tool production, involving simple modifications or unmodified tools, as Mode 1, which corresponds to the Oldowan tradition. The next stage, the Acheulean tradition, was characterized by more advanced bifacial tools, which Clark designated as Mode 2. Unlike the Oldowan tradition, which primarily includes cores, unmodified flakes, and simple large choppers, the Acheulean tradition encompasses handaxes that exhibit both morphological standardization and functional versatility. This distinction highlights a fundamental difference between these two stages of stone tool technology: deliberate planning in stone tool production and the presence of a longitudinal axis of weight and form in the morphology of tools within the Acheulean tradition.

During the development of the Acheulean stone tool tradition, two technological innovations emerged, both of which contributed to refinements in the form of the handaxe. First, around one million years ago, handaxes made from large flakes appeared – a significant advancement. Some scholars refer to this innovation as the "Large Flake Acheulean" (Sharon, 2009, 2010). Such techniques for raw material preparation resulted in Acheulean handaxes with much flatter and more efficient cutting edges compared to earlier forms. Among the handaxes found in the HIRB, including at the Chongokni site, those made from large flake exhibit a higher degree of standardization and cutting efficiency. Moreover, these techniques eventually became essential for the production of cleavers.

During the later stages of the Acheulean period, another significant technological innovation occurred: controlled percussion for refining handaxes. Handaxes crafted using this technique feature a thin cross-section, often resembling a lens shape, and are meticulously worked along their edges, resulting in a symmetrical flat surface on both sides. A great cognitive advancement took place in this stage of stone tool development on the basis of the patterned appearance of symmetrical forms (White and Fould, 2018). This innovation allowed for the creation of handaxes with a more refined and standardized appearance. Indeed, this technique, known as Levallois, in addition to the pre-prepared striking platform method, played a crucial role in shaping the typical forms of handaxes found in regions where this innovation was prevalent. At present, the Levallois technique has not been confirmed in the East Asian region (Lycett, 2007). While there might be isolated instances in the region, there has not been enough evidence to suggest that the technique was widespread nor that it contributed to the shaping of stone tool cultures in the same way as it did in other regions. Certainly, there is a clear correlation between the distribution pattern of the Levallois technique and the standardization of handaxe forms (Clark, 1998; Lycett, 2007). However, the reason why the Levallois technique failed to spread further into East Asia, beyond Mongolia, requires further research in spite of claimes of occaisional or pseudo-levallois findings. The current geographical distribution pattern suggests a clear correlation between the two tool making techniques: prepared flaking and elaborate handaxe production. It is necessary to discuss whether the Levallois technique failed to spread due to certain unkonwn reason of diffusion or difficulties in its application or whether there were specific reasons for its limited adoption in the region. Further studies and discussions are needed to address these questions.

In both African and European regions, handaxes prior to the emergence of the Levallois technique exhibit significantly lower levels of standardization compared to those in later periods. Indeed, even within the Acheulean period, distinct technological stages should be recognized due to these clear differences in the forms and techniques of handaxe production. This finer level of classification is crucial for understanding the evolving nature of stone tool technologies and their implications for human cultural and technological development (Gowlett, 1990). With respect to the chronological aspects of Clark's stone tool manufacturing technology, if we were to refine the classification of Acheulean tools further, categorizing them into two sub-stages, "Mode 2A" and "Mode 2B," would certainly necessary. Using Clark's system of description of technological development in prehistory would provide a better perspective to understanding evolution of regional culture without any emotional bias which may caused by the terminology devised in early stage of western archaeology.

Considering the developmental stages of lithic technology, identifying the early stage of the Acheulean tradition as Mode 2A and the evolved typical form as Mode 2B could be useful for better understanding the evolution

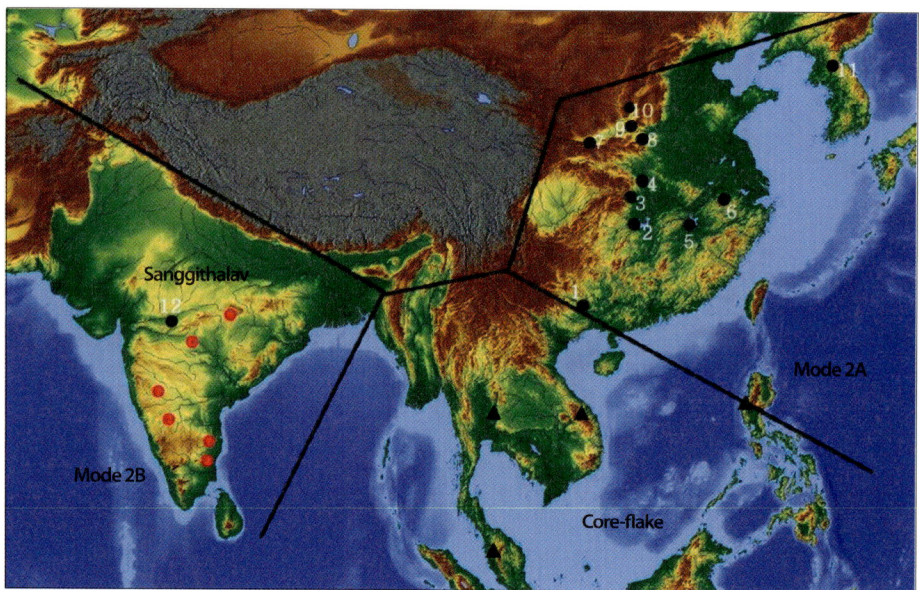

Fig. 12 Handaxe Sites in Asia Mode 2A and Mode 2B

have been one of the popular topics in Paleolithic archaeology of the World. However, debates of Acheulean in East Asia continue in different phrase, for example 'Movius line sensu latto'. Without any paradign shifting in archaeological perspective in approaching cultural diversity in prehistoric times, no resolution from existing debates could be made in near future. Current data of Paleolithic archaeology and Paleoanthropological data in East Asia have been increased radically and raise many critical issues to understand diversity of hominin's behavior.

of lithic cultures (Fig. 12). The production of handaxes at the Chongokni and other sites in the HIRB ultimately falls within the Mode 2A stage, and the variations in forms and compositions observed in each lithic production stage can be understood as manifestations of diverse phenomena within this stage. Descriminating among handaxes in East Asia (e.g., Shipton and Petraglia, 2010)–that is, Acheulean and 'less' Acheulean in case of applying Acheulean-like–may not be relevant in modern Archaeology, because it might appear to be an uni-linear evolutionism of handaxe centered on western terminology in describing regional variations.

In the case of handaxes from East Asia, as indicated by the initial designation of "Large Trihedral" by Chinese archaeologists, it is common to find axes with triangular or isosceles triangular cross-sections for the distal edge. This is also a characteristic pattern of handaxes observed in the HIRB. However, the finely crafted, oval-shaped handaxes observed at sites like Chongokni are not commonly seen in other regions of East Asia. This could be interpreted as a regional developmental process in handaxe production. On the other hand, as mentioned earlier, this regional pattern might also be temporary for the time being and could be changed by reseaches with new perspective to more elaborate ones. In this regard, given the diversity of East Asian Acheulean Mode 2A, the proposed term "Chongoknian" could be highly productive for comprehensively describing handaxe industries in comparison to those in the Western Hemisphere.

Not only few handaxes but rare early Paleolithic have been found in tropical and sub-tropical Southeast Asia in spite of early presence of *Homo erectus*, while number of sites of handaxes is increasing in temperate zone of East Asia, central part of the Chinese mainland and the Korean peninsula. Comparative researches of the morphological and temporal characteristics of handaxe cultures in these regions is a significant task in East Asian Paleolithic archaeology. Doing so could help shed light on the cultural and technological evolution of early human populations in this part of the world and potentially hint at the currently dabating genetic evolution of hominins in East Asia through further researches of cultural movements during the Middle and Upper Pelistocene.

Regional pattern of Mode 2A handaxe industries found in the Korean peninsula could be called "Chongoknian". This new concept of regional variation of handaxe industry may introduce discussion of global pattern of Paleolithic culture with new perspectives of cultural diversity, leaving 'Acheulean' in the meantime.

Morphological and technological variations among handaxe industries in East Asia have also been observed. Based on current observations of early stone tool industries, a multilinear evolutionary approach in conjunction with ecological considerations pertaining to subsistence patterns should be adopted.

7. Conclusive remarks

Numerous handaxe finds in East Asia after first recognition of Acheulean-like handaxe at the Chongokni site in 1978,

References

Bae, K.D., 1988. *The significance of the Chongokni stone industry in the tradition of Paleolithic culture in East Asia.* Ph.D.

Dissertation, Berkeley: University of California.

Bae, K.D., 2021. *Human Evolution and Paleolithic Cultures in Asia*, Hanyang University Press.

Bae, K.D., Mi-young Hong, Han-yong Lee, Young-yeon Kim. 2001. *Chongok Paleolithic Site 2000-2001*. Comprehensive Excavation Report. Yeoncheon County · Cultural Heritage Research Institute, Hanyang University.

Clark, G., 1977. *World Prehistory in New Perspective* 3rd ed., Cambridge University Press.

Clark, J.D., 1998. The Early Paleolithic of the eastern region of the World in comparison to the West. M.D. Petraglia and R. Korisettar eds., Early Human Behavior in Global Context. *One World Archaeology* 28, Routledge, 437-450.

Dennell, R., 2015. Life without the Movius Line: The structure of the East and Southeast Asian Early Palaeolithic. *Quaternary International* 400, 14-22.

Gowlett, J.A.J., 1990. Technology, skill and the psychosocial sector in the long term of human evolution. *Cambridge Archaeological Review* 9, 82-103.

Hou, Ya-Mei. 2014. Palaeolithic sites in China: perspectives on human evolution, significance to the understanding of adaptations and dispersals, and research priorities in the framework of the World Heritage Convention. in Nuria Sanz ed., *Human origin sites and the World Heritage Convention in Asia*, 120-144.

Hou, Y., Potts, R., Baoyin, Y., Zhengtang, G., Deino, A., and Wei, W., 2000. Mid-Pleistocene Acheulean-like stone technology of the Bose Basin, South China. *Science* 287, 1622-6.

Hutterer, K.L., 1977. Reinterpreting the Southeast Asian Paleolithic. In: Allen, J., Golson, J., Jones, R. eds., *Sunda and Sahul*, Orlando: Academic Press, 31-72.

Kim, G., 2017. A Study on the Formation Process and Chronology of Paleolithic Sites in the Imjin-Hantan River Basin. *Korean Journal of Paleolithic Archaeology*, 36, 5-27.

Kim, J., J. Kwon, S. Hong, Y. Choi, H. Lee, T. Lee. 2023. Geochronology and stratigraphy of Quaternary sediments at the Jeongokri archaeological site, South Korea. *Proceeding of the Asian Paleolithic Association the 11th International Symposium*, P. 106.

Kim, W. & Chung, Y.W., 1979. A Preliminary Report on the Bifacial Core Tools from Chongok-ri Assemblages. *The Journal of Diagnostics* 46/47.

Kim, W. ed., 1983. *Chongok-ri*, Cultural Heritage Administration.

Kim, W. & Bae, K. 1983. *Excavation at Chongok-ri*, Seoul National University·Cultural Heritage Administration.

Lebatarda, Anne-Elisabeth, Didier L. Bourlèsa, Samir Khatib, Thibaud Saos, Pierre Rochettea, Régis Brauchera, Kidong Bae. 2018. Preliminary dating of the Mansu-Ri and Wondang-Jangnamgyo Early Paleolithic sites. *C. R. Palevol* 17, 143-151.

Lee, H., Y. Choi, T. Lee and J. Kim. 2023. Stratigraphy and age dating on the Jeongokri Archaeological Site. *Proceeding of the Asian Paleolithic Association the 11th International Symposium*. P 92.

Lee, J., 2010. *A Study on the Production Pattern of Handaxes using 3D Scanning Techniques: Focused on Handaxes from the Imjin-Hantan River Basin*. Master's thesis, Seoul National University Graduate School

Li, H., Li, C.R., Kuman, K., Cheng, J., Yao, H.T., Li, Z., 2014. The Middle Pleistocene handaxe site of Shuangshu in the Danjiangkou Reservoir Region, central China. *Journal of Archaeological Science* 52, 391-409.

Lycett, S.J., 2007. Why is there a lack of Mode 3 Levallois technologies in East Asia? A phylogenetic test of the Movius-Schick hypothesis. *Journal of Anthropological Archaeology* Vol. 26(4), 541-575.

Lycett, Stephen J. & John A. J. Gowlett. 2008. On questions surrounding the Acheulean 'tradition'. *World Archaeology* 40(3), 295-315.

Lycett, C.J. and Norton, C.J., 2010. A demographic model for Palaeolithic technological evolution: The case of East Asia and the Movius Line A demographic model for Palaeolithic technological evolution: The case of East Asia and the Movius Line. *Quaternary International* Vol. 211, 55-65.

Mastufuji, K. 2008. New Progress of the Geology and Radiometric Dating in the Chongok Basin, Korea: Chongokni International Seminar 2006. in K. Mastufuji ed. *Loess Paleosol and Paleolithic Chronology in East Asia*, Yuzankaku, 33-41. (Japanese text, English summary)

Mastufuji, K., K. Bae, T. Danhara, T. Naruse, A. Hayashida, K.M. Yu. N. Inoue, S. Hwang. 2008. New Progree of Studies at the Chongokni Paleolithic Site, Korea: Korea-Japan Cooperative Project in 2001-2004. in K. Mastufuji ed., *Loess Paleosol and Paleolithic Chronology in East Asia*, Yuzankaku, 13-32. (Japanese text, English summary)

Movius, H.L., 1948. The Lower Palaeolithic cultures of southern and eastern Asia. *Transactions of the American Philosophical Society* Vol. 38, 329-420.

Norton, C.J., Bae, K., Harris, J.W.K. and Lee, H., 2006. Middle Pleistocene handaxes from the Korean Peninsula. *Journal of Human Evolution* Vol. 51, 527-536.

Norton, Christopher J. and Kidong Bae. 2008. The Movius Line sensu lato (Norton et al., 2006) further assessed and defined.

Journal of Human Evolution 55, 1148-1150.

Schick, K.D., 1994. The Movius Line reconsidered. R.S. Corruccini and R.L. Ciochon eds., *Integrative Paths to the Past*. Englewood Cliffs, NJ, Prentice Hall, 569-596.

Seo, I.S., 2019. Blade and microblade from the Upper Paleolithic sites in the Middle and Upper reach of the Hantan river basin. In, *People in the Upper reach of the Hantan River from the Chongokni. Newly discovered Paleolithic sites near the DMZ of Gyeonggi Province*. Jeongok Prehistory Museum, 156-195.

Sharon, G., 2009. Acheulean giant-core technology. A worldwide perspective. *Current Anthropology* Vol. 50, 335-367.

Sharon, G., 2010. Large Flake Acheulean. *Quaternary International* Vol. 223, 226-233.

Shipton, C. and M. D. Petraglia. 2010. Inter-continental variation in Acheulean biface, Asian Paleoanthropology: from Africa to China and Beyond. *Vetebrate Paleontology and Paleoanthropology*, Springer.

Wang, S.J., Zhang, X.B., Xing, L.D., Zhang, G.K., Lu, H.Y., Sun, X.F.,

Zhang, W.C. and Liu, T., 2013. *The Acheulean tool assemblage with handaxe and cleaver was found in Luonan*, Shaaxi Province.

Wang, S. and G. Zhang. 2023. The Yeyuan Site in the Luonan Basin in Central China: A Clear Track of Human Occupation Over Million Years. *Proceeding of the Asian Paleolithic Association the 11th International Symposium*, P. 93.

White, M., & Foulds, F., 2018. Symmetry is its own reward: On the character and significance of Acheulean handaxe symmetry in the Middle Pleistocene. *Antiquity* 92(362), 304-319.

Yang, S.X., Wei-Wen Huang, Ya-Mei Hou, Bao-Yin Yuan. 2014. Is the Dingcun lithic assembly a "chopper-chopping tool industry", or "late Acheulean"?. *Quaternary International* 32, 3-11.

Yi, Seonbok and Clark, G.A., 1983. Observations on the Lower Palaeolithic of Northeast Asia. *Current Anthropology* 24, 181-202.

Yi, Seon-Bok. 2011. Handaxes in the Imjin Basin. Yi, S.B. ed., *Handaxes in the Imjin Basin*, SNUPress, 3-21.

Before the Emergence of Acheulean :
New Archaeological Evidence from Jinshuihe River Valley in the Hanzhong Basin, Central China

Jingjing BIE[1,2,3], **Wenting XIA**[4], **Shejiang WANG**[1,2]

[1] Key Laboratory of Vertebrate Evolution and Human Origins of Chinese Academy of Sciences, Institute of Vertebrate Paleontology and Paleoanthropology, China ; bie_jj@163.com
[2] CAS Center for Excellence in Life and Paleoenvironment, China
[3] University of Chinese Academy of Sciences, China
[4] School of History and Administration, Yunnan Normal University, China

ABSTRACT

Recent discoveries have provided evidence of the existence of Acheulean assemblages in East Asia. However, due to the significant chronological gap in the Acheulean industry in the western part of the Old World, as well as its dispersal and transmission route, the progression of East Asian Acheulean remains uncertain. The core-and-flake technology revealed from Jinshuihe River lithic assemblages in the Hanzhong Basin in Central China has shed new light on the technological practices of ancient humans prior to the emergence of the Acheulean in East Asia.

국문초록

최근 동아시아에서 아슐리안 석기군이 존재한다는 증거들이 나오고 있다. 그러나 유라시아 서부인 유럽의 아슐리안 석기공작, 확산과 전파 경로의 편년상의 심각한 격차로 인해 동아시아 아슐리안 공작은 더 발전하지 못하고 불확실한 상태로 남아 있다. 중국 중부 한중분지 남서부의 롱강시 유적 3지점에서 1.2-0.7 Ma 전에 제작된 소형 격지와 격지 도구가 나타나 진수이허강 유역의 석기공작이 한중분지의 전기와 중기 갱신세 몸돌-격지 기술과의 비교가 이루어지고 있다. 그러나 2009년 이후, 여러 구석기 유적에서 이루어진 심도있는 발굴조사와 편년을 종합해본 결과, 한중분지 아슐리안 공작이 약 25만 년 전보다 더 올라가지 않으며, 약 7만 년 간 지속된 것으로 밝혀졌다. 진수이허강 유역 석기군에서 밝혀진 몸돌-격지 기술은 동아시아에 아슐리안 공작이 출현하기 전 구석기 인류의 석기 기술체계를 밝히는 데 새로운 길을 열어주고 있다.

Keywords : Core-and-flake technology, Acheulean, Hanzhong Basin, Middle Pleistocene, Central China

1. Introduction

For many years, the Acheulean techno-complex has been a focus of Paleolithic research due to its production of bifacially retouched large cutting tools (LCTs), which represent an important component of technological advancement in human history (Leakey, 1971; Sharon, 2009; Corbey et al., 2016; de la Torre, 2016; Pargeter et al., 2019). Within the last two decades, various Acheulean assemblages have been identified in China, providing solid evidence for the existence of the Acheulean industry in East Asia (Hou et al., 2000; Wang, 2005; Li et al., 2014; Wang et al., 2014; Yang et al., 2016; He et al., 2022). However, the existence of a significant chronological gap between the duration of the Acheulean industry in the West and East raises more questions, such as the diffusion of early hominin technology, cultural exchange pathways across various regions, and the migration and adaption of hominin (Lepre et al., 2011; Bae et al., 2012; Beyene et al., 2013; Wang et al., 2014; Wang and Lu, 2016; Deino et al., 2018; Yoo and Lee, 2022). Therefore, understanding the developmental trajectory of the East Asian Acheulean culture is crucial. The upper reach of the Hanjiang River, located south of the Qinling Mountains, is a vital region for paleoanthropological and Paleolithic studies. In this region has been unearthed *Homo erectus* craniums, modern human teeth, and diversified lithic assemblages, including Acheulean-type tools and other Paleolithic remains dated to the Early/Middle/Late Pleistocene (Li and Etler, 1992; Chen et al., 1997; Sun et al., 2012; Kuman et al., 2014; Wang and Lu, 2014; Wang et al., 2014, Pei et al., 2015; Li et al., 2016; Sun et al., 2017; Xia et al., 2018). These discoveries offer essential references for answering the aforementioned questions.

The Jinshui River is located on the north side of the Hanjiang River in Yangxian County, east of the Hanzhong Basin. In the 1980s, Paleolithic artifacts and animal fossils indicative of human activities during the Middle Pleistocene were discovered along the river (Tang et al., 1987). However, as all of the remains were collected from the surface, the lack of stratigraphic context hindered further investigation into the technological and adaptive behaviors of ancient humans. To address this issue, a series of systematic archaeological excavations were conducted along the Jinshuihe River from 2014 to 2021, which provided new evidence for understanding lithic technology predating Acheulean cultures (Bie et al., 2019, 2023). This paper presents the most recent study of archaeological finds in the Jinshuihe River Valley.

2. Materials and methods

From 2014 to 2015, our team, in collaboration with the national key construction project "Hanjiang River to Weihe River Water Diversion Project," carried out systematic excavations at three Paleolithic sites along the Jinshuihe River: the Jinshuihekou and Lyudouliang sites on the fourth terrace, and the Jinlingsi site on the third terrace (Fig. 1). As archaeological analysis of Jinlingsi is still ongoing, the results of this analysis will be published at a later time.

The Jinshuihekou site (N33°15′56.2″, E107°51′50.6″) is located

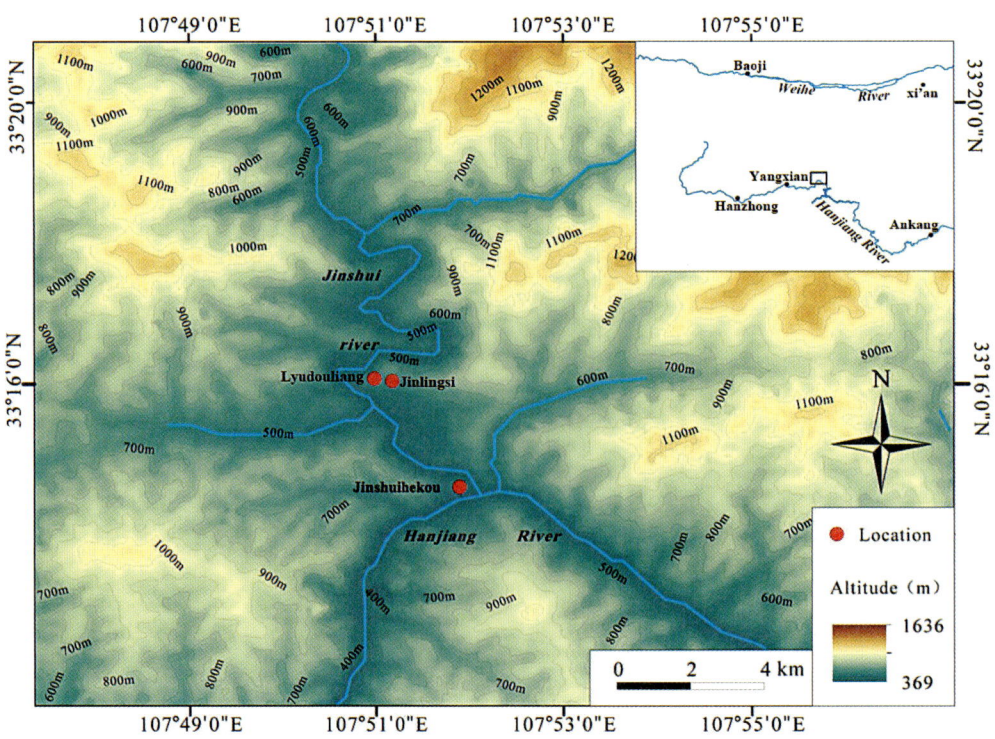

Fig. 1 Location of the Paleolithic sites in Jinshuihe River valley

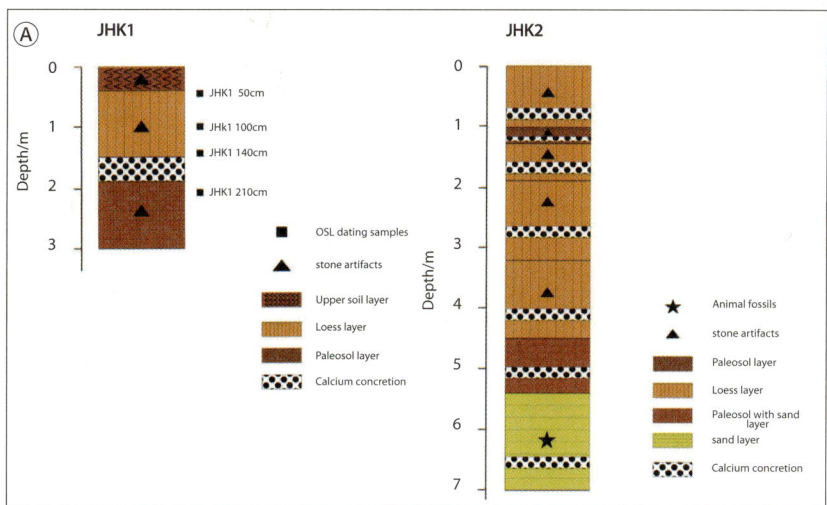

Fig. 2 Ⓐ Pedostratigraphy of the Jinshuihekou site (from Bie et., 2019), Ⓑ Stratigraphic section of the Lyudouliang site (from Bie et., 2023)

in Yangxian County. The site was excavated in two locations, with an exposed area of 236m² and 134m². The stratigraphic sections of the two excavated areas have been labeled JHK1 and JHK2. Four units were identified at JHK1, while seven units were identified at JHK2 (**Fig. 2**Ⓐ). Based on the correlation of the calcium concretion layers at the two sites, the JHK1 section is located above that of JHK2, with the calcium concretion layer resting at the bottom of JHK1 and the top of JHK2.

The Lyudouliang site (33°16′48.3″N, 107°51′6.5″E), to the north of the town of Jinshui, is situated on a slope that gradually increases in height from south to north. The excavation at the Lyudouliang site occurred on the southern side of the G5 Expressway (Beijing-Kunming), covering six grids with a total area of 126m². A total of 1210 lithic artifacts were discovered in the excavation area. Another 30 lithics collected in the vicinity of the site were not included in the study. The site comprises 10 stratigraphic units (**Fig. 2**Ⓑ), with units 1–6 located in the T4 profile and units 7–10 located in the T1 profile.

Comprehensive chronological studies conducted at the three sites revealed that the layer containing stone tools at Jinshuihekou dates back to earlier than 150 ka. Although no date was obtained from the Lyudouliang site, the layers above the Jinlingsi site on the third river terrace were estimated to date to earlier than 100 ka. Therefore, it can be inferred that the Paleolithic occupation of the Jinshuihe River Valley occurred at least during the Middle Pleistocene.

3. Results

3.1. The Lithic assemblage at Jinshuihekou site

The excavation of the Jinshuihekou site produced a total of 1210 lithic artifacts, including cores (n=67), flakes (n=327), retouched tools (n=590), hammers (n=6), chunks (n=590), debris (n=60), and manuports (n=38) (**Fig. 3**). Most of these artifacts were originally fashioned from cobbles and still retain a distinct cortex on their surfaces. The majority were made from quartzite (n=533, 44.04%) or quartz (n=487, 40.25%), followed by siliceous limestone (n=176, 14.55%). Quartzite and quartz are readily found in the Hanzhong Basin, and their high frequency of use in the lithic assemblage suggests no specific selection for high-quality materials for lithic production.

At the Jinshuihekou site 67 cores were found, accounting for 5.54% of the total lithic assemblage. The primary flaking

Fig. 3 The lithic artifacts from Jinshuihekou site : 1 : core, 2 : flake, 3 : light-duty scraper, 4 : awl, 5 : notch, 6 : pick, 7 : chopper, 8 : heavy-duty scraper (from Bie et al., 2019)

technique utilized at the site was hard hammer percussion. Based on an analysis of the striking platform, the cores were categorized as single-platform (n=32), double-platform (n=27), and multi-platform (n=8). single-platform cores had unidirectional and unifacial flaking patterns, while multidirectional patterns were observed on the remaining cores. Most cores had one reduction face (n=33) and three or fewer removals, indicating low utilization efficiency. The size of the cores varied considerably, with lengths ranging from 20.64mm to 243.87mm and mean dimensions of 66.76mm in length, 71.38mm in width, and 51.22mm in thickness.

A total of 327 flakes were recovered from the site, comprising 205 complete flakes and 122 broken flakes. The complete flakes were further categorized into six groups based on the characteristics of the butt and dorsal patterns (Toth, 1985). These groups included type III (n=69), type II (n=48), type VI (n=44), type V (n=29), type I (n=11), and type IV (n=4). The majority of the flake assemblage consisted of small-sized flakes, accounting for 75.61% of the total assemblage, while the rest were medium-sized flakes. On average, the flakes had a length of 40.78mm, a width of 36.6mm, and a thickness of 14.89mm.

The typological analysis identified a total of 122 retouched tools from the site, which consisted of 100 scrapers, 17 choppers, two awls, two notches, and one pick. Of the 100 scrapers, 92 were light-duty scrapers with small sizes, while eight were classified as heavy-duty scrapers with lengths exceeding 100mm. Most of the scrapers have a single edge with unifacial retouching. The choppers are large in size, with an average length of 115.63mm, an average width of 114.09mm, and an average thickness of 90.89mm. The awls were made from small quartz flakes, and the notches have concave edges produced by unifacial retouching. The pick was modified from a large cobble by flaking along two sides, forming an endpoint with a triangular cross-section.

3.2. The lithic assemblage at the Lyudouliang site

A total of 656 lithic artifacts were discovered at the Lyudouliang site, consisting of 626 artifacts excavated from T1–T6 and an additional 30 artifacts found nearby (**Fig. 4**). This discussion focuses on the lithics retrieved from the stratigraphic layers. The majority of the artifacts (53.96%) were made from quartz, with quartzite accounting for 39.63% of the total. Siliceous limestone and quartzite sandstone were infrequently used.

The assemblage includes 10 cores, comprising three single-platform cores, four double-platform cores, and two multi-platform cores. All of these cores were produced using direct hammer percussion. The majority of the cores were exploited from one or two faces and had fewer than four removals (n=8), indicating low core reduction intensity. The size of the cores varies widely, ranging from 28.82mm to 101.31mm in length, with mean dimensions of 60.48mm in length, 77.01mm in width, and 62.8mm in thickness.

The flake assemblage at the Lyudouliang site is composed of 57 complete flakes and 51 broken flakes. Complete flakes include type VI (n=27), type III (n=12), type I (n=6), type II (n=6), type V (n=5), and type IV (n=1). Most of the flakes are small, with mean dimensions of 41.55mm in length, 37.02mm in width, and 17.75mm in thickness.

A total of 21 retouched tools were found at the site, including 17 scrapers, two choppers, one awl, and one point. The scrapers were made from flakes, with 13 serving as light-duty scrapers and four as heavy-duty scrapers. Choppers were modified from cobbles via unifacial retouching. A quartzite flake with two retouched edges that converge and

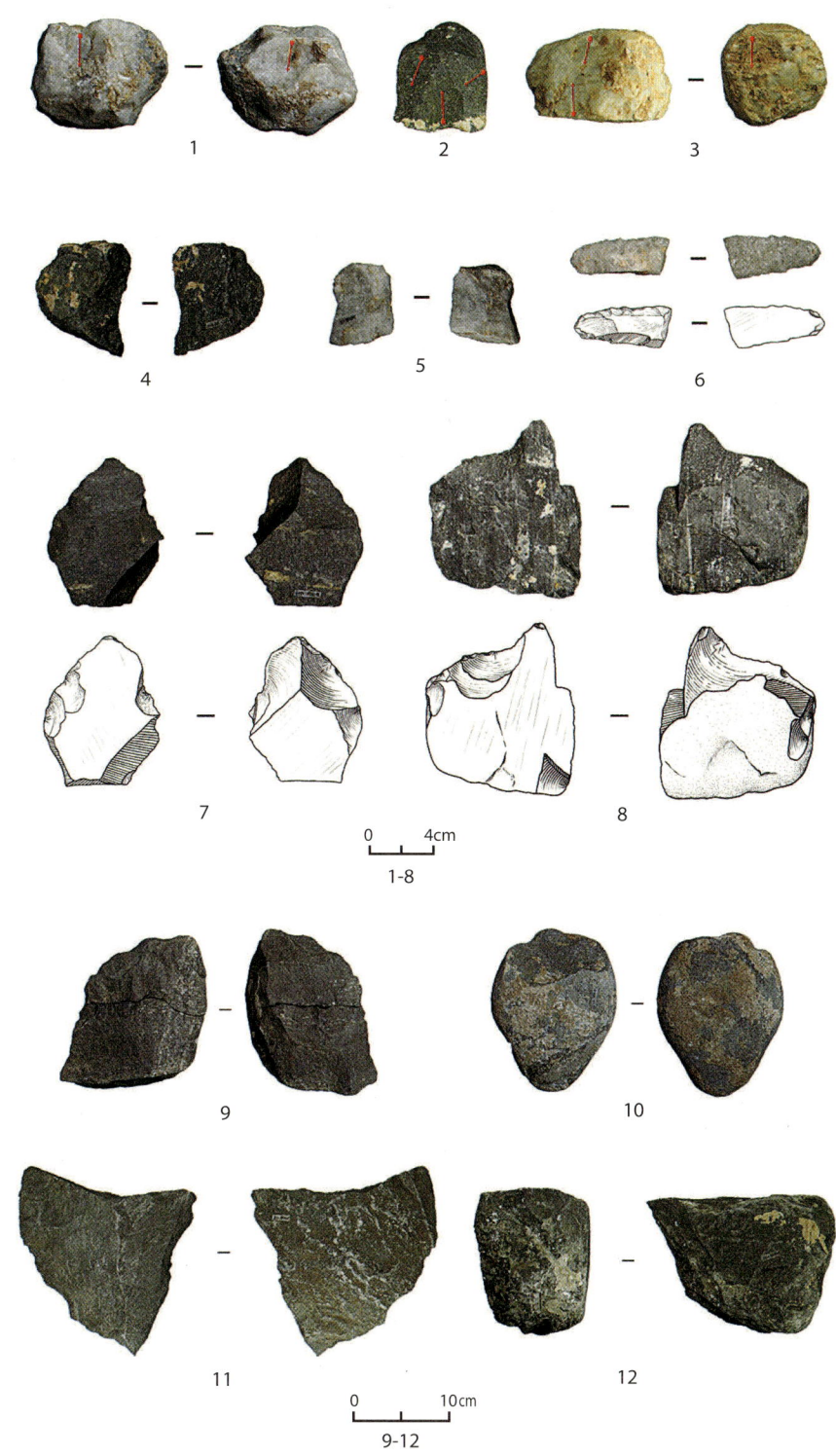

Fig. 4 Lithic artifacts from Lyudouliang site :
1-3 : cores, 4-5 : flakes, 6 : scraper, 7 : point, 8 : awl,
9·11 : heavy-duty scraper, 10·12 : chopper (From
Bie et al., 2023)

meet at one extremity was identified as the point. The awl was manufactured by knapping an elongated point on the right side with alternating removals.

4. Discussion and Conclusion

The lithic assemblages found at the Jinshuihekou and Lyudouliang sites provide evidence for Middle Pleistocene lithic technology in the eastern Hanzhong Basin predating 100 ka. Analysis of the core and flake products indicated an absence of the prepared-core technique in flake knapping. The assemblages were characterized by large flake tools or small flake tools with limited pebbles. A pebble pick identified at the site is similar to those found in the Pebble-Tool Industry of Southern China and is distinct from the typical trihedral picks found in the Acheulean assemblage. The lithic industry of the Jinshuihe River valley is comparable to the core-and-flake technology system that evolved from the Early–Middle Pleistocene in the Hanzhong Basin, as evidenced by Locality 3 of the Longgangsi site, located along the southwestern edge of the basin and dating to 1.2 to 0.7 Ma, which yielded thousands of small flakes and flake tools (Xia et al., 2018). However, differences were observed in the selection of raw materials and the size and composition of the tools. It appears that tool size increased alongside composition, becoming more diverse in the Late–Middle Pleistocene.

Since 2009, integrated chronological studies of several Paleolithic sites (identified through comprehensive surveys) have determined that the Acheulean industry in the Hanzhong Basin existed no earlier than 250,000 years ago and persisted until around 70,000 years ago (Sun et al., 2012; Wang et al., 2014; Sun et al., 2017; Sun et al., 2018). The discovery of sites at Dingcun (Yang et al., 2014; Yang et al., 2016), the Baise Basin (Hou et al., 2000; Wang et al., 2014), the Luonan Basin (Wang, 2005; Xing et al., 2015; Yu et al., 2017), the Danjiangkou Reservoir area (Kuman et al., 2014; Li et al., 2014), and the southwestern edge of the Qinghai-Tibet Plateau (He et al., 2022) has confirmed not only the existence of the Acheulean industry in East Asia but also a significant temporal gap between the Acheulean industry in East Asia and in the West. Excavations at the southwestern edge of the Qinghai-Tibet Plateau also indicate a cultural development sequence from core-and-flake stone technology to the Acheulean techno-complex (He et al., 2022), similar to the sequence observed at the Hanzhong Basin. Discoveries at the Jinshui River Valley suggest that before the emergence of the Acheulean industry in the Hanzhong Basin, core-and-flake technology was prevalent. However, further research is required to determine whether the Acheulean industry in East Asia was caused by population migration or cultural convergence

References

Bae, K., Bae C.J., Kim, K., 2012. The age of the Paleolithic handaxes from the Imjin–Hantan river basins, South Korea. *Quaternary International* 281, 14-25. https://doi.org/10.1016/j.quaint.2012.06.021

Beyene, Y., Katoh, S., WoldeGabriel, G., Hart, W. K., Uto K., Sudo, M., Kondo M., Hyodo M., Renne, P. R., Suwa, G., 2013. The characteristics and chronology of the earliest Acheulean at Konso, Ethiopia. *Proceedings of the National Academy of Sciences* 110(5), 1584-1591. https://doi.org/10.1073/pnas.1221285110

Bie, J.J., Wang, S.J., X.N., Lu, H.Y., Wang, X.Y., Yi, S.W., Xia, W.T., Zhang, G.K., Fox, M.L., Zhang, H.Y., Zhuo, H.X., Zhang, W.C., 2019. Lithic artifacts excavated from the Jinshuihekou site in the Hanzhong Basin, Shaanxi Province, China. *Acta Anthropologica Sinica* 38(3), 344-361. https://doi.org/10.16359/j.cnki.cn11-1963/q.2019.0040

Bie, J.J., X. N., Wang, S.J., Yi, S.W., Lu, H.Y., Xia, W.T., Zhang, G.K., Li, J.M., 2023. Paleolithic artifacts excavated from the Lyudouliang site at Yangxian County, Shaanxi Province. *Acta Anthropologica Sinica* 42(1), 15-24. https://doi.org/10.16359/j.1000-3193/AAS.2022.0059

Chen, T.M., Yang, Q., Hu, Y.Q., Bao, W.B., and Li, T.Y., 1997. ESR dating of tooth enamel from Yunxian *Homo erectus* site, China. *Quaternary Science Reviews* 16(3-5), 455-458. https://doi.org/10.1016/S0277-3791(96)00095-9

Corbey, R., Jagich, A., Vaesen, K., Collard M., 2016. The acheulean handaxe: More like a bird's song than a beatles' tune?. *Evolutionary Anthropology: Issues, News, and Reviews* 25(1), 6-19. https://doi.org/10.1002/evan.21467

De la Torre, I., 2016. The origins of the Acheulean: past and present perspectives on a major transition in human evolution. Philosophical Transactions of the Royal Society B: *Biological Sciences* 371(1698), 20150245. https://doi.org/10.1098/rstb.2015.0245

Deino, A.L., Behrensmeyer, A.K., Brooks, A.S., Yellen, J.E., Sharp, W.D., Potts R., 2018. Chronology of the Acheulean to Middle Stone Age transition in eastern Africa. *Science* 360(6384), 95-98. https://doi.org/10.1126/science.aao2216

He, J.N, Zheng, Z.X., Feng, Y., Tan, P.Y., Wang, Y.P., 2022. A preliminary report of the Piluo Paleolithic site in Daocheng county, Sichuan. *Archaeology* 7, 3-14. https://doi.org/10.1515/char-2023-0001.

Kuman, K., Li, C.R., and Li, H., 2014. Large cutting tools in the Danjiangkou Reservoir Region, central China. *Journal of Human Evolution* 76, 129-153. https://doi.org/10.1016/j.jhevol.2014.08.002.

Leakey, M.D., 1971. *Olduvai Gorge: Vol. 3, excavations in beds I and II, 1960-1963*, Cambridge University Press.

Lepre, C.J., Roche, H., Kent, D.V., Harmand, S., Quinn, R.L., Brugal, J.P., Texier, P.J., Lenoble, A., Feibel, C.S., 2011. An earlier origin for the Acheulian. *Nature* 477(7362), 82-85. https://doi.org/10.1038/nature10372

Li, H., Li, C.R. and Kuman, K., 2014. Rethinking the "Acheulean" in East Asia: evidence from recent investigations in the Danjiangkou Reservoir Region, central China. *Quaternary*

International 347, 163-175. https://doi.org/10.1016/j.quaint.2014.03.059.

Li, H., Li, C.R., Kuman, K., Cheng, J., Yao H.T., and Li, Z., 2014. The Middle Pleistocene handaxe site of Shuangshu in the Danjiangkou Reservoir Region, central China. *Journal of Archaeological Science* 52, 391-409. https://doi.org/10.1016/j.jas.2014.08.033

Li, Y.H., Zhou Y.D., Sun X.F., Li, H., 2016. New evidence of a lithic assemblage containing in situ Late Pleistocene bifaces from the Houfang site in the Hanshui River Valley, Central China. *Comptes rendus - Palevol* : S1631068316300331. https://doi.org/10.1016/J.CRPV.2015.12.005.

Pargeter, J., Khreisheh, N., Stout, D., 2019. Understanding stone tool-making skill acquisition: Experimental methods and evolutionary implications. *Journal of Human Evolution* 133, 146-166. https://doi.org/10.1016/j.jhevol.2019.05.010.

Pei, S.W., Niu, D.W., Guan, Y., Nian, X.M., Yi, M.J., Ma, N., Li, X.L., Sahnouni, M., 2015. Middle Pleistocene hominin occupation in the Danjiangkou Reservoir Region, Central China: studies of formation processes and stone technology of Maling 2A site. *Journal of Archaeological Science* 53, 391-407. https://doi.org/10.1016/j.jas.2014.10.022.

Sharon, G., 2009. Acheulian giant-core technology: a worldwide perspective. *Current Anthropology* 50(3), 335-367. https://doi.org/10.1086/598849.

Wang, S.J. and Lu, H.Y., 2014. Current perspectives on Paleolithic archaeology in the upper Hanjiang River valley, central China. *Acta Anthropologica Sinica* 33(03), 315. https://doi.org/10.3969/j.issn.1000-3193.2014.03.001.

Wang, S.J, Sun, X.F, Lu, H.Y, Yi, S.W., Zhang, G.K., Xing, L.D., Zhuo, H.X., Yu, K.F., Wang, W., 2014. Newly discovered Paleolithic open-air sites in Hanzhong Basin in upper valley of Hanjiang River and their ages. *Acta Anthropologica Sinica* 33(02), 125. https://doi.org/10.16359/j.cnki.cn11-1963/q.2014.02.006

Sun, X.F., Lu, H.Y., Wang, S.J., Xu, X.H., Zeng, Q.X., Lu, X.H., Lu, C.Q., Zhang, W.C., Zhang, X.J., Dennell, R., 2018. Hominin distribution in glacial-interglacial environmental changes in the Qinling Mountains range, central China. *Quaternary Science Reviews* 198, 37-55. https://doi.org/10.1016/j.quascirev.2018.08.012.

Sun, X.F, Lu, H.Y., Wang, S.J., Yi, L., Li, Y.X., Bahain, J.J., Voinchet, P., Hu, X.Z., Zeng, L., Zhang, W.C., Zhuo, H.X., 2017. Early human settlements in the southern Qinling Mountains, central China. *Quaternary Science Reviews* 164, 168-186. https://doi.org/10.1016/j.quascirev.2017.04.005

Sun, X.F., Lu, H.Y., Wang, S.J., Yi, S.W., 2012. Ages of Liangshan Paleolithic sites in Hanzhong basin, central China. *Quaternary Geochronology* 10, 380-386. https://doi.org/10.1016/j.quageo.2012.04.014

Tang, Y.J., Zong, G.F., Lei Y.L., 1987. A New Discovery of Paleolithic artifacts in the upper reaches of the Hanjiang River. *Acta Anthropologica Sinica* 6(1), 55-60. https://doi.org/10.16359/j.cnki.cn11-1963/q.1987.01.007

Li, T.Y. and Etler, D. A., 1992. New Middle Pleistocene hominid crania from Yunxian in China. *Nature* 357(6377), 404. https://doi.org/10.1038/357404a0

Toth, N., 1985. The Oldowan reassessed: a close look at early stone artifacts. *Journal of Archaeological Science* 12(2), 101-120. https://doi.org/10.1016/0305-4403(85)90056-1.

Wang, S.J., 2005. *Perspectives on hominid behaviour and settlement patterns: a story of the Lower Palaeolithic sites in the Luonan Basin, China*. Oxford: Archaopress. https://doi.org/10.30861/9781841718491.

Wang, S.J., and Lu H.Y., 2016. Taphonomic and paleoenvironmental issues of the Pleistocene loessic Paleolithic sites in the Qinling Mountains, central China. *Science China (Earth Sciences)* 59(8), 1519-1528. https://doi.org/10.1007/s11430-016-5298-4

Wang, S.J., Lu, H.Y., Xing, L.D., 2014. Chronological and typo-technological perspectives on the Palaeolithic archaeology in Lantian, central China. *Quaternary International* 347(9), 183-192. https://doi.org/10.1016/j.quaint.2014.07.014.

Wang, W., Bae, C. J., Huang, S.M., Huang, X., Tian, F., Mo, J.Y., Huang, Z.T., Huang, C.L., Xie, S.W., Li, D.W., 2014. Middle Pleistocene bifaces from Fengshudao (Bose Basin, Guangxi, China). *Journal of Human Evolution* 69, 110-122. https://doi.org/10.1016/j.jhevol.2013.11.002

Xia, W.T., Wang, S.J., Xia, N., Lu, H.Y., Wang, X.Y., Sun, X.F., Zhang, H.Y., Zhang, W.C., Zhuo, H.X., Xing, L.D., 2018. Lithic artifacts excavated from locality 3 of the Longgangsi site in Hanzhong Basin, Shaanxi province. *Acta Anthropologica Sinica* 37, 529-541. https://doi.org/10.16359/j.cnki.cn11-1963/q.2017.0078

Xing, L.D., Wang, S.J., Zhang, G.K., Yu, Q.Y., Zhang, X.B., Tuo, L., 2015. Newly discovered paleolithic artifacts from the Yeyuan open-air site in the Luonan basin, Central China. *Acta Anthropologica Sinica* 34(01), 1. https://doi.org/10.16359/j.cnki.cn11-1963/q.2015.0001

Hou Y.M., Potts, R., Yuan, B.Y., Guo Z.T., Deino A., Wei, W., Clark, J., Xie. G.M., Huang, W.W., 2000. Mid-Pleistocene Acheulean-like stone technology of the Bose basin, South China. *Science* 287(5458), 1622-1626. https://doi.org/10.1126/science.287.5458.1622

Yang, S.X., Hou Y.M., Pelegrin, J., 2016. A Late Acheulean Culture on the Chinese Loess Plateau: The techno-economic behavior of the Dingcun lithic industry. *Quaternary International* 400, 73-85. https://doi.org/10.1016/j.quaint.2015.10.043

Yang, S.X., Huang, W.W., Hou, Y.M., Yuan, B.Y., 2014. Is the Dingcun lithic assembly a "chopper-chopping tool industry", or "Late Acheulian"?. *Quaternary International* 321, 3-11. https://doi.org/10.1016/j.quaint.2013.05.012

Yoo, Y., and Lee, J., 2022. Late Pleistocene handaxes from the Korean Peninsula: New discoveries from the Unjeong District Site Complex (UDSC). *Archaeological Research in Asia* 30, 100354. https://doi.org/10.1016/j.ara.2022.100354

Yu, Q.Y., Wang, S.J., Shen C., Lu, H.Y., Cosgrove, R., Zhang, X.B., Zhang, H.Y., Zhang, W.C., Wei, M., Wang, X.Y., Liu, Q.Y., Sun, X.F., Xing, L.D., Xia, W.T., 2017. A preliminary report on the 2013 excavation of the Huaishuping Paleolithic site in Luonan Basin, Shaanxi Province. *Acta Anthropologica Sinica* 36(2), 154-164. https://doi.org/10.16359/j.cnki.cn11-1963/q.2017.0035

A comparative study of Bose and An Khe industries

Guangmao XIE [1,2], **Qiang LIN** [2], **Yan WU** [3]

[1] Professor, School of History and Cultural Heritage, Xiamen University, China ; gmxie92@sina.com
[2] Guangxi Institute of Cultural Relic Protection and Archaeology, China
[3] China Three Gorges Museum, China

ABSTRACT

The Palaeolithic industry in the Bose Basin, Guangxi, South China, is well known in the international scientific community for its Early-Middle Pleistocene handaxes. Recently, a bifacial industry was discovered in An Khe, in the Central Highlands of Vietnam, which was dated to 806 ka BP. The Bose and An Khe bifacial industries are important to the study of Lower Palaeolithic cultures in East and Southeast Asia. This paper presents a comparison of these two industries and discusses some related issues.

국문초록

남중국 광시 좡족(Guangxi Zhuang) 자치구 보세 분지의 보세 구석기유적 제4 단구층에서 출토된 중기 플라이스토세 이른시기까지 올라가는 양면떼기 주먹도끼의 석기공작이 국제 과학계에 잘 알려져 있다. 또한 최근 몇 년 동안 남베트남 기아 라이(Gia Lai) 지역 바강(Ba river) 분지 안케(An Khe) 유적에서도 전기구석기(약 806ka BP)로 거슬러 올라가는 양면떼기 공작이 발견되었다. 위의 보세와 안케 양면떼기 공작은 동아시아와 동남아시아의 전기구석기 문화를 연구하는 데 중요하다. 보세 유적은 역층, 사질층, 양토층으로 이루어진 하성퇴적층으로 구성되며, 이에 비해 안케 유적은 선상지성 퇴적층과 하성 퇴적층으로 구성되는데, 이 두 유적에 공통된 석기공작으로 찍개류, 주먹찌르개, 주먹도끼, 긁개, 찌르개를 들 수 있다. 남중국과 동남아시아의 양면떼기 석기공작은 유사성을 보이며, 유럽에서 약 650~600ka BP에 출현한 아슐리안 복합체(Acheulean Complex)에 대비된다. 이러한 지역적 석기공작의 유사성은 고인류의 환경적응이 문화의 진화와 발달을 가져온다는 가설의 연구사례이다.

Keywords : bifacial industry, cultural comparison, Lower Paleolithic, Southern China, Southeast Asia

1. Introduction

Handaxes, the most typical tool in the Acheulean industrial complex, have been discovered throughout East and Southeast Asia. In China, handaxes have been reported from the Bose (Baise) Basin in Guangxi (Huang, 1987, 1993; Hou et al., 2000; Xie, 2002; Xie et al., 2003; Xie and Bodin, 2007; Xie and Lin, 2008; Wang et al., 2008, 2014; Zhang et al., 2010), the Lishui area in Hunan (Huang, 1987, 1993; Wang, 1997), the Danjiangkou Reservoir Region (DRR) in Hubei (Li et al., 2009, 2012, 2013, 2014a, 2014b, 2017), Dadong Cave in Guizhou (Huang et al., 2012), the Luonan and Hanzhong Basins in Shaanxi (Huang and Qi, 1987; Wang et al., 2005; Lu et al., 2006; Wang, 2005, 2010, 2014; Xing et al., 2015), Dingcun in Shanxi (Huang, 1987), the Shuiyangjiang area in Anhui (Dong, 2020), and the Nanjiang Basin in Guangdong (Liu, 2015, 2017). Handaxes have also been recovered from many Paleolithic sites in Korea, especially in the Hantan–Imjin River Basin (HIRB) (Norton, 2000; Norton et al., 2006; de Lumley et al., 2011). In Southeast Asia, an increasing number of handaxe-yielding sites have been reported since the first discovery of the Pacitanian site in Indonesia (Movius, 1948). These include various Indonesian sites (Simanjuntak et al., 2010), Bukit Bunuh in Malaysia (Saidin, 2006), and Arubo in Luzon, Philippines (Pawlik, 2002). In Vietnam, handaxes were found not only at Nui Do, Thanh Hoah Province (Ciochon and Olsen, 1986; Olsen et al., 1990) but also, in recent years, at An Khe, Gia Lai Province, north of southern Vietnam, which may be the most important Palaeolithic discovery in Southeast Asia this century (Nguyễn et al., 2015; Nguyễn, 2017; Derevianko et al., 2016, 2018).

Comparative studies of the bifacial industries east and west of the Movius Line have been conducted by many scholars (Schick, 1994; Hou et al., 2000; Leng and Shannon, 2000; Norton, 2000; Keates, 2002; Corvinus, 2004; Wang, 2005; Norton et al., 2006; Lycett, 2007; Lycett and Gowlett, 2008; Wang et al., 2008, 2012; Norton and Bae, 2009; Petraglia and Shipton, 2009; Brumm, 2010; Lycett and Bae, 2010; Lycett and Norton, 2010; Norton and Lycett, 2010; Shipton and Petraglia, 2010; Bar-Yosef et al., 2012; Dennell, 2016). There are two points of view on the origin of bifacial tools found in East and Southeast Asia. The first is that they resulted from cultural exchange between west and east, with the bifacial industry in the east originating in the Acheulean complex (Huang, 1993; Wang, 2005; Kuman et al., 2014; Li et al., 2014a, 2014b; Dennell, 2016). The other view is that eastern bifacial tools developed independently: a phenomenon of cultural convergence (Lycett et al., 2008, 2010a, 2010b; Norton et al., 2009, 2010; Gao, 2012). However, no attempt has yet been made to undertake a comparative study of the bifacial industries in East and Southeast Asia. Consequently, the relationship among these industries remains unclear.

The Middle Pleistocene Bose industry is the best-known bifacial industry in eastern Asia, whereas the An Khe industry is considered one of the most important bifacial industries in Southeast Asia. In this paper, we present a comparative study of the Bose and An Khe industries and discuss some related issues.

2. Bose industry

The Bose (Baise) Paleolithic sites are located in the Bose Basin in the western part of the Guangxi Zhuang Autonomous Region, Southern China (23°33′–24°18′ N, 106°7′–106°56′ E). Since the first site was discovered in 1973, more than 110 additional sites associated with the Bose Palaeolithic industry have been identified, 20 of which have been excavated. These excavations have led to the recovery of over 20,000 stone artifacts. Based on the dating of tektites found in situ in association with handaxes and other stone artifacts, the Bose Palaeolithic industry has been dated to 803 ka (Li et al., 1975; Qin et al., 1983; Zeng, 1983; Huang et al., 1990, 2012; Hou et al., 2000; Xie et al., 2003, 2008, 2010; Xie and Bodin, 2007; Pei et al., 2007; Zhang et al., 2010; Wang et al., 2014).

2.1. Geological background

The Bose Basin, covering 800km², is surrounded by low-elevation mountains ranging from 500 to 1,500m above sea level. The basin is bisected by the Youjiang River, flowing from northwest to southeast. The basin features seven river terraces dating to the late Pliocene and Pleistocene, which are associated with the uplift of the Qinghai-Tibetan Plateau (Yuan et al., 1999). Terrace 1 (T1) is the most extensive and stable stratum. The upper part of T1 contains Neolithic artifacts, such as those found at Gexinqiao (Xie et al., 2003), suggesting that the age of T1 should be terminal Pleistocene and/or Early Holocene. The second and third terraces (T2 and T3) are also exposed across the basin, but not as extensively as either T1 or T4. Paleolithic deposits have been identified in both T2 and T3 (Xie, 2015). T4 is the best known due to the presence of handaxes within the tektite-bearing deposits. This terrace comprises an upper sedimentary unit 7–10m thick with poorly developed latosols underlain by reticular mottled red clay, typical of laterites, and a lower unit 5–20m thick with a well-sorted cobble conglomerate. Three additional platforms have been identified on the higher elevations of the surrounding hills. These consist of gravel beds that unconformably overlie the Eocene beds and dispersed pebbles and fragments of iron pan and tubercular iron-manganese. These platforms, which constitute the earliest terraces in the Bose Basin (Yuan et al., 1999; Huang et al., 2012; Xu et al., 2012), may have developed at the end of the Pliocene.

2.2. Stone artifacts

Stone artifacts from the Bose Basin include cores, flakes,

Fig. 1 Stone tools from Bose :
1 : Scraper, 2 : Chopper, 3·5·6·9 : Handaxes, 4·8 : Picks, 7 : Unifacial handaxe (uniface)

choppers and chopping tools, handaxes, picks, scrapers, cleavers, hammers and chunks. Raw materials used for tool making are cobbles composed mainly of quartzite and sandstone, which were derived from the Youjiang River Valley. Most of the tools were manufactured from cobbles, the shapes of which were selected in order to simplify the manufacture of the desired final forms. As a result, many tools found at the site are only partially worked, as demonstrated by their large cortical areas. Direct hammer stone percussion and the direct anvil technique (block-on-block) were used in the production of the tools. Apart from handaxes, the tools are mostly unifacially flaked and retouched (Fig. 1).

Raw materials Raw materials used for tool making are almost always quartzite or sandstone cobbles, which occur abundantly in the basal conglomerates of T5 through T7 in the Youjiang River Valley, followed by quartz, silicified rock, chert, and, rarely, basalt. In most cases, the materials are not of good quality, as there are many faults in the rock, especially quartz, or the cobbles had been weathered long before they were employed for tool making. These factors played an important role in determining the technology applied to the tools. Selectivity has been observed in terms of the choice of raw materials, which vary based on the type of tool.

Flakes and cores In contrast with the other tool types, flakes are rare. Some flakes might be the byproducts of tool making, as many are amorphous. Most are 3-5cm in length. Large, even massive, flakes (over 20cm) have also been retrieved. These discoveries, alongside the absence of percussion bulbs, indicate the use of the anvil technique. None of the flakes show marks of platform preparation, and their cortices remain relatively intact on their backs, especially the large flakes. The dorsal surfaces of most of the flakes, especially the small ones, have flake scars, which were usually struck from the same direction as the flake itself. The edges of most of the large flakes show definite signs of use wear. Retouched flakes are rare.

Cores are also rare. Those that have been found are usually large in size – some are enormous. The most common cores have one or two platforms. The cores appear to have been infrequently used, and, like the tools, have a relatively intact pebble cortex on the surface.

Fig. 2 Stone tools from An Khe :
1 : Scraper, 2·3 : Choppers, 4–6·9 : Handaxes, 7·8 : Picks, 10 : Unifacial handaxe (uniface) (1-9 : photo by Phan Thanh Toan, 10 : after Nguyen, 2017)

Choppers Choppers are the most common tool at the site, comprising 37.8% of the total assemblage. Nearly all are made from cobbles. In most cases, flaking is characterized by large flakes and fairly regular but stepped scars. Large unflaked surfaces that exhibit the original exterior cortex of the cobbles are present on the tools. Both unifacial and bifacial types have been found. The former are much greater in number than the latter, comprising 95% of the total assemblage. Most of the choppers are 12-16cm long and weigh 1,000-1,500g. The unifacial types are often made of cobbles with a flat surface that was left unflaked. Some retouched scars can be found on the working edges, but few traces of use can be observed. Single-edged choppers are the most common, constituting 82% of the total assemblage (**Figs. 1**:2).

Handaxes Handaxes are rare, comprising 6.6% of the lithic assemblage. Raw materials are mainly quartzite and sandstone. The handaxes vary between 10cm and 18cm in length, and weigh between 500g and 1,000g. Handaxes made of cores (cobbles) are much greater in number than those made of flakes. The knapping and trimming technology are Acheulean-like. Flake scars are shallow. The presence of a cortical surface near the butt is common. The edges of the handaxes are straight or only slightly zigzagged. Their lower ends often display a thick "butt." Handaxe subtypes are triangular, elongate ovate, lanceolate, cordiform, kidney-form, and ovate. Triangular handaxes are the most common, followed by elongate ovate. Cross-sections are triangular, plano-convex, bi-convex and trapezoid. Triangular and plano-convex handaxes dominate. In general, Bose handaxes are characterized by simple modification, stepped flake scars, and relatively large thickness in cross-section (**Fig. 1**: 3, 5–6, 9). This is mainly due to the cobble materials, which are coarse-grained, have many textures, and, in some cases, had been weathered long before they were used for tool making.

Picks Picks are characteristic of the Bose industry, accounting for a large number in the lithic assemblage (18.0%). Many picks are very similar to the hand-axes in material, shape and size except that the former are flaked unifacially while the later are bifacial. In fact, picks with shallow scars and thin tips are virtually identical with the unifacial handaxe category as seen in Africa (Beyene et al., 2013; Kuman, 2019). Nearly all of them are made on cobbles, and in most cases are worked on the upper surface only. They have a plano-convex or triangular cross section. The tips are often in the shape of a tongue. Only in a few instances has the upper surface been flaked all over, and the butt-end normally exhibits large areas of cortex. On the tip, the retouch has been carefully executed. Enormous picks also occur but they are rare. In a word, picks are one of the distinguishing features in Bose industry (**Fig. 1**:4,8).

Scrapers Scrapers comprise the second-largest number of tools in the lithic assemblage of the Bose industry. Most are rather large and heavy. They are primarily made of cobbles, with just a few made of flakes. The scrapers differ from heavy-duty tools such as choppers and picks by being made of fine-grained sandstone or silicified rock. Those made of cobbles often have a flat base that has been left unflaked. In many cases, use traces can be observed on their edges. The scrapers range in length from 3cm to 10cm. Side-scrapers and end-scrapers are common (**Fig. 1**:1).

Cleavers Cleavers are rare. Those that have been found are made of cobbles or flakes. Raw materials are limited to sandstone and quartzite. Those made of cobbles are only flaked on their upper part, producing a transverse edge. The flake cleavers are made of large flakes, with their ventral surface constituting a single flake scar. In most cases, secondary working was restricted to the butt-end and/or the lateral borders. The cleavers are usually U- or V-shaped. The cleavers found at the Bose Basin are mainly crude and are atypical compared to those found in the West.

3. The An Khe industry

In recent years, a number of Lower Paleolithic sites have been discovered in the Ba River Basin, in the town of An Khe, Gia Lai Province, Vietnam. This is a transitional area between the Pleiku Plateau and the coastal plain of Binh Dinh Province in north of southern Vietnam. Since its first discovery in 2014, archaeological surveys and excavations have been carried out by Russian–Vietnamese expeditions. As a result, 23 Lower Paleolithic sites have been discovered,, producing approximately 1,200 stone artifacts and nearly 150 tektites. Almost all of the sites are concentrated on flat river terraces about 430-450m above sea level. The excavation of Roc Tung 1 and Go Da yielded not only bifaces but also tektites in association with stone artifacts, including bifaces in situ, indicating that they belong to the same period. Tektites found with the lithics have been dated by the 40K/38Ar method to 806±22 and 782±20 ka BP (Derevianko et al., 2016, 2018; Nguyễn, 2017).

3.1. Geological background

The Paleolithic sites are located on an elevated, hilly plateau. The landscape is strongly affected by erosion. The bedrock comprises basalt, acidic tuffs, and granite, while overlying sediments are primarily lacustrine and riverine, including alluvial fans. Soft sediments accumulated mainly during the Early and Middle Pleistocene. Before these sediments were formed, the bedrock had been exposed to prolonged weathering, following which a relatively thick and weathered crust developed. Artifacts have been found in situ in similar contexts. Cultural layers belong to a single stratigraphic horizon, and all localities reveal similar lithics in terms of their technology and typology.

The stratigraphy of Roc Tung and Go Da differ. At Roc Tung and other sites on the left bank of the Ba, cultural horizons are located within a laterite overlying, and partially included in, the weathering crust on the granite bedrock. At Go Da, the cultural horizon was found directly in the weathering crust and slope wash sediments. No distinct red laterite layers have been found at Go Da (Derevianko et al., 2018).

3.2. Stone artifacts

Stone artifacts recovered from An Khe can be classified into eight main categories: cores and bifaces, picks, spurred tools, carinated end-scrapers, side-scrapers, choppers and chopping tools, denticulate tools, and notched tools (Derevianko et al., 2016). Raw materials for tool making include cobbles mainly of quartz and quartzite, which were transported from the Ba River Valley. Most tools are made of cobbles, with a few fashioned from flakes. Apart from handaxes, tools are mostly unifacially flaked and retouched. Cores and tools vary in size and shape, with unretouched flakes occasionally being utilized (**Fig. 2**).

Cores and flakes Cores and flakes from An Khe are rare. Cores present at the site can be divided into two types: one with a single platform, and the other with a double platform. The former type dominates. A cortex striking platform and single-scar striking platform have been identified, with the cortex striking platform dominating. Most of the cores have 2-3 flake scars. The flakes are mostly primary. Flakes with a length of 10-15cm dominate, and massive flakes (over 20cm) are very rare. The direct hard percussion and anvil techniques were used to detach the flakes, with the former technique dominating.

Handaxes Handaxes are especially typical in the tool assemblage. They appear at nearly all of the Palaeolithic sites in An Khe, but are not abundant. All were manufactured from quartzite pebbles. These handaxes were flaked and retouched bifacially with the cortex remaining on the round butt end. Flaked scars are concentrated on two-thirds of the body and run from the edge to the center, creating a raised line from the pointed end to the handle. Most of the handaxes are rather large and triangular in plan (**Fig. 2**: 4–6, 9).

Picks   Picks account for a large number of tools in the assemblage. Most are made of cobbles of quartzite and quartz, with quartzite dominating. The picks were mainly unifacially worked, with only the pointed working edge being subjected to secondary reduction, while the rest of the surface retains the original cortex. The body cross-section is triangular. The picks are normally large and heavy, and they are similar to handaxes in terms of shape and degree of treatment. Unlike the bifaces, the pointed ends of these tools are more clearly defined and, in some cases, asymmetrical (**Fig. 2**: 7–8).

Choppers and chopping tools   Choppers and chopping tools constitute the heavy-duty tools in the assemblage. These tools are made of cobbles and, rarely, chunks of mainly quartzite or quartz. The tools can be divided into two subtypes: one with a transverse edge, and the other with a longitudinal edge. Some specimens exhibit a sharpened tip. Some chopping tools show signs of retouching on one surface of the working edge, while others show signs on both surfaces. Secondary reduction was focused largely on the working edge, whereas other areas retain their cortex (**Fig. 2**: 2–3).

Scrapers   Scrapers from An Khe can be classified according to their longitudinal and transverse working edges. These tools can be further characterized as having a convex, concave, undulating, or serrated working edge. Most of the scrapers are made of flat pebbles, with some made of flakes or pebble fragments. The scrapers are mostly unifacially flaked, and, in addition to two or three-row small flake removals, they were additionally treated by retouching. The back opposite to the working edge always retained its cortex (**Fig. 2**: 1).

Spurred and nosed tools   This group differs from bifaces and pick-type tools in that their points were fashioned by additional retouching and small flake removals, which sometimes form so-called "shoulders." In the tool kit, denticulate-notched tools are present. Their working edges are shaped by detaching large flakes on their longitudinal and transverse lateral surfaces.

4. Comparison

4.1. Common characteristics

Both industries belong to the Pebble/Cobble Industry. Most of the tools were made of cobbles, with a few made of flakes. Raw materials used for tool making include mainly quartzite and quartz. Direct hard percussion was the main method used for flaking and retouching. Most tools were unifacially worked, although bifacially working also occurred, especially with handaxes.

Tool types at An Khe and Bose include chopper/chopping tools, picks, handaxes, scrapers, and, rarely, cleavers. At An Khe the tool categories differ (Derevianko et al., 2016, 2018) and can be classified into eight main categories: cores and bifaces, picks, spurred tools, carinated end-scrapers, side-scrapers, choppers and chopping tools, denticulate tools, and notched tools. Nguyễn Khac Su's categories (Nguyễn, 2017) include choppers, bifacial tools, handaxes, picks, triangular picks, unifacial tools, knives, cleavers, chopping tools, cores, chopping stone tools with chopped traces, and flakes. In 2015, most of the stone artifacts from An Khe were housed in the An Khe Museum, most of which were observed by the first author of this article.[1] According to the categories applied to the Bose industry, the An Khe collection includes choppers/chopping tools, handaxes, picks, scrapers, cleavers, hammer stones, cores, flakes, and chunks. Tools with a deliberately fashioned spur (or a "nose-shaped" point) from An Khe also occurred in Bose and were classified into the handaxe group (bifacially worked) or pick group (unifacially worked) (**Fig. 1**: 3; **Fig. 2**: 9).

Handaxes and picks are the most characteristic tools at An Khe and Bose. At An Khe, handaxes are Acheulean-like in terms of technology and typology, although they are not abundant. They were made of quartzite cobbles with the cortex remaining on the rounded butt end. This is nearly the same as at Bose. In addition, unifacially worked handaxes (unifaces), one of the subtypes of African handaxes, also occurred at An Khe, although few in number (**Fig. 2**: 10). These were made unifacially, with flaking and retouching restricted to their ventral face. Their dorsal face formed naturally with a shape like the ventral face. This kind of tool also occurred in Bose (**Fig. 1**: 7). The tips of both An Khe and Bose handaxes are of two types–round tip and pointed tip–with the former dominating.

A large number of picks occur in the tool assemblage of both An Khe and Bose. These picks were nearly all made from cobbles and were flaked unifacially, with retouching concentrated on the point and the cortex remaining on the back, with a thick handle. In An Khe picks, when the cobble

---

[1] In 2015, Xie Guangmao was invited to attend an international conference on the An Khe industry held in Pleiku, Gia Lai. After the conference, honored by the invitation of Professors Nguyễn Khắc Sử and Nguyễn Gia Doi, Xie had the opportunity to see most of the collection in An Khe Museum and to visit several sites, including Roc Tung 1 and Go Da. Xie later discussed the An Khe industry with Professor Nguyễn Khắc Sử in Hanoi.

has two natural faces forming an obtuse angle, only one more face was made; when the cobble has one flat side, two more were made (Nguyễn, 2017). This is the same in the Bose industry. At An Khe, triangular picks are notable in the tool assemblage: They are not only large but also have a longitudinal ridge on the back, and therefore their cross-sections are triangular. This kind of tool also occurred at Bose (**Fig. 1**: 8). In addition, rarely, massive picks have been found at both An Khe and Bose. There are two types of Khe picks: round (tongue-shaped) and pointed, with the former dominating. This is the same with Bose picks. Other types of tools at An Khe are similar to those found at Bose and comprise similar percentages of the tool assemblage.

4.2. Differences

Apart from their common characteristics (mentioned above), differences between An Khe and Bose also exist. Geomorphologically, the Bose and An Khe Basins are different. In the former, seven terraces developed. Palaeolithic sites are mainly situated on T4; those on T3 and T2 are uncommon. Terraces in the Bose Basin are typically fluvial deposits, forming mainly two parts, with the lower comprising basal gravels and the upper sandy clays and loams. In T4, the gravel stratum lies on a Tertiary sandstone bedrock overlain by Pleistocene deposits of sandy clays and loams. The Pleistocene deposits can be divided into two units: the lower unit is primary laterite formed by the Youjiang River; the upper unit is secondary deposit produced by slope wash and erosion processes and lies discontinuously on the lower unit. The boundary line between them is often uneven, indicating that erosion occurred before the formation of the upper unit deposits. Stone artifacts were found in both the primary and secondary deposits (Xie et al., 2018, 2020). In the An Khe Basin, however, the bedrock is composed of basalt, acidic tuffs, and granite, while overlying sediments are primarily lacustrine and riverine, including alluvial fans. Soft sediments accumulated mainly during the Early and Middle Pleistocene. Before these were formed, the bedrock had been exposed to prolonged weathering, following which a relatively thick weathering crust developed. The stratum containing the main cultural horizon was produced by slope wash and erosion processes (Derevianko et al., 2018).

At Bose, Palaeolithic stone artifacts were discovered not only on different terraces but also from different stratigraphic layers in the same terrace, especially in T4. Excavations of over 10 sites in the basin between 2005 and 2014 show that handaxes and tektites occurred in situ only in the primary laterite of the lower unit deposit of T4. The excavations also revealed that the Bose industry included four phases, with Phase 1 occurring 803 ka and Phase 4 occurring as late as 10

ka (Xie et al., 2018, 2020). At An Khe, however, cultural layers belong to a single horizon, and all localities reveal similar lithics in terms of their technology and typology (Derevianko et al., 2018).

Raw materials favored at Bose are more varied than those at An Khe. at Bose, raw materials for tool making include quartzite, sandstone, quartz, silicified rock, chert, and basalt, with quartzite sandstone dominating. Quartz and silicified rock are common, while chert and basalt were rarely used. At An Khe, however, quartzite and quartz are the main raw materials, with few other rocks being identified.

In addition, stone tools from An Khe are generally larger than those from Bose, although massive tools also occur at Bose. Handaxes from An Khe were nearly all made of cobbles. At Bose, however, some handaxes were made of flakes, and, rarely, handaxes were flaked all over their body without any cortex remaining. The shapes of Bose tools are more varied, and the subtypes of handaxes and picks are more numerous, than those from An Khe.

5. Discussion and conclusion

5.1. The bifacial industries in Southern China (Lingnan) are similar to those in Southeast Asia

The comparison of the An Khe and Bose stone tool industries revealed many common characteristics. The production of flakes, the tool making techniques, and the tool types are nearly the same at both sites. Minor differences between the sites include the types of raw materials used, tool size, and the time span. Raw materials for tool making depend on rock types and their availability, as hominins in the Lower Palaeolithic often selected local stones as raw materials. However, rocks in different areas may be of different types, and this variability can impact stone tool industries in different regions in terms of technology and typology. However, the main raw materials used for tool making at An Khe and Bose are quite similar (although sandstone also played an important role in Bose). Sandstone and quartzite have similar properties. They are hard, and they belong to the middle quality in Clark's (1994) category of rocks for tool making. In another words, the influence of sandstone and quartzite on tool making technology and typology are nearly the same. The size of tools is mainly due to available raw materials. If cobbles are large and of a suitable size for making tools, then the tools are often large, as in the case of Bose. Tools found in the upper reaches of the Youjiang River in the Bose Basin are often larger than those found in the lower reaches of the river because the cobbles used for making tools are larger, whereas those in the lower reaches are smaller. The same situation may apply to An Khe–that is, cobbles used for tool making at An Khe are larger than those at Bose. Concerning the difference in time span between these two industries, it can be theorized that different phases will be identified at An Khe with further fieldwork. At Bose, for instance, one phase of the stone tool industry was in question until large-scale excavations were conducted at many sites in the basin, which resulted in the discovery of Paleolithic stone artifacts from several stratigraphic layers and even on different terraces.

Technologically and typologically, bifacial industries in Southern China (Lingnan) and Southeast Asia are very similar. In recent years, in the Nanjing Basin of Guangdong, southern China, a new bifacial industry has been identified. In 2012, the Guangdong Institute of Cultural Relics and Archaeology conducted an archaeological survey in the basin, ultimately discovering over 60 Paleolithic sites. In 2014, an excavation carried out at Modaoshan by the Institute produced 400 stone artifacts, including handaxes and picks. In addition, several hundred stone artifacts were collected during one survey in the basin (Liu, 2017). Dating back to the early Middle Pleistocene, this industry is nearly the same as that at Bose. The Lower Paleolithic assemblage found at Pacitanian, Indonesia, included the initial discovery of a bifacial industry in East and Southeast Asia. Bifacial industries were also found in the Philippines and Malaysia (Pawlik, 2002; Saidin, 2006; Simanjuntak et al., 2010). These industries are also similar to those identified at Bose in terms of technology and typology (Xie, 1990). Based on the form of their tips, handaxes and picks found in Southeast Asia and southern China (Lingnan) can be divided into two subtypes: pointed end and round or tongue-shaped end, with the latter dominating. Therefore, the bifacial industries identified in Southeast Asia, including Lingnan, share many common characteristics and belong to the same techno-typological complex.

5.2. Bifacial industries in East and Southeast Asia belong to the Acheulean complex

Migration out of Africa, Acheulean technology spread into Eurasia. However, Acheulean industries in other regions are somewhat different from those in Africa. The Arabian Peninsula is one of the most important routes through which Acheulean technology penetrated into Eurasia. The Acheulean of Arabia is characterized by the presence of bifaces, found together with choppers, and a lack of cleavers. In Europe, Acheulean industries appeared around 600-650 ka BP. Although handaxes are common in tool assemblages in Europe, cleavers are rare, except for in Spain (Beyene et al., 2013).

In East and Southeast Asia, bifacial industries also differ from those in Africa. In general, bifacial industries in this region are characterized by a low percentage of handaxes and few cleavers, as in the case of Bose. At Bose, handaxes are rare, comprising just 6.6% of stone artifacts. Cleavers are also rare and atypical (Xie et al., 2003). The same pattern applies to An Khe. This is, however, not always the case. At Luonan, handaxes are rather common, while cleavers are not only common, but typical (Wang, 2005; Wang et al., 2005; Wang, 2006). In fact, bifacial industries in East and Southeast Asia are not fundamentally different from the Acheulean tradition–indeed, they belong to the Acheulean complex. The characteristics of the bifacial industries in East and Southeast Asia resulted from cultural evolution and development as hominins adapted to new environments in this region.

Aknowledgements

We thank Prof. Charles Higham (University of Otago) for improving the English used in this work. This research was supported by the Major Program of the National Social Science Foundation of China (22 & ZD246).

References

Brumm, A., 2010. The Movius Line and the bamboo hypothesis: early hominin stone technology in Southeast Asia. *Lithic Technology* 35, 7-24.

Bar-Yosef, O., Eren, M.I., Yuan, J.R. et al., 2012. Were bamboo tools made in prehistoric Southeast Asia? An experimental view from South China. *Quaternary International* 269, 9-21.

Beyene, Y., Katohc, S., WoldeGabriel, G. et al., 2013. The characteristics and chronology of the earliest Acheulean at Konso, Ethiopia. *PNAS* 110,1584-1591.

Ciochon R.L., Olsen J.W., 1986. Paleoanthropological and archaeological research in the Socialist Republic of Vietnam. *Journal of Human Evolution* 15, 623-631.

Clark, J.D., 1994. The Acheulean industrial complex in Africa and elsewhere. In: Corruccini, R.S., Ciochon, R.L. eds., *Integrative Paths to the Past: Paleoanthropological advances*, Englewood Cliffs: Prentice Hall, 451-469.

Corvinus, G., 2004. Homo erectus in East and Southeast Asia, and the questions of the age of the species and its association with stone artifacts, with special reference to handaxe-like tools. *Quaternary International* 117, 141-151.

de Lumley, H., Lee, Y.J., Park, Y.C., Bae, K.D., 2011. *Les industries* *lithiques du Paléolithique ancien de la Corée du Sud dans leur contexte stratigraphique et paléoécologique*, Paris: CNRS Editions.

de Lumley, H., Xie, G.M., Feng, X.B., 2020. *Les industries lithiques du Paléolithique ancien du Bassin de Bose*, Paris: CNRS Editions.

Dennell, R., 2016. Life without the Movius Line: The structure of the East and Southeast Asian Early Palaeolithic. *Quaternary International* 400, 14-22.

Derevianko, A.P., Nguyễn, K.S., Tsybankov, A.A. et al., 2016. *The Origin of Bifacial Industry in East and Southeast Asia*, Novosibirsk: IAET SB RAS Publishing.

Derevianko, A.P., Kandyba, A.V., Nguyễn, K.S. et al., 2018. The Discovery of a Bifacial Industry in Vietnam. *Archaeology, Ethnology and Anthropology of Eurasia* 46(3), 3-21.

Dong, Z., 2020. *Study on the lithic technology of early hominins at Chenshan site in Shuiyangjiang Catchment, Anhui Province*. Unpublished PhD dissertation. Institute of Vertebrate Paleontology and Paleoanthropology.

Gao, X., 2012. Characteristics and Significance of Paleolithic Handaxes from China. *Acta Anthropologica Sinica* 31, 97-112. (in Chinese with English abstract)

Huang, W.W., 1987. Bifaces in China. *Acta Anthropologica Sinica* 6, 61-68. (in Chinese with English abstract)

Huang, W.W., Qi, G.Q., 1987. Preliminary observation of Liangshan Paleolithic site. *Acta Anthropologica Sinica* 6, 236-244. (in Chinese with English abstract)

Huang, W.W., Leng, J., Yuan et al., 1990. Advanced opinions on the stratigraphy and chronology of Bose stone industry. *Acta Anthropologica Sinica* 9, 105-112. (in Chinese with English abstract)

Huang, W.W., 1993. Typology of the heavy-duty implements in the East and Southeast Asian Lower Paleolithic and a comment on the Movius typological system. *Acta Anthropologica Sinica* 12, 297-304. (in Chinese with English abstract)

Hou, Y.M., Potts, R., Yuan, B.Y., Guo, Z.T., Deino, A., Wang, W., Clark, J., Xie, G.M., Huang, W.W., 2000. Mid-Pleistocene Acheulean-like stone technology of the Bose Basin, south China. *Science* 287, 1622-1626.

Huang, S.M., Wang, W., Bae, C.J., Xu, G.L., Liu, K.T., 2012. Recent Paleolithic field investigations in Bose Basin (Guangxi, China). *Quaternary International* 281, 5-9.

Leng, J., Shannon, C.L., 2000. Rethinking early Paleolithic typologies in China and India. *Journal of East Asian Archaeology* 2, 9-35.

Li, C.R., Feng, X.W., Li, H., 2009. A study of the stone artifacts discovered in the Danjiangkou Reservoir area in 1994. *Acta Anthropologica Sinica* 28, 337-354. (in Chinese with English abstract).

Li, H., Li, C.R., Feng, X.W., 2012. A study of the stone artifacts from 2004 field investigation in Danjiangkou Reseroir area, Hubei and Henan, China. *Acta Anthropologica Sinica* 31, 113-126. (in Chinese with English abstract)

Li, H., Li, C.R., Kuman, K., 2013. A preliminary report on the excavation of the Guochachang II Paleolithic site in the Danjiangkou Reseroir Region, Hubei Province. *Acta Anthropologica Sinica* 32, 144-155. (in Chinese with English abstract)

Li, H., Li, C.R., Kuman, K., Zhou, X.M., Wanf, G., 2017. Field inveatigation report of the Paleolithic sites discovered in the fourth terrace of the Danjiangkou Reseroir Region. *Acta Anthropologica Sinica* 36, 145-153. (in Chinese with English abstract). *Vertebrata Palasiatica* 13, 225-228. (in Chinese)

Liu, S.Q., 2015. A breakthrough in prehistoric archaeology of Guangdong: Discovery and achievement of Modaoshan site and other sites in Nanjiang Basin. *China Cultural Relics News* December 30. (in Chinese)

Liu, S.Q., 2017. A preliminary report of the excavation of Modaoshan Palaeolithic site in Yunan, Guangdong. *Archaeology* 5, 3-13. (in Chinese with English abstract)

Lu, N., Huang, W.W., Yin, S.P. et al., 2006. A New Study on the Paleolithic Materials from Liangshan Site. *Acta Anthropologica Sinica* 25, 143-152. (in Chinese with English abstract)

Lycett, S.J., 2007. Why is there a lack of Mode 3 Levallois technologies in East Asia? A phylogenetic test of the Movius-Schick hypothesis. *Journal of Anthropology and Archaeology* 26, 541-575.

Lycett, S.J., Gowlett, J.A.J., 2008. On questions surrounding the Acheulean 'tradition'. *World Archaeology* 40, 295-315.

Lycett, S.J., Bae, C.J., 2010. The Movius Line controversy: the state of the debate. *World Archaeology* 42, 521-544.

Lycett, S.J., Norton, C.J., 2010. A demographic model for Palaeolithic technological evolution: the case of East Asia and the Movius Line. *Quaternary International* 211, 55-65.

Li, H., Li, C.R., Kuman, K., 2014a. Rethinking the "Acheulean" in East Asia: evidence from the recent investigations in the Danjiangkou Reservoir Region, central China. *Quaternary International* 347, 163-175.

Li, H., Li, C.R., Kuman, K., Chen, J., Yao, H.T., Li, Z., 2014b. The Middle Pleistocene Acheulean site of Shuangshu in the Danjiangkou Reservoir Region, central China. *Journal of Archaeological Science* 52, 391-409.

Keates, S.G., 2002. The Movius Line: fact or fiction?. *Bulletin of Indo-Pacific Prehistory Association* 22, 17-24.

Kuman, K., Li, C.R., Li, H., 2014. Large cutting tools in the Danjiangkou Reservoir Region, central China. *Journal of Human Evolution* 76, 129-153.

Kuman, K., 2019. Acheulean Industrial Complex. In: Smith C. ed., *Encyclopedia of Global Archaeology*, Springer Nature Switzerland AG, 1-12.

Movius, H.L., 1948. The Lower Palaeolithic cultures of southern and eastern Asia. *Transactions of the American Philosophical Society* (New Series) 38(4), 329-420.

Nguyễn, K.S., Nguyễn, G.D., 2015. System of the Paleolithic locations in the Upper Ba River. *Vietnam Social Sciences* 4, 47-63.

Nguyễn, K.S., 2017. Early Paleolithic industry of An Khe and primitive period in Vietnam. *Archaeology* 12, 13-25.

Norton, C.J., 2000. The current state of Korean paleoanthropology. *Journal of Human Evolution* 38, 803-825.

Norton, C.J., Bae, K.D., Harris, J.W.K., Lee, H.Y., 2006. Middle Pleistocene handaxes from the Korean peninsula. *Journal of Human Evolution* 51, 527-536.

Norton, C.J., Bae, K.D., 2009. Erratum to "The Movius Line sensu lato (Norton et al., 2006) further assessed and defined" Journal of Human Evolution 55 (2008) 1148-1150. *Journal of Human Evolution* 57, 331-334.

Norton, C.J., Lycett, S.J., 2010. The Movius Line. In: *Yearbook of Science and Technology*, New York: McGraw-Hill, 248-250.

Olsen J.W., Ciochon R.L., 1990. A review of evidence for postulated Middle Pleistocene occupations in Vietnam. *Journal of Human Evolution* 19, 761-788.

Pei, S.W., Chen, F.Y., Zhang, L. et al., 2007. Preliminary report on the excavation of the Liuhuaishan Paleolithic site at Baise, south China. *Acta Anthropologica Sinica* 26, 1-15. (in Chinese with English abstract)

Pawlik, A.F., 2002. Acheulean in Nueva Ecija? A report from the 2001 ASP Fieldschool in Arubo, General Tinio, Nueva Ecija, Central Luzon. *Hukay* 4(1), 1-22.

Petraglia, M.D., Shipton, C., 2009. Erratum to "Large cutting tool variation west and east of the Movius Line" Journal of Human Evolution 55 (2008) 962-966. *Journal of Human Evolution* 57, 326-330.

Qin, S.M., Qin, C.L., Liang, X.D., Luo, K.X., 1983. Paleolithic investigation in Xinzhou, Guangxi. *Archeology* 10, 865-868.

Schick, K.D., 1994. The Movius line reconsidered. In: Corruccini, R.S., Ciochon, R.L. eds., *Integrative Paths to the Past: Paleoanthropological advances*, Englewood Cliffs: Prentice Hall, 569-596.

Saidin, M., 2006. Bukit bunuh, Lenggong, Perak: Sum-bangannya kepada arkeologi dan geologi Negara. *Jurnal Arkeologi Malaysia* 19, 1-14.

Santonja, M., Villa, P., 2006. The Acheulian of Western Europe. In: Goren-Inbar, N., Sharon, G. eds., *Axe Age Acheulian Toolmaking from Quarry to Discard*. London, Equinox Publishing Ltd., 429-478.

Shipton, C.B.K., Petraglia, M.D., 2010. Inter-continental variation in Acheulean bifaces. In: Norton, C.J., Braun, D. eds., Asian Paleoanthropology: From Africa to China and Beyond. *Vertebrate Paleobiology and Paleoanthropology Series*, Dordrecht: Springer Press, 49-55.

Simanjuntak, T., Se'mah, F., Gaillard, C., 2010. The palaeolithic in Indonesia: Nature and chronology. *Quaternary International* 223-224, 418-421.

Toth, N., 1985. The Oldowan reassessed: a close look at early stone artifacts. *Journal of Archaeological Science* 12, 101-120.

Wang, Y.P., 1997. *Pleistocene environment and developement of Palaeolithic cultures in South China*. Beijing: Peking University Press. (in Chinese)

Wang, S.J., Shen, C., Hu, S.M. et al., 2005a. Lithic Artefacts Collected from Open-air Sites during 1995-1999 Investigations in Luonan Basin, China. *Acta Anthropologica Sinica* 24(2), 87-103. (in Chinese with English abstract)

Wang, S.J., 2006. Cleavers Collected from the Open-air Sites in Luonan Basin, China. *Acta Anthropologica Sinica* 25, 332-342. (in Chinese with English abstract)

Wang, S.J., 2005b. *Perspectives on Hominid Behaviour and Settlement Patterns: A Study of the Lower Palaeolithic Sites in the Luonan Basin, China*. British Archaeological Reports International Series. Oxford: Archaeopress.

Wang, S.J., 2010. Hushilang Vol.: *The Palaeolithic Open Air Sites in the Luonan Basin China*. Beijing: Science Press. (in Chinese with English summary)

Wang, S.J., SUN, X.F., Lu, H.Y. et al., 2014. Newly Discovered Paleolithic Open-air Sites in Hanzhong Basin in Upper Valley of Hanjiang River and Their Ages. *Acta Anthropologica Sinica* 33, 125-136. (in Chinese with English abstract)

Wang, W., Mo, J.Y., Huang, Z.T., 2008. Recent discovery of handaxes associated with tektites in the Nanbanshan locality of the Damei site, Bose basin, Guangxi, South China. *Chinese Science Bulletin* 53, 878-883.

Wang, W., Lycett, S.J., von Cramon-Taubadel, N., Jin, J., Bae, C.J., 2012. Comparison of handaxes from Bose Basin (China) and the western Acheulean indicates convergence of form, not cognitive differences. *PLoS One* 7, e35804.

Wang, W., Bae, C., Huang, S.M. et al., 2014. Middle Pleistocene bifaces from Fengshudao (Bose Basin, Guangxi, China). *Journal of Human Evolution* 69, 110-122.

Xie, G.M., 1990. The relationship between the stone tools from Bose and the Lower Palaeolithic cultyres in South and Southeast Asia (in Chinese with English abstract). *Southern Ethnology and Archaeology* Vol. 3, 237-247.

Xie, G.M., 2002. A discussion of handaxes from Bose. *Acta Anthropologica Sinica* 21, 65-73. (in Chinese with English abstract)

Xie, G.M., Lin, Q., Huang, Q.S., 2003. *Bose Palaeolithic industry*, Beijing: Cultural Relics Press. (in Chinese with English summary)

Xie, G.M., Bodin, E., 2007. Les industries paléolithiques du bassin de Bose (Chine du Sud) Paleolithic industries of the Bose Basin (South China). *L'Anthopologie* 111, 182-206.

Xie, G.M., Lin, Q., 2008. A preliminary report on the excavation of the Shangsong site. *Acta Anthropologica Sinica* 27, 13-22. (in Chinese with English abstract)

Xie, G.M., Lin, Q., Huang, X., 2010. A preliminary report on the excavation of the Baidu site in the Bose basin, south China. *Acta Anthropologica Sinica* 29, 355-371. (in Chinese with English abstract)

Xie, G.M., 2015. Damei site at Youjiang in Baise City (Bose Basin), Gunagxi. In: *Important discoveries from the rescued excavations in Guangxi*, Nanning: Guangxi Scientific and Technological Press, 2-4. (in Chinese)

Xie, G.M., Lin, Q., Chen, X.Y. et al., 2018. Stratigraphie et chronologie du site de Gaolingpo dans le bassin de Bose, sud de la Chine. *L'anthropologie* 122, 1-13.

Xie, G.M., Lin, Q., Yu, M.H. et al., 2020. Stratigraphy and chronology of the Gaolingpo site in the Bose Basin, South China. *Acta Anthropologica Sinica* 39, 106-117. (in Chinese with English abstract)

Xing, L.D., Wang, S.J., Zhang, G.K. et al., 2015. Newly discovered Paleolithic artifacts from the Yeyuan open-air site in the Luonan Basin, Central China. *Acta Anthropologica Sinica* 34, 1-13. (in Chinese with English abstract)

Xu, G.L., Wang, W., Bae, C.J., Huang, S.M., Mo, Z.M., 2012. Spatial distribution of Paleolithic sites in Bose Basin, Guangxi, China. *Quaternary International* 281, 10-13.

Yuan, B.Y., Hou, Y.M., Wang, W., Potts, R., Guo, Z.T., Huang, W.W., 1999. On the geomorphological evolution of the Bose basin, a lower Paleolithic locality in south China. *Acta Anthropologica Sinica* 18, 215-224. (in Chinese with English abstract)

Zeng, X.W., 1983. New discovery of stone artifacts in Bose region, Guangxi. *Prehist. Res.* 2, 81-88. (in Chinese)

Zhang, P., Huang, W.W., Wang, W., 2010. Acheulean handaxes from Fengshudao, Bose sites of south China. *Quaternary International* 223-224, 440-443.

Statistical comparison of the lithic industries from the Far East and Caune de l'Arago in France; as the Central Point of Loc. 1, Mansuri Site in Korea

Kazuharu TAKEHANA[1], Kazuto MATSUFUJI[2], Yung-jo LEE[3]

[1] Institute of Human Paleontology in France, Japan ; kazu-f19@sea.ncv.ne.jp
[2] Doshisha University, Japan
[3] Institute of Korean Prehistory (IKP), Korea

ABSTRACT

Professor Henry de Lumley devised the techno-typological analysis for statistical method for researching the lithic industries at the Caune de l'Arago site in France since 1964. This techno-typological research convinced us that it is the most precise and systematic study of Lower and Middle Paleolithic industries worldwide. In this paper, we apply this analytical method to six lithic industries in China, South Korea, and France. The lithic industries at the Caune de l'Arago site, which have primitive aspects that coexist with the middle Acheulean in Western Europe, have been knapped on quartz with 70% of the recovered pieces. They lack typical Acheulean tools, such as bifaces and cleavers, and use debris as a blank for flake tools that appear in a completely different aspect from Western Europe. This is common to the principal phase of earlier Paleolithic cultures in the Far East.

국문초록

이 논문은 석기공작(lithic industry)에 대한 통계 수치와 관련한 기술-형식학적 연구를 제시한 것이다. 극동에서 가장 오래된 단계는 마주앙고(Majuangou) 유적 Ⅲ문화층 석기공작이며, 이 문화는 아슐리안의 윤시안(Yunxian) 유적과 보세(Bose) 유적보다 더 이른 시기를 지시하며 찍개 같은 대형석기의 출토 비율이 높다. 두 번째 단계는 중국의 전형적 주구점 문화에서 전통적인 아슐리안 이후 단계로, 만수리 유적 1지점 3문화층, 링징(Ling-Jing) 유적과 후쟈야오(Houjiayao) 유적 하부문화 석기공작이며 황토 고토양 대비 MIS 5로 본다. 세로날 긁개와 톱니날 석기의 형태적 다양성, 높은 찍개 비율, 여러면석기와 사냥돌이 나타난다. 이 단계는 프랑스 캉 드 라라고 H층 고기 타야시안(Protro-Tayacian)과 대비할 수 있으나 형식학적 특징은 잘 일치하지 않는다. 세 번째 단계는 중국 주구점 문화가 발전한 단계로서 시베이마이잉(Xibeimaying) 유적의 석기공작과 동일하며, 석기 돌감은 일부 석영을 사용하기도 하였으나 주로 다양한 퇴적암 계통의 돌감을 사용하였다. 몸체로 만든 격지는 대개 짧고 작으며, 세로날 긁개와 톱니날 석기의 다양성이 증가한다. 이 단계는 전반적으로 타야시안 찌르개와 톱니날 석기가 우세하며 형식학적 특징상 서유럽 중기구석기 무스테리안(Mousterian) 톱니날 석기공작 단계에 대비된다.

Keywords: lithic industries, techno-typological analysis, Mansuri site, Typical Acheulean

1. Outline of the focal sites

1.1. Mansuri Location 1 Site

The Paleolithic open site of Mansuri is close to the city of Osong, in the locality of Cheongju city, Chungbuk Province, 108km south of Seoul. The site is situated on a gentle slope 42-43m above sea level and 12m above the Miho River, a branch of the Geum River, on its right bank. Five Paleolithic cultural layers have been stratigraphically found in the 6m thick sediments (Institute of Korean Prehistory, 2010). The sediments are largely divided into three parts. The upper 2.5m is made of minute aeolian loess. The middle 3.5m comprises alternating sediments of weathered granite sand of basal rock and aeolian loess. The lower segment is composed of sand and fluvial gravel. All of the sediments have a normal magnetic polarity above the Matsuyama-Bruhnes boundary (780 ka). Three types of volcanic ash from the Japanese Archipelago-AT (30 ka), Aso-4 (90 ka), and K-Tz (95 ka)–were found in the upper segment. The lithic industry analyzed in this paper was unearthed from the paleosol of MIS 5c-e, just below K-Tz. Although several OSL dates show ages between 44 ka to 104 ka, these ages are not concordant with the stratigraphy of the site (Lumley et al., 2011) **(Fig. 1, 2)**.

1.2. Houjiayao Site

This site is situated in the Nihewan Basin, on the border of the provinces of Shanxi and Hebei in northern China. The original name of the site was Xujiayao, but it has recently been changed to Houjiayao. Since 1970, many archaeological studies have been conducted in the Nihewan Basin. The Institute of Vertebrate Paleontology and Paleoanthropology (IVPP) was the first to perform a systematic survey and excavations at the location, which resulted in the discovery of several archaeological sites. The Houjiayao site, discovered by the IVPP team in 1974, is situated on the western bank of the Liyigou River, a branch of the Sanggan River. In 1976 and 1977, the IVPP team unearthed several human skull fragments and more than 20,000 lithic artifacts made of quartz and other materials (Lampo et al., 1979; Ning et al., 2011). At first, the geological age of the cultural layer could not be precisely confirmed. In 2007-2008, the Cultural Relics and Archeology Research Institute of Hebei Province systematically excavated the site and determined that a series of cultural layers was included in the younger deposits, in which the second terrace had eroded.

Several U-Th ages were determined for the mammalian teeth found in the superior archaeological level. These ages

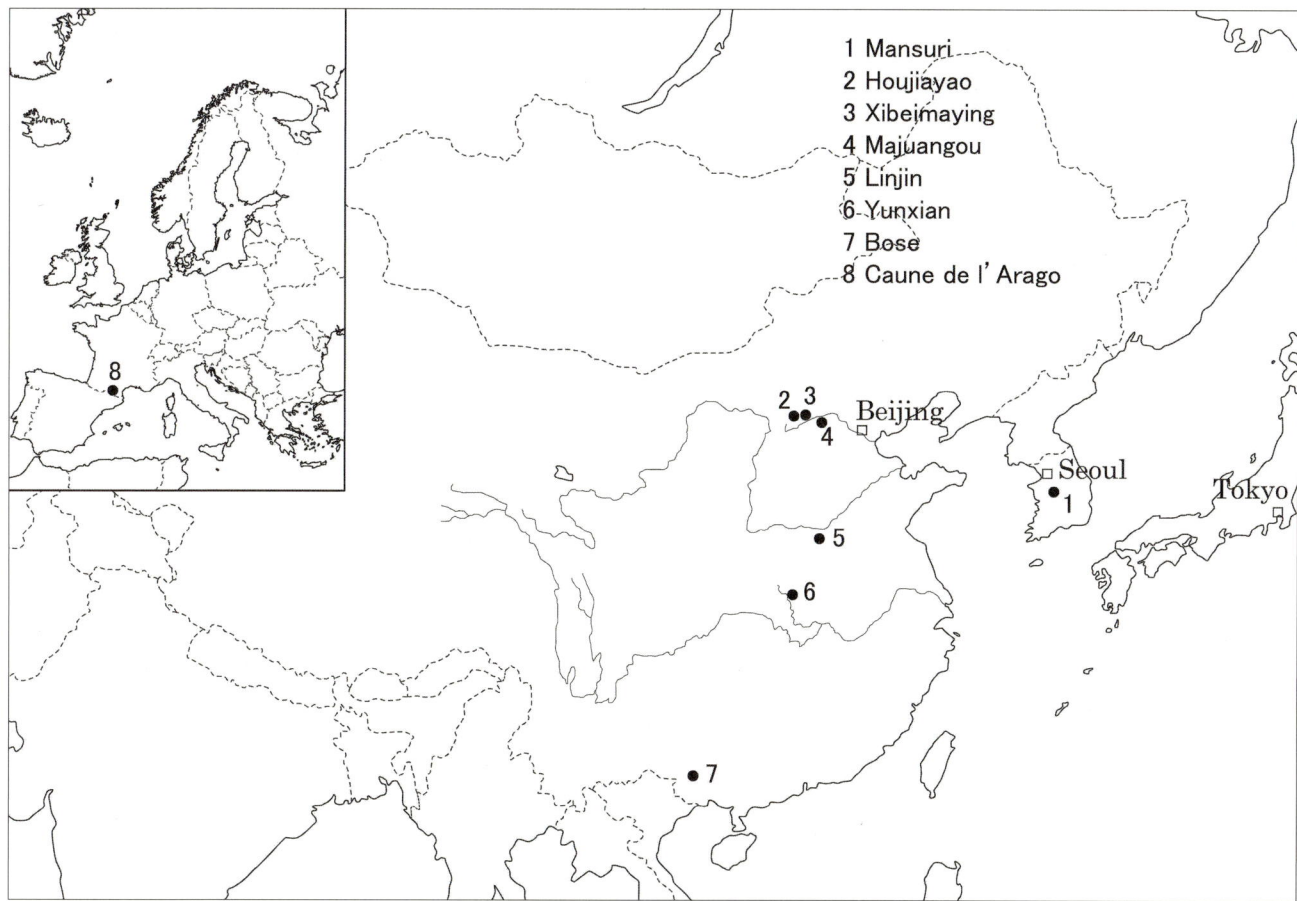

Fig. 1 Concerned sites

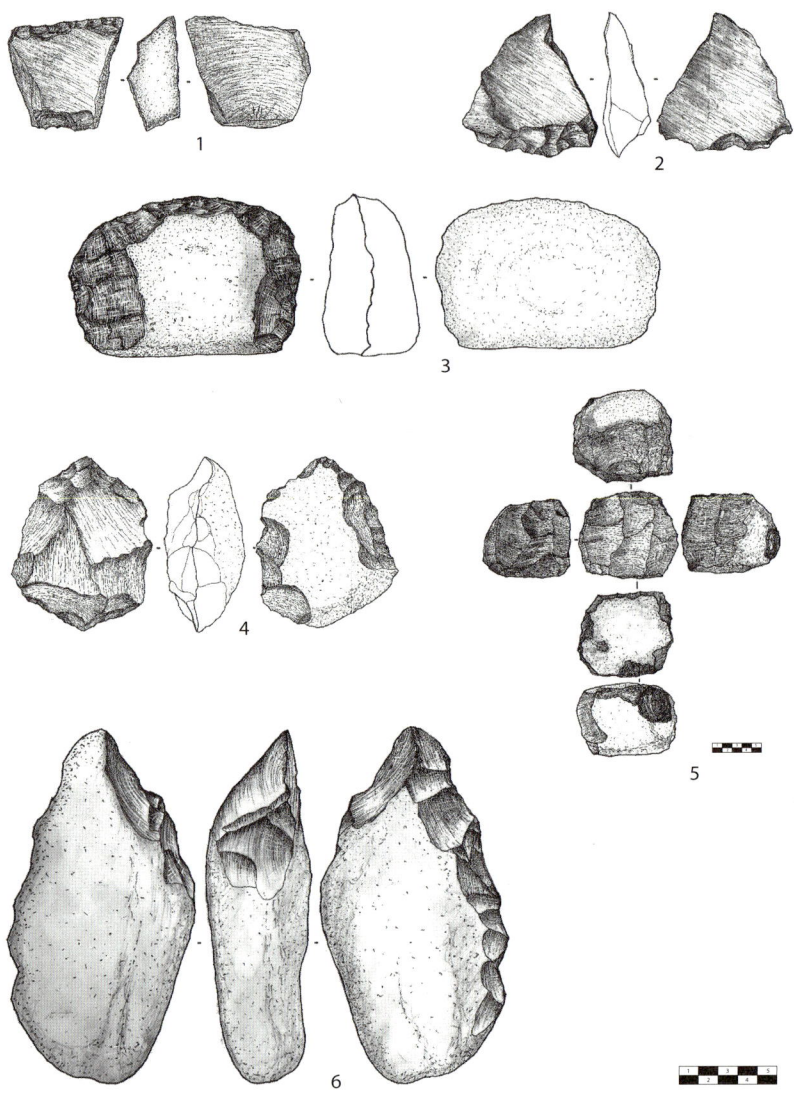

Fig. 2 Tools from the layer III of Mansuri Location 1 :
1 : simple side-scraper on flake in quartz, 2 : simple denticulate on debris in quartz, 3 : triple choppers on pebble in quartz, 4 : Atypical biface in quartz, 5 : polyhedron en quartz, 6 : pick on pebble in quartzitz-sandstone

were between 100 ka and 120 ka, which conforms with the paleontological data. The ages correspond to the beginning of the Upper Pleistocene. The IRSL age for the artifact horizon at the Houjiayao site excavated in 2007-2008 is 69±8 ka (Nagatomo et al., 2009).

However, the geological and topographical research conducted at the Houjiayao site in 2011 by a joint Chinese-Japanese team indicates that the cultural layers were reformed during the last glacial period after MIS4 (Watanabe et al., 2013). Recently, pollen analysis at the Houjiayao site estimated the cultural layers to be ages between 160-185 ka (Li Zhengtao et al., 2014). While the exact ages of these layers remains in dispute, we analyzed the lithic industry (613 pieces) unearthed in 2007-2008 by the Cultural Relics and Archeology Research Institute of Hebei Province (**Fig. 1, 3**).

1.3. Xibeimaying Site

This site, also in Hebei Province, is located 80km east of the Houjiayao site and belongs to the same geological configuration. It was discovered during systematic prospecting carried out in 1985 and subsequently excavated by the Cultural Relics and Archeology Research Institute of Hebei Province in 1986. A total of 1546 artifacts have been retrieved from a layer of lacustrine deposit in the superior part of the Nihewan formation. These artifacts were found alongside mammalian fossils at a level of 3 to 6m below the surface. Some U-Th ages were determined for the mammalian teeth at this level. These ages were 18,000±1,000 BP and 15,000±1,000 BP. Recently, a sample from the organic sediment was dated to 28,240±120 BP by AMS method (Hayase, 2013).

Here, we observed all artifacts kept in the Cultural Relics and

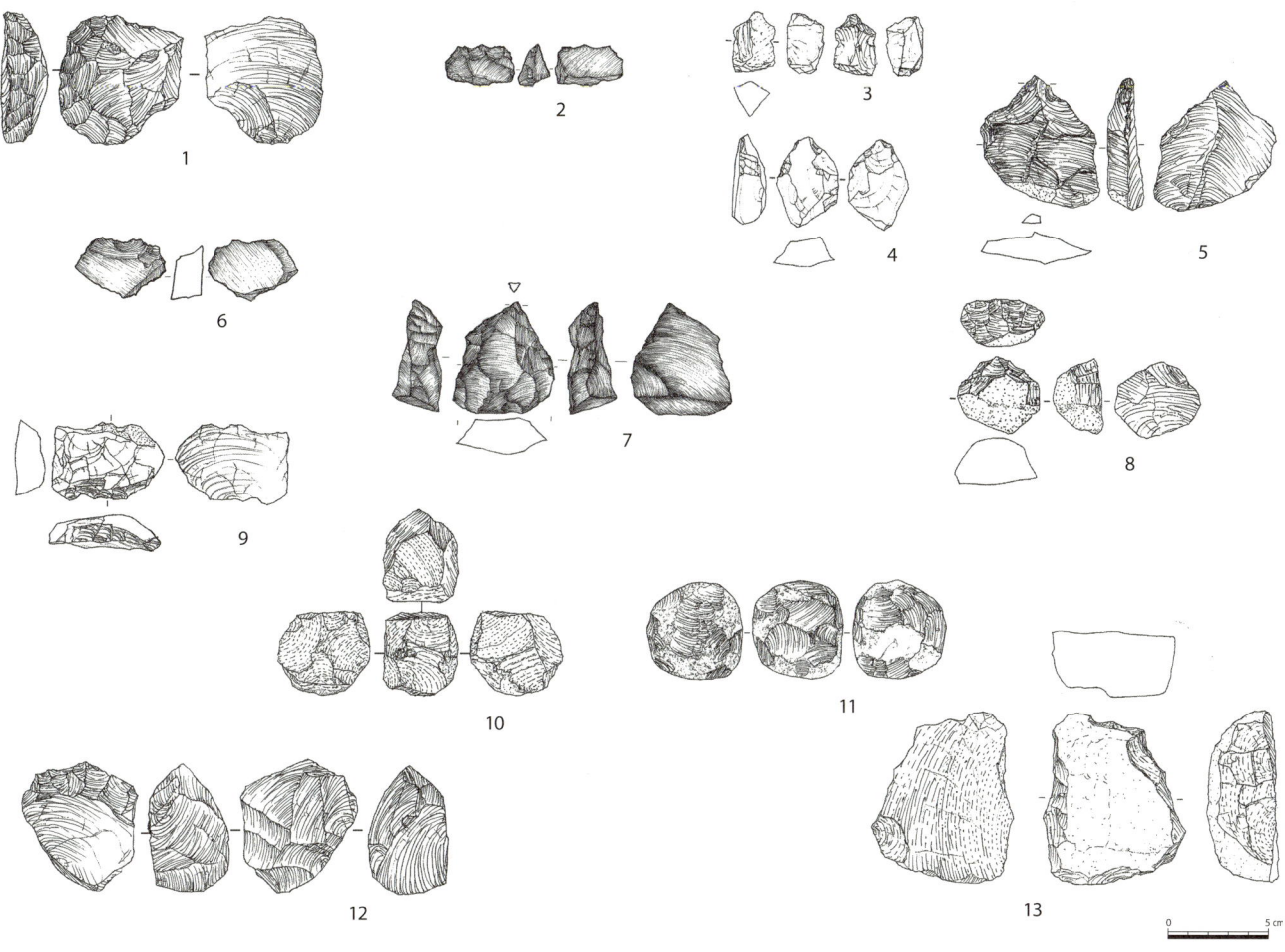

Fig. 3 Tools from the Houjiiayao site
1 : simple convex side-sraper, 2 : simple transversal denticulate, 3-5 : becs, 6 : notch & bec, 7 : convergent scraper, 8 : atypical end-scraper, 9 : double retouched notchs, 10, 11 : polyhedrons, 12, 13 : choppers

Archeology Research Institute of Hebei Province (**Fig. 1, 4**).

1.4. Majuangou Site

The Majuangou site is situated on the right bank of the Sanggan River in the Nihewan Basin in Hebei Province, which features deposits of Lower and Middle Pleistocene concentrate. The Majuangou site was discovered in 1992 during systematic surveys. Prof. Wei Qi, among others, found three archaeological levels among the 22 geological layers present at the site. In the eroded valleys, about 20 sites dating to the Lower Pleistocene (1 ma) can be found. Among them, the Majuangou site is one of the most important. In 2011-2013, we observed and recorded 593 artifacts preserved at the Cultural Relics and Archeology Research Institute of Hebei Province. Here, we comparatively examine those from cultural level III (359 pieces). Cultural level III is younger than the Olduvai Normal Event of 1.8 Ma, which is the earliest site in the Nihewan Basin. Concerning the elephant fossils discovered at level III of the Majuangou site, a Chinese paleontologist identified it a step-mammoth (*Mammuthus trogontherii*), which is a more ancient specimen from the Pliocene, at least older than 1.36 Ma (**Fig. 1, 5**).

1.5. Ling-jing Site

This site is situated in Xuchang, in Henan Province, China. Two different industries have been stratigraphically discovered at the site. The upper is microlithic, while the lower is a small flake tool industry. A large number of mammalian fossils, tools made of quartz, arranged pebble tools, and other artifacts were found in 1965. This site is therefore notable among researchers. Since 2005, the Cultural Relics and Archeology Research Institute of Henan Province has been conducting research at the site.

In 2007, a whole human skull, characterized by a prominent orbit indicative of a type of *Homo erectus*, was discovered at the site. This important discovery attracted anthropological attention from all over the world, with the skull being dubbed "Xuchang Man." This well-preserved skull was unearthed from paleosol S_1 (MIS5). In this paper,

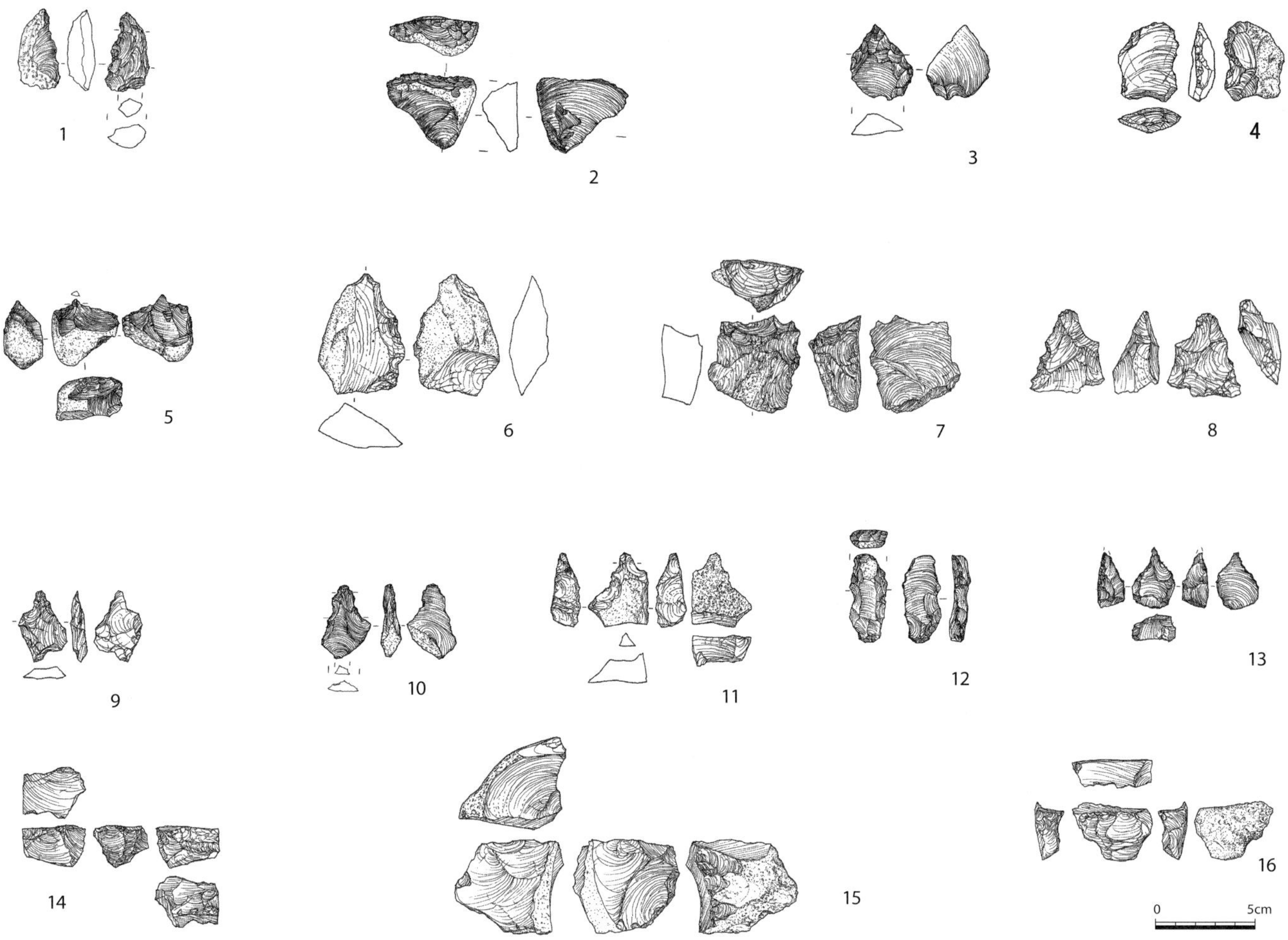

Fig. 4 Tools from the Xibeimaying site :
1 : denticulate, 2 : piece with steep retouch, 3 : '*racloir déjeté*', 4 : retouched notch, 5 : bec by two mixed notchs, 6 : denticulated side-scraper, 7 : simple denticulate, 8-11 : Tayac type point, 12 : double denticulated side-scraper, 13 : atypical drill, 14-16 : cores.

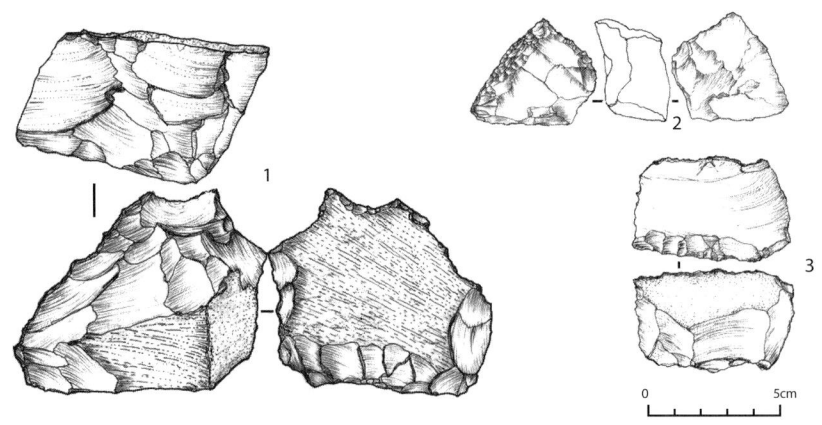

Fig. 5 Tools from the cultural layer III of Majuangou site :
1 : multiple tool (side-scraper, bec & chopper), 2 : '*racloir jdéjeté*', 3 : simple transversal side-scraper by an inverse retouch

we examine the stone materials, recovered from the site in 2012 and 2013, that the Cultural Relics and Archeology Research Institute of Henan Province permitted us to observe.

1.6. Caune de l'Arago site

The Caune de l'Arago site is situated in the village of Tautavel, a Pyrenees-oriental Prefecture in France. This immense limestone cave has a very thick deposit, more than 13m in depth, that was formed after the reversed Matsuyama paleomagnetic polarity epoch (from 2.5 Ma to 780 ka). In this paper, we examine a series of quartz objects (6,431 pieces) from layer H of the Lower Ensemble at the site, dated to 500 ka. The data have already been referenced by Takehana (1991).

2. Technical observation and results

2.1. Raw materials

With regard to the raw materials comprising the six lithic industries mentioned above (**Table 1**), the results from observation permit us to interpret two distinctly different activities at the time the raw materials were acquired. The industries observed can be divided into two major groups. The first group is characterized by the extreme dominance of quartz, sand quartz, and other minerals, which are composite minerals that universally exist in the Earth's crust. The second group is mainly characterized by fine grained silicified rocks, for example, flint, jasper and other rocks of similar materials. The quartz from the first group can cause unforeseeable fractures at the time of blank production for lithic tools occurs–nevertheless, they are extremely frequent at the sites of Caune de l'Arago, Mansuri Location 1, Ling-Jing, and Houjiayao. The second shows very different nature of rock material for lithic production. These rocks are capable of controlling fractures at the time of debitage and tool making in general. This characteristic was confirmed at the Xibeimaying and Majuangou sites and typically appears in flakes detached as blanks. At Mansuri Location 1, the flakes detached in the process of debitage are all made of quartz and quartz sandstone. At layer 10 of Zhoukoudian Location 1 in Beijing, vein quartz accounts for 88% of the raw materials in the lithic industry (Theillard de Chardin, 1932).

2.2. Type of butt

A technical characteristic of the striking platform of the lithic industries discussed in this paper is dominant of the cortical butt (19 to 51%) and flat butt (31 to 51%) types, while extremely few are symmetrical faceted butt (0 to 2%) and a symmetrical dihedral butt (0 to 1%). Therefore, we can infer that the debitages of all the lithic industries discussed in this paper began directly from a cortical surface core without any preparation for a platform, and that the debitages themselves were not successive (**Table 2**).

2.3. Disposition of flake removals

This observation permits us to detect the presence of the predetermined preparation on the core surface. The 38 to 68% of the total number of debitages the debitage were held in the same direction without changing the platform position in most cases. A few debitages, 8 to 16%, show flake scars with orthogonal directions and none of the centripetal removals is observed. Therefore, predetermined preparation at the time of debitage in all of the lithic industries did not exist. With regard to the materials from the Majuangou site, we have not executed this observation (**Table 3**).

2.4. Different states of debitage

We observed the residual cortex of a flake, which permitted us to know the original state of the core surface at the time of detachment from the blank. At first, this required complicated and systematic observations. Here, we only observed the essential and important points. Group I is completely characterized by the cortical surface on the flake. Group II is characterized by a largely cortical surface and some rare removals. Group III is characterized by a large shell-shaped flake with few cases of some cortex. Group IV is completely characterized by a flake without a cortex.

Group I varies between 3% and 11% in the concerned lithic industries. Group II occupy some between 7% and 15%. Group III is dominant in all lithic industries, representing 40 to 55%. Group IV is frequent enough, from 20 to 46% among them. The data indicate that the blocks of raw material were acquired in a cortical state and were introduced without any preparation into the camp or site. In blank production, "debitage" is all continuation–nevertheless, this debitage was not as successive or the detached flakes were only of a limited quantity. This tendency is typical at the site of Caune de l'Arago, and is more remarkable at Mansuri Location I and Ling-Jing. Therefore, we can conclude that these sites were quite close to the location at which the raw materials were extracted (**Table 4**).

2.5. Flake morphology

Regarding the length of a flake, the length of its long axis is especially important among the technical measures of the tool blank. We measured the technical length of flakes superior to 20mm. The detached flakes were all small in the observed lithic industries. No piece corresponded directly to the standard size of recovered bifaces and cleavers. Their mean lengths were between 32mm and 65mm, respectively. The longest flake was 65mm long and was found at the Ling-Jing site, but the total sample number was not sufficient to evaluate it statistically. The Caune de l'Arago

Table 1 Raw material of the analysed lithic industries

rock type / sites	T: all discoveried pieces						F: flakes						I: tools					
	Arago	Xbmyng	Hjy	Mnsr-1	LngJng	Mjng	Arago	Xbmyng	Hjy	Mnsr-1	LngJng	Mjng	Arago	Xbmyng	Hjy	Mnsr-1	LngJng	Mjng
① Quartz	85.9	19.9	74.5	94.7	73	0.2	59.6	7.3	52.4	98.4	55	0	65	16	77	95	91	0
② Crystal	0	0	0.7	0	0	0	0	0	0	0	0	0	0	0	0	0	0	0
③ Qrtz.-sandstone	0	0	0	1.2	6	0	0	0	0	0	9	0	0	0	0	0	0	0
④ Quartzite	3.1	5.7	6.7	3	18	0.5	12.3	9.7	18.8	1.6	27	2	6	6	8.4	5	7	3
⑤ Slcfd. Sandstone	0	0.4	0.3	0.2	0	0	0.1	0.4	0.9	0	0	0	2	0.6	0	0	2	0
⑥ Limestone	1.9	10.1	6.4	0	0	56.8	1.1	7.9	5.6	0	0	23	0.5	3	2.5	0	0	21
⑦ Slcfd. Limestone	0	26.4	0	0	0	24.7	0	23.8	0	0	0	50	0	19	0	0	0	45
⑧ Flint	6.8	14.5	4.6	0	0	10	20.9	23.2	12.1	0	0	11	23	29	8.4	0	0	28
⑨ Chert	0	1.5	0	0	0	1.9	0	1.1	0	0	0	3	0	1	0	0	0	0
⑩ Jasper	0.6	1.5	0.5	0	0	1.1	2.3	2.3	0.9	0	0	3	3	2	0	0	0	3
⑪ Chalcedony	0	12.24	0.8	0	0	0	0	16	2.8	0	0	0	0	18	0	0	0	0
⑫ Petrified wood	0	0	0	0	0	0	0	0	0	0	0	0	0	0	0	0	0	0
⑬ Andesite	0	3.7	0.7	0	0	3	0	4.3	2.8	0	0	6	0	3	0	0	0	0
⑭ Volcanic rock	0	2.3	2	0.2	1	0.8	0	3.2	2.8	0	0	2	0	0.6	2.5	0	0	0
⑮ Sandstone	0.6	1.6	1.6	0.5	0	0.2	0	0.4	0	0	0	0	0.5	0.3	0.8	0	0	0
⑯ Granite	0	0.06	1	0	2	0	2.4	0	0.9	0	9	0	0	0	0	0	0	0
⑰ Schist	0	0	0	0.08	0	0	0	0	0	0	0	0	0	0	0	0	0	0
⑱ Slate	0.3	0	0	0	0	0	0.2	0	0	0	0	0	0	0	0	0	0	0
⑲ Indeterminate	0.8	0.1	0.2	0.12	0	0.8	1.1	0.4	0	0	0	0	0	1.5	0.4	0	0	0
percentage	100	100	100	100	100	100	100	100	100	100	100	100	100	100	100	100	100	100
Total number	6,431	1,507	613	1258	108	359	627	557	107	258	11	62	334	286	118	86	43	29

Table 2 Different types of butt

Types / sites	All observed flakes					
	Arago	Xibeimaying	Houjjayao	Mansuri	Ling-jing	Majuangou
① Smooth butt	43	48.5	49.6	35	45	51
② Cortical butt	41	29.6	18.7	43	55	42
③ Dihedral butt	1	1.1	0.9	0	0	0
④ facetted butt	1	1.8	0.9	0	0	0
⑤ reduced butt	3	8.5	3.7	2	0	0
⑥ Void butt	3	0.9	5.6	8	0	2
⑦ Indeterminate	8	9.6	20.6	12	0	5
Percentage	100	100	100	100	100	100
Total number	646	557	107	258	11	53

Table 3 Disposition of removals on a flake

Disposition type / sites	Arago	Xibeimaying	Houjiayao	Mansuri-1	Ling-jing	Majuangou
① Longitudinal unidirection	68	59.2	38	56	36	-
② orthogonal disposition	8	15.8	15	11	18	-
③ Transversaly unidirection	2	3.8	8	2	0	-
④ Transversaly bidirection	0	1.3	0	1	0	-
⑤ Longitudinal bidirection	3	8.3	7	2	18	-
⑥ Criss-cross direction	1	1.4	8	3	0	-
⑦ Centripetal direction	0	0	1	0	0	-
⑧ Non removal or cortical	8	4.8	4	11	18	-
⑨ Indeterminate	10	5.4	19	14	10	-
Percentage	100	100	100	100	100	-
Total number	650	557	107	258	11	-

Table 4 State of debitage

Different state / sites	All observed flakes					
	Arqgo	Xibeimaying	Houjiayao	Mansuri-I	Ling-jing	Majuangou
① Group-I (cortical surface)	6	2.6	7.4	10.5	9	6
② Group-II (rarely removals)	7	8.6	7.9	14.8	18	8
③ Group-III (rarely cortex)	41	43.4	41.6	54.6	46	40
④ Group-IV (without cortex)	46	45.4	43.1	20.1	27	46
Percentage	100	100	100	100	100	100
Total number	820	557	107	258	11	53

Table 5 Data concerning the archeometry of flakes

Different methods / sites	Arago	Xibeimaying	Houjiayao	Mansuri-I	Ling-jing	Majuangou
① Length minimum of flake	20	20	20	20	21	21
② Length maximum of flake	94	112	79	104	138	59
③ Length average of flake	39	31.7	38.7	41.6	65.4	35.8
④ Width minimum of flake	1	20	20	12	12	13
⑤ Width maximum of flake	6	109	84	101	120	59
⑥ Width average of flake	unknown	27.1	34.5	39.4	54.1	31.9
⑦ Ratio minimum of width to length	0.42	0.5	0.5	0.4	0.9	0.7
⑧ Ratio maximum of width to length	2.5	2.9	2.1	2.7	1.8	2.5
⑨ Ratio average of width to length	1.21	1.25	1.18	1.14	1.27	1.26
⑩ Percentage of blade ration	4	5.6	0.9	7.9	0	3.7
⑪ Minimum flaking angle	79	90	90	90	95	76
⑫ Maximum flaking angle	135	145	131	139	115	148
⑬ Average flaking angle	110	109.1	108.6	103.3	103.7	111.7
Total number	627–680	449	96–107	241	6–11	46–53

site, however, possesses a sufficient quantity of artifacts, with an average length of 39mm. With an exception of the data of the Ling-Jing site, average length oof the other lithic industries are approximately same as that of the Caunes de L'Arageo. It is likely that this was caused by the occurrence of raw materials sizable enough to restrain the size of detached flakes. Proportion of length and width of flakes of all lithic industries observed is calcurated to 1.2. This tendency means that the flakes are short rather than elongated. In morphology, a blade is defined as a flake whose length is twice that of its width. This quantitative particularity has often led to technological discussion. It varies in the concerned lithic industries, from 0 to 5.6%. Accordingly, they cannot be considered as blade technique.

Detailed arguments are occasionally made about flaking angles. However, these angles are influenced by the different natures or shapes of raw materials. Despite this, it is important to understand flaking angles as a general tendency. The average flaking angle varies between 103° and 112° among the concerned lithic industries, which represents all angles in general, obtuse or open (**Table 5**).

3. Observations of typological aspects

Our point of departure in this research was based on the study of the Acheulean in western Europe, where various types of flint were exclusively used as a raw material. The characteristic blank possesses a kind of generalized property as an elongated and thin flake that is essentially used for refined tool fabrication. Flakes evolved gradually to phase of patternized with variations.

As a result, François Bordes developed a new techno-typological method in the 1950s. In the Far East, a clearly different cultural tradition emerged contemporaneous with the Acheulean of Europe. A lithic industry found at Zhoukoudian Location 1 in the suburbs of Beijing, China, represents this tradition. This lithic industry is characterized by vein quartz, which accounts for 88% of the raw materials at the site. Blanks from the small tools at the site are short and thick, and a number of chips were also used as blanks. Although the number of tool types at this site is fewer than at comparable European sites, it contains side-scrapers, front scrapers, awls, notches, bolas (spheroids), picks, choppers, and chop-

Table 6 Application of flake for the small tooling

All sorts of index deta / sites	Arago	Xibeimaying	Houjiayao	Mansuri-1	Ling-jing	Majuangou
① Tool on flake's percentage among the small toolong	56.5	51.9	31.2	27.5	12.1	24.1
② Tool on debris percentage among the small toolong	38.8	48	68.7	72.4	87.8	75.8
③ Percentage of small tooling among every tools	92.9	93.8	79.4	39	63	69
④ Flake tool number against the total fake number	35.6	24.2	32.7	9.3	45	13.2
⑤ Pebble tool number against the total tool number	7.1	6.2	20.6	61	37	31
⑥ Total tool number	438	277	141	223	65	42

ping tools, among others. Theillard de Chardin defined this lithic industry as Choukoutian or Zhoukoudian (1932).

3.1. Blank type of small tools

We have discussed six lithic industries mentioned above: Caune de l'Arago, Xibamaying, Houjiayao, Mansuri Location 1, Ling-Jing, and Majiangou. The ratio of flake tools in the small tools is between 12.1% and 56.5%. First, we show the lithic industries of Ling-Jing (12.1%) and Majiangou (24.1%), although their total numbers are limited. The other four industries are steady in quantity, yet only represent from 27.5% to 56.5%. Except flakes, the tool-blank replaces debris (chips) or small cobbles. The flakes obtained from the blank production (debitage) were hardly used as blanks of the flake tools, and were instead used as is or discarded. The ratio of true flake tools is from 9.3% to 35.6% of all flakes among the concerned lithic industries (**Table 6**). In other words, almost all of the non-retouched flakes were not used or abandoned. At Caune de l'Arago, the ratio of non-retouched flakes (brute flakes) and retouched flakes (flake tools) are, respectively, 64.4% and 35.6%, which is more balanced than the other lithic industries.

3.2. Raw materials of tool

We noticed some differences in the rocks used among the concerned lithic industries. In short, we thought that the lithic industry of Caune de l'Arago depended on quartz, constituting 65% of the total, and we considered it a particular example. However, at Mansuri Location 1 (95%), Ling-Jing (91%), and Houjiayao (77%), quartz is more numerous than at Caune de l'Arago. The former three sites nearly monopolized all of their raw materials. Besides, Xibeimaying and Majiangou used flint, silicified limestone, chert, jasper, and calcedony, which we called a group of flint, and was representative of the lithic industries of Xibeimaying (61%) and Majiangou (76%). Refer to Table 1- I for more information.

3.3. Two different categories of tool making

We can classify the observed tools into two categories according to different types of blanks. On the one hand, there are large tools, such as pebble tools. On the other, there are small tools, such as flake tools. It is well known that the first type only represents 5% to 10% of traditional knowledge in general. In actuality, this type corresponds to only 7.1% of the tools found at Caune de l'Arago, and 6.2% of the tools found at Xibeimaying. Nevertheless, pebble tools constitute 20.1% to 61% of all tools found at the other sites in the Far East covered in this paper. In particular, the lithic industry at Mansuri Location 1 is characterized by a considerable quantity of bolas and choppers–42.1% and 15.8% of the tools, respectively–and 61% at Mansuri Location 1, including bifaces (* cf. **Table 7**).

3.4. Small tool making (flake-tool group)

Small tools account for only 39% of those found at Mansuri Location 1. The small tool or flake-tool group is dominant in the other lithic industries discussed in the present work, from 63% to 93.8% of all tools found. Concerning Mansuri Location 1, no meaningful difference between small tools and pebble tools with regard to raw materials was found. Surplus materials were knapped on debris and small cobbles, representing 74% of the total tools, while tools made from flakes accounted for only 26% of tools. In comparison, flake tools comprise 56.5% of small tools at Caune de l'Arago (* cf. to the **Table 7**).

3.5. Proportion of small tool making

Small tool making dominated at Xibeimaying (93.8%) and Caune de l'Arago (92.9%). Small tool making was also prominent in the lithic industries of Houjiayou (79.4%), Majiangou (60%), and Ling-Jing (63%)–nevertheless, these industries were characterized by the importance of pebble tools. These two groups are typologically variable in terms of different types of tools. The percentage of small tools made at Mansuri

Location 1 (39%) is extremely low, with no precedent (* cf. to the **Table 7**).

3.6. Side-scraper Group

Among the five lithic industries from the Far East covered in this paper, side-scrapers were relatively uncommon, ranging from 15.2% to 25.5% of total tools found. Simple lateral side-scrapers (10% to 20%) and simple transversal side-scrapers (0% to 14%) are two main types in this group. Composite side-scrapers, such as convergent scrapers (from 0% to 2.1%), "racloir-déjeté" (from 0% to 2.5%), and double side-scrapers (from 0% to 1.5%), were rare. True points are observed in the lithic industry of the Xibeimaying site, but it it represents only 0.4%. Authentic Mousterian point with unifacial retouch is not observed in the lithic industries (* cf. to the **Table 7**).

3.7. Denticulate group

This group shows considerable presences between 20.2% and 63.1% in all lithic industries, in particular those of Xibeimaying and Houjiayao. Notch is present variably among them from 0% to 12.7%, and those of Xibeimaying, Houjiayao and Majiangou represent more 10% remarkably.

The 'bec' (beak) can subdivide into some subcategories (* cf. **Table 7**) which represents from 11.3% to 46.1% as their obvious presences in their lithic industries. Especially, it is very important in those of Xibeimaying and Houjiayao. The authentic denticulate occupies small ratio of 3% to 7.1% in the concerned lithic industries. Above all, those of Xibeimaying (4.7%) and Houjiayao (7.5%) are so remarkable. The type is characterized by two denticulated sides that convergent, in other words the Tayacian point which surely present in some lithic industries, particularly, those of Xibeimaying (1.8% of the total) and Houjiayao (0.7% of the total) are well remarkable.

3.8. Upper Paleolithic group

This group only represents 2% to 5% among them. There are concrete types like continuation: the muzzle front scraper (0% to 2.7%), the frontal scraper (0% to 2.1%), the awl (0% to 1.9%) and other. However, these classified pieces are atypical that their facture and retouch are completely different in relation to the original types at the Upper Paleolithic (* cf. to the **Table 7**).

3.9. Pebble tool

Pebble tools are excessively rich between 20.6% and 61% among the lithic industries of the Far East, except Xibeimaying (6.2% of the total). As for the lithic industry of Majuangou, which the chopper represents 31% of the found tools, the choppers with sharp edge without pointing by the continuous removals occupies not to reach half (39% of the choppers). The badly characterized choppers without retouching by the continuous removals are numerous with 61% of the choppers.

In case of the lithic industry of Mansuri Location 1, the discovered choppers occupies 16.7% of the total tools, which they are enough varied typologically and most of them are mainly a plain type and to sharp without pointing. With regard to choppers of Ling-Jing, they can be classified also in two types that the plain type to sharpen without pointing (5% of the tools) and choppers badly characterized on fracture without retouching (3%). Although the choppers from Houjayou are not so numerous, we can distinguish in two types. The one of ordinary type have a sharp without pointing (0.7% of the tools) and another type is a badly characterized chopper on a fracture without retouching (2.8% of the tools). Finally, the lithic industry of Xibeimaying possesses a little quantity to chopper among it (0.4% of the tools).

There is an obvious type distinguishable itself among the concerned lithic industries. It is the polyhedral type, bolas, without retouching sharp edge. We meet it very rarely in the Lower Paleolithic in Western Europe. However, it is frequent enough in certain cultural facies of the Mousterian in the Middle Paleolithic, the denticulate facies and the Quina facies for example. Remarkably, the bola is absent in the lithic industry of Majuangou. The concerned type represents respectively between 4.7% and 42.1% in four lithic industries of the Far East. In particular, it is extremely numerous in the lithic industry of Mansuri Location 1 which it occupies 42% of the discovered tools. About the tool-making of the bolas, we noted to distinguish several stages and different ways by a lot of superficial removals on the pebble. However, all possess no retouched sharp edge, which they have been shelled completely by the numerous superficial removals in totally or partially. The bolas often has some percussion marks in spot either in a belt that suggests distinctly their use (* cf. **Fig. 1**-4). To the term of the typological observation, it is going without saying that the biface is a characteristic type of the Acheulean and Mousterian. We noted this type of tool in the lithic industries of Xibeimaying (0.4%), Houjayou (0.7%) and Mansuri Location 1 (0.9%). These lithic industries possess more numerous pieces.

4. Diagnosis on the concerned lithic industries

Through analysis of observed data, we need find out deductive and important facts of each industry. However, based on anthropological view point, it requires

Table 7 Variability of different types among the concerned lithic industries

Type group	Individual type	Arago layer H (group)	Arago layer H (type)	Xibeimaying (group)	Xibeimaying (type)	Houjiayao (group)	Houjiayao (type)	Mansuri-1 LIII (group)	Mansuri-1 LIII (type)	Ling-jing Lwr (group)	Ling-jing Lwr (type)	Majuangou L3 (group)	Majuangou L3 (type)
Rac : Side-scraper group	① Lateral simple side-scraper	53	28.7			15.6	10	15.2	9.2	21.5	20	30	12
	② Transversal simple side-scraper		8.5		4		1.4		3.6		0		14
	③ Bifacial retouch piece		0.2		0.4		0		1.3		0		0
	④ Double side-scraper		5.1		1.1		0		0		1.5		0
	⑤ Convergent scraper		1.4		1.1		2.1		0.8		0		2
	⑥ Racloir déjeté		7.3		2.5		0.7		0.4		0		2
	⑦ Point (Mousterian point)		2.2		0.4		0		0		0		0
	⑧ Quinson point		0		0.7		0.7		0		0		0
	⑨ Pointe de limace		0		0		0.7		0		0		0
Dent : Denticulate group	① Clactonian notch	24	4.1	63.1	2.9	56.8	5.7		2.2	28	5	30	0
	② Retouched notch		9		5.1		3.5		2.2		6		0
	③ Double clactonian notchs		0		2.2		0.7		0.8		0		0
	④ Double retouchec notchs		0		0		2.1		0		0		0
	⑤ Double mixed notchs		1.2		0		0.7		0		0		0
	⑥ Bec by a clactonian notch		0.9		19.7		9.3		5.9		1.5		5
	⑦ Bec by a retouched notch		2.7		5.4		7.8		0.4		1.5		2
	⑧ Bec by two clactonian notchs		1.9		12.3		12.9		1.3		5		12
	⑨ Bec by two retouched notchs		0		2.2		0.7		1.3		1.5		2
	⑩ Bec by two mixed notchs		0.2		2.2		0.7		1.3		0		0
	⑪ Double becs by mixed notchs		0		4.3		2.8		0.4		1.5		2
	⑫ Multiple becs by mixed notchs		0		0.4		2.1		0		3		2
	⑬ Simple denticulate by clactonian nochs		2.4		2.9		5		2.7		1.5		0
	⑭ Simple denticulate by retouched notchs		0.2		0.7		0		0		0		0
	⑮ Simple denticulate by mixed notchs		0.9		0.7		2.1		0.8		1.5		5
	⑯ Double lateral denticulates		0.2		0.4		0		0		0		0
	⑰ Tayac type point		0.7		1.8		0.7		0.4		0		0
P.S. : Type of Upper Paleolithic group	① Muzzle end-scraper (grattoir à museau)	12	7.6	2.9	0.7	5	2.1	2.7	0.4	3	0	2	2
	② End-scraper		2.4		0		2.1		1.8		0		0
	③ Atypical drill		1.9		1.8		0.7		0.4		1.5		0
	④ Atypical backed knife		0.4		0		0		0		1.5		0
	⑤ Multiple tool (bec, drill, scraper etc.)		0		0.4		0		0		0		0
Drs. : Divers types group	① Kombewa flake	2	0	2.9	0	3.5	0	1.8	0.9	13.5	0	7	0
	② Cleaver "type 0"		0		0		0		0		1.5		0
	③ Pièce esquillée		0		0.4		1.4		0.9		1.5		0
	④ Fragment of tool (indeterminate type)		1.6		2.5		2.1		0		10.5		7
Bfc : Biface group (biface)	① Typical biface (Covered retouch on 2 faces)	0	0	0.4	0	0.7	0	0.9	0	0	0	0	0
	② Atypical biface (patial retouch)		0		0.4		0.7		0.9		0		0
Glt. : Pebble tool group	① Chopper without point	9	1.7	5.1	0.4	18.4	0.7	59.2	10.9	34	5	31	12
	② Pointed chopper		2.2		0		0		0		0		0
	③ Bad characteristic chopper		1.2		0		2.8		3.6		3		19
	④ Double side-choppers		2.4		0		0		0.9		0		0
	⑤ Unilateral retouched pic		0		0		0		0.9		0		0
	⑥ Chopper of "Rostro-caréné" type		0.4		0		0		0.4		0		0
	⑦ Chopping-tool without point		0.2		0		0		0.9		5		0
	⑧ Pointed chopping-tool		0.2		0		0		0		0		0
	⑨ Polyhedral tool or bola		0		4.7		8.6		42.1		18		0
	⑩ Fragment of bola		0		0		6.4		0		3		0
percentage		100	100	100	100	100	100	100	100	100	100	100	100
Total number		407	407	277	277	141	141	223	223	65	65	42	42

circumspection as we argue cultural products of the mankind belonging to one or two older evolutionary stages, but we have to make a logic and bold inference too.

4.1. Caune de l'Arago

The blank production is based on a non-blade technique and non-prepared debitage. Regarding the raw material, kinds of sedimentary rocks with fine quality have also been used, but quartz has been mainly used which occurs around the site. In general, the non-continual debitage provides proportionally short and thick flakes. The produced blank possesses less advantageous morphologically in relation to the other contemporary lithic industries. In consequence, the debris was often used in this lithic industry. Therefore, the finishing of the retouched tools is less good, though the type of the small tools is varied enough typologically. Pebble tool is a small number, but chopper is merely present. Biface is absent entirely. True point and convergent scraper exist certainly, and side-scrapers on large flake are also included. It means that the life style was based on true hunting rather than scavenger. This lithic industry was called the Proto-Tayacian formerly, but it may be related to the lithic industry discovered at the Zhoukoudian Location 1 cave site in the Middle Pleistocene to the first half of the Upper Pleistocene in the Far East.

4.2. Xibeimaying

Regarding the raw material, the Xibeimaying site contains quartz to a certain extent. However, it was rather served for making and use of pebble tool. For the blank production and the trimming of the small tool, the sedimentary rocks with fine quality were used mainly. The exploited technique is non-blade technic and non-prepared debitage, but the debitage shows the most continual flake reduction and frequent platform changing on the core in the concerned lithic industries. Although it has these features, the detached flakes are the smallest among the concerned lithic industries. On the other hand, their advantageous morphology is well clean in relation to those, consequently the tools on debris are in the smallest number. Therefore, the finishing of the small tooling is improved relatively more ameliorate. The small tool making is characterized by the dominance of the denticulate group. On the other hand, the side-scraper group is relatively poor. The pebble-tool like chopper is rare but a certain number of the bolas exists. The true point on flake and the convergent scraper are distinctly poor, besides the side-scraper on large-flake is also in small number. It would reveal the life style is rather scavenger than hunter. We cannot find out such any techno-typological feature as support 28,240±120 BP dated recently by the radioactive dating method. Rather than we can relate to the lithic industry discovered at the Zhoukoudian Location 1 Cave site in the Middle Pleistocene to the first half of the Upper Pleistocene in the Far East. we could follow a report of the lithic industry discovered at the Zhoukoudian Location 1 Cave site. The lithic industry is characterized by the dominance of the denticulate group with the presence of Tayacian-point. It evokes a typological lineage with the cultural face of Mousterian Denticulate in western Europe.

4.3. Houjiayao

Regarding the raw material it composes quartz mainly, while the sedimentary rocks including flint are in small number. The quartz is a selected rock in the limit of the debitage and the trimming of tools, though this unfit rock occupies more half of the raw material. In most cases, the core platform is removing the natural surface, but it is always non-blade technique and non-prepared debitage. We notice a big continuity on the debitage and the frequency of changing platform after the lithic industry of Xibeimaying. The flakes of this site are more short and thick in general. Therefore, they have some advantageous morphology relatively comparing to the other concerned lithic industries. However, the tools on debris are distinctly majority in the small tool making. It looks like the tendency of the lithic industries of the Mansuri Location 1, Ling-Jing and Majuangou. Accordingly the finishing of the small tool making is not refined, which is characterized by the dominance of the denticulate group and it occupies the majority within the total tools. This typological tendency is obviously familiar to the one of Xibeimaying. The chopper is rare among the large tools, but the bolas occupy relatively large ratio in the sites of the Mansuri Location 1 and Ling-Jing. Both true point on flake and the side-scraper on large-flake are absent.

In consequence, the life-style was rather the scavenger with numerous bolas and becs than the hunter. According to the techno-typological analyses of this lithic industry, it does not agree with radioactive ages dated recently. It allows us to remember a lineage with the lithic industry discovered at the Zhoukoudian Location 1 cave site. As mentioned above, this lithic industry is characterized by the dominance of the denticulate group with the Tayacian point like the one of Xibeimaying. It evokes a typological lineage with the cultural phase of Mousterian Denticulate in western Europe.

4.4. Mansuri Location 1

The usage of the raw material among the concerned lithic industries gives us a strong shock, which it hardly lacks sedimentary rocks like flint and quartz is only object for trimming. With regard to blank production and trimming of tool, quartz monopolizes to prevent the introduction of other rocks. The debitage has often been executed from the core platform with cortex that was non-continual flaking. Therefore, the used technique is non-blade technique without any preparation on the core surface. The continuity on the debitage is the lowest among the concerned lithic industries and very little to change some positions for the platform. These features look like the industry of Ling-Jing. However, the detached flakes are relatively big size, though their morphologies are proportionally short and thick that is unfit as the blank of the small-tool. Most of the core surface and platforms are covered with cortex, and the core reduction is a single without continuous flaking. Changing of the platform on the core is rare, which is alike to the Ling-Jing site. Although the size of the flake is large comparatively, the shape is short and irregular. The detached blank is the most inferior among the concerned lithic industries. Therefore, small tools made on debris occupy the majority, which is similar to the lithic industries of Ling-Jing and Majuangou. The finishing of the tools is mediocre, and the variation of the various tool types is poor on the contrary to its huge quantity recovered. With regard to the typology of this lithic industry, the side-scraper is relatively a few. On the other hand, the denticulate group is predominant and varied in different types. Regarding to pebble-tools, the chopper is especially enormous number and typologically varied in subcategories. The discovered bolas shows also so high proportion. This characteristic exceeds the numbers of Houjiayao and Ling-Jing. On the other hand, the true point on flake is completely lacking, and convergent side-scraper is very rare. Moreover, the side-scraper on large-flake is not contained at all. This composition of the lithic tools suggests that the life style was not probably based on the true hunting. To the contrary, it is characterized by a large quantity of becs, notches and bolas, in addition these lithic tools have not pointed tip and sharp cutting edges. The bolas shows especially the largest quantity in the concerned industries. There is no point and large side-scraper, though a few convergent scrapers is contained. This tool assemblage indicates that the life style was not directed for full-scale hunting. It evokes us a kind of life style as scavenger rather than hunting. Besides biface and pic with retouch on one-side existed certainly. This would indicate the cultural contact with other human groups in contemporary. The techno-typological feature does not certainly agree with its more recent age dated by the radiometric method. In this connection, we compares this lithic industry with the one of the Caune de l'Arago in France which we remember the older Mode 2 or the Mode 1. This lithic industry was recovered by a systematic and modern method where the archaeological pieces were kept well in the thick paleosol of

MIS 5c-e. Finally, the dominance of quartz and the phase of predominance of the denticulate group closely resemble to the industry of Ling-Jing.

4.5. Ling-Jing

In the composition of the raw material, quartz is the majority but quartzite is also contained a considerable quantity. These two kinds of rocks are oligopolistic in the raw material. Sedimentary rock like flint is nearly absent. As for the blank production, quartzite makes higher its importance, but quartz monopolizes the raw material in the small tool making. The platform on the core is often in cortex, which the flakes have been not detached continuously from there. The used technique is non-blade technique and non-prepared debitage. Accordingly, the continuity of debitage is relatively low among the concerned lithic industries, in spite of changing of the platform positions that was frequent enough. The technical length of flake is the biggest among them, though the proportion between the length and the width is short. The detached flakes have not the morphological advantage comparing to the other concerned lithic industries. The rate of the tools made on debris is more numerous. It shows a similar tendency to the industries of Mansuri Location 1 and Majuangou. The typological characteristic shows the denticulate group is superior, but the side-scraper group is little. The percentage of the pebble-tools is high, in particular, choppers are relatively numerous. In particular, the big bolas shows high percentage. This typological particularity is evaluated between the lithic industries of Houjiayao and the Mansuri Location 1. Both true point on flake and convergent scraper are absent. However, a few side-scrapers on large-flake made of quartzite exist certainly. It evokes us a life style of hunting more or less. As we had a limit as to number of the observed pieces, we can not know more in detail. Besides, there are a lot of becs, notches, denticulates and bolas. It shows analogy with those of Houjiayou and Mansuri Location 1 on typology.

4.6. Majuangou

The composition of the raw material is very unique, because it does not nearly contain quartz and quartzite. The used rocks are some silicified limestone, limestone, flint, chert, jasper and kinds of sedimentary rocks. The limestone is a destined rock to pebble-tool, silicified limestone and flint were often used for the debitage. This suggests that Majuangou Man has had enough knowledge as to the nature of their rocks. As for the debitage, the core platform is more often in non-cortex than in cortex. However, the butt and the flake surface are often covered with cortex while the core always remains the residual of cortex. However, the platform has frequently changed its positions at the time of the debiatge in general. The technique used in the blank production is non-blade technique and non-prepared debitage. The average length of the blank flakes is small and short after that of Xibeimaying. The flake tool made on debris is the most numerous after Ling-Jing. As the result, the finishing of tools is not quite refined. With regard to the typology, the small tool making of the side-scraper group and the denticulate group is superior. These compose the majority of the total of the tools. The chopper is in large number among the pebble-tools. In particular, atypical chopper which used directly fractured surface exceeds to the typical one. In fact, both bolas and biface are completely absent. The true point on flake is also absent. Although convergent scraper exists in atypical, the side-scraper on large-flake is rare. Therefore, the life style was rather scavenger than true hunting. The techno-typological analysis shows its particularities that are not so obvious in relation to its very old age which indicated by the paleontological method and paleomagnetic dating. Nevertheless, this lithic industry would correspond to the older Oldowan in the Far East, it is very important as archaeological evidence of the earliest human diffusion in these concerned regions.

5. Conclusion

The five lithic industries from the Far East have been dated between 1.6 Ma and 30 ka by the several different dating methods. However, we hesitate to say that the techno-typological studies for these lithic industries have been executed in detail, in particular regarding those numeric data on the statistics. Showing our tentative results at last, we would like to expect more development of the statistical analysis in future.

The oldest phase in the Far East is the industry of the cultural level III in the Majuangou site that preceded the Acheulean phase in China represented on the Yunxian and Bose sites. The acquirement means of the raw material have been already established and enough familiarized. The production of flake as a blank was done, but obvious secondary retouch for small flake tool is poor. Massive tools such as chopper account for very large ratio, but bolas or spheroid and biface are absent entirely. The edge of chopper is atypical without more retouching.

The distinguished second stage, so-called the phase of the typical Zhoukoudian culture, seem to have developed after the phase of the classic Acheulean in China. The lithic industries of the cultural layer III of the Mansuri Location I site, the lower culture of Ling-Jing and Houjiayao are compared to the second stage. The former two industries are certainly dated to MIS 5 by the loess-paleosol chronology. Only quartz as the raw material was used entirely. The blank production is very active, but all blank is thick and short commonly. However, they were hardly used as blank with intentional secondary retouch. Although their industries lack typical or true point and large side-scraper on flake, side-scraper and denticulate groups show variety in morphology. Large massive tool is so remarkable, and especially chopper shows high ratio. Bolas or spheroid without any sharp edge is composed of majority in this stage. A few bifaces exist certainly in this group. It is possible that we can compare this phase with the Protro-Tayacian of the layer H at the Caune de l'Arago, in France, though their typological features are not accord with the Protro-Tayacian always.

The third distinguished phase is so-called the developed stage of the Zhoukoudian lithic industries. It could appear after the second phase described above. This industry is equivalent to the lithic industry of Xibeimaying. The raw material shows a diversity of the sedimentary rocks vastly, despite of quartz survives well in a part. The production of the blank by flaking is more active than the previous stage, and the detached flake is always short and small. Although such blanks are frequently used as tool, the half of the tool blanks is debris. True unifacial retouched point and side-scraper on large flake are in small number. On the other hand, both side-scraper group and denticulate group are important with various types. Although the quantity of the pebble-tools is a few, they are comparable to examples of other regions of the world. Chopper is rare too, but bolas is an important tool as always. In the same way, biface is rarely present in its typological composition. As a result, this phase show more developed one than the second distinguished phase above, though these two phases are in even cultural lineage. The denticulate group including the Tayacian point is predominant as a whole. These typological features evoke us the Mousterian denticulate phase in the Middle Paleolithic in Western Europe.

Acknowledgements

First of all, this study is based on the project of the scientific subsidy of the Japanese government (Assigment No.21251010 in 2009-2012) and represented by Professor Kazuto Matsufuji (University of Doshisha, Kyoto Japan). The project permitted to prospect in China and in South Korea, ten times during a number total of more than hundred days. During that time, Professor Matsufuji achieved a scientific environment according to the meticulous plans and his negotiations. Professor Yung-Jo Lee, President of the Institute of the Korean Prehistory that made good welcome in a friendly way to us, and he opened us generously his very important materials from the recent excavation. Director Xie Fei of Archaeological Institute of Hebei Province and the Institute of Nihewan in Hebei Province, China welcomed us kindly and he showed us his very precious Archaeological materials. Finally we received a good welcome very amiably at Professor Zhanyang LI of Institute of Archaeological Research of Cultural Relics of the Henan Province, China. He opened us his lately discovered lithic industry. As for our visiting in China, Doctor Shinji Katô of Nara National Research Institute for Cultural Properties guided us every times prospectively. We express our gratitude to the concerned ladies and gentlemen. Accomplishing our studies, we put forward the techno-typological method devised by Professor and director Henry de Lumley of the Human Paleontology Institute in Paris, who recommended me to study the lithic industries of the Middle Pleistocene in my staying in France. We express all our acknowledgments for Professor Henry de Lumley.

References

Institute of Korean Prehistory. 2010. *Report on the Excavation of Mansu-ri Paleolithic Site (Loc. 1·2·3)*, Cheongwon, 495p.

Jia Lampo, Wei Qi and Li Chaorong., 1979. Report on the excavation of Hsuchiayao man site in 1976. *Vertebrata Palasiatica* 17-4, 277-293.

LI Zhengtao et al., 2014. Study on stratigraphic age, climate changes and environment background of Houjiayao Site in Nihewan Basin. *Quarternary International* 349, 42-48.

Lumley H. de et al., 2011. *Les industries du Paléolithique ancien de la Corée du Sud dans leur contexte stratigraphique et paléoécologique*, Paris: C.N.R.S., 631p.

Ma Ning, Pei Shu-wen and Gaoxing. 2011. A Preliminary Study on the Stone Artifacts Excavated Locality 74093 of the Xujiayao Site in 1977. *Acta Anthropologica Sinica* 30-3, 275-288.

Matsufuji, K. ed., 2013. *Basic Studies of the Paleoenvironmental Changes and Paleolithic Chronologiy in Northeast Asia*, Scientific Research Fund by the government of Japan: Basic Study A (Subject number : 21251010), 207p.

Nagatomo, T., Shitaoka, Y., Namioka, H., Sagawa, M. and Wei Qi. 2009. OSL Dating of the Strata at Paleolithic Sites in the Nihewan Basin. China. *Acta Anthropologica Sinica* 28(3), 276-284.

Theillard de Chardin P., 1932. The little industry of the Sinanthropus deposits in Choukoutien. *Bull. Geol. Soc. China* 11(4), 315-358.

Wang Fagang, Liu Lianqiang and Xi Fei. 2013. Results of the excavations at the Houjiayao site in 2007-2008. In Matsufuji, K. ed., *Basic Studies of the Paleoenvironmental Changes and Paleolithic Chronology in Northeast Asia*, 61-64.

Watanabe, M. and Kikuchi, K., 2013. Morphological and Sediment-environmental Examination for Houjiayao site. In Matsufuji, K. ed., *Basic Studies of the Paleoenvironmental Changes and Paleolithic Chronology in Northeast Asia*, 73-78.

Xie Fei et al., 1989. The Study of the Upper Paleolithic from the Xibeimaying site at Yangyuan County in Hebei Province. *Wenwuchunqiu* 1989(3), 13-26.

Chrono-typological studies of lithic industries from the Mansuri Paleolithic Site Locality 1 in Korea

Kazuharu TAKEHANA[1], Yung-jo LEE[2], Kaoru OTANI[3]

[1] Institute of Human Paleontology in France, Japan ; kazu-f19@sea.ncv.ne.jp
[2] Institute of Korean Prehistory(IKP), Korea
[3] Tokyo Metropolitan University, Japan

ABSTRACT

The lithic industry of Mansuri Paleolithic site Locality 1 (MPSL1), Cheongju, Korea, was systematically analyzed by using methods and archeological materials derived from Professor Henry de Lumley, which he developed for Middle Pleistocene lithic industries from Caune de l'Arago in France. MPSL1 does not have real convergent scrapers (points) or retouched large flakes. On the other hand, it does have numerous polyhedrons and choppers, among other tools. With regard to evaluating raw materials, the lithic industry at the site is dominated exclusively by quartz, which was acquired nearby. In addition, a large number of natural pebbles or tested pebbles can be found at MPSL1. These quartz blocks or pebbles were eventually used to manufacture bolas, polyhedrons, or choppers. They were not exploited systematically for the production of blanks – in other words, for flaking (debitage) in relation to silicic rock, as in flint. In many cases, silicious rocks are commonly preferred to produce stone tools. However, this rock type has served for flaking (debitage), whose quartz occupies a monopolistic position; otherwise, two types of quartzite are rarely present. The observation of flake butts (a part of the striking platform) revealed that the flakes often retained some of their residual cortex on the flake surface which means no conitnuation of flaking at the same spot. The flakes are generally short and large. The flaking process (debitage) hardly contributed to tool making in these lithic industries. The debitage is either quite non-Levallois or non-blade techniques considering common residual cortex on blanks.

국문초록

이 논문은 프랑스 중기구석기 유적의 유물 분류와 석기공작 체계를 적용하여 극동아시아 중기구석기 시대 대표 유적인 만수리 1지점 석기공작을 평가한다. 만수리 유적은 기술형태적 석기공작 특성상 과감한 사냥도구로서 찌르개나 동물 해체를 위한 비가공의 대형격지는 없으며, 서구유럽의 동시기 유적의 소형석기에 비해 덜 발달된 양상을 보이는 대신 여러면석기, 찍개류가 월등히 우세한 분포 양상을 보인다. 석기공작에 사용된 돌감은 석영제가 우세하며 유적에 인접한 지역에서 조달된 재료로 보고 있다. 석영제 자갈돌이나 자연면 제거가 시도된 자갈돌이 수없이 많은 점이 주목되는데 이들 자갈돌은 사냥돌, 여러면석기, 찍개 제작에 사용되었다고 보며, 플린트(flint) 같은 규산질 돌감에서 보이는 체계적 격지기술에 의한 몸체(blank) 생산은 나타나지 않는다. 또한 후기구석기를 대표하는 돌날제작 기술 측면에서 보면 많은 수의 격지가 존재하지만 전통적 격지 연모로 성형되지는 않았고 돌조각으로 만들어진 도구가 대부분이다. 석기 몸체로는 소형 자갈돌이 이용되었지만 석기제작에서 전형적 르발루아 기술 혹은 돌날 기술에 속하지 않는다. 소형 자갈돌 석기제작에서 대부분 자연면이 남아 있는(residual cortex) 몸체들로 구성된다.

Keywords : Mansuri Paleolithic Site Locality 1 (MPSL1), pebble tool, flaking (debitage), quartz, raw materials, blanks

1. Introduction

For one of the early Paleolithic industry in the Far East, we focused on Mansuri Paleolithic site Locality 1, Cheongju, Korea (Lee Y. et al. and Institute of Korean Prehistory, 2010). As far as the method used for these studies, we applied the systematic method and archeological materials from Professor Henry de Lumley as he developed for Middle Pleistocene lithic industries at Caune de l'Arago in France (de Lumley, 1979) (**Fig. 1**).

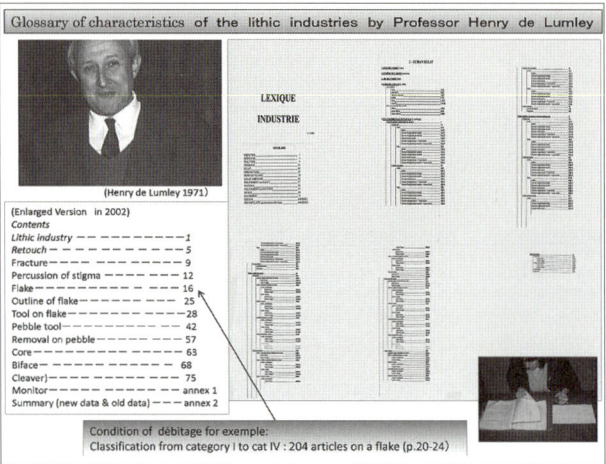

Fig. 1 Used methods on the concerned studies

Of course, we used only the data group which filled statistical quantity fundamentally. The method for the observation that is the above three viewpoints about fabrication of tool blank technique(debitage), typological study(typology), and the acquisition of Raw Material (archeo-petrography). By this consequence, we are accumulating very detailed data information. This result is data corresponding to the Middle and the Lower Paleolithic in the Occidental Europe. In fact, we are increasing the data corresponding to the former region studies. This directive action is clarifying the coincidence on the different regions by human-beings culture, and evolution. We are sure that this tentative can greatly evoke the argument in a study of prehistory from East Asia to the world (Kakehana, 2016; Takehana, 2022).

This method has been used for the analysis of Lower Paleolithic lithic industries that have yielded a large quantity of data, such as the Baume-Bonne cave site (Gagnepain and Gaillard, 2005) and the Terra-Amata site (de Lumley et al., 2015). The method has generated systematic results for lithic industries from the Middle and Lower Paleolithic on several continents. Specifically, it has been applied to industries from Paleolithic sites in several monographs of Paleolithic sites in Spain, Ethiopia, India and Southern China published by Professor Henry de Lumley in his scientific capacity for comparative anslysis (de Lumley et al., 2010).

F. Bordes' method(Bordes, 1950, 1953) is used for techno-typolocial observation of limited numbers of lithic industires from different areas (**Fig. 2**).

Of course, we only used data that is expected enough quantity to get meaningful statistical results. The method designated from the three viewpoints described above was applied to make observation of the fabrication of blanks (debitage), typological study (typology), and the acquisition of raw materials (archeo-petrography) (**Fig. 3**). Consequently, we accumulated very detailed data. This resulted in data corresponding to the Middle and Lower Paleolithic in Occidental Europe. In fact, we are increasing the amount of data corresponding to the former regional studies. This purpose for this action is to clarify the coincidence of the different regions by human culture and evolution. We are certain that this tentative analysis could evoke an argument in a study of prehistory of East Asia to rest of the world (Kakehana, 2016; Takehana, 2022) (**Fig. 4**).

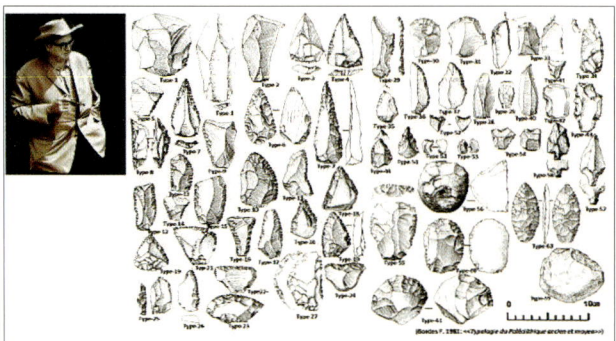

Fig. 2 Typology of Middle and Lower Paleolithic by François Bordes

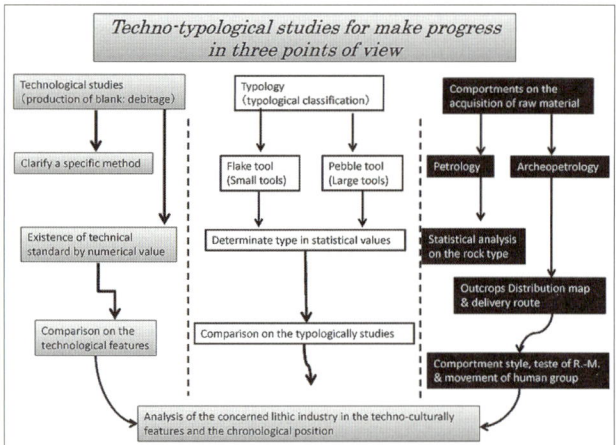

Fig. 3 Three points of view on the techno-typological observation four these studies

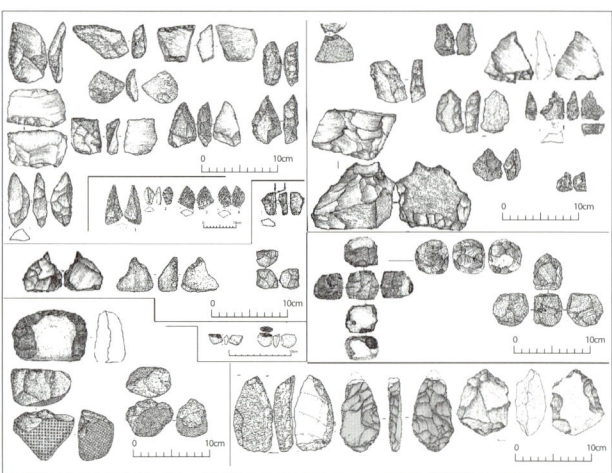

Fig. 4 The encountered types in those studies in the Far East

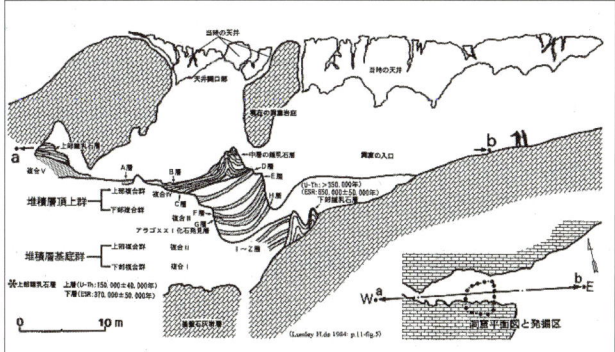

Fig. 5 The cave of La Caune de l'Arago is situated in France, dated 450,000 years. In short, 90% of other flakes didn't have any retouching that was abandoned on the camp site. To this subject, in the stratigraphy of the Lower Ensemble at La Caune de l'Arago in the layers H and J, dated by 500, 000 years ago, in France. The non retouched flakes (natural state) and retouched flakes (flake tool) represent respectively 80% and 20% in a concerned lithic industry.

2. Techno-typological features and raw materials

2.1. Techno-typological features

Here, we pay attention to technological and typological studies of lithic industries from Mansuri Paleolithic site Locality 1 in a chronological and cultural framework. An important characteristic is that the production of flakes was not frequently chosen as a tool blank by authentic retouching. It only represents 10% of this lithic industry, especially in layer III (Takehana, Matsufuji et al., 2013).

In short, 90% of flakes without any retouches was abandoned at the camp site. The stratigraphy of the Lower Ensemble, layers H and J, at Caune de l'Arago, have been dated to 500 ka BP. The non-retouched flakes (natural state) and retouched flakes (flake tools) represent 80% and 20% of the concerned lithic industry, respectively (**Fig. 5, 6**).

2.2. Raw materials

We classified four types of rock. However, they are different types of quartz originated from pebbles at channel bed. These similar rocks of quartz constitute the majority of raw materials among the lithic instruments at the site, accounting for 96% of the total. At Caune de l'Arago, 67% of the flake tools in the lithic industry are made of quartz. With regard to the discovered tools, they are typologically classified into four categories: pebble tools (59%), flake tools (38%), bifaces (1%), and diverse types (2%). The flake tools, including tools made of small debris, count themselves 86% that are relatively in large number in relation to the pebble tools. In this category, the following two types of rock were used: quartz (95%) and quartzite (5%). Flake tools and pebble tools show same proportion of raw materials. The blanks of tools are dominated extensively by debris, pebble

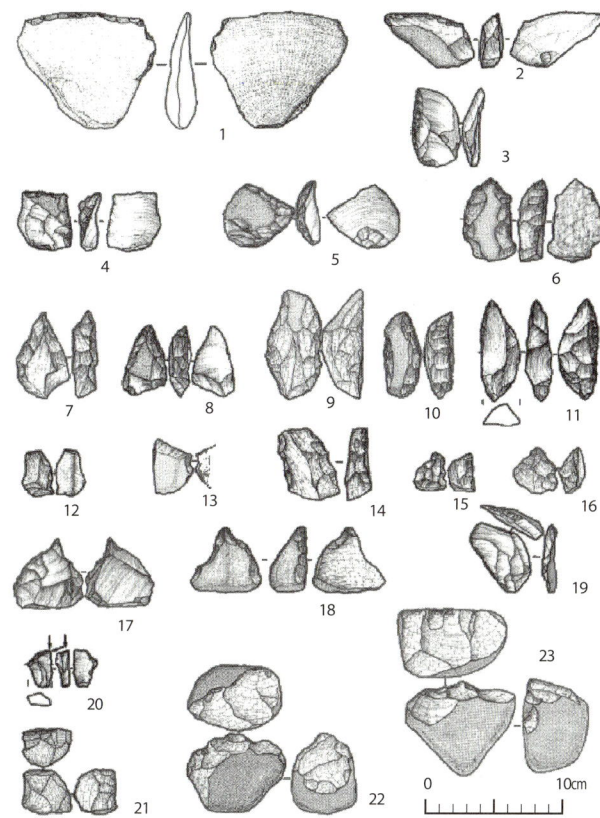

Fig. 6 Linthic industris of La Caune de l'Arago cave in France our standard site as technotypological index.

fragments, and cobbles, representing 74%, while flakes are only composed 26%. To this look, flake represents 50% in relation to the tools on debris in layers in La Caune de l'Arago cave (**Table 1**).

3. Flake tools and pebble tools

3.1. Flake tools (Small tools)

The different types of tools are characterized by some typological features. First, the composition of the scrapers is relatively modest, comprising 15% of the total.

It is composed of simple lateral scrapers (9%), simple transverse scrapers (4%), convergent scrapers (1%), double-sided scrapers (1%), and lopsided scrapers (racloir-déjeté; 0.4%). It is characterized by the absence of authentic uniface points. With regard to the denticulate group, it appears to have a large typological presence, with 20% of the total. It contains some becs (11%), simple denticulate (9%), notches (5%), and Tayac points (0.4%). Concerning the Upper Paleolithic tool group, it contains only end-scrapers (2%), nosed end-scrapers (0.4%), and drills (0.4%).

Table 1 Raw Material of the Analysed lithic industries

rock type / sites	Total of pices		Total of flakes		Total of tools	
	Arago	Mansuri-1	Arago	Mansuri-1	Arago	Mansuri-1
① Quartz	85.9	94.7	59.6	98.4	65	95
② Crystal	0	0	0	0	0	0
③ Qrtz.-sandstone	0	1.2	0	0	0	0
④ Quartzite	3.1	3	12.3	1.6	6	5
⑤ Slcfd. Sandstone	0	0.2	0.1	0	2	0
⑥ Limestone	1.9	0	1.1	0	0.5	0
⑦ Slcfd. Limestone	0	0	0	0	0	0
⑧ Flint	6.8	0	20.9	0	23	0
⑨ Chart	0	0	0	0	0	0
⑩ Jasper	0.6	0	2.3	0	3	0
⑪ Chalcedony	0	0	0	0	0	0
⑫ Petrified wood	0	0	0	0	0	0
⑬ Andesite	0	0	0	0	0	0
⑭ Volcanic rock	0	0.2	0	0	0	0
⑮ Sandstone	0.6	0.5	0	0	0.5	0
⑯ Granite	0	0	2.4	0	0	0
⑰ Schist	0	0.08	0	0	0	0
⑱ Slate	0.3	0	0.2	0	0	0
⑲ Indeterminate	0.8	0.12	1.1	0	0	0
percentage	100	100	100	100	100	100
Total number	6,431	1,258	627	258	334	86

3.2. Pebble-tools (Large tools)

Pebble tools predominant in this lithic industry, representing 18% of the total. The group of pebble tools includes choppers without points (11%), non-characterized choppers (4%), double choppers (1%), chopping tools (1%), picks (1%), and "Rostro-Caréné" (0.1%). It is important that some bifaces were also identified that were partially retouched on two faces (1%). Lastly, one of the strongest points in this lithic industry was found: the "bola," which is a polyhedral type without a sharp edge. The quantity of this type is very important, as it reached nearly one-half of the total number of tools.

4. Comparison

We statistically compared Mansuri Paleolithic site Locality 1 with other sites to determine the chronological position while using techno-typological indications. However, not enough data is available at present since we have just begun. We would like to first present the data from the Lower Ensemble of Caune de l'Arago cave in France. This lithic industry deferred distinctly in the geographical and cultural measure. Nevertheless, it should be noted that it was essentially knapped on quartz as the one of the site concerned in the Occidental Europe. However, this comparison has great significance in that it permits us to determine the technical and typological characteristics of the focal lithic industry (**Fig. 7**).

5. Observation of boals and some polyhedral pieces

5.1. Raw materials

Bolas and related pieces in the concerned lithic industry are counted 93 pieces of this type from layer III. They were resulted from toughness of raw material to make intended fracture. Quartz is dominant (88%), followed by quartzite (8%), sandstone quartzite (3%), and sandstone (1%).

5.2. Types of blank

With regard to the blanks of the polyhedral pieces, they originate in pebbles, amazingly comprising 95% of the total. In this case, pebbles that were thick, angular, and short were chosen, as these are crucial to making bolas.
The highest frequency was thick, round, and short pebble

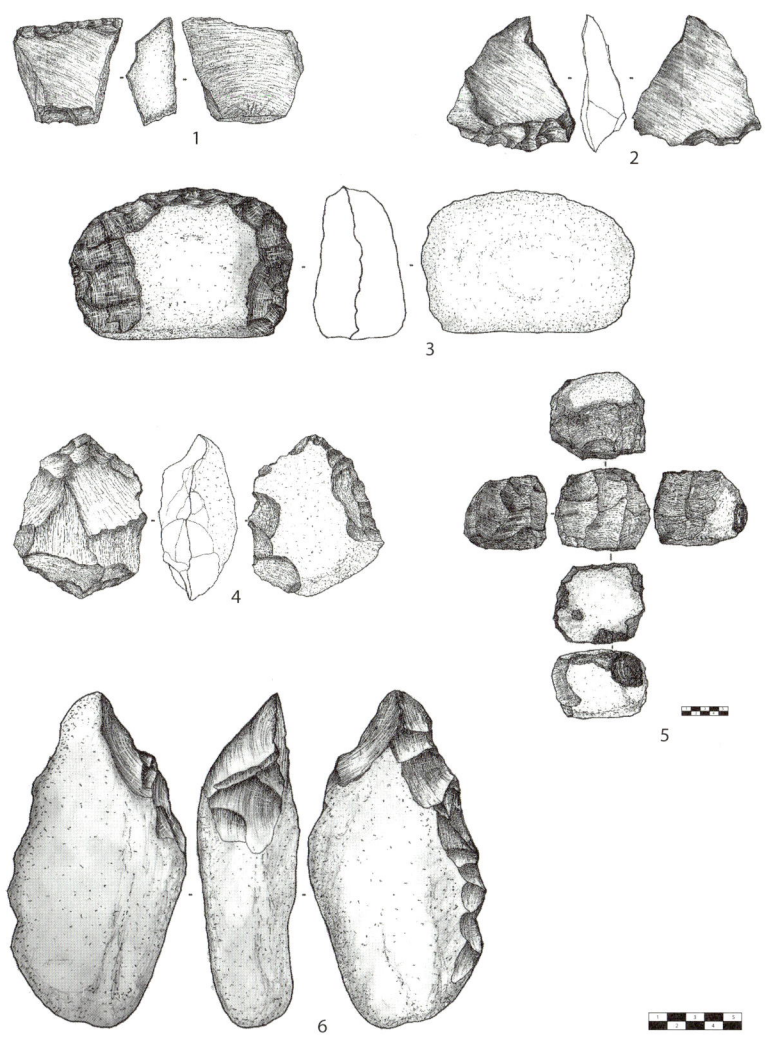

Fig. 7 Lithic industry of the Mansuri Paleolithic site Locality 1 (layer 3)

(17%). Next were pebbles that were thick, round, and long (8%). And there are a type of thick pebble that doesn't permit its shape and its length (10%). However, that may be, thickness was the most important at the time of acquierment of the raw material.

5.3. Number of removals on the surface

We observed some removals varying from 1 (minimum) to 21 (maximum), and a bola possesses nine removals on average. These are various; however, the number shows a tendency toward a large number of removals.

5.4. Different platforms of removal

If we observed their platforms one by one, we would have different compositions above. In the first place, some pieces with all platforms in the cortex that were more important represented 52% of the total. On the other side, some pieces owned some platforms in the cortex and in the non-cortex (15%), and some pieces with some platforms totally in the non-cortex (4%) were well recessive.

5.5. Number of retouched faces on a bola

If we considered this bola like a regular tetrahedron, we could have some different features according to some facial retouches. Some pieces with a retouched face only (5%), with two retouched faces (27%), with three retouched faces (14%), with four retouched faces (10%), with five retouched faces (2%) and with six retouched faces are present. These fractures are unknown by reason of damage. In any case, the polyhedral pieces were retouched on only a few faces on those surfaces.

5.6. Percussion of stigmata (number)

We very often observed some traces of beating on the ridges and flat faces of this piece. First, we examined every piece and counted number of stigma.on his number of stigmas while counting it. Some pieces with only a simple stigma were more numerous, representing 28% of the total. In continuation, some pieces with two represented 15%, and some pieces with three only represented 3%. We noticed that the polyhedrons without a stigma were rare. However, 42% of the pieces had a posterior break and as such we did not know much about this characteristic.

5.7. Localization of percussion stigmata

We notice that this characteristic is the most often on the edges forming by two built faces with 29% of the percussion marks examined, or on the forming angles by three built faces with 10% in the same way. On the other hand, the percussion marks on the cortical flat faces (6%) and on the smooth flat faces (3%) are distinctly in small number.

5.8. Convexity on the removal section

We also observed the composition of the different types of removals on this tool. In short, we distinguish some negative, flat or positive removals. The 35% of tools are shaped by the retouch of the mixed removals (negative and positive) and beating. Not only those, a mixed composition by some flat and positive removals that represent 10%. On the other hand, those by some retouch of the negative removals (6%)

and finally, those of a retouch of beating (5%) which are respectively rare enough.

5.9. Spherical finishing on this type

We classified above, a beautiful sphere (8% of the tools), a good spere (30%), a rather sphere (26%) and weakly sphere (36%). Therefore, we suppose that a spheric finishing was not morphologically a goal on the consequence.

5.10. Size of the tool (maximum diameter)

With regard to a diameter of the tools that varies themselves from 53mm to 126mm. Their average is of 90mm. This variation is considerable that we can subdivide in three groups. We can define the large group (from 96mm to 126mm), the middle size group (from 71mm to 95mm) and the small size group (from 50mm to 70mm). They represent themselves respectively 46%, 42% and 12%.

5.11. Weight of the tool

They vary themselves from 169 to 1,563g whose average is 840g. The variation of their weights is also very large which we can regroup also like the size in three categories as the size of tools. The category heavy weights are from 1,001 to 1,600g while representing 34% of this tool. The one of middle weight is from 601 to 1,000g with 34% among those and the one of light weight is in the same way from150 to 600g with 32%. Each of three categories makes considerably a balance.

5.12. Morphology of the blank

About the choice of support that the thick pebble made of quartz. This rivers pebbles had been sought-after according to the model of use which owns a rough section. It is not a nature what was sought-after for the small tools it, some sedimentary rocks, especially the flint for example.

5.13. Discussion

The retouching of this type tool is formed on average nine flat or superficial removals. Concerning frequency of facial work that is carved from 2 to 4 faces and more often from the cortical platform on a pebble. This decorticated flaking is essentially different in relation to the debitage or the tool edge flaking. Because it is not quite a same intention on the fabrication of flake-tool. Concerning this process of decorticated facial flaking, If we compared it to nibbling of a whole apple. We would eat while making the tour of skins below in upper parts and under remaining the two tips and in top. Finally, it remains some that as the core of an apple. As it is mentioned higher than we can classify them in three categories, big, middle and small sizes. Another point of view we can classified in the same way as, heavy, middle and light weights. These features could come from the capacity of exercise on a paleolithic man side and different objects of use. Among the tools of a big ensemble in a lithic industry at the Lower Paleolithic in the Far-East that we didn't find more take notice with the polyhedron tools as the choppers and chopping-tools accompanied. However, a number of discovered polyhedrons possesses some percussion stigmas which their traces himself is characterized by constant features. Therefore, we would be able to suppose like an instrument destined to serve that one breaks dead flesh bone etc. objects, brittle and less resistance of rubbing rather than a cutting tool.

6. Conclusion

We appreciated the lithic industries of the Mansuri-Loc.1 Paleolithic site that is highly regarded as a representative site of the Middle Pleistocene in the Far East (**Fig. 8**).
Thereafter techno-typologically analyses that we analyzed these lithic industries are characterized by some aspects of the underdevelopment on the small tools that are far quite than the contemporaries sites in Occidental-Europe.
That is, it doesn't have a real convergent scraper(point) for the daring hunting, non- retouched large flake for butcher etc. On the other hand, it composes numerous polyhedrons, choppers etc. that they are distinctly predominant. It is cultural facies that appear as the lithic industry of the very old Paleolithic supposedly the Mode-1 rather than the actual Lower Paleolithic the Acheulean or the Mode-2. That cultural facies could be estimate a different lifestyle. However, with regard to the typological composition of the different types on the small tool in the typological debate, we confirm some bifaces in small number. We confirmed a predominance of the denticulate group to start with the Tayac-point including. However, that allows us to be not able to think that this characteristic would be seemed to the industrial facies of the Middle Paleolithic identified in France, particularly the Mousterian of denticulate.
As regards evaluation of the raw material, it is quite dominated exclusively by quartz in this lithic industry. To the point of view at the acquerment of the raw material that there is at the immediate proximity of the site that we are convinced that.
We paid attention to the existence of a large number of natural pebbles or tested pebbles by removals in quartz, those to tested some abductions etc. These blocks or pebbles in quartz which were destined to the manufacture

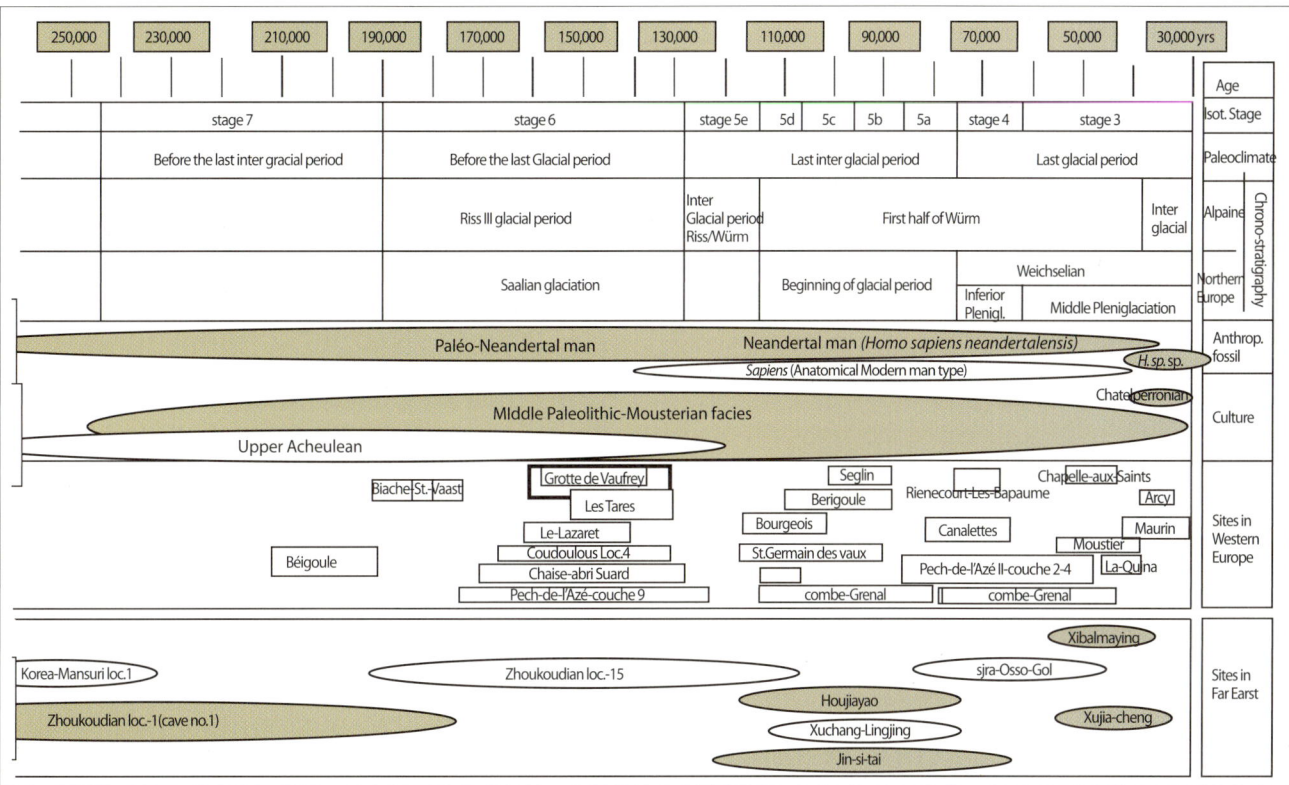

Fig. 8 Chronology of the concerning sites on the studies

of the bolas or polyhedrons, and choppers. It was not exploited systematically for the production of the blanks, in other words the flaking (debitage) in relation to the silicic rock, as the flint for example.

With regard to the raw material for the lithic industry of the layer 3 in the Locality-1 of the Mansuri Paleolithic sites in South Korea where it presents as representative of the concerned localities. Its raw material has been dominated almost completely by quartz.

In many case that is an extreme tendence that it has sedimentary rock only that it suits the production of tool blanks. However, this rock type have been served for the flaking (debitage) whose quartz occupies a monopolistic position and otherwise, two types of quartzite rarely present. According to the observation of the flake butts (a part of striking platform) that permits to note the plans of striking platform of core non prepared. And we confirm that the core surface doesn't have any predetermined preparation.

The flakes keep often some residual cortex on the flake surface what their flaking (debitage) was non continuous quantitatively. It is well possible that it would be inefficient in a place close to one point of acquisition of the raw material. The flakes are less long and proportionally non slender, which they are in general short and large.

The presence of blade qualified for the Middle Paleolithic that the flake has a length which tackles two times bigger than his width which it is rare enough in this site. And as the blade qualified for the Upper Paleolithic that is completely absent. Concerning a feature of technology, this lithic industry is characterized enough by a presence of a number of product flakes in general. However, they are not in many case transformed for authentically flake tools. We pay attention also an existence of important characteristic that persists in the tools on debris reach in majority. As well as the small pebbles were often utilized as a blank for the small tools. The flaking process(debitage) hardly contributes for the tool making in these lithic industries. The debitage is quite non-Levallois and non-blade technique that these produced blanks very often have residual cortex in large majority.

Acknowledgement

We did not come to accept it but they had us welcomed very fraternally. In South Korean investigation, Dr. Kaoru Otani of the South Korean study-of-prehistory measured the communication of Japanese and Korean, and she was able to do smooth investigation each time.

Moreover, we were allowed to use the data of Professor H.de Lumley of the human-beings paleontology research institute in France, and his method of inquiring.

As mentioned above, in addition, I received many fellow researchers' cooperation and advice.

We appreciate these relation Gentlemen deeply respectfully.

References

Lee Y. et al., 2010. *Chongwon-Mansuri Paleolithic Site (Localities 1,2,3)*. Institute of Korean Prehistory, Chongju, the Republic of Korea, 495p. (in Korean)

Lumley H. de. 1979. *Lexique des caractéristiques des galets aménagés et du petit outillage*. Laboratoire de Paléontologie Humaine et de Préhistoire, Marseille.

Gagnepain, J. et Gaillard, C., 2005. La grotte de la Baume Bonne (Quinson, Alpes-de-Haute-Provence) : synthèse chronostratigraphique et séquence culturelle d'après les fouilles récentes (1988-1997). in: *Données récentes sur les modalités de peuplement et sur le cadre chronostratigraphique, géologique et paléogéographique des industries du Paléolithique inférieur et moyen en Europe*. Molines, N., Moncel, M.-H. et Monnier, J.-L. éds., BAR International Series 1364, Actes du Colloque International de Rennes, 22-25 septembre 2003, 73-85.

Lumley H. de, Coche D. et al., 2015. *Terra Amata, Nice, Qlpes-Martimes, France Tome IV Facicule 1, Les industries acheuléennes*. Etude de l'outillage, Planches de dessins et de photographies de l'industrie lithique, CNRS édition, Paris, 806p.

Lumley H. de, Isidro Toro Moyano et al., 2010. *Les industries lithiques archaïqueq de Bqrrqnco Léon et de Fénte Nueva 3, Orce, bassin de Guadix-Baza, Andalousie*. CNRS édition, Paris, 306p.

Bordes F., 1950. L'évolution buissonnante desindustries en Europe Occidentale. Considérations théoriques sur le Paléolithique ancien et moyen (1). *Anthropologie* Tome 54, Paris, 393-420.

Bordes F., 1953. Test of classification of the industries "moustériennes." *Bull. Soc. préhist. fr.*, Paris, 457-466.

Takehana K., 2016. Statistically Sudies on the Middle and Lower Paleolithic From the China and Republic of Korea. *Archeological Journal* No. 687, Tokyo, 26-31. (in Japanese)

Takehana K., 2022. The thecno-typological Method on the lithic industries of Pleistocene in the Far East, especially the typology. *Paleolithic Archeology* No. 86, Kyoto, 1-19. (in Japanese)

Geneste, M., 1985. *Analysis lithique of industries, moustériennes of the Périgord: A technological approach of the behavior of the human groups to the middle Paleolithic*. Thesis of state doctorate, presented June 8, University of Bordeaux I, Vol. 1, 342.

Lumley, H., Lee, J., Park, Hp. Bae and K., 2009-2010. *The industries of the old Paleolithic of South Korea in their stratigraphic context: Their place among the cultures of the old Paleolithic in Eurasia and in Africa*. CNRS Edtions, Paris, 631.

Lumley de H. et al., 2004. Premiers hommes de Chine, *Dossiers d'Archéologia* No. 293. Edition Faton, Quétigny France, 6-85.

Matsufuji K. et al., 2013. *Fundamental Studies on the Paleoclimatology Changes and Paleolithic chronologies*. Grant-in-Aid for Scientific Research of the Japanese government A21251010, Kyoto, 207. (in Japanese and English)

Xiè Fei et al., 2005. *Paleolithic in Niheiwan*. Edition of Hua-shan-wen-yuan, Shijiazhuang, Hebei province, China, 271. (in Chinese)

Lumley H. de. 1976. Les premières industrie humaines en Provence, Les grottes du Vallonnet. *La Préhistoire Française, Tome I: Les civilisations paléolithiques et Mésolithiques de la France*. Editions du C.N.R.S., Paris, 765-770.

Lumley H. de, Fournier A., Kerzepkowska J. et Echassoux A., 1988. L'Industrie du Pléistocene inférieur de la grotte du Vallonnet, Roquebrune-Cap-Martin, Alpes-Maritimes. *L'Anthropologie* Tome 92, No. 2, Paris, 501-614.

Lumley H. de et al., 2004a. *Les sites préhistoriques de la région de Féjej, Sud-Omo, Ethiopie, dans leur contextestratigraphique et paléontologique*. Préfaces de Dominique de Villepin et de Teshome Toga. ADPF, Association pour la diffusion de la pensée française. Editions Recherche sur les civilisations. Ministère des affaires Etrangères. Direction générale de la Coopération internationale et du dévelopement, sous-direction des Sciences sociales et de l'Archéologie, 18 articles, 635p.

Lumley de H., 2004b. Premiers hommes de Chine. *Dossiers d'Archéologia* No. 293. Edition Faton, Quétigny France, 6-85.

LumLey H. de, Lor dkipanidze D. et al., 2005. Les industries lithiques préorldowayennes du début d'un Pléistocene inférieur du site de Dmanisi en Géorgie. *L'Anthropologie* janvier-mars 2005, Vol. 109, No.1, Paris, 182p.

Lumley H. de. 2006. Il y a 2.5 Ma. Un seuil majeur de l'Hominisation. L'émergence de la pensée conceptuelle et des stratégies maîtrisées du débitage de la pierre. *Comptes Rendus Paleovol* Vol. 5, 119-126.

Lumley H. de et al., 2009. Les premières étapes de la colonisation de l'Europe et l'arrivée de l'Homme sur les rives de la Méditerranée. *L'Anthropologie* No. 113.

Takehana K., 1991. *Etudes Techno-Typologique de load'industrie lithique du Pléistocène moyen des Enembles inférieurs (I et II) du Complexe stratigraphique moyen de la Caune de l'Arago (Tautavel, Pyrénées-Orientales, France)*. Doctorat de Muséum Nationale d'Histoire Naturelle (Institut de Paléontologie Humaine), Paris, 4 Dec. 1991, 607, 314.

Takehana K., 2012. Topological todays Studies on the Middle and Lower Paleolithic in the Indian Sub-Continent. *Paleolithic*

Archeology No. 77, Kyoto, 31-52.

Teilhard de Chardin P. et Pei W.-C., 1934. New Discoveries in Choukoutien 1933-1934. *Bull. Geol. Soc. China* XIII, Beijing.

Movius L. Jr., 1944. Early Man Pleistocene Stratigraphy in Southern and Eastern Asia. *Papers of the Peabody Museum* 19(3).

Movius L. Jr., 1948. The Lower Paleolithic Culture of Southern and Eastern Asia. *Transactions of the Philosophical Society New Series* IV, 330-420.

Movius L. Jr., 1957. Pebble Tool Terminology in India and Pakistan. *Man in India* 37(2), 149-156.

Gaillard Cl. and Mishra S., 2001. The Lower Paleolithic in South Asia. In: Sémah F., Falguères Ch., Grimaud- Hervé D. et Sémard A.-M. éds., *Origine des pleuplements dans le sud-est asiatique.* Semenanjung-Arrcom, Paris, 73-91.

Dennell R.Z. et al., 1988a. Late Pleistocene Artefacts from Northern Pakistan. *Current Anthropology* 29, 69-72.

Dennell R.Z. et al., 1988b. Early Tool-making in Asia: Two Million Year Old Artefacts in Pakistan. *Antiquity* 62, 98-106.

Leroi-Gourhan A., 1988. *Dictionnaire de la Préhistoire*. Paris: Presse Université de France, 1220p.

Lordkipanidze, D. et al., 2005. Anthropology: The Earliest Toothless Hominin Skull, *Nature* 434(7034), 717-718.

The place of humankind in the biomechanical evolution of living organisms according to A. Leroi-Gourhan

Marcel OTTE

Professor Emeritus, Liège University, Belgium ; marcel.otte@uliege.be

ABSTRACT

According to André Leroi-Gourhan (ALG), the evolutionary process that culminated in current vertebrates involved the combination and coordination of various factors. These factors include standing in an erect posture, a reduction in the size of the face, and the liberation of the hands. General verticality is linked to fast and distant modes of locomotion, guided by observations made at the top of the head. Shorter faces resulted from a reduction in dentition by compensation to the activities that have become manual. The liberation of the techniques expanded the capabilities of prehension and manipulation of the hands. This liberation also encouraged symbolic expression, initially by shaped objects, external to the anatomy, and then by the design of gestures preliminary to their execution. Words, languages, and consciousness would have emerged at the very end of this evolutionary process, following major anatomical and mechanical modifications, infinitely older and more important. According to ALG, our evolution started with the feet, as we will consider in this work. Cerebral development was a phenomenon secondary to the origins of social systems, which, over time, took the place of biological systems. The reduction of face size was linked to prehension of the hands, which permitted food preparation and initiated a feedback loop between seizure, manipulation, and preparation. Mechanical tilting occurred between the back and front of the skull, favoring the neocortex, and thus abstract symbolic activities. The acquisition of the vertical station was a fundamental phenomenon that triggered all of the others by retroactive effects. Tools became complementary extensions of the hands, while language became a natural complement of the face in regression of its first food function. During this process, social phenomena supplanted biological functions. Ethnic units generate and preserve collective memories, which are transmitted in a form similar to initial genetic baggage. The particular personalities and characteristics of ethnic groups are thereafter defined by alternations of values and rhythms, which make them truly autonomous and distinct, in the same way as biological species. The social body henceforth assumes symbolic value, external to the biological body: It has become abstract, if not materially realized.

국문초록

앙드레 르와-구르앙은 현존 생명체의 생물역학적 진화 관점으로 인류 진화를 설명한다. ALG 이론은 신체적 직립 자세, 얼굴의 축소, 손의 해방을 통해 진화를 설명하고 있다. 대뇌 발달은 시간 경과에 따라 생물학적 시스템을 대신하는 사회시스템의 변화 과정으로의 진화 현상이다. 직립 자세는 신체를 수직으로 확보하는 기초 동작이며 소급효과에 의해 다른 진화 현상을 설명할 수 있다. 얼굴의 축소는 잡기, 조작, 준비라는 피드백 과정을 통한 음식의 장만과 손의 잡기 동작과 연결된다. 이에 따라 두개골 앞뒤 사이에서 역학적 경사로 인해 신피질을 발달시키고, 추상적이고 상징적인 활동이 발달한다. 그리고 도구 사용은 손 기능의 부차적 확장으로 보며, 이에 반해 언어 사용은 입을 통한 음식물 섭취라는 1차 기능의 퇴화에 따라 얼굴에 나타난 자연적 보완 현상이다. 종족집단 내 집단의 집합기억체가 형성되고 이것이 최초 유전자와 같은 방식으로 후대로 전달된다는 측면에서 볼 때 언어 사용을 통해 신체의 생물학 진화를 넘어 사회적 진화로 변천해 간다.

Keywords: evolution, feedback mechanism, consciousness, mind tools

1. Introduction

Everything begins with the separation of bodies and liquid elements whose laws are infinitely less constraining than those in the air. The density of water does not require the forces of traction and resistance that gravity conditions in an irremediable way, leading to later evolutions. As soon as the head is upright in the air, forces of traction are imposed from the spinal column to the top of the skull, like a modern construction crane (**Fig.1**). The hands continue their adaptation, with five fingers for fast locomotion in open environments or in trees. Face size is reduced by the lack of vital mechanical activity, and the cranial cavity opens because it is no longer mechanically solicited on one side or the other: The brain can then slide its nervous mass into it.

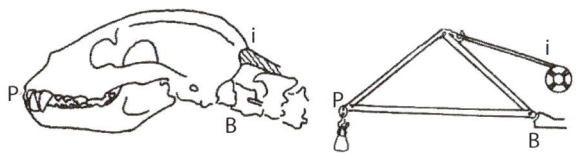

Fig. 1 Suspension of the head of the erect quadruped compared to a lifting device (from *Mécanique vivante*, 1983, Fayard, p. 42. Fig. 83)

This series of interlocking developments along a single track accelerates according to a complex and combinatorial process in which nutritional needs, locomotion, and vivacity are balanced. This represents but one ascending progression of the living world, although some species have barely evolved over hundreds of millions of years, without notable modifications. Other species, such as oysters and jellyfish, have attained perpetual longevity, as opposed to the evolutionary mechanisms of vertebrates, including humanity. Species with an axial bone structure move about in search of food, playing on the relationship between space, time, and mobility. Their brains benefit from locomotor progress because the cranial cavity develops as mechanical constraints disappear in the search for food. Two animal structures developed from the very beginning: a radial and fixed structure that captured food as it passed through, and a mobile and aggressive structure based on the axial model. Bilateral symmetry imposed itself on the lineage of vertebrates, which is defined by a food orifice located toward the front, with anterior polarization with a mouth and organs for gripping. This fundamental condition shaped later animal life via the strict bilateralization of current vertebrates (**Fig. 2**).

2. The fundamental mechanisms

In vertebrates, the internal skeleton includes an anterior cranial box opposed to an articulated skull at the back. This box contains cells sensitive to light and vibrations. However, between the cranial box and the body are articulated fins related to prehension, which were subjected to radical expansion: Our future hands were contained there. In the mouth, articulated jaws developed two functions complementary to locomotion and feeding. These two functions determined the evolution of both the skull and the body.

These adaptive tendencies culminated in a remarkable phenomenon of convergence, similar to how a dolphin, a marine mammal, anatomically resembles a fish. Convergence is universal in the functional activities of the extinct hipparion or extant marsupials, whose diversity would appear to make them part of different phyla.

3. Cerebral box

In aquatic and aerial environments, the development of the nervous systems takes the place left by the osseous framework and soon to the intelligence which is only the prolongation of it in terrestrial environment . The anterior field manifests these new evolutionary tendencies: one attends to the combination of the face and the hands, two poles collaborating in elaborate techniques of locomotion

Fig. 2 Fields of visual relations (*Le geste et la parole*, 1964, p. 51, fig. 7).

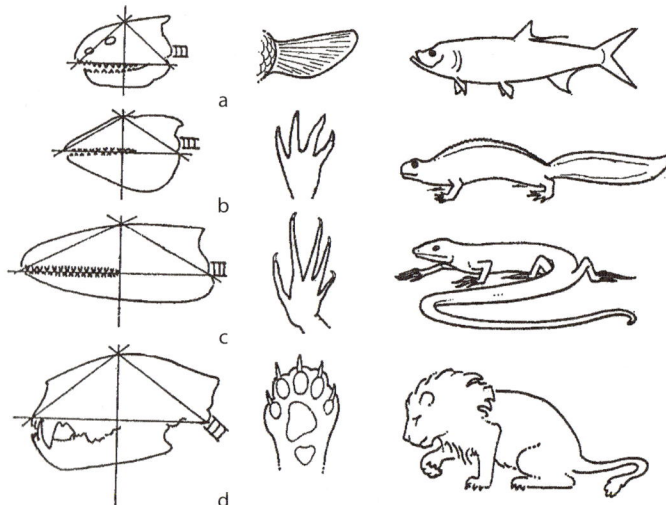

Fig. 3 Axial arrangement in propulsion and prehension in the course of evolution. The angle of the head closes and the hands have different types of functions (*Le geste et la parole*, Albin Michel)

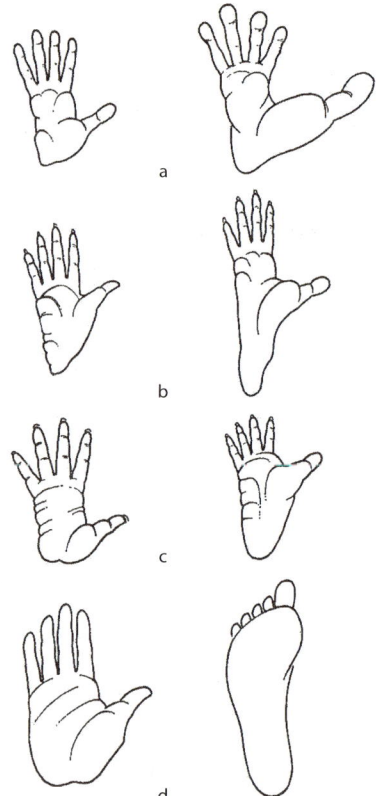

Fig. 4 Arrangement of feet in large primates. The thumb of the foot will never be used again for prehension (*Le geste et la parole*, p. 91, fig. 28)

of capture. The forelimbs possess these two combined operations, like the facial appendages of fish in deep marine environments or the use of claws in birds of prey, both used for prehension and nest building (**Fig. 3**).

In mammals, the distinction is even clearer and determines the continuation of evolution. One can easily distinguish between ungulates feeding on cellulose and primates feeding on fleshy food, animal or vegetable. These food

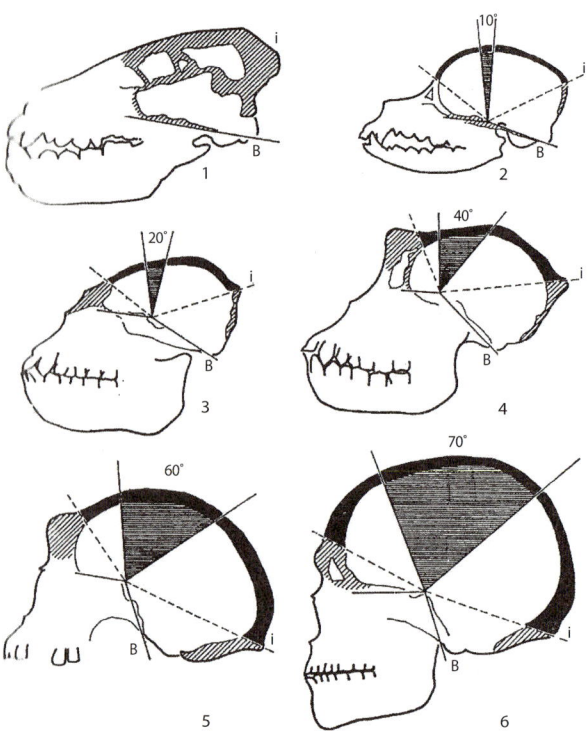

Fig. 5 Opening of the cortical fan and liberation of the cranial vault (*Le geste et la parole*, p. 111, fig. 42)

modalities also determine the modes of locomotion. In primates, the bipolarity of the anterior fields favors prehension and manipulation. And in humans, the absence of mobility in the anterior polarity prohibits any locomotor intervention whose actions will be focused on manual and symbolic activities (**Fig. 4**). In ungulates, the absence of hands implies the absence of language, and all functions are oriented toward mobility. There is an immense variety of activities involving the face, as in rhinoceroses or elephants. There is no relationship between hands and language, even in a rudimentary form, because the limbs are like pillars that support the horizontal body.

From fish to man, functional paleontology is established as evolution proceeds according to a few significant axes that concern all vertebrates since they existed in an aquatic environment. The mode of locomotion inflects the vertebral column to which the limbs are attached as an organic and global structure. The passage of nerve impulses from the medulla to the brain determines the disposition of the occipital foramen, which goes from a subhorizontal position to a vertical orientation vaguely acquired with hominids. The masticatory functions undergo fundamental inflections by distinguishing the different activities of prehension: cutting and grinding.

Each element takes its own measure and establishes itself relative to the others as well as to the sustentation of the cranial cavity (**Fig. 5**). In short, the length is reduced insofar as

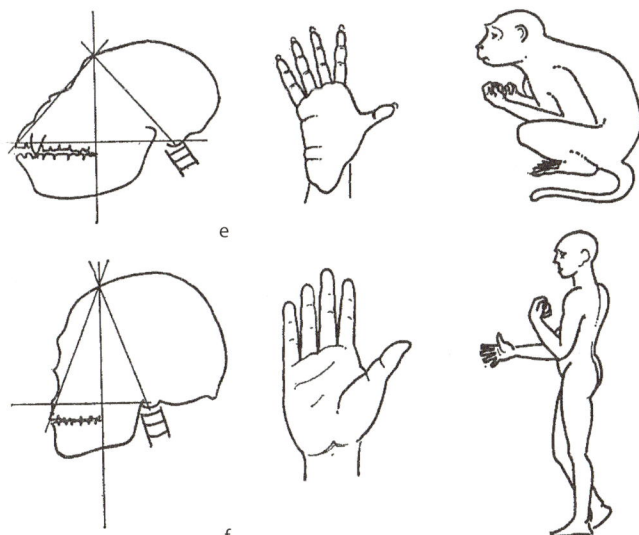

Fig. 6 Liberation of the hand. The relations between the stature and the prehension diversify (*Le geste et la parole*, p. 59, fig. 8)

the progression passes by the anterior limbs: The geometry of the whole cranium is then put into action in correlation to the other activities. The anterior limbs are naturally linked to these modifications because they seize, modify, and prepare food, concomitant to an atrophy of the mandible. In coordination, the brain is now housed in a cavity that grows as it loses its function of supporting the mechanical functions of food. The brain thus becomes the tenant of this cavity, in which all coordinations between the other members will be established. In short, from the moment of the passage from the aquatic to the aerial environment, the saurian, the quadruped, and the rectified man have followed only natural antagonistic forces between gravity and vital associative necessities. No more than a school of herrings, humanity could not have substituted by its only performance: It must be stimulated and guaranteed by the success of its social environment, which thus takes advantage of the other modes of subsistence (**Fig. 6**).

4. Struggle against gravity

Liberation was first a matter of opposition to gravity by the use of a lever of sustentation linked to the dorsal column and whose variants set the stage for the evolution of the vertebrates, constraints linked to the mechanical suspension of the mandible, and the framework according to which it diversified (**Fig. 7**). In such a way, the teeth and the postures are earthy because they represent different solutions of this evolution of all vertebrates with reduced teeth and whose face, progressively lightened, gave rise to the anthropomorphs. Conversely, jaws that remain attached to the ground have a mandible of which only the summit acts as in certain reptiles of which only the skull rises. The modes of displacement are thus closely integrated with the modes of subsistence: Posture and dentition are linked, and the movements of the jaw are reversed in one or the other mechanical situation – either the mandible in sustentation, or the maxilla, which reduces the prey on the lower dental surface (**Fig. 8**).

From the reign of saurians, including our current lizards, a new mechanical balance adapted to terrestrial environments. The column forms a kind of beam to which limbs and the

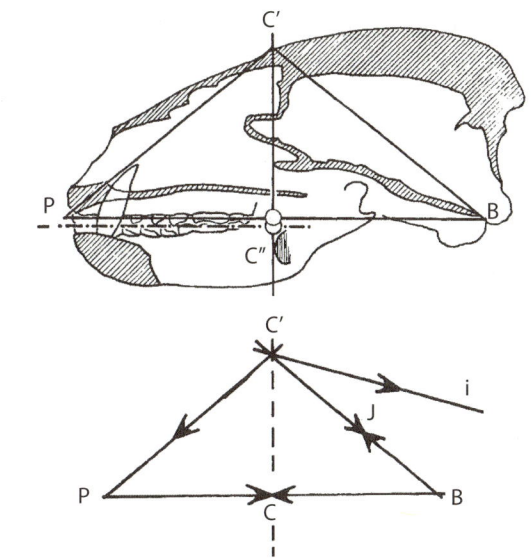

Fig. 7 Axes of the forces on the skull of the badger (*Living Mechanics*, p. 44, fig. 4)

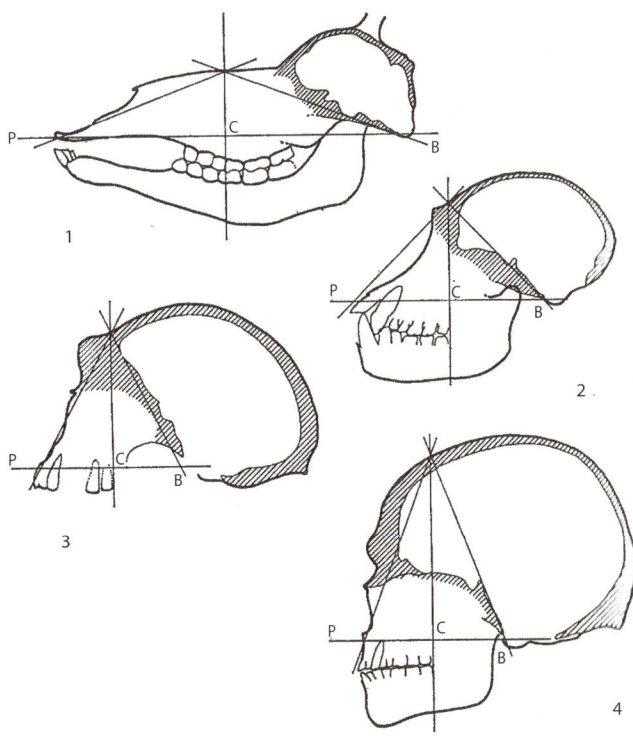

Fig. 8 Softening of the cranial base from cervids to hominids (*Le geste et la parole*, p. 106, fig. 41)

head are attached or suspended. The head and the body are now placed above the ground, and a neck separates them, offering all the possibilities of autonomy between observation and posture or feeding. The size of the brain remains limited to the mechanical constraints of suspension and traction. The hyoid bones are inserted in the muscular actions, offering phonatory possibilities. The brain is installed in a cavity left free by mechanics but already has a complex structure. But the processes are first related to the ossature: the framework being initially determined by osteo-muscular mechanical laws.

In the formula of the theromorphs (mammals), locomotion becomes quadrupedal and elevated. The limbs are columns holding the body high above the ground. The spinal column becomes free to allow for an elongated and flexible neck. Enlarged cervical vertebrae increase relational possibilities, observations, and forecasting. Dentition includes different elements related to specialized functions, such as crushing or cutting. These actions can be observed in their dispositions, and the balance point of the skull rests on the last molars, completely modifying the mechanics through new mechanical lines. In the sitting position, these dispositions free the upper limbs and develop the cranial box. These various mechanical tendencies are now acquired and will diversify according to their particular functions until the rise of the anthropomorphs (**Fig. 9**).

5. The feet

In groups of mammals, two general tendencies are distinguished: the development of the feet, or that of the hands. An example of the first tendency are, for example, primates that feed by prehension and whose cranial box increases accordingly. An example of the second tendency are herbivores that use their legs to run quickly to ensure their survival. The quadrumans establish the link between the sitting and arboreal positions (**Fig. 4, 6**). In the sitting position, the new operations allow prehension and manual operations, as well as the development of the brain. The facial block becomes autonomous with respect to the vertebral framework; the geometrical balance is established by the presence of the suborbital bulge, much like the top of a compass that links the last molars to the first incisors. This structure was borrowed by the human species, which used more powerful means by a particular distribution of the bony masses.

6. The cranial fan

The primates thus developed their cognitive possibilities by the search for contacts, as much by displacements as for food. The evolution of the personal structure and the nervous system took place jointly as soon as the brain structure was unlocked from the mechanical constraints that bound it to a horizontal column (**Fig. 8, 9**). Thus, thanks to mechanical improvements in the cranial cavity, it opened widely, with neuronal masses developing for a second time. This permitted the use of the hands and therefore the elaboration of concepts (**Fig. 6**). The reduction of mechanical constraints allowed for the liberation of the cranial cavity, and therefore of its own capacities, such as foresight and immediate lucidity.

In anthropomorphs, the pelvis widened and supported the entire weight of the body, which distinguishes us from other mammals. As soon as the biped walked, the body structure was radically modified in the distribution of masses and modes of balance. The feet were arranged in rays, and the evolution of the stature was conditioned from the tarsus to the pelvis. The spinal column tended toward verticality in a series of compensatory curves with a vertical result. It is from this formula, which obeys mechanical laws, that the great apes and our own species have evolved, with cultural and physical contributions becoming integrated into new formulas in continuous transformation.

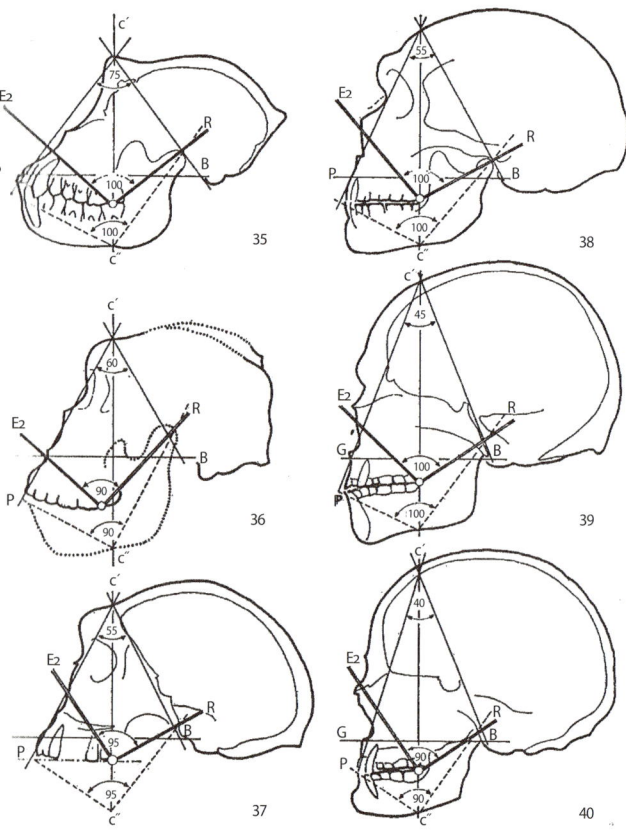

Fig. 9 Support of the jugal teeth and closure of the angles of the face (*Le geste et la parole*, p. 103, fig. 37)

7. The stages of human evolution

Australopithecines (4-3 million years old) have distinctly human characteristics with straight femurs, a wide pelvis open from bottom to top, fully supported feet and a vertically downward facing foramen magnum. The face is long, surmounted by a prominent orbital visor that serves as a rocker between the front and back of the skull (**Fig. 9, 10**). The absence of a forehead and a dentition with large molars show a diet that remained essentially vegetable. A sagittal ridge serves as an attachment to powerful lateral muscles that enclose the development of the skull. Upright posture as well as the use of hands reduce the use of teeth in other large primates. The temporal muscles are high and justify a high cranial cavity. All these criteria definitively distance this lineage from non-human primates and announce the definitive orientation towards our species, all the more so as shaped tools were discovered in association.

Paleontologically, the Archanthropians ("*Homo erectus*") follow and are already clearly distinguished from the lineage of other primates. They have an enormous face, a small and squat skull, with a strong orbital visor at the top of the face compass and the back of the skull. The skulls are reduced in volume but the arrangements are the necessary step towards later humanization (**Fig. 10**).

The following stage belongs to the Paleanthropians which constitute the complete continuity of the latter, including the African or Chinese specimens, at the same evolutionary stage (e.g., Broken Hill). Leroi-Gourhan establishes a coherent evolutionary stage from erectus to sapiens, the European branch of which is represented by the Neanderthals. The architecture of the cranium continues its evolution towards the present-day men who have taken refuge in marginal areas. No racism is to be denounced here but simply successive evolutionary stages, always in the same lineages, whatever the regions considered. Geographical isolation accentuates characteristic traits without offering them a specific status: Australian Aborigines for example, Bushmen, Ainu, Tierra del Fuego. Isolation creates or maintains archaic facies within a single lineage that is already perfectly human in the biological and cultural sense.

The main features are known: receding forehead, suborbital bulges, massive face, no chin, very large brain, strong chewing mandibles. This mechanical arrangement seems to be blocked precisely by its balance between the front and rear masses, the whole being supported by the "compass" (**Fig. 10**) of the powerful and determining orbital arches. However, recent specimens suggest a retreat of the face, thus of the masticatory apparatus and a progressive overhang of the cranial cavity on a face which retreats and reduces. We then witness the closing of the "compass" between incisors and mandibles. This process is especially visible in comparison with later populations where it accelerates so rapidly that it seems difficult to imagine it being deployed any further. The orbital mass is reduced because it no longer serves as a foundation for the facial edifice, the brain extends to the laterally cleared areas so that the cranial capacity is identical to ours but arranged on the sides and to the rear, rather than towards the front as in modern humans.

In the absence of mechanical constraint, the forehead rises and becomes more graceful; it no longer participates in the lock that has held the entire skull together since the first primates. The anterior teeth, freed from the orbital lock, move back, causing a feedback of the chin propelled forward without having done anything but stay where it has always been. The plasticity maintained between the forces, tendencies and hard bone tensions slowly stabilizes in a new geometrical pattern, which is still continuing before our eyes. The first lower molar becomes the pillar of the face and the orbital bulge enters the game of creating the frontal sinuses, in opposition to the development of the brain in the same direction in all Paleanthropians. All the Paleanthropians, whatever the place or the date, proceed in the same way, within the same species, towards the gracialization that will characterize modern man everywhere, but from very different paleontological foundations.

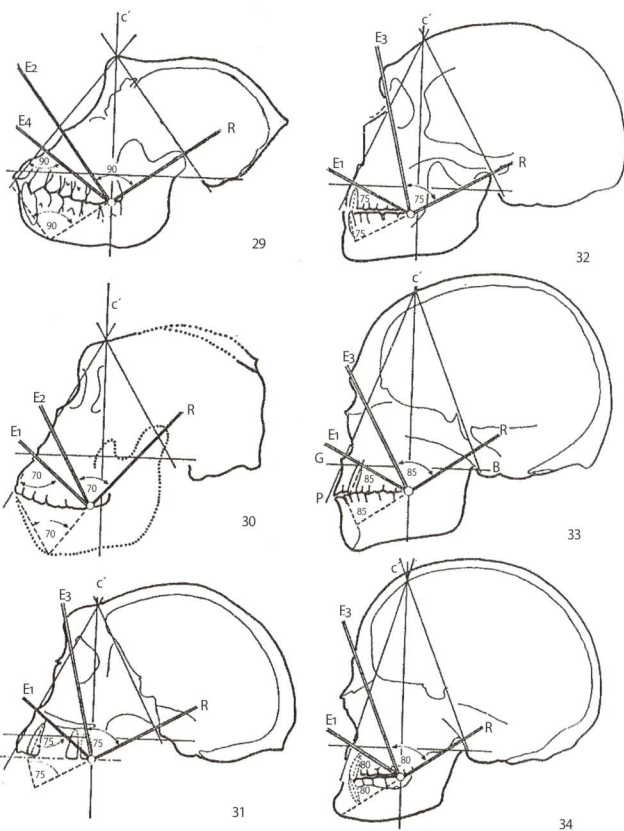

Fig. 10 Evolution of the support of the teeth towards the suborbital bead (*Le geste et la parole*, p. 96, fig. 31)

Leroi-Gourhan has often ironized on what humanity owes to its feet rather than to its brain. In fact, it is a question of complex retroactive processes that could only have been triggered by standing and with all the cascading consequences that it caused, not only at rest but especially when walking or running, where a new supply of oxygen is required: the foot alone does not explain our entire metamorphosis, it participates in it like a starting point. At the same time, the liberation of the hands has opened up the "cortical fan", that is to say the back and front parts of the brain, which then communicate information of a very different nature: instinctive, imaginative or survival. This is surely where the human particularity lies, although it is not limited to it. The cranial box (thus the mass that it contains) is progressively freed from the constraints of mechanical suspensions.

The organization of the different parts of the brain is radically modified, at the same time as the total volume occupied by the neurons is largely amplified. In a reductionist form (from which ALG does not always escape) one could be led to think that this distribution of cerebral functions would be outside the means offered by paleontology; however, all archaeology is there to prove the contrary from the very beginning. A flexion of the cerebral mass seems to correspond to it, when this brain presents an angled aspect, due to the withdrawal of the face. The cranial vault then took a rolled up form as were the dispositions of the brain.

This cerebral curl indicates an increase in the neuronal mass of which one can find the trace by the endocranial casts. The increase of the cortex is then manifested in the frontal and middle regions. However, the regions best adapted to transmissions are located in the intermediate area which opens up like a fan but in a late phase called "middle cortex" (**Fig. 10**). The different areas correspond to the different functions whose coordination is assumed by this intermediate area (called "neocortex") which will appear only late in the cerebral evolution of humans. As much as we can distinguish the functions of prehension (a feline for example), the verticality of the human brain is manifested in its technicality, in its memory and in its imagination.

The human brain is at the maximum of its mechanical capacities: it is thus able to transfer the continuation of its history in the artificial assets which tend to escape to him. In short, in humans as in apes, analogous aptitudes are relegated to the feet and hands, but in different proportions and according to social uses sometimes in opposition. In humans, the face functions in linguistic terms, including mimics, but also for manufacturing. The coordination of the two and of the associated set allows the comprehension of the world via the verbal range. Language, writing tools are all equally coordinated by the interactions between fabrication and language.

8. Development of the cervical fan, and the balancing of the vertical cranium

Human motor skills, the grip of technicality, as well as the functioning of the brain, stretch this range to the maximum at each stage in order to use the tools in their raw and specific form within the panoply offered by the range of language. The ability to symbolize sounds, whether listening or broadcasting, is part of a very significant intellectual activity, as well as a very instructive one. One cannot imagine a tradition of identically shaped tools without the use of speech, which somehow reflects the minimalist means for their execution and use. A skeleton of living thought is involved at every moment of our history. The extension of the manual field is equivalent to the mechanical consequences of its actual applications. A veil of this cervical understanding justifies and supports what the humblest material data brings us.

The extension of the manual field constitutes the proof of the unblocking of the middle cortex, where the two other fields join: knowledge and action. Now, these two distinct fields have been present since the Australopithecus without the slightest doubt: they were never apes, they are not yet men, but they will become so. The most rudimentary archaeological data indicate examples of the clearest gestural and verbal associations. Sounds and gestures are found coordinated since the earliest witnesses, which implies the existence of an abstract language, however rudimentary it may have been. From the first Australopithecines, the areas of verbal and gestural associations testify to the ability to think and communicate. This intellectualization is linked to the mechanical aptitudes evident in the archaeological data. The manual field and the cervical field developed jointly thanks to the unblocking of the middle cortex. The language thus acquired by the association of the two modalities has triggered an ever more rapid evolution that can be observed, for example, in posture: animals can create standing, sitting or quadrupedal movements, which releases the constraints exerted on the cortex and triggers the mechanisms of language and brain.

The most vulnerable of the fossil primates, the Australopithecus, was also the one that conquered the African continent because it was able to produce tools outside its natural anatomy. From then on, social rules were imposed: observation, forecasting, slaughter and hunting of a fleeting game. His remains are associated with the bones of antelopes but also of the pig and the zebra for example. He builds artificial shelters and arms himself with tools shaped according to the image produced by his imagination. It is as if his tools, extending the anatomy, were the result of a secretion of the body and the brain of the anthropians. He knows how to give constant forms to objects that are now stereotyped, recognizable in their forms, their intentions and their functions. The intelligence impregnates the lithic raw material by the meeting of the mechanical laws and the thought in order to reach certain vital objectives. These requirements imposed by man on matter have lasted for hundreds of millennia without any change being detectable. It is as if ideas had been imposed on materials and not the other way around: humanity was already there, transforming matter into spirit and perceptible in the regularity of forms.

9. Archanthropians

With the Archanthropians, the tools reflect at best the acquired flexibility and intelligence. The striking is tangential and the forms are divided into distinct categories which announce their realization: the thought had initially conceived them in all their smoothness and their particularity (**Fig. 11**). The cerebral volume locked by the orbital massifs thus extends laterally or towards the back of the skull. The predictions in the categories of signs and techniques illustrate the parallel deployment of the mind. From this stage, methods and thoughts are manifested in the same way: it is the basis of later complete humans and thought.

Among the Paleanthropians (200 to 300,000 years old) we observe a perfect continuity on the whole earth where they could be studied. They are thus of regional origin but by parallel ways (**Fig. 9, 10**). Of Java, China or Europe, the evolutionary tendencies follow the same trajectory, as much as the technical and spiritual assets. The case of Europe is the best known because it was studied very early and that the vestiges abound there: they are the Neanderthals (near Düsseldorf). Their technical intelligence was the most elaborate, with the ingenious invention of the Levallois method, which made it possible to give a shape prior to the extraction of a block on a chip. Its diversifications and specializations evoke the numerous activities that were to be encountered there according to rigorous and constant operating schemes. For the most part, the tools actually used for hunting must have been made of wood, as rare discoveries demonstrate, as well as the traces left on the stone tools.

The technicality illustrates cerebral aptitudes equivalent to ours, inscribed in a symbolic mode which projected towards the future the assets of a memory which had become ephemeral. The Neanderthals proceeded by symbolic images like all humanity since then. These pre-frontal territories testify to an aptitude for abstraction through their symbolic reactions to the unknowable, such as the care given to the deceased and certain animal remains (skulls, mandibles) selected and arranged in the habitat.

Language skills must have been equivalent to ours: they establish the link between the hands and the facial organs. Tools and language are of the same evolutionary and gradual stage : we can observe the conception of tools before their realization and their use : their symbolic value was more important than their technical functions. These chains of technical operations upstream of use provide a kind of paleontology of language. The technical chains are both flexible and fixed because the concepts are there in operation, but the means adapt to each new situation. The methods are thus external to the concrete: they are organized in syntax like a forecasted narrative (**Fig. 11**). These imprecise but formal feelings are the sources of spirituality and soon of beliefs and religions. In such a way that the social rules took from now on the place which was due to the phylogenesis.

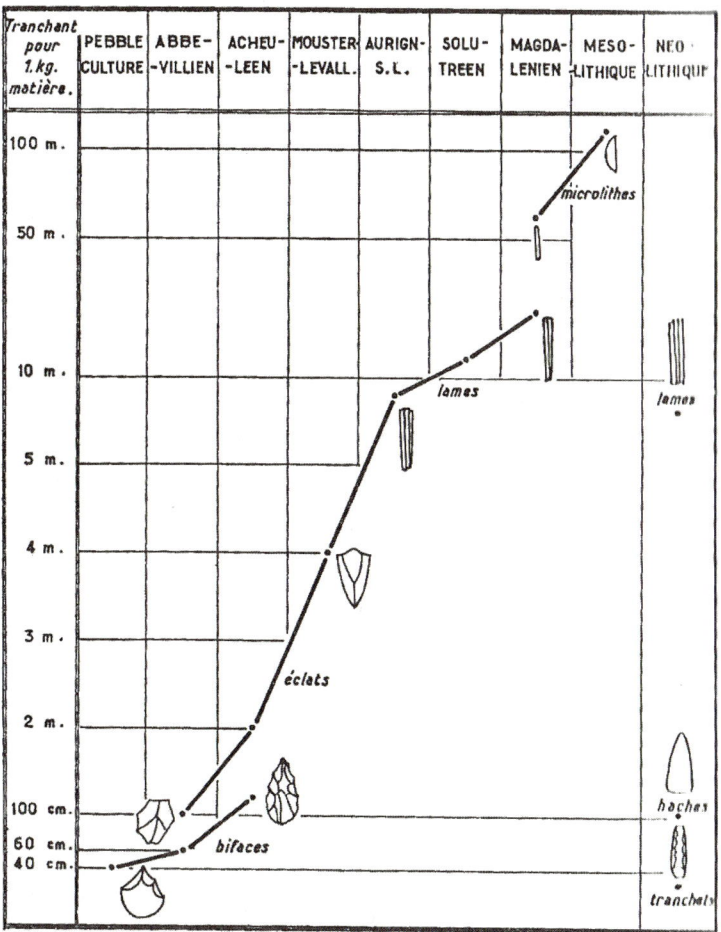

Fig. 11 Length of edges estimated for one kilo of raw material, according to time and the evolutionary biological stages (*Le geste et le parole*, 1964, fig. 64, p. 192)

10. Paleanthropians

Everything suggests that Neanderthals possessed the same neurological capacities as our own, with the same plasticity that allowed them to predict and adjust their behavior. The absence of apparent specialization suggests that all actions were already possible in each of them. The balancing act induced by the erect position had given a skull carried backwards, opposite to a prominent face. The canines are reduced and the cerebral volume increases. The reduction of the facial structure is absolutely universal by the reduction of the canines and the increase of the volume occupied by the brain. The entire phylum of this macroevolution is manifested wherever the remains are available: it was an indispensable biomechanical phase in our evolution, even if it did not take place everywhere at the same rhythm or at the same time. However, the equilibrium patterns observed on the whole earth during this immense period correspond exactly to the initial straightening due to bipedal walking and its consequences. Now, in the long term, the enlargement of the cranial cavity was higher in Neanderthals than in any other period.

In the mind of André Leroi-Gourhan, there are no "races" today in the mechanical sense of the term: these modifications have affected all of humanity at different speeds and by isolating parts of the world where allochthonous exchanges hardly occur. However, these general observations appear immediately in the globality of measurements, evoking tendencies, and based on regional populations of Archanthropians. According to him, the distinction was made only according to a formula of "tendencies" and thus far from the specifications as it was believed for a long time before him (and still now besides).

This is how we see regional processes appearing in isolation, as well as global phenomena that affect our entire species, regardless of location. From there, the traditional opposition between races and civilizations so dear to the schools of the last century. André Leroi-Gourhan tried to show this double tendency with the help of skulls and measurements that he had at his disposal at the time. We see there appear distinct but always parallel evolutionary profiles. The whole results in striking convergences in spite of the distinct origins, precisely because it is the same retroactive process between prehension, language and locomotion (as much as a bat resembles a bird). However, apparently, since the Paleanthropians, the same retroactive tendencies act on the human morphological constitution since it is the tool (therefore the concept) that made it progress. The general and most widely spread tendency therefore logically corresponds to what is called *Homo Sapiens* (without really knowing why) and to which Leroi-Gourhan prefers the expression Neanthropians in order to preserve this flexibility in nomenclature and systematics. From the Neanderthals onwards, Leroi-Gourhan sees the precursor traits of modern humanity appearing, as at Broken Hill in East Africa. Conversely, he shows Neanderthal traces on the remains of the Gravettian of Moravia (Predmost), much more recent. The barrier is therefore not closed, except in the minds of the prehistorians themselves.

11. Transition to Neanthropians

The uniformity of the Neanderthals must be sought in the effects of very ancient trends, the rebalancing of the skull towards the first molar and the regression of the mandible, which isolate distinct populations but undergoing the same evolutionary trends towards modernity. The density of these particular populations creates subspecies or fossil "races" in spite of the weight of convergences: they will be the foundations of the current anatomical diversity. The overhanging forehead and the dental reduction, which are universal, have been called "neoteny", during which the childlike traits continue longer than in other primates, inducing a long period of learning without feedback from the child as in other species. A sort of equilibrium point will soon be reached between the opposing forces that suspend the cranium and maintain the whole body in an upright position. Everything happens as if our goal would already be reached with the Neanthropians which immediately follow by reaching the same evolutionary laws.

12. Neanthropians

With the Neanthropians, the gain in prefrontal connections enriches the cellular networks and their density. This gain extended to the frontal territories is due to the unlocking of the cranial cavity: the fan opens and the neuronal masses extend much more widely towards the front of the skull. Moreover, the back and front areas come together through the control of the main areas: from mastery in the prefrontal cortex to affective regulation in the back of the brain. Between the areas, there is a regulation of the affects that controls the forecast and regulates the feelings. This device, initiated with the Neanthropians, constitutes the foundation of our humanity since then and ensures by the lucidity and the conscience the link with the hold of the judgment on the action.

13. Biology and society

The relation to the biological context is thus quite distant in this world where emotions and rules participate in the shaping of the prefrontal and elevated brain known most often in the current populations. From there start indeed the new techniques always more mastered but also the regulation of the feelings, their judgment and their control. The major creative function in this theoretical base holds in the connection between intelligence and action. To which are added, from the Neanderthals at least, the modes of interaction between individuals belonging to the same social groups. From now on, social rules prevail over those due to biology alone. The values themselves can be of an extreme variety as long as they are reduced to these tendencies where biology and culture are combined. In this sense, the Paleanthropians belong to the hinge between these two worlds, one biological, the other social. From them the processes as much as the arts are going to diversify and even to be detached from the nature where are plunged its individuals: because it is the image which is going to prevail on the trophy of the Paleanthropians. The real animal will be reduced to a graphic allusion with only referential value, thus symbolic.

André Leroi-Gourhan's audacity could have stopped there, but he took the decisive step of underlining the relationship between gestures (anatomy), thought and creation as we still find it difficult to conceive of today. Curiously, deeply rooted in human nature, he sought to justify obvious adventures that have nothing to do with it and that determine him on the contrary. Leroi-Gourhan was suspicious of dogmas, but he was perhaps inclined to have others in addition: the causality in matters of sciences and the harmony. A humanist to whom humanity displeases.

Taking up the theories in vogue where the passages from the mineral life to the one of the existence continue, he reduced the first ones to simple means to make the second one work. A rather rudimentary demonstration shows indeed that the mass of tools required for each period decreases as time passes: it was another way of treating the mineral according to new formulas (**Fig. 11, 12**). However, every theory is based on a before and after that justifies it. One of the most rudimentary means was to oppose a mass to a cutting edge. This relationship varies enormously, like a liberation, by the spirit, of the mechanical constraints opposed by the matter. But it can just as well be justified by the ambition of a thought, freed from mechanical constraints and whose essential values are situated between materials and activities, precisely where consciousness is constituted and where the greatest flexibility offers to man the whole range of his possibilities, without having to apply them but in a way "held in reserve" as soon as their necessity will impose itself.

This reduction of the mass to the cutting edge constitutes for the author the key to the passage from nature to culture, which can be clearly envisaged and understood through the evolutionary mechanisms offered by the technical inventions, prolonging those of nature. It is here that the conception becomes more and more debatable, because why would it have been necessary to change about 500,000 years ago for the destiny of humanity to be given over to other forces than its own? A connection between stone tools and conceptual attitudes is so obvious that to speak about it would be vain (**Fig. 12**). But it is not a question of direct connection, it is a question of maintaining stimulating dialogues, always directed towards a destiny, which although unknown of all, does not remain of it less obvious and evokes a creative impulse, initially natural then human. In this end of evolution, from nature to culture, ALG moves away from the status of neutral thinker to a kind of absolute fatalism: there would be nothing to understand! However, all his work has demonstrated the most complete coherence

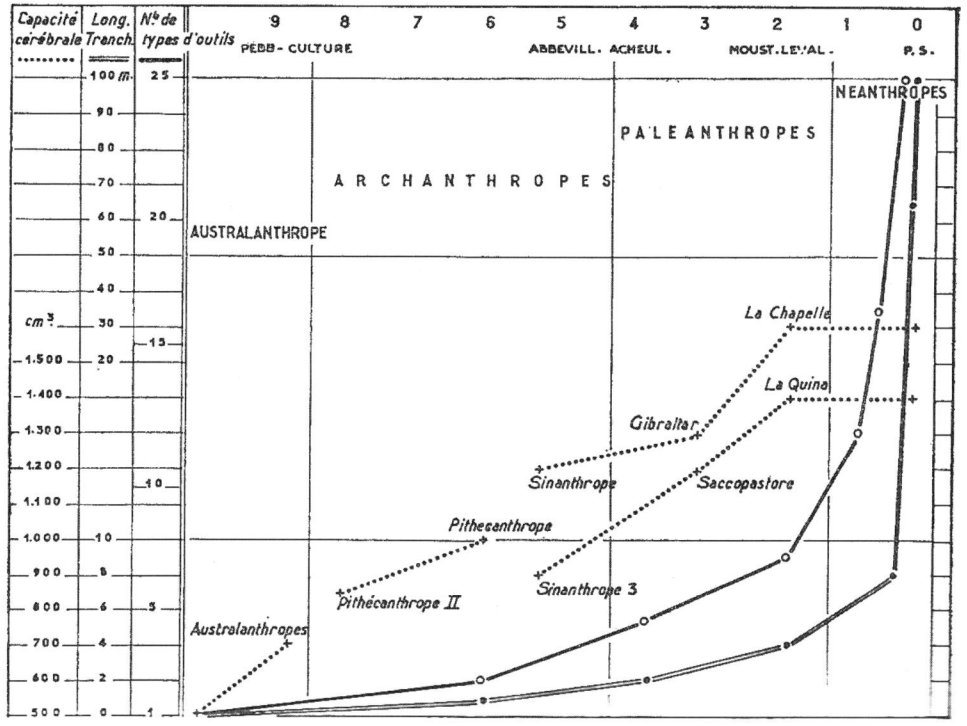

Fig. 12 Evolution of the cutting edge of the tools and reduction of the cranial cavity during the same period. The biological and the cultural tend to counterbalance (*Le geste et la parole*, 1964, p. 196)

in the evolutionary mechanisms. Whatever the driving force behind it, it is undoubtedly the result of a completely different approach that he did not want to outline. He never touched (in public at least) the inevitable question: why was this evolutionary coherence so harmonious, so logical and so regular?

References

André Leroi-Gourhan. 1964. *Le geste et la parole. Technique et langage*, Paris: Albin Michel édit.

André Leroi-Gourhan. 1983. *Mécanique vivante. Le crâne des vertébrés du poisson à l'homme*, Paris: Fayard, 1983.

Archaeological studies on the origin of modern humans in China

Xing GAO

Professor, Institute of Vertebrate Paleontology and Paleoanthropology, Chinese Academy of Sciences, China ;
gaoxing@ivpp.ac.cn

ABSTRACT

Recent paleoanthropological and Paleolithic archaeological discoveries have drastically altered our theoretical perspectives on modern human origins, evolution, and adaptations. China, a vast geographic region in East Asia, has emerged as a hot spot for such studies. New human fossils and stone tool assemblages have been reported from the area that challenge the "Recent Out-of-Africa" model, based mostly on the African and western Eurasian records. New paleoanthropological research results indicate that early modern humans appeared in South China around 100 ka and may have at least partially evolved from aboriginal populations in this region. Some archaic *Homo sapiens* exhibit mosaic or transitional features and possible admixture with Neanderthals and Denisovans. Associated lithic industries exhibit the complexity of early modern human technologies and behaviors. While small flake tools in northern China and large pebble tools in Southern China dominated throughout most of the Pleistocene, beginning from ca. 40 ka, blade-based techno-complexes appeared at some sites in northern and high-altitude China, followed by the emergence of polished bone tools and personal ornaments slightly later, indicating possible technological ties with lithic industries in Siberia and Central Asia and possible northwest-to-southeast migrations in Northeast Asia during the late Upper Pleistocene. Human fossil remains and archaeological evidence cumulatively suggest that the trajectories of modern human origins and adaptations in China may be different from those of western Eurasia. In this paper, new archaeological discoveries and research progress on the origin and evolution of modern humans in China were compiled and reported, a predominantly archaeological perspective on these critical issues was adopted, and everal suggestions for future studies were offered.

국문초록

최근 고인류학 및 구석기 고고학적 발견으로 현생인류의 기원, 진화 및 적응에 대한 이론적 관점이 급격하게 변화되고 있으며, 동아시아의 넓은 면적을 차지하는 중국이 연구 중심지로 부상하고 있다. 아프리카와 서부 유라시아 연구자료를 통해 주장되는 최근 아프리카 기원설에 반하는 새로운 인류 화석과 석기군이 중국에서 보고되고 있다. 새로운 고인류학 연구결과에 따르면, 초기 현생인류는 약 10만 년 전 중국 남부에 나타났으며 적어도 부분적으로 그곳 원주민 집단에서 진화했을 가능성이 있고, 일부 고대 호모사피엔스는 모자이크상 또는 과도기적 특징을 보이면서 네안데르탈인 및 데니소바인과의 혼혈 가능성을 보여준다. 공반하는 석기공작으로 볼 때, 초기 현생인류의 기술과 행태는 복잡했음을 알 수 있다. 즉, 중국 북부는 소형격지, 중국 남부는 대형 자갈돌석기들이 갱신세 전 기간에 우점했으나, 약 4만 년 전에는 대규모 돌날 복합기술이 중국 북부 일부 유적에서 나타나며, 약간 늦은 시기에는 같은 지역에서 뼈 연모와 개인 장신구도 등장하였다. 이는 후기갱신세 동안 동북아시아 석기공작이 시베리아, 중앙아시아, 북서부~동남아 지역 등지로 이동하면서 석기기술이 연계되었을 가능성을 시사한다. 결론적으로 중국 현생인류 화석과 고고학적으로 누적된 증거를 통해 중국 인류 기원과 적응의 흔적이 서부 유라시아와 다를 수 있음을 제시하고 있다.

Keywords : modern human origins, Paleolithic archaeology, cultural traditions, continuity with hybridization, China

1. Introduction

For more than three decades, the origins and evolution of modern humans have been the most important and broadly inclusive issue in paleoanthropological research worldwide as well as one of the major topics of popular media. Discussions and debates on these topics have long been focused on two competing theoretical models: the "Recent Out-of-Africa" (also Single-Place Origin or Total Replacement) hypothesis and the "Multiregional Evolution" paradigm (Wolpoff et al., 1984; 2000, Cann et al., 1987; Wu, 1998; Stringer, 2002; Wu, 2006; Gao et al., 2010). Recently, as more fossil, genetic, and cultural evidence have been accumulated, it has been realized that the origin and evolution of modern humans was an exceedingly complicated process, one in which some archaic hominin groups, such as the Neanderthals and Denisovans, thought to be totally extinct and essentially irrelevant to our species, were found to have contributed certain specific and identifiable genetic material to our gene pool (Green et al, 2010; Fu et al., 2014; 2015; Vernot and Akey, 2014), and that interbreeding played a very important role in the emergence of early modern humans. As a result, models of the origins of modern humans have been revised accordingly, and the so-called Assimilation Model has generated increasing interest and support (Smith et al., 1989, 2005; Gao et al., 2017). From an archaeological point of view, modern behavior documented in material culture appeared in various regions at different times and was not always synchronous with the fossil and genetic records. Thus, behavioral modernity is not exclusively associated with anatomically modern humans. Consequently, some scholars have shifted their research focus toward behavioral variability (Shea, 2011).

Recently, a great progress has been made at the intersection of paleoanthropology, archaeology, and molecular biology in China. While mainstream Chinese geneticists still insist that the modern Chinese population descended directly from African groups that arrived in South China about 50 ka, fossil evidence demonstrates that archaic to modern human evolution in China was more-or-less continuous and, most importantly, mosaic process: Certain modern human morphological characteristics appeared quite early, as revealed by hominin fossils dating to the late Middle Pleistocene and early Late Pleistocene (Liu et al., 2010; Li et al., 2017). Fossil hominins with fully modern *H. sapiens* morphology were living in south and Central China as early as ca. 100 ka (Liu et al., 2009; 2013; 2015).

The DNA sequences reconstructed for an early modern human from Tianyuan Cave, near Beijing in North China, revealed that this individual belonged to a population that was ancestral to many present-day Asians and Native Americans but postdated the divergence of Asians from Europeans (Fu et al., 2013). Evidence from Paleolithic archaeology also indicates a continuous development of lithic technology in China and greater East Asia since the Early Paleolithic. No obvious gap existed from 50-100 ka, as has been proposed by some geneticists who used the Chinese fossil and archaeological records to support the "Out-of-Africa" hypothesis (Ke et al., 2001). This implies that no total population replacement occurred during this period in China (Gao, 2014). These new discoveries and research advances, especially achievements gained through interdisciplinary and transdisciplinary studies, have made the origins and evolution of modern humans in the region much clearer as more details have been revealed (Gao et al., 2017). However, controversies about models of modern human origins and some missing links in fossil and genetic evidence remain, and varying interpretations of the same body of evidence occasionally occur.

2. Archaeological evidence for regional continuity of human evolution in China

Archaeologists in China were largely silent early in the debate over modern human origins. As an evolutionary gap in China occurring roughly 100-50 ka was proposed by some geneticists to support a population replacement model, some paleoanthropologists began to seek evidence from the Paleolithic archaeological record to invalidate such a claim (Wu, 2005; Wu and Xu, 2016). As a result, archaeologists began to contribute to this lively, if not contentious, discussion (Gao et al., 2010; 2017; Gao, 2014). Following a systematic synthesis of Pleistocene cultural remains collected in China, Gao noted that the development of Paleolithic industries in China occurred in one uninterrupted trajectory, indicating that Pleistocene hominids survived and evolved continuously in the region (Gao, 2014). Through the study of the emergence of so-called "Western cultural elements," such as Levalloisian products, Acheulean-like assemblages, and blade tools in the Chinese Paleolithic, it is apparent that such elements never became the mainstream in stone tool production, let alone a replacement for local techno-complexes. Rather, they were probably assimilated into the extant local material culture. Such evidence has provided archaeological support for the evolutionary continuity of Pleistocene hominins in China and the continuity with hybridization hypothesis instead of the "Recent Out-of-Africa" model. The hypothetical occupation hiatus in China between 100 ka and 50 ka proposed by some molecular biologists has been invalidated through archaeological research because some sites have now been dated to within this temporal window as a result of improved chronometric techniques, especially the optically stimulated luminescence (OSL) method. Moreover, paleoenvironmental reconstruction in China demonstrates that the region was not as harsh as what supporters of the "Recent Out-of-Africa" model have suggested, especially in central and Southern China.

Numerous archaeological materials unearthed from the Shuidonggou (SDG) site complex in Ningxia provide a large body of information to fuel discussions of cultural continuity, behavioral modernity and variability, and the influence of in-migrated populations in certain areas. The Shuidonggou site complex is located on the southwestern edge of the Ordos Desert, 28km southeast of Yinchuan and 10km east of the Yellow River. Here, a total of 12 localities bearing Late Pleistocene archaeological materials buried in sandy silt deposits have been discovered and investigated. Since 2003, renewed multidisciplinary research has been carried out at various SDG localities. This cumulative body of research has demonstrated that human groups utilized the SDG area over a much longer time range than was previously suspected via complex but successful behavioral and technological strategies (Gao et al., 2013; Peng et al., 2018; Li et al., 2019).

This aggregated information has yielded a complex story of the adaptation, migration, cultural exchange, and technological evolution of hominins in East Asia since ca. 40 ka (Gao et al., 2013; Li et al., 2019). Beginning roughly 45-40 ka, blade technology with Levallois features (the so-called Initial Upper Paleolithic industry, or IUP) emerged in this area, unearthed from the lower cultural horizon of SDG 1, 2, and 9. Technological comparisons with similar finds in Siberia and Central Asia indicate population dispersals from the west or north of the site. However, this techno-complex did not persist in the area, played little role in shaping the local lithic technology, and was eventually replaced by a local core-flake technology (Li et al., 2013; 2014; Peng et al., 2014).

Most of these core-flake tools were unearthed from the middle and upper horizons of SDG 2, overlying the IUP cultural layer. These tools appeared in the region around 33 ka and persisted until ca. 27 ka. Lithic assemblages during this period show consistent technological and morphological features, including comparatively simple flake production and side-scraper-dominated tool assemblages. These core and flake assemblages contain no evidence of the systematic production of blades or Levallois elements. However, some technological changes and innovations are evident from the sequence of core-flake reduction (Li et al., 2019). For instance, in addition to stone tools manufactured from river pebbles, some artifacts made of high-quality chert with an unrolled cortex were also discovered in Archaeological Layer 2 (AL2). Investigations in the area show that pebble raw materials are easily found on riverbanks and old terrace gravel deposits near the site, but fine chert cannot be sourced near the site; such materials must have come from a primary source at some distance away from the site, and soft-hammer percussion may have been used for the reduction of this latter material. Finely retouched end-scrapers, made mainly on flake blanks, are present in assemblages from the top cultural levels (AL1 and 2) but not in earlier strata. These features demonstrate a clear trajectory of continuous development and the refinement of longstanding core-flake industries in the region.

In addition to various lithic technological complexes, the SDG site cluster has yielded abundant additional cultural remains and behavioral characteristics, including bone tools, ornaments, fireplaces, complex spatial organization, heat treatment of lithic raw materials, and plant food gathering and processing (Guan et al., 2011; 2012; Peng et al., 2012; Zhou et al., 2013; Wei et al., 2016; Martía et al., 2017). Such advanced cultural behaviors, including the manufacture of bone artifacts, systematic use of body decorations, extensive use of earth-pit hearths, distinct functional spatial organization within habitation sites, and extensive exploitation of plant foods, are generally attributed to modern human behavior or behavioral modernity; they provide clues and perspectives for the analysis of early modern human origins and evolution in China and greater East Asia. The emergence of such modern human behavioral evidence within the domain of local core-flake techno-complexes may imply that no replacement occurred in this area. Instead, at least some local populations managed to embark upon and maintain their forward momentum on the evolutionary pathway toward modern humans.

A cluster of newly discovered Paleolithic sites in the Zhengzhou area of Henan Province in central China provide additional evidence for the regional continuity of cultural development and the emergence of behavioral modernity in China. Sites in this group include Zhijidong, Laonainaimiao, and Zhaozhuang, among others. Rich lithic and faunal materials and hearth remains have been unearthed from these sites dating to ca. 50-35 ka. These archaeological remains indicate that human behavior underwent remarkable changes at the beginning of MIS 3, as seen in the long-distance transport of raw materials and the diversity of toolkits, as well as the enlargement of activity areas. However, the technology of lithic reduction itself did not change much; a simple core-flake technology continued to be used as in the previous period (Wang and Qu, 2014).

One notable feature at the Zhaozhuang site is worth mentioning here. Adjacent to a lithic workshop where over 5,000 quartz and quartz sandstone artifacts were collected, a pile of quartz sandstone blocks was uncovered with an elephant skull on top. When it was recovered, the elephant skull was in a fragmented condition as a result of either post-depositional processes or human activity. Most of these quartz sandstone blocks underlie the elephant skull, but some were also distributed around it. It is believed that the stone pile was purposefully erected to support the elephant skull. These large blocks of purple-red quartz sandstones were extracted and carried to the site from a bedrock outcrop about 5km distant . It is blieved that the transport of these rocks was intended for the construction of the stone "foundation" or plinth rather than for the production of stone artifacts, possibly indicating some kind of ritual activity (Wang, 2017, Zhengzhou Archaeological Institute and Beijing University, 2020).

In order to explain the feasibility and dynamics of the continuity of human evolution in China, a Behavioral Model has been proposed (Gao and Pei, 2006; Gao, 2014) that has strengthened the argument in favor of aboriginal populations' capacity for survival and evolution into modern humans. This model offers the following observations and explanations for the stable development and unique features of Paleolithic industries in China:

2.1. Stable environments and continuity of human evolution

During the Pleistocene, China was under the influence of a monsoon climatic regime. Studies of the loess depositional sequence and faunal assemblages suggest that even though climatic fluctuations occurred periodically, environmental conditions were relatively stable in the region, and most of the area was suitable for human habitation.

2.2. Low-intensity resource exploitation and high mobility

Most Paleolithic sites found in the region represent seasonal, short-term occupations and associated artifacts that are mostly simple and share basic features of technology, typology, and morphology, which may indicate that human groups living in the region maintained a simple and "easy" foraging lifestyle. In other words, they kept their exploitation of natural resources at a rather low level of intensity and seldom felt the pressure to develop innovative new lithic technologies to increase their efficiency or procure more difficult to exploit resources.

2.3. Great flexibility in tool technology and adaptation

The scarcity of high-quality stone raw materials and suitable quarrying sites forced Paleolithic humans living in the area to use poor-quality and locally available raw materials. In dealing with such raw materials exhibiting great variability in lithology and morphology, they learned to be highly flexible and to use simple but suitable and effective ways to produce tool blanks and fabricate stone tools. Examples include the bipolar technique, which was employed to make use of otherwise intractable quartz nodules that were abundant in the nearby riverbed at Zhoukoudian, and the specialized "Throw and Collision Method" invented to exploit highly polished and rounded river pebbles in the Three Gorges Region of the Yangzi River.

Observations and analyses of unique behavioral patterns and social attributes of human beings also provide useful insights into issues such as the nature of geographic isolation of different human groups and the possibility of maintaining a single biological species of human groups living in different regions through time (Gao, 2014). Archaeology demonstrates that the biological isolation of human populations did not necessarily preclude cultural interaction or the sharing and possible convergence of technologies.

3. Evidence for human migrations and interaction in North China

Considering that China is a vast area with large topographic and environmental variation, regional continuity cannot comprise the whole story of the origins and evolution of modern humans in China. Migrations and interbreeding must have also played important roles.

In the past, a south-to-north route of early modern human dispersals in China was proposed based principally on genetic studies (Chu, et al., 1998). The human fossil record from China seems to support this assumption (Martinón-Torres et al., 2017) in terms of chronology. For instance, all known localities yielding the earliest modern human fossils are found in south and Central China – sites like Fuyan Cave (Liu et al., 2015), Luna Cave (Bae et al., 2014), and Huanglong Cave (Liu et al., 2009) – and all have provisional dates falling between 120 ka and 50 ka. The earliest known modern human fossils found in North China are from Tianyuan Cave, directly dated to 40 ka (Shang et al., 2007). A recently revised age for Zhoukoudian Upper Cave (ZKD UC) indicates that the modern human remains excavated there minimally date to 35-33 ka (Li et al., 2018).

However, comparative studies of human fossils from ZKD UC and Tianyuan Cave suggest relations with coeval groups from western Eurasia (Harvati, 2009). A recent genetic study found that a Tianyuan individual shared alleles with a 35,000-year-old European individual from Belgium (Yang et al., 2017). Combining apparent similarities between hominin paleontology and archaeology, It was proposed that ZKD UC and, probably, Tianyuan modern humans were part of dispersal events across Eurasia following a northern route, as others have suggested (Fu et al., 2014; Bae et al., 2017; Li et al., 2018). Recently, possible pathways for a northern migration route, eastward toward Siberia and eventually south into northern China, have been proposed (Li et al., 2019).

Other evidence potentially indicating modern human dispersal through a northern route comes from the Shuidonggou, Ningxia, and Nwya Devu, Tibet sites. An assemblage reflecting large blade production was found in the lower cultural horizon of the SDG site complex (Li et al., 2013; 2014). This blade techno-complex, dating to approximately 35 to 45 ka, has been associated with the Initial Upper Paleolithic in eastern Eurasia in that it combined Levallois and prismatic techniques to produce blades. Considering similar and earlier finds from localities west of the Shuidonggou area, some scholars have concluded that this techno-complex intruded from the Siberian Altai region and/or northern Mongolia (Li et al., 2013; 2014; 2016). Interestingly, IUP assemblages lasted for only a short time with an area of distribution in China limited to the northwest and never appearing in eastern North China. Instead, the core and flake technology dominated the Late Paleolithic record in the region until the emergence of microblade technology after roughly 25 ka. Based upon the geographical distribution of blade and core-flake industries, some scholars (e.g., Li et al., 2014; 2016) proposed a demographic model of diverse lithic technologies in the late Upper Pleistocene: Early Upper Pleistocene assemblages indicate that human groups dispersed from the west, while core-flake assemblages imply the continuous evolution of local groups in northern China. The blade assemblage at the Nwya Devu site in Tibet reflects mainly the prismatic production of blades, typical of the Upper Paleolithic. Due to the scarcity of this technology in northern China, scholars have linked the blade assemblage at Nwya Devu with similar finds in the Siberian Altai region and Mongolia, where prismatic blade production appeared earlier (Zhang et al., 2018).

In addition, population interactions across Eurasia have been inferred based upon the presence of Neanderthal DNA in and morphological similarities with the Tianyuan Cave individual (Shang et al., 2007; Fu et al., 2013). Recent finds from Jinsitai Cave, Inner Mongolia (Li et al., 2018) and Tongtian Cave, Xinjiang (Institute of Archaeology and Cultural Relics of Xinjiang, 2018) have added additional evidence of Middle Paleolithic (Mousterian) dispersal by means of tracing lithic technology. Mousterian assemblages have been found in these cave sites, including a typical Levallois component and Mousterian-style retouched tools. Classic Mousterian industries are associated with Neanderthal remains at dozens of sites in Europe, the Caucasus, and Central Asia (Stringer, 2002). Comparison of the Jinsitai assemblages with those from the most closely adjacent regions, such as the Siberian Altai, suggests that Mousterian assemblages in northern China were probably also made by Neanderthals (Li et al., 2018). Complex genetic interactions among modern humans, Neanderthals, and Denisovans have been revealed recently in the Altai region (Krause et al., 2010; Reich et al, 2011; Prüfer et al., 2014; Slon et al., 2017; 2018). Although the determination of the presence of Neanderthals in northern China awaits fossil or molecular evidence, the discoveries of Mousterian assemblages and the presence of Neanderthal morphological features on some human fossil specimens (such as fossils from Lingjing and Xujiayao) indicate a complex picture of Late Pleistocene hominin dispersals and possible physical and technological interactions among different groups in northern China.

3.1. Bone tools and personal ornaments as expressions of behavioral modernity

Polished bone tools and personal ornaments have been taken as cultural markers of modern humans. Such cultural remains have been unearthed from several Late Paleolithic sites in China in association with traditional core-flake and pebble tools, which has added more fuel to discussions of the nature of modern human behavior and the complex relationships between behavioral modernity and cultural variability.

The Upper Cave at the Zhoukoudian site complex in North China is a good example of the complexity of archaeological discoveries and the emergence of behavioral modernity in the area. Polished bone tools, engravings on antlers, personal ornaments, and the use of ocher were found in the cave in association with early modern human skulls and simple core-flake tools. Bone tools include delicately polished bone needles, attesting to the sophistication of bone tool manufacture there. Personal ornaments include perforated pebbles, mammal teeth, tubular bones, and perforated shells (Pei, 1939). The cultural horizons at the site have been recently reliably dated to at least 35.1-33.5 ka, which is associated with the earliest known polished bone tool and ornaments in China (Li et al., 2018). The association of archaic and simple lithic artifacts with early modern human fossils, bone tools, antler engravings, personal ornaments, and the use of ocher in one cultural horizon clearly indicates that lithic industries alone may not be sufficient to ascertain the identity of particular human groups, including archaic hominins versus modern humans. Once again, we are reminded that the human co-evolutionary pathways of biology and culture tell separate stories that require illumination and reconciliation in order to fully comprehend the nature of human origins and development. Items of personal ornament have also been collected from the Shuidonggou site complex. The earliest ornament unearthed from the site is a perforated freshwater shell bead from CL 3 at SDG 2, dated to ca. 33-34 ka (Wei et al., 2016). A total of 93 ostrich eggshell (OES) beads were found in slightly younger cultural horizons at SDG 2, 7, and 8 (Martía et al., 2017; Wei et al., 2017). Most of these beads were derived from CL 2 at SDG 2, which is dated to ca. 31-33 ka. Both well-made and poorly crafted OES beads were produced at SDG 2. Detailed morphological and technological analyses have made it clear that these OES beads were derived from the extinct ostrich *Struthio anderssoni*. Based on microscopic examination, morphometric analysis, and experimental replication, clear differences in morphology, size, technology, and style have been identified. Research results indicate that the technology of bead making at SDG is similar to that used in most Middle and Later Stone Age sites in Africa and recorded ethnographically. Drilling experiments have demonstrated that hafted stone points were probably used to make the perforations. A few beads show traces of deliberate polishing on their inner and outer surfaces. The morphology and technology of these OES beads suggest that distinct types of beads may have been made by different individual craftspeople, and that several human groups may have visited the SDG site and made and used such OES beads during the Late Paleolithic (Wei et al., 2017). These people were certainly modern humans in every sense, yet they still made and used core-flake tools, obviously improved in comparison with earlier, simpler core-flake tools that dominated the technological repertoire in North China for a very long time.

An early occurrence of sophisticated polished bone tools was discovered in the Ma'anshan Cave site in Guizhou Province, South China. At least 17 bone tools were unearthed from three cultural horizons at the site. From Stratum 6, dated to ca. 35 cal ka, three sharpened bone awls were collected; and from Stratum 5, dated to ca. 34 cal ka, six probable spear points, awls, and a cutting tool were discovered. Stratum 3, dated ca. 23-18 cal ka, yielded two types of barbed points. These bone tools were fabricated by scraping, grinding, and polishing. This site features one of the oldest formal bone tool industries in China and provides among the oldest known indisputable evidence of the manufacture of barbed points outside of Africa (Zhang et al., 2016).

Formal bone tools are ubiquitous at Upper Palaeolithic archaeological sites in Europe, and their production has long been regarded as an innovation introduced by anatomically modern humans from Africa colonizing this region ca. 40 ka (Klein, 2009). Occurrences of polished bone tools in China dating to roughly 35 ka exhibit rates of cultural turnover comparable to those observed in the Upper Palaeolithic of Europe, indicating that the emergence of this key cultural innovation is better understood as a complex, discontinuous process that took place at different times and in different regions. This process, which may be the outcome of both diffusion and independent invention, must be documented on a regional scale (Zhang et al., 2016). The two cases of the early appearance of polished bone tools in the Upper Cave at Zhoukoudian in North China and the Ma'anshan site in South China reflect a similar cultural pattern – that is, sophisticated bone tools found in association with lithic technology that remained relatively unchanged for a long period of time. This pattern once again testifies to the complexity of Late Paleolithic cultures in China and to the ambiguity of the material expression of human behavioral modernity.

3.2. Evidence of the unprecedented capacity for adaptation of early modern humans

Modern humans developed rapidly during the Late Pleistocene. Alongside improvements in their physical capabilities, cognition, technology, and social organization, these humans engaged in successful biogeographic expansions, eventually spreading even to extreme high-altitude environments. Successful adaptations to high altitudes have always presented humans with severe biological challenges. The Tibetan Plateau is the highest and one of the most challenging environments inhabited by humans. The combination of high altitude, atmospheric hypoxia, cold year-round temperatures, and low rainfall creates an extremely challenging environment for human habitation. Archaeological evidence indicates that this area was one of the last terrestrial habitats colonized by *Homo sapiens*. Today, the Tibetan Plateau is the third least-populous spot on the planet (after Antarctica and Greenland). The peopling of the Tibetan Plateau provides compelling evidence for the unprecedented capacity for adaptation of early modern humans.

Until recently, there has been no concrete evidence of people inhabiting the interior of the Tibetan Plateau before the Holocene epoch, and only a few reliably dated Pleistocene archaeological sites have been discovered around the Plateau's margins (Brantingham et al., 2003). In 2013, the Nwya Devu open-air site was discovered. The site is located on an ancient lacustrine terrace of Co Ngoin, in the Nagqu district of interior Tibet. Formal excavations of the site were carried out in 2016-2018. Fieldwork and laboratory analyses yielded multiple reliable dates in direct association with buried artifacts, extending the history of human occupation of the region back to 40-30 ka. The site, situated nearly 4,600 masl, is the highest Paleolithic archaeological site yet identified globally. A total of 3,683 stone artifacts were recovered from an excavated area of 20m². The lithic assemblage comprised 91 blade cores, 57 flake cores, 499 blades, 1,814 flakes, 195 tools, and 1,027 chunks. The slate raw material was sourced nearby on Nwya Devu Hill, where an outcrop is exposed on the surface. Based on the analysis and comparison of thin sections of unearthed artifacts and rocks collected at nearby outcrops, researchers concluded that the ancient inhabitants of Nwya Devu exploited the fine-grained slate exposed on the west slope of Nwya Devu Hill and knapped it exclusively (Zhang et al., 2018).

The Nwya Devu lithic complex is distinguished by the production of blades from prismatic rather than Levallois cores. Comparing the length×width of the flaking face with the length×width and length×thickness of blade cores, the results show that prehistoric people intended to detach blades from the long narrow face. Unidirectional flaking dominates the Nwya Devu assemblage, while blade size varies considerably. The Nwya Devu assemblage principally comprises flakes, blades, cores, and chunks; formal tools are comparatively rare (5.3% of the collection). Finely retouched formal tools are scarce, and most retouching is expedient. The abundance of prismatic blade cores at Nwya Devu is therefore nearly unique in China. Technologically, the Nwya Devu lithic assemblage most closely resembles those classified as Early Upper Paleolithic (EUP) in southern Siberia and northern Mongolia and is differentiated from the core-flake assemblages common in northern China. The blade cores, blades, and tools from Nwya Devu, which include unidirectional as well as bidirectional nuclei for the production of medium-large size blades, share similarities with artifacts from Early Upper Paleolithic sites in the Siberian Altai region, such as Kara Bom (Variant 1), and Tolbor-21 (Layer 3a) in Mongolia (Derevianko et al., 2000; Derevianko, 2011; Rybin et al., 2015; Khatsenovich et al., 2017).

Research on the Nwya Devu site considerably deepens the history of the peopling of the "Roof of the World" and the antiquity of human high-altitude occupation more generally. The research demonstrates that despite cold temperatures and low-oxygen conditions at least 30-40 ka, hunter-gatherers colonized extreme high-altitude Tibetan Plateau environments in the Late Pleistocene. Thus, the Nwya Devu site establishes a new record for the prehistoric conquest of one of the most challenging environments in the history of modern human evolution, much earlier than current evidence for high-altitude colonization in the Andes (Rademaker et al., 2014).

3.3. Discussion and conclusions

In the past 30 years, hypotheses concerning the origins of modern humans have been intensively debated, and two competing models, the "Recent Out-of-Africa" and "Multiregional Evolution" paradigms, have dominated research and academic discussions for decades. Evidence from China has played a fundamental role in this debate: Regional continuity and replacement by populations in- migrated from Africa have both been suggested and supported mainly by paleoanthropologists and geneticists, respectively. Recent discoveries of new human fossils, Paleolithic archaeological materials, and ancient DNA evidence in China have yielded a large body of information regarding the origins and evolution of modern humans in this region, and concrete progress has been made in this broad and rich field.

New paleoanthropological and Paleolithic archaeological discoveries have drastically changed our theoretical perspectives on modern human origins, evolution, and adaptations. From an anatomical point of view, some archaic *Homo sapiens* groups found in China, such as those represented by fossils from the Hualongdong, Dali, Jinniushan, Dadong, Xujiayao, and Xuchang sites (Chen et al., 1994; Liu et al., 2013; Wu et al., 2014; Li et al., 2017; Athreya and Wu, 2017; Gao, 2017; Wu et al., 2019), exhibit mosaic or transitional features, while some (i.e., Xujiayao and Xuchang) indicate possible admixture with Neanderthals and Denisovans. Together with the continuous development of traditional core-flake technologies in North China and the pebble tool techno-complex in South China, such evidence lends credence to a "continuity with hybridization" model of modern human evolution in China. However, the morphological and genetic evidence of early modern humans from Zhoukoudian Upper Cave and Tianyuan Cave reveals a very complicated history of genetic inheritance and hybridization with other hominin groups in western Eurasia, including both modern and archaic groups. A blade-based techno-complex appeared at some sites in northern China by ca. 40 ka, indicating possible technological ties with lithic industries in southern Siberia and Central Asia as well as possible human migration and interbreeding. When we aggregate available information from archaeological discoveries, including the association of refined traditional core-flake tools with bone tools and ornaments in North China and the persistence of a pebble-based industry in combination with the development of bone tools in South China, a very complex picture of modern human origins and evolution emerges.

Nevertheless, many problems could impinge on the validity of this model, including inadequate data relating to research on modern human origins and dispersals in northern China, the virtual hiatus in China's human fossil record between roughly 100-50 ka, and the uncertain relationship between archaeological assemblages and specific fossil human groups. It is clear that one of the major tasks that must be undertaken in northern China is the search for more archaeological sites and human fossils dating to 100-30 ka.

The study of modern human origins and evolution is a joint venture, one including many research fields. Every discipline engaged in this study is characterized by its own inherent strengths and weaknesses (Gao, 2017). Archaeological material is abundant and much richer than the human fossil record, but only the latter can provide morphological and genetic information. Material cultural remains, on the other hand, can provide a large body of information that can help answer questions such as when hominins first appeared in a certain region, to where they dispersed, whether human evolution in a certain region was continuous, what ecosystems and adaptation strategies were exploited, and whether interactions among ancient human groups occurred. However, the weakness of this dataset is its association with particular human ancestral groups or hominin evolutionary stages. Moreover, cultural behavior can be shaped by the environment and the availability of raw materials, indicating great variability in the mechanisms of change, and are very weakly correlated with anatomical and genetic evolution. Consequently, strengthening communication and interaction among traditional paleoanthropological and archaeological fields and the burgeoning molecular biological fields, understanding each discipline's specialties and limitations, and carrying out interdisciplinary and integrative research is the right direction to follow in pursuing research on human origins and evolution in the future.

References

Athreya S., Wu X., 2017. A multivariate assessment of the Dali hominin cranium from China: morphological affinities and implications for Pleistocene evolution in East Asia. *American Journal of Physical Anthropology* 164, 679-701.

Bae C.J., Petraglia M.D., Douka K., 2017. On the origin of modern humans: Asian perspectives. *Science* 358. DOI: 10.1126/science.aai9067

Bae C.J., Wang W., Zhao J. et al., 2014. Modern human teeth from Late Pleistocene Luna Cave (Guangxi, China). *Quaternary International* 354, 169-183.

Brantingham J., Ma H.Z., Olsen J. et al., 2003. Speculation on the timing and nature of Late Pleistocene hunter-gatherer colonization of the Tibetan Plateau. *Chinese Science Bulletin* 48(14), 1510-1516.

Cann R.L., Stoneking M., Wilson A.C., 1987. Mitochondrial DNA and human evolution. *Nature* 325, 31-36.

Chen T.M., Quan Y., En W., 1994. Antiquity of Homo sapiens in China. *Nature* 368, 55-56.

Chu J., Huang W., Kuang S. et al., 1998. Genetic relationship of populations in China. *PNAS* 95, 11763-11768.

Derevianko A.P., 2011. *The Upper Paleolithic in Africa and Eurasia and the Origin of Anatomically Modern Humans*, Novosibirsk: Institute of Archaeology and Ethnography SB RAS Press.

Derevianko A.P., Petrin V., Rybin E., 2000. The Kara-Bom site and the characteristics of the Middle-Upper Paleolithic transition in the Altai. *Archaeology, Ethnology and Anthropology of Eurasia* 2, 33-52.

Fu Q., Hajdinjak M., Moldovan O.T. et al., 2015. An early modern human from Romania with a recent Neanderthal ancestor. *Nature* 524, 216-219.

Fu Q., Li H., Moorjani P. et al., 2014. Genome sequence of a 45000-year-old modern human from Western Siberia. *Nature* 514, 445-449.

Fu Q., Meyer M., Gao X. et al., 2013. DNA analysis of an early modern human from Tianyuan Cave, China. *PNAS* 110, 2223-2227.

Gao X., 2014. Archaeological evidence for evolutionary continuity of Pleistocene humans in China and East Asia and related discussions (in Chinese with English abstract). *Acta Anthropologica Sinica* 33, 237-253.

Gao X., 2017. Collaboration and Integration among Paleoanthropology, Archaeology and Genetics (in Chinese with English Abstract). *Acta Anthropologica Sinica* 36(1), 131-140.

Gao X., Pei S.W., 2006. An archaeological interpretation of ancient human lithic technology and adaptive strategies in China. *Quaternary Sciences* 26, 504-513.

Gao X., Peng F., Fu Q.M. et al., 2017. New progress in understanding the origins of modern humans in China. *Science China (Earth Sciences)* 60(12), 2160-2170.

Gao X., Wang H.M., Pei S.W. et al., 2013. *Shuidonggou: Archaeological Excavations and Research Reports for 2003-2007* (in Chinese with English abstract), Beijing: Science Press.

Gao X., Zhang X.L., Yang D.Y., SHEN Chen & WU XinZhi. 2010. Revisiting the origin of modern humans in China and its implications for global human evolution. *Science China (Earth Sciences)* 53, 1927-1940.

Green R.E., Krause J., Briggs A.W. et al., 2010. A draft sequence of the Neandertal genome. *Science* 328, 710-722.

Guan Y., Gao X., Li F. et al., 2012. Modern human behaviors during the late stage of the MIS3 and the broad spectrum revolution: Evidence from a Shuidonggou Late Paleolithic site. *Chinese Science Bulletin* 57, 379-386.

Guan Y., Gao X., Wang H.M. et al., 2011. Spatial analysis of intra-site use at a Late Paleolithic site at Shuidonggou, Northwest China. *Chinese Science Bulletin* 56, 3457-3463.

Harvati K., 2009. Into Eurasia: a geometric morphometric reassessment of the Upper Cave (Zhoukoudian) specimens. *Journal of Human Evolution* 57, 751-762.

Hublin J.J., 2007. What can Neanderthals tell us about Modern Origins? In: Mellars, P., Boyle, K., Bar-Yosef O, Stringer C. eds., *Rethinking the Human Revolution: New Behavioural and Biological Perspectives on the Origin and Dispersal of Modern Humans*, Cambridge: McDonald Institute for Archaeological Research, 235-248.

Institute of Archaeology and Cultural Relics of Xinjiang, School of Archaeology and Museology of Peking University. 2018. Tongtiandong site in Jimunai, Xinjiang (in Chinese). *Archaeology (Kaogu)* 18(7), 723-734.

Ke Y., Su B., Song X. et al., 2001. African origin of modern humans in East Asia: A tale of 12,000 Y chromosomes. *Science* 292, 1151-1153.

Khatsenovich A., Rybin E., Gunchinsuren B. et al., 2017. New evidence for Paleolithic human behavior in Mongolia: the Kharganyn Gol 5 site. *Quaternary International* 442, 78-94.

Klein R.G., 2009. *The Human Career: Human Biological and Cultural Origins* (the third edition), Chicago: University of Chicago Press.

Krause J., Fu Q., Good J.M. et al., 2010. The complete mitochondrial DNA genome of an unknown hominin from southern Siberia. *Nature* 464, 894-897.

Li F., Bae C.J., Ramsey C.B. et al., 2018. Re-dating Zhoukoudian Upper Cave, northern China and its regional significance. *Journal of Human Evolution* 121, 170-177.

Li F., Chen F.Y., Wang Y.H. et al., 2016. Technology diffusion and population migration reflected in blade technologies in northern China in the Late Pleistocene. *Science China (Earth Sciences)* 59, 1540-1553.

Li F., Kuhn S.L., Bar-Yosef O. et al., 2019. History, chronology and techno-typology of the Upper Paleolithic sequence in the Shuidonggou area, Northern China. *Journal of World Prehistory* 32(2), 111-141.

Li F., Kuhn S.L., Chen F.Y. et al., 2018. The easternmost Middle Paleolithic (Mousterian) from Jinsitai Cave, North China. *Journal of Human Evolution* 114, 76-84.

Li F., Kuhn S.L., Gao X. et al., 2013. Re-examination of the dates of large blade technology in China: A comparison of Shuidonggou Locality 1 and Locality 2. *Journal of Human Evolution* 64, 161-168.

Li F., Kuhn S.L., Olsen J.W. et al., 2014. Disparate stone age technological evolution in North China. *Journal of Anthropological Research* 70, 35-67.

Li F., Vanwezer N., Boivin N. et al., 2019. Heading north: Late Pleistocene environments and human dispersals in central and eastern Asia. *PLoS ONE* 14(5), e0216433.

Li Z.Y., Wu X.J., Zhou L.P. et al., 2017. Late Pleistocene archaic human crania from Xuchang, China. *Science* 355, 969-972.

Liu W., Jin C.Z., Zhang Y.Q. et al., 2010. Human remains from Zhirendong, South China, and modern human emergence in East Asia. *PNAS* 107, 19201-19206.

Liu W., Martinón-Torres M., Cai Y.J. et al., 2015. The earliest unequivocally modern humans in southern China. *Nature* 526, 696-699.

Liu W., Schepartz L.A., Xing S. et al., 2013. Late Middle Pleistocene hominin teeth from Panxian Dadong, South China. *Journal of Human Evolution* 64, 337-355.

Liu W., Wu X.Z., Li Y.Y. et al., 2009. Evidence of fire use of late Pleistocene humans from the Huanglong Cave, Hubei Province, China. *China Science Bulletin* 54, 256-264.

Martía A.P., Wei Y., Gao X. et al., 2017. The earliest evidence of coloured ornaments in China: the ochred ostrich eggshell beads from Shuidonggou Locality 2. *Journal of Anthropological Archaeology* 48, 102-113.

Martinón-Torres M., Wu X., Castro JMBD et al., 2017. Homo sapiens in the eastern Asian Late Pleistocene. *Current Anthropology* 58, S434-S448.

Pei W.C., 1939. On the Upper Cave industry. *Palaeontologica Sinica* 9, 1-59.

Peng F., Gao X., Wang H.M. et al., 2012. An engraved artifact from Shuidonggou, an Early Late Paleolithic Site in Northwest China. *Chinese Science Bulletin* 57, 4594-4599.

Peng F., Guo J., Lin S. et al., 2018. The onset of Late Paleolithic in North China: An integrative review of the Shuidonggou site complex. China. *L'Anthropologie* 122(1), 74-86.

Peng F., Wang H.M., Gao X., 2014. Blade production of Shuidonggou Locality1 (Northwest China): A technological perspective. *Quaternary International* 347, 12-20.

Prüfer K., Racimo F., Patterson N. et al., 2014. The complete genome sequence of a Neanderthal from the Altai Mountains. *Nature* 505, 43-49.

Rademaker K., Hodgins G., Moore K. et al., 2014. Paleoindian settlement of the high-altitude Peruvian Andes. *Science* 346(6208), 466-469.

Reich D., Patterson N., Kircher M. et al, 2011. Denisova admixture and the first modern human dispersals into Southeast Asia and Oceania. *The American Journal of Human Genetics* 89, 516-528.

Rybin E., Zwyns N., Gunchinsuren B. et al., 2015. Issledovanija mnogoslojnoj paleoliticheskoj stojanki Tolbor-21 (severnaja mongolija) (Investigation of the multilayered Paleolithic site, Tolbor 21). In: Derevianko A., Molodin V. eds., *Problems of Archaeology, Ethnography and Anthropology in Siberia and Neighboring Territories 21*, Novosibirsk: Institute of Archaeology and Ethnography SB RAS Press, 152-156.

Shang H., Tong H.W., Zhang S.Q. et al., 2007. An early modern human from Tianyuan Cave, Zhoukoudian, China. *PNAS* 104, 6573-6578.

Shea J.J., 2011. Homo sapiens is as Homo sapiens Was. *Current Anthropology* 52, 1-35.

Smith F.H., Falsetti A.B., Donnelly S.M., 1989. Modern human origins. *American Journal of Physical Anthropology* 32, 35-68.

Smith F.H., Janković I., Karavanić I., 2005. The assimilation model, modern human origins in Europe, and the extinction of Neandertals. *Quaternary International* 137, 7-19.

Slon V., Hopfe C., Weiß C.L. et al., 2017. Neandertal and Denisovan DNA from Pleistocene sediments. *Science* 356, 605-608.

Slon V., Mafessoni F., Vernot B. et al., 2018. The genome of the offspring of a Neanderthal mother and a Denisovan father. *Nature* 561, 113-116.

Stringer C., 2002. Modern human origins: Progress and prospects. *Philosophical Transactions of the Royal Sciety of London B* 357, 563-579.

Vernot B., Akey J.M., 2014. Resurrecting surviving Neandertal lineages from modern human genomes. *Science* 343, 1017-1021.

Wang Y.P., Qu T.L., 2014. New evidence and perspectives on the Upper Paleolithic of the Central Plain in China. *Quaternary International* 347, 176-182.

Wang Y.P., 2017. Late Pleistocene Human Migrations in China. *Current Anthropology* 58 (Supplement 17), s504-s513.

Wei Y., d'Errico F., Vanhaeren M. et al., 2016. An Early Instance of Upper Palaeolithic Personal Ornamentation from China: The Freshwater Shell Bead from Shuidonggou 2. *PLoS ONE* 11(5), e0155847.

Wei Y., d'Errico F., Vanhaeren M. et al., 2017. A technological and morphological study of Late Paleolithic ostrich eggshell beads from Shuidonggou, North China. *Journal of Archaeological Science* 85, 83-104.

Wolpoff M.H., Hawks J., Caspari R., 2000. Multiregional, not multiple origins. *American Journal of Physical Anthropology* 112, 129-136.

Wolpoff M.H., Wu X.Z., Thorne A.G., 1984. Modern Homo sapiens origins: A general theory of hominid evolution involving the fossil evidence from East Asia. In: Smith F.H., Spencer F. eds., *The Origins of Modern Humans: A World Survey of the Fossil Evidence*, New York: Alan R Liss Inc., 411-483.

Wu X.J., Crevecoeur I., Liu W. et al., 2014. Temporal labyrinths of eastern Eurasian Pleistocene humans. *PNAS* 111(29), 10509-10513.

Wu X.J., Pei S.W., Cai Y.J. et al., 2019. Archaic human remains from Hualongdong, China, and Middle Pleistocene human continuity and variation. *PNAS* 116(20), 9820-9824.

Wu X.Z., 1998. Origin of modern humans of China viewed from cranio-dental characteristics of Late Homo sapiens in China (in Chinese). *Acta Anthropologica Sinica* 17, 276-282.

Wu X., 2005. Discussion on the results of some molecular studies concerning the origin of modern Chinese (in Chinese with English abstract). *Acta Anthropologica Sinica* 24(4), 259-269.

Wu X.Z., 2006. Evidence of multiregional human evolution hypothesis from China (in Chinese with English abstract). *Quaternary Sciences*, 702-709.

Wu X.Z., Xu X., 2016. The origin of modern humans in China viewed from the Paleolithic data and Daoxian human fossils (in Chinese with English abstract). *Acta Anthropologica Sinica* 35, 1-13.

Yang M.A., Gao X., Theunert C. et al., 2017. 40,000-Year-Old Individual from Asia Provides Insight into Early Population Structure in Eurasia. *Current Biology* 27, 3202-3208.

Zhang S.Q., d'Errico F., Backwell L.R. et al.,2016. Ma'anshan cave and the origin of bone tool technology in China. *Journal of Archaeological Science* 65, 57-69.

Zhang X.L., Ha B., Wang S.J. et al., 2018. The earliest human occupation of the high-altitude Tibetan Plateau 40-30 thousand years ago. *Science* 362(6418), 1049-1051.

Zhengzhou Archaeological Institute and the Peking University. 2020. *Report on excavations at the Paleolithic site of Zhaozhuang in Zhengzhou*, Beijing: Science Press.

Zhou Z.Y., Guan Y., Gao X. et al., 2013. Heat treatment and associated early modern human behaviors in the Late Paleolithic at the Shuidonggou site. *Chinese Science Bulletin* 58, 1801-1810.

Chronological aspects concerning the Middle and Late Pleistocene hominin presence in Sudanese Nubia, NE Africa

Mirosław MASOJĆ

Professor, Laboratory for Non-European Archaeology, Institute of Archaeology, University of Wroclaw, Poland;
miroslaw.masojc@uwr.edu.pl

ABSTRACT

This paper presents evidence for Middle and Late Pleistocene Eastern Saharan hominin activity based on research results from *Middle Pleistocene hominins* Sudanese areas referred to as the Eastern Desert Atbara River (EDAR) and Bayuda Desert. The results of chronological and archaeological analyses highlight several aspects regarding hominin presence in this part of Africa, which will be discussed in this article, including the earliest traces of *Homo erectus* activity (oldest Acheulean) the presence of the latest *Middle Pleistocene hominins* (the youngest Acheulean) as well as the oldest traces of the presence of *Homo sapiens* (the oldest traces of Middle Stone Age). The existing evidence supports the long presence of *Homo erectus* in the Eastern Sahara, possibly even from the Early Pleistocene (MIS >13-11) to the end of the Middle Pleistocene (MIS 7a/6), as well as the early appearance of *Homo sapiens* (MIS 9<), which shows the long coexistence of these two human species in a relatively small area of the deserts of contemporary Sudan. It is no less important to describe the Eastern Sahara as an area that cyclically played an important role in the dispersion, through green corridors, of hominins–and thus human culture–in the Pleistocene.

국문초록

본 논문은 수단의 동부사막 아트바라강(Eastern Desert Atbara River)과 바유다사막(Bayuda Desert)으로 알려진 수단지역의 연구결과를 통해 중기와 후기 갱신세 동안 동부 사하라 고인류의 활동증거를 제시하고 있다. 연대학적 고고학적 분석결과, 아프리카 수단지역에서 고인류 존재에 대한 다양한 양상이 전개되고 있는데 본 논문에서는 첫째, 최고기 아슐리안으로서 호모 에렉투스의 가장 이른시기 활동 흔적, 둘째, 최후기 아슐리안으로서 중기갱신세 최말기 고인류 활동 흔적, 셋째, 중기구석기 가장 이른시기로서 호모 사피엔스 활동 등을 각각 살펴보았다. 현재까지 알려진 고인류 활동 증거는 동부 사하라지역에서 초기 갱신세(MIS 〉13-11)부터 중기 갱신세 말(MIS 7a/6)에 걸친 호모 에렉투스 활동, 호모 사피엔스 최초 출현(MIS 9〈)으로 나타난다. 이러한 연대학적 증거가 뒷받침되면서 현재 수단에서는 비교적 협소한 사막지역에서도 호모 에렉투스와 호모 사피엔스라는 두 종류의 인류가 장기간 공존했음을 알 수 있다. 따라서 동부 사하라지역은 갱신세 고인류와 고인류 문화의 확산이 주기적으로 일어나는 녹색통로(green corridor) 역할을 한 중요한 지역임을 시사하고 있다.

Keywords : Africa, Eastern Sahara, Sudan, Pleistocene, hominin presence, dispersals

1. Introduction

A simple nonparametric estimator was presented in a recent study of ancestor spatial location that used the coordinates of descendants of a node combined with the structure of a tree sequence to provide an estimate of ancestors' geographic position (Wohns et al., 2022). Tree sequence-based analysis of ancient samples allows for the characterization of patterns of recent descent. Although the inferred geographic center of gravity of the 100 oldest ancestral haplotypes (which have an average age of ~2 million years) is located, according to Wohns et al., 2022 in Sudan, in northeastern Africa (at 19.4°N, 33.7°E), this is an area where hominin remains are in fact exceptionally rare, with lithic inventories serving as primary evidence for an early hominin presence (Grine, 2016; Masojć, 2021; Masojć, in press).

Only a few sites from Nubia (southern Egypt and Sudan) have yielded Pleistocene human remains, attributed, without exclusion, to *Homo sapiens* from the MIS 6-2 period (marine isotopic stages) (Grine, 2016). Outside Nubia, in a neighboring area known as the Northern Danakil (Afar) Depression, in Eritrea, a hominin cranium preceding *Homo sapiens* was found (Abbate et al., 1998; Bruner et al., 2016). The discovery of a well-preserved Homo cranium with a mixture of characteristics typical of *Homo erectus* and *Homo sapiens* was found in a layer near the top of the lower normal magnetozone, which was identified as the Jaramillo subchron (Abbate et al., 2004). Consequently, human remains at the site can be dated to ~1 million years BP.

The only Middle Pleistocene find from Nubia is a considerably mineralized partial human cranium discovered in 1924 together with artifacts protruding from a calcrete deposit in Singa, along the west bank of the Blue Nile, ca. 320km southeast of Khartoum. It was enclosed in a block of limestone calcrete (Woodward, 1938; Arkell et al., 1951). The calcrete matrix that enclosed the cranium was dated by U-Th to ca. 133 ka, a date supported by less precise dating from isochron analyses of other samples of calcrete and from electron spin resonance (ESR) measurements of indirectly associated animal teeth (McDermott et al., 1996). Because the calcrete formed on the cranium after it was deposited, the cranium itself is older–its most probable age is within the range of 145-133 ka (MIS 6) (Millard, 2008; Grine, 2016). Morphological studies indicated a mixture of archaic and more modern human traits, but such analyses are complicated by the possibility that the vault is pathologically deformed (Spoor et al., 1998). Associated fauna and artifacts were collected at both Singa and the comparable site of Abu Hugar, ca. 15km to the south (Arkell et al., 1951). The artifacts from Singa and Abu Hugar have been variously interpreted as non-diagnostic (Marks, 1968), Middle Paleolithic (McBurney, 1977), or perhaps even Acheulean (Bräuer, 1984) in affinities.

This paper presents evidence for Middle and Late Pleistocene Eastern Saharan hominin activity based on research results from Sudanese areas referred to as the Eastern Desert Atbara River (EDAR[1]) (Masojć et al., 2021a) and Bayuda Desert (Masojć et al., 2017) (**Fig. 1**). The results of chronological and archaeological analyses highlight several aspects of hominin presence in this part of Africa, which will be discussed as follows: 1. Earliest traces of *Homo erectus* activity (oldest Acheulean); 2. The presence of the latest *Middle Pleistocene hominins* (the youngest Acheulean); 3. The oldest traces of the presence of *Homo sapiens* (the oldest traces of Middle Stone Age).

Given that the entire Acheulean industrial complex cannot be unambiguously associated with *Homo erectus* (also referred to as *Homo ergaster* in Africa) and that the anthropological picture of the functioning of this cultural phenomenon varies, *Homo erectus* term , in the absence of human remains from EDAR sites, should be employed very generally as a human species associated with the Acheulean,

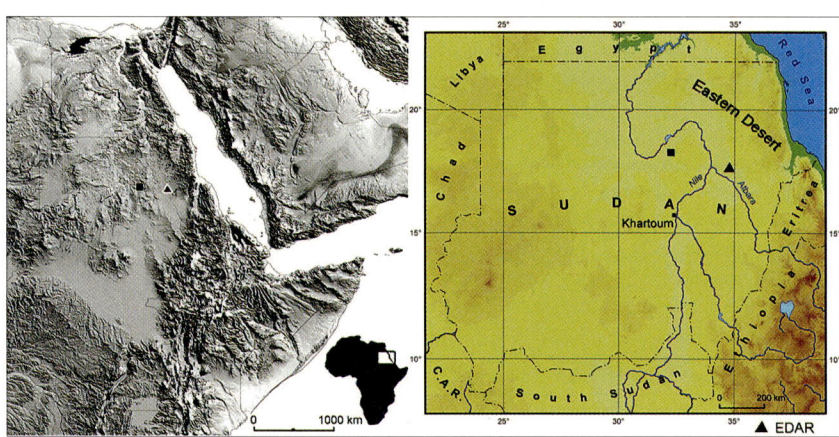

Fig. 1 Location of Eastern Desert Atbara River (EDAR) area (black triangle) and site BP 177 in the Bayuda Desert (black rectangle) Left: NE Africa with the EDAR area and BP 177 marked. Right: map of Sudan with the location of EDAR within the Eastern Desert and BP 177 in Bayuda Desert. Grey-shaded Digital Elevation Model (DEM) derived from Shuttle Radar Topography Mission elevation data (SRTM)

---

1) Research in the EDAR region of Sudan has been carried out since 2017 in cooperation with many Korean colleagues, possible thanks to an invitation to the author of this text by Professor Yung-jo Lee, President of the Institute of Korean Prehistory (IKP) and Professor Lucyna Domańska, of the Institute of Archeology at the University of Łódź, for the annual Suyanggae and Her Neighbors Symposium. The geoarchaeological work in the project is being coordinated by Dr. Ju Yong Kim from the Korea Institute of Geoscience and Mineral Resources (KIGAM), to whom special thanks is due for their commitment to fieldwork, publication, and the involvement of colleagues from KIGAM and other Korean scientific institutions.

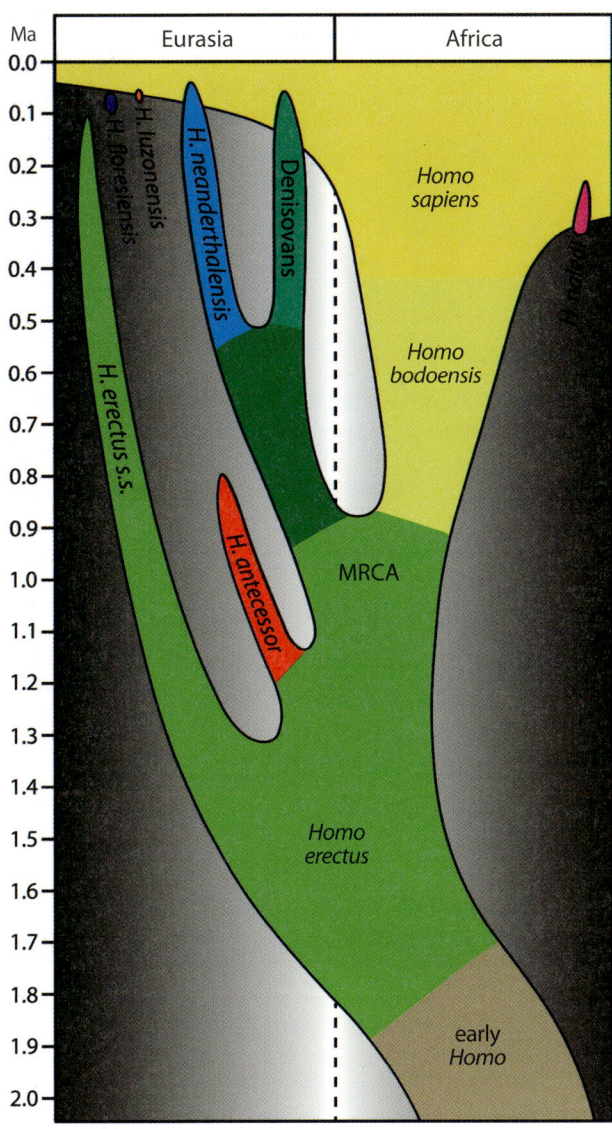

Fig. 2 A simplified model for the evolution of the genus Homo over the last 2 million years MRCA – most recent common ancestor (acc. Roksandic et al., 2022)

Fig. 3 EDAR 7, Eastern Desert, Sudan Cleavers on flakes (Rhyolite) from the Acheulean horizon dated to (MIS >13-11) (acc. Masojć et al., 2021b)

proceding the *Homo sapiens*. Hominins originating from *Homo erectus* in Africa, younger than 1 Ma, have also been called the most recent common ancestor (MRCA) or *Homo bodoensis*–a new Middle Pleistocene (i.e., Chibanian Age/Stage, 774-129ka) hominin species based on the Bodo skull (Conroy et al., 1978) that represents the direct ancestor of *Homo sapiens* (Roksandic et al., 2022) (**Fig. 2**).

2. Earliest traces of *Homo erectus* activity (oldest Acheulean) from Nubia

The earliest traces of *Homo erectus* activity in the studied region-i.e. the oldest Acheulean assemblages – come from site EDAR 7. At EDAR 7, a stone industry of the Acheulean culture, unique to East Saharan Africa, was examined (Masojć et al., 2021b). The significance of this inventory of nearly 1,000 artifacts results from the presence of, apart from handaxes, specific bifacial products in the form of cleavers produced using the Kombewa technique. Massive flakes and cleavers made with the Kombewa technique were also discovered nearby, at the heavily eroded EDAR 6 site (Masojć et al., in press). The occurrence of this type of Acheulean inventory has not yet been confirmed for the Saharan part of Northeast Africa. However, Acheulean tools are known from areas located, e.g., in southern Sudan, in the Great Rift Valley, such as the Gombore II site: Melka Kunture, Upper Awash, Ethiopia (Gallotti et al., 2010). Such developed Acheulean technologies of large flake production and high values of standardized made-on-large flake cleavers and handaxes first appeared in Africa around 1.0 Ma and continued into the Middle Pleistocene, labeled the "Large Flake Acheulean" stage (Sharon, 2007, 2010). This is not a characteristic feature of other Acheulean Nubian sites dated to ~300-200 ka. Therefore, a wide possible chronology for the EDAR 7 inventory could fall into the Large Flake Acheulean phase (**Fig. 3**).

The Acheulean horizon at the EDAR 7 site occurs within fluvial formations and is associated with the UNIT IA stratigraphic horizon in the EDAR region (Masojć et al., 2019). The age of the geological sediment above the Acheulean horizon at EDAR 7 was determined via optically stimulated luminescence (OSL) to be 280±27 ka. However, more than a dozen meters away, at the EDAR 135 site, a sample taken directly above the UNIT IA level was dated to 391±30 ka. This indicates that the Acheulean artifacts from the UNIT IA level of EDAR 7 may be related to the MIS 11 period but could be from MIS 13 or older, as indicated by the technological analogies presented above. Both the OSL dating and the morphological features of the Acheulean assemblage from EDAR 7 indicate that it is the oldest recognized archaeological site for Middle Pleistocene hominin activity in the Eastern Sahara discovered so far, with a chronology determined by absolute methods indicating its age as MIS 11-13 or earlier. The site also provides evidence of hominin activity in the green corridors of the Sahara Desert during their dispersal throughout the African continent. Indirectly, EDAR 7 also provides evidence for migration outside the African continent, as artifacts at the site are related to Acheulean surface collections from the Red Sea Mountains (Kobusiewicz et al., 2018). In addition, the paleohydrographic system in this region, visible on satellite maps, clearly indicates a northwesterly direction for the potential dispersion of *Homo erectus* (or more generally *Middle Pleistocene hominins*), toward the Red Sea and nearby mountains. The fact that assemblages from the Acheulean phase containing cleavers are not known from areas north of Atbara (the Nile Valley in Sudan and Egypt) but are present in the Middle East, e.g., Gesher Benot Ya'akov in Israel (Goren-Inbar et al., 2018), confirms the dispersion of this species up to 0.5 Ma along the coastlines of Eastern Africa.

3. The presence of the latest *Middle Pleistocene hominins*, represented by the youngest Acheulean assemblages

In the Eastern Desert of Sudan, in the EDAR area (EDAR 135), a stratified sequence was investigated, yielding evidence for the presence of *Middle Pleistocene hominins* and *Homo sapiens* in a chronological range of approximately 200-100 ka (Michalec et al., 2021; Ehlert et al., 2022) (**Fig. 4**). The upper level of the site is associated with *Homo sapiens* communities. The assemblage bearing Levallois artifacts, which were fashioned from locally available quartz and rhyolite, was excavated from a layer bracketed by OSL dates of 116±13 and 125±11 ka. This dating places the layer

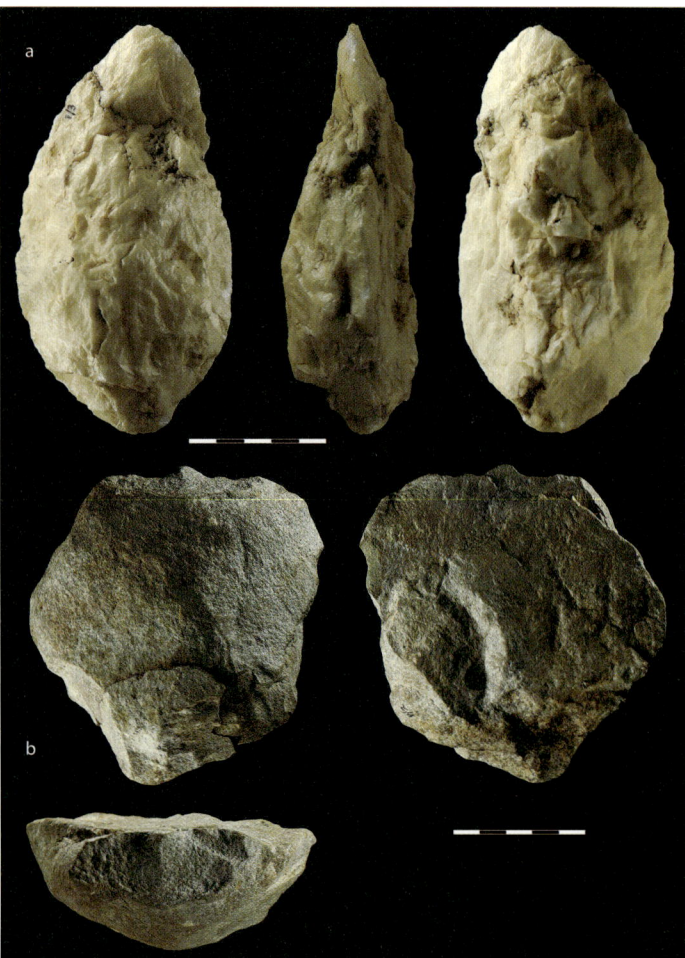

Fig. 4 EDAR 135, Eastern Desert, Sudan. Large Cutting Tools a: handaxe, quartz; b: chopper made from a rhyolite cobble from the Acheulean horizon dated to MIS 7a/6 (acc. Michalec et al., 2021)

within Marine Isotope Stage 5e-5d. About half a meter deeper, a lithic assemblage was discovered, within a layer of gravel sediments formed by a paleostream during a humid period in the Middle Pleistocene. This layer was dated by OSL to between 220±12 and 145±20 ka (MIS 7a/6). These dates indicate that the assemblage could be the youngest evidence of the Acheulean in northeastern Africa. Bearing in mind the evolutionary processes and anthropological and cultural changes experienced by *Homo erectus* during its existence, from about 2 Ma to 100 ka, the evidence at this site represents the activity of the last representatives of African *Homo erectus* (alternatively, *Middle Pleistocene hominins* or *Homo bodoensis*), with the caveat that the youngest *Homo erectus* remains, dated to 117-108 ka, come from outside Africa (Ngandong, Java; Rizal et al., 2020).

The discovery of an Acheulean horizon dated to ca. 220-140 ka demonstrates the fairly prolonged coexistence (at least 100,000 years) of the last representatives of *Homo erectus* sensu largo and the earliest representatives of archaic *Homo sapiens* in the African continent, as evidenced at Jebel Irhoud, Morocco, a site dated to 315±34 ka (Richter et al., 2017). This coexistence also occurred on a regional scale, such as in the Bayuda Desert in Sudan, where the lower level of site BP 177 (Masojć et al., 2017) contains early Nubian Levallois artifacts TL (thermoluminescence) dated to 322 ±106 ka *terminus post quem*. This indicates the early presence of *Homo sapiens* in the region. The results of research at the EDAR and Bayuda Desert (BP 177) sites show that the Eastern Sahara Desert was shared by different Homo species for a very long time.

4. The oldest traces of the presence of *Homo sapiens* (the oldest traces of Middle Stone Age)

Research in the Bayuda Desert in Sudan has resulted in the discovery of unique, stratified lithic assemblages associated with the so-called Nubian variants of the Levallois method, confirming the presence of early *Homo sapiens* in this part of Africa. For instance, site BP 177, located within a niche at the top of a volcanic hill, yielded more than 60,000 stone artifacts (Masojć, 2018). Within the area researched thus far, a kind of natural stone shelter was found, with an open, oval course, and containing numerous artifacts. Thermoluminescence dating (IRSL/OSL) for two archaeological levels at the site indicated that it functioned as a settlement from 60-20 ka (Masojć et al., 2017). These findings were verified by a re-analysis of a sample taken directly below the lower horizon of the Nubian Middle Stone Age (MSA). As mentioned above, the site was then TL dated to 322±106 ka *terminus post quem*. Such a chronological position is confirmed by the specificity of the complex of stone artifacts from the lower cultural level of the site. The complex includes a few handaxes, massive bifacial foliates characteristic of the initial phases of MSA, and so-called type 1 Levallois Nubian cores. The lower "Nubian" level from site BP 177 therefore belongs to one of the oldest archaeological assemblages providing evidence of the activity of *Homo sapiens* in the Eastern Sahara (Fig. 5).

Both the large number of artifacts, especially from the younger level of the site, and the age of the younger horizon (dated to ca. 24-17 ka) indicate intensive activity by human groups using the Nubian variant of the Levallois method. This evidence also confirms the presence of these groups from the end of the Middle Pleistocene to the end of the Late Pleistocene. Located several dozen kilometers east of the Nile Valley, the site BP 177, like the complex of EDAR sites, provides evidence of the dynamics of human dispersion beyond large river valleys and settlement enclaves during favorable climatic conditions. Despite a rather opportunistic attitude toward raw material resources (a significant share of artifacts are made of volcanic rocks available within the volcanic cone on which the site is located), there is also

Fig. 5 BP 177, Bayuda Desert, Sudan. Bifacial foliates from the Nubian Levallois horizon dated to 322±106 ka *terminus post quem* (acc. Masojć, 2018)

evidence for the careful selection of raw materials and the penetration and use of the area (searching for deposits of petrified wood for stone production). The early dating of the lower level of the site indirectly confirms the thesis of a complicated, non-uniform evolution of *Homo sapiens* within a single population and/or region of Africa (Stringer, 2016; Scerri, 2018).

5. Conclusion

The existing evidence supports the long presence of *Homo erectus* in the Eastern Sahara, possibly even from the Early Pleistocene (MIS >13-11) to the end of the Middle Pleistocene (MIS 7a/6), as well as the early appearance of *Homo sapiens* (MIS 9<), which demonstrates the prolonged coexistence of these two human species in a relatively small desert region of contemporary Sudan. It is no less important to depict the Eastern Sahara as an area that cyclically played an important role in the dispersion of hominins through the green corridors of the Eastern Sahara and thus the development of human culture in the Pleistocene.

Acknowledgments

The research conducted in the EDAR area (http://sudan.archeo.uni.wroc.pl/) was funded by the National Science Centre in Poland, a government agency supervised by the Ministry of Science and Higher Education (grant nr. NCN 2022/45/B/HS3/01262). Investigations were conducted by the University of Wrocław (Poland) and Al Neelain University (Sudan). Besides these two leading institutions, a team of scholars from various institutions participated: Shendi University (Sudan), Gdańsk Archaeological Museum (Poland), the Korean Institute of Geoscience and Mineral Resources (KIGAM; Republic of Korea), and Gyeongsang National University (Republic of Korea). Laboratory analyses were conducted by KIGAM, Royal Holloway, and the University of London (GB), as well as by several Polish laboratories.

References

Abbate E., Albianelli A., Azzaroli A., Benvenuti M., Tesfamariam B., Bruni P., Cipriani N., Clarke R.J., Ficcarelli G., Macchiarelli R., Napoleone G., Papini M., Rook L., Sagri M., Medhin Tecle T., Torre D., Villa I., 1998. A one-million-year old Homo cranium from the Danakil (Afar) depression of Eritrea. *Nature* 393, 458-460. https://doi.org/10.1038/30954

Abbate E., Beraky W., Bruni P., Falorni P., Papini M., Sagri M., Simret G., Tewolde M.T., 2004. Geology of the Homo-bearing Pleistocene Dandiero basin (Buia region, Eritrean Danakildepression). *Riv Ital Paleont Strat* 110, 5-34.

Arkell A.J., Bate D.M.A., Wells L.H., Lacaille A.D., 1951. *Fossil Mammals of Africa* 2, 1-50.

Bräuer G., 1984. Acraniological approach to the origin of anatomically modern Homo sapiens in Africa and implications for the appearance of modern Europeans. In F. Smith and F. Spencer eds., *The Origins of Modern Humans*, New York: Alan Liss, 327-410.

Bruner E., Bondioli L., Coppa A., Frayer D.W., Holloway R.L., Libseka, Y., Medin T., Rook L. and Macchiarelli R., 2016. The endocast of the one-million-year-old human cranium from Buia (UA 31), Danakil Eritrea. *American Journal of Physical Anthropology* 160, 458-468. https://doi.org/10.1002/ajpa.22983

Conroy G.C., Jolly C.J., Cramer D., Kalb J.E., 1978. Newly discovered fossil hominid skull from the Afar depression, Ethiopia. *Nature* 1978; 276, 67-70.

Ehlert M., Kim J.Y., Sohn Y.K., Cendrowska M., Krupa-Kurzynowska J., Andrieux E., Armitage S.J., Michalec G., **Dreczko E., Alkhidir H.M., Szmit M. & Masojć M.,** 2022. The Middle Stone Age in the Eastern Desert. EDAR 135–a buried early MIS 5 horizon from Sudan. *Azania: Archaeological Research in Africa* 57(2), 155-196. https://doi.org/10.1080/0067270X.2022.2078561

Gallotti R., Collina C., Raynal J-P., Kieffer G., Geraad D., Piperno M., 2010. The Early Middle Pleistocene site of Gombore II (Melka Kunture, Upper Awash, Ethiopia) and the issue of Acheulean bifacial shaping strategies. *African Archaeological Review* 27(4), 291-322. https://doi.org/10.1007/s10437-010-9083-z

Goren-Inbar N., Alperson-Afil N., Sharon G., Herzlinger G., 2018. The Acheulian Site of Gesher Benot Ya'aqov, Vol. IV. The Lithic Assemblages. Delson E., Sargis E.J. eds., *Netherlands*: Springer. https://doi.org/10.1371/journal.pone.0190804

Grine F.E., 2016. The Late Quaternary Hominins of Africa: The Skeletal Evidence from MIS 6-2, (in:) Jones S.C. & Stewart B.A. eds., Africa from MIS 6-2, Population Dynamics and Paleoenvironments, Springer. *Vertebrate Paleobiology and Paleoanthropology Series*, 323-381.

Kobusiewicz M., Bobrowski P., Jórdeczka M., Chłodnicki M., 2018. Gebel Karaiweb and Bir Nurayet (Sudan). *The Oldest Settlement in the Red Sea Mountains*. In: Kabaciński J., Chłodnicki M., Kobusiewicz M., Winiarska-Kabacińska M. eds., *Desert and the Nile. Prehistory of the Nile Basin and the Sahara*. Papers in honour of Fred Wendorf. Poznań: Poznań Archaeological Museum; 2018. 483-514. https://doi.org/10.5114/ada.2018.77617

Marks A.E., 1968. The Khormusan: an Upper Pleistocene industry in Sudanese Nubia. In: Wendorf, F. ed., *The Prehistory of Nubia* Vol. I, Dallas: Fort Burgwin Research Center and Southern Methodist University Press, 315e391.

Masojć M. (in press), Eastern Desert Atbara River (EDAR), In: Beyin A., Wright D.K., Wilkins J. and Olszewski D.I. eds., *Handbook of Pleistocene Archaeology of Africa*, Springer Nature, Cham, Switzerland.

Masojć M., 2021. Palaeolithic Hunters-Gatherers of Nubia, In: Emberling, G. & Williams, B.B. eds., *The Oxford Handbook of Ancient Nubia*, Oxford: Oxford University Press, 81-100. https://doi:10.1093/oxfordhb/9780190496272.013.58

Masojć M. 2018. *Lithic Materials from a Late Nubian Complex Middle Stone Age Site in the Bayuda Desert: Goat Mountain.* (In:) Lohwasser A., Karberg T., Auenmüller eds., *Bayuda Studies. Proceedings of the First International Conference on the Archaeology of the Bayuda Desert in Sudan*. Harrassowitz Verlag, Wiesbaden, Meroitica 27, 503-536.

Masojć M., Kim J. Y., Michalec G., Nassr A.H., Szmit M., Lee S.Y., Ahn H. S., Kim J. Ch., Sohn Y. K., 2022. (in press) EDAR 6 - Acheulean site in the Eastern Desert, Sudan. In: Chłodnicki J.,

Kabaciński J. eds., *XI Poznań African Symposium Proceedings*, Poznań Archaological Museum.

Masojć M., Nassr A., Kim J.Y., Krupa-Kurzynowska J., Sohn Y.K., Szmit M., Kim J.Ch., Kim J.S., Choi H.W., Wieczorek M., Timmermann A., 2019. Saharan green corridors and Middle Pleistocene hominin dispersals across the Eastern Desert, Sudan. *Journal of Human Evolution* 130, 141-150. https://doi.org/10.1016/j.jhevol.2019.01.004

Masojć M., Nassr A., Kim J.Y., Ehlert M., Michalec G., Krupa-Kurzynowska J., Sohn Y.K., Andrieux E., Armitage S.J., Szmit M., Kim J.C., Kim J.S., Cendrowska M., Dreczko E., Moska P., Kim K.J., & Choi Y., 2021a. Gold Miners on the Trail of the Earliest Humans in Eastern Saharan Africa. Investigating the Acheulean and Middle Stone Age in Sudanese Nubia. *Journal of African Archaeology* 19(2), 235-244. 10.1163/21915784-20210003

Masojć M., Kim J.Y., Krupa-Kurzynowska J., Sohn Y.K., Ehlert M., Michalec G., Cendrowska M., Andrieux E., Armitage S.J., Szmit M., Dreczko E., Kim J.Ch., Kim J.S., Lee G-S., Moska P. & Jadain M.A., 2021b. The oldest Homo erectus buried lithic horizon from the eastern Sahara, Africa. EDAR 7–an Acheulean assemblage with Kombewa method from the Eastern Desert, Sudan. *PLoS ONE* 16(3), e0248279. doi.org/10.1371/journal.pone.0248279

Masojć M., Kusiak J., Standzikowski K., Paner H., Kuc M., Parafiniuk M., Szmit M., 2017. OSL/IRSL estimation for Nubian Complex Middle Stone Age settlement from Bayuda Desert in Sudan. *Journal of Archaeological Science: Reports* 16, 391-396. https://doi.org/10.1016/j.jasrep.2017.10.026

McBurney C.B.M., 1977. *Archaeology and the Homo sapiens sapiens Problem in Northern Africa*, Netherlands Museum for Anthropology and Prehistory.

McDermott F., Stringer C., Grün R., Williams C.T., Din V.K., Hawkesworth C.J., 1996. New late Pleistocene uranium-thorium and ESR dates for the Singa hominid (Sudan). *Journal of Human Evolution* 31, 507-516.

Michalec G., Cendrowska M., Andrieux E., Armitage S.J., Ehlert M., Kim J.Y., Sohn Y.K., Krupa-Kurzynowska J., Moska P., Szmit M. & Masojć M., 2021. A Window into the Early–Middle Stone Age Transition in Northeastern Africa–A Marine Isotope Stage 7a/6 Late Acheulean Horizon from the EDAR 135 Site, Eastern Sahara (Sudan). *Journal of Field Archaeology* 46(8), 513-533. https://doi.org/10.1080/00934690.2021.1993618

Millard A.R., 2008. A critique of the chronometric evidence for hominid fossils: I. Africa and the Near East 500-50 ka. *Journal of Human Evolution* 54(6), 848-874.

Richter D., Grün R., Joannes-Boyau R. Steele T.E., Amani F., Rué M., Fernandes P., Raynal J-P., Geraads D., Ben-Ncer A., Hublin J-J. & McPherron S.P., 2017. The age of the hominin fossils from Jebel Irhoud, Morocco, and the origins of the Middle Stone Age. *Nature* 546, 293-296 (2017). https://doi.org/10.1038/nature22335

Rizal Y., Westaway K.E., Zaim Y., van den Bergh G.D., Bettis III E.A., Morwood M.J., Huffman O.F., Grün R., Joannes-Boyau R., Bailey R.M., Sidarto, Westaway M.C., Kurniawan I., Moore M.W., Storey M., Aziz F., Suminto, Zhao J-X., Aswan, Sipola M.E., Larick R., Zonneveld J-P., Scott R., Putt S. & R.L. Ciochon. 2020. Last appearance of *Homo erectus* at Ngandong, Java, 117,000-108,000 years ago. *Nature* 577, 381-385. https://doi.org/10.1038/s41586-019-1863-2

Roksandic M., Radović P., Wu X-J., Bae C.J., 2022. Resolving the "muddle in the middle": The case for *Homo bodoensis* sp. nov. *Evolutionary Anthropology* 31, 20-29. https://doi.org/10.1002/evan.21929

Scerri E.M.L., Thomas M.G., Manica A., Gunz P., Stock J.T., Stringer C., Grove M., Groucutt H.S., Timmermann A., Rightmire G.P., d'Errico F., Tryon C.A., Drake N.A., Brooks A.S., Dennell R.W., Durbin R., Henn B.M., Lee-Thorp J., deMenocal P., Petraglia M.D., Thompson J.C., Scally A., Chikhi L., 2018. Did our species evolve in subdivided populations across Africa, and why does it matter?. *Trends in Ecology and Evolution* 33(8), 582-594. https://doi:10.1016/j.tree.2018.05.005

Sharon G., 2007. *Acheulian Large Flake Industries: Technology, Chronology, and Significance*, Oxford: Archaeopress.

Sharon G., 2010. Large flake Acheulian. *Quaternary International* 223, 226-33. https://doi.org/10.1016/j.quaint.2009.11.023

Spoor F., Stringer C.B., Zonneveld F., 1998. Rare temporal bone pathology of the Singa calvaria from Sudan. *American Journal of Physical Anthropology* 107, 41-50.

Stringer C., 2016. The origin and evolution of *Homo sapiens*. *Phil. Trans. R. Soc. B* 371: 20150237. http://dx.doi.org/10.1098/rstb.2015.0237

Wohns A.W., Wong Y., Jeffery B., Akbari A., Mallick S., Pinhasi R., Patterson N., Reich D., Kelleher J., McVean G., 2022. A unified genealogy of modern and ancient genomes. *Science* 375. https://doi.org/10.1126/science.abi8264

Woodward A.S., 1938. A fossil skull of an ancestral Bushman from the Anglo-Egyptian Sudan. *Antiquity* 12, 193-195.

The first discovery of Plio-Pleistocene mammalian faunal sequence and suspected artifacts from Jinyuan Cave of Luotuo Hill, Dalian, Northeast China

Changzhu JIN [1,2], **Yuan WANG** [1,2,3], **Wenhui LIU** [4]

[1] Professor, Key Laboratory of Vertebrate Evolution and Human Origins of Chinese Academy of Sciences, Institute of Vertebrate Paleontology and Paleoanthropology, Chinese Academy of Sciences, China ; jinchangzhu@ivpp.ac.cn
[2] CAS Center for Excellence in Life and Paleoenvironment, China
[3] State Key Laboratory of Palaeobiology and Stratigraphy, Nanjing Institute of Geology and Palaeontology, Chinese Academy of Sciences, China
[4] National Museum of China, China

ABSTRACT

Here we introduce the history of Jinyuan Cave, Luotuo Hill, Dalian, Northeast China and our work at the site. The Plio-Pleistocene mammalian complex at the site can be divided into four types: Luotuoshan fauna, Jinyuan Lower fauna, Jinyuan Upper fauna and Wanghai fauna. In this paper, we provide revised mammalian lists and compare them with related mammalian fauna of Northeast Asia. The suspected artifacts from Jinyuan Cave were also photographed.

국문초록

이 논문은 2014년 중국 고척추고동물여고인류연구소와 다롄자연사박물관이 공동으로 루오투오산 진유안 동굴 유적에서 조사된 지질학과 고생물학 결과를 설명한다. 진유안 유적의 고동물화석 발굴 자료를 보면, 초기에 돼지(Sus lydekkeri), 양(Cervus grayi), 산양(Ovis sp) 등을 수습한 이후, 원숭이(Macaca robustus), 점박이하이에나(Pachycrocuta brevirostris sinensis), 검치호랑이(Megantereon inexpectatus), 코끼리(Palaeoloxodon cf. namadicus), 말(Equus sanmeniensis), 코뿔이(Stephanorhinus kirchbergensis), 큰뿔사슴(Sinomegaceros pachyosteus), 물소(Bubalus teilhardi), 호랑이(Trogontherium cuvieri)를 포함하여 약 30여 종의 선신세-갱신세(3.60-0.35 Ma)의 포유동물을 확인하였다. 동물군은 후기 선신세(3.6-2.6 Ma) 루우투오산, 전기 이른시기 갱신세(2.6-1.7 Ma)의 하부 진유안(Jinyuan Lower), 전기 늦은시기 갱신세(1.7-0.78 Ma)의 상부 진유안(Jinyuan Upper), 중기 갱신세(0.78-0.35 Ma)의 왕하이(Wanghai)를 포함하는 4개 동물군으로 구분된다. 독특하고 연속적인 진유안 동물화석군은 동북아시아 다른 유적의 포유동물군을 비교하는 중요한 기준이 된다. 특히 왕하이 동물군과 관련하여 이곳에서도 인류화석이 발견될 가능성을 시사하는 유물이 발견되었다.

Keywords : Luotuo Hill, Luotuoshan fauna, Jinyuan Lower fauna, Jinyuan Upper fauna, Wanghai fauna, Plio-Pleistocene

1. Introduction

Jinyuan Cave (39°23′59.01″N, 121°41′20.28″E) is located on Luotuo Hill (Luotuoshan) in the town of Fuzhouwan, Dalian Puwan Economic Zone, Liaoning Province, southwest of the Liaodong Peninsula and, in turn, the southern tip of Northeast China (Fig. 1).

In December 2013, the first two authors, from the Institute of Vertebrate Paleontology and Paleoanthropology, Chinese Academy of Sciences (IVPP, CAS) and researchers from the Dalian Natural History Museum (DNHM) carried out geological and paleontological investigations on Luotuo Hill, leading to the discovery of a new fossiliferous cave site, which was named "Jinyuan Cave" (Liu et al., 2017a; Jin et al., 2021). Fossils of *Sus lydekkeri*, *Cervus* (*Sika*) *grayi* and *Ovis* sp. were collected during short-term investigations (Liu et al., 2017; Jin et al., 2021).

Luotuo Hill was the site of large-scale commercial quarrying operations by a cement works company, which seriously damaged Jinyuan Cave and made it difficult to recognize. In August 2014, an IVPP (CAS) team conducted rescue excavations at the cave in collaboration with colleagues from the DNHM. Large mammalian remains were unearthed from cave deposits and small mammalian fossils were also collected by the screen-washing method. The initial excavation yielded hundreds of vertebrate fossil specimens, including fish, reptiles (turtles, lizards and snakes), birds and mammals. The mammalian assemblage was composed of over 30 species of mammals, such as *Macaca robustus*, *Pachycrocuta brevirostris sinensis*, *Megantereon inexpectatus*, *Palaeoloxodon* cf. *namadicus*, *Equus sanmeniensis*, *Stephanorhinus kirchbergensis*, *Sinomegaceros pachyosteus*, *Sus lydekkeri*, *Bubalus teilhardi* and *Trogontherium cuvieri*.

The faunal and ecological characteristics of Jinyuan Cave are very similar to those of the Middle Pleistocene Peking Man Site (Zhoukoudian Loc. 1) in Beijing (Liu et al., 2017a). Furthermore, the first discovery of *Palaeoloxodon* cf. *namadicus* and *Megantereon inexpectatus* in Northeast China also indicates the relative antiquity of this fauna, in contrast to discoveries of typical Late Pleistocene *Mammuthus-Coelodonta* fauna in other parts of Northeast China (Kahlke, 2014).

At the beginning of 2015, the limestone covering the southwest wall of Jinyuan Cave collapsed due to demolitions by Donghai Cement Works, resulting in the further exposure of large-sized cave deposits. The rescue excavation area in 2014, which was 3m in height and 4m in width, was merely a part of the upper deposits of Jinyuan Cave. Although mostly destroyed by extensive quarrying, Jinyuan Cave is evidently enormous in size, with a sedimentary thickness of more than 40m. Since 2015, the entire site has been exposed, revealing that the sediments at Jinyuan Cave are composed of five calcareous concretion layers and six fossiliferous layers (Liu et al., 2017).

From 2015 to 2016, researchers from the IVPP (CAS) and DNHM collaborated in systematic excavations of the upper to lower deposits at Jinyuan Cave. Surprisingly, an abundance of typical Early Pleistocene remains, including *Pachycrocuta brevirostris licenti*, *Megantereon nihowanensis*, *Sinicuon* cf. *dubius*, *Hipparion* (*Proboscidipparion*) *sinense*, *Coelodonta nihowanensis*, *Paracamelus gigas* and *Bison palaeosinensis*, were discovered from the middle/lower deposits. The faunal characteristics resembled those of typical Early Pleistocene Longdan fauna and Zhoukoudian Loc. 18 fauna, in North China (Qiu, 2006).

Since 2017, a new research team co-organized by the

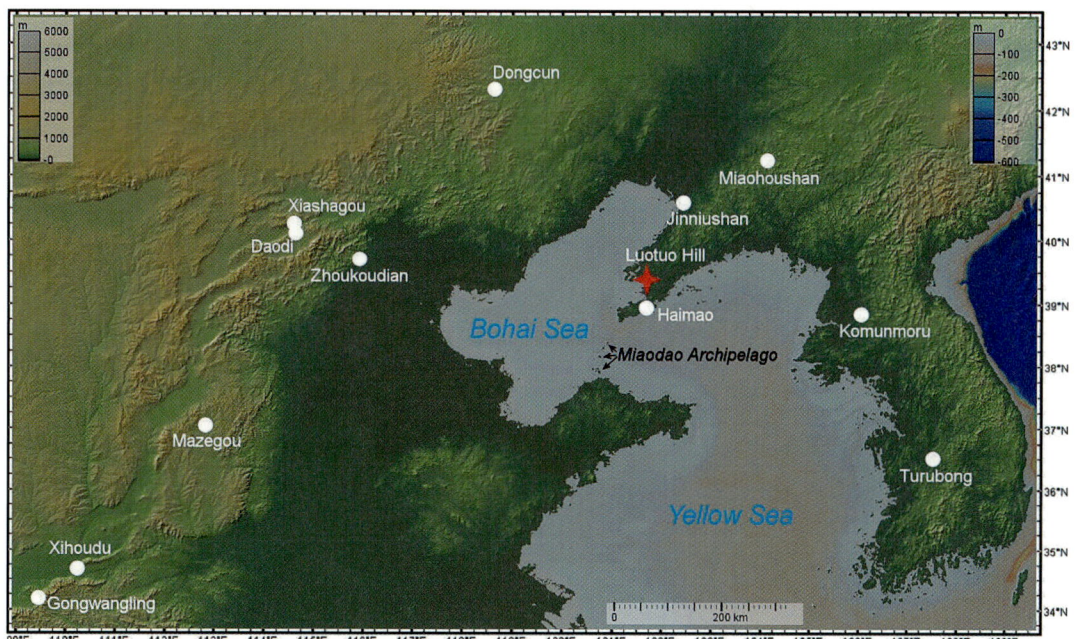

Fig.1 The location of Luotuo Hill and other related mammalian faunas in Northeast Asia

IVPP (CAS), the DNHM and local authorities (Dalian Puwan Economic Zone) have conducted paleontological investigations and systematic excavations at Luotuo Hill and the adjacent area. The annual duration of fieldwork exceeds four months. Intact skulls and skeletons belonging to *Pachycrocuta brevirostris licenti*, *Paracamelus gigas* and *Coelodonta nihowanensis* have been recovered from the middle/lower deposits of Jinyuan Cave. Moreover, several typical Pliocene species have been retrieved from the lowermost deposits of the cave, such as *Hipparion* (*Proboscidipparion*) *pater*, *Apodemus zhangwagouensis*, *Chardinomys nihowanicus*, *Villanyia fanchangensis* and *Mimomys nihewanensis*. These finds mark the first discovery of large mammalian fauna belonging to the Late Pliocene in Northeast China.

For nearly a decade, systematic excavations at Jinyuan Cave have yielded many well-preserved vertebrate fossils from multiple fossiliferous layers. Since the stratified fossiliferous deposits at Jinyuan Cave bear very little discontinuation in sedimentation sequence from top to bottom, the successive faunal finds from the cave hold enormous potential as a Plio-Pleistocene mammalian biochronological standard for Northeastern China. These finds present the unparalleled opportunity to conduct a thorough synthesis combining systematic paleontology, community-level faunal analysis, geochronology via magnetostratigraphic (Ge et al., 2021) and radiometric methods and paleoenvironmental analysis with palynology (Shen et al., 2021) and stable isotopes.

2. Stratigraphy of Jinyuan Cave

The original appearance of Jinyuan Cave has been seriously damaged and is difficult to recognize due to continuous large-scale quarrying operations at the site over many years. Jinyuan Cave deposits mainly consist of brown-red clay and mild clay, five well-developed calcareous concretion layers and six richly fossiliferous layers with distinct mammalian fossils. The deposits can be divided into seven layers from top to bottom based on lithology and the status of calcareous concretion and fossiliferous layers (Jin et al., 2021) (**Fig. 2**).

Based on a combination of faunal differences and geochronological evidence, the enormous deposits at Jinyuan Cave can be roughly divided into three fossiliferous deposit units. The bottom deposit unit comprises layer 7 and has a visible thickness of about 3-7m. The lower part of layer 3 and layers 4, 5 and 6 constitute the middle-lower deposit unit, which is 25.5-32.5m thick. The upper deposit unit includes layers 1 and 2 and the upper part of layer 3, with a thickness of 5.7-7.8m.

3. The Plio-Pleistocene mammalian faunal sequence from Jinyuan Cave

Abundant and diversified vertebrate fossils have been excavated from different fossiliferous layers of Jinyuan Cave. Although some of these finds have been described elsewhere (Bai et al., 2017; Jiangzuo et al., 2017; Liu et al., 2017b; Jiangzuo et al., 2019; Pan et al., 2020; Ge et al., 2021; Jiangzuo et al., 2021; Jin et al., 2021; Liu et al., 2021; Qin et al., 2021; Shen et al., 2021; Stidham, Smith, Li et al., 2021; Sun et al., 2021a; Sun et al., 2021b; Wang et al., 2021; Yang et al., 2021; Jiangzuo et al., 2022; Sun et al., 2022a; Sun et al., 2022b; Jiangzuo et al., 2023), most are still being researched.

The fossil assemblages from Jinyuan Cave have been divided into three successive faunal types: (1) Luotuoshan fauna from the bottom fossiliferous deposit unit; (2) Jinyuan fauna from the middle-lower deposit unit; and (3) Wanghai

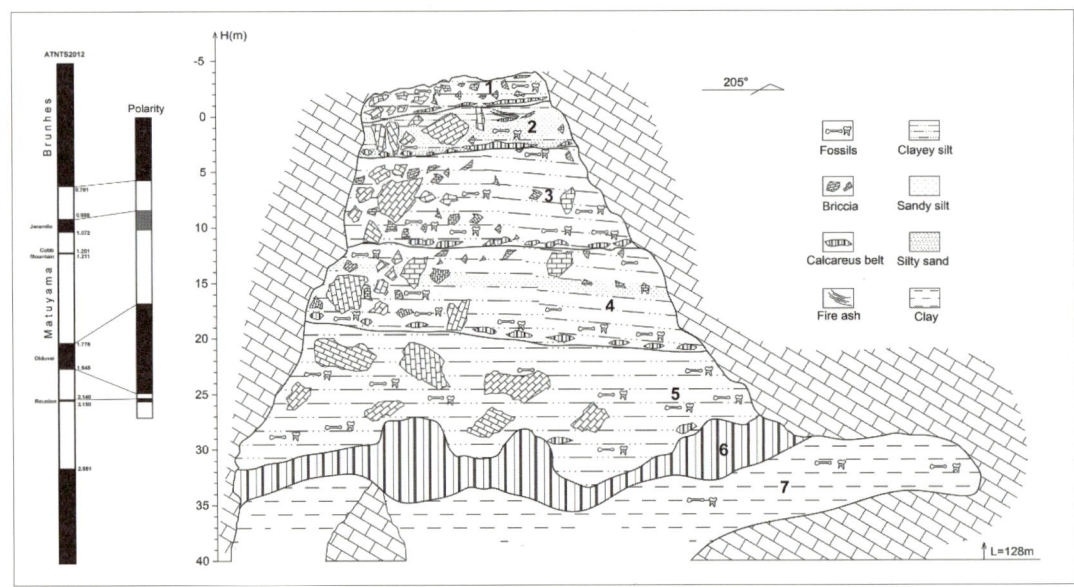

Fig. 2 The stratigraphic sections and magnetostratigraphy of Jinyuan Cave of Luotuo Hill (copy from Jin et al., 2021)

fauna from the upper deposit unit (Jin et al., 2021).
The middle-lower deposit unit from which the Jinyuan fauna were retrieved has a thickness of around 30m, which constitutes the main structure of Jinyuan Cave. This mammalian assemblage contains 58 genera and 72 species (see revised lists below) and spans a long period of the Early Pleistocene. The paleomagnetic evidence shows that the geomagnetic polarity column from the lower part of layer 3 and upper part of layer 4 is covered mainly by Matuyama reverse polarity, whereas the geomagnetic polarity column from the lower part of layer 4 and layer 5 has a normal polarity, which roughly corresponds to Olduvai and Reunion Normal Events (Ge et al., 2021; **Fig. 2**). Considering this difference between the mammalian assemblage and the paleomagnetic data, the Jinyuan fauna has been further divided into Jinyuan Lower fauna and Jinyuan Upper fauna (Jin et al., 2021). The middle part of layer 4 is regarded as the boundary between Jinyuan Lower fauna and Jinyuan Upper fauna.

The mammalian faunal sequence from Jinyuan Cave is composed of four faunal types. Here, we will provide a revised list of these four faunal types and discuss their characteristics and ages.

3.1. Luotuoshan fauna: Late Pliocene (3.6-2.6 Ma)

The Luotuoshan fauna comes from the bottom deposit unit of Jinyuan Cave (layer 7, see **Fig. 2**) and is named after the main site, "Luotuo Hill." The sediments, which have a visible thickness of 3-7m, are composed of solid purple-red clay with limestone breccias. Abundant mammalian fossils were collected after trial excavation and the screen-washing method. After preliminary identification, the Luotuoshan fauna were found to contain at least 11 mammalian species (Jin et al., 2021; Qin et al., 2021; and the *Leptobos*). This fauna is dominated by extinct genera and species. Most of the species are common to the Daodi local fauna and Mazegou fauna of North China (**Table 1**).

Daodi local fauna were recovered from the Laowogou section near Daodi village, Nihewan Basin, Hebei Province. These fauna are famous for micromammals, containing 25 (Zhang et al., 2003) or 29 (Li et al., 2008) species in total (Cai et al., 2013, p. 221) restricted the Daodi Formation to layers 3~9 of the Laowogou section. If so, Daodi local fauna (*sensu stricto*) consist of 18 micromammalian species: *Sorex* sp., *Paenelimnoecus chinensis*, *Ochotona* sp., *Sinocricetus progressus*, *Nannocricetus mongolicus*, *Ungaromys* spp., *Mimomys nihewanensis* (=*Mimomys* sp. and *Mimomys* sp.2), *Mesosiphneus praetingi*, *Pliosiphneus daodiensis* (=*Pliosiphneus* sp.2), *Pseudomeriones complicidens*, *Dipus fraudator*, *Paralactaga anderssoni*, *Micromys tedfordi*, *Apodemus zhangwagouensis*, *Chardinomys yusheensis*, *Chardinomys nihowanicus*, *Karnimata* sp. and *Saidomys* sp. (Li et al., 2008; Cai et al., 2013; Zheng et al., 2019). Five macromammalian species from layer 9 of the Laowogou section remain undescribed: *Hipparion*, *Chilotherium* sp., *Axis shansius*, *Cervus* sp. and *Antilospira* sp. (Cai et al., 2004). The exact horizon of *Apodemus* cf. *A. atavus* from Daodi (Cai and Qiu, 1993) is unstated; Li et al. (2008) and Cai et al. (2013) listed *Apodemus zhangwagouensis* from layers 2-11 of the Laowogou section rather than *Apodemus* cf. *A. atavus*. The *Hypolagus schreuderi* from the Daodi local fauna mentioned by Qiu et al. (2013) is likely *H. schreuderi* from Hongya Nangou, Qijiazhuang and Qianjiashawa, as described by Cai (1989). Despite these two doubtful forms (*Apodemus* cf. *A. atavus* and *Hypolagus schreuderi*), Daodi local fauna (*sensu stricto*) comprise the complex most similar to that of Luotuoshan fauna. The Myospalacinae of these two fauna show few differences, but all the zokors are very primitive and mainly spread in the Pliocene. The Daodi local fauna from the Daodi Formation of the Nihewan Basin is considered Late Pliocene: ~3.4-2.6 Ma (Cai et al., 2013).

Mazegou fauna, especially the micromammalian fauna, has been described by Flynn and Wu (2017). This fauna shares

Table 1 Comparison of Luotuoshan fauna with other Late Pliocene faunas from Northern China

	Fauna composition	Luotuoshan fauna	Daodi Local fauna	Mazegou fauna
	Age (Ma)	3.6-2.6	~3.4-2.6	3.6-2.6
△	*Hypolagus mazegouensis*	+	* *H. schreuderi*	+
△	*Nannocricetus mongolicus*	+	+	
△	*Sinocricetus progressus*	+	+	
△	*Episiphneus dalianensis*	+		
△	*Pliosiphneus daodiensis*		+	*P. lyratus*
△	*Mesosiphneus praetingi*		+	+; *M. intermedius*
△	*Mimomys nihewanensis*	+	+	*M. gansunicus* *M.* cf. *youhenicus*
★	*Apodemus zhangwagouensis*	+	+	+
★	*Apodemus atavus*	cf.	* cf.	
△	*Chardinomys nihowanicus*	+	+	+
△	*Villanyia fanchangensis*	+		+
△	*Hipparion (Proboscidipparion) pater*	+	sp.	* Youhe
△	*Leptobos*	sp.		

Note : ◎ extant species; ★ extinct species; △ extinct genus. * uncertain

some typical species with the Daodi local fauna and Luotuoshan fauna (Table 1). According to Qiu et al. (1987), *Hipparion* (*Proboscidipparion*) *pater* does not occur in the Mazegou Formation of the Yushe Basin, but it does appears in the Youhe fauna of Shaanxi Province. The Youhe fauna ranges in age from 3.15 to 2.6 Ma, while the Mazegou fauna is correlated to chron C2An. 3n to C2An.1n, 3.6-2.6 Ma (Qiu et al., 2013).

Depending on the biostratigraphy analysis, the Luotuoshan fauna is correlated with the Daodi Formation of the Nihewan Basin and the Mazegou Formation of the Yushe Basin. It is chronologically correlated to MN16 (Late Pliocene, ca. 3.6-2.6 Ma). A detailed study of Luotuoshan fauna will be published elsewhere.

In particular, from the Luotuoshan fauna, horns and mandibles definitively belonging to *Leptobos* have recently been found. This is the earliest *Leptobos* in East Asia and the only Pliocene record of this genus outside of Europe. *L. stenometopon* from Dusino, Italy, is a taxon characteristic of the early Villafranchian LFAs and is the only evidence that a *Leptobos* event occurred in the late Pliocene rather than at the beginning of the Pleistocene (Cherin et al., 2013; Masini et al., 2013). However, Masini et al. (2013) admitted that it is difficult to ascertain whether the type specimens were collected from the Late Pliocene or younger deposits. The type specimens were first described by Sismonda in 1846 and their exact location remains unknown. In this case, the *Leptobos* from the Luotuoshan fauna will be most significant in clearing the *Leptobos* event at MN16.

3.27. Jinyuan Lower fauna: Early Pleistocene (2.6-1.7 ma)

Jinyuan Lower fauna was recovered from the lower deposit unit of Jinyuan Cave (layer 5 and lower part of layer 4, see Fig. 2). The Jinyuan Lower fauna covering the Olduvai and Reunion Normal Events (Ge et al., 2021) contains 50 mammalian genera and 55 species (Jin et al., 2021; revised fauna list in Table 2) and is characterized by the co-occurrence of *Mammuthus meridionalis* and primitive *Equus* (e.g., *E. eisenmannae* and *E. teilhardi*).

The so-called elephant-*Equus* event or *Mammuthus-Equus* event is generally considered to have occurred at the beginning of the Quaternary (Azzaroli, 1977, 1983). However, this is a misleading term in that it depicts a diachronous biochronological event and as such merits caution when invoked. Elephantids, including early species of *Mammuthus* (e.g., *M. rumanus*), are now convincingly known to have appeared in Eurasia during the Late Pliocene (3.6-3 Ma) interval (Wei et al., 2010; Patnaik, 2013; Rabinovich and Lister,

Table 2 Comparison of Jinyuan Lower fauna with other early Early Pleistocene faunas from Northern China (micromammals and Carnivora)

	Fauna composition	Jinyuan Lower fauna	Longdan fauna	Zhoukoudian Loc. 18 fauna	Xihoudu fauna
	Age (Ma)	2.6-1.7	2.5-2.2	>2	2-1.8
★	*Erinaceus sp.*	+		+	+
△	*Sericolagus brachypus*	+	+	+	
△	*Ochotonoides complicidens*	+		+	
★	*Ochotona nihewanica*	+			
★	*Sciurotamias praecox*	+		+	
△	*Trogontherium cuvieri*	+			sp.
△	*Episiphneus dalianensis*	+			
△	*Mimomys gansunicus*	cf.	cf.		
△	*Borsodia chinensis*	+			
△	*Villanyia fanchangensis*	+			
△	*Allophaiomys terraerubrae*	+		+	
△	*Chardinomys nihewanicus*	+			
★	*Diplothrix yangziensis*	cf.			
★	*Apodemus zhangwagouensis*	cf.			
★	*Macaca anderssoni*	+	cf.		
★	"*Nyctereutes sinensis*"	+			
△	*Sinicuon dubius*	cf.	cf.	+	
★	*Canis chihliensis*	cf.		cf.	
★	*Canis teilhardi*	cf.	+		
★	*Ursus minimus*	cf.			
★	*Ursus etruscus*	cf.		cf.	
★	*Martes crassidens*	+		sp.	
★	*Meles teilhardi*	+	+		
△	*Chasmaporthetes progressus*	+	+		
△	*Pachycrocuta brevirosris licenti*	+	+	sp.	sp.
★	*Crocuta honanensis*	+	+		
△	*Homotherium crenatidens*	+	+		
△	*Megantereon nihowanensis*	+	+		
△	*Sivapanthera linxiaensis*	+			
★	*Panthera palaeosinensis*	+	+		

Note : ◎ extant species; ★ extinct species; △ extinct genus.

Table 2 (Continued)
(Proboscidea, Perissodactyla and Artiodactyla)

	Fauna composition	Jinyuan Lower fauna	Longdan fauna	Zhoukoudain Loc. 18 fauna	Xihoudu fauna
	Age (Ma)	2.6-1.7	2.5-2.2	~2	
△	*Mammuthus meridionalis*	+	+		+
△	*Hipparion (Proboscidipparion) sinense*	+	+		+
△	*Hipparion (Plesiohipparion) shanxiense*	+			
★	*Equus eisenmannae*	+	+	*E.* cf. *sanmeniensis*	*E. sanmeniensis*
★	*Equus teilhardi*	+			
△	*Coelodonta nihowanensis*	+	+		+
★	*Dicerorhinus yunchuchenensis*	+			*D.* cf. *kirchbergensis*
△	*Elasmotherium sp.*	+			
★	*Sus lydekkeri*	+	sp.		cf.
△	*Paracamelus gigas*	+			
★	*Muntiacus bohlini*	sp.		+	
★	*Axis shansius*	+			+
★	*Cervus (Sika) magnus*	+		sp.	
△	*Eucladoceros boulei*	+			+
★	*Ovis shantungensis*	+			
△	*Sinocapra sp.*	+			
★	*Budorcas sp.*	+			
△	*Euceratherium sp.*	+			
△	*Megalovis piveteaui*	cf.			
△	*Spirocerus wongi*	+			
★	*Gazella sinensis*	+			
★	*Gazella blacki*	+	cf.		cf.
◎	*Gazella subgutturosa*	cf.			
△	*Leptobos brevicornis*	+	+		*L. crassus*
△	*Proamphibos sp.*	+			

Note: ◎ extant species; ★ extinct species; △ extinct genus.

2017); whereas no credible record of Eurasian *Equus* (*sensu lato*) pre-dates the earliest Pleistocene (Rook et al., 2019; Sun and Deng, 2019). That said, *Mammuthus meridionalis* has been suggested to have originated in northern China around 2.6 Ma (Wei et al., 2010). As immigrants from North America, *Equus* entered Eurasia around 2.6 Ma (Sun and Deng, 2019), together with *Mammuthus meridionalis* and spread rapidly from East Asia into Europe (Bernor et al., 2019; Rook et al. 2019). The period ~2.6 Ma was critical as it was marked by major global events, including the great expansion of the Arctic ice sheet, the beginning of large-scale loess deposition induced by the intensification of the monsoon system and the extinction of large numbers of typical *Hipparion* fauna (Qiu, 2006). The Jinyuan Lower fauna includes many taxa that made their first Asiatic appearance during the Pleistocene, such as *Pachycrocuta brevirostris licenti*, *Megantereon nihowanensis*, *Sinicuon* cf. *dubius*, *Canis* cf. *teilhardi*, *Meles teilhardi*, *Coelodonta nihowanensis*, *Eucladoceros boulei*, *Euceratherium*, *Proamphibos* and *Bison palaeosinensis*. Several relic Neogene taxa continue to occur in the fauna, including *Villanyia fanchangensis*, *Chardinomys nihewanicus*, *Hipparion (Proboscidipparion) sinense* and *Stephanorhinus yunchuchenensis*. The 28 extinct genera account for 56% of the mammals, while 54 extinct species represent 98% of all mammalian species. Paleomagnetic analyses yielded an estimated age of Jinyuan Lower fauna of 2.6-1.7 Ma (Ge et al., 2021).

The characteristics of the Jinyuan Lower fauna are mostly similar to those of typical Early Pleistocene fauna from Longdan, Dongxiang, northwest China, Zhoukoudian Loc. 18 from Huiyu, Beijing and Xihoudu (=Hsihoutu), Ruicheng County, Shanxi Province (Qiu, 2006; Deng et al., 2019).

The Longdan fauna (Dongxiang, Gansu) is considered to be the earliest Quaternary mammalian fauna, with abundant mammalian fossils and paleomagnetic dating so far known in northwest China. This fauna was discovered from the basal part of the "Wucheng loess." Thirty-one mammalian species were described by Qiu et al. (2004). Later, *Castor anderssoni* and *Ursus (Protarctos) yinanensis* were additionally described by Wang (2005) and Qiu et al. (2009). Still, *Sus*, *Postschizotherium* remain undescribed (Qiu, 2006). Recently, newly collected elephant molars, whose provenance can be traced to the Longdan fauna, have been indisputably identified as *Mammuthus meridionalis* (Wang Shi-Qi and Deng Tao, personal communi- cation). Thus, in total, 36 mammalian species in the Longdan fauna have been identified. The fauna has been paleomagnetically dated to 2.5-2.2 Ma (Zan et al., 2016). The Longdan fauna is mostly similar to the Jinyuan Lower fauna with regard to whole faunal characteristics shared with typical early Early Pleistocene species, such as *Sericolagus brachypus*, *Macaca anderssoni*, *Pachycrocuta brevirostris licenti*, *Crocuta honanensis*, *Chasmaporthetes progressus*, *Sivapanthera linxiaensis, Megantereon nihowanensis, Homotherium crenatidens, Panthera palaeosinensis, Meles teilhardi, Coelodonta nihowanensis* and *Leptobos brevicornis*. The co-occurence of *Mammuthus meridionalis* and *Equus eisenmannae* in both the Longdan and Jinyuan Lower faunas echoes the contemporaneous Khapry Faunal Unit in the Russian Black Sea region, where *Mammuthus meridionalis* coexists with another gigantic dolichocephalic stenonid horse: *Equus* liventsovensis (Titov, 2008; Kahlke et al., 2011). Such a faunal association, found in both northern China and Ciscaucasian Russia, indicates that the *Mammuthus-Equus* event occurred very rapidly across the entirety of Northern Eurasia at the beginning of the Quaternary (around 2.6 Ma). The Zhoukoudan Loc. 18 fauna (Huiyu, Beijing) is one of the most classical Early Pleistocene mammalian faunas in North China. It was first described by Teilhard de Chardin (1940) and consists of 27 mammalian forms. This fauna comprises mainly micromammals. Based on faunal analysis, Qiu (2006) considered its age to be around 2.0 Ma. This fauna is marked by the appearance of primitive *Episiphneus youngi* with rooted molars, the ancestor of the living Palearctic zokor, *Myospalax*, with rootless molars. In addition, several primitive species of Arvicolidae (e.g., rooted *Mimomys* cf. *gansunicus*, *Borsodia chinensis* and *Villanyia fanchangensis*) have been replaced by the more derived rootless *Allophaiomys terraerubrae*, showing that the age of this fauna is slightly younger than those of the Longdan and Jinyuan Lower faunas. The lagomorph remains in the Zhoukoudian Loc. 18 fauna are both abundant and diversified, including *Alilepus annectens, Hypolagus schreuderi, Sericolagus brachypus, Ochotona thibetana* and *Ochotonoides complicidens*, representing an important dispersal event of rabbits during the Early Pleistocene.

The Xihoudu fauna is associated with stone and bone artifacts from the Paleolithic site at Ruicheng, Shanxi. It was first described by Jia and Wang (1978). It consists of 21 forms and is dominated by large mammals. Since most of the good specimens are housed at the Shanxi Museum, most of their elements have not yet been revised. Wei (2004) referred to the elephantine material as *Mammuthus meridionalis* and concluded that Xihoudu was older than the classical Nihewan fauna. Therefore, its age is estimated at 1.8-2 Ma (Qiu, 2006). Depending on our observation, "*Elaphurus chinnaniensis*" should be transferred to *Arvernoceros chinnaniensis*, which is comparable to *A. ardei* from Europe. *A. ardei* is a characteristic species of early Villafranchian, MN 16a, about 3.6-2.58 Ma (Stefaniak et al., 2020). Recently, the Xihoudu site was dated to about 2.43 Ma by Isochron 26Al/10Be burial dating (Shen et al., 2020).

The Xiashagou complex animals (classical Nihewan fauna) were recovered from more than 32 localities around Xiashagou village. The assemblage is somewhat farraginous. The third author of this work focused on the Xiashagou complex during his doctoral work. By synthesizing original field records by Licent (*Comptes rendus de Onze Années* [1923-1933]), a scientific report by Teilhard de Chardin and Piveteau (*Les mammifères fossils de Nihowan* [China]), relevant collections housed in Paris, Tianjin and Beijing, as well as field investigations, he built a rather complete database for Licent's collections from Nihewan and then demonstrated how the classical Nihewan fauna was mixed. He then separated the total "fauna" into at least six levels, which occupied a period from the lower boundary of the Quaternary to the end of the Early Pleistocene or the beginning of the Middle Pleistocene (Liu, 2019). Since his work has not yet been published, we have not yet compared the "Xiashagou Fauna."

3.3. Jinyuan Upper fauna: Late Early Pleistocene (1.7 - 0.78 Ma)

The Jinyuan Upper fauna was retrieved from the middle deposit unit of Jinyuan Cave (layer 5, upper part of layer 4 and lower part of layer 3, see **Fig. 2**). The Jinyuan Upper fauna above the Olduvai Normal Event is composed of 24 mammalian genera and 26 mammalian species (**Table 3**) and represents a transitional fauna from the Early to Middle Pleistocene.

The distinctive features of the fauna have been outlined by Jin et al. (2021). We summarize this outline as follows: (1) Several ancient taxa of the early Early Pleistocene (e.g., *Pachycrocuta brevirosris licenti, Mammuthus meridionalis, Stephanorhinus yunchuchenensis* and *Episiphneus dalianensis* with rooted molars) were replaced by descendant forms (e.g., *Pachycrocuta brevirostris brevirostris* [Liu et al., 2021], *Mammuthus trogontherii, Stephanorhinus kirchbergensis* and *Myospalax prosilurus* with rootless molars). (2) Several species that make their first appearance in the Pleistocene, such as *Ursus deningeri, Canis* cf. *mosbachensis, Equus qingyangensis* (Sun et al., 2021b), *Equus sanmeniensis* and *Bubalus teilhardi*. (3) Some primitive species continued to occur, such as *Ursus* cf. *etruscus* (Jiangzuo, et al., 2017), *Proboscidipparion sinense* (Sun et al., 2021a) and *Spirocerus wongi*. The appearance of the steppe mammoth *Mammuthus trogontherii* at Jinyuan Cave is almost simultaneous with that of the Majuangou Paleolithic site in Nihewan Basin, marking the earliest record of steppe mammoths globally (Wei and Lister, 2005). The nine extinct genera account for 37.5% of the mammals, while 24 extinct species represent 92% of all mammalian species. Both of the two ratios are obviously higher than those of Wanghai fauna (19% and 67%) and Zhoukoudian Loc. 1 fauna (21% and 64%), indicating that the age of Jinyuan Upper fauna should be earlier than the Middle Pleistocene. The Jinyuan Upper fauna from the middle/late Early Pleistocene (ca.

Table 3 Comparison of Jinyuan Upper fauna with other late Early Pleistocene faunas from Northern China

	Fauna composition	Jinyuan Upper fauna	Haimao fauna	Chutou-lang fauna	Gongwangling fauna
	Age (Ma)	1.7–0.78	1.6–1.2	1.6–1.4	1.6–1.35
★	*Crocidura wongi*	+	+		
◎	*Sorex minutus*	sp.	+; *Sorex* sp.		
△	*Trogontherium cuvieri*	+			
△	*Allocricetus ehiki*	+	sp.1		
△	*Allocricetus bursae*	+	sp.2		
★	*Myospalax propsilurus*	+	+		sp.
◎	*Meriones* sp.	+	+		+
★	*Vulpes chikushanensis*	+	*V. corsac*; *V. tchiliensis*	sp.	
★	"*Nyctereutes sinensis*"	+		+	
★	*Canis mosbachensis variabilis*	cf.	*C. lupus*	+	+
★	*Ursus etruscus*	+	*U. arctos*	sp.	cf.
★	*Ursus deningeri*	+			
△	*Pachycrocuta brevirostris brevirostris*	+			+
△	*Mammuthus trogontherii*	+			
△	*Hipparion (Proboscidipparion) sinense*	+		+	
★	*Equus qingyangensis*	+			
★	*Equus sanmeniensis*	+	*E. dalianensis*	+	+
★	*Dicerorhinus kirchbergensis*	+		cf.	
★	*Sus lydekkeri*	+		+	+
△	*Protoryx* sp.	+			
★	*Ovis shantungensis*	+			
△	*Sinocapra* sp.	+			
△	*Spirocerus wongi*	+	cf.; *S. peii*	cf.	
★	*Gazella sinensis*	+		+	
△	*Leptobos crassus*	cf.			sp.; *L. brevicornis*
★	*Bison palaeosinensis*	+		+	

Note : ◎ extant species; ★ extinct species; △ extinct genus.

1.70–0.78 Ma by paleomagnetic dating; Ge et al., 2021) can be compared with Gongwangling fauna in Shaanxi, northwest China and Haimao fauna, in Dalian, northeast China (**Table 3**).

The Haimao fissure site is situated in Dalian, just 70km south of Jinyuan Cave on Luotuo Hill. The Haimao fauna, studied by Sun et al. (1992), is composed of 28 micromammalian species, once the oldest Quaternary micromammalian fauna in northeast China. Based on faunal analysis, Haimao fauna contains seven extinct genera accounting for 30% of the mammals and 16 extinct species representing 67% of all mammalian species. Both of the two ratios are similar to those of Gongwangling fauna (29% and 62%) and Jinyuan Upper fauna, indicating that the age of Haimao fauna should be the late Early Pleistocene (ca. 1.2 - 1.6 Ma). The Haimao fauna is characterized by the co-occurrence of *Beremendia pohaiensis* and rootless *Myospalax prosilurus*, *Microtus*, *Pitymys* and *Allophaiomys*, indicating that they lived during the glacial period (Jin et al., 2021).

The Chutoulang fauna from Chifeng, Inner Mongolia, was described by You and Zhang (1989), Zhang (1989a, 1989b) and Dong et al. (2017). This fauna is composed of over 30 mammalian taxa and can be compared with Jinyuan Upper fauna. The age of the Chutoulang fauna is estimated to be between 1.4-1.6 Ma based on faunal comparison (Dong et al., 2017).

Furthermore, the Gongwangling fauna is the associated mammalian fauna from the Gongwangling *Homo erectus* site (Lantian, Shaanxi). It consists of 41 mammalian forms except for *Homo*, with 40 forms having been systematically described by Hu and Qi (1978) (*Apodemus* cf. *sylvaticus* is only listed in Table 1 of Hu and Qi, 1978). The elements of this fauna have been revised elsewhere. "*Megamacaca lantianensis*" was revised as *Rhinopithecus lantianensis* (Jablonski and Gu, 1991). "*Apodemus* sp." was revised as *A. agrarius* (Zheng and Han, 1993). "*Hystrix* cf. *subcristata*" was revised as *Hystrix kiangsenensis* (Wang, 2019). "*Cricetulus varians*" was revised as *Allocricetus teilhardi*, while *Cricetulus* cf. *griseus* is identical to *C. griseus* (Wang et al., 2020). "*Allophaiomys terraerubrae*" and "*Microtus epiratticeps*" were both transferred to *Proedromys bedfordi* (Zheng, 2020a). *Gerbillus* sp. was replaced by *Meriones* sp. (Qiu, 2020). "*Myospalax tingi*" and "*Myospalax fontanieri*" were revised as *Yangia tingi* and *Eospalax fontanieri*, respectively (Zheng, 2020b). "*Canis variabilis*" was revised as *C. mosbachensis variabilis* (Jiangzuo

Table 4 Comparison of Wanghai fauna with other Middle Pleistocene faunas from Northeast Asia (Micromammals)

	Wanghai Fauna	Zhoukoudian Loc.1 fauna	Miaohoushan fauna	Jinniushan fauna	Komunmoru fauna
Age (Ma)	0.78-0.35	0.69-0.42	0.8-0.4	0.26-0.19	? 0.6-0.2
Erinaceus olgae	+	+		+	
Crocidura wongi	+	sp.	+	+	
Rhinolophus pleistocaenicus	+	+	+		
Miniopterus	sp.	sp.	sp.		
Lepus wongi	+	+	+	*L. oiostolus*; *L. mandshuricus*	
Ochotona koslowi	+	+	+	*O. hyperborea*	
Marmota complicidens	+	+	*M. bobak*	*M. bobak*	
Trogontherium cuvieri	+	cf.	*Castor fiber*	+	
Hystrix kiangsenensis	sp.	+	+		
Cricetulus varians	+	+	+	+	
Myospalax propsilurus	+	*M. wongi*			
Myospalax psilurus	+	sp.	sp.	+	
Microtus branatioiaes	+	+	*M. brandti*	*M. brandti*	
Clethrionomys rufocanus	+	+	+	*C. rutilus*	
Gerbillus roborowskii	+	+			
Apodemus sylvaticus	+	+	*A. peninsulae*	*A. peninsulae*; *A. agrarius*	
Macaca robustus	+	+	+	+	sp.

et al., 2018). "*Hyaena sinensis*" was revised as *Pachycrocuta brevirostris brevirostris* (Liu et al., 2021). "*Megantereon lantianensis*" was revised as *M. inexpectatus* (Li and Sun, 2022). Thus, the revised Gongwangling fauna consists of 39 or 40 forms in total.

3.4. Wanghai fauna: Middle Pleistocene (0.78-0.35 Ma)

This fauna was recovered from the upper deposit unit of Jinyuan Cave (layer 1 to upper part of layer 3, see **Fig. 2**) and is named after the Wanghai Cave at Luotuo Hill. The sediments, with a total thickness of around 9m, are composed of limestone breccias, sandy silt and silty sand clayey silt from the top to bottom interbedded with a calcareous lens series. A prodigious quantity of mammalian fossils, representing a diverse range of species, was collected after systematic excavation. Preliminary identification revealed 39 species belonging to 36 genera (**Table 4**). It is interesting that a great number of tubular bones of deer and wild boars accumulated at the site in a nest shape.

The main characteristics of the Wanghai fauna (Liu et al., 2017a; Jiangzuo et al., 2019) are summarized by Jin et al. (2021). We summarize these characteristics as follows. (1) Many typical Early Pleistocene species are totally extinct, including *Pachycrocuta brevirostris licenti*, *Megantereon nihowanensis*, *Canis teilhardi*, *Coelodonta nihowanensis*, *Leptobos brevicornis* and *Sinomegaceros konwanlinensis*. (2) The fauna includes taxa that make their first appearance during the Pleistocene, such as *Pachycrocuta brevirostris sinensis*, *Megantereon inexpectatus*, *Canis mosbachensis variabilis*, *Ursus arctos*, *Enhydrictis melina*, *Palaeoloxodon* cf. *namadicus*, *Coelodonta antiquitatis yenshanensis*, *Myospalax psilurus* and *Sinomegaceros pachyosteus*. (3) Several species that first appeared during the Early Pleistocene continued to occur, such as *Myospalax prosilurus*, *Vulpes chikushanensis*, *Ursus deningeri*, *Equus sanmeniensis* and *Bubalus teilhardi*. Seven were extinct genera and 26 were extinct species, accounting for about 19% and 67% of the total mammalian taxa, respectively. The Wanghai fauna represents a typical Middle Pleistocene fauna in northern China.

Both the paleomagnetic and U-series dating methods were used to yield the age of Wanghai fauna. A series of secondary carbonate fragments from different depths, including calcareous belts and stalagmites from the upper deposit unit, were sampled and dated using the MC-ICPMS U-series dating method. The results showed that the ages of these speleothems ranged from 350 ka to 560 ka, suggesting a maximum end age of the sediments of Jinyuan Cave of ~350 ka (Ge et al., 2021). The paleomagnetic analysis showed that the upper fossil-bearing deposit unit of Jinyuan Cave had a normal polarity, which is best correlated to the Brunhes normal chronology due to the age constraints of the U-series dating results. The age of the Wanghai fauna is, therefore, estimated to be about 780-350 ka, during the

Table 4 (Continued) (Macromammals)

	Wanghai fauna	Zhoukoudian Loc.1 fauna	Miaohoushan fauna	Jinniushan fauna	Komunmoru fauna
Age (Ma)	0.78–0.35	0.69–0.42	0.8–0.4	0.26–0.19	? 0.6–0.2
Prochycrocuta brevirostris sinensis	+	+	+	*Crocuta ultima*	
Megantereon inexpectatus	+	+		*Homotherium ultimum*	
Panthera gombaszogensis	+	+	+	*Acinonyx cf. jubatus; P. tigris*	*P. tigris*
Vulpes chikushanensis	+		+; *V. corsac*	*V. corsac*	
Canis mosbachensis variabilis	+	+	+	+	
Ursus deningeri	+	+	+	*U. spelaeus*	*U. spelaeus*
Ursus arctos	+	+	+	+	+
Meles leucurus	+	+	+	*M. meles*	*M. meles*
Enhydrictis melina	+				
Lutra melina	sp.	+			
Lynx sp.	sp.				
Palaeoloxodon namadicus	cf.	+		-inae	-idae
Equus sanmeniensis	+	+		sp.	*E. sangwonensis*
Coelodonta yenshanensis	+	+		sp.	
Dicerorhinus kirchbergensis	+	+	+	+	+
Sus lydekkeri	+	+	+	sp.	
Sus scrofa	+				+
Cervus (Sika) grayi	+	+	+	cf.	+
Cervus elaphus					+
Sinomegaloceros pachyosleus	+	+	+	+	sp.; *Megaloceros sangwonensis*
Paracamelus praebactrianus		cf.			
Bubalus teilhardi	+	+			sp.
Ovibos	sp.				
Bison	sp.	+			
Bos primigenius					+

Middle Pleistocene (Ge et al., 2021).

Since the Wanghai fauna list has changed little since 2021, it is not necessary to discuss it in more detail, as Jin et al.'s (2021) description is sufficient. The most representative faunal localities in Northeast Asia during the Middle Pleistocene are Zhoukoudian Loc. 1, Jinniushan, Miaohoushan and Kommunmoru (Bae, 2007; Norton et al., 2007). Although we sought to provide fauna lists of these faunas, it proved to be too difficult because these classical faunas have been revised elsewhere. Table 4 in this work thus constitutes a provisional list and is not to be considered conclusive. The Zhoukoudian Loc. 1 fauna have been listed by many authors (e.g., Zdansky, 1928; Young, 1932; Black et al., 1933; Pei, 1934; Young, 1934; Teilhard de Chardin, 1939; Teilhard de Chardin and Pei, 1941; Liu, 1973; Chow, 1979; Zheng, 1984). The Miaohoushan fauna was listed in a monograph by Miahoush, published in 1986. The Jinniushan fauna was listed by Zheng and Han (1993) and Jiangzuo et al. (2018), among others. Data concerning the Komunmoru fauna of North Korea were generated by Norton (1999). It is unfortunate that we do not have the original report published in the Korean language, as without it we cannot outline the micromammalian species in this faunal group.

4. Suspected artifacts from the upper part of Jinyuan Cave

During recent excavations, dozens of suspected lithic artifacts made of flint, sandstone and vein quartz as well as tubular bones with visible hacking marks have been unearthed from the upper deposits of Jinyuan Cave. The discovery of many burnt stones, bones and charcoal along with possible fire ash implies the use of fire by ancient

Fig. 3 Parts of suspect artifacts from Jinyuan Cave (according to Professor Huang Wei-Wen, IVPP)

humans in this area (**Fig. 1**). Most of these artifacts were recovered from Layer 1-2 (**Fig. 3**) of Jinyuan Cave and can be associated with the Wanghai fauna described above. The Wanghai fauna in Dalian and corresponding faunas from Zhoukoudian Loc. 1 in Beijing, the Miaohoushan hominid site in Benxi, the Jinniushan hominid site in Yingkou and the Komunmoru site in Hugu-ri, North Korea, all belong to important Middle Pleistocene faunas, including human remains around the Bohai Sea circle. Therefore, their geological sequence has a relatively high degree of comparability (**Table 4**).

5. Conclusion

In conclusion, the fossil assemblages from Jinyuan Cave, Luotuo Hill, can be roughly divided into three successive faunas spanning the Late Cenozoic (ca. 3.60-0.35 Ma) based on combined evidence from biostratigraphy, geochronology and geomorphology. The four faunas of Jinyuan Cave are as follows (from oldest to youngest): the Luotuoshan fauna (Late Pliocene, 3.6-2.6 Ma), the Jinyuan Lower fauna (early Early Pleistocene, 2.60-1.7 Ma), the Jinyuan Upper fauna (late Early Pleistocene, 1.7-0.78 Ma) and the Wanghai fauna (Middle Pleistocene, 780-350 ka). The faunas at Jinyuan Cave provide a uniquely continuous faunal and sedimentary sequence from the Late Pliocene to the Middle Pleistocene, which is significant for establishing the Quaternary Mammal Fauna Sequence of Northeast Asia for the first time. Associated with the Wanghai fauna, some suspect artifacts were also found, which implies the possibility of finding human fossils here as well.

References

Azzaroli A., 1977. The Villafranchian stage in Italy and the Plio-Pleistocene boundary [J]. *Giornale di Geologia* 41(2), 61-79.

Azzaroli A., 1983. Quaternary mammals and the "end-Villafranchian" dispersal event: A turning point in the history of Eurasia [J]. *Palaeogeograph, Palaeoclimatology, Palaeoecology* 44, 117-139.

Bae K., 2007. Peopling in the Korean Peninsula [C]// Norton C.J., Braun D.R. eds., *Asian Paleoanthropology: from Africa to China and Beyond*, Springer, 181-190.

Bai Wei-Peng, Dong Wei, Liu Jin-Yuan, Wang Yuan, Jin Chang-Zhu, Liu Si-Zhao, Liu Li. 2017. New material of *Axis shansius* (Mammalia, Artiodactyla) and phylogenetic consideration of *Axis* [J]. *Quaternary Sciences* 37(4), 821-827. (in Chinese with English abstract)

Bernor R.L., Cirilli O., Jukar A.M., Potts R., Buskianidze M., Rook L., 2019. Evolution of Early *Equus* in Italy, Georgia, the Indian Subcontinent, East Africa and the Origins of African Zebras [J]. *Frontiers in Ecology Evolution* 7, 166.

Black D., Teilhard de Chardin P., Young Chung-Chien, Pei Wen-Chung. 1933. Fossil man in China [J]. *Memoir of the Geological Society of China* Series A 11, 38-39.

Cai Bao-Quan. 1987. A preliminary report on the late Pliocene micromammalian fauna from Yangyuan and Yuxian, Hebei [J]. *Vertebrata PalAsiatica* 25(2), 124-136. (in Chinese with English summary)

Cai Bao-Quan. 1989. Fossil Lagomorphs from the Late Pliocene of Yangyuan and Yuxian, Hebei[J]. *Vertebrata PalAsiatica* 27(3), 170-181. (in Chinese with English summary)

Cai Bao-Quan, Qiu Zhu-Ding. 1993. Murid rodents from the late Pliocene of Yangyuan and Yuxian, Hebei [J]. *Vertebrata PalAsiatica* 31(4), 267-293. (in Chinese with English summary)

Cai Bao-Quan, Zhang Zhao-Qun, Zheng Shao-Hua, Qiu Zhu-Ding, Li Qiang, Li Qian. 2004. New advances in the stratigraphic study on representative sections in the Nihewan Basin, Hebei [J]. *Professional Papers of Stratigraphy and Palaeontolog* 28, 267-285. (in Chinese with English abstract)

Cai Bao-Quan, Zheng Shao-Hua, Liddicoat J.C., Li Qiang. 2013. Review of the Litho-, Bio- and Chronostratigraphy in the Nihewan Basin, Hebei, China [C]// Wang Xiao-Ming, Flynn L.J., Fortelius M. eds., *Fossil Mammals of Asia: Neogene Biostratigraphy and Chronology*, New York: Columbia University Press, 218-242.

Cherin M., D'Allestro V., Masini F., 2019. New Bovid remains from the Early Pleistocene of Umbria (Italy) and a reappraisal of *Leptobos merlai* [J]. *Journal of Mammalian evolution* 26, 201-224.

Chow Ben-Shun (=Zhou Ben-Xiong). 1979. The fossil Rhinocerotides of Locality 1, Choukoutien [J]. *Vertebrata PalAsiatica* 17(3), 236-258. (in Chinese with English summary)

Deng Cheng-Long, Hao Qing-Zhen, Guo Zheng-Tang, Zhu Ri-Xiang. 2019. Quaternary integrative stratigraphy and timescale of China [J]. *Science China (Earth Sciences)* 62, 324-348.

Deng Tao. 2012. A skull of *Hipparion* (*Proboscidipparion*) *sinense* (Perissodactyla, Equidae) from Longdan, Dongxiang of Northwestern China–Addition to the Early Pleistocene Longdan Mammalian Fauna (3) [J]. *Vertebrata PalAsiatica* 47(4), 245-264.

Dong Wei, Zhang Li-Min, Liu Wen-Hui. 2017. New material of the Early Pleistocene mammalian fauna from Chutoulang, Chifeng, eastern Nei Mongol, China and binary faunal similarity analyses [J]. *Vertebrata PalAsiatica* 55(3), 257-275.

Flynn L.J., Wu Wen-Yu. 2017. Late Cenozoic Yushe Basin, Shanxi Province, *China: Geology and Fossil Mammals*. Vol. II: Small Mammal fossils of Yushe Basin [M]. Springer, 208-209.

Ge Jun-Yi, Deng Cheng-Long, Shao Qing-Feng, Wang Yuan, Tang Rui-Ping, Zhao Bo, Cheng Xiao-Dong, Jin Chang-Zhu. 2021. Magnetostratigraphic and uranium-series dating of fossiliferous cave sediments in Jinyuan Cave, Liaoning Province, northeast China [J]. *Quaternary International* 591, 5-14.

Hu Chang-Kang, Qi Tao. 1978. Gongwangling Pleistocene mammalian fauna of Lantian, Shaanxi [J]. *Palaeontologia Sinica* New Series C 21, 1-64.

Jablonski N.G., Gu Yu-Min. 1991. A reassessment of *Megamacaca lantianensis*, a large monkey from the Pleistocene of north-central China [J]. *Journal of Human Evolution* 20, 51-66.

Jia Lan-Po, Wang Jian. 1978. *Hsihoutu– A culture site of Early Pleistocene in Shansi Province* [M], Beijing: Wenwu Press, 1-85. (in Chinese with English summary)

Jiangzuo Qi-Gao, Gimranov D., Liu Jin-Yuan, Liu Si-Zhao, Jin Chang-Zhu, Liu Jin Yi. 2021. A new fossil marten from Jinyuan Cave, northeastern China reveals the origin of the Holarctic marten group [J]. *Quaternary International* 591, 47-58.

Jiangzuo Qi-Gao, Liu Jin-Yi, Wang Yuan, Jin Chang-Zhu, Liu Si-Zhao, Liu Jin-Yuan, Chen Jin. 2017. New materials of *Ursus etruscus* from Jinyuan cave of Luotuo Hill, Dalian and a brief review of *Ursus* cf. *etruscus* in China [J]. *Quaternary Sciences* 37(4), 828-837. (in Chinese with English abstract).

Jiangzuo Qi-Gao, Liu Jin-Yi, Wagner J., Dong Wei, Chen Jin. 2018. Taxonomical revision of fossil *Canis* in Middle Pleistocene sites of Zhoukoudian, Beijing, China and a review of fossil records of *Canis mosbachensis variabilis* in China [J]. *Quaternary International* 482, 93-108.

Jiangzuo Qi-Gao, Liu Jin-Yuan, Jin Chang-Zhu, Song Ya-Yun, Liu Si-Zhao, Lü Sheng, Wang Yuan, Liu Jin-Yi. 2019. Discovery of *Enhydrictis* (Mustelidae, Carnivora, Mammalia) cranium in Puwan, Dalian, Northeast China demonstrates repeated intracontinental migration during the Pleistocene [J]. *Quaternary International* 513, 18-29.

Jiangzuo Qi-Gao, Wang Yuan, Ge Jun-Yi, Liu Si-Zhao, Song Ya-Yun, Jin Chang-Zhu, Jiang Hao, Liu Jin-Yi. 2023. Discovery of jaguar from northeastern China middle Pleistocene reveals an intercontinental dispersal event [J]. *Historical Biology* 35(3). https://doi.org/10.1080/08912963.2022.2034808

Jin Chang-Zhu, Wang Yuan, Liu Jin-Yuan, Ge Jun-Yi, Zhao Bo, Liu Jin-Yi, Zhang Han-Wen, Shao Qing-Feng, Gao Chun-Ling, Zhao Ke-Liang, Sun Bo-Yang, Qin Chao, Song Ya-Yun, Jiangzuo Qi-Gao. 2021. Late Cenozoic mammalian faunal evolution at the Jinyuan Cave site of Luotuo Hill, Dalian, Northeast China [J]. *Quaternary International* 577, 15-28.

Jiangzuo Qi-Gao, Wang Yuan, Song Ya-Yun, Liu Si-Zhao, Jin Chang-Zhu, Liu Jin-Yi. 2022. Middle Pleistocene *Xenocyon lycaonoides* Kretzoi, 1938 in northeastern China and the evolution of *Xenocyon-Lycaon* lineage [J]. *Historical Biology*. published online: https://doi.org/10.1080/08912963.2021.2022138

Kahlke R.D., 2014. The origin of Eurasian Mammoth Faunas (*Mammuthus-Coelodonta* Faunal Complex)[J]. *Quateernary Scieences Reviews* 96, 32-49.

Kahlke R.D., García N., Kostopoulos D.S., Lacombat F., Lister A.M., Mazza P.P., Spassov N., Titov V.V., 2011. Western Palaearctic palaeoenvironmental conditions during the Early and early Middle Pleistocene inferred from large mammal communities and implications for hominin dispersal in Europe [J]. *Quateernary Scieences Reviews* 30, 1368-1395.

Li Qiang, Zheng Shao-Hua, Cai Bao-Quan. 2008. Pliocene biostratigraphic sequence in the Nihewan Basin, Hebei, China [J]. *Vertebrata PalAsiatica* 46(3), 210-232. (in Chinese with English summary)

Li Yu, Sun Bo-Yang. 2022. *Megantereon* (Carnivora, Felidae) in the late Early Pleistocene in China and its implications for paleobiogeography [J]. *Quaternary International* 610, 97-107.

Liu Hou-Yi. 1973. The fossil horse of Peking Man Site [J]. *Vertebrata PalAsiatica* 11(1), 86-97. (in Chinese with English abstract)

Liu Jin-Yi, Liu Jin-Yuan, Zhang Han-Wen, Wagner J., Jiangzuo Qi-Gao, Song Ya-Yun, Liu Si-Zhao, Wang Yuan, Jin Chang-Zhu., 2021. The giant short-faced hyena *Pachycrocuta brevirostris* (Mammalia, Carnivora, Hyaenidae) from Northeast Asia: A reinterpretation of subspecies differentiation and intercontinental dispersal[J]. *Quaternary International* 577, 29-51.

Liu Si-Zhao, Dong Wei, Wang Yuan, Li Hong-Long, Liu Li, Liu Jin-Yuan, Jin Chang-Zhu. 2017b. New materials of *Cervus (Sika) magnus* from Luotuoshan Locality of Dalian, Liaoning Province [J]. *Quaternary Sciences* 37(4), 838-844. (in Chinese with English abstract)

Liu Si-Zhao, Wang Yuan, Dong Wei, Liu Jin-Yuan, Liu Yi-Hong, Gao Chun-Ling, Liu Jin-Yi, Jin Chang-Zhu, Zhao Bo. 2017a. Preliminary report on the 2016's excavation at Luotuoshan Locality of Dalian, Liaoning Province [J]. *Quaternary Sciences* 37(4), 908-915. (in Chinese with English abstract)

Liu Wen-Hui. 2019. *Nyctereutes* from Hongya Yangshuizhan locality at Nihewan Basin and the systematic revision on the Genus *Nyctereutes* [D]. *Doctor Dissertation of the University of Chinese Academy of Sciences*, 1-402. (in Chinese with English abstract)

Masini F., Palombo M.R., Rozzi R., 2013. A reappraisal of the Early to Middle Pleistocene Italian Bovidae [J]. *Quaternary International* 288, 45-62.

Norton C.J., Jin Chang-Zhu, Wang Yuan, Zhang Ying-Qi. 2007. Rethinking the Palearctic-Oriental Biogeographic Boundary in Quaternary China [C]// Norton C.J., Braun D.R. eds., Asian Paleoanthropology: from Africa to China and Beyond. *Springer*, 81-100.

Norton C.J., 1999. The current state of Korean paleoanthropology [J]. *Journal of Human Evolution* 38(6), 803-825.

Pan Yue, Liu Si-Zhao, Dong Wei, Wang Yuan, Liu Jin-Yuan, Jin Chang-Zhu. 2020. New materials of *Eucladoceros* (Artiodactyla, Mammalia) from Luotuoshan Locality of Dalian, Liaoning Province[J]. *Quaternary Sciences* 40(1), 275-282. (in Chinese with English abstract)

Patnaik R., 2013. Indian Neogene Siwalik mammalian biostratigraphy: an overview [C]// Wang Xiao-Ming, Flynn L.J., Fortelius M. eds., *Fossil Mammals of Asia−Neogene Biostratigraphy and Chronology*, New York: Columbia University Press, 423-444.

Pei Wen-Chung. 1934. On the Carnivora from Locality 1 of Choukoutien [J]. *Palaeontologia Sinica* Series C 8(1), 1-165.

Qin Chao, Wang Yuan, Liu Si-Zhao, Song Ya-Yun, Jin Chang-Zhu. 2021. First discover of fossil *Episiphneus* (Myospalacinae, Rodentia) from Northeast China [J]. *Quaternary International* 591, 59-69.

Qiu Zhan-Xiang. 2006. Quaternary environmental changes and evolution of large mammals in north China [J]. *Vertebrata PalAsiatica* 44(2), 109-132.

Qiu Zhan-Xiang, Deng Tao, Wang Ban-Yue. 2004. Early Pleistocene Mammalian fauna from Longdan, Dongxiang, Gansu, China [J]. *Palaeontologia Sinica* New Series C 27, 1-193.

Qiu Zhan-Xiang, Deng Tao, Wang Ban-Yue. 2009. First Ursine bear material from Dongxiang, Gansu− Addition to the Longdan Mammalian Fauna (2) [J]. *Vertebrata PalAsiatica* 47(4), 245-264.

Qiu Zhan-Xiang, Huang Wei-Long, Guo Zhi-Hui. 1987. The Chinese hipparionine fossils [J]. *Palaeontologia Sinica* New Series C 25, 1-243. (in Chinese with English summary)

Qiu Zhan-Xiang, Qiu Zhu-Ding, Deng Tao, Li Chuan-Kui, Zhang Zhao-Qun, Wang Ban-Yue, Wang Xiao-Ming. 2013. Neogene Land Mammal Stage/Ages of China: Toward the goal to establish an Asian Land Mammal Stage/Age Scheme [C]// Wang Xiao-Ming, Flynn L.J., Fortelius M. eds., *Fossil Mammals of Asia: Neogene Biostratigraphy and Chronology*, New York: Columbia University Press, 76.

Qiu Zhu-Ding. 2020. Family Gerbillidae [C]// Qiu Zhu-Ding, Li Chuan-Kui, Zheng Shao-Hua eds., Glires II: Rodentia I. *Palaeovertebrata Sinica* Vol. III Fascicle 5(2), Beijing: Science Press, 278-296.

Rabinovich R., Listerm A.M., 2017. The earliest elephants out of Africa: Taxonomy and taphonomy of proboscidean remains from Bethlehem [J]. *Quaternary International* 445, 23-42.

Rook L., Bernor R.L., Avilla L.S., Cirilli O., Flynn L., Jukar A., Sanders W., Scott E., Wang Xiao-Ming. 2019. Mammal Biochronology (Land Mammal Ages) Around the World from Late Miocene to Middle Pleistocene and Major Events in Horse Evolutionary History [J]. *Frontiers in Ecology Evolution* 7, 278.

Stidham T.A., Smith N.A., Li Zhi-Heng. 2021. A Pleistocene raven skull (Aves, Corvidae) from Jinyuan Cave, Liaoning Province, China [J]. *Quaternary International* 591, 80-86.

Shen Guan-Jun, Wang Yi-Ren, Tu Hua, Tong Hao-Wen, Wu Zhen-Kun, Kuman K., Fink D., Granger D.F., 2020. Isochron 26Al/10Be burial dating of Xihoudu: Evidence for the earliest human settlement in northern China [J]. *L'anthropologie* 124, 1-25.

Shen Hui, Zhao Ke-Liang, Ge Jun-Yi, Zhou Xin-Ying, Song Ya-Yun, Liu Si-Zhao, Wang Yuan, Jin Chang-Zhu, Gao Chun-Ling, Huang Wen-Juan, Li Xiao-Qing. 2021. Early and Middle Pleistocene vegetation and its impact on faunal succession on the Liaodong Peninsula, Northeast China [J]. *Quaternary International* 591, 15-23.

Stefaniak K., Ratajczak U., Kotowski A., Kozłowska M,. Mackiewicz P., 2020. Polish Pliocene and Quaternary deer and their biochronological implications [J]. *Quaternary International* 546, 64-83.

Sun Bo-Yang, Deng Tao. 2019. The *Equus* Datum and the Early Radiation of Equus in China [J]. *Frontiers in Ecology Evolution* 7. https://doi.org/10.3389/fevo.2019.00429

Sun Bo-Yang, Liu Si-Zhao, Song Ya-Yun, Liu Yan, Wang Shi-Qi, Shi Qin-Qin, Zhang Feng-Jiao, Wang Yuan. 2021a. *Hipparion* in Luotuo Hill, Dalian and evolution of latest *Hipparion* in China [J]. *Quaternary International* 591, 24-34.

Sun Bo-Yang, Liu Wen-Hui, Liu Jin-Yuan, Liu Li, Jin Chang-Zhu. 2021b. *Equus qingyangensis* in Jinyuan Cave and its palaeozoogeographic significance [J]. *Quaternary International* 591, 35-46.

Sun Bo-Yang, Yan Ya-Ling, Jin Chang-Zhu, Dai Xi-Chao, Wang Yuan. 2022a. New material of *Stephanorhinus* (Rhinocerotidae, Mammalia) from Jinyuan Cave, Luotuo Hill in Dalian, Northeast China [J]. *Historical Biology*. published online: https://doi.org/10.1080/08912963.2022.2130793

Sun Bo-Yang, Zhu Min, Dai Xi-Chao, Jin Chang-Zhu. 2022b. Early Pleistocene *Equus* community from Jinyuan Cave, Luotuo Hill in Dalian, Northeast China and its palaeoecological significance [J]. *Historical Biology*. published online: https://doi.org/10.1080/08912963.2022.2077647

Sun Yu-Feng, Wang Zhi-Yan, Liu Jin-Yuan, Wang Hui, Xu Qin-Qi, Jin Chang-Zhu, Li Yi, Hou Lian-Hai, Huang Yu-Zhen. 1992. *Dalian Haimao fauna* [M], Dalian: Dalian University of Technology Press, 1-137. (in Chinese with English abstract)

Teilhard de Chardin P., 1939. On two skulls of Machairodus from the Lower Pleistocene beds of Choukoutien. *Bulletin of the Geological Society of China* (= Acta Geologica Sinica) 19(3), 235-256.

Teilhard de Chardin P., 1940. The fossils from Locality 18 near Peking [J]. *Palaeontologia Sinica* New Series C 9, 1-94.

Teilhard de Chardin P., Pei Wen-Chung. 1941. The fossil mammals from Locality 13 of Choukoutien [J]. *Palaeontologia Sinica* New Series C 11, 101-102.

Titov V.V., 2008. Late Pliocene large mammals from Northeastern Sea of Azov Region [M]. *Rostov-on-Don: SSC Rusian Academy of Sciences* Publishing, 1-262. (in Russian, with English summary)

Wang Ban-Yue. 2005. Beaver (Rodentia, Mammalia) fossils from Longdan, Gansu, China—Addition to the Early Pleistocene Longdan Mammalian Fauna (1) [J]. *Vertebrata PalAsiatica* 43(3), 237-242. (in Chinese with English summary)

Wang Ban-Yue, Wu Wen-Yu, Qiu Zhu-Ding. 2020. Family Cricetidae [C]// Qiu Zhu-Ding, Li Chuan-Kui, Zheng Shao-Hua, eds. Glires II: Rodentia I. *Palaeovertebrata Sinica* Vol. III Fascicle 5(2), Beijing: Science Press, 10-152.

Wang Yuan. 2019. Family Hystricidae [C]// Li Chuan-Kui, Qiu Zhu-Ding eds., Glires II: Rodentia I. *Palaeovertebrata Sinica* Vol. III Fascicle 5(1), Beijing: Science Press, 327-341.

Wang Yuan, Ge Ju-Yi, Zhao Ke-Liang, Liu Wen-Hui. 2021. Cave deposits from Luotuo Hill, Northeast China: A geochronologically calibrated mammalian biostratigraphic standard for the Quaternary of Eastern Asia [J]. *Quaternary International* 591, 1-4.

Wei Guang-Biao. 2004. *Taxonomy and biostratigraphy of the Middle Pliocene-Early Pleistocene Mammuthus of Northern China, with discussion on the evolution of Eurasian mammoths* [D], Doctor Dissertation of Osaka: City University, 1-112.

Wei Guang-Biao, Hu Song-Mei, Yu Ke-Fu, Hou Ya-Mei, Li Xin, Jin Chang-Zhu, Wang Yuan, Zhao Jia-Xin, Wang Wen-Hua. 2010. New materials of the steppe mammoth, *Mammuthus trogontherii*, with discussion on the origin and evolutionary patterns of mammoths [J]. *Science China (Earth Sciences)* 53, 956-963.

Wei Guang-Biao, Lister A.M., 2005. Significance of the dating of the Majuangou site for understanding Eurasian mammoth evolution [J]. *Vertebrata PalAsiatica* 43, 243-244. (in Chinese, English abstract)

Young Chung-Chien. 1932. On the Artiodactyla from the Sinanthropus Site at Chouk'outien [J]. *Palaeontologia Sinica* Series C 8(2), 1-100.

Young Chung-Chien. 1934. On the Insectivora, Chiroptera, Rodentia and primates other than Sinanthropus from Locality 1 at Choukoutien [J]. *Palaeontologia Sinica* Series C 8(3), 1-139.

Yang Yang-He-Shan, Li Qiang, Ni Xi-Jun, Cheng Xiao-Dong, Zhang Jie, Li Hong-Long, Jin Chang-Zhu. 2021. Tooth micro-wear analysis reveals that persistence of beaver *Trogontherium cuvieri* (Rodentia, Mammalia) in Northeast China relied on its plastic ecological niche in Pleistocene[J]. *Quaternary International* 591, 70-79.

You Yu-Zhu, Zhang Wen-Shan. 1989. An Early Pleistocene mammalian fauna at Dongcun, Chifeng district, Nei Monggol [J]. *Quaternary Sciences* 9(1), 48-55. (in Chinese with English abstract)

Zan Jin-Bo, Fang Xiao-Min, Zhang Wei-Lin, Yan Mao-Du, Zhang Tao. 2016. Palaeoenvironmental and chronological constraints on the Early Pleistocene mammal fauna from loess deposits in the Linxia Basin, NE Tibetan Plateau [J]. *Quaternary Science Reviews* 148, 234-242.

Zdansky O., 1928. Die Säugetiere der Quartärfauna von Chou-K'ou-Tien [J]. *Palaeontologia Sinica* Series C 5(4), 1-146. (in German)

Zhang Wen-Shan. 1989a. The discovery and stratigraphic bearing of the Mammalian fauna in Dongliang, Chutoulang,

Chifeng City (1) [J]. *Journal of Hebei College of Geology* 12(1), 69-80. (in Chinese with English abstract)

Zhang Wen-Shan. 1989b. Zhang W.S., 1989. The discovery and stratigraphic bearing of the mammalian fauna in Dongliang, Chutoulang, Chifeng City (2). *Journal of Hebei College of Geology* 12(2), 175-182. (in Chinese)

Zhang Zhao-Qun, Zheng Shao-Hua, Liu Jian-Bo. 2003. Pliocene micromammalian biostratigraphy of Nihewan Basin, with comments on the Stratigraphic division [J]. *Vertebrata PalAsiatica* 41(4), 306-313. (in Chinese with English summary)

Zheng Shao-Hua. 1984. Revised determination of the fossil Cricetine (Rodentia Mammalia) of Choukoutien district [J]. *Vertebrata PalAsiatica* 22(3), 179-197. (in Chinese with English summary)

Zheng Shao-Hua. 2020a. Family Arvicolidae [C]// Qiu Zhu-Ding, Li Chuan-Kui, Zheng Shao-Hua eds., *Glires II: Rodentia I. Palaeovertebrata Sinica* Vol. III Fascicle 5(2), Beijing: Science Press, 152-228.

Zheng Shao-Hua. 2020b. Family Myospalacidae [C]// Qiu Zhu-Ding, Li Chuan-Kui, Zheng Shao-Hua eds., *Glires II: Rodentia I. Palaeovertebrata Sinica* Vol. III Fascicle 5(2), Beijing: Science Press, 313-378.

Zheng Shao-Hua, Han De-Fen. 1993. Mammalian fossils [C]// **Zhang Sen-Shui** et al. eds., Comprehensive study on the Jinniushan Paleolithic Site. Memoirs of Institute of Vertebrate Paleontology and Palaeoanthrology. *Chinese Academy of Science* 19, Beijing: Science Press, 1-163.

Zheng Shao-Hua, Zhang Ying-Qi, Cui Ning. 2019. Five new species of Arvicolinae and Myospalacinae from the Late Pliocene–Early Pleistocene of Nihewan Basin [J]. *Vertebrata PalAsiatica* 57(4), 308-324.

Chapter 2.
Late Paleolithic Culture of Siberia and the Far East

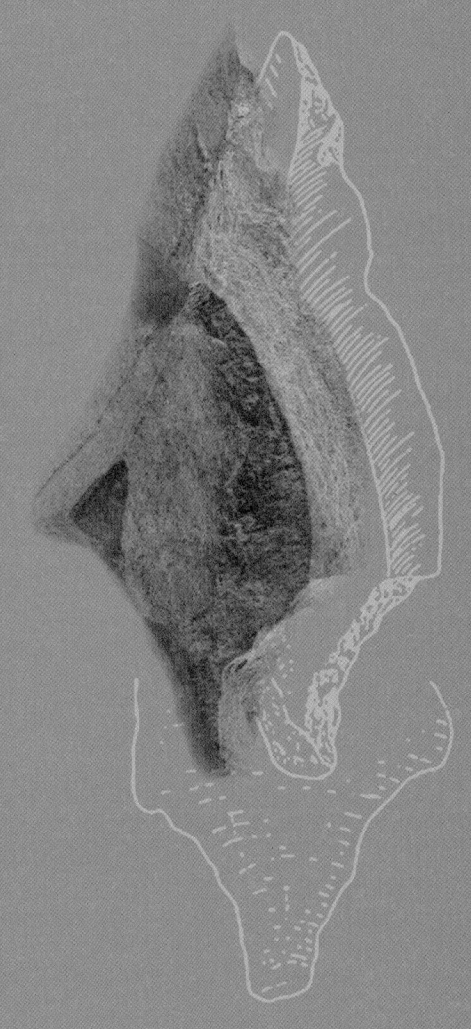

The study of blade tool industry in Korea

Heon-jong LEE[1], **Sang-seok LEE**[2]

[1] Professor, Mokpo National University, Korea ; ruslee@mokpo.ac.kr
[2] Jeonnam Provincial office, Korea

ABSTRACT

Typical artifacts of Korean blade tool industry, which prevailed around 35 - 30 ka BP, are found across the country, while emergent relics of microblade industry expanded around 30 - 20 ka BP. The artifacts of blade tool industry coexisted with the microblade industry, when it pervaded the Korean Peninsula, around 20 ka to 15 ka BP. Stone tools, typical byproducts of blade tools, are were found along with pebble tools. This suggests the possibility that the cultural environment centered on blade tool industry, which spread widely in Northeast Asia, influenced the pebble tool tradition developed by Middle to Upper Paleolithic people around 45 - 25 ka BP. In short, in the Korea Peninsula, around 30 ka BP, blade tool industry appeared, influencing the pebble tool tradition that had existed since the late Middle to Early Upper Paleolithic.

국문초록

한국의 여러 유적에서 발견되는 다양한 돌날 문화를 입증하는 전형적 석기류는 중기구석기 말에서 후기구석기 이른시기까지 지속된 자갈돌 석기의 전통, 돌날기술로 제작된 몸돌과 돌날, 긴 격지들을 들 수 있다. 한국의 전형적인 돌날 석기문화는 고례리 유적, 진그늘 유적, 호평동 유적, 용산동 유적, 화대리 유적, 죽내리 유적, 오지리 유적에서 나타나며(30-35ka BP), 좀돌날 석기문화는 호평동 유적, 용산동 유적, 화대리 유적에서 나타난다(30-20ka BP). 후기구석기 유적에서 많은 석기가 45-25ka BP 시기에 발견되는데, 격지 석기문화와 돌날 석기문화가 다중적 문화층 유물로 나타난다. 정장리 유적, 노봉 유적, 기곡 유적, 그리고 촌곡 유적에서는 자갈돌 석기전통이 발견되며 중심연대는 30-25ka BP로 보고 있다. 결론적으로 한반도에는 자갈돌 석기 전통의 영향을 받는 가운데 약 30ka BP경에 돌날 석기문화가 출현하며 이 석기전통은 시베리아의 초원길을 따라 극동으로 이주한 문화의 특성으로 간주된다.

또한 돌날 석기문화가 확산되는 가운데 좀돌날 석기문화가 유입되어 정착되었으며, 오지리 유적과 죽내리 유적에서는 20-15ka BP경에 좀돌날 문화가 공존하였다.

Keywords : blade tool industry, Middle - Upper Paleolithic transition, persistence, cultural variety

1. Introduction

Discussions related to the blade tool industry of Korea vary from support for the continuity of the pebble tool tradition and the steady use of heavy-weight tools throughout the Upper Paleolithic (Lee, 2002a, 2002b; Lee and Lim, 2008) to the opinion that the flake tool tradition was shaped based on the technology with which heavy-weight tools continued to be made (Lee, 1997, 1998). There is also a discussion undertaken to understand the blade-making technique adopted by the people of the Paleolithic, who were exposed to the cultural environment of the Upper Paleolithic in Northeast Asia, among other stone artifacts of the flake tool tradition, blade industry as a migrated industry, the emergence of the microblade industry, and the continuity of blade tool industry (Lee, 2004, 2008a, 2008b). The typical artifacts of Korean blade tool industry are found across the country, as well as artifacts of the pebble tool tradition, which continued from the Middle Paleolithic through the early part of the Upper Paleolithic. In addition, core and blade tools made with the blade technique and elongated flake have been verified. These local characteristics demonstrate the diversity of the blade tool industry of Korea (Fig. 1).

2. The emergence of blade tool industry

The typical relics of blade tool industry around 30 ka BP include the Koreri site (Seo et al., 1999; Jang, 2000a, 2000b), Jingeunul site (Lee, 2004), Hopyongdong site (Hong et al., 2008), Yongsandong site (Cental Institute of Cultural Heritage, 2007), Hwadaeri site (Choi et al., 2005), Jungnaeri site (Lee et al., 2000), and Ojiri site (Lee, 2008). Of the blade tools, those that are chronologically found in 35~30 ka BP include the Hwadaeri site, Hopyongdong site, and Yongsandong site (Fig. 2). The relics that emerged with the microblade industry as the blade tool industry expanded in 30~20 ka BP include the Jingeunul site and Koreri site (Fig. 3). The artifacts of blade tool industry that coexisted with the microblade industry when it pervaded the Korean Peninsula in 20 ka to 15 ka BP include the Jungnaeri site and Ojiri site (Fig. 4). The stone tools found at these sites are related to the typical blade tool industry and are made of volcanic rocks. The stone tools excavated appear different and are, in general, primary products, like blade cores, blades, and technical flakes and scrapers, end-scrapers, burins, and tanged points. These stone tools, typical byproducts, and stone tools made mainly of blade tools are found along with pebble tools.

3. Blade-making technique and stone tools in the pebble tool tradition

From the Upper Paleolithic, many artifacts with an absolute dating of 45 ka to 25 ka BP have been found. Among the stone tools from this period, the stone tools of the flake tool industry and the blade tool industry, at once multi-layered relics and based on pebble tools, are found as well. Meanwhile, the representative stone tools with an absolute chronology that maintained the pebble tool tradition of 30 to 25 ka BP include the Jeongjangri site, Nobong site, Gigok site, and Chongok site (Lee, 2010). In an increasing number of cases, blade-making techniques or blade tools are found at the stone tools of the Upper Paleolithic that maintained the pebble tool tradition as at these sites (Fig. 5). The representative sites are the Jeongjangri site (Paleolithic site at Jeongjang-ri of Geochang I, 2004) and Chongok site (Lee et al., 2004). They are dated from 40 to 25 ka BP. This shows the possibility that the cultural environment centered on blade tool industry that spread widely in Northeast Asia influenced the Paleolithic people who used the pebble tool tradition (Lee, 2004).

4. The regional characteristics of the blade tool industry in the Korean Peninsula

As mentioned above, we can see that around 30 ka BP, blade tool industry appeared in the Korean Peninsula, while the Paleolithic industry had an earlier influence on the pebble tool

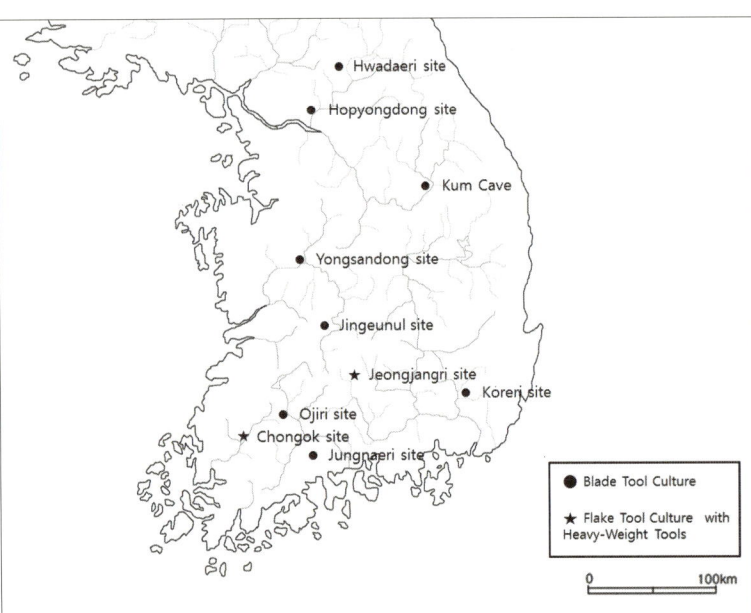

Fig. 1 Distribution Map of Blade Tool Culture

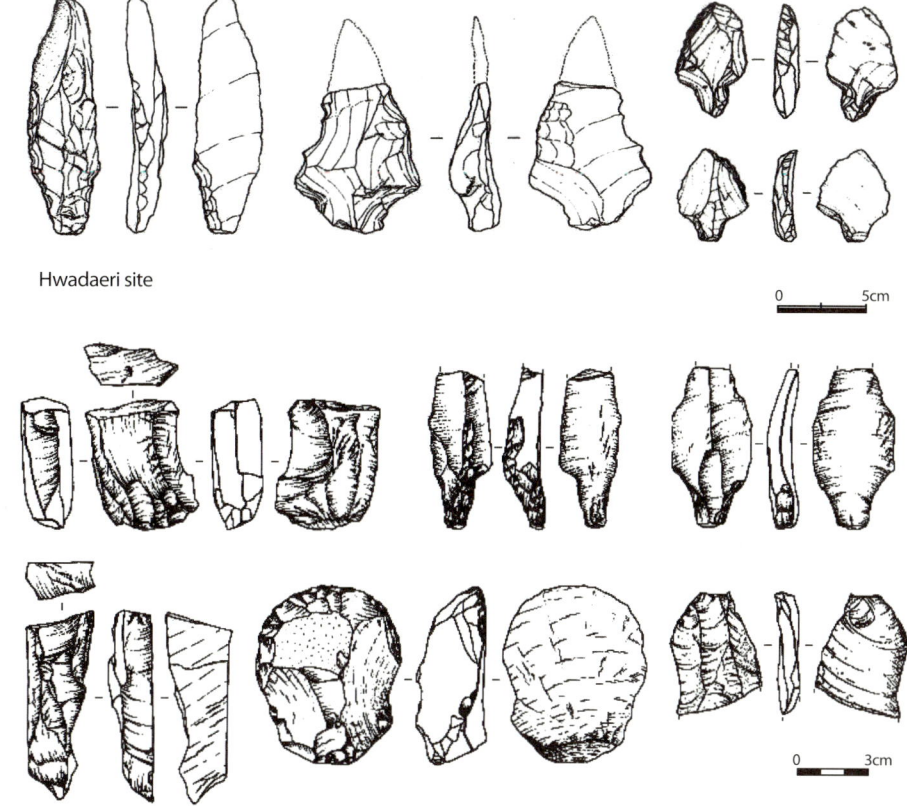

Hwadaeri site

Hopyongdong site

Fig. 2 Blade tool of 35 - 30 ka site

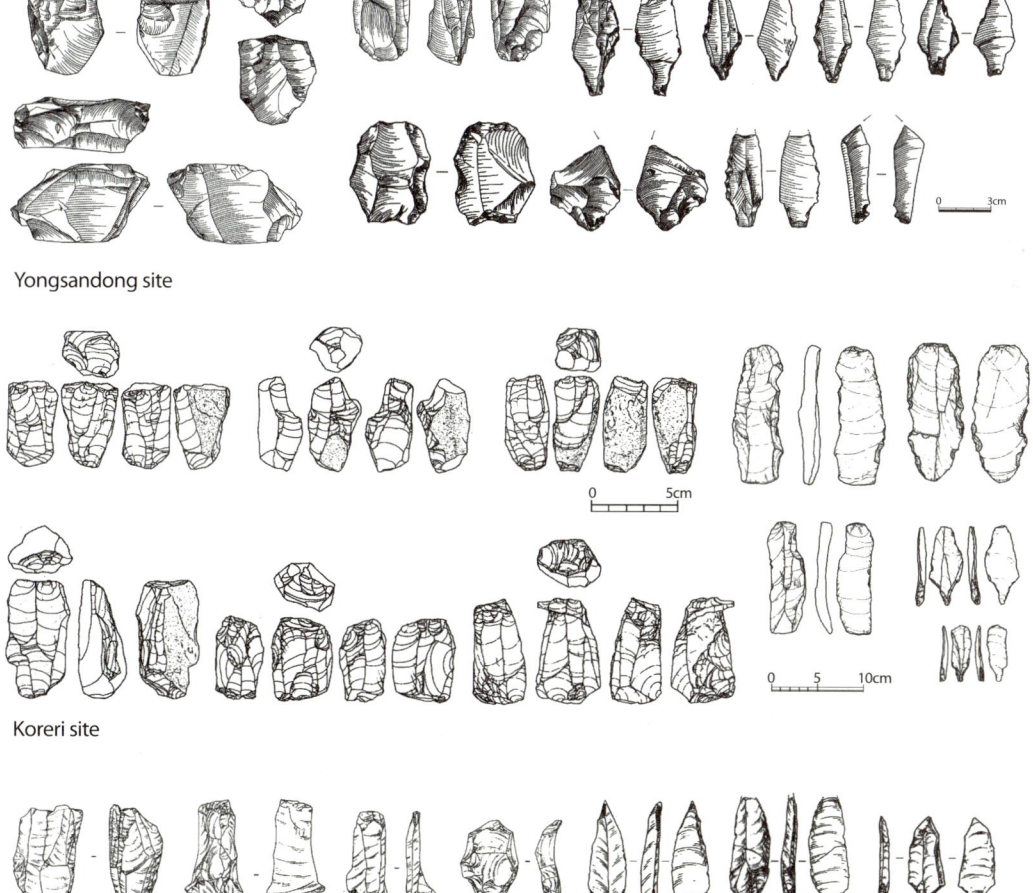

Yongsandong site

Koreri site

Jingeunul site

Fig. 3 Blade tool of 30 - 20ka site

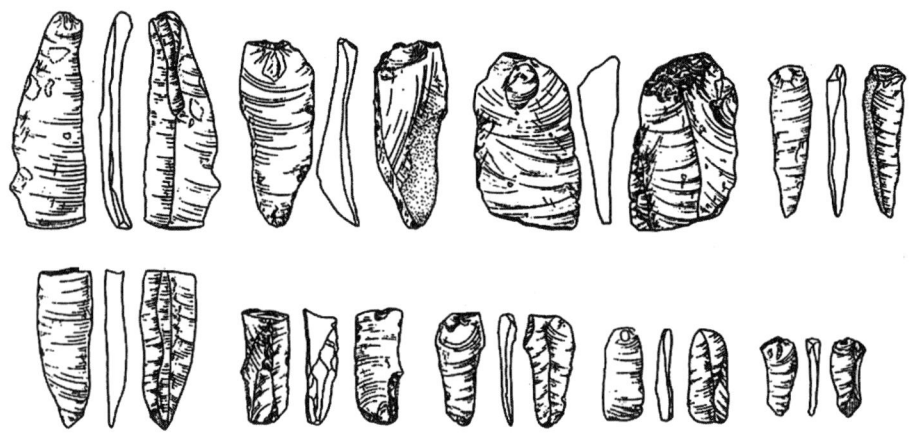

Jungnaeri site

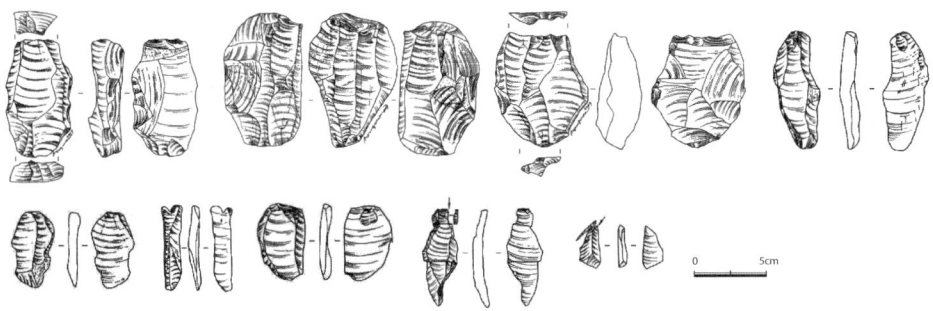

Ojiri site

Fig. 4 Blade tool of 20 - 15ka site

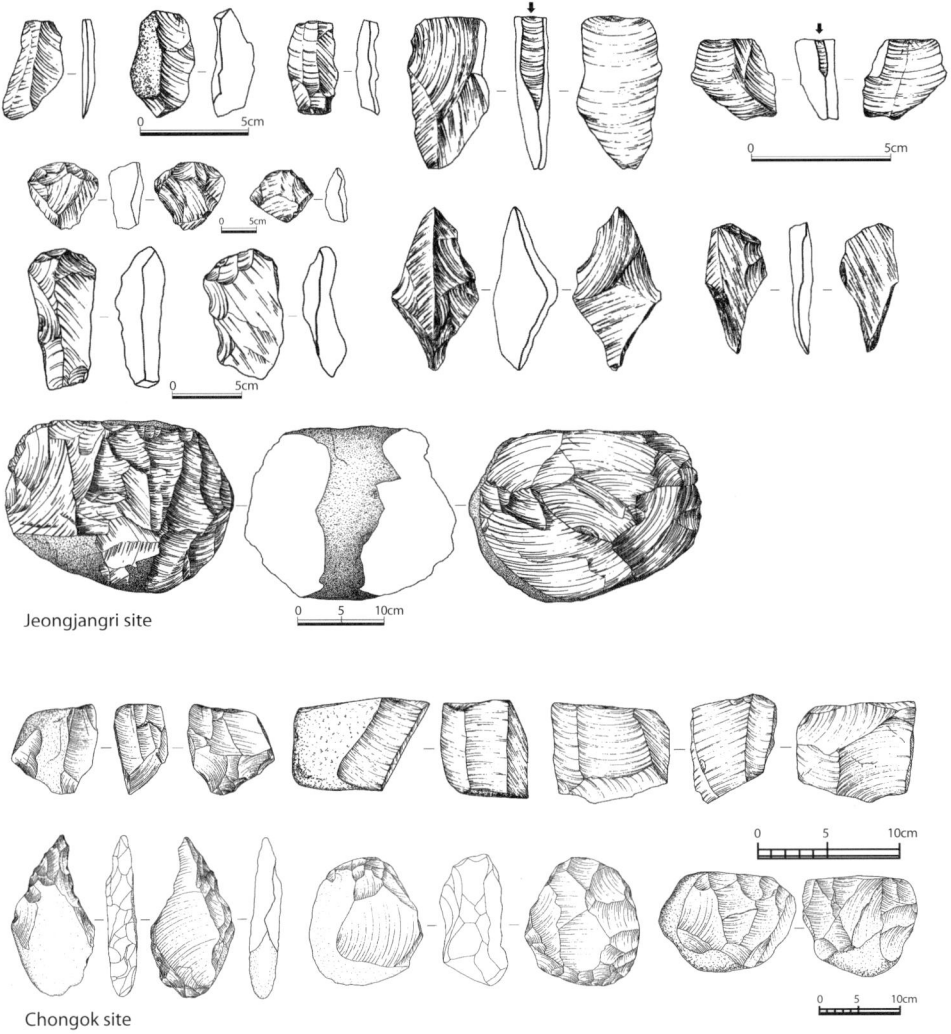

Jeongjangri site

Chongok site

Fig. 5 Blade tool of the pebble tool tradition site

tradition. What is remarkable is that at the stone tools where typical blade tools are excavated, almost no heavy-weight stone tools of the pebble tool tradition are found . These consistent characteristics demonstrate that the blade tool industry migrated from Siberia (steppe route from Altai to Russian Far East) as suggested by Derevianko's hypothesis (Derevianko, 2005).

On the other hand, there is no evidence that the microblade industry replaced the blade tool industry or that there was a regional transition from the blade tool industry to the microblade industry. Rather, the two industrys were products of populations that migrated into the Korean Peninsula during the Upper Paleolithic. It is not that blade tool industry was replaced by microblade industry, but rather that as the blade tool industry spread, the microblade industry moved and settled into the Korean Peninsula. In fact, at the Chulwon Jangheungri site, Sinbuk site, Hopyoungdong site 3a, and Jinju Jiphyun site, based on absolute dating, the earliest date for the microblade industry has been verified as 25 ka to 20 ka (Lee, 2004). It has been confirmed that the Ojiri site and Jungnaeri site coexisted in the development of the microblade industry of 20 ka to 15 ka (Lee, 2008).

References

Cental institute of Cultural Heritage. 2007. *The Paleolithic Site at Yongsandong of Daejeon.*

Center of History & Culture, Gyeongnam Development Institute. 2004. *The Paleolithic Site at Jeongjang-ri of Geochang I.*

Choi, B.K., Yu H.J., 2006. *The Hwadae-ri shimteo Paleolithic Site in Pocheon-si, korea*, Kangnwon National University Museum.

Derevianko A.P., 2005. Formation of Blade Industries in Eastern Asia. *Archaeology, Ethnology & Anthropology of Eurasia* Vol. 4, No. 24.

Hong M.Y., Kim J.H., 2008. *Hopyeong-dong Paleolithic site (Namyangju, Gyeonggi Province, Korea) II*, Korea Land Corporation Gyeonggi Cultural Foundation Gijeon Institute of Cultural Properties.

Jang Y.J., 2001a. *The study of core from Milyang Koreri site in Paleolithic age*, Pusan National University.

Jang Y.J., 2001b. Core Reduction Technology During the Upper Palaeolithic focusing on the Goryeri Collection Milyang Korea. *Hanguk GuseokgiHakbo* No.4.

Lee G.K., 2004. The Jingeuneul Upper Palaeolithic Site In Jinan County od Submerged Area around the Yongdam Dam and Its Significance. *Honam Gogohakbo* 19.

Lee G.K., Choi M.N., KiM E.J., 2000. *Soonchon jungnae-ri site*, Kwangju: Chosun University Museum, korea.

Lee H.J., 1997. The variousness of Upper Paleolithic tool making tradition in Korea. the *2nd international symposium: Suyanggae and her neighbours.*

Lee H.J., 1998. Chronology of Upper Paleolithic in Korean Peninsula. the *3rd international symposium: Suyanggae and her neighbours.*

Lee H.J., 2002a. Change of making stone tool technique of Korean Paleolithic. *Paleolithic culture of Korea*, Yensei University press.

Lee H.J., 2002b. A study of the conservative character and persistence of the Pebble Tool Tradition in Korea. *Hanguk Sanggosa Hakbo* 38.

Lee H.J., 2003. The Middle to Upper Paleolithic tradition and the tradition of the flake tool manufacturing on the Korean Peninsula. *Archaeology, Ethnology & Anthropology in Eurasia* 1(13).

Lee H.J., 2004. Correlation of chronology and techno-typological character of Upper Paleolithic in Korea. *Hanguk SanggosaHakbo* 44.

Lee H.J., 2008a. A study of GokseongOjiri site and Blade Tool culture of Late Upper Paleolithic. *Yeoksahak Yeongu* 33.

Lee H.J., 2008b. Study of comparison of microblade core technical system of Upper Paleolithic in Northeast Asia. *Dongbuka Mumhwa Yeongu* 16.

Lee H.J., Lim H.S., 2008. New point of view of Blade culture of Siberia and persistence of Pebble Tool tradition in Korean Peninsula. *Hanguk Siberia Yeongu* 2(12).

Lee H.J., 2009. Study of appearance of *Homo sapiens* and regional adaptation of Hunting tool in Northeast Asia. *Hanguk GuseokgiHakbo* No. 20.

Lee H.J., No S.H., Lee H.Y., 2004. *Report on the Excavation of Dangga Site·Chongokri site, Naju*, Mokpo National University Museum.

Seo Y.N., Kim H.J., Jang Y.J., 1999. Upper Paleolithic culture of Goryeri site, in Milyang-si, Kyengnam province. *youngnamJibang Guseokkimunhwa.*

The Lithic Assemblages and Chronology of Nosan-ri Paleolithic site, Cheongju, Korea

Byeong-il YUN[1], Kaoru OTANI[2], Yung-jo LEE[3]

[1] Senior Researcher, Institute of Korean Prehistory (IKP), Korea ; mercury0323@hanmail.net
[2] Tokyo Metropolitian University, Japan
[3] Institute of Korean Prehistory (IKP), Korea

ABSTRACT

The Nosan-ri Paleolithic site is located in the midstream area of the Geum River in Cheongju, surrounded by mountainous terrain to the north and bordered to the south by the Geum River flowing in a U-shape. Lithic assemblage from 7 localities with well-preserved Paleolithic cultural layers were analyzed. As a result, the Paleolithic culture of the Nosan-ri area was divided into five phases. During Phase 1, around 50,000 years ago in the Late Middle Paleolithic. Most of the flake-tools had naturally formed narrow edges or were made from thin flakes or fragments. In Phase 2, Early Upper Paleolithic culture, 40,000 years ago, made small handaxes and scrapers that were retouched on both sides of the edge or on a round edge. Phase 3, Middle Upper Paleolithic culture, 30,000 years ago, made light-duty tools made from flakes, which became increasingly more common and diversified. In addition to existing tool production systems with quartz and quartzite, a new method with fine-grained raw materials, such as tuff, rhyolite, and shale. In Phase 4, Upper Paleolithic cultural layers, around 20,000 years ago, blade tool production was beginning and the pebble tool production system was gradually declining. Fine-grained raw materials, like tuff and hornfels, were actively used for making tools. Also, tanged points appeared. Phase 5, The blade production technique became more developed, and microblade technology emerged, and after edge-ground stone axe was found. It is of keen interest to estimate the elements of the cultural transition from the Late Upper Paleolithic to the initial Neolithic Period in Northeast Asia.

국문초록

금강 중류의 청주 노산리 구석기유적 7개 지점에서 구석기 문화층의 석기 및 문화층에 대한 분석 결과, 노산리 유적 구석기문화를 5기로 구분하였다. 1기는 5만년 전 중기구석기 말기로 주먹도끼, 주먹찌르개, 찍개, 여러면석기 같은 몸돌 석기, 격지와 홈날 같은 격지 석기가 확인된다. 대부분 격지 석기는 가장자리가 자연적으로 좁은 면이 형성된 얇은 격지나 조각을 이용하고 있다. 2기는 주먹도끼의 크기가 작아지고, 양쪽 또는 둥근 가장자리를 손질한 긁개류가 출토된다. 3기는 3만년 전 후기구석기 중기로 격지 석기의 도구가 증가하고 다양해지며, 긴 격지로 제작된 부리날, 뚜르개, 새기개와 같은 도구들이 나타나기 시작한다. 여러면석기는 감소하며 석영과 규암을 이용한 기존의 생산시스템에 더해 응회암, 유문암, 셰일과 같은 세립질 돌감을 이용한 새로운 제작방법이 등장한다. 4기는 돌날 생산 개시, 자갈돌석기 생산시스템 감소, 응회암과 혼펠스와 같은 돌감의 도구 제작 사용, 그리고 슴베찌르개의 등장이 이루어진다. 5기는 돌날 생산기술이 더욱 발전되고, 좀돌날 기술도 나타나며, 두 기술이 동일 문화층에서 발견된다. 자귀형 도끼도 확인되어 후기구석기에서 초기신석기로 이행되는 문화적 변이를 확인할 수 있다. 노산리 구석기유적에 대한 고고학적 분석을 통해 중기구석기부터 후기구석기 말기의 석기 제작기술과 금강 주변 문화의 특성 및 유적 구조의 변화 양상을 이해할 수 있다.

Keywords : Nosan-ri Paleolithic sites, Geum River, lithic assemblages, Late Middle Paleolithic, Upper Paleolithic

1. Introduction

Geum River is an important river that crosses the central and southwestern parts of the Korean peninsula. The upper stream area is surrounded by the Noryeong and Charyeong mountain ranges, and forms a deep river course with meanderings between steep mountainous terrain, while the middle stream area is formed as a small alluvial plain that is almost straight. In addition, the lower stream area is widened and a wide plain is formed, and a granary area is spread out. In the Geum River basin with these geographical conditions, many Paleolithic sites have been discovered.

The one of largest number of sites excavated in the Geum River basin is the Nosan-ri site in Cheongju. Nosan-ri Paleolithic sites are located near the middle basin of Geum River. Paleolithic artifacts were collected at the surface of the sites in 1976 by Chungbuk National University Museum, and Loc. 1 was excavated through some test pits dug in January 2002. Excavation procedure is as follow Table 1.

Table 1 Excavation Procedure

Loc.	Trial-excavation	Excavation	Research Team
1	2002.1.		CBNUM
2	2005.8. – 9.	2005.12. – 2006.2.	IKP
3	2007.9. – 11.	2008.4. – 10. 2009.7. – 8.	IKP
4		2008.4. – 10.	IKP
5			IKP
41-3	2017.2. – 11.	2017.3. – 2017.12.	JCPI
873	2018.11.	2019.1. – 3.	HCHI

2. Paleolithic relics and formation process of Nosan-ri sites

Nosan-ri sites are divided into seven localities within a 1km range, located on the side of a Guem River terrace. Loc. 1, and Loc. 3 to Loc. 5, Loc. 873 are situated on the west side, and Loc. 2 and Loc. 41-3 are located on the east side. Each locality appeared from about over 50,000 BP to 20,000 BP(**Fig. 1**).

At Loc. 1, cultural layers were found in the western part of the excavation area. CL 1 yielded cores, hammer stones, choppers, and a plane, while CL 2 yielded a chopping tool, a blade, and a flake. Many carbon samples were also found in CL 1 and were dated to 31,700±900 BP by Accelerator Mass Spectrometry (AMS).

At Loc. 2, The site was divided into two areas (A, B-1). Most of the artifacts were found in the dark-brown layer with first soil wedge, including Upper Paleolithic cultural layers. Samples of soil and charcoal were found at the site and analyzed by AMS and optically stimulated luminescence (OSL). The dating results were 20,240±120 BP (OSL), 25,200±200 BP and 22,700±700 (AMS).

Most of the assemblage is composed of flakes, debris, cores, and blades, which are all related to tool production. Tools were also found, including side-scrapers, end-scrapers, tanged points, and microblades. Hornfels, tuff, and shale were mainly used for blade tools. On the other hand, some quartz and quartzite were used for making pebble tools, like choppers and chopping tools, and occasionally for small flake tools(**Fig. 2**).

The stratigraphy of Loc. 3 was classified into 13 layers, and two Paleolithic cultural layers were discovered, from which 1,780 artifacts were excavated; 1,642 from CL 1 and 84 from CL 2. Most of the raw materials used for the stone tools were quartz and quartzite, although porphyry was also employed. A large amount of the assemblage comprises cores, flakes, and debris, with retouched tools rarely present. Numerous refitted artifacts (100 pieces refitted into 26 individual groups) were found in CL 1, drawing much attention(**Fig. 3**).

Loc. 4 has nine layers, five of which are Paleolithic cultural layers. Tools such as choppers, chopping tools, and side-scrapers were found at the location. Heavy-duty tools, such as handaxes, picks, polyhedrons, and planes, were excavated intensively, and some light-duty tools, including denticulated tools, notched tools, and awls, were also found. Moreover, six concentrated areas of pebbles and seven hearths were unearthed. These seemed to be used as cooking spaces or fireplaces(**Fig. 4**).

The sedimentary condition of Loc. 5 is simple, with three

Fig. 1 Nosan-ri site Locations Satellite Picture

Fig. 2 Cultural layers and excavated artifacts from Nosan-ri site Loc. 2

layers and one cultural layer. The cultural layer was deposited on the upper part of the gravel layer, known as the 2nd terrace, and most of the artifacts, comprising cores, flakes, and polyhedrons, were excavated in this layer(**Fig. 5**).

Loc. 41-3 is located at the end of a low ridge slope between the 2 area of the Loc. 2. Paleolithic cultural layers were found in 4 clay layer, with 96 Paleolithic artifacts. Loc. 873 is discovered in a single cultural layer in a dark brown clay layer including soil wedges, and a total of 100 Paleolithic artifacts were excavated. Most of the raw materials used for the stone artifacts were quartz and quartzite in both sites.

3. Cultural phases of Nosan-ri sites

Through an analysis of the assemblage of artifacts and the dating of the cultural layer at Nosan-ri, Paleolithic culture in the whole Nosan-ri area was determined to consist of five cultural phases(**Fig. 6-9**).

Phase I : Late Middle Paleolithic culture, over 50,000 years ago, mainly used large pebble tools such as handaxes, picks, choppers, chopping tools, and polyhedrons, but also used light-duty tools, such as scrapers and notches. Most of the light-duty tools were made from thin flakes or debris with a natural narrow side edge. The cultural layers from this phase–i.e., CL 1 at Loc. 5 and CL 1 and 2 at Loc. 4–have some differences but also exhibit similar characteristics.

Phase II : Early Upper Paleolithic culture, 40,000 years ago,

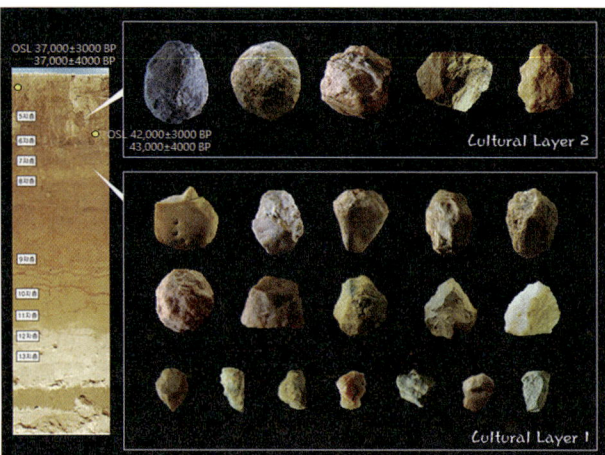

Fig. 3 Cultural layers and excavated artifacts from Nosan-ri site Loc. 3

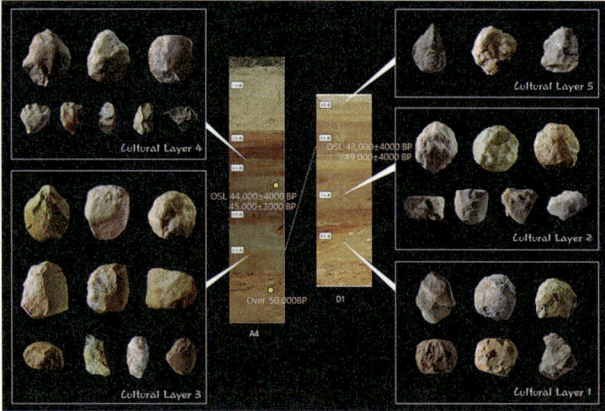

Fig. 4 Cultural layer and excavated artifacts from Nosan-ri site Loc. 4

Fig. 5 Cultural layer and excavated artifacts Nosan-ri site Loc. 5

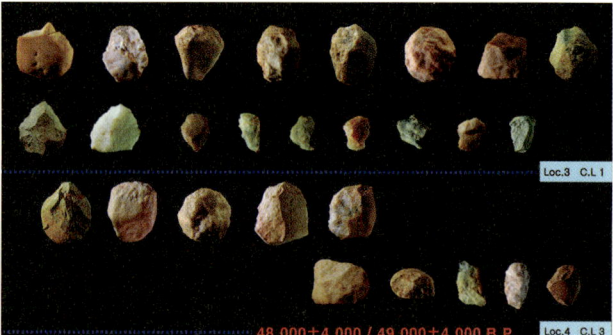

Fig. 6 Late Middle Paleolithic era 50,000 years ago artifacts

Fig. 7 Eary Upper Paleolithic era 40,000 years ago artifacts

Fig. 8 Middle Upper Paleolithic era from 30,000 years ago artifacts

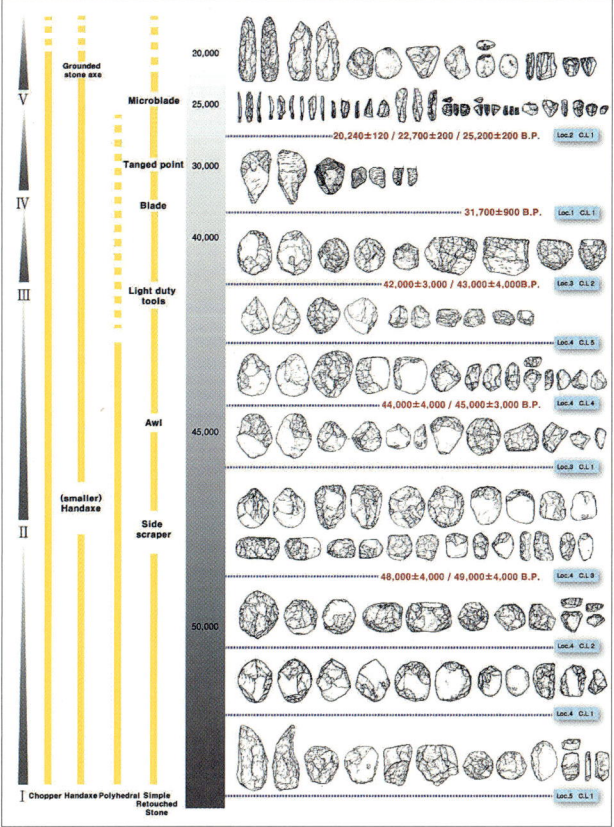

Fig. 9 5 cultural phases at Nosan-ri Paleolithic sites

made small handaxes and scrapers that were retouched on both sides of the edge or on a round edge. These stone tools were found in CL 3 at Loc. 4 and CL 1 at Loc. 3.

Phase III : Middle Upper Paleolithic culture, 30,000 years ago, made light-duty tools made from flakes, which became increasingly more common and diversified. Some tools especially, such as awls, becs, and burins, made from elongated flakes began to appear in this phase. On the other hand, polyhedron tools decreased. In addition to existing tool production systems with quartz and quartzite, a new method with fine-grained raw materials, such as tuff, rhyolite, and shale, appeared in CL 4 at Loc. 4 and CL 2 at Loc. 3 and are associated with this phase.

Phase IV : In this phase, blade tool production was beginning and the pebble tool production system was gradually declining. Fine-grained raw materials, like tuff and hornfels, were actively used for making tools. Also, tanged points appeared.

Phase V : The blade production technique became more developed, and microblade technology emerged. Both technologies were found together in the same cultural layer at Loc. 2. Moreover, an edge-ground stone axe was found at Loc. 2. It is of keen interest to estimate the elements of the cultural transition from the Late Upper Paleolithic to the initial Neolithic Period in Northeast Asia.

4. Conclusion

The Paleolithic culture of the Nosan-ri area, In the Late Middle Paleolithic (over 50,000 years ago), flake tools had naturally formed narrow edges or were made from thin flakes. By the Early and Middle Upper Paleolithic (40,000–30,000 years ago), small handaxes, scrapers, and diverse light-duty tools became more common, with the use of fine-grained raw materials like tuff and rhyolite. In the later Upper Paleolithic (20,000 years ago and beyond), blade tool production advanced, pebble tool use declined, and technologies like microblades and edge-ground stone axes emerged.

Various cultures were influenced by each site, and have distinctive characteristic. Therefore, archaeological analysis of the Nosan-ri Paleolithic sites can not only provide fundamental data on tool production techniques from the Middle Paleolithic to the end of the Late Paleolithic, but also serve as an important source for understanding changes in cultural characteristics and site structures around the Geum River Basin.

References

Ambiru, M., 2007. Japanese Paleolithic culture and Korean peninsula, *Archaeology Quaarterly* 100, Yuzankaku Press, 23-27. (in Japanese)

Anderfsky, Jr. William. 1998. *Lithics–Macroscopic approaches to analysis*, Cambridge University Press.

Gongju national museum. 2005. *The Paleolithic age culture of the Guemgang*. (in Korean with English abstract)

Kim, H.I., 2004. Yongsandong Paleolithic site, Daejon–with focus on the preliminary excavation–. *Journal of the Korean Palaeolitihc society* 10, The Korean Palaeolithic society, 83-94. (in Korean with English abstract)

Lee, H.J., 2008. Study of comparison of microblade core technical system of Upper Paleolithic in Northeast Asia. *Journal of North-East Asian cultures* 16, The Association of North-east Asian Cultures, 83-108. (in Korean with English abstract)

Lee, Y.J., Lee, S.W., Otani, K., 2011. *Nosanri Paleolithic site (Loc. 3, 4, 5), Cheongwon*, Institute of Korean Prehistory.

Lee, Y.J., Lee, S.W., Otani, K., 2014. *Nosanri Paleolithic site (Loc. 2), Cheongwon*, Institute of Korean Prehistory.

Otani, K., 2010. Microlithic culture in the Korean Peninsula. *Journal of the Japanese Paleolithic Archaeology* 73, 1-12. (in Japanese with English abstract)

Otani, K., 2012. Microlithic technology and raw materials use in Korea. *Journal of the Hoseo Archaeological Society* 26, 4-37. (in Korean with English abstract)

Otani, K., 2014. Paleolithic culture in Korean Peninsula. *Archaeology Quarterly* 126, 45-48. (in Japanese)

Otani, K., 2021. Site Formation and Cultural Characteristic of Paleolithic Site in the Middle Guem River Basin : Focus on the Nosan-ri Loc. 2. *Journal of the Korean Palaeolithic Society* 43, 71-106. https://doi.org/10.52954/kps.2021.1.43.71

Park, Y.A., Gong, U.S., Im, D.I., Kim, J.Y., Yun, S.O., Hwang, S.I., Chang, J.H., Cho, H.R., 2001. Stratigraphy and environment of the late quaternary. *Korea. Environment of the late Quaternary in Korea*, Seoul National University press, 3-155. (in Korean)

Yun, B.I., 2014. *The Analysis of Cores to the Aspects of Production and the Making Process in Nosan-ri Paleolithic Site Loc. 3, 4.* Dissertation of Ph. M. of University of Seoul.

Growth and Status of Paleolithic Research in Southwestern Korea

Gi-kil LEE

Professor Emeritus, Chosun University, Korea ; kklee@chosun.ac.kr

ABSTRACT

Paleolithic research in southwestern Korea (the Honam region) commenced only in the late 1980s, more than 20 years later than in other regions in Korea. However, over the past 30 years, Paleolithic research has developed rapidly; the accumulated achievements are impressive. Many Paleolithic sites have been discovered and excavated, and a great deal of archaeological materials, such as artifacts, features, and ecofacts (e.g., Pleistocene deposits) have been retrieved. Subsequent research has broadened our understanding of the lithic assemblage and technologies of the MIS 4~MIS 2 stages and established a chronology based on absolute dates and stratigraphic data. Site geographical types and functions have been described, as have human behaviors that persist today, such as decorations, long-distance networking, and cultural exchange between the Korean Peninsula and the Japanese Archipelago.

국문초록

1986년에 시작된 호남 구석기 고고학은 어느덧 37주년을 맞이하였다. 그동안 많은 유적과 함께 석기제작소, 돌화덕, 집자리 등의 유구, 그리고 10만 점 이상으로 추산되는 다양한 유물이 확보되었다. 이를 바탕으로 호남 구석기시대의 편년과 석기군의 변천, 석기의 형식과 제작 기술, 유적의 성격, 백두산과 고시다케산 흑요석기에 근거한 원거리교류망, 붉은 안료인 철석영이 암시하는 정신세계, 나아가 현생인류의 행위 요소 등 다양한 분야의 연구에서 진전이 있었다. 남부지역 구석기인의 일본열도로 이주, 그리고 지속적인 교류의 증거들이 증가하는 상황에서 인접한 일본열도의 구석기문화를 이해하고 새로운 성과와 연구 동향을 주시할 때, 구석기시대의 호남이 가지는 가치가 객관적으로 평가되고 향후 조사와 연구의 지향점을 제대로 설정할 수 있을 것이다.

Keywords: Honam Paleolithic research, continuity of cultural tradition, Japanese Archipelago, cultural exchange, modern human migration

1. Growth of Paleolithic research

1.1. Discovery of many Paleolithic sites

By 2017, the number of reported Paleolithic sites in the Honam region numbered 405, in great contrast to the four or five sites known just 30 years ago (Lee, 2017). However, the number of sites is estimated to be more than 600. This remarkable achievement is attributable to the dedicated surface surveys of major basins of the Boseonggang, Yeongsangang, Seomjingang, and Geumgang rivers and various islands by Paleolithic researchers from Chosun, Mokpo National, and Chonbuk National Universities in the 1990s and 2000s (Lee, 1997a, 2020; Lee, 1997, 2015; Lee et al., 2009).

Pleistocene deposits with rich information on the natural environment are important when establishing a relative chronology. Such deposits generally feature layers of gravel, silty sands, and clay that may be red, yellow, or dark or light brown. The gravel and silty sand layers formed during the last interglacial period, and the clay layer formed during the last glacial period. Most cultural information is contained in the clay and silty sand layers; from one to five cultural layers have been found at each site. The deposits of representative sites, such as the Juknae-ri, Dosan, Gusan, Wolpyeong, and Jingeneul sites, are important records when reconstructing the Korean environment over the last 100,000 years (Lee, 2018a, 2020; Lee et al., 2020) (Fig. 1).

Geographical conditions and site sizes were important criteria when Paleolithic people selected campsites. For example, 85 sites have been found in the Boseonggang River basin and can be classified as "waterfront hill," "independent hill," "basin hill," and "moat hill" types. The sites may be small (around 17,500m²), medium (about 35,000m²), large (around 70,000m²), or extra large (over 100,000m²) (Lee, 2020). Many sites are of the waterfront hill type. Of all sites, about 50% are small and about 25% are medium. Both the extra-large Sinbuk site of the basin hill type and the large Wolpyeong site of the moat hill type could accommodate many people and are assumed to have been base camps. On the other hand, the Jingeuneul site on the sun-starved northern slope of an anonymous mountain is presumed to be a hunting camp given the limited kinds of stone tools, although 99 tanged points were recovered. In addition, prey

Fig. 1a Stratigraphy of Dosan site

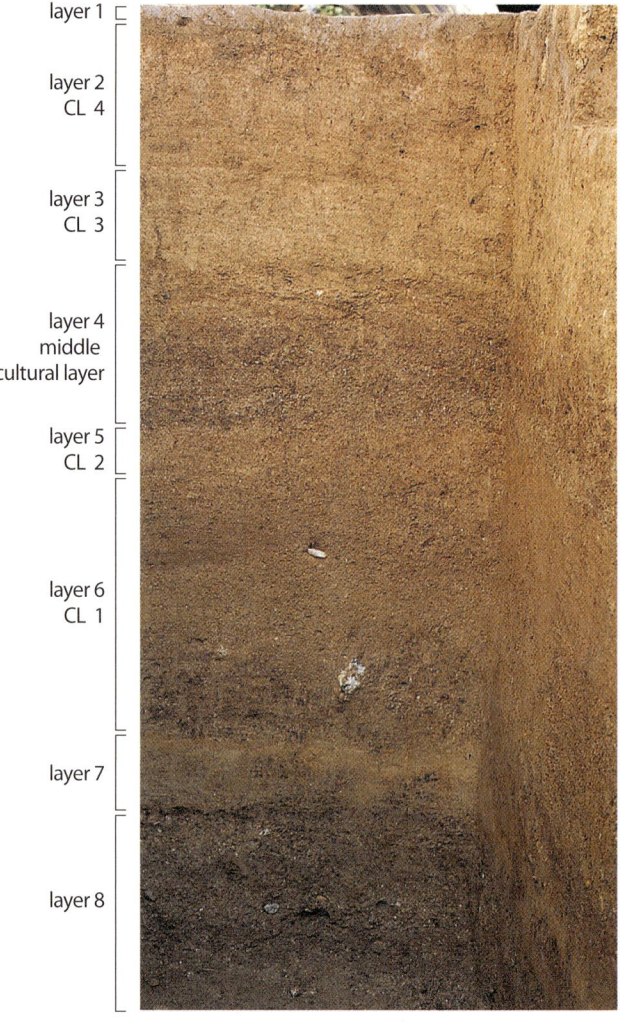

Fig. 1b Stratigraphy of Wolpyeong site

Fig. 2a The basin hill type (Sinbuk site)

Fig. 2b The moat hell type (Wolpyeong site)

Fig. 2c The waterfront type (Jingeuneul site)

could be driven through the narrow valley (Lee and Sano, 2019) (**Fig. 2**).

Of all sites, more than 70 have been excavated. The Chipyeong-dong and Jingeuneul sites were the first to be excavated in the Yeongsangang River basin and Jeollabuk-do, respectively. The Wolpyeong site has been designated a National Historical Site, while the Juknae-ri, Sinbuk, and Haga sites are considered monuments; these sites honor the Paleolithic culture of southwestern Korea (Lee, 1997b, 2017, 2018a, 2020).

1.2. Artifacts and features

Artifacts and features were collected during surface surveys and excavations. Up to 2010, the artifacts numbered 68,900 (Han, C.G., 2010). However, it is estimated that the number will increase to more than 100,000 because some surface surveys and excavations performed in the last 13 years have remain uncalculated. The artifacts include various heavy-duty and light-duty tools, hammers, anvils, and ground stone tools. The heavy-duty tools contain choppers, chopping tools, handaxes, picks, cleavers, polyhedrons, spheroids, bolas, heavy scrapers, heavy end-scrapers, heavy notches, heavy denticulates, and heavy awls. The light-duty tools are composed of scrapers, end-scrapers, notches, denticulates, awls, burins, backed knives, tanged points, knife-shaped tools, and leaf-shaped points. Also present are mortar-shaped stone tools and grinded boulders with parallel fine striations, which were used for processing various materials (Lee ed., 2009; Lee, 2018b) (**Fig. 3**).

Lithic workshops and hearths have also been found. Workshops with conjoining stone artifacts, either cores and flakes or tools and flakes, have been unearthed at the

Fig. 3a Mortar-shaped stone tool (Haga site)

Fig. 3b Grinded boulder with parellel fine striations (Wolpyeong site)

Juknae-ri, Dosan, Wolpyeong, Haga, Jingeuneul and other sites (Lee et al., 2000; Lee et al., 2008; Lee and Kim, 2009; Lee, 2018a; Lee, ed., 2021) (**Fig. 4**). Analyses have revealed the shapes and sizes of the raw materials preferred by Paleolithic knappers, the manufacturing processes of stone tools, and the intention of knappers during the Middle to Upper Paleolithic.

Stone hearths have been excavated at Upper Paleolithic sites, including the Sinbuk, Sinwol, Wolpyeong and Maejuk-ri sites (Lee et al., 2008; Dongguk Institute of Cultural Properties, 2018, 2019; Lee et al., 2020; Nara Institute of Cultural Heritage, 2020). There are two types of round hearth: an enclosure type with a diameter of about 1m, and a stacked type with a diameter of about 60cm. The former type was found at the Maejuk-ri site, and the latter type was found at the Sinbuk, Sinwol, and Wolpyeong sites (**Fig. 5**).

Seven hearths were found at the Sinbuk site, of which four were in an area of 4.5×13.2m. On the other hand, at the Maejuk-ri site, four hearths were located in an area of 7×19m separated by distances of about 2-15m. Stone hearths are advanced compared to bonfires. Although no post-holes were detected around the hearths, it is possible that simple huts were located near the hearths. The several hearths at one site suggest that the number of residents was relatively large and that the sites served as base camps.

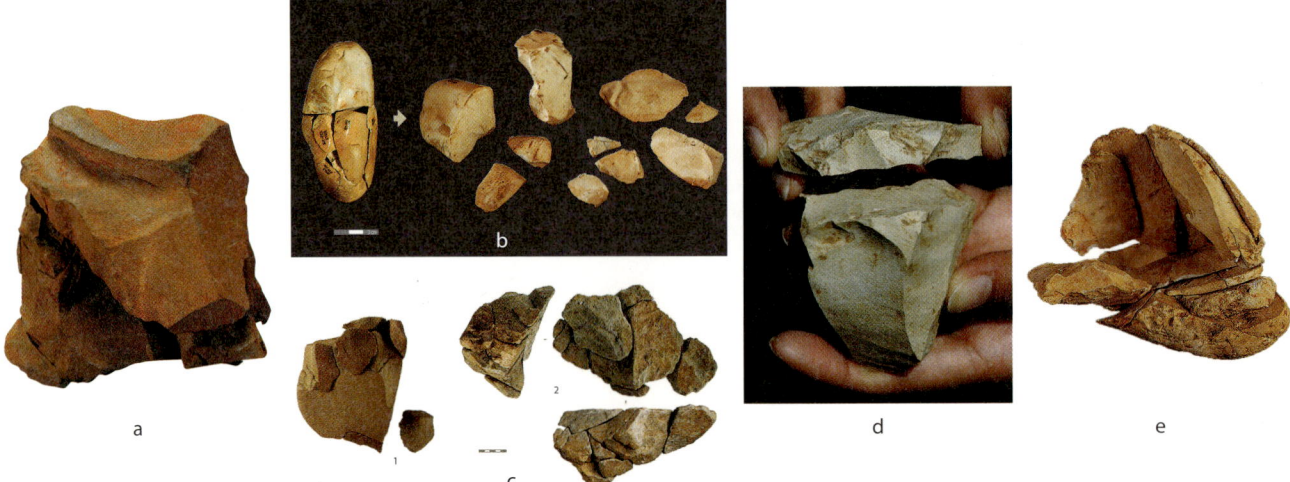

Fig. 4a Conjoining core and flakes (1st Cultural layer of the Jucknaeri site)
Fig. 4b Conjoinung core and flakes (4th Cultural layer of the Jucknaeri site)
Fig. 4c Conjoining core and flakes (Sinbuk site)
Fig. 4d Conjoining bladecore and rejuvenation flake
Fig. 4e Conjoining microbladecore and flakes (Wolpyeong site)

Fig. 5a Enclosure type hearth (Maejuckri site)

Fig. 6 Lithic assemblage of 2nd culturlal layer of Dosan site

Fig. 5b Stacked type Hearth (Sinbuk site)

Fig. 7 Lithic assemblage of Middle cultural layer of Wolpyeong site

1.3. Paleolithic industry and chronology

Four stratified cultural layers have been unearthed at the Dosan, Jucknaeri and Seokpyeong sites (Lee et al., 2000; Kim and Song, 2012; Lee, 2018a). At Dosan, the four cultural layers span about 5m of the Pleistocene deposit, allowing reliable absolute dating of each layer. Juknae-ri is similar to Dosan but, unfortunately, the absolute dates were not measured. The Pleistocene deposit at Seokpyeong is only about half as thick as that at other sites, and the reliability of absolute dating is very low. Therefore, currently, Dosan is the most suitable site when studying the basic Paleolithic chronology of southwestern Korea. The Paleolithic sites in Honam correspond to MIS 4~MIS 2, or the late Middle to Upper Paleolithic (**Table 1**).

The lithic assemblages of the first and second cultural layers at Dosan feature heavy-duty and light-duty tools, with about twice as many of the former than the latter (**Fig. 6**). Of the heavy-duty tools, heavy scrapers and end-scrapers are the most common, accompanied by heavy notches and denticulates. Such heavy-duty tools may have been used to trim branches and make spear shafts. Some light-duty tools are very finely retouched and are thus difficult to distinguish from those of the Upper Paleolithic. The second cultural layer at Seokpyeong is similar, as is the first cultural layer at Juknae-ri, but the latter site includes many large tuff flakes that served as the blanks for heavy-duty tools.

The third cultural layer at Dosan yielded only a few stone tools but included heavy-duty tools such as picks. The middle cultural layer at Wolpyeong also yielded heavy-

Table 1 Published books on Honam Paleolithic culture

Year	Title	Author
2006	Illustrated Book of the Paleolithic Sites in the Honam Region: Jucknaeri, Dosan, Wondang, and Wolpyeong sites	Lee, G.K.
2006	The Paleolithic Archaeology and Quaternary Geology in Yeongsan River Region	Lee, H.J. et al.
2009	Splendid Relics of Honam Region from 100,000 years ago	Lee, G.K.
2015	Island Archaeology: Appearance and Sea Development of Paleolithic Humam Being in the Southwest Coast of Korea	Lee, H.J.
2018	The Study of Paleolithic Culture in Southwestern Korea	Lee, G.K.
2018	Paleolithic Paradise, Boseong River	Lee, G.K.
2020	Paleolithic Culture of the Boseong River basin in Southwestern Korea: Survey and Research since 1986	Lee, G.K.

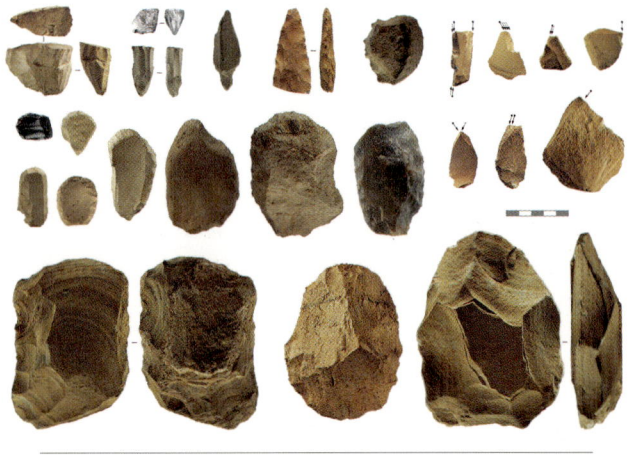

Fig. 8b Lithic assemblage of Haga site

Fig. 8a Lithic assemblage of Sinbuk site

Fig. 8c Lithic assemblage of the 4th cultural layer of Wolpyeong site

duty and light-duty tools, principally the latter, and long rectangular flakes of vein quartz cobble, but no blade or microblade tools (Lee and Kim, 2009) (Fig. 7).

The lithic assemblages of Sinbuk, Jingeunuel, Haga, and the third and fourth cultural layers at Wolpyeong yielded light-duty tools that were more standardized and sophisticated than the earlier tools and, for the first time, blade and microblade tools; heavy-duty tool numbers declined. This era was characterized by various hunting tools, end-scrapers, burins, and awls. In addition, a few polished axes and U-shaped flaked axes were found (Lee, 2020; Lee, ed., 2021) (Fig. 8).

In summary, heavy-duty tools predominated, accompanied by some light-duty tools, in the lithic assemblages of MIS 4 to the first half of MIS 3. However, in the second half of MIS 3 to MIS 2, light-duty tools were dominant, and new blade and microblade tools appeared, together with Neolithic elements such as polished axes. Thus, the Upper Paleolithic was characterized by innovation and the decline of tradition; elements that would become popular in the next era began to appear (Fig. 9).

1.4. Long-distance networking and cultural exchange

At the Sinbuk site only, obsidian from Mt. Paektusan and Mt. Koshidake of the Korean Peninsula and the Japanese

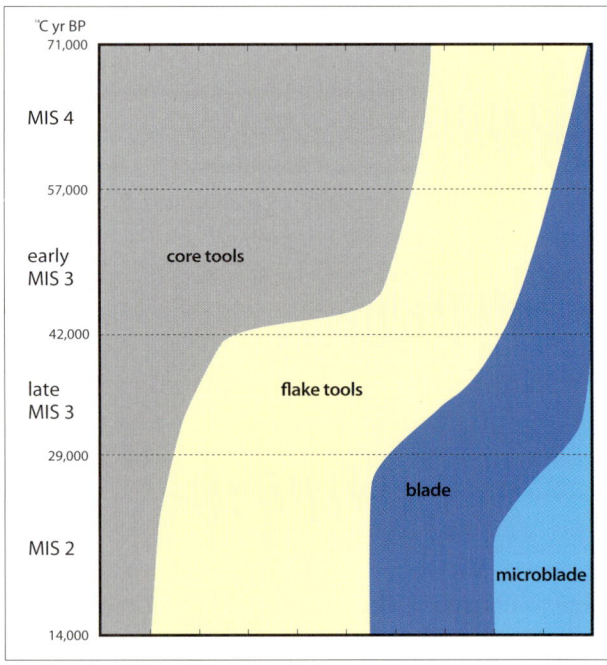

Fig. 9 Development of Lithic assemblagages during MIS 4- MIS 2 stages

Archipelago, respectively, were discovered (Lee and Kim, 2015) (Fig. 10). Thus, Paleolithic people in the Boseong River basin were connected to both the northern part of the Korean Peninsula and Japan. Networking extended over a straight-line distance that exceeded 800km, and Sinbuk was a major base of southwestern Korea where people exchanged information, raw materials, and so on from distant areas. Such long-distance networking may have ensured the viability of the Paleolithic people (Fig. 11). Haga has yielded knife-shaped tools and "Kakusuijyo-sekki," which were thought to be uniquely Japanese tools. These tools were found together with Korean tanged points (Lee, 2011) (Fig. 12). Kakusuijyo-sekki appeared 21,000 years ago in the Japanese Archipelago, but those of the Haga site were radiocarbon dated to 23,500 BP. Thus, it is now interpreted that the tools originated on the Korean Peninsula and were exported to Kyushu (Sato, H., 2018). Light-duty tools and flakes made of not only Koshidake obsidian but also Taku Sanukite have been excavated in southwestern Korea, and tanged points were popular in Kyushu for thousands of years after 29,000 BP (Fig. 13). Thus, cultural exchange between the Korean Peninsula and the Japanese Archipelago continued during the Upper Paleolithic. Clearly, people crossed the Korean Strait (Matsufuji, 1987; Oppenheimer, 2009; Ikeya, 2015; Ambiru, 2020).

Korean Paleolithic sites feature very few mineral pigments. Black graphite was excavated at Hopyeongdong and red ferruginous quartz pebble was found at Sinbuk (Hong and Kim, 2008; Lee et al., 2008) (Fig. 14). In Eurasia, red ochre was used in funeral ceremonies during the Upper Paleolithic. Today, the Himba people of Namibia apply ochres to their skin and hair. The red ferruginous

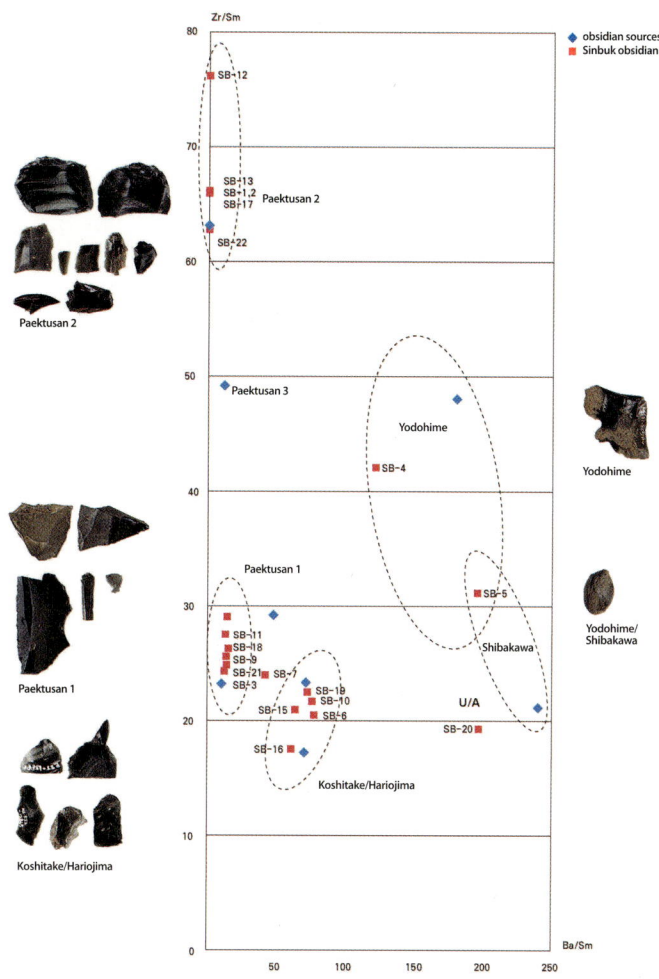

Fig. 10 Obsidians from Mt. Paektusan and Mt. Koshidake

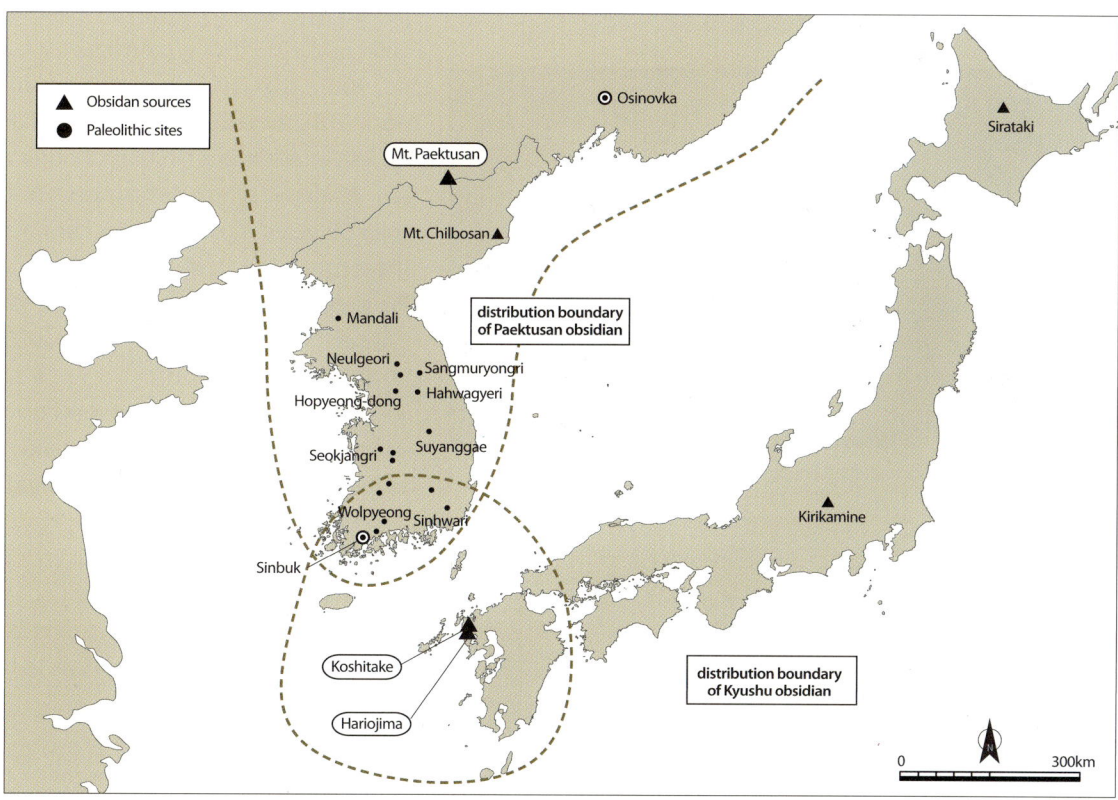

Fig. 11 Long-distance network extended over 800km during Upper Paleolithic Age

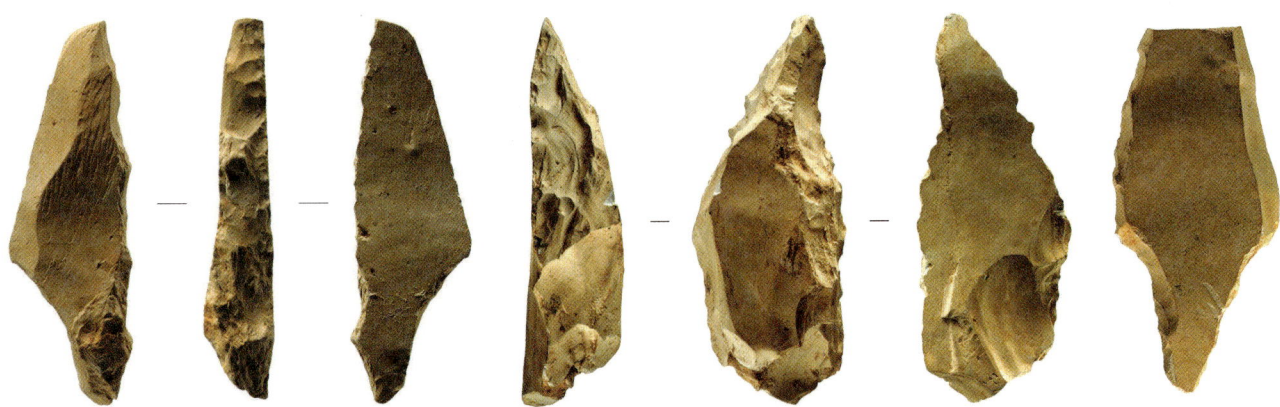

Fig. 12a Knife-shpaped tools (Haga site) **Fig. 12b** Kakusuijyo-sekki (Haga site) **Fig. 12c** Tanged-point (Haga site)

Fig. 13 Obsidian tools made of Koshidake obsidian and flake made of Takku sanukite (Wolpyeong and Naeu sites)

Fig. 14 Red ferruginous quartz pebble and black graphite

in domestic and overseas academic journals, and 23 dissertations have been completed (Lee, 2018). Most papers have reported on newly discovered artifacts and sites, enhancing our understanding of the lithic industry and the local chronology. Some studies have adopted novel perspectives or used advanced methods to determine the provenances of raw materials (Lee, 2018).

The Honam Archaeological Society and the Korean Paleolithic Society held conferences on the Paleolithic Age of southwestern Korea in 2001 and 2018, respectively. The Honam Archaeological Society treated the Paleolithic period as a session of the annual meetings of 2004 and 2013 (Honam Archaeological Society, ed., 2001, 2004, 2013; Korean Paleolithic Society, ed., 2018). Although Paleolithic archaeology is no less interesting than that of other eras, only four academic symposia have been held in more than 30 years. However, four commemorative international symposia on the Sinbuk, Wolpyeong, and Haga sites were hosted by Chosun University Museum (Lee, ed., 2004, 2014, 2018, 2020) **(Table 2, Fig. 15)**.

The following quotes from a number of researchers writing over 20 years reflect the changes in status of the Paleolithic Age in the Honam Region:

quartz may have been part of their group identity and spiritual beliefs during the Korean Paleolithic (Lee, 2021).

2. Status of Paleolithic research

Over the past 30 years, more than 100 articles on the Paleolithic culture of the Honam region have been published

"The Honam region is emerging as the most important area for new Paleolithic research…. The biggest achievement is the discovery of sites scattered in the river basin, and research on these lithic tools and sites is a task to be started in the future" (Bae, 2001).

"The Paleolithic research in Honam region has seen remarkable growth over a short period of time. It would not

Table 2 Conferences on Paleolithic Age and Sites in the Honam Region

Year	Title	Host
2001	Paleolithic Culture of Honam Region	Honam Archaeological Society
2004	The achievements and Issue of Honam Archaeology seen from the outside	Honam Archaeological Society
2004	Evaluating the Cultural Features of the Sinbuk Upper Paeolithic Site in the Northeastern Asia	Jangheung County, Jeollanam-do, The Residents' Group for Preservation of the Sinbuk Paleolithic Site, and Chosun Univ. Museum
2013	20 years of Honam Archaeological Society, its retrospect and prospect	Honam Archaeological Society
2014	Academic Value and Creative Application of the Wolpyeong Historic Site	Chosun Univ. Museum and The Residents' Group for Preservation of the Wolpyeong Paleolithic Site
2018	The Value of Cultural Heritage and Application Plan of Haga Site in Imsil County	Imsil Culture Center and Chosun Univ. Museum
2018	Achievement and Status of Paleolithic Research in Honam Region	Korean Paleolithic Society
2020	From Paleolithic to Future: The Value and Application of the Paleolithic Culture of the Sinbuk Site and Boseong River Basin	Jangheung County and Dept. History of Chosun Univ.

Fig. 15 Conferences on Paleolithic Age and Sites in the Honam Region

be an exaggeration to say that it is now taking a pioneering position not only in terms of the number of sites and the quality of the accumulated data, but also in terms of the level of research" (Bae, 2004).

"The excavation and research results made in a short period of more than 20 years are considered to have a very remarkable archaeological value in Korean paleolithic research. In particular, the achievements accumulated through co-work with the natural science are expected to contribute greatly to the study of Paleolithic in Korea" (Han, 2010).

"The level of Paleolithic research in Honam region is evaluated as a time of understanding beyond the discovery period.... With the increase of sites discovered and excavated around major water systems, a new trial of understanding of human behavior is being sought beyond simply identifying the existence of sites. Currently, many Paleolithic records found in Honam region is becoming valuable data and an attractive research subject for Paleolithic research in East Asia as well as the Korean Peninsula" (Lee, 2013).

"In the middle of the Upper Paleolithic... At that time, it seems that people and materials frequently moved between the southern part of the Korean Peninsula and the Kyushu area. The obsidian native to Koshidake excavated from the Boseonggang River basin and the tanged points made in large quantities at the origin of Taku and Ogi andesite provenance must be evidence of this.... In this way, the Paleolithic history of Korea and Japan, which is the contact point between the Boseonggang River basin and the Koshidake-Taku·Ogi area, will be understood. In this sense, the Boseonggang River basin and the Koshidake-Taku·Ogi area are the long-standing origin of the "Korea-Japan Exchange" that dates back to the Paleolithic Age" (Ambiru, 2020).

To date, seven books by local researchers have described the outcomes of research on the Yeongsangang River basin, the southwest coast and islands, and the Boseonggang, Seomjingang, and Geumgang River basins (**Table 3, Fig. 16**).

3. Future challenges

Honam Paleolithic studies have proceeded for nearly 40 years, since 1986. Many lithic workshops and hearths, and more than 100,000 stone artifacts, have been discovered at a number of sites. The developments include a better understanding of the chronology of the Paleolithic Age, the identification of various lithic assemblages, and an understanding of manufacturing techniques, the functions of sites, long-distance networking, and modern human behaviors.

However, archaeologists have not found sites older than about 70,000 years or those of the Early Upper Paleolithic

Table 3 Published papers on Honam Paleolithic culture

Year	Title	Author
2001	A Study on the Paleolithic Research Results and Current Issues in Honam Region	Park, Y.C.
2004	Achievements and Prospects of Paleolithic Archaeology in Honam Region	Bae, K.D.
2010	20 Years of Excavation of Paleolithic sites in Honam Area	Han, C.G.
2010	Paleolithic Age and Culture in Honam Region from the Perspective of Japanese Archipelago	Ambiru, M.
2013	A Study on the Paleolithic Age in Honam: Summary and Prospects	Lee, H.W.
2014	The Status of Wolpyeong Site from the Perspective of the East Asian Paleolithic Age	Ambiru, M.
2014	Meaning and Value of Wolpyeong Site in Korean Paleolithic Research	Lee, H.J.
2017	Review on Paleolithic Survey and Research in Honam Region since 1986	Lee, G.K.
2018	International Status of Imsil Haga Paleolithic site	Sagawa, M.
2018	Paleolithic Culture of Honam Region of the Korean Peninsula from the Perspective of Japanese Archipelago	Sato, H.
2018	Performance and Prospect of Paleolithic Research in Honam Region	Lee, H.W.
2020	The Long-standing "Korea-Japan Exchange" with the Paleolithic People in the Boseonggang River Basin	Ambiru, M.

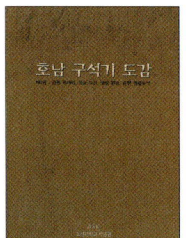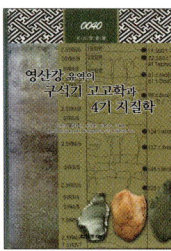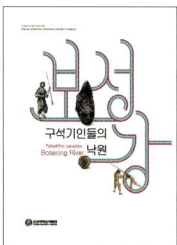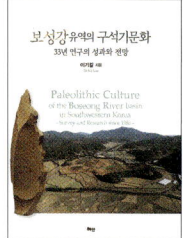

Fig. 16 Books on Paleolithic culture in the Honam region

in southwestern Korea. The early cultural layer of the Upper Paleolithic must be somewhere. In addition, where are the early stages of the Middle Paleolithic? Surface surveys must continue.

In the past, South Korean scholars suggested that the Korean Peninsula was vacant for about 3,000–4,000 years after the last glacial period and that Paleo-Asia and Tungus ethnic groups were the occupants during the Neolithic and Bronze Ages, respectively. North Korean scholars have explained that the nation originated in the Upper Paleolithic, and the blood-related, linguistic, regional, and cultural commonalities of the Korean people formed during the Bronze Age (Kim, W.Y., 1983; Kim, J.B., 1973; Jang, W.J., 2009). Evidence bearing on the continuity of cultural tradition has been discovered in the Paleolithic records of the Honam and other regions. For example, Upper Paleolithic leaf-shaped points excavated at Sinbuk and Wolpyeong were also found at the Early Neolithic Gosan-ri site of Jeju Island (Lee et al., 1998; Go et al., 2014, 2016) (**Fig. 17**). The bifacial arrowhead termed "Yugyeong Cheomdugi" was discovered at the

Fig. 17a Leaf-shaped bifacial points (Wolpyeong and Sinbuk sites)

Fig. 17b Leaf-shaped bifacial points (Gosanri site)

Fig. 18 Yugyeong cheomdugi (Stemmed point, Seoduri 2 site)

Seoduri 2 site in Iksan city and at early Jomon sites in the Japanese Archipelago (Han et al., 2013) (Fig. 18). At locality C of the Osan-ri site, the Upper Paleolithic and the Early Neolithic cultural layer were adjacent; the former was on top (Jeong, Y.W. et al., 2010). Such findings suggest that the ethnic group originated after the Upper Paleolithic.

In 2003, the Japanese Archeology Society claimed that the Lower and Middle Paleolithic sites were fakes; in other words, the Japanese Archipelago was empty before the Upper Paleolithic (Japanese Archaeological Association, ed., 2003; Ono, A. and Yamada, M., 2012). To overcome this potential embarrassment, the Japanese Paleolithic Society focused on research on modern humans. Projects titled "Replacement of Neanderthals by Modern Humans: Testing Evolutionary Models of Learning" and "Cultural History of Paleo Asia" ran from 2010 to 2020 (Akazawa, T. ed., 2012; Nishiaki et al. eds., 2018). Japanese researchers became more interested in the neighboring Korean Paleolithic, particularly that of the Honam region. For example, Sagawa Masatoshi of Tohoku Gakuin University was a visiting scholar at Chosun University for one year from 2011 and published several papers (Sagawa, M., 2018).

Today, the major issues are the migration of modern humans to the Japanese Archipelago from the southern part of the Korean Peninsula and the cultural exchanges between the two regions. Paleolithic researchers of the Honam region must approach their local Paleolithic study from a global perspective, with a particular focus on Japanese Paleolithic culture and research achievements. It will then be possible to recognize the significant potential of the Paleolithic culture of southwestern Korea and reset the desirable research directions.

References

Akazawa, T. ed., 2012. *Replacement of Neanderthals by Modern Humans: Testing Evolutionary Models of Learning*. Research Institute, Kochi University of Technology.

Ambiru, M., 2010. Paleolithic Age and Culture of Honam Region from the Japanese Archipelago. *Splendid Relics of Honam Region from 100,000 years ago*, Chosun Univ. Museum, 128-149. (In Japanese)

Ambiru, M., 2014. The Status of Wolpyeong Historic Site from the perspective of East Asian Paleolithic Study. *Academic Value and Creative Application of Wolpyeong Historic Site*, Chosun Univ. Museum, 25-38. (In Japanese)

Ambiru, M., 2020. Paleolithic People in Boseong River Basin and Long-lasting Korea-Japan Exchange. *From Paleolithic to Future: The Value and Application of the Paleolithic Culture of the Sinbuk Site and Boseong River Basin*, Chosun Univ. Museum, 60-77. (In Japanese)

Bae, K.D., 2001. Discussion about the Review on the Results and Issues of Paleolithic Research in Honam Region. *Paleolithic Culture of Honam Region*, Honam Archaeological Society, 95-96. (In Korean)

Bae, K.D., 2004. The Achievements and Prospects of Paleolithic Archaeology in Honam Region. *The achievements and Issue of Honam Archaeology seen from the outside*, Honam Archaeological Society, 15-21. (In Korean)

Dongguk Institute of Cultural Properties. 2018. *Preliminary excavation report on Bukkyori Sinwol site in Jangheung county*. (In Korean)

Dongguk Institute of Cultural Properties. 2019. *Additional Preliminary excavation report on Bukkyori Sinwol site in Jangheung county*. (In Korean)

Go, J.W. et al., 2014. *The Jeju Gosan-ri site*, Jeju Cultural Heritage Institute. (In Korean)

Go, J.W. et al., 2016. *The Jeju Gosan-ri site II*, Jeju Cultural Heritage Institute. (In Korean)

Han, C.G., 2010. 20 Years of Paleolithic Excavation in Honam Region. *Splendid Relics of Honam Region from 100,000 years ago*, Chosun Univ. Museum, 108-127. (In Korean)

Han, S.Y., Kim, M.R., Lee, C.S., 2013. *Iksan Seoduri 2 · Bosamri Site*, Honam Cultural Property Research Center. (In Korean)

Honam Archaeological Society ed., 2001. *Paleolithic Culture of Honam Region*. (In Korean)

Honam Archaeological Society ed., 2004. *The achievements and Issue of Honam Archaeology seen from the outside*. (In Korean)

Honam Archaeological Society ed., 2013. *20 years of Honam Archaeological Society, its retrospect and prospect.* (In Korean)

Hong, M.Y. and Kim, J.H., 2008. *Hopyeong-dong Paleolithic site (Namyangju, Gyeonggi Province, Korea)* II, Gijeon Institute of Cultural Properties. (In Korean)

Ikeya, N., 2015. Maritime Transport of Obsidian in Japan during the Upper Paleolithic. *Emergence and Diversity of "Modern" Human Behavior in Paleolithic Asia*, Texas A&M University Press, 362-375.

Jang, W.J., 2009. *The Origin and Formation of Korean*, Social Science Publishing Co. (In Korean)

Japanese Archaeological Association ed., 2003. *Inspection of the Early and Middle Palaeolithic Problem in Japan*, Simoda Printing Co., Ltd. (In Japanese)

Jeong, Y.W. et al., 2010. *Yangyang Osanri Site: Excavation Report at Road construction area from Yeounpo to Songjeon in Yangyang County*, Yemaek Culture Research Center. (In Korean)

Kim, J.B., 1973. *Origins of Korean National Culture*, Korea Univ. Press. (In Korean)

Kim, J.Y., and Song, J.S., 2012. *Report on the Excavation of the Doan-ri Seokpyeong III Site in the Boseong*, Mahan Culture Research Center. (In Korean)

Kim, W.Y., 1983. *Introduction to Korean Archaeology* 2nd ed., Iljisa publishing co. (In Korean)

Korean Paleolithic Society ed., 2018. *Achievement and Status of Paleolithic Research in Honam Region.* (In Korean)

Lee, C.G. et al., 1998. *Jeju Gosan-ri site*, Jeju Univ. Museum. (In Korean)

Lee, E.J., An, H.S., Lee, D.S., 2020. Jeongeup Maejukri Paleolithic Site. *Paleolithic Research and Natural Science Analysis*, The Korean Paleolithic Society, 83-95. (In Korean)

Lee, G.K., 1997a. Preliminary Report on the newly discovered Paleolithic Sites on the Boseong River Basin. *Hanguk Koko-Hakbo* No. 37, 7-62.

Lee, G.K., 1997b. *Kwangju Chipyeongdong Paleolithic Site*, Chosun Univ. Museum. (In Korean)

Lee, G.K., Choi, M.N., Kim, E.J., 2000. *Soonchon Jungnae-ri site*, Chosun Univ. Museum. (In Korean)

Lee, G.K. ed., 2004. *Evaluating the Cultural Features of the Sinbuk Upper Paeolithic Site in the Northeastern Asia*, Chosun Univ. Museum. (In Korean)

Lee, G.K., 2006. *Illustrated Book of the Paleolithic Sites in the Honam Region*, Chosun Univ. Museum. (In Korean)

Lee, G.K. et al., 2008. *The Sinbuk Upper Paleolithic Sites in Jangheung County, Jeollanam Province, Korea*, Chosun Univ. Museum. (In Korean)

Lee, G.K., Cha, M.A., Kim, S.A., 2008. *Imsil Haga site vol. 1: Excavation in 2006*, Chosun University Museum. (In Korean)

Lee, G.K. and Kim, S.A., 2009. *Historic site No. 458 Suncheon Wolpyeong Site vol. 3: Excavation in 2005*, Chosun Univ. Museum. (In Korean)

Lee, G.K. ed., 2009. *Splendid Relics of Honam Region from 100,000 years ago,* Chosun Univ. Museum. (In Korean)

Lee, G.K., 2011. Upper Paleolithic interaction between Korean peninsula and Japanese archipelago: based on new discovered data. *The Archaeological Journal* No. 618, New Science Co., 27-31. (In Japanese)

Lee, G.K. ed., 2014. *Academic Value and Creative Application of the Wolpyeong Historic Site*, Chosun Univ. Museum. (In Korean)

Lee, G.K. and Kim, J.C., 2015. Obsidians from the Sinbuk archaeological site in Korea; Evidences for strait crossing and long-distance exchange of raw material in Paleolithic Age. *Journal of Archaeological Science: Reports* 2, 458-466.

Lee, G.K., 2017. Review on Paleolithic Survey and Research in Honam Region since 1986. *Honam Gogohakbo* No. 55, 4-31. (In Korean)

Lee, G.K., 2018a. *The Study of Paleolithic Culture in Southwestern Korea*, Hyean Publishing Co. (In Korean)

Lee, G.K., 2018b. *Paleolithic Paradise, Boseong River*, Chosun Univ. Museum. (In Korean)

Lee, G.K. ed., 2018. *The Value of Cultural Heritage and Application Plan of Haga Site in Imsil County*, Chosun Univ. Museum. (In Korean)

Lee, G.K. and Sano, K., 2019. Were tanged points mechanically delivered armatures? Functional and morphometric analyses of tanged points from an Upper Paleolithic site at Jingeuneul, Korea. *Archaeological and Anthropological Sciences* No. 11, 2453-2465.

Lee, G.K., 2020. *Paleolithic Culture of the Boseong River basin in Southwestern Korea: Survey and Research since 1986*, Hyean Publishing Co. (In Korean)

Lee, G.K. ed., 2020. *From Paleolithic to Future: The Value and Application of the Paleolithic Culture of the Sinbuk Site and Boseong River Basin*, Chosun Univ. Museum. (In Korean)

Lee, G.K., 2021. Multiple sources of the archaeological evidences from the Sinbuk Upper Paleolithic site and their relation in the Northeast Asia. *Hanguk Guseokgi Hakbo* 43, 49-70. (In Korean)

Lee, G.K. ed., 2021. *Imsil Haga Site; Basecamp of Paleolithic Inhabitants 23,500 years ago*, Imsil Culture Center. (In Korean)

Lee, H.J., 1997. New discovered Paleolithic Sites in the Yeongsangang River Basin. *Honam Gogohakbo* No. 5, 103-147. (In Korean)

Lee, H.J. et al., 2006. *The Paleolithic Archaeology and Quaternary Geology in Yeongsan River Region*, Hakyeon Printing Co. (In Korean)

Lee, H.J., 2014. The Meaning and Value of Wolpyeong Historic Site in Korean Paleolithic Studies. *Academic Value and Creative Application of Wolpyeong Historic Site*, Chosun Univ. Museum, 39-45. (In Korean)

Lee, H.J., 2015. *Island Archaeology: Appearance and Sea Development of Paleolithic Humam Being in the Southwest Coast of Korea*, Minsokwon. (In Korean)

Lee, H.W., Lee, C.S., Song, E.Y., 2009. The Paleolithic Culture of Imsil Province, in Cheonbuk region. *Hanguk Guseokgi Hakbo* 19, 19-44. (In Korean)

Lee, H.W., 2013. Paleolithic Research in Honam Region: Summary and Prospects. *20 years of Honam Archaeological Society, its retrospect and prospect*, Honam Archaeological Society, 14-24. (In Korean)

Lee, H.W., 2018. Achievements and Prospects of Paleolithic Research in Honam Region. *Achievement and Status of Paleolithic Research in Honam Region*, Korean Paleolithic Society, 67-73. (In Korean)

Lee, Y.M. et al., 2020. *Report on the Excavation of Suncheon Gusanri Gusan site*, Research Centre of Dolmens in Northeast Asia. (In Korean)

Lisiecki, L.E. and Raymo, M.E., 2005. A Pliocene-Pleistocene stack of 57 globally distributed benthic $\delta 18O$ records. *Paleoceanography* Vol. 20.

Matsuhuji, K., 1987. Paleolithic tool across the Sea: Tanged-point. *Hanazonosigaku* No. 8, 8-19. (In Japanese)

Nara Institute of Cultural Heritage. 2020. *Preliminary excavation report on Wolpyeong site in Suncheon city*.

Nishiaki, Y., Kadowaki, S., Kondo, Y. eds., 2018. *PaleoAsia 2018: The International Workshop Cultural History of PaleoAsia–Integrative Research on the Formative Processes of Modern Human Cultures in Asia*, The University Museum of Tokyo.

Ono, A. and Yamada, M., 2012. The Upper Palaeolithic of the Japanese Islands: An Overview. *Archeometriai Mühely*, 219-228.

Oppenheimer, S., 2009. The great arc of dispersal of modern humans: Africa to Australia. *Quaternary International* 2002, 2-13.

Park. Y.C., 2001. A Review on the Results and Issues of Paleolithic Research in Honam Region. *Paleolithic Culture of the Honam Region*, Honam Archaeological Society, 87-94. (In Korean)

Sagawa, M., 2018. The international status of the Imsil Haga Site–Characteristics of Spheroids, Tanged-points, and Microblade technique of Haga Site from the Perspective of Northeast Asia. *The Value of Cultural Heritage and Application Plan of Haga Site in Imsil County*, Chosun Univ. Museum, 45-55. (In Japanese)

Sato, H., 2018. Paleolithic culture of Honam region from the Perspective of Japanese archipelago. *Achievements and status of Paleolithic Research in Honam region*, Korean Paleolithic Society, 7-19. (In Japanese)

Environmental fluctuation in the Northern Circum Japan Sea Area in the Upper Paleolithic and subsistence adaptation of prehistoric hunter-gatherers

Hiroyuki SATO

Professor Emeritus, Center for Evolving Humanities, Graduate School of Humanities and Sociology, The University of Tokyo, Japan; hsato@l.u-tokyo.ac.jp

ABSTRACT

The Northern Circum Japan Sea Area (NCJSA) is the northern part of the Circum Japan Sea Area, comprising the Russian Far East (Primorye, Sakhalin Island, and southern Khabarovsk Territory), northeast China, the Korean Peninsula, and the Japanese Archipelago. The prehistoric Circum Japanese Sea Area was obviously formed as one of the archaeological cultural areas. And, in NCJSA, high cultural mutuality archaeologically is recognized such microblade industries, because the Paleo-Hokkaido Peninsula connected through Sakhalin with the Continent and southern Krill Islands under the continental climate in glacial age, Upper Paleolithic, before the Japanese Archipelago becoming to the oceanic climate in Early Holocene. These archaeological phenomena proceed from a human technological and adaptation behavior response to the natural resource structure yielded by the common environmental condition and its fluctuation in Late Pleistocene NCJSA. Upper Paleolithic hunter-gatherers of the Paleo-Hokkaido Peninsula revealed that culture change and subsistence adaptation to environmental change in accordance with climate fluctuation, by research results of the human ecosystem approach composed of climate, landscape, fauna, flora and cultures in those days, on the basis of the characteristics and resolution ability of their archaeological data.

국문초록

북환동해역은 러시아 극동(연해주, 사할린 섬, 하바롭스크 남부 영토), 중국 북동부, 한반도 및 홋카이도를 포함한 환동해역의 북부이며, 이 지역에도 선사시대 동안 확실한 고고문화가 형성되었다. 이 해역은 지리적으로 홀로세 초기의 일본열도가 해양성 기후로 변하기 이전 후기구석기의 대륙성 기후 하에서 고 홋카이도가 사할린을 통해 대륙이나 남부 크릴 제도로 연결되어 있고 이 해역 내에 좀돌날 공작을 통해 고고학적으로 문화적인 상호작용이 있었다. 이런 고고학적 현상은 갱신세 말기 이 해역의 공통적인 환경 조건과 변동으로 인해 생기는 자연자원 구조 변동에 대한 인류의 기술적 적응과 행태적 반응으로 본다. 고 홋카이도의 후기구석기 당시 기후, 지형, 동물군, 식물군, 문화로 구성된 인간 생태계적 접근, 즉 고고학 자료의 특성과 해석을 통해 볼 때, 당시 수렵-채집인은 기후변동에 따른 환경변화에 대응하여 문화적 변화와 생태적 적응을 잘 했던 것으로 나타났다.

Keywords : Northern Circum Japan Sea Area, Upper Paleolithic, environmental fluctuation, Late Pleistocene, human ecosystem

1. Introduction

Northern Circum Japan Sea Area (NCJSA) is the northern part of the Circum Japan Sea Area composed of the Russian Far East (Primorye, Sakhalin Island and southern Khabarovsk Territory), northeast China, the Korean Peninsula and the Japanese Archipelago. Prehistoric Circum Japanese Sea Area, where was different with the present geographic division, is obviously formed as one of the archaeological cultural areas (Onuki,1998; Sato, 2000, 2005a, 2005b). During the Upper Paleolithic (UP: 38-10 ka) this area had a high cultural similarity based on the mutual paleoenvironment in the glacial age (Sato ed., 2009, 2011; Morisaki & Sato, 2015; Morisaki et al., 2015). In this paper, I discuss what and how the prehistoric people respond to the intensive environmental fluctuation during the UP of NCJSA by the analyses of the human ecosystem factors as landscape, fauna, flora and human cultures.

2. Paleoenvironmental settings of the Late Pleistocene of the Japanese Archipelago

2.1. Physiographic setting

The UP in the Japanese Archipelago correspond to the late Late Pleistocene, characterized by a cold, dry climate of the glacial period, when sea level drop down remarkably, since water fixed on the land as a ice sheet or glacier. Although present Japanese Archipelago consists of four major islands as Hokkaido, Honshu, Shikoku and Kyushu, and incidental many small islands, it is clear that it consisted of two major landmasses and one archipelago (Paleo-Okinawa Islands) in the Pleistocene by the recent studies of the sea regression/transgression and sea bottoms topography of channels along the Japanese Archipelago (Sato, 2005b, 2018). In the glacial period the Sakhalin Island, Hokkaido, and the southern Kuril Islands were combined into the Paleo-Hokkaido Peninsula connected to the Asian Continent, while Honshu, Shikoku and Kyushu formed a single landmass called the Paleo-Honshu Island because of glacial eustasy (Sato et al., 2011) (Fig. 1).
For the research of prehistoric archaeology, it is much important that narrower Tsugaru Straight had remained between these two landmasses. Because, both suggested to be held different cultural dynamisms basically at least UP except a few common features. Besides, the interrelationship of technology, information, culture and human group were presented basically between the Paleo-Hokkaido Peninsula and the Paleo-Honshu Island (Sato et al., 2011).

Also, narrower Korean Straight had remained between the Paleo-Honshu Island and the Paleo-Korean Peninsula where composed of a part of eastern coast of the Asian Continent in the Pleistocene. This paleo-geographic condition was much influence with the characters of the Japanese Paleolithic cultures (Sato, 2000). Although, in the Japanese UP, the Paleo-Honshu Island had independent cultures, the Paleo-Hokkaido Peninsula had not and something similar with the Continent one, because the latter connected to the Continent and expanded Asian Continent. Through these two routes, the Paleo-Korean Peninsula and the Paleo-Hokkaido Peninsula, various information and human groups sometime came into the Japanese Archipelago in UP.

The Paleo-Okinawa Islands, however, had been insisted on the connecting to the Taiwan and Continent in the Pleistocene based on the biogeographic evidences so far, it become clear that each island still had been island in spite of expanding the island area in the Pleistocene by the recent research results of the sea bottom topography and geology (Sato, 2005b).

2.2. Paleo-climatic condition

Although it is well known that the fundamental climate of Upper Paleolithic was a dry and cold, it was not continued

Fig.1 Paleo-geography and vegetation of the LGM in the Japanese Archipelago (Iwase et al., 2010)

uniformly and unstable. From 1950s to the present, the analysis of ice sheet core in Greenland, Antarctic, Andes mountains and so on demonstrates to the mutation of Pleistocene ice sheets. Since the mutation of these correspond to the change of climate, warm and cold, fundamentally, it is developed that climatic environments of Pleistocene and Holocene are much deferent each other contrastively on the boundary of 11 ka. Before 11 ka, Paleolithic period is not only dry and cold, but also much unstable for the sever fluctuation of climates as called Dansgaard-Oeschger cycle. After that, this environmental fluctuation is confirmed everywhere on the world including the bottom cores of the Japan Sea, so that presently we know this fluctuation is universal (Morisaki, 2010) (**Fig. 2**).

This fluctuation changed drastically after the end of glacial period, 11 ka, and to be stable, warm and wet in the Japanese Archipelago. In Holocene under the stable climate, it is possible that agricultural settlements or urban civilizations emerged on the world for the first time. In the Japanese Archipelago, the geographic condition like present emerged by the transgression.

In the Pleistocene, because of very narrow straights remained in the Korean Straight and the Tsugaru Straight, oceanic currents were unable to flow into the Paleo-Japan Sea, so that it was closed sea system which had a freshwater zone in the upper level of sea like present Okhotsk Sea. This condition of the Paleo-Japan Sea brought to the dry and cold climate to the Japanese Archipelago. After the Holocene, however, the warm tributary current became to inflow into the Japan Sea, so the climatic condition of the Japanese Archipelago changed from the continental, dry, cold and unstable in the glacial period, to the maritime, warm, wet and stable during the Holocene.

And, since a land area became to decrease, the oceanic currents such as Kuroshio Current and the Kuril Current, which were flown in the offshore in Pleistocene, flowed along the shores of the Pacific Sea side. That is also contributed to this climatic change. This warm, wet and stable maritime climate brought to the Jomon forest landscape yielded many fruitful plant edible resources, which Jomon people depended on mainly.

Each Paleolithic cultural era shown in Fig. 2 does not always correspond to the timing of climatic change rigidly. These phenomena are the fundamental characteristics of relationship between the natural environments and human cultures people respond to.

2.3. Flora and plant resources

Vegetation history of Japanese Upper Paleolithic has mainly restored by the pollen or seeds analyses from the good preservative deposits such as a wetland or buried river sediment. Since the full restoration of it completely, however, was not obtained yet, vegetation map of the Last Glacial Maximum (LGM), which is most known, can be representative (**Fig. 1**), and the research result of paleoenvironmental history during past 72 ka in the Lake Nojiri (Kumon et al., 2009) is corroborated in this problem. Although each researcher in the world has different opinions about the duration of LGM based on the data everywhere, in Japan it is most predominant opinion that LGM is from 18-20 ka.

In the northeastern area of Paleo-Hokkaido, the coniferous forest and grassland called the 'Mammoth Steppe', where were favorable to the Mammoth Fauna, were flourished (Igarashi, 2011). The cool-temperate coniferous forest in the south-western Paleo-Hokkaido and northeastern part of the Paleo-Honshu Island, and the temperate Pan-mixed forest in the western part of the Paleo-Honshu Island distributed mainly. These three vegetation zones were mainly in the late Late Pleistocene Japan. In addition, it should be noticed that as the forth vegetation zone the warm-temperate deciduous or the evergreen broadleaf forest distributed along the southern coastal area of the Paleo-Honshu Island. Because, only this vegetation zone, plant edible resources were plentiful exceptionally, Paleolithic people of this zone

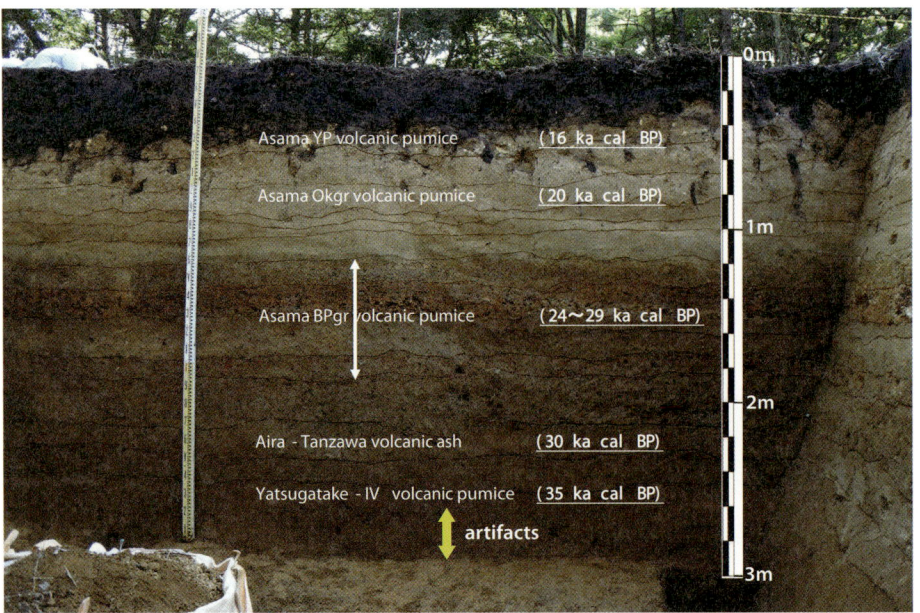

Fig. 2 Climatic fluctuation during past 100 ka and archaeological periods of the Japanese Archipelago (modified after Morisaki, 2012)

had the different subsistence adaptation to plant resources than the other areas. Presently this vegetation zone is distributed widely in the western part of Japan, however, three vegetation zones as mentioned above is not almost confirmed in present Japanese Archipelago, because the plant species from these three zones were mainly adapted to dry and cold climate in the Pleistocene. Especially, the cool-temperate coniferous forest is not distributed in Japan at all. This vegetation zone distributed presently in the Lower Amur River Basin, where dry and cold continental climate is dominant (Tsuji, 2004).

The research group including the author has carried out the ethnoarchaeological research projects in the Russian Far East past 20 years (Onuki and Sato ed., 2005), and investigated in the wild edible resources in the Northeast Asia including the Amur River Basin (Onuki, 2005). Forest of this area composes of Pan-mixed and cool-temperate coniferous forest (Ono and Igarashi, 1991). Such forests can not be confirmed in present warm and wet Japanese Archipelago, however, the forest of Japanese Paleolithic most be composed of a dry forest like this. Although several kinds of deer and wild boar distributed to the south area to the Amur River estuary, the northern area from the Amur River estuary is belong to Siberian environment and reindeer is distributed at the most as a middle-sized animal. In the Amur River Basin chestnut is not distributed at all, and acorn and walnut are seldom distributed in the estuary. Some kinds of berries are flourished but major food such as nuts which were main stable resources in Jomon Era. In these two vegetation zones, the plant resources that people can use as a stable main food are seldom (Sato, 2005b).

That is, in the Upper Paleolithic Japanese Archipelago the stable and edible plant resources as a main food were seldom originally, because main vegetation zones adapted to continental dry and cold climate were predominant. So that, it is sure that the fundamental subsistence strategy of the Paleolithic Japanese people was the terrestrial mammal hunting. In addition, since the climate was unstable and changed cyclically in short term, animal hunting strategy was more advantageous than edible plant gathering. Because animal can avoid the influence of the fluctuation of the climatic change to be moved, while plant resources are uncertain when the climate is unstable. This environmental and vegetation condition is supposed to be one of utmost reasons that the subsistence strategy used the plant resources was not developed originally in the Paleolithic Japanese Archipelago without the southern coast area of the Paleo-Honshu Island (Sato et al., 2011).

As mentioned above, forest environment was predominant in the Paleolithic Japanese Archipelago except the coniferous forest and grassland of the northeastern area of Paleo-Hokkaido, and provided for the basic subsistence strategy of Japanese Paleolithic human groups. Japanese Upper Paleolithic archaeological remains mainly composing hunting weapons such as various points support obviously to this response (Sato, 1992, 2005a).

2.4. Fauna and mammal resources

Once large mammals in the Paleolithic as wooly mammoth (*Mammuthus primigenius*), Naumann's elephant (*Paleoloxodon naumanni*), Giant deer (*Sinomegaceros yabei*), Bison (*Bison priscus*) were thought vaguely to be extinct at the end of glacial period. Although, recently the author's grope compiled large mammal fossil examples found from the Pleistocene Japanese Archipelago and analyzed the chronological fate of these, including the re-measurement of radiocarbon dating, if need. As a result, it is highly possible that the terrestrial large mammals were extinct at the 25 ka of LGM in the Paleo-Honshu Island, and 20 ka of the beginning of the Later Glacial in the Paleo-Hokkaido Peninsula (Takahashi, 2008; Iwase et al., 2012, 2015). Terrestrial mammal fauna in the Late Pleistocene Japanese Archipelago should be divided into two gropes, which the one was the mammoth fauna derived through Paleo-Hokkaido Peninsula from Siberia and the other was the *Palaeoloxodon-Sinomegaceroides* complex through Paleo-Korean Peninsula from northern China1). Within these two mammal gropes large mammals as mentioned above were extinct at the transition from Pleistocene to Holocene, so that in Holocene present mammal fauna composed of middle-sized and small-sized animals was established. These two Pleistocene mammal fauna were supposed to move over north to south or in reverse according to the change of cold and warm in the glacial age. In the comparative warm period the *Palaeoloxodon-Sinomegaceroides* complex should be moved into the Paleo-Hokkaido Peninsula, while in the cold period Mammoth fauna into the northern Paleo-Honshu Island (**Fig. 3**). Since Upper Paleolithic human gropes adopted mainly the hunting strategy for large and middle-sized animals, it is well likely that they adopted the behavioral strategy with wide range movement according to the mammal gropes movement (Sato et al., 2011).

By the way, while some researchers including environmental studies insist on that Pleistocene extinction of the large mammals depend mainly on the over kill by prehistoric hunters, in according with recent archaeological reassessment for this problem in details, Pleistocene extinction was thought not to be based on the human but environmental factors fundamentally. In North America and Australia, over kill hypothesis was insisted strongly as far, however, there are no archaeological evidences for the over kill in the archaeological sites of both areas in fact (Sato, 2011).

Fig. 3 Change of two major mammal fauna during past 500 ka in the Japanese Archipelago (Takahashi, 2008)

3. Human ecosystem of the NCJSA : How human response to the nature?

What and how the interrelationship between human and natural environment and resources is in the Pleistocene NCJSA? In order to resolve this problem, the authors organized the international project with Russian researchers (Sato ed., 2008, 2011). In four areas of the NCJSA as Hokkaido, Sakhalin, Amur River Basin, and Primorye (Russian Maritime Province), main factors of the human ecosystem composed of dates, climate, landscape, fauna, flora, and cultures

Table 1 Correlation of fauna, flora and human cultures in NCJSA (Sato ed., 2011)

Age (KaBP)	Climatic stage (MIS)	Flora				Fauna			Culture			
		Hokkaido	Sakhalin	Amur	Primorye	Hokkaido	Sakhalin	Amur & Primorye	Hokkaido	Sakhalin	Amur	Primore
6	1	Pan mixed forest composed of cool temperate broad leaf trees and some alpine trees	Taiga(Picea, Larix, Pinus, Abies)	Picea, Quercus, Ulmus, Abies	Broad leaf-Coniferus (Korean pine) forest	Fauna with Brown bear	(formation of Sakhalin island)	Fauna with Brown bear and Amur Tiger	Early Jomon	Middle Early Neolithic	Early and Middle Neolithic (biface and blade technology)	Middle Neolithic(biface and blade technology)
7				Dark coniferus forest with some broad leaf species								
8										Early Neolithic	?	?
9							Fauna with Brown bear Equus, Panthera, Bos, Bovis		?	?	Osipovka culture	Microblade and blade industries
10				Larch, Betula						Microblade technology, and Tachikawa point		
11												
12	2	Open larch-pine taiga with grassland	Open larch-pine taiga with mire	Taiga(Larch, Pine, Picea, Birch) with open grassland	Taiga(Larch, Pine, Picea, Birch) with open grassland	Fauna with Mammoth	Fauna with Mammoth	Fauna with Mammoth	Various Microblade industries	Microblade technology, the same with Hokkaido	Microblade culture, Pebble tool technology, and Blade technology	?
13												
14												
15												
16												
17										?		
18										Blade technology (prismatic core) polished stone, scraper, adze/beginning of microblade technology		
19									Microblade, Blade, and Flake industries			
20												
21												
22												
23												
24												
25	3	Taiga(Picea, Abies, Larch, Pinus)	Taiga(Picea, Larix, Pinus) with grassland	Taiga(Picea, Abies, Larch)	Taiga(Picea, Abies, Larch)	Fauna with Nauman's elephant			Trapizoidal and Blade Industries	?	?	Pebble technology (Geographic society cave)
26												
27												
28												
29												
30												
31												
32												
33												

... relatively warm period

are evaluated (Table 1). Main tree in Pleistocene forest of these areas was Larix, which is one in taiga forest presently except Hokkaido. Change of vegetation in these four areas was to be linked each other and homogeneous, and respond to the climatic change sensitively, while the change of fauna was not respond to immediately in reverse. Generally speaking, in the NCJSA the Pleistocene mammoth fauna change over to the Holocene middle and small-sized mammal fauna in the transition form Pleistocene to Holocene. This timing of changing over on fauna between Sakhalin-Hokkaido and Amur Basin-Primorye was slightly different, and appeared earlier than the climatic change. Around the beginning of Later Glacial, when was the biggest climatic change in last Pleistocene, change of main fauna was done. Pollen analyses show that Later Glacial was the biggest climatic change in the Pleistocene northern hemisphere (Igarashi, 2011).

Fig. 4 Correlation of Paleolithic industries and paleoenvironmental change in Hokkaido (Izuho and Takahashi, 2005)

Human culture shows the drastic fluctuation. Since Paleolithic people adopted the hunting behavioral strategies with wide range mobility to hunt large and middle-sized animals, main lithic assemblages composed of hunting weapons changed basically, being linked with the change of fauna, but that is not all. The dynamism of each archaeological cultures were diversified and, especially, the archaeological features became not to be clear at the initial Holocene, 10 to 8 ka in the NCJSA without the Japanese Archipelago, when severe glacial age was finished and Holocene mild climate had started. Although in some case the opinion which people did not lived in these regions at the initial Holocene was insisted, the reason why is not sure in detail. Probably it was enormous impact than we anticipate that not only the large change on fauna and flora, but also on landscape such as landform or geological environments affected to human activities and cultures.

4. Upper Paleolithic in Hokkaido

Before the Upper Paleolithic (>35 ka, Early MIS3) of Hokkaido, it was cold stage flourishing Mammoth fauna but human activity was unknown. The Early Upper Paleolithic (35-25 ka) was correspond to Late MIS3 and, in reverse, it became to warm when Naumman's elephant lived and oldest human remains in Hokkaido appeared. Oldest archaeological assemblage of Hokkaido is the small flake industry with trapezoid. This assemblage is not found in Sakhalin and common to the Early Upper Paleolithic industry in southern Paleo-Honshu Island. So that, the cultural genealogy of this assemblage is supposed to be one of the Paleo-Honshu Island. It is high possibility that oldest archaeological culture formed by the immigration from the southern Paleo-Honshu Island (Izuho and Takahashi, 2005; Sato, 2005a) (Fig. 4). In next stage of 25 ka, when MIS2 and Late Upper Paleolithic were begun, the climate became cold again and Mammoth fauna had reappeared. While in the beginning of MIS2 the blade industry from the Paleo-Honshu Island was presented, in 21 ka of LGM the microblade industries from the north emerged suddenly. After the microblade industries emerged, the industries from southern Paleo-Honshu Island were disappeared and the microblade industries had continued till Holocene. This cultural dynamism is much different from the Paleo-Honshu Island. Paleolithic people from the north had immigrated to pursuit for the Mammoth fauna in the LGM of Early MIS2, however, they did not move to the south, Paleo-Honshu Island immediately. Tsugaru Strait between Paleo-Hokkaido Peninsula and Paleo-Honshu Island was thought to be a cultural barrier.

Generally speaking, in the Upper Paleolithic Hokkaido, it is likely that in the early stage, EUP and mild Late MIS3, the combination southern fauna with southern assemblage, and in the late stage, LUP and cold Early MIS2, northern fauna with northern assemblage were presented.

People having microblade industries dispersed from the north in the LGM had distributed the northern Eurasia. It is possible to be said that this microblade cultures had emerged firstly around the Baikal Lake in the 30-25 ka and they dispersed to the east and the northern end of the Japanese Archipelago through Paleo-Hokkaido Peninsula. After 5,000 years later, this human group with microblade industries in Hokkaido began to move to the south Paleo-Honshu Island in the terminal UP. This dispersal also expanded to the north and east in Asia, and through the Northeast Asia and Beringia, reached to the New World finally. It is likely that this human and cultural dispersal was concerned in the first peopling of the America (Sato, 2010; Morisaki et al., 2018a).

5. Cultural dynamics of Holocene NCJSA

As mention above, after the transition from Pleistocene to Holocene, cultural dynamics in the NCJSA was much different from the one of Pleistocene, because of large climatic and geographic change (Morisaki et al., 2018b). While in the terminal Pleistocene East Asia northern microblade industries and southern small flake and pebble tool industries confronted each other, this cultural composition became to change after rice cropping emerged in China. Although, accompanying the emergence of cultivation, sedentism was emerged in Central China, in the northern and southern areas than Central China, hunting and gathering activity remained and mobile life was continued after. But, in the Far East including the Japanese Archipelago, semi-sedentary Neolithic culture, such as Jomon in Japan, which developed large settlements composed of a lot of pit-dwellings, was emerged, because of rich wild food procurement comparatively based on the stable wild edible resources (Onuki, 1998).

In the Holocene Hokkaido was divorced from the Continent and became island due to the transgression. At the same time, the Japanese Archipelago changed over the warm and wet climatic resource environment, and became to be much different from contemporary resource environment of the Continent where dry climate continued. So that, on the border of the southern end of Sakhalin, after the beginning of Holocene Hokkaido and Sakhalin belonged to distinctive system of cultural dynamics each other (Fukuda et al., 2022). Cultural relationship was not going away at all between them. Distinctive cultures each other were confronted basically. The reoccurrence of cultural interrelationship between both areas was after the Okhotsk culture, AD 5th to 10th century, of ancient sea animal hunters was appeared.

Note:

(1) Based on mammalian fossils from Siberia, Sakhalin, and Hokkaido, the mammoth fauna ranged throughout the Paleo-Hokkaido Peninsula, and included woolly mammoth (*Mammuthus primigenius*), brown bear (*Ursus arctos*), steppe bison (*Bison priscus*), reindeer (*Rangifer tarandus*), snow sheep (*Ovis nivicola*), leopard (*Panthera* sp.), wolf (*Canis lupus*), and Arctic fox (*Alopex lagopus*). *Palaeoloxodon-Sinomegaceroides* complex was mainly composed of Naumann's elephant (*Paleoloxodon naumanni*), giant deer (*Sinomegaceros yabei*), Cervid (*Cervus* sp.), brown bear (*Ursus arctos*), black bear (*Ursus tibetanus*), wild boar (*Sus scrofa*), badger (*Meles meles*), raccoon dog (*Nycteretes procyonoides*), least weasel (*Mustela nivalis*), marten (*Martes melampus*), fox (*Vulpes vulpes*), wolf (*Canis lupus*), and Japanese monkey (*Maccaca fuscata*) (Iwase et al., 2012). Since some common species between Siberia and North China, where were original distribution area of both faunas, presented, there are some same species in two lists.

Reference

Fukuda, M. Morisaki, K. and Sato, H., 2022. Synthetic perspective on prehistoric hunter-gatherer adaptaion and landscape change in northern Japan. *The Maritime Prehistory of Northeast Asia*, Springer, 73-95.

Igarashi, Y., 2011. LGM vegetation in Hokkaido and Sakhalin: development of grassland. *Environmental History of Grassland*, Tokyo: Bunichi Sougo Shuppan, 17-39. (in Japanese)

Iwase, A., Hashizume, J., Izuho, M., Takahashi, K. and Sato, H., 2012. Timing of megafauna extinction in the late Late Pleistocene on the Japanese Archipelago. *Quaternary International* 255, 114-124.

Iwase, A., Takahashi, K. and Izuho, M., 2015. Further study on the Late Pleistocene megafaunal extinction in the Japanese Archipelago. *The Emergence and Diversity of Modern Human Behaviors in Paleolithic Asia*, Texas M&A University Press, 325-344.

Izuho, M. and Takahashi, K., 2005. Correlation of Paleolithic industries and paleoenvironmental change in Hokkaido (Japan). *Current Research in the Pleistocene* 22, 19-21.

Kumon, F., S. Kawai and Y. Inouchi. 2009. High-resolution reconstruction of paleoclimate during the last 72 ka on the basis of the drilled sediments from Lake Nojiri, central Japan. *Palaeolithic Research* 5, 3-10. (in Japanese)

Morisaki, K., 2012. The evolution of lithic technology and human behavior from MIS3 to MIS2 in the Japanese Upper Paleolithic. *Quaternary International* 248, 56-69.

Morisaki, K. and Sato, H., 2015. Hunter-gatherer responses to abrupt environmental change from the terminal Pleistocene to the early Holocene in the Lower Amur region. *Forgotten Times and Spaces: New Perspectives in Paleoanthropological, Paleoethnological and archaeological studie*, Brono: Masaryk University & Institute of Archaeology of the Czech Academy of Science, 418-434, reference 549-598.

Morisaki, K., Izuho, M., Terry, K., Sato, H., 2015. Lithics and climate: technological responses to landscape changes in Upper Paleolithic northern Japan. *Antiquity* 89-345 ; 554-572.

Morisaki, K., Izuho, M., Sato, H., 2018a. Human adaptive responses to environmental change during the Pleistocene-Holocene transition in the Japanese Archipelago. *Lithic Technological Organization and Paleoenvironmental Change: Global and Diachronic Perspective*, Springer, 91-122.

Morisaki, K., Kunikita, D., Sato, H., 2018b. Holocene climatic fluctuation and lithic technological change in northeastern Hokkaido (Japan). *Journal of Archaeological Science: reports* 17, 1018-1024.

Ono, Y. and Y. Igarashi. 1991. *Natural History of Hokkaido: Traveling into the Ice Age Forest*, Sapporo: Hokkaido University Press. (in Japanese)

Onuki, S., 1998. *Archaeology in the Northeast Asia*, Tokyo: Doseisha. (in Japanese)

Onuki, S., 2005. Wild food resource basis. *Ethnoarchaeology in the Russian Far East: Subsistence and Residential System of Temperate Forest Hunter-Fishers*, Tokyo: Rokuichi Shobo, 263-294. (in Japanese)

Onuki, S. and H. Sato eds., 2005. *Ethnoarchaeology in the Russian Far East: Subsistence and Residential System of Temperate Forest Hunter-Fishers*, Tokyo: Rokuichi Shobo. (in Japanese)

Sato, H., 1992. *Structure and Evolution of Japanese Paleolithic Cultures*, Tokyo: Kashiwa Shobo. (in Japanese)

Sato, H., 2000. Flame of Upper Paleolithic Japanese Archipelago and Hokkaido and Kyushu Island. *Paleolithic Kyushu* 4, 71-82. (in Japanese)

Sato, H., 2005a. Overview to the Hokkaido Paleolithic: Hokkaido and its surroundings. *Hokkaido Paleolithic Research* 10, 137-146. (in Japanese)

Sato, H., 2005b. Natural history and human in the Japanese Archipelago. *Topography of Japan* Vol. 1, Tokyo: Asakura Shoten, 80-94. (in Japanese)

Sato, H., 2005c. Plant resource utilization in Kondon village and Russian Far East. *Ethnoarchaeology in the Russian Far East: Subsistence and Residential System of Temperate Forest Hunter-Fishers*, Tokyo: Rokuichi Shobo, 118-133. (in Japanese)

Sato, H. ed., 2008. *Proceedings for the International Symposium on Human Ecosystem Changes in the Northern Circum Japan Sea Area (NCJSA) in Late Pleistocene*, Tokyo: The University of Tokyo.

Sato, H. ed., 2009. *Research on the Settlement and the Formation of Cultures in Transition from Pleistocene to Holocene in Northern Japanese Archipelago*, Kitami: Tokoro Field Laboratory, The University of Tokyo. (in Japanese)

Sato, H., 2010. Dispersal of wedge-shaped microblade core industries in the East Asia. *Perspective in Comparative Archaeology*, Tokyo: Doseisha, 895-904. (in Japanese)

Sato, H., 2011. Emergence of modern humans in Australia. *Paleolithic Archaeology* 75, 101-108. (in Japanese)

Sato, H. ed., 2011. *Research on the Relationship between Human and Environmental Fluctuation in the Northern Circum Japan Sea Area (NCJSA) in Late Pleistocene*, Kitami: Tokoro Field Laboratory, The University of Tokyo. (in Japanese)

Sato, H. and K. Iinuma eds., 2011. *Environmental History of Grassland*, Tokyo: Bunichi Sougo Shuppan. (in Japanese)

Sato, H., M. Izuho and S. Yamada. 2011. Hunting and animal resources in Paleolithic. *Environmental History of Grassland*, Tokyo: Bunichi Sougo Shuppan, 51-71. (in Japanese)

Sato, H., 2018. Three Paleolithic cultures in the Japanese Archipelago. *Proceedings of the 23rd Suyanggae International Symposium in Malaysia "Suyanggae and Lenggong: Prehistory Adaptation"*, Malaysia: Penang, 23-33.

Takahashi, K., 2008. Transition of large mammal faunas in the Sea of Japan area during the Late Pleistocene. *Proceedings for the International Symposium on Human Ecosystem Changes in the Northern Circum Japan Sea Area (NCJSA) in Late Pleistocene*, Tokyo: The University of Tokyo, 68-79.

Tsuji, S., 2004. Environmental history in the global age. *Issues of Environmental Studies*. Sakura: National Museum of Japanese History, 40-70. (in Japanese)

Geological requirement for the Paleolithic site in the volcanic area

Hisao KUMAI

Professor Emeritus, Osaka City University, Japan; hkumai@sakai.zaq.ne.jp

ABSTRACT

Many Paleolithic sites are located around the volcanoes in Japan. Especially, a lot of the sites are located around the Yatsugatake Volcanic Area. Almost of them are belong to the Middle to Late Paleolithic sites (about 60 ka BP to 10 ka BP). After the Paleolithic age, So many Jomon sites have been formed at the lower place than the Paleolithic sites. And the Middle Jomon sites are located on the volcanic skirt lower than Early Jomon sites. Number of sites of the Middle Jomon had increased than older one. Almost of them situate near the stream. However, before the beginning of the Late Jomon Age, all of them have been disappear. Reason of that estimated for the moving to the valley plain because of stat of rice crop. Concerning on the Paleolithic site, almost of them are located in the deep mountain area such as upstream of the valley and on the mountain ridge near the spring. Especially, the camp sites are located near the spring. It is estimated for the convenience on the hunting. Amount of the water flow in the revers on the volcanic area are very rich than other area. It is corroborated by the rich fountain water from the volcanic rocks. Almost of the fountainhead of the rivers on the volcanic area are supported by the groundwater fountained from lava aquifer. Especially, the young lavers are excellent aquifer. One of them is the Ikenotaira Lava situated on the east slope of the Middle Yatsugatake volcanic range. The sites situate on the Late Pleistocene lava flow erupted from central part of Yatsugatake volcanic chain, altitude of about 1,700m to 1,300m. The slope on the lava flow is gentle compare to surrounding mountainside and visibility is very well. It is covered mainly Betula. Also, the sites distributed along the narrow lava flow surface less than 1km in wide. Seemingly forming a route to the quarry site exposing obsidian and many obsidian gravels distributed in the streams that situate at the both edge of lava flow. On account of the assemblage, the Komade-ike site might be assignet as a campsite complex during the Last Glacial Maximum Stage. The culture reconstructed from the yielded tools indicates that the age of the site is correlated with the last stage of Paleolithic age and the site seems to be a life center of many ancestor generations (Kumai, 2011).

국문초록

일본 화산체 주변 구석기 유적지 중 야쓰가타케 화산지대는 중기와 후기 구석기(약 60~10ka BP) 유적들이 많다. 후기구석기 이후에는 낮은 고도에 조몬(Jomon) 유적이 많이 분포하며, 조몬중기 유적은 조몬전기 유적보다 고도가 더 낮고 화산체 하단부에 위치한다. 조몬중기 유적은 이전 유적에 비하여 유적 숫자가 증가하고 곡지하천 근처에 있었지만 조몬후기 시작 전에는 벼농사를 위해 곡지평원으로 많이 이주했다. 구석기 유적지는 깊은 산간의 계곡 상류부와 사냥 용이성으로 인해 정천이 있는 구릉산지에 널리 분포하며, 특히 사냥터는 용암대수층 지하수가 유출되는 정천 부근에 분포한다. 유적은 해발 약 1,700-1,300m 야쓰가타케 화산 중앙부에서 후기갱신세 동안 분출된 용암 위에 있다. 용암대지는 주변 산맥에 비해 경사가 완만하며 가시성이 매우 좋고 자작나무로 덮여 있다. 폭 1km 이하의 좁은 용암 지표면을 따라 고고 유적이 분포한다. 용암대지의 양쪽 가장자리에 위치한 하천에는 흑요석과 흑요석제 자갈돌이 많이 노출되어 있고, 하천변을 따라 채석장 가는 길이 있다. 출토된 석기군을 통해 코마데-이케 유적 문화를 복원해 보면, 이 유적은 LGM 시기 야외숙영지로서 후기구석기 말 생활유적의 중심지로 추정된다.

Keywords : Yatsugatake Volcanic Area, Jomon sites, ground water spring, quarry site, camp site complex

1. Introduction

It is said that the volcanic area is a big water reservoir. The Yatsugatake volcanic range is also excellent groundwater reservoir. The range situated at center part of Honshu Island, northward from Mt. Fuji. The Yatsugatake volcanic range consist of many volcanic cones and domes, arranged in two arcuate rows. Formed by successive effusive centers, they have migrated from north to south, and then from south to north again throughout the whole of the Pleistocene. The Early Pleistocene volcanic activity began in the north part of the volcanic range. The thick effusive sediments i. e., the Yachiho Group, laid down into the lake basin which had been formed at the north and northeast volcanic foot area. In this Group, some of lava beds intercalated at upper part of the mountain (Fig. 1).

After about 400 thousand years from the finish of volcanic activity during the sedimentation age of Yachiho Group, new volcanic activity began in the middle Middle Pleistocene, in the south part of the range. As a result a new lake basin appeared near the area. The Minamisaku Group is the name given to the sediments of this lacustrine. Volcanic clastic, fluvial and lacustrine deposits with volcanic products fill up the basin. In this Group, also many lava flows are intercalated.

In the Late Pleistocene, volcanic activity took place again in the north part of the range. Several lava domes swelled up on the west side of the older volcanic range. A small, bog-like sedimentary basin was formed on the west foot of the range.

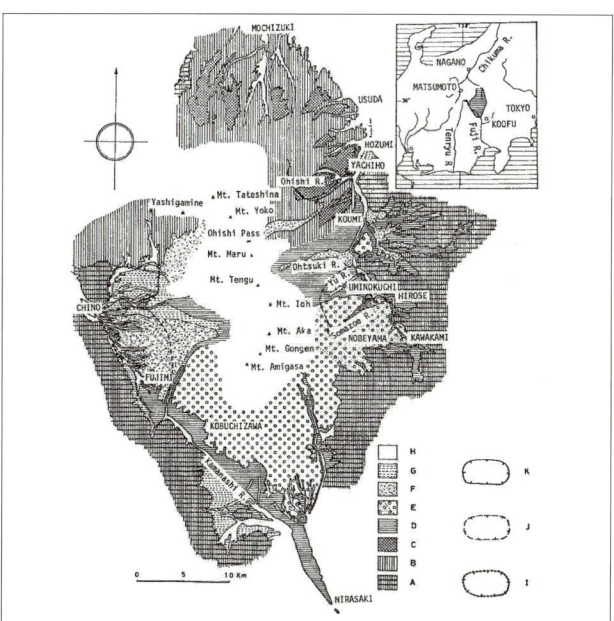

Fig. 1 Geological outline map on the foot area of Yatsugatake volcanoes (Kumai,1982) A: Basement rock, B: Yachiho G., C: Matsui decayed gravel bed, D: Hirose G., E: Upper most Hirose G., F: Late Pleistocene lava, G: Late Pleistocene sediments, H: Lacustorine area of Yachiho G., I : Lacustrine area of Hirose G., J: Lucustrine area of Upper Pleistocene

2. Groundwater condition on the volcanic terrain

Groundwater condition of the Yatsugatake volcanic range is generally richer than those of other area, because this type of land is made up of aquifers with excellent reservation capacity. However, the mechanism of groundwater aquifers and flow process have not been made clear yet. For instance, it is difficult to explain the presence of springs halfway up some volcanoes. To investigate these points, the author studied at the Yatsugatake volcanic terrain quantitatively for its groundwater storages mechanism and
A: Basement rock, B: Yachiho G., C: Matsui decayed gravel bed, D: Hirose G., E: Upper most Hirose G., F: Late Pleistocene lava, G: Late Pleistocene sediments, H: Lacustorine area of Yachiho G., I: Lacustrine area of Hirose G., J: Lucustrine area of Upper Pleistocene relationship between the surface water and groundwater.

The five groundwater zones in the Yatsugatake terrain show different characteristic of groundwater and are divided from the volcanic body to the piedmont.

(1) Volcanic body recharge zone: This is a recharge zone made by precipitation. There is no base flow in to the valley.
(2) Middle recharge zone: This zone is located in the upper part at 1,600m altitude, where the springs groups in the valley from a line along the contour line. About 10% of the groundwater flowing from the upper part is discharged along this line.
(3) Middle spouting zone: This zone has many springs on the piedmont planation surface. About 40% of the groundwater flows from the discharges of the upper zone.
(4) Lower leak zone: This zone is situated on the piedmont planation surface and faces the deep valley which marks the edge of the terrain. The potential of confined groundwater is about 10m lower than the unconfined groundwater in the area.
(5) Lower spouting zone: This zone is found in the deep valley which marks the edge of the volcanic terrain. All of the recharged groundwater of the terrain is discharged in this area.

3. Distribution of a groundwater fountain

The geological situation of the groundwater fountain is restricted with geological rock facies such as lava and intercalated sand. In the case of northern area of Yatsugatake foot area, the representative fountains distribute at valley. The groundwater spouted out from such kind of fountain come from intercalated sandy bed or lava. Most big spouted volume is more than 6,000m³ / day (Fig. 2).

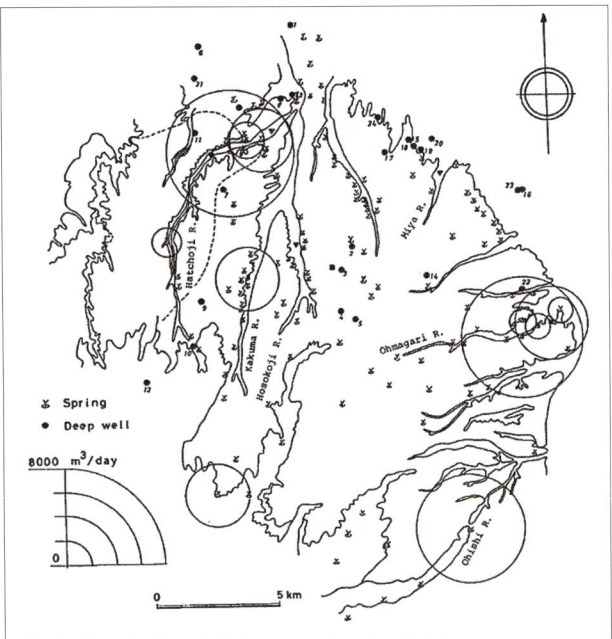

Fig. 2 Distribution of groundwater fountain on the Northern Part of Yatsugatake Volcanic Range (Kumai, 1982)

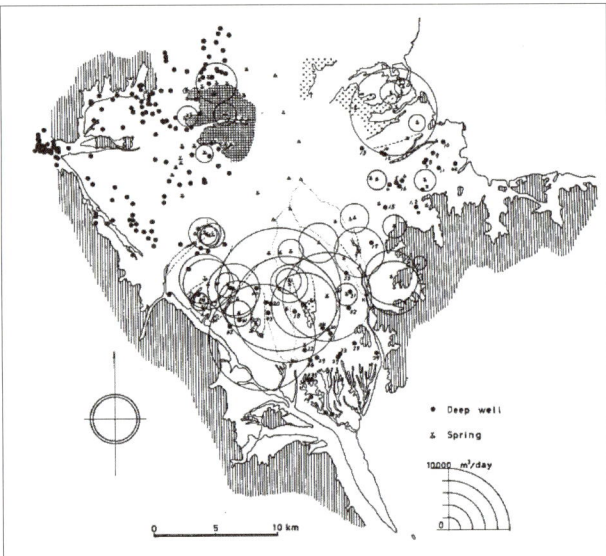

Fig. 3 Distribution of groundwater fountain on the Southern Part of Yatsugatake Volcanic Range (Kumai, 1982)

Concerning on the big fountains distributed at south area of Yatsugatake Volcanic Area, almost of them distributed at the flow end of lava. Which are belong to the Hirose Group. Most big spouted volume is more than 10,000m³ / day (**Fig. 3**).
Almost of the groundwater fountain on the Yatsugatake range are spouted from the flow end of the lava. The effective porosity in lava is rather high. So, it is useful for the groundwater flow. It is about 2 to 4% and coefficient of permeability is around 10^{-6} to 10^{-5} m/sec. It is rather lower than sedimentary deposits, however the groundwater speed is high because the passage is very narrow.

Fig. 4 Distribution of the remain sites on the Yatsugatake Volcanic Area (Nakamura, 2001)
○ : Quarry Site ● : Paleolithic site Enclosed area is site group

4. Relationship between Paleolithic sites and the groundwater fountain

Many Paleolithic sites located on the Yatsugatake Range (**Fig. 4**). Almost all of them are so-called camp sites. However, some of them are also quarry sites. The quality obsidian outcrop and gravel are located in this area, and many Paleolithic sites are located around them. Typical cases of such kind of site were reported (Kumai, 2011). In this case, the elevation of quarry site is 2,100m and cam site is about 1,300m. On the way to quarry site to camp site, they stop by arbor. Where is about 1,700m in elevation, and made some tool such like the point. It is some of the working yard.

5. Distribution of the Paleolithic sites in the Yatsugatake Range

So many Paleolithic sites located in the Yatsugatake area. Almost of the sites located at high place near the obsidian quarry site are correcting sites of obsidian and the sites to camp site are processing place of the stone tools. The camp site located in the forest near the waterside such like the spring. The Paleolithic sites distributed at the foot area of mountain located near the big groundwater fountains. The relationship between the big groundwater fountains indicated at Fig. 3 and location of the Paleolithic sites indicated at Fig.4 has close

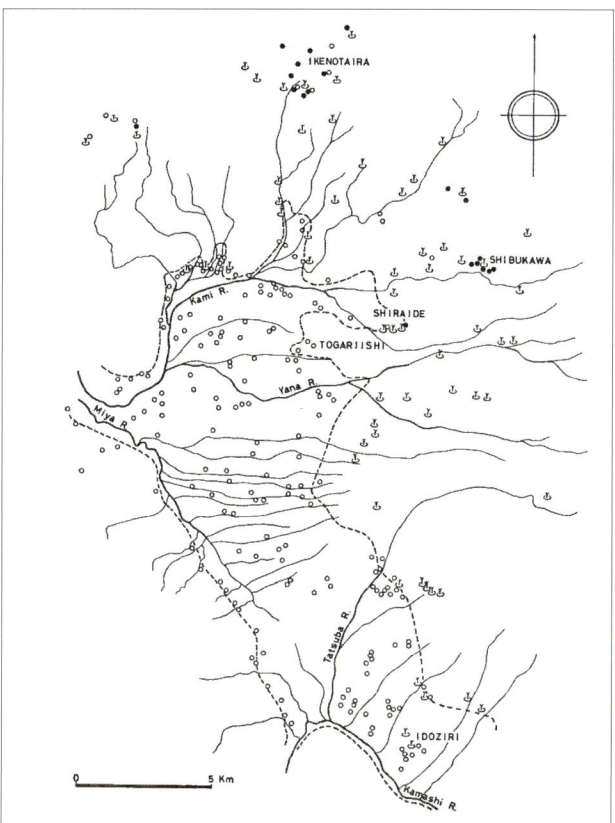

Fig. 5 Distribution of the remain sites and groundwater table on the Western Foot area of Yatsugatake Volcanic Area (Kumai,1982)
● : Paleolithic site, ○ : Neolithic site, ♨ : Spring - - : Spring line

relation. So much kind of the Paleolithic tools were found at the sites near the water front. And the sites indicate that the camp site had been used rather long time. However, it may mean not inhabitant but some seasonal camp site. Because the remains indicate not all season and living plain is not so long continue.

The relationship between the obsidian quarry site and camp site is supposed in the case of the Ikenotaira Site. In this case, the obsidian quarry site locates at altitude 2,100m, the camp site at altitude 1,300m. The processing site locates at altitude about 1,700m on the way from quarry site to the camp site. The Paleolithic human track is on the lava flow which formed about 0.1 Ma before. The land surface is rather frat and covered with white birch. So that, the visibility is good and walking is rather easy for human.

6. Neolithic site

The relationship on the location of the sites between the Paleolithic and Neolithic Sites on the Yatsugatake area is quite different. Because, the location of Neolithic (so called Jomon Period) sites located lower place such as the foot area of volcano to flood plain. It is indicated one of the example of the case of west foot area of the Yatsugatake range (**Fig. 5**).

In the figure, the Paleolithic sites are located along the spring line. It is indicated the Groundwater spouting place. This place is the cross point of ground surface and groundwater table level. Especially, the cross point at the lava flow, it is formed big fountain spring. And the many the Paleolithic sites were formed. The other hand, the Neolithic Sites distributes under the spring line. It is indicated that the Jomon peoples possible to live at the grassland. Of course, they had been take water at the near stream.

References

Kumai, H., 1982. Hydrogeological Study of the Yatsugatake Volcanic Terrain. *Journal of Faculty of Science* Vol. 17, Shinshu University, 31-115. (Japanese with English abstract)

Kumai, H., 2011. Stone Tool Manufacturing Site on the High Volcanic Mountain, Central Japan. *Suyanggae and, Her Neighbours in Nihewan,* 193-202.

Nakamura, Y., 2001. Paleolithic Sites and Quarries of Obsidian around Mts. Yatsugatake. *Daishiki* No. 33, 93-104. (Japanese)

New achievements of Paleolithic research in Zhengzhou and related issues

Youping WANG[1,2], **Wanfa GU**[2], **Yue FENG**[3]

[1] Professor, School of Archaeology and Museology, Peking University, China ; ypwang@pku.edu.cn
[2] Zhengzhou Municipal Institute of Relics and Archaeology, China
[3] School of Archaeology and Museology, Peking University, China

ABSTRACT

Since 2000, the School of Archaeology and Museology of Peking University, together with Zhengzhou Municipal Institute of Cultural Relics and Archaeology, have been cooperating to excavate the sites of Zhijidong Cave, Laonainaimiao, Zhaozhuang, Huangdikou, Fangjiagou, Xishi, Dongshi, and Lijiagou, in the Zhengzhou area. These works have made significant progress from three aspects: first, establishing the sequence of cultural development in the Middle and Late Paleolithic Central Plain; second, discovering substantial evidence for the emergence and development of modern humans; third, filling the research gap concerning the transition of the Paleolithic to the Neolithic, as well as the origin of farming in the region. New achievements in Paleolithic archaeology in the Zhengzhou region are of great importance and have provided fresh and valuable materials that shed new light on the study of the development of Paleolithic cultures and the emergence of modern humans in both China and East Asia.

국문초록

2,000년부터 베이징대학교 고고학박물관은 정저우시 문물고고연구소와 협력하여 정저우 지역의 Zhijidong, Laonainaimiao, Zhaozhuang, Huangdikou, Fangjiagou, Xishi, Dongshi, Lijiagou 동굴 유적들을 발굴 조사하였다. 중국 중앙평원지역 발굴을 통해 세 가지 측면의 큰 진전을 이루었다. 첫째, 중기 말~후기 초 구석기(약 50-30ka BP, MIS 3)에 해당하는 Laonainaimiao, Fangjiagou, Zhaozhuang 유적들의 격지-몸돌 제작기술 범주의 석기문화 양상을 정립하였다. 둘째, 북중국처럼 중앙평원지역에서 상대적으로 온난한 기후에서 출현한 현생인류들이 중앙평원과 하천유역을 따라 전개되어 왔던 다양한 고고학적 증거가 발견되었다. 셋째, 구석기~신석기 전환기의 Lijianggou 문화와 Peiligang 문화로 이어지는 좀돌날과 좀돌날몸돌 문화는 점차 감소하고, 식물 씨앗 보존용 도자기와 연마도구가 많이 나타나며 농업 기원에 관한 연구 공백이 메워지고 있다. 정저우지역 구석기 고고학의 새로운 성과는 매우 중요하며, 중국 중부와 동아시아의 구석기 문화 발전과 현생인류의 출현 연구를 조명해주는 새롭고 아주 귀중한 자료를 제공하고 있다.

Keywords: Middle Paleolithic, Late Paleolithic, Paleolithic to Neolithic transition, modern human origins, Zhijidong Cave, Laonainaimiao, Zhaozhuang, Fangjiagou, Xishi, Lijiagou

1. Introduction

Zhengzhou, located in the eastern piedmont of the Songshan Mountains (core area of Central China), is one of the key regions for the origin and development of Chinese civilization. Zhengzhou is also the center of development of early hominins and their cultures, especially in the period from the emergence of modern humans to the origin of agriculture, when a series of crucial changes occurred. From 2,000 onward, the School of Archaeology and Museology of Peking University and the Zhengzhou Municipal Institute of Relics and Archaeology cooperated to excavate a series of sites dated to the Middle to Upper Paleolithic and Paleolithic-Neolithic transition, including the Zhijidong Cave site at Xingyang, the Lijiagou site at Xinmi, the Zhaozhuang and Huangdikou site at Xinzheng, Xishi, Dongshi, and the Fangjiagou site at Dengfeng, as well as the Laonainaimiao site in the Erqi District in Zhengzhou. These sites are of great importance, with the findings providing fresh and valuable materials that shed new light on the study of the development of Paleolithic cultures and the emergence of modern humans in both China and East Asia.

As early as the 1980s, the local administrations of cultural relics and research institutes were already paying much attention to Paleolithic archaeology in the Zhengzhou area. Professionals initiated excavations and field surveys, searching for clues of Paleolithic sites, and discovered a number of important localities, such as the Honggou site in Gongyi County and the Zhijidong Cave site in Xingyang County, representing a very promising start for Paleolithic studies in the region. During the last decade, the Zhengzhou Municipal Institute of Relics and Archaeology, in cooperation with the School of Archaeology and Museology of Peking University, have carried out a series of excavations and archaeological research focusing on key topics, such as the origin of modern humans in East Asia, the Paleolithic–Neolithic transition in Central China, and the origin of agriculture in this area. This work demonstrates recent progress in the Paleolithic archaeology of the Eastern Songshan Piedmont, as described below (Fig. 1).

2. Middle and Upper Paleolithic cultural sequence in Zhengzhou

The establishment of a regional cultural sequence is the foundation of archaeological research for a specific area under study. Given its central location, the Paleolithic cultural sequence of Central China is of great importance for fundamental research in the area, especially during the Middle to Upper Paleolithic period. It also serves as a key enabler of studies on essential topics in prehistoric archaeology, such as Chinese Paleolithic cultural development in general, the emergence of modern humans in this region as well as in East Asia, and their developmental trajectories, and the origin of agriculture in Central China. In the last decade, benefiting from new details about paleo-environmental characteristics and chronology through research on Late Pleistocene loess, as well as substantial data from AMS radiocarbon and OSL dating, newly excavated sites have yielded a rather complete picture of the development of regional Paleolithic cultures since the Late Pleistocene, especially during the middle and late period.

A number of excavated sites in this region were dated to MIS 3, such as Laonainaimiao site in the Erqi District of Zhengzhou, the Fangjiagou site in Dengfeng, and the Zhaozhuang site in Xinzheng, with dates ranging around 45-30 ka BP, and their lithics all falling into the typical core-and-flake technology. The core reductional sequence is simple and used to produce flake blanks for making tools of different shapes and edges, which shows a clear connection with the long-term small-flake industry prevalent in northern China. However, lithics at these sites utilized quartz from distant locations, and their flaking industry was more developed, with unidirectional flaking using a back wedge to produce elongated flakes. Retouching on edges was more evenly distributed, and the number of tools with a more regular shape also increased, which reflected the characteristics of Paleolithic cultures during this time (Fig. 2).

With the arrival of MIS 2, at about 26 ka BP, a distinct change was observed in the regional lithic industry. Primarily due to the environmental change caused by the cooling of the climate, the number of sites decreased drastically. The selection of raw materials also changed from quartz to chertin at the sites that have been discovered. A more important change was that the dominant flaking technology gave way to blade and microblade technology. For example,

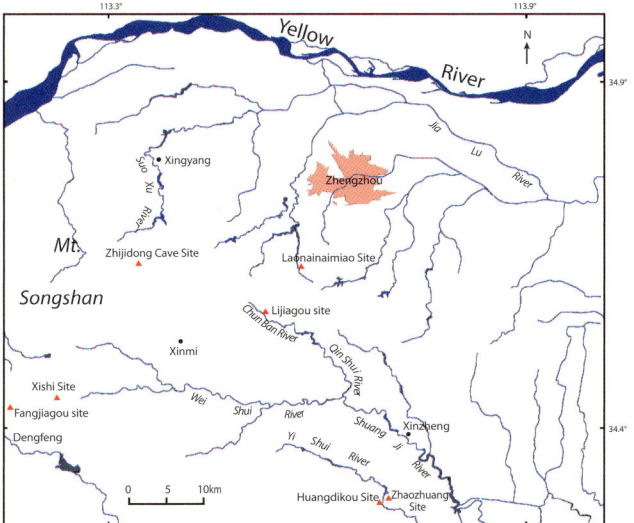

Fig. 1 The map of mentioned Paleolithic sites in Zhengzhou region

Fig. 2 Flake cores from Zhaozhuang site

Fig. 4 Microblade cores from Lijiagou site

3. The emergence of modern humans in the eastern Songshan piedmont

The emergence of modern humans has always been the central issue of prehistoric archaeology and paleoanthropology. Different hypotheses, whether it be the "Multiregional Evolution" or "Recent Out-of-Africa" hypotheses, remain to be tested by solid archaeological materials. Archaeological findings in Central China, the core area of China, and mainland East Asia are of great significance in discussing this topic. For those who advocate for the "Multiregional Evolution" paradigm, it is necessary to demonstrate the continuity of cultural developments in China and East Asia, and thus the Paleolithic cultures in Central China are undoubtedly the most crucial part. For those who propose the replacement of modern humans in East Asia by groups migrating from Africa via the northern or southern route, their hypothesis should be tested with new Paleolithic evidence. Recent Paleolithic discoveries in the Zhengzhou area have provided valuable new evidence to advance this discussion.

As mentioned above, the flake tool tradition long prevalent in northern China continued to be the mainstream from 40–50 ka BP to around 30 ka BP in Central China. Local inhabitants utilized simple flaking techniques to produce tools for daily use. Because of the relatively warm and wet environment of MIS 3, Central China, during this time, became the core area for human activities. Different human groups were distributed in plains and river valleys, in habitable locations. These spots were later turned into long-term base camps, with temporary localities radially distributed around the camps. These local localities were used for hunting, gathering, raw material procurement, tool making, or even symbolic behaviors, such as piling stone blocks atop which was placed the head of a *Palaeoloxodon antiquus*. Such settlement patterns demonstrate the success of human occupation in the eastern Songshan piedmont

Fig. 3 Blade cores from Xishi site

the Dongshi site and the eastern part of the Xishi site in Dengfeng both yielded typical blade products. Moreover, at the Dongshi site, it is possible to reconstruct the whole *chaîne opératoire* of blade and microblade production. These findings indicate that regional Paleolithic culture changed with fluctuations of the global environment. During the cold interval of MIS 2, local culture transited to a blade-microblade industry suitable for specialized hunters with higher mobility. However, this period was still dominated by blade production, while microblade technology was still immature and not capable of completely separating from blade technology (**Fig. 3**).

At about 10 ka BP, local microblade technology became mature, with findings from the lower cultural layer of the Lijiagou site presenting new traits of this period. Although core-and-flake and blade technology still existed during this period, typical boat-shaped and conical microblade cores were completely dominant. Moreover, new cultural traits, such as partly polished stone tools and pottery, also emerged. Recent discoveries in Zhengzhou have demonstrated a clear cultural sequence from the Middle to Upper Paleolithic, i.e., typical flake tools prevailed during 40–30 ka BP, blade and simple microblade technology appeared later, around 20 ka BP, and typical microblade technology became dominant and new cultural traits emerged in 10 ka BP (**Fig. 4**).

during the Late Pleistocene, which also clearly evidences the continuity of Paleolithic cultures in China, as opposed to the interruptive mode repeatedly proposed by some scholars, especially hypotheses suggesting that the cooling of the environment due to the Last Glacial Maximum (LGM) or Toba eruption led to the extinction of Paleolithic cultures in China. These hypotheses do not appear to withstand the testing of new archaeological materials in the Zhengzhou area. New discoveries in Zhengzhou not only demonstrate the continuity of Paleolithic cultures in the region but also indicate that the producers of flake tools exhibited very complex behaviors, e.g., the emergence of symbolic behaviors that are unique to modern humans. At the Laonainaimiao site, well-organized settlement patterns, the long-distance transportation of high-quality raw materials, and improvements in lithic technology all evidence modern human behaviors (**Fig. 5**). In particular, at the Zhaozhuang site, pink sandstone blocks were transported from a distance and piled up as a pedestal, and a huge skull of *Palaeoloxodon antiquus* was placed upon it. Such sophisticated, non-utilitarian activity had clear symbolic meanings, be it out of fear or reverence for giant animals or for praying for a bountiful hunting harvest, serves as definitive evidence for the emergence of modern humans in Central China. The stone mounds topped with an elephant head at the Zhaozhuang site were the first of their kind not only in China but in East Asia more broadly. Lithics found at this site were also of the quartz flake industry, which was prevalent in Northern and Central China at the time, demonstrating the emergence and cultural traits of modern humans in East Asia (**Fig. 6**).

The blade-microblade industry at the Xishi site and Dongshi site of Dengfeng distinctly reflect the influence of global climate fluctuations in the Late Pleistocene on lithic technology and subsistence strategy, and also provide evidence for human dispersal and cultural exchange in China and the central part of East Asia. Different from the long-term core-and-flake technology prevalent in northern China, blade-microblade technology was clearly exotic. Its appearance was more likely the result of the southward migration of specialized hunters in Northern and Central Asia at the time of climate cooling during the LGM. Such dispersal of lithic technology and human groups demonstrate that influence from the north affected Central China, but also that the dispersal happened much later than the emergence of modern humans in this area. The above

Fig. 5 Laonainaimiao site

Fig. 6 Lateral view of the Elephant skull and the pile of pink sandstone at Zhaozhuang site

finding further suggests that external influence during the emergence and development of modern humans in East Asia would evidently leave distinct traces on archaeological materials.

4. The Paleolithic–Neolithic transition in Lijiagou

The excavation of the Lijiagou site in Xinmi in 2009 found the Lijiagou Culture, which was older than the Peiligang Culture and beneath the microblade cultural layer. This finding was another important breakthrough in Central China prehistory after the discovery of the Peiligang Culture in the 1970s, hailed by some scholars as "a long-awaited discovery." The subsequent excavation of the northern and southern parts of the Lijiagou site in 2010 further expanded knowledge about the site. Pottery sherds of the Peiligang Culture were found above the typical Lijiagou

Culture layer, which further confirmed the development from microblades to the Lijianggou Culture and then to the Peiligang Culture, and suggests that groups with different cultural traditions should have been living around the Lijiagou site for a long time during the Paleolithic–Neolithic transition. Their remains have provided vital evidence useful for understanding the transition from the Paleolithic to the Neolithic and from hunting and gathering to agriculture in Central China.

Similar to findings in surrounding areas, such as the Dagang site in Wuyang, Henan, and the Shizitan site in Jixian, Shanxi, microblades discovered in the lower layer of the Lijiagou site mainly fall within the boat-shaped and conical microblade core system, indicating common traits of regional Upper Paleolithic cultures. Products of simple core-and-flake technology and blade technology coexisted with microblade products, with the former accounting for a limited proportion and functioning as a supplement to microblade assemblages. Notably, aside from stone tools and related raw materials, boulders were found to have been artificially transported to the lower cultural layer of the Lijiagou site and might have been used for building residential structures, such as tents or fireplaces. These features were rarely discovered at campsites of earlier hunter-gatherers with higher mobility but, in the later period of the Lijiagou Culture, more transported boulders can be found and their distribution was more concentrated around fireplaces or residential areas. In the 2010 excavation of the south portion of the Lijiagou site, a non-decorated pottery sherd and a partly polished stone adze were also discovered, indicating the complexity of the Paleolithic–Neolithic transition in Central China (Fig. 7).

The period of the Lijiagou Culture witnessed the gradual decline of microblades. Compared with earlier periods, the percentage of microblade products in this layer was reduced, and the technique appeared to be simpler and more casual. At the same time, the number of products from grinding technology increased – in particular, grounding stones. Products of simple core-and-flake technology were still in use. Broken bones were common at the site, but large-sized animals were very rare, as opposed to an abundance of small-sized mammals, indicating the decline of specialized hunting of large-sized animals. The capture of small-sized mammals might have been merely a supplement to subsistence at the Lijiagou site. Although plant remains were

Fig. 7 Pottery sherd of the Lijiagou Culture

absent, the large quantities of pottery sherds demonstrate the prevalence of pottery in this period. As studies of the function of early pottery suggest, sherds found at the Lijiagou site were likely related to the consumption and preservation of plant seeds. Combining findings at the two cultural layers of the Lijiagou site, it is clear that the local inhabitants were gradually changing from highly mobile large-game hunters to settlers relying more on plant resource, which initiated the transition from the Paleolithic to the Neolithic and from hunting and gathering to sedentism and agriculture.

References

Wang Youping et al., 2022. *The Development of Late Pleistocene Human Society and Culture in the Central Plains*, Beijing: Science Press. (in Chinese with English abstract)

Zhengzhou Municipal Institute of Relics and Archaeology & School of Archaeology and Museology, Peking University. 2020. *Zhaozhuang Site: Excavation Report of Paleolithic Site*, Beijing: Science Press.

School of Archaeology and Museology, Peking University & Zhengzhou Municipal Institute of Relics and Archaeology. 2020. *Excavation Report of Fangjiagou Site in Dengfeng*, Beijing: Science Press.

Wang Youping et al., 2018. *Lijiagou Site and the transition of the Paleolithic to Neolithic Age: a study on the origin of agriculture in the eastern foot of Mount Song*, Beijing: Science Press.

The Search for the Paleolithic in the Republic of Khakassia (Southern Siberia)

N.I. DROZDOV[1,2], **D.N. DROZDOV**[1], **V.I. MAKULOV**[3]

[1] Professor Emeritus, International Innovation University, Russia ; kfurao@mail.ru
[2] Siberian Federal University, Russia
[3] St. Petersburg State Budgetary Professional Educational Institution "Polytechnic College of Urban Economy", Russia

ABSTRACT

As the result of exploration work held in 2015-2017 on the right bank of the Abakan River valley in the South of Khakassia, in the vicinity of Matkechik village new Paleolithic localities were discovered: Matkechik 1, 2, 3. At the Matkechik site 1 two cultural layers were found in the prospecting shafts. The artifacts of the first layer were represented with a single- platform pebble core and flakes; of the second cultural layer – with two pebble cores, core blanks, a flat axe made of a flat alongated pebble, scrapers made of big flakes, flakes, blades, chips and cracked animal bones. The material can be referred to Late Paleolithic. At the Matkechic site 2 stone inventory was found in the cultural layer and along the slope of the Abakan River right- bank terrace. The collection consists of flakes and chips with traces of retouching, unprocessed flakes. On some tools there is a carbonaceous crust and traces of corrosion. Typologically the material of Matkechik 2 locality can be preliminarily referred to the time of Middle and Late Paleolithic. At Matkechik locality 3 stone inventory was collected from water galls. The artifacts include a scraper made of flake, a knife with an oval working edge made of flake, pebble flakes which can be referred to the time of Late Paleolithic. In the vicinity of Ust-Sos and Bolshoy Manok settlements several new Paleolithic localities were found. The archeological material consists of stone inventory, and it was discovered in the outcrops of sand blowouts, on the surface and along the slope of the right bank of the Abakan River. The collection consists of subprismatic cors, core blanks, scraper-shaped and knife-shaped tools made of blades and flakes. Typologically the material can be referred to Late Paleolithic.

국문초록

2015-2017년 하카시아 남부 아바칸강 우안 부분에서 진행한 탐사 결과, Matkechik 마을 부근에서 새로운 구석기 유적 Matkechik 1, 2, 3 이 발견되었다. Matkechik 유적 1은 탐색구덩 조사에서 2개 문화층이 발견되었는데, 첫 번째 문화층은 단일 작업면의 자갈돌 몸돌과 격지가 대표적 유물이며, 두 번째 문화층은 두 개 자갈돌 몸돌, 몸돌 밑감, 길죽한 자갈돌로 제작된 도끼, 대형 격지로 만든 긁개, 격지, 돌날, 돌조각, 균열된 동물뼈로 구성되며, 이러한 유물상을 볼 때 후기구석기로 간주된다. Matkechic 2 유적은 문화층과 아바칸강 우안 단구면 상의 문화층에서 두 가지 석기 유형이 발견되었으며, 수습한 유물은 재가공된 격지와 돌조각, 격지로 구성되고, 일부 도구에는 탄소 피박과 부식 흔적이 있다. 본 유적의 유물상으로 볼 때 후기구석기로 간주된다. Matkechik 3 유적에서 수습된 석기유물은 격지로 제작된 긁개, 격지를 이용해 타원형 모서리를 만든 칼, 자갈돌 격지가 포함되며, 유물상으로 볼 때 후기구석기로 간주할 수 있다. 그리고 Ust-Sos와 Bolshoy Manok 정착지 부근의 구석기 유적 석기 유물상은 아각주상 몸돌, 몸돌 밑감, 격지와 돌날로 제작된 긁개류와 칼유형 도구이며, 형식학적으로 볼 때 후기구석기로 간주된다.

Keywords : Khakassia, Abakan River, Matkechik location, travelling expenses fees, Ust-SoS, Bolshoy Manok, Krasny Kamen town, sand blowouts, Middle Paleolithic, Late Paleolithic

1. Introduction

In 2015-2017, the Krasnoyarsk detachment of the IAET SB RAS (Novosibirsk, Russia) together with the staff of the Chongqing Research Institute of Cultural Heritage (Chongqing, China) and the Siberian Federal University (Krasnoyarsk, Russia) conducted archaeological research in the south of the Republic of Khakassia. During the work, several Paleolithic sites were discovered, including stratified ones. In the 40s-80s of the last century, researchers Levashova, Rygdylonom, Z.A. Abramova, S.N. Astakhov, Y.S. Khudyakov in the vicinity of pp. Ust-Sos and Matkechik on the dune blowouts were found several locations of stone tools, among which there was a Paleolithic (Rygdilon, 1953; Abramova et al., 1991; Khudyakov, 1980). But today their geographical links have been lost. There are no pre-existing field roads, livestock farms to which they were tied, many local names have been forgotten (Fig. 1).

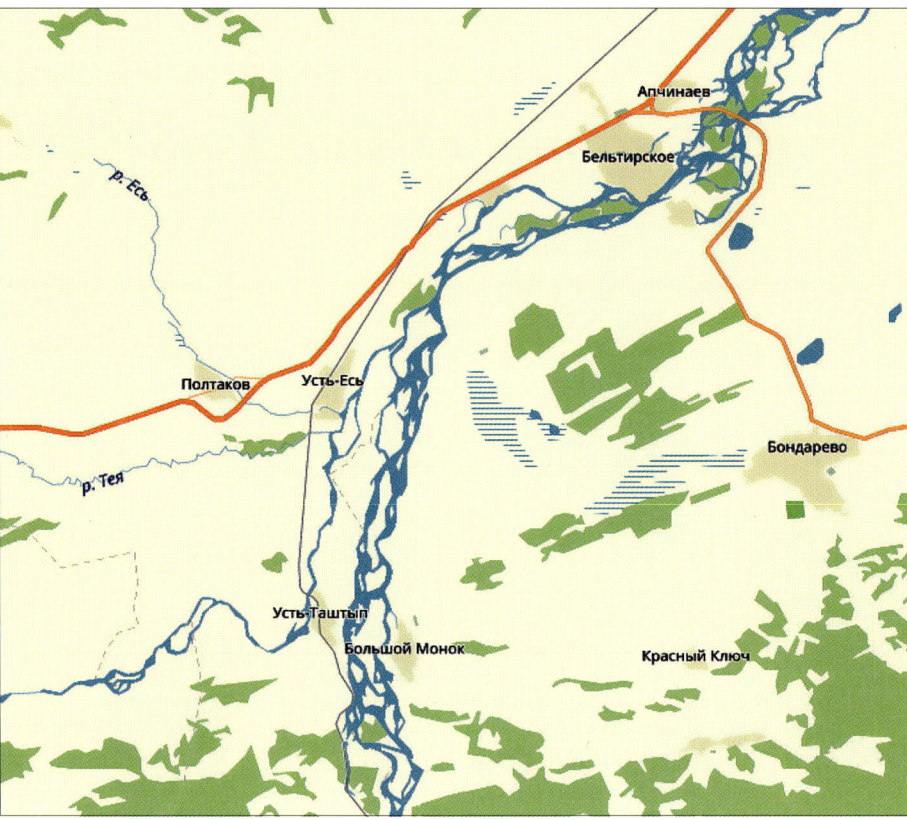

Fig. 1 Area of the field work in the Republic of Khakassia. Location. 1 : Maketchik-1, 2 : Maketchik-2, 3 : Maketchik-3, 4 : Ust-Sos, 5 : Ust-Sos-1, 6 : Ust-Sos-2, 7 : Ust-Sos-3, 8 : Bolshoi Monok

2. Archaeological research on Paleolithic sites

2.1. Location Ust-Sos

It was found at the upper point of the watershed surface and on its western slope between the settlements of Ust-Sos and Bondarevo. The archeological material was collected on the bottoms and slopes of depressions and hollows formed by powerful blowouts. The surrounding surface is slightly blackened, in many places there are small depressions of both formed and old blackened blowouts. The archaeological material was found on the surface of sand blasts, in the form of small accumulations of stone inventory and is represented by: large single-site subprismatic nuclei, blanks of nuclei, chips of various shapes and sizes, plates (some of them have traces of part-time work), crushed pebbles (Fig. 2). The gun set is represented by flat knife-shaped tools made on plates of a sub-rectangular shape, with a working edge at the ends (3 copies). Knife-scrape on a large primary chip from the pebbles. The chip

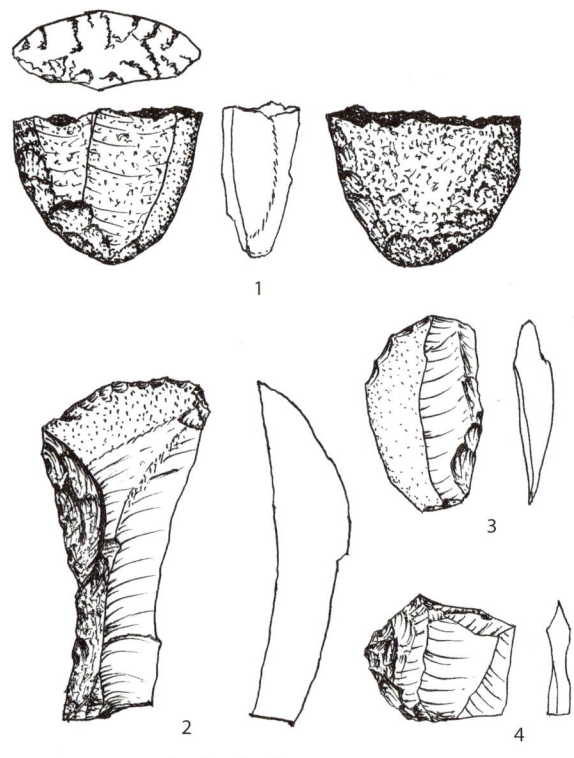

Fig. 2 Location of Ust-Sos. Lifting material 1 : nucleus, 2, 3, 4 : scraping tools

is of a subtriangular shape with oval edges. The pebble surface has been completely preserved on the back. The

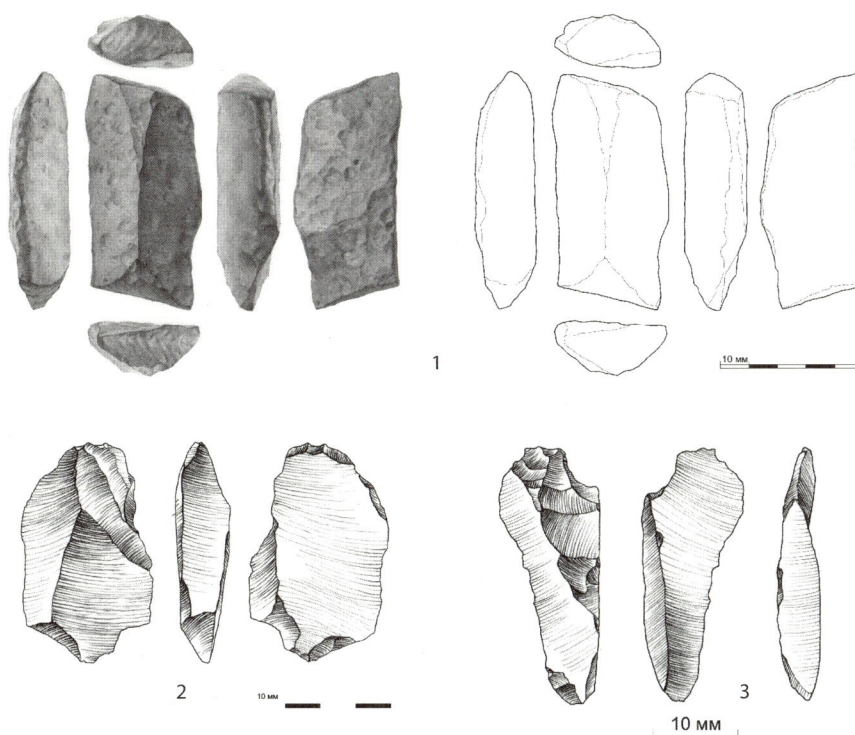

Fig. 3 Location Ust-Sos 2. Carraded plastic

oval working edge is oval, decorated on both sides with multifaceted retouching. Some products have a carbonate crust. The archaeological material has been repositioned. The raw materials were pebbles from the floodplains of the Abakan and Sos rivers, flint, granitoids. Technical and typological material is characteristic of the Late Paleolithic of the Khakasko-Minusinsk basin.

2.1.1. Location Ust-Sos 1

It was revealed on the right-bank estuary section of the Sos River, on the surface of the deluvial gentle southern slope of the Red Stone Mountain, adjacent to the mountain in the form of a terraced approach. A bump was found on the blackened surface, made on a small oval slightly flattened quartzite pebble. There are spot marks of clogging along the perimeter of the artifact. Dating is difficult. On the vertical friezes of the southern slope of the mountain, there are ancient rock carvings of the Bronze and early Iron Ages, made including in the technique of spot embossing. It is possible that the detected bump was used when applying them. Also, on the top of the Red Stone Mountain, the location of a stone inventory of Paleolithic appearance was revealed. Perhaps the bump has rolled off this location.

2.1.2. Location Ust-Sos 2

It was revealed on the top of the Red Stone Mountain. There is a small sample of rock in the place of the exit of the bedrock. At the southern wall of the sample, among the fragments of rock, a single-site nucleus blank was found, made on greenish-colored pebbles, elongated-elongated shape. The playground is decorated with large chips. A flint plate was also found here without additional side work (**Fig. 3**). Typologically, the material can be tentatively attributed to the Late Paleolithic.

2.1.3. Location of Ust-Sos 3

It was revealed on the gentle south-eastern slope of the hill adjacent to the SE slope of the town of Krasny Kamen. Archaeological material, represented by stone inventory. Preparation of a subprismatic single-site nucleus on a small pebble. The working area is decorated with several chips. The surface of the artifact is coveted. A large obbito-retouched chip made of black siliceous rock. The surface is partially carbonated. Typologically, the material can be attributed to the Late Paleolithic.

2.2. Location of the Big Monoc

The location was revealed in the south part of the basin, in the narrow valley of the Bolshoy Monok River, on the southern outskirts of the Bolshoy Monok village on a deluvial terrassoup. Its surface is destroyed by powerful dune blowouts, up to 8-10m deep. The archaeological material is collected at the bottom of the blowouts and is represented by stone inventory: a large subprismatic single-site nucleus, a large tool billet, a knife-shaped tool on a flint plate, plates, flakes and chips. There is a carbonate crust on some artifacts. The technical and typological characteristics of the material allow us to attribute it to the Late Paleolithic. A survey of the right-bank section of the Abakan River in the vicinity of the village of Matkechik at the automobile bridge, above which the river forms a large bend ending in a cape-shaped rocky cliff, was carried out. The surface of the terrace is blackened, its highest point is marked in the area of the bridge crossing, from which it gently descends into and upstream of the river. The side of the terrace is steep, cut by numerous natural washouts, small ravines. Three Paleolithic sites, named Matkechik 1, 2, 3, were identified on the surveyed territory with a length of up to 3km.

Fig. 4 Location of Matkechik 1. Stratigraphic section of pit No. 1. Levels 3.4. contain Late Paleolithic artifacts.

2.3. Location of Matkechik

2.3.1. Location of Matkechik 1

It was found in 4km of the SSZ of Matkechik village during the survey of the right-bank 8–2-meter terrace of the Abakan River, 1.2-1.5km upstream from the bridge. Lifting archaeological material: pebble single-site and double-site nuclei, blanks of nuclei, scrapers and scrapers on large chips, chips and flakes. In the pit, two cultural layers were recorded in a layer of gray-brown light powdery sandy loam (**Fig. 4**). The first cultural layer was detected at a depth of 0.58-0.64m from the modern surface. The archaeological material of the layer is represented by: a blank of a single-site nucleus on a pebble; a chopping tool on a flattened oval-elongated pebble, with a beaten-retouched working edge and a sharpened rim; a plate and flakes. The fauna is represented by small fragments of animal bones. The second cultural layer was found at a depth of 0.74-0.80m from the daytime

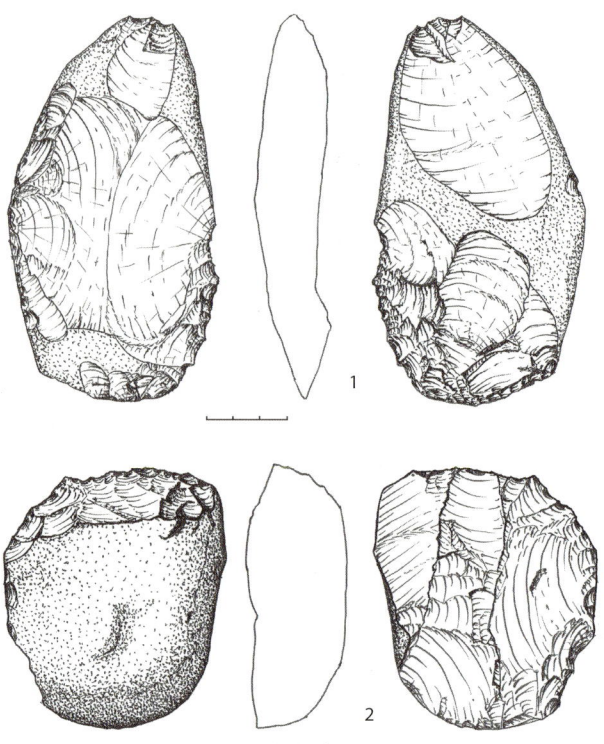

Fig. 5 Location Matkechik 1. 1 : adze, 2 : side-scrapper

surface. The archaeological material is represented by stone inventory. Single-site pebble nuclei with single removal of plates from one end and laterals. Work sites are decorated with large chips. Billets of single-site nuclei on small pebbles. A chopping tool on an elongated-elongated pebble with narrowed ends, on one of which the working edge of a maneuver-oval shape is decorated. The processing was carried out on both sides with rough chips (**Fig. 5**-1). The chopping tool is on a pebble, lenticular one-sided convex in cross-section. Processed with multifaceted retouching (**Fig. 5**-2). The end scrape on a large flat sandstone chip. The working edge is decorated with a cool large retouch. A large chip with retouching, chips and flakes of various shapes and sizes, some have traces of industrial retouching. The surface of most of the artifacts is partially covered with a carbonate crust. Faunal remains are represented by small carbonated fragments of crushed animal bones. The technical and typological characteristics of the stone inventory of the location allow us to pre-date it to the time of the Late Paleolithic. The location is stratified and is promising for stationary excavation studies.

2.3.2. Location of Matkechik 2

It was found on the site of the right-bank terrace of the Abakan River at 350m. from the location of Matkechik 1. Archaeological material was found at several points along the slope of the terrace and in the outcrops of the

Fig. 6 Abakan River, right bank. Location of Matkechik 2. The place of finds of Aeolian-carraded artifacts.

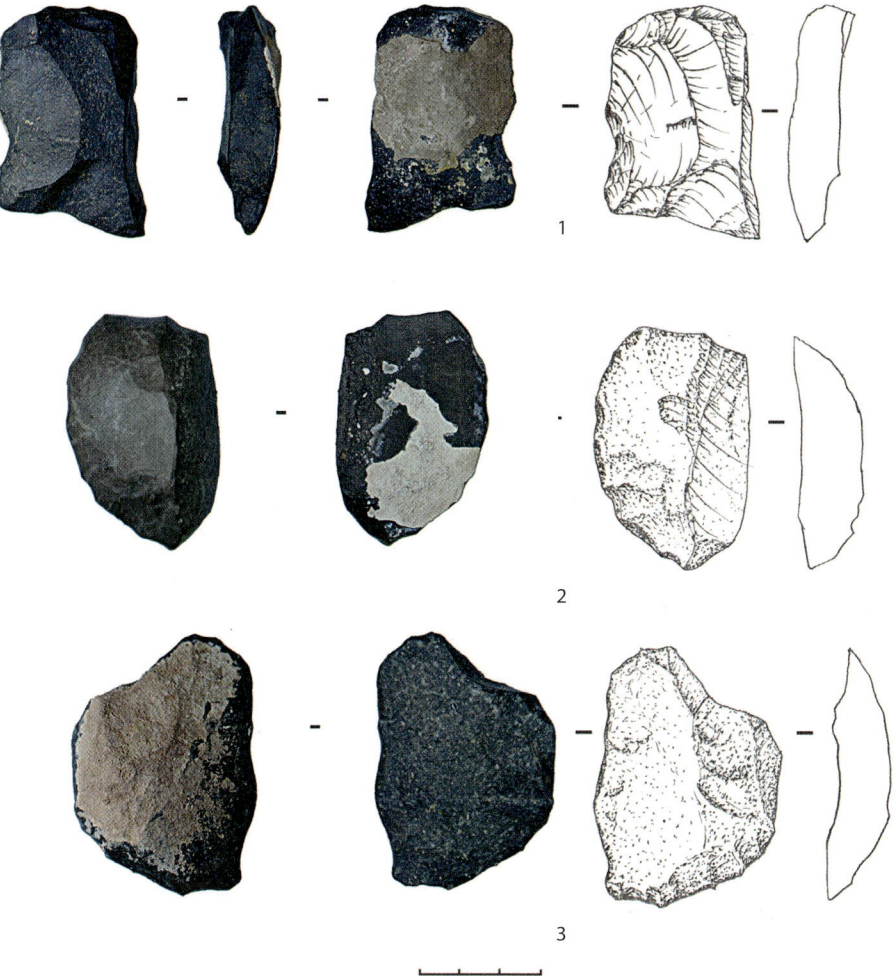

Fig. 7 Location Matkechik 2. 1 : blade-like flake, 2 : end-scrapper on a flake, 3 : retouching flake

geological layer along its side, for about 300m. (Fig. 6). The archaeological material found closest to the location of

Matkechik 1 was made in the outcrop of the geological layer. On the border of greenish-gray sand and continental rock - red weathered siltstone, at a depth of 0.53m. from the daytime surface, a lamellar flake with the edges of the preceding chips along the back was revealed. There is a steep shallow retouch on both edges, and a carbonate crust on the abdomen. 4.5m to the east, in the wall of a small precipitous outcrop at a depth of 0.47-0.53m from the surface, 3 small flakes of flint without side work with a carbonated crust on the surface and a small lobular chip with the remains of a pebble surface were found. 0.40m from the surface. On the border of grayish sandy loam and carbonated weathered bedrock of red-brown alleurolites, a plate chip without processing, with a carbonate crust on the surface, was found. At 20m from the first find, on a cape-shaped ledge in a steep outcrop, in a whitish decomposed carbonate structure, at a depth of 0.33m from the surface, a chip with a fragment of a pebble surface and a shallow working retouch along one edge was found. There is a carbonate crust on the abdomen. The next find was made after 70m. in a steep outcrop in light gray sandy loam. At a depth of 0.20m. from the daytime surface, a small siliceous chip was found without treatment. After 120m. downstream of the river, a large flint flake was found on the surface of the side of a small ravine. There is a scraper retouch around the perimeter. The surface is strongly smoothed by weathering. There is a carbonate crust on its surface. 7 meters away, in a ravine, another large plate flake was found, with a completely smoothed surface. There is a working retouch around the perimeter. There are traces of various degrees of

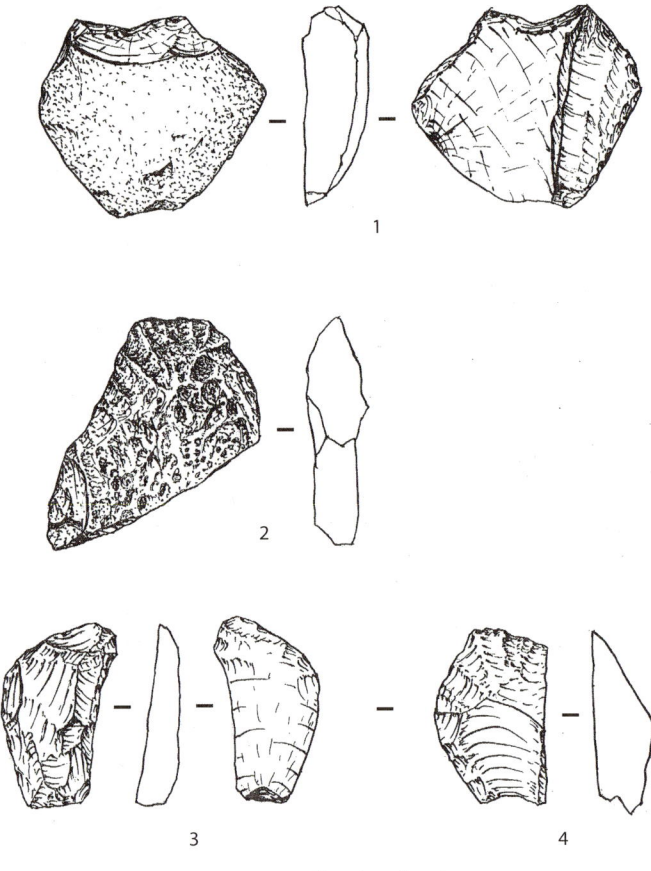

Fig. 8 Location Matkechik 3. 1 : blade-like flake, 2 : flake, 3 : retouching blades

carrasia and lustrage on individual artifacts on the surface (Fig. 7). The technical and typological characteristics of the archaeological material of the location of Matkechik 2 allow us to attribute individual artifacts (with the presence of carrasia and lustrage on the surface) to the Middle Paleolithic period, and the main collection belongs to the Late Paleolithic. The location is stratified, promising in terms of further stationary excavation studies.

2.3.3. Location of Matkechik 3

It was found on the right bank of the Abakan River at 500-600m below the bridge crossing. The surface of the terrace is slightly blackened, cut by small washouts, and sand dune blowouts, in which archaeological material presented by stone inventory was discovered. A bump on a large flattened oval-elongated large pebble of green-gray color. It is decorated at both ends with large double-sided chips forming sharp protrusions on which there are clear traces of clogging. A fragment of a lamellar flake with a strong degree of carrasia. It was broken in ancient times, and fine-meshed corrosion can be traced on the surface of the break. On one edge there are traces of scraper retouching, almost completely removed by carrasia (Fig. 8-1). A flake of a sub-triangular shape, with the remains of a platform, such as "shapo de gandarm". There are traces of working retouching along the edges, except for the remains of the site. The back is a natural pebble surface (Fig. 8-2). A knife on a siliceous plate with an oval blade, which is decorated with fine-scaled retouching. There are traces of a chandelier on the surface of the artifact (Fig. 8-3). The combined end-scraper is a screwdriver on a plate chip. At the proximal end there is a screwdriver, at the distal end there is a scraper retouch. A surface with faint traces of carrasia. Plate chipping of siliceous rock without additional processing. Large pebble chips, large and small flakes. The technical and typological characteristics of the archaeological material of the location of Matkechik 2 allow us to attribute individual artifacts (with the presence of carrasia and lustrage on the surface) to the Middle Paleolithic period, and the main collection belongs to the Late Paleolithic. The location seems promising for conducting stationary excavation studies.

3. Conclusion

We note that the identified Paleolithic sites in the valleys of the pp. Sos and Bolshoy Monok and the village of Matkechik allow us to talk about the prospects of searching for stratified monu- ments of the Middle and Late Paleolithic in the valley of the Abakan River, in the area adjacent to its exit from the mountainous taiga area into the steppe zone of the southern outskirts of the Khakass-Minusinsk basin, the study of which will make it possible to restore the pages of the history of the initial settlement and further development by ancient man this region of Khakassia.

References

Абрамова З.А., Астахов С.Н., Васильев С.А., Ермолова Н.М., Лисицын Н.Ф. Палеолит Енисея. - Ленинград: Наука. - 1991. - 160 с.

Рыгдылон Э.Р. Новые следы поселений каменного века в бассейне Среднего Енисея// МИА, 1953, № 39. - С. 276-285.

Худяков Ю.С. Работы Хакасского отряда в 1975 г.// Источники по

археологии Северной Азии (1935-1976 гг.). - Новосибирск: Наука, 1980. С. 97-122.

Towards the roots of Eurasia : The Moravian stone discs

Jiří SVOBODA

Professor Emeritus, Academy of Science of the Czech Republic, Czech; j.svd@volny.cz

ABSTRACT

Using the case of Moravian stone discs, this paper addresses the possibility of long-term persistence of archaic patterns of human behavior in ethnographic and historial records of North Eurasia. Several Gravettian sites in Moravia have provided large, heavy, centrally perforated discs made of soft marlstone plaques. In two cases (Předmostí and Brno 2), these objects were associated with human burials. Discs identical in size and weight, made of metal or jade, are also known from later Siberian and Chinese contexts. Approaches derived directly from comparative anthropology and/or diffusionism may lead to simplicist conclusions. To avoid the risks of comparing unrelated patterns and objects, this paper aims to place them in the context of the Northern Eurasian landscape and its long-term intellectual record.

국문초록

이 논문은 석재 원반 사례를 이용하여 북유라시아의 민족지 및 역사기록에서 이른시기 호모사피엔스 행동 패턴이 장기간 지속되었을 가능성을 다루고 있다. 모라비아에서는 그라베시안(Gravettian) 시기의 프레드모스티(Předmostí)와 브루노 2(Brno 2) 유적에서 부드러운 이회석(Marlstone)으로 제작된 크고 무겁고 중앙부에 천공된 원반이 출토되었고, 이 유물은 인간 매장과 관련 있는 것으로 본다. 석재 원반은 크기와 무게가 동일하고 금속이나 옥으로 만들어졌으며 나중시기의 시베리아와 중국 유적에서도 나타나는 것으로 알려져 있다. 비교인류학이나 확산주의적인 직접적 접근방법을 사용하면 단순한 결론으로 이어질 위험이 있다. 따라서 관련 없는 대상 유물과 유물 형태의 직접 비교라는 위험성을 피하기 위해 이 논문에서는 이 유물을 북유라시아 자연경관과 장기적으로 기록된 인간 지성이라는 맥락의 접근을 목표로 하고 있다.

Keywords : Eurasia, Moravia, Upper Paleolithic, China, stone discs, ethnoarchaeology, symbolism

1. Introduction

Since its beginning in the late 19th century, Paleolithic archaeology and paleoethnology borrowed analogies from ethnology and history, and Russian Paleolithic archaeology specifically profited from the North Asian record. The application of ethnological observations to the past was purely empirical at the time. Later, in the early 20th century, positivist researchers critisized the non-systemic approach and random selection of data. In the later 20th century, as ethnoarchaeology was being formed as a discipline equipped with its own methodology, this type of reasoning, especially in the context of the post-processualist concern for archaic symbolism, was being reconsidered.

Discussions of early shamanism make an important contribution to these discussions. Diffusionists and comparative anthropologists argue that shamans share similar techniques, ideas, and rituals worldwide and stress distant analogies in human behavior, while evolutionists argue that features recorded today result from a long-term process of progressive development from proto-shamanism to actual shamanism.

2. Contextual framework : The Eurasian steppe

Approaches derived directly from diffusionism and comparative anthropology may lead to simplifications. To avoid the risks of comparing unrelated patterns and objects, this paper aims to place them in the context of the Northern Eurasian landscape and its long-term intellectual record. In another words, analogies and parallels become meaningful within a defined spatio-temporal context.

The cultural unity of Northern Eurasia during the Upper Pleistocene was framed by landscapes and climates. To the north, this zone was bordered by continental glaciers with areas of open tundra; meanwhile, to the south, the zone was demarcated by more or less continuous mountain chains: the Alps, Carpathians, Caucasus, Tian-Shan, Altai, and Sayans. The cold and vast steppe, patterned by mosaics of bushes and patches of conifer forests, housed large herds of reindeer, horses, mammoths, and rhinoceros, and was open to long-distance movements of both animals and humans. It is likely that the richess in biomass, meat, fat, and protein offered by animal herds attracted early modern humans from their southern homelands to these otherwise hostile periglacial zones (where, in addition, they risked conflict with Neanderthals and other archaic humans).

The northern steppes encouraged the collective hunting of large animal herds. When led by a common strategy, hunting was usually successful and allowed for the seasonal coexistence of larger human groups. When meat storage was implemented well, these groups could have coexisted over longer timespans throughout the year. Large aggregation sites in the Eurasian steppe were places for the creation and use of symbolic and decorative objects (such as the typical female figurines; Abramova, 1995).

3. The discs : Contexts of discovery, description, raw material, function

In 1891, Alexander Makowsky salvaged the remains of a male burial during engineering work along Francouzská Street in Brno, Czech Republic. Given the rich equipment found in this burial, it is believed that the buried man was of special significance, perhaps a sorcerer or shaman (Valoch, in Jelínek et al., 1959; Oliva, 1996). In his orginal report, Makowsky (1892) mentioned two marlstone discs found in the burial, one of which was apparently not preserved in the assemblage curated at the Technical High School. Therefore, it was presumed to be lost. However, the other disc, which was curated in the Moravian Museum collection, is horizontally split into two conjoining pieces, and thus it is possible that Makowsky simply did not realize that they fit together (**Fig. 1**). The diameter of the disc is 140mm, with an aperture 45-50mm, a thickness of 24mm, and a weight of 715g (the second one, following Makowsky, should have been

Fig. 1 Brno 2. Stone disc, coll. Moravian Museum Brno, photo by M. Frouz

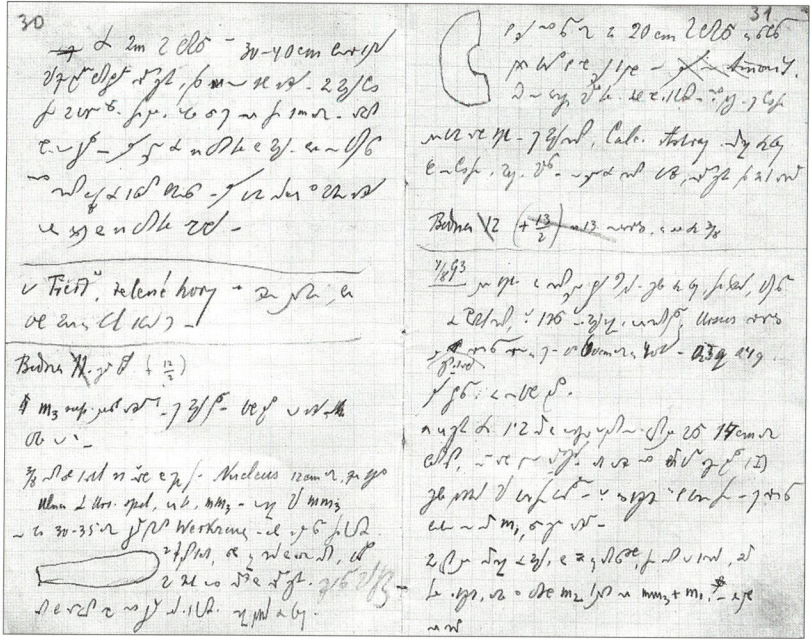

Fig. 2 Předmostí I, Diary of K.J. Maška, 3rd August 1894, mentioning the discovery of a fragment of stone disc. Institute of Archaeology, AS CR, Dolní Věstonice.

larger – 150mm in diameter). Valoch and Oliva described traces of abrasion in the aperture and red spots and dendrites on the surface (Valoch, in Jelínek et al., 1959; Oliva, 1996).

Three years later, in August 1894, Karel J. Maška discovered objects of the same type at the site of Předmostí (Fig. 2). At this site, he conducted an excavation in concentric bands in order to stay in the shade of an elm in the northern part of the surveyed area as long as possible. These bands stretched from the north to the east but, on August 3rd of that year, he turned southward, reaching the upper layer of a human burial area "so that any of the workers, the numerous watchers and I myself could realise that just a shallow depths below the stones something important lay." (Maška, 1895). On that day, he found a fragment of a disc, making a simple sketch of it on page 31 of his diary. The burial area, consisting of more than 20 buried individuals, was fully excavated between August 7th and September 10th (Maška, 1895; Svoboda, 2008). A complete disc from the excavation is curated in the Moravian Museum collection, but it unfortunately lacks a clear indication of when and how it was found. The diameter of the disc is 140mm (Fig. 3). A note from August 3rd suggests an association with the human burial area, at least for the fragment. In this context, Absolon (Absolon and Klíma, 1977) mentioned fragments of various circular stones discovered during his excavation at Dolní Věstonice.

Additional perforated discs from various south Moravian sites, not exactly of the same type as those described above and roughly elaborated, are curated in the Moravian Museum collection. These are listed and described by Oliva (Oliva, 2007; Jiřice, Měnín, Telnice, Židlochovice), while others are indicated in earlier Museum records (Bořetice, Brumovice). In one case, several discs were even placed one on the other "like a chimney" (A. Jílek, unpubl. report in the Moravian Museum, 1934). However, all of these discs were found during early surveys and thus without clear archaeological contexts.

Finally, the excavation at Pavlov I by Bohuslav Klíma yielded part of a comparable disc (Fig. 4) and another, smaller fragment (Klíma, 1984; Svoboda and Přichystal, 2005). In terms of petrography, the raw material was determined to be marlstone or marl slate (determined by Štelcl jun., Mrázek, Přichystal). This material occurs as grey, dark-grey, brownish,

Fig. 3 Předmostí I, Stone disc, coll. Moravian museum Brno, photo by M. Frouz

Fig. 4 Pavlov I, part of a stone disc, coll. Institute of Archaeology, AS CR, Dolní Věstonice, photo by M. Frouz

or yellowish lithified calcareous claystones, gradually transforming into clay limestones. It may originate from several outcrops in south Moravia – e.g., as intercalations in the Ždánice-Hustopeče Formation, in parts of the Menilite Formation (Dynow) or Klentnice Formation (Stráník et al., 1999). Although widely used for flake and blade production (especially at Pavlov I), the occurrence of this material as thin bands or solid crusts within clayish or silty Tertiary sediments is advantageous for producing plaques or discs (Klíma, 1984; Svoboda and Přichystal, 2005). With the exception of Předmostí, all items mentioned above are from sites not too far from the raw material outcrops.

Discussing the practical functions of these discs provided no convincing results. All of the discs have identical or similar dimensions (diameter of around 140mm). Grinding or any other function related to the rotation of a heavy object is unlikely because the material is soft and easy to break, the shape of the circle is slightly asymmetrical, and no use-wear traces are observed on the expected grinding surfaces. Use as a throwing weapon, as suggested by Absolon (Absolon and Klíma, 1977) based on analogies from India (tshkran), does not seem likely due to the significant weight of the object and other practical reasons. Finally, its use in games, as practiced by certain Northwest American Indian tribes, is difficult to consider in this context.

4. Analogy I : Siberian ethnology

In the Siberian ethnological record, shamans were equipped with discs of similar shape and weight, made mostly of metal in this case. They were attached to the body at various places, and additional figurative pendants could be tied to these circles. One common idea in shamanism is that there are multiple worlds, superimposed over each other, and that shamans are capable of traveling from one to another. In this context, the discs, especially their central aperture, symbolize ascent to another world (Czaplicka, 1914; Zelenin, 1935; Potapova and Levina, 1956; Anisimov, 1958; Dioszégi, ed., 1968; Alekseev, 1980).

5. Analogy II : Ancient China

The influence of northern (so-called "barbarian") traditions in the formation of Chinese mythology is generally accepted. From the Chou period ownward, discs of the same shape and size, here mostly of jade, were called *pi*. They symbolized the circular sky, and their central hole represented the *lie-chhiu*, through which lightning flashes (**Fig. 5**, Christie, 1968). These discs were used in rituals by kings or in investitures of princes. Evidence from a protohistoric Korean burial

Fig. 5 Jade disc of Chinese origin, coll. Museum Tokio, photo by J. Svoboda

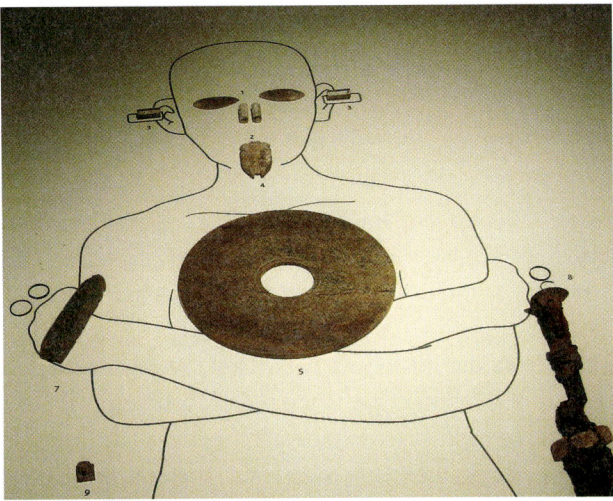

Fig. 6 Disc used as a pectoral in a Korean protohistoric burial. National Museum Soeul, photo by J. Svoboda

illustrates the use of these discs as a pectoral, on the chest of a diseased warrior (**Fig. 6**). If these objects symbolized "gates" to other worlds, than this meaning may be derived from older "barbarian" traditions in the north.

6. Conclusion

As Karel Absolon put it (in Absolon and Klíma, 1977): "Here, again, we face the old secret of a significative relationship of numerous paleolithic or other prehistoric cultural objects with those of the ancient Orient".

Archaeological and ethnological record offers numerous formal analogies across the world, be it Orient or elsewhere. Here we raise the case of North Eurasian stone discs. To gain credibility to formal and symbolic relationships among these specific objects, we emphasize the unique nature of the Eurasian steppic belt and climates as a potential framework for the formation of common mythological and religious background.

References

Abramova, Z.A., 1995. L´art paléolithique d´Europe orientale et de Sibérie, Grenoble: Jerome Millon.

Absolon, K., Klíma, B., 1977. Předmostí. Ein Mammutjägerplatz in Mähren. *Fontes Archaeologiae Moraviae* 8, Praha.

Alekseev, N.A., 1980. *Ranniye formy religiyi tyurkojazychnych narodov Sibiri*, Novosibirsk: Nauka.

Anisimov, A.F., 1958. Religiya Evenkov v istoriko-geneticheskom izucheniyi i problemy priskhozhdeniya pervotnykh verovaniy. *Izdatelstvo AN SSSR*, Moskva-Leningrad.

Christie, A., 1968. *Chinese mythology*, Feltham: Paul Hamlyn.

Czaplicka, M.A., 1914. *Aboriginal Siberia: A study in social anthropology*, Oxford: Clarendon Press.

Dioszégi, V. ed., 1968. *Popular Beliefs and Folklore Tradition in Siberia*, Budapest: Akadémiai Kaidó.

Jelínek, J., Pelíšek, J., Valoch, K., 1959. Der fossile Mensch Brno II. *Anthropos* 9, Brno.

Klíma, B., 1984. Sonderbare Rohstoffe der paläolithischen Steinindustrie aus Pavlov (ČSSR). In: *IIIrd Seminar in Petroarchaeology, Reports*, Plovdiv, 201-213.

Makovsky, A., 1892. Der diluviale Mensch im Löss von Brünn. *Mitteilungen der Anthropologischen Gesellschaft Wien* 22, 73-84.

Maška, K.J., 1895. Diluviální člověk v Předmostí. *Časopis Vlastivědeného spolku musejního Olomouc* 12, 4-7.

Oliva, M., 1996. Mladopaleolitický hrob Brno II jako příspěvek k počátkům šamanismu. *Archeologické rozhledy* 48, 353-383.

Oliva, M., 2007. Gravettien na Moravě. *Dissertationes archaeologicae* 1, Brno-Praha.

Potapova, M.G., Levina, A.P., 1956. Narody Sibiri. *Izdatelstvo Akademii Nauk SSSR*, Moskva-Leningrad.

Stráník, Z., Čtyřoký, P., Havlíček, P., 1999. Geological history of the Pavlovské vrchy Hills. *Journal of Geological Sciences* 49, 5-32.

Svoboda, J., 2008. The Upper Paleolithic burial area at Předmostí: Ritual and taphonomy. *Journal of Human Evolution* 54, 15-33.

http://hdl.handle.net/11104/0160302

Svoboda, J., Přichystal, A., 2005. Non-flint and heavy-duty industries. In: J. Svoboda Ed., Pavlov I-Southeast: A window into the Gravettian lifestyles. *The Dolní Věstonice Studies* 14, Brno, 148-166.

Valoch, K., 1960. Bemerkenswerte jungpaläolithische Steingeräte aus Předmostí in Mähren. *Časopis Moravského muzea* 45, 21-26.

Zelenin, D.K., 1935. Ideologiya sibirskogo shamanstva. *Izvestiya Akademii nauk SSSR*, Moskva: Nauka.

Chapter 3.
Late Paleolithic Site of Suyanggae

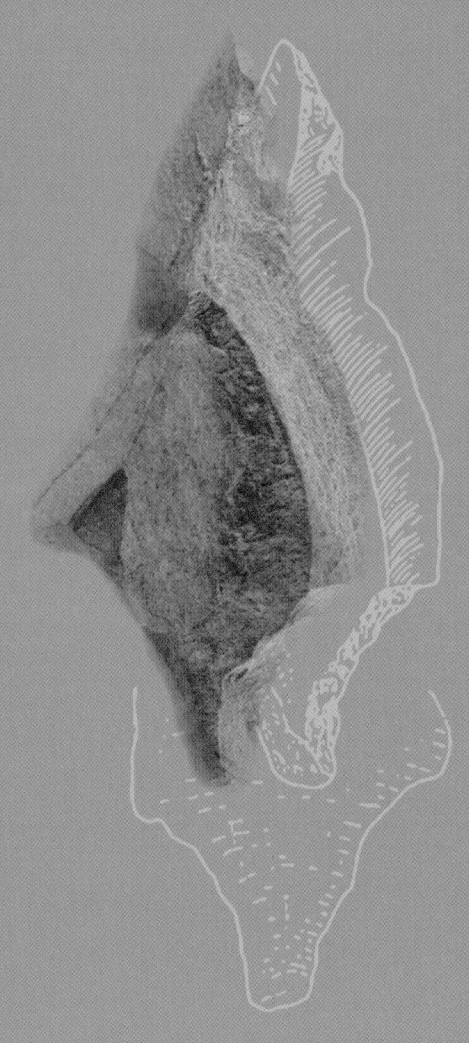

Upper Paleolithic site-forming process and chronostratigraphy of the Suyanggae sites (Loc. 1, Loc. 3, Loc. 6), Danyang County, Korea

Ju-yong KIM[1], Yung-jo LEE[2], Jong-yoon WOO[2], Ho-seong SUH[3], Seung-won LEE[2], Keun-chang OH[4]

[1] Honorary researcher, Korea Institute of Geoscience and Mineral Resources (KIGAM), Korea ; kjy@kigam.sci.kr
[2] Institute of Korean Prehistory (IKP), Korea
[3] Korea Research Institute of Standards and Science, Korea
[4] Quaternary and Paleo-environmental Research (QPR), Korea

ABSTRACT

Suyanggae Paleolithic sites, including Loc. 1, Loc. 3, and Loc. 6, are located above the 2nd (Loc. 1 and 6 and the 3rd fluvial terraces [Loc. 3]). Sedimentary deposits in representative profiles typically consist of fluvial gravels and flooding muds in the lower part of the section, transitioning to pedogenized sandy muds or simply muds in the upper part of the profile. The analysis revealed that the C-M patterns of the fine-grained sediments at the Suyanggae sites are characterized by two distinct sedimentary deposits. This indicates that fluvial sediments in the lower part were derived from both traction and suspension processes, but pedogenized deposits near the surface or toward the upper part were mainly transported by slope mudflow processes. The stone tools found at the Suyanggae sites include tang points, cores, flakes, blades, microblades, end-scrapers, and other items, primarily made from metamorphosed mudstones. Particularly, a line-engraved cobblestone, serving as a metrological tool, was discovered in CL 3 of Suyanggae Loc. 6 and may be regarded as an important indicator for the development of cognitive ability in Late Paleolithic *Homo sapiens*. Radiocarbon dating undertaken to determine the ages of cultural layers at the Suyanggae sites revealed that a typical cultural layer of Suyanggae Loc. 1 is less than 15 ka (Late Upper Paleolithic), cultural layer 2 (CL 2) of Suyanggae Loc. 6 is approximately 20 ka, and CL 3 and 4 (CL 3 and CL 4) are about 36–42 ka, respectively. Lastly, as a result of optically stimulated luminescence (OSL) dating of Suyanggae Loc. 3, the ages of reddish-brown paleosoils converge at approximately 40.8 ka, while those of the yellowish-brown paleosoil range around 33.5–40 ka. This may indicate that the age of cultural layers at Suyanggae Loc. 3 ranges from 33 ka to 40 ka (Early Upper Paleolithic).

국문초록

수양개 구석기 유적 1, 3, 6지구(Loc. 1, 3, 6)는 남한강의 제2, 제3 하안단구 위에 위치하며, 대표단면을 보면 하부에는 하성역층과 범람성 니질층이 우세하게 분포하며 상부로 가면서 토양화된 니사질 내지 니질층이 분포하고 있다. 수양개 1지구와 6지구는 남한강 제2 하안단구, 수양개 2지구는 남한강 제3 하안단구 위에 각각 분포한다. 수양개 구석기 유적의 퇴적층은 입도 C-M 양상이 2개의 서로 다른 퇴적물로 구성되어 있음이 밝혀졌다. 하성기원 퇴적물은 하천 유수(fluvial flow)의 견인작용(traction)이나 부유작용(suspension)으로 이동된 퇴적물이 우세하며, 지표면 혹은 상부로 갈수록 사면작용으로 이동된 니류성(mudlow deposits) 퇴적물이 우세하게 분포한다. 수양개 유적에서 주로 출토되고 있는 구석기 유물은 변성 니질암류가 우세한 슴베찌르개, 몸돌, 격지, 돌날, 좀돌날, 밀개 등을 포함하는 다양한 종류의 석기가 많이 출토되었다. 특히 수양개 6지구 3문화층에서 계측도구로 추정되는 눈금새긴돌(line-engraved cobble stone)이 최초로 출토되었으며, 이는 후기 구석기시대 호모사피엔스의 인지발달 특성을 지시하는 주요한 유물로 인식되고 있다. 수양개 유적의 문화층 시기를 규명하기 위해 방사성탄소연대 측정 결과, 수양개 1지구의 대표적 문화층은 후기구석기 말(약 2만년 전후), 수양개 6지구 2문화층은 후기구석기 말(약 2만년 전), 그리고 3문화층과 4문화층은 후기구석기 초(약 3.6–4.2만년 전)로 각각 밝혀졌다. 또한 수양개 3지구에 대한 OSL 연대측정 결과, 적갈색 고토양층이 약 40.8 ka, 황갈색 고토양층이 33.5–40 ka로 나타나므로 고토양층의 연대를 감안하면 수양개 3지구 문화층은 후기구석기 초(33–40 ka)를 지시하고 있다.

Keywords: Suyanggae Loc. 1, Loc. 3, Loc. 6, Upper Paleolithic (UP), Line-engraved cobblestone, Fluvial–slope processes, Fluvial terrace, Geosols

1. Introduction

Suyanggae Paleolithic sites (Cultural Heritage Site no. 398) are located near Aegog-ri (Suyanggae Loc. 1 and Loc. 3) and Hajin-ri (Loc. 6), Danyang County, in Chungbuk Province. Three excavation localities include Suyanggae Loc. 1, Loc. 3., and Loc. 6 (Lee, 1989, 1999, 2000, 2001, 2007; Lee et al., 1992, 1993, 1999, 2004, 2013a, 2013b; Kim et al., 2005, 2006, 2017, 2020; Oh et al., 2018). Suyanggae Paleolithic sites are geomorphologically associated with the marginal parts of the river valley and the flooding banks of the Namhan River (Fig. 1).

In particular, the river terrace located higher than the present river bottom was developed along the foothills of steep mountains, frequently showing meandering cores along the Namhan River. Suyanggae sites are related to the old river-bottom sand and gravel deposits, as shown in Loc. 1, Loc. 3, and Loc. 6. Among the three sites, Suyanggae Loc. 3 is the highest in terms of topographic elevation. Specifically at Suyanggae Loc. 1, the old riverbed sands and gravels are distributed on the lower terrace (2nd FT) at a level of about 125–127m (asl) above the present river bottom (asl 115m). Meanwhile, at Suyanggae Loc. 6, the old riverbed sands are dominant at a level above 122m (asl) (Fig. 2).

At the Suyanggae sites, geosols overlies fluvial deposits or slope sediments. Geosols are defined as soil-stratigraphic units, typically found as soil wedges formed under the freezing and thawing process of the glacial period. Geosols are ubiquitously developed and observed at Paleolithic sites in Korea (Kim et al., 2016). As a mesoscale site-forming context, it may be important to consider morpho-, pedo-, and sedimentary processes in the Suyanggae Loc. 1, Loc. 3, and Loc. 6. The purpose of this research was to compare both site-forming processes and artifact productions in the geoarcheological context of Suyanggae sites, particularly related to Loc. 1, Loc. 3, and Loc. 6.

2. General Background

Suyanggae Loc. 1 was initially excavated between 1983 and 1985, although the main excavation site was submerged by the present Chungju Dam. The type section has been known and designated by Representative Profile-1 (RP1-1) (Fig. 3). Suyanggae Loc. 1 was excavated again at the submerged part of the Chungju Dam, which is located very close to the downstream part of the initial Suyanggae Loc. 1. The type section, north-facing wall of GRID 6DE, was designated Representative Profile-2 (RP1-2) (Fig. 4). As RP1-2

Fig. 1 Landscape settings of Suyanggae Paleolithic sites, including Loc. 1, Loc. 3., and Loc. 6.

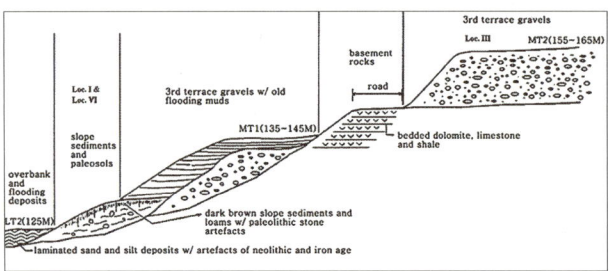

Fig. 2 Morph-sedimentary system of Loc. 1, Loc. 3, and Loc. 6 at the Suyanggae Paleolithic sites.

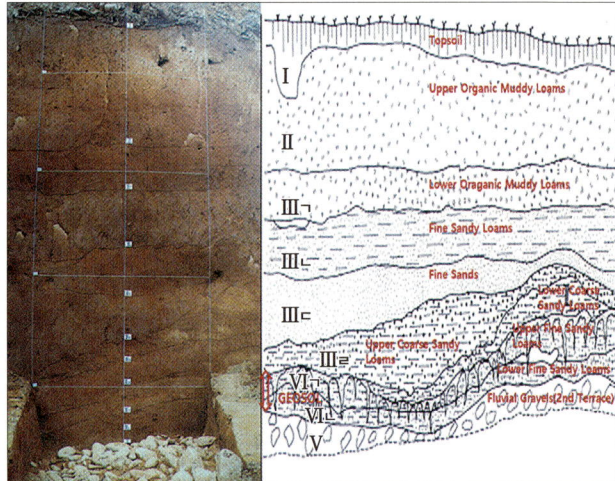

Fig. 3 Litho-profile (RP1-1) of the Suyanggae site Loc. 1, showing fluvial Gravels, Sand and Muds derived from fluvial origin, associated with cryoturbated Geosol.

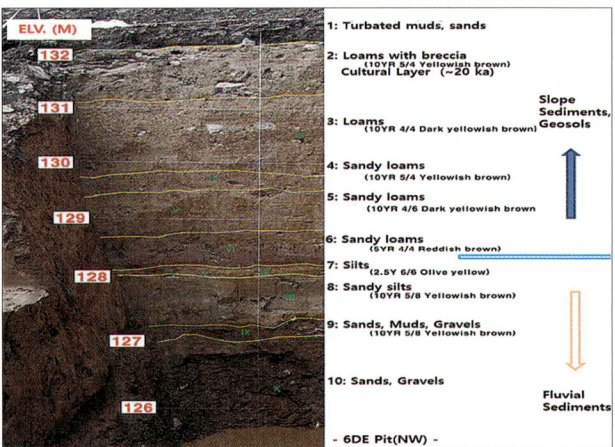

Fig. 4 Representative litho-profile (RP 1-2) at '–6DE pit' (northwest wall) of Loc. 1 at the Suyanggae site, showing lower fluvial muds, sands and gravels overlying pedogenized slope sediments as Geosols.

is near the valley mouth and slope margin, it is characterized by slope sediments, as well as flooding muds, sands, and gravels as channel lag.

At Suyanggae Loc. 3, sedimentary deposits consist of sand and gravel at the bottom, slope deposits containing angular to rounded gravels in the middle, and geosols with frost cracks on top (Fig. 5). The geosols, which have polygonal patterned grounds, are interpreted to have formed under the periglacial process. A thick layer of gravels as lag deposits was developed just above the middle fluvial terrace. Most stone artifacts, however, were found at the interfaces between either fluvial gravel and sand deposits or fluvial deposits and slope deposits, or in reddish-brown geosol (Grb) to dark-brown geosol (Gdb) or brown geosol (Gb). Some handaxes were also found at Loc. 3. The formation age of the middle terrace has been considered for the last two decades (Lee et al., 1992; Kim et al., 1998, 2001, 2006, 2008; Kim, 2001). The age of the lowermost part of the sand and gravel formed on the middle fluvial terrace may extend as far back as 300 ka, equivalent to MIS 9 (Martinson et al., 1987). However, the ages of other interfaces, including slope deposits and geosols above the middle fluvial terrace, are much younger than the formation age of the fluvial terrace as a geomorphic process.

Lastly, at Suyanggae Loc. 6, sedimentary deposits are characterized by mudflows with debris toward the slope and fluvial sands and flooding muds toward the Naham River (Kim et al., 2017, Fig. 6).

Three reference pits (-5D, 1E, -1D) with representative profiles show slightly different lithological features (Kim et al., 2023). Below 123.7m (asl), sandy muds are the main components, which were derived from the frequent inundation of the old Namhan River. In the lithological profile of the "-5D pit," mudflows intercalated with debris flow are dominant at an elevation higher than 127.3m, while slope-derived deposits and fluvial sedimentary deposits both prevail between elevations of 127.3m and 123.7m. Below 123.7m, sandy muds are the main components, which were derived from frequent inundation of the old Namhan River. But in the lithological profile of the "1E pit," slope-derived deposits and flooding muds both prevail between elevations of 129.3m and 126.5m. Below an elevation of 126.5m, sandy muds are the main components, which were derived from frequent inundation of the old Namhan River. Finally, in the lithological profile of the "-1D pit," mudflows and debris flows are dominant at elevations higher than 127.5m. Slope-derived deposits and flooding muds both prevail between elevations of 127.5m and 126.5m. Below an elevation of 126.5m, sandy muds from old flooding are the dominant sedimentary matrix (Kim et al., 2023).

3. Site-Forming Processes of Suyanggae sites

3.1. Suyanggae Loc. 1

Suyanggae Loc. 1 is located at 182-1 Aegog-ri, Jeokseong-myeon, Danyang, Chungbuk Province. This site was initially excavated from the 2nd to the 4th sessions between 1983 and 1985, with the main excavation site now submerged by the Chungju Reservoir Dam. The original lithologic profile has been known and designated as the initial representative profile (Kim et al., 2020). Suyanggae Loc. 1 was re-excavated from the submerged part of the Chungju Reservoir Dam, which is located very close to the downstream part of the initial representative profile of Suyanggae Loc. 1. Suyanggae Loc. 1 was newly re-excavated in 2013, and the profile (GRID 6DE, north-facing wall) was designated as a new representative profile of Suyanggae Loc. 1 (Lee et al., 2018; Oh et al., 2018), which is adjacent to the valley mouth and slope margin. The sedimentary deposits of Suyanggae Loc. 1 are characterized by slope sediments,

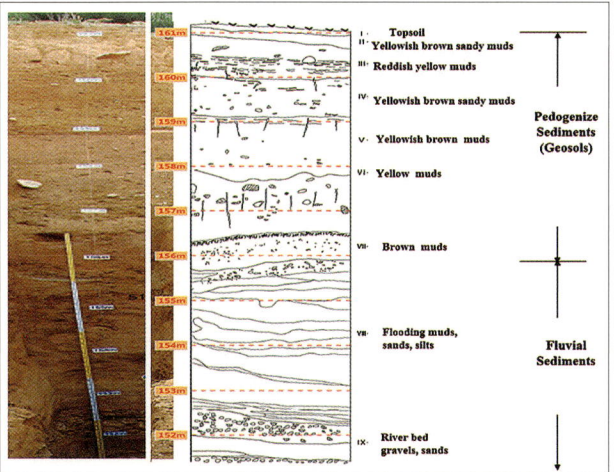

Fig. 5 Representative litho-profile (1Ga west wall) of Loc. 3 at the Suyanggae site, showing Pedogenized muds as Geosols overlying flooding muds, sands and gravels of fluvial origin. Gravels are originated from the 3rd Fluvial terrace in the Namhan River Basin.

Fig. 6 Transversal (left, right) and longituninal (central) lithological profiles of Loc. 6 at the Suyanggae Paleolithic site

fluvial flooding muds and sands, and river-bottom gravels as stream-channel deposits (**Fig. 4**). The C-M patterns (Passega, 1964) of fine-grained sediments obtained from the new representative profile of Suyanggae Loc. 1 are typified by two different processes in terms of transported particles. They were transported by either mudflows derived from slope processes or suspended loads and/or bed loads (Kim et al., 2020). Gdb or Gb prevail at Suyanggae Loc. 1. Overlying the fluvial sands and gravels of the 2nd terraces along the Namhan River Valley are cultural layers, which are associated with artifactual layers. The submerged initial profile of Suyanggae Loc. 1 shows that the geosols (Layers IVㄱ and IVㄴ) were formed above the riverbed sands and gravels of the 2nd fluvial terrace at a level of about 125–127m (asl) (**Fig. 3**).

Radiocarbon average age of the Geosol is 18,690 cal BP (ranging between 18,240–18,997 cal BP) for two samples obtained 270cm below the excavation suface (Lee and Kim, 2004). Stone tools such as handaxes, tanged points, microblades, microblade cores, end-scrapers, and so forth were excavated in the cultural layer of the initial profile of Suyanggae Loc. 1 (**Fig. 7**). In addition, the new representative profile (6DE pit, north wall) of the site indicates that fluvial flooding sandy muds are distributed at a level between 128m and 130.5m below the yellowish-brown geosols (Gyb). The artifactual layer at a level of about 135m (asl) produced such lithic artifacts as cores, blades, tanged points, cleaves, and so forth (Lee et al., 2018) (**Fig. 8**). Radiocarbon ages of the fluvial deposits and Gyb below the artifactual layer range between 26,420±200 BP and 31,140±280 BP, which may belong to the early part of the Last Glacial Maximum (LGM). Radiocarbon ages of the fluvial deposits below yellowish brown Geosols (Gyb) as the artifactual layer range between 26,420±200 BP and 31,140±280 BP (128.3–128.7m, ASL), which may belong to the late Last Glacial. In short, in the Loc. 1 at the Suyanggae Paleolithic site, it is reasonable to assume that the artifactual layer of RP1-2 is approximately 20 thousand years BP, which is equivalent age of cultural layer in RP1-1.

3.2. Suyanggae Loc. 3

Suyanggae Loc. 3 is located at San 24-19 Aegog-ri, Jeokseong-myeon, Danyang, Chungbuk Province. This site has been excavated several times, including the 7th test survey (1996), the 8th test survey (2001), the 9th academic survey (2008), and the 10th survey (2011). Before the construction of the Chungju Reservoir Dam, the riverbed of Namhan River at Suyanggae was located at approximately 110m (asl). After the construction of the dam, the average water level rose to a level of 130–140m (asl). The excavation site at Suyanggae Loc. 3 is situated between 155m (asl) and 160m (asl), where the representative lithologic profile (1Ga, west wall) is characterized by both fluvial sediments and geosols. The representative profile shows that the fluvial deposits are composed of muds, sands, and gravels as a fining-upward sequence up to a level of 156m (asl) on the 3rd fluvial terrace (3rd TrB).

The C-M pattern of fine-grained sediments in the representative profile is notably typified by mudflow deposits derived from slope processes with some admixture of suspended sand or silt loads originating from fluvial processes (Kim et al., 2020). Rounded pebbles and cobbles prevail at the bottom of the representative profile, and matrix-supported gravelly sands with muddy sands dominate in the middle part of the profile below 156.5m (asl). Toward the upper part of the profile, geosols become more dominant. Prevalent geosols, as soil-stratigraphic units, can be enumerated as Gdb, Gb, yellow geosols (Gy), Grb, and Gyb. The geosols are assumed to have formed under the dry and cold climatic condition because geosols are commonly associated with polygonal patterned grounds and soil wedges of tens of centimeters to meters in depth.

Concerning the age of the lower part of the middle fluvial terrace, it may be as old as 300 ka, equivalent to MIS 9.

Fig. 7 Stone artifacts discovered in Loc. 1 (RP1-1) during the 1st, 2nd, 3rd 4th sessions (1983–1985), producing handaxes, tanged points, microblade, blade, end-scrapers, and scraper.

Fig. 8 Stone artifacts discovered in Loc. 1 during the 11th session (2013), showing tanged points, cores, blade cores hammers, blade, flake, and tools.

However, the ages of the interfaces between the 3rd fluvial terrace (3rd TrB) and the geosols may be considered younger than the formation of the 3rd fluvial terrace (3rd TrB). This is due to episodic erosion processes and pedogenic processes that followed after the formation of the landscape surface of the 3rd fluvial terrace. It can be inferred that the geosols were mainly derived from slope sediments and their ages are much younger than the formation of the 3rd fluvial terrace.

The OSL ages of the geosols can be summarized as follows: The age of Gb or Grb (12GA pit, the east wall) is approximately 40.8 ka, and the age of the Gb or Gyb ranges from 33.5 ka to 40 ka, when considering the ages of CL-1, CL-2 and CL-4 of Grid 10Na(south wall) (**Fig. 9**).

All of these ages are indicative of the age ranges of artifactual layers 2 and 3 of Suyanggae Loc. 3. CL 2 and 3 are characterized by small stone artifacts, such as flakes, cores, blades, scrapers, and points (Lee et al., 2013a, 2013b) (**Fig. 10**). These artifacts may be interpreted to have formed during the interstadial period of the Last Glacial Period (approximately 33–41ka, MIS 3), belonging to the Early Upper Paleolithic.

3.3. Suyanggae Loc. 6

Suyanggae Loc. 6 is located at 302 Hajin-ri, Jeokseong-myeon, Danyang, Chungbuk Province. Suyanggae Loc. 6 is adjacent to two distributary streams (Sangri-cheon from the north and Danyang-cheon from the south) of the Namhan River. The Namhan River in this area is typified by incised meandering and longitudinal bars in the riverbed. Suyanggae Loc. 6 was excavated consecutively over three sessions (2013, 2014, 2015) prior to the construction of the underwater embankment or dyke, up to a level of about 132m (asl). During the excavation survey, the water level of Chungju Reservoir Dam was maintained at around 125m (asl). The excavation site was situated approximately between 125m (asl) toward the Namhan River and 132m (asl) toward the hillslope margin. Suyanggae Loc. 6 is situated above the 2nd fluvial terrace (2nd Tr) of the Namhan River. The representative lithologic profile of Suyanggae Loc. 6 is defined in the "-5D" pit toward the hillslope margin, where fluvial deposits and mudflows intercalated with debris are conspicuously dominant. Sandy muds are more abundant between 123.7m (asl) and 122m (asl), which may have been derived from flooding episodes of the paleo-Namhan River. The C-M patterns of the fine-grained sediments in the representative profile of Suyanggae Loc. 6 indicate that the sediments were derived from both suspension processes of the paleo-Nanhan River and mudflows linked to the slope process. In particular, below the level of 127.3m (asl), suspension loads of flooding muds and fine sandy muds are dominant, while above the 127.3m (asl) mudflow is a conspicuous transporting process, mostly derived from the western hillslope margin. Sandy muds, known as geosols, are mainly distributed at an elevation between 128m (asl) and 130m (asl). These muds were transported primarily by mudflows originating from hillslope processes rather than the fluvial processes of the paleo-Namhan River. Artifactual layers II and III are linked to Gyb, but artifactual layer IV belongs to Grb. From the

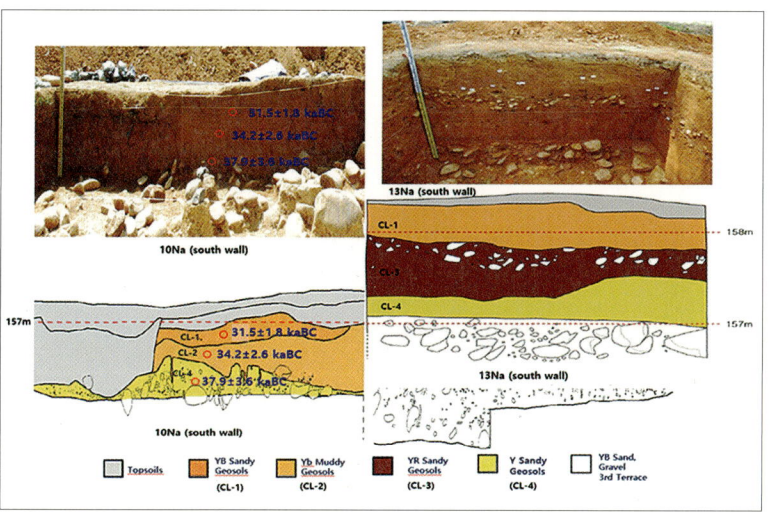

Fig. 9 OSL ages of Geosols in the representative lithological profile(10Na, south wall) of the Loc. 3 at the Suyanggae site excavated during 2000, 2008 and 2011 (8th-10th sessions).

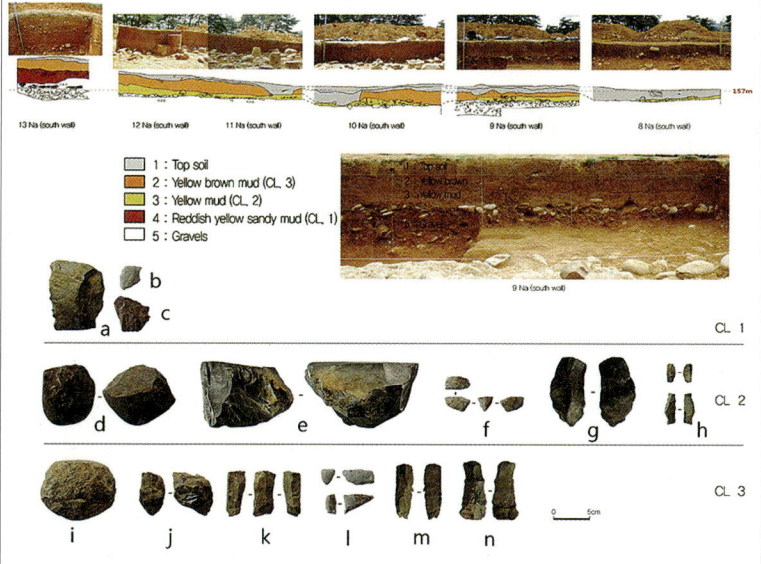

Fig. 10 Cultural layer (CL 1, CL 2, CL 3) were approximately dated between 33.5 ka and 40.8 ka in the Loc. 3, producing side scraper (a), notch (b), flake (c), plane (d), core (e), micro-blade core (f, m, n), blades (g, h), bola stone (i), and blade cores (j, k).

projection diagram (artifact production vs elevation) in the direction perpendicular to the NNW-SSE grids of Suyanggae Loc. 6 (Lee et al., 2018), it can be observed that artifactual layer IV is predominantly separated from artifactual layer III in the direction of the hillslope above the level of approximately 128m (asl) (Grids C-4 – A-6), but mixed with artifactual layer III at the level between 126m (asl) and 128m (asl) (Grids A-3 – C-1). Below the level of about 126m (asl) (Grids B1 – G3), artifacts are predominantly produced in association with artifactual layer III, but artifacts derived from artifactual layer IV abruptly disappear(Kim et al., 2023).

The C-M patterns of the fine-grained sediments in the representative profile of Suyanggae Loc. 6 indicate that the sediments were derived from both suspension processes of the paleo-Nanhan River and mudflows linked to the slope process. In particular, below the level of 127.3m (asl), suspension loads of flooding muds and fine sandy muds are dominant, while above the 127.3m (asl) mudflow is a conspicuous transporting process, mostly derived from the western hillslope margin. Sandy muds, known as geosols, are mainly distributed at an elevation between 128m (asl) and 130m (asl). These muds were transported primarily by mudflows originating from hillslope processes rather than the fluvial processes of the paleo-Namhan River. Artifactual layers II and III are linked to Gyb, but artifactual layer IV belongs to Grb. From the projection diagram (artifact production vs elevation) in the direction perpendicular to the NNW-SSE grids of Suyanggae Loc. 6 (Lee et al., 2018), it can be observed that artifactual layer IV is predominantly separated from artifactual layer III in the direction of the hillslope above the level of approximately 128m (asl) (Grids C-4 – A-6), but mixed with artifactual layer III at the level between 126m (asl) and 128m (asl) (Grids A-3 – C-1). Below the level of about 126m (asl) (Grids B1 – G3), artifacts are predominantly produced in association with artifactual layer III, but artifacts derived from artifactual layer IV abruptly disappear (Kim et al., 2023). The radiocarbon age of artifactual layer II, found in the matrix of muddy Gyb, ranges between 17,550±80 BP and 20,470±70 BP (average age: 18,410±70 BP, or 22,467–22,023 cal BP), related to the initial cold and dry period of the LGM. The radiocarbon age of artifactual layer III, composed of Gyb, ranges widely between 30,360±350 BP and 44,100±1,900 BP (average age: 35,180±450 BP, or 40,172–39321 cal BP). On the other hand, the radiocarbon age of artifactual layer IV, composed of Grb, ranges between 34,620±190 BP and 46,360±510 BP (average age: 36,980±350 BP, or 41,874–41,254 cal BP), which is approximately 2,000 years older than the age of artifactual layer III based on the average radiocarbon age (Lee et al., 2018; Kim et al., 2020; Kim et al., 2021; Kim et al., 2023) (**Fig. 11**).

Lithic artifacts, such as microblade cores, scrapers, and blades, were found from artifactual layer II (CL 2) at Suyanggae Loc. 6. Artifactual layers III and IV (CL 3 and CL 4) are associated with blades and tanged points. Particularly, a line-engraved cobblestone was found in artifactual layer III, where flooding muds dominate at a level of about 126.057m (asl) (Grid C5) (**Fig. 12**). The two radiocarbon ages of charcoal obtained from the same horizon of Grid 5C (126.057m, asl) are 34,020±400 (OTg141001, KIGAM-2014) and 36,600±1,100

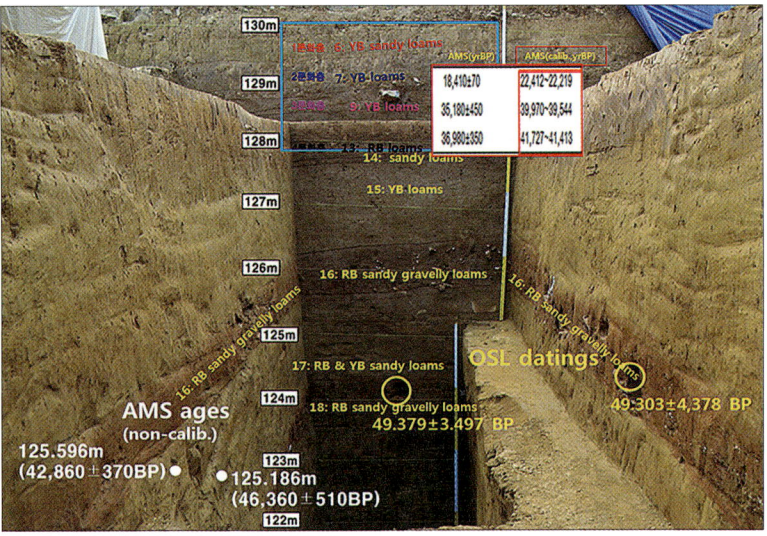

Fig. 11 Average radiocarbon ages of CL 2, 3, and 4, showing alternating layers of yellowish brown and reddish brown Geosols and OSL ages(~49 ka) of sandy gravelly loams (units 16 and 18) in the representative profile (-5D grid) at the Loc. 6.

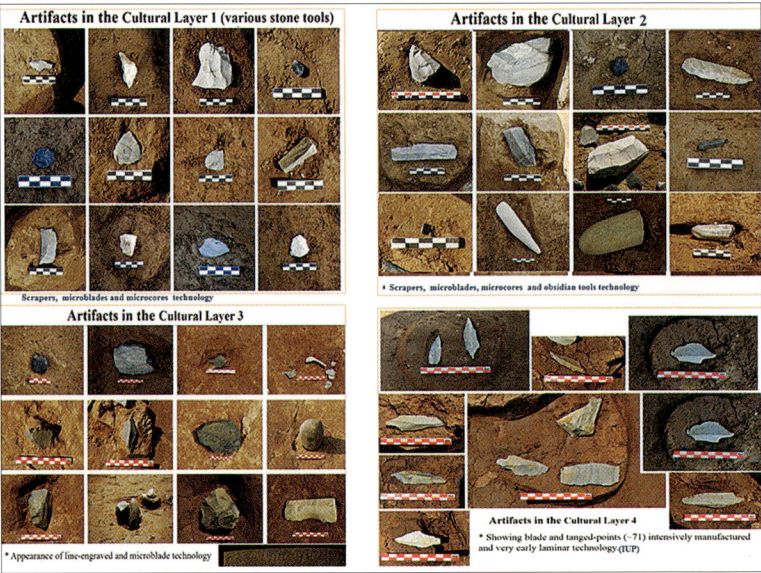

Fig. 12 Production of stone artefacts in the Cultural Layers (CL1 – CL4) at the Suyanggae Loc. 6, indicating the Upper Paleolithic culture.

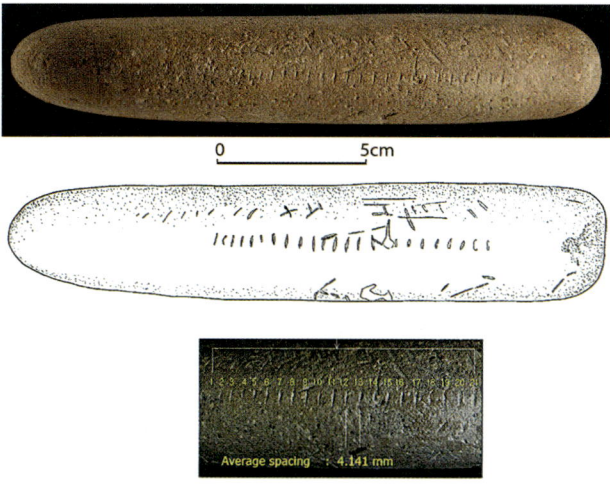

Fig. 13 Line-engraved cobblestone discovered in CL 3 of Loc. 6, showing 23 regular lines with equal spacings.

(AA105103, UA-2014). The average calibrated ages (2σ calibrated) are 38,046–35,681 cal BP and 40,536–37,281 cal BP (Kim et al., 2020; Kim et al., 2021; Kim et al. 2023). Based on the line-engraved cobblestone from artifactual layer III (with an average age of 37–39 ka), anatomically modern humans, who lived during the Early Upper Paleolithic, might have had some knowledge of metrology for the purpose of reproducing blade tools and creating line-engraved stones (Fig. 13). Finally, it can be inferred that artifactual layer II is indicative of the Late Upper Paleolithic, which was marked by severe paleoclimatic conditions, while artifactual layers III and IV are representative of the initial to Early Upper Paleolithic under interstadial conditions.

4. Summary and Conclusion

Along the riverbank of the Chungju Dam, submerged parts of the Suyanggae site constitute Suyanggae Loc. 1 and Loc. 6, but Suyanggae Loc. 6 was formed on the emergent fluvial terrace of the Namhan River Valley. The site-forming process of geomorphic, stratigraphic, pedo-sedimentary, and geochronological contexts was taken into consideration. Concerning the site-geomorphic forming process, the Namhan River Valley in Danyang County underwent excessive denudation, which may have significantly lowered the base level of old riverbeds toward 115m (asl). The average altitude difference between the gravel beds of the middle fluvial terrace (3rd FT) and present riverbeds at Suyanggae Loc. 3 is about 45m, so the geomorphic formation age of the middle fluvial terrace can be calculated as approximately 300 ka, when we apply a general uplift rate of around 0.14–0.15m/ka, the rate of which is one of the lowest in the Korean Peninsula (Kim et al., 2008). Regarding the morpho-stratigraphic background, Suyanggae Loc. 1 (RP1-1) and Loc. 6 were developed above the low fluvial terrace (Fluvial Terrace II), but Suyanggae Loc. 3 is located above the middle fluvial terrace (Fluvial Terrace III), at least 25m higher than the low fluvial terrace (Fluvial Terrace II). The former (Suyanggae Loc. 1 and Loc. 6) was formed much later than the latter (Suyanggae Loc. 3). Suyanggae Loc. 1 (RP1-1 and RP1-2), Loc. 3, and Loc. 6 are typified by fluvial sand and gravel, slope deposits such as mud flows and debris flow, and geosols as pedo-sedimentary deposits. These are the main lithological units constituting Suyanggae site-forming materials. Concerning the pedo-sedimentary perspective, the representative profiles of Suyanggae Loc. 1 (RP1-2) (Aegog-ri site) and Loc. 6 (Hajin-ri site) are dominated by sands and gravels at the bottom and sands and flooding muds with occasional intercalations of reddish-brown slope mudflows and debris flows in the middle. Debris flows are composed of subrounded to subangular cobbles or boulders. Suyanggae Loc. 3, however, is typified by rounded pebbles and cobbles at the bottom and matix-supported gravelly sands with muddy sands up to the middle part of the representative profile 1GA (below 156.5m, asl). Toward the upper part of profile 1GA, Gb, Grb, and Gyb are dominant. At Suyanggae Loc. 1 and Loc. 6, CL 2 and CL 3 are confined to between the middle and upper parts of the representative profiles of Suyanggae Loc. 1 (RP1-2) (Aegog-ri site) and Loc. 6 (Hajin-ri site); while, at Suyanggae Loc. 3, CL 2 is associated with the matrix of Gb or Gyb to Grb, and CL 3 is associated with a matrix of Gyb or Gb, particularly in the excavation profiles 10NA, 12 GA, and so forth.

From a geochronological viewpoint, specifically from the now-submerged RP1-1 of Suyanggae Loc. 1, the slope deposits and geosols above the old riverbed sands and gravels, constituting the lower terrace (2nd FT) at a level of about 125–127m (asl), are the matrix of a cultural layer producing handaxes, tanged points, microblades, microblade cores, end-scrapers, and so forth. On the other hand, from RP1-2 of Suyanggae Loc. 1 (5C, north wall), it was shown that the fluvial sandy muds, as flooding deposits, were distributed between 128m and 130.5m, and radiocarbon ages ranged between 26,420±200 BP and 31,140±280 BP. The Gyb above the flooding muds is regarded as an early part of the LGM. The stone artifacts are enumerated as cores, blades, tanged points, cleavers, and so forth. In addition, CL 2 and CL 3 at Suyanggae Loc. 6 are well established by numerical dating. A number of radiocarbon datings, conducted on the charcoal collected from the excavations at Suyanggae Loc. 6, indicates that CL 2 was formed during the Late Upper Paleolithic, and CL 3 belongs to the Early Upper Paleolithic. And the chronology of CL 2 at Suyanggae Loc. 6 is applicable to the main cultural layer of Suyanggae Loc. 1 (RP1-1 and RP1-2), designating the Late Upper Paleolithic Culture, converging after the LGM. At

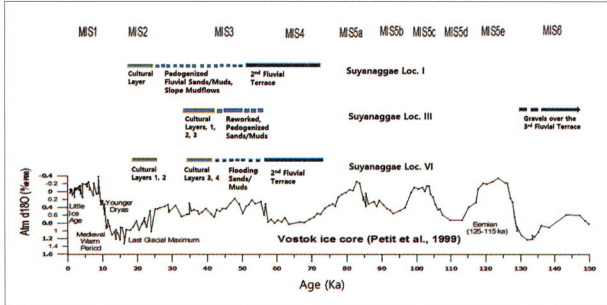

Fig. 14 Integration of chronology for artefactual layers in Loc. 1, Loc., 3, Loc. 6 at the Suyabaggae Paleolithic sites (modified from Petit et al., 1999).

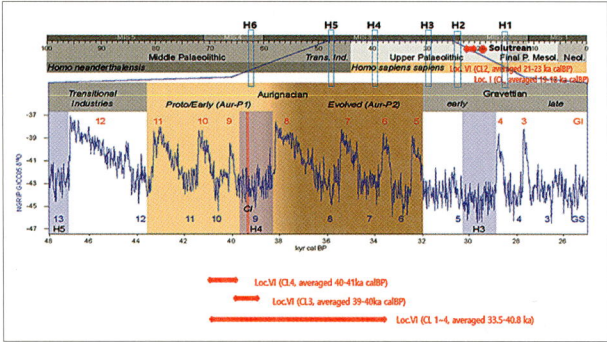

Fig. 15 Correlation of Paleolithic Chronostratigraphy for artifactual layers (cultural layers) at the Suyanggae sites (Loc. 1, 3, 6) in the Upstream Namhan River Basin (modified from Kim., et a., 2024; Shao et al., 2021).

Suyanggae Loc. 3, the OSL ages were measured at about 40.8 ka in the Gb or Grb of the profile of 12GA (east wall) and range from 33.5 ka to 40 ka in the Gb or Gyb, which indicates that the stone artifacts found in CL 2 an CL 3 converged at the interstadial of the Last Glacial Period, indicative of MIS 3–2 (**Fig. 14**).

Finally it can be concluded that the morpho-sedimentary site-forming processes, as well as the chronology of site-material formation, indicate that the main cultural layers of Suyanggae Loc. 1 (RP1-1, RP1-2), Loc. 6, and Loc. 3 were both formed since MIS 3. The pedo-sedimentary features of the main cultural layers of Suyanggae Loc. 3 were formed much later, as late as 40–45 ka, even though Suyanggae Loc. 3 was formed geomorphologically since approximately 300,000 years ago. This implies that there may be a rather long lapse between the gravelly fluvial terrace deposits and slope sediments as geosols. The latter are the main cultural layers of stone artifacts at Suyanggae Loc. 3.

In the context of Paleolithic chronostratigraphy, it is presumed that both cultural layers 3 and 4 of the Loc. 6, and cultural layers 2 and 3 of Loc. 3, are characterized by such distinct culture as producing tanged points, flake and blade tools, which can be correlated with the early Aurignacian (Dansgaard-Oeschger (D/O) event 10). Cultural layer 2 of Loc. 6, representing microblade production, can be correlated generally with the Solutrean (D/O event GI, or Heinrich Event 2) (**Fig. 15**). In general both the cultural layers 2 and 3 of Loc. 3 and the cultural layer 4 of the Loc. 6 in the Suyanggae open site can be assigned to the later stage of those in the Gunang Cave site, and the early stage of those of the Maedun Cave site (Kim et al., 2024, 2023; Yi, et al., 2021).

Acknowledgement

This paper was supported by funding from the Korea Institute of Geoscience and Mineral Resources (KIGAM). Authors greatly acknowledge the collaboration with the Institute of Korean Prehistory (IKP), Korea Research Institute of Standards and Science, and Quaternary Paleoenvironment Research (QPR).

◆ This paper is prepared by summarizing and modifying previous article (Kim et al., 2023), with supplementation of figures and renewed text.

References

Kim J.C., Han M., Ahn H.-S., Yoon H.H., Lee J.Y., Park S., Cho A., Kim J.Y., Nahm W.H., Choi H.W., Lim J., Yang D.Y., Hong S.S. and Yi S., 2024. Quaternary environmental studies in South Korea. *IUGS-Episodes*, published online. https://doi.org/10.18814/epiiugs/2024/02403s09

Kim Ju-yong and Lee Yung-jo. 2006. Stratigraphy of the Upper Pleistocene and Paleolithic in Korea. *L'anthropologie* 110, 119-138.

Kim J.Y., Lee K.W., Suh H.S., Choi W.H., Yang H.J., Kim K.J., Woo J.Y. and Lee Y.J., 2017. Sedimentary matrix-forming processes of the engraved stone-bearing Suyanggae Site(LOC.6) of the Upper Paleolithic, Danyang county, Korea (S1-3-R03). *Conference abstract book of the 3rd Asian Association for Quaternary Research* (www.asqua2017.org).

Kim Ju-yong and Lee Yung-jo. 2005. Morpho-stratigraphy and Pedo-sedimentological Formations of Suyanggae Site of the Namhan River, Danyang County, Korea. *Proceedings of the 10th Symposium of Suyanggae and her Neighbours*, 43-56.

Kim J.Y., Lee Y.J., Woo J.Y., Lee S.W., Suh H.S., Kim K.J., Yang H.J., Lee K.W., Choi W.H., Oh K.C., 2023. Morpho-Stratigraphy, Sedimentology, and Radiocarbon Chronology of Suyanggae Sites, Focusing on Loc. 6, South Korea. *Archaeology, Ethnology & Anthropology of Eurasia* 51/3, 96-108.

Kim Ju-Yong, Oh Keun-Chang, Yang Dong Yoon, Choi Weon Hack, Hong Sei Sun and Lee Jin Young. 2008. Stratigraphy, chronology, and implied uplift rate of coastal terraces in the southeastern part of Korea. *Quaternary International* 183, 76-82.

Kim Ju-yong, Suh Ho-seong, Oh Keun-chang, Lee Seung-won. 2020. Geoarcheology and Quaternary formation of Suyanggae sites in danyang County of Korea. *Journal of Museum Studies* No. 39, 53-82.

Kim J.Y., 2001. Quaternary geology and assessment of aggregate resources of Korea for the national industrial resources exploration and development. *Quaternary International* 82, 87-100.

Kim J.Y., Lee D.Y. and Choi S.G., 1998. A research on Pleistocene stratigraphy. *The Korean Journal of Quaternary Research* 12, 77-87.

Kim J.Y. and Yang D.Y., 2001. Geomorphology and geology of Palaeolithic Sites of Korea. In: Yonsei Press ed., *Palaeolithic Culture of Korea*, Seoul: Museum of Yonsei University Academia 1.

Kim J.Y., Suh H.S., Oh K.Ch., Lee S.W., 2020. Geoarcheology and Quaternary formation of Suyanggae sites in Danyang County of Korea. *Journal of Museum Studies* Vol. 39, 53-82.

Kim K.J., Kim J.Y., Lee K.W., Lee S.W., Woo J.Y., Lee Y.J., Jull A.J. Timothy. 2021. Radiocarbon ages of Suyanggae palelithic sites in danyang, Korea. *Radiocarbon* 63(5), 1429-1444.

Lee, D.Y., Kim, J.Y., 1992. Review on the Quaternary Stratigraphy of the Korean Peninsula. Sino-Korean *Symposium of Quaternary and Prehistory*, 69-99.

Lee, Yung-jo. 1989. Report on the upper Paleolithic Culture of Suyanggae Site, Korea. Presented paper at the *'89 World Summit Conference on the Peopling of the America*, 40p.

Lee, Yung-jo. 1999. Suyanggae Micro-blade Core Industry in Korea. Presented paper to INQUA 15th International Congress: *The Environmental Background to Hominid Evolution in Africa*, 20.

Lee, Yung-jo. 2000. On the Significance and Role of Suyanggae Culture in East Asia. Presented paper to *Society of East Aisa Archaeology: The 2nd World Wide Conference*, 20.

Lee, Yung-jo. 2001. Suyanggae Culture: Its Significance and Role. Presented paper to *International Symposium Modern Problem of Eurasian Paleolithic*, 14.

Lee, Yung-jo. 2007. SUYANGGAE: Why so important? Presented paper to *The 12th International Symposium SUYANGGAE and Her Neghbours: Prehistory Migrations in Euraisa and America*, 9.

Lee, Yung-jo and Kim, Jong-chan. 2004. Report on the dating results of the Suyanggae Paleolithoc site. *The Paleolithic Culture of Jungwon Region*, Korea. ed. by Jung-jo Lee, Institute of Jungwon Culture-Chungbuk National University, 299-303.

Lee, Yung-jo and Kong, Sujin. 2004. Spatial Distribution Analysis of Suyanggae Site, Korea. Presented paper at the *International Symposium of Paleoanthropology in Comemoration of the 100th Anniversary of the Birth of Prof. Pei Wenzhong and the 75th Anniversary of the Discovery of the First Pekingman Skull*, 10.

Lee, Yung-jo, Woo, Jong-yoon and Kong, Sujin. 1999. Suyanggae Tanged-Point in Korea. Presented Paper to *International Symposium on Paleoanthropology : In Commemoration of the 70th Anniversary of the Discovery of the First Skull of Peking Man*, 14.

Lee Yung-jo and Yoon Yong-hyun. 1992. Micro-blade Cores from Suyanggae Site, Korea. *International Symposium on Chronostratigraphy of North, Central, East Asia and America*, 135-146.

Lee Yung-jo and Yoon Yong-hyun. 1993. Tanged-point and Micro-blade Core from Suyanggae Site, Korea. *The Origin and Dispersal of Micro-blade Industry in Northern Eurasia*, 52-67.

Lee Yung-jo, Woo Jong-yoon, Lee Seung-won, Kang Kim-kyu, Yun Byeong-il, Otani Kaoru, Kim Mi-ra. 2013a. *Progress Report of Suyanggae Site LOC. III, Danyang-2008 Year Excavation(9th)*, IKP, Korea, 149p.

Lee Yung-jo, Woo Jong-yoon, Lee Seung-won, Ahn Ju-hyun, So Dong-young, Shin Seung-chul, Noh Hye-sun. 2013b. *Progress Report of Suyanggae Site Loc. III, Danyang-2011 Year Excavation (10th)*, IKP, Korea, 255p.

Lee Yung-jo, Woo Jong-yoon, Lee Seung-won, Ahn Ju-hyun, Yun Byeong-il, Park Jeong-mi, Otani Kaoru, Kim Mi-ra, Kim Eun-jeong, Han Seung-chul, Jang Hyeong-il, Choi Dong-hyuk. 2018. *Report on the excavation of Suyanggae Site (LOC. I and VI)*, Danyang, IKP, Korea, 821p.

Oh Keun-chang, Kim Ju-yong. 2018. Formation and environment of Quaternary deposits of Suyanggae Loc. 1 and VI in Danyang County. IKP *Report on the excavation of Suyanggae Site (Locs. I and VI)*, Danyang, IKP, Korea, 5-93.

Martinson, D.G., Pisias, N.G., Hays, J.D., Imbrie, J., Moore, T.C., and Shackleton, N.J., 1987. Age dating and the orbital theory of the ice ages: development of high- resolution 0-300,000 years chronostratigraphy. *Quaternary Research* 27, 1-29.

Passega, R., 1964. Grain size representation by CM patterns as geological tool. *Journal of Sedimentology* 34(4), 830-847.

Petit J.R., Jouzel J., Raynaud D., Barkov N.I., Barnola J.-M., Basile I., Bender M., Chappellaz J., Davisk M., Delaygue G., Delmotte M., Kotlyakov V.M., Legrand M., Lipenkov V.Y., Lorius C., Pepin L., Ritz C., Saltzmank E. and Stievenard M., 1999. Climate and atmospheric history of the past 420,000 years from the Vostok ice core, Antarctica. *Nature* Vol. 399, 429-436.

Shao Y., Limberg H., Klein K., Wegener C., Schmidt I., Weniger G.-C., Hense A., Rostami M., 2021. Human-existence probability of the Aurignacian techno-complex under extreme climate conditions. *Quaternary Science Reviews* 263, 1-20.

Yi, S., Han, C.G., Oh, K.-C., Seo, I.S., Kim, D., Lee, J., Han, M., Choi, H., Lim, J., Park, S., Jun, C.-P., and Cho, T., 2021. A preliminary study of natural environmental change and its impact on early Late Paleolithic people in the northeast central Korean Peninsula during Marine Iso- tope Stage 3 (40-30k cal a BP). *Journal of Quaternary Science* Vol. 37, 100-113.

Characteristics of the blade technology in the Korean Peninsula with a focus on CL 4 and CL 3 at Suyanggae 6 (SYG 6)

Kaoru OTANI[1], Jong-yoon WOO[2], Yung-jo LEE[2]

[1] Assistant Professor, Tokyo Metropolitan University, Japan ; kaoru_31@naver.com
[2] Institute of Korean Prehistory(IKP), Korea

ABSTRACT

The lithic assemblages from Early Upper Paleolithic reveal two distinct reduction sequences: one involving pebble tools or flake-based reduction, predominantly using quartzite or quartz, which appears to reflect a continuation of earlier stone tool traditions; and the other one blade-based reductions, utilizing fine-quality raw materials, which seems to represent a newly adopted technology. Combined with other lines of evidence, local archaeologists suggest that the EUP marks a significant cultural shift in the Korean peninsula, potentially associated with the arrival of modern humans. At the Suyanggae site Loc. 6 (Suyanggae 6), reveals clear differences in terms of lithic reduction pattern and raw material utilization. From the cultural layer (CL) 4, an exceptional lithic assemblage was identified, featuring tanged-points and the reduction of large-sized blades. In CL 3, a decline in large-sized blades and tanged-points was observed, along with the increase of small blade or bladelet reduction. By CL 2, intensive microblade production and diversification were evident, accompanied by an increase in the lithic reduction pattern of retouched tools such as scrapers, with no tanged-points present. It is remarkable that the small blade or bladelet reduction found at CL 3 is associated with tanged-points. The small blade cores were not modified into a wedge shape but instead retained simple characteristics that utilized the original shape of the cores, making it possible to compare them to a primitive type of microblade core. These small blade core technique found at every CL of Suyanggae VI closely corresponds to microblade cores. These lithic aspects discovered at Suyanggae VI are not limited to the particular geographical condition as a local phenomenon. Although we must consider differences with regard to the abundance of raw materials and landscapes, the phenomenon is thought to represent changes in Upper Paleolithic cultures in the Korean Peninsula.

국문초록

수양개 6지구(Loc. 6) 문화층은 석기의 도구 제작과 원석 활용에서 뚜렷한 차이를 드러내고 있다. 4문화층(CL 4)은 대형 돌날과 슴베찌르개 생산, 3문화층(CL 3)은 돌날과 슴베찌르개 감소와 좀돌날 관련 기술 등장, 그리고 2문화층(CL 2)은 집중적 좀돌날 생산, 슴베찌르개가 사라지고 생활도구로서 긁개 다양화와 급증이 나타난다. 특히 4문화층(CL 4)은 후기 구석기 출현을 알리는 돌날과 슴베찌르개를 포함한 석기군을 보여주며 후기 구석기 현생인류 도래에 대한 귀중한 정보를 제공한다. 3문화층(CL 3)의 좀돌날 공작은 슴베찌르개와 관련되어 있으며 좀돌날 몸돌은 쐐기모양의 변형이 아닌 몸돌 원형을 활용하는 단순한 형태이므로 몸돌의 시발점으로 볼 수 있다. 수양개 6지구 전체 문화층에 나타나는 좀돌날-몸돌 관련 기술은 소형 돌날-몸돌 기술이다. 수양개 6지구 유적은 석기의 돌감 조성과 원석 변화 측면에서 원산지 특성이나 경관 특수성과 같은 지리적 환경 측면을 고려할 수 있으며, 특히 한반도 후기구석기의 미세한 문화적 변동 측면에서 볼 때 수양개 유적은 한반도를 대표하는 유적에 속한다. 요컨대 수양개 6지구 유적은 연속적 지층 내에서 후기 구석기 초기에서 말기까지 석기가 집중적으로 포함된 문화층이 분포하며 원석 확보와 선택 및 활용, 석기 제작과 기술 발전과정을 순차적으로 확인할 수 있는 많은 정보를 제공하는 유일하고 중요한 유적이다.

Keywords : Suyanggae 6, lithic reduction pattern, raw materials utilization, Early Upper Paleolithic, Tanged-points, blades, small blades, microblades

1. Introduction

The Korean Peninsula, located at the eastern end of Eurasia, is elongated in a north-south direction and has geological features that differ greatly from east to west (**Fig. 1**).

The Suyanggae Paleolithic site is located in Danyang County, Chungbuk Province, Korea. All six localities are within about 5km of each other along the upper South Han (Namhan) River (**Fig. 2**). The Suyanggae basin has been investigated through 13 full-scale excavations conducted from 1983 to 2015 by Chungbuk National University Museum and the Institute of Korean Prehistory. Paleolithic cultural layers were discovered at three localities: Locality (Loc.) 1, Middle and Upper Paleolithic culture, from 1st to 4th, 7th and 11th excavation. Loc. 3, Lower or Middle to Upper Paleolithic culture, from the 8th to 10th excavation. And, most recently, Loc. 6, which was investigated in 2013 with the 11th excavation and in 2015 with the 13th excavation (Lee et al, 2018).

More than 100,000 stone tools were excavated from all localities at the site, and consequently the site is considered

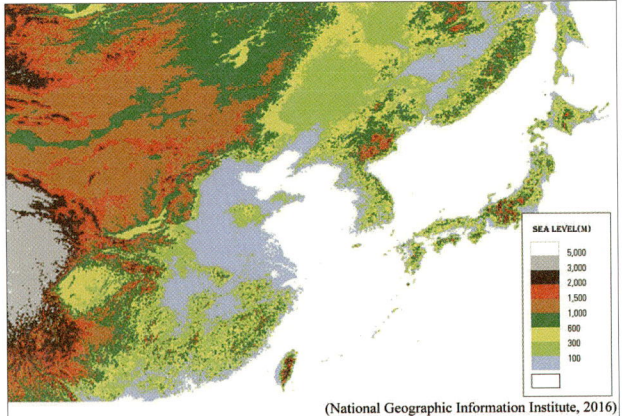

Fig. 1 Geological map of East Asia

representative of the Upper Paleolithic industry in Korea. Loc. 1 is particularly famous for having yielded the largest number of blade and microblade artifacts in Korea. This locality is also considered characteristic of Korean Upper Paleolithic culture. In 1983, the Suyanggae site yielded a large lithic assemblage, including blade and microblade industries. More than 250 microblade cores and about 50

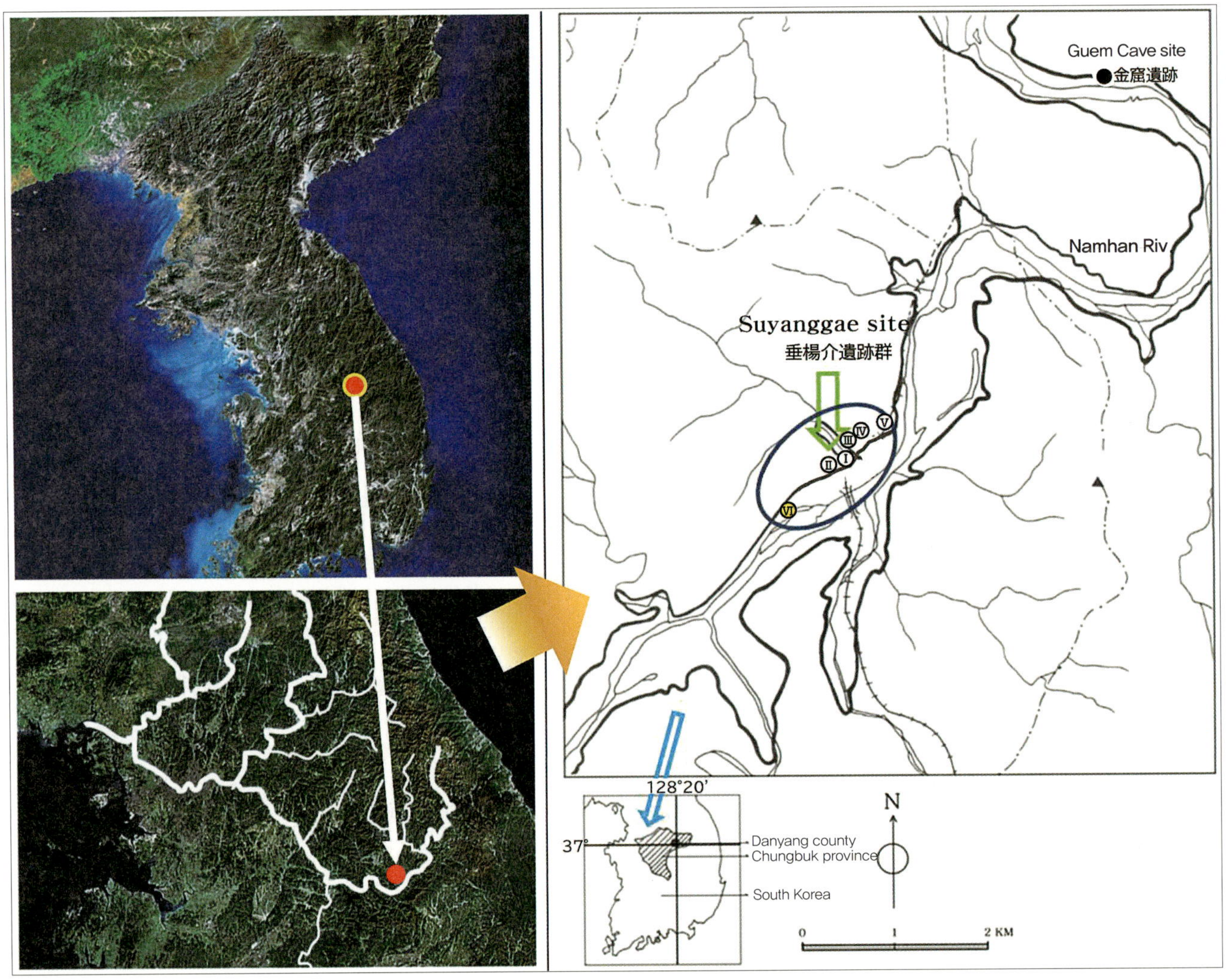

Fig. 2 Location of the Suyanggae site

tanged-points were found, and amount of blades or flakes were refitted. Especially, the microblade core reduction process was reconstructed based on their morphological and technical characteristics (Lee, 1985).

The Loc. 6, contains four cultural layers dating to the Upper Paleolithic, corresponding to MIS 3 to MIS 2. When all 40,679 artifacts had been unearthed, there were identified as belonging to a variety of lithic clusters from each CL, showing distinctive aspects of lithic composition.

2. Site formation

At the Suyanggae site, Quaternary sedimentary formations are characterized by mudflows of sloping debris, fluvial sands, and flooding muds toward the South Han River (Kim, 2008). The South Han River is a tributary of the Han River, where the branch and main stream unite to form a shallow waterflow and which flows westward in the middle of the Korean Peninsula. This River basin contains the second terrace of Loc. 1 and the third terrace of Loc. 3, both of which formed 250 to 300 ka ago. Loc. 6 is located on the second terrace alongside Loc. 1, at a sea level of about 125m to 132m. This second terrace was situated with upper sedimentation composed of colluvial deposits from the mountain slope, and lower sedimentation formed from fluvial deposits from the river.

Loc. 6 is located on a wide and thick paleosoil deposited. Sedimentation was formed with a gentle slope from north to south. The deposits comprise yellowish-brown and reddish-brown clay. Each layer is separated by sandy clay that contains angular pebbles and yields four cultural horizons named from the surface downward. The matrix of these cultural layers is associated with the flooding muds on the low fluvial terrace of the paleo-South Han River below 127m (msl).

In the lithological profile of the "-5D pit," mudflows intercalated with debris are dominant at an elevation higher than 127.3m, while slope-derived deposits and fluvial sedimentary deposits both prevail between televations of 127.3m and 123.7m. Below 123.7m, sandy muds are the main components, which were derived from frequent inundation of the old South Han River (**Fig. 3**).

3. Materials and method

3.1. Lithic assemblage

At Suyanggae 6, yielding more than 40,000 artifacts. Most of these lithic artifacts were concentrated on the central part of a grid, and the distribution of lithic scatters appears to be different in each cultural layer. A large number of tool-making debitage associated with blade, scrapers, tanged-points, microblades, and small-blade redction (**Table 1**).

As the first cultural layer, CL 1 is distributed in the middle and northeastern part of the grid, and 582 lithic artifacts were found. While most of the artifacts are debitage of microblade or blade reducion process, the number of retouched tools is relatively low.

The second cultural layer, CL 2 yielding 21,744 pieces – the largest number among the cultural layers. Most of the artifacts are related to microblade or blade reduction. Given the various types of microblade cores, microblades,

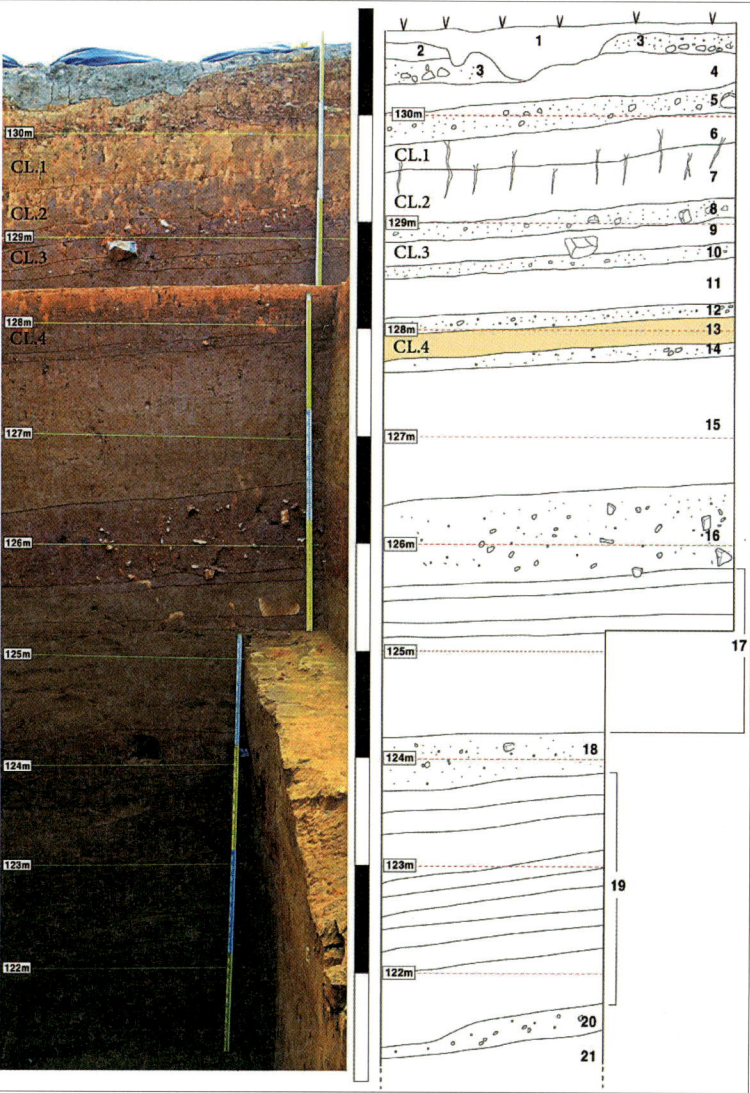

Fig. 3 Sedimentary structure of Suyanggae Loc. 6 (-5D pit)

Table 1 Tool composition at Suyanggae Loc. 6

Artifacts	CL 1	CL 2	CL 3	CL 4	All
Cores	17	447	254	160	878
Blade cores	1	83	53	149	286
Bladelet cores		19	9	4	32
Microblade cores	2	134			136
Microblade core blanks		148	4		152
Blades	4	917	578	2,253	3,752
Microblades	1	264	16		281
Bipolar	5	9	50		64
Core reduction flakes		573	13	29	615
Flakes	247	15,288	4,813	7,845	28,193
Chips	215	2,583	1,306	167	4,271
Hammer	13	157	77	59	306
Anvil stones	10	18	10	4	42
Pebbles	5	55	153	32	245
Pebble tools	4	2	2	1	9
Handaxes		1	2		3
Tanged-points			13	73	86
Points		11	1		12
Side scrapers	26	279	27	24	356
End scrapers	8	332	14	1	355
Burins		42	3	4	49
Drills	4	7	2	3	16
Notched tools	2	13	2	1	18
Becs	1	2	2	1	6
Denticulated tools		8	1	2	11
Chisel shaped tools		58	1		59
Composited tools	1	9	1		11
Retouched flakes	16	264	57	71	408
Engraved gravels			6		6
Polished tools		21			21
All	582	21,744	7,470	10,883	40,679

the western part of the grid. 7,470 artifacts were discovered, including related to blade reduction. And emergence of tanged-points is a new characteristic feature of this CL, while other retouched tools decrease significantly such as side-scrapers, end-scrapers, and burins. The application of bladelet or small blade technology was observed in this layer, which can be closely connected to microblade production in CL 2.

CL 4 was found in the north-western part of the grid, where a single lithic scatter yielded 10,883 artifacts in total. Tanged-points were intensively manufactured, while other retouched tools were relatively rare, forming an uncomplicated lithic composition. Shale accounts for the vast majority of utilized raw materials (94.8%), which is much more dominant compared to other CLs (Fig. 4, 5). In each cultural layer, the main raw materials were shale and quartz. However, the ratio of raw material utilization was different in each layer. Other raw materials accounted for only 5% of artifacts in CL 4, with the proportion of shale decreasing in the upper layer alongside the more frequent exploitation of other materials like quartz and rhyolite, demonstrating more diverse raw material utilization. Obsidian was recovered only from CL 1 and CL 2, and provenance analysis (Kim, 2018) revealed that some of it originated from the Baekdu (Paektu) volcanic system. This suggests a strong association

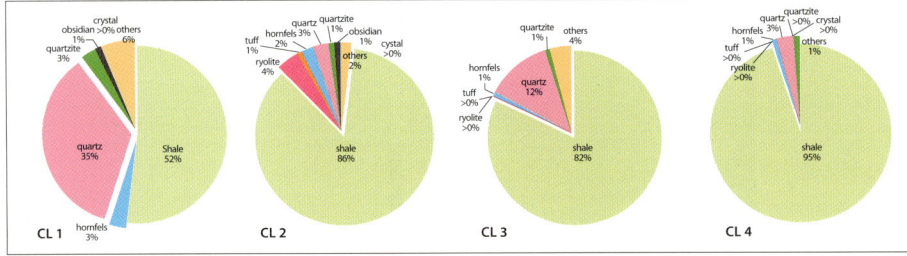

Fig. 4 Raw material compositions at Suyanggae Loc. 6

and spalls, the site is expected to provide crucial data for reconstructing microblade technology. While most of the tools were made of blades, the ratio of end-scrapers with steep edges on the distal end of the blade is noticeably large. In addition, a large number of complex retouched side-scrapers, burins, points, stone bowls, chisel-typed tools, and partially ground-axes were found in this layer.

CL 3 has an elongated distribution north and south in

with microblade assemblages and likely represents a shift in human behavior patterns involving more extensive long-distance migration.

In the case of tool assemblages, debitages of tool manufacturing, such as cores and flakes, account for more than 90% of materials from all cultural layers. Blade reduction decreases as the layers progress from CL 4 to CL 1, as evidenced by the declining proportion of blade cores.

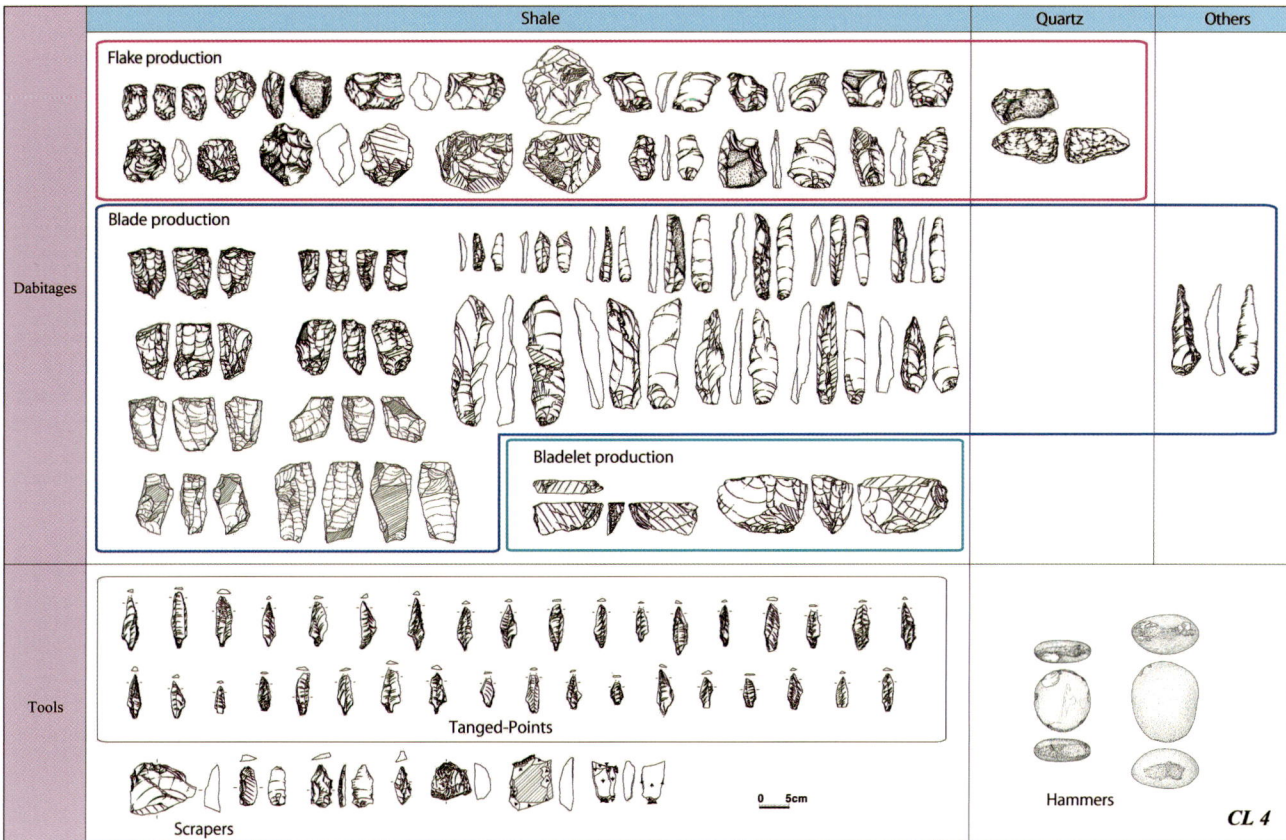

Fig. 5 Lithic assemblage of CL 4, Suyanggae Loc. 6

In contrast, microblade reduction emerges in CL 2 and CL 1, indication a shift in the reduction system from vlades to microblades. As retouched tools, tanged-points, which are the most typical tools used in the Korean Upper Paleolithic, shows a dramatic difference in each layer: Although comprising more than 60% of tools in CL 4, only 20% of tools in CL 3 are tanged-points, with none in CL 2. End-scrapers, on the other hand, constitute 31% of tools in CL 2, while only four pieces were found in CL 3 and one piece in CL 4.

3.2. Radiocarbon dating

The dates for 34 charcoal samples were calculated by AMS and OSL (AMS: 32, OSL: 2). In the AMS era, from the bottom to the top strata, two pieces in the 16th layer, six pieces in the 13th layer (CL 4), 14 pieces in the 9th layer (CL 3), and 10 pieces in the 7th layer (CL 2). The samples for layer 16 (muddy gravel) were collected from the reference section, but all other samples were collected from the lithic concentrations (Fig. 6). The samples from layer 13 were detected in the area overlapping the debitages for blade production at the -B3 grid; for layer 9, they were distributed at the southern part of the survey area with a lithic concentration (Fig. 7). The samples from layer 7 were detected from the eastern to southern grids within the debitage concentration for microblade production.

None show clear signs of combustion remains, such as a hearth, but no charcoal was detected outside the range of the lithic concentration, and a small number of heated artifacts were unearthed. It can be determined that it is a carbide associated with lithic industry.

The distribution of median dating (calibrated) for each layer is as follows: 48,755–45,335 cal yr BP for layer 16, 44,740–39,750 cal yr BP for layer 13 (CL 4), 43,285–34,815 cal yr BP for layer 9 (CL 3), and 24,620–21,190 cal yr BP for layer 7 (CL 2). In addition, the OSL dating of two pieces is 47,379±3,497 BP (Layer 17, 125.35m) and 49,303±4,378 BP (Layer 16, 126.46m), which is consistent with the AMS dates.

The values for each geological monolayer are generally consistent, but there are many overlapping age intervals in CL 4 and CL 3. In terms of the plane distribution of debitages, CL 4 and 3 debitages are distributed in the same direction as the long axis of the slope. The sedimentary layer is thin through the southern part of CL 4 to the northern part of CL 3, and the distribution of the lithic concentrations is partially overlapped. We confirmed the existence of two cultural layers. From the above, it was determined that the two cultural layers have slightly different survival datings and can be recognized as a blade industry from the early Upper Paleolithic. It is the oldest date of tanged-points not only in Korea, but in all of Asia. This shows that tanged-point culture in the Korean Peninsula had already been established

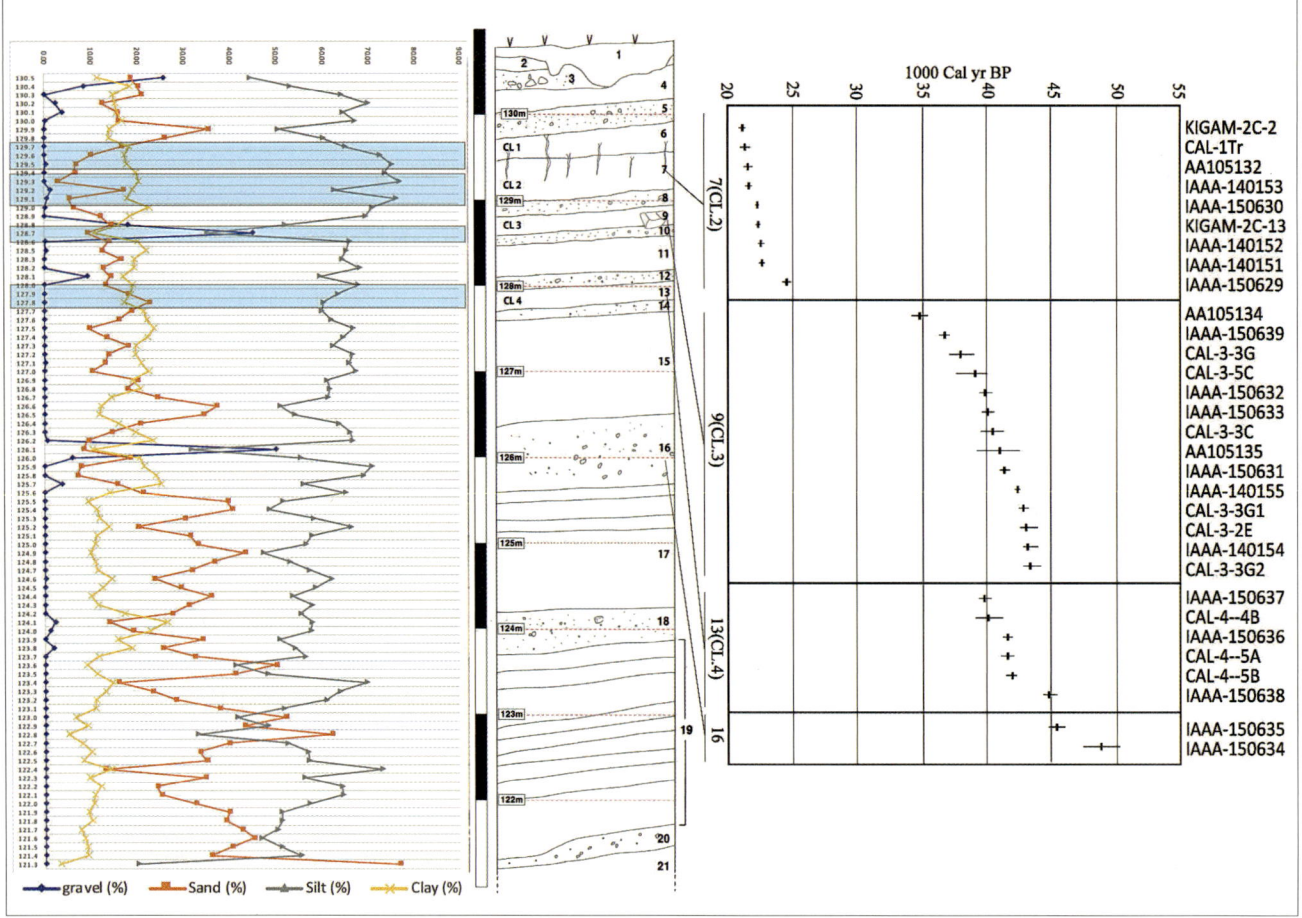

Fig. 6 Radiocarbon dating and particle size distribution of soils at Suyanggae Loc. 6

in the very early phase of the Upper Paleolithic. The typical artifacts were made from blades, the production of which was performed systematically for the largest pieces.

4. Lithic analysis

4.1. Blade technology

The size of the blade becomes smaller, and raw material utilization becomes more varied in the latter CL. Compared to cases from CL 3 and Loc. 1, the tanged-points from CL 4 have a wider distribution in length of edge and tang. Especially, they show the greatest ratio of edge to tang, while the ratio of thickness to width in tang is smallest.

In addition, while the width of tang appears similar at every site, the index of the width of barb is greater in CL 4 compared to other sites. That is, these tanged-points contained different utilizations of blanks according to the characteristics of the lithic assemblage and the temporal condition, even though they shared same techno-morphological aspects. This can be thought to reflect different functions.

It was observed that blades were utilized as a main preform of tanged-points. From CL 4, 149 blade cores and 2,253 blades were excavated. Most of the blade cores were measured at 7–8cm in length, 5cm in width, and 3cm in thickness on average. Among the blades, 154 large blades bigger than 10cm were found, 527 medium blades from 10cm to 6cm were found, and 336 small blades of less than 6cm were found. This difference appears clearer compared to other CLs. In other words, it is apparent that blade cores became smaller and the ratio of large to small blade cores decreased in the upper layers.

Most of the blade cores were measured at 7–8cm in length, 5cm in width, and 3cm in thickness on average, and variable types of core reduction were found in 149 pieces from CL 4. On blade cores, an elaborate preparation process of preforming for blade knapping was observed, such as the modification of platforms and ridges on the ventral surface, producing repetitive blade knapping through a change of platforms. Given the repetition of modification on the platform, a systematic and strategic reduction of cores was reconstructed. The sequence from preparation to blade knapping is considered practicable due to the favorable geographical conditions and the abundant availability of high-quality raw materials.

On the other hand, traces of small blade or bladelet reduction, though limited, were found in all CLs. Unlike blade

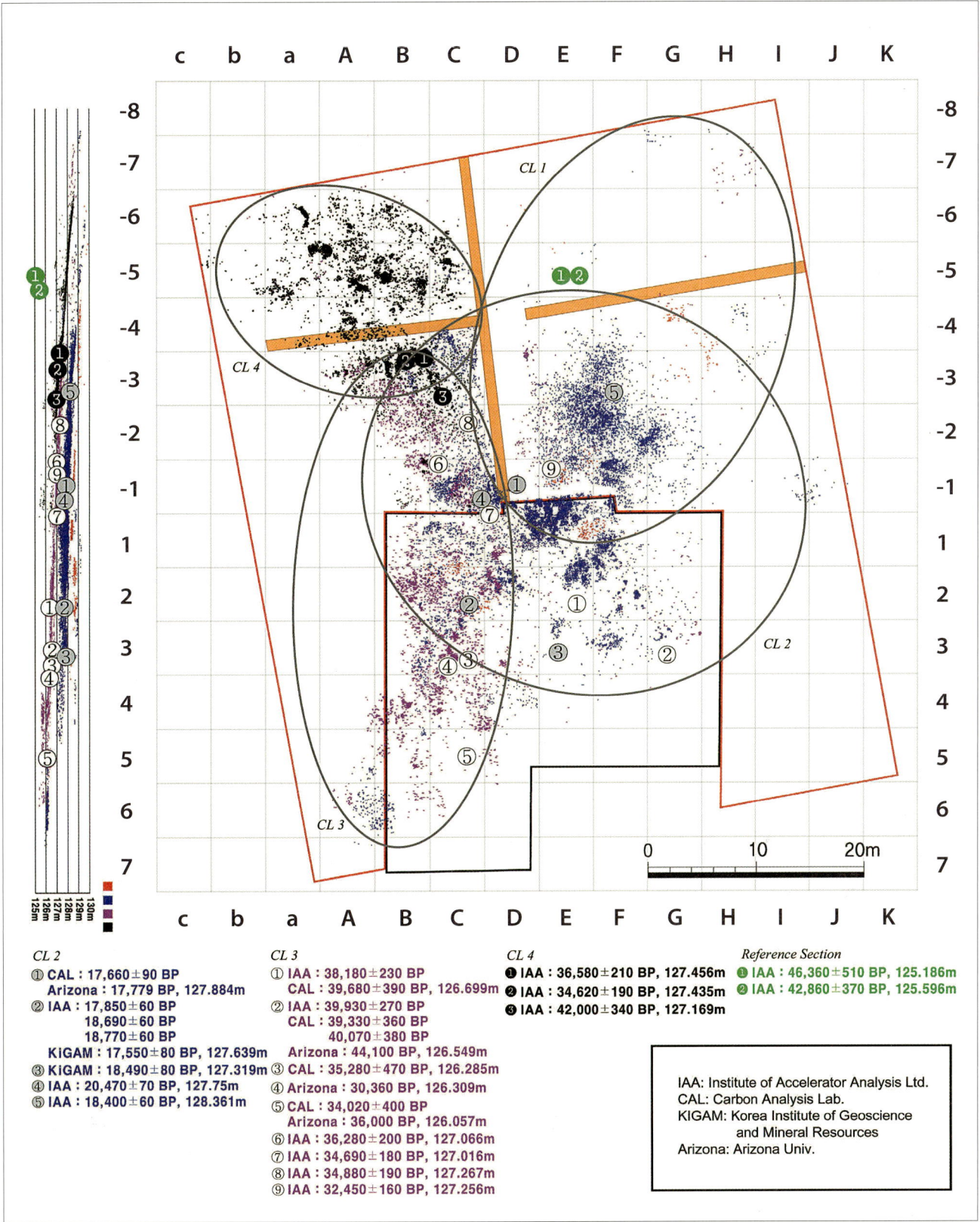

Fig. 7 Distribution of artifacts from Suyanggae Loc. 6

reduction, these were not systematic, and their shapes were irregular. However, in some instances of small blade reduction, a process very similar to the microblade reduction that appears from CL2 onward was employed. This involved shaping blanks using a bifacial technique, creating platforms through spall flaking, and then progressing with small blade flaking from the edge. While the technical relationship between the two is unclear, it is evident that these two reduction systems developed at Suyanggae share many commonalities (**Fig. 8**).

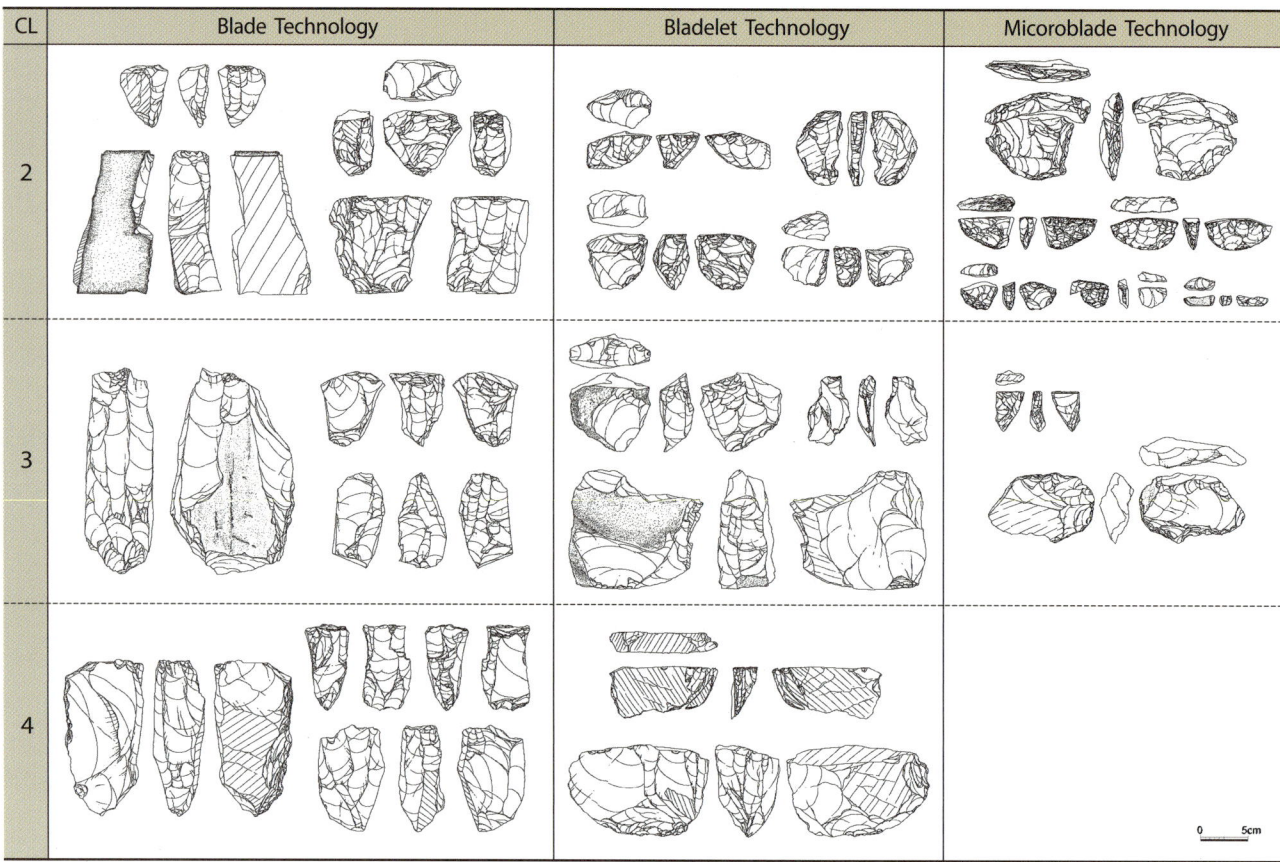

Fig. 8 Blade-bladelet-microblade cores from CL 4 to CL 2

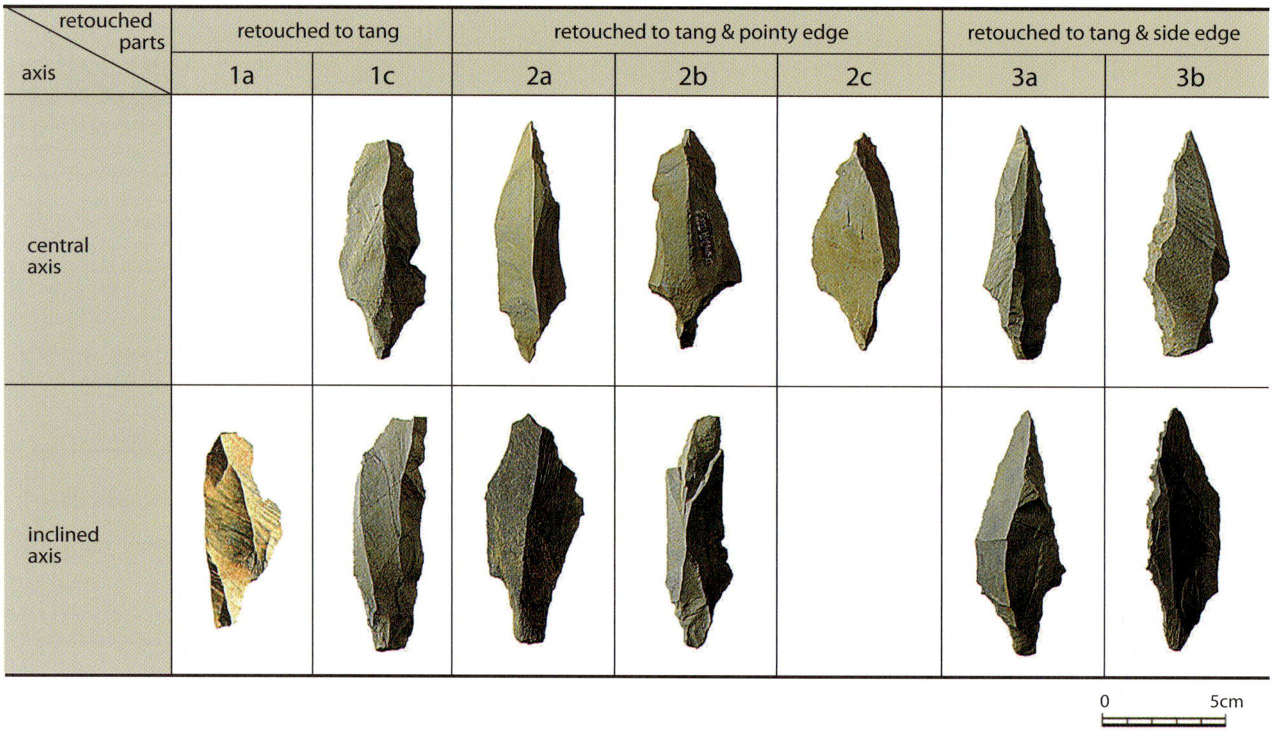

Fig. 9 Classification of tanged-point based on retouched parts and axis positions at CL 4

4.2. Tanged-point production

Tanged-points are found in CL 4 and 3, but not in CL 2 and 1. Instead, other retouched tools, such as scrapers and burins, were made intensively in CL 2 via microblade reduction. From CL 4, 73 tanged-points were found. Among them, 62 were well preserved and their retouched parts were investigated. When these tanged-points were classified

Table 2 Classification result according to Fig. 9

	tang			tang+ pointy edge			tang+ side edge			all
	1a	1b	1c	2a	2b	2c	3a	3b	3c	
central axis			18	5	4	1	4	2		34
inclined axis	1		11	4	5		6	1		28
all	1	0	29	9	9	1	10	3	0	62

based on the shape and position of the retouching edge, they could be divided into 9 types (Fig. 9). As a result, more than half (29 pieces) were retouched only on the tang portion. Additionally, 18 were retouched on both the tang and the tip (9 on the left tip and 9 on the right tip), 13 pieces were retouched on both the tang and the lateral edges (10 on the right edge and 3 on the left edge), and 1 piece was retouched only on the right tang (Table 2).

For the axis of tools, given 27 pieces with a central axis and 29 pieces with an inclined axis, a tendency was found that only those retouched on the tang part had a central axis, whereas others retouched on the whole edge had an inclined axis. To attest to the symmetry of the tanged-points, Flip Test v.0.9 was chosen to yield an Index of Asymmetry (IA). Eighteen tanged-points were in a symmetrical range, while another 30 pieces (62.5%) showed low symmetry. Basically, asymmetry appears because of an inclined axis between the tang and edge. Even in cases with overall retouching, the degree of symmetry was very low because the opposite edge of the retouched part had a natural sharp edge, which may imply that they served some other purpose than as a projectile point.

5. Results

The tanged-points from CL 4 have a wider distribution in terms of length of edge and tang. Especially, they exhibit the greatest ratio of edge to tang, while the ratio of thickness to width in tang is the smallest. In addition, while the width of tang appears to be similar at every site, the index of the width of barb is greater in CL 4 compared to other sites. That is, tanged-points utlized blanks differently according to the characteristics of the lithic assemblage and the temporal condition, even though they shared the same techno-morphological aspects. This can be thought to reflect different functions.

The small blade production process proceeded from a narrow side, after striking platform preparation by longitudinal knapping as spall. Most small blade cores found in CL 3 and 4 utilized their original shapes without modification. On the other hand, small blade cores in CL 2 utilized bifacial flaking with a spall striking platform, such as a microblade core. The technological innovation marked by the transition from large-sized blades to small-sized blades, and finally to microblade production, was revealed by the difference in assemblages from CL 4 to CL 2. This is one of the key issues when analyzing the interaction between small blade technology, large blade technology, and microblade technology. As lithic reduction varied, the raw materials also showed differences in each layer. Shale predominated in CL 4, quartz was intensively used in CL 3, and obsidian was appeared in CL 2. Especially, it is thought that obsidian was introduced with the regularization of microblades by developing a long-distance source to obtain high-quality material, implying a major technical change before and after CL 2. Similarly, a change in raw material exploitation reflected the composition of main tools and their production. It can be thought that the tool-making technique and the circumstances related to obtainable raw materials are the most crucial conditions fro determining a lithic assemblage.

Radiocarbon dating yields reliable data. The oldest date generated was for the tanged-point assemblage in CL 4, around 42,000 to 40,000 cal BP. This is the oldest date for the tanged-point industry not only in Korea, but in East Asia. This shows that the tanged-point industry based on large-sized blade reduction indicated that it had already been established during the Early Upper Paleolithic on the Korean Peninsula. In addition, the prototypes of microblade cores or small blade cores that appeared in CL 3 were dated to 40,000 to 39,000 cal BP. Although it is unclear where the borderline is between microblade and small blade or bladelet technology, these artifacts are thought to represent the technological transition from blade to microblade industry.

6. Conclusion

Each cultural layer of Suyanggae Loc. 6 revealed a clear difference in tool manufacturing and raw material utilization. The large blades reduction and tanged-points production in CL 4, a decline in blades and tanged-points and the emergence of a new technique related to microblades in CL 3, intensive microblade production and diversification and an increase in living tools, such as scrapers, with no tanged-points in CL 2. Notably, while small blade reduction is found in each CL, there is a clear trend of increasing technological similarity with the microblade reduction system over time. In particular, the small blade cores excavated from CL3 closely

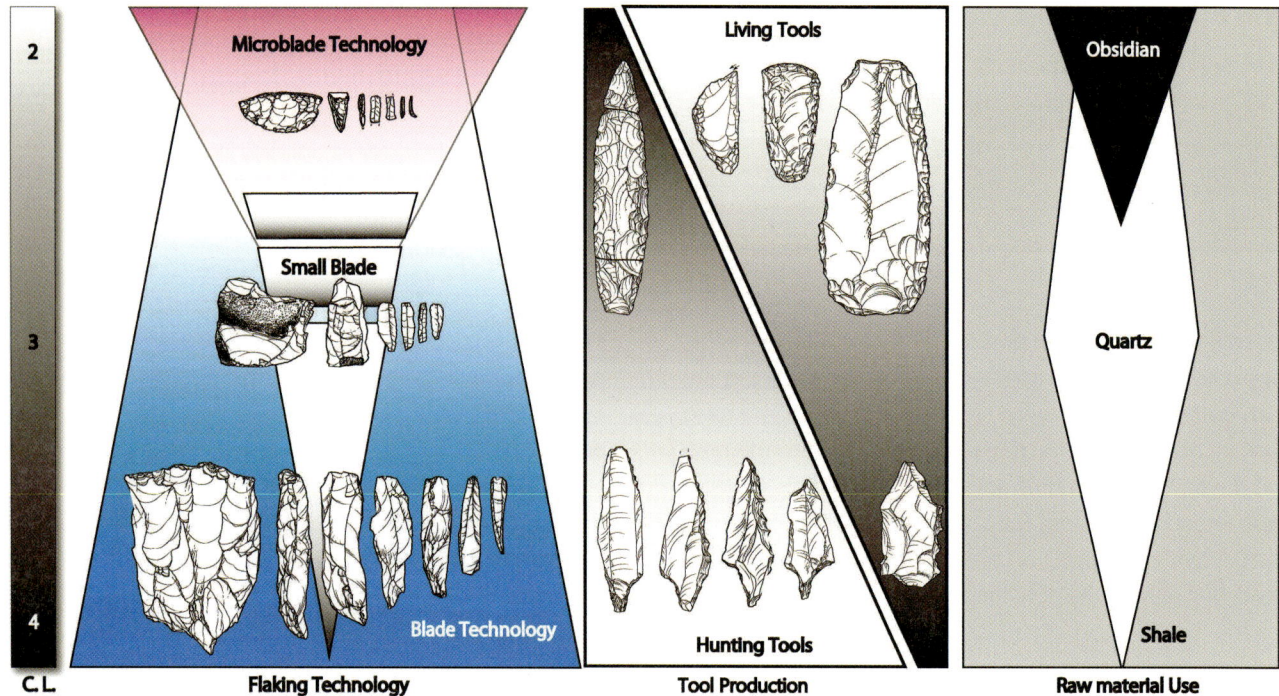

Fig. 10 Lithic assemblage transition from CL 4 to CL 2

resemble elements of microblade technology. Moreover, in CL2, small blades and microblades were reduced on the same core, further highlighting the gradual integration of these two technologies (Fig. 10).

Changing aspects of lithic composition and raw materials found at Suyanggae Loc. 6 were not limited to local phenomena. Even though particular surrounding conditions, like raw material source and landscape, should be considered, it is thought to be one of the most important sites that represents minute cultural change during the Paleolithic in the Korean Peninsula. It is the only significant case where Upper Paleolithic assemblages were found concentratedly, forming distinctive cultural layers. These layers allow for the reconstruction of lithic technology and the process of raw material utilization across sequential phases, from the early to the Late Upper Paleolithic. Suyanggae Loc. 6 is the only site containing a huge lithic assemblage in concentration with well-defined stratification. It is expected to provide critical information crucial to understanding how lithic technology developed alongside the selection and acquisition of raw materials. Especially, CL 4 yielded an exceptional lithic assemblage with tanged-points and blades in the Early Upper Paleolithic, which had been unknown before its excavation. It is expected to provide invaluable data on the emergence of the Upper Paleolithic and on modern humans more generally.

References

Kim Jong-Chan. 2018. Provenance Analysis of Obsidian Artifacts Excavated from the Suyanggae Site Loc. VI in Danyang, Lee, Y.J., Woo, J.Y., Lee, S.W., An, J.H., Yun B.I., Park, J.M., Otani, K., Kim, M.R., Han, S.C., Jang, H.G., Choi, D.H., 2018. *Report on the Excavation of Suyanggae Site (Loc. I and VI)*, Danyang, Institute of Korean Prehistory, 185-198. (in Korean)

Kim Ju-Yong, Keun-Chang Oh, Dong Yoon Yang, Weon Hack Choi, Sei Sun Hong, Jin Young Lee. 2008. Stratigraphy, chronology and implied uplift rate of coastal terraces in the southeastern part of Korea. *Quaternary International* 183, 76-82.

Kim, J.Y., Lee, H.J., Yang, D.Y., 2002. Quaternary formation, environment and chronology of some Palaeolithic sites of South Korea. *Journal of the Korean Palaeolithic Society* 6, 165-180.

Lee, Y.J., 1985. *An excavation report on the Palaeolithic site of Suyanggae, Danyang, in Chungju Dam Submerging Area Archaeological Reports*: 101-251. ed., Chungbuk National University Museum, Cheongju: Chungbuk National University Museum. (in Korean)

Lee, Y.J., Kim, J.C., 2005. Report on the dating results of the Suyanggae Paleolithic site. In: Lee, Y.J. eds., *The Paleolithic Culture of Jungwon Region, Korea*, Institute for Jungwon Culture and Chungbuk National Univ., 299-306. (in Korean with English abstract)

Lee, Y.J., Yun, Y.H., 1992. Tanged-points and Micro-blade Cores from Suyanggae Site, Korea. *Micro-blade Industry in Northern*

Eurasia and Northern North America, Sapporo University, Japan.

Lee, Y.J., Woo, J.Y., Lee, S.W., Kang, M.K., Otani, K., Yun B.I., Kim, M.R., 2013a. *Progress Report of Suyanggae Site Loc. III, Danyang–2008 Year Excavation (9th)–*, Institute of Korean Prehistory. (in Korean with English abstract)

Lee, Y.J., Woo, J.Y., Lee, S.W., Ahn, J.H., So, D.Y., Shin, S.C., Noh, H.S., 2013b. *Progress Report of Suyanggae Site Loc. III, Danyang–2011 Year Excavation (10th)–*, Institute of Korean Prehistory. (in Korean with English abstract)

Lee, Y.J., Woo, J.Y., Suh H.S., Lee, S.W., An, J.H., Park, J.M., 2014. New Findings from Loc. VI, Suyanggae Site, Korea. *International Symposium on Paleoanthropology in Commemoration of the 85h Anniversary of the Discovery of the First Skull of Peking Man*.

Lee, Y.J., Woo, J.Y., Lee, S.W., An, J.H., Yun B.I., Park, J.M., Otani, K., Kim, M.R., Han, S.C., Jang, H.G., Choi, D.H., 2018. *Report on the Excavation of Suyanggae Site (Loc. I and VI)*, Danyang, Institute of Korean Prehistory. (in Korean with English abstract)

Lim Jaesoo, Ju-Yong Kim, Seon-Ju Kim, Jin-Young Lee, Sei-Sun Hong. 2013. Late Pleistocene vegetation change in Korea and its possible link to East Asian monsoon and Dansgaard–Oeschger (D–O) cycles. *Quaternary Research* 79, 55-60.

Otani, K., 2016a. The Characteristic Change of Microlithic technology in Korea. *Journal of Korean Ancient Historical Society* 91, 4-41. (in Korean with English abstract)

Otani, K., 2016b. Analysis of Hunting-tool production and Raw material strategies in the Late Paleolithic of Korea. *Journal of the Hoseo Archaeological Society* 35, 4-37. (in Korean with English abstract)

Otani, K., 2020. *Tool Production and Raw material Consumption of Microlithic Cultural Stage; Korean Peninsula and Japanese Archipelago*, Meiji University. (in Japanese with English and Korean abstract)

The Emergence of Microblade culture at the Suyanggae site

Seung-won LEE[1], Yung-jo LEE[2]

[1] Assistant Director, Institute of Korean Prehistory (IKP), Korea ; arch152@hanmail.net
[2] Institute of Korean Prehistory (IKP), Korea

ABSTRACT

Cultural layers 1 to 3 in Loc. 3 of the Danyang The Upper Paleolithic in our country is divided into the early period of Upper Paleolithic and later period of Upper Paleolithic based on the appearance of the blade and the microblade and its boundary is known as the period around 25 ka. In Suyanggae Loc. 6, which was investigated recently, four cultural layers from early period of Upper Paleolithic to later period of Upper Paleolithic, corresponded to 42-22 ka were investigated, through which the data to be able to identify the aspect of change in the stone tool making technique were secured. Among them, the CL 3 and 4 are corresponded to the early period of Upper Paleolithic together with the CL 1 to 3 of Suyanggae Loc. 3. These cultural layers are the blade culture-based cultural layers and the blade making technique and the tanged point using that were made. Particularly, in the CL 3 of Loc. 6, it attracts the attention as the microblade cores, microblades, etc. were unearthed together with new type of culture such as stone engraved with lines including "Suyanggae stone ruler" and "Face-engrave sculpture," etc. The microblade cores unearthed in the CL 3 of Loc. 6 are not wedge type, which the core was adjusted, but show the simple aspect that the microblade was taken off utilizing original shape as is without repairing the core. For the microblade cores unearthed in the CL 2 and 3 of Loc. 3, the core was adjusted partly but no separate preparation work in the working face was made and was disposed after taking off microblade once or twice. These are the aspect showing difference from the standardized microblade core enearthed in the CL 2 of Loc. 6 and Loc. 1, which are corresponded to the later period of Upper Paleolithic. As such, the artifacts to the microblade making unearthed in the CL 3 of Loc 6 and Loc. 3 can be considered that they are showing the early period of microblade making.

국문초록

단양 수양개 유적 3지구 1-3문화층과 6지구 3-4문화층은 후기구석기 초(40,000-34,000년 전)를 나타내며 수양개 1지구와 6지구 1문화층과 2문화층에 비하여 석기의 구성과 제작기술에서 차이를 보여주고 있어 후기구석기 문화의 변화를 이해하는 데 중요하다. 특히 6지구 4문화층에서는 약 20cm의 크고 두꺼운 돌날을 포함하여 다양한 크기의 돌날 생산을 보여주며, 또한 돌날을 이용한 전문적 슴베찌르개 제작을 시사하고 있어 한국 돌날문화의 시초를 보여준다. 3문화층에서는 4문화층에 나타난 돌날과 슴베찌르개 제작이 지속되면서 돌날 관련 유물과 함께 새로운 유형의 유물로서 눈금돌(돌자)과 얼굴새긴돌이 출토되었다. 좀돌날몸돌은 3지점 2-3문화층에서 발견되며, 후기구석기의 일반적 좀돌날몸돌과 돌날에 비하여 몸체 조정, 작업 준비, 타격면 등이 없으며 즉시 좀돌날을 생산하는 좀돌날 생산 초기단계를 보여준다. 또한 좀돌날몸돌과 함께 출토된 소형 몸돌은 후기구석기의 일반적 좀돌날몸돌과 유사한 제작기술을 보여주고 있어, 후기구석기 초의 좀돌날 생산체계를 이해하는 좋은 자료이다.

Keywords : Suyanggae site, microblade, microblade core, tanged point, Upper Paleolithic, Paleolithic

1. Introduction

The Suyanggae site is considered an important site for studying the Upper Palaeolithic culture of Korea because of the large number of typical Upper Palaeolithic stone tools, such as tanged points and microblade cores, found at the site. One to four cultural layers were identified in the excavated areas of Suyanggae Loc. 1, 3, and 6. Absolute age dating revealed that Loc. 1 was formed during the Late Upper Paleolithic, Loc. 3 during the Early Upper Palaeolithic, and Loc. 6 during the early to Late Upper Paleolithic.

In general, the emergence of blade technology in Korea is considered to be in the Early Upper Paleolithic and microblade technology in the Late Upper Paleolithic, with the boundary being around 25,000 years ago. In CL 3 and CL 4 of Suyanggae Loc. 6, a large number of blades and tanged points were excavated, showing the upper limit of blade culture. In CL 2 of Loc. 1 and 6, the proportion of artifacts related to the production of formalized microblades increased, indicating a change in cultural patterns in the Upper Paleolithic.

Meanwhile, the early Palaeolithic ruins of CL 2 of Suyanggae Loc. 3 and CL 3 of Loc. 6 are notable for the presence of artifacts related to microblade technology, which are mainly found in the Late Upper Paleolithic. In this study, I will discuss the nature of the microblades recovered from the Early Upper Palaeolithic cultural layers of Loc. 3 and 6 at the Suyanggae site.

2. Remains overview

The Suyanggae site is located in Aegok-ri (Loc. 1 to 5) and Hajin-ri (Loc. 6) in Jeoksung-myeon, Danyang-gun, Chungbuk Province. The Namhan River flows to the south of the site. Loc. 1 and 6 are separated by 3.5km in a straight line, and cultural layers have been identified around 130m above sea level at the end of the mountain slopes bordering the Namhan River. Loc. 3 is located at the top of a ridge (150–165m above sea level) to the north of Loc. 1. The lowest part of the sedimentary layer in Loc. 3 shows an elevation difference of more than 40m from the river bed of the Namhan River, indicating that it is likely to be the third terrace. The terrace was exposed to the surface 40,000 years ago, and the Paleolithic cultural layers was formed subsequently (Fig. 1).

Suyanggae Loc. 1 and 6, located along the Namhan River, have similar landforms. Loc. 1 is adjacent to the confluence of the Aegok and Jukryeong stream, and Loc. 6 is adjacent to the confluence of the Danyangcheon stream and Sangricheon stream. It is located on a protected slope that is subject to sedimentation rather than erosion by river

Fig. 1 Suyanggae site

activity. Both sites have good views of the surrounding area, and their natural environment and location would have been suitable for hunting, gathering, and fishing for the Paleolithic people.

2.1. Loc. 3 of the Suyanggae site

Loc. 3 of the Suyanggae site revealed three Paleolithic cultural layers during excavations in 2008 and 2011. The layer of the site consists of topsoil (layer 1), yellow-brown clay (layer 2, CL 3), yellow clay (layer 3, CL 2), reddish-yellow clay that is sandy (layer 4, CL 1), and gravel (layer 5) from top to bottom. The artifacts were identified in the sediment layer formed between the topsoil and gravel layers and named CL 1, CL 2, CL 3, and CL 4 in the order of bottom to top (**Fig. 2**).

The proportion of stone tools in each cultural layer tends to be higher for artifacts related to stone tool production, such as cores, blade cores, flakes and hammer-stones. The proportion of small tools, such as scrapers, end-scrapers, notchs, and awls, which were retouched by flakes, and blades, is higher than the proportion of heavy-duty tools using core stones or pebble stones as the body. Quartzes and shales were mainly used for making stone tools. In particular, microblade cores in CL 2, shale blade in CL 3, and tanged points and microblade cores were excavated.

Absolute age dating for the cultural layers was determined using OSL. CL 1 dated at 38,800±3,400 BC, CL 2 at 37,900 ±3,600 BC, and CL 3 at 34,200±2,600 BC This suggests that the artifacts were formed in the Early Upper Palaeolithic date overall.

2.2. Loc. 6 of the Suyanggae site

Loc. 6 of the Suyanggae site was excavated between 2013 and 2015. The site's layers consist of repeated deposits of yellowish-brown and reddish-brown clay, with a reddish-brown, sandy clay layer containing 10 to 100cm rock fragments washed down from the top of the slope between each cultural layers (**Fig. 3**).

Four Upper Palaeolithic cultural layers were identified, and a total of 40,679 artifacts were excavated. The cultural layers at the top, CL 1, was damaged by erosion. However, CL 2 to CL 4 remained intact, and a wide range of stone tools were identified in each cultural layers. The distribution of artifacts and the analysis of use traces on individual stone tools suggest that both stone tool production and use of the tools.

Absolute age dating was performed on each cultural layer. The result revealed CL 4 to be between 41,874 to 41,254 BP, CL 3 to be between 40,172 to 39,321 BP, and CL 2 to be between 22,467 to 22,023 BP (anomaly corrected). This places CL 3 and CL 4 in the Early Upper Palaeolithic, and CL 1 and CL 2 in the Late Upper Palaeolithic.

Looking at the characteristics of each cultural layers, the lowest cultural layers, cultural layers 4, shows the production of large blades that are almost 20cm made through a systematic production process. The cultural layers is characterized by the production of tanged point using blades. In CL 3, the ratio of blades to tanged point is lower than in CL 4 ; however, microblade technology emerged. It shows a new cultural pattern different from the previous period that involves the production of artworks, such

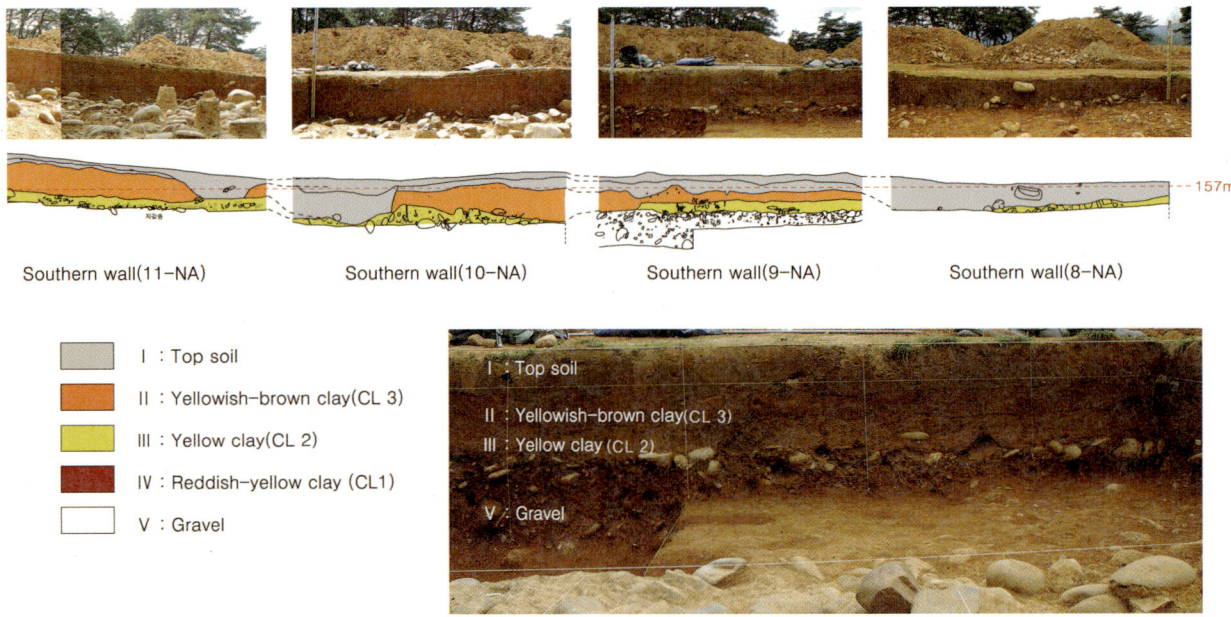

Fig. 2 Stratigraphy of Suyanggae Loc. 3

as "stone ruler" and "face-engrave sculpture," which has engravings at regular intervals on pebble stones.

While the proportion of blades decreased, the production of microblades increased in CL 2. Although tanged point, which was found in large quantities in CL 3 and CL 4, was not found, leaf-shaped points, chisel-typed tools, stone bowls, and ground stones were characteristically identified, along with formalized end-scrapers. As in previous cultural layers, shale was the dominant material for stone tools. However, the use of higher quality stones, such as obsidian, rhyolite, tuff, and hornfels, increased.

As such, differences in the production and use of stone tools by different cultural layers have been identified in Suyanggae Loc. 6, which allows an understanding of the flow and changes in stone tools throughout the Upper Paleolithic period.

3. The emergence of microblade culture at the Suyanggae site

The cultural layers corresponding to the Early Upper Paleolithic at the Suyanggae site are CL 1 to CL 3 in Loc. 3 and CL 3 and CL 4 in Loc. 6. The cultural layers were formed in the following order: CL 4 in Loc. 6, CL 3 in Loc. 6, CL 1 in Loc. 3, CL 2 in Loc. 3, and CL 3 in Loc. 3. These cultural layers are based on blade technology, and blades and tanged points were excavated in the layers.

Twenty-two artifacts related to microblade technology were excavated from CL 3 in Loc. 6, including two microblade cores, three microblade cores, one microblade core spall, and 16 microblades. In Loc. 3, seven artifacts were excavated from CL 3, including four microblade cores, one microblade core, and two microblades, and one microblade core from CL 2. Shale and quartz were mainly used, and the artifacts are characterized in that the microblades were made by grinding the stone surface or striking the surface of a broken surface without any special adjustment to the body (**Fig. 4-6**).

It is known that the systematic microblade technology emerged around 24,000 to 25,000 years ago from Korean Paleolithic remains, including Jangheung-ri in Cheolwon, Sinbuk in Jangheung, and Hopyeong-dong Loc. 3 in Namyangju. Lee Heon-jong classified the emergence, spread, peak and transition periods of the microblade culture into three periods : the first (25-20 ka),

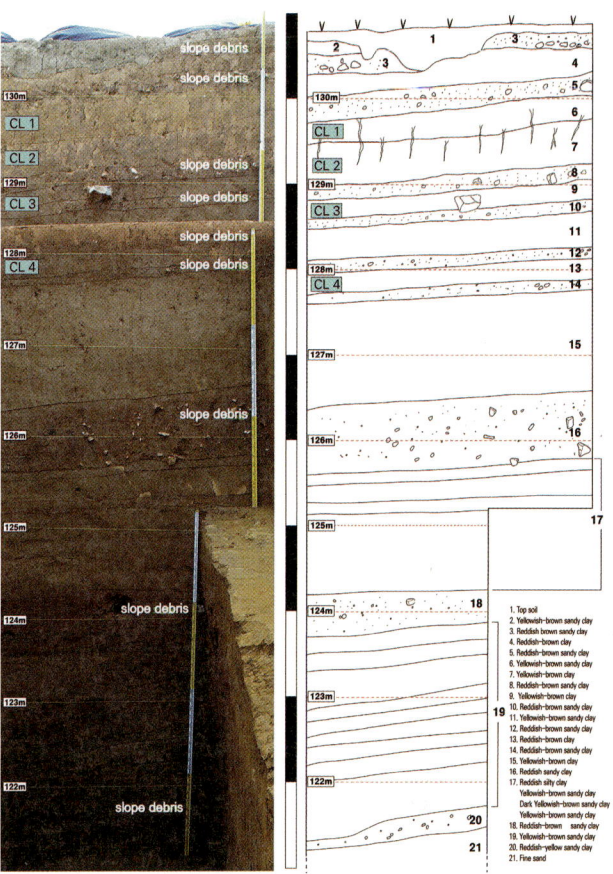

Fig. 3 Stratigraphy of Suyanggae Loc. 6

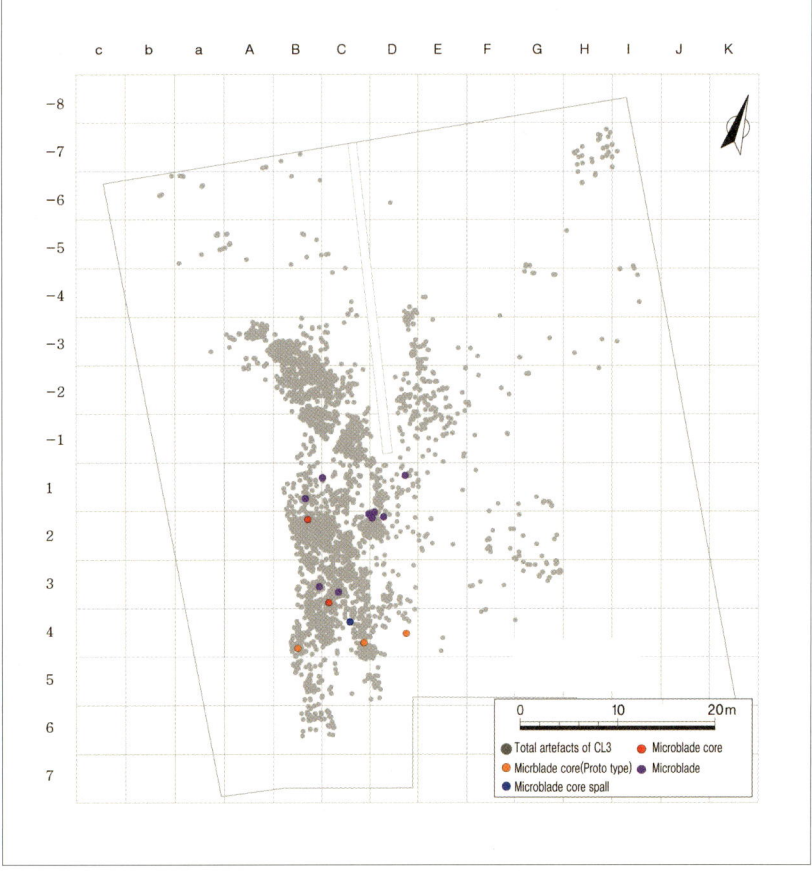

Fig. 4 Distribution of artefacts related to microblade in Suyanggae Loc. 6

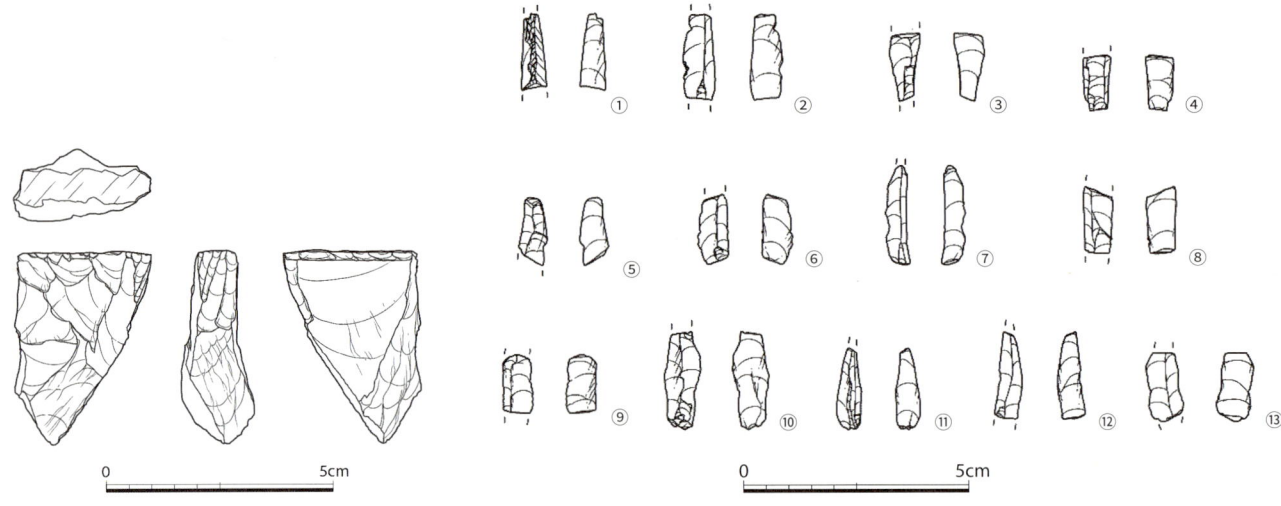

Fig. 5 Artifacts of Suyanggae Loc. 6 (CL 3)

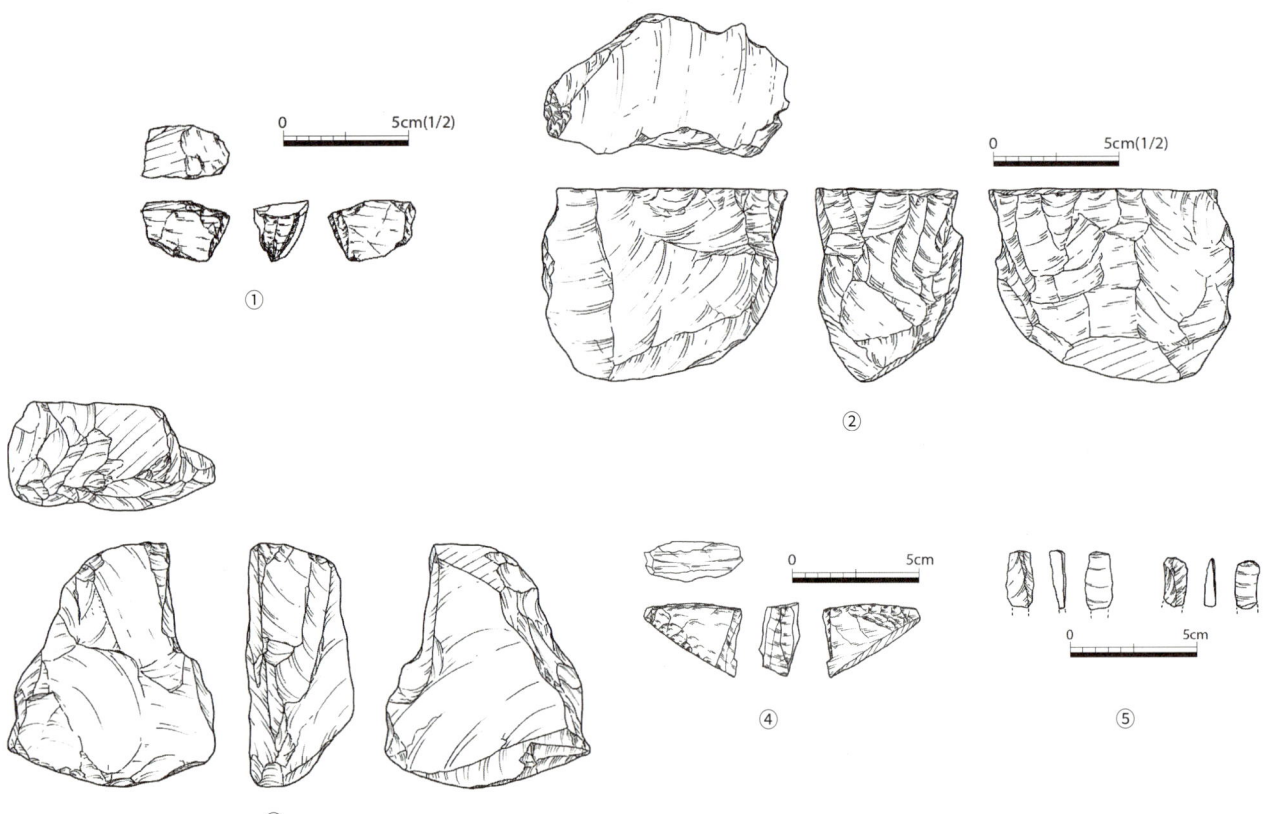

Fig. 6 Artifacts of Suyanggae Loc. 3 (① CL 2, ②–⑤ CL 3)

the second (20–15 ka, Seokjang-ri, Imsil Haga, Suyanggae, and Wolsung-dong), and the third (15–10 ka, Hahwagye-ri, Sangmuryong-ri, Gokcheon, Okgwa, Hwasun Daejeon, Minrak-dong, etc.). Compared with CL 2 (21,000–19,000 years ago) and 3 (17,000–13,000 years ago) of Selemdja in the middle Amur River, he explained the development of the microblade culture based on the techniques of bifacial chipping principle and grid utilization principle. He also examined the artifacts excavated with the identification of stone tool production techniques. Among these periods, he noticed that the typical stone tools of the Late Paleolithic period that appeared in the first period, in which microblades appeared including the microblade cores, which reflect the principle of bifacial chipping, were characterized by the blades and flakes (**Fig. 7**).

However, CL 3 of Loc. 6, where the microblades first appeared in the Suyanggae site, is based on blade culture. The microblade culture appeared while coinciding with the use of tanged points. The microblade cores of CL 3 do not have an wedge shaped, and their bodies are not adjusted. These cores show simple technical features that utilize the original shape of the body without any modification.

Later, in CL 2 and 3 of Loc. 3, which dates from 39,000 to 34,000 years ago, some of the microblade cores were modified in their bodies bifacial chipping; however, they do not show a preparation of a separate working surface. Shale and quartz were used for the stone, but the quartz microblade cores excavated in CL 2 and 3 of Loc. 3 do not show a series of microblade chipping due to the nature of the stone. The microblades were discarded after one or two rounds of production.

As such, the microblade cores excavated from the Upper Palaeolithic cultural layers of Loc. 6 and 3 of Suyanggae site show different production compared to that of the later period, which uses the bifacial chipping principle. Also, these, unlike the microblade cores that used shale and obsidian, which were found in CL 2 of Loc. 6 and in Loc. 1 in the later period, show various attempts made to use quartz, which is relatively unsuitable for chipping in the early stages of stone tool production.

Meanwhile, the "small blade cores" found alongside the microblade cores were found in both CL 2 and 4 in Loc. 6 (**Fig. 8, 9**). They are less regular than the microblades and are made from small blades that fall somewhere between the

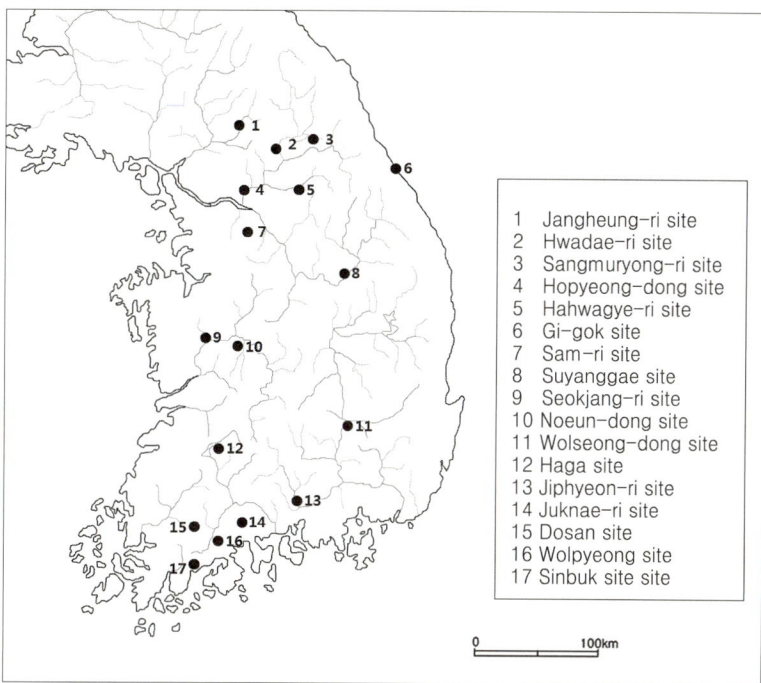

Fig. 7 Microblade sites in South Korea (LEE, H. J., 2015)

size of a blade and a microblade. The chipping technique is very similar to that used to make microblade cores.

In other words, the small blade core is made by removing the flake in a longitudinal direction to prepare a striking surface and preparing a blade at one end, which is similar to the spall chipping technique. In the small blade cores of CL 3 and 4, the small blades were chipped using the original form of the bodies without any modifications, which is similar to the technique used in microblade cores excavated in the

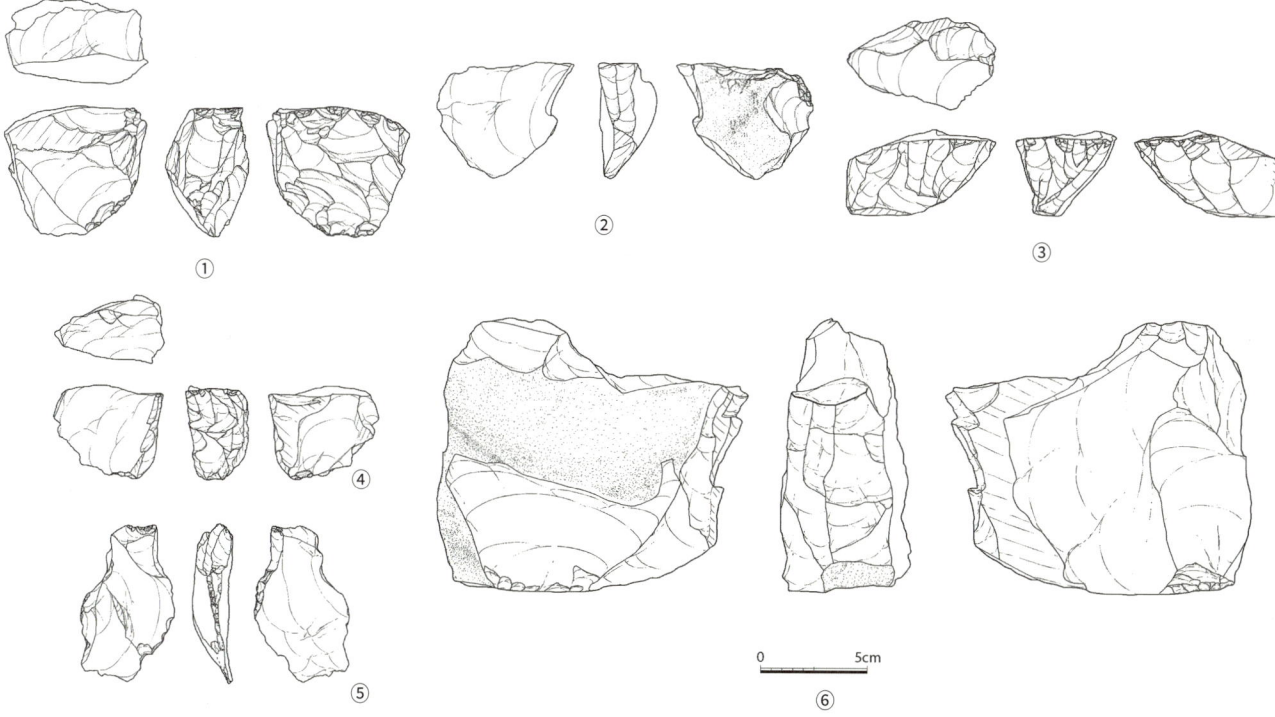

Fig. 8 Small blade core of Suyanggae Loc. 6 (①–④ CL 2, ⑤–⑥ CL 3)

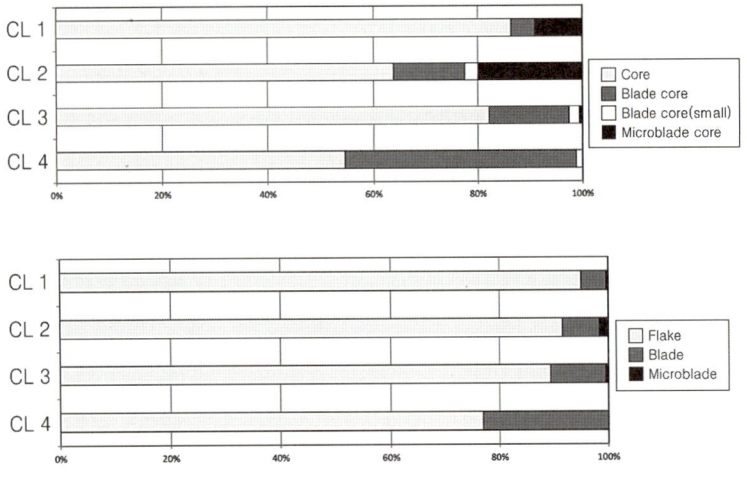

Fig. 9 Ratio of cores and flakes

4. Conclusion

CL 1 to 3 in Loc. 3 of the Danyang Suyanggae site and CL 3 and 4 in Loc. 6 reflect the Early Upper Paleolithic period (40,000-34,000 years ago). They have become a good source for understanding the changes in Upper Paleolithic culture as they show differences in the composition and production techniques of stone tools compared to the later layers 1 and 2 in Suyanggae Loc. 1 and 6.

In particular, CL 4 of Loc. 6 shows the production of blades of various sizes, including large and thick blades of about 20cm. This layer also displays the professional production of tanged points using blades, showing the Upper limit of Korean stone blade culture. In CL 3, the production of blades and tanged points that appeared in CL 4 continued, and new types of artifacts, such as stone rulers and face stones, were excavated along with artifacts related to blades.

These microblade cores were also found in CL 2 and 3 of Loc. 3, and compared to typical microblade cores blades the Upper Palaeolithic, they show aspects of the early stages of microblade production, such as the immediate production of microblades without a body adjustment and preparation of the working and striking surfaces. In addition, the small stone cores excavated with the microblade cores display production techniques similar to those of typical microblade cores in the Upper Palaeolithic age, and are a good source for understanding the production of mciroblades in the Early Upper Palaeolithic age.

◆ This paper is prepared by summarizing and modifing previous article (LEE, Seongwon. 2020. *Journal of Museum Studies* 39).

same layers.

In CL 2, which corresponds to the Late Upper Paleolithic, the blades were removed after modifying the body and preparing the working surface using a bifacial flaking technique similar to the technique used in microblade cores. In the end, the blades made in the layers are bigger than microblades; therefore, they cannot be classified as microblades. However, they were made using the same technique as the one used in microblades. This distinction suggests that small blade techniques converged with systematic microblade techniques in the Late Paleolithic age to produce blades of different sizes as needed. In this way, the emergence of microblade making techniques based on the stone blade culture in CL 3 of Suyanggae Loc. 6, dated around 40,000 years ago, is the earliest to be dated in Korea. However, the ratio of the microblade-related artifacts from CL 3 is very low in the distribution ratio of cores and flakes, and the production techniques of the stone tools are not systematic; therefore, it cannot be concluded that the production of microblades at this time was specialized.

According to Lee Heong-jong, the conditions for the full-scale emergence of microblades are as follows: First, there must be a 'need' to mass-produce microblades. Second, there must be a 'new form of adaptation process' due to changes in ecological conditions at the time. Third, there must be an accumulation of technical 'know-how'. Lastly, the 'ability to select good quality stone' must be found. In CL 3 of Suyanggae Loc. 6, the microblade culture emerged based on the ability to select high-quality stones and production techniques, which were used to product delicate tools such as tanged points. It can be concluded that the conditions for the production of microblades have been satisfied based on the stone rulers and face stones excavated from the same layer, which suggest a new cultural change different from the previous period.

References

Kim Kyeong J., Kim Ju Y., Lee Kyong W., Lee Seung W., Woo Jong Y., Lee Yung J., Jull A.J. Timothy. 2021. Radiocarbon ages of Suyanggae Paleolithic Site in Danyang, Korea. *RADIOCARBON* Vol. 63(5), 1429-1444. https://doi.org/10.1017/RDC.2021.77

Kim J.Y., Lee Y.J., Woo J.Y., Lee S.W., Suh H.S., Kim K.J., Yang H.J., Lee K.W., Choi W.H., Oh K.C., 2023. Morpho-Stratigraphy, Sedimentology, and Radiocarbon Chronologyof Suyanggae Sites, Focusing on Loc. VI, South Korea. *Archaeology Ethnology and Anthropology of Eurasia* 51(3), 96-108. https://doi.org/

10.17746/1563-0110.2023.51.3.096-108

Lee Heonjong. 2015. Study of origin and distribution of blade and microblade industry in Korea. *Journal of the Korean Palaeolithic Society* 31, 84-115.

LEE Yung-jo, Woo Jong-yoon, LEE Seung-won, AHN Ju-hyun, SO Dong-young, SHIN Seung-chul, NOH Hye-sun. 2013. *Progress Report of Suyanngae Site Loc. III, Danyang - 2011 Year Excavation(10th)*, IKP, p. 256.

LEE Yung-jo, Woo Jong-yoon, LEE Seung-won, AHN Ju-hyun, YUN Byeong-il, PARK Jeong-mi, OTANI Kaoru, KIM Mi-ra, KIM Eun-jeong, HAN Seung-chul, JANG Hyeong-gil, CHOI Dong-hyuk. 2018. *Report on the Excavation of Suyanggae Site(Loc. I and VI), Danyang*, IKP, p. 824.

LEE Yung-jo, Woo Jong-yoon, LEE Seung-won, KANG Min-kyu, YUN Byeong-il, OTANI Kaoru, KIM Mi-ra. 2013. *Progress Report of Suyanngae Site Loc. III, Danyang –2008 Year Excavation(9th)*, IKP, p. 150.

Otani, K., 2020. *Tool Production and Raw material Consumption of Microlithic Cultural Stage; Korean Peninsula and Japanese Archipelago*, Meiji University.

An analysis of end-scrapers by manufacturing technology in the Upper Paleolithic from the Suyanggae site, Loc. 6, in Danyang, Korea

Eunjeong KIM[1], Seung-won LEE[2], Jong-yoon WOO[2], Yung-jo LEE[2]

[1] Department Director, RADPION Inc., Korea ; ejkim@radpion.com
[2] Institute of Korean Prehistory (IKP), Korea

ABSTRACT

As a result of comparing the morphology of end-scrapers excavated at Suyanggae site Loc. 6 by cultural layer in more detail, the tendency for their length to gradually become smaller can be seen, from CL 4 to CL 1. Thus, earlier end-scrapers were larger and heavier. Regarding their width and thickness, end-scrapers from CL 4 and CL 3 are larger, with those in CL 2 and CL 1 becoming narrower and thinner. End-scrapers in CL 2 especially clearly show they were concentrated in a certain section, and were the smallest in terms of width, thickness, and weight. We can look at the standardization trend that manufactured the end scraper by choosing a certain size of flakes in this respect. In addition, end-scrapers in CL 2 feature nearly uniform retouching on both side edges of the long flakes. Therefore, the standardization of end-scraper manufacturing was revealed to be clearly and definitely associated with the process of preparing the blank.

국문초록

수양개 유적 6지구, 후기구석기 4개 문화층에서 출토된 밀개는 총 355점으로 1문화층 8점, 2문화층 332점, 3문화층 14점, 가장 아래 4문화층 1점이며, 후기구석기 늦은시기의 2문화층에 밀개 제작이 집중되어 있다. 이 논문에서는 문화층별 밀개의 형태 및 속성을 비교하고 보다 집중적으로 제작된 2문화층의 밀개 제작기법을 분석하여 제작과 사용에 따른 형태적 변화를 고찰하였다. 문화층별 밀개의 형태 및 속성 비교 결과, 길이는 4-3-2-1문화층 순으로 감소하는 경향을 볼 수 있다. 이른시기 밀개가 더 크고 무거운 반면 늦은시기로 가면서 점차 작아진다. 밀개 너비와 두께는 4, 3문화층 밀개가 더 크고 2, 1문화층에서는 좁고 얇아짐을 볼 수 있다. 특히 2문화층 밀개는 너비와 두께, 그리고 무게가 가장 작고 일정 구간에 집중 현상이 뚜렷하다. 이는 일정 크기의 격지 선택과 밀개 제작의 규격화 경향을 의미한다. 2문화층은 밀개의 압도적 출토 수량, 규질 석재, 규격화된 몸체 선택성, 정형화된 몸체 조정기법 등으로 볼 때, 다른 문화층과 차이가 뚜렷하며, 밀개 제작이 특화된 전문성을 보여준다. 아울러 일정 크기 및 형태의 몸체 준비 공정이 도구 제작에 가장 중요한 요소임을 확인했다. 날 형태의 평면과 단면 모습의 차이에 기반하여 제작-수리 및 재생-폐기의 3단계 변화 과정이 추정되며 정형화된 유형의 밀개 제작과 재생 양상을 유추할 수 있다.

Keywords : Upper Paleolithic, end-scraper, blank of standardization, edge condition, edge management

1. Introduction

The Milgae (end-scraper) was classified into a living tool of the Paleolithic Age. This word by being stemmed from the work of making the terms of the Paleolithic into the Korean language, which had taken place in the latter half of the 1960s, it reaches the now (Sohn, 1968). In the Republic of Korea, research has departed from classification according to the shape of the end-scraper edge and focused instead on classification of the morphology based on the manufacturing technology and shape of the edge (Sohn, 1968; Park, 1990; Lee and Kong, 2001; Kim, 2006). Although it had been easy in grasping the special feature of end-scrapers, regarding the meaning of the morphological diversity of end-scrapers and regarding the connection to the diverse formal modification according to the use method and the function of end-scrapers, indeed, there had been a limitation.

In the 2010's, after a technological approach of the lithic analysis from France had been introduced, while the concept about the lithic manufacturing process and the work chain (chaîne opératoire) got recognized widely (Seo, 2010; Kim, 2012; Kim 2020; Kim and Yun, 2020). Thereafter a research that had looked at the end-scrapers manufacturing process from the aspect of the lithic production was announced. On the one hand, in terms of lithic consumption, the research reports regarding the examination of the function of end-scrapers and regarding the functional divisions by the morphology had continued through a use-ware analysis.

Technological approach of the lithic analysis, which was stated earlier, as a thing that reorganizes the arrangement of the technological activities according to the lithic manufacturing method, it is the confirmation of the manufacturing process from the aspect of lithic production. Indeed, it is a research methodology that comprehensively includes from the acquisition of raw material to the process of producing a tool that was the purpose after obtaining the blank (Seo, 2010). As a result, the research ever since 2010, the meaning is big because the research direction was converted to a lithic manufacturing process. In this writing, by receiving the direction of the research toward a lithic technological analysis, it is intended to look at the end-scrapers manufacturing process.

As for the object of the research, it is intended to examine the Suyanggae site Loc. 6, where four cultural layers of the Paleolithic Age had been excavated. The morphology and the property of the end-scrapers by each cultural layer are compared. And, furthermore, in terms of the lithic assemblages of CL 2, it is intended to have the end-scrapers of the standardization group that captures the superiority overwhelmingly as the main object of the analysis. Especially, it is intended to look at the morphological change resulting from the manufacturing and the use. And it is intended to understand the method of manufacturing of end-scrapers, which had been standardized by extracting the special features of the manufacturing technique.

2. The morphology and the property of end-scrapers by the cultural layer

In an investigation of the 6 District, which had taken place over 30 years from the excavation of the Suyanggae site Loc .l, 21 sedimentary layers were confirmed. Inside them, four cultural layers that belong to the Upper Paleolithic were confirmed (Lee et al., 2018). Especially, in CL 4 (The excavations of 10,883 artifacts) that is below the most and in CL 3 (7,470 pieces) above it, based on the blade technique, because lithic artifact of the tanged point was confirmed, it can be seen as a first half of the Upper Paleolithic. In contrast, in CL 2 (21,744 pieces) and CL 1 (582 pieces), including the micro-blade core and the micro-blade that have the micro-blade technique as the basis, the end-scraper, the side-scraper, the burin, the axe-shaped stone tool, etc. excavated. That come from the latter half of the Upper Paleolithic.

The artifacts were excavated in four cultural layers of Loc. 4, the by-products that are related to the lithic manufacturing, including the cores, the flakes, the debris, etc. basically, capture the most to the extent of being 39,000 pieces (Around 96%). Furthermore, among the tools, the end-scrapers (355 pieces) and the side-scrapers (356 pieces) excavated the most. Especially, among the artifacts of the Upper Paleolithic of Korea, the end-scrapers are the artifacts that had been excavated the most. Therefore, in this analysis, it is intended to look at the change of the end-scraper by the time in the Upper Paleolithic, by comparing and analyzing the morphology and the property of end-scrapers by each cultural layer.

2.1. The blank and raw materials

Regarding the end-scrapers excavated from four cultural layers corresponding to the Upper Paleolithic, all of them are 355 pieces. If it is aggregated by each cultural layer, it is eight pieces on the cultural layer 1 right below the surface, 332 pieces in CL 2, 14 pieces in CL 3, one piece in CL 4, which is at the bottom (Table 1). Especially, in CL 2 which pertains to the late of Upper Paleolithic, the manufacturing of the end-scrapers are concentrated on. Among the end-scrapers in CL 2, the things of broken edge (37 pieces), the things of which only one part of the edge remains (9 pieces), around a half of the entire size being refitted with each other while being broken (18 pieces of the 9 pairs), etc. are observed. Not only get the manufacturing process, but damage also due to

Table 1 Comparison of the blanks and the raw materials of end-scrapers excavated from Suyanggae site Loc. 6 by cultural layers

Cultural layer	excavated	observe	The blanks		The raw materials						
			flake	debris	quartz	rhyolite	shale	tuff	hornfels	obsidian	chert
1	8	8	4	4	8	-	-	-	-	-	-
2	332	275	262	13	15	122	111	22	1	3	1
3	14	12	6	6	5	-	6	1	1	-	-
4	1	1	1	-	-	-	1	-	-	-	-
Total	355	296	273	23	28	122	118	23	2	3	1

the use confirmed. As a result, without stopping at only the intensive manufacturing of the end-scraper in CL 2, even the appearance of the actual use, too, can be portrayed.

Meanwhile, in CL 2, 48 pieces that had the limitations in extracting the basic data, including 37 pieces with damaged edges, nine pieces with only part of the edge remained, two pieces with weathered things, etc., were excluded from the objects of the observation. Accordingly, the analysis of objects from CL 2 were restricted to 284 pieces. And the nine pairs in which two pieces are refitted as one end-scraper are analyzed in the refitted condition, the number of the end-scrapers that become the objects of an analysis is 275 pieces. Also, 2 pieces from CL 3 was difficult to observe the property due to severe weathering of the raw material, only 12 pieces had been the objects of the analysis (**Table 1**).

If the ratios of the use of the blank by the cultural layer are compared, CL 1 and CL 3 are similar with flakes and debris, being four pieces and six pieces each (**Fig. 1**). And, as for the end-scraper in CL 4, the flakes had been used for the blank. Compared to this, in CL 2, in contrast to the fact that the debris were 13 pieces, the remaining 262 pieces show a difference that is 20 times or more by using the flakes. In CL 2, which had intensively produced and used the end-scrapers, it can be known that the flakes had been preferred with the blanks of the end-scrapers. Meanwhile, among the flakes or the flakes of broken that had been used as the blanks of the end-scrapers, because it can, also, be seen as the blades or the blades of broken, we can know that the blades are included in the blank.

The raw material that was used for an end-scraper can be largely distinguished into the siliceous stone and the ordinary stone. For the ordinary stone, quartz had been

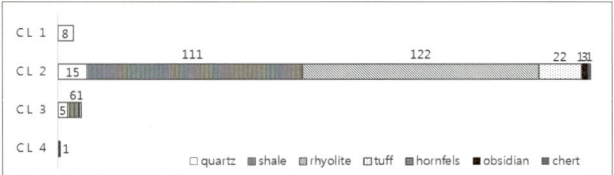

Fig. 2 Comparison of raw material by cultural layer

used. Regarding the siliceous stone, rhyolite, shale, tuff, hornfels, etc. had been used. And obsidian and chert are included.

If I look at the usage ratio of the raw material by the cultural layer, in CL 4, shale had been used. In CL 3, five pieces of quartz, six pieces of shale, and one piece each was used for tuff and hornfels. Indeed, with eight pieces of the siliceous stone and five pieces of the ordinary stone, a big difference was not recognized regarding the degree of the preference. In contrast, in CL 2, contrary to the fact that the quartz was only 15 pieces, regarding the remaining 260 pieces, because the siliceous stones were used for all, we can clearly and definitely confirm the degree of preference regarding the siliceous stone. What is even more, from the siliceous stones, because rhyolite (122 pieces) and shale (111 pieces) had been capturing around 90%, we can know that there had been a stone selection for the end-scrapers. Afterwards, at the phase of CL 1, too, the degree of preference regarding the stone was recognized. Except, all of the eight pieces had used only the quartz, which is an ordinary stone (**Fig. 2**).

2.2. The morphology, the size, and the weight

To measure the size of the tool, the end-scraper edge was put on top. In addition, by considering even an axis that gets connected from the central point of the distal part to the proximal part central point, it had been arranged so that the overall balance does not get disorderly (**Fig. 3**). In this condition, the length, the width, the thickness, and the weight were measured.

In terms of the length and the width, the end-scraper is a long shape (**Fig. 4**_left). Especially, in CL 2, it shows the tendency of getting concentrated in a narrow and long. And, compared to the length, the width gets integrated into

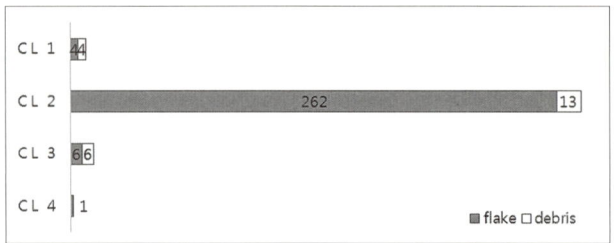

Fig. 1 Comparison of blank by cultural layer

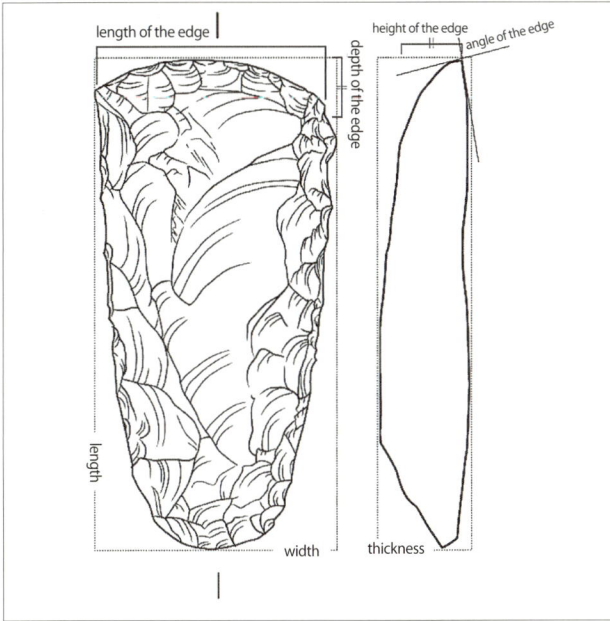

Fig. 3 Criteria for observation

a specific range. More specifically, if we take a look at the size of the end-scraper by the cultural layer, firstly, the end-scrapers from CL 4 are close to a square at 64x67x26mm, and the weight is 115g.

Next, the 12 pieces of end-scrapers in CL 3 are distributed with the length of 36-75mm, the width of 19-68mm, and the thickness of 16-37mm. And the weights are 12-125g. The end-scrapers in CL 3, too, showed a tendency that is close to a square. Again, this was distinguished into a thing (6 pieces) that had used the flake and a thing that had used the debris (6 pieces). The end-scraper that had used the flakes as the blank has the relationship of the length ≧ the width, in other words the length is the same as the width, or it is the morphology of being a little longer. In contrast, regarding the end-scraper that has the debris as the blank, the length and the width are similar.

In CL 2, to the extent that the most end-scrapers of 275 pieces had been excavated, the distribution is wide. There are distributed at the length of 13-114mm, the width of 15-88mm, the thickness of 3-41mm, and the thickness of 1-306g. Especially, the length is concentrated on 29-45mm, the width is concentrated at 20-27mm, the thickness is concentrated on 7-12mm, and the weight is concentrated on 4-14g. End-scrapers in CL 2 have a long from the basic size. While the size distribution is wide, it clearly shows the tendency of concentrated on a certain value.

If this is looked at by distinguishing by the blank again, regarding the things that had the flakes as the blank, there were 262 pieces, which captures the most. The things that had the debris as the blank are merely 13 pieces. Although, regarding the things that had used the flakes, compared to the width, the length is much longer, the things that had used the debris are nearly similar in terms of the length and the width. And, regarding the thing that had used the debris, it is thicker and heavier compared to the end-scraper of the blank of the flakes. Indeed, although, regarding the end-scrapers of the blanks of the flakes in CL 2, mostly, they are long and thinner, the morphological difference that the debris' blank is close to a square and closer gets recognized.

The end-scrapers (8 pieces) that came from CL 1 right below surface are distributed at the length of 25-40mm, the width of 24-40mm, the thickness of 13-25mm, and the weight of 6-38g. When looking at this, the end-scrapers from CL 1 have a morphology that is close to a square. This was distinguished again into the things (4 pieces) that used the flakes and the things (4 pieces) that used the debris with the blank as the standard. Although the length and the width by the flakes and the debris did not have a big difference, in terms of the thickness, the flakes are much thinner.

If the morphology of the end-scrapers are compared by the four cultural layers (**Fig. 4**_right), the length shows the tendency of becoming smaller gradually in the order of CL 4–CL 3–CL 2– CL 1. When looking at this, mostly, the end-scrapers of an early time is bigger and heavier. In contrast, it was confirmed that it had become smaller gradually while the time has passed. And, regarding the width and the thickness, in contrast to the fact that the end-scrapers of CL 4 and CL 3 are bigger, CL 2 and CL 1 get narrower and thinner. Especially, the end-scrapers of CL 2 clearly show the phenomenon of being concentrated in a certain section while the values of the width, the thickness, and the weight are the smallest. When looking at this, by selecting the flakes of a certain size, the expertise of having manufactured the end-scrapers can be peeped

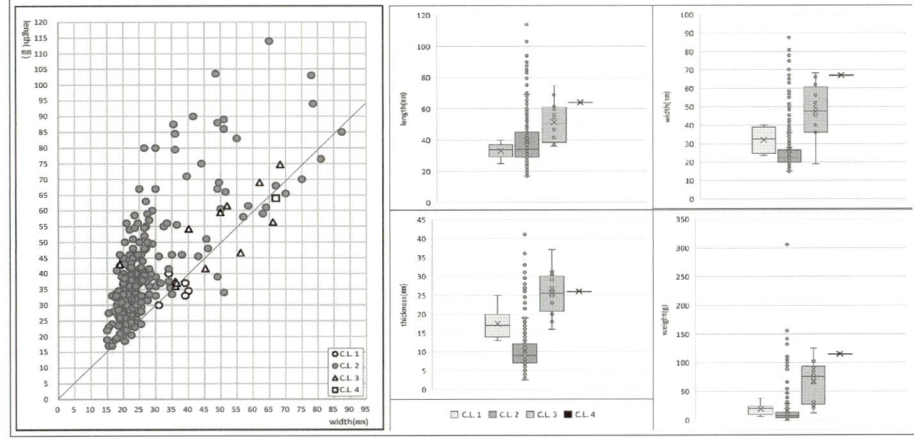

Fig. 4 Comparison of morphology and size by cultural layer

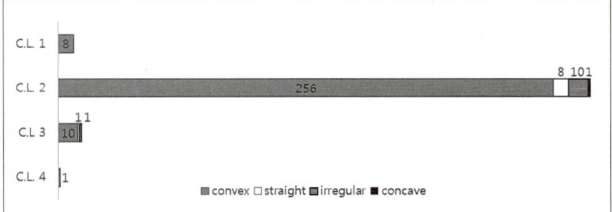

Fig. 5 The position of edge by cultural layer

into.

2.3. The property of edge

If we take a look at the functional definition of 'end-scraper', it has been known that, although it is used for trees or hard animal materials, mostly, it had been used in processing the dried leather (Demars and Laurent, 1992; Kim, 2018). In order to understand the properties of the edge that is in charge of the actual function of the tool, the following had been intended to look at consecutively: The position of the edge of the end-scraper, the length of the edge, the height of the edge, the depth of the edge, the angle of the edge, the curvature of the edge by the cultural layer and by the blank. Firstly, regarding the end-scraper (1 piece) from CL 4, the flakes had been used as the blank. And at the side corner on the right side of the dorsal, by retouching in the dorsal direction, an edge of nose shape had been retouched. The direct line length of the edge was 47.0mm. The height of the retouching is 21.0mm. The depth of the retouching is 13.0mm, and the angle of the edge retouching is 75°. With the edge of convex as the object, in order to objectify the extent of the roundness of the edge, the curvature was measured (www.handymath.com). Then, the value was 29R(mm). It is a relatively gentle edge of convex.

Regarding the end-scrapers (12 pieces) of CL 3, the things that had the flakes as the blank and the things that had the debris as the blank were six pieces each. Regarding the position of the edge that had the flakes as the blank, other than one piece regarding which the side had been retouched with an edge, all of them have the edges on the distal parts (**Fig. 5**). Regarding the things that had used the debris as the blanks, there were 4 pieces that retouched the edges on the short sides. And, regarding the remainder, it is 1 piece each at the long side and the corner part. Mostly, the edges were retouched in the short range of the blank. Regarding the shapes of the edges, 10 pieces had the edges of convex. And the edge of straight and the irregular are 1 piece each (**Fig. 6**). Most of the

edges of convex are rounds. And, among them, the sharp type gets confirmed by 1 piece each at the debris blank and the flakes blank.

If the sizes of the edges are compared, the end-scraper by the flakes as the blank has the length of 16-55mm, the height of the edge at 5-25mm, the depth of the edge is 2-14mm, the angle of the edge is 65-96°. And the curvature of the edge is 15-58R(mm). Meanwhile, regarding the end-scraper by the debris, the length of the edge is 27-49mm, the height of the edge is 11-28mm, the depth of the edge is 2-17mm, and the angle of the edge is 60-90°, and the curvature of the edge is 14-39R(mm). To the extent of the retouching of the edge resulting from the blank, there is no big difference. Except, on the length of the edge and the height of the edge of the flakes, a smaller value gets confirmed. It can be thought that this is a result in which the special feature of the blank, regarding which it is said that the flakes are narrower and thinner than the debris, is reflected. It can be considered that, regarding the difference, too, that is seen in the maximum value of a curvature, it is related with the size of the blank.

In CL 2, among the 275 pieces that had been the objects of the analysis, the things that had the flakes as the blanks were 262 pieces. And the things that had the debris as the blanks were 13 pieces. First, regarding the position of the edge of a thing that had the flakes as the blanks, the distal part was 254 pieces. And the retouch of an edge on a proximal part (1 piece) and the retouch on the side (7 pieces), etc. were confirmed. Meanwhile, using the debris for the blanks, they were diversely confirmed as the things that retouched the edges on the short sides (7 pieces), the things that retouched at the corner parts (3 pieces), the things that were retouched on the long sides (2 pieces), the thing that retouched while going around a circumference (1 piece), etc. Even so, mostly, the edges had been retouched at the short parts in a limited way. Regarding the shapes of the edges, 256 pieces were the convex edges. And, other than them, there are the straight edges (8 pieces), the irregulars (10 pieces), the concave edges (1 piece), etc.

If the sizes of the edges are taken a look at, the length of

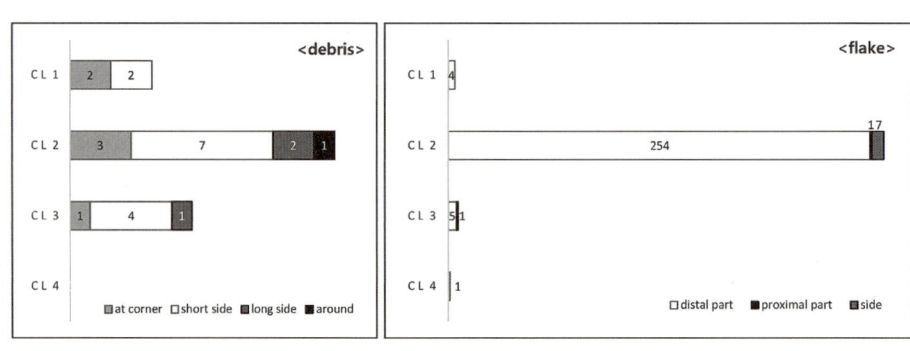

Fig. 6 The shape of edge by cultural layer

the edge is 9-68mm, the height of the edge is 2-23mm, the depth of the edge is 1-17mm, and the angle of the edge is 31-130°. And the curvature of the edge is 5-37R(mm). Among these, regarding the end-scrapers (13 pieces) by the debris, the length of the edge is 16-58mm, the height of the edge is 1-23mm, the depth of the blade is 1-14mm, and the angle of the edge is 65-110°. And the curvature of the edge is 12-33R(mm). When comparing the sizes of the edges by the blank above, a smaller value is distributed in the lengths of the edges of the flakes. Regarding this, it can be considered that the special feature of the width of the flakes being narrower was reflected. Especially, it can be considered that the width value of the end-scraper in CL 2 is related with the aspect of it being concentrated in a certain section. Also, when the angle of an edge is seen, among the things that had used the flakes as the blanks, because there is an example of the retouching with the acute angle, it catches the eye. In addition, when seen with the numerical value of the curvature, it can be seen that an edge of round with an angle that is more rapid than the end-scraper that uses the flakes as the blank had been retouched.

Right below the surface, the end-scrapers from CL 1 (8 pieces) are four pieces each in terms of the flakes blank and the debris blank. Regarding the position of the edge by the flakes, all of them are the distal parts. And, regarding the debris blanks, it is two pieces for the short side and two pieces for the corner part. Mostly, the edges were retouched in a short range of the blanks. The shape of the edges is convex at all eight pieces. Most of the convex edges are in a round shape. Among them, limited to the narrower parts, the edge of the nose shape that had been retouched get confirmed by 1 piece each in the blank of the flakes and in the blank of the debris.

If the sizes of the edges are compared, the end-scrapers by the flakes as the blank, the lengths of the edges were 17-35mm, the heights of the edges were 8-15mm, the depths of the edges were 1-12mm, and the angles of the edges were 70-105°. And the curvatures of the edges were 5-12R (mm). All of the raw materials are the quartzes. The fact that, compared to the cultural layer at an early time, the blank becomes small was confirmed above.

In addition, either the short side of the small blank or the corner part by retouching only in the restricted range, mostly, the size and the extent of the retouching of the edges became smaller.

If the properties of the edge of the end-scraper by the cultural layer are compared (**Fig. 7**), mostly, the positions of the edges had been retouched on the distal part of the flakes or the short sides of the debris. Commonly, it can be peeped into the fact that, by restricting to a short range, it had been retouched. In addition, the shape of the edge on the end-scraper are rotating roundly. So, nearly all edges are convex by retouching. But, in CL 2, several pieces of the straight edges and concave edges, too, were confirmed.

If the sizes of the edges are compared, firstly, the lengths of the edges, we can see the tendency of them getting smaller gradually in the order of CL 4–CL 3–CL 2–CL 1. The length of the edge, because there is a relationship with the size of the blank, it has a thread of connection with the tendency of the blank getting smaller the more that one comes down from an early time to a later time. Such an aspect is the same way regarding the height of the edge and the depth of the end. Especially, in CL 2, it clearly shows the length of an edge concentrated more than a specific value. Because the height, the depth, and the angle of the edge collected as a certain value, we can infer that there was a certain pattern in the manufacturing of the end-scrapers.

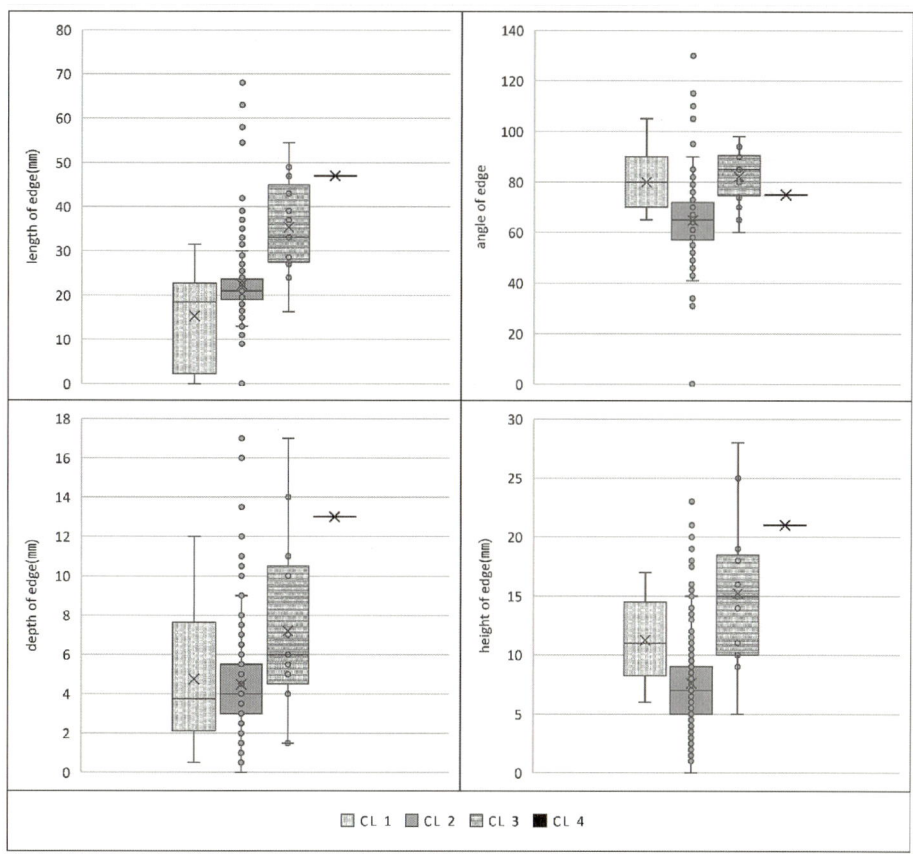

Fig. 7 The property of edge by cultural layer

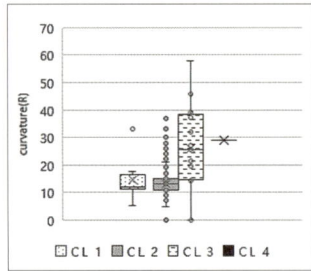

Fig. 8 The curvature of edge by cultural layer

Also, the curvature of the end-scraper edge, too, the more the time passes, it gets converted closely inside a certain section. Especially, in CL 2, it is concentrated on the certain value more (**Fig. 8**). When looking at this, it can be confirmed once again that in the case of CL 2, it is a time of showing the expertise in manufacturing of the end-scrapers, not only the shape and the size of the blanks and the raw materials, but also the edge property.

3. An analysis of the manufacturing technique of end-scrapers from CL 2

As a result of comparing the morphologies and the properties of the end-scrapers that were excavated from four cultural layers, it was confirmed that the following were recognized: regarding the end-scrapers from CL 2, the selection of the siliceous stone, the preference of the long flakes (Including the blades) with a certain width as a blank that is suitable for the manufacturing of the end-scrapers, the size of the edge, the uniformity of the curvature, etc. Based on this, it can be inferred that, during the two cultural layers time, the expertise of the manufacturing of the end-scrapers had taken place.

Among the end-scrapers in CL 2, regarding the 275 pieces that became the objects of the analysis, according to the raw materials, the selection of the blank, the special formal feature, and the technique of manufacturing, by dividing largely into 236 pieces and 39 pieces, it can be distinguished as two groups. Firstly, regarding the raw materials of the group that shows the commonalities of the 236 pieces, the siliceous stones-including rhyolite, shale, tuff, etc.- are the most (**Table 2**). However, there is not even one piece that had used the quartz. All of the bodies are the flakes (Including the blades). Regarding the shape, mostly, while the width being narrow, the length is longer. Especially, if it is looked at from the aspect of the manufacturing technique, regarding 78% or more, at the side edges, while the retouching had remained, because the width has been collected inside a

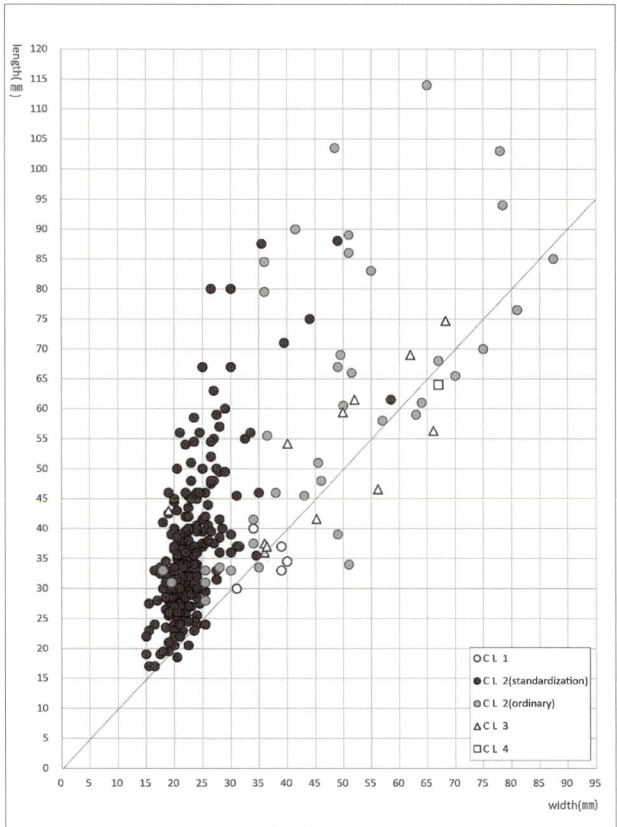

Fig. 9 Distribution of size by cultural layer and group of CL. 2

certain category, it was classified as 'the standardization' group (**Fig. 9**).

On the other hand, the raw material of the group that pertains to the remaining 39 pieces, although the siliceous series was also used. However, what is most characteristic is that all of the quartz's things pertain to here. In addition, there are the flakes and the broken flakes as the blanks, all of the 13 pieces of the end-scrapers that had been used the debris as the blanks included in this group. Moreover, the morphologies are diverse. In order to distinguish this from the group at the front, it was distinguished as the 'ordinary' group.

If reobserving after dividing the excavated end-scrapers from CL 2, it is a standardization group that more clearly shows the expertise of the manufacturing of the end-scrapers. Therefore, afterwards, the standardization group (236 pieces, 86%) among the 275 pieces of analysis will be analyzed in more detail, and the characteristics of the manufacturing technique and the meaning of the morphological change.

Table 2 Comparison of the blanks and the raw materials of end-scrapers excavated from Suyanggae site Loc. 6, cultural layer 2

classify		excavated	observe	The blank		The raw materials						
				flake	debris	quartz	shale	rhyolite	tuff	hornfels	obsidian	chert
cultural layer	ordinary	332	275	39	26	13	15	21	1	1	1	-	-
	standardization			236	236	-	-	90	121	21	-	3	1

210

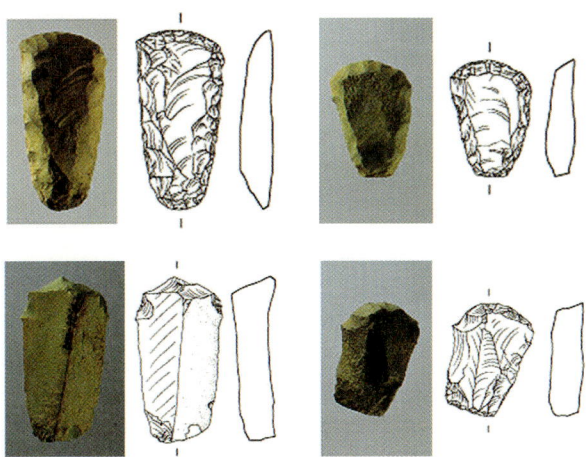

Fig. 10 Classify of type in standardization group (up : standard type, down : non-standard type)

3.1. The blank and the raw material

The most remarkable special feature of the end-scraper that belongs to the standardization group is long compared to the width without any relationship of size of the tool itself. Also, the width gets collected in a certain category (**Fig. 10**). In contrast, the range of the change of the length is big. Indeed, it can be peeped into the fact that the width is more restricted than the length. Such a special, formal feature can be connected with the manufacturing technique. At the edges of the both sides or the one side of the end-scrapers, mostly, the even retouching remains. In contrast, there is an example, too, of remaining in the condition of the edge without any retouching at the edge of the tool while belonging to the standardization group.

In this way, the end-scrapers (236 pieces) of the standardization group, too, get divided into two kinds of types according to the manufacturing technique. One is there being an adjustment retouching at the edges of both sides that remain long. And the other one is there being no adjustment retouching. Regarding the former, as the 'standard' type, 183 pieces (78%) pertain. And the 'non-standard' type, which is the latter, is 53 pieces (22%). Because the standard type is overwhelmingly a lot, we can infer that doing the adjustment retouching of the edge on the side is a more basic manufacturing method (**Fig. 11**). Although the difference of the score of the analysis is big, the standard type is more concentrated. In contrast, the non-standard type is more sporadic. Indeed, the standard type gets concentrated in a certain size. Especially, compared to the length, the width gets concentrated in a specific range.

All of the blanks of the end-scrapers of the standardization group are the flakes (Including the blades). Among these, the things of the proximal part of the flakes remaining and the things of being broken are confirmed together. The case of the former was distinguished into the flakes of the complete

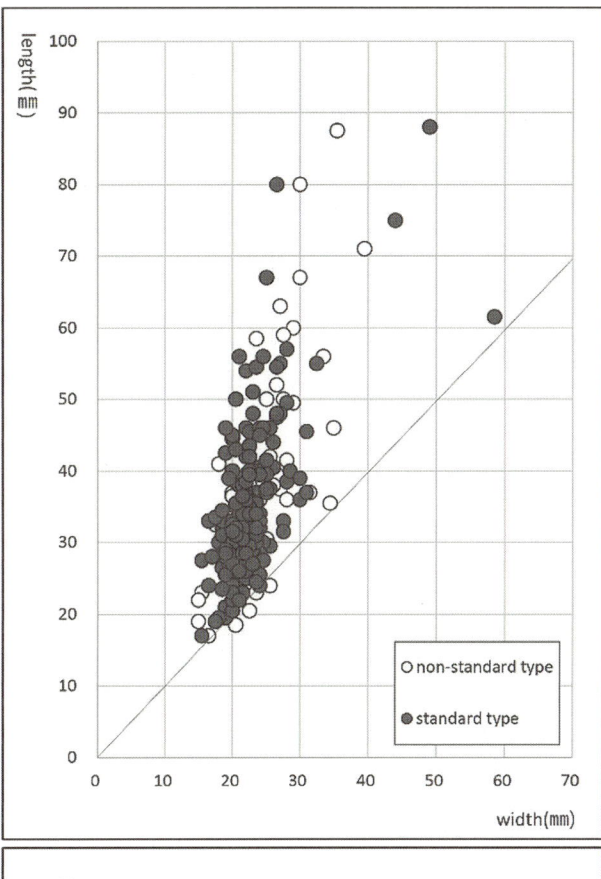

Fig. 11 The size of standard type and non-standard type in standardization group

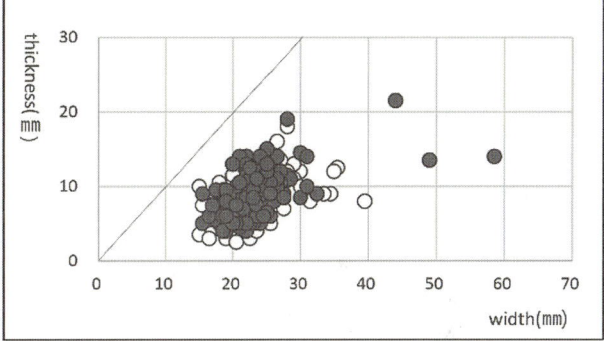

Fig. 12 The blank by type in standardization group

morphology. And the case of the latter was distinguished as the debris of the flakes that were damaged. Let us take a look at the standard type regarding which the side edges of the flakes were adjustment retouched. The end-scrapers that were made by having the complete morphology flakes as the blanks were 135 pieces. And the end-scrapers that were made with the flake fragments that were damaged were 48 pieces. It is a lot to the extent of being two times the debris of which the completed morphology was damaged (**Fig. 12**).

In contrast, regarding the non-standard type that did not have an adjustment retouching, the end-scrapers of the completed morphology flakes were 23 pieces, and the end-scrapers of the flakes that were damaged were 30 pieces. Because there were more damaged things, it shows an aspect that is different from the standard type.

3.2. The size and the weight

Regarding the end-scrapers of the standardization group (236 pieces) inside CL 2, they are distributed at the length of 17-88mm, the width of 15-59mm, the thickness of 3-22mm, and the weight of 1-70g. It is intended to compare the sizes by each and every type inside this (**Fig. 13**).

Firstly, for the length, both the standard type (183 pieces) and the non-standard type (53 pieces) is distributed at 17-88mm. But, if a section that is more concentrated is tried finding inside this, in the case of the standard type, it concentrated at 28-40mm. In contrast, the non-standardized type is gathered at 29-48mm.

Regarding the width, the standard type is 16-59mm. And, regarding the non-standard type, by being distributed at 15-40mm, as for the area, the standard type is wider. But, if the concentration range is looked at, the non-standard type is distributed at 20-28mm. In contrast, the standard type is distributed a smaller range at 20-24mm.

Regarding the thickness, the standard type is distributed at 4-22mm. The non-standard type is distributed at 3-18mm. And, regarding the concentration range, they are 6.5-10mm and 7-12mm, respectively. In the same way as the width, regarding the standard type, while the entire distribution area is wide, regarding the concentrated section, also, that is distributed a smaller range.

Lastly, the weight is distributed with the standard type at 2-70g and the non-standard type at 2-35g. The range that gets concentrated inside this is 4-10g and 4.5-15g, respectively.

If the sizes of the end-scrapers by the type inside the standardization group are compared, overall, the distribution range of the standard type is wider. This can be seen as being because the thing that belongs to the standard type has a much more amount at 183 pieces (78%). In contrast, if the concentration range of each item, including the length, the width, the thickness, the weight, etc., is taken a look at, all of the standard type are concentrated in a narrower range. Indeed, it can be said that the special characteristic of the standard type that gets concentrated in a certain section was reflected.

Also, regarding the size of the standard type, it gets collected more at the length of 28-40mm, the width of 20-40mm, the thickness of 6.5-10mm, and the weight of 4-10g. In contrast, regarding the type of the non-standard, it is distributed

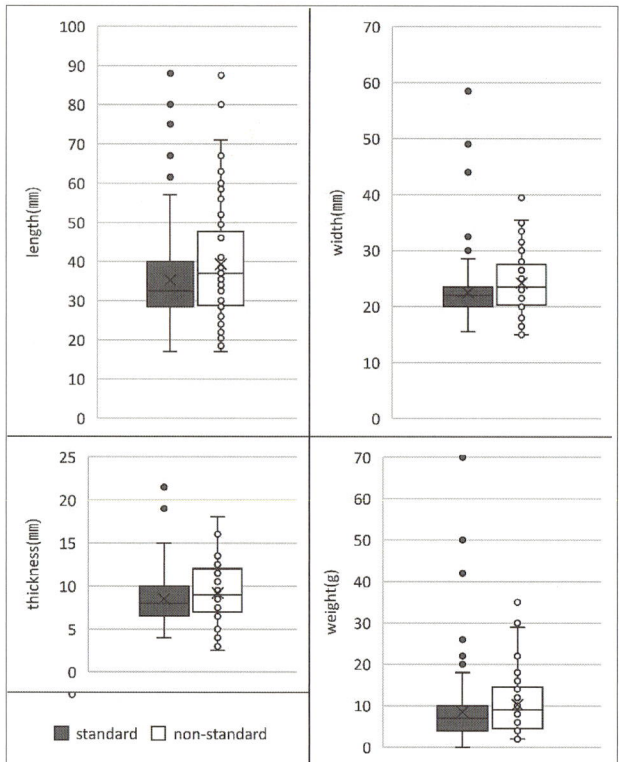

Fig. 13 The size by type in standardization group from CL 2

more at the length of 29-48mm, the width of 20-28mm, the thickness of 7-12mm, and the weight of 2-25g. When seen with the size by the type, the equation of the standard type $\leqq$ the non-standardized type gets established. Indeed, the non-standard type is the same as, or bigger than, the standard type.

3.3. The property of the edge

Regarding the end-scrapers in the standardization group (236 pieces) inside CL 2, from which the most end-scrappers were excavated, all of them used the flakes (Including the blade) of the siliceous stone. Regarding the positions of the edges, most of them remain at the distal part. In the case of the standard type (183 pieces), only one piece was on a side. And, in the case of the non-standardized type (53 pieces) there were two pieces, the edges were retouched on a side and on a proximal part. Regarding the shape of the edge, mostly, there were convex. Other than it, the edge of straight (6 pieces) and the edge of irregular (10 pieces) were confirmed. When looking by the type, in the standard, the edge of straight was five pieces and the edge of irregular was six pieces. In contrast, regarding the non-standard, they are one piece and four pieces each. In other words, it was confirmed that the edges were convex basically without any relation to the type.

It is intended to take a look at the properties of the edges by the type of the standardization group inside CL 2. Firstly, the length of the edge, although the standard type is distributed

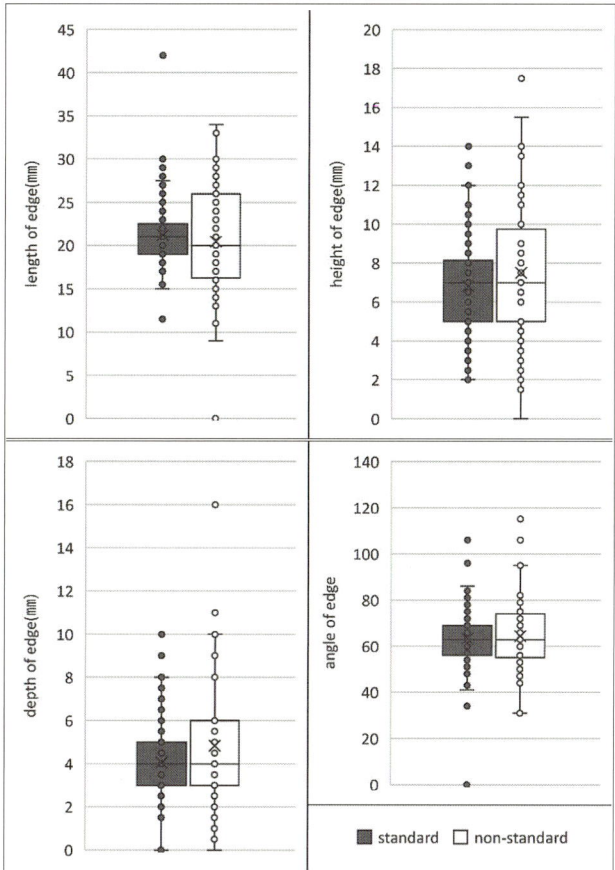

Fig. 14 The property of edge by type in standardization group from CL 2

at 12-42mm, it is more concentrated at 19-23mm (Fig. 14). In contrast, the lengths of the edges of the non-standardized type are distributed at 9-34mm. And, inside, too, they are more gathered at 16-26mm. The lengths of the edges of the non-standardized type are distributed more widely. It can be seen that, inversely, regarding the length of the edge of the standard type, the collection at a certain value can be seen.

On the height and the depth, regarding which an edge was retouched, are seen, in the case of the standard type, the height of the edge is concentrated at 5-8mm, and the depth of the edge is concentrated at 3-5mm. The non-standardized type is gathered more at the height of the edge at 5-10mm and at the depth of the edge at 3-6mm. Regarding the height and the depth of the edge that had been retouched, the difference according to the type does not get recognized.

Regarding the angles of the edges, in the case of the standard type, by being distributed at 34-106°, and, regarding the type of the non-standard, by being distributed at 31-115°, a big difference is not shown. In addition, the angle of the edge that is concentrated more is 55-74°.

Regarding the curvature(R) of the edge, the standard type is distributed at 5-29R(mm) (Fig. 15). The non-standardized type is distributed at 7-29R(mm). Regarding the curvature that gets concentrated regarding each, the standard type is 12-15R(mm) and the non-standard type is 11-16R(mm). So, there is no big difference.

In summary, including a blades, regarding the end-scrapers of the standardization group (236 pieces) inside CL 2 that had used only the flakes as the blank, all of them used only the siliceous stones. Except, excluding three pieces, all of them retouched the edges at the distal part on the flakes. Other than 16 pieces of the irregular edges and the straight edges, all of them are the edges of convex. Regarding the length of the end-scraper edge, the type of the non-standard is distributed more widely. And, relatively, the standard type gets concentrated more on a certain value. Other than these, regarding the height and the depth of the retouched edge, the angle of the edge, the curvature, etc., a big difference by the type does not get recognized. When looking at this, in the case of the standard type, in the phase oof the adjustment of the blank, it had been concentrated on a certain value. Regarding the retouching of an end-scraper edge, there was no difference by the type. It was confirmed that, indeed, the expertise regarding the manufacturing of the end-scrapers, rather than the direct retouching of an edge, the expertise is clearly and definitely revealed in the phase of the preparation of the blank.

4. The considerations: The changes of manufacturing technique on the end-scraper in the Upper Paleolithic

As a result of the investigation of the Suyanggae site Loc. 6, from the four cultural layers that pertain to the Upper Paleolithic, all of the end-scrapers were excavated. If the amount of excavations by each cultural layer is confirmed, from CL 1 right below surface, eight pieces came out. From CL 2, 332 pieces came out. Fourteen pieces came out of CL 3. And, from CL 4 at the bottom, one piece came out. In total, 355 pieces came out. When comparing the amounts of the excavations, the end-scrapers were excavated overwhelmingly from CL 2. Looking at the raw materials that had been used, in CL 2, rhyolite and shale capture 84% of the entirety. Additionally, the siliceous stones, including tuff, hornfels, obsidian, etc., had been used together. Quartz had been merely 15 pieces. In contrast, at the other cultural layers, a lot of quartz had been used. And, especially, in CL 3 and CL 4, shale was confirmed.

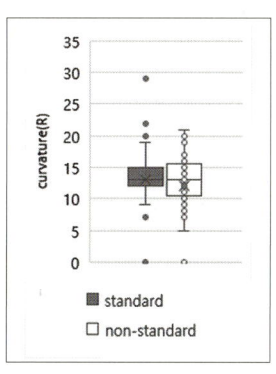

Fig. 15 The curvature of edge by type in standardization group from CL 2

If the types of the blanks are distinguished, in CL 2, the flakes, including the blades, had captured 96% of the

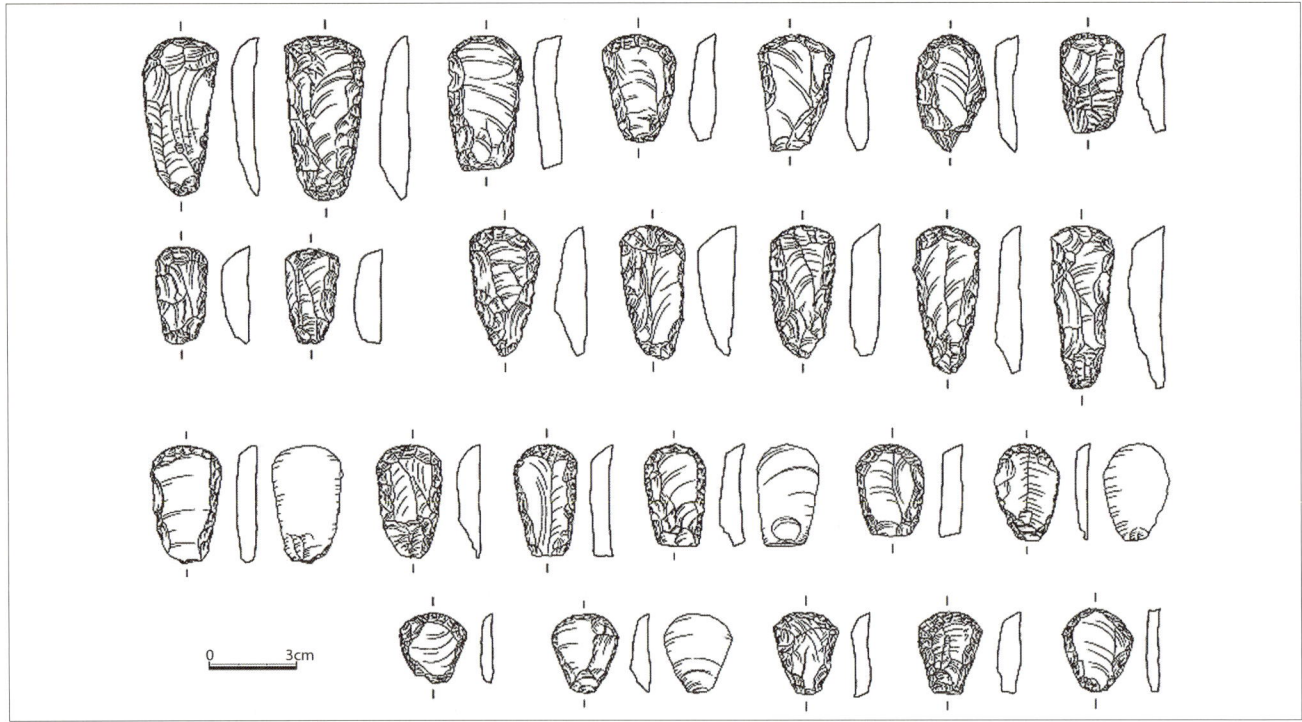

Fig. 16 The standard type end-scraper in standardization group from CL 2 on Suyanggae site Loc. 6

entirety. And the things that had used the debris were merely 13 pieces. In contrast to this, on a different cultural layer, the debris and the flakes had been used at the same ratios.

If the size is simply compared with the length and the width, all of the end-scrapers from CL 2 are in the long. However, regarding a different cultural layer, mostly, the length and the width have the similar sizes. It is a thicker thing while being close to a square.

As a result of comparing the morphology of the end-scrapers by the cultural layer in more detail, the tendency of the length getting smaller gradually can be seen, including CL 4–CL 3–CL 2–CL 1, in that order. When looking at this, mostly, the end-scrapers at the early time are bigger and heavier. In contrast, while the time had been passing by, becoming smaller gradually was confirmed. And, regarding the width and the thickness, the end-scrapers from CL 4 and CL 3 are bigger. In the opposite way, CL 2 and CL 1 become narrower and thinner. Especially, the end-scrapers from CL 2 clearly show the phenomenon of getting concentrated in a certain section while the values of the width, the thickness, and the weight are the smallest. When looking at this, by selecting the flakes with a certain size, the standardization tendency that had produced the end-scrapers can be looked at.

In addition, if the manufacturing technique is examined, regarding the end-scrapers from CL 2, the retouch remains nearly uniformly at both side edges of the long flakes. And the tendency of getting concentrated on a certain width according to this can be seen. Indeed, it can be said that the standardization is revealed clearly and definitely in the phase of the preparation of the blank (**Fig. 16, 17**).

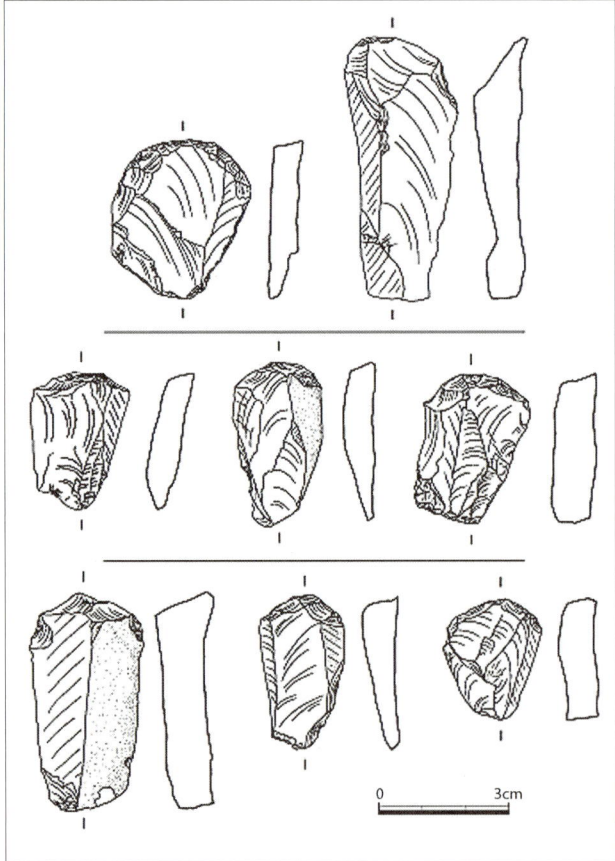

Fig. 17 The non-standard type end-scraper in standardization group from CL 2 on Suyanggae site Loc. 6

As above, regarding the end-scrapers from CL 2, when looking at the overwhelming amount of the excavation, the siliceous stone, the selectivity of the blank that had been standardized, the technique of adjusting the blank that had been standardized, etc., the clear difference from a different cultural layer can be confirmed. Regarding such a difference, it can be considered to be one side that was specialized more regarding the manufacturing of the end-scrapers of the group on the cultural layer, in other words, it can be seen as a material that shows the expertise. In addition, it was able to confirm that the process of preparing a blank with a certain size and morphology is the most important element. In order to complete the results of the expertise research of the manufacturing of the end-scrapers in the latter part of the Upper Paleolithic, which could be seen in CL 2 of the Suyanggae site Loc. 6, the objects of the research must be expanded to the different artifacts of the same time. As a result, while leaving the comparative researches that must be continued in the future as the tasks, I intend to end this writing.

◆ This paper is prepared by summarizing and modifing previous article (Kim, Eunjeong and Yun, Byeongil. 2020. *Journal of Museum Studies* 39).

References

Ambiru M., 1979. The morphology and function of lithic. *Study the Japanese archeology* (2), Tokyo: Yuhikaku, 17-39.

Ambiru M., 2010. *History of the Japanese Archipelago in the Paleolithic Period*, Tokyo: Gakuseisha.

Ambiru M., 2013. *The wisdom of Paleolithic people*, Tokyo: Shinnihon shyuppansha.

Binford, L., 1980. Willow smoke and dog's tails: Hunter-gather settlement systems and archaeological site formation. *American Antiquity* 45-1.

Bordes F., 1961. *Typologie du Paléolithique Ancien et Moyen*, Bordeaux: L'Université de Bordeaux.

Brézillon, N. Michel. 1983. *La dénomination des objets de pierre taillée, IVe supplé ment à "Gallia Préhistoire"*, Paris: C.N.R.S.

Choi S., 2016. A study on the site function and end-scraper from the Songho-dong Upper Paleolithic Site, Wonju City. *Journal of The Paek-san Society* 104, 5-30.

Demars P.Y. and Laurent P., 1989. Types d'outils lithiques du Paleolithique superieur en Europe. *Cahiers du Quaternaire n°14*, Paris: edition du CNRS.

Hong, M., and Nina Kononenko, 2005. Obsidian tools and their use excavated from the Hopyeong-dong Upper Paleolithic Site, Korea: Preliminary progressice report(1). *Jorunal of the Korean Palaeolithic Society* 12, 1-30.

Inizan, M.-L., Reduron-Ballinger, M., Roche, H., and Tixier, J., 1999. *Technology and Terminogy of Knapped Stone*, Nanterre: CREP.

Kim, E. and Yun, B., 2020. An analysis on the manufacturing process of end-scraper in the Upper Paleolithic on Suyanggae Site Loc. VI. *Journal of Museum Studies* 39, 133-160.

Kim, K., 2018. A study on the function of end-scraper in Paleolithic, Korea. *Journal of the Korean Palaeolithic Society* 37, 63-85.

Kim, S., 2006. *A study on end-scraper of Wolpyeong Upper Paleolithic Site, Suncheon*. Master's thesis at Chosun University Graduate School.

Kim, S., 2012. A study on end-scraper of Hopyeong-dong Upper Paleolithic Site, Namyangju, Korea. *Journal of the Korean Palaeolithic Society* 26, 23-47.

Kim, T., 2020. End scraper morphology and reduction process: focusing on the Upper Paleolithic collections from the Imjin-Hantan river area. *Journal of the Korean Archaeological Society* 114.

Lee, Y., 1985. *Report on the excavation of Suyanggae Paleolithic Site, Danyang*, Chungbuk National University Museum.

Lee, Y. and Kong, S., 2001. End-scrapers from the Upper Palaeolithic layer of the Suyanggae site, Danyang, Korea. *Prehistory and Ancient History* 16, 39-72.

Lee, Y., Woo, J., Lee, S., An, J., Yun, B., Park, J., Otani, K., Kim, M., Kim, E., Han, S., Jang H., and Choi, D., 2018. *Report on the excavation of Suyanggae Site(Loc. I and VI), Danyang*, Institute of Korean Prehistory.

Midoshima T., 2005. *A study on use-wear of lithic*, Tokyo: Douseisha.

National Research Instutite of Cultural Heritage eds., 2013. *Dictionary of Korean Archaeology: The Paleolithic Age*.

Park, H., 1990. *A study on the Upper Palaeolithic Culture at Changnae, Korea*. Doctoral thesis at Yonsei University Graduate School.

Seo, I., 2010. Epistemology and methodology of prehistoric archaeology in France. *Hangang. Journal of Hangang Institute of Cultural Heritage* 4, 47-73.

Sohn, P., 1968. Pebble chopping-tool industry of the stratified Palaeolithic cultures at Sŏk-chang-ni, Korea. *Journal of Korean History* 1, 1-62.

Sohn, P., 1970. The burin-grattoir industry of the stratified Palaeolithic cultures at Sŏk-chang-ni, Korea. *Journal of Korean History* 5, 1-46.

Tsutsumi T., 2011. *Archeology of the Archipelago: The Paleolithic Age*, Tokyo: Kawade Shobo Shinsha.

On the use-wear analysis of tanged points from Loc. 1 and 6, Suyanggae site, Korea

Kaoru AKOSHIMA[1], Hyewon HONG[2], Seung-won LEE[3], Jong-yoon WOO[3], Yung-jo LEE[3]

[1] Director, Tohoku History Museum, Japan ; akoshima-ka927@pref.miyagi.lg.jp
[2] Okayama University of Science, Korea
[3] Institute of Korean Prehistory (IKP), Korea

ABSTRACT

The paper investigates the function of tanged points excavated from the Suyanggae site locality 1 and 6. It was revealed by use-wear analysis that these tanged points were actually utilized as "multi-functional tools" rather than simple projectile weapons by one of the first arrival groups of *Homo sapiens* into the Korean Peninsula. Our method of use-wear analysis combines three different techniques, that is, Low-power, Mid-power, and High-power observation. By synthesizing results from three types of microscopic devices, usage patterns of the tanged points were reconstructed. The tang portion of the tool was produced to secure actual hafting. Implications of the present study include new insights into the behavioral meaning of secondary retouch of lithic artifacts, and conceptual recognition of composite tools that requires deep planning depth by early Modern Humans. The successful application of microwear analysis to Korean prehistory also testifies wider potential of this technique for East Asian archaeological research.

국문초록

슴베찌르개는 한반도 후기 구석기의 중요한 도구 중 하나이다. 유물이 퇴적 이후 다양한 석기 표면의 변형도와 석기 돌감의 상대적 다양성에 관하여 4개 측면 요소들을 조합하여 상세한 기능 결정은 어렵지만 일반적 경향은 제시될 수 있다. 즉, 석기 표면에서 사용 여부(사용, 비사용), 석기의 사용 부위, 사용시의 동작 형태(세로, 가로, 혼합, 식별불가), 작업에 사용한 재료 유형(부드러움, 중간, 단단함 또는 뼈, 녹용, 목재)와 같이 4개 측면 적용에 대해 구체적으로 설명한다. 수양개 유적에서 출토된 96점의 슴베찌르개 중 돌감 종류와 녹쓴 정도에 무관한 47점의 유물에 대해 쓴자국을 분석하였다. 수양개 유적 슴베찌르개 기부 가공 부분은 오목하며 심하게 둥글게 처리되어 있어 일종의 석기 결합 행위와 접합식 도구 출현을 시사한다. 슴베찌르개 측면은 다양한 작업에 활용되었고, 톱니 모양의 측면 날은 자르는 행위로 활용되었다. 슴베찌르개의 끝날 활용과 충격 파쇄 유형도 드물게 나타난다. 이것은 도구 사용에 있어 더 깊은 의도를 가지고 융통성 있는 사용을 시사한다. 쓴자국 분석 연구 결과는 한반도 후기 구석기 초 고인류의 기능적 행위 특성을 나타내며, 일본 열도 동북부의 후기 구석기 초 기저부 재가공 석기와 비교를 통해 동아시아 현생인류의 문화 적응에 대한 통찰을 갖게 한다.

Keywords : traceology, use-wear analysis, tanged point, function, Suyanggae site

1. Introduction

This work reports a microwear analysis of tanged points. There are three fundamentally important realms of stone tool analysis: typological, technological, and functional analysis. Each of these realms is key to understanding stone tool assemblages. From the early stage of prehistoric science in the 19th century, prehistorians worldwide have had a keen interest in the use of stone tools. Although it is important to include stone tool analysis in excavation site reports, thus far, compared to typology and technology, functional aspects of stone tools have been underrepresented in these reports. This is partially due to technical difficulties and a relative lack of specialists needed to conduct such research. The present report seeks to address this issue by presenting not only the results of functional analysis but also the associated procedures and basis of such functional inferences.

As archaeological records contain static facts, robust criteria are needed to make inferences about past dynamics (e.g., Binford, 1981). Binford termed these types of research for archaeological inferences the "Middle Range Theory." In the case of use-wear analysis, the basis of reliable inferences comes mostly from experimental archaeology. From the pioneering work of Semenov (1964) to the methodological breakthroughs of Keeley (1980) to the present state of prehistoric science, experimental reference work has played a critical role in functional reconstruction. The Tohoku University Microwear Research Team (TUMRT) has held the same theoretical position since 1976 when the late Professor Emeritus Chosuke Serizawa launched a large-scale experimental project. The present research sought to apply the methodology of TUMRT to Suyanggae site artifacts for the first time, as a cooperative endeavor between Korea and Japan.

2. Methods and procedures

An analysis was conducted at the Institute of Korean Prehistory (IKP) from July to September 2017 based on The Agreement for Cooperation between Laboratory of Archaeology, Tohoku University (TU), and Institute of Korean Prehistory (IKP), signed on August 4, 2017.

A total of 96 tanged points were examined for functional interpretation. Eighty-three specimens were excavated from Locality 6, and 13 specimens were excavated from Locality 1 All of these specimens were unearthed during excavations carried out by the IKP between 2013 and 2015.

Experimental data provided by TUMRT were adopted as functional references for the cooperative research. The analytical procedure integrated both a "low power" approach and a "high power" approach for observation of both microflaking and microwear polish. The identification of use-wear patterns was based on the long-term experimental program. The methods and techniques of microwear analysis used by TUMRT have been described mainly in the Japanese literature (e.g., Akoshima, 1981; Kajiwara and Akoshima, 1981; Serizawa et al., 1982; Akoshima, 1989). An English discussion of these methods and techniques can be found in Akoshima (1987), Akoshima (2010, with Korean summary), Akoshima and Kanomata (2015), and Akoshima and Hong (2017a). For a discussion of projectile impact fractures, please refer to Sano (2012) and Sano et al. (2016).

An English description of the identification criteria for tool usage were published as a database by the Tohoku University Museum and are discussed in, for example, Akoshima and Hong (2014, 2016) for microflaking, and Akoshima and Hong (2017b, 2018) for microwear polish.

The main lithic raw materials were shale, both fine-grained and coarse-grained. Their surface conditions were also variable, from a seemingly relatively fresh surface to an apparently patinated surface. Analytical methods were specifically designed for the Suyanggae artifacts. The low power method, which emphasizes the observation of microflaking, and the high power method, which emphasizes the observation of microwear polish, are integrated in the present analysis.

The strength of our analytical method for the Suyanggae artifacts is its capacity for cross-checking datasets obtained with two different types of microscope and two different clues about how the same specimen was actually used. The interpretation of use was also the combined result of different criteria – that is, microflaking scar patterns (also called "microchipping") and microwear polishes plus striations. There has been a tendency in past use-wear studies for researchers to emphasize either a low power or high power approach. In our opinion, this strategy is imbalanced and should be revised as a more synthetic, integrated approach.

Our analytical procedure was as follows: In the first stage, a basic screening process for microwear was conducted. Specimens potentially suitable for microwear analysis were selected for more detailed analysis. These specimens included tanged points that exhibited microflaking scars at very low magnifications. Hand magnifiers (up to 12x times) were used by two analysts independently for all 96 points. Forty-eight tanged points were selected for further analyses. Macrophotographs of edges, both ventral and dorsal face, were taken for most of these artifacts.

On the other hand, surface conditions for high-power analysis were evaluated under relatively high magnifications (from 50x to 200x), and tanged points were classified according to rock type and degree of patination. Of the 96 artifacts, 44 were considered promising for high-power analysis. Later, however, it became clear that many of these artifacts were actually covered with slight patination and were thus unsuitable for micropolish identification.

Consequently, 47 tanged points were subjected to microwear analysis. For the low-power analysis, a stereoscopic microscope with 30x magnification (Vixen Microboy SL-30cs) was used to observe microflaking scar patterns. Among the fundamental criteria in this analysis were the shape, size, termination of feather or step, distribution patterns, and continuity of these scare patterns.

Worked materials were interpreted as soft, medium, or hard. Motion was interpreted as longitudinal, transverse, or a mix of the two. For the high-power analysis, a metallurgical microscope (Olympus BH-FM) was used to observe micropolish and microscopic striations, at magnifications of 50x, 100x, and 200x with incident light attachment. The polish type was a reliable clue about the type of worked material – for example, plant, hide, wood, bone, or antler. The directions of the striations yielded important clues about the type of motions, such as cutting or scraping .

In the following sections, analytical results for each artifact are presented. In the first section, nine artifacts are described in detail with respect to the integrated results of both the high-power and low-power analyses. These specimens had relatively good surface conditions. In the second section, 26 artifacts are comprehensively described, based mainly on the results of low-power analysis. For these specimens, high-power analysis was not very effective for functional reconstruction, due primarily to their surface conditions and lithic raw material type. However, even for these specimens, inferential interpretation was possible to some extent, evidencing the strength of the employed methodology. In both sections, descriptive texts and interpretative figures with independent use zones (IUZs), direction of motion, and worked materials, many with microphotographs, are referred to by the artifact number assigned during the IKP excavations. IUZ is an analytical concept developed by Vaughan (1985) to denote the portion of a tool considered to have been utilized.

Lastly, concerning the methodology section, it should be emphasized that these results are inferences, not necessarily determinations. That said, these inferences were derived from experimental frames of reference. Of course, it is possible that the results will be revised in the future with the further development of programs for controlled experimentation, especially at sites yielding the same lithic raw materials as the Suyanggae artifacts.

Fig. 1 Analytical Result (High Power and Low Power) : Artifact No. 29078

3. Analytical results, Part 1: Combined high-power and low-power analysis

3.1. Artifact No. 29078 (Fig. 1)

This knife-shaped tool is made of medium-grained shale, banded dark grey in color. Its surface condition permitted high-power analysis. It has one IUZ.

The left lateral side (part A) was used in a longitudinal motion on relatively soft materials. On the ventral face, polished areas can be found, but they are arranged in small patches, not widely distributed. The polish type is unclear, but some striations extend in longitudinal direction. On the dorsal face, along the edge, are weakly polished patches of an unidentified type. Microflaking scars are found on both faces. These scars are scalar, micro, deep type, and, occasionally, trapezoidal, step type. These microchipping scars are distributed in alternating patterns between the two faces. They are mostly tiny with some small step fractures. Some edge rounding can also be seen. This is the pattern of longitudinal movement on softer materials.

The right lateral side (part B) shows no microflaking scars except for one dorsally notched depression. This part was probably a retouched edge but may not have been used.
 The base of this knife-shaped tool shows heavy rounding on the retouch of both lateral sides. This rounding is probably related to some hafting behavior.

3.2. Artifact No. 33928 (Fig. 2)

This tanged point is made of black shale. The texture of the raw material is wavy and slightly banded. The rock type resembles andesite in quality and is coarse-grained. The

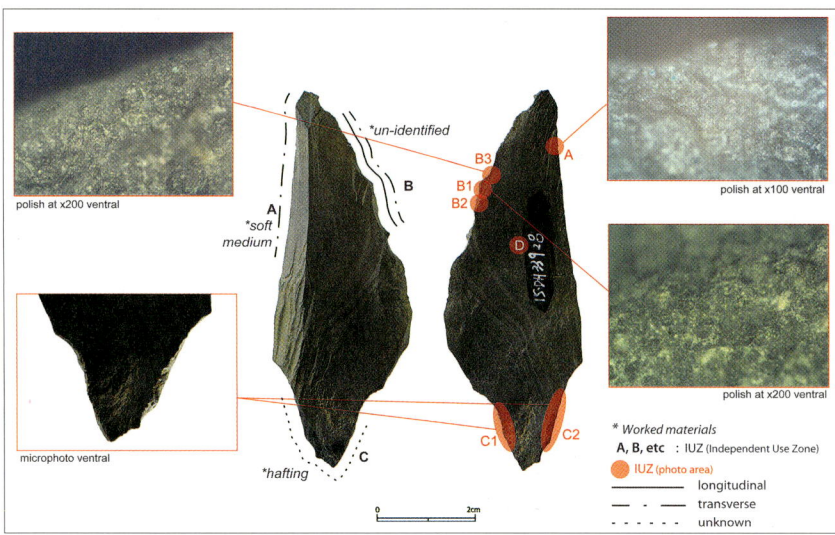

Fig. 2 Analytical Result (High Power and Low Power) : Artifact No. 33928

Fig. 3 Analytical Result (High Power and Low Power) : Artifact No. 34265

surface was unpatinated and thus good for high-power analysis. It has two IUZs.

The left lateral edge (part A) was used in a transverse motion, with the ventral surface as its leading face. Worked materials were possibly of soft to medium hardness. The sharp unretouched lateral side retains microflaking scars toward the tip of the point. These scars are intermittently rectangular or scalar, with microtypes on the ventral face, and continuous scalar, micro, deep types on the dorsal face. However, along the proximal half of the left lateral edge microflaking scars are not found in large numbers. Clear striations can be observed perpendicular to the sharp edge on the ventral face. Microwear polish is not clear, however.

The right lateral edge (part B) was used in both a transverse and longitudinal motion along the same edge. Worked materials for the dorsally denticulated edge were likely mixed. Edge rounding can be found on the ventral face at overhanging projections. Striations can be observed both parallel and perpendicular to the edge with connected micropolish patches of a granular texture.

The base portion exhibits traces of haft-related behavior. The artifact has base rounding parts toward the proximal half of the tang on a ventral overhang, rather than in notched concavities. The tip of the point tool has a break caused in modern times.

3.3. Artifact No. 34265 (Fig. 3)

This tanged point is made of banded colored shale. The rock is fine-grained, and the surface condition was suitable for high-power analysis. The surface patination on the point is slight.

It has two IUZs along its lateral sides.

The right lateral edge (part B) is denticulated dorsally. This part was used mainly in a transverse motion. Generic weak polish and perpendicular faint striations can be found on the ventral face. The micropolish, of an E1 or F2 type, can be observed as tiny patches on the projecting parts of the denticulate. Microflaking scars are micro-scalar and of a rectangular-continuous type on the dorsal face. Some rounding can be observed ventrally on projections of the denticulated edge. The worked materials have not been identified.

The left lateral edge was used in both longitudinal and transverse motions (part D). Generic weak polish patches and some perpendicular faint striations can be found on both the ventral and dorsal faces. Microflaking scars are mainly of scalar and some of rectangular types, micro sized, and continuous on both faces along the sharp unretouched edge . The worked materials have not been identified. The use-intensity can be inferred to be relatively light from the generic nature of the polish and the density of the microflaking scars.

The base portion of the tanged point (part A, C) exhibits some rounding at the retouch initiation edge on the ventral face, suggesting some haft-related behavior. However, no clear micropolish was found on the ventral face along the retouched area.

The tip of the point was probably not used. No clear polish, no evident striations, and no impact fractures were found around the tip portion.

3.4. Artifact No. 34708 (Fig. 4)

This knife-shaped tool is made of black shale of a granular texture. The surface condition was relatively suitable for high-power analysis. The tool has three IUZs, but the use-intensity was not heavy, judging from the general weakness of the traces.

The right lateral edge (part A) was likely used in various motions, including both transverse and longitudinal. The worked materials were not hard. On the ventral face, intermittent weak polish patches can be observed. These patches are faint and of a generic type. Some striations can also be found perpendicular to the edge. Microflaking scars can be found on both faces. On the dorsal part, scalar, microtype scars are distributed continuously. On the ventral part, scalar and rectangular, microtype scars were found. Step fracture scars are also visible. The distal part of right lateral side near the tip area shows some modern nibbling on dorsal face.

The right-side proximal portion (part B) was slightly used on the denticulated depression area of consecutive notches. The motion was possibly transverse. The worked materials were not identified due to the rock texture and the weakness of the traces. On the ventral face at the notch depression edge, small patches of weak polish, of an unknown type, are visible. Some rounding can also be found on the retouch overhang.

The left lateral edge (part C) was slightly used. Neither the direction of motion or the worked materials were identified. On the ventral face, along the denticulated portion, occasional intermittent weak polish patches can be observed, but striations or rounding were not detected. Some microflaking scars were also found. These scars are intermittent, scalar and rectangular, micro, or shallow type.

3.5. Artifact No. 35033 (Fig. 5)

This tanged point is made of banded colored shale. The surface condition is relatively suitable for high-power analysis. The point has two IUZs.

The left lateral edge (part B) was used in a transverse motion, with its ventral surface leading face forward. The worked materials were medium to hard, possibility made of wood.

Fig. 4 Analytical Result (High Power and Low Power) : Artifact No. 34708

Fig. 5 Analytical Result (High Power and Low Power) : Artifact No. 35033

Small patches of polish are found intermittently on the ventral face. The polish is bright and rounded, resembling type B of the Tohoku University classification. Faint striations are found perpendicular to the edge. Microflaking scars can be observed on both faces. On the dorsal surface, there is relatively heavy rounding of the edge toward the tip. Microflaking scars are continuous toward the tip, of micro to small size, and of varied shape, such as scalar, rectangular, or trapezoidal. Many step fracture terminations exist. A characteristic pattern on this point are wide scars with step flaking and overlapping step fracture scars. On the ventral side, heavy edge rounding can be seen, stronger on the distal half of part B, but virtually no microflaking scars, except for occasional tiny scalar or microtype scars.

The right lateral edge (part C) was used in a transverse motion, with its dorsal surface leading face forward. The worked materials were medium to hard. Microflaking scars can be found on the ventral face. These scars comprise overlapping step flaking in addition to relatively heavy rounding. Toward the point tip, microflaking scars are smaller

Fig. 6 Analytical Result (High Power and Low Power) : Artifact No. 35043

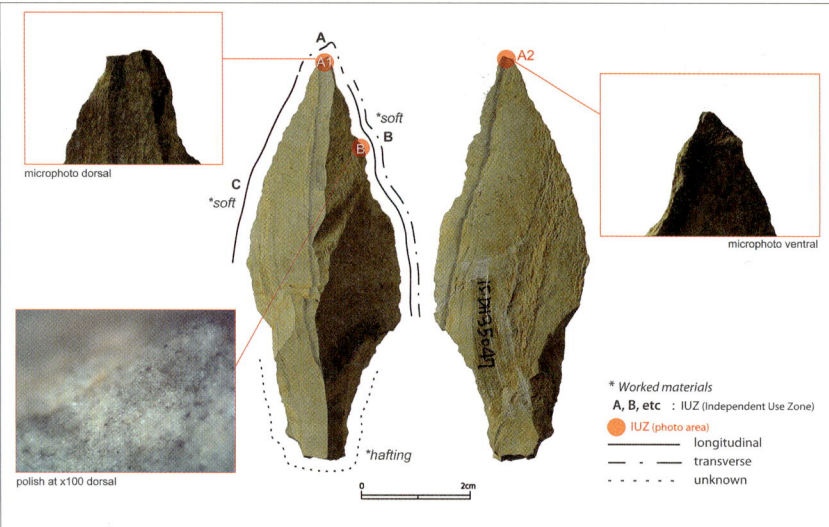

Fig. 7 Analytical Result (High Power and Low Power) : Artifact No. 35047

and of a scalar, microcontinuous pattern. On its dorsal face, virtually no microflaking scars can be seen, but slight to moderate edge rounding can be observed. Clear polish or striations were not found along part C.

The base exhibits some hafting-related traces. The base is unifacial and dorsally retouched to produce its pointed base. There are rounded portions at depressions on the ventral overhang. The tip retains no trace of usage.

3.6. Artifact No. 35043 (Fig. 6)

This tanged point is made of coarse-grained shale with some band structure. The surface of the point is patinated. The point has two IUZs.

The left lateral side (part B) is a sharp edge but it was used in a transverse motion on medium to hard worked materials. The leading face forward of scraping or whittling motion was its ventral surface. Continuous microflaking scars comprising an overlapping step fracture in trapezoidal and scalar shapes can be found on the dorsal face. On the ventral face, sporadic microflaking scars of tiny scalar types are visible. These patterns are signs of transverse motion.

The right lateral edge (part C) is denticulated. Slight rounding occurs at both the projection and depression of the denticulated notches. The edge was used in a transverse motion, with its ventral surface serving as the leading face. Occasional polish patches and perpendicular striated features can be found on the battered rock surface. The polish types resemble Tohoku University type B. The worked materials were of a soft to medium hardness, likely some type of wood. However, the surface patination and coarse-grained rock type prevented a detailed reconstruction of use.

The base retouch is unifacial on the dorsal face. The base also exhibits heavy rounding, especially on the retouch overhang, suggesting haft-related behavior. The tip of the point shows no trace of use.

3.7. Artifact No. 35047 (Fig. 7)

This tanged point was made of coarse-grained banded colored shale. The point has three IUZs. The tip part was pointed by dorsal retouches. This part shows traces of a possible impact fracture. Flaking scars can be seen in the axial direction, with some tiny crushed microchipping.

The right lateral edge (part B) is denticulated on the dorsal face. The edge was used in mixed motions, transverse and longitudinal, on soft worked materials. Some occasional rounding is visible on projections and depressions on overhanged portions. Microflaking scars of various types can also be found. On the ventral face, the distal half of part B retains a continuous scalar, micro, deep type, and a triangular, micro, step type. On the dorsal face, scars of a scalar, micro, deep type can partially be seen. No clear polish patches were found along part B, but some striated features can be seen on the denticulate in perpendicular distributions.

The left lateral edge (part C) is sharp. This part was used

mainly in a longitudinal motion on soft worked materials. Microflaking scars are distributed on both the dorsal and ventral faces. These are of a scalar, micro, shallow type and often alternate along both faces. Some dorsal polish-like areas exist but they are unclear due to the surface conditions.

The base part was alternately retouched, either ventrally or dorsally, between the left and right. This part shows some rounding on the retouch overhang points, suggesting haft-related behavior.

3.8. Artifact No. 36497 (Fig. 8)

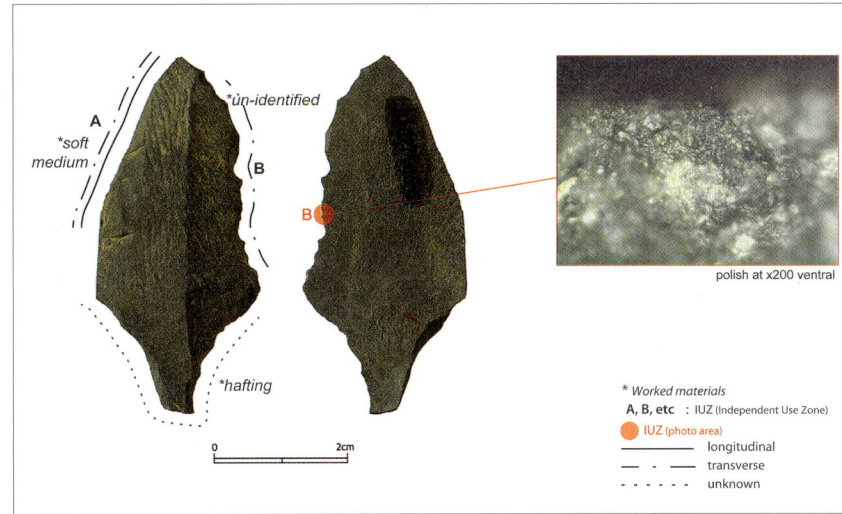

Fig. 8 Analytical Result (High Power and Low Power) : Artifact No. 36497

This tanged point was made of medium-grained blackish grey shale. The patination is slight, making high-power analysis possible. The point has two IUZs. The left lateral edge (part A) was used in mixed motions – i.e., both longitudinal and transverse motions. The worked materials were likely of soft to medium hardness. Microflaking scars exist on both faces. These scars are tiny (observable only at 30x) to micro, scalar and rectangular, and distributed continuously or intermittently. Weak polish patches can be found on both faces. These are generic and were difficult to identify. They do not extend to wider areas. Striated features, although faint, are visible in multiple directions.

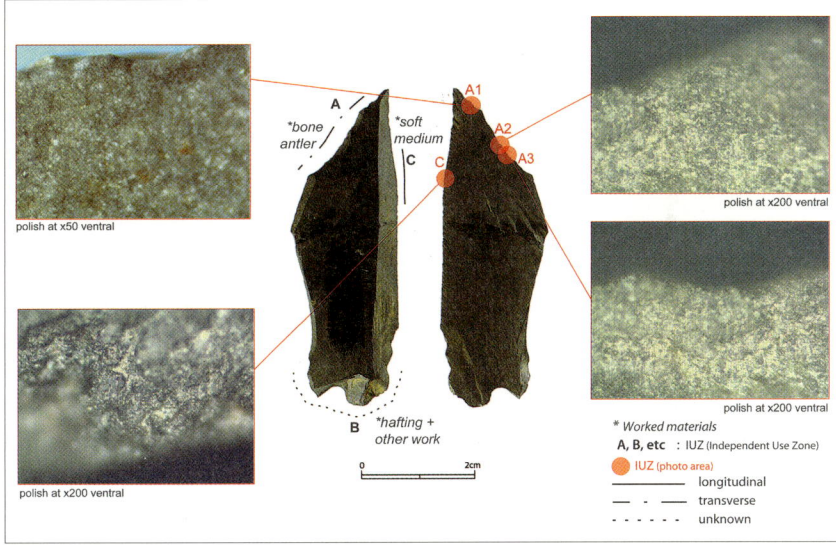

Fig. 9 Analytical Result (High Power and Low Power) : Artifact No. 39356

The right lateral edge (part B) was dorsally denticulated. This part was used mainly in a transverse motion. The worked materials are unknown, as the polish is of a weak, generic type. Faint striated features are visible in a perpendicular direction. Edge rounding can be seen on the ventral surface, with some microflaking of a micro, scalar type, and of a sliced type.

The base part was retouched unifacially to the dorsal face. This part exhibits rounding on the ventral face, especially on the notched depression part at the overhang. There are also traces of hafting.

The tip of the point shows no clear traces of use, with no impact fractures or rounding.

3.9. Artifact No. 39356 (Fig. 9)

This specimen is made of fine-grained black shale. Its surface condition is good, and thus high-power analysis was possible. The backed knife on the blade has two IUZs.

The left lateral edge (part A) was used in a transverse motion, with the ventral surface of the tool as a leading face. The worked materials probably included bone/antler. Microwear polish of D1 type was found. The polish, although somewhat unclear, exists in weak patches. Perpendicular striations can be seen on the retouched denticulated backing parts, indicating transverse movements. The ventral face shows slight rounding of the edges at the retouch scars. Technologically, this side was unifacially dorsally retouched or notched, considered lateral backing.

The right lateral edge (part C) was used in a longitudinal motion, on worked materials of soft to medium hardness. Polish patches of an unidentified type can be found on elevated portions. These patches are rough and bright but were difficult to classify according to Tohoku University categories. Microflaking scars of a scalar, micro, deep type were found in a continuous alternating fashion on both

Fig. 10 Analytical Result (Mainly Low Power) : Artifact No. 358

Fig. 11 Analytical Result (Mainly Low Power) : Artifact No. 1843

4. Analytical results, Part 2: Mainly low power

4.1. Artifact No. 358 (Fig. 10)

This tanged point is also considered a knife-shaped tool. It is made of coarse-grained banded shale with a laminar texture. Its entire periphery is rounded but the degree is variable. Low-power and supplementary high-power analysis detected two IUZs: the point tip and the right lateral side.

The right lateral side, distal half, was possibly used in a longitudinal motion on relatively soft materials. This portion (part A) exhibits microflaking scars on both the ventral and dorsal faces. They are continuous, scalar or rectangular, and tiny to microsized, Scars partially alternate between the faces. However, clear polish or striations are not found on the patinated surface.

The tip (part B) shows some dorsal chipping scars to its tool body direction. The flaking has the possibility of an impact fracture. Striations can be seen parallel to the body from the tip (50x observation) on the dorsal face.

The base (part C) shows heavy rounding on the ventral overhang and base retouch. Some hafting-related behavior can be inferred.

4.2. Artifact No. 1843 (Fig. 11)

This tanged point is also considered a knife-shaped tool, with one side base having been retouched dorsally. It is made of fine-grained grey banded shale. The surface is seemingly suitable for high-power analysis, but it is actually patinated, as seen at the dark colored tip break from modern nibbling (part B). The tip macrophoto shows patination effects. However, low-power analysis detected one IUZ, with supplementary high-power observation.

The right lateral side (part A) was probably mainly used in a longitudinal motion. Worked materials remain unidentified. Microflaking scars can be found on both the ventral and dorsal faces. These are continuous to intermittent, scalar (often a wide shape), micro, deep type. When viewed from the edge side direction, they are distributed alternatingly between the faces, suggesting parallel mobility to the edge. The edge is also rounded. Microwear polish or striated features are not clear, however.

4.3. Artifact No. 28600 (Fig. 12)

This tanged point is made of fine-grained banded shale. The distal portion of the point is broken. The base retouch is dorsally unifacial to the form of the tang. The surface is heavily patinated, as revealed by modern nibbling at the right side. However, the possibility of an impact fracture resulting from the use of the point as a projectile has been

faces.

The base (part B) shows some hafting-related traces but also exhibits more intense traces of use on the proximal portion at the end. Technologically, the base retouch was partial and on alternating sides. There is slight rounding of the edges on the initiation face of the alternate retouch.

highlighted for this specimen.

The distal breakage portion (part B) shows a very irregular scar pattern, suggesting an impact from the tip direction. Flaking scars are large. Further research is necessary, including experimental references. At high magnifications, some striated features are detectable at the dorsal corner with the right lateral side. Striations are perpendicular to the break line – that is, parallel to the point tool body shape. Surface conditions prevent a precise identification. No clear polish was found.

The base portion (part A) exhibits rounding at notch depressions on the ventral face overhang. Some hafting-related behavior can be inferred.

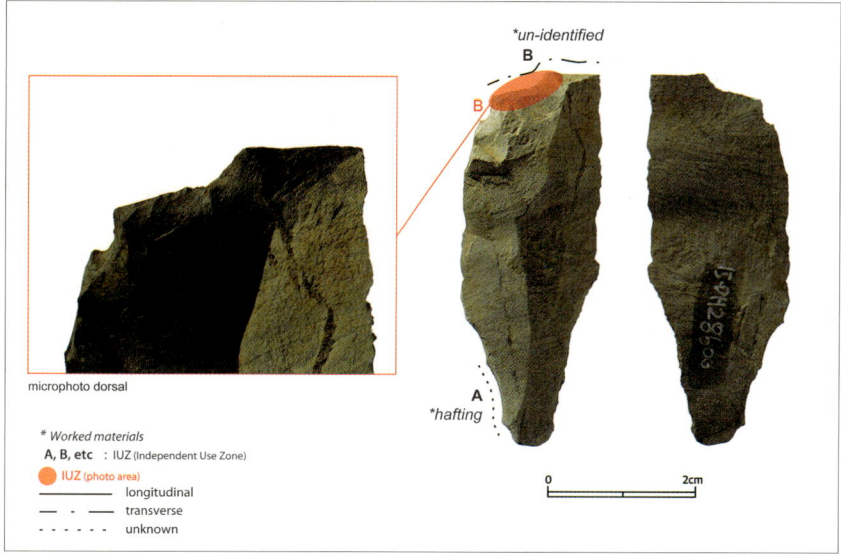

Fig. 12 Analytical Result (Mainly Low Power) : Artifact No. 28600

4.4. Artifact No. 30779 (Fig. 13)

This tanged point is made of coarse-grained shale of a white color. The rock has a tuff-like texture. Low-power analysis detected two IUZs. Both lateral edges were used in similar activities.

The left lateral side (part A) was used mainly for its distal half, possibly in a longitudinal motion on relatively soft materials. Microflaking scars are found on both faces, dorsal and ventral. On the dorsal face, scalar, micro, deep-type scars are distributed continuously. On the ventral face, rectangular, micro, shallow-type scars are distributed intermittently. The proximal half of the left lateral side is battered by modern nibbling, and use-wear cannot be observed.

The right lateral side (part B) was also used mainly for its distal half, possibly in a longitudinal motion on relatively soft materials. Microflaking scars are found on both the ventral and dorsal faces. These are scalar, micro, deep type and are distributed continuously with edge rounding. Modern nibbling overlaps on the edge, but use-wear scars are observable.

The base (part C) retains wear from some hafting-related behavior. Some rounding can be found at the notch concavities of both sides on the ventral overhang. The base is dorsally unifacially retouched to make a rectangular shape.

4.5. Artifact No. 31625 + No. 31627 (Fig. 14)

This tanged point is made of very coarse-grained shale

Fig. 13 Analytical Result (Mainly Low Power) : Artifact No. 30779

(tuff-like rock). The surface is patinated and not suitable for high-power analysis. Low-power analysis identified two IUZs. The point was broken into two pieces and refitted. It is noteworthy that the same lateral edge shows two different use episodes. This means some usage after tool breakage.

The left lateral side has two IUZs (part A1 and part A2) across the break line. Part A1 (distal half edge) exhibits heavy rounding on the refit line after breakage. Rounding occurred differently across the break. Microflaking scars are found intermittently on both the ventral and dorsal faces, with heavy rounding. The scars include three types, that is, triangular, micro, stepped and scalar, micro, deep, and rectangular, micro, deep types.

The left lateral side, proximally halfway from the break (part A2), shows heavy rounding on the ventral side. Worked materials are not known for either IUZ (parts A1 or A2). The motion possibly includes transverse kinematics.

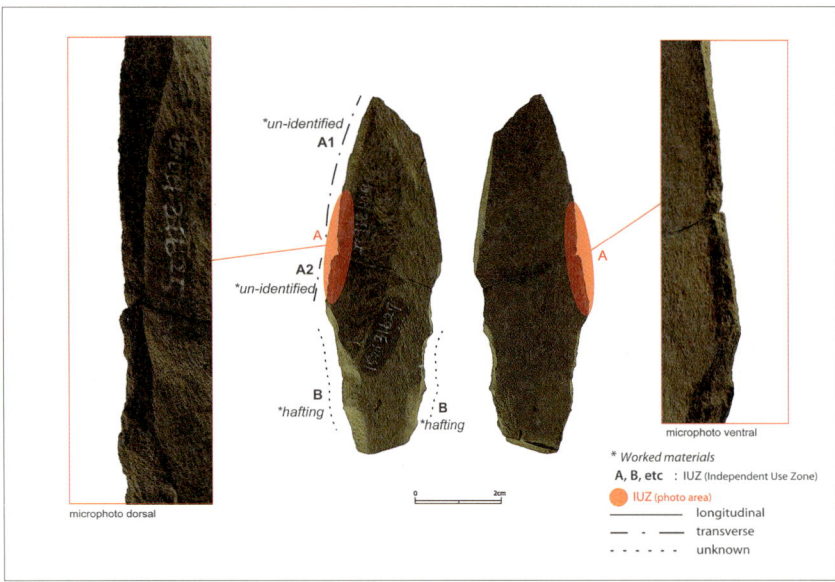

Fig. 14 Analytical Result (Mainly Low Power) : Artifact No. 31625+31627

Fig. 15 Analytical Result (Mainly Low Power) : Artifact No. 31891

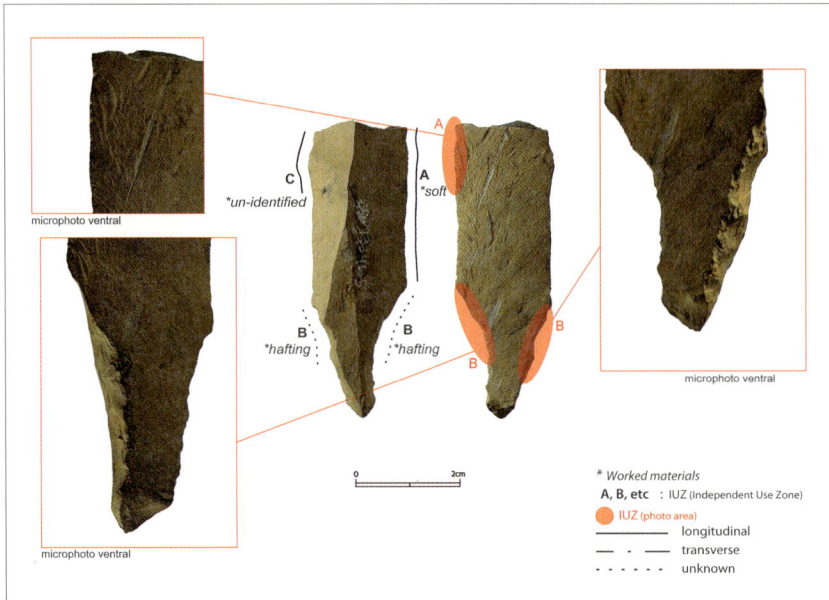

Fig. 16 Analytical Result (Mainly Low Power) : Artifact No. 33965

The right lateral side shows no clear microflaking scar patterns. This side has an acute-angled blank blade edge and is partially snapped off at a steep angled edge. The base (part B) exhibits some hafting-related traces. Heavy rounded parts can be found along both the right and left side of the base, at acute-angled portions of the base retouch. The base retouch is dorsally unifacial (left side) and bifacial (right). The bulb of percussion of the blank blade remains and the tang is rectangularly shaped. The tip of the point shows no clear trace of use.

4.6. Artifact No. 31891 (Fig. 15)

This tanged point is made of very coarse-grained shale with a tuff-like texture. The surface is patinated to a white color and is not suitable for high-power analysis. However, the low-power method identified one IUZ.

The left lateral side (part A) was possibly used in a longitudinal motion, but the worked materials remain unknown. Microflaking scars are found intermittently on both the ventral and dorsal faces along the sharp edge with no retouch. The blank blade is very thin. The scars are scalar, micro, step type, and scalar, micro, deep type. They are distributed in an alternating fashion between the two faces, suggesting longitudinal movements.

The right lateral edge exhibits some scars, but they are sporadic and insufficient as microflaking scar group for use-wear .

The base parts show some rounding. However, the raw material is very soft and differentiation between natural surface grinding and use-wear or manufacture wear is unclear. The identification of haft-related traces has not yet occurred for this specimen (i.e., hafting unidentified).

4.7. Artifact No. 33965 (Fig. 16)

This tanged point is made of shale but the surface is heavily patinated and its color has turned to yellow; as such, it is unsuitable for high-power analysis. Patination can be seen from its modern breakage part toward the point tip. The tip portion is lost. However, the low-power method detected two IUZs.

The right lateral side (part A) was possibly used mainly in a longitudinal motion on relatively soft worked materials. Microflaking scars can be found. On the right-side distal portion on the ventral face, scalar, micro, deep-type scars can be found continuously. On the right-side proximal portion, a partial continuous pattern of tiny to microsize scars can be found on both faces. They are distributed intermittently with the pattern of alternating scars between the ventral and dorsal faces, suggesting parallel movement to the edge.

The left lateral side (part C) was possibly used in a longitudinal motion. The IUZ part was cut off by a modern break toward the distal portion. Microflaking scars can be found on both ventral and dorsal faces. These scars are mainly scalar, micro to small, deep or stepped types. Edge rounding accompanies the microchipped edge up to the breakage point.

The base (part B) exhibits possible hafting-related behavior. The base tang was produced with a dorsal unifacial retouch. Edge rounding can be found on the concave portions of the ventral face. The rounding exists next to a neighboring sharp edge area of the tool's lateral side.

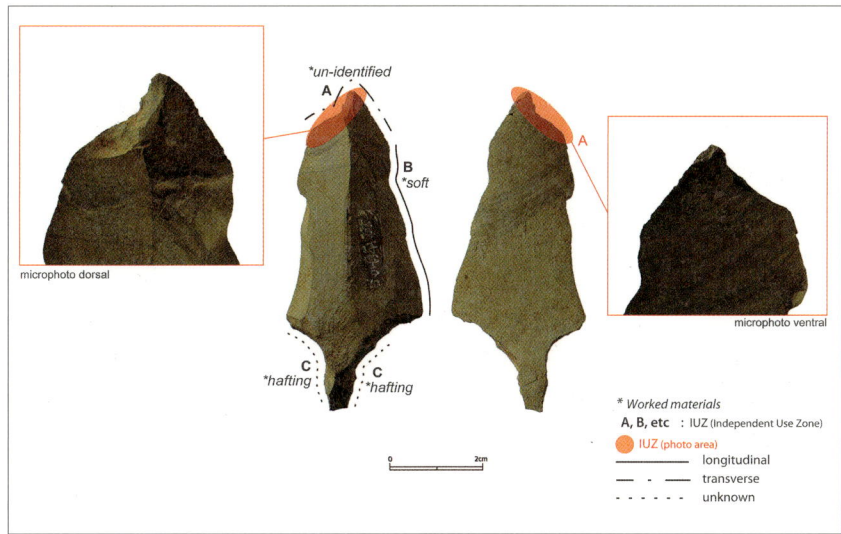

Fig. 17 Analytical Result (Mainly Low Power) : Artifact No. 34144

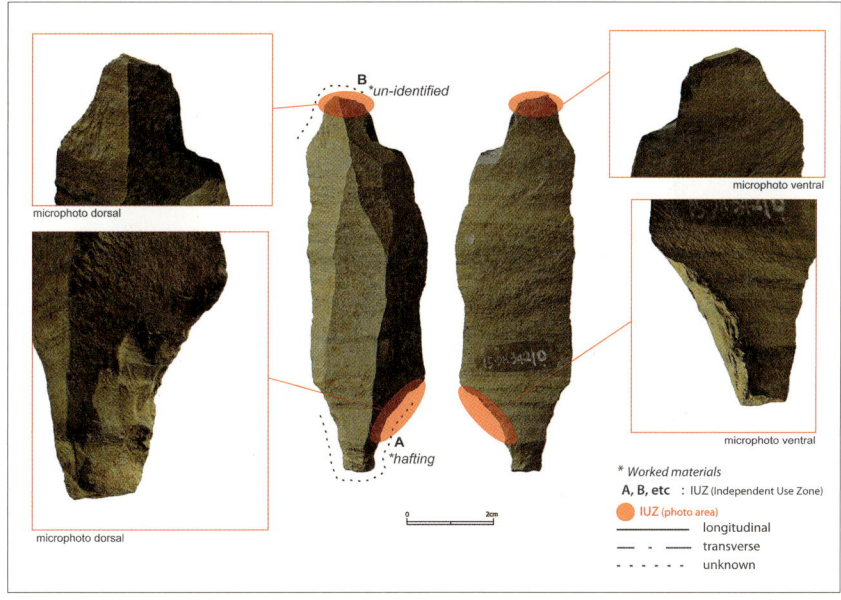

Fig. 18 Analytical Result (Mainly Low Power) : Artifact No. 34210

4.8. Artifact No. 34144 (Fig. 17)

This tanged point is made of fine-grained banded shale, but it is patinated to a whitish grey color, known from modern nibbling. It is unsuitable for high-power analysis, but low-power observation identified two IUZs.

The tip portion (part A) has traces of a possible impact fracture. Some scar facets are visible on the dorsal face from the tip to an interior direction. The right lateral tip shows microflaking scars of a continuous, triangular, small, step type.

The right lateral side (part B) was possibly used in a longitudinal motion on relatively soft materials. The side is an unretouched sharp edge. Sporadic microflaking scars of a scalar, micro, deep type are visible on both the ventral and dorsal faces. These scars partially alternate between the two faces, suggesting parallel movements to the edge. The base portion (part C) exhibits possible wear from haft-related behavior. The base is dorsally notch retouched along both sides. Rounding is visible on the ventral overhang of the notches on both sides.

4.9. Artifact No. 34210 (Fig. 18)

This tanged point is made of medium-grained shale of a grey color. The surface is heavily patinated, known from modern nibbling. It is unsuitable for high-power analysis, but low-power observation detected one IUZ.

The tip portion (part B) exhibits the possibility of some utilization (IUZ). The tip is faceted dorsally. The blank blade curvature is strong, so simple inference as an impact fracture is doubtful. Here, the existence of tip faceting is evident. Neither use method nor worked materials are known.

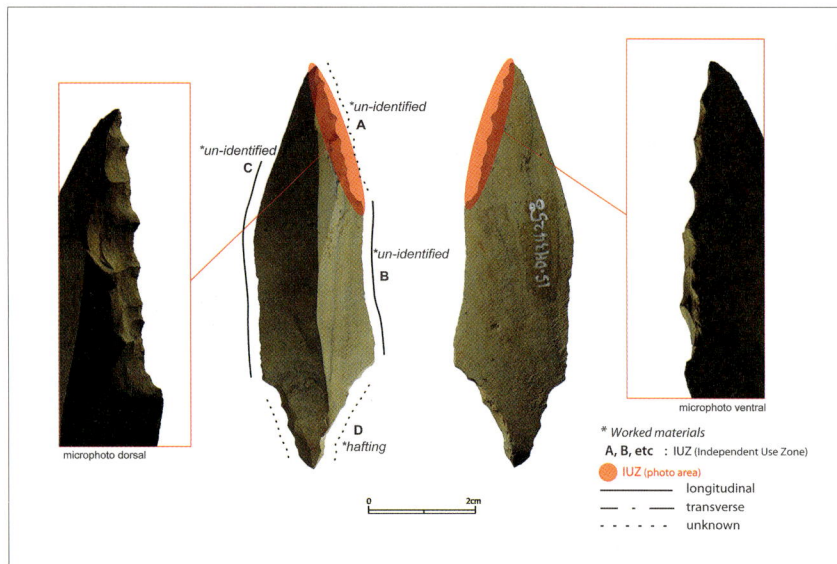

Fig. 19 Analytical Result (Mainly Low Power) : Artifact No. 34258

Fig. 20 Analytical Result (Mainly Low Power) : Artifact No. 34394

power observation detected three IUZs. Its lateral sides were utilized, but the tool was not used as a projectile.

The right lateral side, distal half (part A), is a dorsally denticulated edge. This part was inferred as a utilized edge, but its motion or worked materials remain unidentified. Some denticulated projections are rounded on the ventral face and side face. Some striations are detectable but, regrettably, low-power observation could not make a clear determination.

The right lateral side, middle portion (part B), was probably used mainly in a longitudinal motion. Worked materials are unidentified. Microflaking scars are found continuously on both the ventral and dorsal faces. These are mostly scalar, micro, deep type, and are often distributed in an alternating fashion between the two faces. Also, rounding accompanies the microflaking edge scars.

The left lateral side (part C) was also probably used mainly in a longitudinal motion. Worked materials remain unidentified. Microflaking scars are found intermittently on the ventral face. Along the distal half can be found trapezoidal, micro, step-type scars; and along the proximal half can be found scalar, micro, deep-type scars. On the dorsal face, microflaking scars are also found intermittently. These are scalar, tiny to micro, and deep and stepped types. When the side is viewed from a lateral direction, the scars are distributed in an alternating fashion between the two faces, suggesting parallel movement of the edge.

The tip part exhibits no clear impact traces consistent with projectile usage. The base (part D) shows some traces from hafting-related behavior.

The right lateral side and left lateral side show very few microflaking scars, even though both sides have sharp, unretouched edges. The lateral sides were not utilized very much and were not identified as an IUZ.

The base (part A) shows heavy rounding on the right-side ventral face. Rounding occurs at the notched vertical depressions. Some hafting-related behavior can be inferred. The base was retouched dorsally. The left base side has modern nibbling.

4.10. Artifact No. 34258 (Fig. 19)

This tanged point is made of fine-grained banded shale. Its surface is heavily patinated and its color has turned to grey. Patination is known from modern nibbling along the dorsal blank ridge. It is unsuitable for high-power analysis, but low-

4.11. Artifact No. 34394 (Fig. 20)

This tanged point is made of banded shale, seemingly good for high-power observation. However, modern nibbling at the point tip and right lateral side revealed its original dark grey to black texture before considerable degrees of patination. One IUZ was identified.

The left lateral side (part A) was possibly used in a transverse motion on relatively soft worked materials. Microflaking scars can be found on the dorsal face. These scars are scalar, microtype, and continuous. At high magnifications (200x), light ventral rounding and faint striated features are detectable perpendicular to the edge, but clear microwear polishes were not found.

The right lateral side has some modern chipped scars. Clear use-wear traces are not detected.

The base retouch was unifacially applied onto the dorsal face to form a tang shape. This portion (part B) exhibits light rounding on ventral overhanged spots of retouching, suggesting some hafting-related behavior. The tip part was broken by modern flaking scars.

4.12. Artifact No. 34474 (Fig. 21)

This tanged point is made of coarse-grained shale. The surface is patinated and unsuitable for high-power analysis. Two IUZs were detected.

The left lateral side (part B) was possibly used in a longitudinal motion on soft materials. On the dorsal face, continuous microflaking scars can be found. These are mainly scalar, with some rectangular, stepped fractures. On the distal ventral face, continuous microflaking scars can be found. These are mainly scalar and micro, with the occasional occurrence of scars of a rectangular type. On the middle part of the side edge, the ventral face shows occasional scalar microtype scars.

The right lateral side (part C) was possibly used in a transverse motion. Worked materials remain unidentified. On the distal ventral face at denticulate projections, rounding can be observed on the overhang edges. There are some microflaking scars on the edge of the retouch.

The tip is broken. It is a snap break and was not identified as an impact fracture.

The base was retouched bifacially. The left ventral portion (part A) is rounded at the overhang. Some hafting-related behavior can be inferred.

4.13. Artifact No. 34627 (Fig. 22)

This tanged point is made of banded shale of a dark grey color. The surface condition is suitable for high-power observation. There are some modern nibbling breaks along

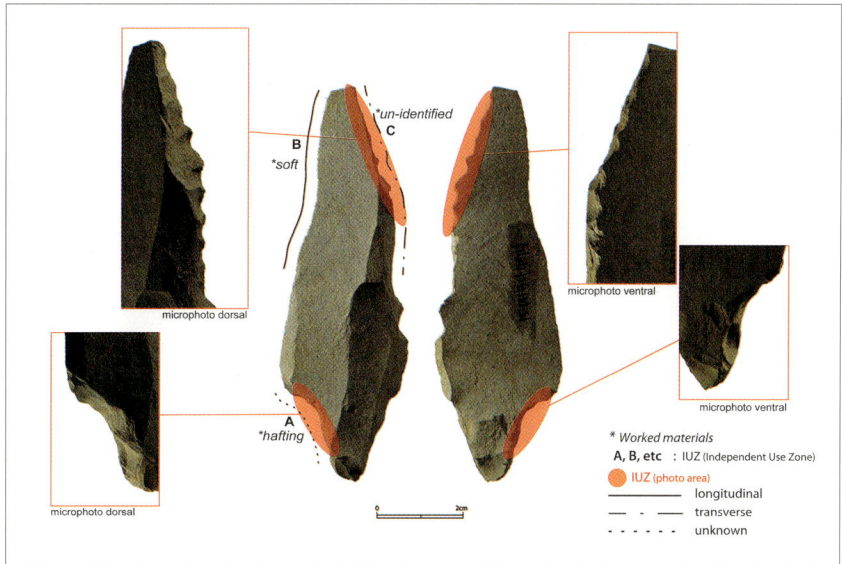

Fig. 21 Analytical Result (Mainly Low Power) : Artifact No. 34474

Fig. 22 Analytical Result (Mainly Low Power) : Artifact No. 34627

the left lateral side, revealing the degree of patination. The tool was interpreted as not having been utilized.

The right lateral side (part B) is dorsally denticulated. On the ventral face at notched depressions only slight rounding is visible. This may represent traces from retouching. The edge is fresh and sharp, and virtually no microflaking was found. This edge was probably un-used.

The left lateral side shows virtually no wear traces under magnifications of 100x and 200x, suggesting no use. No rounding, striations, or polish patches were detected.

The base (part A) exhibits edge rounding on the ventral face (100x) at the base retouch, distal portion. However, the other side (right side) of the base is sharp and shows no rounding. The base was inferred to have been hafted, but without much movement or contact.

The tip retains no wear traces of possible use. The tanged point was denticulately retouched, prepared, and hafted,

Chapter 3. Late Paleolithic Site of Suyanggae

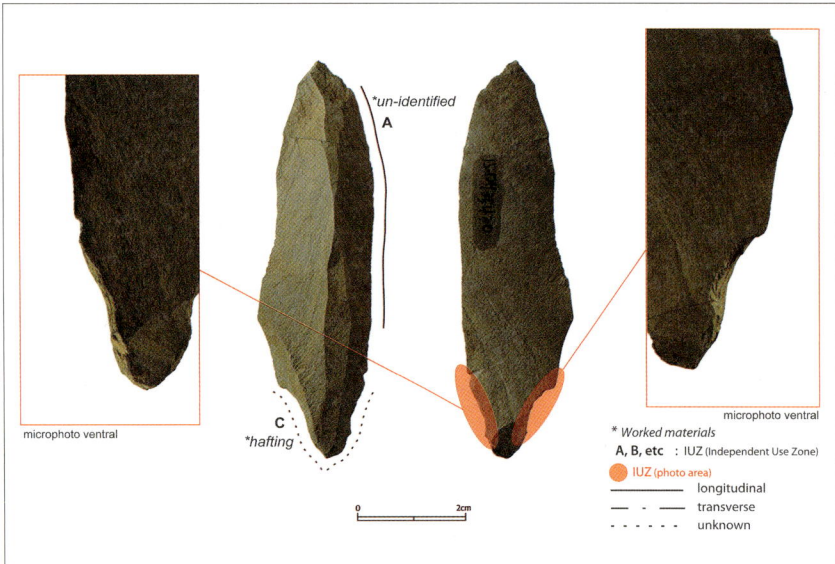

Fig. 23 Analytical Result (Mainly Low Power) : Artifact No. 35430

Fig. 24 Analytical Result (Mainly Low Power) : Artifact No. 35602

trapezoidal, tiny to micro size, but mostly deep with some stepped fractures. Edge rounding was not seen.

The left lateral side exhibits sporadic microflaking scars: scalar, triangular, micro, deep, and stepped. There is insufficient evidence to identify an IUZ used edge.

The tip of the point was not retouched but retains its original blank blade shape. There is no trace of diagnostic impact fracture (DIF).

The base (part C) was produced with dorsal unifacial retouching. Retouched portions are heavily rounded on the projections and overhang of the ventral face. Some hafting-related behavior can be inferred.

4.15. Artifact No. 35602 (Fig. 24)

The tanged point is made of medium-grained shale. The surface is patinated and brown stain patches are seen. The tool is not suitable for high power analysis, but low power observation could reconstruct its usage. There are 2 IUZs.

Right lateral side (part A) shows traces of use. The part A was probably used in longitudinal motion, on relatively soft worked materials. Microflaking scars are found along the side on both faces with slight rounding of edge. The scars are mainly on ventral face in the middle portion of part A, while they are mainly on dorsal face in the distal and proximal portions of part A. Shapes of scars are variable, scalar, trapezoidal, triangle, both deep and stepped, micro sized. Their distribution is partially alternating.

Left lateral side (part B) was probably used in transverse motion, possibility being on relatively hard (medium to hard) worked materials. Its moving direction was the ventral face as its leading aspect. Microflaking scars of various shapes (trapezoidal, rectangular, scalar) and sizes (small to middle), some with stepped termination are found mainly on dorsal face. The pattern indicates movement in perpendicular direction to the edge. Edge rounding is not found along part B. Striations in perpendicular direction are also found along part B edge on both faces, ventral and dorsal (observable at 30X), again suggesting transverse motion on relatively hard materials.

but was probably not used.

4.14. Artifact No. 35430 (Fig. 23)

This tanged point is made of fine-grained banded shale of a grey color. The surface is heavily patinated and unsuitable for high-power analysis. Surface modification (PDSM, that is, post-depositional surface modification) is known from modern nibbling on the tip and base parts. One IUZ was identified.

The right lateral side (part A) exhibits traces of some utilization. The motion was possibly in a longitudinal direction, but worked materials remain unidentified. The edge remains sharp as retouching was not applied. There are intermittent microflaking scars on both the ventral and dorsal faces. These are various, including scalar and

The base retains wear traces from some hafting related behavior. There are slight rounding edges on ventral concavities of tang notches which were made unifacially on both sides.

The point tip is broken. The break is of snapped off type and not clear as DIF (diagnostic impact fracture). The tool was made from a thin blade as blank and both lateral sides are not retouched, retaining sharp edges.

4.16. Artifact No. 36021 (Fig. 25)

The tanged point is made of banded shale, patinated to grey. Its blank was a crested blade and the base is shouldered one side. There is one IUZ.

Left distal sharp edge (part A) was the main use area of this shouldered point. Various motions are inferred, probably mixed with longitudinal and transverse. Worked materials are not identified due to rock patination. Microflaking scars are found. A pattern of flat, small to medium, shallow type is found on a part of ventral face. Another pattern of scalar, micro, deep type is found alternating on both ventral and dorsal faces with some edge rounding.

Left lateral side and right lateral side exhibit sporadic micro- flaking scars, but they are not enough as evidence of IUZs.

The base (part C) retains wears from some hafting related behavior. There is rounding of straight side edge on retouch. Right lateral side shows rounding ventrally even though the part was not concave. Left lateral notch of base is rounded at distal concavity on ventral face.

Fig. 25 Analytical Result (Mainly Low Power) : Artifact No. 36021

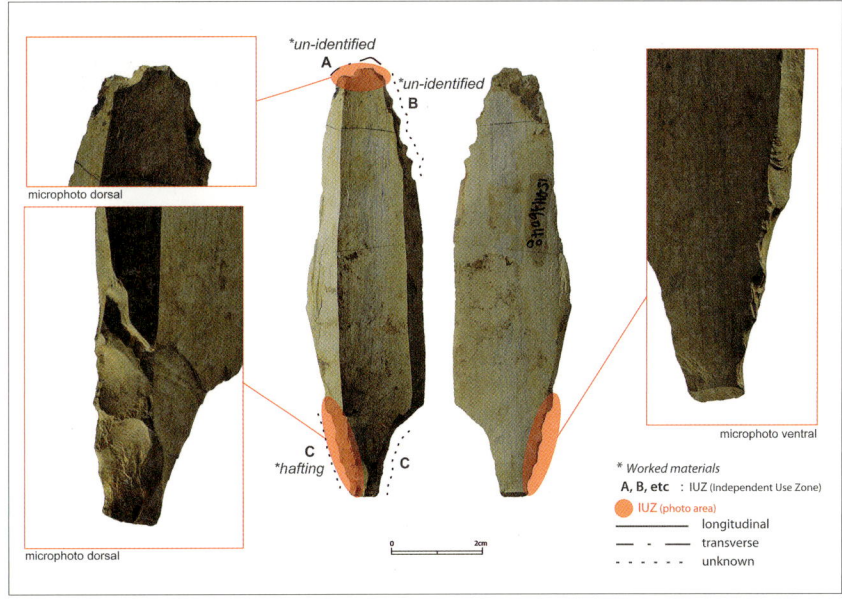

Fig. 26 Analytical Result (Mainly Low Power) : Artifact No. 36048

4.17. Artifact No. 36048 (Fig. 26)

The tanged point is made of fine-grained shale of banded texture. Its blank is a large long blade. The surface was patinated to grey color. Modern nibbling at the tip left reveals its original black andesite type rock texture. Stain patches of dark brown to black scatter around tip and both faces. There are 2 IUZs.

The point tip area (part A, IUZ) exhibits some fracture scars on dorsal face with flaking axis from tip to interior. Possibility of impact fracture needs further examination. Striations are not detectable due to surface patination.

Right lateral distal side (part B) which is a dorsally denticulated portion shows moderate rounding on projections of edge on ventral face. No microflaking scars are seen on ventral face. Part B was possibly put to use, but motion or worked materials are not clear.

Right lateral side proximaly next to the denticulated area and left lateral side of long sharp edge show some microflaking scars. They include trapezoidal, micro, step type. But they are sporadic and not continuous, so not enough evidence as IUZ.

The base (part C) is shouldered with unifacial retouch. Both left and right lateral proximal sides are rounded on ventral face. The rounding is at corresponding spots between right and left. The wear is possibly from hafting related behavior.

Fig. 27 Analytical Result (Mainly Low Power) : Artifact No. 36158

Fig. 28 Analytical Result (Mainly Low Power) : Artifact No. 36456

4.18. Artifact No. 36158 (Fig. 27)

The tanged point is made of medium-grained shale of dark grey color. Surface patination is not heavy. Retouch was limited to its base area where unifacial work was dorsally applied with platform lip remaining. There are 2 IUZs along lateral sides. The tool was possibly hand held and was used as cutting and whittling knife.

Left lateral side near distal portion (part A) exhibits continuous microflaking scars which distribute on both dorsal and ventral faces in alternate way. The scars are mainly scalar, micro, deep type, with some rectangular, step, type as well. The scar types and distribution pattern suggest longitudinal motion on relatively soft materials.

Along left lateral side in proximal half, some microflaking scars are seen but only sporadic and not enough evidence as IUZ recognition.

Along right lateral side in proximal half (part B), microflaking scars are found continuously on dorsal aspect. They are scalar, micro, deep type and trapezoidal, micro, step type. On ventral aspect, the same portion of lateral side show striations perpendicular to edge (30X observation with oblique lighting). Part B was probably utilized in transverse motion with ventral face as leading aspect. But the worked materials are un-identified.

The base part shows little rounding on either side, or no positive traces for hafting is detected.

4.19. Artifact No. 36456 (Fig. 28)

The tanged point is made of coarse-grained banded shale. The surface is heavily patinated (known from modern nibbling near distal end) and not suitable for high power analysis. One IUZ is detected on this point made of long, large flake with undulating wavy ventral and dorsal faces. The base part was deeply notched to concavity and retains wear traces as hafting related behavior.

Right lateral side (part A) shows continuous microflaking scars of small and middle sized, scalar types on dorsal face. Slight rounding is seen along the part A including the microchipped area. Motion or worked materials are not identified.

The sides of base (part B) exhibit heavy rounding on ventral and dorsal face and also side aspect, on projections (protruded portions). There are notable heavy abrasion wear.

4.20. Artifact No. 36801 (Fig. 29)

The tanged point is made of medium-grained shale. The surface is patinated and not suitable for high power analysis. Stains of brown to black color are on various parts of the artifact. The base tang is pointed by retouch. Lateral sides remain sharp with no retouch. Two IUZs are recognized.

Left lateral side (part B) was probably used in longitudinal motion, worked materials are unidentified. Along the sharp edge, microflaking scars of scalar, micro, deep type continuously distribute on both faces of ventral and dorsal alternating.

Right lateral side exhibits no clear use-wear traces. Microflaking scars exist but only sporadic.

The point tip (part C) exhibits possible wear traces as

Fig. 29 Analytical Result (Mainly Low Power) : Artifact No. 36801

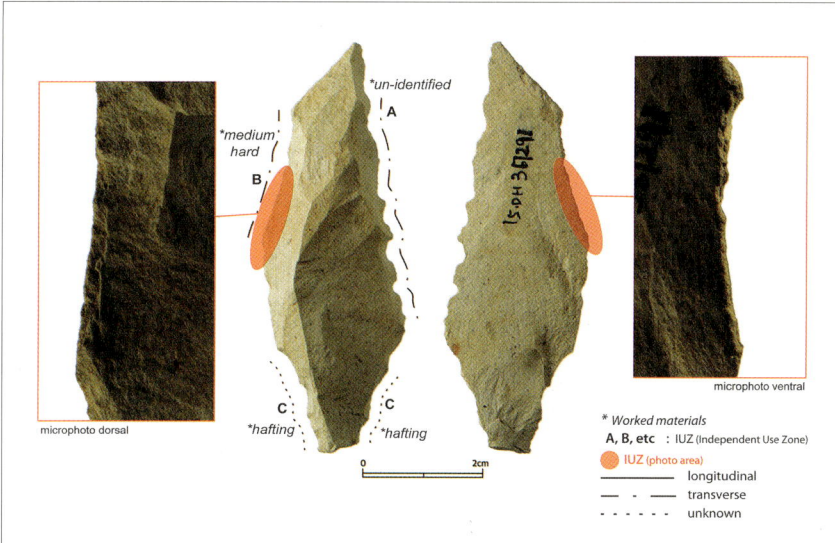

Fig. 30 Analytical Result (Mainly Low Power) : Artifact No. 37291

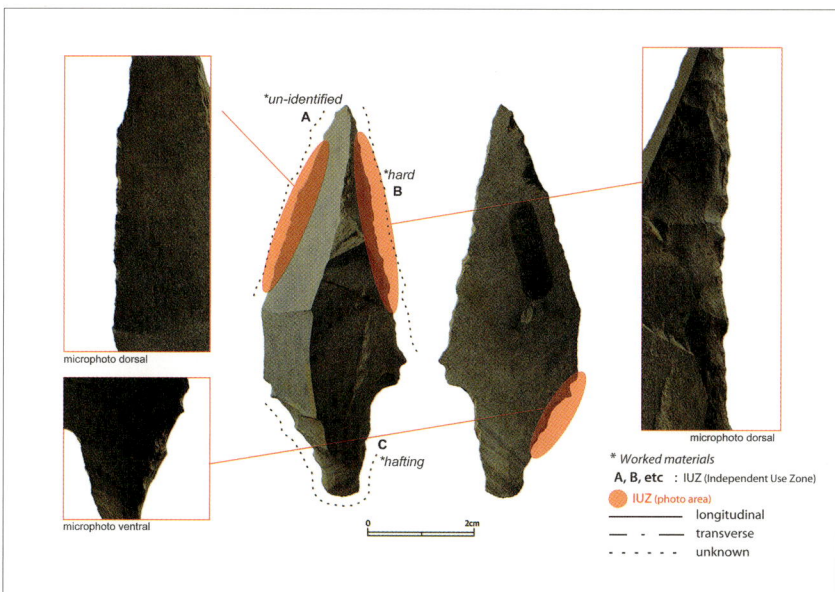

Fig. 31 Analytical Result (Mainly Low Power) : Artifact No. 37499

projectile use. There are three small burin-like fractures from the tip. There are also irregular angular chipping scars near the tip on the left lateral side (more distal portion than part B aforementioned). They need closer examination as DIF (diagnostic impact fracture) by Sano (2012) or not. Here, only the possibility is noted.

The base partially shows heavy rounding on the concavity of base notch retouch (ventral to side face) at part A.

4.21. Artifact No. 37291 (Fig. 30)

The tanged point is made of coarse-grained tuff-like shale. The surface is heavily patinated to yellow, white color. The point was used on both lateral sides (2 IUZs) and the base was hafted.

Right lateral side (part A) was probably used in transverse motion with its ventral face as leading aspect, but worked materials are un-identified. On ventral face, moderate rounding of projection parts of denticulate is found. Also, striations are detected perpendicular to edge.

Left lateral side (part B) was probably used in transverse motion with its ventral face as leading aspect, on medium to hard worked materials. On ventral face, heavy edge rounding and also striations perpendicular to the edge are detected (at 30X with oblique spotlight). On dorsal face microflaking scars of overlapping step fracture, including rectangular type, are found with edge rounding.

The base (part C) on both side areas, exhibits ventral face rounding on edge, interpreted as haft related behavior traces. The unifacial base retouch was around the bulb of percussion area of blank blade.

4.22. Artifact No. 37499 (Fig. 31)

The tanged point is made of medium-grained shale of banded texture. The surface is patinated to dark grey color. Modern nibbling reveals its original black texture. Not suitable for high power

Fig. 32 Analytical Result (Mainly Low Power) : Artifact No. 37689

Fig. 33 Analytical Result (Mainly Low Power) : Artifact No. 38592

4.23. Artifact No. 37689 (Fig. 32)

The tanged point is made of coarse-grained shale. The surface is patinated to light grey to yellow, and not suitable for high power analysis. The tool is typologically irregular in that the blank blade tapers toward the tip. Its bulb of percussion area is wavy with ripples. There is one IUZ. The tool was probably hand held and a few parts were lightly utilized.

The middle part of left lateral side (part A) was used, including transverse motion. Worked materials were possibly relatively soft. Continuous microflaking scars are found on dorsal face. There are various types, scalar, trapezoidal, and rectangular, micro to small sizes. On ventral face, only sporadic distribution of microflaking is seen. No rounding is seen on ventral edge.

Right lateral side shows sporadic microflaking scars of micro, scalar type. They are not enough evidence for IUZ recognition.

The base is irregular in that there is bifacial denticulated retouch along right side (no rounding), and unifacial retouch along left side (slight rounding on ventral projections). Clear traces are not found to indicate hafting related behavior.

4.24. Artifact No. 38592 (Fig. 33)

The tanged point is made of fine-grained shale. The surface is heavily patinated to yellowy light-grey color. Modern nibbling at the base right side dorsally reveals heavy patination of this specimen. Original surface was black to dark blue, fine-grained andesite-like texture. There are 2 IUZs and the tip also retains possible use-wear.

Right lateral side (part B) was probably used in longitudinal motion on relatively softer worked materials. Microflaking scars are found on both ventral and dorsal faces. They are mainly micro, scalar and rectangular, deep or stepped types. They distribute alternatingly on both faces and as the result, they are continuous. There is some rounding along the edge. Left lateral side (part D) is identified as IUZ, but motions or worked materials are unknown due to heavy patination. The used portion retains sharpness.

The tip (part A) was possibly put to use as a projectile, but needs more reference experiments to be sure. The tip has

analysis. The point has 2 IUZs.

Left lateral side (part A) was used, but motion and worked materials are not identified. There is a possibility of varied (mixed) utilization. Microflaking scars are found on both dorsal and ventral faces. Their distribution is intermittent, and types are variable, mainly micro to small, scalar and trapezoidal.

Right lateral side (part B) of denticulated edge was also used. There is a possibility of relatively hard materials. On ventral face, varied degrees of rounding are found along the denticulate especially at projection parts. On dorsal face, however, microflaking analysis is difficult due to the retouch. The base (part C) exhibits heavy rounding on ventral face along both left and right sides. The traces at the base are interpreted as hafting related behavior.

scars of possible impact fracture, but not necessarily DIF (diagnostic impact fracture) by Sano (2012). The tip was not retouched for point.

The base shows heavy rounding along both sides. The base is interpreted as hafted. The base was produced by retouch which reduced thick proximal bulb of percussion part of its blank blade.

4.25. Artifact No. 38798 (Fig. 34)

The tanged point is made of grey colored shale. Its surface is heavily patinated and not suitable for high power observation. The distal half of the point is broken and missing. Along left lateral base side, modern nibbling reveals its original black color texture of the shale. There are brown stain patches on surface. There is one IUZ.

Right lateral side (part A) exhibits intermittent microflaking scars on both faces. They are tiny to micro, scalar and triangular shapes. However, modern nibbling blurs microflaking scar patterns. Use motion or worked material types are unknown.

Left lateral side also show some intermittent microflaking scars, but modern nibbling and surface patination prevents identification as an IUZ.

The base part was unifacially retouched dorsally. The part shows moderate rounding on sides of the base, but they are overlapped by modern nibbling plus modern grinding. Some haft related behavior is inferred.

4.26. Artifact No. 38920 (Fig. 35)

The knife shaped tool is made of fine-grained banded shale. Its surface is heavily patinated and not suitable for high power observation. There is one IUZ and possible two parts of wear traces.

Left lateral side is dorsally denticulated (part A). Denticulate retouch continues to its base part. The denticulated edge shows rounding. Motion or worked materials are un-identified due to heavy patination.

Right lateral side is sharp as the typological edge of knife shaped tool. There are sporadic microflaking scars but not clear as evidence of use (not recognized as IUZ).

The base (part B of both sides) exhibits heavy rounding

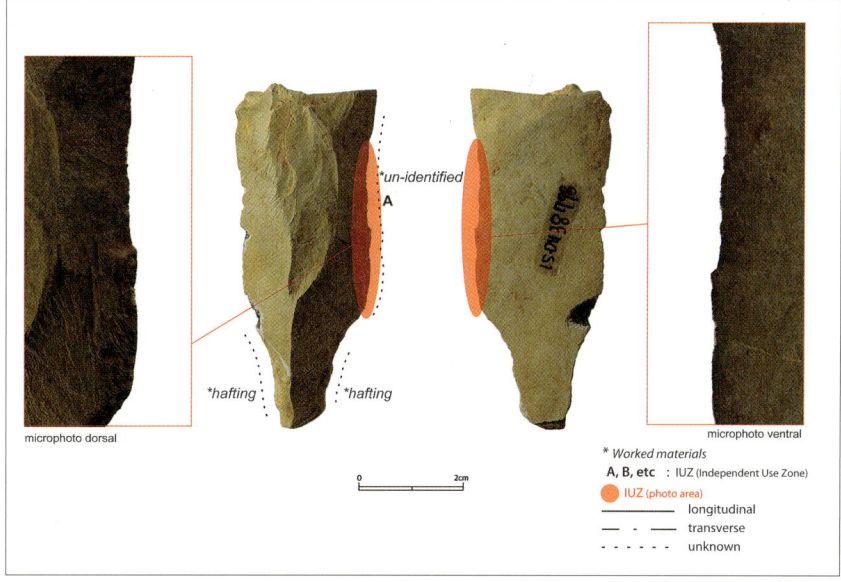

Fig. 34 Analytical Result (Mainly Low Power) : Artifact No. 38798

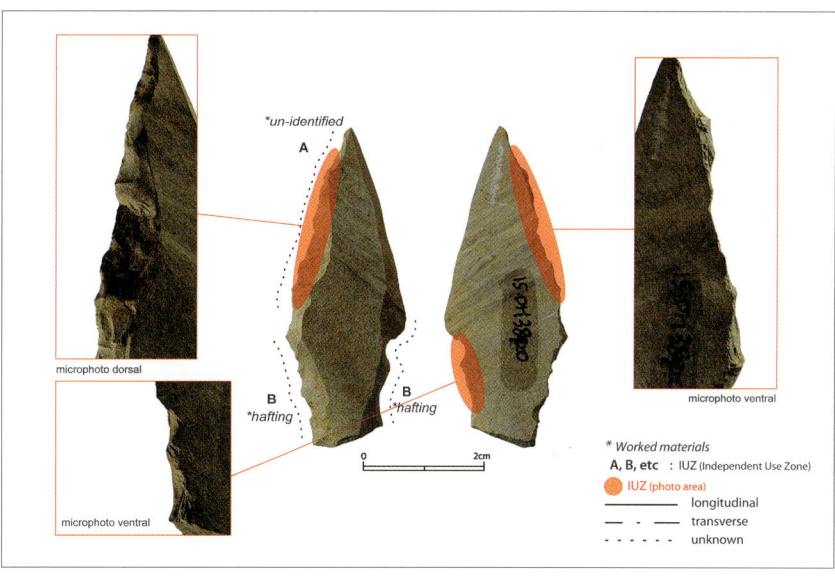

Fig. 35 Analytical Result (Mainly Low Power) : Artifact No. 38920

especially on ventral face along denticulated edges of both sides. The wear is interpreted as some hafting related traces.

5. Conclusions

The tanged point was one of the most important formal tool types in the Upper Palaeolithic period in the Korean Peninsula. We sincerely believe this cooperative research between Korea and Japan also will open a new perspective on the Palaeolithic of East Asia in general. Even though various degrees of post-depositional surface alteration and relative variabilities of lithic raw materials detract from detailed functional determinations, the integrated combination of two analytical methods revealed important results including the following general tendency.

1. The results are obtained as inferences, in terms of four dimensions. That is, 1) used, unused or unknown, 2) which part of the artifact was used (identified as IUZ), 3) for what kind of motions they were used, longitudinal, transverse, mixed, or un-identified, 4) on what type of worked materials they were used, soft, medium, hard, or more specific type such as bone/antler or wood.

2. Out of 96 tanged points from the Suyanggae site, most of the analyzed specimens yielded clues to their functions to a certain extent. Forty seven specimens were analyzed and the majority of them are suitable for use-wear analysis, irrespective of their rock type, or the degree of patination. This is because our methodology is a combination of "low power analysis" and "high power analysis". However, surface conditions from the post depositional surface modification processes (also termed as PDSM) prevented from identification of microwear polish types in many cases. Microwear polish is the most reliable clue to the worked materials inference. Only relatively fresh surface shale of dark colors provided some information on the type of polishes.

3. The method of use exhibits diversity. The tanged points were not necessarily projectile weapons, but they were utilized in a variety of tasks, such as cutting/sawing, scraping/whittling.

4. The tips of tanged points do not show traces as point projectiles in the majority of cases. Rather, lateral sides were often utilized as tool edges. Both right lateral edges and left lateral edges were utilized. In many cases, both sides were utilized, not only along the sharp side, but also the denticulated side and/or retouch blunting side. Some denticulated lateral sides were used in transverse motion of use. Some sharp lateral sides were used in both longitudinal and transverse motions.

5. The base of tanged points exhibits a particular clear pattern of use. The concave parts of the base show microwears of rounding. They are notable especially on their overhanged parts of retouch edges. Whether the rounding was the result of use, or hafting preparation such as grinding, is not clear. However, the rounding at the base is evident in the majority of analyzed cases. The phenomena are interpreted as related to some kind of hafting behavior. The tanged points were hafted.

6. Above observations are from about a half of the tanged points. They were selected as the result of initial screening process using very low magnifications of the hand lenses. However, some cases which do not show microflaking scars under the hand magnifier do exhibit clear microwear traces under higher magnifications. Due to time limitations we could not, but if all specimens were examined with high power method, unused tools could possibly be identified as related to site structural and behavioral analysis.

To summarize our project results, the base retouched parts of tanged points were often heavily rounded on concavity, suggesting some sort of hafting behavior and the emergence of composite tools. Lateral sides of the tanged points were often utilized for a variety of tasks. Denticulated side edges were often used in transverse motions. The tips of points were less frequently utilized. Impact fracture patterns are rare. All these suggest the deeper planning depth and flexibility of tool usage.

The observed facts and interpretation thereof indicate some important behavioral characteristics of the Early Upper Palaeolithic population in the Korean Peninsula. Future comparative researches with base retouched tools in the EUP of Northeastern Japanese Archipelago and further functional analysis of various artifacts in Korean Peninsula throughout the Upper Palaeolithic period, will bring more insights into cultural adaptations by Modern Humans in East Asia.

Acknowledgments

The authors are very grateful to Dr. Lee Yung-jo and Dr. Woo Jong-yoon for their generous approval of this truly excellent opportunity of cooperative research, as well as their heartful hospitality during our stay in Cheongju. Great thanks are also to the members of the Institute of Korean Prehistory for their assistance and cordial support for our joint project. Our research and trips were partially supported by Grant-in-aid for Scientific Research by JSPS (KAKENHI), granted to Akoshima (No.17K03204). The metallurgical microscope was provided by JSPS grant No.25370885.

References

Akoshima, K., 1981. An Experimental Study of Microflaking. Kokogaku Zasshi. *Journal of the Archaeological Society of Nippon* Vol. 66, no. 4, 1-27. (in Japanese)

Akoshima, K., 1987. Microflaking Quantification. *The Human Uses of Flint and Chert*. edited by Sieveking, G. de G., and M. H. Newcomer, Cambridge University Press, 71-79.

Akoshima, K., 1989. Use-wear of Stone Tools. *Archaeological Library* 56, New Science Co. (in Japanese)

Akoshima, K., 2010. Lithic Use-wear Analysis: Method and Theory Now and Then. *The 15th International Symposium: SUYANGGAE and Her Neighbours.* edited by Yung-jo Lee and Jong-yoon Woo, Institute of Korean Prehistory and Danyang County Office, 99-115. (English with Korean summary)

Akoshima, K. and H. Hong. 2014. Standard Use-wear Chart of TUMRT (1): Microflaking (1). *Bulletin of the Tohoku University Museum* No.13, 43-76.

Akoshima, K. and H. Hong. 2016. Standard Use-wear Chart of TUMRT (2): Microflaking (2). *Bulletin of the Tohoku University Museum* No.15, 127-193.

Akoshima, K. and H. Hong. 2017a. Toward the Standardized Identification of Lithic Use-wear, for Universal East Asian Criteria. *The 22 (2nd) International Symposium: SUYANGGAE and Her Neighbours in Sakhalin*, 44-51.

Akoshima, K. and H. Hong. 2017b. Standard Use-wear Chart of TUMRT (3): Microwear Polish (1). *Bulletin of the Tohoku University Museum* No.16, 69-86.

Akoshima, K. and H. Hong. 2018. Standard Use-wear Chart of TUMRT (4): Microwear Polish (2). *Bulletin of the Tohoku University Museum* No.17, 115-138.

Akoshima, K. and Y. Kanomata. 2015. Technological Organization and Lithic Microwear Analysis: An Alternative Methodology. *Journal of Anthropological Archaeology* vol. 38, 17-24.

Binford, L.R., 1981. *Bones: Ancient Men and Modern Myths*, Academic Press.

Keeley, L.H., 1980. *Experimental Determination of Stone Tool Uses*, University of Chicago Press.

Kajiwara, H. and K. Akoshima. 1981. An Experimental Study of Microwear Polish on Shale Artifacts. *Kokogaku Zasshi* Vol. 67, no. 1, 1-36. (in Japanese)

Serizawa, C., H. Kajiwara and K. Akoshima. 1982. Experimental Study of Microwear Traces and Its Potentiality. *Archaeology and Natural Sciences* No.14, 67-87. (in Japanese)

Sano, K., 2012. *Functional Variability in the Late Upper Palaeolithic of North-Western Europe*. Universitatsforschungen zur prahistorischen Archaologie, Band 219. Verlag Dr. Rudolf Habelt GmbH, Bonn.

Sano, K., Y. Denda and M. Oba. 2016. Experiments in Fracture Patterns and Impact Velocity with Replica Hunting Weapons from Japan. *Multidisciplinary Approaches to the Study of Stone Age Weaponry.* edited by K. Sano and R. Iovita, Springer, 29-46.

Semenov, S.A., 1964. *Prehistoric Technology.* translated by M.W. Thompson, Moonraker Press.

Vaughan, P.C., 1985. *Use-wear Analysis of Flaked Stone Tools*, The University of Arizona Press.

The Paleolithic survey in Danyang, South Korea : Focusing on the results and future tasks

Jungchul LEE

Associate professor, Hallym University Museum Dohyeon Academy, Korea ; Jungchullee@hallym.ac.kr

ABSTRACT

Danyang County has attracted attention because it contains of the earliest Paleolithic sites in Korea. In order to establish features of Korean Paleolithic culture in Danyang County, eight Paleolithic sites have been excavated so far, including three localities at Suyanggae, which are open, cave, and rock shelter sites. Among them, the Suyanggae sites and the Gunang Cave site can be evaluated as key sites because they have been repeatedly excavated since their initial excavation. A large amount of new research data have been generated, including data on site-formation processes, stone tool-making processes by Paleolithic humans, the identification of representative artifacts of the Early and Late Paleolithic, and the recovery of plant and animal fossils, bone tools, and artwork from caves and rock shelter sites. This led to a better understanding of the site-formation process, paleoclimate, and paleoenvironmental implications of the area, as well as the associated behaviors and ritual systems of the Paleolithic humans who lived there.

국문초록

단양에서 발굴된 구석기 유적은 하나의 유적군인 수양개 3개 지구를 포함하여 총 8곳이며, 한데, 동굴, 바위그늘 유적으로 구분된다. 현재까지 이루어진 단양 구석기 조사성과는 (1) 토양과 퇴적물에 대한 자연과학적 분석을 통해 유적 형성 과정을 이해할 수 있는 자료 축적, (2) 고인류 석기 제작 행태를 이해할 수 있는 자료 확인, (3) 이른 구석기와 늦은 구석기를 대표하는 유적과 유물 확인, (4) 동굴과 바위그늘 유적의 고인골 출토, (5) 다양한 종류의 동물 화석 출토, (6) 식물 화석 확인, (7) 뼈 도구 및 예술품 조사이다. 이를 통해 유적의 형성과 시기, 고기후와 고환경, 구석기인과 그들의 행동 및 상징체계, 구석기 문화 양상을 파악하는 데 있어 중요한 자료를 제공한다. 특히 수양개 유적군과 구낭굴 유적은 핵심 유적으로 평가된다. 단양 구석기의 핵심 가치는 기후변화와 고환경 복원을 가능케 하는 연결고리이자 우리나라 후기구석기 문화를 대표하는 성격을 제시하는 데 있다. 지금까지의 연구성과를 발전시켜 우리나라 구석기인이 생활했던 당시 자연환경과 동식물을 복원하고 다양한 자연과학적 분석을 통해 그들의 생존방식과 도구제작 등 인간활동을 이해할 필요가 있다. 또한 후기 구석기시대 석기 제작기법의 출현과 발전, 도구 제작과정의 재구성, 인간의 인지 구조와 상징을 표현한 유물 해석 등에 대한 지속적 연구가 이루어져야 한다.

Keywords : Danyang, Paleolithic, excavation, Suyanggae sites, Gunang Cave site

1. Introduction: History of survey and excavation sites

Danyang County is located in northeast Chungbuk Province, bordered by Jecheon City, Chungbuk Province, Yeongwol County, Gangwon Province, and the cities of Yeongju and Mungyeong, Gyeongbuk Province. Danyang covers an area of 780,17km², with the Namhan River running through the center of the county from northeast to southwest. Except for the Namhan River and its tributaries, the area is relatively high and mountainous, with the Sobaek Mountains forming the border with Gyeongbuk Province. A fluvial terrace is developed around the Namhan River, and karst features, such as doline, uvale, polje, and limestone caves, are widely found in the county (Table 1, Fig. 1).

The upper part of the fluvial terrace and the limestone caves were very important for human life in the ancient past. The upper part of the fluvial terrace was important for human habitation from the past to the present because it was easy to drain and thus prevent flooding, while the caves provided protection from the surrounding environment in prehistoric times when human power was limited.

Due to this topographical and geological background, it has been speculated that human habitation may have begun relatively early in Danyang County, which has been continuously and actively investigated since the beginning of Korean Paleolithic research. As a result, several open, cave, and rock shelter sites have been identified. In particular, the Suyanggae sites have become one of the most important sites for Paleolithic research in Korea, Northeast Asia, and the world.

In Danyang, the surface survey of the Dwitteul Cave in 1957 was the beginning of Paleolithic studies (Kim, 1958). In 1967, a Yonsei University research team explored caves in the karstic areas of Jecheon and Danyang, identifying Gosu Cave, Danyang Cave, and Dodam Geum Cave in Danyang, and finding possible Paleolithic sites (Sohn, 1984a). In 1974, a rock shelter site was discovered at Sangsi-ri in Danyang (Sohn, 1984a). Later, in 1979 and 1980, surface surveys were conducted in the submerged area of the Chungju Dam, and a number of Paleolithic sites and possible caves and rock shelters were identified in Danyang (Chungbuk National University Museum, 1980). A number of stone tools were found in Sangjin-ri and Aegok-ri, and the Dodam-ri cave was also suggested as a possible Paleolithic site.

An excavation survey began in earnest in the 1980s. In 1981, an additional rock shelter site was discovered and excavated at Sangsi-ri (Sohn, 1984a). Three rock shelters were excavated at the Sangsi site, with those associated with the Paleolithic designated No. 1 and 3. Based on a surface survey of the submerged area of Chungju Dam, intensive excavations in the area were conducted from 1983 to 1985. During this period, Geum caves and Suyanggae sites were also excavated (Lee, 1983, 1984, 1985; Sohn, 1984b, 1985). Also, in 1986, the Gunang Cave site was discovered, and excavations were conducted in 1986 and 1988 (Lee et al., 1991).

In the 1990s, additional excavation surveys were conducted at the previously excavated sites. First, in 1995 and 1996, additional excavations were conducted at the Suyangae sites (Lee and Woo, 1995; Lee et al., 1996; Chungbuk National University Museum and Danyang County, 2001), and new Paleolithic artifacts were identified. Accordingly, the site was divided into localities according to the location and historical period of the artifacts. Therefore, the previously excavated site is referred to as Suyanggae Loc. 1. In 1998, the third excavation of Gunang Cave was conducted (Lee et al., 1999). From the 1990s to the mid-2000s, surface surveys were actively conducted. In this process, the Sangsi-ri, Hajin-ri, and Agok-ri rock shelters, the bat caves of Dodam-ri and Dodam-ri, Sangjin-ri Cave, Hari, and Gadae-ri were identified as Paleolithic sites (Cheongju University Museum, 2000; Chungbuk National University Museum, 2002; Chungbuk Research Institute of Cultural Heritage, 2007). In particular, a number of cave sites were identified in surface surveys and were described as having a high probability of prehistoric sites–if future excavations are conducted, some will likely unearth Paleolithic sites.

In the 2000s, excavation surveys continued around previously excavated sites along with the Suyanggae sites where the locality was divided. In 2001, during the construction of the Suyanggae Prehistory Museum, Suyanggae Loc. 3 was excavated (Lee et al., 2003a), about 200m away from Loc. 1, at an altitude of more than 20m. In 2008, excavations of the museum's southern hills were conducted (Lee et al., 2013a). In 2007, add an excavation survey at Gunang Cave was performed (Lee and Kim, 2007).

The the 2010s, excavation surveys of Suyanggae Loc. 1 and 3 and Gunang Cave continued, as well as excavations of new sites and the discovery of new localities at the Suyanggae sites. First, in 2011, the Hyeoncheon-ri Hahyeoncheon site and Dwitteul Cave were excavated (Institute of Korean Prehistory, 2011; Sohn et al., 2013). In addition, Suyanggae Loc. 3 was excavated by expanding the scope of the 2008 survey (Lee et al., 2013b). Gunang Cave was excavated again in 2011 and yet again in 2013 (Lee et al., 2013c, 2015), and the Gunang I cave, situated at the bottom of the east side of Gunang Cave, was additionally excavated. The core project in the 2010s was Suyanggae Loc. 6, which was excavated from 2013 to 2015 (Woo et al., 2018). The site is located 3.5km downstream from Suyanggae Loc. 1 along the Namhan River. Artifacts were concentrated in four cultural layers, with a greater number of artifacts than were recovered from Suyanggae Loc. 1.

Table 1 List of the Paleolithic sites excavated in Danyang

No.	Site Name	Site Type	Excavation Year	Excavation Agency
1	Sangsi rock shelter	Rock shelter	1981	Yonsei University Museum
2	Geum cave	Cave	1983, 1984, 1985	Yonsei University Museum
3	Suyanggae Loc. 1	Open	1983, 1984, 1985, 1996, 2013	Chungbuk Nat'l University Museum, Institute of Korean Prehistory
4	Gunang cave	Cave	1986, 1988, 1998, 2007, 2011, 2013	Chungbuk Nat'l University Museum, Institute of Korean Prehistory
5	Suyanggae Loc. 3	Open	2001, 2008, 2011	Chungbuk Nat'l University Museum, Institute of Korean Prehistory
6	Heoncheon-ri Haheoncheon	Open	2011	Institute of Korean Prehistory
7	Dwitteul Cave	Cave	2011	Institute of Korean Prehistory
8	Suyanggae Loc. 6	Open	2013, 2014, 2015	Institute of Korean Prehistory

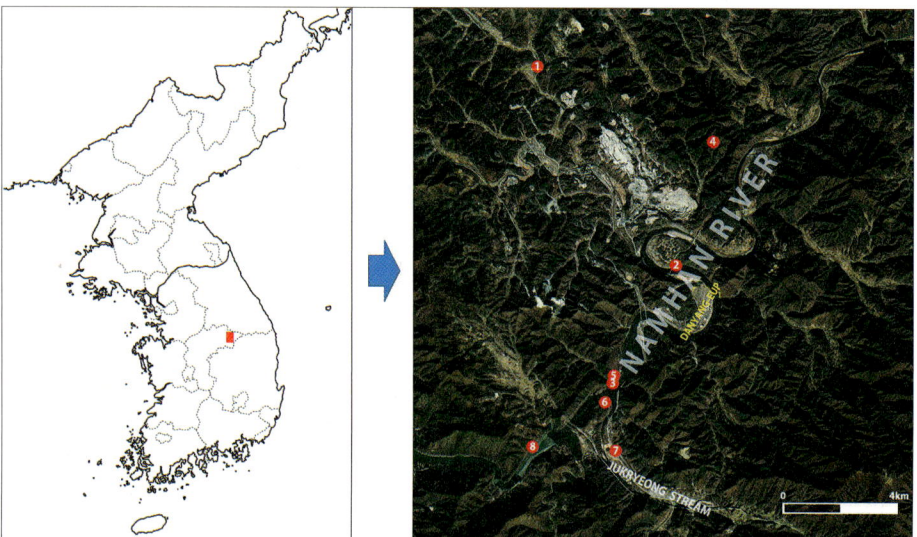

Fig. 1 Distribution of excavated Paleolithic sites in Danyang (site numbers are from No. of Table 1)

Fig. 2 View of Suyanggae Loc. 1 - 5 sites (Woo et al., 2013b)

2. Excavation sites

2.1. Open sites

2.1.1. Suyanggae sites

The Suyanggae sites were discovered by the Chungbuk National University Museum in 1980 during a surface survey in the submerged area of Chungju Dam. Starting with the first excavation in 1983, 13 excavations were conducted, ending in 2015 (**Table 2**). The Suyanggae sites are divided into six localities, from Loc. 1 to 6. Of these, excavations have been conducted at Loc. 1, 2, 3 and 6. Paleolithic sites have been identified at Loc. 1, 3, and 6 and Iron Age dwellings have been uncovered at Loc. 2.

2.1.1.1. Suyanggae Loc. 1
This site was discovered during a surface survey in the submerged area of Chungju Dam, with subsequent excavations conducted from 1983 to 1985 (Lee, 1983, 1984, 1985) (**Fig.3-4**). Additional excavations were conducted in 1996 to determine the extent of the cultural layers and artifact distribution (Lee et al., 1996; Chungbuk National University Museum and Danyang County, 2001).

The site is located at the end of a slope at about 132m in altitude. It is bordered by the Namhan River to the southeast and a small stream that joins the Namhan River to the west. In terms of stratigraphy, the lower part is dominated by

Since 2015, no excavation survey has been conducted. However, considering the places where previous surveys have been conducted, it is highly likely that new Paleolithic sites will be identified and excavated in the area of the Namhan River and its tributaries, and the survey of previously excavated sites will thus be repeated.

Table 2 Status of excavations at the Suyanggae sites

Excavation Order	Excavation Date	Excavation Locality	Excavation Agency
1st excavation	1983.07. – 08.	Loc. 1	Chungbuk Nat'l University Museum
2nd excavation	1984.10. – 11.		
3rd excavation	1985.02. – 03.		
4th excavation	1985.04. – 07.		
5th excavation	1995.07. – 08.	Loc. 2	
6th excavation	1996.06. – 07.		
7th excavation	1996.09. – 11.	Loc. 1 and 2	
8th excavation	2000.01. – 03.	Loc. 3	
9th excavation	2008.10. – 12.		Institute of Korean Prehistory
10th excavation	2011.03. – 05.		
11th excavation	2013.04. – 06.	Loc. 6	
12th excavation	2014.04. – 06.		
13th excavation	2015.03. – 10.		

Fig. 3 Excavation view in Suyanggae Loc. 1 site (Lee and Woo eds., 2005)

Fig. 4 Lithic workshop in Suyanggae Loc. 1 site (Lee and Woo eds., 2005)

fluvial deposits consisting of sand and gravel, while the frequency of slope deposits increases toward the upper part. However, in areas close to the Namhan River, the depositional pattern of the river's flooding is evident. Paleolithic artifacts were mainly found in the upper clay layer and lower gravel layer, and were divided into Late and Middle Paleolithic cultural layers.

The artifacts recovered from the Middle Paleolithic cultural layer are dominated by large core tools made by direct striking using cobble, with only minor touching. These artifacts include points, choppers, chopping tools, planes, and side-scrapers, which are few in number.

More than 50 lithic workshops have been identified in the Late Paleolithic cultural layer. More than 30,000 artifacts were recovered in total, including cores, blade cores, microblade cores, flakes, blades, microblades, debitage, hammers, anvils, and other artifacts associated with stone tool making, as well as shaped tools, such as tanged points, side-scrapers, end-scrapers, notches, denticulates, and burins. The raw materials of these stone tools are mostly shale, but also rhyolite, hornfels, obsidian, and crystal.

The site is dated to between 18,000 and 15,000 ka based on absolute dating of the Late Paleolithic cultural layers (Lee and Kim, 2006).

2.1.1.2. Suyanggae Loc. 3

This site was excavated in 2001 in conjunction with the construction of the Suyanggae Prehistory Museum (Lee et al., 2003a), with subsequent excavations in the area surrounding the museum conducted in 2008 and 2011 (Lee et al., 2013a, 2013b). The site is located about 200m north of Suyanggae Loc. 1 at the end of a sloping ridge at an elevation of 150m to 165m (**Fig. 5**).

In terms of the stratigraphy of the site, fluvial deposits are observed in the lower part, while the upper part is influenced by slope deposition. From the top, the site is divided into topsoil, a clay layer, a sandy clay layer, a gravel layer, with the clay layer divided into yellowish brown soil above and yellow with a developed soil wedge below. Artifacts were recovered from the yellowish brown (CL 3) and yellow clay layers(CL 2) and from the sandy clay layer (CL 1).

About 700 artifacts with a stratigraphic context were recovered, most of which were concentrated in CL 3, while CL 1 yielded a small number of artifacts, making it difficult

Fig. 5 Excavation view in Suyanggae Loc. 3 site (Lee et al., 2013b)

Fig. 6 View of Suyanggae Loc. 6 sites (Woo et al., 2018)

Fig. 7 Strata in Suyanggae Loc. 6 site (Woo et al., 2018)

to discuss their characteristics. On the other hand, the lithic composition of CL 2 and CL 3 is similar, with cores, flakes, and debris, all of which are artifacts of the stone tool-making process, and stone tools related to the production of blades and microblades using shale. Shaped tools include choppers and chopping tools, which are heavy-duty tools, and side- and end-scrapers, which are light-duty tools.

The absolute dates (OSL) of the site are 31,500±1,800 BP and 34,200±2,600 BP for CL 3, 37,900±3,600 BP for CL 2, and 38,800±3,400 BP for CL 1.

2.1.1.3. Suyanggae Loc. 6

Suyanggae Loc. 6 was excavated from 2013 to 2015 (Woo et al., 2018). It is located 3.5km downstream from Suyanggae Loc. 1 along the Namhan River. The site is located on a gentle slope at an elevation of 130m and stretches in a a southeast direction from the summit of the mountain in the north (**Fig. 6**).

The stratigraphy of the site consists entirely of slope deposits, with some indications of fluvial deposition. In other words, in the upper part, there are repeated deposits of sandy clay and clay layers associated with slope deposition. Below, the slope deposits are sandy layers, comprising fluvial deposits. There are four cultural layers. Based on the clay layer (CL 2) with a developed soil wedge, the upper layer is CL 1 and the lower layers are CL 3 and CL 4 (**Fig. 7**).

A total of 40,679 artifacts were recovered: 582 from CL 1, 21,744 from CL 2, 7,470 from CL 3, and 10,883 from CL 4. Artifact concentrations were identified in all cultural layers, with many conjoined artifacts. In CL 1, artifacts related to the production of lithics were primarily excavated, and small shaped tools, such as side- and end-scrapers, borers, and burins were recovered. In CL 2, various small tools, such as side- and end-scrapers, notches, borers, burins, points, and denticulates were produced, and a large number of microblade cores reflecting the microblade technique were excavated. In CL 3, quartz-quartzite tools and artifacts related to the blade technique were excavated, and a large number of flakes, blades, and debris were utilized to make tools such as tanged points, side- and end-scrapers, notchs, borers, and burins. In addition, several artifacts were found with regularly spaced stripes on cobble. CL 4, like CL 3, contains both quartz-quartzite tools and artifacts related to the blade technique. In particular, large blades and tanged tools, such as tanged points, were recovered. In all cultural layers, the raw material for lithic making was shale. However, obsidian is found in CL 1 and CL 2, and rhyolite, tuff, and hornfels were also found in CL 2 (**Fig. 8**).

The absolute dates (AMS) of the cultural layers cover the entire Late Paleolithic (Kim et al., 2021). CL 2 is 17,550±80 BP to 20,470±70 BP, CL 3 is 30,360±350 BP to 39,680±390 BP, and CL 4 is 34,870±540 BP to 42,000±340 BP.

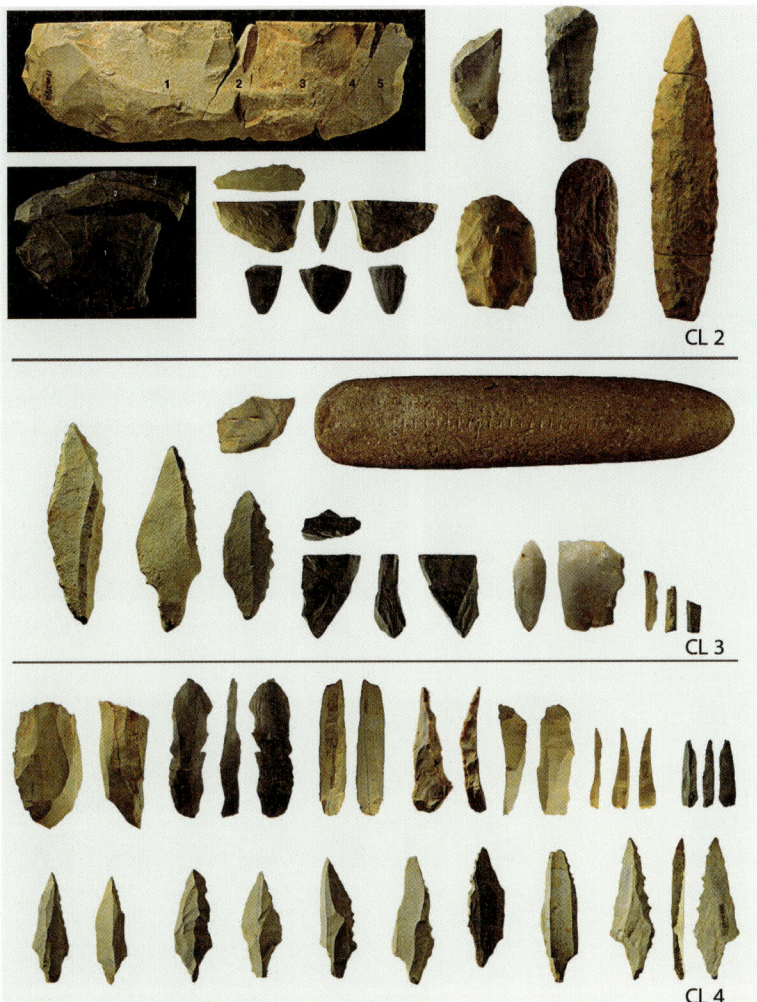

Fig. 8 Important Artifacts in Suyanggae Loc. 6 site (Woo et al., 2018)

2.1.2. Heoncheon-ri Haheoncheon site

This site was excavated in 2011 due to road construction (Sohn et al., 2013). It is located at the end of a ridge leading north from Deokjeol Mountain (780.2m in elevation). To the north of the site is Namhan River, and to the east is Jukryeong Stream, which joins the Namhan River (**Fig. 9**). Looking at the stratigraphy of the site, fluvial deposits are thickly developed in the lower part, and only in the part close to the surface are clay layers deposited by slope deposition. The clay layers are brown, yellowish brown, and reddish yellow, with parts of a soil wedge observed in the yellowish brown clay layers. Artifacts were identified in the yellowish brown clay layer, with only five artifacts being recovered so far.

2.2. Cave and rock shelter sites

2.2.1. Geum Cave site

This site was excavated from 1983 to 1985 as part of a survey of the submerged area of Chungju Dam (Sohn, 1984b, 1985). The entrance to the cave is adjacent to the Namhan River (**Fig. 10**). The Geum Cave slopes from the inside out at about 12 degrees. The cave is 8m in height and over 85m in length, with a width of 7-10m in the wider part.

The cave is divided into 11 sedimentary layers, of which Paleolithic artifacts were found in Layers ㄷ and ㄹ of Layer II, and Layers IV, V, VI and VII. In particular, animal fossils were found in large quantities in Layers IV and VII. Based on this, five cultural layers were established. The artifacts changed from large tools to small tools from the bottom to the top.

The site was dated using ESR on animal fossils, with values of 180,000 ka for CL 2 and 140,000 to 150,000 ka for CL 3. CL 4 and CL 5 belong to the Late Paleolithic, based on the artifacts recovered.

2.2.2. Gunang Cave site

The Gunang Cave site was excavated six times between 1986 and 2013 (Lee et al., 1991, 1999, 2013c, 2015; Lee and Kim, 2007). The site is located in an area where the mountains behind the Namhan River form narrow valleys

Fig. 9 View of Heoncheon-ri Haheoncheon site (Sohn et al., 2013)

Fig. 10 View of Geum Cave site (author's photo)

Fig. 11 View of Gunang Cave site (Lee et al., 2015)

Fig. 12 Strata in Gunang Cave (Lee and Woo eds, 2005)

and ravines. It is located at the midpoint (312m in altitude) of a mountain range that extends south from Samtae Mountain (Fig. 11). The Gunang Cave site is divided into the original cave and the Gunang 1 cave. The Gunang 1 cave is located at the lower eastern end of the original cave and was excavated in 2011. Based on the depositional patterns and artifact frequency within the cave, the original cave is the core site. The original cave measures 5.1m in height, 4.6m in width, and 150m in length at the entrance, and 5.4m in height and 9.5m in width in the center plaza. The sediments are thinner at the entrance and thicker in the center plaza, and the ceiling and floor of the cave become lower as one ventures deeper into the cave.

The stratigraphy of Gunang Cave consists of 10 layers, based on the center plaza. Layers 2, 5, and 7 are lime floor layers, while Layer 3, a mixture of yellowish brown clay and fallen stones, and Layer 6, a mixture of red clay and small fallen stones, are cultural layers. In particular, Layer 3 is the core layer. Layer 3 is subdivided alphabetically from the top, with Layer 3a being a reddish yellow clay, Layer 3b being a yellowish brown clay, Layer 3c being a red clay, Layer 3d being a dark red clay, and Layer 3e being a red silt. Layers 3b and 3c are dominated by clay with fewer fallen rocks and contain a high concentration of animal fossils (Fig. 12).

More than 40 stone tools were recovered from Layer 3, including side-scrapers and burins, and large tools such as picks. Human bones included a phalange, metatarsal and metacapal bones, and a calcaneus (Park et al., 2018). In addition, a number of animal fossils have been identified, including deer (*Cervus* sp.), tiger (*Panthera tigris* L.), bear (*Ursus* L.), badger (*Meles meles*), and monkey (*Macaca* sp.) The frequency of deer was very high. The deer were young and old based on the teeth. On the other hand, pollen

Fig. 13 View of Dwitteul Cave site (Institute of Korean Prehistory, 2011)

analysis showed that Layer 3 was subjected to repeated warm and cold climates, and the charcoal analysis identified tree species that reflected a temperate humid climate in Layers 3a and 3b (Park et al., 2003; Kim et al., 2007). This is in contrast to the survival climate of the animal fossils.

The core cultural layer is Layer 3, which was dated by AMS to be MIS 3 (Lee et al., 2003b, 2015; Yum et al., 2004; Kim et al., 2005). This is a reflection of the date for animal fossils and charcoal samples, as follows the Layer 3b are 35,070 ± 170 BP, 36,230 ± 180 BP, 36,400 ± 900 BP, the Layers 3d and 3e are >51,000 BP.

2.2.3. Dwitteul Cave site

After a surface survey in 1957, excavations were carried out in 2011 due to road construction (Institute of Korean Prehistory, 2011). The site is located at an elevation of 145-148m, under a cliff on the edge of a ridge that leads southwest from Seulum Mountain (671.1m elevation) (Fig. 13). In front of the cave entrance, Jukryeong Stream flows to

Fig. 14 View of Sangsi No. 1 Rock Shelter site (Sohn, 1984a)

the right and joins the Namhan River. The cave deposits are divided into 15 layers, of which Layers 2-5 are cultural layers. The upper cultural layer belongs to the Holocene, while the lower CL 3 and CL 4 belong to the Paleolithic.
In CL 3, stone tools and small animal fossils were excavated; and in CL 4, deer (*Cervus* sp.) were identified.

2.2.4. Sangsi rock shelter site (No. 1 rock shelter)

The Sangsi rock shelter site was discovered in 1974 with two rock shelters, and one additional rock shelter was identified in 1981. Excavations were carried out in 1981 (Sohn, 1984a). Three rock shelters were excavated, of which No. 1 and 3 are associated with the Paleolithic, although evidence for No. 3 is limited (Hong, 2009).
The No. 1 rock shelter corresponds to the end of a branch ridge that slopes southwest from a ridge leading southeast from the top of Gab Mountain (732.4m in elevation), with a view of Maepo Stream to the northwest. The rock shelter measures 2.5m from east to west and 6m from north to south, with about 3.5m of sediment deposited inside (**Fig. 14**).
There are a total of 11 layers at the site. Animal fossils were found in Layers 2, 3, 5, 7, 8, 9, and 11, with the highest number of species found in Layer 2, and deer (*Cervus* sp.) fossils found in all layers. Human bones were found in Layer 5, including a skull, scapula, radius, and ulna. Stone tools were excavated from Layers 5, 7, and 9. Meanwhile, pollen analysis was conducted for each layer, and it was found that the lower Layers 5-11 reflected a cooler climate, while Layers 2 and 3 reflecting a warmer climate.
Uranium-series dating at the site using animal fossils from Layers 5-7 yielded an age of 30,000 BP for Layer 5, 32,000 BP for Layer 6, and 37,000 BP for Layer 7.

3. The results of excavation survey

As mentioned above, eight Paleolithic sites have been excavated in Danyang County, including three localities within the Suyanggae sites. In particular, the Paleolithic sites in Danyang County include open, cave, and rock shelter sites, making it easier to understand the environment and the way humans adapted to it during the Paleolithic. In other words, animal and plant fossils that can be used to reconstruct the paleo-environment have been intensively excavated from the cave and rock shelter sites. In addition, a large number of artifacts based on characteristic lithic techniques have been excavated, mainly at the Suyanggae sites. These aspects provide a very good source for exploring Korean Paleolithic culture (**Fig. 15**).
The results of the survey on the Paleolithic sites in Danyang can be summarized as follows:
First, natural science analyses were conducted on soils and sediments to accumulate data to understand site-formation process. At various sites, soil grain size analysis, magnetic susceptibility analysis, mineral analysis, and absolute dating were conducted, which enabled the interpretation of the origin and age of the sediments and the artifacts in the sediments. Especially, in-depth analysis of the site-formation process is being conducted through soil and sediment analysis at the cave and rock shelter sites. In addition, during the excavation of Paleolithic sites in Danyang, absolute dating was performed on soil samples, charcoal, and bones. The results provided important data about the Paleolithic of the Namhan River Basin and the chronology of Korean Paleolithic culture.
Second, clear evidence has been generated about the behavior of Paleolithic humans. A number of lithic workshops have been identified at Suyanggae Loc. 1 and 6, which provide insights into the process and aspects of stone tool making. Many anvils, hammers, cores, blade cores, microblade cores, flakes, blades, microblades, and debris have been observed in the stone tool production process, and many shaped tools have been identified.
Third, sites and artifacts belonging to the Early and Late Paleolithic have been identified–particularly, sites representing the Late Paleolithic are definitely Suyanggae Loc. 1 and 6, where more than 70,000 artifacts have been excavated. The artifacts recovered from these sites reflect the entire Late Paleolithic and represent Korean Late Paleolithic culture. The sites also constitute a key resource for the study of Paleolithic culture in Northeast Asia and the world.
Fourth, human bones were identified in cave and rock shelter sites. There are very limited cases of Paleolithic human bones excavated in Korea. In this situation, human bones from the Sangsi rock shelter site and Gunang Cave site provide an anthropological approach to paleo-humans in the Korean Peninsula (**Fig. 16**).
Fifth, a number of fossilized animals that lived in Korea

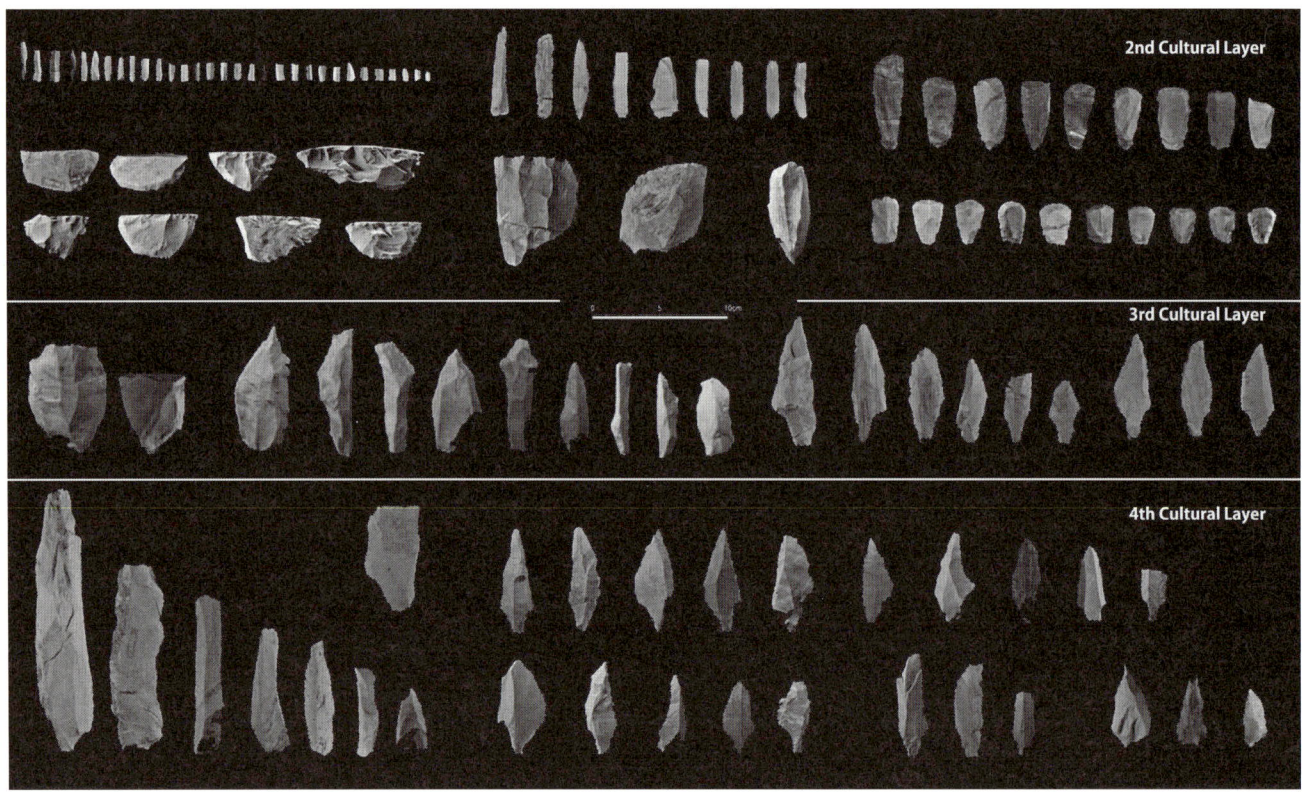

Fig. 15 The main artifacts of Suyanggae Loc. 6 site by cultural stratum (Lee, 2018a)

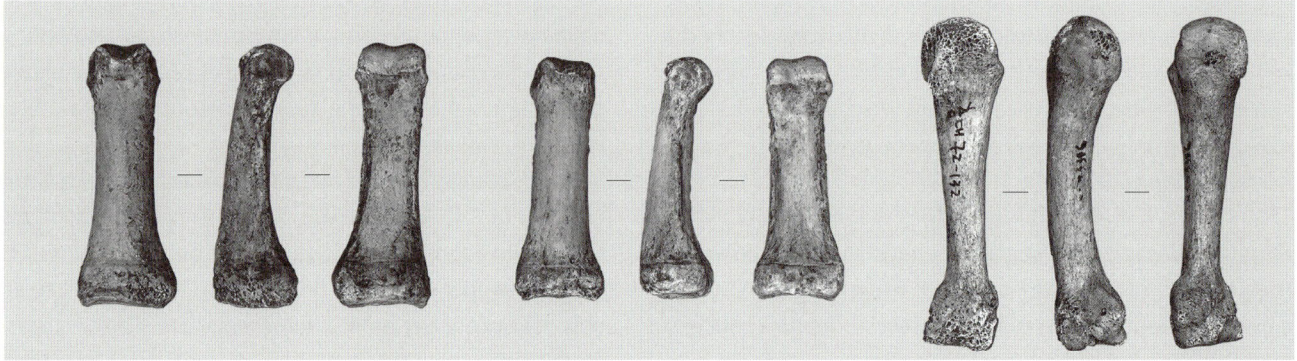

Fig. 16 Human bones excavated from Gunang Cave site (Lee et al., 2013c)

during the Quaternary Pleistocene have been identified, which can be used to infer relative age settings and paleo-environments. Among the animal fossils excavated from cave and rock shelter sites, a large number of extinct species were identified, and the higher the percentage of extinct species, the higher the age of the site, making it possible to establish a relative age between sites with animal fossils. In addition, species analysis of animal fossils can be used to infer paleo-climatic environments. In other words, by analyzing the species of animals that lived in cold and hot climates, we can infer the paleo-climate at the time of the site's formation. This suggests that there was a colder climate in the Late Pleistocene compared to the mid-Pleistocene, but not a drastic change (Cho, 2008). It also allows us to understand the living ecology around the site (Cho, 2002) (**Fig. 17**).

Sixth, like animal fossils, plant fossils have also been studied, providing data useful for reconstructing the Paleolithic environment. Pollen analysis was conducted at Geum and Gunang Cave, Suyanggae Loc. 1, and the presence of various pollens was identified. In addition, tree species were

Fig. 17 An excavation of animal fossils from Gunang Cave site (Lee and Woo eds., 2005)

Fig. 18 Stone with lines engraved at regular intervals in Suyanggae Loc. 6 site (Woo et al., 2018)

identified through analysis of charcoal excavated from the site. In other words, pollen and tree species can be used to identify climate changes during the Paleolithic.

Seventh, bone tools and artwork were reviewed, and their study opened a new chapter in Paleolithic studies. Bone tools were once viewed negatively in the West, but have since been recognized as tools that reflect human behavior through numerous studies and excavations. Therefore, it is significant that the analysis of these tools has pioneered a new field of research. In addition, the discovery of artwork is also a source for understanding the consciousness of Paleolithic humans. In particular, stone carved with lines at regular intervals found in Suyanggae Loc. 6 are of great interest (**Fig. 18**).

As such, the results of the Paleolithic sites in Danyang provide important data on the site formation and time, paleo-climate and paleo-environment, Paleolithic humans and their behavior and ritual systems, and aspects of Paleolithic culture.

4. Future tasks

Most of Korea's Paleolithic sites are concentrated in the Late Pleistocene. In Korea, research on the climatic environment of the Pleistocene is relatively active in the natural sciences– and in the case of the Paleolithic, the focus has been on soils and sediment analysis of sites. However, since most of the excavated sites are open sites, it is common for the sites to be transformed by repeated erosion and deposition as time advances. Therefore, researchers have turned their attention to cave sites, where sedimentation is relatively stable compared to open sites.

At cave sites, fallen rock layers develop in colder climates, while lime floor layers form in warmer, wetter climates. Through this, it is possible to confirm the aspect of climate change. Meanwhile, many animal and plant fossils are found in the sedimentary layers between these layers, which can be used as important data for climate change and paleo-environmental reconstruction. In this respect, the cave site at Danyang has a core value for Korean paleolithic studies. However, the study of animal and plant fossils is still at a basic level, with plant analysis focusing on the identification of species through pollen and tree species analysis, and animal fossils being studied at the level of inferring the climatic environment through the identification and number of species and judgment of extinct species. Therefore, in the future, it is necessary to conduct scientific analyses of animal and plant fossils excavated from cave sites to reconstruct the Pleistocene environment and ecosystem of the Korean Peninsula. In other words, the natural environment and animal and plant systems with which Paleolithic humans interacted in the Korean Peninsula during the Paleolithic must be better understood to gauge their survival methods and stone tool-making activities.

Meanwhile, climate change during the Late Pleistocene caused changes in the ecological environment. In the process, humans created and developed their tools. Several researchers have proposed hypotheses for the development of the stone industry in the Korean Paleolithic (Lee, 2000, 2004, 2015; Yi, 2000, 2001; Jang 2006; Seong, 2006a, 2006b; Choi, 2010; Kim, 2011; Lee, 2012, 2018b). These hypotheses center on the sequential emergence and spread of large tools, including chopping tools and handaxes, quartz-quartzite small tools, and the blade and microblade technique. In general, large stone tools are associated with the Early Paleolithic, quartz-quartzite small tools with the Early to Late Paleolithic, and blade and microblade techniques with the Late Paleolithic.

The Paleolithic artifacts from Danyang are important because they provide a clear picture of the flow of the stone industry in the Late Paleolithic in Korea, which began around 40,000 years ago. In other words, the appearance, development, and decline of the blade and microblade techniques have been clearly shown, and tools completed based on such characteristic lithic techniques have been identified.

CL 4 at Suyanggae Loc. 6 yielded the earliest evidence for Korea's blade techniques, including a number of artifacts related to blade techniques. In particular, large blades have been identified CL 4 and their appearance has been compared to the stone industry in Altai, Russia (Lee, 2015; Sato, 2017; Lee, et al., 2020). However, if the blade technique originated and spread from Altai, at least some of it would have traveled through the northern part of the peninsula, and yet no large blades have been identified earlier than or around the same time as the Suyanggae sites. Therefore, rather than emphasizing the diffusion of the lithic technology and human migration, we should focus on changes in the global ecological environment during MIS 3 (57-29 ka). In other words, it is possible that innovations in blade techniques occurred simultaneously in several places in Northeast Asia, mainly in areas with high-quality raw materials (Lee, 2018a). Based on this, the Suyanggae sites at Danyang can be considered a cutural center related to the blade technique for the Korean Peninsula and Northeast Asia. In addition, the blade technique of the Suyanggae sites, combined with the raw material of shale, survived until the end of the Late Paleolithic, suggesting that it may have spread outside Danyang. Of course, in order to verify the above, it is necessary to closely analyze the results of surveys conducted in North Korea and the surrounding area in Danyang in the future.

A large number of artifacts related to the microblade technique have also been excavated, leading to the classification and supplementation of types according to production methods (Lee, 2002; Otani and Lee, 2020). In addition to the results from Suyanggae Loc. 1, the excavation of Suyanggae Loc. 6 is providing data that can be used to chronologically identify the process from the emergence to the decline of the microblade technique (Lee, 2020). In particular, ongoing research and interpretation of artifacts related to the emergence of the microblade technique is needed, as well as on the decline of blade-related tools, the overwhelming utilization of the microblade technique, and the relationship between lithic techniques and raw materials.

In addition, a closer examination of the site-formation and post-depositional process is needed to overcome the differences in the context of artifact excavation between Suyanggae Loc. 1 and 6, as is the reconstruction of the stone tool-making process through artifacts excavated from workshops within each cultural layer and the interpretation of artifacts that represent human cognitive structures and symbols.

5. Conclusion

The topographic and geologic background of Danyang County has attracted attention since the early days of Korean Paleolithic studies. Since the initial surface survey of the Dwitteul Cave in 1957 until recently, continuous and active surveys have been conducted, and sites from the Early to Late Paleolithic have been identified.

So far, eight sites have been excavated, including three localities at one Suyanggae site, which are open, cave, and rock shelter sites. In addition, about 10 Paleolithic artifact recovery points and a number of cave sites that may have been used in prehistoric times were identified. Among the excavated sites, the Suyanggae sites and the Gunang Cave have been repeatedly excavated since the first excavation, and new research data have been generated.

The results of the excavation of Paleolithic sites in Danyang County to date include (1) the accumulation of data to better understand the site-formation process by conducting natural science analysis of soils and sediments, (2) the identification of data to understand the stone tool-making behavior of Paleolithic humans, (3) the identification of sites and artifacts that can represent the Early and Late Paleolithic, (4) the excavation of human bones from caves and rock shelter sites, (5) the excavation of various types of animal fossils, (6) the identification of plant fossils, and (7) the examination of bone tools and artwork. All of these accomplishments provide important data for understanding site formation and when it occurred, as well as the paleo-climate and paleo-environment, Paleolithic humans and their behavior and ritual systems, and aspects of Korean Paleolithic culture. In particular, the Suyanggae sites and the Gunang Cave site can be evaluated as key sites.

The core value of the Paleolithic in Danyang can be established as a link to climate change and paleo-environmental restoration, and as a representative of the stone culture of the Late Paleolithic in Korea. Therefore, it is necessary to conduct further research, and, in the future, through the results of various natural sciences, to reconstruct the natural environment, flora, and fauna with which Paleolithic humans interacted in Korea to understand their survival methods and activities such as stone tool making. In addition, it is hoped that research will be conducted on the emergence and development of new lithic technologies in the Late Paleolithic, the reconstruction of stone tool making processes, and the interpretation of artifacts that represent human cognitive structures and symbols.

References

Cheongju University Museum. 2000. *Cultural Heritage in Danyang*, Cheongju. (in Korean)

Cho, T.-S., 2002. A Syudy on Paleolithic Animal Bone Remains: Overview and Perspective. *Journal of the Korean Palaeolithic Society* 5, 99-120. (in Korean with English Abstract)

Cho, T.-S., 2008. Faunal change during the Quaternary in Korea. *Journal of the Korean Palaeolithic Society* 17, 63-73. (in Korean with English Abstract)

Choi. S., 2007. Development of Marine and Fluvial Terraces and Related Environmental Changes in the Late Pleistocene along the East Coast of Korea. *Journal of the Geomorphological Association of Korea* 14 (2), 17-28. (in Korean with English Abstract)

Choi, S.-Y., 2010. *A Study on the Paleolithic Culture in Gangwon Province, Korea*. Doctoral Dissertation of Kangwon National

University. (in Korean with English Abstract)

Chungbuk National University Museum. 1980. *Surface Survey Report on Cultural sites in the Submerged Area of Chungju Dam*, Cheongju. (in Korean)

Chungbuk National University Museum and Danyang County. 2001. *Suyanggae site: 5th-7th Excavation*, Cheongju. (in Korean)

Chungbuk National University Museum. 2002. *Surface Survey Report on Limestone Mine Prearranged Development Area for Sungshin Cement in Danyang*, Cheongju. (in Korean)

Chungbuk Research Institute of Cultural Heritage. 2007. *The Site Map of Danyang*, Cheongju. (in Korean)

Hong, H.-S., 2009. *A Study on Sangsi rockshelter no.3, Chungbuk Munwhaje Yeongu* 2, 5-40. (in Korean with English Abstract)

Institute of Korean Prehistory. 2011. *Brief Report on Excavation of Dwitteul Cave Site in the Danyang IC-Daegang Road Construction Section*, Cheongju. (in Korean)

Jang, Y.-J., 2006. *A Study on Techniques and Chronology of Upper-Paleolithic Age in Korea: Centered on the history of the Blade and Micro-blade Artifacts*, Doctoral Dissertation of Pusan National University. (in Korean with English Abstract)

Kim, J.-H., 1958. The Problem of Paleolithic Culture in Korea. *Munrinonjib* 3, 1-25. (in Korean)

Kim, J.-Y., Lee, Y.-J., Yang. D.-Y, Oh, K.-C., Kim, J.-C., 2005. A Research on Formation Process and Chronology of Gunag Cave Deposits in Danyang County, Korea. *Prehistory and Ancient History* 22, 117-130. (in Korean with English Abstract)

Kim, K., Kim., J., Lee, K., Lee, S., Woo, J., Lee, J., Jull, T., 2021. Radiocarbon Ages of Suyanggae Paleolithic sites in Danyang, Korea. *Radiocarbon* 63(5), 1429-1444. https://doi.org/10.1017/RDC.2021.77

Kim, K.-H., Kim, S.-C., Kim, Y.-J., Sohn, B.-H., Lee, Y.-J., Park. W.-K., 2007. Paleoclimate Reconstruction from Species Charcoals Excavated at Gunang Cave, Dayang in central Korea. *Journal of the Korean Palaeolithic Society* 15, 19-41. (in Korean with English Abstract)

Kim, S., 2011. *A Study on the Lithic Assemblages of the Lower-Middle Palaeolithic in Korea*, Doctoral Dissertation of Kangwon National University. (in Korean with English Abstract)

Lee, H.-J., 2000. A Study of Middle Paleolithic Culture in Northeast Asia. *Journal of Korean Ancient Historical Society* 33, 7-48. (in Korean with English Abstract)

Lee, H.-J., 2004. Correlation of Chronology and techno-typological Character of Upper Paleolithic in Korea. *Journal of Korean Ancient Historical Society* 44, 5-22. (in Korean with English Abstract)

Lee, H.-J., 2015. Study of origin and distribution of blade and microblade industry in Korea. *Journal of the Korean Palaeolithic Society* 31, 84-115. (in Korean with English Abstract)

Lee, H.-J., Woo, J.-Y., Lee, Y.-J., 2020. A Study of Blade Technological System of Initial Upper Paleolithic in 4th Cultural Layer of Suyanggae Loc. VI. *Journal of Museum Studies* 39, 83-112. (in Korean with English Abstract)

Lee, J., 2012. Geoarchaeological Chronology of the Paleolithic Sites in the Namhan-River Basin. *Archaeology* 11(1), 5-24. (in Korean with English Abstract)

Lee, J., 2018a. Characteristics and Significations of the Recently Excavated Paleolithic Sites in the Namhan River Basin. *The Peak-San Hakpo* 111, 75-107. (in Korean with English Abstract)

Lee, J., 2018b. Regionality of the Paleolithic Industry in Central Korea. *Archaeology* 17(2), 5-44. (in Korean with English Abstract)

Lee, S., 2020. Emergence of Microblade Culture in Suyanggae paleolithic site. *Journal of Museum Studies* 39, 113-131. (in Korean with English Abstract)

Lee, Y.-J., 1983. *Brief Report on Excavation of Suyanggae Paleolithic Site in Danyang, Brief Report on Excavation of Cultural Relics in the Submerged Area of Chungju Dam: 1983*, Cheongju: Chungbuk National University Museum, 45-66. (in Korean with English Abstract)

Lee, Y.-J., 1984. *Excavation Report on the Suyanggae Paleolithic Site, Synthesis Report on Excavation of Cultural Sites in the Submerged Area of Chungju Dam: Field of Archaeology and Mounds(I)*, Cheongju: Chungbuk National University Museum, 101-186. (in Korean with English Abstract)

Lee, Y.-J., 1985. *Excavation of Suyanggae Site, Report on Extension Excavation of Cultural Sites in the Submerged Area of Chungju Dam*, Cheongju: Chungbuk National University Museum, 101-252. (in Korean with English Abstract)

Lee, Y.-J., Park, S.-J., Woo, J.-Y, 1991. *Gunang Cave(I): Excavation of Pleistocene Site in 1986 and 1988, Tanyang, Korea*, Cheongju: Chungbuk National University Museum. (in Korean)

Lee. Y.-J. and Woo, J.-Y., 1995. Introduce Excavation of Suyanggae Site, Danyang. *Annual Bulletin* 4, Cheongju: Chungbuk National University Museum, 111-121. (in Korean)

Lee, Y.-J., Woo, J.-Y., Lee, J.-D., 1996. Introduce Excavation of Suyanggae Site, Danyang(6th and 7th), *Annual Bulletin* 5, Cheongju: Chungbuk National University Museum, 197-214. (in Korean)

Lee, Y.-J., Cho, T.-S., Kim, J.-Y., Kang, S.-J., 1999. *Progress Report of Kunang Cave Site, Tanyang: 1998 Year Excavation*, Cheongju: Chungbuk National University Museum. (in Korean with English Abstract)

Lee, Y.-J., 2002. Suyanggae Micro-blade Core Industry in Korea. *Journal of the Hoseo Archaeological Society* 6·7, 27-45.

Lee, Y.-J. and Woo, J.-Y. eds., 2005. *Paleolithic Sites of the Jungwon Region, Korea*. Cheongju: Chungbuk National University Museum.

Lee, Y.-J. and Kim, J.-C., 2006. Report on the dating results of the Suyanggae Paleolithic Site. *The paleolithic Culture of the Jungwon Region, Korea*, Institute for Jungwon Culture, Cheongju: Chungbuk National University, 299-306. (in Korean with English Abstract)

Lee, Y.-J. and Kim, H.-R., 2007. *Progress Report of Gunang Cave Site, Danyang: 2007 Year Excavation*, Cheongju: Institute of Korean Prehistory. (in Korean with English Abstract)

Lee, Y.-J., Kim, J.-Y., Woo, J.-Y., Yang, D.-Y., Cho, T.-S., Kong, S.-J., Lee, S.-W., 2003a. *SUYANGGAE Paleolithic Site (Locality III): Test Excavation Report before the Construction of the SUYANGGAE Museum*, Cheongju: Chungbuk National University Museum. (in Korean with English Abstract)

Lee, Y.-J., Kim, J.-C., Cho, T.-S., Yum, J.-K., 2003b. The Carbon Age Dating ad Origin of Travertine Layer in Kunang Cave. *Journal of the Korean Palaeolithic Society* 8, 57-66. (in Korean with English Abstract)

Lee, Y.-J., Woo, J.-Y., Lee, S.-W., Kang, M.-K, Otani, K., Yun, B.-I., Kim, M.-R., 2013a. *Progress Report of Suyanggae Site Loc. III, Danyan: 2008 Year Excavation(9th)*, Cheongju: Institute of Korean Prehistory and Danyang County. (in Korean with English Abstract)

Lee, Y.-J., Woo, J.-Y., Lee, S.-W., Ahn, J.-H., So, D.-Y., Shin, S.-C, Noh, H.-S., 2013b. *Progress Report of Suyanggae Site Loc. III, Danyang: 2011 Year Excavation(10th)*, Cheongju: Institute of Korean Prehistory and Danyang County. (in Korean with English Abstract)

Lee, Y.-J., Woo, J.-Y., Lee, S.-W., Yun, B.-I., Park, J.-Y., 2013c. *Progress Report of Gunang Cave Site, Danyang(IV): 2011 Year Excavation(5th)*, Cheongju: Institute of Korean Prehistory and Danyang County. (in Korean with English Abstract)

Lee, Y.-J., Woo, J.-Y., Lee, S.-W., Seo, D.-W., Park, J.-Y., 2015. *Progress Report of Gunang Cave Site, Danyang(V): 2011 Year Excavation(6th)*, Cheongju: Institute of Korean Prehistory and Danyang County. (in Korean with English Abstract)

Otani, K. and Lee, Y.-J., 2020. Microblade Technology and Working Process of Suyanggae Loc. VI, C.L. 2 in Korea. *Journal of Museum Studies* 39, 161-195. (in Korean with English Abstract)

Park, S.-J., Kim, J.-Y., Lee, Y.-J., Woo, J.-Y., 2018. A Late Pleistocene modern human fossil from the Gunang Cave, Danyang county in Korea. *Quaternary International* 519, 82-91. https://doi.org/10.1016/j.quaint.2018.12.013

Park, W.-K., Kim, Y.-J., Lee, Y.-J., 2003. Species Identification of Charcoals Excavated at the Late Paleolithic Site of Suyanggae, Danyang. *Journal of Conservation Science* 12(1), 26-30. (in Korean with English Abstract)

Sato, H., 2017. Recent advances of the Initial Upper Paleolithic study in Asia: Estimating the lithic assemblages of third and forth cultural layers in the Locality 6 of the Suyanggae Site. *Journal of the Korean Palaeolithic Society* 35, 5-20. (in Japanese with Korean and English Abstract)

Seong, C., 2006a. A Comparative and Evolutionary Approach to the Korean Paleolithic Assemblages. *Journal of Korean Ancient Historical Society* 51, 5-41. (in Korean with English Abstract)

Seong, C., 2006b. Structure and Evolution of Late Paleolithic Assemblages in Korea. *Journal of The Korean Archaeological Society* 59, 4-37. (in Korean with English Abstract)

Sohn, M.-S., Shin, S.-C., Lee, S.-W., 2013. *Report on the Excavation of Heoncheon-ri Haheoncheon Site, Danyang*, Cheongju: Institute of Korean Prehistory and Danyang County. (in Korean with English Abstract)

Sohn, P., 1984a. *Early Man at Sangsi Rockshelter No.1*, Laboratory of Prehistory, Seoul: Yonsei University. (in Korean with English Abstract)

Sohn, P., 1984b. *Early man in Prehistoric Korea-Lower Paleolithic to Bronze Age culture: The case of Kumgul Cave Site at Todam-ri, Maepo-up, Tanyang-Gun Chungchongpukto, Synthesis Report on Excavation of Cultural Sites in the Submerged Area of Chungju Dam: Field of Archaeology and Mounds(I)*, Cheongju: Chungbuk National University Museum, 15-99. (in Korean with English Abstract)

Sohn, P., 1985. *1985 Excavation of Kum Cave Site, Report on Extension Excavation of Cultural Sites in the Submerged Area of Chungju Dam*, Cheongju: Chungbuk National University Museum, 5-100. (in Korean with English Abstract)

Woo, J.-Y., Lee, S.-W., Ahn, J.-H., Yun, B.-I., Park, J.-M., Otani, K., Kim, M.-R., Han, S.-C., Jang, H.-G., Choi, D.-H., 2018. *Report on the Excavation of Suyanggae Site(Loc. I and VI), Danyang*, Cheongju: Institute of Korean Prehistory. (in Korean with English Abstract)

Yi, S., 2000, For chronology and stratigraphy of Korean palaeolithic. *Journal of The Korean Archaeological Society* 42, 1-22. (in Korean with English Abstract)

Yi, S., 2001, Middle-Upper Paleolithic Transition in Korea: A Brief Review. *Journal of the Korean Palaeolithic Society* 4, 17-24.

Yum, J.-G., Kim, J.-C., Cho, T.-S., Kim, J.-Y., Lee, Y.-J., Kim, I.-C., 2004. Age dating and paleoenvironmental changes of the Kunang cave paleolithic site. *Journal of the Geological Society of Korea* 40 (2), 203-211. (in Korean with English Abstract)

A review of the Late Pleistocene hominid fossil remains in the southern part of Korea

Sun-joo PARK[1], Yung-jo LEE[2]

[1] Professor Emeritus, Chungbuk National Univeristy, Institute of Human Evolutionary Studies, Korea ; sjpark@cbnu.ac.kr
[2] Institute of Korean Prehistory (IKP), Korea

ABSTRACT

In South Korea, cave human fossils are associated with the *late Homo sapiens* discovered from the Sangsi rock shelter, Hungsu Cave, and Gunang Cave. Among them, Gunang cave man fossils were interpreted as a descendent of *Homo sapiens*. By means of correlation with AMS datings of cervid bone fossils associated with human fossil bones, *Homo sapiens* of Gunang cave arrived and scattered around Danyang County at about 30,000–40,000 yr BP, and the Gunang man and Sangsi rock shelter man likely inhabitated the area in the Early Upper Paleolithic, exhibiting similar social activity of athleticism and reflecting a hunting-gathering lifestyle. In contrast, the Hungsu Juvenile, Cheongju City, was assumed to be a late Upper Paleolithic man in the Korean Peninsula. Suyanggae Paleolithic sites and Paleolithic humans flourished in the early Upper to late Upper Paleolithic culture near the paleo-Namhan River valley.

국문 초록

한반도 남부지역의 중기 및 후기 구석기시대의 고인류 화석은 동굴유적(구낭굴, 두루봉)과 바위그늘(상시) 유적에서 발견되었다. 방사성탄소 연대측정법을 통해 구낭굴 연대가 30,000–40,000년 전으로 나타나 후기 갱신세 말의 구낭굴에 살았던 고인류는 충북 단양지역에서 흩어져 살았던 호모사피엔스로 구낭굴과 상시 바위그늘 고인류는 한반도 후기구석기 초기의 고인류 중 한 무리이며, 청주의 흥수아이는 한반도 후기구석기 말기의 고인류 중 한 무리로 가늠된다. 단양지역의 후기 갱신세에 살던 구낭굴 출토 고인류와 상시 출토 고인류는 비슷한 사회적 활동능력을 지녔으며, 이들은 단양지역의 한데유적인 수양개 유적 등에 살던 고인류처럼 수렵채집 생활을 하였으며 한반도 남부지역의 후기구석기 초기의 문화 주인공으로 가늠된다.

Keywords : cave human fossils, late *Homo sapiens*, Sangsi rock shelter, Hungsu Cave, Gunang Cave, Suyanggae Paleolithic site, upper Paleolithic

1. Introduction

When did *Homo sapiens* first appear in the Korean Peninsula, especially in the southern part of Korea? Although the best contemporary prospects for breakthrough discoveries lie in genetic research, traditional disciplines, like human anatomy and paleo-osteology, offer tantalizing clues. The morphological study of Pleistocene hominid fossils especially should still be considered a useful method for answering this question.

The discovery of hominid fossils contributes to the reconstruction of Middle and Upper Paleolithic culture in Korea. The first finding of Pleistocene hominid fossil remains in Korea was reported during the mid-1970s. From this period, a total of eight caves, one rock shelter, and one open site yielded hominid fossils from the Korean Peninsula (Park, 1991, 1993, 2003, 2006; Norton, 2000; Park et al., 2002; Kuzmim et al., 2014; Park et al., 2018) (Fig. 1). Reports on such findings are available; however, fossil remains in the northern part of Korea are inaccessible at present time. Therefore, a comprehensive analysis and observation can be conducted on the basis of currently available reports rather than the direct comparison of unattainable fossils. Studies such as tool type and dating method show that all sites yielding fossils remains might belong to the Upper Paleolithic.

In this paper, the general features of Late Pleistocene humans residing on the southern part of the Korean Peninsula are described. The typical Late Pleistocene hominid fossil remains in the southern part of Korea have come from the Sangsi rock shelter, Hungsu Cave, and Gunang Cave. All of these locations are limestone sites, indicating the unique environment of Late Pleistocene humans in Korea, particularly associated with animals hunted near sites.

2. The Pleistocene sites yielding hominid fossil remains in Korea

Hominid fossils in Korea have been classified as early *Homo sapiens* and late *Homo sapiens*. Early *Homo sapiens* are reported from Ryo'kpo (Kim et al., 1985a), Sungrisan (Institute, 1978), and Yonggok (Chon et al., 1986) Caves in the north, whereas fossils associated with late *Homo sapiens* were discovered from the Sangsi rock shelter (Sohn, 1981, 1987; Sohn, 1988) and Hungsu Cave (Park et al., 1990; Lee et al., 1991) in the south. Mandal-ri (Kim et al., 1985b) and Gumchon (Jang et al., 1988) in the north might also be classified as late *Homo sapiens*. Phylogenetic classification of Hawdae Cave remains (Jang, 2002) in the north are not yet available. In the south, new fossil remains have been reported from Gunang Cave (Lee et al., 2007; Park et al., 2013). Although the dates of Gunang are the same as those of Ryonggok, it is just classified as *Homo sapiens* only (Table 1).

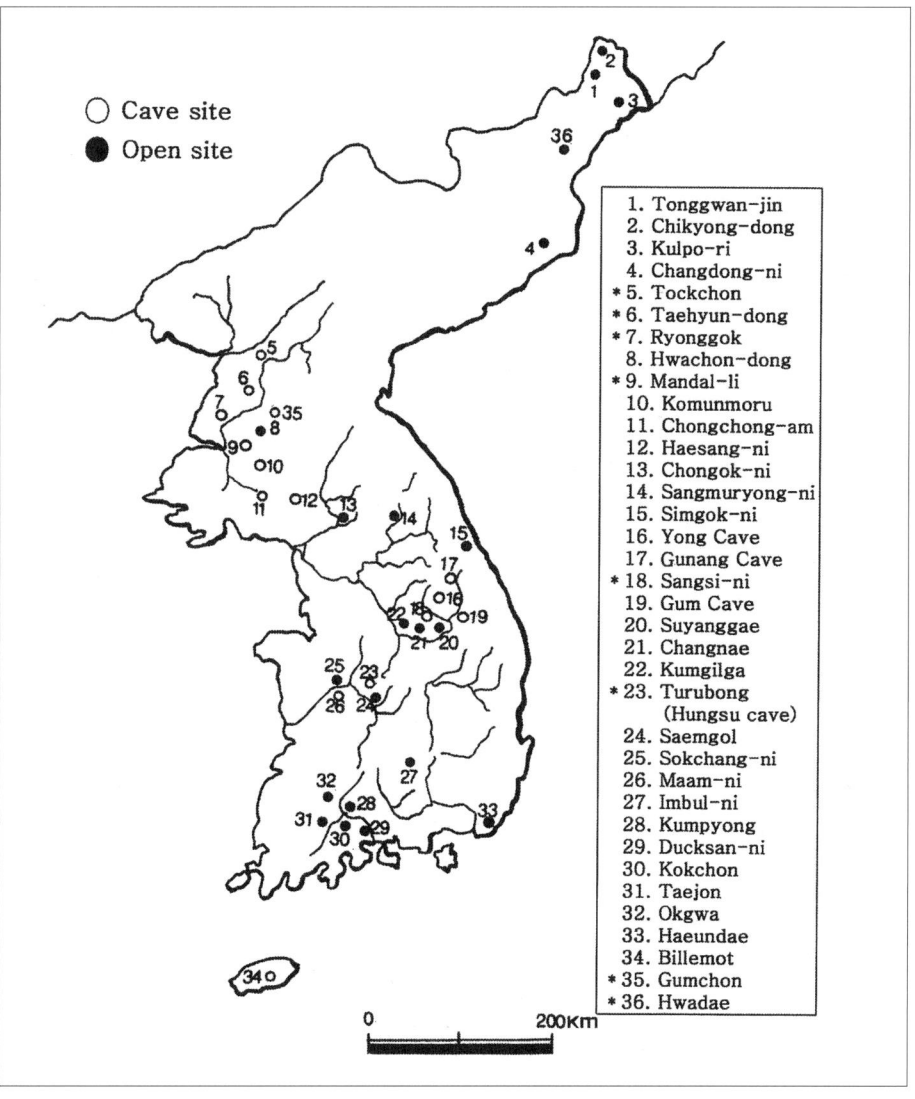

Fig. 1 Paleolithic Sites in Korea
* Hominid Fossil Yielding Sites (Reprinted from Park Sunjoo, 2006, The Upper Pleistocene Hominid Fossils in Korea)

Table 1 Pleistocene Sites Yielding Hominid Fossils in Korea

Site	Type		Specimen	Date	Reference
Northern Part of korea					
Yonggok	cave	layer 9 10 11 12	skull, mandibles skull, mandibles, femur parts of cranium, mandible, humerus, innominate, femurs maxilla	46-48 ky (U-Th)	Chon et al., 1986
Ryokpo	cave		part of cranium	middle pleistocene	Kim et al., 1985a
Sungrisan	cave		mandible, molars	late m. pleistocene-early l. Pleistocene	Institute, 1978.
Mandal	cave		parts of cranium, mandible, humerus, femur, innominate	late l. pleistocene	
Gumchon	cave			early l. pleistocene	Jang et al., 1988
Hawdae	cave			300 ky (FL) ?	Jang, 2002
Southern Part of Korea					
Sangsi	rock shelter		parts of skull, sacpular, radius	30 ky (gamma ray)	Sohn, 1981
Hungsu	cave		an almost complete juvenile skeleton	40 ky	Lee et al, 1991
Gunang	cave		big toe, talus	40-50 ky	Park et al., 2017

3. Late Pleistocene hominid fossil remains in the southern part of Korea

Late Pleistocene hominid fossil remains in the southern part of Korea have been discovered from Sangsi rock shelter, Hungsu Cave, and Gunang Cave. These sites are situated in the limestone regions of Chungbuk Province.

3.1. Sangsi fossil remains

In the southern part of Korea, hominid fossil remains were initially found in the Sangsi limestone rock shelter (1974) and were excavated in 1980. This site exhibits 11 geological layers, with hominid fossils found in Layer 5 (**Fig. 2**). Also, some stone tools (choppers) and bone tools have been discovered together. By the gamma-ray dating method, the age of the fossil-containing layer is approximately 30,000 BP (Sohn, 1987, 1988).

From this site, parts of a left parietal bone, part of an occipital bone, a right scapula, a left radius, and a right ulna were found. The main characteristics of Sangsi fossils can be found in the axillary border of the scapula. The shape of the axillary border of the scapula is similar to that of early *Homo sapiens*, such as the Skhul fossil, which exhibits bisulate (**Fig. 3**). This means that Paleolithic humans in Korea exhibited social activity similar to that of living athletes. In 1987, the excavator of this rock shelter named this fossil *Homo sapiens sangsiensis* (Sohn, 1987).

Fig. 3 Sangsi scapular showing Bisulate Axillary Border

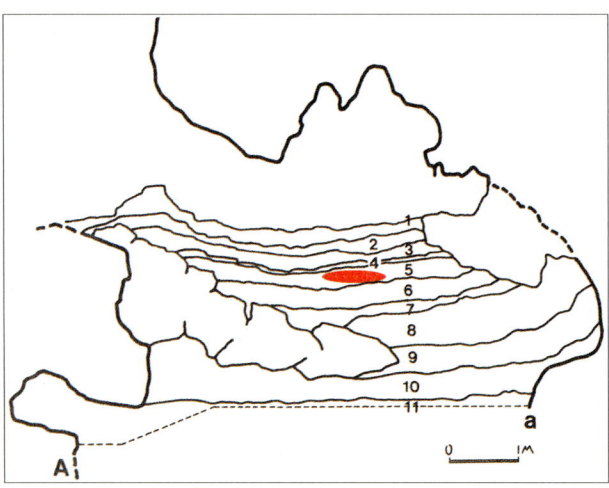
Fig. 2 Cross-Section of the Rock shelter (● : Layer Yielding Hominid Fossil)

3.2. Hungsu juvenile fossil

Hungsu Cave, a part of the Turupong limestone cave complex, yielded a partially complete juvenile skeleton in 1982 (**Fig. 4, 5, 6**). This cave consists of 12 geological layers, with the hominid fossil coming from Layer 3 (**Fig. 7**).

Although the excavator believed that the age of the site might date to 40,000–50,000 BP based on the stone tool type (**Fig. 8**) and depositional layer, the true age remains uncertain; that said, it likely belonged to the late Upper Pleistocene period (Lee, 2011).

The age of the Hungsu child is 5-6 years old. Although the Hungsu child is differentiated by the superiority in the size of the skull, cranial length, height, and, most significantly, a greater parietal arc, the child falls within the modern juvenile

Fig. 4 A Distant View of Turupong Cave Complex

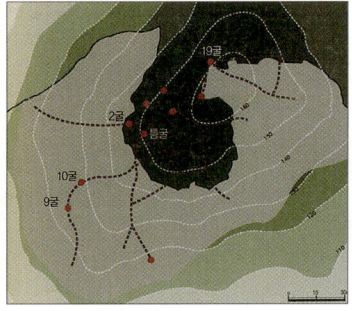
Fig. 5 Distributional Map of Turupong Cave Complex

Fig. 6 Hungsu Juvenile Skeleton

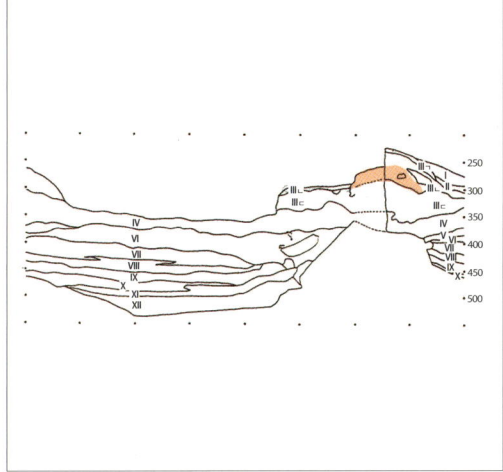
Fig. 7 Cross-Section of Hungsu Cave Ⅲㄴ. Layer Yielding Hominid Fossil

Fig. 8 Stone tools from Hungsu Cave

range of variation, metrically and non-metrically.

3.3. Gunang Cave man

Gunang Cave, a limestone cave, was one of the living sites of Late Pleistocene hominids in Korea. The cave is located in Danyang County, Chungbuk Province, in the middle region of the Korean Peninsula (Fig. 9). From 1986 to 2013, Gunang cave was excavated five times, revealing 13 geological layers and containing three cultural layers (Lee et al., 1991; Lee et al., 2007; Lee et al., 2013) (Fig. 10).

Among the three cultural layers, CL 3 is important due to the presence of the Late Pleistocene man and fauna, including cervid, felid, and urusid bone remains. In addition, and significantly, stone tools and man-made bone fragments were found in this layer (Fig. 10). Most ^{14}C dating ages of CL 3 have been examined by the cervid bone samples (Kim et al., 2011).

Hominid bones, such as a metatarsal, a talus, and foot phalanges, have also been found between 120-127cm in depth in this layer (Park et al., 2013), which date to between 28,000–38,000 BP by the AMS dating method (Kim et al., 2011; Lee et al., 2013). Also, bones came from the same layer, meaning they may have belonged to the same individual (Fig. 11, 12).

Fig. 9 Enterance View of Gunang Cave

First of all, studies have focused on the MT1 to obtain general anthropological information about the Late Pleistocene man in Korea. After examining the first metatarsal bone (big toe) from Gunang Cave, and based on the shape and size of MT1, the Gunang Cave man can be placed in the morphological spectrum of an adult male. Based on the size and shape of MT1, the examination demonstrated that the bones from Gunang Cave must have belonged to a man who was approximately 163-169cm in height (Byers et al., 1989).

The date of this site shows that the ^{14}C ages of CL 3 containing animal bones range from 28,910 ± 200 yr to 48,090 ± 1050 yr BP (Park et al., 2019). Recently, average

Chapter 3. Late Paleolithic Site of Suyanggae

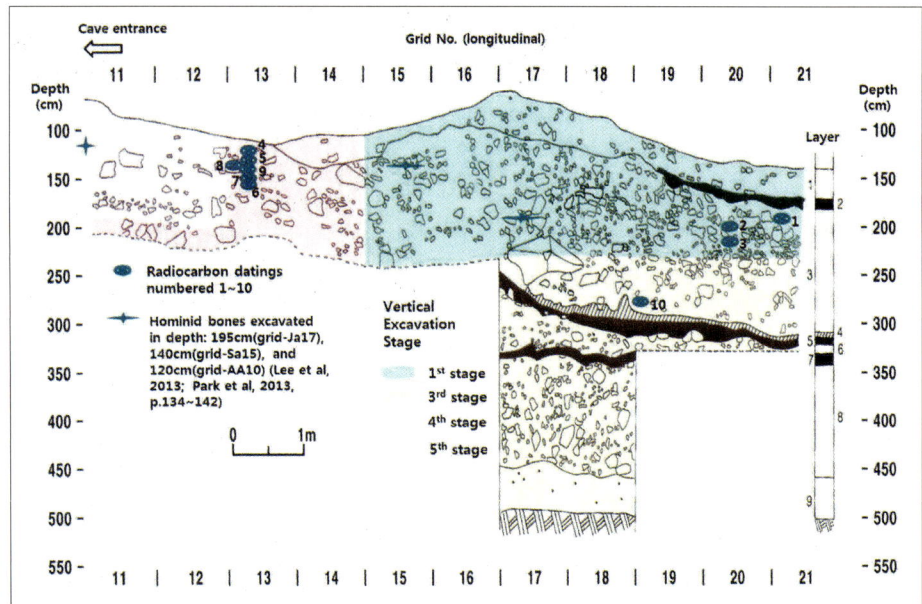

Fig. 10 Geological Section-Map of Gunang Cave

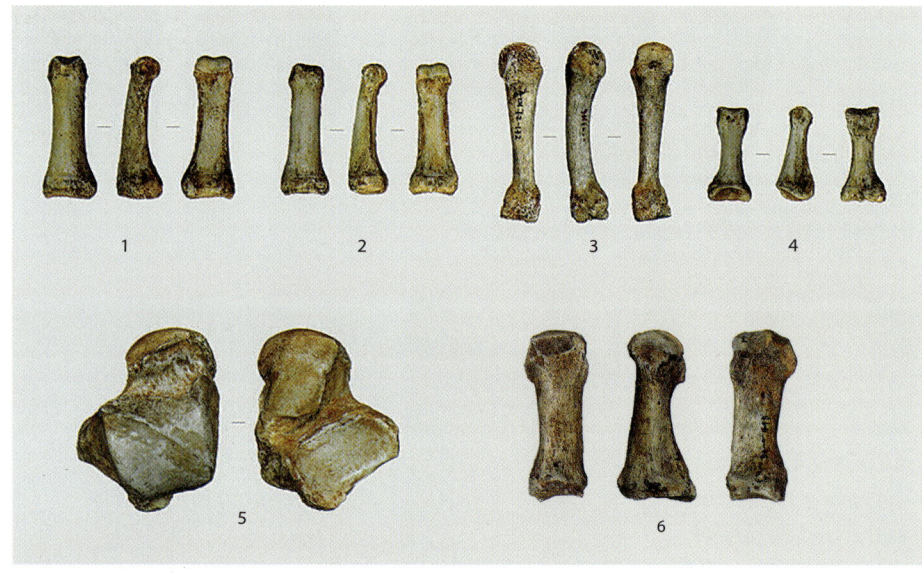

Fig. 11 Human Bones from Gunang Cave

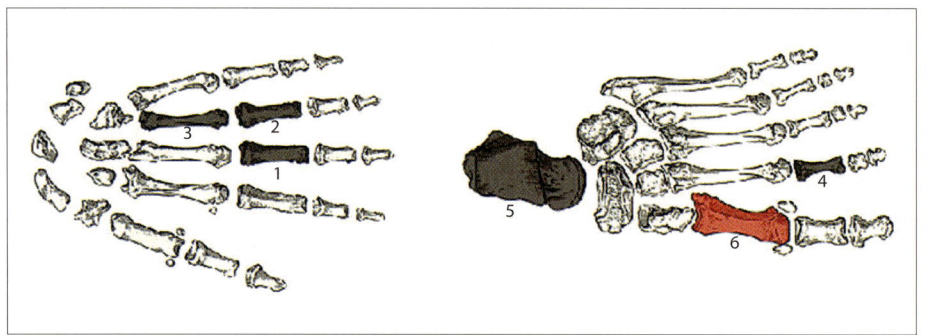

Fig. 12 Bones Belonged to The Same Hand and Foot

3.4. Some questions on the origin of *homo sapiens* in Korea

In Danyang county, two well-known Upper Paleolithic sites – Suyannggae open site and Sangsi rock shelter site – are approximately 10km away from the Gunang Cave site. Gunang Cave's age is nearly the same as CL 3 of Loc. 6 of Suyanggae site. Mechanical influences on the bone are often both localized and functionally interpretable. Also, mechanically based analyses can be valuable in reconstructing past behavioral patterns from skeletal materials. The social activity of Pleistocene man in Korea can be evaluated by using bone materials such as the scapula from the Sangsi rock shelter.

Although no hominid fossils appeared from CL 3 of Loc. 6 of the Suyanggae site, during 2013 and 2015 excavations, many cultural remains, such as tanged points, and a pebble-stone tool with engraved lines, were uncovered. Based on these discoveries, the excavator believed that the age of the site was around 45,000 yr BP (Lee et al., 2014: Woo et al., 2017; Sato, 2017).

Based on these dating results, hominid fossils from the Gunang and Sangsi sites can be classified as representing Early Upper Paleolithic *Homo sapiens*, and Hungsu Juvenile bones as representing Late Paleolithic *Homo sapiens*, from the southern region of Korea. It is possible that many Late Pleistocene hominid living sites would have been disbursed around Danyang

radiocarbon ages of human bones obtained by calibrating the depth (grid-JA1) of CL 3 in Gunang Cave were computed to 43,000 cal yr BP, ranging between 40,900 and 44,900 cal yr BP (Park et al., 2021, corrigendum to our paper) (**Fig. 13**).

County and may have exhibited similar social activities of athleticism and reflected a more hunting-gathering lifestyle. The overall cranial characteristics of the Late Pleistocene hominid fossils in Korea exhibit similar connections to the

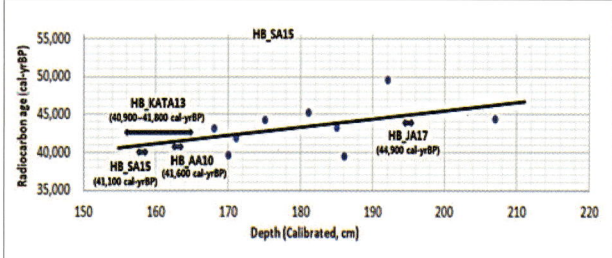

Fig. 13 Average radiocarbon ages of human bones (HB) by calibrating depth of the layer 3 in Gunang Cave

morphological spectrum of *Homo sapiens*. Therefore, most, if not all, Late Pleistocene hominid fossils in Korea should be classified as a single specices, *Homo sapiens*, who flourished in the Upper Paleolithic culture in the Korean Peninsula (Park, 2006, 2013).

Recent advances in paleoanthropological, geological, molecular, biological, and human behavioral research provide some clues about the emergence and dispersion of modern humans. There is an emerging consensus among many western paleoanthropologists that evidence from the Far East must be reconciled with the emerging unified theory of modern human origins. But if the dual African-Asian ancestry hypothesis is more acceptable, then the unique Asian features could not have been inherited from the Peking Man (Park, 2013) Recent archaeological, geological, and hominid fossil evidence in Korea, China, and Japan may shed some light on the emergence and dispersion of modern humans in the Far East.

4. Conclusion

The age of Gunang Cave by the AMS dating method demonstrates that it is likely Late Pleistocene humans who descended from *Homo sapiens* who arrived and scattered around Danyang County about 30,000–40,000 yr BP. Up until now, it has been plausible to suggest that the Gunang and Sangsi rock shelter men should have been Early Upper Paleolithic humans and the Hungsu Juvenile should have been a late Upper Paleolithic human in the Korean Peninsula. Also, it is plausible that the Gunang and Sangsi men may have been part of a group of Late Pleistocene hominids who might have scattered around Danyang County, exhibiting similar social activity of athleticism and reflecting a hunting-gathering lifestyle similar to that of Suyanggae man, who flourished in Early Upper Paleolithic culture.

Acknowledgement

The authors are greatly indebted to both the Museum of Chungbuk National University, Municipal Administration Office of Danyang County, and the Institute of Korean Prehistory for funding a series of excavations and academic reporting on the Hungsu and Gunang Cave sites. We pay tribute to the late Professor Sohn Pokee for the recovery of the Sangsi rock shelter.

References

Byers, S.N., Churchill, S., Curran, B., 1989. Determination of stature from metatarsals. *American Journal of Physical Anthropology* 79, John Wiley & Sons Inc., 275-279.

Cheon, J.H., Yoon J., Kim, G.S., Yun, J.G., 1986. *Yonggok Cave Site*, Pyungyang: Kim Ilsung University Press. (In Korean)

Institute of Archaeology. 1978. *An Excavation Report of Sungrisan Site, Tockch'on* (Bulletin of Excavation Report 11), Pyungyang: Science and Encyclopedia Publishing Co. (In Korean)

Jang, U.J., Kang M.W., 1988. Hominid Fossil from Gumchon Cave. *Choson GoGo YonGu* 1, 6-10. (In Korean)

Jang, U.J., 2002. Hominid Fossil in Lava: Hawdae Man. *Chosun GoGo YonGu* 124, 2-7. (In Korean)

Keates, S.G., 2010. The Chronology of Pleistocene Modern Humans in China, Korea, and Japan. *Radiocarbon* 52(2-3), 428-465.

Kim, J.Y., Lee, Y.J., Yang, D.Y., K, C., Kim, J.C., 2006. A research on formation process and chronology of Gunang Cave deposits in Danyang County, Korea. In Lee, Y.J. ed., *The Paleolithic Culture of Jungwon Region, Korea*, Institute for Jungwon Culture, Chungbuk National University. (In Korean)

Kim, K.J., Hong, W., Park, J.H., Woo, H.J., Hodgins, G., Jull, A.J.T., Lee, Y.J., Kim, J.Y., 2011. Development of Radiocarbon Dating Method for Degraded Bone Samples from Korean Archaeological Sites. *Radiocarbon* 53(1), 129-135.

Kim, S.K., Kim, K.Y., Baek, K.H., Jang, U.J., Sea, G.T., 1985. A excavation report of Daehyundong site at Yeokpo Region. *The Exacavation Reports of Cave Sites in Pyungyang Region: Archaeological Report 14,* Pyungyang: Science and Encyclopedia Publishing Co. (In Korean)

Kuzmin, Y.V., Keates S.G., 2014. Direct Radiocarbon Dating of Late Pleistocene Hominids in Eurasia: Current Status, Problems, and Perspectives. *Radiocarbon* 56(2), 753-766.

Lee, Y., Park, S.J., Woo, J.Y., 1991. *Excavation Report of Gunang Cave Site, Danyang (I)–1986 · 1988 Year Excavation–*, Chungbuk National University Museum. (In Korean)

Lee, Y.J., Park, S.J., 1991. *An Excavation Report of Hungsu Cave at Turupong, Cheongwon*, Chungbuk National University Museum. (In Korean)

Lee, Y.J., Kim, H.R., 2007. *Progress Report of Gunang Cave Site, Danyang–2007 Year Excavation–*, Institute of Korean Prehistory. (In Korean with English abstract)

Lee, Y.J., 2011. Grotte de Heungsu-Gul(Drubong) In: de Lumley H., Lee Y.J., Park Y.C., Bae K. eds., *Les Industries du Paleolithique Ancien de Coree du Sud dans Leur Conttexte Straigraphique et Paleoecologique*, Paris: CNRS Edition, 286-297.

Lee, Y.J., Woo, J.Y., Lee, S.W., Yun, B.I., Park, J.Y., 2013. *Progress Report of Gunang Cave Site, Danyang(IV)–2011 Year Excavation(5th)*, Danyang County: Institute of Korean Prehistory, 134-142. (In Korean with English abstract)

Lee, Y.J., Woo, J.Y., Suh, H.S., Lee, S.W., An, J.H., Park, J.M., 2014. New Findings from Loc. VI. Suyanggae Site, Korea. Recent Discoveries and Interpretations from Korean Paleolithic Sites (V). *International Symposium on Paleoanthropology in Commemoration of the 85th Anniversary of the First Skull of Peking Man* 2014. 10. 20-27, Beijing, China. (In English)

Norton, C.J., 2000. The current state of Korean paleoanthropology. *Journal of Human Evolution* 38(6), 803-25.

Park, S.J., Lee Y.J., 1990. A new discovery of the Upper Pleistocene child's skeleton from Hungsu cave (Turubong Cave Complex), Chongwon, Korea. *The Korean Joural of Quaternary Research* 4(1), 1-14. (in English)

Park, S.J., 1991. Current aspects and problems on the origin of *Homo sapiens*. *Bak Mul Kwan Ki Yo* 7, Dankuk University Museum, 121-146. (in English)

Park, S.J., 1993. Brief Comment: The Plesitocene Hominid Fossils in Korea. *GoGo Misul Saron* 3, 8-92. (In Korean)

Park, S.J., 2003. The Pleistocene Hominids in Korea. *Journal of Korean Paleolithic* 7, 41-51. (In Korean)

Park, S.J., 2006. L'hominide du Pleistocene superieur en Corée. *L'anthropologie* 110, 162-174. (In French)

Park, S.J., 2013. *Trace of Humankind*, Gaeshin Publishing Corp.

Park, S.J., Lee, Y.J., Lee, Y.M., 2013. Analysis of Human bones from Gunang Cave. In Lee, Y.J., Woo, J.Y., Lee, S.W., Yun. B.I., Park, J.Y., *Progress Report of Gunang Cave Site, Danyang(IV) –2011 Year Excavation(5th)*, Danyang County: Institute of Korean Prehistory, 134-142.

Park, S.J., Kim, J.Y., Lee, Y.J., Woo, J.Y., 2019. A Late Pleistocene modern human fossil from the Gunang Cave, Danyang county in Korea. *Quaternary International* 519, 82-91.

Park, S.J., Kim, J.Y., Lee, Y.J., Woo, J.Y., 2021. Corrigendum to A Late Pleistocene modern human fossil from the Gunang Cave, Danyang county in Korea. *Quaternary International* 519, 82-91.

Sato, H., 2017. Recent Advances of the Initial Upper Paleolithic Study in Asia : Estimating the lithic assemblages of third and fourth cultural layers in the Locality 6 of the Suyanggae Site. *Journal of Korean Paleolithic* 37, 5-20.

Sohn, P.K., 1981. A preliminary report of Sangsi Rockshelter. *The Dawn of Ancient History of Korea*, Cheongju: Chungbuk National University. (In Korean)

Sohn, P.K., 1987. *Homo sapiens sangsiensis*. *L'Anthropologie* 89(1), 147-150.

Sohn, S.Y., 1988. Contribution a Etude des Restets des Os Parietaus Deecouverts a Sangsi, Coree du Sud. *Archaeological and Anthtopological Bulletin of Memoir for Professor Sohn Pokee*. (In French)

Woo, J.Y. et al., 2017. Excavation Report of Suyanggae Locality 6 in the Upper Paleolithic. Presented Paper to *the 3rd ASQUA Conference 2017*, Jeju, Korea.

Chapter 4.
Culture of the Holocene Transition

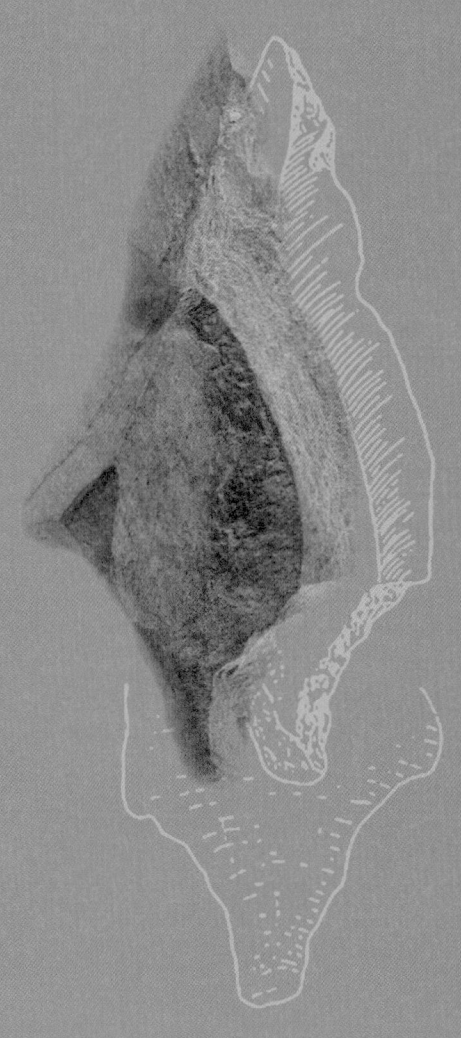

Evidence of a pointed bifacial flake in Tool Workshop 12 ka at the Tingkayu site, Sabah, Malaysia

Mokhtar SAIDIN

Former Director, Centre For Global Archaeological Research, University Sains Malaysia, Malaysia ; mokhtarsaidin@gmail.com

ABSTRACT

Bifacial stone tools were produced in Malaysia more than 1.83 ma, represented by the handaxes and bifacial pebble tools found at the Bukit Bunuh site, Lenggong, Perak. Bifacial pebble tools then became dominant in all prehistoric sites in Malaysia and even in Southeast Asia from 14–6 ka, which are known as the Hoabinhian culture. Meanwhile, microliths were only present during the Neolithic. However, research at the Tingkayu site has revealed its own uniqueness. At this site, the only one in the country, a pointed bifacial stone tool manufacturing workshop, dating to 12 ka, has been found. Therefore, this article focuses on this site and its contribution to Paleolithic culture in the Late Pleistocene.

국문초록

말레이시아에서 생산된 양면가공 석기는 183만 년 이전부터 시작되었으며, 페락 렝공(Lenggong, Perak) 지역 부킷 부누(Bukit Bunuh) 유적에서는 주먹도끼와 양면가공 자갈돌 석기가 대표적이다. 양면가공된 자갈돌 석기는 약 1.4만-6천 년 전부터 말레이시아 전 지역과 동남아시아에 이르는 선사유적에서 우점하고 있으며, 이른바 호아비니안(Hoabinhian) 문화로 잘 알려진 반면, 소형석기는 신석기 동안에만 출현한다. 말레이시아 팅카유 유적에서는 약 1.2만 년 전의 나뭇잎 모양 첨두형 양면가공(Pointed Bifacial) 격지 제작기술이 유일하게 나타나고 있다. 팅카유 유적의 첨두형 석기는 원재료, 어란형 형태, 전면 가공한 격지기술, 크기를 기준으로 볼 때 일본의 노가와(Nogawa), 매하라(Maehara) 유적(약 1만-1.8만 년 전)의 첨두형 석기와 동일한 것으로 간주된다. 말레이시아 내에서 동일 시기에 속하는 구아 하곱 빌로(Gua Hagop Bilo), 만술리(Mansuli), 구아 사망 부아(Gua Samang Buat) 등의 다른 유적에서는 첨두형 석기가 왜 발견되지 않는지에 대한 문제제기가 있는데, 팅카유 유적은 호수 주변의 삶을 영위하는 가운데 기술적으로 고립되었을 가능성을 암시한다.

Keywords : Late Pleistocene Culture, Pointed bifacial stone tool, Late Palaeolithic workshop, Tingkayu Site

1. Introduction

The Tingkayu site is located in eastern Sabah, bounded by longitude 117°4' to 118°5' E and latitude 4°40' to 4°45' N. An open site, Tingkayu was first discovered in 1975 by John Morris, a British soil scientist, who reported the discovery of a special stone tool known as a pointed bifacial type of flake tool. Peter Bellwood then carried out a detailed study involving excavation, artifact analysis, and paleoenvironmental reconstruction, and proposed a relative dating of the site to around 28–18 ka, especially at the TIN 2 site (Fig. 1). Bellwood (1988), in his studies in the Tingkayu Valley, discovered and mapped 11 sites named TIN 1 to TIN 11. However, his excavations focused more on the TIN 2 site, where he found a pointed bifacial flake tool and gave a relative dating.

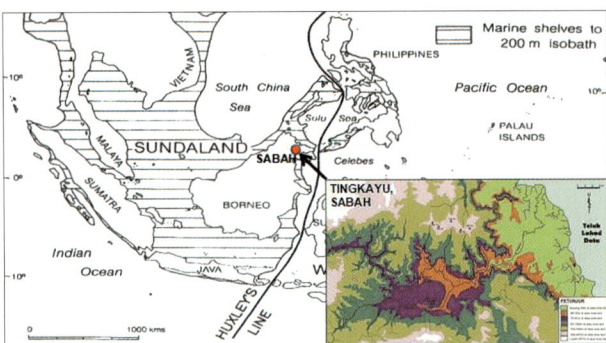

Fig. 1 Topography of the Binuang-Tingkayu Valley showing the location of TIN 1-TIN 17 (after Mokhtar, 1997)

The author then continued his research in Tingkayu in 1993 and found six new sites, designated TIN 13 to TIN 17 (Mokhtar, 1997). The author carried out subsequent excavations at TIN 2 and TIN 13 (Fig. 2). Both sites are at a height of around 90m asl and have yielded pointed bifacial flake tools. The results of optically stimulated luminescence (OSL) dating of a soil sample taken from one of the trenches in TIN 2 gave a date of 12 ka.

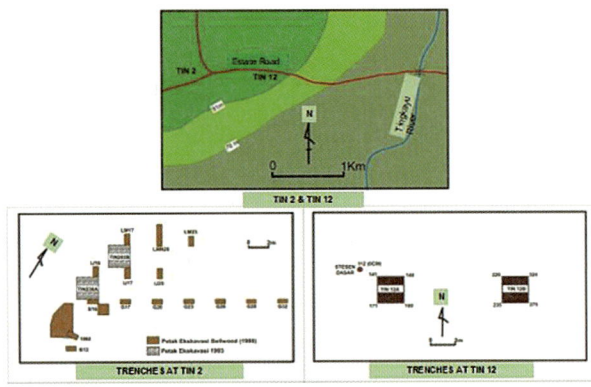

Fig. 2 1993 Excavation Plan at TIN 2 and TIN 12 sites

2. Dating of the Tingkayu site

Bellwood (1988, p. 78) suggested that the Paleolithic culture in Tingkayu occurred around 28–18 ka. This dating was based on the date of the existence of the ancient lake Tingkayu, 28,300±750 BP (ANU3444a), and the earliest dating of the Hagop Bilo Cave, located in the Tingkayu Valley: 17,900±200 BP (ANU2560). Bellwood (1988) used the date at Gua Hagop Bilo because, in the deepest layer, representing the earliest culture at the site, he found no pointed bifacial flake tools. Bellwood believed that the earliest culture in Hagop Bilo Cave occurred when the ancient lake Tingkayu began drying out. Therefore, Bellwood (1988) suggested that the bifacial tool industry in Tingkayu must have taken place before the Hagop Bilo Cave was inhabited.

A soil sample was taken at a depth of 25cm in an excavation trench at the TIN 2 site for dating via the OSL method. The general principle of the OSL dating method is to determine when the soil was last exposed to sunlight. Therefore, the sample should be taken in complete darkness. The TIN 2 soil sample was sent to the Korea Basic Science Lab to be dated. Because of this, the soil samples that arrived at the laboratory were stripped of their outer parts to ensure that only samples that were not exposed to light were analyzed for dating. This work was also completed in the absence of light. A sample of sand-sized grains (90-250μm) was removed from the final sample through a wet sieving method with the use of acid 10% HCl and 10% H_2O_2. It was then put in HF (40%) for one hour to obtain the original quartz grains.

These quartz grains were then checked for the presence of feldspar through infrared (IR) tests and post IR-Blue methods (Wallinga et al., 2002). OSL measurements were made using the Risø TL/OSL measurement tool available at the Korea Basic Science Lab. The device was equipped with a blue-LED stimulation light source (470±30 nm), which applied -30mW. cm-2 to the sample. The instrument was also equipped with a 90Sr/90Y beta source that charged 0.101050±0.002469 Gy.s-1 to the sample. Photon determination was performed through a Hoya U-340, 7mm filter. The balancing dose was estimated using the existing single-aliquot regenerative (SAR) dose standard as found in Murray and Wintle (2000) and Choi et al. (2003). The determination of the dose rate was accomplished according to the recommendations of Olley et al. (1996) and Zimmerman (1971), with an estimated water content of 10±10% using the Beta factor 0.93±0.03, and cosmic radiation was estimated at a rate of 0.13±0.03 Gy/ka. Table 1 shows the OSL scientific data generated from the Tingkayu sample in the process of dating it.

Table 2 shows the final OSL dating results for the Tingkayu sample, which gave a date of 12 ka. This soil sample was

Table 1 OSL scientific analysis data on Tingkayu samples

Sampel	Regeneration Doses	Preheating	Test Dose	Cut-heat	Optical Stimulation
TIN2/25 (90-250μm)	5 Gy, 10 Gy, 30Gy, 50 Gy	240°C, 10s	5 Gy	220°C, 0s	125°C, 40s

Table 2 OSL dating results of Tingkayu samples

No. Sample	(Gy/ years ago)	Water (%)	(Gy)	(n/N)*	Age, KA, 1σSE
TIN 2/25	2.63 + 0.21	10 ± 10	31 ± 2	16/16	12 ±1

taken in the middle of the culture layer, at a depth of 25cm from the surface. This absolute dating indicates that the stone tool workshop at Tingkayu in TIN 2 is 12 ka, which represents an industry at the end of the Late Pleistocene. This finding resolves issues concerning the dating of the Tingkayu site, which had not had absolute dating since it was discovered in 1975.

3. Tingkayu stone tool industry

The 1993-1994 excavation at the TIN 2 site found 3,182 stone artifacts (Table 3) through two trenches (TIN 2A and TIN 2B), each two square meters in size (Fig. 2). The Tingkayu Paleolithic community at the TIN 2 site was found to have quarried purple-gray chert rock, which they brought to the site, as their basic material to make flake tools. No pebbles were produced.

In general, they used stone equipment, such as cores, hammerstones, and anvils, to produce flake tools. The purplish-grey chert-type core, which was the choice at the TIN 2 site, was found around 0.5km to the west of the site. The paleoenvironmental study found that the location of TIN 2 was chosen as a place to make flake tools because it was at the mouth of the ancient Tingkayu lake. Not many anvils (n=2) were found in the excavation trenches. This is likely because the residents directly used the sandstone bedrock as anvils. In fact, sandstone (n=13) was also found to have been dominantly used as hammerstones, in addition to chert (n=3). Since the TIN 2 site functioned as a center for making flake tools, debris or debitages (Fig. 3) have been widely found (n=3106, 97.71%). Here, we discuss the end product of the industry 12 ka in Tingkayu, which is a flake

Fig. 3 Purplish-gray friable debris (chunks, flakes and chips) found at spit 3, quadrant 3, TIN trench 2A

tool, especially a pointed bifacial flake tool, known as a Tingkayu point.

3.1. Flake tools (n=38)

Flake tools are the only tool produced at the Tingkayu site. This is in accordance with the Tingkayu site, whose basic materials were obtained from other places nearby, i.e., through quarrying. Therefore, quarrying activities only allowed the Tingkayu Paleolithic community to produce flake tools. Tingkayu flake tools can be distinguished from other artifacts by two attributes, namely (1) clearly a flake, having either a platform, a bulb of percussion, ripples, or fissures, and (2) having edges with traces of use or trimming. Excavations at TIN 2 have revealed 38 flake tools. The classification of Tingkayu flake tools was made using morphological and technological criteria. The classification does not include functional elements, such as scrapers,

Table 4 Flake Tools from TIN 2

Flake Tools		Quantity	Noet
1. Pointed bifacial (bifacial points-Tingkayu Point)		9	Figure 4
2. Notched			
	I. single notched	7	Figure 5
	ii. denticulate	3	Figure 6
	iv. serrated	10	Figure 6
3. Straight and steep-edge		2	Figure 6
4. Burin		2	Figure 6
5. Combination edge		2	
6. Miscellaneous		3	

Table 3 Stone artifacts found in the excavation of the TIN 2

	Core	Hammerstone	Anvil	Flake Tools	Debitage			Total
					Chunk	Flake	Chip	
TIN 2A	11	16	2	11	8	226	346	614
TIN 2B	6	-	-	27	20	840	1,669	2,562
Total	17 0.53%	16 0.51%	2 0.06%	38 1.19%	28 0.88%	1,066 33.50%	2,015 63.33%	3,182 100.0%

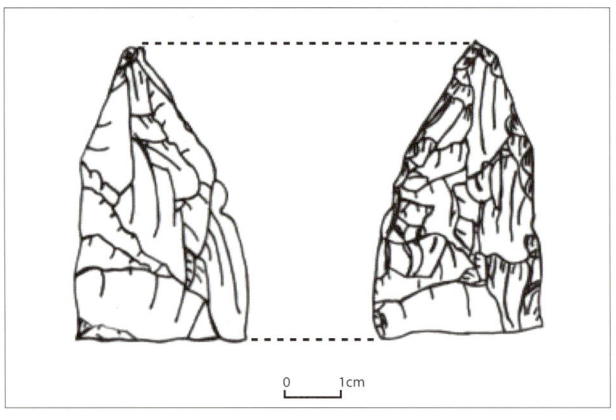

Fig. 4 Pointed Bifacial Flake Tools

Fig. 7 Tingkayu Points

Fig. 5 Single Notched Flake Tools

because it is believed that Tingkayu flake tools were multipurpose. There are six types of Tingkayu flake tools as listed in Table 4. All of them were found to be retouched except for the serrated type. This shows that there is a possibility that serrated tools were formed through use (utilized), while others, which are clearly edged, describe the Paleolithic community of Tingkayu 12 ka, which thought about the desired shape of their stone tools.

and (iii) stone tools – finished and semi-finished. In-situ evidence includes (i) the same cultural layer for all excavation trenches, located on top of the sandstone layer, (ii) the presence of several stone tools classifications that indicate manufacturing activities took place here, and (iii) a clear association of artifacts.

The Tingkayu site was the only site that produced pointed bifacial flake tools, not just in Malaysia but in the surrounding Asian region as well. The Tingkayu points are characterized as (i) flakes trimmed almost completely on both sides of the surface of the artifact, (ii) being leaf-shaped and pointed, and (iii) not having a notch on their perimeter (**Fig. 7**).

Nine Tingkayu points (**Fig. 8**) were found during the excavation of TIN 2 in 1993. The presence of the Tingkayu points shows that the community at the time planned and aimed to produce this tool in a bifacial manner with a pointed shape at the end. So, it is believed that tools of this type were produced for a specific function, perhaps like

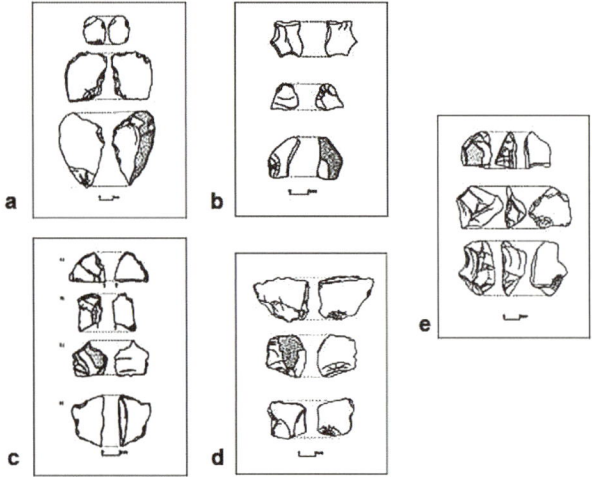

Fig. 6 a: denticulate, b: burin, c: combination-edge, d: serrated and e: straight and steep-edge

3.2. Tingkayu points

Excavations at TIN 2 in 1993 uncovered evidence of an in-situ Paleolithic stone tool workshop. Only stone artifacts were found. Evidence of a workshop include the presence of artifacts representing (i) stone tool equipment, i.e., core hammerstones and an anvil, (ii) debitage or work residue,

Fig. 8 Tingkayu Points

Fig. 9 The results of the Tingkayu Points experiment a: Tingkayu Point that was break into two, b: debitage by using a horn, and c: debitage by using the hammerstones

Fig. 10 Tingkayu Points a: excavation result in TIN 2 which has been broken into two in the middle and split into several parts, b: experimental result also broken in two and c: also found in the excavation

arrowheads, in their activities around the ancient Tingkayu lake.

Tingkayu points are bifacially flaked on both surfaces. Framing was accomplished by focusing on the resulting edge points and the final shape. The final shape was oval-like and pointed at the end. All of the cores used to make these bifacial flake tools were found to be in the shape of a slab or tabular. This kind of core is easier to flake because it has a uniform thickness, thereby making bifacial flaking easier. This observation shows that the Tingkayu Paleolithic community thought about the final form of the necessary tools and adapted them to the core.

The experiment of making Tingkayu points shows that the splitting of the biface can be accomplished with either a hammerstone or organic materials, such as horns (**Fig. 9**). Although Whittaker (1994, pp. 185-190) reported differences in flaking results using hammerstones and horns, the experiment of making Tingkayu points did not show clear differences between the two.

The experiment of making a Tingkayu points involves several stages of work, the first of which is choosing a suitable core. Since the flaking process causes the core to become thinner, the thickness needed to match the desired end result is very important. Tabular-shaped cores or slabs are the most suitable type, as found in TIN 2. The second stage involves marking the required final shape on the core, followed by flaking on one surface to prepare it for the next stage of work.

The third stage involves flaking on the other side. At the end of the third stage, the rock has formed a biface. The fourth stage involves finer flaking on both surfaces to form an oval shape and point at the tip. Finally, the fifth stage involves trimming by removing some small fragments on both sides of the surface to stabilize the shape of the tool and straighten the edges. This last stage usually employs pressure techniques (pressure flaking), especially when forming the pointed part at the end of the tool.

Experiments revealed that the tools can easily break into two in the final stages of their formation because the tool becomes thinner. Thus, this may be the reason for the discovery of many halved Tingkayu points at the excavation site (**Fig. 10**).

4. Conclusion

Apart from the Tingkayu site, there is no record of the discovery of pointed bifacial flake tools in the whole of Southeast Asia. Glover (1981) reported the discovery of a Levallois point in Leang Burung 2, Sulawesi, in a layer aged 20-30 ka. However, the retouched effect was only found on one side of the tool, while the entirety of Tingkayu points demonstrate this effect. Therefore, these points cannot be compared directly. Sulawesi also revealed a pointed chip tool that was produced during the Neolithic, namely the Maros pointed tool, which dates to around 6-3 ka (Mulvaney and Soejono, 1970a, 1970b). The Maros tool is triangular in shape, like an arrowhead, with a dented base that is only bifaced on the side, while Tingkayu points are more leaf-shaped and are bifaced around the tool. Therefore, Tingkayu points represent a unique stone tool industry in this region. The closest comparison can be found in Japan, at open sites such as the Nogawa, Sengawa, and Maehara sites, which have been dated to around 10-18 ka (Akazawa et al., 1980; Pearson, 1992). The pointed tools found at these sites are known as bifacially retouched points. These pointed tools resemble the Tingkayu points in terms of basic materials, shape (oval leaf), technology (flaked and trimmed biface throughout the tool), and size. Therefore, the OSL dating of the Tingkayu site to 12 ka is very accurate when compared to the dating of similar tools in Japan. Their presence in Tingkayu 12 ka raises the question of why the same date was not found in Gua Hagop Bilo, Mansuli, Gua Samang Buat, and other sites nearby in Sabah. Could this represent an isolated group with its own technology and lifestyle around the lake? Answering this question requires further studies of various sites to obtain a more complete picture.

Reference

Akazawa, T., S. Oda and I. Yamanaka. 1980. *The Japanese Palaeolithic: a techno-typology study*, Rippu Shobo Publishing Company.

Bellwood, P., 1988. Archaeological research in south-eastern Sabah. *Sabah Museum Monograph* 2.

Choi, J.H., A.S. Murray, M. Jain, C.S. Cheong and H.W. Chang. 2003. Luminescence dating of well-sorted marine terrace sediments on the southeastern coast of Korea. *Quaternary Science Reviews* 22, 407-421.

Glover, I.C., 1981. Leang Burung 2: an Upper Palaeolithic rock shelter in south Sulawesi, Indonesia. *Modern Quaternary Research in Southeast Asia* 6, 1-38.

Mokhtar Saidin. 1997. *Palaeolithic Culture in Malaysia-contribution s of sites Lawin, Perak dan Tingkayu, Sabah.* PhD Thesis Universiti Sains Malaysia. (unpublished)

Mulvaney, D.J. and R.P. Soejono. 1970a. Archaeology in Sulawesi, Indonesia. *Antiquity* 177, 26-33.

Mulvaney, D.J. and R.P. Soejono. 1970b. The Australian-Indonesian archaeological expedition to Sulawesi. *Asian Perspective* 13, 163-177.

Murray, A.S. and A.G. Wintle. 2000. Luminescence dating of quartz using an improved single-aliquot regenerative–dose protocol. *Radiation Measurements* 32, 57-73.

Olley, J.M., A.S. Murray and R.G. Roberts. 1996. The effects of disequilibria in the uranium and thorium decay chains on burial dose rates in fluvial sediments. *Quaternary Science Review* 15, 751-760.

Pearson, R., 1992. *Ancient Japan*, Washington D.C: Smithsonian Institution.

Wallinga, J., A.S. Murray and L. Botter-Jensen. 2002. Measurement of the dose rates in quartz in the presence of feldspar contamination. *Radiation protection dosimetry* 101, 367-370.

Wittaker, J.C., 1994. *Flintknapping: making and understand stone tools*, University of Texas Press.

Zimmerman, D.W., 1971. Thermoluminescence dating using fine grains from pottery. *Archaeometry* 13, 29-52.

Modeling the islanders' behavior in the insular world of the Far East during the Pleistocene/Holocene transition within the Terminal Paleolithic/Incipient Neolithic boundaries

Vyacheslav A. GRISHCHENKO[1], Kimura HIDEAKI[2], Alexander A. VASILEVSKI[3]

[1] Professor, Museum of Archaeology, Sakhalin State University, Principle, Russia ; v.grishchenko@mail.ru
[2] Sapporo University, Japan
[3] Chairof Russian and World History, Sakhalin State University, Russia

ABSTRACT

This article models the behavior of islanders in Northeast Asia during the Pleistocene/Holocene transition after 13,000 years ago. The researchers focus on the spread of Neolithic culture to the North across the islands of Sakhalin, the Kurils, Hokkaido, and potentially beyond. Key innovations of this period include subsemiterranean houses, deep sea fishing, polished stone tools, distinctive pottery and the family rituals. The Iturup Island sites of Kitovyi 2 and 4, dated to 13–8.5 ka BP, provide crucial evidence for these developments, including unique boat-shaped long barrows suggesting elaborate funerary practices. The model presented considers four factors driving this expansion: geographic (environmental changes forcing migration), psychological (aspirations of leaders and individuals), social (motivating events and societal pressures), and technological (newly acquired skills). The authors emphasize that while geographic factors were external, the others were internal, suggesting a purposeful, willed migration rather than simply a reaction to environmental pressures.

국문초록

섬 주민의 행동 모델링은 고인류의 삶을 알아내는 확실한 수단으로서 이 모델링을 통해 북태평양 연안을 따라 사할린 해협을 건너 북일본 열도, 쿠릴 열도, 캄차카 반도, 그리고 북미 신대륙에 이르는 항로를 따라 인류의 정착 흔적을 찾고자 한다. 구석기 종말기에서 신석기 초창기에 이르는 관련 문화로는 이른시기의 토기, 간석기, 좀돌날 기술을 들 수 있다. 이러한 문화 흔적을 보이는 유적으로는 러시아 극동의 오시포브스카야(Osipovskaya) 유적과 그로마츄킨스카야(Gromatukhinskaya) 유적, 사할린의 돌린스크(Dolinsk) 17 유적과 타코예(Takoye) 2-6 유적, 일본 홋카이도의 조몬문화를 보이는 타이쇼(Taisho) 3과 6 유적, 그리고 쿠릴열도 4개 도서 중 이투루프섬(Iturup Island)의 키토브이(Kitovyi) 2와 4 유적 등이다. 이들 유적에서는 13-8.5 ka 기간에 걸치는 반지하식 가옥, 어로 흔적, 석재연마제, 양면가공 도구 및 많은 토기류, 배모양 긴무덤 등이 발견되었다. 이는 북태평양 연안을 따라 고인류의 삶이 확장된 흔적으로서 자연적·사회적 위협을 피하고 부유함을 얻고자 미지세계를 개척하는 도전적인 욕망에 대한 반응으로 보고 있다.

Keywords : Islanders, Pleistocene, Holocene, Terminal Paleolithic, Incipient Neolithic, Northeast Asia, Neolithic culture

On the island of Iturup, the sites of Incipient Neolithic Kitovyi 2 and 4 dated to 13–8.5 ka BP are characterized by innovations such as semi-subterranean houses, fishing, stone polishing, bifacial retouched tools, linear-relief pottery vessels, and long barrows in the shape of boats (Grishchenko et al., 2022). The factors that caused the expansion of the Late Pleistocene–Early Holocene people along the northern coasts of the Pacific should have always been conditioned by deadly threats of a natural and social nature, as well as the indomitable desire of humans to prosper and explore the unknown (**Fig. 1, Table 1**).

Modeling human behavior, in our opinion, is one of the most promising methods of studying ancient human life. The process of making a decision to travel is a subject of great interest. As for the case of a dangerous sea passage, it was only taken as a result of extreme needs, or as a result of a decisive act of will. The current level of knowledge makes it possible to model the behavior of the inhabitants of the coast of the North Pacific only in general terms, especially the reasons that prompted groups of Upper Paleolithic–Incipient Neolithic people to settle on the big islands of Sakhalin and the Japanese Archipelago; next, to traverse the straits, inhabit chains of smaller Kuril Islands, the Kamchatka Peninsula and finally to reach and explore the New World by boat.

The necessity to understand and model the behavior of the Terminal Palaeolithic–Incipient Neolithic islanders when moving through the straits of the Northern Pacific islands emerged because of the very important recent discovery of Neolithic cultures of insular Northeast Asia. To date, dozens of sites associated with the Incipient and Initial Neolithic are known in the south of the Far East of Russia, including sites of the Osipovskaya and Gromatukhinskaya cultures, dated to the Pleistocene/Holocene transition period. In Sakhalin, there are several sites, such as Dolinsk 17 and Takoye 2-6, where early pottery, polished stone tools, and microblade technologies were found adjacent to each other. Daigo

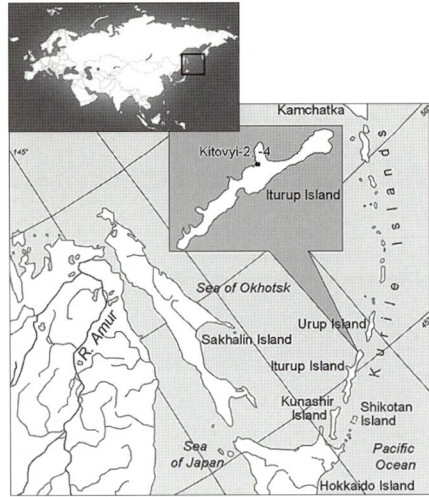

Fig. 1 Area of study Recent geographical condition and the sites of the Incipient Neolithic–settlements of Kitovyi 2 and 4 in Iturup Island of the Big Kuril chain

Natsuki underlined, that in Japan, at least 2,400 sites of the origin of Jomon, which are widespread from the island of Kyushu in the south, are attributed to this period, to Hokkaido in the north (Natsuki, 2021). There are several Incipient Neolithic sites dated to the period between 13-11 ka BP in Hokkaido. Among them are at least two sites—Taisho 3 and 6–characterized by typical Neolithic cultural features, including semi-subterranean houses, fishing, stone polishing, bifacial retouched tools, and high-quality pottery vessels. For us, it is important to underline that the Neolithic people in Hokkaido coexisted with populations that still lived as they did in the Terminal Paleolithic (Takakura, 2020; Natsuki, 2021).

Very important field results were generated on the island of Iturup, where Incipient Neolithic settlements Kitovyi 2 and 4 have been studied in the excavated area of more than 5000 square meters (Grishchenko et al., 2022). These sites include dwellings of two types–terranean with wooden frames not dug into the ground, and semi-subterranean dwellings (**Fig. 2**). Artifacts include linear-relief pottery and retouched bifacial stone tools made of flakes and entire singularities,

Table 1 Radiocarbon dates of the sites of the Incipient Neolithic – settlements of Kitovyi 2 and 4 in Iturup Island
Data of radiocarbon analysis of samples from the sites of Incipient Neolithic of Kitovyi 2 and 4, Iturup island. After Grishchenko et al., 2022

Lab code	Sample description	Date, yrs BP	
		Noncalibrated 1σ (68%)	Calibrated 2σ (95.4%)
Kitovyi-2			
IGAN-8034	Charcoal from hearth in dwelling 5	9,800 ± 130	11,647 – 10,758
IGAN-7916	Charred remains from ceramic vessel, scrape from the outside Charred remains from	8,140 ± 35	9,139 – 8,998
IGAN-7917	ceramic vessel, scrape from the inside	7,940 ± 40	8,985 – 8,639
Kitovyi-4			
IGAN-8774	Charcoal from the terranean dwelling 3	10,775 ± 30	12,757 – 12,720
IGAN-8775	Charcoal from the floor of terranean dwelling 3 Charcoal from the hearth depression	11,115 ± 30	12,950 – 12,926
IGAN-8773	of dwelling 1	7,375 ± 30	8,142 – 8,035
SOAN-9988		7,990 ± 120	9,264 – 8,543
SOAN-9989	Charcoal from the hearth depression of dwelling 2 Charcoal from the filling of the pit	7,005 ± 175	8,182 – 7,515
IGAN-8776	at ritual object 1	7,570 ± 30	8,415 – 8,343

the perimeter were detected. These structures with evidently non-utilitarian enclosures made of plates, identified as places for cremation burials and funerary rites, indicate symbolic behavior. Stratigraphic evidence, supported by radiocarbon analysis, allowed us to establish the incipient stages of the Kuril Neolithic, dating to 13.0–8.5 cal ka BP. Thus, the Incipient Neolithic of this period is now known on the sea route to Kamchatka, about 300km to the north from Hokkaido.

Long barrows in the shape of long boats evoke thoughts that the new inhabitants of the Kuril Islands engaged in funeral rituals in which they sent their dead back to the homeland of their ancestors in boats in memory of their great migration from the south through the stormy straits of the northern Pacific islands.

Let us consider the factors that caused the expansion of people along the northern vector of the Upper Paleolithic ecumene of Eurasia, traveling through inclement conditions and overcoming insurmountable obstacles: stormy sea straits, arctic cold, ice, and extremely bad weather. The decision to take an extreme trip and risk the unknown is contrary to the logic of everyday modern human behavior. It is possible to construct a model that is understandable to us only by taking into account factors that are understandable to all people.

The first factor is geographic. This is the natural human environment of the Late Pleistocene and Early Holocene in all its dynamics in Northeast Asia 23-7 ka BP. Nature in the cruelest ways possible left Paleolithic people with a difficult choice: leave and fight for life or die by remaining in place. The second factor of the movement to the unknown lands may be characterised as the psychological. It appeared each time when there were an extreme need to inspire people for unusual breakthrough activity. And the society leaders, the individual fighters, or groups of them passionately revealed their desire to conquer the fear of the unknown new areas and their personal thirst

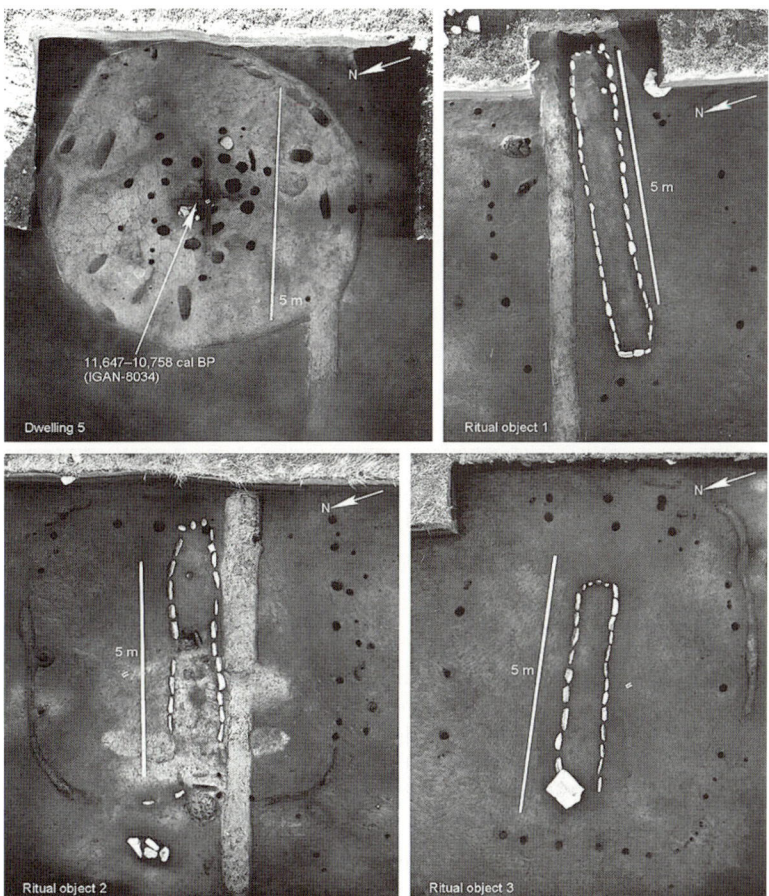

Fig. 2 A pit dwelling #5 floor and the long barrows – ritual objects 1-3 in the site of the Incipient Neolithic – settlement of Kitovyi 4 in Iturup Island of the Big Kuril chain (after V. Grishchenko et al., 2022)

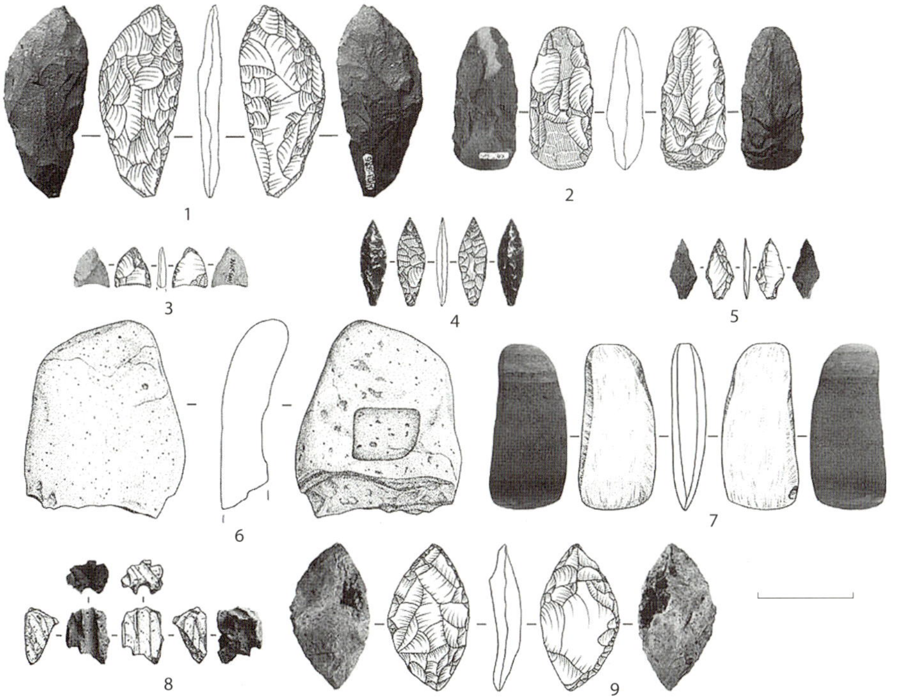

Fig. 3 Stone tools of Incipient Neolithic in Iturup Island 1-4 : Kitovyi-2, dwelling 5 and inter-dwelling area, 5-9 : Kitovyi-4, dwelling 1 and inter-dwelling area (After V. Grishchenko et al., 2022)

processed by advanced polishing (**Fig. 3, 4**). For the first time on the Kurils, long barrows encircled by basalt plates along

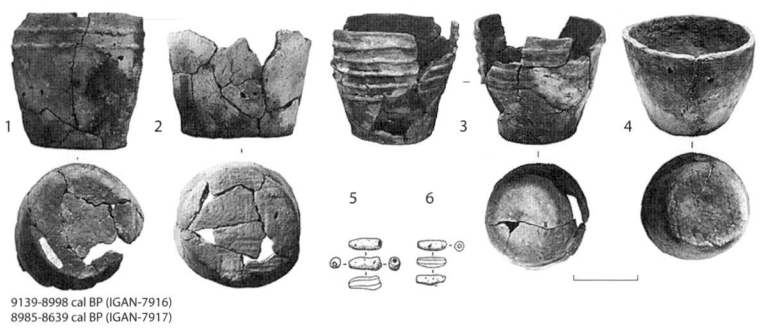

9139-8998 cal BP (IGAN-7916)
8985-8639 cal BP (IGAN-7917)

Fig. 4 Incipient Neolithic ceramics from Kitovyi -2 (1, 2, 5, 6) and - 4 (3, 4) (After V. Grishchenko et al., 2022)

for new knowledge. And the third factor is social. This includes elements such as a specific historical moment with associated motivating events, threats, and developmental trends. What matters are the characteristics of the reconstructed society and the rules of behavior in it. In addition, we consider specific historical events that force a group of people to make a choice in favor of migration or, it may be better to say, "escape." And, finally, the fourth–and no less important–factor is technological. In this vein, the acquired capabilities and skills of people, created and achieved by them as a result of innovative processes, are important. We must note that for people, only one of the four factors–namely geographic–was external. The other three were internal, related to the group interactions and their social environment. This alone makes it possible to believe that the process associated with the development of coasts and islands, and the movement of a people overcoming obstacles, was completely meaningful and directed by their own will. It is this that allows us to consider the early human development of peninsular and island territories on the verge of critical survival as an objective and irreversible historical and psychological phenomenon.

Environment, as an Objective Cause and Driving Factor of Movement. The natural habitats of prehistoric *Homo sapiens* undoubtedly played a primary role in their lives, it determined the rules of behavior, traditions, life cycles, the strategy of survival and development, and often their very fate. The most important factors determining the dynamics of mammals, including humans, in the Japanese Islands were changes in the environment of the Pleistocene with accompanying glacial-interglacial cycles and sea level fluctuations (Honda et al., 2019; Vasilevski, 2008b). Starting from 34 to 28 ka BP the Paleo-SHK Peninsula was inhabited by modern humans (Buvit et al., 2014). Before the straits cut off Sakhalin, Hokkaido, Kunashir and the Lesser Kuril Islands from the Asian mainland, and from each other, the resources of this huge peninsula with a diverse environment were renewed due to the direct contact and interaction with the Asian mainland and through the constant renewal processes of the Pacific Ocean. The same applies to the islands of Paramushir and Shumshu, which were part of the northern paleo peninsula of Northern Kurils and Kamchatka. Accordingly, a significant part of the terrestrial bioresources exploited by human hunters became inaccessible at the transition of the Pleistocene and Early Holocene due to the inundation of the straits and termination of the direct renewal process. The response to this crisis in the hunting model of the economy on the islands at the end of the TUP 2 period was a forced reaction of societies in favor of coastal adaptations. Alternative resources available for the population of Sakhalin, Hokkaido and the Kuril Islands was the richness of the marine resources capable of feeding the inhabitants of coastal villages throughout the year. The extinction of mammoths and corresponding megafauna at the MIS 3-MIS 2 boundary predetermined the need for a very early orientation towards ocean resources in the period no later than 16-15 ka BP. Crisis compelled hunters of the Upper Paleolithic to look for alternative resources in the Pacific Ocean. This, in our opinion, explains the early process of Neolithization on the Japanese Islands, Sakhalin and the Kurils.

Rhythms of the Environment as a reason for migration. A sharp change in the environment that could fundamentally affect the life of the Upper Paleolithic population of the Paleo-SHK is a temporary warming of the climate and the spread of broadleaf vegetation in the south of the peninsula 37-28 ka ago (MIS 3-2). The spectrum of pollen from the loam layer underlying the cultural layer at the Ogonki 5 settlement is characterized by just such features. On the other hand, in the layer from the floor of the dwelling in this settlement, the spectra corresponded to a cold, treeless space. Already at 16 ka BP the first waves of global change in climate and the entire natural environment of man began to have direct impacts after the maximum period of glaciation. For the post-Paleolithic population of the disintegrating peninsula, abrupt climate changes in the 15-11 ka BP period became especially noticeable. The emergence and expansion of the La Perouse Strait, and all the Kuril straits, the change in the regimes of the Japanese, Okhotsk and Bering Seas and the redesign of the islands is an incomplete list of Dryas period catastrophes. All this fundamentally changed the life of all creatures, including people of the insular world. The Dryas catastrophe was especially important for coastal populations that depended on the sea. Undoubtedly, the contrast of climatic and environmental changes in coastal conditions is always somewhat less than on the continent. But in the conditions of the islands, the possibility of an adequate response to natural changes is more difficult as a result of limited space and natural barriers that limit the movement and renewal of terrestrial resources. Another feature of island life is a limitation of choice of consumable resource due to limited adaptive availability within the endemic environment. The population of the coast, however, like the entire nature of the islands, is always guided by the extraction of the most abundant and always seasonal resources. These are migratory fish, such as salmon.

Expansion is both a response and a way of self-preservation, and a characteristic way of a society's actions in an aggressive environment. The struggle for resources in the limited space of islands is a rather important incentive for the expansion of primitive collectives. Raw materials are an objective marker by which the stages and routes of exchange within the island arcs of the Pacific North had been restored. The functioning of several Stone Age resource centers in the region has been reliably proven. (Hall & Kimura, 2002; Vasilevski & Grishchenko, 2011; Kimura & Girya, 2016). Firstly, was access to obsidian from dozens of deposits on Hokkaido Island and the Kamchatka Peninsula that was sought after. Secondly, there were the jaspers sources of the East Sakhalin Mountains that were highly valued. Thirdly, were the basalt deposits of South Sakhalin and the basalt plateau at the foot of the Bogdan Khmelnitsky volcano on Iturup Island that were utilized. Fourth, were the valued bitumen lakes of Northern Sakhalin and the outcrops of natural bitumen in Aomori (Honshu Island). No less significant are the amber deposits on the Krilyon Peninsula and on the coast of the Okhotsk Sea near the village of Starodubskoye, in the south of Sakhalin. Already in the Upper Paleolithic, starting from 30 to 27 ka BP, the so-called "obsidian exchange" took place in Honshu, Hokkaido, and later reached Sakhalin, as first indicated by Hideaki Kimura (1992, 1998). In the dwellings of the Ogonki-5 settlement and in the cultural layer of a number of Upper Paleolithic sites, including Sokol, Olympia 5, Starorusskoye 3, and others, obsidian from the deposits of Hokkaido Island were identified. This means that no later than 23-21 ka BP, exchange processes involving obsidian raw materials covered both the south and the middle part of the Paleo-SHK Peninsula. Not later than 9 ka BP, exchange processes expanded to the north of Sakhalin Island. In the Holocene, the exchange of obsidian connected Hokkaido with Kamchatka through the Kuril Islands, as well as with the northern part of Sakhalin Island and the mouth of the Amur River (Glascock et al., 2000; Colby & Speakman, 2009; Vasilevski & Grishchenko, 2011). The movement of bitumen to Hokkaido Island and Honshu Island from the deposits of Northern Sakhalin (Kato et al., 2008) too place, probably in exchange for Hokkaido obsidian, which was proven for the first millennium B.C. For the Upper Paleolithic period in the insular world this subject has yet to be studied. It should be noted that another very important product for exchange along the entire length, from the mouth of the Amur to the central regions of Hokkaido Island, was amber from the Starodubskoye and Krilyon outcrops on Sakhalin Island. In our studies, amber, along with obsidian, were typical valued exchanged goods for all periods, beginning with the MUP of Sakhalin Island. In addition, an examination of museum collections of the excavated artifacts from Hokkaido and Northern Sakhalin, revealed the items made of red Sakhalin amber that were widely represented. Traveling a distance of up to thousands of kilometers, or more, in one direction for exchange purposes, as well as for seasonal fisheries, was typical of the ancient and historical populations of the island chains of Northeast Asia. Presumably, the distances of the exchange routes gradually increased from 400 to 500km in the Upper Paleolithic to 1000 and more kilometers in the Neolithic. The intense traffic on the island territories is well known from the ethnography of the Ainu and the Koryaks peoples of the eighteenth and nineteenth centuries. The history of the Kuril Islands shows that the Kuril Ainu, having exhausted the resources of one island, always left with their families to another, even if they had to go by boat through the entire Kuril ridge, from north to south. But this was especially pronounced due to the appearance of a strong enemy (Vasilevski & Potapova, 2017). However, this can also be attributed to the mechanisms of their adaptation, if we take the entire Kuril Archipelago as a single ecosystem of Kuril tribes, in which each access to specific resources had their own master controlled by a specific clan or tribe.

Periodic Migrations as a Type of Adaptative Behavior Small periodic migrations in the insular world were a sort of adaptative behavior. Seasonal fishing routes to small islands were typically part of strategy for the Ainu and Nivkhs native people of Sakhalin and the Kuril Islands. In the Neolithic period, all-natural niches suitable for an appropriating economy on Sakhalin, Hokkaido, and the Kuril Islands were filled in the regime of a seasonal fishing territory. The only question was about the number of inhabitants who could exploit this, or that, territory. The second, no less important circumstance is semi-sedentary movement or mobility on the coasts and islands and the associated exploitation of resources of a large aquatic territory by small mobile teams. The basis of their survival depended upon their watercraft, the practice of navigation, fishing, and sea mammal hunting. This also characterizes the Neolithic, Paleometal and Early historical times in the Kuril Islands.

Catastrophe as a Cause of Migration was another driving force behind the movement of people. Such disasters in Hokkaido, the Kuril Islands and the Kamchatka Peninsula were tsunamis, strong volcanic eruptions, powerful typhoons and ecological destruction from the blanketing of tephras (ash layers) that destroy or impoverish the ecosystem and were the causes of hunger and disease. The history of the Pleistocene and Holocene demonstrates the variability of the environment and a combination of long-term changes and unexpected abrupt collapses of climates, vegetation, fauna, etc. For living organisms, unexpected but often short-term dramatic changes in the environment were exceptionally dangerous.

These catastrophic events on the islands of the northern Pacific during and after the end of Younger Dryas were characterised by substantial change in hunter-gatherer socioeconomy as it was underlined by Nakazawa et al. (2011). To the above opinion of colleagues from the point of view of general historical evolution, there are no objections. However, if we assume the possible discreteness, which is the discontinuity of human habitation at each specific place, the process of adaptation on the islands does not seem to be so perfect. For us, the discreteness and variability of archaeological sources characteristic of the boundary periods is explained rather by the movement of societies than by the process of adaptation of the population that has experienced a crisis on the spot. A striking example of significant climate fluctuations and changes in vegetation and fundamental changes in landscapes was fourfold in the restructuring of the Holocene environment on Iturup Island. Two adjustments were associated with global climate change. The two largest disasters that undoubtedly completely changed the historical and cultural situation in the South Kuril Islands, east of Hokkaido and in Southern Sakhalin, were the two Plinian eruptions of the L'vinaya Past (Lion's Mouth) paleo-volcano (Japanese–Moekeshiwan). They occurred sequentially, with an interval of several hundred years between ~13 and ~12.3 ka BP. The southern part of Iturup Island was buried under the multimeter strata of pyroclastic deposits. A complete restructuring of the landscape took place over an area of more than 100km². As a result of the eruption, a caldera with a diameter of ~9km and a depth of ~1km was formed (Degterev et al., 2014). Earlier in the twentieth century, the eruption date of 9.4 ka BP was published. The dates ~13–12 ka BP, allowed researchers to consider both disasters as the most important dramatic events of the Dryas in the southern Kuril Islands, east of Hokkaido and Southern Sakhalin.

The boundary characteristics of the described events on Iturup Island is confirmed by a break in the Neolithization process on the ocean coast of Hokkaido. During the warm period in the Late Pleistocene, 15–13 ka BP, as a result of migration from Honshu Island in the ocean coast of the Paleo-SHK, we see the rise of Neolithic fishing settlements. This process is illustrated by materials from excavations in the Incipient Neolithic site of Taisho 3 and Kitovyi 2 and 4. According to AMS dating, these sites are dated to 14.7-11.55 and 12.95-8.5 ka BP, respectively, when, the communities of the Neolithic (Incipient phase) and Paleolithic (TUP 2) coexisted. But during the coldest period of about 13-11.55 ka BP: "subsistence and settlement strategies adopted by the Incipient Jomon people could not continue… TUP people's mobile lifestyle might have enabled them to adapt to the late glacial cold environment. In the Incipient Holocene, there was a change in subsistence strategies evident in the increase in pottery vessels and the emergence of tools for processing of plant foods. The dramatic warming at the beginning of the Holocene is thought to have significantly changed the TUP people's subsistence strategies and lifestyles" (Natsuki, 2022b). The instability, constant changes and discontinuity of natural processes in the coastal and insular world of the Far East led to the typical discontinuity and instability of historical and cultural processes. Archaeologists record these changes by observing a layerby-layer change in the material culture against the background of natural events, including catastrophic changes at the borders of the Pleistocene and Holocene of the island world (Rudaya et al., 2013; Vasilevski et al., 2010). Over the entire period from the Upper Paleolithic to the seventeenth century, we have recorded more than 25 changes in the historical and cultural situation. During the period covered by written sources (700-1900 CE (current era)), seven island tribes were mentioned on Sakhalin, not counting the Russians, Japanese, Chinese and Europeans. Indigenous tribes were recorded in the seventh century CE as one tribe of the Luguei, in the thirteenth century three tribes of the Kuwei, Tzilemi and the Iliyui. In the nineteenth century–four tribes, three of which, the Uilta, the Evenk and the Ainu, clearly remembered their arrival to the island. The Nivkhs positioned themself as the indigenous population of Sakhalin. At the same time, the Ainu and the Nivkhs remembered the mythical tribe of their predecessors, the Tonchi. Both ethnographers and archaeologists have recorded the mobility of island tribes, moving between continent and islands, from island to island, and along the large islands of Sakhalin, Hokkaido and Honshu quite intensely. The calculated lifespan of one archaeological culture for Sakhalin was no more than 300–400 years for the Neolithic, and about 700–800 years for the Paleometal, the Middle Ages and the New History Age. The emergence of a new culture is usually associated with an abrupt change in climate, such as a warming, but more often, a cooling event (Vasilevski et al., 2010), because northern ocean currents bring the waters rich in biomass. Periodic breaks between dates are evident for several time periods, both, in stratigraphic sedimentation and in prehistorical records. Probably, the most frequent chronological occurrences illustrate favorable periods, characterized by a maximum increase in the island population. Conversely, the absence of radiocarbon dates indicates periods of desolation, outflow and population decline. We also note several intervals for Sakhalin and Kurils which are poorly understood through archaeological data (Vasilevski et al., 2010)

References

Colby, P.S., & Speakman, R., 2009. Initial source evaluation of archaeological obsidian from the Kuril Islands of the Russian Far East using portable XRF. *Journal of Archaeological Science* 36(6), 1256-1263.

Degterev, A.V., Rybin, A.V., Arslanov, Kh. A., Koroteyev, I.G., Chibisova, M.V., & Romanyuk, F.A., 2014. Caldera-forming eruption of Lion's Jaws (Iturup Island, South Kuril Islands): Stratigraphy and age (report) (Kal'deroobrazuyushcheye izverzheniye L'vinoy Pasti (o. Iturup, Yuzhnyye Kuril'skiye ostrova): stratigrafiya i vozrast (doklad)). In *VII Siberian Scientific and Practical Conference of Young Scientists on Geosciences: Proceedings of the Conference (Sibirskaya nauchno-prakticheskaya konferentsiya molodykh uchenykh po naukam o Zemle: Materialy konferentsii)*, 14-15. http://www.ipgg.sbras.ru/ru/science/publications/publ-kalderoobrazuyuschee-izverzhenie-lvinoy-pasti-o-iturup-2014-y2014006 (in Russian)

Glascock, M.D., Shackley, M.S., Kuzmin, Y.V., Popov, V.K., Gorbunov, S.V., Vasilevski, A.A., & Shubina, O.A., 2000. Obsidian geochemistry from the obsidian sources and archaeological sites of Sakhalin. In *Volcanic glasses of the Russian Far East: Geological and archaeological aspects* (Chap. 5). Russian Academy of Sciences, Far Eastern Branch, Far Eastern Geological Institute, 88-106. (in Russian)

Grishchenko V.A., Pashentsev P.A., Vasilevski A.A., 2022. The Incipient Neolithic of the Kurile Islands: The Culture of Long Barrows. *Archaeology, Ethnology & Anthropology of Eurasia* 50(2), 3-12.

Hall, M., & Kimura, H., 2002. Quantitative EDXRF studies of obsidian in Northern Hokkaido. *Journal of Archaeological Science* 29, 259-266. https://doi.org/10.1016/j.quaint.2015.04.015

Kato, K., Miyao, A., Ito, J., Soga, N., & Ogasawara, M., 2008. The search for the origin of bitumen excavated from archaeological sites in the northernmost island in Japan by means of statistical analysis of FI-MS date. *Archaeometry* 50(6), 1018-1033.

Kimura, H. ed., 1992. *Reexamination of the Yubetsu technique and study of the Horokazawa Toma Lithic culture*, Sapporo University.

Kimura, H., 1998. Obsidian, humans, technology. *Paleoecology of the Pleistocene and the Stone Age cultures of North Asia and contiguous territories (Paleoekologiya Pleistotsena i Kul'turi Kamennogo Veka Severnoi Azii I Sopredel'nyikh Territorii)*, 302-314. IIAESO RAN

Nakazawa Yuichi, Iwase Akira, Akai Fumito, Izuho Masami. 2011. Human responses to the Younger Dryas in Japan. *Quaternary International* Vol. 242, Issue 2, 416-433.

Natsuki, D., 2021. Migration and adaptation of Jomon people during Pleistocene/Holocene transition period in Hokkaido. *Quaternary International*. https://doi.org/10.1016/j.quaint.2021.01.009. https://www.sciencedirect.com/science/article/abs/pii/S1040618221000240

Takakura, J., 2020. Rethinking the disappearance of microblade technology in the terminal Pleistocene of Hokkaido, Northern Japan: Looking at archaeological and paleo environmental evidence. *Quaternary* 3(21). https://doi.org/10.3390/quat3030021

Natsuki. 2021. Migration and adaptation of Jomon people during Pleistocene/Holocene transition period in Hokkaido, Japan. *Quaternary International* 608-609(4), 49-64. DOI: 10.1016/j.quaint.2021.01.009

Rudaya, N.A., Vasilevski, A.A., Grishchenko, V.A., Mozhaev, A.V., 2013. Environmental conditions of the Late Paleolithic and Early Neolithic sites in Southern Sakhalin. *Archaeology, Ethnology and Anthropology of Eurasia* 41(2), 73-82.

Vasilevski, A.A., & Grishchenko, V.A., 2011. The definition of raw-material centers during the Late Paleolithic, Neolithic and Paleometal Ages of Sakhalin Island, Eastern Russia. *Current Research in the Pleistocene* 28, 11-15.

Vasilevski, A.A., & Potapova, N.V., 2017. *Essays on the history of the Kuriles Islands (Ocherki istorii Kuril'skikh ostrovov)*, IAET SORAN: SakhGU. (in Russian)

Vasilevski A.A., Grischenko V.A., Orlova L.A., 2010. Periods, boundaries, and contact zones in the far eastern insular world of the Neolithic: (Based on the Radiocarbon Chronology of Sites on the Sakhalin and Kuril Islands). *Archaeology, Ethnology and Anthropology of Eurasia* 38 (1), 10-25.

A specter from the Lithic Stone Age to the Non-Lithic Fur and Bone Age

Ole GRØN[1], Torunn KlOKKERNES[2]

[1] Professor, Institute of Geophysics and Natural Resource Management (IGN), University of Copenhagen, Denmark; olegron111@gmail.com
[2] Museum of Cultural History, University of Oslo, Denmark

ABSTRACT

Knapped lithics are generally assumed to reflect the territorial configurations of cultural groups, as well as their cultural interactions. Some Mesolithic and Neolithic groups, however, show archaeologically worrying deviations from this pattern. While in some areas they are represented by reasonable numbers of worked lithics, in other parts of their cultural territories they are characterized by features such as pits and hearths, which can be of substantial size and appear in significant concentrations with little or no content of knapped lithics. This permits the consideration of whether we have a problem with the absence from the archaeological record of extensive prehistoric "Stone Age" groups that do not employ knapped lithics at all. Furthermore, it is worth considering the extent to which our understanding of the cultural dynamics and interactions of prehistoric groups, as well as their subgroups, informed by preserved knapped lithics, can be misleading. Even though variation between the material cultures of different cultures is is evident, observations from modern hunter-gatherer societies indicate that the organic aspects of their material culture generally appear to serve as the dominant marker of such differences relative to their knapped lithics component. This is most likely because the organic aspects of material culture are the easiest to mark/shape with identifying and characteristic elements (ornaments, etc.). Important are skins and furs, for clothing, covers for dwellings and boats etc., while bark, plant fibers, and sinew are also important in many cultures. Bone and antler have a role in the production of points and cutting edges, and wood can also be important for making various artifact types, including shafts. Knapped lithics do not always form part of the inventory, even though suitable material is locally available. It is clear that the "currents of cultural influence" may vary for different types of objects/materials – for example, artifact types, hafting methods, clothing ornamentation, and burial customs. Even though such complex, multilayered, cultural interaction patterns will, in most cases, be impossible to reconstruct archaeologically due to the poor preservation of organic material culture, it is nevertheless important to keep in mind that they do not automatically follow the patterns of interaction distinguishable in the well-preserved knapped lithics.

Keywords : Mesolithic, Neolithic, organic material, knapped lithics, cultural variation, cultural interaction

국문초록

뗀석기 문화집단은 지리적 영역과 문화 상호작용을 반영하나 중석기와 신석기 그룹에서는 그렇지 않다. 한 지역에서 합당한 석기문화가 문화 지리적으로 다른 유적에서는 상당히 규모가 크고 밀도가 높은 구덩이와 불땐자리 유적일지라도 뗀석기는 거의 나타나지 않는 수가 있다. 이 경우 뗀석기가 없다 해서 광범위한 석기집단이 고고학적으로 없는지는 의문의 여지가 있다. 따라서 뗀석기가 보존된 선사집단과 그 하위집단의 문화적 역동성과 상호작용을 잘못 이해하는 일이 없도록 제대로 된 고찰이 필요하다. 상이한 문화에서 물질문화 간에 차이는 분명 존재하지만, 현생인류의 수렵채집 사회를 보면, 유기물을 사용하는 집단의 물질문화는 뗀석기를 사용하는 집단에 비하여 현저한 차이를 보인다. 유기물 사용 집단의 물질문화는 특징적 요소(장식 등)를 식별하여 표시하고 성형하기 쉽기 때문이다. 유기물 사용 집단의 문화에서는 가죽, 모피, 의류, 주거용 덮개, 보트, 나무껍질, 식물 섬유, 힘줄 등이 중요한 물질 요소다. 뼈와 뿔은 찌르개와 절삭 날을 만들고, 목재는 손잡이를 비롯한 다양한 목기를 만드는 데 중요하다. 유기물은 보존이 어려워 복잡하고 다층적 문화 상호작용 양상을 고고학적으로 재구성하기 어렵다. 그렇다고 잘 보존된 뗀석기에서 식별된 문화 상호작용 양상을 유기물 문화 양상에 자동으로 적용해선 안 될 것이다.

1. Introduction

Prehistoric Stone Age hunter-gatherers are archaeologically defined and distinguished by their knapped lithics, which are generally assumed to reflect the territorial configurations of cultural groups, as well as their cultural interactions. In Europe, however, further research has revealed that some Mesolithic and Neolithic hunter-gatherers exhibit deviations from this pattern. While, in some areas, they are signaled and represented by reasonable numbers of worked lithics, in other parts of their cultural territories, they are characterized by features such as pits and hearths. The latter may be of substantial size and appear in significant concentrations with little or no knapped lithic content. This confronts us with a more complicated archaeological reality than that traditionally perceived and compels us to investigate the wider implications of such observations. Does the absence from the archaeological record of extensive prehistoric "Stone Age" groups that do not employ knapped lithics at all constitute a problem? Furthermore, how significant is the problem we may face in our understanding of the cultural dynamics and interactions of prehistoric groups, and subgroups, if the knapped lithics on which we tend to base our interpretations merely represent an unstable and, in some cases, unimportant fraction of the various prehistoric groups, and in some areas only poorly reflect their cultural dynamics?

Even though variation between the different cultures is evident, observations from modern hunter-gatherer societies indicate that the organic elements of their material culture generally appear to dominate significantly relative to the knapped-lithics component. This applies in terms of both the time invested in manufacture and the role in cultural dynamics and interaction. The most important organic elements appear to be skins and furs, for clothing, covers for dwellings and boats etc., while bark and plant fibers are also important in many cultures. Bone and antler have a role in the production of points and cutting edges, and wood can also be important for making various artifact types, including shafts. Knapped lithics do not always form part of the inventory, even though suitable material is locally available.

With regard to the dispersal or development of new cultural features (i.e., diffusion or independent invention), it is clear that the "currents of cultural influence" may vary for different elements of a cultural group's material culture—for example, their knapped lithics technology, hafting methods, clothing ornamentation, and burial customs. Even though such complex, multilayered, cultural interaction patterns will, in most cases, be impossible to reconstruct archaeologically, it is nevertheless important to keep them in mind. We must not allow ourselves to be deceived by the illusion that patterns distinguishable in knapped lithics are automatically representative of all other patterns of cultural influence, too, which we are then able to reconstruct in some detail.

2. Knapped lithics in living hunter-gatherer cultures: A few examples

The ethnographic record shows that different cultures, due either to the lack of locally available lithic raw materials or, in some cases, to their cultural traditions, place a different emphasis on the use of organic materials, such as bone, antler, wood, and shell, than that placed on lithics used for producing tools for cutting, piercing, drilling, etc.

For instance, the Andaman Islanders used knapped flakes of quartz for an extremely limited spectrum of activities: shaving, tattooing, and skin scarring. The remainder of their tool use relied on shells, bone, wood, and plant materials, but not on knapped lithics, despite good local access to quartz – and obsidian, in some areas (Radcliffe Brown, 1922; Man, 1932; Cipriano, 1966).

The Wik of Cape York, northern Australia, where no local stone suitable for knapping is available, employed ground stone axes made of imported material as their only stone implement type. Their material culture was based on wood, bark, grass stems, leaves, sap, animal bones, teeth, feathers, shells, spines, wax, and hair (Sutton, 1994). They had the opportunity to import lithic materials suitable for knapping, but they chose to employ local alternatives.

The Halakwulup and the Yamana of Tierra del Fuego made projectile points of knapped lithics, slate, bone, and wood, and, to shave the shafts for these, they used quartz flakes and shells. Otherwise, they made no use of knapped lithics, and their material culture was mainly based on bone, wood, and shell, as well as a various materials of plant origin (Gusinde, 1937; 1974).

That bone can be satisfactorily substituted for lithics as a cutting material is demonstrated by several North American indigenous groups, such as the Thaltan and the Iglulik. They used knives made exclusively of bone or antler for skinning, butchering, and removing fat from sinew, even though they had access to lithic materials suitable for knapping. The Thaltan even employed butchering knives with obsidian inserts in parallel with butchering knives of bone for the same tasks (e.g., Mathiassen, 1928; Albright, 1948). The Wola of New Guinea reduced their need for a wide range of functionally specialized flake tools by employing bamboo as an alternative material (Sillitoe and Hardy, 2003).

It is important to note that it is not only a lack of local access to lithic materials suitable for knapping that can prompt the use of alternative materials for drilling, penetration, and cutting. Cultural traditions related to ideological or religious ideas may, in some cases, play a decisive role. Even hunter-gatherer cultures appear to operate such that they acquire a resource surplus that provides them the capacity to behave irrationally (Grøn, 2012).

3. Time spent on knapping lithics

Compared to activities associated with organic materials, the manufacture and use of stone tools, seen by many archaeologists as a central and defining feature of Stone Age cultures, most likely involved much less of people's active time than is generally imagined. For an area with easy access to large quantities of good flint, such as Denmark, lithics specialist Bo Madsen estimated that a Late Paleolithic or Mesolithic family, not using bifacial techniques for making, for example, arrowheads, spent about 1-2 hours knapping flint per week (Madsen pers. comm. 2021). A similarly low estimate for the general duration of knapping activities was also suggested by Eigeland (2015). Furthermore, it is consistent with ethnoarchaeological observations that the knapping of lithics in some small-scale cultures is undertaken in brief sessions when needed, at a routine level of consciousness, like when one ties one's shoelaces (e.g., Gould, 1968; Hayden, 1979; Binford and O'Connell, 1984; Sillitoe and Hardy, 2003; Jochim, 2015).

The idea that the more or less constant sound of flint knapping at Stone Age sites "embodied a range of sensory experiences and provided a means through which prehistoric people gained expression and negotiated social strategies" (Mills and Pannett, 2009) seems rather excessive. It ignores the importance of a multitude of experiences associated with the processing and use of other materials, each of which demanded a considerable level of expertise and investment of time. Today's intense focus on flint knapping and refitting seems to have thrown us back to the silent assumption made in some traditional typological studies (e.g., Kozłowski, 1975; Stout, 2011; Sørensen et al., 2013) that all cultural traits are reflected in their lithic tools. Such views are today often enveloped in a cultural landscape perspective.

"Regardless of geographical location or time period, it may be argued that lithic materials reflect the knowledge and exploitation of the landscape and the social organisation required to promote and facilitate that exploitation" (Blades and Adams, 2009).

In our opinion, the "lithic dimension" of material culture in the exploitation of the landscape, and its broader role in social interaction, is generally overestimated in comparison to perspectives related to other, often more important materials. The requirement for skins and furs for clothing and tents, for example, involves a range of activities related to their acquisition, processing, manufacture, decoration, and maintenance. Satisfying this requirement must have been extremely time consuming. The replacement of worn-out items had to be planned well in advance so that animals with the appropriate skin and fur specifications could be killed, their hides processed, and garments sewn and decorated. Depending on their size, tents could have comprised many smaller skins or a few (about 10 or more) larger skins (bison, buffalo, elk, or the like). The processing of one of these larger, thicker skins would have taken at least 100 hours of work (Reilly, 2015; Klokkernes, 2022). The production of baskets, tents, clothes, boats, and so on from bark, plant fibers, etc., would have required well-prepared materials and must also have been quite time consuming with regard to acquisition, production, decoration, and maintenance (e.g., Vasilevich and Smolyak, 1964; Turnbull, 1965a; Emmons and de Laguna, 1991; Anderson, 2000; Adney and Chapelle, 2014).

4. Knapped lithics as a medium for communication of social and cultural signals

According to Sackett's concept of "isochrestic" aspects of style, organic artifacts are easier to modify and use for the display of dynamically changing signals of social differences and similarities at all levels of scale (e.g., within the family, within the clan, between clans) than is the case for knapped lithics (Sackett, 1982). Furthermore, it is obvious that socially significant stylistic elements applied to the human body (e.g., the clothing itself and/or elements applied to it and painting, tattooing, or scarring of the skin) constitute direct and powerful social signals, compared to stylistic elements applied or related to lithic artifacts, which only indirectly perform a "social expression" of relationships (e.g., Strathern and Strathern, 1971; Ebin, 1979; Krutak, 2015). Consequently, the generally difficult-to-modify but well-preserved knapped lithics are not well suited to mirroring the social reality of the past, with its highly dynamic currents of social and cultural impulses; while organic objects, which are mostly not preserved, would have done so in a much more comprehensive way.

If one could assume that all cultural impulses communicated via both organic materials and knapped lithics moved along the same trajectories and behaved in roughly parallel ways, then one would have the possibility of reconstructing the patterns of diffusion that carried cultural impulses to specific sites or areas, based on the vague reflections of these impulses that can be identified in knapped lithics. But ritual and linguistic aspects of living hunter-gatherer cultures display a much greater degree of small-scale variation in space and time than we are able to distinguish in the "lithic dimension" of most prehistoric hunter-gatherer cultures as defined by archaeologists (e.g., Donner, 1926; Krause, 1956; Bird Grinnell, 1962; Turnbull, 1965b; Croes, 1989; Oakes and Riewe, 1992; Svensson, 1992). A strong tendency can be observed in living hunter-gatherer cultures to modify, and thereby personalize, incoming cultural trends through inventive behavior at the small-scale social level, such that the resulting cultural features tend to vary in a dynamic way from clan to clan, and even among subgroups consisting of just a few families. This variation seems, to a large extent, to result from conscious but quite unpredictable choices and from local invention or modification within the various small groups, to mark their individuality within their own group and toward other groups, so as to reinforce their identity (Donner, 1926; Shirokogoroff, 1935; Barth, 1987; Grøn et al., 2009; Tanner, 2014; Grøn, 2016).

The slow, gradual changes over time, as well as the low spatial variation observable in most Mesolithic and Palaeolithic knapped lithics inventories, concurs poorly with the high spatio-temporal dynamics observable in living hunter-gatherers (Grøn et al., 2009). Even cultural transmission theory, despite its focus on all types of cultural transmission, in the case of prehistoric hunter-gatherers, appears to be trapped in the "knapped lithics pitfall" due to the lack of information on the organic materials employed (e.g., Bettinger and Eerkens, 1999; Eerkens et al., 2014). There is therefore good reason to believe that the typo-technological changes in lithic artifacts over time represent, at best, a very distant and poorly representative echo of the sociocultural processes operating among prehistoric hunter-gatherers. At worst, these changes may be of a totally different nature and spatial configuration than the main trajectories of their cultural dynamics and interaction, and may therefore be directly misleading with regard to an understanding of the potentially multifaceted development of living and dynamic prehistoric societies (**Fig. 1**; e.g., Turnbull, 1965b).

5. Knapped lithics and landscapes

In landscapes of high relief, as well as those dominated by wetlands, it is natural for the main transport corridors and contact routes to follow the river valleys and lake shores, because it is easier to use these routes rather than crossing mountainous areas or extensive marshlands. But even in such landscapes, as well as those less directionally oriented, lines of contact and, consequently, channels of sociocultural interaction (e.g., trade or exchange, the search for marriage partners, visits prompted by curiosity) will deviate from the most simplistic linear corridor models and form rather fine-meshed local networks (e.g., Rogers, 1969; Townsend, 1978; Cavalli-Sforza and Hewlett, 1982; Fischer, 1982; Hewlett et al., 1982; Swagerty, 1988; Stiles, 1993; Brown, 2001; Tykot, 2004; Bar-Yosef, 2005; Fitzgerald et al., 2005; Grøn et al., 2005; Floss, 2014; Grøn, 2019). Exchange systems must have varied in character according to their different purposes and must therefore have conveyed a varied or differently weighted spectrum of cultural impulses (local redistribution of hunted or gathered food, exchange related to intermarriage, exchange of exotic materials from distant places, etc.) (Rogers, 1969; Ericson, 1977; Cavalli-Sforza and Hewlett, 1982; Layton, 1986; Joiris, 2003). We cannot therefore not assume that cultural impulses related to lithics necessarily followed the same geographical routes as most other sociocultural impulses in play. It is obvious that if lithic material for knapping could only be obtained through long-distance exchange systems, access to it would be embedded in cultural exchange contexts of quite a different character than if it could be obtained via short-range networks or locally by the end-users themselves. The character of cultural exchange related to lithics therefore probably varied significantly in prehistory, and the role of lithics in sociocultural interaction and local modification or invention will, accordingly, be difficult to generalize in relation to all of the other in- and out-going signals.

A basic problem in understanding the economy and exchange related to prehistoric settlement systems, as well

Fig. 1 Nisga'a chiefs of Gitlaxt'aamiks, British Columbia, Canada, with ceremonial equipment. From left to right: three children; Andrew Nass, wearing shirt with coppers and ermine-decorated headdress; John Nass, in light-coloured skin robe, holding a rattle, his dance headdress showing a carved frontlet; James Skean, wearing a Chilkat blanket and decorated leggings and dance apron; Philip Nass, wearing a Chilkat blanket, neck ring, three-ringed headdress and dance apron decorated with puffin beaks; two children; Charlie Brown, in shirt with inverted face holding a painted drum; Eliza Brown, in button blanket with neck ring; Matilda Peal, in button blanket; one child. Both women have down in their hair. On display are masks, frontlets, dance headdresses and carved wooden boxes. Photo: possibly C.H. Orme, approximately 1903.

as in being able to predict likely settlement locations, relates to sites of low "lithic visibility." Our current understanding and theories are based on sites that have sufficient lithics or other preserved artifacts for them to be observed and recorded in surveys. Investigations in France, the Netherlands, Norway, Sweden, etc., of numerous sites with substantial pits and hearths, and even dwellings, dated to the Mesolithic period and related to cultural contexts that, in many cases, have very few or no knapped lithics appear to raise serious questions about how close to, or far away from, the truth the existing theory of the Mesolithic landscape takes us (Achard-Corompt et al., 2017; Živaljević et al. 2021; Achard-Corompt et al., 2022; Dugstad, 2022; Fretheim, 2022; Grøn and Peeters, 2022; Hernek, 2022; Vogt et al., 2022).

Several wetland and lake sites with good preservation of organic materials provide solid evidence for the existence in some prehistoric cultures of elaborate dwelling structures of considerable size but of such low "lithic visibility" that they most likely would not qualify as sites meriting investigation, and possibly not even recording, according to typical survey and recording criteria. The most archaeologically visible of these wetland sites are those with remains of elaborate pile dwellings from the Neolithic Age and Bronze Age, known today from various parts of Europe (Haffner et al., 2020). Many of these sites are characterized by a remarkably low density of knapped lithics derived from their occupation phases. The Lake Zurich site of Meilen-Schellen, for example, has an accumulation of cultural material approximately 500m long, up to 80m wide, and several meters thick that includes remains of wooden pile dwellings from several Neolithic phases, as well as from an extensive Bronze Age habitation. The 430m² portion of this material excavated in 1975–1977 revealed a sequence of deposits with a thickness of up to 1.2m, representing Neolithic Cortaillod, Pfyner, Horgener, and Corded Ware cultures, as well as the Early and Late Bronze Age. The density of knapped lithics was approximately 0.5-1 pieces per m² (Altorfer and Conscience, 2005; Grøn et al., 2021)–which corresponds to about 0.1-0.2 pieces of knapped lithics per m² per culture, each of which may have had several settlement phases. Taking into consideration that this is an accumulated total from several extended habitation phases, and that this total might well be even smaller were the Early and Late Bronze Age to be excluded, it is obvious that the material representing the individual cultures at a similar site on dry land, with no preservation of organic material, would not have qualified for a site record based on the knapped lithics in a survey relying on surface observations. A slightly greater total density, of about 2.5 pieces of knapped lithics per m², was recorded during the excavation of c. 3,600m² of a c. 80cm thick "sandwich" of Neolithic cultural deposits representing a pile dwelling settlement (Early Neolithic, Horgener and Corded Ware cultures) at Zürich-Parkhaus Opéra. The density was obviously considerably lower for the individual cultural layers (Kienholz and Affolter, 2016; Bleicher and Harb, 2017; Harb et al., 2017). A central question is how great a problem do these low-visibility sites represent for archaeology? Does it totally undermine our current understanding of prehistoric hunter-gatherer landscapes, and consequently our possibilities for modeling potential settlement locations and areas, as well as demographic processes? Is its effect of equal importance from one cultural context to another?

We are presently unable to answer these questions due to a lack of reliable quantitative information. A more systematic effort to record and document "lithic-less" Mesolithic sites has only just begun in some areas. At a qualitative level, however, we can begin to list known sites and site types with low lithic visibility as the first step in a more targeted approach to determining how radical a revision of our archaeological thinking is required.

6. Conclusions

There is no standard procedure for how to obtain a better understanding of the organic elements of prehistoric material culture. An increased strategic focus on wetland and underwater sites with good preservation of organic materials would help (e.g., Croes, 1989), while the development of improved survey and excavation methods would also increase the chances of finding and salvaging organic objects (e.g., Grøn and Hermand, 2015; Grøn et al., 2021, 2022b). It is necessary to carefully consider how much energy and money should be invested in the investigation of Stone Age sites where only the lithic artifacts are preserved, in contrast to sites with good preservation of organic remains, which typically involve more expensive and relatively more time-consuming processing, documentation, and conservation of finds. Submerged sites are especially important and can sometimes offer surprising preservational conditions, which offer promising material for future studies (e.g., Skaarup and Grøn, 2004).

On the theoretical front, a conceptual reorientation is required. We must include the broad spectrum of signals related to organic material culture, which is normally much more dynamic than the developments observable in "slow-reacting" knapped lithics. Since the latter formed the basis for the development of Stone Age archaeology, the initial focus on this material is understandable. But with the knowledge we possess today, there are no valid grounds for maintaining this intense focus on the typology and technology of lithics. In all probability, these were only a relatively minor aspect of the material culture, and consequently not a good indicator of either the interaction between different sociocultural groups or their internal cultural inventiveness (e.g., Grøn et al., 2009).

Geographical modeling of zones with a high probability of Stone Age settlement, as well as a range of other major methodological challenges (e.g., Kamermans, 2010; Grøn et al., 2022a), tends to take as its point of departure the topographical positions of known sites with high lithic visibility, while ignoring their original associated organic component. Regarding the landscape aspects of these sites, in addition to their topographical positions, the landscape dynamics at different spatial and temporal scales must be considered as well (Peeters, 2007; Grøn et al., 2022a). The modeling of demographic features and processes in Stone Age cultures based on radiocarbon dates, which has in itself serious methodological issues (e.g., Riede, 2009), must also be seen as relatively meaningless in the absence of dates for the large numbers of "missing" sites of low lithic visibility. Furthermore, the negative consequences of the lack of data from areas that are now submerged, with their highly attractive coastal resources, must be regarded as significant (Carleton and Groucutt, 2020).

How can we cope with such a mismatch between basic archaeological method and theory focusing on knapped lithics, on the one hand, and sociocultural interaction in modern cultures on the other? One obvious way to reconcile this incongruity is to intensify our focus on the organic elements of the prehistoric cultures in question. This could be done by prioritizing fieldwork in areas with the potential for the preservation of organic materials and environmental data, as well as ancient DNA–notably wetlands and submerged landscapes. The development of improved technologies and procedures for efficient recording and analysis of organic materials during excavations and the subsequent processing of information from wetland or underwater sites would facilitate significant advances. Principal excavation methodologies employed today have, however, been primarily developed to cope with dryland sites, characterized by large quantities of knapped lithics. These sites likely only represent the tip of the iceberg in an ocean of sites that were originally mainly characterized by organic remains. If the latter had, in general, been better preserved, they would likely provide a quite different, and much more detailed and dynamic, narrative to that which we have today. An increased focus on sites with good preservation of organic remains may provide access to at least some fragments of this different prehistoric cultural reality. Equally important is a wider and better acceptance of ethnoarchaeology as a tool to generate ideas about what we are seeing archaeologically and to give us clues to the reality of organic materials in prehistory.

References

Achard-Corompt, N., E. Ghesquière, C. Laurelut, C. Leduc, A. Rémy, I. Richard, V. Riquier, L. Sanson & J. Wattez. 2017. Des fosses par centaines, une nouvelle vision du Mésolithique en Champagne: Analyse et cartographie d'un phénomène insoupçonné, in: N. Achard-Corompt, E. Ghesquière & V. Riquier eds., *Creuser au Mésolithique. Digging in the Mesolithic.* Actes de la séance de la Société préhistorique française de Châlons-en-Champagne (29-30 mars 2016). Société préhistorique française, 2017, Paris: Séances de la Société préhistorique française 12, 11-25.

Achard-Corompt, N., E. Ghesquière, C. Laurelut, C. Leduc, A. Rémy, I. Richard, V. Riquier, L. Sanson & J. Wattez. 2022. Dozens of large and (almost) empty pits: towards a new geography for the French Mesolithic?. in: O. Grøn & H. Peeters eds., *Hidden Dimensions. Aspects of Mesolithic hunter-gatherer landscape use and non-lithic technology*, Leiden: Sidestone Press, 83-112.

Adney, E.T. & H.I. Chapelle. 2014. *The Bark Canoes and Skin Boats of North America*, Washington D.C.: Smithsonian Institution National Museum of History and Technology.

Albright, S.L., 1984, *Tahltan Ethnoarchaeology*, Burnaby, British Columbia (Department of Archaeology Publication 15, Simon Fraser University).

Altorfer, K. & A.-K. Conscience. 2005. *Meilen-Schellen. Die neolithischen und Spätbronzezeitlichen Funde und Befunde der Untersuchungen 1934-1996*; Seeufersiedlungen, Zürich : Zürcher Archäologie 18. Baudirektion Kanton Zürich, Hochbauamt Kantonsarchäologie.

Anderson, K., 2000. California Indian Horticulture: Management and Use of Redbud by the Southern Sierra Miwok. in: P.E. Minnis ed., *Ethnobotany: A Reader, Norman*, Oklahoma : University of Oklahoma Press, 29-40.

Bar-Yosef, D.E., 2005. The Exploitation of Shells as Beads in the Palaeolithic and Neolithic of the Levant. *Paléorient* 1, 176-185.

Barth, F., 1987. *Cosmologies in the Making: A Generative Approach to Cultural Variation in Inner New Guinea*. Cambridge: Cambridge University Press.

Bergsvik, K.A. & E. David. 2015. Crafting Bone Tools in Mesolithic Norway: A Regional Eastern-Related Know-How. *European Journal of Archaeology* 18(2), 190-221.

Bērziņš, V., 2008. *Sarnate: Living by a Coastal Lake During the East Baltic Neolithic*, Oulu, Latvia: Faculty of Humanities, General Archaeology, University of Oulu.

Bettinger, R.L. & J. Eerkens. 1999. Point Typologies, Cultural Transmission, and the Spread of Bow-and-Arrow Technology in the Prehistoric Great Basin. *American Antiquity* 64(2), 221-242.

Binford, L.R. & J.F. O'Connell. 1984. An Alyawara Day: The Stone Quarry. *Journal of Anthropological Research* 40(3), 406-432.

Bird Grinnell, G., 1962. *The Cheyenne Indians: Their History and Ways of Life* Vol. 1, New York: Cooper Square.

Blades, B.S. & B. Adams. 2009. Introduction: Lithics, Landscapes, and Societies. in: B. Adams & B.S. Blades eds., *Lithic Materials and Palaeolithic Societies*, Oxford: Wiley-Blackwell, ix-xiii.

Bleicher, N. & C. Harb. 2017. Rück- und Ausbliche. in: C. Harb & N. Bleicher, *Zürich-Parkhaus Opera. Eine neolithische Feuchtbodenfundstelle Band 3: Naturwissenschaftliche Analysen und Synthese*, Zürich: Monographien der Kantonsarchäologie Zürich 49, 263-279.

Brown, J.S.H., 2001. History of the Canadian Plains Until 1870. in: R.J. DeMaille ed., *Handbook of North American Indians* Vol. 13, Plains, Washington, D.C.: Smithsonian Institution, 300-312.

Carleton, C. & H.S. Groucutt. 2021. Sum Things Are not What They Seem: Problems with Point-Wise Interpretations and Quantitative Analyses of Proxies Based on Aggregated Radiocarbon Dates. *The Holocene* 31(4), 630-643.

Cavalli-Sforza, L.L. & B. Hewlett. 1982. Exploration and Mating Range in African Pygmies. *Annals of Human Genetics* 46, 257-270.

Cipriani, L., 1966. *The Andaman Islanders*. London: Weidenfeld and Nicolson.

Croes, D.R., 1989. Prehistoric Ethnicity on the Northwest Coast of North America: An Evaluation of Style in Basketry and Lithics. *Journal of Anthropological Archaeology* 8, 101-130.

Crombé, P., 1998. *The Mesolithic in Northwestern Belgium: Recent Excavations and Surveys*, Oxford: BAR International Series 716, Hadrian Books.

Donner, K., 1926. *Bei den Samojeden in Sibirien*, Stuttgart: Strecker und Schröder.

Dugstad, S., 2022. A Mesolithic bark mat on Kvitsøy in south-western Norway. in: O. Grøn & H. Peeters eds., *Hidden Dimensions. Aspects of Mesolithic hunter-gatherer landscape use and non-lithic technology*, Leiden: Sidestone Press, 27-53.

Ebin, V., 1979. *The Body Decorated*, London: Thames and Hudson.

Eerkens, J.W., R.L. Bettinger & P.J. Richerson. 2014. Cultural Transmission Theory and Hunter-Gatherer Archaeology. in: V. Cummings, P. Jordan & M. Zvelebil eds., *The Oxford Handbook of the Archaeology and Anthropology of Hunter-Gatherers*, Oxford: Oxford University Press, 1127-1142.

Eigeland, L.C., 2015. Maskinmennesket i steinalderen. *Endring og kontinuitet i steinteknologi fram mot neolitiseringen av Øst-Norge*, Oslo: PhD thesis, University of Oslo.

Emmons, G.T. & F. de Laguna. 1991. *The Tlingit Indians*, Seattle: University of Washington Press and American Museum of Natural History.

Ericson, J.E., 1977. Egalitarian Exchange Systems in California: A Preliminary View. in: T. Earle & J. Ericson eds., *Exchange Systems in Prehistory*, New York: Academic Press, 109-126.

Fischer, A., 1982. Trade in Danubian Shaft-Hole Axes and the Introduction of Neolithic Economy in Denmark. *Journal of Danish Archaeology* 1, 7-12.

Fitzgerald, R.T., T.L. Jones & A. Schroth. 2005. Ancient Long-Distance Trade in Western North America: New AMS Radiocarbon Dates from Southern California. *Journal of Archaeological Science* 32, 423-434.

Floss, H., 2014. Rivers as Orientation Axes for Migrations, Exchange Networks and Transmission of Cultural Traditions in the Upper Palaeolithic of Central Europe. in: M. Yamada & A. Ono. *Lithic Raw Material Exploitation and Circulation in Prehistory: A Comparative Perspective in Diverse Palaeoenvironments*; International Symposium, Sat 27-Sun 28 October 2012; Meiji University (Tokyo); Organized by Akiro Ono, Tokyo (Series ERAUL 138. Meiji University), 11-22.

Fretstad, S.E., 2022. No knapping on the floor! Norwegian examples of (mainly) Mesolithic dwellings with few associated lithics. in: O. Grøn & H. Peeters eds., *Hidden Dimensions. Aspects of Mesolithic hunter-gatherer landscape use and non-lithic technology*, Leiden: Sidestone Press, 27-53.

Gehlen, B., E. Eckmeier, K. Gerken, W. Schön & A. Zander. 2020. Mesolithic pits in Germany–a first compilation. in: A. Zander & B. Gehlen eds., *From the Early Preboreal to the Subboreal period–Current Mesolithic research in Europe. Studies in honour of Bernhard Gramsch*, Kerpen-Loogh, 243-313.

Gould, R.A., 1968. Chipping Stones in the Outback. *Natural History* 77(2), 42-49.

Gross, D., H. Lübke, U. Schmölcke & M. Zanon. 2018. Early Mesolithic Activities at Ancient Lake Duvensee, Northern Germany. *The Holocene* 29(2). DOI.org/10.1177/0959683618810390

Grøn, O., 1987. Seasonal Variation in Maglemosian Group Size and Structure. *Current Anthropology* 28(3), 303-327.

Grøn, O., 1995. *The Maglemose Culture: The Reconstruction of the Social Organisation of a Mesolithic Culture in Northern Europe*, Oxford: BAR International Series 616, Hadrian Books.

Grøn, O., 2012. Our grandfather sent the elk–some problems for hunter-gatherer predictive modelling. *Quartär* 59, 175-188

Grøn, O., 2014. Human Spatial Behaviour in Dwellings and Social Psychology. in: M. Svart Kristiansen & K. Giles. *Dwellings, Identities and Homes: European Housing Culture from the*

Viking Age to the Renaissance, Aarhus: Jutland Archaeological Society, 29-38.

Grøn, O., 2016. Yakut Food Producers Colonising Areas Occupied by Evenk Hunter-Gatherers: Fragments of a Process of Cultural Change Caused by Migration. In: L. Melheim, H. Glørstad & Z. Tsigaridas Glørstad eds., *Comparative Perspectives on Past Colonisation, Maritime Interaction and Cultural Integration*, Bristol: Equinox, 73-83.

Grøn, O., 2019. Mammoth-Hunter Camps in the Scandinavian North Sea Sector during the Late Weichselian?. *Vestnik of Saint Petersburg University: History* 64(2), 555-583. DOI.org/10.21638/11701/spbu02.2019.209

Grøn, O., C. Nellemann & N. Røv. 2005. Die Auswirkungen von Transportkorridoren auf indigene Kultur und kulturelles Erbe. Annäherung an eine Definition von Einflusszonen. in: P. Schweitzer ed., *Beiträge zum zirkumpolaren Norden/Contributions to Circumpolar Studies*, Vienna and Fairbanks, AK: University Wien and University of Alaska, 172-183.

Grøn, O., T. Klokkernes & M.G. Turov. 2009. Cultural Small-Scale Variations in a Hunter-Gatherer Society: Or 'Everybody Wants To Be a Little Bit Different!' An Ethnoarchaeological Study from Siberia. In: S. McCartan, R. Schulting, G. Warre & P. Woodman. *Mesolithic Horizons*. Papers presented at the Seventh International Conference on the Mesolithic in Europe, Belfast 2005, Oxford: Oxbow, 203-209.

Grøn, O. & J.-P. Hermand. 2015. Settlement Archaeology Under Water: Practical, Strategic and Research Perspectives. *2015 IEEE/OES Acoustics in Underwater Geosciences Symposium (RIO Acoustics)*. DOI.org/10.1109/RIOAcoustics.2015.7473591

Grøn, O., L.O. Boldreel, M.F. Smith, S. Joy, R. Tayong Boumda, A. Mäder, N. Bleicher, B. Madsen, D. Cvikel, B. Nilsson, A. Sjöström, E. Galili, E. Nørmark, C. Hu, Q. Ren, P. Blondel, X. Gao, P. Stråkendal & A. Dell'Anno. 2021. Acoustic Mapping of Submerged Stone Age Sites—A HALD Approach. *Remote Sensing* 13(3), 445. DOI.org/10.3390/rs13030445

Grøn, O. & H. Peeters. 2021. Mesolithic 'Ghost' Sites and Related Stone Age Problems with Lithics. in: D. Borić, D. Antonović & B. Mihailović. *Foraging Assemblages*. Belgrade and New York: Serbian Archaeological Society and the Italian Academy for Advanced Studies in America, Columbia University, 233-239.

Grøn, O., A. Hansson, J. Cook Hale, C. Phillips, A. Zander, D. Groß, & B. Nilsson. 2022a. Mapping Stone Age Sites by Topographical Modelling: Problems and Possibilities. in: S. D'Amico & V. Venuti eds., *Handbook of Cultural Heritage Analysis*, Cham, Switzerland: Springer Nature, 1595-1642.

Grøn, O., L.O. Boldreel, R. Tayong Boumda, P. Blondel, B. Madsen, E. Nørmark, D. Cvikel, E. Galili & A. Dell'Anno. 2022b. Acoustic Detection and Mapping of Submerged Stone Age Sites with Knapped Flint. in: S. D'Amico & V. Venuti eds., *Handbook of Cultural Heritage Analysis*, Cham, Switzerland: Springer Nature, 901-933.

Grøn, O., H. Peeters. 2022. Cultural dynamics in Stone Age hunter-gatherers: hidden dimensions. in: O. Grøn & H. Peeters eds., *Hidden Dimensions. Aspects of Mesolithic hunter-gatherer landscape use and non-lithic technology*, Leiden: Sidestone Press, 9-24.

Gusinde, M., 1937. *Die Feuerland Indianer*. Ergebnisse meiner vier Forschungsreisen in den Jahren 1918 bis 1924 unternommen im Auftrage des Ministerio de Instruccion Publica de Chile. Band II, Die Yamana. Vom Leben und Dencken der Wassernomaden am Kap Hoorn, Mödling bei Wien: Verlag der Internationalen Zeitschrift Anthropos.

Gusinde, M., 1974. *Die Feuerland Indianer*. Ergebnisse meiner vier Forschungsreisen in den Jahren 1918 bis 1924 unternommen im Auftrage des Ministerio de Instruccion Publica de Chile. Band III/I, Die Halakwulup, Mödling bei Wien: Verlag St. Gabriel.

Haffner, A.M., A. Hinz, E. Mazurkievich, E. Dolbunova & E. Pranckenaite. 2020. Introduction: Neolithic and Bronze Age Pile Dwellings in Europe: An Outstanding Archaeological Resource with a Long Research Tradition and Broad Perspectives, in: A. Haffner, E. Dolbunova, A. Mazurkievich, E. Pranckenaite & M. Hinz eds., *Settling Waterscapes in Europe: The Archaeology of Neolithic and Bronze Age Pile-Dwellings*, Heidelberg: Propylaeum, Heidelberg University Library, 1-6. DOI.org/10.11588/propylaeum.714

Harb, C., N. Bleicher, E. Jochum Zimmermann, A. Kienholz, B. Ruckstuhl & M. Weber. 2017. Handwerk und Technologie, in: C. Harb & N. Bleicher, Zürich-Parkhaus Opera. *Eine neolithische Feuchtbodenfundstelle Band 3: Naturwissenschaftliche Analysen und Synthese*, Zürich: Monographien der Kantonsarchäologie Zürich 49, 238-262.

Hayden, B., 1979. *Palaeolithic Reflections: Lithic Technology and Ethnographic Excavation among Australian Aborigines*, Canberra: Australian Institute of Aboriginal Studies.

Hernek, R., 2022. Mesolithic sites with no or few finds: some examples from the west coast of Sweden. in: O. Grøn & H. Peeters eds., *Hidden Dimensions. Aspects of Mesolithic hunter-gatherer landscape use and non-lithic technology*, Leiden: Sidestone Press, 69-82.

Hewlett, B., J.M.H. van De Koppel & L.L. Cavalli-Sforza. 1982. Exploration Ranges of Aka Pygmies of the Central African Republic. *Man* 17(3), 418-430.

Jochim, M., 2015. Beyond Stone: Contributions of Bone and Antler Technology to Stone Age Archaeology. in: Y.-j. Lee, J.-y. Woo, S.-w. Lee & K.-W. Lee eds., *Proceedings of the 20th*

International Symposium: Suyanggae and Her Neighbours in Korea, Seoul: Institute of Korean Prehistory, 39-48.

Joiris, D.V., 2003. The Framework of Central African Hunter-Gatherers and Neighbouring Societies. *African Study Monographs, Suppl* 28, 57-79.

Kammermans, H., 2010. The Application of Predictive Modelling in Archaeology: Problems and Possibilities. in: F. Niccolucci & S. Hermon eds., *Beyond the Artefact: Digital Interpretation of the Past*. Proceedings of CAA204, Prato 13-17 April 2004, Budapest: Archaeolingua, 273-277.

Khlopashev, G.A. & E.J. Giria. 2010. *Secrets of Ancient Bone Carvers in Eastern Europe and Siberia: Methods of Processing Mammoth Tusk and Reindeer Horn in the Stone Age* (According to Archaeological and Experimental Data), Saint Petersburg: Nauka. (in Russian)

Kienholz, A. & J. Affolter. 2016. Sileces, in: C. Harb & N. Bleicher eds., *Zürich-Parkhaus Opera: Eine neolithische Feuchtbodenfundstelle Band 2: Funde*, Zürich: Monographien der Kantonsarchäologie Zürich 49, 109-233.

Klokkernes, T., 2007. *Skin Processing Technology in Eurasian Reindeer Cultures*, Copenhagen: Royal Danish Academy of Fine Arts, The School of Conservation.

Klokkernes, T., 2022. What is not there? Skin and fur objects in prehistoric hunter-gatherer societies. in: O. Grøn, H. Peeters eds., *Hidden Dimensions. Aspects of Mesolithic hunter-gatherer landscape use and non-lithic technology*, Leiden: Sidestone Press, 153-175.

Krause, A., 1956. *The Tlingit Indians: Results of a Trip to the Northwest Coast of America and the Bering Straits*, Seattle: University of Washington Press.

Krutak, L., 2015. The Cultural Heritage of Tattooing: A Brief History. *Current Problems in Dermatology* 48, 1-5.

Kozłowski, S.K., 1975. *Cultural Differentiation of Europe from 10th to 5th millennium B.C.*, Warsaw: Warsaw University Press.

Larsson, L., 1975. A Contribution to the Knowledge of Mesolithic Huts in Southern Scandinavia. *Meddelanden från Lunds Universitets Historiska Museum* 1973-1974, 5-28.

Layton, R., 1986. Political and Territorial Structures Among Hunter-Gatherers. *Man* 21(1), 18-33.

Man, A.F., 1932 (2nd edition. first published in 1885). *On the Aboriginal Inhabitants of the Andaman Islands with Report of Researches Into the Language of the South Andaman Island*, London: Royal Anthropological Institute of Great Britain and Ireland.

Mathiassen, T., 1928. *Material Culture of the Iglulik Eskimos*, Copenhagen: Nordisk Forlag.

Mills, S. & A. Pannett. 2009. Sounds Like Sociality: New Research on Lithic Contexts in Mesolithic Caithness. in: S. McCartan, R. Schulting, G. Warren & P. Woodman eds., *Mesolithic Horizons: Papers Presented at the Seventh International Conference on the Mesolithic in Europe, Belfast 2005*, Vol. 2, Oxford: Oxbow, 717-721.

Oakes, J. E. & R. Riewe. 1992. A Comparison of Historical and Contemporary Skin Clothing Used in North Greenland: An Ethnohistorical Approach. *Clothing and Textile Research Journal* 10(3), 76-85.

Peeters, J.H.M., 2007. *Hoge Vaart-A27 in Context: Towards a Model of Mesolithic–Neolithic Land-Use Dynamics as a Framework for Archaeological Heritage Management*, Amersfoort, Netherlands: Rijksdienst voor Archeologie, Cultuurlandschap en Monumenten.

Peeters, H. & M.J.L.Th. Niekus. 2017. Mesolithic Pit Hearths in the Northern Netherlands: Function, Time-Depth and Behavioural Context. in: N. Achard-Corompt, E. Ghesquière & V. Riquier eds., *Creuser au Mésolithique. Digging in the Mesolithic*. Actes de la séance de la Société préhistorique française de Châlons-en-Champagne (29-30 mars 2016). Société préhistorique française, 2017, Paris: Séances de la Société préhistorique française 12, 225-239.

Peeters, H., D.C.M. Raemaekers, I.I.J.A.L.M. Devriendt, P.W. Hoebe, M.J.L.Th. Niekus, G.R. Nobles & M. Schepers. 2017. *Paradise Lost? Insights into the Early Prehistory of the Netherlands from Development-Led Archaeology*, Amersfoort, Netherlands: Cultural Heritage Agency of the Netherlands.

Radcliffe Brown, A.R., 1922. *The Andaman Islanders: A Study in Social Anthropology*, Cambridge: University Press.

Reilly, A., 2015. *Women's Work, Tools, and Expertise: Hide Tanning and the Archaeological Record*. MA thesis, Calgary: Department of Anthropology, University of Alberta.

Riede, F., 2009. Climate and Demography in Early Prehistory: Using Calibrated ^{14}C Dates as Population Proxies. *Human Biology* 81(2-3), 309-337.

Rogers, E.S., 1969. Band Organization among the Indians of Eastern Subarctic Canada: Contributions to Anthropology. in: D. Damas ed., *Band Societies*. Proceedings of the Conference on Band Organization, Ottawa, August 30 to September 2, 1965, Ottawa: Bulletin 228. Anthropological Series 84. National Museum of Canada, 21-55.

Sackett, J.R., 1982. Isochrestism and Style: A Clarification. *Journal of Anthropological Archaeology* 5(3), 266-277.

Schönweiss, W. & H. Werner. 1974. Mesolithische Wohnanlagen von Sarching, Ldkr. Regensburg. *Bayrische Vorgeschichtsblätter* 39, 1-29.

Shirokogoroff, S.M., 1935. *Psychomental Complex of the Tungus*, London: Kegan Paul, Trench, Trubner.

Skaarup, J., O. Grøn. 2004. *Møllegabet II. A submerged Mesolithic settlement in southern Denmark*, Oxford: Langelands Museum/BAR International Series 1328.

Sillitoe, P. & K. Hardy. 2003. Living Lithics: Ethnoarchaeology in Highland Papua New Guinea. *Antiquity* 77(297), 555-566.

Sjöström, A., 2011. *Mesolitiska lämninger I Rönneholms mosse: Arkeologisk förundersökning 2010*, Lund. Sweden: Rapporter från Institutionen för arkeologi och antikens historia Lunds Universitet 4.

Sjöström, A., 2012. *Mesolitiska lämninger I Rönneholms mosse: Arkeologisk förundersökning 2011*, Lund, Sweden: Rapporter från Institutionen för arkeologi och antikens historia Lunds Universitet 5.

Sjöström, A., 2013. *Mesolitiska lämninger I Rönneholms mosse: Arkeologisk förundersökning 2012*, Lund, Sweden: Rapporter från Institutionen för arkeologi och antikens historia Lunds Universitet 8.

Sjöström, A., 2014. *Mesolitiska lämninger I Rönneholms mosse: Arkeologisk förundersökning 2013*, Lund, Sweden: Rapporter från Institutionen för arkeologi och antikens historia Lunds Universitet 12.

Sjöström, A., 2015. *Mesolitiska lämninger I Rönneholms mosse: Arkeologisk förundersökning 2014*, Lund, Sweden: Rapporter från Institutionen för arkeologi och antikens historia Lunds Universitet 14.

Stiles, D., 1993. Hunter-Gatherer Trade in Wild Forest Products in the Early Centuries A.D. with the Port of Broach, India. *Asian Perspectives* 32(2), 152-167.

Stout, D., 2011. Stone Toolmaking and the Evolution of Human Culture and Cognition. *Philosophical Transactions of the Royal Society B* 366, 1050-1059.

Strathern, A. & M. Strathern. 1971. *Self-Decoration in Mount Hagen*, London: Gerald Duckworth.

Sutton, P., 1994. Material Culture Traditions of the Wik People, Cape York Peninsula. *Records of the South Australian Museum* 37(1), 30-52.

Svensson, T., 1992. Clothing in the Arctic: A Means of Protection, a Statement of Identity. *Arctic* 45(1), 62-73.

Swagerty, W.R., 1988. Indian Trade in the Trans-Mississippi West to 1870. in: W.E. Washburn ed., *Handbook of North American Indians Vol. 4: History of Indian–White Relations*, Washington, D.C.: Smithsonian Institution, 351-374.

Sørensen, M., T. Rankama, J. Kankanpää, K. Knutsson, H. Knutsson, S. Melvold, B. Valentin Eriksen & H. Glørstad. 2013. The First Eastern Migrations of People and Knowledge into Scandinavia: Evidence from Studies of Mesolithic Technology, 9th-8th Millennium BC. *Norwegian Archaeological Review*, 1-38.

Tanner, A., 2014. *Bringing Home Animals: Mistissini Hunters of Northern Quebec*, St. John's, Newfoundland: ISER Books, Memorial University of Newfoundland.

Townsend, P.K., 1978. The Politics of Mobility among the Sanio-Hiowe. *Anthropological Quarterly* 51(1), 27-35.

Turnbull, C.M., 1965a. *The Mbuti Pygmies: An Ethnographic Survey*, New York: Anthropological Papers of the American Museum of Natural History 50(3).

Turnbull, C.M., 1965b. *Wayward Servants: The Two Worlds of the African Pygmies*, New York: Natural History Press/Garden City.

Tykot, R.H., 2004. Neolithic Exploitation and Trade of Obsidian in the Central Mediterranean. in: le Secrétariat du Congrès eds., *Acts of the XIVth UISPP Congress*. University of Liège, Belgium, 2-8 September 2001. Section 9: The Neolithic in the Near East and Europe, Oxford: BAR International Series 1303. Archaeopress, 25-35.

Vasilevich, G.M. & A.V. Smolyak. 1964. The Evenks. In: M.G. Levin & L.P. Potapov. *The Peoples of Siberia*, Chicago: University of Chicago Press, 620-654.

Vogt, D., O. Grøn, H. Peeters, R Hernek, É. David. 2022. Mesolithic landscapes and where to hunt big game: everywhere or ???. in: O. Grøn & H. Peeters eds., *Hidden Dimensions. Aspects of Mesolithic hunter-gatherer landscape use and non-lithic technology*, Leiden: Sidestone Press, 113-150.

Živaljević, I., Dimitrijević, V., Jovanović, J., Blagojević, T., Pendić, J., Putica, A., Uzelac, V., Bulatović, J., Spasić, M., Jončić, N., Penezić, K., Anđelić, D., Bajčeta, M., Stefanović, S., 2021. Revealing the "hidden" Pannonian and Central Balkan Mesolithic: new radiocarbon evidence from Serbia. *Quaternary International* 574, 52-67. https://doi.org/10.1016/j.quaint.2020.11.043

The Mesolithic in Poland in light of field research of the Institute of Archaeology, University of Lodz

Lucyna DOMAŃSKA[1], Marcin WĄS[2]

[1] Professor, Institute of Archaeology, University of Lodz, Poland ; lucyna.domanska@uni.lodz.pl
[2] Institute of Archaeology, University of Gdańsk, Poland

ABSTRACT

A team from the Institute of Archaeology, University of Lodz excavated three Mesolithic sites, including Dabrowa Biskupia 71, Deby 29, and Jastrzebia Gora 4. The last one is located on the Baltic coast, with the other two located in the Kuyavia region of the Polish Lowlands. From the results of archaeological studies, climatic and environmental changes were interpreted in relation to the migration of peoples in the Mesolithic sites. A significant climatic change at the transition between the Pleistocene and Holocene caused enormous changes in the environment in the European Lowlands. At the beginning of the Holocene, birch forest appeared in these areas; and later, birch-pine forest with elm, hazel, and oak. Together with the environmental changes, Mesolithic populations settled vast areas of western, central, and northern Europe. The first Mesolithic groups emerged in western Poland in the second half of the Preboreal period. The most important event at the end of the Boreal period is linked with flooding by sea transgressions of the west Baltic land bridge occupied by the Maglemose peopl. It is believed that this event caused the migration of these groups southeastward and their appearance in the northern part of the pre-valley zone of the Polish Lowlands. Dabrowa Biskupia 71 is one of the Maglemosian sites discovered in the Polish Lowlands. The main features of the late Mesolithic (Atlantic and Subatlantic stages of the Holocene) in the territory of Poland are, on the one hand, the continuation of the Early Mesolithic cultural tradition, and, on the other, the appearance of new cultural units connected with the Mesolithic of the Black Sea region. The first cultural tradition is represented by so-called Post-Maglemosian groups; the second, by Janislawice culture.

국문초록

이 논문은 우찌대학교 고고학연구소에서 발굴한 발트해 연안과 폴란드 저지대 쿠야비아(Kuyavia) 일대의 중석기 유적을 소개하고 있다. 갱신세–홀로세 전환기 기후변화는 유럽 저지대 환경 변화를 초래했는데 홀로세 초 자작나무 숲에서 점차 느릅나무, 개암나무, 참나무와 공생하는 자작나무–소나무 숲이 나타났다. 이 시기에 중석기 인류가 유럽의 서부, 중부, 북부에 널리 정착하게 되었으며 폴란드 서부에서도 프리보리얼(Preboreal) 후반기에 최초 중석기가 출현했다. 보리얼 말기에는 마글레모스(Maglemose) 집단이 살고 있던 서부 발트 육교, 그리고 북해 도거랜드(Doggerland) 일대에는 해침으로 인해 범람이 일어났고 이에 연동하여 중석기 마글모즈 집단이 남동으로 이동함으로써 폴란드 저지대로 이주한 마글모즈 집단에 의한 다브로와 비스쿠피아 71 유적 등이 나타나고 있다. 폴란드에서 홀로세 아틀란트기와 서브아틀란트기에 해당하는 늦은시기의 중석기 시대에는 이른 중석기 문화전통이 연속되었으며, 흑해지역의 새로운 중석기 대표집단인 후기마글레모시아(Post-Maglemosian) 집단과 야니스라비체(Janislawice) 집단이 출현하고 있다.

Keywords : Poland, Mesolithic, cultures, lithic analysis, Post-Maglemosian, Janislawice culture

1. Introduction

In our article, we present three Mesolithic sites excavated by a team from the Institute of Archaeology, University of Lodz. These sites are as follows: Dąbrowa Biskupia 71 (DB 71), Dęby 29 (D 29), and Jastrzębia Góra 4 (JG 4). The last site is located on the Baltic coast, with the other two located in the Kuyavia region of the Polish Lowlands (Fig. 1).

Significant climatic changes at the turn of the Pleistocene and Holocene caused enormous changes in the environment of the European Lowlands. At the beginning of the Holocene, birch forest appeared in these areas; later, birch-pine forest with elm, hazel, and oak. Together with the environmental changes, Mesolithic populations settled vast areas of western, central, and northern Europe. The first Mesolithic groups emerged in western Poland in the second half of the Preboreal period.

The Mesolithic covers the period from the Preboreal to the Subatlantic stage of the Holocene. It is divided into two phases: the Early and Late Mesolithic (Kabaciński, 2016; Masojć, 2016). The end of the early phase is connected with Atlantic warming and the spread of deciduous forest.

The most important event at the end of the Boreal period is linked to flooding by sea transgressions of the west Baltic land bridge occupied by the Maglemose people (Astrup, 2018). It is believed that this event caused the migration of these groups southeastward and their appearance in the northern part of the pre-valley zone of the Polish Lowlands. Only a few Maglemosian sites dated to the Boreal period are known from the territory of Poland (Kabaciński, 2016).

One of the Maglemosian sites discovered in the Polish Lowlands is DB 71 site. In 2001-2003, excavations were conducted with the aim of fully identifying the site and defining the character of the spatial distribution of its artifacts (Domańska and Wąs, 2009; Domańska, 2016).

The main features of the Late Mesolithic in the territory of Poland are, on the one hand, the continuation of the Early Mesolithic cultural tradition, and, on the other, the appearance of new cultural units connected with the Mesolithic of the Black Sea region. The first cultural tradition is represented by so-called Post-Maglemosian groups; the second, by Janisławice culture.

Of particular importance in the study of the Post-Maglemosian groups were excavations conducted at the JG 4 site in 1975-1980 (Wąs, 2018). On the other hand, important data for studies on the Janisławice culture in Poland were provided by excavations at the site of Deby 29 carried out in the years 1984-1987 (Domańska, 1991).

In the origin of the Janisławice culture the impulse from the areas of the Black Sea steppes played a vital role. It has been confirmed, among other things, by the presence of pencil-shaped cores (Fig. 4: 1) at Janisławice culture sites (Domańska, 1990, 1991). Long-distance interregional contacts are a characteristic feature of these communities. Artifacts made of chocolate flint confirm such contacts (Cyrek, 1995; Wąs, 2006b). Single products made of this raw material were found at Janisławice culture sites in the Pripyat River basin in the Ukraine. In the middle Vistula River basin, long-distance distribution of chocolate flint has been confirmed by materials recovered from the D 29 site. All products from this site were made of this raw material, whereas the nearest outcrops of chocolate flint are situated about 250km from the site.

The excavations carried out at DB 71, JG 4, and D 29 yielded important information not only for the reconstruction of the settlement processes of the Polish Lowlands in the Mesolithic but also for research on changes in flint production among the Early Holocene hunting-gathering societies in Poland. Different cultural affiliations as well as different chronologies of flint inventories from DB 71, JG 4, and D 29 reveal specific conditions for the identification and comparison of the specificity of Mesolithic flintworking.

Flint assemblages from DB 71, JG 4, and D 29 are currently one of the best recognized technologically Mesolithic sites in Poland. The results obtained from the analysis of these sites (including the refitting method) shed new light on flint processing and particularly on the

Fig. 1 Location of the Mesolithic sites: JG4, DB71 and D29.

identification of relationships between the raw materials and technologies occurring in various traditions of the Mesolithic in Central Europe (Domańska and Wąs, 2009; Wąs, 2018 ; Wąs and Domańska, 2023).

The inventories from DB 71, JG 4, and D 29 represent different traditions of flint technology that resulted not only from their different cultural affiliations and chronologies. A very important factor is the geographic spread of these sites and the availability of local sources of raw materials. The impact of raw materials – their quality and nodule size – on Mesolithic flint production is well illustrated by the materials from JG 4 and D 29.

2. Site Dąbrowa Biskupia 71 (DB 71)

In 2001, sondage excavations were conducted at DB 71 by digging four trenches of 1m² each in the area of the site. These trenches yielded single Mesolithic artifacts – exclusively microliths and bladelets. During the following two seasons, in 2002-2003, broader excavations were conducted with the aim of fully identifying the site and defining the character of the spatial distribution of the artifacts (Domańska and Wąs, 2009).

Over the course of the excavations, 482 flint artifacts were discovered. The artifacts were concentrated mainly in the central part of the explored area, with no distinctive concentrations.

All Mesolithic artifacts were made of local flint – so-called Baltic flint. Among them, two categories predominate: tools (39.8% of the entire inventory) and blades (32% of the materials). Within the group of tools, microliths are the most numerous products – 189 such specimens were distinguished, comprising 98.5% of the tools (**Fig. 2**).

Several types of microliths were distinguished. Narrow scalene triangles (**Fig. 2:** 1-20) and microliths with a retouched base (**Fig. 2:** 25-26) predominate among them. Despite the typological differentiation, the discussed group of artifacts is marked by considerable stylistic similarity. All of the microliths were made of slender, regular bladelets.

Blades are the second most frequent category of products in the inventory. All of the blades exhibit similar morphological features, which makes it possible to treat them as a technologically homogeneous assemblage. Among them, the frequency of flat butts and abrasion is almost the same as among the microburins and the microliths.

A separate case is the flint inventory from DB 71 dated to the Early Mesolithic, which has a different structure than the assemblages from JG 4 and D 29. It does not have typical workshop elements and is probably a remnant of a small hunting camp. The research on flints from DB 71 yielded insights into the method of blade production and the further selection of geometric microliths (Sørensen, 2012). Importantly, the entire inventory is based only on the local Baltic flint, the resources of which are not very rich in the vicinity of the site and the quality of which is rather bad. This factor surely determined a very economical core reduction strategy and the method of forming hunting tools like microliths.

3. Site Jastrzębia Góra 4 (JG 4)

JG 4 contains only materials made of local raw materials, so-called Pomeranian flint, which occurs in the form of very small (mainly 4-6cm) pebbles. Both the poor sources of raw material in the neighboring area of the site and the specific – oval – form of concretions determined the chaines operatoires related to its exploitation (Wąs, 2018). Research on the assemblage from JG 4 makes it possible to state that the dominant aim of production was a blade technology based on the exploitation of microlithic cores. The form of the exploited egg-shaped nodules of raw material influenced the method of exploitation of the microlithic blade cores. A clear example of this was the limitation of the preparation of striking platform by removing a single cortex flake for the formation of a flat surface. Also, the further exploitation of the core and the production of microblades were carried out with the use of a very economical pressure technique (**Fig. 3:** 29-32). The obtained blades were transformed mainly into geometric microliths, the tips of which were formed with a microburin blow (**Fig. 3:** 7, 9-11), or small punctiform butts were left as a microlith point (**Fig. 3:** 1-22). Slightly wider blades were transformed into trapeze-shaped microliths (**Fig. 3:** 23). Scraping tools were formed from small, oval, and cortical flakes, mostly coming from the striking platform preparation. The special regime and local conditions of raw materials determined the necessity to re-utilize the exhausted or damaged blade cores via the splintering method. Thus, within one lump of raw material, the blade production trend was changed to the flake production trend.

4. Site Dęby 29 (D 29)

The flint processing technology at Late Mesolithic D 29 developed differently than at JG 4. The inventory from this site is entirely based on a non-local raw material called chocolate flint, outcrops of which are located more than 200km SE from the site. Research on flint production at D 29 provided important information on how the local Mesolithic hunter-gatherer societies developed the strategy of using

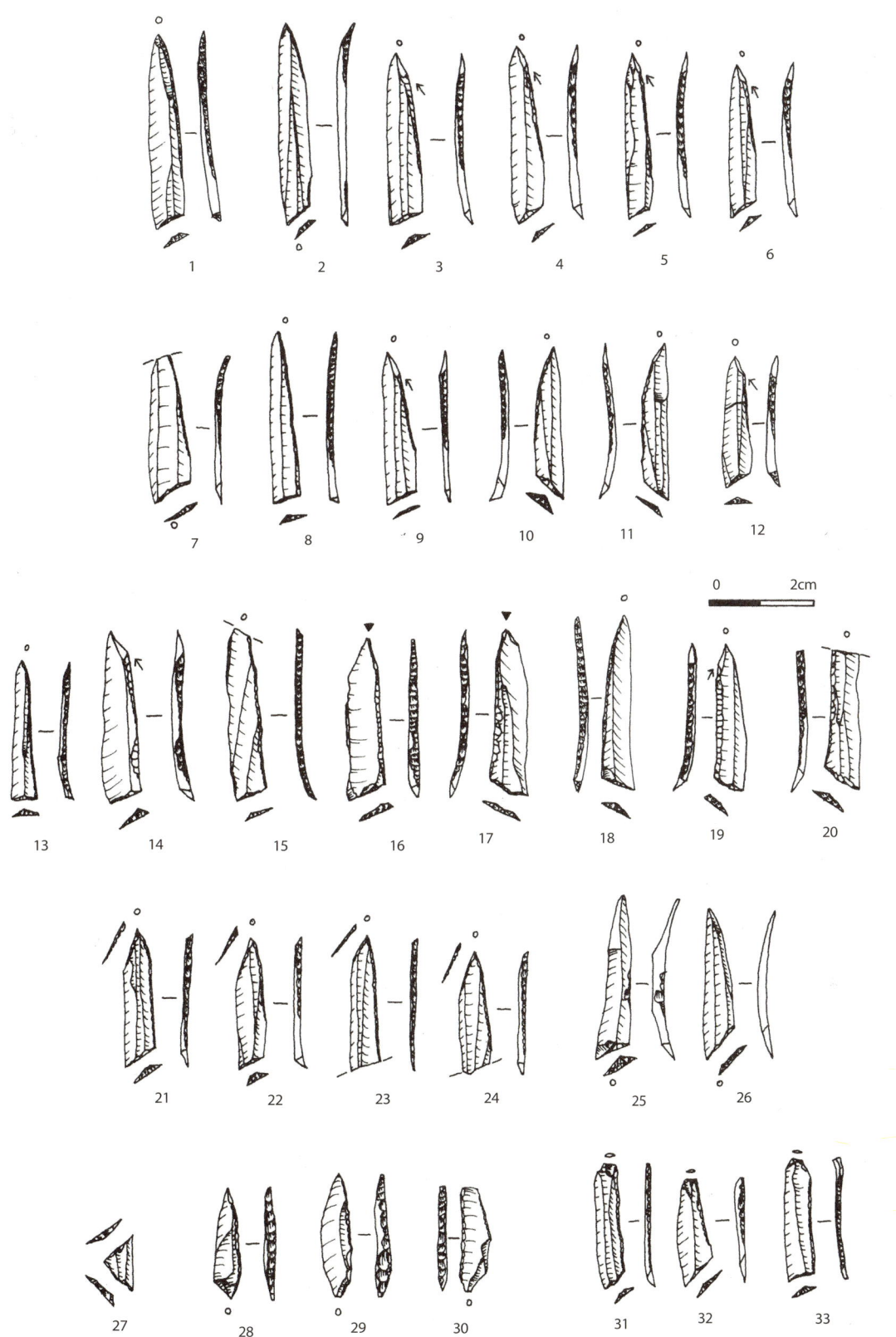

Fig. 2 Dąbrowa Biskupia 71. Microliths.

imported flint in areas located far from its outcrops and in areas poor in local flint resources. Particularly, valuable information for the identification of flint technology at this Late Mesolithic site was generated by the use of the refitting method (Wąs, 2006a). The results of this research are important because only one exhausted blade core (a so-called pencil-shaped core) was found at the site. The obtained refittings clearly indicate that several blade cores were processed at the site. Each of these cores was reduced using one of two techniques: indirect percussion

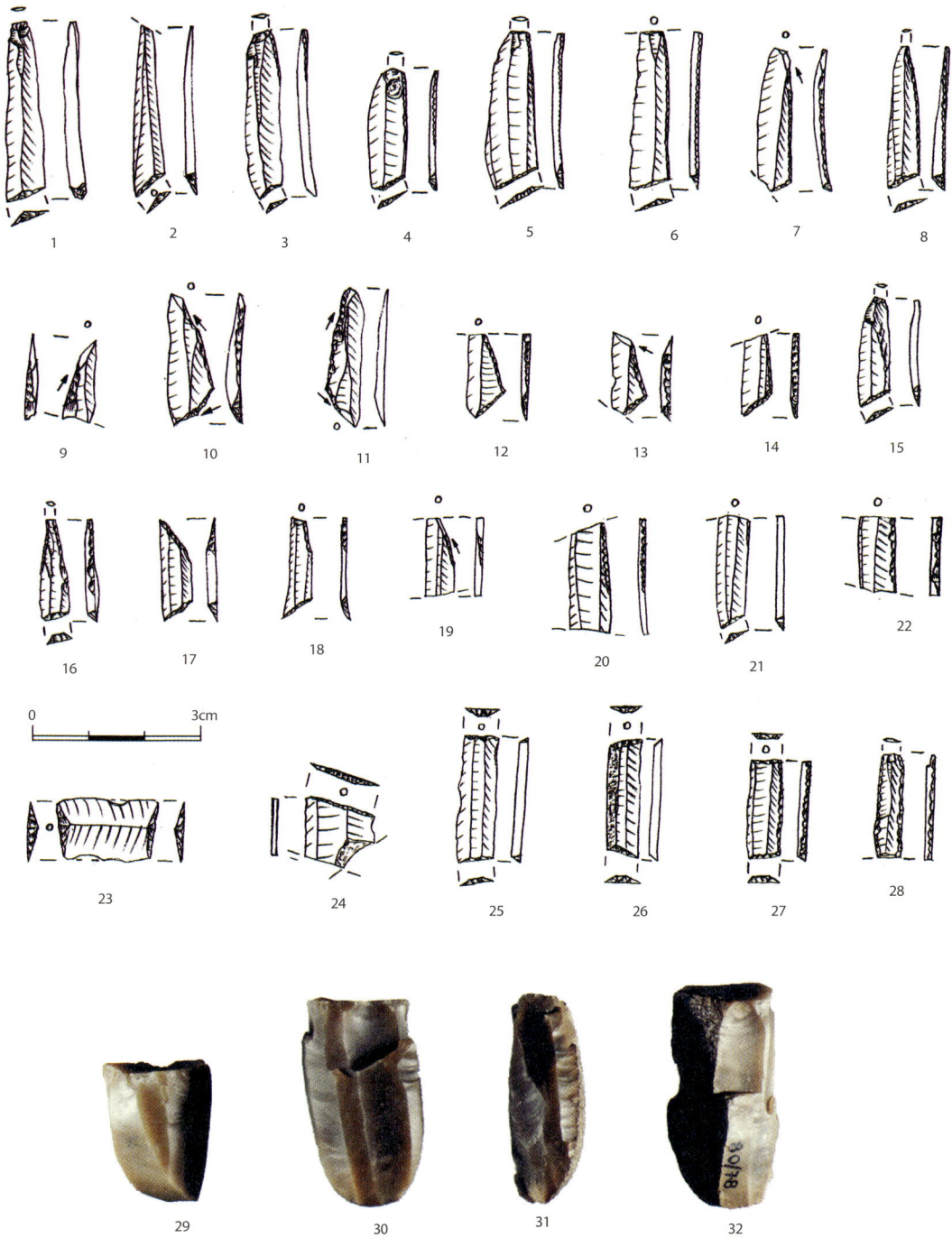

Fig. 3 Jastrzębia Góra 4. Microliths and cores.

(for medium-sized blades) and the pressure technique (for microlithic regular blades) as shown by the results of experimental research (Migal and Wąs, 2006; Pelegrin, 2012). Both techniques required the frequent preparation and correction of the striking platforms (mostly the rejuvenation of the flaking angle), which resulted in a large number of small- and medium-sized flakes. Therefore, it was not necessary to exploit separate flake cores. As a result of such an organized method of processing blade cores, some of the flakes removed from their striking platforms were used to form tools such as scrapers and other retouched flakes. The main purpose of production – i.e., blades – was transformed into microliths (**Fig. 4**) and larger specimens of blades for other tools, like burins. Geometric microliths in the type of half-becked points (so-called Wieliszew points) (**Fig. 4:** 7-11, 15-17) and very narrow long triangles (so-called long janislavician triangles) (**Fig. 4:** 12-14) were always formed by using the microburin blow technique (**Fig. 4:** 1-6) to sharpen their tips and by transversal breaking to shape the base of microliths.

It is also worth mentioning that thanks to the analysis of flint materials using the refitting method, important information

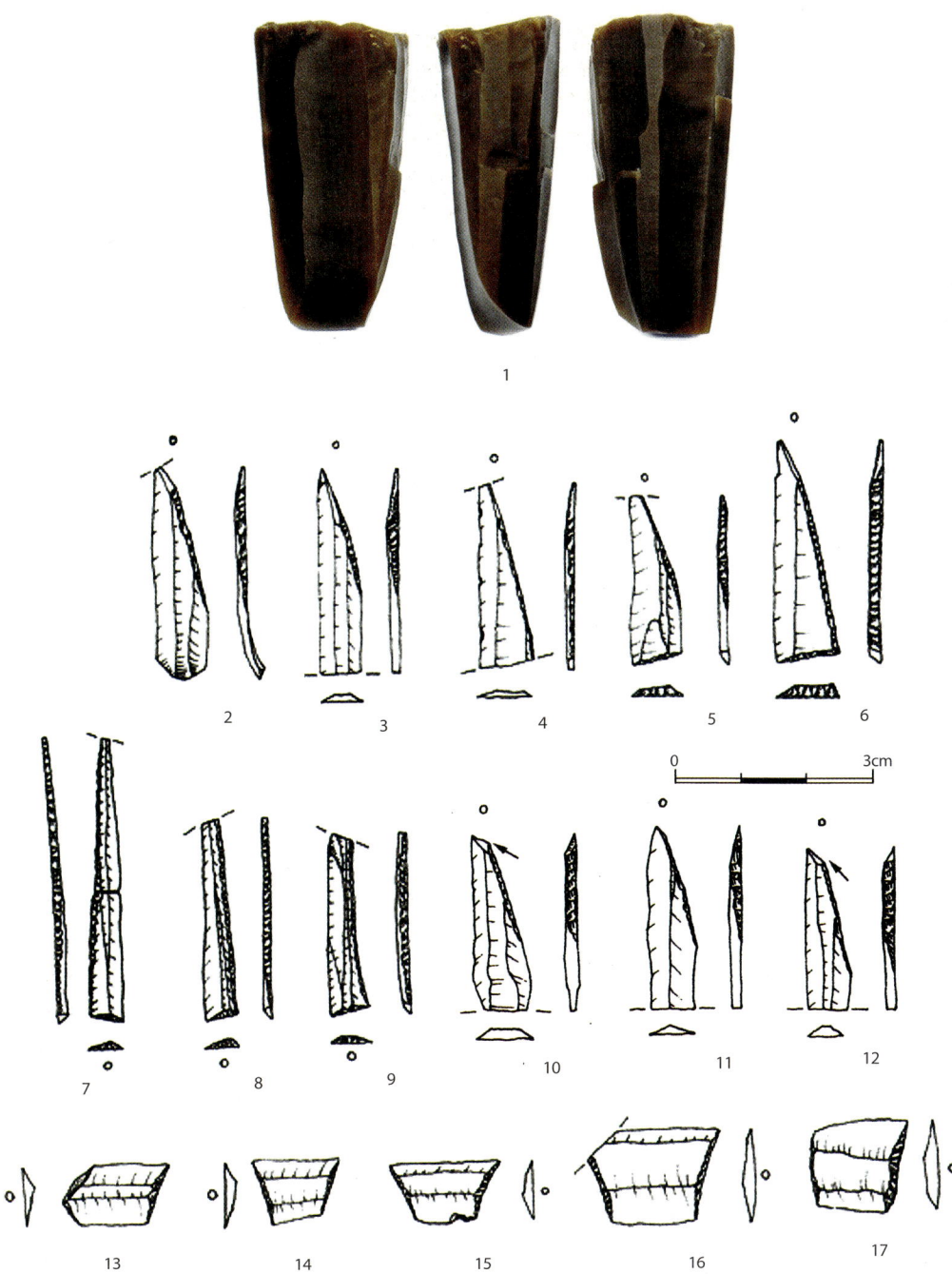

Fig. 4 Dęby 29. Microliths and core.

was obtained on the distribution of chocolate flint in the Janisławice culture, and indirectly also conclusions on interregional contacts between the late mesolithic societies in the Vistula river basin (Wąs, 2006b, 2008).

5. Conclusions

The sites presented above put the problem of the origin of the Mesolithic cultures in the Polish Lowlands in a new light. The Early Mesolithic in Poland was associated with the coming of hunting, fishing and gathering communities from western and north-western Europe, which brought with them already developed cultural models. At the end of the Boreal period this process was caused by the submergence of the west-Baltic land bridge through sea transgression, which forced the groups of the Maglemose culture to migrate south and south-eastwards in search of new areas to settle. The site Dąbrowa Biskupia 71 confirms this process. In the late Mesolithic, significant differences can be observed between western and eastern regions of Poland. In north-western Poland, local contacts are becoming more important. The result of these contacts are the so-called Post-Maglemosian groups to which the site Jastrzębia Góra

4 belongs. In turn, in central and eastern Poland, contacts with the areas of today's Ukraine are becoming particularly important. The effect of these contacts is the appearance of the new cultural unit (so-called Janisławice culture) connected with the Mesolithic of the Black Sea region. The site Dęby 29 represents this culture.

To sum up, it should be emphasized that the short characteristics of the sites from Dabrowa Biskupia 71, Jastrzebia Gora 4 and Deby 29 presented above do not include all the results achieved by the team of researchers from the Institute of Archaeology of the University of Lodz under the direction of Lucyna Domańska at sites dating to the Mesolithic. The ones we have described here undoubtedly make an important contribution to the understanding of the Mesolithic in Poland, both thanks to many years of excavations as well as thanks to various analyses and studies, such as use-wear analyses of flint tools or research on flint technology using the refitting method (e.g. Winiarska-Kabacińska, 2007; Pyżewicz, 2022). Currently, the DB 71, JG 4 and D2 9 sites belong to the group of the most important Mesolithic sites in Poland, therefore they are often cited and mentioned in publications and the most important syntheses on the Middle Stone Age in Central Europe (e.g. Kozłowski, 1989, 2009; Kabaciński, 2016; Masojć, 2016).

References

Astrup, P.M., 2018. *Sea-level Change in Mesolithic Southern Scandinavia*, Aarhus: Jysk Arkaeologisk Selskab.

Cyrek, K., 1995. On the distribution of chocolate flint in the Late Mesolithic of the Vistula basin. *Archaeologia Polona* 33, 99-109.

Domańska, L., 1990. *Kaukasko-nadczarnomorskie wzorce kulturowe w rozwoju późnomezolitycznych społeczeństw niżu strefy pogranicza Europy Wschodniej i Środkowej*. Uniwersytet im, Inowrocław: Adama Mickiewicza w Poznaniu.

Domańska, L., 1991. *Obozowisko kultury janisławickiej w Dębach, woj: Włocławskie, stanowisko 29*. Uniwersytet im, Inowrocław: Adama Mickiewicza w Poznaniu, Poznań.

Domańska, L., 2016. Change and continuity. *Traditions of the flint processing from the perspective of the Tążyna river valley*, Łódź: Instytut Archeologii Uniwersytetu Łódzkiego.

Domańska, L., Wąs, M., 2009. The site Dąbrowa Biskupia 71– specialized camp from the Maglemose culture. in: McCartan, S., Schulting, R., Warren, G., Woodman, P.C. eds., *Mesolithic Horizons*. Papers presented at the seventh international conference on "The Mesolithic in Europe", Belfast 2005, Oxford: Oxbow Books, 259-266.

Kabaciński, J., 2016. After the Ice Age. in: Kabaciński, J. ed., *The Past Societies. Polish lands from the first evidence of human presence to the Early Middle Ages* Vol. 1, 500,000-5,500 BC, Warszawa: Wydawnictwo IAE PAN, 249-270.

Kozłowski, S.K., 1989. *Mesolithic in Poland. A new approach*, Warszawa: Wydawnictwa Uniwersytetu Warszawskiego.

Kozłowski, S.K., 2009. *Thinking Mesolithic*, Oxford: Oxbow Books.

Masojć, M., 2016. Mesolithic hunter-gatherers of the Atlantic forests. in: Kabaciński, J. ed., *The Past Societies. Polish lands from the first evidence of human presence to the Early Middle Ages* Vol. 1, 500,000-5,500 BC, Warszawa: Wydawnictwo IAE PAN, 271-291.

Migal, W., Wąs, M., 2006. Microblade pressure technique at the Late Mesolithic site Dęby 29. Experimental approach. in: Wiśniewski, A., Płonka, T., Burdukiewicz, J.M. eds., *The Stone– Techniques and Technologies*, Wrocław: Instytut Archeologii Uniwersytetu Wrocławskiego, 179-188.

Pelegrin, J., 2012. New Experimental Observations for the Characterization of Pressure Blade Production Techniques. in: Desrosiers, P.M. ed., *The Emergence of Pressure Blade Making. From Origin to Modern Experimentation*, New York: Springer Science Business Media, 465-500.

Pyżewicz, K., 2022. *Przykłady strategii produkcji i użytkowania paleolitycznych oraz mezolitycznych narzędzi krzemiennych*, Warszawa: Wydawnictwo Uniwersytetu Warszawskiego.

Sørensen, M., 2012. The Arrival and Development of Pressure Blade Technology in Southern Scandinavia. in: Desrosiers, P.M. ed., *The Emergence of Pressure Blade Making. From Origin to Modern Experimentation*, New York: Springer Science Business Media, 237-259.

Wąs, M., 2006a. Raw materials and flint processing strategy in the Late Mesolithic in Poland. Results of refitting. in: Wiśniewski, A., Płonka, T., Burdukiewicz, J.M. eds., *The Stone– Techniques and Technologies*, Wrocław: Instytut Archeologii Uniwersytetu Wrocławskiego, 173-178.

Wąs, M., 2006b. Some remarks on contacts between Late Mesolithic hunters–gatherers societies as reflected in their flint technology: a case study from Central Poland. in: Apel, J., Knutsson, K. eds., *Skilled Production and Social Reproduction. Aspects of Traditional Stone-Tool Technologies*, Uppsala: Societas Archaeologica Upsaliensis, 315-322.

Wąs, M., 2008. O dystrybucji „czekolady" w kulturze janisławickiej z perspektywy technologii krzemieniarstwa. in: Borkowski, W., Libera, J., Sałacińska, B., Sałaciński, S. eds., *Krzemień czekoladowy w pradziejach*, Warszawa: Państwowe

Muzeum Archeologiczne w Warszawie, 171-184.

Wąs, M., 2018. *Późny paleolit i mezolit w północnej części Pomorza Gdańskiego*, Łódź: Łódzka Fundacja Badań Naukowych.

Wąs, M., Domańska, L., 2023. Dęby 29 mniej znane. Mezolityczny inwentarz z krzemienia bałtyckiego ze stanowiska 29 w Dębach, woj. kujawsko-pomorskie. *Fontes Archaeologici Posnanienses* 59, 202-218. https://doi.org/10.34868/fap.59.004

Winiarska-Kabacińska, M., 2007. Dąbrowa Biskupia 71: Mesolithic hunters' camp?. in: Masojć, M., Płonka, T., Ginter, B., Kozłowski, S.K. eds., *Contributions to the Central European Stone Age*, Wrocław: Instytut Archeologii Uniwersytetu Wrocławskiego, 153-160.

Hell Gap: Then and now

Marcel KORNFELD[1], Mary Lou LARSON[2]

[1] Professor, University of Wyoming, USA; Anpro1@uwyo.edu
[2] University of Wyoming, USA (Deceased)

ABSTRACT

First excavated in the 1960s, the Hell Gap site serves as the backbone of North American Paleoindian chronology. Numerous Paleoindian complexes were defined over the previous 30 years, but their temporal relationships remained uncertain. The advent of radiocarbon dating was brought to bear on the chronological problem, but the solid carbon dating was too inexact to enhance our understanding of cultural sequencing of this early period. The 10 cultural complexes, found superimposed on each other at Hell Gap, demonstrate the cultural succession of the complexes at the site, several of which were newly defined. Sixty years later, renewed site investigation demonstrates the reliability of the original results and contributes to current debates of Paleoindian lifeways.

국문초록

1960년대에 처음 발굴되었고 1990년대에 추가 발굴 조사된 헬갭 유적을 통하여 북미 최초 거주민으로서의 고인디안 문화연대기가 마련되었다. 그러나 약 30년 이상 조사를 통해 많은 고인디안 유적들이 확인되었으나 시간적 관계성은 불확실했다. 1960년대 최초 유적조사에서 연대층위(11,000-8,000년 전)가 확립되었고, 구슬, 바늘, 주거지 발견을 통하여 최초 인디안 문화계통이 수립되었다. 1990년대 유적조사에서는 고고학적 자료들을 통하여 문화층과 지질층의 형성과정 모델링을 실시하였고, 고정밀 자료 분석을 통해 헬갭 유적이 고인디안의 단기간 정착(약 3,000년간) 유적임을 밝혔다. 방사성탄소연대측정법으로 연대문제는 해결되었지만, 이는 초기 문화적 계통의 이해를 증진시킬 정도로 정확한 것은 아니었다. 헬갭 유적에서 서로 겹쳐진 10개 문화층을 통해 문화적 연속성을 확인했다. 1990년대에 새롭게 실시된 현장조사를 통해 1960년대 조사결과에 대한 신뢰성이 재입증되었으며, 고인디안 의생활 양식에 대해서도 열띤 논쟁이 가능하게 되었다.

Keywords : North America, Paleoindian chronology, Hell Gap site, site formation, Paleoindian lifeways

1. Introduction

The Hell Gap site was discovered in 1958 and brought to the attention of professional archaeologists in 1959 (Agogino, 2009; Duguid, 2009). Agogino's attention was aroused by an amateur discovery of a projectile point that appeared to be of Paleoindian age, but of as yet undefined type (Agogino, 1961). Pursuing this discovery, Agogino's test excavations located a number of previously defined Paleoindian complexes in stratigraphic position. Given the state of Paleoindian studies, in particular the problem of yet undefined cultural sequence, the site seemed like a promising location to contribute data for solving this problem (see Wormington, 1957 about the proposed Paleoindian cultural sequence).

In 1927 the Pleistocene age of human occupation of the Americas was demonstrated on the basis of geologic association of Folsom points (as they became known later) and other stone tools with extinct species of bison (B. bison antiquus) (Figgins, 1927). Subsequently a myriad of such discoveries were made, forming the initial period of Paleoindian studies (e.g., Roberts, 1935, 1943; Schultz, 1932; Sellards et al., 1947). In the early 1950s radiocarbon dates began to show that the Paleoindian period dated to approximately 10,000 plus or minus about 2,000 years ago. However, more specific radiocarbon dating to temporally differentiating artifact types such as Folsom from others (such as Plainview, Eden, Agate Basin), was unreliable at the time, hence the understanding of temporal relationships or sequences of objects could only be based on stratigraphic sequences and similiary seriation (Uhle, 1903; Wormington, 1957). Because of the nature of the sites identified as Paleoindian, mostly bison bone beds that represent relatively brief moments in time rather than camp sites, temporal sequences of human occupation at any one location were relatively rare or represented short periods of prehistory. Consequently some dozen artifacts types (projectile point styles) were known to be of Late Pleistocene or Early Holocene age (based on association with extinct bison), but whether or how they were temporally related to each other remained unknown. Then came Hell Gap, located at the edge of the Hartville uplift a Ponderosa Pine savanna setting and adjacent to the open plains to the east.

2. Hell Gap and Paleoindian Chronology

The Hell Gap site was destined to bring chronological order to Paleoindian period, however, its first contribution was to define a new Paleoindian complex, Hell Gap, assigned on the basis of a new projectile point style identified at the site (Agogino, 1961). Several other new complexes were defined during the early investigations of the 1960, based on new projectile point styles occurring throughout the geologic sequence, the Goshen and Frederick projectile

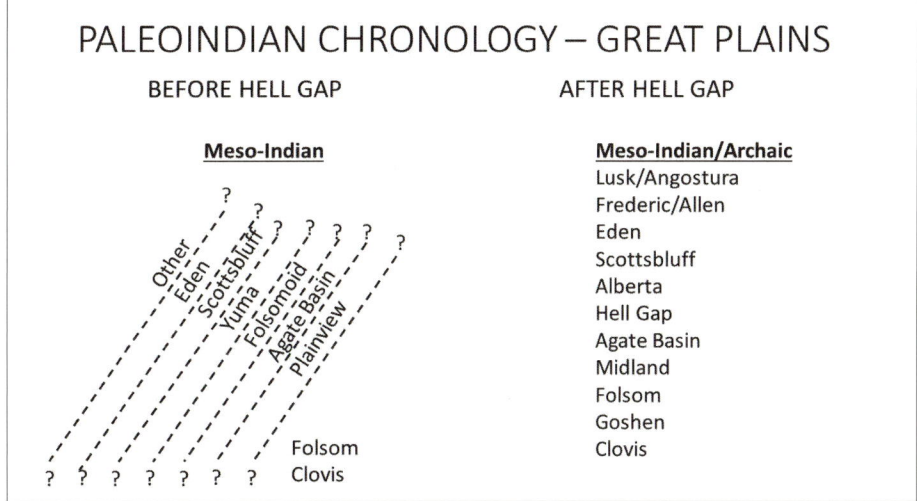

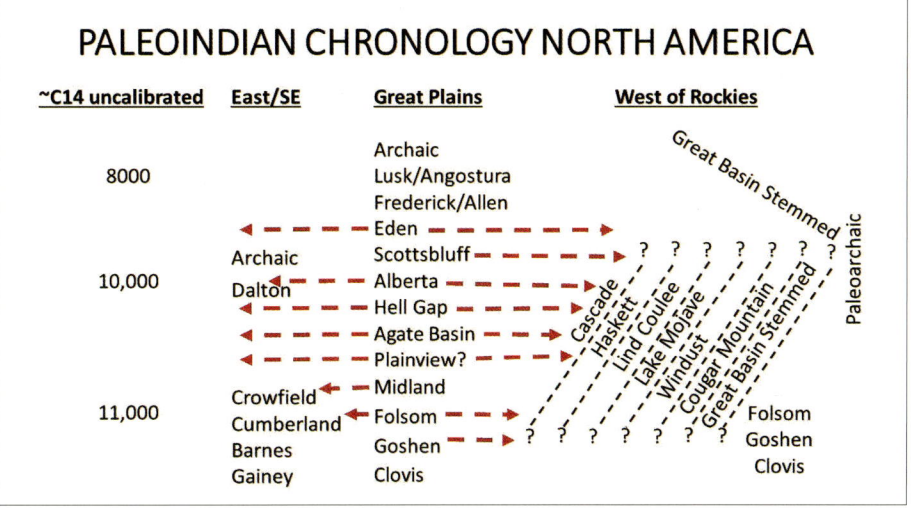

Fig. 1 Paleoindian chronology in the Great Plains before and after the excavations at the Hell Gap site (top) and relationship of Hell Gap chronology to Paleoindian cultural sequence of North America (bottom). Before excavations at Hell Gap, the relative temporal relationships of diagnostic artifacts was unknown (top left); Hell Gap excavations solved this chronological conundrum (top right).

points (Irwin, 1968; Irwin-Williams et al., 1973). At the close of the early investigations of Hell Gap, 10 cultural complexes were shown to be overlying each other (**Fig. 1** top). This sequence of Paleoindian 'cultures' holds in general for the wider Great Plains region of North America and in some instances beyond. Folsom, for example extends through the Rocky Mountains, Great Basin and beyond to the west as well as eastward and southeastward where associated complexes of Cumberland and Crowfield may represent variants. Likewise, stemmed points such as Hell Gap and the several Cody varieties have variants to the west and possibly eastward as well. The Paleoindian cultural sequence was the main reason for investigation of Hell Gap in the 1960s, but the results proved even more remarkable by demonstrating other firsts, or nearly so, for the period. The 1960s investigations yielded much additional and sometimes unique data regarding Paleoindian lifeways (see below).

2.1. The first round – 1960s

After some initial testing, Agogino began collaboration with two young archaeologists, one of whom (Henry Irwin), was in search of data for his doctoral dissertation. Siblings, Henry and Cynthia Irwin from Denver, Colorado, but now graduate students at Harvard University, developed a research project along with George Agogino and their mentor J.O. Brew of Harvard University to investigate the site in the coming years (Knudson, 2009:20). Well-funded by the Peabody Museum at Harvard, National Geographic Society, and the American Philosophical Society, a four year project ensued (1962-1966). The results were reported annually, although sometimes belatedly, in National Geographic Society Research Reports (e.g., Agogino and Irwin-Williams, 1971; Irwin, 1969, 1970a, 1973; Irwin and Brew, 1968), Henry Irwin's dissertation (1968), a summary report in Plains Anthropologist (Irwin-Williams et al., 1973), and a series of specialized papers that used the Hell Gap data to address a broad range of Paleoindian topics (e.g., Irwin, 1970b, 1971; Irwin and Wormington, 1970). Results of the 1960 investigations made a significant contribution to the Paleoindian database at the time and continue to do so to this very day.

2.1.1. Site setting

The Hell Gap site is located in a small previously unnamed valley, now known as the Hell Gap arroyo, draining eastward from the Haystack Range of the Hartville Uplift (**Fig. 2**). The arroyo appears to drain a particularly large area of the Uplift, perhaps resulting in less fluctuating and more reliable water supply. The site is situated just inside the canyon before the valley exits the Hartville Uplift and enters the open plains to the east, perhaps an advantageous ecological position for hunter-gatherers for their subsistence pursuits. Hartville Uplift is a ponderosa pine savanna vegetation community, while the open plains to the east are short grass prairie (Knight et al., 2014: 83). The two provide an exceptional complement of resources for a foraging population. On a very general level, various grasses, prairie potato (Psorealea lanceolata), pronghorn (Antilocapra americana), buffalo (Bison sp.), and Jackrabbit (Lepus townsendii) reside on the open grassland. The Hartville Uplift on the other hand is populated by yucca (yucca glauca), sago lily (Calochortus sp.), wild onion (Allium sp.), current (Ribes sp.), chokecherry (Prunus sp.), deer (Odocoileus hemionus), elk (Cervus elaphus), and rabbits (Sylvilagus floridanus), species that also exist or on the ecotone between the open plains and the Uplift.

2.1.2. 1960s Results

The 1960s investigations identified four stratified Paleoindian localities over an approximately 1.5km of the Hell Gap arroyo (Irwin-Williams et al., 1973). Cumulatively, the localities yielded 21 components of 10 superimposed Paleoindian complexes (see **Fig. 1** top). Missing from the stratified sediments was the earliest American cultural complex, Clovis. However, one of the newly defined complexes, Goshen, was found below Folsom, hence, between Clovis and Folsom in terms of age (Irwin, 1968). The other new complex, Hell Gap, was erroneously first described as pre-dating Agate Basin (Agogino, 1961:558), however, the error was subsequently corrected showing the complex to be between Agate Basin and Alberta (Agogino, 2009: 318). The third new complex defined at Hell Gap, Frederick, followed Eden-Scottsbluff component, hence it dates to the Late Paleoindian period.

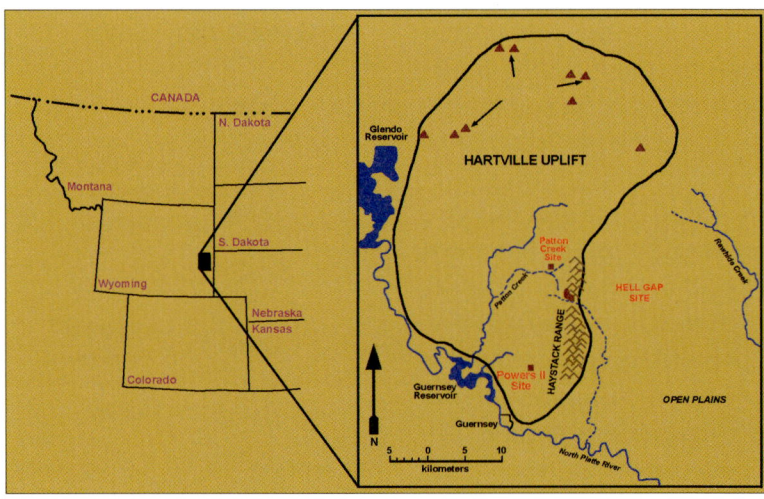

Fig. 2 Location of the Hell Gap site and the Hartville Uplift on the western Great Plains and Rocky Mountain interface. (Courtesy of D.N. Walker)

Frederick likely represents a variant of the James Allen projectile point style (Mulloy, 1959) and both should likely be subsumed under the Frontier complex defined by Holder and Wike (1949; see also Bradley, 2009). The excavations also yielded a series of radiocarbon dates, placing several of the identified components in an absolute time frame between 10,840±200 to 8,600±600 (Haynes, 2009; Irwin-Williams et al., 1973; Knudson, 2009). However, the burned material, yielding these series of ages, was assayed using the early, solid carbon method, with some composite samples for a stratigraphic layer, which yielded large standard errors and dates of limited reliability. Nevertheless, the dates provided a framework for an understanding North American Paleoindian cultural sequence (**Fig. 1** bottom).

The 21 Paleoindian components in the Hell Gap Valley essentially represent a minimum of 21 Paleoindian occupations or sites. However, each of the 21 components may represent a single or multiple occupations, as each component is essentially a vertically restricted artifact concentration in a single geological unit. How such a concentration accumulated as a single or multiple events over a period of time remains to be demonstrated. Hence, Hell Gap valley may have been occupied hundreds of times by the earliest Americans. Whether each component represents a single occupation or multiple, the overall density of Paleoindian occupation in the Hell Gap arroyo, presents a unique archaeological record of this early period of American prehistory anywhere in North America. One goal of our reinvestigation of the Hell Gap site is to better understand the nature of the episodic reoccupations of the valley. This goal remains elusive, although we will discuss the current evidence.

The 1960s investigations of Hell Gap yielded much additional and sometimes unique data regarding Paleoindian lifeways. Beads, needles, ochre, post holes, tent rings were all recovered at Hell Gap in the 1960s. As Irwin-Williams (1973) noted, Hell Gap was a campsite, unlike most Paleoindian localities investigated up to that time. Consequently, these discoveries should not surprise us, nevertheless they remain rare in the Paleoindian archaeological record to this day. Needles were recovered from Lindenmeier and Allen sites, and from Horn Shelter, the former two prior to Hell Gap investigations, but remained unreported or underreported until much later (Wilmsen and Roberts, 1978; Schultz and Frankforter, 1948; Redder and Fox, 1998). The situation is identical with beads. Although recovered early at Arch Lake (Texas), Blackwater Draw (New Mexico), Horn Shelter (Texas), and Lindenmeier (Colorado), reporting, especially detailed descriptions did not occur until after their recovery at Hell Gap (e.g., Hester, 1972; Jodry, 2010; Redder and Fox 1988; Wilmsen and Roberts 1978). Subsequentl to investigations of the Hell Gap site, the number of Paleoindian localities with needles and beads grew substantially. However, compared to 1,000s of Paleoindian sites across the continents, the discoveries remain unique (~140 total Paleoindian beads, Holliday and Killick 2013; ~90 total Paleoindian needles, Lyman 2015).

Remains of dwelling, interpreted as closed domestic space, are also unique and rare in the Paleoindian archaeological record. Until the recent proliferation of Folsom structures (Steiger, 2006; Surovell, 2022; Surovell and Waguespack, 2007) and earlier descriptions by Frison (1982; Frison and Bradley, 1980), only Bull Brook had been suggested to exhibit such features (Robinson et al., 2009; see also Jodry, 1987 for another instance, but that long follows the 1960s excavations at Hell Gap). The post holes of the Midland (essentially Folsom age) and overlying Agate Basin component have been interpreted as evidence of lean-to type structures at Hell Gap (Irwin, 1968). At the time of discovery they were "the earliest known definite remains of Plains Indian dwellings" (Irwin-Williams, 1973: 47). If, in fact, they are such facilities, they may represent the only cases of lean-tos in North America. Also among the dwellings represented is a ring of stone, presumably a tent or tipi ring. Although common during later periods on the Plains and in the Asian Paleolithic, the Hell Gap specimen is the oldest example known in the Americas of this type of facility.

Along with such spectacular finds, the 1960s excavations, like any archaeological project, recovered enormous amounts of mundane objects or objects of everyday life of hunter-gatherers, namely chipped stone debitage and animal remains. At the time of recovery neither were analyzed or only so very superficially. So from the fauna we learn that two taxa are present (bison and deer) in addition to small animals and shellfish, presumably constituting the diet of site occupants. Furthermore, bison was the predominant species through much of the Hell Gap occupations, with only the Frederick component having substantial quantity of deer (Irwin-Williams et al., 1973). The chipped stone debitage remained completely unanalyzed, only being mentioned in vicinity of hearths and having possible spatial significance ('workshop debris' Irwin-Williams et al., 1973: 49 and elsewhere).

In addition to defining the Paleoindian cultural sequence, a more theoretical goal of the 1960s was to define the Paleoindian complexes (or cultures), beyond just the chronologically diagnostic artifacts. With that goal in mind, Irwin and Wormington (1970; also in Irwin, 1968), constructed cumulative graphs of 'formal' stone tools for consecutive components of the site. These showed differences in artifact inventories between successive complexes of the Paleoindian periods. Whether such variation is a mark of cultural identity, functional differences between components, or some other characteristic is debatable.

2.2. The 1990s and after

Were chronologically diagnostic artifacts the only yields from the Hell Gap archaeological record, the site would hold some significance. However, other objects constitute most of the archaeological record, increasing that significance manifold. After some decades following initial site investigations in the 1960s, we returned to reinvestigate the site and collection with the goal of writing a full report on previous work (Larson et al., 2009), still a work in progress. The approaches taken by archaeologists in the 1960s, coupled with a critique of interpretation of the Hell Gap cultural sequence (Sellet et al., 2009), pointed to new questions to ask of the Hell Gap archaeological record. Hence a re-evaluation of the proposed sequence and Paleoindina sociocultural and socioecological dynamics drove the analysis and field studies from the early 1990s until today.

For the first question, the re-evaluation of the Paleoindian cultural sequence, our studies have confirmed the 1960s results. Six of the 10 projectile point styles were found in stratigraphic order as suggested during the early investigations of the site (Irwin-Williams et al., 1973). Additionally, a component below Folsom is in the position of the Goshen component. Although we did not find a chronologically diagnostic artifact, a Goshen point, little doubt exists that the occupation(s) below Folsom pertain to this period of prehistory. Separating Folsom from Goshen components in the witness wall at Locality I is problematic and further analyses are required. The complicated nature of site history is well illustrated by the vertical artifact distribution (**Fig. 3** top). Successive occupations are alternatively characterized by dense concentrations of bone, chipped stone, or ochre. In some occupations bone is the main object in others it is chipped stone, or some combination of both artifact classes and ochre.

However, the east block in which only lower cultural components remain, the separation of the lowest occupation is clear. In this area, the 1960s excavations removed components overlying Agate Basin mechanically. The mechanical removal was warranted because an erosional cut, originating at the Cody component extended into sub-cultural geologic units in the eastern corner of Locality 1, resulted in loss of early Paleoindian components. The 1960 investigators appear to have known this, although they never explicitly said so. Why the mechanical removal was all the way to the Agate Basin component, rather than to Cody, is unknown.

Regardless of the logic of the 1960s investigators, the lower components east of the witness block left intact were Agate Basin and below (Agate Basin, Midland, Folsom, and Goshen). These three components (Midland is likely not separate from upper Folsom) are best separated by cultural objects point provenienced with two points (**Fig. 3** bottom). Only elongated objects were point provenienced with two points and the most visible of these are bones, although a large number of smaller pieces of chipped stone were also apparently elongated and treated the same way. The bone being generally larger provides a better sense of separation of the components and site integrity. The bones are shown to be flat lying and in three clearly separated layers, corresponding to Agate Basin, Folsom, and Goshen (below Folsom as no diagnostic artifacts were recovered) cultural components. The Midland component is not clear and it may have been obscured in the 1960s excavations as well. As Midland is likely related to Folsom or perhaps closely following Folsom in time, Midland may simply be part of the upper Folsom component.

The elongated artifacts provenienced with two points, however, fail to show the full structure of the early Paleoindian components in the east block of Locality 1. This is because ochre and chipped stone are less likely to be elongated and thus be provenienced with two points. Conversely, rocks are generally not elongated and are most often provenienced with multiple points. Thus, few or none of these objects are visible in the backplot (**Fig. 3** bottom). To get a sense of the distribution of all of these objects relative to each other, we use a single provenience of each object (first provenience point taken at the deepest point of each object; **Fig. 3** middle). A backplot clearly shows a low gravel lens on the north edge of the east block. The gravel lens slopes upward to the north. The Goshen component begins/abuts this lens and continues to the south in the form of two chipped stone concentrations (see **Fig. 3** middle) and the flat lying bone (see **Fig. 3** bottom).

The Folsom component, between Goshen and Agate Basin, contains some flat lying bone to the north of the southernmost portion of the east block, but it's strongest signature is the large ochre concentration in the northern portion of the east block. In the southern portion of the east block, a large chipped stone pile marks the Folsom component. That the pile consists of large, early stage production, with many elongated flakes is demonstrated by the fact that many of these specimens show up with objects provenienced with two points. A preliminary analysis also suggests that many of the recently recovered bone needles are part of the Folsom assemblage from the northern ochre concentration.

The uppermost component in the east blocks is Agate Basin. This component is marked by an ochre concentration in the southern portion of the block, a chipped stone concentration in the center of the block, and some scattered natural rock (gravel). The Agate Basin component largely thins out in the northern part of the east block. Whether some of the Agate Basin component at the north end of the

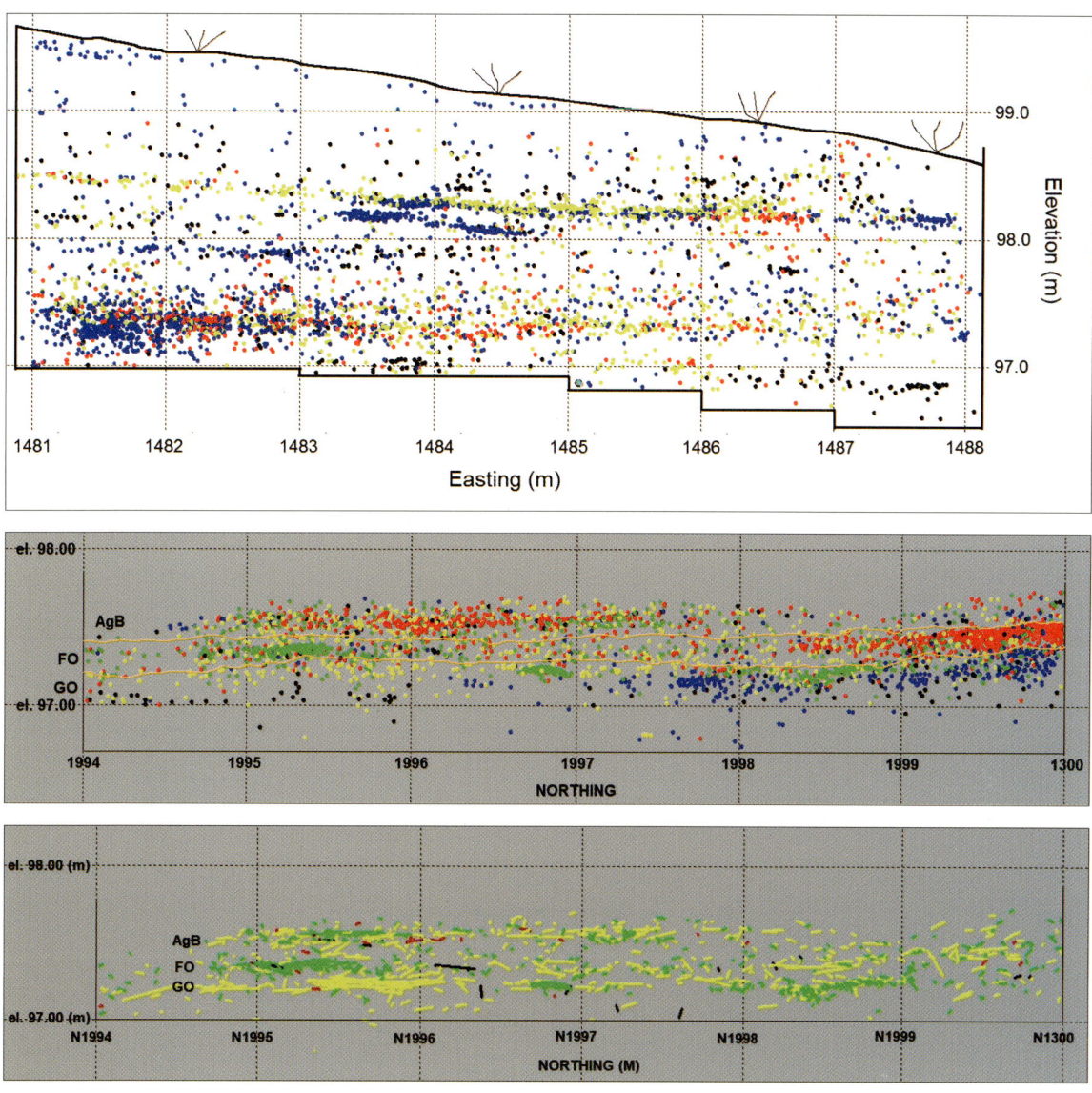

Fig. 3 Backplots of Locality I. South side of witness block (top), east side of east block (middle and bottom); top and middle show single point provenienced per artifact, bottom shows artifacts provenienced by two points. Yellow = bone, red = ochre in all plots; blue = chipped stone in top plot and black = charcoal. In bottom two plots green = chipped stone and blue = rock.

block has been truncated by mechanical means of removal of the overlying sediment in the 1960s is unclear at this time. By discontinuous horizontal distributions of small overlapping pockets of individual artifact concentrations, the backplots (Fig. 3) suggest small scale repeated occupations over the Paleoindian Period. However, at least some components point to possible larger scale, high spatial integrity, occupation surfaces. The Folsom component may signal a single occupation of some time depth. A preliminary analysis of the entire Folsom component excavated since the 1990s, appears to show spatial patterning reminiscent of horizontal space use at hunter-gatherer camps (e.g., Tanaka, 1980; Yellen, 1976), rather than a palimpsest of spatially overlapping occupations. A preliminary map of the Folsom component (Fig. 4 top) shows two ochre and three chipped stone concentrations along with variation in the distribution of bone. None of these concentrations overlap and the distances between them are relatively consistent. The chipped stone concentrations are about 6-7m apart, while the two ochre concentrations are about 10m apart. All these observations are first impressions currently under scrutiny and analysis.

Such horizontal site integrity is inexorably linked to vertical integrity. Understanding vertical integrity of the Hell Gap site is a critical component of further analysis and interpretation of horizontal use of camp space. This is especially important for multi-component sites such as Hell Gap. Vertical travel of artifacts from the point of original deposition is a fact at all archaeological sites. Distance of that travel, however, is highly dependent on the kind of sediment (sand or clay), and its compaction (lose or compact), time, and sub-surface earth moving biotic processes. A recently developed theoretical model of site integrity (Todd et al., 2022), based on earlier work (Brantigham et al., 2007), used one excavation unit

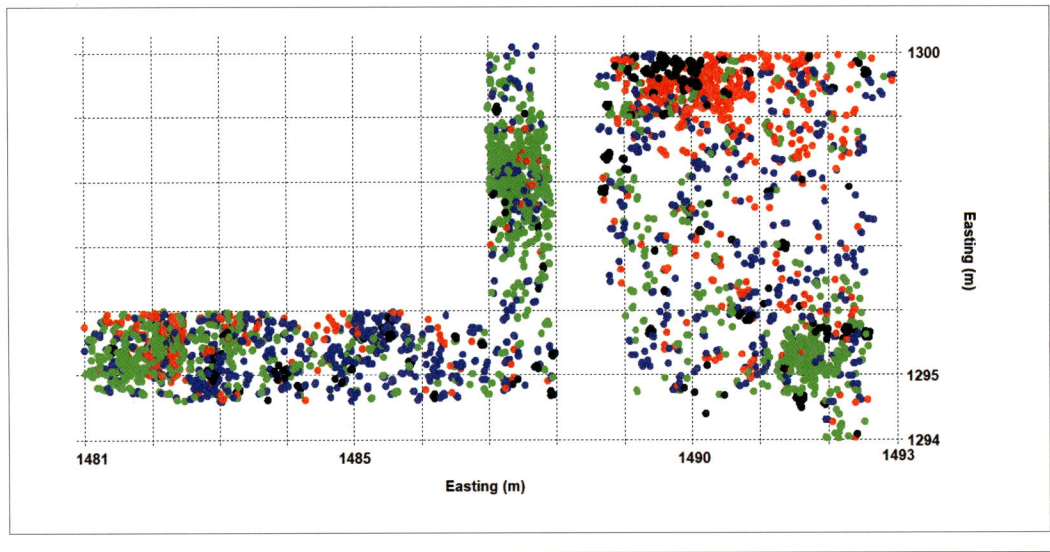

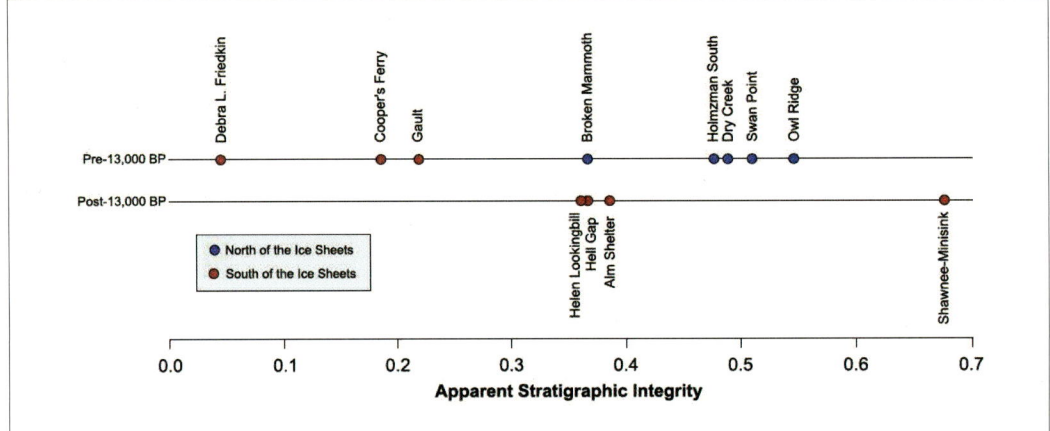

Fig. 4 Folsom component excavated since the 1990s (top) and apparent stratigraphic integrity of the Hell Gap site relative to other early North American localities (bottom). Folsom component plan view Green = chipped stone, red = ochre, blue = bone, black = other. (site integrity model Courtesy T.A. Surovell)

from the Hell Gap site and compared it with a number of other sites. The result suggests that Hell Gap falls in the middle of the pack of several other sites (**Fig. 4** bottom). We should remember that the model, the integrity index, is a single calculation for the entire 2.5m deposit containing 10 components at Locality I of Hell Gap. Breaking this down into various vertical slices could produce different integrity indices for different sets of components. Likewise we do not know what integrity index would show for adjacent units or for different parts of the site. Thus, while some overall units show middle range integrity, other parts of the site could show much higher integrity. In fact, the Hell Gap excavation, used in Todd et al. (2022) is from a particularly messy unit from the perspective of vertical stratigraphic component separation.

Along with affirming the cultural sequence is the refinement of absolute dating. The 1960's investigations yielded a limited number of age determinations, due to costs and available analytical methods. Improved methods, especially AMS dating, additions of optical stimulated luminescence (OSL) techniques, and age depth modeling, provide for more reliable age estimates of the Hell Gap stratigraphy and in particular the cultural components. Whereas four cultural complexes, or rather their sedimentary context, were directly dated during the 1960s, we now have all components radiocarbon dated and some radiocarbon dates added or confirmed by OSL technique.

More interesting, however, are studies of Paleoindian subsistence and technology. The perspective that views Paleoindian as big-game hunters, based on associations of diagnostic projectile points with mammoth or bison bone, persisted to the 1960s and still does today. However, cracks began to form in this perspective and although much of Hell Gap fauna is dominated by bison, nuances in the use of this resource have emerged (e.g., Speth et al., 2013). As stated above, deer was introduced as a subsistence resource late in the Paleoindian period and became an important part of the diet. More important however, is what we have learned from the bison bones of the earlier Paleoindian times. Hell Gap site zooarchaeology has shown how a campsite assemblage complements kill sites. In fact, the Hell Gap faunal assemblage is enhancing our current understanding

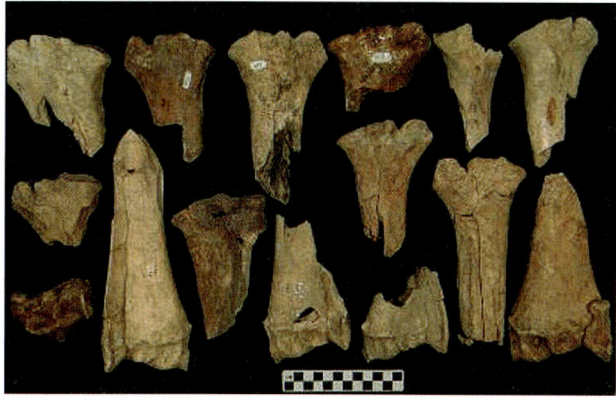
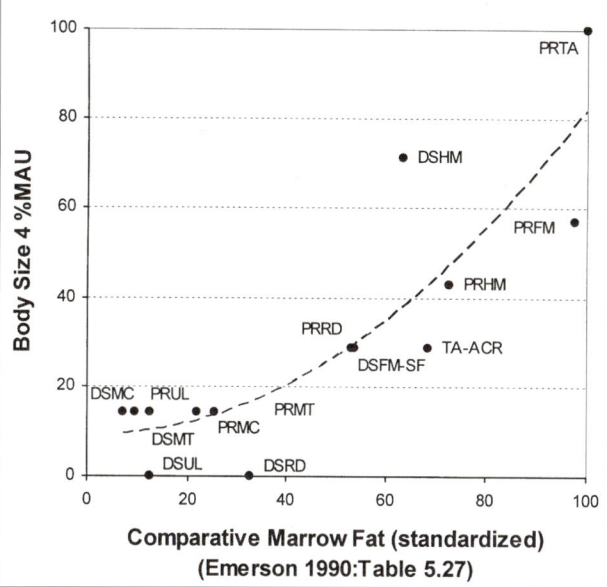

Fig. 5 Cracked meaty and fat rich bones, bison radii processed for bone marrow and relationship of %MAU and morrow fat index. (Courtesy of D.J. Rapson)

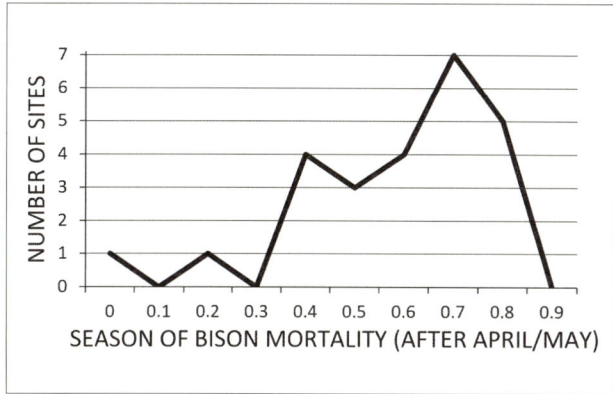
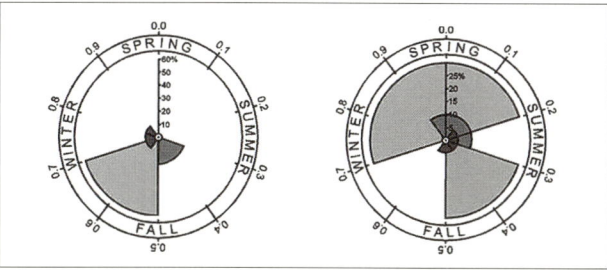

Fig. 6 Season of bison mortality at northern Plains Paleoindina bison bone beds (top) and season of mortality of Hell Gap bison localities (bottom). Locality 1 (bottom left) and Locality II (bottom right). (bottom courtesy D.J. Rapson)

of early bison procurement and use. Not only do we have bison bone beds, identified as kill sites, but finer behavioral nuances are possible between kill and consumption: kill → primary butchering → secondary butchering → consumption. The taphonomic studies of the Hell Gap assemblages have allowed us to demonstrate the import into camps of meaty and fat rich animal portions and heavy processing of bison products at camps (**Fig. 5**), patterns that contrast with better-known kill/butchery sites, where distal limb bones are used as snacks during butchering (Rapson and Niver, 2009).

The faunal assemblage further provides for more comprehensive inferences about Paleoindian seasonal behavioral variation. Paleoindian bison kill/butchery sites are invariably winter/early spring events (**Fig. 6** top). Hell Gap zooarchaeological analysis has demonstrated occupation at all seasons of the year (**Fig. 6** bottom). Given the likely need for labor to accomplish mass animal procurement and processing of animal products, and hence social fusion, we can suggest that campsites were the season(s) of social fission. That is Paleoindians likely lived in small, family size or several related family groups (e.g., Lee, 1979) and aggregated periodically into bands.

Paleoindian technology, beyond the projectile points used to procure animal products has been another result of our re-analyses. Unusual for the Paleoindian period, occupation(s) of most components at the site relied on local Hartville Uplift raw material to manufacture tools (e.g., Kornfeld, 2009; Larson, 2009). The use of local raw material is at odds with much of Paleoindian literature (e.g., Meltzer, 2009; Speth et al., 2013); however, regional source availability is variable and is an underappreciated part of understanding the raw material procurement strategies. One exception to local material use at Hell Gap is the Alberta component at Locality I of the site. In this component the majority, sixty percent of raw material originates more than 200km from Hell Gap in the Green River Basin (Knell, 2009:183). We do not think the disproportionately high use of Bridger chert signals a major change in settlement strategy, rather the Alberta component is one of many intermittent occupation of the Hell Gap site that happens to follow some sort of a direct or indirect contact of the population with southwest Wyoming. Another contact with southwest Wyoming is based on one obsidian object from the Agate Basin component discovered recently (Cory et al., 2021:Appendix 4).

3. Conclusion

The Hell Gap site has endured over half century of research and continues to yield new insights into the Frist Americans. The site investigations took place in the 1960s, were revived by a new slate of investigators 30 years later in the 1990s, and continue to this day. The 1960s yielded many firsts of Paleoindian prehistory: beads, needles, dwellings, and an impeccable stratigraphic record. The latter provided a means of constructing the first Paleoindian cultural sequence from nearly 11,000 to less than 8,000 years ago. Investigations starting in the 1990s have provided much needed support for the established cultural sequence, but more significantly are beginning to yield data for modeling cultural and natural formation processes of the archaeological record. That Hell Gap is the location of many short-term occupations, over some 3,000 radiocarbon years (or approximately 5,000 years), is suggested by analysis of high resolution data collected since the 1990s. However, some site components may be the remnants of more intense and longer campsites, representing village life of the First Americans.

Acknowledgements

Several generations, hundreds of field and laboratory technicians and field school students have contributed to the data used in this paper. This summary paper relies heavily on analysis and results presented by authors in the first Hell Gap monograph as well as technical reports from annual investigation since 2001.

References

Agogino, G.A., 1961. A New Point Type from Hell Gap Valley, Eastern Wyoming. *American Antiquity* 26(4), 558-560.

Agogino, G.A., 2009. The Frist Two Years of Investigation, 1959-1961: The Discovery and How the Later Excavations Leadership Developed. In *Hell Gap: A Stratified Paleoindian Campsite at the edge of the Rockies.* edited by M.L. Larson, M. Kornfeld, and G.C. Frison, Salt Lake City: University of Utah Press, 316-320.

Agogino, G.A. and C. Irwin-Williams. 1971. Archeological Investigations at the Hell Gap Site, Guernsey, Wyoming, 1965. *National Geographic Society Research Reports* 1965, 11-13.

Bradley, Bruce A., 2009. Bifacial technology and Paleoindian projectile points. In *Hell Gap: A Stratified Paleoindian Campsite at the Edge of the Rockies.* edited by M. L. Larson, M. Kornfeld, and G. C. Frison, Salt Lake City: University of Utah Press, 259-273.

Brantingham, P.J., T.A. Surovell and N.M. Waguespack. 2007. Modeling post-depositional mixing of archaeological deposits. *Journal of Anthropological Archaeology* 26, 517-540.

Cory, McKenzie J., Rachael L. Shimek, L.F. Berg, Laurie Cale, Tony A. Fitzpatrick, Liana Flecker, Molly Herron, Briana Houghton, Shane P. McDonnell, Matt T. Morris, Falon Norford, Lee Olinger, Kim Sutherland, Allison White, Clifford White, Brayden Wirick, Kenneth Humphrey, Mary Lou Larson, and Marcel Kornfeld. 2021. *Preliminary Results of the 2021 Investigations at the Hell Gap Site,* APPENDIX 4 Geochemical Analysis of 14X20005-91. Technical Report No. 71, Paleoindian Research Lab, Department of Anthropology, University of Wyoming.

Duguid, James O., 2009. In *Hell Gap: A Stratified Paleoindian Campsite at the edge of the Rockies.* edited by M.L. Larson, M. Kornfeld, and G.C. Frison, Salt Lake City: University of Utah Press, 316-320. In *Hell Gap: A Stratified Paleoindian Campsite at the edge of the Rockies.* edited by M.L. Larson, M. Kornfeld, and G.C. Frison, Salt Lake City: University of Utah Press, 313-315.

Figgins, Jesse D., 1927. The antiquity of man in America. *Natural History* 27(3), 229-239.

Frison, George C., 1982. Folsom Components. In *The Agate Basin Site* by George C. Frison and Dennis J. Stanford, New York: Academic Press, 37-76.

Frison, George C., and Bruce A. Bradley. 1980. 1980 *Folsom Tools and Technology of the Hanson Site, Wyoming.* Albuquerque: University of New Mexico Press.

Haynes, C. V. Jr., 2009. Geochronology. In *Hell Gap: A Stratified Paleoindian Campsite at the edge of the Rockies.* edited by M.L. Larson, M. Kornfeld, and G.C. Frison, Salt Lake City: University of Utah Press, 39-52.

Hester, James J., 1972. *Blackwater Locality No. 1,* New Mexico: Fort Burgwin Research Center, Southern Methodist University, Ranchos de Taos.

Holder, P., and J. Wike. 1949. The Frontier Culture Complex: A Preliminary Report on a Prehistoric Hunters' Camp in Southwestern Nebraska. *American Antiquity* 14(4), 260-265.

Holliday, Vance T., and David Killick. 2013. An Early Paleoindian bead from the Mockingbird Gap site, New Mexico. *Current Anthropology* 54(1), 85-95.

Irwin, H.T., 1968. *The Itama.* Unpublished Ph.D. dissertation, Department of Anthropology, Cambridge: Harvard University.

Irwin, H.T., 1969. Archaeological Investigations at the Hell Gap Site, Guernsey, Wyoming, 1964. *National Geographic Research Reports-1969,* 113-116.

Irwin, H.T., 1970a. Archaeological Investigations at the Hell

Gap Site near Guernsey, Wyoming, 1962. *National Geographic Research Reports-1961-1962*, 127-130.

Irwin, H.T., 1970b. Effects of Excavation on Seriation at a Palaeo-Indian Site. In *Mathematics in the Archaeological and Historical Sciences*. edited by F. R. Hodson, D. G. Kendall and P. Tátu. Proceedings of the Anglo-Romanian Conference, Romania: Mamaia, 209-214.

Irwin, H.T., 1971. Development in Early Man Studies in Western North America. *Arctic Anthropologist* 8(2), 42-67.

Irwin, H.T., 1973. Archaeological Investigations at the Hell Gap Site, Guernsey, Wyoming, 1966. *National Geographic Research Reports-1966*, 131-136.

Irwin, H.T. and J.O. Brew. 1968. Archaeological Investigations at the Hell Gap Site near Guernsey, Wyoming. *National Geographic Research Reports-1963*, 151-156.

Irwin, H.T. and M. Wormington. 1970. Paleo-Indian tool types in the Great Plains. *American Antiquity* 35(1), 24-34.

Irwin-Williams, C., H.T. Irwin, G.A. Agogino, and C.V. Haynes, Jr., 1973. Hell Gap: Paleo-Indian occupation on the High Plains. *Plains Anthropologist* 18(59), 40-53.

Jodry, Margaret A., 1987. *Stewart's Cattle Guard Site: A Folsom Site in Southern Colorado; a report of the 1981 and 1983 Field Seasons*. Unpublished Master's thesis, Department of Anthropology, Austin: University of Texas.

Jodry, Margaret A., 2010. Walking in Beauty: 11,000-Year-Old Beads and Ornaments from North America. *The Bead Forum* 57(1), 6-9.

Knell, Edward J., 2009. Cody Complex at Locality I. In *Hell Gap: A Stratified Paleoindian Campsite at the edge of the Rockies*. edited by M.L. Larson, M. Kornfeld, and G.C. Frison, Salt Lake City: University of Utah Press, 180-194.

Knight, Dennis H., George P. Jones, William A. Reiners and William H. Romme. 2014. *Mountains and Plains: The Ecology of Wyoming Landscapes*, New Haven: Yale University Press.

Knudson, Ruthann. 2009. The Early Expeditions: University of Wyoming, Harvard University, and Peabody Museum. In *Hell Gap: A Stratified Paleoindian Campsite at the edge of the Rockies*. edited by M.L. Larson, M. Kornfeld and G.C. Frison, Salt Lake City: University of Utah Press, 14-35.

Kornfeld, Marcel. 2009. Modified Chipped Stone and Implications for Paleoindian Technology and Adaptation. In *A Stratified Paleoindian Campsite at the edge of the Rockies*. edited by M.L. Larson, M. Kornfeld and G.C. Frison, Salt Lake City: University of Utah Press, 243-258.

Larson, Mary Lou. 2009. Site formation and technological organization at Locality I. In *A Stratified Paleoindian Campsite at the edge of the Rockies*. edited by M.L. Larson, M. Kornfeld and G.C. Frison, Salt Lake City: University of Utah Press, 229-242.

Larson, Mary Lou, Marcel Kornfeld and George C. Frison editors. 2009. *Hell Gap: A Stratified Paleoindian Campsite at the edge of the Rockies*, Salt Lake City: University of Utah Press.

Lee, Richard. 1979. *The !Kung San: Men, Women, and Work in a Foraging Society*. Cambridge: Cambridge University Press.

Lyman, R. Lee. 2015. North American Paleoindian Eyed Bone Needles: Morphometrics, Sewing, and Site Structure. *American Antiquity* 80(1), 146-160.

Mulloy, W.T., 1959. The James Allen Site, Near Laramie, Wyoming. *American Antiquity* 25, 112-116.

Redder, Albert J. and John W. Fox. 1988. Excavations and positioning of the Horn Shelter's burial and grave goods. *Central Texas Archeologist* 11, 2-15.

Roberts, Frank H.H., 1935. A Folsom Complex: A preliminary report on investigations at the Lindenmeier site in northern Colorado. *Smithsonian Miscellaneous Collections* 94, 1-35.

Roberts, Frank H.H., 1943. A new site. *American Antiquity* 8, 100.

Robinson, Brian S., Jennifer C. Ort, William A. Aldridge, Adrian L. Burke, and Bertrand G. Pelletier. 2009. Paleoindian Aggregation and Social Context at Bull Brook. *American Antiquity* 74(3), 423-447.

Schultz, C. Bertrand. 1932. Association of artifacts and extinct mammals in Nebraska. *Bulletin* 1(33), Nebraska Sate Museum, 271-282.

Schultz, C. Bertrand and W.D. Frankforter. 1948. Preliminary report on the Lime Creek sites: New Evidence of Early Man in southwestern Nebraska. *Bulleting* Vol. III, No. 4, Part 2, University of Nebraska State Museum, 43-62.

Sellards, E.H., Glen L. Evans, and Grayson E. Meade. 1947. Fossil bison and associated artifacts from Plainview, Texas. *Bulletin* 58, Geological Society of America, 927-954.

Sellet, Frederic, James Donohue and Matthew G. Hill. 2009. The Jim Pitts site: A stratified Paleoindian site in the Black Hills of South Dakota. *American Antiquity* 74(4), 735-758.

Speth, John D., Khori Newlander, Andrew A. White, Ashley K. Lemke, Lars E. Anderson. 2013. Early Paleoindian big-game hunting in North America: Provisioning or Politics?. *Quaternary International* 285, 111-139.

Stiger, Mark. 2006. A Folsom Structure in the Colorado Mountains. *American Antiquity* 71(2), 321-351.

Surovell, Todd A., 2022. *The Barger Gulch Site*, Tucson: University of Arizona Press.

Surovell, Todd A, Sarah A. Allaun, Barbara A. Crass, Joseph A. M. Gingerich, Kelly E. Graf, Charles E. Holmes, Robert L. Kelly, Marcel Kornfeld, Kathryn E. Krasinski, Mary Lou Larson, Spencer R. Pelton, Brian T. Wygal. 2022. Late Date Human Arrival to North America: Continental Scale Difference in the Stratigraphic Intergrity of pre -13,000 BP Archaeological Sites. *PLOSOne* 17(4), e026409.

Surovell, Todd A., and Nicole M. Waguespack. 2007. Barger Gulch Locality B. In *Frontiers in Colorado Paleoindian Archaeology*. edited by R.H. Brunswig and B.L. Pitblado, Boulder: University Press of Colorado, 219-259.

Tanaka, Jiro. 1980. *The San Hunter-Gatherers of the Kalahari*. Translated by David W. Hughes, University of Tokyo Press.

Tanaka, Jiro. 2022. Late Date of Human Arrival to North America: Continental Scale Differences in Stratigraphic Integrity of pre-13,000 BP Archaeological Sites. *PLOSOne*. doi.org/10.1371/journal.pone.0264092

Uhle, Max. 1903. *Pachacamac*, Philadelphia: University of Pennsylvania Press.

Wilmsen, Edwin N., and Frank H.H. Roberts, Jr., 1978. *Lindenmeier 1934-1974*, Washington, D.C.: Smithsonian Institution Press.

Wormington, H.M., 1957. *Ancient Man in North America*, Denver Museum of Natural History, Popular Series No. 4.

Yellen, John E., 1977. *Archaeological Approaches to the Present*, New York: Academic Press.

The IFD Model of Palaeolithic and Mesolithic Sites on the Federsee, Germany

Michael JOCHIM

Professor Emeritus, Department of Anthropology, University of California, USA; mjochim@ucsb.edu

ABSTRACT

Various approaches to the study of settlement patterns in different regions have been used in archaeology. Little attention, however, has been given to the investigation of the processes of colonization and expansion, including the issue of the choices of settlement location. In hunter-gatherer research, environmental factors have played a major role in understanding site distributions, but the role of different factors, and how this role changed through time, has rarely been discussed. Models such as the Ideal Free Distribution (IFD) allow examination of the role of these various factors, determining their importance and their relative ranking by developing predictions that can be compared to actual site distributions. This facilitates a greater and more precise understanding of the uneven distribution of sites, of the processes of decision-making underlying site locations, and how these change through time. An application of this model is presented examining the colonization of the Federsee Lake in southern Germany in the Palaeolithic and Mesolithic periods.

국문초록

고고학에서는 서로 다른 지역 간 정착유형 연구를 위해 다양한 접근방법을 사용하고 있으나 정착지 선정을 포함한 집단의 이주와 팽창 과정 조사에는 관심이 없는 편이다. 이상적 자유분포(Ideal Free Distribution, IFD) 모델은 생태학 용어로서 고고학 연구에서는 유적위치의 분포 연구에 적용되고 있다. 수렵채집인 연구에서 환경요인이 유적지 분포 이해에 중요하지만 다양한 환경요인의 역할과 그 시간 변화에 따른 역할은 거의 논의된 적이 없다. 이상적 자유분포 모델을 사용하여 이러한 다양한 요인의 역할 검토와 현장 유적분포의 비교를 통해 분포위치를 예측함으로써 유적의 중요성과 상대적 순위를 정할 수 있다. 이에 따라 불균형한 유적분포, 유적위치에 따른 의사결정 과정, 시간에 따른 변화에 대해 더 확장된 정확한 이해가 가능하다. 본 연구에서는 이 모델을 적용하여 구석기와 중석기 시대 독일 남부 페데르 호수의 집단이주를 검토한 결과, 페데르 호수 일대 유적은 후기구석기(약 12,000-9,700cal BC) 동안 실질적 집단이주가 일어났으며, 중석기(약 9,700-700cal BC) 동안에도 유적 숫자의 증가와 호안을 따라 일정한 정착 형태의 출현을 보여주고 있다.

Keywords: Palaeolithic, Mesolithic, Germany, Settlement patterns, Ideal Free Distribution

1. Introduction

The Federsee Lake in southwestern Germany has a long history of research spanning the period from the Late Palaeolithic to the Iron Age. Work that focused specifically on the Palaeolithic and Mesolithic occurred at various times, especially in the 1920s and 1930s (Reinerth, 1929) and by various private collectors in the period of the 1960s to 1980s (Eberhardt et al., 1987). My colleagues and I began research in 1980 and continued until 2014. This work involved extensive surface collecting on the lakeshores and in its hinterlands, test excavations in a number of sites, and large excavations of five sites, as well as the study of collections from earlier research (Jochim, 1998, Jochim et al., 1998, Jochim and Kind, 2015).

Based on this work, it has become clear that the initial, substantial colonization of the Federsee occurred during the Late Palaeolithic (ca.12,000-9,700 cal BC), with a number of shoreline sites identified, most of which are surface sites in plowed fields (**Fig. 1**). For the subsequent Early Mesolithic (ca. 9,700-7,000 cal BC) the number of known sites shows a significant increase (**Fig. 2**), a pattern seen also on a neighboring lake (Jochim, 2007). Little attention, however, has been given to the investigation of the processes of colonization and expansion, especially the issue of the choices of settlement location. A notable feature of the Late Palaeolithic sites is that their distribution is not random, but shows a number of clusters, primarily in the southeastern, southwestern and northwestern portions of the lake, while other areas have few to no sites. What underlies this pattern? What features were important in the selection of these locations?

2. A Model of Colonization

A recently developed model adopted from ecology appears to be useful in addressing these issues. For investigating the distribution of sites, the Ideal Free Distribution Model (Fretwell and Lucas, 1969) and its variants have recently been usefully adopted into archaeology. At its most basic, the model predicts that upon entering a new area as pioneers, people are free to settle first in the locations most suitable for their economy–the "best" locations from an adaptive perspective. These locations are specified and determined using various characteristics, especially those thought to be economically important, and allow prediction of where such sites should be situated. Actual site locations can then be compared to them in an attempt to understand the colonization process. If actual settlement patterns deviate significantly from the predictions of the model, then other factors underlying locational choices must be

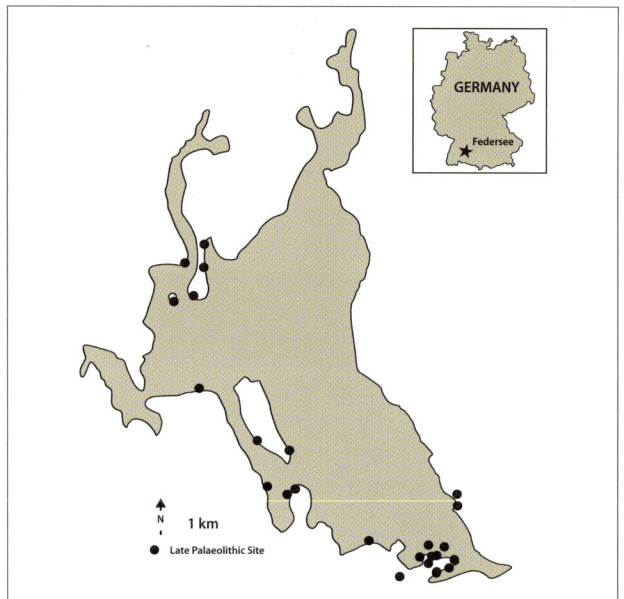

Fig. 1 Federsee Late Palaeolithic Sites

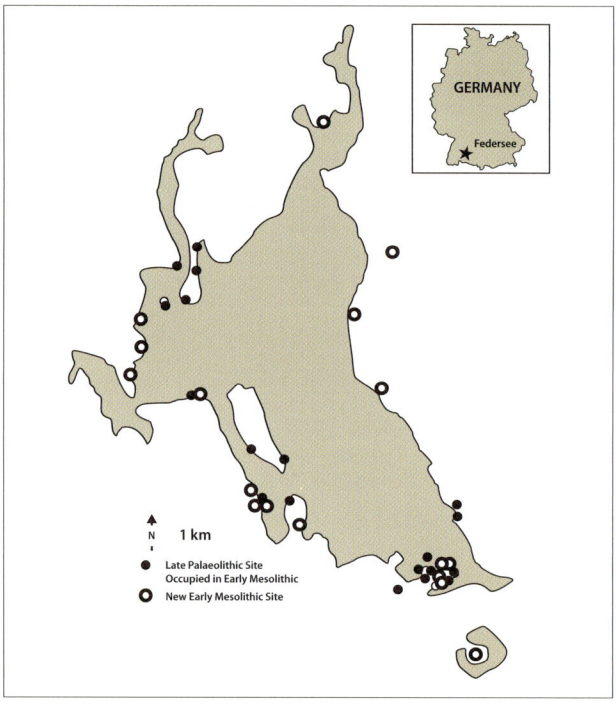

Fig. 2 Federsee Early Mosolithic Sites

investigated. This approach has several requirements for use in archaeology. First, sufficient knowledge of the economy is necessary in order to specify the suitable environmental characteristics. Second, a decision must be made about how to measure and combine these characteristics to calculate a location's suitability.

3. The Late Palaeolithic of the Federsee

Late Palaeolithic subsistence in this region is known to have emphasized the hunting of large game, including moose and red deer, together with beaver and smaller mammals, and some use of fish and waterfowl as well (Jochim, 1998). A number of locations around the Federsee Lake may have offered significant advantages for these economic activities (Jochim, 2020). Moose are closely associated with lakes and ponds and particularly with bays and shallows with abundant lake vegetation. Similarly, beaver often frequent shallow bays and their shores as they feed. Red deer occupy a variety of habitats, but often use protected lakeshores and stream inlets and outlets for travel, drinking and for feeding on sedges and grasses. Many smaller mammals, including otters, pine marten, weasel and ermine show some preference for stream edges and sheltered lakeshores, especially because of the diverse vegetation and cover. Narrows are commonly places of animal crossings and could provide locations for scouting and intercept hunting. Depending on the season, fish may congregate around inlets or shallows, and a find of a barbed harpoon at the Late Palaeolithic site of Kappel suggests that spearing in shallows may have been practiced. Shelter and shallow water are often found in lake narrows, off peninsulas and islands, and in other areas of complex shoreline such as bays. Access to the water as well as views of nearby shores for hunting may be facilitated by settlement placement close to the lakeshore, which may also allow views for strangers, if that was a consideration.

Consequently, in developing an IFD model of the best settlement locations, a number of landscape features seem appropriate. In this application the "best" locations include shoreline proximity, complexity of shore (with peninsulas, islands, and bays), proximity of narrows, proximity of shallow bays, and proximity to lake inlets and outlets. Numerous other features were surely important, such as level ground and local vegetation, but these are not easily reconstructed and cannot be included. This application assumes that all of the locational features are of equal importance and assigns each a value of 1. For example, a location that is directly on the lakeshore and on an island has a score of 2. A location meeting all criteria has a score of 5, the highest possible.

There are 24 known Late Palaeolithic sites around the Federsee. Of these, 23 are directly on the shore, 23 are on a complex shore, 21 are near a shallow bay, 17 are near a lake inlet or outlet, and 16 are near lake narrows. The average score for these locations is 4.2 (out of 5). It appears that the pioneering Late Palaeolithic people were utilizing the locational features used in the model in selecting the "best" locations for settlement. Furthermore, among the types of complex shoreline, location on a peninsula was selected for 15 of the sites, with islands and location within a bay each accounting for 4. Although these sites were surely not occupied simultaneously, the important point is that whenever a new site was occupied, the best locations were sought.

The model as presented here gives equal weight to each of the locational criteria, but this is not likely to have been the case. Models of decision-making can help determine the differential importance by ranking the criteria. A common approach to decision-making involving multiple variables is the use of decision trees. This approach is founded upon the work of Tverski (1972), who formulated the decision strategy of Elimination by Aspects. As concisely described in the APA Dictionary of Psychology (2015), "a choice is reached through a series of eliminations. At each stage the decision maker selects an attribute or aspect perceived to be important and eliminates alternatives lacking that attribute. The next most important attribute is then selected, and the process continues until only one alternative is left." Tverski (1972, p. 488-489) characterizes this approach as "easy to apply, it involves no numerical computations, and it is easy to explain and justify in terms of a priority ordering defined on the aspects," particularly "since man's intuitive computational facilities are quite limited." By examining variables individually and sequentially rather than attempting to deal with them simultaneously, this reduces computational complexity.

These results also allow some consideration of the relative importance of the locational factors. The Late Palaeolithic data from the Federsee suggest that a location directly on shore (23 sites) and on a complex shoreline (23 sites) are most important in situating settlements. Among the latter, a location on a peninsula is of greatest importance. A location near a bay is somewhat less important, followed by locations near narrows and near inlets and outlets. All of the landscape features are important but their importance varies, reflected by the frequency with which they were chosen.

4. A Relationship between Site Location and Function?

Very few of the Late Palaeolithic sites have been excavated, but two of these show considerable similarity, suggesting that they may have had similar functions and shared locational scores of 3. Sattenbeuren is a small site located directly on the shore of a small peninsula on the lake (Kind, 1995). It contained an assemblage of 959 lithic artifacts. The larger site of Kappel, with an assemblage of 3,638 lithic artifacts, is situated on the shore of a sandspit jutting into the lake adjacent to a shallow bay (Jochim and Kind, 2015). Tables 1 and 2 list some of the characteristics of these assemblages. Notable are the similarities in the percentages of the cores and blank categories, the mean length of blades, the percentages of the various raw materials, the percentage of artifacts with cortex, and the percentage of heat-treated artifacts. The percentages of

Table 1 Two Late Palaeolithic Sites : Technology

CATEGORY	SATTENBEUREN	KAPPEL
% BROWN CHERT	88.6	79.5
% WITH CORTEX	34.1	34.5
MEAN BLADE LENGTH	26.4	25.8
% BLADES	30.4	28.3
% FLAKES	64.0	64.3
% CHUNKS	4.2	4.6
% CORES	1.4	1.9

Table 2 Two Late Palaeolithic Sites : Typology

CATEGORY	SATTENBEUREN	KAPPEL
% SCRAPERS	12.8	13.6
% BURINS	41.0	26.0
% END/LATERAL RETOUCH	11.5	10.2
% BACKED PIECES	20.5	25.3
% BORERS	2.6	13.0
% OTHER	11.6	11.9
% HUNT/BURCHER TOOLS	32.0	35.4
% MANUFACTURE TOOLS	68.0	64.6

the various retouched tool categories are quite similar, but differ somewhat, largely in the case of burins and borers. However, if the tools are grouped into the general categories of hunting/butchering tools versus maintenance/manufacturing tools, the similarities are obvious. It appears that two sites are comparable in terms of raw material use, technology, and activities, with both representing residential camps. These features differ significantly from those of another, smaller excavated Late Palaeolithic site, Henauhof West, which contains relatively more and larger blades, a different spectrum of raw material, and a relatively greater proportion of hunting and butchering tools, suggesting a function as hunting camp (Jochim, 1998). Notably, this site has a locational score of 4, indicating that the criteria for "best" location were sufficiently general to apply to sites of different function.

5. The Early Mesolithic of the Federsee

One of the predictions of the IFD model is that as populations grow, locations of lower suitability will be utilized due to competition for the best places. During the Early Mesolithic the number of known sites is considerably higher than in the preceding Late Palaeolithic. A total of 38 Early Mesolithic sites around the Federsee are known. Applying the same Ideal Free Distribution Model to these sites reveals significant changes in site locations. Among the 38 sites, 21 are situated at the same locations as earlier Late Palaeolithic settlements, and therefore share the same locational advantages. The other 17 new sites, however, have an average score of only 2.9, much lower than the average of 4.2 during the Late Palaeolithic. Most of these are directly on the lakeshore, but two are situated on top of cliffs overlooking the lake and another is well inland from the shore. Only 14 are located on complex shorelines, while two are on small streams feeding into the lake and one is on a straight section of shore. Ten sites are near bays and five are near narrows and inlets. The locations would appear to have a lower suitability according to the model's criteria. In terms of ranking of the criteria in importance, the pattern of these sites is much the same as in the Late Palaeolithic: on shore and shore complexity are the most important, but the other factors (near bay, narrows and inlets) are much lower in importance. Again, these sites were surely not contemporary. Instead, they no doubt represent a collection over time of periodic occupations of various short-term camps. Consequently, it is unlikely that direct, simultaneous competition over the best locations, as envisioned in the IFD model, was operating. The greater number of Early Mesolithic sites in comparison to those of the Late Palaeolithic may indeed reflect a higher population but also possibly a more frequent use of the lake. The latter situation might be the result of changes in subsistence or simply the longer time span of the Early Mesolithic (ca. 2,700 years) in comparison to that of the Late Palaeolithic (ca. 2,300 years). Although the "best" locations according to the original criteria were still favored, the selection criteria for choice of locations were somewhat relaxed. One reason for this may be that the "best" locations were overused.

Studies of modern forest campsites document significant impacts brought about by human occupation (Cole, 2014; Smith et al., 2012). Considerable alterations in campsite areas can be caused by trampling, creation of trails, and collection of branches and saplings for bedding and wood for fuel. Foot traffic in campsites and trails tends to favor the growth of grasses, sedges and rushes. As a result, in one ethnographic study, for example, Savishinsky (1978) cites the depletion of firewood and other resources as a disadvantage of reusing old campsites by the Cree of Canada. Consequently, lakeshores may have been used repeatedly by prehistoric groups, but with frequent occupation of new locations.

Paradoxically, the changes created by human occupation may have enhanced their attractiveness to grazing animals. Studies of modern lake edges in Sweden, Finland and Canada suggest that natural clearings may have been scarce (Harper and Macdonald, 2001; Komonen, 2009; Timbal et al., 2005). Near-shore areas tend to have high densities of trees, very few wind-downed trees, and only single-tree gaps. Deadwood, however, tends to be relatively abundant. Initial clearance of vegetation for camping, together with collection of branches and saplings would have led to a decline in trees in the immediate camp area, while trampling would have favored the growth of grasses, sedges and rushes. Thus, small clearings would have been created that, after abandonment, attracted largely grazing animals such as aurochs and red deer. Avoiding occupation of these locations would have allowed their transformation into prime areas for hunting, but would have required the hunters to camp in other locations. Over the course of hundreds of years, the alternation of occupation and abandonment of the best locations may have forced the use of less desirable sites.

6. Conclusions

A variety of approaches to the study of settlement patterns have been used in archaeology. In hunter-gatherer research, environmental factors have played a major role in understanding site distributions. Certain areas such as river valleys and coastlines for example, often stand out for concentrations of settlement, usually explained by their abundant resources and positional advantages for travel and exchange. More specifically, such habitats may have particular locations that offer substantial advantages. In coastal settings, for example, details of coastline structure and nature of offshore resources have been given priority in understanding site locations (Kennett et al., 2009). Along rivers and streams, other factors including the presence of tributary mouths, shoals, and valley width and slope may be significant.

On regional scale, I have argued that, in contrast to surrounding areas, lakes offer the important benefits of vegetational and animal diversity that attract settlement (Jochim, 2020). On a finer scale, the configuration of lakeshores, shallows, and inlets may play an important role. Models such as the IFD allow these factors to be included into predictions that can be compared to actual site distributions. These approaches allow examination of the role of these various factors in determining their importance and relative ranking. This facilitates a greater and more precise understanding of the uneven distribution of sites and of the processes of decision-making underlying the distributions of sites on the landscape.

Acknowledgement

On the occasion of celebrating his 80th birthday, I want to congratulate Dr. Yung-jo Lee and express my gratitude for his many accomplishments and tireless efforts in creating and directing the impressive series of Suyanggae symposia. I have known him for over 20 years and have witnessed the creation of a true "Suyanggae Family" of international scholars. In the process, Palaeolithic researchers from all over the world have come together to share ideas and investigations and to build friendships that transcend national boundaries. He and his wife have been gracious hosts who welcomed us and made exceptional accommodations for our participation. We not only have learned about exciting research around the world, but also have been able to experience the cultural diversity of our host countries. This is a magnificent accomplishment that has enriched the lives of all participants

References

American Psychological Association. 2015. *APA Dictionary of Psychology* (2nd ed.).

Cole, D., 2014. *Impacts of hiking and camping on soils and vegetation : A review.* http://www.leopold.wilderness.net/research/fprojects;docs12/ecotourism.pdf

Eberhardt, H., Keefer, E., Kind, C., Rensch, H., Ziegler, H., 1987. Jungpaläolithische und mesolithische Fundstellen aus der Aichbühler Bucht. *Fundberichte aus Baden-Württemberg* 12, 1-51.

Fretwell, S., Lucas, H., 1969. On territorial behavior and other factors influencing habitat distribution in birds. *Acta Biotheoretica* 19, 16-36.

Harper, K., Macdonald, S., 2001. Structure and composition of riparian boreal forest: new methods for analyzing edge influence. *Ecology* 82, 649-659.

Jazwa, C., Kennett, D., Winterhalder, B., 2016. A test of ideal free distribution predictions using targeted survey and excavation on California's northern Channel Islands. J. Archaeol. *Method and Theory* 23, 1242-1284.

Jochim, M., 1998. *A Hunter-gatherer Landscape*, Springer.

Jochim, M., 2007. One more bog. In B. Hardh et al. eds., *On the Road, Studies in Honour of Lars Larsson*, Lund, Sweden: Almqvist & Wiksell International, 207-211.

Jochim, M., 2020. A lacustrine revolution: adaptive shifts in the late-glacial of south-central Europe. *Mitteilungen Der Gesellschaft für Urgeschichte* 29, Tübingen, 81-92.

Jochim, M., Kind, C., 2015. Eine spätpaläolithische Fundstelle am Ufer des Federsees: Bad Buchau-Kappel, Flurstück Gemeidebeunden. *Fundberichte aus Baden-Württemberg* 35, Germany, Stuttgart, 37-134.

Jochim, M., Glass, M., Fisher, L., McCartney, P., 1998. Mapping the stone Age: an Interim report on the South German Survey Project. In Aktuelle Forschungen zum Mesolithikum/Current Mesolithic Research ed., N. Conard. *Urgeschichtliche Materialhefte* 12, Tübingen: Mo Vince Verlag, 121-32.

Kennett, D. Winterhalder, B., Bartruff, J., Erlandson, J., 2009. An ecological model for the emergence of institutionalized social hierarchies on California's northern channel islands. In S. Shennan ed., *Pattern and Process in Cultural Evolution*, Berkeley: University of California Press, 297-314.

Kind, C., 1995. Ein spätpaläolithischer Uferrandlagerplatz am Federsee in Oberschwaben. *Fundberichte aus Baden-Wurttemberg* 20, 159-194.

Komonen, A., 2009. Forest characteristics and their variation along the lakeshore-upland ecotone. *Scandinavian Journal of Forest Research* 24, 515-526.

Reinerth, H., 1929. Das Federseemoor als Siedlungsland des Vorzeitmenschen. *Führer zur Urgeschichte* 9, Augsburg.

Savishinsky, J., 1978. Trapping, survival strategies, and environmental involvement: A case study from the Canadian sub-arctic. *Human Ecology* 6, 1-25.

Smith, A., Newsome, D., Enright, N., 2012. Does provision of firewood reduce woody debris loss around campsites in southwest Australian forests?. *Australasian Journal of Environmental Management* 19, 108-121.

Timbal, J., Bonneau, M., Landmann, G., Bouhot-Delduc, L., Trouvilliez, J., 2005. European non-boreal conifer forests. In F. Anderson ed., *Ecosystems of the World 6: Coniferous Forests*, 131-162.

Tverski, A., 1972. Elimination by aspects: a theory of choice. *Psychological Review* 79, 281-299.

Chapter 5.
Sorori, Cheongju and Ancient Rice in East Asia

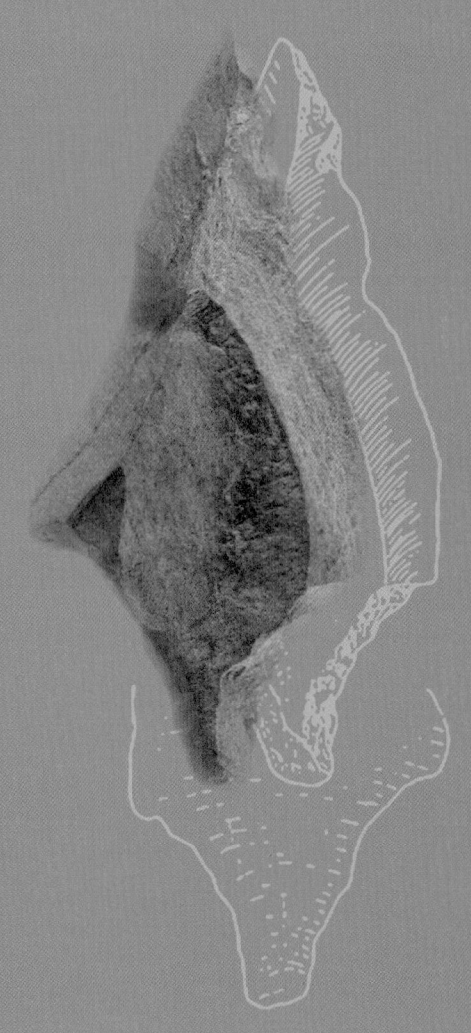

Radiocarbon age of the Cheongju Sorori rice and its significance in understanding human environmental settings

KyeongJa KIM[1], Yung-jo LEE[2], Ju-yong KIM[2]

[1] Center chief, Korea Institute of Geoscience and Mineral Resources (KIGAM), Korea ; kjkim@kigam.re.kr
[2] Institute of Korean Prehistory (IKP), Korea

ABSTRACT

Sorori ancient rice is reported to be the oldest ancient rice to date. It is important to explore other geographic regions associated with rice culture to determine whether there is any cultural similarity concerning the origin of the ancient rice culture. This will allow for a better understanding of Asian Paleolithic culture. Ancient culture is established by the natural environmental setting. In order to better understand rice cultivation, it is important to know the geological and anthropological situation at the time. Sorori ancient rice is believed to be an interim evolutionary stage between ancient rice and modern rice species. This is likely possible due to the fact that, currently in the Korean Peninsula, both *Japonica* and *Indica* types of rice are cultivated; however, much more *Japonica*-type rice is grown throughout the Korean Peninsula. Sorori rice is at least 2,000 years older than Chinese ancient rice, whereas Japanese ancient rice has not been reported to be as old as rice types from either China or Korea. This could be related to the geographic environment at the time rice spread naturally or by early humans, around 15,000 years ago. This paper introduces the Sorori rice culture and geographic background along with evidence of Paleolithic cultures of East Asian countries.

국문초록

소로리 고대벼는 현재까지 가장 오래된 볍씨로 보고되고 있는데, 벼 문화와 관련된 다른 지리적 지역을 탐색하여 문화적 유사성을 알아보고, 고대벼의 문화 기원을 비교하는 것이 중요하며 이를 통해 아시아 구석기 문화를 이해할 수 있다. 고대문화는 자연환경에 지배를 받으며 벼재배 사실을 이해하기 위해서는 당시의 지질학적, 인류학적 상황을 이해하는 것이 중요하다. 소로리 고대벼는 고대벼와 현대벼의 중간 진화단계로 여겨진다. 중간 진화단계는 현재 한반도에서 자포니카 품종과 인디카 품종 벼가 모두 재배된다는 사실과 한반도 전역에서 훨씬 더 많은 자포니카 유형의 벼가 재배된다는 사실로 인해 가능한 것으로 본다. 소로리 벼는 연대측정된 중국 고대벼보다 최소 2,000년 더 오래된 것으로 보고된 반면, 일본 고대벼는 중국이나 한국의 벼 만큼 오래되지 않았다. 소로리 벼는 지리적 환경과 관련되어 약 15,000년 전 자연적으로 내륙으로 전파되었거나, 초기 인류에 의해 내륙으로 전파되었을 가능성이 있다. 본 논문은 소로리 벼 문화와 더불어 지리적 배경 및 동아시아 여러 국가의 구석기문화 증거를 소개하고 있다.

Keywords : Cheongju Sorori rice, oldest ancient rice, rice culture, Japonica rice, Indica rice

1. Introduction

Korea has nearly 50 Paleolithic sites, which are either open or cave sites (Lee and Woo, 2000). Sorori rice is reported to be the oldest ancient rice to date. The ancient rice excavated in the Sorori rice field is located in Cheongju County, Chungbuk Province, Korea. This area was the construction site for the Ochang industrial complex. A number of field surveys were accomplished during 1994-1998. From this site, not only rice grains but also Paleolithic stone artifacts, such as choppers, scrapers, points, and other artifacts, were also excavated (Lee and Woo, 2002). The area of the rice field site is located near the Kum River in Kongju. A total of 51 rice grains were collected from the site. A number of radiocarbon dating results were obtained at three AMS laboratories: Geochron (GX), Seoul National University (SNU), and NSF Arizona AMS Laboratory (NSF). The ages of the rice grain itself was determined as 12,500±200 for quasi rice and 12,520±150 ^{14}C (BP) for ancient rice, respectively. Both rice grains are different with respect to their shape and genetic information. However, the identical radiocarbon ages confirm that these two kinds of rice species were available at the time. Not only the ancient grain but also the peat layer surrounding the grain have identical radiocarbon ages. This serves as convincing evidence that the rice grain had not been moved since its deposition in the layer. The radiocarbon dating results from the three organizations, taken at various layers for both peat and rice grains, confirmed that the ancient rice culture in the Sorori region was well established around 12,520±150 BP (15,283–14,194 years ago) and categorized as two types of rice samples–quasi rice and ancient rice–by Korean rice specialists (Lee and Woo, 2000; Park and Lee, 2004). Fewer ancient rice samples were available for dating, and the ancient rice samples were reported to be smaller and rounder. At the Sorori excavation site, not only rice grains but also stone artifacts that could have been used as tools for scraping rice grains from the stem of the rice plant were excavated.

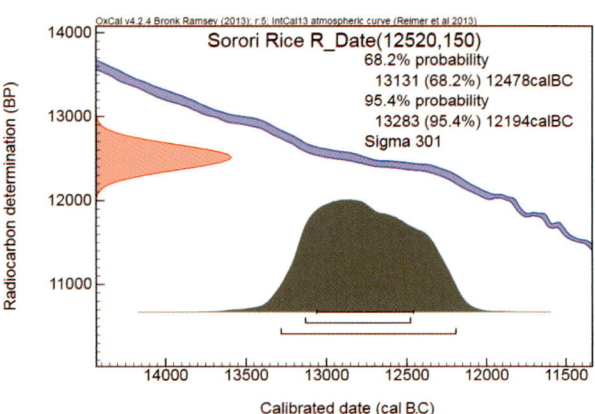

Fig. 2 Calibrated age of the Sorori rice by OxCal.

Before machines were built, rice grains were collected from rice plants much more efficiently only with the proper tools. The stone artifact which could have been used to scrape rice grains and put them into a basket. The two different stone artifacts excavated at the Sorori site possibly explain the suggested activities (**Fig. 1**). The ancient Sorori rice is more likely categorized as the *Japonica* type, which is distinctively different when it is compared with quasi rice with respect to its shape, scanning electron microscopy (SEM) images, and DNA analysis (Kim et al., 2013).

The investigated soil depths of the Sorori site were from 34.6–35 to 26.0–27.1m MSL. In the middle layer, from 30.5 to 32.1m MSL, both quasi and ancient Sorori rice grains were found. The dark layer at 32m MSL was the locality where the ancient rice grain was found. This layer's age ranges from 12,780 to 14,800 years BP. Another peat layer below this layer is located at 28.2 and 29.3m MSL. The peat layer was found to be 16,300 to 17,300 BP years old (**Table 1**). With the previous investigation of both radiocarbon age and stone artifacts, we can deduce the establishment of an ancient rice culture in Korea. This does not confirm whether rice was cultivated or not. However, the consumption of rice could be highly convincible. Because of this possibility, it is important to investigate geographic information around the time when early humans started to use rice. At present, rice is consumed by mostly Asian countries, especially along coastal regions. In this study, we examined ancient rice culture and geographic information around 12,500 years BP. This will guide us to understand rice culture within Asian countries.

2. Rice culture in Korea

Rice culture could have been established throughout the Korean Peninsula over the last 10,000 years. It is important to check the characteristics of the Sorori ancient rice grains against other Korean old rice examples, as well as against current Korean rice types. Sorori is located in the middle of

Fig. 1 Sampling location in Sorori, rice sample, and stone artifacts which could have been used for scraping rice grains from rice stems (Lee and Woo, 2002).

Table 1 Radiocarbon ages of Sorori rice from three AMS laboratories (Lee and Woo, 2002; Mannion, 2006).

No	Depth (MSL)	Deposit layer	¹⁴C date(BP)			
			Geochron (1988)	Geochron (2001)	SNU (2001)	NSF AZ (2009)
1	34.6–35	Disturbed later				
2	33.6–34.6	Paleo-soil				
3	33–33.6	Muddy sand 1			8,800 ± 90	
4	32.8–33	Upper peat		9,450 ± 40 9,580 ± 40		
5	32.1–32.8	Muddy sand 2				
6	30.5–32.1	Middle peat Quasi rice and ancient rice were found in this layer.	13,010 ± 190 14,820 ± 250	12,780 ± 170-13,270 ± 180 13,420 ± 180 14,000 ± 190-14,020 ± 190 14,800 ± 210	★12,500 ± 200 (quasi rice) 12,930 ± 400 13,490 ± 150 13,600 ± 300 13,700 ± 200 13,920 ± 200	*12,520 ± 150 (ancient rice) 12,552 ± 90 (peat) *modern(W/preservatives)
7	29.3–30.5	Old riverine sand				
8	28.2–29.3	Lower peat	17,310 ± 310	16,250 ± 50 16,680 ± 50	17,320 ± 200 17,300 ± 150	
9	27.1–28.2	Old riverine sand				
10	26.0–27.1	Old riverine pebble				

the Korean Peninsula, near the border between North and South Korea. A Neolithic rice field in Koyang City, Kyunggi Province, has been unearthed. The rice grains between Sorori and Koyang City were compared. The rice from Koyang is called "Gawaji." The Sorori rice and Gwaji rice are comparable with respect to their grain sizes. The 13 Sorori ancient rice grains can be compared to the three types of modern rice and reflect *Japonica* (62%), *Javanica* (7.5%), and *Indica* (7.5%), outside of these three types (23%). This implies that the distribution of Sorori rice might be a progenitor of the current Korean rice types. Park (2009) compared the Sorori rice with Gawaji rice found in Koyang using two groups of rice grains dated to 5,000 BP (10 grains, Gawaji I) and 3,000 BP (287 grains, Gawaji II). In Fig. 3, we can see that if we compare Sorori rice (12,500 BP) with other archaeological rice, such as from Gwaji I (5,000 BP) and Gawaji II (3,000 BP), the variation of these samples overlap with Sorori rice. When we consider the change of the rice grain distribution pattern from Sorori to Gawaji II, we can be confident that Sorori rice shows the dominant Korean rice type (*Japonica*) (Park, 2009). Interestingly, when these rice types from South Korea are compared with the modern rice distribution in North Korea, we can conclude that evidently both *Japonica*- and *Indica*-type rice have been cultivated in North Korea. *Japonica*-type rice is the dominant rice type in North Korea. However, in the western area of North Korea, where fertilized rice fields are available, *Indica*-type rice has been cultivated to date. One study showed that only *Japonica*-type rice is cultivated in the Korean Peninsula, Japan, and a northeastern area of China, while *Indica*-type rice is cultivated in Korea, China, Malaysia, and Inida (Koo et

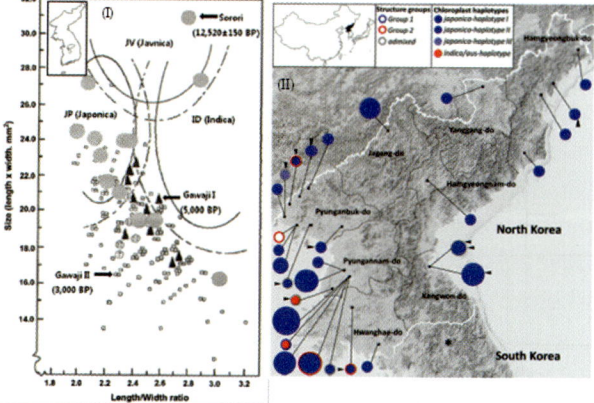

Fig. 3 (I) Rice grain distribution in association with grain size and ratio of length/with from 300 grains from Koyang city (square and triangle) and 13 well preserved grains from Sorori (circle), as well as Gawaji I and II (Park, 2009). The Sorori rice (circle) has much wide variation in size compared to Gawaji (triangles) dated as 5,000 BP. much wide variation in size compared to Gawaji (triangles) dated as 5,000 BP. (II) Rice type distribution in North Korea (Kim et al. 2014).

al., 2013). This pattern could support a possible theory in the evolution and origin of rice culture with Sorori rice, which is reported to be the oldest to date, with the possibility of an ancestor of the three current dominant rice types of the world. The adaptation of rice type in different regions could be related to climatic regions as well as to the preference of rice type in each human society, associated with the characteristics of the rice type itself and the specific humans living in the climatic zone.

3. Rice culture in China and Japan

The ancient cultivated rice culture of China is not evidently known. However, in the Xianrendong, Wannian County, Jiangxi, Yuchanyan site of Dao County, Hunan, Miaoyan of Guilin, Guangxi and other cultural sites, the unearthed rice remains are dated to 13,000–19,000 years old. It is assumed that the cultivated rice sample in Xianrendong is as old as 19,000 years and could possibly be wild rice. In China, a cultivated rice husk that was 8,000 years old was found at the Jiahu site of Wuyang Country, Henan Province, and 7,000-year-old cultivated rice was found at the Hemudu site of Yuyao, Zhejian Province. This study indicated that the ancient rice in Yuchanyan, Dao County, was the most primitive cultivated rice and evolved into the early cultivated rice. This has characteristics of wild rice, *Indica* rice, and *Japonica* rice. This ancient cultivated rice of Yuchanyan is about 13,000 years old (http://cofcorice.com/en/nutritions/1063.aspx). Keally (2004) reported that in the case of Japan, the calibrated age of the Jomon period is 15,650 years old. Some other uncalibrated radiocarbon ages for a few other pottery examples, such as the Kannoki linear-relief pottery and the Fukui Cave linear-relief pottery, were known to be 13,000 years old (Oda and Keally, 1979) and 12,700±500 years old (Kigoshi, 1967c; Kamaki and Serizawa, 1967). It is known that there are three Late Jomon sites with reported rice ages: the Minami Mizote site, Okayama Prefecture, Fukuda Shell mounds, Okayama Prefecture (Fukuda Kaizuka, 1992), and Kazahari site, Hachinohe City, Aomori Prefecture (Odoroki, 1992).

Based on the Chinese and Japanese rice cultural histories, the strong evidence of Chinese rice culture seems much older than that for Japanese. At present, it is hard to know whether the origin of rice culture is from China or Korea. However, the oldest rice excavated with characteristics of modern rice would be evidently appeared for the Sorori ancient rice based on the genetic information and SEM images. Based on the Chinese rice report, the rice from Yuchanyan, Dao County, may have similar characteristics as the indication of Sorori rice features associated with the combination of characteristics of *Japonica* and *Indica* reported by Kim et al. (2013). In the case of Sorori rice, highly *Japonica* and much more recent ancient rice (Kawaji, 3,000 BP) are mixed in its characteristics while the Chinese ancient rice has combined characteristics of wild rice, *Japonica* and *Indica* rice.

4. Geographical information of the Korean Peninsula around 12,500 BP

The radiocarbon age of the Sorori rice is 12,500 years BP. It is important to know geographic information around 12,500 years BP. Fig. 4 indicates that the sea level at the time in the Yellow Sea was found to be about 64m below the present surface. There are four different models plotted in the right side of Fig. 4 (Yang et al., 2009). This also clearly indicated

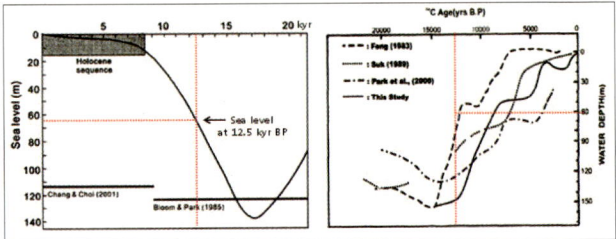

Fig. 4 Sea level estimation at 12,500 BP, modified after Yang et al., 2009.

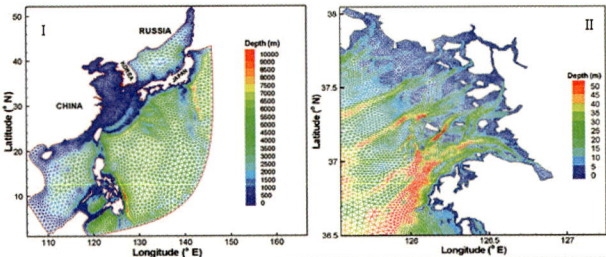

Fig. 5 Water depth maps of the East Asia (I) and the western area of the Korea (II) (Shu and Kim et al. 2011)

the estimated sea level at the time of 12,500 years BP could be lower than 60m for all four models. Fig. 5 demonstrates the water depths in both the Korean Peninsula and Yellow Sea. All areas of the Yellow Sea are shallower than 50m in water depth (Shu et al., 2011). From Fig. 4 and 5, we can conclude that all areas of the Yellow Sea areas were above the water and everywhere was reachable by walking. In the case of the water depth between Korea's southern coastal region and Japan, the range of water is from mostly 100 to 150m (Choi et al., 2002). Thus, around 12,500 years BP, Japan was not reachable by walking from Korea. This geographic difference could impact on early rice culture associated with human settlement relatively much more in the region between Korea and China than that between Korea and Japan. The large human habitat could have been formed from the Korean regions to the Yangtz River passing though the Yellow Sea. The uncalibrated Sorori radiocarbon age of the ancient rice is 12,520 BP, which is estimated as within cal 15,283–14,194 years ago. This age is at least 2,000 older than the reported age from the Chinese rice cultural area. Considering the large area of this rice cultural area from Korea to Chinese region, the area must have been developed as an early human settlement, one which could have evolved as a large union of human occupation.

5. Summary

The ancient Sorori rice is the oldest rice reported to date. The ancient Sorori rice has similarity with *Japonica* and Kawaji rice (3,000 BP). This implies that ancient Sorori rice could represent an evolutionary stage of an ancient rice type between the *Japonica* and modern cultivated rice grown in 3,000

BP, which is a similar age as Yayoi Japanese rice culture. It is important to know the geographic information of the time of ancient rice cultures established in order to understand the early human settlement and cultural environment. The spread of rice culture was also found to be involved in geographic settings within Asian regions. Presently, the areas with the heaviest rice cultivation are coastal regions, such as Korea, Japan, China, Taiwan, and Indonesia. When we consider the fact that rice culture was established along coastal regions at present, the ancient rice cultural site could been similar. The oldest Sorori rice indicates that rice culture started from the area of Sorori and spread to the western region of the Korean Peninsula, but not greatly to the Japanese region, because of the difficult terrain in that direction and the sea depth between Korea and Japan.

References

Bon-Hyuk Koo, Soo-Cheul Yoo, Joon-Woo Park, Choon-Tak Kwon, Byoung-Doo Lee, Gynheung An, Zhanying Zhang, Jinjie Li, Zichao Li, and Nam-Chon Paek. 2013. Natural Variation in OsPRR37 Regulates Heading Date and Contributes to Rice Cultivation at a Wide Range of Latitudes 2013. *Molecular Plant* 6(6), 1877-1888.

Choi, B.H., Kim, K.O. and Eum, H.M., 2002. Digital bathymetric and topographic data for neighboring Seas of Korea. *Journal of Korean Society of Coastal and Ocean Engineers* 14(1), 41-50. (in Korean)

Fukuda Kaizuka (Kurashiki) de hakken doki no konseki, ine no momi ato to hanmei: Jomon Koki no inasaku urazuke [Identified as a rice-grain impression on a potsherd from the Fukuda Shellmound [Kurashiki City]: Support for Late Jomon rice farming). 1992. *San'yo Shinbun*, July 26. Reprinted in: *Gekkan Bunkazai Hakkutsu Shutsudo Joho*, September 1992, 109.

HyunJung Kim, Eung Gi Jeong, Sang-Nag Ahn, Jeffrey Doyle, Namrata Singh, Anthony J. Greenberg, Yong Jae Won and Susan R. McCouch. Nuclear and chloroplast diversity and phenotypic distribution of rice (*Oryza sativa* L.) germplasm from the democratic people's republic of Korea (DPRK; North Korea). *Rice* 7, 7.

Kamaki Y. & Serizawa C., 1967. Nagasaki-ken Fukui Doketsu (The Fukui Cave, Nagasaki Prefecture). In Nihon no doketsu iseki (Cave sites of Japan), ed. *Nihon Kokogaku Kyokai Doketsu Iseki Chosa Tokubetsu Iinkai*, Tokyo: Heibonsha, 256-265.

Keally, Charles T., 1990. The third-millennium B.C. Uedomari 3 site, Rebun Island, Hokkaido: Life at a far northern outpost of the Ento peoples from Tsugaru. *Sophia International Review* 12, 19-33.

Keally, C.T., 2004. Bad science and the distortion of history: radiocarbon dating in Japanese archaeology. *Sophia International Review* 26, 1-16.

Kigoshi K., 1967. *Radiocarbon* 9(1), 43-62.

Kyeong Ja Kim, Yung Jo Lee, Jong Yoon Woo, A.J. Timothy Jull. 2013. Radiocarbon ages of Sorori ancient rice of Korea. *Nucl. Instr. Method* B294, 675-679.

Lee, Y.J. and Woo, J.Y., 2000. *The 4th Int. Rice Genetics Symp.*, Manila, Philippines, 15.

Lee, Y.J. and Woo, J.Y., 2002. Publication, *Dept. of Archaeology and Art*, Chungbuk University.

Li, F., Petraglia, M., Roberts, P., Gao, X., 2020. The northern dispersal of early modern humans in eastern Eurasia. *Sci. Bull.* 65(20), 1699-1701.

Mannion, A.M., 2006. *The History and Consequences of Carbon Domestication, Carbon and its Domestication*, Springer, Dordrecht, 140.

Oda, S. and Charles T. Keally, C.T., 1979. *Japanese Palaeolithic cultural chronology*. Privately published monograph. (Reprinted with Japanese translation: International Christian University Archaeology Research Center, Tokyo, 1999)

Odoroki. 1992. Odoroki to tomayoi to: "Jomon" saiko no keiki ni mo (Surprise and confusion: A good chance to rethink the meaning of "Jomon"). 1992. Mainichi Shinbun (Seibu), August 30. Reprinted in: *Gekkan Bunkazai Hakkutsu Shutsudo Joho*, October 1992, 17.

Park, T.S. and Lee, Y.J., 2004. Origin of Early domesticated Rice in Korea Excavated by the Unhulled Rice(Oryza sativa L.) Grains(15,000BP) from Sorori Site. *Korea Agriculture Hist. Assoc.* 3(2), 119 -132.

Park T.S., 2009. Reconsideration on the importation pathway of ancient Korean rice (*Oryzar sativar* L.). Journal article: *Korean Journal of Crop Science / Hanguk Jakmul Hakhoe Chi* Vol. 54, No. 1, 119-123.

Shu, S. and Kim, S.I. et al., 2011. Storm Surges in West Coast of Korea by Typhoon Bolaven (1215). *Journal of Korean Society of Coastal and Ocean Engineers* 26(1), 41-48.

Yang D. Y., 2009. The abrupt climate change for the prediction of extreme geo-hazards and sea level change around the Korean peninsula, *KIGAM annual report, Ministry of Knowledge Economy*.

Geomorphic background and pedo-sedimentary matrix formation of the Sorori Paleolithic site in Miho River, Korea

Ju-yong KIM[1], Yung-jo LEE[2], Jong-yoon WOO[2], Keun-chang OH[3], Seung-won LEE[2]

[1] Honorary Researcher, Institute of Geoscience and Mineral Resources (KIGAM), Korea ; kjy@kigam.re.kr
[2] Institute of Korean Prehistory (IKP), Korea
[3] Quaternary and Paleo-environmental Research (QPR), Korea

ABSTRACT

The Sorori Paleolithic site in the Cheongju area is located above the 2nd fluvial terrace of the Miho River. The alluvial plain is developed at a lower topographic level, exhibiting sandy muds or muds derived from fluvial backswamp. According to representative trench profiles and borehole data, the Sorori Paleolithic (SP) site is characterized by fluvial gravel and sands in the lower part. However, toward the upper part, pedogenized sandy mud or muds progressively dominate, showing stiff and hardened layers (Fragipan) associated with spots of iron-manganese oxides, vertical cracks or soil wedges, and horizontal laminae. These pedogenized layers (Geosol or Paleosoil) can be correlated in the field and therefore designated as geosols, which are soil-stratigraphic units. Based on AMS radiocarbon dating of organic muds, it was revealed that fluvial deposits formed prior to 36 ka, belonging to the Old Fluvial Deposits (OFDs) during the Last Glacial Period (late Upper Pleistocene). On the other hand, toward the alluvial plain of the Miho River, organic-rich mud is predominantly developed and dated as old as 20 ka, based on radiocarbon dating of the plant relics within the organic mud. This is regarded as Younger Fluvial Deposits (YFDs) of the Last Glacial Period. Ancient rice seeds were specifically excavated from the organic peaty muds in the YFDs, and the AMS radiocarbon age of the Sorori rice seeds ranges from 12,500 to 17,300 years BP. This seed is known as one of the oldest rice seeds in the world. As global warming and a wet climate prevailed in the mid-latitude region after the Last Glacial Maximum (LGM) (approximately 18,000-20,000 years ago), it is reasonable to assume that the same type of warm and wet environment periodically occurred in the Sorori site of the Cheongju area. Cheongju-Sorori rice seeds are significant for yielding a deep understanding of the growing environment and characteristics of rice during the transition from wild rice to cultivated rice.

국문초록

청주 소로리 구석기 유적은 미호천의 제2 하안단구 퇴적 층위에 분포하며, 고도상 더 아래로 내려가면서 미호천 충적대지가 발달하며 배후습지성 니사질과 니질층이 우세한 양상을 보이고 있다. 트랜치 단면과 시추자료를 통해 퇴적층을 구분해 보면, 소로리 구석기 유적은 하부에 하성역층과 사질층이 분포하며, 상부로 가면서 철망간 산화물이 점철되고, 수직 토양쐐기(Soil wedge) 구조, 수평의 엽상조직, 토층경반화(fragipan)가 현저한 토양화된 니사질층과 니질층이 우세하게 분포하고 있다. 이러한 토양 특성을 가진 지층(혹은 고토양층)은 야외에서 층서 대비가 가능하며 토양층서 단위로서 지질토층(Geosol)으로 규정될 수 있다. 유기 니질층에 대한 방사성탄소 연대분석 결과, 갱신세 말 최종빙기에 속하는 약 3.6만년 이전에 형성된 고기 하성퇴적층(Old fluvial deposits)으로 밝혀졌다. 제2 하안단구보다 고도상으로 더 낮은 지점으로 내려가면 퇴적단면상 하부에는 하성역층과 사질층이 분포하지만, 상부로 가면서 유기 니질층(토탄질 니질층)이 여러 매 협재하는 저습지성 하성퇴적층이 분포한다. 한편, 미호천 충적대지로 가면서 유기물이 많이 포함된 니질층(organic muds)이 넓게 발달하며 여기에 포함된 식물유체의 방사성탄소 연대측정을 통하여 약 2만년 이후 형성된 신기하성층(Younger fluvial deposits)로 간주되고 있다. 특히 신기하성 퇴적층 내에 협재된 유기 니질층 내에서 볍씨가 출토되었으며, 볍씨가 출토된 유기 니질층과 볍씨에 대한 AMS 방사성탄소 연대측정결과, 12,500–17,300 BP로 나타났으며, 소로리 출토 볍씨는 세계적으로 가장 이른 시기를 알리는 볍씨의 하나로 간주되고 있다. 전 지구적으로 최종빙기 최성기(LGM) 이후 중위도 지역을 중심으로 기후온난화가 현저하게 나타나며 특히 청주 소로리에서도 온난다습한 환경이 반복적으로 나타났음을 의미한다. 청주 소로리 볍씨는 향후 야생벼에서 재배벼 전환기의 벼 생육환경이나 특성을 이해하는 데 중요하다.

Keywords : Fluvial wetland, Old fluvial deposits, Young fluvial deposits, Radiocarbon age, Soil wedge

1. Introduction

The Sorori Paleolithic (SP) site is situated near Namcheonri and Sorori, Oksan-myeon, Heungdeok-gu, in Cheongju City, Chungbuk Province (see **Figs. 1**-A and **1**-B). The study area is characterized by a Holocene alluvial plain, an upper Pleistocene low fluvial terrace, and a backslope at the margin of a gently undulating landscape of Jurassic Daebo Granite. To explain the Sorori landscape and sedimentary deposits, it is important to consider fluvial morphostratigraphy and pedo-sedimentary formation as crucial surface processes for understanding the site-matrix formation and chronology of the SP site. This paper explains the SP site-forming process in the Miho River (Cheongju area) as an illustration of the fluvial terrace system and soil-sedimentary formations of the Upper Paleolithic in Korea.

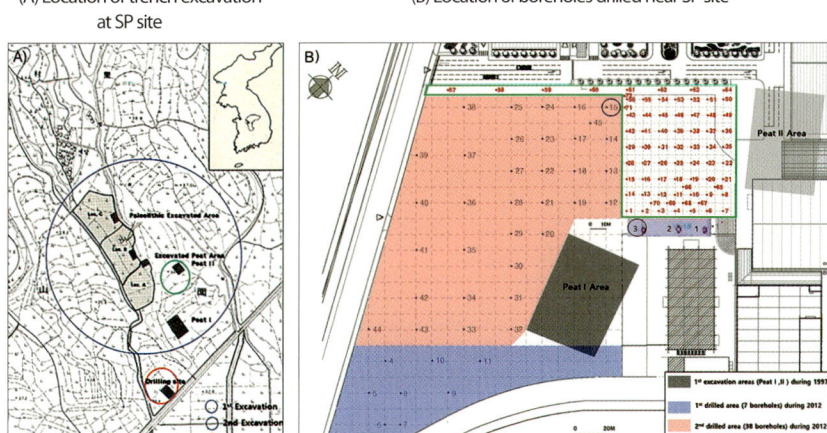

Fig. 1 Location of excavations, trenches, and drilling locations at the Sorori Paleolithic (SP) sites (Kim et al., 2000, 2008, 2015b; Lee et al., 2012).

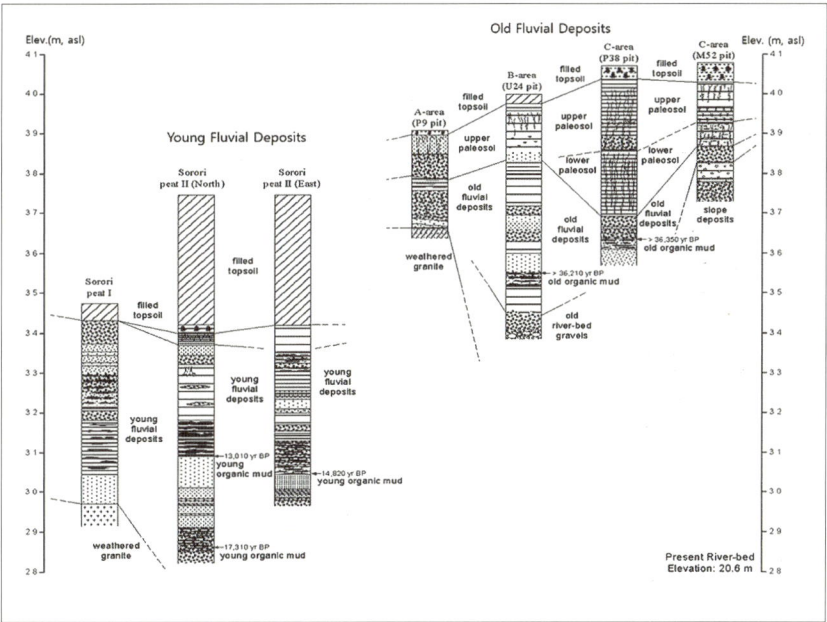

Fig. 2 Distribution of the Old Fluvial Deposits (OFDs) and Young Fluvial Deposits (YFD) based on lithological profiles of trench excavations in the Sorori Paleolithic sites (Kim et al., 2000; Kim et al., 2008b; Kim et al., 2015a, 2015b; Lee et al., 2015).

2. Fluvial terrace and sedimentary sequences

2.1. Old Fluvial Deposits (OFDs)

In the SP site, Old Fluvial Deposits (OFDs) illustrate pre-Last Glacial Maximum (LGM) fluvial processes. The OFDs (pre-LGM) typically consist of sands and gravels on the surface of low terraces, which are distributed at an elevation of around 30 to 35m (asl). Low terrace surfaces are assumed to have formed during the earliest part of the Last Glacial Period or after the Last Interglacial Period (approximately 80,000 years ago). From P38 and U24 pits of the SP site (**Fig. 2**), it is evident that the OFDs are linked to earlier backswamp organic muds (the 4th peaty layer) dating back to at least 36,000 years BP, as determined by the ^{14}C age of the organic muds found above the sands and gravels of the OFDs (**Fig. 2**). From borehole BH-15, drilled during the second session in 2012 (**Fig. 1**-B), black peat layers were found OFDs and were dated between 43,600 BP and 48,540 BP. The base level of the OFDs ranges from 30.2m (asl) to 36.9m (asl), indicating that it is higher than that of YFDs in SP (**Fig. 4**). Based on a sedimentation rate of 0.4m/yr in the OFDs, the bottom of the OFDs can potentially be estimated as old as 70,000 years ago in U24 pit of the B area (**Fig. 2, 3**). The data from the OFDs suggest

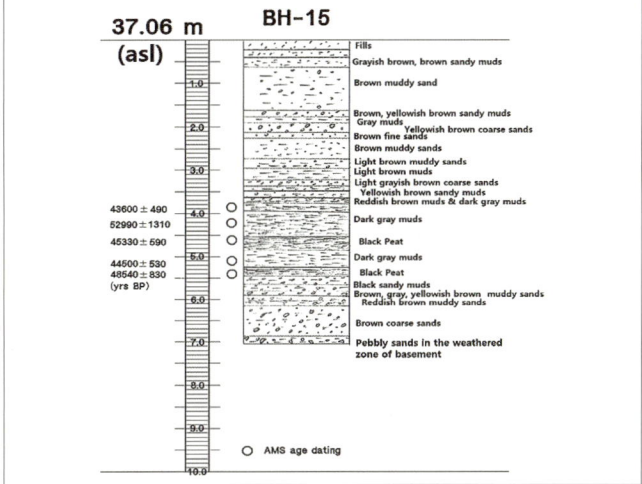

Fig. 3 The peaty layers of Old Fluvial Deposits (OFDs) in the borehole BH-15 dated 43,600-48,540 BP, and the base level ranges from 30.2m (asl) to 36.9m (asl), before forming YFD in SP.

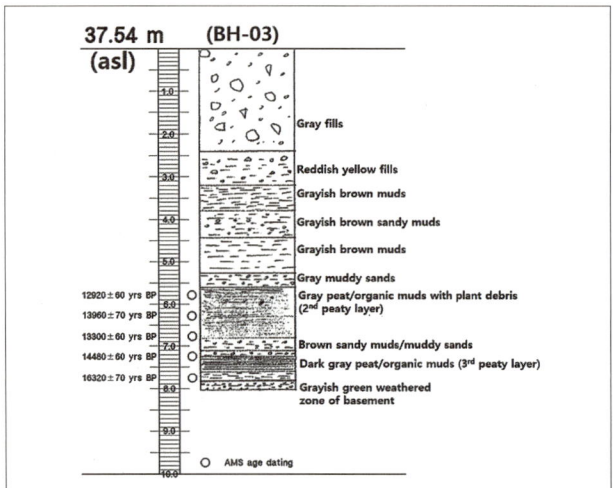

Fig. 4 The 2nd and 3rd peaty layers of Young Fluvial Deposits (YFDs) in the BH-03 dated 12,900-16,320 BP, and the base level was lowered to the range from 29.5m (asl) to 34.4m (asl), after forming OFDs in SP site

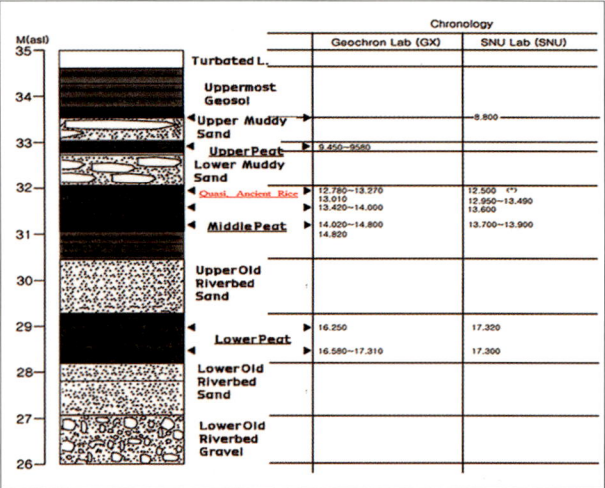

Fig. 5 AMS Radiocarbon dating (non-calibrating) results for soil organic matter, peat, and seeds collected from the YFDs in SP site.(Kim et al., 2000, 2006, 2008b; Lee et al., 2015; Kim et al., 2012). (*) representing 12,520 yrBP (ancient rice) and 12,552 yrBP (peat) (Kim et al., 2012), which is synchronous with old Bølling period.

that as the elevation of the peaty layer increases, the age of the peaty layer also increases.

2.2. Young Fluvial Deposits (YFDs) and Peaty Layers

The most recent Pleistocene Young Fluvial Deposits (YFDs) (post-LGM) can be distinguished and elucidated by the lithology and sedimentary facies of YFDs. According to the lithofacies and radiocarbon ages (Fig. 4, 5), these deposits consist of young fluvial sands and gravels at the bottom, and backswamp organic muds in the middle and upper parts of the YFDs. The lower part of the YFDs, formed after the LGM, is characterized by sand and gravel. The middle part of the YFDs, however, is characterized by organic muds, particularly formed after approximately 17,000 BP, when local backswamps flourished with grasses, leading to the formation of peaty layers (Fig. 4, 5). The second and third

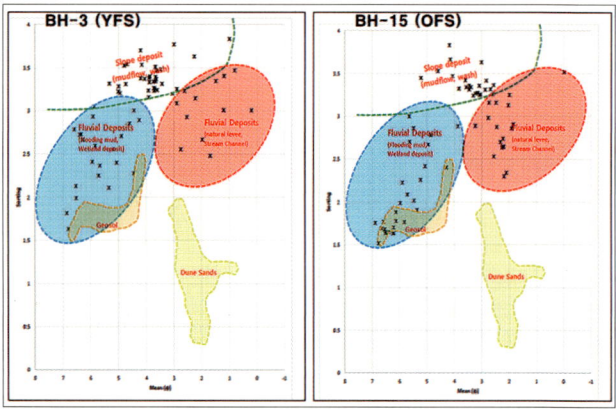

Fig. 6 Classification of sedimentary environmental conditions at SP sites based on borehole cores (BH-3, BH-15)

peaty layers of (YFDs) in the BH-03 dated 12,900-16,320 BP, and the base level was lowered to a range between 29.5m (asl) and 34.4m (asl), after formation of the OFDs in SP site. The primary fluvial processes include those resulting from stream channel dynamics, flooding, backswamp formation, and slopewash from the foothills at the SP site (Fig. 6).

In the YFDs, three organic muds and peaty layers formed between 17,300 to 9,450 years BP (Fig. 5). It can be interpreted that after the LGM, fluvial bed-load sands were associated with organic mud derived from the backswamp along the old Miho River. The ancient seeds, discovered in the second Sorori excavation site, yielded radiocarbon dates of 12,500 years BP (14,600 cal-yrs BP) from the middle peaty layer. Geological drilling surveys (Fig. 1-B), aimed to uncover the extent of Sorori peaty layers that may contain ancient rice seeds, result that no rice seeds were identified in the drilling core samples. The AMS ages of core samples BH-3 were dated to 12,920 to 16,320 BP, which may be corroborated by the same age interval obtained from the 1st and 2nd excavation works at the SP site in 1997. Based on a sedimentation rate of 0.5mm/yr in the YFDs, the bottom of the YDFs could potentially be dated as old as 29,650 years ago (approximately 25.5m, asl). The boreholes BH-66 and BH-70 indicate that as the elevation of the peaty layer increases, the age of the peaty layer decreases in the YFDs. The ages of the old rice seeds are mainly synchronous with the Bolling and Allerod periods (approximately after 14,700-13,000 years ago) (Fig. 5).

3. Geosol formation in Old Fluvial Deposits

Geosols (or paleosoils) are generally prevalent along the Miho River Basin, and the excavation profiles in the SP site reveal a number of geosol remains in the OFDs. One of the typical geosols is dark brown, characterized by soil wedges, Fe-Mn nodules, and a variably turbated structure resulting from episodic freezing and thawing of the sedimentary

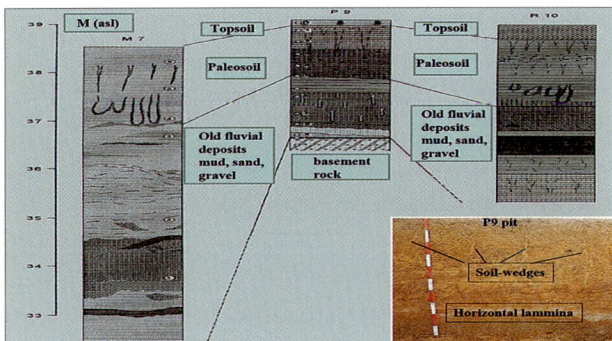

Fig. 7. Soil-sedimentary matrix of OFDs in SP site, adapted from excavation pits of the Chungbuk National University (Kim et al., 2000, 2015b)

matrix (Fig. 7). Geosols commonly formed during the Interstadial and two Stadial periods. In the SP site, the low geosol with soil-wedge structures and polygonal patterns on the weathered basement was formed during the period equivalent to Marine Isotope Stage 4 (MIS 4) (approximately 65 ka), while the upper geosol corresponds to MIS 2 (20 cal-ka in the SP site). The Interstadial geosol is not distributed ubiquitously but rather in patches of dense brown geosol (middle geosol) found between the low geosol associated with a disturbed pattern in the weathered basement of the MIS 4 (approximately 65 cal-ka) period and the dark brown upper geosol of the LGM period.

4. Summary and conclusion

4.1. Fluvial deposits and chronology

The Pleistocene terraces have formed in the middle of the Miho river basin. The terrace gravel is located at an elevation below 30m asl and is assumed to have been formed by geomorphic processes resulting from climatic change and/or sea level change. Along the Miho-cheon River, a low terrace prevails in the downstream part from the confluence of the Musim River near Cheongju City. The low terrace is situated at an elevation of 20-25m asl. It is mainly composed of subrounded gravels, channel sands with intercalations of backswamp organic muds, or peat layers (Kim et al., 2000; Kim et al., 2015a, 2015b). At the SP site, fluvial gravels are generally distributed up to a level of 35m asl. The last interglacial thalassostatic terrace could not be reached at the SP site. The paleo-shoreline of MIS 5e in the western part of the Korean Peninsula may reach approximately 26.5m asl when we apply the uplift rate of 0.14 to 0.21m/ka (Kim et al., 2008a) in the terrestrial part of the Korean Peninsula. Paleoshoreline indications may not extend to the SP site, so it makes sense that the low fluvial terrace gravels formed after the highest sea-level stand during the MIS 5. Around 80,000 years ago, major rivers prograded toward the Yellow Sea in the western part of the Korean Peninsula. Particularly, the Yellow Sea mostly disappeared during the earliest part of the Last Glacial Period and the LGM. During the latter period, the coastline dropped to about 120m below the present level, and the majority of the Yellow Sea emerged above sea level. After the LGM, however, the sea level abruptly rose due to the rapid melting of polar ice.

The chronology of the OFDs can be interpreted using the AMS radiocarbon dates of organic muds (4th peaty soil) obtained from borehole BH-15, and excavation trenches U24 and P38. The age of the OFDs may indicate that they are older than 50 ka, when the interstadial periods were prevalent at the SP site. Many stone artifacts are associated with the Upper Paleolithic period, ranging between LGM and MIS 4 in OFDs.

The YFDs, which contain intercalations of backswamp organic muds or peat layers, are predominant below the base level of the OFDs along the Miho River. The Sorori peat muds were dated to 12,930-17,300 years BP, indicating a post-LGM period during which there was a repetition of warm-humid and cool-dry conditions prevailing in the SP site. It is commonly accepted that the latest Pleistocene fluvial deposits are mainly associated with the YFS, which prevails along the major fluvial systems in the Korean Peninsula (Kim et al., 2008b; Kim and Lee. 2006).

Along the Miho River, the Gramineae (Poaceae) of the YFDs were dominant and associated with evergreen conifers (Betula-Abies-Piceas) and broad-leaved deciduous trees (Alnus-Quercus). This suggests that the forestry transitioned from fluvial backswamps to wetland bogs. It may be concluded that the Bølling and Allerød (B/A) Interstadial favors the abundant growth of early grain grasses (such as rice, barley, maize, buckwheat, etc.). The hypothesis may be supported by the discovery of prototype rice seeds (O. sativa, prototype) as the ancestor of cultivated Asian rice (Gross et al., 2014; Huang et al., 2012). This discovery is closely linked to peaty layers and is primarily found between the B/A Interstadial (Kim et al., 2015a, 2015b; Lee et al., 2015).

4.2. Geosols as a geochronological time scale

At the low terrace in the SP site and surrounding areas along the Miho River, three typical geosols (paleosoils) have been identified (Fig. 7). The Lower Geosol (LG) is characterized by yellow or brownish yellow soil sediments. The LG is characterized by frost cracks dating back to 60,000-65,000 years ago in the OFDs (Fig. 8). The Middle Geosol (MG) exhibits a rather reddish brown to dense brown color, while the Upper Geosol (UG) is characterized by a dark pinkish brown color. The MGs and UGs are assumed to have originated from different landscape-forming processes during the middle and upper parts of the Last Glacial Period. Several open Paleolithic sites, regardless of the

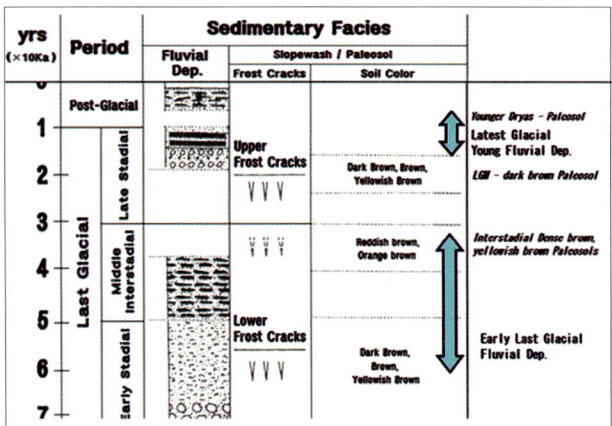

Fig. 8 Scheme of sedimentary facies and Geosols formation during the Last Glacial Period, depicting OFD and YFD, as well as Geosols as the pedo-sedimentary layers (adapted from Kim and Lee., 2006; Kim et al., 2008b, 2015b; Cho, 2006).

origin of deposits (fluvial, eolian, slopewash, or coastal), are characterized by the presence of MG and UG as crucial site-forming matrix types.

In chronological terms, the MG can be attributed to the middle of the Last Glacial Period (possibly MIS 3, 55 to 30 ka). The UG, which extensively shaped surficial soil formation in the Korean Peninsula, is distinguished by numerous polygonal structures in its horizontal view and ground veins or frost cracks in its vertical view as seen in excavation profiles. The UG exhibits a dark pinkish brown loamy texture that is relatively stiffer than the MG below. The vertical length of cracks ranges from several tens of centimeters up to several meters. The branching of cracks is more pronounced in the tangential direction than in the radial direction of the undulating foothill. The infilling materials within the cracks exhibit glossy textures, are vertically continuous, and range in color from light yellow to pale bluish gray. The microscopic texture is characterized by clay coatings and cappings, nodules, or patches of aggregates resulting from the concentration of Fe-Mn hydroxides, as well as a number of clay fills in the interstices of the pedo-sedimentary matrix. Chronologically, the UG, found mostly on slope deposits, is characterized by frost cracks (soil-wedges) or desiccation cracks with fragipan texture, indicating very cold and dry climate conditions during the formation of the UG in the Korean Peninsula and the Japanese island arc (Cho et al, 2006).

5. Conclusion

Regarding the Upper Paleolithic implications of the site-matrix forming process at the SP site, it is important to emphasize that the UG can be notably characterized by the presence of typical microblades and blades, representing the general culture. The subdivision of the Upper Paleolithic culture suggests that the OFDs of the SP site can be assigned to the Early Upper Paleolithic (EUP) and Middle Upper Paleolithic (M2UP), while the YFS may belong to the Late Upper Paleolithic (L3UP) and the latest Upper Paleolithic. The Sorori Paleolithic site will hold a significant position among the Upper Paleolithic sites along the Miho and Keum River Basin as it encompasses the entire Upper Paleolithic culture. Lastly, it may also be presumed that during the Last Glacial Period, the East Asian Winter Monsoon was more active than the Summer Monsoon. This could have led to seasonal freezing and thawing grounds even in the mid-latitudes, leaving remnants of surface processes that formed geosols. These are indicative of a unique geochronological time scale of the Last Glacial Period in the Korean Peninsula.

Acknowledgement

This paper was supported by the Korea Institute of Geoscience and Mineral Resources (KIGAM), the Institute of Korean Prehistory (IKP), and Quaternary Paleoenvironment Research (QPR).

◈ This chapter was prepared by summarizing and modifying the preceding paper (Kim et al., 2016).

References

Cho Chul-jae. 2006. Comparative study on the formation mechanisms of frost cracks and desiccation crack, cause of stratigraphic disturbance, during the last Glacial Stage. *Basic Research(B) Report of Cultural Association of Osaka City* (Project Funding No. 15300298), 59-62.

Gross Briana L., Zhao Zhijun. 2014. Archaeological and genetic insights into the origins of domesticated rice. *Proceedings of the National Academy of Sciences* 111(17), 6190-6197.

Huang Pu, Molina Jeanmaire, Flowers Jonathan M., Rubinstein Samara, Jackson Scotta A., Purugganan Michael D., Schaal Barbara A., 2012. Phylogeography of Asian wild rice, *Oryza rufipogon*: a genomewide view. *Molecular Ecology* 21(18), 4593-4604.

Kim Ju Yong, Yang Dong Yoon, Lee Dong Young, Bong Pil Yun, Choi Sung Ja. 2000. Quaternary Geology of Sorori Paleolithic Site in Cheongwon County, Korea. *Museum of the Chungbuk National University Research Report* 68, 17-163.

Kim Ju-Yong, Lee Yung-Jo. 2006. Stratigraphy of the Upper Pleistocene and Paleolithic in Korea. *L'anthropologie* 110, 119-

138.

Kim Ju-Yong, Keun-Chang Oh, Dong Yoon Yang, Weon Hack Choi, Sei Sun Hong, Jin Young Lee. 2008a. Stratigraphy, chronology and implied uplift rate of coastal terraces in the southeastern part of Korea. *Quaternary International* 183, 76-82.

Kim Ju Yong, Dong Woon Yang, Wook-Hyun Nahm, Sangheon Yi, Jeong Chan Kim, Sei-Sun Hong, Hyun-Su Yun, Jin-Young Lee, Jin-Kwan Kim, Keun-Chang Oh and Don-Won Choi. 2008b. Last Glacial and Holocene fluvial wetland sedimentary stratigraphy: Comparison between Soro-ri and Jangheung-ri archeological sites, Korea. *Quaternary International* 176-177, 135-142.

Kim Ju-Yong, Lee Yung-jo, Woo Jong-yoon, Lee Seung-won, Oh Keun-Chang. 2015a. Analysis and Implication of Geological Environment of the World's Oldest Sorori Rice Seed. *Proceeding of the International Conference on the Cheongju Sorori Rice and Bio-cultural Cheongju City*, 41-58.

Kim Ju-Yong, Yang Dong-Yoon, Lee Yung-jo, Woo Jong-yoon, Hong Se-Sun, Yi Sangheon, Nahm Wook-Hyun, Lee Jin-Yong, Bong Phil-Yoon, Oh Keun-Chang, Lee Seung-won. 2015b. Quaternary Geological Environment and Stratigraphy of Paleolithic sites in the middle Keum River Basin. *Journal of Korean Paleolithic Society* 32, 2-36.

Kim Ju-yong, Lee Yung-jo, Woo Jong-yun , Lee Seungwon, Oh Keun Chang. 2016. Landscape and Soil-Sedimentary Matrix-Forming Processes of Sorori Paleolithic Site in the Miho River since MIS 5, Korean Peninsula. Program and *Proceedings of the 21st Suyanggae and Her Neighbors International Symposium, titled Suyanggae and Hell Gap*, 118-129.

Kim Kyeong Ja, Yung-Jo Lee, Jong-Yoon Woo, A.J. Timothy Jull. 2012. Radiocarbon ages of Sorori ancient rice of Korea. *Nuclear Instruments and Methods in Physics Research B* 294, 675-679.

Lee Yung-jo, Woo Jong-yoon. 2015. The oldest Cheongju Sorori Rice for the City of Life and Culture. *Proceeding of the International Conference on the Cheonghu Sorori Rice and Bio-cultural Cheongju City*, 11-35.

Rice (*O. sativa*) remains excavated in China

Shengxiang TANG[1], Yung-jo LEE[2]

[1] Professor, China National Rice Research Institute, China ; sxtang93@163.com
[2] Institute of Korean Prehistory (IKP), Korea

ABSTRACT

According to incomplete statistics, until now, more than 255 rice remains, including rice grains, brown grains, hulls, stems, leaves, opals, old paddy fields, as well as stone and bone tools for primitive rice cultivation, have been excavated from different sites in China. More than 179 of these rice remains have been dated to 12,300–3,500 BP. Most of these remains are situated in the region between the middle-lower reaches of Yangtze River and the upper reaches of Huai River, and a few in Southwest China. The most ancient rice remains are as follows: Hemudu (6,950±130 BP), Jiahu (8,285–7,450 BP), Shangshan (11,400–8,600 BP), Huxi (9,000 BP), Bashidong (9,000–8,000 BP), Yuchanyan (12,300–10,000 BP), Neulandong (12,000 BP), Xianrendong (14,000–10,000 BP), Diaotonghuan (12,060–10,000 BP). The observation of opals, bi-peak-tubercles on hulls, and grain shapes and their dimensions, showed that primitive *indica-japonica* differentiation occurred 8,000-11,000 BP in China. The various evidence indicates that the beginning of primitive rice (*O. sativa*) cultivation in China could be traced to, at least, before 10,000 years.

국문초록

통계자료에 따르면 현재까지 볍씨, 현미, 껍질, 줄기, 잎, 규소체, 고대 경작논, 중국의 여러 유적에서 발굴된 초기 벼 재배에 사용된 석기와 골기 등을 포함하는 볍씨 출토유적이 255개 이상 집계되었다. 중국 179개 이상 유적에서 볍씨 흔적에 대한 연대측정 결과 12,300-3,500년 전으로 나타났다. 대부분 볍씨는 양쯔강 중·하류, 황하~회강 상류 사이 지역에 남아 있고, 일부 지역은 중국 남서부에 위치하고 있다. 중국의 문헌에서는 16개 지역에 야생벼(wild rice, *O. rufipogon*) 혹은 잡초벼(weedy rice)가 있고, 이들이 자연적으로 매년 씨앗이 뿌려지며 생장하는 것으로 알려져 있다. 중국의 가장 오래된 고대 볍씨(ancient rice) 출토유적으로는 Hemudu(6,950±130 BP), Jiahu(8,285-7,450 BP), Shangshan(11,400-8,600 BP), Huxi(9,000 BP), Bashidong(9,000-8,000 BP), Yuchanyan(12,300-10,000 BP), Neulandong(12,000 BP), Xianrendong(14,000-10,000 BP), Diaotonghuan(12,060-10,000 BP)을 들 수 있다. 볍씨 흔적으로 규소체, 껍질의 유봉돌기, 볍씨 모양, 크기 등을 관찰해 보면 중국에서는 초기 인디카-자포니카(*indica-Japonica*)의 분화가 8,000-11,000년 전에 발생했음을 알 수 있다. 다양한 증거에 따르면 중국에서 초기 벼 재배는 적어도 10,000년 전에 시작되었다고 볼 수 있다.

Keywords : *O. sativa*, rice remain, rice origination, *indica-japonica* differentiation, China

1. Common wild rice (*O. rufipogon*) remains

At present, common wild rice (*O. rufipogon*) is widely distributed from Taiwan (Taoyuan County, 121°15′E) in the east to Yunnan Province (Jinghong County, 100°47′E) in the west, and from Hainan Island (Sanya area 18°09′N) in the south to Jiangxi Province (Dongxiang County 28°14′N) in the north. But according to old Chinese writings, there were 16 areas for growing wild rice, showing automatic seed shattering and growing year by year in natural conditions. The old wild rice was distributed wider and more northerly during the Neolithic Period, including all of South China, the current territories of southern Sichuan, Chongqing, southern Hubei, a large part of Shandong, and Anhui, Jiangsu Province (You, 1992). However, is the above self-perpetuating rice true of *O. rufipogon* or of weedy rice? No final conclusions have yet been made.

The direct evidence is that four *O. rufipogon* carbonized grains (6,950±130 BP) with long awns and other common wild rice features were discovered from the population of 146 rice carbonized grains excavated at the Hemudu site (29°58′N, 121°22′E), Zhejiang Province, in East China. By scanning electronic microscope (SEM) examination, these four wild grains showed following characteristics: (1) more dense bristles on the long awn compared with other Hemudu carbonized rice grains, as well as modern cultivated varieties; (2) smooth traces of natural shedding during maturity in spikelet rachis at the base point when compared with relative rough traces of other Hemudu ancient grains shed by external force; and (3) a narrow grain shape with a width-length ratio of 2.88–3.10 (Sato, 1991; Tang, 1994). It was revealed that *O. rufipogon* had been growing in East China about 30°N at least 7,000 years ago. *O. rufipogon* grains from a mixed population dating to before 7,000 years were also found. *O. rufipogon* might be growing near or be mixed with primitive cultivated rice *O. sativa* in primitive rice fields in the region of the Low-Yangtze River.

An analysis of the excavated rice grains and rice opals from the soil of the Jiahu archaeological site (8,285-7,450 BP, 33°36′N, 113°40′ E) indicated that some of Jiahu's ancient rice grains had some *O. rufipogon* characteristics (Wang, 1996).

2. Rice (*O. sativa*) grain remains

According to incomplete statistics, 255 rice remains (grains, brown grains, hulls, stems, leaves, opals, etc.) with an age >1,500 years were excavated from various sites in Central, South, and Southwest China. Of these, 179 rice remains were dated to 12,300–3,500 BP. The most ancient 24 rice remains, dated to about 7,000 BP–12,300 BP, were situated in the

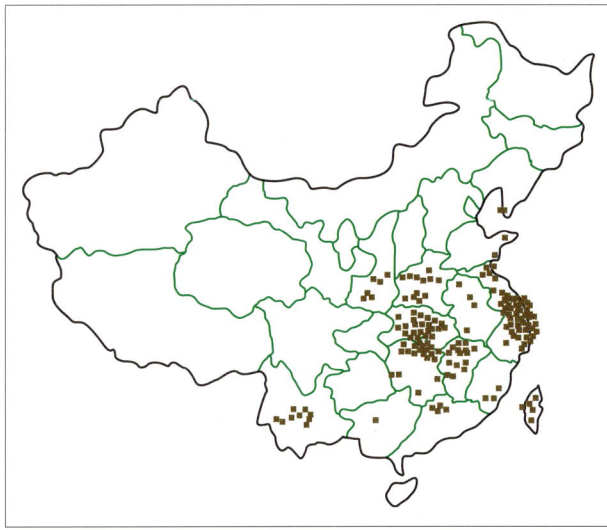

Fig. 1 Distribution of 161 late Paleolithic-Neolithic sites (12,300 - 3,500 BP) where various rice remains have been excavated.

region between the middle-lower reaches of Yangtze River and the upper reaches of Huai River, with a few in South China (**Fig. 1**).

In the 1970s, a great quantity of rice remains, together with many bone and stone tools used primarily for land preparation and harvesting, as well as many sub-tropical plants and animals, were excavated from the Hemudu site (6,950±130 BP, 29°58′N, 121°22′E), located in the delta of the lower Yangtze River, Zhejiang Province. A stacked area of rice remains around 400m², with a thickness ranging 10–40cm was found. Thousands of carbonized rice grains were excavated together with rice leaves and straws from this relic (**Fig. 2**). Many Hemudu rice grains showed a straw-yellow color when just excavated from the air-tight layer and then changed immediately to carbonized black. Most of the Hemudu grains had awns. The dimensions of the carbonized grains vary considerably in length and width, being judged as a mixed population of primitive *japonica* rice, primitive *indica* rice, and a few common wild rice (*O. rufipogon*) based on grain length, width, shape, size, and awn bristles, as well as the characteristics of bi-peak-tubercles on hulls (Tang, 1994, 1999). At the Tianluoshan site, 7km from the Hemudu site, a number of carbonized rice grains dated to 6,900-6,600 BP were found together with many kinds of clay pots, bone and stone tools, plant seeds, and animal bones.

In Zhejiang Province, many old rice remains from different sites were unearthed. In 2001-2002, thousands of carbonized rice grains and hulls with many primitive farming stone and bone tools, dated to 8,220–7,660 BP, were excavated from the Kuahujiao site. Looking at grain shape, ratio of length-width, and opal shape, Kuahujiao rice was considered the primitive cultivated rice more close to *japonica*. In 2010, at the Huxi site, some brown rice grains were excavated and dated to 9,000 BP. Recently, some carbonized ancient rice, as well as rice hulls in pottery, dated to 11,400-8,600

Fig. 2 Ancient rice grains (6,950±130 BP) excavated from Hemudu site in Zhejiang province

BP, were found at the Shangshan site (29°31'N, 119°52'E), Pujiang County. An analysis of grain shape, opals, and rachillas showed that Shangshan ancient rice had a shorter grain length and a wider width than common wild rice, closed to *japonica*, but possibly with some characteristics of tropic *Japonica* (*javanica*) in an opal shape. It was revealed Shangshan that rice grains might be of the most ancient rice remains to be find in the East China. But some colleagues argue whether these Shangshan rice grains and hulls belong to old common wild rice, or to primitive cultivated rice. It is not well judged today. Besides, some important rice remains in Zhejiang Province are as follows: Luojiajiao site (7,040±150 BP), Tongjiaao site (about 7,000 BP), and Xiaohuangshan site (about 9,000 BP).

The bi-peak-tubercles on lemma were studied on three grains of Hemudu and four grains of Luojiajiao, as well as eight *indica* and eight *japonica* local varieties by SEM. The significant differences in the bi-peak-tubercle between *indica* and *japonica* varieties have been observed. According to judgement criterion of the peak angle 80°, col angle 150°, and ratio of bi-peak distance/col depth 10, the bi-peak-tubercles of Hemudu rice could be classified into two types as '"acute" of *indica* and "obtuse" of *japonica*. The bi-peak-tubercles of three Hemudu and four Luojiajiao ancient grains were identified as "obtuse" although the grain shape of the six from these seven grains trended to *indica*. Therefore, the Hemudo and Loujiajiao ancient rice could be deeply convinced as a group of "differentiating," "non-*indica*," "non-*japonica*" primitive cultivated rice (**Fig. 3**) (Tang, 1999).

From Jiahu village (33°36'N, 113°40'E) of Henan Province, located near the southern region of Huai River, hundreds of carbonized rice grains dated 8,942–7,868 BP were excavated in the early 1990s. The studies of morphological and bi-peak-tubercles indicated that Jiahu ancient rice was considered a pro-*japonica* primitive type with some characteristics of common wild rice and *indica-japonica* identity not being fully differentiated (Wang, 1996).

In the 1980s, many carbonized rice grains and hull in earthenware dated 8,200–7,450 BP were discovered, with many bones and stone tools roughly in same layer from Pengtoushan, Hunan Province near southern basin of the middle Yangtze River. In 2018, carbonized rice grains have been found in the middle cultural layer of Gaomiao culture 7,400 years ago in Hunan Province, and starch grains of rice and Pearl barley have been found on the stone tools of the ancestors of Gaomiao site, which have been confirmed by testing and analysis. In 1996, hundreds of Bashidong rice grains dated 9,000–8,000 BP were found from Li County, Hunan Province. Differing to Jiahu ancient rice, Bashidong rice was an independent and complicated colony with great variations, more closed to *indica* and *O. rufipogon*. Therefore, Bashidong rice was deduced to be an original type of cultivated rice which had completely developed

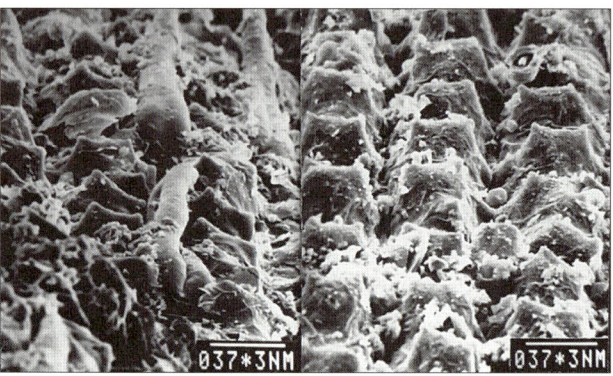

Fig. 3 The bi-peak-tubercles on lemma of Hemudu ancient grains

in nature without any artificial selection (Zhao, 2000). In 2014, more than 100 brown-rice grains of Songjiagang site were excavated dated 9,000 BP also in Li county of Hunan Province. In the mid-1990s rice hulls and several rice opals dated 12,000–10,000 BP from Yuchanyan site (25°30′N, 110°30′E) were excavated from cultural soil layer of Dao county, Hunan Province, together with many plants, animals, primitive stone and bone tools. In 2004 in the same Yuchanyan site, five carbonized rice grains and the primitive earthenware dated 12,300–10,000 were discovered. These five carbonized rice grains showed an overall characteristics with indica/japonica/common wild rice, therefore was deduced as the most ancient and primitive cultivated rice in Central China (Table 1).

3. Rice opal remains

A large number of ancient *O. rufipogon* opals in G layer (14,000-11,000 BP), and the opals both ancient *O. rufipogon* and ancient cultivated rice (*O. sativa*) in D layer (12,060–10,000 BP), and the opals major in primitive cultivated rice in C layer were found in Diaotonghuan site (28°44′N, 117°09′E), which meaning primitive rice (*O. sativa*) cultivation had taken place in the Early Neolithic period in Central China.

In the soil cultural layer of Kuahujiao site (8,220–7,660 BP) in Zhejiang Province, a number of rice opals was found in 2001–2002. As comparing with the opals of present *japonica* and *indica* rice, Kuahujiao's opals were closed to *japonica* ones.

In 2012, a large number of rice opals was discovered together with amount of various animal bones, pieces of earthenware and polishing stones etc in Neulandong site. These opals (12,000 BP) were judged as sector opals of primitive rice with the characters of '*indica*-like' in opal's handle length and '*japonica*-like' in opal's thicknes.

The rice opals in six ancient sites of Caoxieshan (5,900–6,200 BP), Guangfucun (6,000 BP), Dongshancun (6,000–8,000 BP), Shaoqingshan (5,000–5,500 BP), Xuecheng (6,000–6,500 BP) and Longqiuzhuang (6,300–7,000 BP) in Jiangsu Province were detected. A large amount of rice opals in all the soil samples from the cultural layers were found and dated back to near 8,000 BP. If the number of rice opals was over 5,000 in one gram soil sample, in general, it illustrated that the

Table 1 Twenty-four excavated rice remains with age ≥ 7000 BP in China

Site	Location	Era	Rice remains
Hemudu, Zhejiang province	29°58′N, 121°22′E	6,950 ± 130 BP	Thousands of carbonized rice grains, stems, leaves, with a few of *O. rufipogon* grains
Luojiajiao, Zhejiang province	30°37′N, 120°27′E	7,040 ± 150 BP	Hundreds of carbonized rice grains, majority in primitive *japonica*
Tongjiaao, Zhejiang province	30°10′N, 121°15′E	About 7,000 BP	A few of Carbonized rice hulls
Huxi, Zhejiang province	28°56′N, 120°05′E	9,000 BP	Many brown rice grains
Shangshan, Zhejiang province	29°31′N, 119°52′E	11,400–8,600 BP	A great number of carbonized brown rice grains rice hulls and opals in pottery
Kuahujiao, Zhejiang province	30°08′N, 120°13′E	8,220–7,660 BP	Thousands of carbonized rice grains and hulls
Tianluoshan, Zhejiang province	30°01′N, 121°11′E	7,000–5,600 BP	Hundreds of Carbonized rice grains
Xiaohuangshan, Zhejiang province	29°33′N, 120°43′E	About 9,000 BP	Rice grains in pottery, rice hulls in sintering red soil
Erjiancun, Jiangsu province	34°50′N, 119°15′E	7,000–6,000 BP	A few of carbonized rice hulls
Longqiuzhuang, Jiangsu province	32°59′N, 119°30′E	7,000–6,300 BP	Hundreds of carbonized rice grains
Jiahu Village, Henan province	33°36′N, 113°40′E	8,285–7,450 BP	Hundreds of carbonized rice grains and opals, primitive pro-*Japonica*
Lijiacun, Shaanxi province	32°58′N, 107°45′E	About 7,600 BP	Vestige of rice grain hulls on burned soil
Pengtoushan, Hunan rovince	29°40′N, 111°39′E	8,200–7,450 BP	Vestige of carbonized rice grains and hull on roughcast of earthenware
Songjiagang, Hunan province	29°37′N, 111°38′E	9,000 BP	More than one Hundred carbonized grains of brown rice
Bashidang, Hunan province	29°45′N, 111°50′E	9,000–8,000 BP	Hundreds of carbonized rice grains, ancient *indica*
Yuchanyan, Hunan province	25°30′N, 113°30′E′	12,300 ± 10,000 BP	5 carbonized rice grains, 4 rice hulls, with some mixed characters of *indica*, *Japonica* and *O. rufipogon*
Shanlonggang, Hunan province	29°40′N, 111°30′E	9,000–8,000 BP	6 carbonized rice grains
Dulinau, Hunan province	26°46′N, 113°32′E	About 7,000 BP	A few of carbonized rice grains
Gaomiao, Hunan province	27°32′N, 110°15′E	About 7400 BP	A few of carbonized rice grains
Chengbeixi, Hubei Province	30°18′N, 111°29′E	8,000–7,000 BP	A few of carbonized rice hulls in pottery
Xianrendong, Jiangxi province	28°44′N, 117°10′E	14,000–10,000 BP	Opals of ancient *O. rufipogen* and ancient primitive rice
Diaotonghuan, Jiangxi province	28°44′N, 117°09′E	12,060–10,000 BP	Opals of ancient *O. rufipogen* and ancient primitive rice
Zhichengbei, Hubei province	30°18′N, 111°29′E	About 7,000 BP	A few of carbonized rice hulls in pottery
Niulandong, Guangdong province	24°20′N, 113°27′E	12,000 BP	Some sector opals of primitive rice

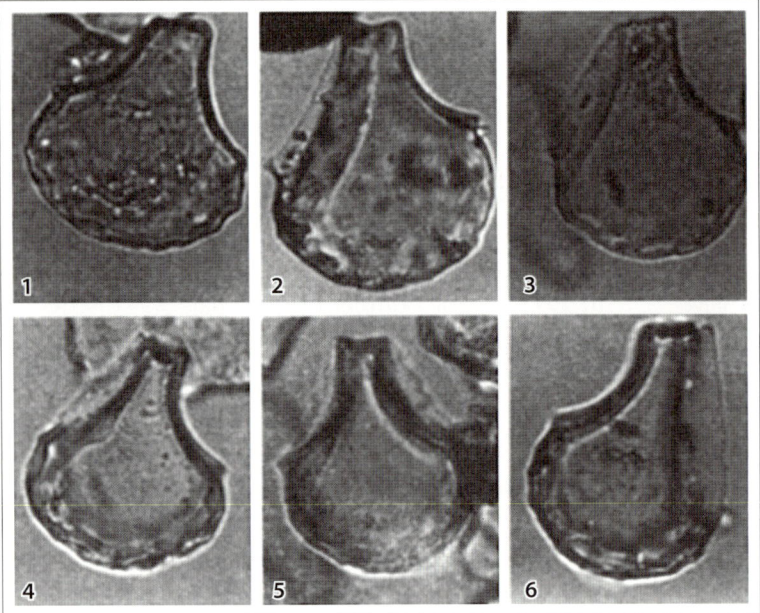

Fig. 4 Rice opals detected from paddy soil of 6 Neolithic ancient sites
1: Caoxieshan site, 2: Shaoqingshan site, 3: the Dongshancun site, 4: Guangfucun site, 5: Xuecheng site, 6: Longqiu zhuang site (Wang, 2000)

ancient field has been grown or cultivated rice in the old years. The morphological analysis of the opals showed the ancient rice cultivated in Taifu area (East China) in Neolithic period were belonged to *japonica* (**Fig. 4**). However, the morphological characteristics of the opals varied in different sites and different cultural layers.

4. Remains of ancient cultivated rice field

The finding of ancient cultivated rice field may have special significance for studying on rice origin and its domestication. In the mid-1990s, archaeologists excavated 33 ancient rice paddy fields back to 6,000 BP in Caohaishan site (31°22′N, 120°47′E), Wu County, Jiangsu Province (low base of Yangtze River). The ancient paddy fields varied in size ranging 0.9m²–12.6m² with the shapes about rectangle, ellipse and irregular in deep of 20–50cm. These rice fields could be connected each other through ditches with small water pools. In Tenghualuo site (3,900–3,500 BP) of Lianyungang, Jiangsu Province, there were not only hundreds of *japonica* ancient rice grains to have been excavated but also ancient paddy field about size of 67m², having rough ridge connecting by water ditch and small water pool.

In 1997, a larger ancient rice field with three ridges has been found in Chengtoushan site (6,629±896 BP, 29°41′N, 111°39′E) of Li County, Hunan Province. Observing on longitudinal section of the paddy field, it was clearly found of many rice plant bases and roots carbonated, showing the seeding type of broadcasting (direct seeding). Besides, the primitive irrigation system with three small water pools and three ditches was also found. The water pools were higher than that of paddy fields, with diameter of 1.2m–1.6m and depth about 1.3m, connecting by the ditches. It is believed that this ancient paddy field and its irrigation system may be the most primitive in rice cultivation. The predominantly old rice paddy field found also indicates that Chinese cultivators exercised great care in water control (irrigation and drainage) from more early days of rice cultivation.

In year 2006, a plenty of carbonized rice grains and branes, huskes, as well as well irrigation system of rice field dated 4,000 BP were discovered in Jijiaocheng site in Li county, Hunan Province.

It is reported in 2020 that the Shiao site of Yuyao county, Zhejiang Province, is an ancient rice field, with a total area of about 80,000m² in exploration, and it is estimated the total area of the ancient rice fields nearby is about 900,000m². This large-scale rice field discovered can be traced back more than 6,500 years of In Hemudu Culture period. After testing, the accumulation of ancient rice fields contained the remains of rice rachillas, grain hulls, and weeds associated. The analysis results showed that the density of rice opals in the accumulation of the rice fields was 10,000–20,000 grains/gram soil, which was much higher than the generally recognized standard that more than 5000 grains/g of rice opals in soil could be judged as paddy fields. The old rice field discovered in the first exploration period is belongs to the early Hemudu Culture, and is definitely dated to about 4,700–4,500 BC. In this rice field, a field ridge about 2.2m wide and an ancient river channel were found. A small number of fragments of clay kettles and clay pots were unearthed in the accumulation. The rice field in the second exploration period have an absolute age of about 3,700–3,300 BC. Eight east-west ridges about 30-100cm wide and three wide north-south ridges were found. One river channel with a general north-south trend was also found in the old rice fields in the western and eastern areas. Many pottery chips, stones, woods, plant seeds were unearthed from the accumulation of rice field ridges and rivers in the western area. Therefore, Shiao "Ancient Rice Field" can be considered the largest, oldest and most well-documented large-scale rice field found in the world.

So far, these evidences such as the distribution of *O. rufipogon* in old time, the excavated rice remains and the opals found in the soils and the potteries, the old paddy fields and irrigation systems, the related primitive stones and bones for farming tools, and human's activities at ancient time for primitive rice cultivation etc, all showed the situation of early rice cultivation in China. The most archaic rice remains found in sites of Hemudu, Huxi, Shangshan, Jiahu, Pangtoushan, Bashidong, Xianrendong, Diaotonghuan, Niulantong, Yuchanyan, etc were not only large in quantity but also the oldest in age. These oldest sites are not only having big amount of rice remains but also many human cultural evidences like bone spades, stone tools, bifacial axes, earthenware, potters, probably being used by ancient people for primitive crop cultivation including rice and living. Considering that domestication from common wild rice to primitive cultivated rice must be a long and a graduating process, it is reasonable to believe that the beginning of primitive rice cultivation in China could be traced to, at least, 10,000 BP.

It is generally consideration that the affirmation of the original place (ancestral home) of cultivated rice should meet at least four necessary conditions. First, progenitor of cultivated rice exists at present or has existed in ancient time in the home area. Second, the conditions of the climate and other environment factors in the Late Paleolithic-Neolithic time or saying old time were suitable for growth and domestication of *O. rufipogon*. Third, there existed motive evidences of old human for domesticating *O. rufipogon* to primitive rice (*O. sativa*) cultivation for food. And fourth, archaeology findings including ancient rice remains together with other possible evidences of early human cultural traces and/or related plants and animals etc.

Recent 50 years, great advances have been made toward the archaeological finding of more old, valuable rice remains and the multidisciplinary studies for well understanding rice origin and dissemination. We still have long way to go.

References

Chang, T.T., 1983. The origins and early cultures of the cereal grain and food legumes. In: *The Origins of Chinese Civilization*, USA: U.C Press, 65-94.

Heu, M.H., Moon, H.P., 2010. History of rice culture in Korea: origin, antiquity and difussion. In: Editor Sharma SD: *Origin, Antiquity and History of Rice*, USA: CRC Press, 85-114.

Sato, Y.I., Tang, S.X., Yang, L.J., Tang, L.H., 1991. Wild rice seeds found in an oldest rice remain. *Rice Genetics Newsletter*, IRRI, 76-78.

Suh, H.S., Cho, J.H., Lee, Y.J., Heu, M.H., 2003. RAPD variation of the carbonized rice aged 13,010 and 17,310 years. In: *The first international symposium: prehistory cultivation in Asia and Sorori rice*, Cheongju, Korea, 79-85.

Lee, Y.J., Woo, J.Y., 2000. Excavation of the Sorori site and its significance. Paper In: *the 4th International Rice Genetics symposium*, IRRI.

Lee, Y.J., Woo, J.Y., 2003. The oldest Sorori rice 15000BP: its finding and significance. In: *The first international symposium: prehistory cultivation in Asia and Sorori rice*, Cheongju, Korea, 33-46.

Lee, Y.J., Woo, J.Y., 2014. The oldest "Cheongju Sorori Rice" 17,000BP : its investigation and significance. In: *International symposium on paleoanthropology in commemoration of the 85th anniversary of the discovery of the first skull of Peking Man*, Beijing, China.

Ling, Q.H., 2012. *Origin of rice and Chinese rice farming culture*, Beijing: Chinese Agri Press, 117.

Liu, Z.Y., 2003. The origin of rice cultivation in China from a comparative analysis between Yuchanyan and Niulantong both Neolithic sites. *Agricultural Archaeology* 69, 76-87.

Sina Hunan. 2018. *The earliest rice in western Hunan was found in Huaihua Gaomia site*.

Tang, S.X., Min, S.K., Sato Y.I., 1993. Exploration on origin of Keng rice (*japonica*) in China. *Chinese J. Rice Sci.* 7(3), 129-136.

Tang, S.X., Sato, Y.I., Yu, W.J., 1994. Discovery of wild rice grains (*O. rufipogon*) from Hemudu ancient carbonized rice. *Agricultural archaeology* 35, 88-91.

Tang, S.X., Zhang, W.X., Liu, J., 1999. The study on the bi-peak tubercle on lemma of Hemudu and Luojiajiao ancient excavated rice grains with electric scanning microscope. *Acta Agri Sinica* 25(3), 320-327.

Tang, S.X., Xuan, S.N., 2010. Domestication of rice in China and its cultural heritage. In: Editor Sharma SD: *Origin, Antiquity and History of Rice*, USA: CRC Press, 85-114.

Wang, C.L., Zou, J.S., Tang, L.H., 2000. Rice cultivation at the Neolithic age in Taihu Valley. *Jiangsu J. of Agri. Science* 16(3), 129-138.

Wang X.K., 1996. New research progresses relating to several main problems about the origin of rice cultivation in China. In: *Origin and Differentiation of Chinese Cultivated Rice*, Beijing: China Agri Univ Press, 2-7.

Wang, X.K., Sun, C.J., Zhang, J.H., 2003. A discussion on the origin of *Oryza japonica* in China and Sorori ancient rice in Korea. *The first international symposium: prehistory cultivation in Asia and Sorori rice*, Cheongju, Korea, 115-123.

Yan, W.M., 2003. The origin of rice agriculture and Sorori excavated rice. In: *The first international symposium: Prehistory Cultivation in Asia and Sorori rice*, Cheongju, Korea, 95-103.

You, X.L., 1992. Origin and cultivation history of rice in China. In: *China Rice*, Beijing: China Agri Press, 1-19.

You, X.L., 2002. Rice origin and *Indica-japonica* differication caused by ancient rices excavated in China and Korea. *Agricultural Archaeology*, 101-103.

Zhao D.L., Pei, A.P., Zhang, W.X., 2000. Restudy of ancient cultivated rice from Bashidang site in Lixian county, Hunan province. *China J. of Rice Sci* 14(8l), 139- 43.

Zheng Y.F., Jiang, L.P., 2007. The ancient rice remain excavated in Shangshan site and its significance. *Archaeology* 19, 19-25.

Yuchanyan ancient rice and generation of rice agriculture of China

Jiarong YUAN

Professor, Hunan Institute of Archaeology of China, China ; Yjrhsh@163.com

ABSTRACT

Yuchanyan ancient rice is the oldest rice specimen discovered in human cultural relics worldwide. Among three sessions of discovery and identification of rice remains in Yuchanyan site, the most important discovery in Yuchanyan site is the unearthed rice husk. In 1993, screening in the first exploration of Yuchanyan site obtained two rice husks. The soil sample containing the rice husk is the bottom cultural lime soil of T1 (3llayer). The rice husk was black. In the second exploration in 1995, two rice in grayish yellow were discovered from the calcium plate bedding of grey white 2B5 and 3B1. The colors of the unearthed rick husk twice had differences, due to the different burial environments of the specimen. The former was buried in the relatively loose ash soil layer and was black due to oxidation after unearthing. The latter was buried in the yellowish white calcite cementation soil layer and was grayish yellow due to calcification, which was closer to the true color of the rice. In 2004, a charring rice grain was discovered during the flotation in the soil sample of T1-D-C-3h layer, and the soil sample was taken from the layer below the unearthed pottery shard in the current year. In the research significance on the origin of the cultivated rice, Yuchanyan ancient rice provides us with information about the evolutionary chain during the domestication process of cultivated rice at the earliest. Through the comparative analysis on the grain length, grain width and length–width ratio of modern *Oryza rufipogon*, *Indica*, *Japonica*, and Yuchanyan ancient rice, the rice grain length unearthed inYuchanyan was in the variation area of the *Oryza rufipogon* and *Indica*, and the average value is approximate to *Oryza rufipogon*. The husk hair length of the unearthed rice is between *Oryza rufipogon* and *Indica*, and shows the trend of longitudinally shortening. Lastly, Yuchanyan ancient rice is the oldest rice specimen discovered in the human cultural relics all over the world, whether or not it is *Oryza rufipogon* or cultivated rice, which is directly related to the research on the origin of the rice agriculture.

국문초록

중국 유찬얀 유적에서 고대벼는 3회의 발굴조사를 통해 발견되었다. 1993년에는 기저부 석회질 문화층(T1, 3층)에서 2개 흑색 볍씨 껍질이 발견되었고, 1995년에는 기저부 회백색 석회질로 고결화된 평탄층2(B5와 3B1층)에서 2개의 회황색 볍씨가 발견되었으며, 2004년에는 토층 시료(T1-D-C-3h층)에서 탄화 볍씨가 발견되었다. 중국 유찬얀 유적에서의 볍씨 발견으로 야생벼에서 재배벼(cultivated rice)로의 순화과정(domestication) 연구와 더불어 후속적으로 중국의 벼농사(rice agriculture)에 대한 심층적 고찰과 토론이 전개되었다. 유찬얀 고대벼(Yuchanyan ancient rice)와 현대의 오리자 루피포곤(*Oryza rufipogon*), 인디카(*Indica*), 자포니카(*Japonica*)의 너비와 길이 비율에 대한 비교분석을 통해 유찬얀 고대벼는 오리자 루피포곤과 인디카의 변종에 근접하지만 평균적으로 보면 오리자 루피포곤에 근접하는 것으로 나타났다. 요컨대 발굴된 유찬얀 고대벼는 오리자 루피포곤의 너비와 길이를 유지하면서 전체 크기가 커지는 벼의 진화 과정을 지시하고 있다. 본 연구에서는 유찬얀 고대벼가 야생벼인 오리자 루피포곤이든 재배벼든 모두 벼농사의 기원과 관련되어 있으며 세계적으로 가장 오래된 볍씨로 보고 있다.

Keywords : Yuchanyan ancient rice, unearthed rice husks, *Oryza rufipogon*, *Indica*, *Japonica* cultivated rice, rice agriculture origin

Fig. 1 Yuchanyan site, Dao County, Hunan Province, China

1. Discovery and identification of rice remains at the Yuchanyan site

The most important discovery at the Yuchanyan site is an unearthed rice husk. In 1993, screening in the first exploration of Yuchanyan site obtained two rice husks. The soil sample containing the rice husk is the bottom cultural lime soil of T1 (3I layer). The rice husk was black. In the second exploration in 1995, two grayish yellow rice grains were discovered from the calcium plate bedding of grey white 2B5 and 3B1. The colors of the unearthed rick husk twice had differences, due to different burial environment of the specimen. The former was buried in the relatively loose ash soil layer and was black due to oxidation after unearthing. The latter was buried in the yellowish white calcite cementation soil layer and was grayish yellow due to calcification, which was closer to the true color of the rice. In 2004, in the third exploration of Yuchanyan site during the cooperation between China and the US, a charring rice grain was discovered during the flotation in the soil sample of T1-D-C-3h layer, and the soil sample was taken from the layer below the unearthed pottery shard in the current year (**Fig. 1**). Meanwhile, we made the soil sample analysis of the phytolith for the cultural layer of the site. Due to serious alkaline corrosion in the cave deposit, the morphology of the phytolith had always been unclear, resulting in difficulty analyzing the phytolith. Even so, *Oryza* sp. phytolith with the doublet mastoid morphological characteristic was discovered in the explored soil sample for testing. In 1995, the fan-shaped and dumbbell shaped phytolith was also discovered in the explored soil sample, and was tentatively called *Oryzoideae* due to unclear morphological corrosion. The specific situation was yet to be analyzed further. The existence of *Oryza* sp. Phytolith was further verified by the fact that the rice existed at the Yuchanyan site.

The serendipitous discovery of the real rice in Yuchanyan site caused the in-depth thought and discussion of the people for the domestication of the rice in China and the origin of the rice agriculture.

Mr. Zhang Wenxu was the inventor of the rice in Yuchanyan site in 1995. He discovered the rice specimen from the cementation bedding of the cultural layer during the process of personally clearing up the calcified plate of the site. After exploring, he went back to Changsha, and began to make analysis and research by borrowing the electron microscope equipment of Hunan Normal University. He specialized in two rice husk specimens discovered in Yuchanyan in 1993 and 1995. He conducted comprehensive research on the unearthed rice of Yuchanyan from three different perspectives of grain length, grain width, and length–width ratio of the rice, the husk hair length and husk shoulder angle characteristics, and the doublet mastoid morphology of the rice husk surface (**Fig. 2**).

Through the comparative analysis on the grain length, grain

width and length- width ratio of modern *Oryza rufipogon*, *Indica*, *Japonica* and Yuchanyan ancient rice, the rice grain length unearthed in Yuchanyan was in the variation area of the *Oryza rufipogon* and *Indica*, and the average value is approximate to *Oryza rufipogon*. The grain width is obviously wider than *Oryza rufipogon* and larger than the high limit of *Indica*, and is in the variation area of the *Japonica*. The average value is wider than *Oryza rufipogon* and *Indica*, and narrower yet approximate to *Japonica*. The average value of length–width ratio is greatly higher than *Japonica*, and lower than *Oryza rufipogon*, and is in the variation area of *Indica* yet slightly higher than the average value of *Indica*. Thus, the unearthed rice of Yuchanyan is a larger grain, and shows a sign of evolving towards the primary grain width on basis of keeping the grain length of *Oryza rufipogon*. It is the variation character that is easily noticed yet selected by the ancestor.

The husk hair length of the unearthed rice is between *Oryza rufipogon* and *Indica*, and shows the trend of longitudinally shortening. The doublet mastoid morphology of the unearthed rice and various indexes are similar to *Japonica*, and it keeps the initial conditions of Jiangyong *Oryza rufipogon*. The lemma top of the unearthed rice is awnless, and totally different from *Oryza rufipogon*, Indicating that it possesses the character of the cultivated rice. According to the signs showed by these characteristics, it can be presumed that the unearthed rice of Yuchanyan is the most primitive ancient cultivated rice type evolving from *Oryza rufipogon* to the early cultivated rice with the comprehensive characteristics of *Oryza rufipogon*, *Indica* and *Japonica*, known as "Yuchanyan ancient cultivated rice." It is necessary to explain that "Yuchanyan ancient cultivated rice" is just the common name, rather than the scientific name in the biological classification significance.

For the unearthed charring rice in 2004, Mr. Zhang Wenxu calculated the original grain length of the charring rice of 7.38mm, grain width of 2.54mm, grain thickness of 2.08mm, grain weight of 17.76mg, and length- width ratio of 2.91 through recovery and morphological index analysis.

Fig. 2 Rice husk, Left: 1995 unearthed, Right: 1993 unearthed

Referring to the grain shape comparison of Jiangyong *Oryza rufipogon*, Chaling *Oryza rufipogon*, Bashidang ancient rice, *Indica*, and *Japonica*, the ancient rice length is very short and even shorter than *Japonica*. The rice width is narrow, and in the variation area of *Oryza rufipogon*. Moreover, the rice thickness is relatively large and approximate to *Indica*. The rice weight is very small and similar to *Oryza rufipogon*. The length–width ratio of the grain shape is relatively large, and in the upper limit of the variation area of *Indica*. According to the grain shape discrimination function measurement, it belongs to *Indica* type comprehensively. Upon the Euclidean distance analysis of form quality in reference system, Yuchanyan ancient rice has the maximum similarity with two *Oryza rufipogon*, and then Bashidang ancient rice, while having dissimilarity with *Japonica*. He held that the unearthed charring rice in 2004 further strengthened the conclusion of the unearthed rice research in 1993 and 1995. Their common characteristic is manifested as the character variation and *Oryza rufipogon* have smaller differences, and Euclidean distance measured value can testify, Indicating that it has more characteristics of *Oryza rufipogon*, with a lot of information of the early evolution, so it possesses the primitiveness. The ancient rice grain width is enlarged, and the grain thickness is increased, whereas the grain length is invariant or shortened. All of these factors demonstrate the evolutionary trend of the cultivated rice. It is approximate to *Oryza rufipogon*, but not *Oryza rufipogon*, with the characteristics between *Oryza rufipogon* and Bashidang ancient rice. So, it is a cultivated rice in early stage of evolution.

2. Status of Yuchanyan ancient rice in the origin of rice agriculture in China

At present, Yuchanyan ancient rice is the oldest rice specimen discovered in human cultural relics worldwide. Whether it is *Oryza rufipogon* or cultivated rice is directly related to the research on the origin of the rice agriculture. Therefore, it has been the focus of the discussion since discovering. Due to the remote epoch, the rarity of the specimen quantity, and the single evidence first discovered, diverse arguments are being expected about the rice from the Yuchanyan site. The unearthed quantity of Yuchanyan ancient rice is very small and the group analysis can not be made, so the character relevant to it still has very great disputes. Due to the single evidence, the dispute will naturally be continuous. The progress of archaeology will constantly change the inherent understandings of the people.

Many experts discussed mostly on the attribute of *Oryza rufipogon* and cultivated rice in the formal and informal occasions, with different opinions. For example, Japanese scholar Zuotengyangyilang carefully observed the rice specimen, and deemed that it was *Oryza rufipogon* early. The different opinions Indicated that Yuchanyan ancient rice possessed the complexity mosaic character of *Oryza rufipogon* and cultivated rice. It was normal to have different opinions and to seek the truth in the atmosphere of the academic discussion. Generally, conventional thought prefers to flatly judge whether it is *Oryza rufipogon* or cultivated rice. It seems that the problem for the origin of the rice agriculture will be clear in the case of the judgment of yes or no. Actually this is not so. In any new research of the origin of species, the simple yes or no is difficult to solve the problem. Because the origin is a gradual evolutionary process, and any mass point during the process can be plausible, the simple yes or no can not reveal the true feature of the origin but will obliterate some important evolution details. Thus, we can not meet the judgment of the simple yes or no, and should grasp various mass points during the process of origin, make the objective and serious analysis, explore the periodical mark, and carry out reasonable interpretation.

The origin of the cultivated rice is actually the process by which *Oryza rufipogon* gradually evolved into cultivated rice under the intervention of human behavior, as well as the domestication process of cultivated rice as has been said generally. The research on the origin of cultivated rice is focused on the domestication process. The research on the origin of the cultivated rice not only researches the social value of the mass point with very specific characteristic of the cultivated rice, but also contains all mass points and links, i.e., evolutionary chain during the domestication process of the cultivated rice. Through the connection of the evolution chain, it discusses the evolution process, evolution phase, and evolution rate of the biological character of the cultivated rice, and the relevancy with the human behavior. In the research significance on the origin of the cultivated rice, Yuchanyan ancient rice provides us with the information of the evolution chain during the domestication process of the cultivated rice at the earliest.

From the biosystematics, Yuchanyan ancient rice can not yet be determined as the category of the cultivated rice at present, and it may be the attribute of *Oryza rufipogon* more. Mr. Zhang Wenxu named it as "Yuchanyan ancient cultivated rice". What counts I considered is to affirm the intervention of human behavior, without symbolizing that the Yuchanyan ancestors have successfully domesticated the cultivated rice and have become the inventor of the cultivated rice. The completion of the domestication of the cultivated rice is a social behavior, which can not be achieved by the behaviors of the individual and local place. Yuchanyan ancestors just made the brave attempt in the entire behavior during the domestication process of the cultivated rice, manifesting the first step that the humans stepped during the domestication process of the cultivated rice. Their behaviors were only the bud of the domestication of the cultivated rice. Taking this step also symbolized that Dao County Basin as the location of Yuchanyan site might be an organic component of the origin region of the cultivated rice.

Dao County Basin is located at north foot of Nanling Mountain, and the upper and middle reaches of Xiao River basin as the secondary tributary of Yangtze River. Xiao River is the largest tributary of Xiang River. In history, the name of Xiaoxiang has mostly stood for Hunan, thus it can be seen the status of Xiao River in Hunan. It was not accidental that Yuchanyan ancestors could firstly attempt to plant *Oryza rufipogon* in Dao County Basin and take out the step of domesticating the cultivated rice, which had the exterior objective conditions.

On the one hand, the modern geographical conditions of Yuchanyan site provide the circumstantial evidence for possibly wide distribution of *Oryza rufipogon* in Dao County Basin at that time. The modern *Oryza rufipogon* is mainly distributed within the geographical location range of the northern latitude 18°15′ to 25°00′. The northernmost natural distribution area is in Dongxiang County of Jiangxi Province and Chaling County of Hunan, and the geographical location is the northern latitude 28°14′. Yuchanyan site is located at the northern latitude 25°30′, which is the geographical range of the natural distribution for *Oryza rufipogon*. Although *Oryza rufipogon* has not been discovered near to Yuchanyan site at present, the distribution of the modern *Oryza rufipogon* has been discovered in the adjacent Taochuan Basin of Jiangyong County, with the distance of only about 40km between both. It Indicates that the distribution of the *Oryza rufipogon* can fully be around Yuchanyan site at that time. Within the geographical range of the natural distribution for the modern *Oryza rufipogon*, the distribution of *Oryza rufipogon* has not been seen in most regions. The main reason may be the development of the humans, resulting in the distribution of *Oryza rufipogon* gradually drawing back to the remote location with small area. Nevertheless, Yuchanyan site belongs to the edge zone, rather than distributing in the heartland of the geographical location for the main distribution of the modern *Oryza rufipogon*. The distribution characteristic is identical to "edge theory of rice origin" proposed by Mr. Yan Wenming in the research on the origin of the rice agriculture of China.

On the other hand, the unearthed animals and plants of Yuchanyan site also fully displayed the survival environment of *O. rufipogon* around the site. *O. rufipogon* grows at the low-lying, wet and sunny zone, and the habitual nature is applicable to the mild and wet tropical and sub-tropical climate. During the growth period, it demands the rainfall season at high temperature. The annual average temperature of the distribution area is generally 19–23 °C. Among all kinds of unearthed animals in Yuchanyan site, there are 35 mammals, including 16 tropical and sub-tropical animals such as macaque, zibet, rasse, Malayan Tapir, and deer, covering 48%, and other 18 animals belong to the species of the extensive climatic adaptation, covering 51%. Among 27 birds, there are 17 migrant birds migrating from the temperate zone to the tropical and sub-tropical zone for wintering. Marabou stork and parrot are the typical tropical and sub-tropical species. Nettapus coromandelianus and bambusicola thoracica is mainly distributed in South China area, and others belong to the species of the extensive climatic adaptation. In the site, a large number of microbody fresh water snails are discovered, and are the common species in the fresh water lake and even riverside and pond under the mild and wet environment in the south of Yangtze River Basin at present. All categories of the animals do not have the cold climate species. Therefore, at the macro level, the climate adaptation characteristic of the fossil fauna in Yuchanyan site fully reflects Yuchanyan site in the tropical and sub-tropical climatic environment. From the micro perspective, there is the wetland environment for breeding of Oryza rufipogon near Yuchanyan site. For the unearthed animals and plants of Yuchanyan site, one part is the aquatic environment, such as fish, snail, mussel, and terrapin etc. The other part is the hydrocole environment, for example, 18 birds are closed related to the waterborne environment, covering about 67% of the bird fossil species in Yuchanyan site. The otter of the mammal is also the hydrocole environment. The survival of these animals is sufficient to describe that the wide lake is near Yuchanyan site at that time. Especially, six birds of ciconiiformes possess the characteristics of long legs and long beaks, mostly live at the marsh land, and often walk in the shallow water or the open ground for foraging and pecking small animals such as fish and shrimp. Various kinds of terrapins of different sizes are good at acting in the shallow mud, Indicating that the wider shallow mud environment is around the lake. The lake and mud environment around Yuchanyan site provides the survival conditions for the survival of Oryza rufipogon at that time.

By the above analysis, we can confirm that the Oryza rufipogon was distributed around Yuchanyan site at that time, and it possessed the objective conditions for Yuchanyan ancestors to develop the collection of Oryza rufipogon and the plantation of Oryza rufipogon.

The fundamental motive power for the collection and plantation of Oryza rufipogon by Yuchanyan ancestors should focus on the demand of the human society. After the Last Glacial Maximum (the year of 23,000–16,000), the global temperature rose again, the ecology was thriving, and the human development was unprecedented. With the increasing population, the food resources were relatively poor, and the "population pressure" was generated in the Late Paleolithic Period. The radical increase of the population density in some region certainly resulted in the motility hunting-gathering economy in local area that could not solve the relatively poor food resources. Some crowds selected the settlement or semi-settlement living style, to expand the new food resources within the limited geographic region as well as strengthen the use ratio of the existing means of livelihood. It was just the reinforcement economic strategy occurred in the Late Paleolithic Period as generally estimated. At present we can not specifically analyze the problem of "population pressure" that Yuchanyan ancestors have been confronted with, yet to be explained by more information in the future. However, in the face of the crisis of the relatively poor food resources, it is an irresistible trend for Yuchanyan ancestors to adopt the reinforcement economic strategy of expanding new food resources. Expanding Oryza rufipogon as the new food resources became very successful and effective coping strategy of Yuchanyan ancestors.

With the motivation of the survival stress, Yuchanyan ancestors utilized the objective conditions for the natural distribution of Oryza rufipogon around Yuchanyan site, and developed the collecting economic mode of Oryza rufipogon. The rice remains discovered in Yuchanyan site firstly told us that Dao County Basin in the Late Paleolithic Period had the collecting economy of Oryza rufipogon (**Fig. 3**). After expanding the collecting economy of Oryza rufipogon and further evolving to the plantation and cultivation of Oryza rufipogon, Yuchanyan ancestors took the initial step for the domestication of the cultivated rice. Mr. Yan Wenming made good explanations for this. He deemed that the differences between winter and summer in the middle reach of the Yangtze River were remarkable. It is cold in winter, and the vegetable food is very rare. Hunting animals is difficult to ensure the gains, and it is necessary to seek a solution of the food supply in winter. Although Oryza rufipogon was few there and the collection and processing were troublesome, people had to care nothing for gathering due to the advantage of storable character. Moreover, due to easily breeding of Oryza rufipogon, people would protect and cultivate with special care. The rice agriculture in the bud in the place of Yuchanyan and Fairy Cave should emerge in this wise. The ambient environment of Yuchanyan site could provide the relatively abundant food resources, but the food resources of every season were unbalanced. In summer and autumn, the resources may be the most abundant, and may be available in addition to meeting the consumption. In winter and early spring, the resources were

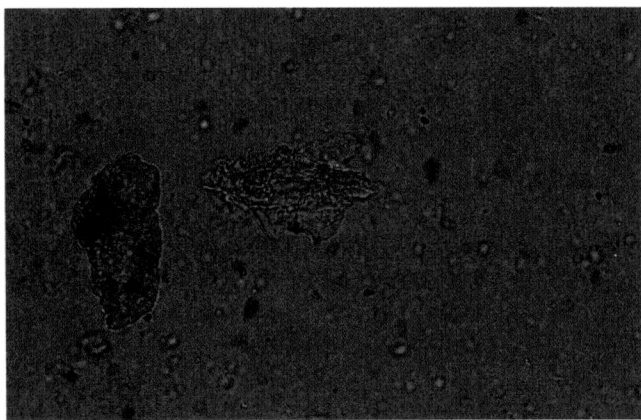
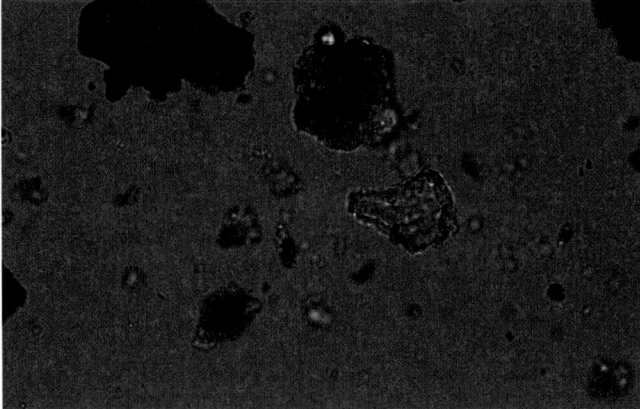

Fig. 3 Rice bimodal mastoid silica bodies (left) and Rice fan-shaped silica bodies (right)
Rice remains unearthed Yuchanyan site

relatively deficient. In order to adjust the relatively poor seasonality of the food resources, it is necessary to store the surplus portions in summer and autumn, as the supplement of the insufficient resources in winter. The storage object and storage mode became a strategy of reinforcement economy by the settlement and semi-settlement crowds in the Late Paleolithic Period. During the process of gathering and eating *Oryza rufipogon*, Yuchanyan ancestors realized the advantage of the storable character of *Oryza rufipogon* after drying, and selected *Oryza rufipogon* as the strategic resource for adjusting the relatively poor seasonal resources. When Yuchanyan ancestors selected to store *Oryza rufipogon* to help coping with the food shortage crisis of winter, it is necessary to pay attention to the protection and care of *Oryza rufipogon*. With the increasing demands for *Oryza rufipogon*, the behavior of expanding the range of *Oryza rufipogon*, planting and selecting *Oryza rufipogon* artificial would naturally occur among Yuchanyan ancestors. On the other hand, Yuchanyan site was located at the northern latitude 25°30´, and was the northern edge zone for the distribution of *Oryza rufipogon*. The distribution of the natural state of *Oryza rufipogon* was limited after all, and was not as extensive as the core distribution area of *Oryza rufipogon* to the south of the northern latitude 25°. The output could not meet the needs of the local crowd, so it urged Yuchanyan ancestors to expand the range of *Oryza rufipogon*, and carry out the artificial planting of *Oryza rufipogon* consciously. The unearthed rice of Yuchanyan with the comprehensive characteristics of *Oryza rufipogon*, *Indica* and *Japonica* was the witness of cultivating *Oryza rufipogon* by Yuchanyan ancestors. The distinguishing feature of "large graininess" of Yuchanyan ancient rice was the reflection for the initial artificial selection of cultivating *Oryza rufipogon* by Yuchanyan ancestors.

Yuchanyan ancient rice is the most primitive ancient rice type evolving from *Oryza rufipogon* to the cultivated rice. It can not be affirmed as the cultivated rice type, but it shows the bud state of the human behavior of domesticating the cultivated rice. The researcher Gu Haibin firstly used the rice embryo morphological research to identify the cultivated rice. Through morphological observation for eight copies of *Oryza rufipogon* of Chaling County and Jiangyong County of Hunan Province and Dongxiang County of Jiangxi Province and 32 copies of the cultivated rice embryo in the ancient local variety from Hunan and Guangdong, she set up the reference standard of the cultivated rice embryo length of 1.58–2.48mm and embryo width of 0.79–1.61mm, and *Oryza rufipogon* embryo length of 1.32–1.98mm and embryo width of 0.82–1.02mm. Select the research results of 60.00%, 70.00%, 78.00% and 87.10% successively as the similarity rate of the charring rice embryo and modern cultivated rice embryo in Bashidang site, Dingjiagang site, Chengtoushan site, and Jijiaocheng site (the age of about 8,000, 7,000, 6,000, and 5,000 years before present successively) at the prehistoric era of Hunan Liyang Plain, and calculate the domestication rate of the cultivated rice as about 8%-10% per millennium. The time for the humans to domesticating the rice was roughly prior to 14,000 years before present. Yuchanyan ancestors took the first step of the rice domestication during about 16,000–14,000 years, which were identical to the research.

The origin and development process of the cultivated rice would be more complex than you think. It is zigzag and repeated, rather than the simple mode of "center – spreading – diffusing" as well as linear origin – development. The final completion of the cultivated rice domestication may possess more extensive sociality, and the territorial range may be more extensive. The initial artificial selection domestication of *Oryza rufipogon* may occur in multiple places with different selected directions, such as success or failure, elimination or inheritance, exchange or reserve. Dongting Lake Plain in middle reaches of Yangtze River is the possible center for finishing the cultivated rice domestication. The current archaeology achievement Indicates that Dongting Lake Plain possessed the relatively developed rice agricultural scale during the period of

Pengtoushan Culture before about 8,000 years. Over ten thousands of unearthed rice grains in Bashidang site of Lixian County would be excellent description. The character of the ancient rice in Bashidang was obviously different from the ancient cultivated rice of Yuchanyan, showed up the additional selected direction, and implied that Dongting Lake Plain had earlier generated source of cultivating the rice.

3. Origin of cultivated rice in China

The origin and development of the agriculture is the worldwide archaeology strategic task. The origin and development of the rice agriculture is one of the focuses of attention in China and even the world for a long time. At present, most scholars can confirm that the middle and lower reaches of Yangtze River of China is the cradle of the rice agriculture of East Asia. The Ganges River of India in South Asia may be the other cradle of the rice cultivation of Asia. It is also the central area for the high development of the prehistoric rice agriculture. Certainly, more extensive and specific relevant details are still discussed and need the in-depth exploration.

The origin of the rice agriculture and the origin of the cultivated rice are two related yet distinguishing concepts. The origin of the rice agriculture is to discuss the human social behavior and economic mode. The origin of the cultivated rice is the evolution process of discussing the biological behavior of the rice. The former is mainly the discussion task of the archaeologist. The latter is mainly the discussion task of the agronomist and paleobotanist. But both are closely connected and interdependent. Without the origin of the cultivated rice, it is far from the origin of the rice agriculture. The origin of the cultivated rice is to research the domestication process of the rice. The domestication of the rice is not purely the natural process of the biology, including the human behavior. The human behavior during the domestication process of the rice is also the social behavior during the process of the origin of the rice agriculture. The unhulled rice and the rice in the prehistoric archaeology site are the most important cultural relics of the primitive rice agriculture, and is the physical evidence of researching the domestication process of the rice. Since the 1930s, the understanding on the origin time and place of the cultivated rice of China had gone through the long course.

Asia is the main production place of the rice in the world, as well as the cradle of the rice agriculture. Before 1930s, Vavilov from the Former Soviet Union put forward the theory of diversity center – variation center origin. From the perspective of the plant taxonomy and genetic evolution, he deemed that the region of centrally distributing a large number of dominant genes of the species might be its center of origin, and advocated that the cultivated rice of Asia was originated from India and the rice of China was introduced from India. Professor Ding Ying as the famous agronomist of China regarded the wide distribution of *Oryza rufipogon* in South China as the basis, and proposed the opinion of "the rice origin of China is related to the ancient South China Sea, i.e. South China today" in 1949. He proposed again that the cultivated rice of our country was originated from South China in the paper of *Origin and Evolution of Cultivated Rice of China* in 1957. In the seventies, Japanese Dubuzhongshi divided the origin place of the cultivated rice of Asia in the semilune zone of Assam of India – Yunnan of China in Road of Rice, and the age for the rice remains discovered by the India archaeology at that time had not exceeded 5,000 years. The proposition of Dubuzhongshi has become the mainstream opinion for a long tme, and influenced the understandings of the academic circle. However, the age for the prehistoric rice remains in Yunnan and Guizhou regions and South China revealed by the archaeological excavation so far is very late, and forms the contradiction difficult to reconcile with the theory of origin. The national *Oryza rufipogon* general survey shows that the modern *Oryza rufipogon* of Yunnan is only distributed in the individual location of the south, rather than the independent distribution area, and is closely related with the distribution area of *Oryza rufipogon* in Indo-China Peninsula. Therefore, the origin argument of the cultivated rice in Yunnan always has larger difficulties.

From 1973 to 1979, Hemudu site of Yuyao, Zhejiang had successively carried out two archaeological excavations. The primitive tribe site prior to 7,000 years before present unearthed many spade-shaped tools for the rice and agricultural production at the earliest in the world, and caused a sensation at home and abroad. People quickly attracted the research focus of the rice agriculture origin to the lower reaches of Yangtze River. The academic circle generally considered that the lower reaches of Yangtze River are the center for the origin of the rice.

In November 1988, Pengtoushan site of Lixian County of Hunan was formally excavated. Among the unearthed pottery shards of site, the rice traces were discovered generally, judging that the rice husks were consciously mixed into the pottery clay as the admixtures. Later, upon ^{14}C age determination, the site was 9,000-7,800 years before present. The rice remains of Pengtoushan site moved up the age of the cultivated rice for more than 1,000 years, and the research on the origin of the rice in the middle reaches of Yangtze River immediately became the focus of attention from the scholars all over the world. In 1995, Bashidang site of Lixian County unearthed over ten thousands of charring rice of Pengtoushan culture, and further enhanced the status of the research on the origin of the rice in the middle reaches of Yangtze River. The academic circle amended the understandings in the past, and regarded the vast areas in the middle and lower reaches of Yangtze River as the center of the origin of the rice.

Meanwhile, Jiahu site of Wuyang of Henan also unearthed the rice before 9,000–7,800 years. The cultural character of Jiahu site belonged to Peiligang culture of the Central China, where the archaeological excavation had been made since 1983 for years. The rice traces were also observed on the unearthed burnt soil of the site. In 1993, analyze the rice silicon plastid and screen the charring rice from the soil sample analysis of the cultural layer successively. The researcher of Jiahu site put forward the viewpoint on the rice origin center of the Huaihe River basin, and expanded the region of the rice origin from the middle and lower reaches of Yangtze River to the Huaihe River basin.

In 2001, Jiang Leping hosted to excavate Shangshan site of Pujiang County of Zhejiang Province, and discovered that the surface of the charring pottery shard in Shangshan site had the husk trace generally, and the embryo soil was mingled with a large number of husks. Upon sampling analysis display, many pottery shards contained the fan-shaped silicate body from the rice leaf. The observed result for the length and shape of the husk in the pottery shard was that the grain was shorter than *Oryza rufipogon* and the grain width is larger than *Oryza rufipogon*. Different from *Oryza rufipogon*, it was the early cultivated rice upon the selection of the humans. ^{14}C determination of Shangshan site was within the scope of 8,000–10,000 years before present. It was generally simultaneous with or earlier than Pengtoushan site of Hunan and Jiahu site of Henan.

So far, the affirmative earliest cultivated rice of China had occurred before 9,000 years, and the distribution range was mainly in the lower reaches of Yangtze River and expanded to the upper reaches of Huaihe River to the north. According to the current archaeological discovery, the rice remains in about 8,000 years of China had been distributed in Hanzhong of Shaanxi, Shandong Yuezhuang site in the lower reaches of the Yellow River, Xijiang River site, and Northern Suzhou Shunshanji site of Huaibei. Thus, the distribution of the rice remains in the Early Neolithic period of China showed that the rice agriculture of China before 8,000 years had possessed the considerable scale. The cultivated rice of the site during this period was the evidence of the early rice agricultural development of China. They were not the source of the cultivated rice. But they provide the clue of the origin of the cultivate rice, and told the people that the origin of the cultivated rice needed seeking towards ten thousand years and even longer time and space.

Through discovery of Hemudu site, Pengtoushan site, Jiahu site and Shangshan site, people put forward the hypothesis of the lower reaches of Yangtze River, the middle reaches of Yangtze River, the middle and lower reaches of Yangtze River, and Huaihe River basin successively. The experts discussed various defined conditions of how to judge the cradle of the cultivated rice.

The primary issue for the research on the origin of the rice agriculture is the origin of the cultivated rice, i.e. the origin of the rice domestication. As for how to judge the cradle of the cultivated rice, the academic circle generally considered two indispensable conditions, involving the natural distribution area of *Oryza rufipogon* and the archaeological discovery of the ancient rice. It was two foremost conditions for researching the origin of the cultivated rice. The archaeological discovery of the most ancient rice could intuitively help the people judge the earliest time and place of the cultivated rice, which was the essential evidence for researching the origin of the cultivated rice. The archaeological discovery of the ancient rice was the fixed index for exploring the origin of the rice agriculture. People could not verify the place without discovering the ancient rice as the origin of the cultivated rice. Obviously, during the process of archaeology, seeking the most ancient crops was the inevitable pursuit and responsibility of the archaeologist while discussing the origin of the agriculture. The evidence of the archaeological discovery was not enough to affirm the cradle. Only the primitive discovery place for the ancient rice as the natural distribution area of *Oryza rufipogon* could be the cradle of the cultivated rice. In the case of the place without the natural distribution of *Oryza rufipogon*, it would not mention the initial domestication of *Oryza rufipogon* to the cultivated rice, and even the cradle of the cultivated rice. The cultivated rice appearing in the place without the natural distribution of *Oryza rufipogon* was obviously the result of spreading of the cultivated rice, because the cultivated rice could not appear at the earliest in the place without the existence of the domestication process of the cultivated rice. But it should be noted that, with the expansion of the cultivated rice, *Oryza rufipogon* would also be expanded to the north and mixed with the cultivated rice under the intervention of the humans. Therefore, the natural distribution of *Oryza rufipogon* was the prerequisite for the origin of the cultivated rice.

China possesses the abundant resources of *Oryza rufipogon*, and the abundant genetic diversity draws the worldwide attentions. The natural distribution areas of the modern *Oryza rufipogon* of China are in the south of the Yangtze River. From 1978 to 1982, our country made a nationwide *Oryza rufipogon* general survey. The general survey showed that China had three kinds of *Oryza rufipogon*, involving *Oryza granulate*, *O. officinalis* and *O. rufipogon*, which were widely distributed in Guangdong, Guangxi, Hainan, Yunnan, Jiangxi, Hunan, Fujian and Taiwan. Among three kinds of

Oryza rufipogon, *O. rufipogon* was the affinis ancestor of the cultivated rice. *O. rufipogon* was mainly distributed within the geographical location range of the northern latitude of 18°15′ to 25°00′. The northernmost natural distribution area was in Dongxiang County of Jiangxi Province and Chaling County of Hunan, and the geographical location was the northern latitude 28°14′. Mr. You Xiuling moved the north bound of the ancient perennial *Oryza rufipogon* to N30° to the north through the *Oryza rufipogon* record analysis during the historical period in the ancient literature of China. The opinion was identical to the climatic change during the warm period. According to Guode Bingxin Record with the most sensitive temperature variation, the climate had been mild during the period of 8,500–8,000 years before present, and the climatic zone could be moved for three latitudes to the north compared with that now. The *Oryza rufipogon* record during the historical period in the north of the Yangtze River in the literature was generally the wild cultivated rice, with a large extent of the uncertainty. *O. rufipogon* grew at the low-lying, wet and sunny zone, and the habitual nature was applicable to the mild and wet tropical and sub-tropical climate. During the growth period, it demanded the rainfall season at high temperature. The annual average temperature of the distribution area was generally 19-23 °C, as the region with the highest temperature in China. Thus, it was supposed that the middle and lower reaches of Yangtze River during the temperature rise process of the late post glacial period as the cradle of the cultivated rice should also be in the area to the south of N30° before 8,000 or 9,000 years.

4. Formation and development of primitive rice agriculture of China

Recently, Mr. Zhao Zhijun summarized the forming process of the rice agriculture of China as breeding phase – early phase – later phase, and accordingly established the rice agricultural production system. At the breeding phase, the economic mode was the gathering-hunting economy, and the plantation behavior of the rice occurred, or it could be called as "quasi-agriculture yet non-agriculture" phase. At present, the discovery of Shangshan site, Fairy Cave site, Diaotonghuan site, and Yuchanyan site belonged to the phase, and their age had been more than 10,000 years before present. The social economic characteristics at the early phase were manifested as focusing on the gathering-hunting (or gathering-fishing and hunting), supplemented by the farming production. Jiahu site, Pengtoushan site, Bashidang site, Kuahuqiao site, and Xiaohuangshan site were the representative of this phase. The later phase was still in the transition period of converting from the gathering-hunting to the agricultural economy. The agricultural economy was gradually prosperous, and the gathering-hunting economy gradually declined in the human economic life. Hemudu culture was the typical example of the later phase. When the rice agriculture displaced the gathering-hunting economy, it became the economic agent of the human society, marking the true establishment of the rice agricultural phase of China. He held that the rice agriculture had displaced the gathering-hunting to become the economic agent in the lower reaches of the Yangtze River during the Liangzhu culture of about 5,000 years before present, and the rice agricultural production system was established in the middle reaches of the Yangtze River during Daxi culture period of about 6,000 years before present or earlier. Chengtoushan site was a good example. The above phase division for the forming process of the rice agriculture of China basically reflected the general outline for the forming process of the rice agriculture of China from the later Pleistocene to 5,000 years before present. The division by Zhao Zhijun was established in occupying position of the rice agricultural economy in the social economy as the judgment standard. During the prehistoric period, the economic sector expressed by various archaeological sites was unbalanced, and the practical situation might be more complex. In the case of the joint analysis of the factor for the domestication degree of the rice, it might be more beneficial to the judgment of the relative phase division during the forming process of the rice agriculture of China. Mr. Gu Haibin selected the research results of 60.00%, 70.00%, 78.00% and 87.10% successively as the similarity rate of the charring rice embryo and modern cultivated rice embryo in Bashidang site, Dingjiagang site, Chengtoushan site, and Jijiaocheng site (the age of about 8,000, 7,000, 6,000, and 5,000 years before present successively) at the prehistoric era of Hunan Liyang Plain, and calculated the domestication rate of the cultivated rice as about 8%–10% per millennium. The time for the humans to domesticating the rice was roughly prior to 14,000 years before present. Meanwhile, we could infer that the cultivated rice with the rice domestication achieved the modern significance might be prior to 4,000 years before present. The judgment was close to the opinion of some agronomists that the rice might be fully domesticated after 5,000 years before present through the research on the ancient rice specimen. At this time, it could indeed meet the standard of the ancient traditional rice agriculture.

The breeding phase during the forming process of the rice agriculture of China was actually the slowly starting phase of the rice agriculture bud, as well as the phase of "cultivated rice" bud of stepping on the domestication. Currently, very few and scattered materials at this phase have been discovered, and now the specific details for the bud domestication process can not be known. But people believed that it was a long and repeating process, and the duration could be as long as 5,000 years. At the breeding phase, the humans had the rice agricultural behaviors involving planting, harvest and storage, with very small development scale. It basically planted *Oryza rufipogon* and the domesticating *Oryza rufipogon*, so it did not form the scale agriculture, and was not the rice agricultural society in the true sense.

For the analysis of the archaeological discovery and research status of China at present, the early phase for the forming process of the rice agriculture of China should step into the primitive rice agricultural society, and generally it should be the primitive rice agricultural society evolving towards the ancient traditional rice agricultural society from 9,000 years to 4,000 years before present. Certainly, there is now larger divergence in such cognition yet to be discussed deeply. At present, for the rice appeared in China prior to 7,000 – 9,000 years before present, the academic circle now is still entangled with the identification conclusion of the cultivated rice or *Oryza rufipogon*. The identification between the modern cultivated rice or *Oryza rufipogon* is not very difficult, while the identification between the prehistoric cultivated rice or *Oryza rufipogon* is expressed complexly due to being in the process of gradually evolving from *Oryza rufipogon* to the cultivated rice. The agronomist and archaeologist attempt to carry out the identification work by multiple means. For example, the grain size ratio, rice phytolith, husk doublet mastoid, rice surface seta, rachilla, rice embryo, DNA analysis and other methods are used for the identification work of the prehistoric cultivated rice or *Oryza rufipogon*. These researches are very positive and fruitful. However, various conclusions still have the divergences. For the reason, on the one hand, these methods show the reasonable feasibility to a certain degree, as well as the uncertainty to a certain degree. On the other hand, during the process of *Oryza rufipogon* evolving towards the cultivated rice gradually, the evolution progress for various signs and characters of the rice species is not synchronous, with the characteristic of the interlaced inlay, and the relatively complex character variation is formed. Therefore, in the identification of the prehistoric cultivated rice or *Oryza rufipogon*, it did not have a determinative method at present. We should respect for the hard working of the identification experts, and can not have blind faith in the determinative conclusion. The author held that, the rice distribution range of China appeared in 7,000 years to 9,000 years before present had been very extensive, and exceeded the scale of the natural distribution of *Oryza rufipogon*. During the period, the site in Hemudu culture, Kuahuqiao culture and Shangshan culture in the lower reaches of the Yangtze River, and Pengtoushan culture and Zaoshi sublayer culture in the middle reaches of the Yangtze River generally had the rice remains, and became the normal state of the primitive rice core area. Not only so, the rice remains expanded to the north substantially. Han River basin in the north bank of the Yangtze River is expanded to the south slope of Qinling Mountains, such as Lijiacun site in Hanzhong region of Shaanxi. The Central China is expanded to Huaihe River basin, such as Jiahu site of Henan. The east is expanded to the Yellow River and Huaihe River area in the south of the Yellow River, such as Shandong Yuezhuang site, Xijiang River site, and Northern Suzhou Shunshanji site. The distribution pattern of the rice remains appeared before 8,000 years or 9,000 years of China could not only be the result of gathering *Oryza rufipogon*. Regardless of the species judgment of these rice remains as the cultivated rice or *Oryza rufipogon*, it should be the human behavior i.e. the result of cultivation and spreading. During this period, the species of the rice remains are in the early phase of *Oryza rufipogon* gradually evolving towards the cultivated rice, with *Oryza rufipogon* as well as "cultivated rice".

"Cultivated rice" is not the cultivated rice in modern sense, and will certainly have the characteristics queried by the people.

Without the seed selection in the strict sense at that time, *Oryza rufipogon* spread to the Yellow River and Huaihe River area together with "cultivated rice" and mixed with "cultivated rice" during the process of rice remains spreading northwards. The geographical location of Jiahu site of Henan is in the northern latitude 33°37′. The geographical coordinate of Shunshanji site in the north of Jiangsu is the northern latitude 33°34′36.5″. Shandong Yuezhuang site is in the northern latitude 36°28′41″. Xijiang River site is in the northern latitude 36°44′17″. All of these obviously exceed the natural distribution range of *Oryza rufipogon* of China. Thus, *Oryza rufipogon* of the rice remains in Yellow River and Huaihe River basin is not native, and may be the cultivated *Oryza rufipogon*. It should be the result of the human cultural transmission. The primitive state of the rice should be the tropic and subtropic environment. But under the cultivation of the humans, the modern distribution can reach at the north border area of Heilongjiang. Before 8,000 or 9,000 years, it is possible to move the cultivated *Oryza rufipogon* distribution for 5–6 latitudes to the north under the effect of the human behavior.

The distribution pattern of the rice remains of China before 8,000 or 9,000 years had reflected the human behavior for cultivation and spreading of the rice. Not only so, the large-scale rice production and spreading are sufficient to express very powerful economic mode regardless of planting *Oryza rufipogon* or "cultivated rice". Although the occupied position for the rice economic mode specifically in every site during the period had great differences, some may not possess the economic advantages. The author deemed that it had possessed the conditions of the rice agriculture at that time and the distance with the ancient traditional rice agriculture, and it was only the primitive rice agriculture.

From the bud and forming process of the primitive rice agriculture of China, we can see that the initial domestication behavior of the cultivated rice had early occurred and slowly evolved before "Climatic Event of Younger Dryas". Younger Dryas (hereinafter referred to as YD) was the most important cold climatic event occurred during the transition from Glacial period to Holocene Post Glacial period. After completion of the Last Glacial Maximum prior to 15,000 years, the global temperature gradually tended to warm up. But the temperature cooled down sharply prior to 12,700 years before present, and rose again quickly after 1,000 years (i.e. prior to 11,400 years before present), known as "Event of Younger Dryas". The most prominent characteristic for the climatic change of Younger Dryas was the mutability at the beginning and end. The scientist surprisingly discovered that it occurred during the time of about 10 years, while it was end only for three years. In other words, the temperature of Northern Europe quickly cooled down within 10 years, and suddenly returned to normal within three years after continuing for more than 1,000 years. The awful change of the mutable weather might destroy the food resource environment of the survival of the humans, urged to rapidly adopt the contingency strategy on basis of the survival economy in the Late Paleolithic Period, and accelerated the selection of the humans on the agricultural economy. Therefore, "Event of Younger Dryas" might become an opportunity of speeding up the formation and development of the primitive rice agriculture of China.

References

CHEN Baozhang·Wang Xiangkun·ZHANG Juzhong. 1995. The Finds and Morphological Study of Carbonized Rice in the Neolithic Site at Jiahu in Wuyang Conunty, Henan Province. *Chinese Journal of Rice Science* 9(3).

Henan Provincial Institute of Cultural Heritage and Archaeology. 1999. *Jiahu Site*, Science Press.

Hunan Provincial Instiyute of Cultural Relics and Archaeology. 2006. *Peng tou shan yu ba shi dang*, Science Press.

JIANG Leping·ZHENG Jianming·RUI Shungan·ZHENG Yunfei. 2003. Early Neolithic Site Found in Pujian County, Zhejiang, Dating Back Around 10,000 Years. *China Culture Relics Newspaper* November 17.

LUAN Fengshi. 2005. The Origin, Development, and Spread of Prehistoric Rice Farming in the Haidai Region. *Journal of Literature, History & Philosophy* 6

QIN Jiaming·YUAN Daoxian et al., 2004. Younger Dryas Event and Early-Middle Holocene Climate Mutation: Oxygen Isotope records of Maolan stalagmite in Guizhou Province, China. *Chinese Science* 34(1).

WU Shiying et al., 2000. The Occurrence of the Xianren Wood Event and Its Global Significance. *Yellow Sea and Bohai Sea Ocean* 18(1).

Wu Xiaohong·Elisabetta·Boaretto et al., 2012. Radiocarbon Dating Study of Early Pottery and Stratigraphic Accumulation at the Yuchanyan Site in Daoxian, Hunan. *Cultural Relics in Southern China* 3.

YAN Wenming. 1997. New Advances in the Research on the Origin of Rice Farming in China. *Archaeology* 9.

YAN Wenming. 2004. *The Dawn of Yangtze River Civilization*, Hubei Education Press

YUAN Jiarong. 1996. Important New Evidence for the Origin of Rice in Yuchanyan. *China Culture Relics Newspaper* March 3, First Edition.

YUAN Jiarong. 1998. Preliminary Study on Ancient Cultivated Rice from the Yuchanyan Site in Daoxian, Hunan. *The Crop Jouranal* 24(4).

YUAN Jiarong. 2000. Rice and Pottery from 10,000 Years Ago at the Yuchanyan Site in Daoxian, Hunan. *The Origin of Rice Farming, Pottery, and Cities*, Cultural Relics Press.

ZHANG Chi. 2000. Early Pottery and Phytolith Remains of Rice at Wannian, Jiangxi. *The Origin of Rice Cultivation, Pottery, and Urbanization*, Cultural Relics Press.

ZHANG Juzhong. 1998. The Origin and Evolution of Rice Farming in China. *Science Bulletin* 43(22).

ZHAO Zhijun. 2013. The Origin Process of Rice Farming, Bulletin of the Research Center for Ancient Civilizations. *Chinese Academy of Social Sciences* 24.

Chapter 6.
Neolithic Age

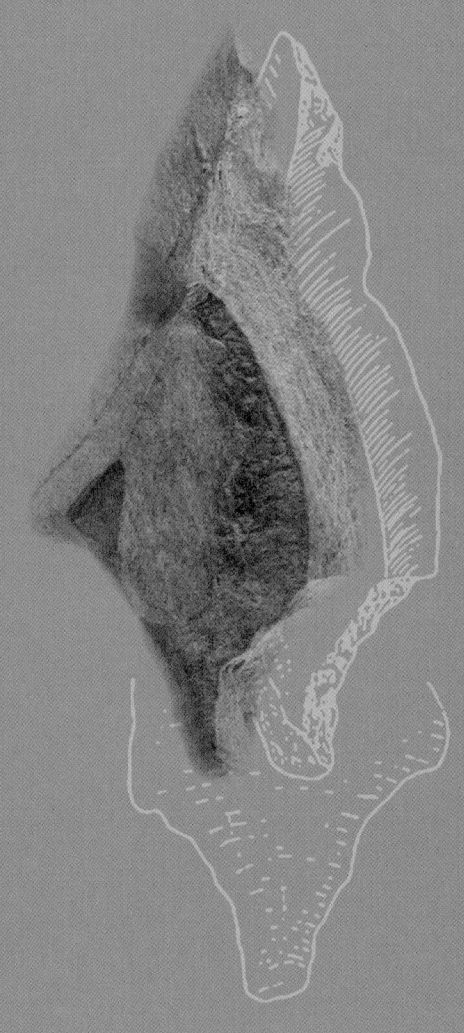

Wilkostowo 23/24: An example of the Neolithic chipped flint inventory from the Polish Lowlands

Lucyna DOMAŃSKA[1], Seweryn RZEPECKI[2]

[1] Professor, Institute of Archaeology, University of Lodz, Poland; lucyna.domanska@uni.lodz.pl
[2] Institute of Archaeology, University of Gdańsk, Poland

ABSTRACT

The aim of this paper is to characterize important changes across the vast expanses of Europe in the 4th millennium BC. Long-range contacts are the main feature of this period. These contacts were testified to by among other things retouched macroblades made of Volhynian flint, which comes from west Ukraine. Particularly impressive results concerning the abovementioned problem were achieved during the investigations of the Wilkostowo 23/24 site from the Polish Lowlands. A multi-farmstead settlement from the period around 3,650-3,400 BC was discovered there. The site of Wilkostowo 23/24, Aleksandrów Kujawski commune, was discovered in 1980, and in the years 1999-2011 it was the target of intensive excavations. As a result, on an area of approx. 1 hectare, the remains of a settlement of the TRB culture from the period around 3,650-3,400 BC were discovered. The remains of 10 houses and hundreds of other farm buildings were identified within it. Tens of thousands of fragments of destroyed vessels and other artifacts were also obtained. In combination with a rich collection of animal bones and obtained radiocarbon dates, the discoveries made in Wilkostowo have been one of the basic sources for learning about the TRB culture in the Polish Lowlands for years. Flint materials from the site form the source basis, which allows us to characterize flint processing in the 4th millennium BC. The result of the comparative analysis of the flint materials from the Wilkostowo 23/24 site and other diagnostic assemblages from the Polish Lowlands was the separation of a flint processing model typical for 4th millennium BC. This model distinguishes: (1) a clear advantage of artifacts made of the local flint, (2) the presence of imported exotic raw materials (among them Volhynian flint played special role), (3) the dominance of splintering technology application, (4) the predominance in terms of the share of retouched blades and flakes, end-scrapers, truncated blades, and retouched macroblades in the group of tools, and (5) the occurrence of projectile points and flint polished axes.

국문초록

이 논문은 유럽의 광활한 지역에서 중요한 변화가 일어난 기원전 4천 년의 문화특징을 규명하고자 한다. 장거리 문화접촉이 이 기간의 주요 특징인데, 이러한 접촉은 무엇보다 서부 우크라이나에서 생산된 Volhynian 플린트로 재가공된 대형 돌날 사례에서 입증되고 있다. 상기 접촉 문제와 관련하여 특히 폴란드 저지대의 Wilkostowo 23/24 유적을 조사하는 가운데 인상적인 결과가 나타났다. 기원전 3,650~3,400년경 다중 농장형 정착지가 발견되었고, 유적 내의 플란트는 기원전 4천 년의 플린트 공정을 특성화할 수 있는 원석으로 활용되었다. Wilkostowo 23/24 유적 현장의 플린트 원석과 폴란드 저지대 여러 지시 유물군을 비교 분석한 결과, 기원전 4천 년의 전형적 플린트 제작 공정 모델이 ① 플린트제 유물의 분명한 장점, ② 외부 유입 원석의 존재(Volhynian 플린트의 특별한 역할), ③ 쪼개기 기술 적용의 우세, ④ 재가공된 돌날, 격지, 밀개, 잘려진 돌날, 재가공된 대형 돌날 점유의 우세, 그리고 ⑤ 발사체 결합 찌르개와 플린트제 마연 도끼 등으로 잘 식별되고 있다.

Keywords : Poland, Late Neolithic, long-range contacts, flint knapping

Fig. 1 Wilkostowo 23/24. Reconstruction of the settlement (according to S. Rzepecki, 2014).

1. Introduction

The aim of the paper is the characteristics of the period of the important changes recognizable across the vast expanses of Europe in the 4th millennium BC. Long-range contacts are the main feature of this period. These contacts were testified among other things by the retouched macro-blades made of Volhynian flint, which comes from the west Ukraine.

Particularly impressive results, concerning above-mentioned problem, were achieved during the investigations of the site Wilkostowo 23/24 from the Polish Lowlands (L. Domańska, 2013, 2016; S. Rzepecki, 2014). A multi-farmstead settlement of so-called the Funnel Beaker culture from the period around 3,650-3,400 BC was discovered there (**Fig. 1**). Flint materials from the site form the source basis which allows to characterize flint processing on the Polish Lowlands during 4th millennium BC.

2. Characteristics of the inventory from the site Wilkostowo 23/24

The analysis of the raw material structure of the inventory is an important element of its characteristics. In the area of the whole Polish Lowlands, erratic Baltic flint is the only locally available flint raw material. Other flints (e.g., chocolate flint) belong to a group of non-local raw materials in relation to the Lowlands. Their outcrops are localized in the south of Poland. The exception is Volhynian flint, outcrops of which occur in the area of west Ukraine.

Local Baltic flint prevails in the inventory from the site Wilkostowo 23/24, 685 pieces of this raw material were identified, which comprises 66.4% of the whole assemblage. Clearly smaller importance than this of local raw material should be ascribed to exotic flints. Volhynian and chocolate flint stand out among them in terms of quantity. Respectively, 89 (8.6%) and 82 (8%) of the artifacts were made of them. Other raw materials occurred in inconsiderable amounts.

About 16% of raw material structure of the inventory from the Wilkostowo 23/24 site belong to tartifacts that are thermally deformed to the extent that an analysis of the raw material composition is impossible. Generally, they were classified as burnt pieces (162 artifacts). It can be suggested that, in vast majority, they are probably burnt pieces of Baltic flint. An acceptance of this diagnosis would additionally increase an occurrence rate of this raw material in the structure of the discussed inventory.

The flint materials discovered at the Wilkostowo 23/24 site include specimens classified within 12 categories of artifacts (**Table 1**). Most of them are technologically connected with two methods: flaking and splintering ones. Only 23 artifacts belong to the blade exploitation.

Products of splintering exploitation form a decidedly dominating group in respect of quantity. Totally, they

Table 1 Wilkostowo 23/24. Quantitative and qualitative structure of the inventory

Artifact category		Quantity	%
Blade cores		2	0.2
Flake cores		4	0.4
Blade-flake cores		1	0.1
Flakes		155	15.0
Blades		21	2.0
Splintered pieces		153	14.8
Splintered flakes		293	28.5
Chunks		158	15.3
	with negative scars	*80*	-
	burnt	*78*	-
Chips		44	4.3
Tools		181	17.6
Axes		2	0.2
Flakes from axes		17	1.6
	common	*13*	-
	splintered	*4*	-
Total		1,031	100

constitute nearly a half of the inventory (43.3%). This group includes splintered flakes - 293 specimens (28.5% of the inventory) and splintered pieces - 153 items (14.8%). Group of splintering exploitation is the most technologically and functionally complex one. Although it contains the artifacts related to the simplest method of flint exploitation, its components carry the most essential information for determining the nature and the direction of the local production.

The main focus of the splintering method application was the working of local Baltic flint. About 80% of all splintered pieces and splintered flakes were made of that type raw material.

The splintering method was commonly used for the scaling of some artifacts. This process encompassed predominantly the macroliths of exotic raw materials. As a result of their scaling, some splintered pieces or splintered flakes were created. The most likely aim of the application of the splintering method was to maximize the use of the imported raw materials.

A distinguished group of flake exploitation includes mainly flakes – 155 items. Four flake cores and, with high probability, one blade – flake core are genetically connected with them. Complete flakes (116 items) were subjected to a detailed analysis. The majority of them are pieces with multidirectional scar patterns in the distal part; with negative butts and distinct bulbs, in the longitudinal section – they are straight or with bend in the distal part.

Unfortunately, the technological origin of the majority of the flakes is most often impossible to determine. Rather, a technological syncretism of the discussed group of artifacts can be indicated here. A large part of the flakes indirectly point to the existence of multiplicity of trends in the flint production within the area of the discussed site, resulting into the occurrence of the flake debitage. This can be evidenced by the flakes having flake scars and blade-flake scars on their distal parts. This type of piece is clearly related to the transformation of blade cores. Another group of flakes is probably related to the process of shaping and repairing axes.

The presence of flake cores in the inventory, including a core made of chocolate flint, also indicates an intentional production of flakes from different raw materials. However, the scale of this process is difficult to estimate.

A group of blade exploitation includes 21 blades and two blade cores, which constitutes merely 2.2% of the whole inventory.

This group includes only blade fragments. Medial parts prevail (9 items), followed by proximal parts (8 items) and distal parts (3 items). In terms of size, this group is fairly well diversified. The thickness of the majority of the blades is placed in an interval 2–5mm, and their width varies between 12–17mm. The tool analysis revealed that some macroblades occurred at the site. Their thickness reached 8mm and their width exceeded 25mm. The length of the blades can be reconstructed only in the case of some well preserved blade tools. The dominant group comprises blades with a length ranging between 30 and 50mm, while

Table 2 Wilkostowo 23/24. Quantitative and qualitative structure of the tool assemblage

Tool category	Quantity	%
End-scrapers	22	12.2
Perforators	3	1.6
Borers	2	1.1
Truncated blades - with single truncation - with double truncation	 9 3	 6.6
Retouched macro-blades with continuous retouch	4	2.2
Trapeze	1	0.6
Projectile points	6	3.3
Blades - retouched - micro-retouched - with use retouch - with polish	 7 10 20 2	 21.5
Odłupki - retouched - micro-retouched - with use retouch	 26 8 18	 28.8
Splintered-based tools - retouched splintered pieces - retouched splintered flakes - splintered flakes with use retouch	 10 17 9	 19.9
Other tools	4	2.2
Total	181	100

the blades with a length of 70–110mm presented a lower proportion.

A fragment of a blade core made of Baltic flint was discovered at the site. More evidence for the presence of blade cores made of this raw material is a piece of blade-flake core and a massive overpassed blade from a single platform core. Except for the mentioned artifacts of Baltic flint, neither cores nor technical forms were connected with the exploitation, preparation, and reparation of blade cores, i.e., crested blades or platform rejuvenation flakes of imported raw materials were registered.

In conclusion, there were no artifacts at the Wilkostowo 23/24 site that might indicate the existence of the local production of blades using exotic raw materials.

A considerable part of the inventory – comparable with the number of flakes – is composed of specimens defined as chunks (15.3%); this category is composed by burnt and faceted chunks. Microdebitage in the form of chips (i.e., flakes of sizes smaller than 5mm) constitutes slightly over 4.3% of the inventory (44 items).

Besides the abovementioned categories in the general structure of the inventory from Wilkostowo 23/24, a tool group was distinguished (**Table 2**). Altogether, 181 tools, which constituted over 17.6% of the whole inventory, were identified.

Due to a degree of retouching, two subgroups of tools were distinguished. The first includes typological (conventional) tools. The other is made up of atypical (utility) tools, i.e., atypically retouched blades, flakes, and artifacts of the splintering group (Conolly, 1996, 1999; Andrefsky, 2001). This group may also include specimens with traces of use in the form of so-called use retouch and polish (Wąs, 2023).

Typological (conventional) tools in the inventory from the Wilkostowo 23/24 site were classified within eight types. Altogether, 50 conventional specimens were distinguished, among which two types prevail with respect to quantity: end-scrapers (22 items – **Fig. 2**) as well as single and doubled truncated blades (altogether 12 items). Secondly, projectile points (6 items – **Fig. 3**), perforators and borers (together 5 items), retouched macroblades with continuous retouching on both edges (4 items) and a trapeze should be listed.

Atypical tools dominate in the materials under analysis (127 items – about 70% of all tools). This group was divided into three subsets, as a criterion of the division half-raw material was used. Therefore, blade, flake and splintered-based atypical tools were distinguished.

Atypical blade tools (39 specimens – **Fig. 4**) were divided into retouched blades (7 items), micro-retouched blades (10 items), blades with use retouch (20 items) and blades with polish (2 items).

Atypical flake tools dominate among utility tools – 52 specimens were discovered. Their further division is based

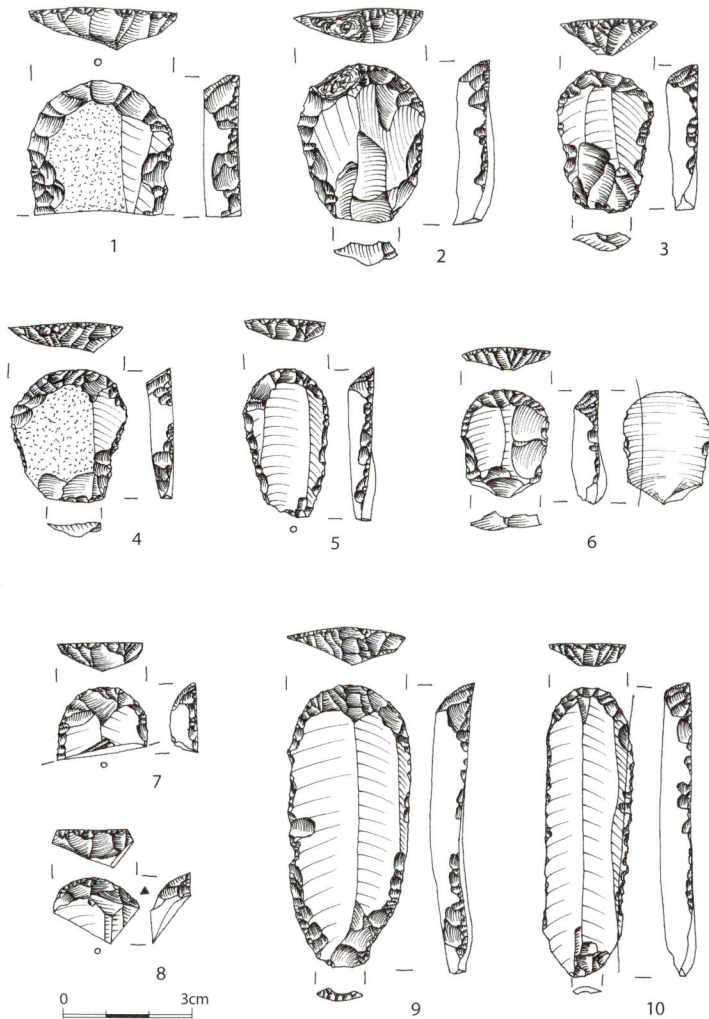

Fig. 2 Wilkostowo 23/24. End-scrapers (1-10). Volhynian flint (1-10).

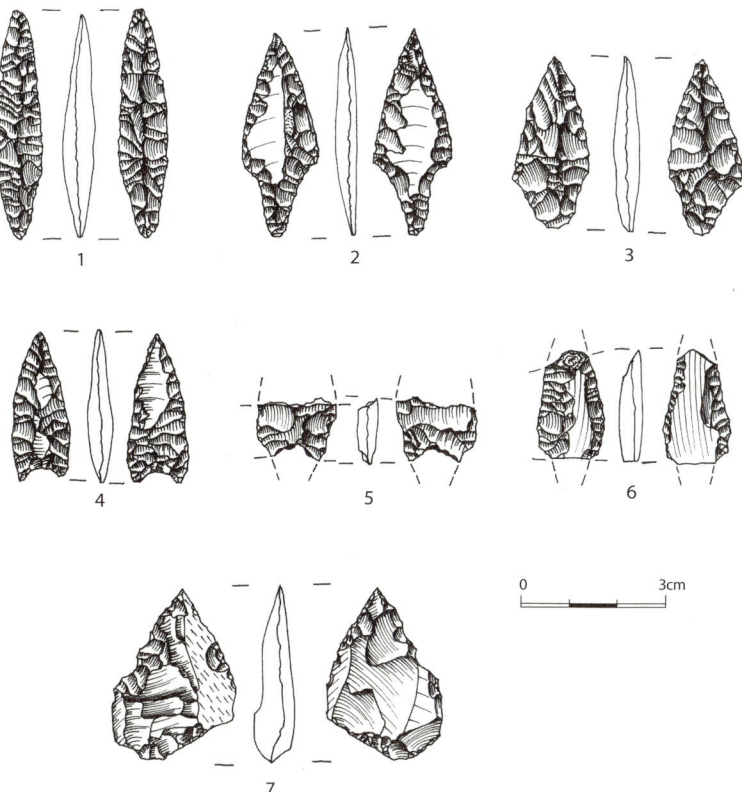

Fig. 3 Wilkostowo 23/24. Projectile points (1-7). Volhynian flint (1, 2, 6), Baltic flint (3-5, 7).

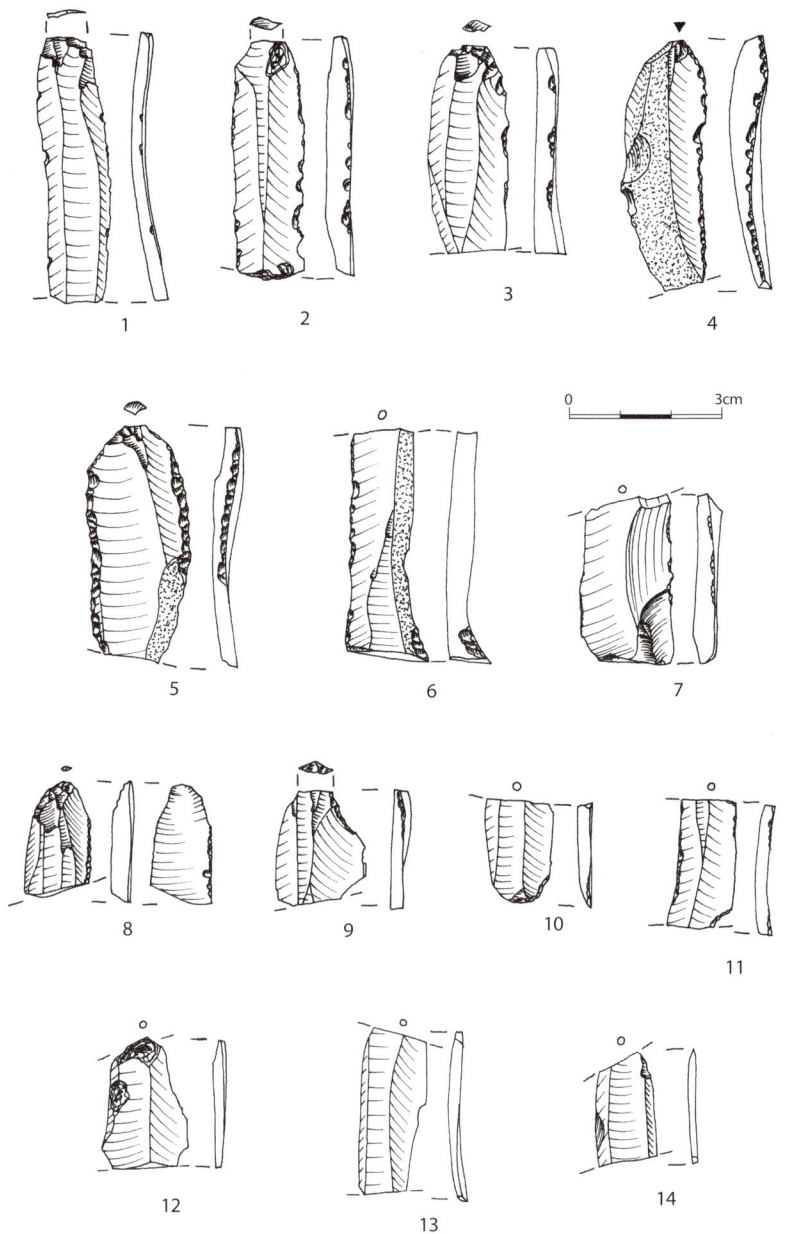

Fig. 4 Wilkostowo 23/24. Retouched blades (4-5), micro-retouched blades (8-11), blades with use retouch (1-3, 6-7), blade fragments (12-14), Chocolate flint (1-14).

on the same criteria used in case of blade tools. Among them most numerous are retouched flakes – 26 such artifacts were discovered. Another place is taken by flakes with use retouch – 18 specimens and micro-retouch – eight pieces.

Atypical splintered-based tools (**Fig. 5**) include retouched splintered pieces – 10 specimens, retouched splintered flakes – 17 specimens and splintered flakes with use retouch – nine flakes. Axes (2 artifacts) and flakes from such forms (17 items) were distinguished as a separate group.

3. Retouched macroblades of Volhynian flint

Four retouched macroblades with continuous retouching on both edges were distinguished in the inventory from the Wilkostowo 23/24 site (**Fig. 6**). One of them has both the proximal and distal edges broken off, due to which its precise classification is not possible. The remaining three specimens were included as so-called convergent retouched macro-blades. Two of them possess spiky distal ends whose shape resembles the tips of perforators. The discussed specimens were made mainly with the use of steep retouch, only one has flat retouch on one side. All of the specimens have polish on their longer sides. A micro-wear analyses (Winiarska-Kabacińska, 2014) showed that these tools were used to cut crops or, generally, for harvesting plants; in one case, the traces of use pointed to the probability of cane cutting.

The thickness of the convergent retouched macroblades

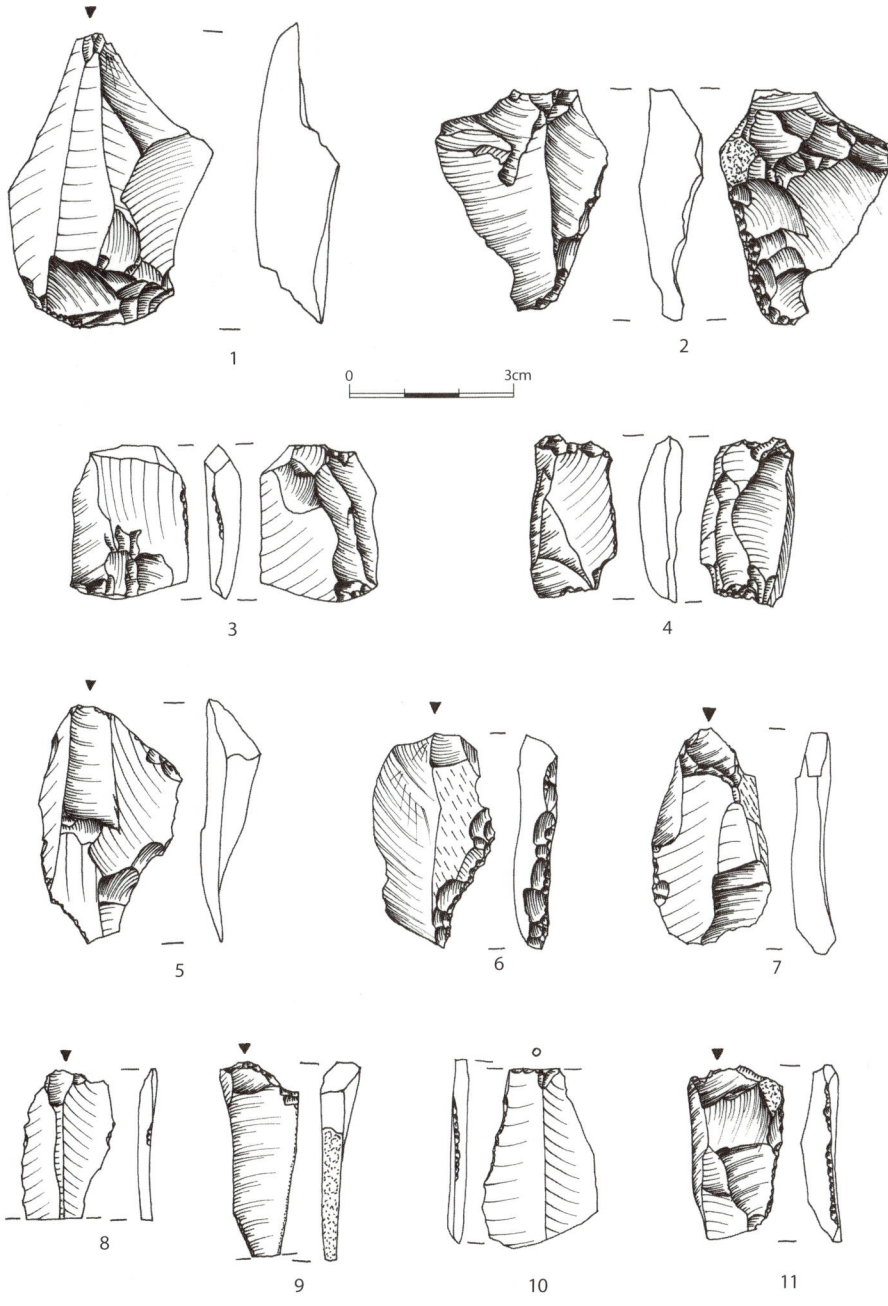

Fig. 5 Wilkostowo 23/24. Splintered flake (1), retouched splintered pieces (2-4), splintered flakes with use retouch (5, 7), retouched splintered flake (6), blade with traces of scaling (8), micro-retouched splintered flakes (9-11). Chocolate flint (1-6, 8-11), Świeciechów flint (7).

from the Wilkostowo 23/24 site is placed in an interval 5–6mm, their width ranges from 24 to 29mm, the length of the specimen with a small fragment broken off is 86mm.

4. Late Neolithic flint production model

The results of the comparative analysis of the flint materials from the Wilkostowo 23/24 site and other diagnostic assemblages from the Polish Lowlands was the separation of a flint production model typical for the 4th millennium BC (Domańska, 2013, 2016, 2022). This model distinguishes the following: (1) a clear advantage of artifacts made of local Baltic flint, (2) the selective presence of imported exotic raw materials (among them Volhynian flint played special role), (3) the dominance of splintering technology application, (4) the predominance in terms of the share of atypical tools over conventional tools, (5) the permanent presence of end-scrapers, truncated blades, and retouched macroblades in the group of typological tools, and (6) the occurrence of projectile points and flint polished axes.

A special position among the mentioned diagnostic features of the Late Neolithic flint production is occupied by tools

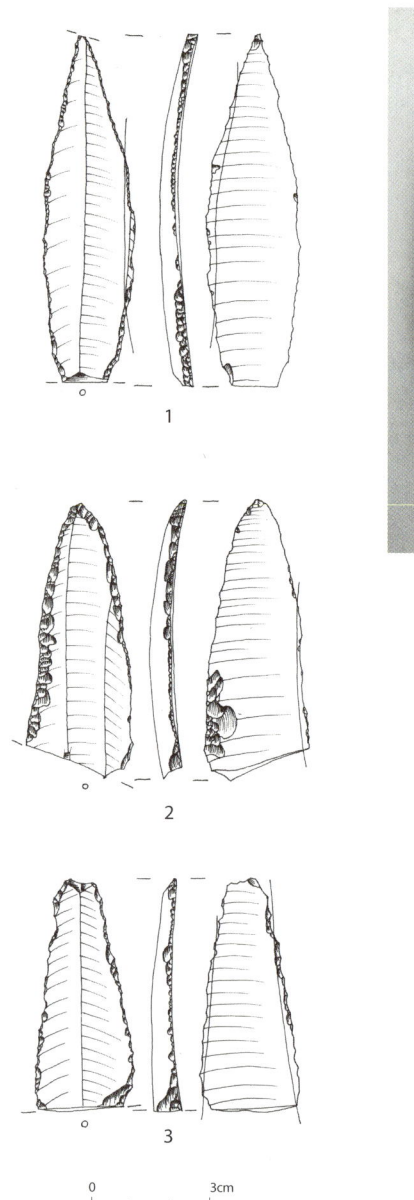

Fig. 7 Wilkostowo 23/24. Tools made of Volhynian flint.

Fig. 6 Wilkostowo 23/24. Retouched macro-blades with continuous retouch on both edges (1-3). Volhynian flint (1-3).

made of Volhynian (**Fig. 7**) and chocolate flints. These indicate the intensification of contacts between Lowlands societies and societies to the south in the 4th millennium BC.

References

Domańska, L., 2016. *Change and continuity: Traditions of the flint processing from the perspective of the Tążyna river valley*, Łódź.

Domańska, L., 2022. Microregional variants of the flint knapping traditions in the Late Neolithic from the perspective of the Prokopiak's Mount. *Sprawozdania Archeologiczne* 74(1), 205-220. https://doi.org/10.23858/SA/74.2022.1.3049

Rzepecki, S., 2015. Wilkostowo 23/24. *A Neolithic Settlement in Kuyavia, Poland c. 3500 BC. Studien zur Archäologie in Ostmitteleuropa* 15.

Wąs, M., 2023. Neolithic Flintworking of the Samborzec-Opatów Group in Lesser Poland in the Light of Settlement Materials from Tonie 9 site, Kraków Commune. *Analecta Archaeologica Ressoviensia* 18, 41-66. https://doi.org/10.15584/anarres.2023.18.3

Winiarska-Kabacińska, M., 2015. Results of microwear analysis of flint artefacts. in: Rzepecki, S., *Wilkostowo 23/24. A Neolithic Settlement in Kuyavia, Poland c. 3500 BC. Studien zur Archäologie in Ostmitteleuropa* 15, 323-336.

Can human behavioral ecology models contribute to understanding the Neolithization of Taiwan? Considering the Ideal Despotic Distribution and Allee Effects Model

Pei-Lin YU

Professor, Boise State University Minpaku/National Museum of Ethnology, Taiwan; pei-linyu@boisestate.edu

ABSTRACT

The Neolithization of Taiwan between 5,500 and 6,000 years ago caused adaptive responses of both immigrating food producers and territory-holding hunter gatherers. The Two Layer Model of Neolithic beginnings in Taiwan describes hunter-gatherers as rapidly marginalized, then completely replaced, by Austronesian farming peoples. Yet, ethnographic information about farmer/hunter-gatherer interactions, as well as the archaeological record of southeastern China, suggest that the process may have been more complex and gradual – with variations arising in different habitats. Human behavioral ecology, as part of the extended evolutionary synthesis, attempts to predict decision making by individuals who seek to maximize fitness: either reproductive fitness, or foraging returns (expressed as the ratio of energy capture to energy output). Foraging niche, or the dietary role played by the organism within its ecosystem, is central to these models. Human behavioral ecology models can be used as conceptual tools to generate testable working hypotheses about past behaviors related to the origins of food production, migrations, inter-cultural encounters, and more. This paper describes and evaluates the "Ideal Despotic Distribution" with Allee Effects Model as it applies to expectations for the archaeological record of the early Neolithization of Taiwan.

국문초록

이 논문은 대만의 초기 신석기화에 대해 고고학 기록에 기대를 갖게 하는 Allee 효과 모델을 이용하여 '이상적 독점적 분포'를 설명하고 평가한다. 5,500-6,000년 전 타이완의 신석기화와 함께 이주해온 식량생산자와 영토를 소유한 수렵채집인 양자 간에 적응 반응이 생겼다. 타이완의 신석기시대 시작은 수렵채집인이 빠르게 밀려나고 오스트로네시아 농경민족에 의해 완전 대체되는 2개 모델로 설명된다. 그러나 농부와 수렵채집인의 상호작용에 관한 민족지지학 정보와 중국 남동부 고고학 기록자료를 보면 그 상호작용 과정은 지역에 따른 다양성으로 인해 더 복잡하고 점진적으로 나타났다. 확장진화론인 인간행동생태학(HBE) 이론을 통해 생존적합성의 극대화라는 개인의 자기결정권, 즉 생식적합성 또는 채집수익률(에너지 출력/에너지 포획 비율)로 표현되는 자기결정권을 예측한다. 틈새 수렵채집 행태나 생태계 내에서 유기체가 행하는 식의 행태가 HBE 모델의 핵심 요소인데, 이 HBE 모델을 개념적 수단으로 삼아 식량생산의 기원, 이주, 문화간 만남 등 과거 행태에 관련하여 검증 가능한 작업가설을 만들 수 있다.

Keywords : Taiwan, hunter-gatherers, Pre-ceramic, Neolithic, human behavioral ecology, Ideal Despotic Distribution, Allee Effects Model, agriculture

1. Introduction and purpose

With the onset of the Neolithic and resulting demographic expansion in East Asia, the phenomenon of food producers moving into areas already occupied by hunter-gatherers occurred many times. Both groups responded adaptively in ways that were influenced by characteristics of the habitat and social organization, ranging from stable coexistence and exchange relations to complete avoidance or out-migration—sometimes in sequence (Higham, 2013; Fujio, 2021; Ikeya, 2021). In particular, the islands of subtropical Southeast Asia are interesting "laboratories" for exploring Neolithization by immigration, as they offer a view into the influence of maritime opportunities and constraints.

The Two-Layer Hypothesis has been advanced in the field of Southeast Asian archaeology, bioarchaeology, and paleogenetics to describe a major Neolithic population replacement event. The "first" layer is anatomically modern hunter-gatherers that colonized Southeast Asia at least 40,000 years ago (termed Australo-Melanesians) and later encountered the "second" layer of food-producing immigrants from North and/or East Asia. These groups eventually combined to form present-day Southeast Asians (Von Koenigswald, 1952; Coon, 1962; Bellwood, 1987, 1997, 2005; Brace et al., 1991; McColl et al., 2018). According to this hypothesis, the first layer—hunter gatherers—were either extinguished or able to persist only in mountain refugia (Matsumura et al., 2011; Higham, 2013; Matsumura et al., 2019; Hung et al., 2022). All else being equal, we may expect that on island habitats, the process was mediated by proximity to other islands and larger land masses, topography, offshore and nearshore currents, and climate.

Taiwan, in its position between East Asia's main landmass and the Pacific Ocean, and south of the Ryuku island chain and the north of the Philippine islands, lies at the intersection of several climatic and environmental zones. The island has a total area of 35,980km² and a total coastline of 1,566km. It is distinctive in the number of high mountains, having 268 peaks greater than 3,000m in height (Fig. 1).

During the Pleistocene, the Taiwan Peninsula experienced multiple overland immigration events by hominins (Chang et al., 2015). During the mid-Holocene, rising sea levels cut off the island from the main landmass. Anatomically modern hunter-gatherers were the sole human occupants of Taiwan until the arrival of food-producing peoples, most likely from the Southeastern China coastlands, at about 6,000 BP. The Two Layer Hypothesis is applied to Taiwan based on the disappearance of archaeological traces of hunter-gatherers by c. 4,800 BP, during a time when Neolithic sites were increasing rapidly (Liu, 2016; Tsang, 2016; Tsang et al., 2018). Yet, the apparently total disappearance of hunting and gathering in Taiwan between 6,000 and 4,800 years

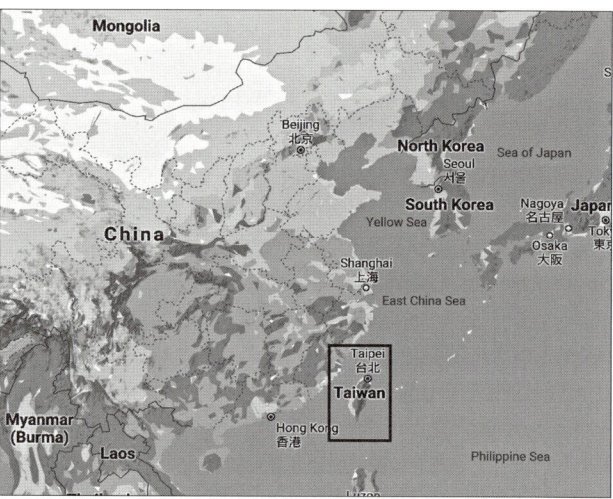

Fig. 1 Geographic location of Taiwan.

ago stands in contrast to persistence of complex aquatic-dependent hunting and gathering in the region, including Kyushu in southern Japan (Hoover and Hudson, 2016) and southeastern China (Jiao, 2016, 2021) until at least 3,000 BP, and mountain hunting and gathering in the Philippines' northern Luzon to the ethnographic present.

Is there something unusual about Taiwan's landscape or climate that made hunting and gathering unsustainable in conjunction with farming neighbors? An enduring question concerns "the timing, source and scale of the dispersal of food-producing people often linked with language family expansion from Southern China or Taiwan, and whether they mixed with or replaced local, extant populations. This issue is of crucial importance with respect to the validity, or otherwise, of the Two Layer model as a means of understanding the population history of Southeast Asia" (Matsumura et al., 2011). With ongoing research and the accumulation of new archaeological evidence, there is an opportunity to develop hypotheses about hunter-gatherer interactions with food producers using concept models from independent, yet relevant, bodies of reference information. In particular, models derived from behavioral ecology of non-human species immigrations into already-occupied territories can provide useful concepts for hypothesis building (Codding and Bird, 2015; Kennett et al., 2006; Weitzel and Codding, 2022).

Human behavioral ecology (HBE) stems from the larger field of evolutionary animal behavior. HBE models consider the goals, opportunities, and constraints faced by individuals seeking to maximize the ratio of energetic returns to costs. In behavioral ecology case studies, energetic yields often serve as the proxy currency for reproductive success because energetic yields are easier to observe and measure in real time (Codding and Bird, 2015). The challenge for archaeologists continues to be clarifying expectations for patterning in material traces of behaviors that occurred at the level of the group rather than individuals, were cumulative over time, and are imperfectly preserved (Codding and Bird, 2015). Additionally, models are not predictions, approximations of past reality, or falsifiable hypotheses. Rather, a good model is a heuristic device for conceptualizing processes so that hypotheses can be tested and refined using archaeological data (Codding and Bird, 2015; Yu, 2020, 2021).

HBE models concerning adaptive ramifications of immigration have recently been derived and tested among non-human species and applied to human cultural change. The models include but are not limited to the following: Prey and Patch Choice Models, which predict foraging based on nutritional yield and rate of return to the forager (MacArthur and Pianka, 1966; Stephens and Krebs, 1986; Gremillion and Piperno, 2009; Yu, 2021), Niche Variation Theory, which describes niche constriction arising from competition between colonizer and colonized (Elton, 1958; Olsson et al., 2009; Bolnick et al., 2010; Yu, 2021), Allee Effects Model, which improve fitness with increasingly dense populations (Allee and Bowen, 1932; Codding et al., 2019; Bliege Bird et al., 2020; Yu, 2021), and the Ideal Free Distribution Model which predicts the serial colonization of unoccupied habitat types in order of preferential ranking (Winterhalder et al., 2010; Jazwa et al., 2016; Kennett et al., 2006; Yu, 2020, 2021), among others. A corollary of Ideal Free Distribution, Ideal Despotic Distribution (Fretwell and Lucas, 1969) factors in the presence of territorial defenders and uneven capabilities between groups (Kennett et al., 2006; Kennett et al., 2009; Winterhalder et al., 2010). In this paper, I briefly summarize the archaeology and bioarchaeology of the Pre-ceramic and incipient Neolithic periods of Taiwan. I then consider the implications of the Ideal Free Distribution, Despotic Distribution, and Allee Effects models of behavioral ecology.

2. Summary of archaeology and bioarchaeology

2.1. Paleolithic and Pre-ceramic periods

Little is currently known about the hunter-gatherers of Taiwan. Although they lived on the island for thousands of years, only a few securely dated Paleolithic sites have been excavated in protected cave and rockshelter sites on the east coast. The earliest evidence is the Baxiandong type site of the Changbin Culture, a multi-cave complex located on rugged terrain along what is now the east coast. During glacial maxima, the caves were likely a longer walk from the ocean. The lithic assemblage of the lower levels includes unifacially flaked choppers and cobble flake tools in the lower levels (c. 20,000–25,000 BP, Tsang et al., 2006; Tsang et al., 2009; Tsang et al., 2011, 2016), made of pebbles sourced from nearby beaches (Tsang, 2013) and knapped on-site based on refit data (Lien, 2015). This cobble tool/chopper complex has been affiliated with the Hoabhinian culture of mainland Southeast Asia (Chang, 1969; Solheim, 1969; Bellwood, 2007). Upper levels (c. 15,000–19,000 BP) are characterized by smaller flake tools of higher-quality raw materials, such as chalcedony (Tsang et al., 2011). Bone needles, hooks, and other tools indicative of hunting and fishing are also present in later occupations (Tsang et al., 2009, 2011; Lien, 2015). Hearths have been found at Baxiandong, but thus far no implements or features associated with plant processing. Faunal remains include fish, shellfish, and cervids (Tsang et al., 2009). No Changbin-era burials have been discovered to date.

After a prolonged evidentiary gap extending from c. 15,000 BP to c. 6,000 BP (Lien, 2015; Tsang, 2016; Chen, 2017; Hung et al., 2022), hunter-gatherer sites re-appear in Taiwan at c. 5,500 BP. At Chaoyin Cave in Baxiandong, Song (1969) described evidence of a culture (termed Chaoyindong Culture) intermediate to the Changbin and Neolithic layers. Lithics are smaller and of higher-quality raw materials, with more evidence for retouch techniques, and there is an increase in bone tools. Prey types continued to be mostly aquatic, with abundant cervid bone. There is as yet no evidence of plant food remains.

Tsang (2016) argued that the temporal position and distinctive artifacts of the Chaoyindong layer are evidence that this Pre-ceramic culture is unrelated to either the Paleolithic Changbin or the Neolithic Dapenkeng (p. 59). Evidence of regionalization of Pre-ceramic cultures includes chipped stone lithic technologies identified in the north near Taipei (Sung, 1980; Liu et al., 2004), in the central-western region near Miaoli and Taichung (Liu, 1989; Liu et al., 2007), at the Xiaoma site in the southeast near Tainan (Sung, 1980; Huang and Chen, 1990; Huang, 1991), on the southern "beak" at O-luan-pi and Longkeng (Li, 1985; Huang, 1991), and in the southwest near Pingtung (Li et al., 1983; Huang et al., 1987) and Taitung (Huang and Chen, 1990). The time period of 6,500–5,000 BP is well-represented in the southern region. Some researchers hold that regionalized Pre-ceramic cultures evolved from Changbin origins despite the gap in the archaeological record, persisting until c. 4,500 BP (Kuo, 2019). Others argue that the c. 9,000-year gap indicates an actual hiatus in human occupation, in which Changbin peoples disappeared (Tsang, 2016; Matsumura et al., 2019; Hung et al., 2022). One possible candidate for a hiatus-era site is the Wangxing culture complex of sites in northwest central Taiwan. The lower stratum includes a flaked chopping tool culture distinctive from Changbin that is colluvium dated to between 47,000 and 8,250 BP (Liu et al., 2007; Liu, 2011). The upper stratum (8,250 and 6,000 years ago) includes small flake and core tools, blades with significant edge wear, and a large amount of debitage. Organic-poor red clays make radiometric dating difficult. Overall, the Changbin/Pre-ceramic hiatus is somewhat remarkable in East Asia (Tsang, 2016), and it i not clear if the gap reflects actual absence or post-depositional processes. Between 15,000 and 6,000 years ago, Taiwan experienced multiple major sea-level rises, tectonic uplift, volcanic activity, and earthquakes, raising the possibility of inundation or geological destruction of small, ephemeral open-air sites.

Current bioarchaeological data suggest that Taiwan's hunter-gatherer populations were diverse. About 140km to the northwest, near China's Min River delta, skeletons of an adult female and male were discovered on Liang island of the Matsu Archipelago. The skeletons lie below shell mounds that contain artifacts such as pottery, stone tools, and bone tools. Direct AMS dating of the bone direct AMS dating of Liangdao 1, a flexed burial of a male, placed it at 6,380–6,204 cal BC (7380 ± 40 BP; Chen, 2013; Chen and Chiu, 2013). This individual has cranio-facial and dental characteristics aligned with Australo-Papuan or Negrito populations (Hung, 2016). Liangdao 2, an extended burial, was dated to 5512–5374 cal BC (6490 ± 30 BP) (Chen, 2013; Chen and Chiu, 2013). The second individual has cranio-facial characteristics of East Asian or Austronesian populations (Hung, 2016).

Ko et al. (2014) analyzed a complete mitochondrial DNA genome sequence of a phalanx from the male Liangdao specimen and compared with 550 sequences from eight mountain Indigenous Taiwan groups and four from lower elevation regions. They found that the Liangdao mitochondrial (mt)DNA sequence has close links with Taiwan Indigenous people – very interesting given the Australo-Papuan cranio-facial traits and Negrito-style flexed burial. Further, the Liangdao male has the most ancestral haplogroup E sequences found among extant Austronesian speakers. Bayesian phylogenetic analysis was used to reconstruct a history of early Austronesians arriving in Taiwan in the north at c. 6,000 years ago and spreading rapidly to the south. This partly agrees with Liu's archaeological summary of first "landfall" near Tamsui in northwest Taiwan and diverging: some moving south toward what would later become the western coastal plains, and some going north up and over what is now Keelung and down to Yilan and Hualien (Liu, 2022). According to a simulation based on the divergence between the highland Formosans and Han, the two groups last shared common ancestry between 8,093 and 10,306 years ago (Ko et al., 2014). Within the Taiwan groups they found evidence of a north-to-south gradient in the patterns of (mt)DNA nucleotide diversity. Higher nucleotide differences in the north tentatively support a north-to-south spatial expansion model. Higher nucleotide diversity among mountain groups matches the expectation that mountainous territories were isolated and highly heterogeneous environments, and that mountain groups split early from other Austronesians and went through genetic bottlenecks. Liu et al. (2023) added lowland Taiwan Indigenous groups in a multifactorial fine scale genomic analysis, and found an affinity between Liangdao Man and today's Rukai people of the south.

Only one instance of a Pre-ceramic hunter-gatherer burial has been documented for Taiwan: a female adult at Xiaoma Cave at between 6,100 and 5,700 BP (Huang, 1991; Hung et al., 2022). Like the Liangdao 1 individual, she was buried in a flexed position. Craniometric and dental traits as well as her small stature strongly indicate affiliation with so-called Australo-Papuan or Negrito peoples of Northern Luzon and the Andaman Islands, supporting the possibility of Philippine origins for some Pre-ceramic Taiwan groups. The Xiaoma woman was found with stone tools typical of other Pre-ceramic sites, including cobble chopping tools, flake tools, and finer-material lithic tools made of quartz, agate or carnelian (mostly less than 4–5cm in length), and marine shells (Huang and Chen, 1990; Huang, 1991).

Taken together, the bioarchaeology and ancient DNA for the Pre-ceramic period indicate that multiple genetically distinct populations were present in or near Taiwan between 9,000 and 5,000 years ago. An ancient connection exists between Taiwan's Indigenous groups today and hunting and gathering ancestors who lived in SE China between 8,000 and 6,000 years ago. It is not clear what happened to the prior Changbin hunter gatherers, but no evidence of them survives to the Pre-ceramic period. By c. 6,000 years ago, hunter-gatherers of Negrito affiliation were present on

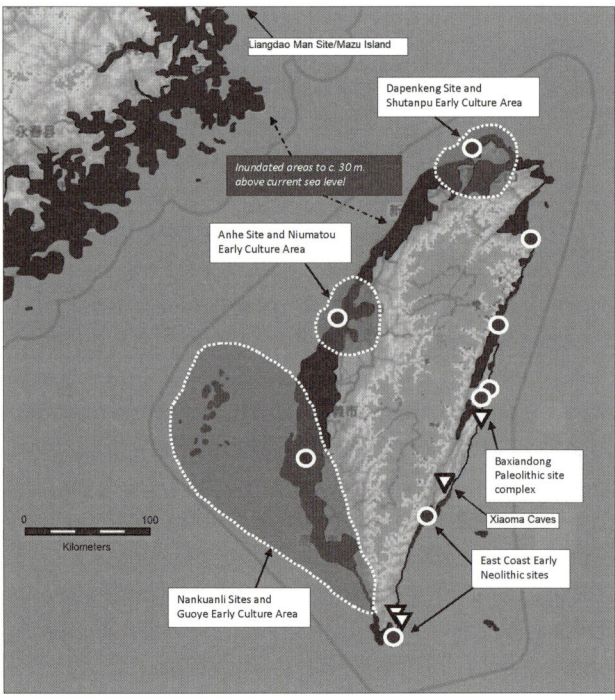

Fig. 2 Early culture areas of Taiwan discussed in the text, showing inundated zones at c. 6,000 BP.

the southeast coast, possibly having arrived by boat from the Luzon region (Hung et al., 2022). Hopefully additional datable archaeological sites associated with hunter gatherers will be discovered, as essential contextual information on the nature of Taiwan's hunter-gatherer adaptations is needed to complement bioarchaeological and genetic data (Tsang, 2016) (Fig. 2).

2.2. Incipient Neolithic Period

The earliest-documented instance of Neolithic culture in Taiwan is the Dapenkeng in the northwest (Chang, 1969, 1989; Chang and Goodenough, 1996), which has since been grouped within the larger Shuntanpu Culture (Chu, 2012; Kuo, 2019). This period of earliest immigrations by cultivators is estimated at c. 6,000–5,000 BP during a major marine transgression that inundated Taiwan up to 35m. higher than today (Chen, 2016). Thus, the earliest Neolithic sites are usually found on hills and terraces inland from the current shoreline (Hung and Carson, 2014; Liu, 2022).

Other regional variants of the incipient Neolithic include Guoye in the south (Tsang and Li, 2018; Kuo, 2019), Niumatou in the central west (Kuo, 2019), National Museum of Natural Science, and Oluanpi in the south (Sung et al., 1969). Incipient Neolithic sites tend not to have easily datable contexts, but in the potentially older sites shell middens and tool assemblages suggest a strong reliance on coastal-marine zones and possibly tuber-based horticulture (Chang, 1969). Although some cultural and technological traits were cited by Kano (1937) as evidence of a Malayan origin, researchers currently agree that the Indigenous peoples of Taiwan today are descended from ancestral populations in what is now SE China (Liu, 2016), with the possible exception of the Yami Tribe of Orchid Island or Lanyu. Thorough summaries of Japanese and early Taiwan research on this question are in Tsang (2016), Hung (2016), and Kuo (2019) among others.

Incipient Neolithic sites are represented by shell middens or located in sand dunes, with no evidence of grain cultivation thus far. The shell middens are often located on slightly elevated ground originally overlooking coastal swamps, now in-filled with alluvium. For example, at the Changguang site (長光) excavated in eastern Taiwan (Hung, 2016), pottery and stone adzes were present but no evidence of stone knives (for crop harvesting) or rice remains (phytoliths or macrobotanical). Evidence indicates that the Dapenkeng culture groups moved rapidly around the island establishing settlements in the northwest, south, and east. In the nearby southern Ryuku islands, the Shimotabaru culture shows some similarities with Dapenkeng Culture such as coastally based subsistence, chipped stone adzes and axes, and crude ceramics (Chiang, 2022). Newly corrected dates from the Ryukyu sites extending back to c. 4,900 BP suggest adaptive if not cultural connections.

By about 4,300 BP, Neolithic regionalization was in full swing. Some settlements like Nankuanli at the Tainan Science Park in the southwest were large, with internal differentiation, irrigation features, and a cemetery containing 14 supine extended burials (Tsang, 2006; Li, 2013; Tsang and Li, 2018; Tsang, 2022). Both millet and rice appear later in the sequence, at c. 4500 BP. Faunal evidence indicates a broad-spectrum diet including sika deer, boar, dog, clouded leopard, rabbit, muntjac, mouse, civet cat, bats, land turtles, snakes, and frogs. Abundant aquatic prey include 23 species of salt, freshwater, and estuarine fish, five species of shellfish, and softshell turtles (Tsang, 2022). The Nankuanli East site yielded evidence of millet and rice (Tsang and Li, 2018; Tsang et al., 2017) – crops that require different cultivation methods (Ibid). Beans and the seeds of Job's Tears (Coix lachrymae jobi) were also found, and geophytes and tree crops also may have been cultivated. Imported lithic raw material from Nankuanli includes olivine basalt from Penghu as well as non-local shellfish remains, indicating ongoing exchange relationships with nearby islands in the strait (Ibid ; Liu, 2022). In sum, recent evidence suggests that between 8,500 and 5,000 BP, multiple ethnic groups of hunter gatherers occupied various areas of Taiwan; at minimum, ancestral Austronesians as indicated by the Liangdao burials in the north and Negrito populations as indicated by the Xiaoma site in the southeast. Taiwan's hunter-gatherer toolkit included cobble tools as well as finer lithic tools. They were proficient in making short boat journeys and connected culturally and economically with southeast China, the Ryukyu Islands, and likely the northern Philippine islands. They preferred aquatic resources while also hunting terrestrial prey, and likely augmented wild plant foods with tubers, tree nuts, and fruit. The dead were buried with personal belongings, in a flexed position. By about 4,800 BP, sites indicative of hunting and gathering were no longer being formed, or became so scarce that they have not been preserved (Liu, 2016; Li, 2016).

Taiwan's Austronesian immigrants were apparently able to swivel between low level food production and hunting and gathering (Jiao, 2007, 2013, 2016). In fact, they shared many subsistence and settlement practices with hunter-gatherers of SE China and the southern Ryukyu Islands. The region was distinguished and united by a lifeway based on largely marine resources and opportunities: "…during the Middle Holocene period, peoples along the southeast coast of the Asian continent and surrounding islands shared similar ways of life, as evidenced from similar compositions of tool assemblages, the presence of shell middens, the lack of cereal cultivation, small settlement size, a shorter term of habitation, and produced ceramic vessels of a variety of styles" (Chiang, 2022). Tsang's (2022) comparison of contemporaneous subsistence remains from across the strait in Matsu islands, Kinmen island, Dongshan Hill site in Fujian, and others in Guangdong, also indicates a regional cultural complex strongly centered on aquatic foods. Although some of the earliest immigrants to Taiwan did not cultivate cereals at all (Hung and Carson, 2014; Hung, 2016) they may have found other species to be useful; K. C. Chang (1969, 1989) proposed that vegeculture and arboriculture were likely practiced on both sides of the strait during the incipient Neolithic. Therefore, although the apparently rapid disappearance of hunter-gatherer sites from Taiwan appears to support the Two Layer Hypothesis, we now turn to behavioral ecology models to consider how or why the immigration of low level food producers might have led to such a dramatic change.

3. The Ideal Distribution Models

Fretwell and Lucas (1969) in a pioneering study described a model of habitat selection with three variants: the Ideal Free Distribution, the Ideal Free Distribution with an Allee effect, and the Ideal Despotic Distribution (originally termed the ideal dominance distribution). The core premise of Ideal Distribution models is that dispersing organisms will settle in the best of habitats that differ in suitability (e.g., availability of preferred resources, exposure to hazards, and other characteristics). The premise is based on density-dependent changes to the suitability of the habitats available to them (Fretwell and Lucas, 1969 ; Weitzel and Codding, 2022). These models, originally developed to conceptualize the ways that non-human organisms distribute themselves across an environment of uneven quality, have been adapted for processes of human colonization and migration (see Codding and Bird, 2015, for a detailed summary).

3.1. Equal capabilities and access to habitats

According to the Ideal Free Distribution, organisms will first select the most resource-rich habitat available. This is a negative density dependent model in which increasing population density due to immigration or local growth leads to overconsumption of resources and deterioration of habitat quality (Fretwell and Lucas, 1969; Kennett et al., 2006; Weitzel and Codding, 2022). When the prime habitat deteriorates to the level of the second ranked habitat, population growth stimulates out-migration and populations will equilibrate between first and second ranked habitats. This repeats for the third ranked habitat, and so forth, as each group relocates to another habitat with better suitability (Fig. 3–5). Eventually the population distribution will

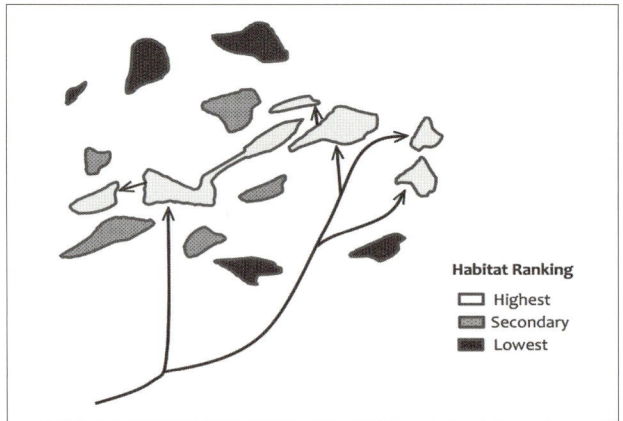

Fig. 3 IFD Phase 1. Free movement into optimal habitats within a hypothetical region.

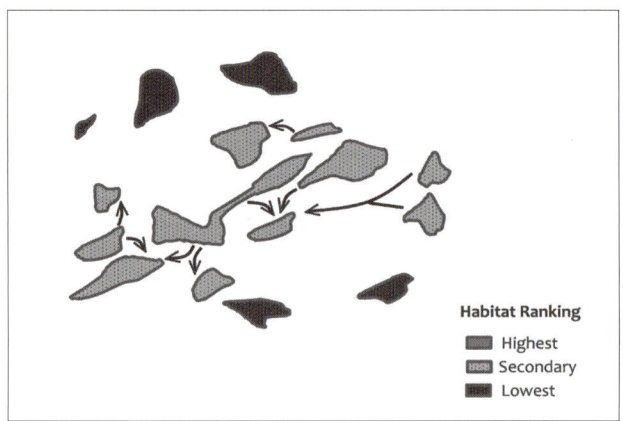

Fig. 4 IFD Phase 2. As optimal habitats become degraded, groups migrate to secondary habitats.

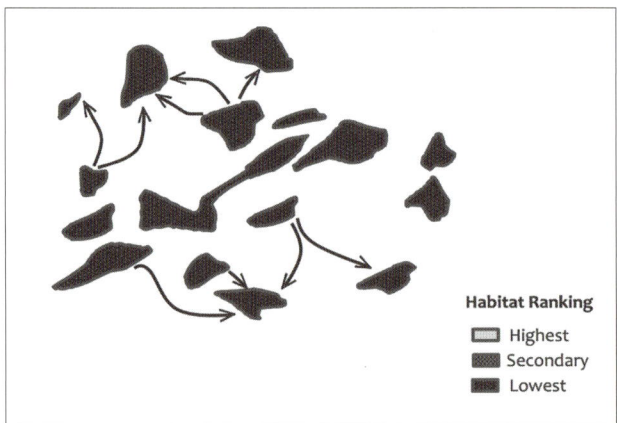

Fig. 5 IFD Phase 3. When primary and secondary habitats degrade further, groups out-migrate to lowest ranked habitats.

equalize marginal qualities across all occupied habitats. This end state, called equilibrium distribution, is a consequence of the marginal equalization of habitat suitability. At completion of the IFD, no group has an incentive to move (Kennett et al., 2006).

The Ideal Free Distribution makes some important assumptions.
(1) Habitats are patchy, and unequal in terms of resource richness;
(2) The dietary niche is unchanging, and all are presumed to

have equal abilities and access to resources;

(3) Habitats are presumed as un-occupied by similar organisms or those with a similar niche, so colonizers do not encounter any defenders;

(4) Colonizers will choose the ideal or best habitat available, and that they are free or unrestricted in their movements; and

(5) The occupied patch quality can only deteriorate over time as population densities grow.

Clearly, the case of Taiwan's incipient Neolithic has characteristics that diverge from assumptions of the IFD model. The island was already occupied by hunter-gatherers; it is likely that their abilities to hold territory were different from those of immigrating cultivators; and habitats were ultimately altered by the labor of increasingly dense populations.

3.2. Unequal capabilities and access to habitats

The Ideal Despotic Distribution (IDD) takes into account differential access to resources and is appropriate when habitats considered optimal by immigrating organisms are already occupied. In the process as summarized by Calsbeek and Sinervo (2002) and Kennett et al. (2006), complexity arises when competitors have unequal abilities. The IDD is further divided into two important variants: negative and positive. "Negative" despotism occurs when the original occupants of a habitat find it worthwhile to defend semi-exclusive use of the territory against newcomers who seek to cohabitate. Superior competitors thus protect access to prime habitats and push inferior competitors and those without territories to poorer habitats. Higher quality territories are expected to be smaller due to greater habitat productivity and lower costs of perimeter defense. Fitness (reproduction and/or energetic returns) are higher in those habitats. Such territoriality can result in skewed population densities, with more rapid dispersals to lower suitability habitats than expected under the IFD (Weitzel and Codding, 2022) (**Fig. 6**).

Under the 'positive' form of despotism, the initial occupants of a habitat find it worthwhile to allow others to occupy their patch by relinquishing some of their control of the habitat (Ibid). Bell and Winterhalder (2014) mathematically demonstrated that despots may choose to reduce their monopoly by making concessions so that others find it more suitable to stay as a subordinate than to disperse to the next most suitable habitat as autonomous individuals (Weitzel and Codding, 2022).

The archaeological record suggests that coastal, shoreline, estuarine, and other wetlands areas with good access to aquatic foods were probably preferred by both immigrating cultivators and defending hunter-gatherers. This agrees with estimates of Taiwan hunter-gatherer subsistence derived

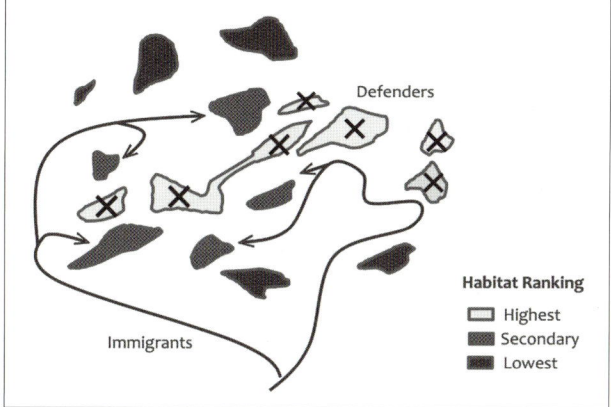

Fig. 6 IDD Phase 1. Original populations defend optimal habitats: immigrants occupy secondary habitats.

from the Lewis Binford Hunter-Gatherer Database (Binford, 2001; Binford and Johnson, 2014; Yu, 2020). Sites attributed to hunter-gatherers in Taiwan are not numerous, and the question of whether this is the result of preservation bias affecting small ephemeral sites or very low hunter-gatherer populations is not settled. Nonetheless, the Despotic Distribution predicts that some of Taiwan's prime coastal habitats would be occupied by hunter-gatherers and potentially defended against incursions by colonizers. Lower ranked habitats were likely less contested; archaeological evidence and Binford's database predict that preferred secondary habitat types for hunter-gatherers were mountain footslopes with abundant terrestrial prey (Yu, 2020) contrast to immigrators' preference for flat, arable lands near coastal areas (Yu, 2020; Tsang and Li, 2018; Tsang, 2022) (**Fig. 7**). Inter-group conflicts could have been minimized by over-use of secondary habitats by both groups, and scheduled or otherwise negotiated access of prime coastal habitats. In this scenario, the 'negative' Despotic Distribution applies.

In considering prime versus secondary habitats of Taiwan c. 6,000-5,000 years ago it is important to consider the effects of the marine transgression (Chen, 2016). During this time sea levels in the area were considerably higher than today, up to 35m. Much of western Taiwan resembled eastern Taiwan with few coastal plains and a close interface between mountain foot slopes and the sea. Therefore, flat lands would have been scanty for Taiwan's first cultivators,

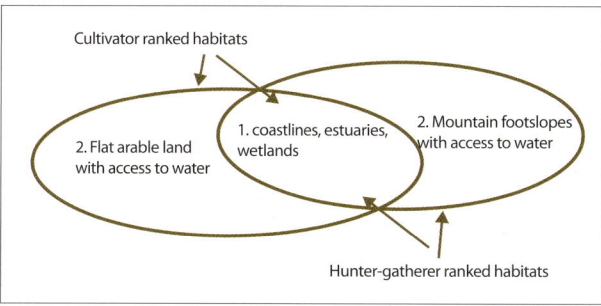

Fig. 7 Concept map of overlapping primary habitats versus non-overlapping secondary habitats, Neolithic cultivators and Pre-ceramic hunter-gatherers of Taiwan.

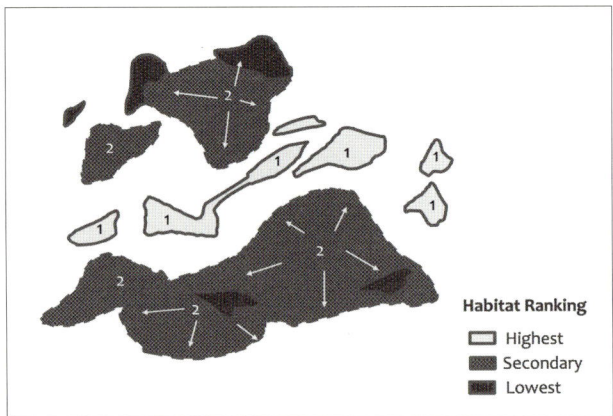

Fig. 8 IDD Phase 2. Occupants of sub-optimal habitats expand their territory in attempt to improve energetic returns. Original populations continue to maintain control over smaller, more productive territories.

potentially leading to inter-group competition among the immigrants rather than with hunter-gatherers.

The next phase predicted by the Despotic Distribution is the expansion of territories located in secondary habitats in order to increase encounter rates with needed resources (**Fig. 8**). A high level of effort would be required to defend boundaries and find food in these larger territories. In contrast, occupants of prime habitats expend less effort to obtain resources, have smaller territories to defend, and enjoy better energetic and reproductive fitness. This pattern has been confirmed experimentally with lizards of the Channel Islands off California (Calsbeek and Sinervo, 2002).

3.3. Positive density dependence and territorial quality

Both the IFD and the Despotic Distribution presume negative density dependence in which growing populations deplete resources and reduce the quality of the habitat. However, some organisms have demonstrated positive density dependence (Allee and Bowen, 1932; Allee et al., 1949) in which more dense populations actually enhance fitness in ways such as greater ease in finding mates, release from inbreeding depression, and opportunities for cooperative predation or defense against predators/invaders (Stephens and Sutherland, 1998). Allee Effects result in larger-than-anticipated group sizes until at some point, a threshold is reached in which those benefits decline (Weitzel and Codding, 2022). Another potential benefit of dense populations is facilitation of cooperative activities that modify habitats for improved productivity. In an example from hunting and gathering societies, anthropogenic fire is cited as having profound and lasting effects on ecosystem function, habitat heterogeneity, and vegetative succession, in turn conditioning beneficial changes to prehistoric mobility, settlement, and socio-political organization (Bliege Bird et al., 2008; Codding et al., 2019; Zeanah et al., 2017).

Allee Effects among cultivators can stabilize, then improve, secondary habitat quality through increasing plant food productivity and early succession habitats that attract prey species such as sika deer (Jiang, 2009; Li et al., 2013).

4. Discussion

Allee Effects can combine with the Despotic Distribution across the Neolithization spectrum. Pre-ceramic hunter-gatherers with access to prime aquatic resource habitats originally had limited incentive to modify them. Fish traps and weirs made of perishable materials were possibly used, as more recent stone weirs are found in Penghu and other gently sloping coastal settings (Tsai, 2009; Kuo and Li, 2018). There is as yet no evidence of anthropogenic fire in Taiwan during the Pre-ceramic period.

Expansive movements of Austronesian immigrants combined with subsequent lowering sea levels and exposure of flat arable lands increased the frequency of encounters between hunter-gatherers and growing populations of cultivators in the west and south. There, Pre-ceramic peoples had incentive (territorial pressure) and opportunity (cultural knowledge exchange) to experiment with small-scale cultivation (Yu, 2020). Information transfer about crops and cultivation might have been direct from cultivators. However, in eastern Taiwan Austronesian incursions occurred later and the need for Pre-ceramic groups to defend territory and experiment with cultivation was delayed. Information transfer about cultivation was likely indirect, via communication with other hunting and gathering groups (Ibid).

The combination of the Despotic Distribution with Allee Effects also makes it possible to predict sequential phases of colonization. Initially, cultivators likely occupied sub-optimal terrestrial habitats as a result of some degree of defense by Pre-ceramic peoples. The improvement of secondary habitats through cultivation practices could, for a time, create an Allee Effects feedback loop of human population growth and continued habitat improvements. Thus initial low-level cultivation and small settlements were followed by increased cultivation and a strong uptick in cultivator population size and density: a pattern consistent with the archaeological evidence of Taiwan's Early to Middle Neolithic described by Liu (2016) and Hung (2016). This territorial expansion could have turned the tide against Pre-ceramic hunter-gatherers, increasing the costs of territorial defense. It is at this point that the Two Layer Hypothesis describes marginalization of hunter-gatherers into habitats that were not contested by cultivators: most likely the central mountains (Higham, 2013; Hung et al., 2022) (**Fig. 9-10**).

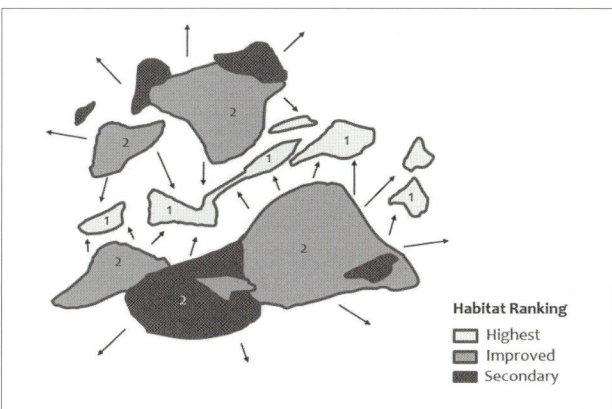

Fig. 9 IDD Phase 3. Colonizers (2) improve productivity of secondary habitats and increase their populations. Territory expands and approaches quality of smaller, high ranked habitats. Original defenders (1) experience increased costs of perimeter defense.

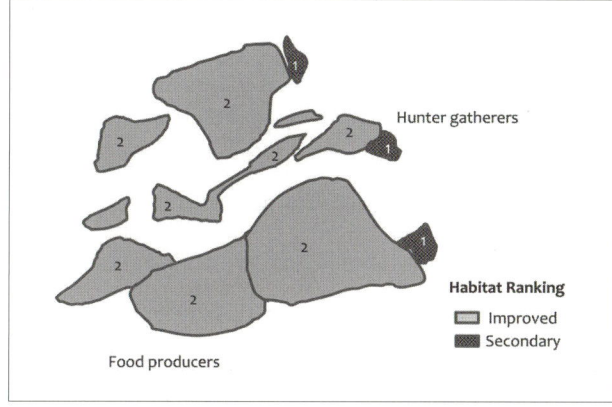

Fig. 11 IDD Phase 5. Descendants of original defenders (1) and colonizers (2) enter into mutualistic relationships involving exchange of goods and services.

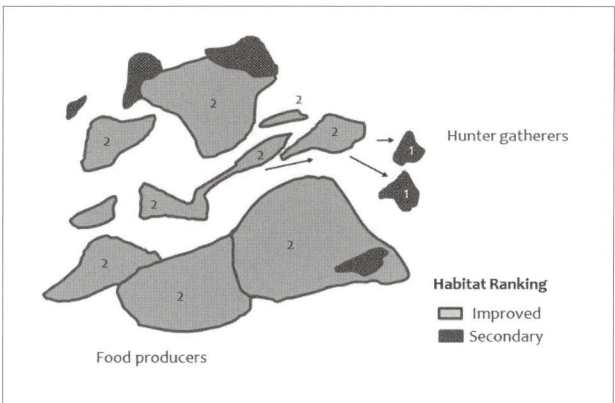

Fig. 10 IDD Phase 4. Descendants of colonizers (2) displace natives (1) throughout most habitats. Original defenders move to secondary or tertiary habitats that can be defended.

4.1. A question of mutualism

It is worth noting that the rapid disappearance of evidence for hunting and gathering is not equivalent to the disappearance of the people themselves. Archaeological evidence suggests that Early Neolithic food producers in subtropical East Asia were not necessarily avoidant or confrontational with hunter-gatherers. The Austronesian homeland of SE China's coast shows archaeological evidence of coastally adapted, semi-sedentized hunter-gatherers who used ceramics as late as 3000 BP (Zhang and Hung, 2012; Hung and Carson, 2014; Jiao, 2016). In this region, wild and semi-domesticated plants from both terrestrial and aquatic settings were consumed alongside fully domesticated crops up to the Middle Neolithic (Liu et al., 2011; Chi and Hung, 2012; Hung, 2016; Jiao, 2013, 2016). Cultivators lived alongside hunting and gathering neighbors for millennia: Along the Fujian coast, Jiao (2016) summarized evidence for a lengthy sequence of coexistence that lasted from c. 6,500–3,500 BP.

Thus, throughout most of the SE China Neolithic, cultivation occurred along a sliding scale within a distinctive mixed economy of low-level food production (Smith, 2001, cited in Jiao 2016). Sparse population density, high dependence on aquatic foods, and delayed development of social hierarchies, make China's warm-temperate coastal regions "a unique zone in China's Neolithization process, both economically and socially" (Smith, 2001). It is reasonable to expect that Taiwan's first farmers already possessed a cultural "template" for interacting with hunting and gathering neighbors, as well as some hunting and gathering themselves. The colonization of Taiwan, rather than a violent or abrupt confrontation, was more likely a series of negotiated relationships that were largely contingent on characteristics of the environment.

Co-existence is suggested by narratives of "little dark people" that are told among Taiwan's current Austronesian Indigenous groups (Adachi, 1906; Torii; 1907; Ogawa and Asai, 1935; Kano, 1937; Li, 1996; Liu, 2015): Some describe a friendly or even intimate relationship, and others, open conflict. The specificity and near universality (15 out of 16 groups) of these traditional narratives support an hypothesis of mutualistic co-existence based on exchange relations long after the disappearance of archaeological evidence for hunter-gatherers more than 4,000 years ago. The benefits of mutualism between hunter-gatherers and cultivators include complementary uses of different ecosystems to maintain exchange relations, which align with the "positive" mode of the Despotic Distribution in which despots share territory and some resources in order to derive benefits from nearby subordinates (**Fig. 11**).

5. Conclusion

Can behavioral ecology models help researchers to understand the process of Neolithization in Taiwan? Potentially. Although the Despotic Distribution combined with Allee Effects tells us nothing new about the archaeological evidence, these concept models have facilitated the development of expectations for the pace and process of Neolithization. The models visualize a slow first phase of Austronesian initial colonization and settlement of second-rate habitats (c. 6,000–4,800 BP) that had a minimal impact on Taiwan's Pre-ceramic hunter-gatherers, especially those in the east. This was followed by a strong growth phase of Austronesian populations resulting from Allee Effects-related habitat improvements (late Early Neolithic at about 4,500 BP). The Neolithic 'growth spurt' pressured hunter-gatherers into yielding prime coastal habitats especially adjacent to arable lands. Their options: retreat to remote mountain habitats, which would lead to hunter-gatherer settlements with no ceramics in Taiwan's remote mountains. The alternative would be to offset the costs of territorial loss by forging mutualistic relationships and experimenting with small-scale cultivation. This would necessitate settlement near cultivation communities, with the expectation of ceramic-using hunter-gatherer camps sited adjacent to farming communities. In both cases, archaeological evidence for hunter-gatherers is likely to be scanty, subtle, and in the latter case hard to separate from cultivators. An ethnoarchaeological analysis of mutualistic relationships should provide useful details for further development of archaeological expectations, the role of gardening, and potential mechanisms for the eventual breakdown of mutualistic relations and the disappearance of full-time hunting and gathering in Taiwan.

References

Adachi, B., 1906. About Taiwanese ancient natives (Negritos). *Journal of the Anthropological Society of Nippon* 22(249), 83-88. (in Japanese)

Allee, W.C., Park, O., Emerson, A.E., Park, T. and Schmidt, K.P., 1949. *Principles of Animal Ecology* (No. Edn 1), Philadelphia: W. B. Saunders Co. Ltd.

Allee, W.C., and Bowen, E., 1932. Studies in animal aggregations: Mass protection against colloidal silver among goldfishes. *J. Exp. Zool* 61, 185-207.

Bell, A.V. and Winterhalder, B., 2014. The population ecology of despotism: concessions and migration between central and peripheral habitats. *Human Nature* 25, 121-135.

Bellwood, P., 2007. *Prehistory of the Indo-Malaysian Archipelago*, Canberra: ANU Press.

Bellwood, P., 1997. Taiwan and the prehistory of the Austronesian-speaking people. *The Review of Archaeology* 18(2), 39-48.

Bellwood, P., 1987. The prehistory of island Southeast Asia: a multidisciplinary review of recent research. *Journal of World Prehistory* 1, 171-224.

Binford, L.R., 2001. *Constructing Frames of Reference: An Analytical Method for Archaeological Theory Building Using Hunter-Gatherer and Environmental Data Sets*, Berkeley: University of California Press.

Binford, L.R. and Johnson, A.L., 2014. *Program for Calculating Environmental and Hunter-Gatherer Frames of Reference* (ENVCALC2.1). Updated Java Version (August, 2014). https://ajohnson.sites.truman.edu/data-and-program/ (accessed 12 April 2023)

Bliege Bird, R., McGuire, C., Bird, D.W., Price, M.H., Zeanah, D., and Nimmo, D.G., 2020. Fire mosaics and habitat choice in nomadic foragers. *Proceedings of the National Academy of Sciences of the USA* 117(23), 12904-12914.

Bliege Bird, R., Bird, D.W., Codding, B.F., Parker, C.H., and Jones, J.H., 2008. The "fire stick farming" hypothesis: Australian Aboriginal foraging strategies, biodiversity, and anthropogenic fire mosaics. *Proceedings of the National Academy of Sciences* 105(39), 14796-14801.

Brace, C.L., Tracer, D.P. and Hunt, K.D., 1991. Human craniofacial form and the evidence for the peopling of the Pacific. *Population Biological Studies, Bulletin of the Indo-Pacific Prehistory Association* 11, 247-269.

Chang, C.H., Kaifu, Y., Takai, M., Kono, R.T., Grün, R., Matsumura, S., Kinsley, L., and Lin, L.K., 2015. The first archaic Homo from Taiwan. *Nature Communications* 6, 6037. Doi: 10.1038/ncomms7037

Chang, K.C., 1989. The Neolithic Taiwan Strait. *Kaogu* 6, 541-569.

Chang, K.C., 1969. *Fengpitou, Tapenkeng, and the Prehistory of Taiwan*, New Haven: Department of Anthropology Yale University.

Calsbeek, R. and Sinervo, B., 2002. An experimental test of the ideal despotic distribution. *Journal of Animal Ecology* 71(3), 513-523.

Chen, C.Y., 2013. *Liangdao Man DNA studies*, Lienjiang: Lienjian County Government. (In Chinese)

Chen, C.Y., and Chiu, H.L., 2013. *The excavation of the Daowei sites on Liangdao Island of Mazu, and the reconstruction plan for "Liangdao Man"*, Lienjiang: Lienjiang County Government. (In Chinese)

Chen, W.S., 2016. *Taiwan Dizhi Gailun*, Taipei: Republic of China Geology Society.

Chi, Z. and Hung, H.C., 2012. Later hunter-gatherers in southern China, 18000–3000 B.C. *Antiquity* 86(331), 11-29.

Chiang, C.H., 2022. Possible relationships between Taiwan and the Southern Ryukyu Islands during the Early Neolithic Period. In *Taiwan Maritime Landscapes from Neolithic to Early Modern Times*. P. Calanca, Y.C. Liu, and F. Muyard eds., Études thématiques 34, Paris: École française d'Extrême-Orient, 103-114.

Codding, B.F., Parker, A.K. and Jones, T.L., 2019. Territorial behavior among Western North American foragers: Allee effects, within group cooperation, and between group conflict. *Quaternary International* 518, 31-40.

Codding, B.F. and Bird, D.W., 2015. Behavioral ecology and the future of archaeological science. *Journal of Archaeological Science* 56, 9-20.

Coon, C.S., 1962. *The Origin of Races*, New York: Alfred Knopf.

Chu, Cheng-yi et al.(with 24 co-authors), 2012. *Dalongdong report of salvage archaeological excavation*, Tainan: Sugu Cultural Foundation. (In Chinese, unpublished report)

Elton, C.S., 1958. *The Ecology of Invasions by Animals and Plants*, Chicago: University of Chicago Press.

Fretwell, S.D. and Lucas, H.L., 1969. On territorial behavior and other factors influencing habitat distribution in birds. *Acta Biotheor* 19, 16-36. Available online: https://link.springer.com/article/10.1007/BF01601953 (accessed on 5 July 2023)

Fujio, S., 2021. Early grain cultivation and starting processes in the Japanese Archipelago. *Quaternary* 4, 1-15.

Gremillion, K.J. and Piperno, D.R., 2009. Human behavioral ecology, phenotypic (developmental) plasticity, and agricultural origins: insights from the emerging evolutionary synthesis. *Current Anthropology* 50(5), 615-619.

Higham, C., 2013. Hunter-gatherers in Southeast Asia: From prehistory to the present. *Human Biology* 85(1-3), 21-44.

Hoover, K.C. and Hudson, M.J., 2016. Resilience in prehistoric persistent hunter–gatherers in northwest Kyushu, Japan as assessed by population health and archaeological evidence. *Quaternary International* 405, 22-33.

Huang, S.C., 1991. Pre-ceramic culture of Taiwan revealed at the cave site of Xiaoma. *Field Archaeology of Taiwan* 2(2), 37-54. (in Chinese)

Huang, S.C. and Chen, Y.B., 1990. *Test excavations in Donghe and reconstruction of prehistoric culture*, Taipei: National Taiwan University. (in Chinese)

Huang, S.C., Chen, Y.B. and Yan, X., 1987. Kending Guojia Gongyuan Kaogu Minzu Diaocha Baogao. *Neizhengbu Yingjianshu Kending Guojia Gongyuan Guanlichu Weituo, Guoli Taiwan Daxue Renlei Xuexi Zhixing*.

Hung, H.C., 2016. The formation and dispersal of Early Austronesian-speaking populations: New evidence from Taiwan, the Philippines, and the Marianas of Western Micronesia. In *Austronesian Diaspora: A New Perspective*. B. Prasetyo, T.S. Nastiti, and T. Simanjuntak eds., Yogyakarta: Gadjah Mada University Press, 125-144.

Hung, H.C. and Carson, M.T., 2014. Foragers, fishers and farmers: origins of the Taiwanese Neolithic. *Antiquity* 88(342), 1115-1131.

Hung, H.C., Matsumura, H., Nguyen, L.C., Hanihara, T., Huang, S.C. and Carson, M.T., 2022. Negritos in Taiwan and the wider prehistory of Southeast Asia: new discovery from the Xiaoma Caves. *World Archaeology*, 1-22.

Ikeya, K., 2021. Ethnoarchaeology of introducing agriculture and social continuity among sedentarised hunter–gatherers: the transition from the Jomon to the Yayoi Period. *Quaternary* 4(3), 28-44.

Jazwa, C.S., Kennett, D.J. and Winterhalder, B., 2016. A test of ideal free distribution predictions using targeted survey and excavation on California's Northern Channel Islands. *Journal of Archaeological Method and Theory* 23, 1242-1284.

Jiang, Z., 2009. *Biodiversity and Sika deer in Taohongling Nature Reserve, Jiangxi, China*, Beijing: Tsinghua University Press. (in Chinese)

Jiao, T., 2021. Archaeology of Southeast China and the search for an Austronesian homeland. *Social Sciences in China* 42(1), 161-170.

Jiao, T., 2016. Toward an alternative perspective on the foraging and low-level food production on the coast of China. *Quaternary International* 419, 54-61.

Jiao, T., 2013. An Economic Perspective of Southeast China's Prehistory–in Memory of Professor Kwang-Chih Chang. In *Rethinking East Asian Archaeology: Memorial Essay Collection for the Tenth Anniversary of Kwang-Chih Chang's Death*. Chen, K.T. ed., Taipei: Institute of History and Philology, Academia Sinica, 21-36.

Jiao, T., 2007. *The Neolithic of southeast China: Cultural Transformation and Regional Interaction on the Coast*, Amherst NY: Cambria Press.

Kano, T., 1932. Legends of Pygmy People in Taiwan. *Journal of the Anthropological Society of Nippon* 47(3), 103-116. (in Japanese)

Kennett, K., Anderson, A. and Winterhalder, B., 2006. The Ideal Free Distribution, food production, and the colonization of Oceania. In *Behavioral Ecology and the Transition to Agriculture*. Kennett, D. and Winterhalder, B. eds., Berkeley: University of California Press, 265-88.

Ko, A.M.S., Chen, C.Y., Fu, Q., Delfin, F., Li, M., Chiu, H.L.,

Stoneking, M. and Ko, Y.C., 2014. Early Austronesians: into and out of Taiwan. *The American Journal of Human Genetics* 94(3), 426-436.

Kuo, C. and Li, C., 2018. Real illustration of continuity in human fishing/hunting cultures from past to present-introduction about the conservation of stone tidal weirs at Taiwan. Paper presented at ICOA1238, Session 3: World Heritage, Regulations and Guidelines, Authenticity and Integrity. Delhi, India.

Kuo, S.C., 2019. *New Frontiers in the Neolithic Archaeology of Taiwan (5600-1800 BP): A Perspective of Maritime Cultural Interaction*, New York: Springer.

Li, C., Ping, X., Lu, X.L., Liu, W.H., Zhu, H.B., Xu, X., Jiang, Z.G., 2013. Current status of the critically endangered South China Sika deer and its dispersal out of the protected area: effects of human activity and habitat alteration. *J. Biodivers. Endanger. Species* 1(3), 1-4.

Li, K.T., 2016. Least cost and decision making: Application of economics to the lifeways of early Neolithic settlers of Taiwan. In *Archaeology, History, and Indigenous Peoples: New Perspectives on the Ethnic Relations of Taiwan*. Hung, L. H. ed., Taipei: Shung Ye Museum of Formosan Aborigines, 139-162.

Li, K.T., 2013. First farmers and their coastal adaptation in prehistoric Taiwan. In *A Companion to Chinese Archaeology*. Underhill, A.P. ed., Hoboken: John Wiley and Sons, 612-633.

Li, K.T., 1985. Duiyu Taiwan Kaogu Yanjiu de Ryogan Renshi. *Taiwan Wenxian* 36(3-4), 15-23.

Li, K.T., Liu, Y.C., and Chang, C., 1983. Eluanbi Gongyuan Kaogu Diaocha Baogao. *Jiaotongbu Guangguangju Kending Fenjing Tedingqu Guanlingchu Weituo*, Guoli Taiwan Daxue Renlei Xuexi Zhixing.

Li, P. J.K., 1996. Legends about Pygmies among the Formosan natives. In *Proceedings of the Conference on Chinese Myth and Legend*. Li, Y.Y. and Wang C. G. eds., Taipei: Center for Chinese Studies, 579-604. (in Chinese)

Lien, C.M., 2015. Chang-pin Culture of Taiwan and Characteristics of Its Lithic Industry. In *Emergence and Diversity of Modern Human Behavior in Paleolithic Asia*. Kaifu, Y., Izuho, M., Goebel, T., Sato, H., and Ono, A. eds., College Station: Texas A & M Press, 239-248.

Liu, D., Ko, A.M.S. and Stoneking, M., 2023. The genomic diversity of Taiwanese Austronesian groups: implications for the" Into and Out of Taiwan" models. *bioRxiv* 2023-01. https://www.biorxiv.org/content/10.1101/2023.01.09.523210v1 (Accessed 12 April 2023)

Liu, L., Ge, W., Bestela, S., Jones, D., Shi, J., Song, Y., and Chen, X., 2011. Plant exploitation of the last foragers at Shizitan in the Middle Yellow River valley, China: Evidence from grinding stones. *Journal of Archaeological Science* 38, 3524-3532.

Liu, Y.C., 2022. Taiwan prehistoric maritime trade networks and their impacts. In *Taiwan Maritime Landscapes from Neolithic to Early Modern Times*. P. Calanca, Y. C. Liu, and F. Muyard eds., Études thématiques 34, Paris: École française d'Extrême-Orient, 65-86.

Liu, Y.C., 2016. Discussion on the distribution and composition of aborigines from the perspective of prehistoric cultural development. In *Archaeology, History, and Indigenous Peoples: New Perspectives on the Ethnic Relations of Taiwan*, Hung. L.H. ed., Taipei: Shung Ye Museum of Formosan Aborigines, 73-107.

Liu, Y.C., 2011. Zhuminzhi Kaogupian. *Taiwan Quanzhi (Juan 3)*, Nantou: Guoshiguan Taiwan Wenxianguan, 51-321.

Liu, Y.C., 1989. Disanzhang: Shiqian Yizhi. *Taizhong Xianzhi (Juan 1) Tudizhi*, Fengyuan: Taizhongxian Zhengfu, 773-849.

Liu, Y.C., Chen, J., Zheng, H., and Li, J., 2007. *Taizhongxian Kaogu Yizhi Pucha yu Yanjiu Jihua Yanjiu Baogao. Taizhongixian Wenhuaju Weituo, Zhongyan Yanjiuyuan Renwen Shehui Kexue Zongxin*, Kaoguxue Yanjiu Zhuanti Zhongxin Zhixing.

Liu, Y.L., 2015. The Study of the Legend of Pygmy from Taiwanese Indigenous Tribes. Unpublished PhD Thesis, Hualien: National Dong Hwa University. (in Chinese)

MacArthur, R.H. and Pianka, E.R., 1966. On optimal use of a patchy environment. *The American Naturalist* 100(916), 603-609.

Matsumura, H., Hung, H.C., Higham, C., Zhang, C., Yamagata, M., Nguyen, L.C., Li, Z., Fan, X.C., Simanjuntak, T., Oktaviana, A.A. and He, J.N., 2019. Craniometrics reveal "two layers" of prehistoric human dispersal in eastern Eurasia. *Scientific Reports* 9(1), 451.

Matsumura, H., Oxenham, M.F., Nguyen, K.T., Nguyen, L.C., Nguyen, K.D., Enfield, N. and White, J., 2011. Population history of mainland Southeast Asia: the Two Layer Model in the context of northern Vietnam. *Dynamics of Human Diversity: the Case of Mainland Southeast Asia* 2011, 153-178.

McColl, H., Racimo, F., Vinner, L., Demeter, F., Gakuhari, T., Moreno-Mayar, J.V., Van Driem, G., Gram Wilken, U., Seguin-Orlando, A., De la Fuente Castro, C. and Wasef, S., 2018. The prehistoric peopling of Southeast Asia. *Science* 361(6397), 88-92.

Ogawa, N., and Asai, H., 1935. *The Collection of Legends of Taiwanese Aborigines Taken down in Their Own Languages*. Taipei: SMC Publishing Inc. (In Japanese)

Olsson, K., Stenroth, P., Nyström, P.E.R. and Granéli, W., 2009. Invasions and niche width: does niche width of an introduced crayfish differ from a native crayfish?. *Freshwater Biology* 54(8), 1731-1740.

Smith, B.D., 2001. Low-level food production. *Journal of Archaeological Research* 9, 1-43.

Stephens, D.W. and Krebs, J.R., 1986. *Foraging Theory* Vol. 6, Princeton: Princeton University Press.

Stephens, P.A. and Sutherland, W.J., 1999. Consequences of the Allee effect for behaviour, ecology and conservation. *Trends in Ecology and Evolution* 14(10), 401-405.

Sung, W.H., 1980. The archaeology of Taiwan. In *Taiwan of China*. Chen, C.L. ed., Taipei: Zhongyang Wenwu Gongyingshe, 93-220. (in Chinese)

Sung, W.H., Huang, S.C., Lien, C.M., and Li, K.C., 1969. O-luan-pi: A Prehistoric Site at the Southern Tip of Formosa. *Annual Bulletin of the China Council for East Asian Studies* 6, 148-149.

Torii, R., 1907. Taiwanese dwarfs are Negritos. *Journal of the Anthropological Society of Nippon* 22(252), 215-219. (in Japanese)

Tsai, H.M., 2009. Co-evolution and beyond: landscape changes in the Penghu archipelago (the Pescadores), Taiwan. In *Asia-Pacific Forum* 44(2), 193-213.

Tsang, C.H., 2022. Cross strait migration during the Early Neolithic Period of Taiwan. In *Taiwan Maritime Landscapes from Neolithic to Early Modern Times*. Calanca, P., Liu, Y. C., and Muyard, F. eds., Paris : Études thématiques 34. École française d'Extrême-Orient, 87-102.

Tsang, C.H., 2016. Archaeological perspectives on the origins of the indigenous peoples of Taiwan. In *Archaeology, History and Indigenous Peoples-New Perspectives on the Ethnic Relations of Taiwan*. Hung, L.W. ed., Taipei: Shung Ye Museum of Formosan Aborigines, 33-71.

Tsang, C.H., Chen, W.S., Li, K.T. and Zeng, Y.X., 2009. *A Progress Report on First Year Results of the Ba Xian Dong Archaeological Survey Research Project*, Taipei: Academia Sinica. (in Chinese)

Tsang, C.H., Chen, W.S., Li, K.T. and Zeng, Y.X., 2011. *Report of the Baxiandong Cave Sites, Changbin, Taidong County (The Second Year)*, Taipei: Academia Sinica. (in Chinese)

Tsang, C.H. and Li, K.T., 2018. *Archaeological Heritage in the Tainan Science Park of Taiwan; National Museum of Prehistory*, Taitung: National Museum of Prehistory.

Tsang, C.H., Li, K.T., Zeng, Y.X. and Chen, W.L., 2018. Baxiandong Archaeological Site. In *Selected Archaeological Reports in Taiwan*. Chen, K.T. ed., Taichung: Bureau of Cultural Heritage, Ministry of Culture, 1-52. (in Chinese)

Tsang, C.H., Li, K.T., Hsu, T.F., Tsai, Y.C., Fang, P.H. and Hsing, Y. I.C., 2017. Broomcorn and foxtail millet were cultivated in Taiwan about 5000 years ago. *Botanical Studies* 58, 1-10.

Tsang, C.H., Li, K.T. and Chu, C.Y., 2006. *Footprints of Ancestors: Archaeological Discoveries in Tainan Science-based Industrial Park*, Tainan: Tainan County Government. (in Chinese)

Weitzel, E.M. and Codding, B.F., 2022. The Ideal Distribution Model and Archaeological Settlement Patterning. *Environmental Archaeology* 27(4), 349-356. DOI: 10.1080/14614103.2020.1803015

Winterhalder, B., Kennett, D.J., Grote, M.N. and Bartruff, J., 2010. Ideal free settlement of California's northern Channel Islands. *Journal of Anthropological Archaeology* 29(4), 469-490.

Yu, P.L., 2022. At the Pacific edge and field's margin: Edible weeds, the Ideal Free Distribution, and Niche Construction in Neolithic Taiwan. In *Archaeology on the Threshold: Studies in the Processes of Change*. Wardle, J., Yu, P., Hitchcock, R.K., and Schmader, M. eds., Gainesville: University Press of Florida, 145-173.

Yu, P.L., 2021. Tempo and mode of Neolithic crop adoption by Paleolithic hunter-gatherers of Taiwan: Ethnoarchaeological and behavioral ecology perspectives. In *Hunter-Gatherers in Asia: From Prehistory to the Present*. Ikeya, K., and Nishiaki, Y. eds., Senri Ethnological Studies 106. Osaka: National Museum of Ethnography, 147-177.

Yu, P.L., 2020. Modeling Incipient Use of Neolithic Cultigens by Taiwanese Foragers: Perspectives from Niche Variation Theory, the Prey Choice Model, and the Ideal Free Distribution. *Quaternary* 4(3), 26-50.

Zeanah, D.W., Codding, B.F., Bliege Bird, R., and Bird, D.W., 2017. Mosaics of fire and water: The co-emergence of anthropogenic landscapes and intensive seed exploitation in the Australian arid zone. *Australian Archaeology* 83(1-2), 2-19.

Preliminary research on the formation and post-depositional processes in Amsa-dong Neolithic site, Seoul

Kiryong KIM[1], Kidong BAE[2]

[1] Senior Researcher, Mirae Institute of Cultural Heritage, Korea ; kiryong76@gmail.com
[2] Institute of East Asia Archaeology, Korea

ABSTRACT

The Amsa-dong site is one of the oldest Neolithic sites in the western part of the Korean Peninsula and is dated to about 4,000 BC. Since archaeological excavations in the 1960s, more than 40 Neolithic settlements have been discovered in sand layers of riverine terrace about 20m above mean sea level. C14 dates indicate the settlement lasted for more than 2,000 years. Comb-patterened pottery from the site changed from the most typical ones to the type of degenerated decoration, late type, partial and irregular pattern of incised decoration. Based on these evidences, it is generally believed that the settlement was continuously occupied without interruption. However, as the settlement was situated on fluvial terrace, it is highly probable that the settlement was damaged by floods and occupation was interrupted for a certain period of time. It is attempted to estimate the length of a single occupation at the site during the Neolithic Age by using hydrological data of the Han River during the last 100 years. Three different cycles of flood have been observed: Major in 125 years, medium in 30 years and minor in 12 years. The most serious one in the record is the one in 1925 when the site was exposed by flood for the first time. At that time, flooded water reached to the Namdaemun Gate in the downtown of Seoul. Subterranean houses were quite likely damaged totally by flood and people had to move away. Considering higher channel bed and poor control of flood in the Neolithic Age, it is quite likely that Neolithic village at the Amsadong was not permanent or long-lasting occupation, but evacuated and rebuilt by repetitive floods with probably shorter intervals than expected.

국문초록

서울 암사동 유적은 기원전 4,000년경의 신석기시대 유적으로 한반도에서 오래된 신석기시대 유적 중 하나다. 본 유적지는 한강 자연제방 위에 위치하고 있으며, 발굴된 거주공간과 토기들은 신석기시대 동안 약 2,000년 이상 장기간에 걸친 고고학적 증거들로 확인되고 있다. 암사동 유적이 위치한 범람원은 생활에 유리한 환경조건을 갖추고 있어 정착지를 이루었지만, 잦은 한강 홍수에 의해 정착지 훼손 양상이 반복되었다. 따라서 홍수 주기는 신석기시대 정착지의 점유기간과 관련될 것으로 추정된다. 고고학적 발굴 자료를 볼 때, 신석기시대 문화층은 두께가 두껍지 않고 중복된 주거지들이 확인되고 있어 유적지 내 점유기간은 길지 않았던 것으로 보인다. 그리고 후퇴적 과정에 의해 시기적으로 다른 유물들이 동일층 내에서 확인되었다. 한강홍수통제소의 1920년부터 기록된 수위와 홍수 자료를 보면 암사동 지역은 12년에서 30년 주기로 홍수가 발생했다. 이러한 홍수 주기는 신석기시대에도 마찬가지였을 것이며, 이에 따라 암사동 신석기인들은 정착지를 이동시켰을 것으로 추정된다. 이처럼 홍수로 인해 이동했다가 재정착하는 과정을 반복함으로써 유적지 점유기간은 길지 않았던 것으로 판단된다.

Keywords : Amsa-dong site, Han River, settlement, site formation process, post-deposits, flooding

1. Introduction

Amsa-dong site, located in the Han River basin in Seoul, is one of the oldest Neolithic sites in the Central West region of Korea. This site dates back to about 4,000 BC in the Early Neolithic period in the Korean Peninsula. Since archaeological excavations in the 1960s, more than 40 Neolithic settlements have been discovered in the sand layer (Kim, 1972; Im, 1985; National Museum of Korea, 1994, 1995, 1999; Cho et al., 2006; Song et al., 2007, 2008; Bae et al., 2018; Ahn et al., 2020).

Many settlements excavated from the Amsa-dong site formed a village in the area, but there are many negative views that the settlements were continuou during the Neolithic (Bae et al., 2018; Yoo, 2020; Hong, 2021; So, 2011). This area is where a major tributary joins the Han River, through which the river passes a narrow valley between Gangjang-dong in the north and the settlement in the Neolithic. Because of these topographical conditions, floods can directly affect the living area.

In the Neolithic, the settlement population preferred to be located in the flood plain for fishing. It is inevitable, however, that the settlement was moved in the temporary rainy season. The settlement was formed in an optimal location for subsistence and moved to other locations with regular flooding. The research preliminarily reviewed the movement and space arrangement of the village to examine sustainability and subsistence strategies in the Neolithic.

2. Neolithic settlements and geological characteristics at the Amsa-dong site

The Amsa-dong site is located at 37° 33′ latitude and 127° 10′ longitude in the central-west part of the Korean Peninsula (**Fig. 1**). Settlements form a cluster on a natural levee (about 20m wide and about 150m long) formed as a flood plain in the southern part of the Han River. The surroundings of the ruins are deposited with the Quaternary alluvial layer, and in Gwangjang-dong located in the north of the site, there is a hill with Precambrian banded gneiss and Jurassic granite as bedrock.

In the Amsa-dong site, more than 40 Neolithic settlements have been discovered, and the flat-form of the Neolithic houses with a hearth in the center is square in shape and circular in shape. The comb-pattern pottery patterns of the Amsa-dong site represent the early Neolithic culture of the Korean Peninsula (Han, 1978; Im, 1983; Lim, 2008; So, 2013), and most of the excavated artifacts are living tools such as pottery and stone tools. Grinding stones and large earthenware for processing and cooking plant resources such as acorns and walnuts were also discovered. A large

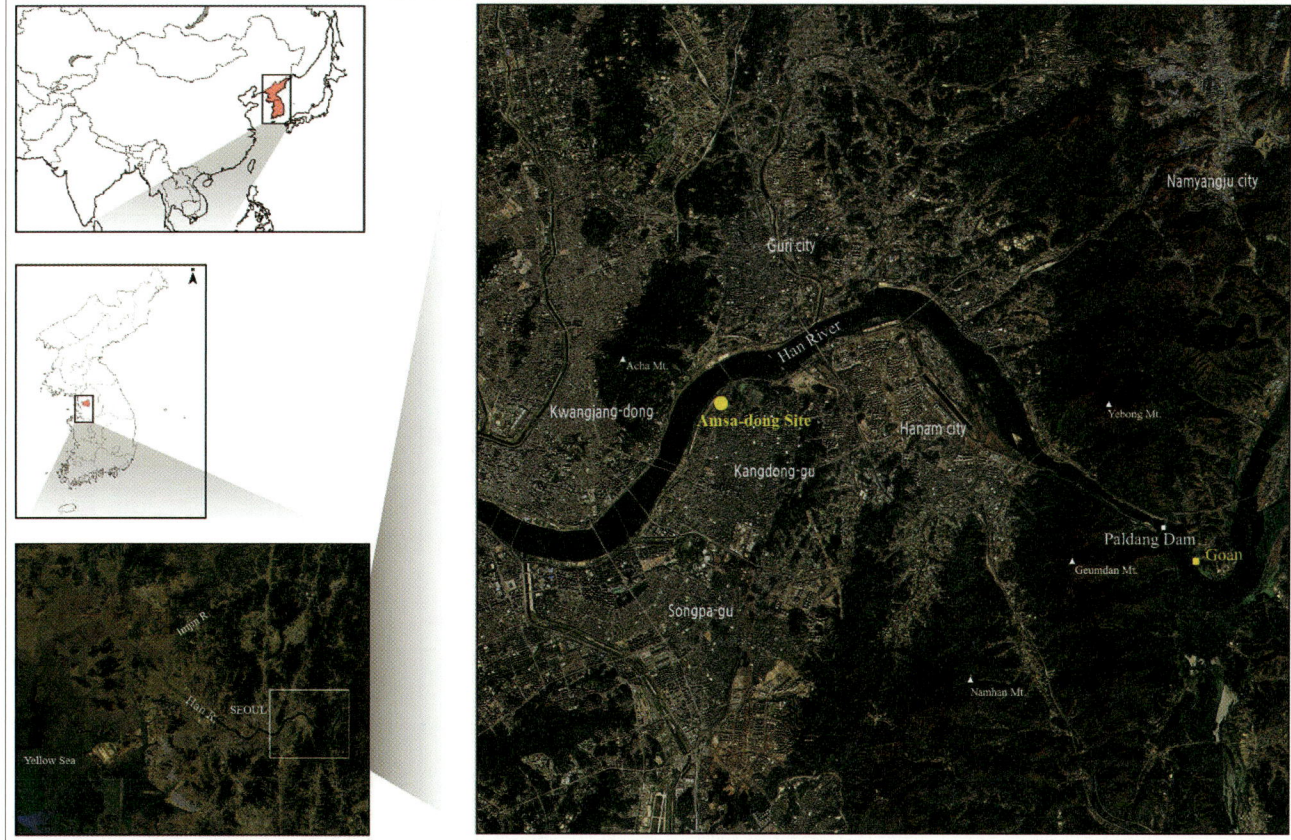

Fig. 1 Location of Amsa-dong site

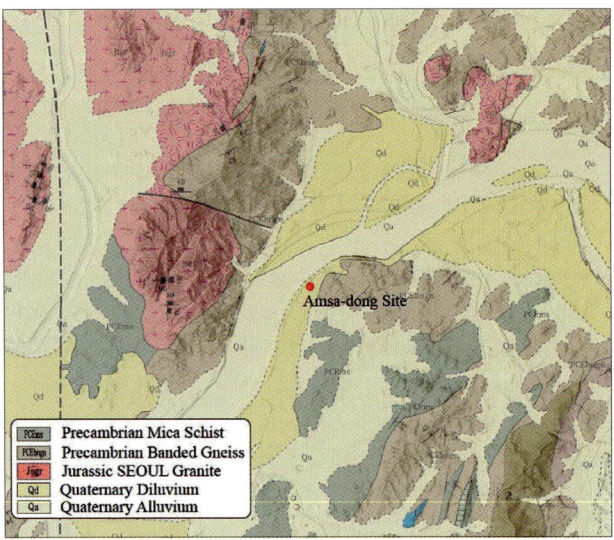

Fig. 2 Geological map around Amsa-dong site

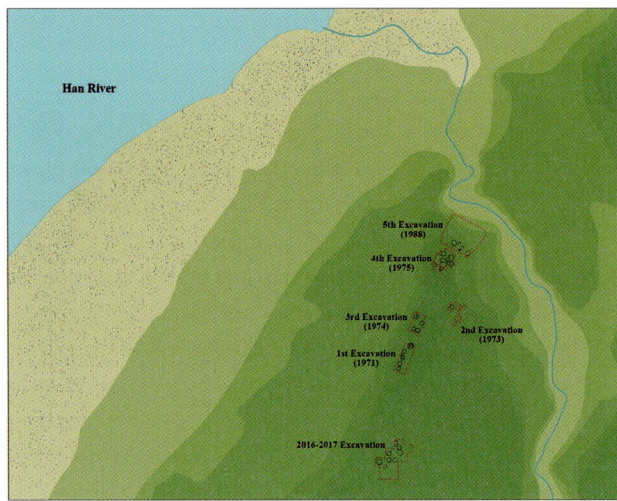

Fig. 3 Distribution map of the settlements in Amsa-dong site

※ The background map was modified and edited from the floor plan drawn during the excavation and topographical map in 1976 (edited).

Table 1 Radiocarbon dates in Amsa-dong site

Settlement Name (Year-Number)	Dates	Sample Source	Analysis Number (Lab No.)	References
1967-?	3,430 ± 250 BP	Charcoal	-	Kim, 1972
1974-5(84-1)	4,610 ± 200 BP	Charcoal	-	Song et al., 2008
1975-1	4,610 ± 70 BP	Charcoal	KCP-135	Song et al., 2008
1975-2	5,000 ± 70 BP	Charcoal	KAERI-189	Song et al., 2008
1975-4	4,730 ± 200 BP	Charcoal	-	Song et al., 2008
1975-10	4,660 ± 70 BP	Charcoal	KAERI-188	Song et al., 2008
1975-?	6,230 ± 110 BP	Charcoal	-	Kim, 1979
1975-?	6,050 ± 105 BP	Charcoal	-	Kim, 1979
2016-1	4,780 ± 30 BP	Charcoal	Beta-44116	Bae et al., 2018
2016-4	4,800 ± 30 BP	Charcoal	Beta-44115	Bae et al., 2018
2016-5	4,810 ± 30 BP	Charcoal	Beta-44117	Bae et al., 2018

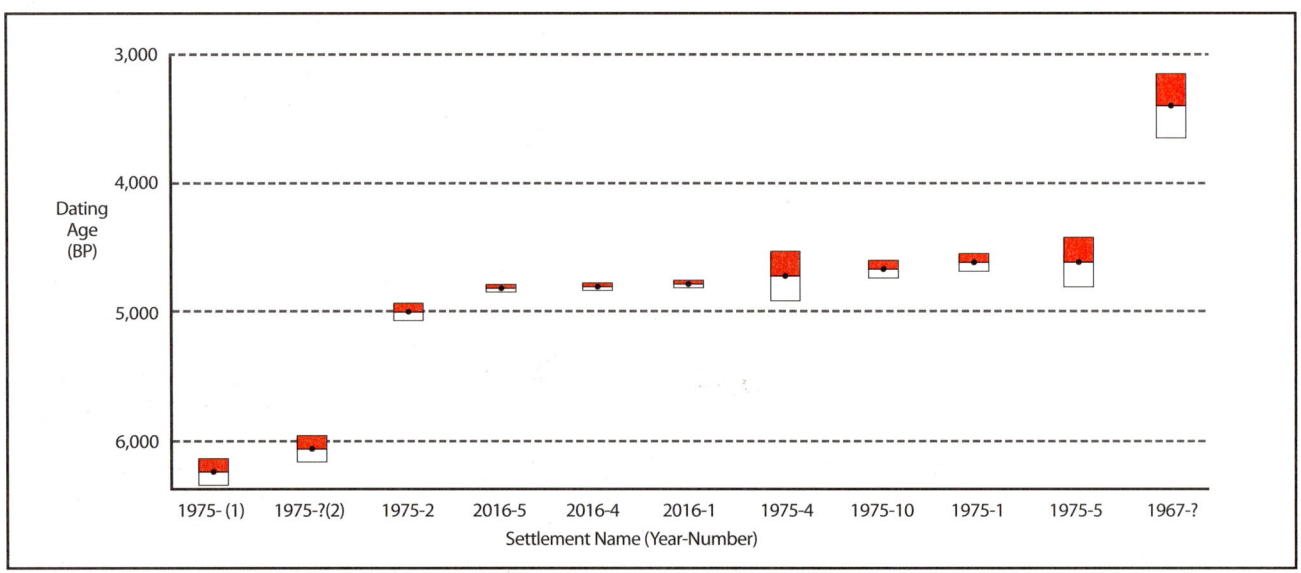

Fig. 4 Distribution of radiocarbon dates in Amsa-dong site

amount of fishing nets were found, which means that river resources were being provided from the Han River (Kim, 2007). In addition, one piece of jade jewelry as a ceremonial item was confirmed at the excavation in 2016 (Bae et al.,

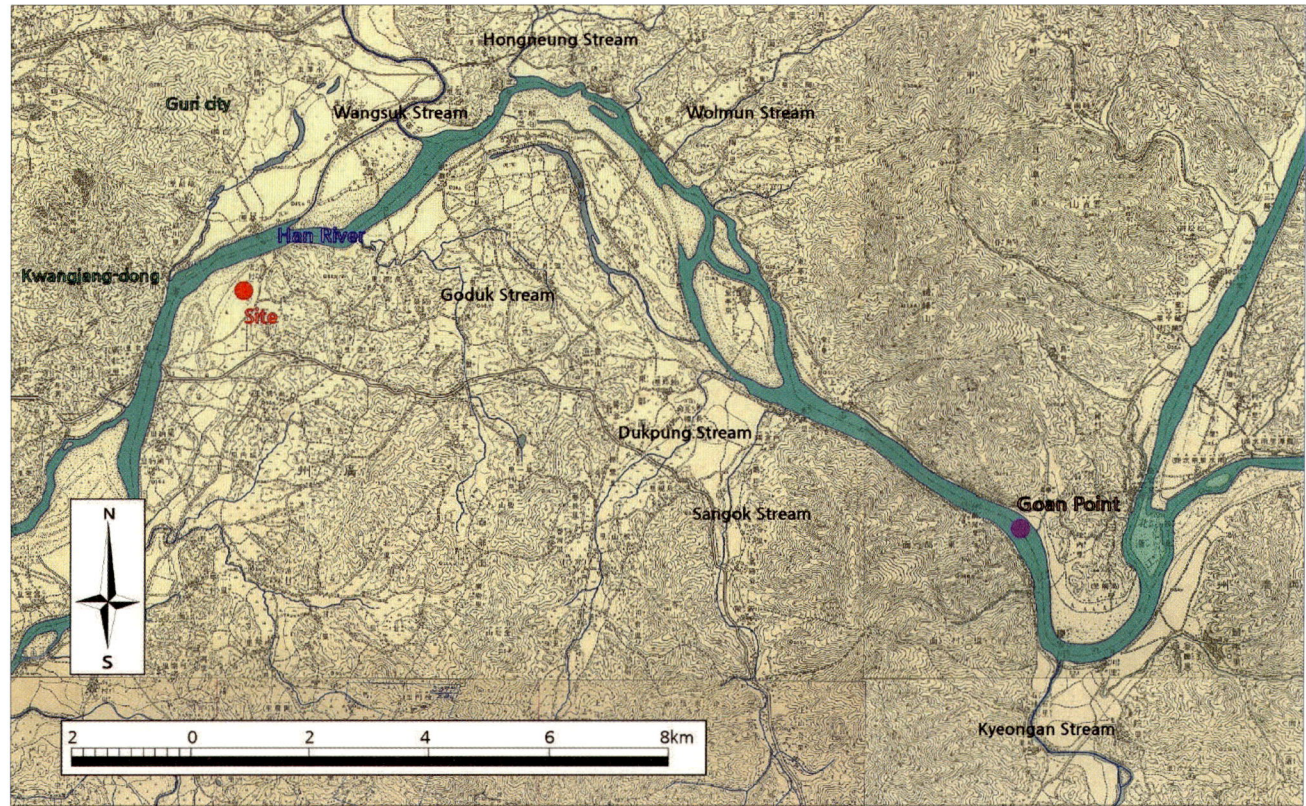

Fig. 5 Study area with the Han River and tributaries
※ The background map is topographical map in 1913

2018). According to the radiocarbon dates, the settlement was formed within 6,500–3,500 BP (Kim, 1972; Kim, 1977; National Museum of Korea, 1994; Bae et al., 2018). Looking at the correctable age, the center age is confirmed to be about 4,500 to 3,500 years ago (Bae et al., 2018).

The site was formed on the sedimentation after the mainstream of the Han River was changed to the Neolithic layer excavated 17.5–20.0m above sea level. Some overlapped houses in excavated areas of more than 40 Neolithic settlements provide possibility that the site had been repetitively used. It is 60km from Mt. Odusan at the mouth of the Han River, near the Yellow Sea, and 15km downstream from the merging point of two major tributaries in Yangsu-ri. Han River was merged by several tributaries upstream from the Amsa-dong site and abraded in much wider and flat plain from the Amsa-dong site. In this region, branches of the Han River flow together including Wangsuk stream, Kyengan stream and Goduk stream between Paldang and Amsa-dong site and passed within valley in the Kwangjang-dong and Amsa-dong (**Fig. 1** and **Fig. 5**).

Regression of stream channels from this area was probably caused by minor climate changes during the Early Holocene (Hwang, 1998; So, 2011; Yoo, 2020). However, settling down with a deep channel bottom at the other side of the river would also be one of the major factors leaving an ancient flood plain in this area without further fluvial actions, which would be very suitable for a fishing village in the Early Neolithic period.

However, the Han River's regular flooding has a major impact, especially in this floodplain where the Amsadong settlements are located. It is assumed that flooding happened more often in the Neolithic due to poor flood control. The cycle of flooding may be related to the occupation period of the settlement, and this research examined this cycle (**Fig. 2, 3**).

3. Methods and analysis

The Neolithic topography of the Amsadong site would have been very different from current condition (Lee, 1972; So, 2011). The Han River joins a tributary upstream of Amsa-dong and its flow increases. This characteristic is that the riverbed, flow path, and flow velocity frequently change due to the influence of floods, and the terrain can change frequently.

In a certain location, the main cause of flooding would be the amount of rainfall and topographical condition. In order to calculate the rate of flow in a certain location in a river, various conditions should be considered. This research focuses on the influence on the Amsa-dong topographical condition by the change of water level in the relation between the amount of rainfall in a certain period and a

Table 2. Data on Past flood water level at the Goan point before 1973 (Yi et al., 1995 [table 2] editing)

Date	Measured Water Level(m)	Radio of Flood (cms)	Reduced Water Level(m)	Date	Measured Water Level(m)	Radio of Flood (cms)	Reduced Water Level(m)
Sep. 5. 1917	7.62	7,400	4.25	Sep. 4. 1940	13.58	23,100	11.44
Aug. 17. 1918	9.45	12,100	6.77	Jul. 12. 1946	6.65	5,300	2.94
Jul. 7. 1919	11.08	16,600	8.83	Aug 8. 7. 1947	10.46	14,900	8.08
Jul. 8. 1920	13.56	23,100	11.44	Jul. 29. 1954	9.02	10,860	6.14
Jul. 7. 1921	8.65	9,900	5.64	Jul. 4. 1955	8.28	9,020	5.17
Jul. 30. 1922	12.75	21,000	10.63	Jul. 16. 1956	9.95	13,350	7.37
Aug. 2. 1923	9.47	12,200	6.81	Jul. 18. 1957	7.76	7,720	4.44
Jul. 25. 1924	10.50	15,000	8.13	Sep. 6. 1958	11.40	17,500	9.22
Jul. 18. 1925	19.38	37,000	16.09	Sep. 1. 1959	11.12	16,760	8.90
Aug. 6. 1926	11.05	16,500	8.79	Jun. 29. 1960	8.20	8,700	4.99
Jul. 15. 1927	10.24	14,200	7.76	Jul. 13. 1961	7.00	5,800	3.27
Sep. 16. 1928	6.79	5,580	3.13	Sep. 8. 1962	8.60	9,800	5.59
Aug. 18. 1929	6.60	5,100	2.81	Jul. 18. 1963	10.44	14,760	8.02
Jul. 14. 1930	12.20	19,700	10.12	Aug. 12. 1964	10.12	13,860	7.60
Aug. 20. 1931	9.00	10,800	6.11	Jul. 16. 1965	15.27	27,000	12.85
Aug. 31. 1932	10.28	14,300	7.81	Jul. 26. 1966	14.42	25,100	12.17
Jul. 30. 1933	9.37	11,900	6.67	Jul. 20. 1967	8.12	8,500	4.88
Jul. 24. 1934	9.10	11,100	6.27	Aug. 24. 1968	8.20	8,700	4.99
Jul. 23. 1935	12.70	20,900	10.60	Jul. 31. 1969	11.30	17,300	9.13
Aug. 12. 1936	14.55	25,500	12.32	Sep. 18. 1970	10.97	16,210	8.66
Jul. 20. 1937	9.03	10,900	10.60	Aug. 12. 1971	8.30	9,100	5.21
Sep. 5. 1938	8.15	8,600	4.94	Aug. 19. 1972	15.94	29,000	13.53
May. 13. 1939	3.50	1,100	-0.29				

[■ : Date of flood in Amsa-dong]

Table 3. Estimation of cycle period for Probable Flood using past flood data (Lee et al. 1995 [Table 8] editing)

Reference Value 23,000(cms)				Reference Value 25,000(cms)			
Year	Ranking	Flow(cms)	Repeat Cycle(year)	Year	Ranking	Flow(cms)	Repeat Cycle(year)
1925	1	37,000	125	1925	1	37,000	126
1984	2	30,130	48	1984	2	30,130	49
1972	3	29,000	30	1972	3	29,000	30
1990	4	28,693	22	1990	4	28,693	22
1965	5	27,000	17	1965	5	27,000	17
1936	6	25,500	14	1936	6	25,500	14
1966	7	25,100	12	1966	7	25,100	12
1920	8	23,100	10	1920	8	23,100	10
1940	9	23,100	10	1940	9	23,100	10
1978	10	19,840	7	1978	10	19,840	7
1976	11	17,880	6	1976	11	17,880	6
1958	12	17,500	5	1958	12	17,500	6

water level in a certain location.

Accordingly, considering the water level and flooding in the past, the research intends to estimate the flooding damage in Amsa-dong in the Neolithic. Perhaps it is possible to estimate flooding in the Neolithic with recent flooding data (Table 1).

Flooding is different depending on hydrological and topographical factors. The research takes advantage of the hydrological data measured in Goan, where Neungnae-ri, Wabu-myeng, and Namyangju are located (Fig. 5), and the data are compared with the flooding in Amsa-dong. With Yi 's data (Yi et al., 1995), a different approach is necessary to estimate the amount of flooding in a certain location.

4. A flood cycle in Amsa-dong site

The scale of the Han River is 23,608km² excluding the Imjin River, Jungrang stream, and Anyang stream. The gauge attitude of Goan location is 8.975m and the flooding level is 6.5m above sea level. The amount of flood water from the Goan location is divided into Paldang Dam construction and the research used the converted data.

In fact, it is necessary to consider the branches of the Han River, but the data is made after the Paldang Dam construction in 1973. The other consideration is increase of water in Amsa-dong because branches flow together. Although variable of the flooding cycle is scale of the cross section and structure of Amsa-dong, the water level could be higher than Goan location in the case of temporary rainfall.

According to the hydrological data about the water amount and cycle of flooding, the greatest flood in 1925 is 37,000cms and cycle is 125 years, and the minor flood is in 1966 and cycle is 12 years. Considering the amount of flooding water in Goan location, the flood happened more than 25,000cms and cycle is 12 years. According to the record in 1972, the cycle is 30years. In addition, the cycle of the great flood is estimated by 125 years. Some locations could be damaged by even the flood in minor cycle. Considering descent of the riverbed by aggregate picking in modern time, it can be expected that flooding had damaged more often in the Prehistoric period.

5. Conclusion: Human migration at the Amsa-dong site

This research focuses on the possibility and cycle of flood for sustainability of the Neolithic settlement in Amsa-dong. In addition, the research examines the movement cycle of the settlement by overlapping Neolithic houses.

In this preliminary research, Amsa-dong is vulnerable to change of the Han River and topography was often changed. As a result, the houses located in flood level could not be avoid damage by flooding. The excavated Neolithic houses in Amsa-dong are located between 17.5–20.0m above sea level. It is true that most of housed had been influenced by flood. As shown in Table 2, modern flooding data also reveal the fact of periodic flooding. Considering the fact that the influence of flood is profounder in the Neolithic, flood had damaged more often than now. In other words, the flow direction of the Han River in Amsa-dong was changed very often.

The current excavation data also shows transformation of topography in Amsa-dong. It is possible to estimate the topographical change model caused by Neolithic floods in that layers of sand were repeatedly deposited, and the direction of deposition was formed by flooding. Although Neolithic houses are overlapped and the date are slightly different, it provides sound ground of flooding damage that longstanding deposited layer is not discovered. It can take advantage for subsistence that the Neolithic settlement is located river basin and it is why the topography is used repeatedly. However, the topography of the reformed settlement also caused the damage by flooding.

The recent archaeological excavation data indicates that the occupation period is not long. According to current data about flooding level, the cycle of flood is from 12 years to 30 years and the movement by flooding can be happened considering the higher riverbed and poor water control in the past.

Perhaps, the temporary rainfall caused the movement of settlement in Neolithic. It is difficult to clearly explain the migration of residents at that time due to the lack of data to investigate past changes in the Han River. However, it is possible to consider the possibility that the Neolithic settlement of Amsa-dong site was repeatedly occupied for a shorter period than generally thought due to the site formation and post-depositional processes causde by flooding.

References

Ahn S.W., Lee H.J., Kim K.R., 2020. *Excavation Report of Seoul Amsadong Site–2018 Excavation Report–*, Seoul: Gangdong-gu and Hanyang University Museum. (in Korean)

Bae K.D., Kim K.R., Lee S.H., 2018. *A Report of Excavation on Amsa site in Seoul–Excavation 2016-2017*, Ansan: Gangdong-gu and the Institute of Cultural Properties in Hanyang University . (in Korean)

Cho H.J., Lee J.H., Yang S.H., Yoo S.N., Chu M., Jeong D., 2006. *Excavation Report of the AMSA-DONG Site 3*, Seoul: National Museum of Korea. (in Korean)

Han Y.H., 1978. The Neolithic culture of central-western Korea: With an emphasis on the pottery chronology. *Journal of the Korean Archaeological Society* 14·15, 17-108. (in Korean)

Hong E.K., 2021., A Speculation on the Temporal Horizon of Amsa-dong Site. *Archeology: Journal of the Jungbu Archaeological Society* 20, 5-28. (in Korean with English abstract)

Hwang S.I., 1998. The Holocene Depositional Environment and Sea-Level Change at Ilsan Area. *Journal of Korean Geographical Society* 33, 143-163. (in Korean with English abstract)

Im H.J., 1983. The Comb-pattern Pottery Cultures in West Shoreline Areas. *Journal of the Korean Archaeological Society* 14·15, 1-18. (in Korean)

Im H.J., 1985. *Amsadong–A Neolithic Village Site on the Han River–*, Seoul: The Museum of Seoul National University. (in Korean)

Kim J.H., 1972. *Archeology in Korea*, Tokyo: Kawade Shobo Shinsha. (in Japanese)

Kim J.S., 2007. Position of Amsa-dong Prehistoric Settlement from the Social Aspect. *Journal of the Korean Prehistoric Archaeological Society* 20, 13-29. (in Korean with English abstract)

Kim W.Y., 1977. *Introduction to Korean Archeology*, Seoul: Iljisa press. (in Korean)

Lee M.C., 1972. Flood and Flood Adjustments to the Han River. *Journal of Korean Geographical Society* 7, 24-39. (in Korean with English abstract)

Lim S.T., 2008. Investigations of the Establishment of Neolithic Pottery Chronology at Central-Western Korea: Historical Perspective. *Archeology: Journal of the Jungbu Archaeological Society* 7, 5-21. (in Korean with English abstract)

NMK. 1994. *Excavation report of the Amsa-dong site I*, Seoul: National Museum of Korea. (in Korean)

NMK. 1995. *Excavation report of the Amsa-dong site*, Seoul: National Museum of Korea. (in Korean)

NMK. 1999. *Excavation report of the Amsa-dong site II*, Seoul: National Museum of Korea. (in Korean with English abstract)

So S.Y., 2011. Changes in the Holocene Environmental and the Location of Neolithic Sites in Central-Western Korea. *Journal of the Korean Neolithic Society* 21, 1-42. (in Korean with English abstract)

So S.Y., 2013. A Study of the Neolithic Chronology of Central-Western Korea through the Use of Radiocarbon Analysis. *Journal of the Korean Archaeological Society* 89, 4-47. (in Korean with English abstract)

Song E.J., Yoon H.W., Kim H.J., 2007. *Excavation Report of the Amsa-dong Site 4*, Seoul: National Museum of Korea. (in Korean with English abstract)

Song E.J., Yoon H.W., Kim H.J., 2008. *Amsa dong Site 5*, Seoul: National Museum of Korea. (in Korean with English abstract)

Yi S.J., Seo K.W., Heo J.H., Cho W.C., 1995. Conversion of Flood Level and Flood Frequency Analysis for Goan Station in Han River. *Journal of Korea Water Resources Association* 28, 191-204. (in Korean with English abstract)

Yoo S.H., 2020. *A Study on the Changing Patterns of Spatial Distribution in Amsa-dong Site Focusing on the Topographic Change of the Neolithic and the Three Kingdom Period*. Dissertation of Ph.M. of Hanyang University. (in Korean with English abstract)

A reconsideration of the chronology of the Bangudae petroglyphs in prehistoric Korea

Bong Won KANG

Professor Emeritus, Gyeongju University, Korea; bongwonkang@naver.com

ABSTRACT

The major purpose of this article is to argue that the chronology of the Bangudae petroglyphs should be dated to the "Neolithic" and that the people who engraved this rock art engaged in whaling. The researchers who discovered and reported this rock art put forward that it was engraved sometime between the Korean Neolithic and Bronze Age. Wonyong Kim (1980), a pioneering Korean archaeologist, however, formulated a completely different date of the rock art. He asserted that the date should be sometime between the Korean Bronze and Early Iron Ages (BC 300 - 100 AD). A Korean National History textbook adopted Kim's chronology without caution. Consequently, most Korean high school students have been significantly influenced by this date.

This chronology has been playing a critical role in Korean archaeological and historical societies. Some Korean rock art researchers have been arguing that people responsible for the rock art were unable to practice whale hunting. They interpret that whale bones discovered at Neolithic shell midden sites are byproducts of collecting and butchering stranded whales. In contrast, there are many other rock art researchers who deny the date generated by Kim. Newly discovered whale bones and whaling tools at many Neolithic shell midden sites convinced these researchers to argue that the rock art may have been created during the Korean Neolithic (ca. 4000-3000 BC). They also assert that whaling was part of Korean Neolithic people's subsistence economies. This paper focuses on three other issues as well. First, although Kim and his followers have argued that this rock art was engraved with iron tools, there is a high possibility that stone tools may have been used to create them. Second, although Kim interpreted the image on top of a whale to be an iron arrowhead, it may be a harpoon. Third, the image placed in the right-hand side of the harpooned whale may not be a crossbow but a float. A few crossbows were excavated in association with many exotic artifacts in Pyeongyang North Korea. It is also pointed out that although many archaeological excavations have been conducted in and in the vicinity of Ulsan where the Bangudae petroglyphs are located, not a single crossbow has been reported so far. Considering this archaeological context, a crossbow was not the material that whalers were capable of possessing.

국문초록

본고는 기존 연구에서 반구대 암각화를 청동기-초기 철기시대로 편년하면서 판독하였던 세 가지에 초점을 맞추어 검토하였다. 첫째, 반구대 암각화가 철제 도구로 제작되었다는 것에 대해서 경도가 강한 돌로도 제작 가능하다는 점을 거론하였다. 둘째, 고래 등에 얹힌 형상을 미늘 있는 철제 화살촉으로 판독한 것에 대해 골제 작살일 가능성이 높다는 점을 강조하였다. 이에 대한 고고학적 증거로서 울산 황성동 유적에서 출토된 작살 맞은 고래뼈를 제시하였다. 셋째, 이 철촉은 그 옆에 있는 형상을 중국 전국시대 혹은 한나라 쇠뇌로 판독하고 거기에서 발사된 것이라고 주장한 것에 대해 이것은 쇠뇌가 아니라 고래사냥 때 사용한 부구(浮具)로 보아야 한다고 해석하였다. 특히, 고고학적 맥락에서 쇠뇌는 화려한 유물들과 공반되어 출토된다는 측면에서 신분지위가 높은 사람들이 소유하였던 물건으로 고래잡이가 소유할 수 있는 물건이 아니라는 견해를 제시하였다. 아울러 이러한 종류의 쇠뇌는 울산 및 인근 지역에서 현재까지 한 점도 발견되지 않았다는 점도 지적하였다. 따라서 반구대 암각화의 최초 조성시기는 신석기시대로 편년되어야 하고 이를 제작한 주민들이 고래사냥을 수행했다고 해석된다.

Keywords : Bangudae petroglyphs, Ulsan, Korea, Neolithic, whaling

1. Introduction

This paper argues that it is necessary to reconsider the chronometric chronology of the Bangudae petroglyphs, located at Ulsan in the southeastern part of Korea. The petroglyphs are composed of aquatic and terrestrial animals, such as whale, sea lion, turtle, deer, tiger, weasel, and boar. In addition, a possible shaman, hunting scenes of whales and terrestrial animals, and hunters, a mask, boats, and either a harpoon/iron arrowhead or a crossbow/float have also been recognized (Fig. 1). It is well known that the Bangudae petroglyphs were superimposed over time and at least four or five different strata have been identified so far. Thus, each layer should be differently dated. The chronology of this rock panel has been a debated research topic among Korean archaeologists and art historians. Yet, the whales and whaling scenes depicted in the rock panel have been considered as the earliest motifs according to the stratigraphy of the rock panel. There is a general consensus about the strata at least.

Overall, there are two pivotal groups about the chronology of the rock panel: one Neolithic, the other Bronze Age. This paper argues that as long as the whaling scenes and whale motifs are concerned, they should be dated to the Neolithic rather than the Bronze Age considering the entire Korean archaeological context. The Bangudae petroglyphs were discovered by three, then-young researchers – Yung-jo Lee, Jung-bae Kim, and Myeong-dae Moon – on Christmas Eve 1971. The discovery was not made by accident but by an enthusiastic field survey conducted by the three energetic and ambitious researchers. This rock art site was the second one identified in the entire Korean Peninsula. The petroglyphs have been playing a critical role for the study of Korean rock art in specific and Korean prehistoric studies in general. Since then a great number of researchers became interested in Korean rock art and so many more rock art sites have been identified in many different places in Korea. A number of articles and books related to Korean rock art one way or another have been published so far. Thus the academic endeavors carried out by the three scholars should be highly appreciated for years to come.

Shortly after this rock art was discovered, it was dated to the Neolithic (Moon, 1973; Hwang and Moon, 1984). However, the rock art was dated to sometime between the Late Korean Bronze Age and Early Iron Age by the pioneering Korean archaeologist Won-yong Kim in 1980. After his paper was published, many Korean history and archaeology textbooks, including Korean National History text books, have been adopting his chronological point-of-view up until today. Although some researchers put forward an idea that the Bangudae petroglyphs must have been engraved much earlier than Kim's chronology, not many people paid attention to the different perspective.

Recently, however, some researchers have been beginning to raise questions about the chronology determined by Kim (1980) based on different archaeological perspectives as well as newly discovered material evidence, such as whale bones, a pot sherd on which a deer is incised, and dug out wooden boat planks (Jeon, 2013). In particular, a couple of harpooned whale bones discovered in the Neolithic site approximately 22km east away from the Bangudae petroglyphs have made a big contribution to speculate the old chronology (Ha, 2013; Kang, 2020, 2022; Ma, 2010). Based on these kinds of archaeological evidence, some researchers have been arguing that Korean Neolithic people may have hunted whales and they were the people who

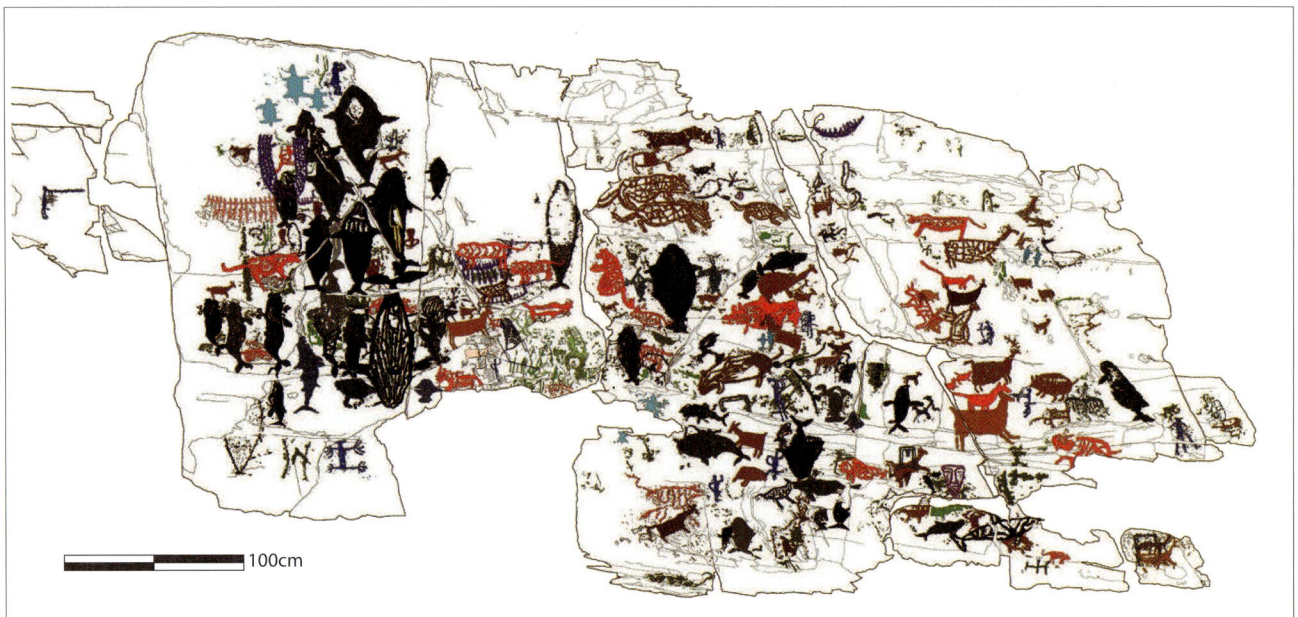

Fig. 1 The Bangudae petroglyphs (Bangudae Petroglyphs Institute, Ulsan University, 2020:75).

engraved the Bangudae petroglyphs.

In spite of the fact, many Korean archaeologists and historians are still not convinced by the newly discovered material evidence as well as a different chronology put forward by some other researchers. As a consequence, some researchers have been still arguing that the Bangudae petroglyphs were engraved by the Korean Bronze Age people (Jang, 2001; Im, 2003; Kim, 2013, 2015, 2021; Kim, 2015). Since some are still assuming that the Bangudae petroglyphs were engraved with sharp metal objects, it is hard, if not impossible, to reevaluate the old chronology. By utilizing some new material evidence discovered in and in the vicinity of the Bangudae petroglyphs, different interpretations about some images, and overall Korean archaeological contexts, this paper reevaluates the old chronology and generates a different chronology.

2. The background for the chronology of the Bangudae petroglyphs

It should be emphasized that the very first thing that we have to do with dating is closely related to "what the motifs appearing on the rock panel are." In fact, it is important to interpret any kind of archaeological material/feature that we come across in the field. Because logically it is a starting point to begin conducting research on the phenomenon of interest. Regardless it is an artifact, archaeological feature, character, symbol or different kinds of art, we have to interpret 'what it is' in the first place. In this sense, it is quite critical to accurately interpret some of the motifs depicted in the Bangudae petroglyphs. This paper focuses on the two questionable images and whaling in conjunction with a different perspective of the date of the rock art.

Especially the two motifs which have been playing a critical role for the determination of the rock panel will be discussed in detail. First, we have to interpret the motif which is located on the very right side of a whale. Second, it is also important to interpret the motif which appears on top of a whale. Kim (1980, 1995) regarded the two motifs as a crossbow and a barbed iron arrowhead which was shot from the crossbow. Unfortunately, based on their physical appearance alone, we do not exactly know if they are really a crossbow and a barbed arrowhead. On the basis of this assumption in terms of the material type (i.e., either bronze or iron) of the two motifs as well as the motifs themselves (i.e., crossbow and arrowhead respectively), Kim (1980, 1995) dated the entire rock panel to between the Late Bronze Age and early Iron Age (see below for details). There are many Korean researchers who have been supporting Kim's chronology of the Bangudae petroglyphs. As a result, the chronology of the rock art was determined significantly younger than

Fig. 2 The controversial images: either crossbow or float or iron arrowhead or harpoon.

Fig. 3 Bronze arrowheads and gilt bronze bells associated with crossbows excavated from Seokam-li cemetery, burial numbers 9 and 219 (National Museum of Korea, 2001: 49, 56).

many Korean rock art researchers have been considering.

In the meantime, some other Korean researchers have been arguing that the motif should not be regarded as a 'crossbow' but a 'float' that may have been used when prehistoric people were whaling (Lee, 2004, 2015; Ha, 2012; Kang, 2020, 2022). Although we cannot rule out the possibility that the depicted motif on top of the whale is a barbed iron arrowhead, it is highly likely that it was either a bone harpoon or an obsidian arrowhead. With this debating research topic, to better understand the date of the Bangudae petroglyphs, this paper examines the two controversial motifs from archaeological and/or anthropological context.

Kim (1980, 1995) regarded the motif depicted on top of a whale not as a harpoon, but as a barbed arrowhead (**Fig. 2**). Kim (1980) also made an assumption that the motif located next to the whale hit by an iron arrowhead was a crossbow manufactured and used by the warriors during Chin (秦) and Han (漢) dynasties in China (**Fig. 3**) (Kim, 1980). He treated them as a set piece in association with whale hunting. Thus, he came to a conclusion that the whale hunting scenes, the whale motifs appearing in the rock panel, and the entire Bangudae petroglyphs were engraved sometime between 300 BC to AD 100 (Kim, 1980).

This interpretation has been causing a lot of problems in terms of the date of the Bangudae petroglyph. One of the biggest problems with the date is that Kim (1980) did not take into consideration overall archaeological context in conjunction with a crossbow as well as an iron arrowhead and whaling at all. He simply paid attention to interpret the motif itself and regarded the two images as if they were a crossbow by its physical appearance alone. That is, he made an assumption about the two motifs without presenting any other convincing material evidence and/or archaeological context. As a consequence, the majority of Korean historians and archaeologists accepted the chronology of Bangudae rock art generated by Kim (1980, 1995) without any further questions. This chronology has not been reconsidered for a little more than 40 years.

In particular, Kim (1980) emphasized the importance of crossbow heavily used by Chin and Han Chinese army when they were engaged in war. Since the northwestern part of Korean Peninsula was occupied by the Lelang Commandery for a little over 400 years (108 BC to AD 313), he assumed that local indigenous people in the southern part of Korean Peninsula were also influenced by Han Chinese culture as well. All the historical interpretation made by Kim (1980) is correct except for diffusion of crossbows. Thus, it is hard, if not impossible, accept that indigenous Korean people also commonly used a crossbow from the archaeological and historical perspectives.

The chronology of the Bangudae petroglyphs established by Kim (1980, 1995) has been effective up until today and a great number of scholars have been supporting it without raising a question (Jang, 2001; Im, 2003; Kim, 2013, 2015, 2021; Kim, 2015). Moreover, Korean National History textbook also has been adopting the date for more than 30 years. It also should be pointed out that some Korean researchers consciously or unconsciously have modified the original chronology generated by Kim (1980) (i.e., the Late Bronze Age or the Early Iron Age) to "the Bronze Age," without presenting any archaeological evidence and/or explanations. Although this is an important issue which requires a further examination, this paper is beyond the scope of the topic.

Meanwhile, some Korean archaeologists began to come up with different ideas about the conventional chronology about the Bangudae petroglyphs. This group of people, including myself, argues that the Bangudae rock art was much older than the Late Bronze Age and it may have been engraved during the early-middle Korean Neolithic period (approximately 5,000 BC) (Lee, 2015).

In order to support their idea they put forward different interpretations about the two images and archaeological evidence. First, they interpret the arrowhead looking motif not as an iron arrowhead but as either a bone harpoon (Ha, 2012, 2013) or an obsidian arrowhead (Jeon, 2013), since some of these kinds of artifacts have been recovered from the Neolithic archaeological sites located 22km east away from the Bangudae petroglyphs (Ma 2010: 122). In particular, many researchers have different interpretations about the motif interpreted as a crossbow in the past by Kim (1980). They consider the motif not as a crossbow but a float that may have been used by prehistoric whalers when they were trying to hunt whales (Jeong, 1996; Jang, 1997; Lee, 2004). At least four more of the motif have been detected in the Bangudae petroglyphs (Lee, 2004, 2015).

3. Interpretation of the motifs : From an archaeological context

It is very important to interpret some of the images in which we are interested. As was mentioned above, although Kim (1980) interpreted the two images depicted near a whale as a crossbow and an embedded barbed iron arrowhead appearing on top of the whale, some researchers put forward a different opinion about them. They have been arguing that it is not a iron arrowhead but a bone harpoon. They also continue to argue that the other image is not a crossbow but a float that might have been used by whalers. In fact, it is not certain whether the two images are a bone harpoon and a float respectively. There is no way of precisely interpreting the two motifs. However, we can take into consideration some other indirect archaeological evidence to interpret the motifs. By examining the archaeological context in association with a crossbow, it is possible to solve the research questions.

There are a few archaeological features that yielded crossbows in North Korea. This archaeological site, located in Pyeongyang North Korea, was a cemetery area. Between 1916 and 1942, Japanese researchers excavated a great number of burials at the site and recovered a tremendous number of artifacts from them. Crossbows were recovered from Seokam-li burial numbers 9 and 219, and Jeongbaek-li burial number 8 respectively (National Museum of Korea 2001: 49) (see **Fig. 3**). Since Pyeongyang once was the central part of the Lelang commandery, some of the owners of the burials may have been Han Chinese government officials who possessed a high status in terms of socio-economics as well as politics.

The entire artifact assemblages in association with the crossbow in both Seokam-li burial number 219 and Jeongbaek-li burial number 8 are brilliant. Especially in the case of Seokam-li No. 9 burial, it is the largest one in terms

Fig. 4 Gold buckle associated with crossbow excavated from Seokam-li Burial No. 9 (National Museum of Korea, 2001:64).

Fig. 5 Gilt bronze crossbow and bronze halberd and its scabbard excavated from Yongejon-li burial, Yeongcheon (Gyeongju National Museum, 2007 : ii-iii).

of the tomb scale. In addition, the quantity and quality of the grave goods recovered from the burial are also superior to any other burials excavated in the Pyeongyang area. The crossbow recovered from the burial was associated with the masterpiece of gold buckle which was designated as Korean National Treasure (then No. 98) (**Fig. 4**). Other than these burials, we do not have many archaeological examples of a crossbow in North Korea.

On the other hand, a gilt bronze crossbow was recovered for the very first time in the vicinity of a wooden coffin tomb in Yongjeon-li, Yeongcheon located in the southeastern part of Korea (Gyeongju National Museum, 2007) (**Fig. 5**). At this site only one wooden coffin tomb was detected and a crossbow was not recovered from the inside but outside and in the immediate vicinity of the main burial. However, according to the archaeological context and investigators who conducted the expedition, it is not unreasonable to consider this crossbow was associated with other artifacts discovered inside of the wooden coffin tomb, particularly because the tomb was the only one in the area (Gyeongju National Museum, 2007). The grave goods recovered from the burial are such as mirrors, spearhead, scabbard, bells, antenna type dagger pommel ornament all made of bronze, and axes, spearheads, halberds, bits, chisel, bell, pommel made of iron, Wuzhu Han Chinese coins (五銖錢), and a few glass beads (Gyeongju National Museum, 2007).

Although some bronze arrowheads that may have been used with a crossbow were recovered from many different archaeological sites in Korea such as Gangwon and Gyeonggi Provinces, Sinchang-dong Gwangju, Gujeong-dong Gyeongju, Neuk-do Island South Gyeongsang Province, and Samyang-dong Jeju Island, Yongjeon-dong is the very first site where a crossbow was discovered in the southern half of the Korean Peninsula (Gyeongju National Museum, 2007).

On the other hand, though a great number of rescue archaeological excavations have been conducted Ulsan area since the 1980s, neither a crossbow nor a single bronze arrowhead has been discovered yet in Ulsan area including the area in which the Bangudae petroglyphs is located. This archaeological context indicates that a crossbow was a valuable material and it was definitely associated with exotic grave goods. The person who possessed a crossbow must have had one of the highest positions in the society. Thus, it is hard, if not impossible, to accept the interpretation (i.e., "…. it may have been used by whale hunters") made by Kim (1980) and his chronology without a caution. As a consequence, the chronology of the Bangudae petroglyphs generated based on the assumption of the presence of a crossbow and a barbed iron arrowhead in the rock panel needs to be seriously reexamined and it is necessary to reconsider the chronology from the very beginning. As mentioned above, that is why it is critical to precisely interpret the motifs engraved on the Bangudae petroglyphs which is the phenomenon of interest in the first place.

Some other archaeological artifacts recovered in the Ulsan area where the Bangudae petroglyphs are situated will play an important role for the determination of the chronology of the rock panel as well. So far, over 10,000 semi-subterranean pithouses with various kinds of artifacts dated to the Bronze Age have been recovered in the vicinity of the Bangudae petroglyphs and in Ulsan region. It should be noted that neither a single crossbow nor a bronze or iron arrowhead has been discovered since large-scale archaeological expeditions have been conducted from the middle of 1980s. Furthermore, neither whaling gears nor whale bones has been reported from those Bronze Age pithouses. The majority of artifacts discovered from the pithouses are pottery, clay net sinkers, and polished stone artifacts, such as arrowheads, daggers, whetstones, spearheads, chisels, mortars, grooved stone adze, and grinding stones (**Fig. 6**).

Stone artifacts, such as semi-lunar shaped reaping knives and stone sickles, and wooden hoe discovered from the Bronze Age residential areas are good indicators of agricultural practices by the Bronze Age people in the Ulsan area (**Fig. 7**). In addition, dry agricultural fields and paddy fields have been also identified in the area as well. These

Fig. 6 Polished stone artifacts (daggers, spearhead, circular-shaped axes, and grooved adzes) (The Ulsan Institute of Cultural Properties, 2010: 74, 76).

Fig. 7 Polished stone semi-lunar shaped reaping knives and sickles (The Ulsan Institute of Cultural Properties, 2010: 78, 80).

kinds of features as well as the overall artifact assemblages strongly suggest that the Bronze Age people who inhabited in the Ulsan area depended on agriculture for their subsistence.

It is important to note that Korean Bronze Age (ca. 1,500 BC) witnessed an abrupt decrease of shell midden sites (Norton, 2007; Ha, 2010). This tells us that shellfish and utilization of other food resources from the sea decreased immensely and the Bronze Age peoples' subsistence patterns switched to agricultural practices more than during the previous period. Agricultural equipment recovered not only in the Ulsan area but also across the entire Korean Peninsula correspond to this food procurement behavior in general. The frequency of deep-sea fishing tools discovered from the Bronze Age residential areas also significantly decreased as well.

As was suggested by Kim (1980), if the Bronze Age peoples had been engaged in whaling, it is expected that some whaling gears and/or ecofacts should have been discovered in the pithouses excavated near the Bangudae petroglyphs in specific and/or in the Ulsan area in general. Furthermore either a crossbow or some bronze and/or iron arrowheads which may have been used in whaling should have been discovered in and in the vicinity of the Bangudae petroglyphs. However, neither a single whaling gear nor a whale bone has been recovered from the Bronze Age pithouses investigated in the Ulsan area. This indicates two things. First of all, the Bronze Age people in the area did not practice whaling. Second of all, as a consequence, the Bangudae petroglyphs were not engraved by the Bronze Age but by the Neolithic people.

This archaeological context suggests that whalers in the Ulsan are used neither a crossbow nor iron arrowheads when they were whaling. Among other things, the Bronze Age people were not involved in whaling to begin with. Therefore, the chronology of the Bangudae petroglyphs generated by Kim (1980, 1995) does not correspond with the purported Korean archaeological contexts.

4. The role of a float in whaling

A float is one of the most critical gears when whalers are engaged in whaling (Jeong, 1996). From cross cultural research perspectives, examining how a float was used when whale hunters in action will provide a clue to appropriately interpret the controversial motifs engraved in the Bangudae petroglyphs (Waterman, 1920; Rousselot et al., 1988; Berenguer and Strecker, 2017). For example, Makah Indians who have resided at Ozette of the Olympic Peninsula in Washington State in the U. S. used floats when they were on whaling (**Fig. 8**). An anthropological and/or ethnographic research concerning the Makah Indians in conjunction with whaling was conducted from as early as in 1920 (Waterman, 1920). A detailed whaling processes including a variety of equipment are described in this monograph. How Makah Indian tribes used floats when they were hunting whales is described as follows:

As he "sounds" and takes out the line, additional floats are bent on, new lines being added as the quarry goes into the depths. As many as thirteen floats may be attached to one line....Last of all a small buoy is added to serve as a "marker," attached by a very light cord. This buoy remains near the surface, and when the whale starts upward from his long submergence, it bobs quickly to the surface, long before the whale himself appears. The canoe races forward

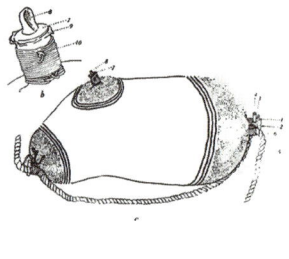

Fig. 8 Makah Indian with his floats and a detailed illustration of a float (Left: http://www.makah.com/whalingtradition.html ; Right: Waterman 1920:35).

to that point, ready to plant another harpoon....He often disappears below the surface, being sustained only by the float (see Plate 4). Upwards of twenty floats are required for that purpose. If the floats are too few in number, the whale is correspondingly deeper in the water (Waterman, 1920. emphasis added).

In addition, the webpage of the Makah Indian Tribal Council also provide a valuable information concerning floats as follows: Floats of sealskin blown up like huge balloons were attached to the harpoon line to slow down the whale....A telltale float at the end of the line acted as a marker so that the whalers could follow their prey, setting additional harpoons and staying out overnight if it was merited (http://www.makah.com/whalingtradition.html).

According to these two citations a harpoon was an important gear when Makah Indians were hunting whales. However, it was a float that certainly played a more critical role in whale hunting than harpoons. If we take into consideration this circumstance in conjunction with whale hunting in Korean prehistoric period, there is a high possibility that the motif presented on the Bangudae rock panel is not a crossbow but a float.

In this sense, it is time to change the research orientation in terms of the chronology of the whales and whaling scenes presented in the Bagudae petroglyphs. Basically we have to accurately interpret a specific motif (s) in which we are interested and we have to logically go from there. The meaning and interpretation become completely different when we interpret the motif as either a "crossbow" or a "float." Ultimately, there will be a significant difference in determining the chronology of the Bangudae petroglyphs.

If this kind of anthropological/ethnographical research outcome in terms of whaling had been incorporated in the past, it would have been much more reasonable to have figured out the presence and importance of a "float." Then the controversial motif would not have been interpreted as a crossbow manufactured with either bronze or iron. Instead, the motif that may have been a float has been regarded as a crossbow, while the motif that may have been a bone harpoon was considered as barbed iron arrowhead. Consequently, the Bangudae petroglyphs were dated to sometime between the late Bronze Age or the Early Iron Age. That is, "the three centuries immediately before the beginning of the Christian Era" (Kim, 1995).

After the chronology of the Bangudae petroglyphs was determined as the Late Bronze Age or the Early Iron Age (Kim, 1980, 1995), two researchers conducted studies from cross cultural ethnographic perspectivess in relation to "float" in whaling (Jeong, 1988; Im, 1991). Both of them pointed out the importance of a "float" when prehistoric people were engaged in whaling. Another important aspect that should be kept in mind is that when the chronology of the Bangudae petroglyphs was being generated, this kind of anthropological and/or ethnographic research outcome was not even considered at all. If this research outcome was incorporated from the beginning, the chronology of the Bangudae petroglyphs turned out to be significantly different from the one currently under discussion.

5. Discussion and conclusion

A few Neolithic archaeological sites were excavated at Hwangseong-dong and Seongam-dong area in Ulsan in 2010 (Ma, 2010). No definite archaeological feature except for a few hearths was identified at the site. Investigators, however, identified a few layers that contained both artifacts and ecofacts. The site was a waterlogged midden from which a number of faunal and floral remains were recovered. The artifacts discovered at the site were composed of lots of typical Korean Neolithic pottery sherd (i.e., geometric design pottery), polished stone axes, mortars, whetstones, and a variety of tools made of bone and antler. On the other hand, deer bones and antlers, shark and tuna bones, abalone, oysters, gastropods, and various kinds of shellfish were also identified. These faunal remains indicate that the inhabitants of the site relied on land and maritime resources at the same time.

It is of interest to note that two whale bones with embedded pieces of bone harpoon were recovered at the site (**Fig. 9**). According to the result of radiocarbon dating, the date turned out to be 3,890–3,870 cal BC (Choi et al., 2012). Some researchers argue that the two pieces of bone embedded in a whale coccygeal vertebra and a shoulder blade could be harpoons (Choi et al., 2012). There are similarities between these artifacts and the gorges recovered by Sample (1964) at the Tongsam-dong shell midden site in Busan Korea, though Sample assumed the gorges may have been used for fishing. However, it is not unreasonable to classify the gorges as slender harpoons. If this is the case, this would support the idea that the residents the Bangudae petroglyphs site practiced whaling rather than mere collecting stranded

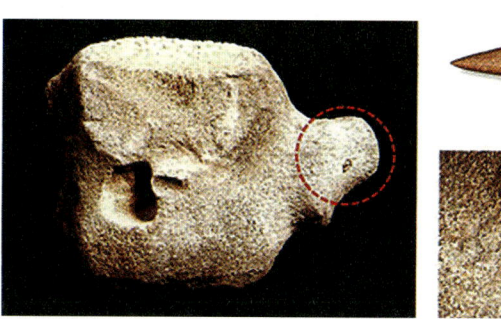

Fig. 9 A harpooned whale bone and a tip of the harpoon excavated from Hwangseong-dong, Ulsan (Ha 2013:217, cited from the Korean Archaeology & Art History Research Institue).

whales (Ma, 2010). This is undeniable evidence to support that the residents of Hwhangseong-dong in Ulsan site practiced whaling. This indicates that there is a high possibility that the Bangudae rock art in which whaling scenes appearing were engraved by the Neolithic people who lived in and in the vicinity of the site.

In the mean time, after examining the harpooned whale bones, Choi (2012) asserts that the two harpoons embedded in the whale bones may not be related to direct whaling. He argues that in order for a harpoon to have penetrated into the whale bone, it must go through the hide, fat, and meat of the whale. Thus, he is skeptical whether there was such a tool in the Neolithic period. He assumes that the whale bones in which a harpoon was embedded may have been a by-product of a ritual ceremony conducted prior to the butchering of stranded whales. On the other hand, taking into consideration the cut marks in skull, lower jawbone, and rib bones and the presence of whaling scenes in the Bangudae petroglyphs, he admits the possibility of whaling using hunting tools such as harpoons and nets (Choi, 2012, 2013). Thus, his arguments are not consistent at all and cause a bit of puzzling. In the case of Choi (2013), who also tookd part in the excavation at Ulsan Hwangseong-dong, argues that the scapula and coccygeal vertebra of whale excavated in association with harpoons are the evidence of whaling, and the whale bones discovered at the site are the result of whaling conducted by the people who may have been responsible for creating the Bangudae petroglyphs.

In addition, some other abstract rock art motifs such as concentric ring, geometric designs, bronze dagger hilt shapes, have been identified on the surface of dolmen which is one of the most abundant burial type during the Korean Bronze Age. So far, some dolmens on which abstract motifs are depicted have been identified at many different sites in Korea. This archaeological context definitely indicates that there was a huge time gap between realistic motifs of the Bangudae and the other abstract motifs of the Bronze Age. In conclusion, the Bangudae petroglyphs should be dated to the Neolithic Age (ca. 7000-4000 BP at least).

References

Bangudae Petroglyphs Institute, Ulsan University. 2020. *Korean Petroglyphs*, Ulsan: Ulsan University Press.

Berenguer, Jose R. and Matthias Strecker. 2017. Representations of whales and other cetaceans in pre-Hispanic rock art of Chile and Peru. in *Whale on the rock*. edited by Sang-mog Lee, Ulsan: Ulsan Petroglyphs Museum, 55-84.

Choi, Eun-ah, Sang-hyeon Kim, and Gyeong-hee Ma. 2012. *Ulsan Hwangseong-dong sinseokgisidae yujeok [Ulsan Hwangseongdong Neolithic Site]*, Busan: Saejong Press. (in Korean)

Gyeongju National Museum. 2007. *The Ancient Site at Yongjeon-ri, Yeongcheon*, Daegu: Seojae Press. (in Korean)

Ha, In-Soo. 2012. Dongsam-dong shell midden site and the petroglyphs of Bangudae. *Journal of the Korean Neolithic Society* 14, 49-74. (in Korean)

Ha, In-Soo. 2013. Bangudae petroglyphs in the archeological contexts: Focusing on the site of Dongsam-dong in Pusan. In *Korean Rock Art III: Bangudae Petroglyph in Daegok-ri, Ulsan*. edited by Ulsan Petroglyph Museum, Ulsan: Advison, 204-224. (in Korean)

Hwang, Soo-yeong and Myeong-dae Moon. 1984. *Bangudae ambyeokjogak [Rock picture at Ban-gu Dae]*, Seoul: Dongguk University Press. (in Korean)

Im, Jang-hyeok. 1991. Examination of Daegok-ri rock art from folklore perspective. *Journal of Korean Folklore Studies* 24, 171-195. (in Korean)

Im, Sae-gwon. 2003. *Korean Rock Art*, Seoul: Daewonsa. (in Korean)

Jang, Myeong-soo. 1997. Subsistence patterns and belief systems of the rock art in Daegok-ri, Ulsan. *Inha Sahak* 5, 65-146. (in Korean)

Jang, Myeong-soo. 2001. A Study on the Cultural Aspect of the Petroglyph in Korea: Focused on the Developmental Shape of Religion. Ph.D. dissertation in the Department of History at In Ha University Graduate School. (in Korean)

Jeon, Ho-tae. 2013. *A Study of Bangudae Petroglyphs in Ulsan*, Seoul: Hollym.

Jeong, Dong-chan. 1988. A study of prehistoric petroglyph in Daegok-ri, Ulju. In *Essays in Honour of Professor Dr. Powkey on His Retirement: Archaeology and Anthropology*, Seoul: Jisiksanueop-sa, 389-434. (in Korean)

Jeong, Dong-chan. 1996, *Dynamic Myth: Rock Art*, Seoul: Haean. (in Korean)

Kang, Bong Won. 2020. Reexamination of the chronology of the Bangudae petroglyphs and whaling in prehistoric Korea: A different perspective. *Journal of Anthropological Research* 76(4), 480-506.

Kang, Bong Won. 2022. A critical review of the chronology of the Bangudae petroglyphs in Korea. *Hanguk Sanggosa Hakboe [Journal of Korean Ancient Historical Society]* 117, 5-32. (in Korean)

Kim, Gwon-gu. 2013. A consideration of the chronology of the Bangudae rock art. *Yeongnam Archaeological Review* 67, 119-129. (in Korean)

Kim, Gwon-gu. 2015. A critical review on the chronology argument of the Bangudae petrography as the Neolithic Age. In *Investigation on the Dating of Bangudae Petroglyphs*. edited by Petroglyphs Institute University of Ulsan, Ulsan: Samchang Press, 63-81. (in Korean)

Kim, Gwon-gu. 2021. The chronology of petroglyphs of Cheonjeon-ri, Ulju and their nature. *Korean Journal of Cultural Heritage Studies* 54 (2), 98-118. (in Korean)

Kim, Jung-Bae. 2015. The cultural and historic meanings of Daegok-ri petroglyphs. In *Investigation on the Dating of Bangudae Petroglyphs*. edited by Petroglyphs Institute University of Ulsan, Ulsan: Samchang Press, 107-124. (in Korean)

Kim, Won-yong. 1980. Prehistoric rock painting at Bangu-dai, Ulchu, South East. Korea. *Journal of Korean Archaeological Studies* 9, 6-22. (in Korean)

Kim, Won-yong. 1995. *Art and Archaeology of Ancient Korea*, Seoul: Taekwang Publishing.

Lee, Sang-mog. 2004. The representation of animals on the prehistoric rock art site of Bangudae. *Journal of the Korean Archaeological Society* 52, 35-68. (in Korean)

Lee, Sang-mog. 2015. Contemplation study on the dating method of Bangudae Petroglyphs. In *Chronology of Bangudae Petroglyphs in Ulsan, Korea*. edited by Bangudae Petroglyphs Institute, University of Ulsan, Ulsan: Samchang press, 83-105. (in Korean)

Ma, Gyeong-hee. 2010. A Neolithic site in Hwangseong-dong: Its excavation and result. *The Journal of Korean Petroglyph* 14, 117-132. (in Korean)

Moon, Myeong-dae. 1973. Prehistoric rock art in Ulsan. *Cultural Properties* 7, 33-40. (in Korean)

National Museum of Korea. 2001. *The Ancient Culture of Nangnang*, Seoul: Sol. (in Korean)

Norton, Christopher J., 2007. Sedentism, territorial circumscription, and the increased use of plant domesticates across Neolithic-Bronze Age Korea. *Asian Perspectives* 46 (1), 133-165.

Rousselot, Jean-Loup, William W. Fitzhugh, and Aron Crowell. 1988. Maritime economies of the North Pacific rim, in *Crossroads of Continents: Cultures of Siberia and Alaska*. Edited by William W. Fitzhugh, and Aron Crowell, Washington D. C.: Smithsonian Institution Press, 151-172.

Ulsan Institute of Cultural Properties. 2010. *The Culture in the Region of Taehwagang, Ulsan*, Yangsan: Yong Design. (in Korean)

Ulsan Petroglyph Museum. 2013. *Bangudae Petroglyph in Daegok-ri, Ulsan*, Ulsan: Advision. (in Korean)

Waterman, T.T., 1920. T*he Whaling Equipment of the Makah Indians*, Seattle: University of Washington Press. http://www.makah.com/whalingtradition.html

Shalabolino's petroglyphs technique analysis : Experience of trace research

N.I. DROZDOV [1], E.G. DEVLET [2], E.Y. GIRYA [3], V.I. MAKULOV [4]

[1] Professor Emeritus, Center of Historical Regionalism of Yenisei Siberia, Siberian Federal University, Russia, Siberian Institute of Higher Education "International Innovation University", Russia ; kfurao@mail.ru
[2] Institute of Archaeology, Russian Academy of Sciences, Russia
[3] Institute of History of Material culture of the Russian Academy of Sciences, Russia
[4] Saint-Petersburg State Budgetary Professional Educational Institution "Polytechnic College of Urban Economy", Russia

ABSTRACT

Several petroglyphs were investigated in the lower level of the Shalabolino rock-art site. The aim of this work was to determine the material of tools for making petroglyphs. A method, previously employed, was used: silicone mass was used to take small impressions of the petroglyph fragments. The positive casts made from the silicon imprints were investigated in the laboratory. Petroglyphs made by stone and metal tool were determined.

국문초록

러시아과학원 산하기관의 공동연구를 통하여 극동 살라볼리노 암각화 유적(Shalabolino rock-art site)의 흔적 분석 연구를 수행했다. 살라볼리노 암각화 유적 하부에 있는 소, 배, 말코손바닥사슴 등이 새겨진 여러 암각화의 조사목적은 암각화 제작도구의 물질적 측면을 규명하는 데 있다. 기존 연구에서는 실리콘 덩어리를 암각화 조각에 압착하는 방법을 사용했다. 실리콘에 새겨진 양각 주물로 사본을 만들어 실험실 연구를 통해 암각화 제작도구가 석기인지 금속기인지를 판단했다. 살라볼리노 암각화를 석기 혹은 금속기로 제작했을 경우, 도구의 차이에 따른 흔적의 특징을 알아보기 위해 흔적을 사암에 안착하여 실험했다. 석재로 석영도구를 사용했을 경우 직경 2.6-11mm 흔적으로 형태와 크기가 불규칙하고, 천공부 외곽선은 각이 지고 구멍 입구가 넓게 나타나는 데 비해, 금속 도구를 사용했을 때는 직경 1-4.5mm 흔적으로 형태와 크기가 규칙성을 보이고, 천공부 외곽선은 둥글고 구멍 입구가 좁고 깊고 U자형으로 나타났다. 끝으로 석기로만 들어진 절개부 흔적이 금속 도구로 제작한 흔적과 구별되는 특징은 석재작업 부분에 신속한 변화를 줄 수 있다는 것인데, 석기로 만들어진 흔적은 둥근형이나 사각형에서 길다란 선형으로의 역동적인 변경이 가능하다.

Keywords : Shalabolino rock-art site, rock art of the Middle Yenisei River basin, petroglyphs, trace analyses.

During joint complex archaeological works of Krasnoyarsk laboratory of archeology and palaeogeography of Central Siberia of Institute of archeology and ethnography of the Siberian office of the Russian Academy of Sciences, Institute of archeology of the Russian Academy of Sciences, Institute of history of material culture of the Russian Academy of Sciences trace analysis research of petroglyphs of the Shalabolino rock-art site was conducted. This rock-art site is located in the Kuraginsky district of Krasnoyarsk Krai, on the right bank of the river Tuba, the right inflow of the River Yenisei (Vyatkina, 1949; Pyatkin, Martynov, 1985). Many ancient images are revealed on this monument in the 2010s thanks to field researches of Krasnoyarsk archeologists (Drozdov, Zaika, Berezovsky, 2002; Drozdov, Zaika, Marchenko etc., 2003; Zaika, Drozdov, Berezovsky etc., 2004; Zaika, Drozdov, Makulov, 2005; Zaika, Drozdov, Berezovsky, 2006). Thus, the most interesting results were received when clearing rocky exits of the lower level: many flatnesses with petroglyphs were in whole or partly closed by bedding of rocky fragments and soil.

Determination of the material of tools by which the petroglyphs are executed was the purpose of the research. Selection of petroglyphs of the lower level was analysed, there both images made with stones and with metal tools were successfully identified. (**Fig. 1-3**) (Girya, Drozdov, Devlet, Makulov, 2011; Devlet, Girya, 2011, 2012).

The technique applied in the field and laboratory analysis of petroglyphs of Shalabolino, was used earlier on materials of the rock drawings of Chukotka (Devlet, 2008, 2012; Girya, Devlet, 2010). A fragment of an incised image with an adjoining natural rocky surface chosen for studying was covered by the protective layer, approved in restoration interfering damage of a stone (Kochanovich, Devlet, 2006). The silicone print (matrix) was taken from this site, the protective layer was washed off. Then a plaster cast forming from the silicone negative print which precisely reproduced a positive relief of a stone with a fragment of the image (**Fig. 1** : 2, 4, 6 ; **2** : 5, 6). The use of the silicone prints taken in the field from rocky surfaces with traces of stationing allowed in the following to investigate features of the technique of incising images in laboratory conditions on macro- and microlevels. Similar copies of stationing traces fully save information on tools with which petroglyphs were incised.

For the characteristic of a microrelief the method of shadow section was used: the microrelief outlined by means of a linear shadow which is cast by the thread located horizontally to a surface of casting, shined on the one hand at an angle in 45°. The linear shadow precisely outlines a surface with processing traces (see **Fig. 2**: 2). Changing the position of a thread it is possible to receive information on any (cross, longitudinal etc.) section of a surface relief, the sizes of traces are measured by means of Altami Studio

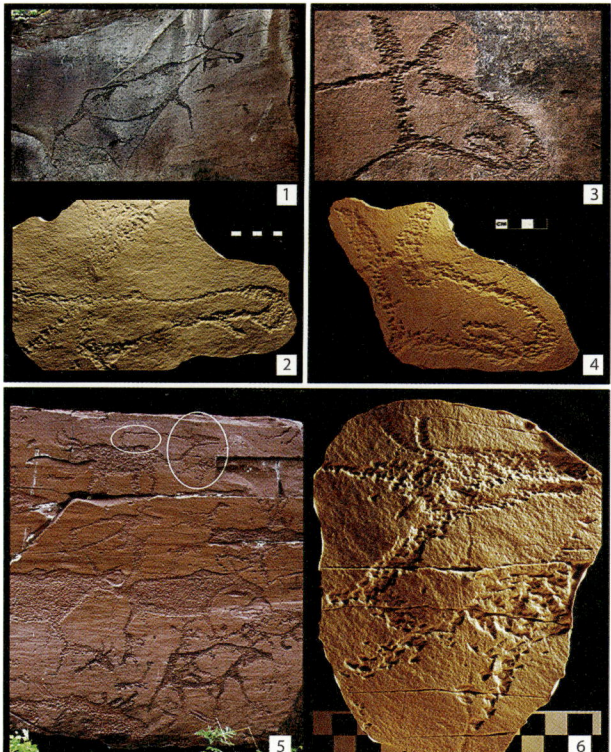

Fig. 1 Shalabolino's rock-art site.

1–2 : The figure of an elk which was made with a mud bit tool, used as an intermediary tool, 3–4 : the image of a deer, made with the metal tool and the copy of stationing traces on the plaster casting with the indication of the sizes of separate hollows, 5–6 : palimpsest from three zoomorphic figures which was made with the metal tool and the plaster casting of a fragment of the image a hoofed, made from silicone mold.

Fig. 2 Shalabolino's rock-art site.

1-2 : traces of work with a stone tool (a fragment of the image of an elk, the copy of stationing traces on the plaster casting with the indication of the sizes of separate hollows) and the shadow section of a stationing surface. 3–4 : the plaster casting of a fragment of the image of the boat with the oarsmen, made with a stone intermediary and the copy of stationing traces with the indication of the sizes of separate hollows. 5 : the image of the tagarsky time made with a metal tool with a pointed working end with a lensoid section used as an intermediary. 6–7 : the casting received from a silicone mold and the copy of stationing traces on the plaster casting with the indication of the sizes of separate hollows.

software.

Gradation on the incise depth from an initial surface was used (superficial/shallow, average, deep stationing) for the technique description, the forms of separate holes were distinguished as roundish, linear and figured stationing types.

Continuous stationing in which traces of incising recover each other, is hardly informative for trace analysis, and the special attention was paid to single outlined holes. Deep and average holes transfer the form contours of the stationing tool quite precisely while superficial stationing in this aspect is less informative. Even if the stationing tool gets rather deeply into the stone, the remaining trace most often doesn't represent an exact negative of its working part. Integrity degree also in many respects defines possibilities of the trace analysis, and the weathered images often are unsuitable for reliable research of a tool material with which it was incised.

The difference between traces made with stone and metal tools was revealed while investigating the petroglyphs of Shalabolino, also there were conducted special experiments on sandstone stationing. The main difference criteria of stationing traces with quartz and iron tools can be formulated this way: iron tools are used when the stationing is regular in a form and sizes, often roundish in outlines of separate holes, deep at rather narrow entrance openings. Quartz tools are used when the stationing is irregular in a form and sizes, angular in outlines of separate hollows, with wide entrance openings. The main diagnosing sign distinguishing traces of incising, left by a stone tool, from traces of work made by an iron tool, – fast change of working part of the stone tool, traces from which are dynamically transform from roundish or square to an extended linear.

The examples of the images made by the stone tool, the analysed selection of Shalabolino's petroglyphs can be some zoomorphic figures, the boat image, etc. (**Fig. 1**: 1; **2**: 3).

One of the most known groups of petroglyphs includes a realistic image of an elk (see **Fig. 1**: 1). There are the visitors' inscriptions, one of them was made in 1936. The stationing traces of the elk's head are different in shape. On the muzzle they are square and roundish, and on a site of horns they have an extended, semi-lunar and irregular linear form (see **Fig. 1**: 2). Hollows of linear and extended semi-lunar forms are very various in length (from 2.5 to 10mm) and width (from 2 to 4.5mm). In profile the stationing relief flat, without sharp differences between peaks and draw-downs. Similar dynamics of form changing of tool traces is observed on the studied fragments of the elk legs: roundish (on the site close to the belly) stationing traces are replaced with extended linear traces when moving off the body to legs, even turning into fine linear traces where the hoofs of the represented animal have to be incised (see **Fig. 2**: 1-2). Such kind of change

of a form of stationing traces is a characteristic feature of work with the stone as an intermediary tool from strong isotropic breed of a stone. The prepared spiked end in process of use quickly was painted, the tool turned into a mud bit. It is impossible to determine whether the ancient artist improved one tool several times or replaced the working part.

One of the images of boats with the people designated by vertical strokes located nearby was analysed. The test print was taken from the fragment, the studies on which showed that this petroglyph is put with the stone intermediary with the spiked blunted working end (**Fig. 2**: 3-4). In spite of the fact that continuous stationing that is perpendicular to the surface prevails in this image and most hollows recover each other, on some sites it is possible to track outlines of separate holes: in the plan it is polygons of different figures. They are rather superficial with the considerable width reaching 5mm on the greatest measurement.

Partial images of bulls are characteristic for the rock art of the Middle Yenisei. The silicone prints were taken from the head and the croup of the image. It is established that the stone intermediary was applied to incise the contour with the mud bit end. Traces of picks are mainly direct, large, reach 11mm in length and 4mm in width, the crescent form of separate hollows prevails. Slight polishing from the muzzle contour to the eyes is noted. Stationing out of the contour line is executed by another tool. These traces represent group of hollows of irregular rectangular outlines of 4–6mm.

Many Shalabolino's rock images were made with the use of metal tools (**Fig. 1**: 3-6; **2**) . The petroglyphs of tagarsky time of the VII-III centuries BC, among which we can find figures of the armed man's characters, the image of a horse, battle scenes can be an example (**Fig. 2**: 5-7; **3**).

The single anthropomorphous armed character is stationed by direct and slanted picks made with a sharp metal intermediary (see **Fig. 2**: 5-7). Judging by stationing traces, the tool had a sharp flattened working end with a lensoid section. Both roundish, and almond-shaped are present among traces of picks in respect of a hollow. The size of the almond-shaped: length is up to 3.4mm, width is up to 1.2mm diameter of the roundish – to 1.4mm. Two tools with various section of the working ends were probably used: one with lensoid section, and another with the roundish. It is impossible to exclude one more variant: after the tool with the flattened working element became blunted, it was regronded in an edge with round section.

The image of two-armed man characters is stationed with direct and slanted picks made with a sharp metal tool (**Fig. 3**). The stationing traces of a roundish form are equable by the size: from 1 to 1.5mm in the diameter. They are rather deep: width of an entrance opening is close in the size to the depth of penetration of the tool. Such traces testify to use

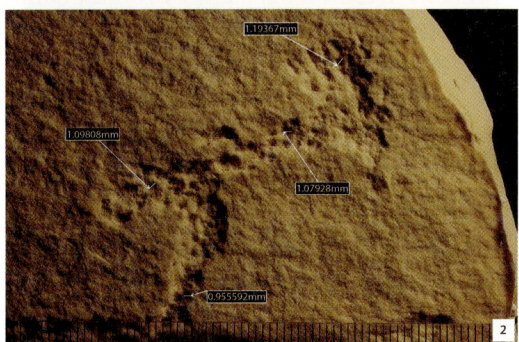

Fig. 3 Shalabolino's rock-art site.

The images of the tagarsky time. Figures of the armed characters, made with a metal tool with a pointed working end with a roundish section applied as an intermediary.

quite thin metal tools with a sharp roundish working end in section. The figure of a horse located below is stationed with a very small and steadily roundish on outlines in the plan of stationing with uniformly flat, concave (U-shaped) bottom. The diameter of the traces is from 1 to 1.5mm. This image also could be stationed by a tool like an awl.

The silhouette image of fish can serve as an example of stationing made by a larger metal tool. The stationing is continuous; traces of picks are monotonously roundish, up to 3mm in the diameter. Narrow, moderately deep, straight lines prevail, but there are also some of them that are picked at an angle. In this case it is possible to assume the use of the metal intermediary with a blunted roundish working end.

The palimpsest of the group, consisting of three figures was investigated: the partial zoomorphic, turned to the right, stationed by picking the contour and a partial silhouette filling of the head and neck. Another zoomorphic image that is partly lost closes up with the front foot of the first image. On the left the silhouette image of the bull that turned its head on the left recovers the zoomorphic image stationed in partial way. (**Fig. 1**: 5, 6). The partial silhouette image located above with partial silhouette filling of area of the muzzle and the neck was tested on two sites. The stationing traces with the diameter from 1.2 to 1.4mm (on the muzzle of the animal) and to 2mm (on the croup) are left with a tool with a very narrow and sharp awl-shaped end. The fragment of lost zoomorphic image (on the right below) is made with a non-standard for petroglyphs of the Shalabolino's rock-art site tool, probably, a tip of a knife or the similar metal tool. Separate hollows in the plan have eigher triangular (occurring from slanted picks), or extended linear (occurring from frontal picks) outlines. Linear hollows are rather narrow and rather deep. The full-figured image of the bull turned to the left located on the left, is stationed with a blunted metal tool. Hollows on a site of the bottom petroglyph are larger, the sizes from 2 to 3.5mm, with more flat U-shaped bottom.

As a whole, the sizes of the stationing traces which for Shalabolino's petroglyphs are interpreted as made by means of stone tools, vary from 2.6 to 11mm on the greatest measurement. The sizes of the traces left the metal tool, – from 1 to 4.5mm. The metal stationing sets apart because of its high extent of standardization of forms and the sizes of traces of the picks relating to one image. They are very uniform by the size (2–2.5mm in the diameter) and in a form: roundish in the plan with smoothly concave, U-shaped bottom. The exceptions are rare examples of very fine stationing. It should be noted that similar forms and the sizes (about 2.3mm) have traces of picks on the visitors' inscription, that served as comparative material.

The essential data which showed prospects of a developed technique of the analysis for studying of sequence of filling of the planes by petroglyphs are obtained in the course of the field and laboratory experimental trace researches of petroglyphs of Shalabolino. Such research direction will allow to come to an understanding about what kind of tool and made of material were made these images and how many various tools were applied.

References

Vyatkina K.V., 1949. Shalabolino (Tessinsky) rock-art. *Collection of Museum of Anthropology and Ethnography*, 417-484.

Gurya E.Y., Devlet E.G., 2010. Some results of development of a equipment studying technique of implementation of stationing petroglyphs. *Ural historical bulletin* No. 1(26), Yekaterinburg, 107-118.

Girya E.Y., Drozdov N.I., Devlet E.G., Makulov V.I., 2011. Works on trace studying of petroglyphs of Shalabolino. *Petroglyphic art in modern society. To the 290 anniversary of a discovery of the Tomsk rock-art. Materials of the international scientific conference* 2, Kemerovo: Kuzbassvuzizdat (Works of the Siberian Association of researchers of primitive art. Edition VIII), 201-207.

Devlet E.G., Girya E.Y., 2011. "Graphic layer" in petroglyphic art and equipment research of petroglyphs implementation of Northern Eurasia. *Ancient art in an archeology mirror. To D.G.*

Savinov's 70 anniversary, Kemerovo (Works of the Siberian Association of researchers of primitive art. edition VII), 186-201.

Devlet E.G., Girya E.Y., 2012. Trace research of petroglyphs of the Middle Yenisei. *Historical and cultural heritage and cultural wealth of Russia*, 60-65.

Drozdov N.I., Zaika A.L., Berezovsky A.P., 2002. Researches of the Shalabolino's rock-art site (by results of works of 2001-2002). *Issues of archeology, ethnography, anthropology of Siberia and contiguous territories*, Novosibirsk, 309-312.

Drozdov N.I., Zaika A.L., Marchenko L.A., Makulov V.I., Berezovsky A.P., Zhuravkov S.P., Yemelyanov I.N., Babina M.S., Churakova E.V., 2003. Results of research of the Shalabolino's rock-art site (results of works of 2002-2003). *Issues of archeology, ethnography, anthropology of Siberia and contiguous territories*, Novosibirsk, 342-345.

Zaika A.L., Drozdov N.I., 2008. New petroglyphs of the Shalabolino's rock-art site. *Works of the II (XVIII) of the All-Russian archaeological congress in Suzdal*, 28-30.

Zaika A.L., Drozdov N.I. Berezovsky A.P., 2006. Results of researches of the Shalabolino's rock-art site in 2005-2006. *Issues of archeology, ethnography, anthropology of Siberia and contiguous territories*, Novosibirsk, 331-260.

Zaika A.L., Drozdov N.I. Berezovsky A.P., Klyuchnikov T.A., Zhuravkov of S.P., 2004. Shalabolino's petroglyphs (results of researches of 2004). *Issues of archeology, ethnography, anthropology of Siberia and contiguous territories*, Novosibirsk, 259-260.

Zaika A.L., Drozdov N.I. Makulov V.I., 2005. Research of Shalabolino's petroglyphs (results of works of 2004). *Archeology of Southern Siberia: ideas, methods, discoveries. The collection of reports of the international scientific conference devoted to the 100 anniversary since the birth of the member correspondent of the Russian Academy of Sciences of S.V. Kiselyov* (Minusinsk, June, 20-26, 2005), Krasnoyarsk, 152-155.

Pyatkin B.N., Martynov A.I., 1985. *Shalabolino's petroglyphs*. Krasnoyarsk, 188p.

Sovetova O.S., 2005. *Petroglyphs of the tagarsky era on Yenisei (plots and images)*, Novosibirsk, 40p.

Devlet E., 2008. Rock Art Studies in Northern Russia and the Far East. *Rock Art Studies. News of the World* 3, Oxbow, 120-137.

Devlet E., 2012. Rock Art Studies in Northern Eurasia. *Rock Art Studies. News of the World* 4, Oxbow, 124-148.

Exploitation beyond subsistence of faunal resources at "RARH" (West Bengal, India) by new settlers during the Ferro-Chalcolithic period

Manomay GHOSH

Ret'd In-Charge Prehistoric Zoology, Zoological Survey of India, India ; ghoshmanomay@yahoo.com

ABSTRACT

It is surmised that some of the early settlers from the Vindhya mountainous region established themselves at the zone of colloquial "RARH" during the Ferro-Chalcolithic period (1450 BC to 200 AD), despite possessing a number of livestock and having knowledge of nominal agriculture. They were very much inclined to a game hunting and snaring economy for their livelihood for two reasons: First, pray or game animals were plentiful; and second, the people were better equipped than their earlier neighbors. Most of the exploited animals, some of which had been exterminated, were the denizen of that patch of deciduous forest and riverine grasslands. Among the terrestrial forms, except the enigmatic extinct *Bos namadicus*, eight were of domesticated animals. Animals like gharials (*Gavialis gangeticus*) and turtles, which used to harbor in the water bodies for living, but which were also exclusively dependent on the land (shore and bank) for breeding, disappeared quickly from the zone. The fate of land animals like nilgai (*Boselaphus tragocamelus*), hog deer (*Axis porcinus*), and samber (*Cervus unicolour*) followed suit. With the disappearance of the species of deer and gallinaceous birds, the sal (*Shorea robusta*) forests soon also dwindled. The extermination was expedited by hunting pressure and human population growth. All of this resulted in the loss of humidity in the atmosphere, less annual rainfall, more infertile soil, and weakening affluence of rivers, aggravated, on the other hand, by increasing average temperature, the denuding of humus-rich subsoils, and the deoxidization of water in water bodies.

국문초록

철기-금석병용기(1.450 BC-200 AD)에 적색토 지대(RARH)인 빈디야산맥 지역에서 생활했던 초기 정착인은 많은 가축을 소유하고 목축업에 대한 지식도 가지고 있었다. 당시 사냥할 동물이 많고 다른 이웃에 비해 금석기로 무장하여 생계를 위한 동물사냥과 함정을 통한 동물포획 경향을 가지고 있었다. 과도한 동물자원 남획으로 인해 활엽수림과 강가 초목지에는 산재되거나 협소한 동물 서식지를 이루든지 혹은 특정 동물은 멸종되기도 했다. 멸종 이유를 알 수 없는 소(*Bos namadicus*)를 제외하면 육상에서 멸종된 동물은 순화(domesticated) 동물로 본다. 주요 멸종동물은 새끼 양육을 위해 물가에 사는 악어(*Gavialis gangeticus*)와 거북이었고, 이들이 빠르게 사라지고 난 뒤 사슴류의 인도영양(*Boselaphus tragocamelus*), 돼지사슴(*Axis porcinus*), 루사사슴(*Cervus unicolour*)과 가금류 등이 식물생태계의 사라수(沙羅樹, *Shorea robusta*) 산림과 함께 사라졌다. 동물의 멸종은 인구 증가, 사냥 압력 증가로 빠르게 진행되었으며, 인위적 요인에 의한 생태계 변화는 대기 습도손실, 강수량 감소, 토양 비옥도 악화, 하천생태의 약화를 초래했다. 더불어 자연현상으로 평균기온 감소, 토양유기물층 삭박, 지표수 탈산성화 등이 수반되면서 동물생태계는 더욱 악화되었다.

Keywords : Early Holocene, Late Neolithic, Ferro-Chalcolithic, dolicocephalic, Proto-australoid, laterite, Rarh region, microcosm

1. Introduction

Decades ago, in one national seminar on the "Environmental Hazards and Archaeological Studies," organized by the School of Studies in Environmental Radiation and Archaeological Sciences, Jadavpur University, I tried to emphasise the role of "archaeozoology" and its significance in revealing the past. In the present topics, I would like to shed some light on how the once prevalent natural deciduous forests and reverine grass lands in West Bengal's latterite soil-enriched "RARH" area started declining during Chalcolithic phase along with entirety of its wild fauna due to overexploitation, probably enhanced after the arrival of some new settlers in the region. Although beginning only after the sixth decade of the present century, of late, the archaeological exploration and excavations in a number of ancient sites in West Bengal, especially in the west-southwestern 'RARH' area – namely the districts of Bankura, Birbhum, and Bardhaman – generated important clues and materials to facilitate archaeozoological research (**Fig. 1**). Analyzing the animal remains unearthed from eight Chalcolithic (or Ferro-Chalcolithic) sites Bahiri, Baneshawardanga, Bharatpur, Hatikra, Kotasur, Mahisadal, Mangalkot, and Pandu Rajar Dhaibi, we can now concede that the maximum faunal resources were exploited by Chalcolithic (or Ferro-Chalcolithic) people in these areas, but can also precisely depict the then socio-economic environment and way of life of the people in that vanished conglomerate of settlements (**Fig. 2, 3**). Most of the skeletal remains belonged to animals exploited for food (flesh and meat) – some, of course, in later development, utilized in labor (draft or transport) or for industries (fleece, leather, bone tools, domestic or ritual implements).

From each of the sites, the archaeological excavations and explorations yielded recognizable animal remains of both wild (natural) and domesticated animals. The excavations unearthed a total of 1,620 samples of animal remains, mainly skeletal fragments and some bone tools. The study and identification of these materials by different experts, including the present author (see the references) revealed the existence of 39 animal species (listed in the following

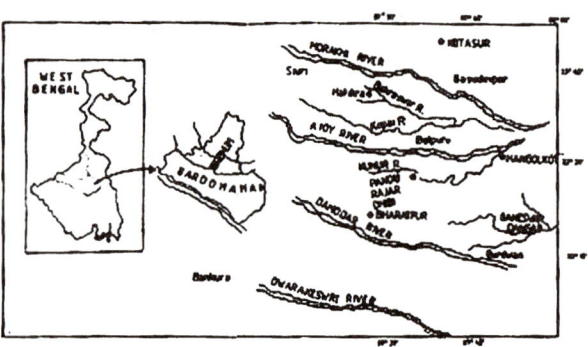

Fig. 1 Some of the Chalcolithic sites in the RARH area of West Bengal

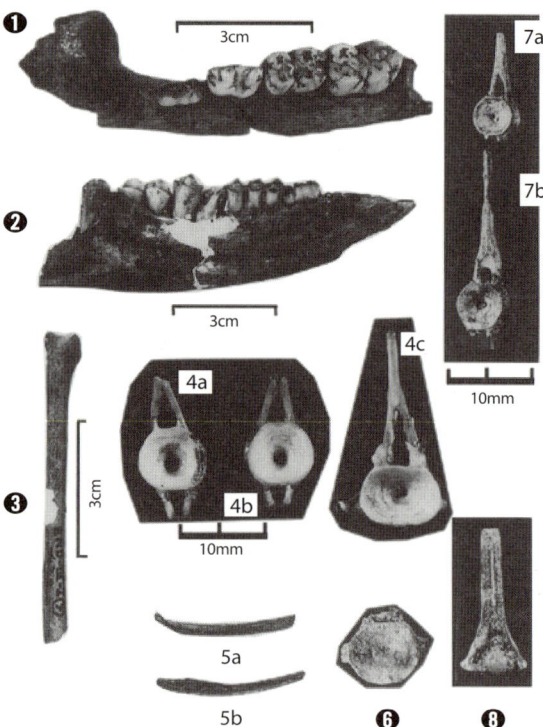

Fig. 2 Some of the Chalcolithic remains RARH area of West Bengal

① Fragment of left mandible with a portion of body, 3rd, 4th premolar, 1st and 2nd molar of Indian wild boar, *Sus scrofa cristatus*, from Baneswrdanga, BND- I.
② Fragment of right mandible with 2nd, 3rd premolar (Milk) and 1st and 2nd molars and a portion of erupting 3rd molar of Bara Singha, *Cervus duvauceli* from Baneswardanga, BND- II.
③ Tibio-tarsal bone of Jungle Fowl, *Gallus gallus murghi* from Baneswardanga, BND- III.
④ Three thoracic vertebrae of Teleost fish, *Labeo rohita* from Bharatpur.
⑤ Pleural ribs of Carp, *Catla catla* from Pandu Rajar Dhibi.
⑥ Proatlas vertebra of Arh fish, *Mystus aor* from Pandu Rajar Dhibi.
⑦ Thoracic vertebrae (centrum) of some Indian major Carp, from Pandu Rajar Dhibi.
⑧ Dorsal spine of Arh fish, *Mystus Sp.* from Baneshwardanga, BND-III.

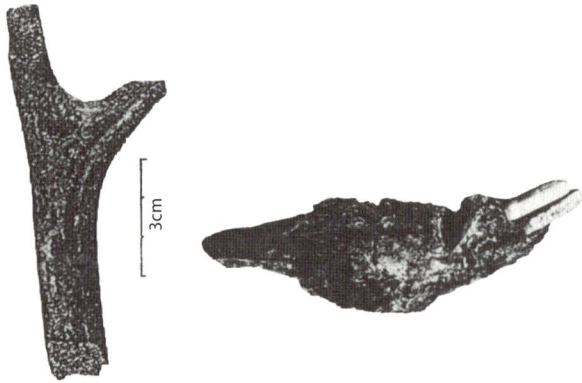

Fig. 3 Fragment of antler of Axis Porcinus(Hog deer) and Fragment of mandible of *Sus scrofa cristatus* (Wild boar) of the Chalcolithic period from Rarh area, West Bengal, India

chart), mostly indigenous denizens of the neighbouring aquatic and terrestrial habitats. Although the era that persisted from 1,450 BC to 200 AD experienced a sea-change later with respect to pristine forests, grasslands, water bodies, or overall ecosystems, we are now able to depict the then environmental conditions, human lifeways, food habits, and trade and import of animals, domestication, and migration by accessing and scrutinizing the analytical results on unearthed remains. In this work, recovered animal figurines, motifs or seals, artifacts like fish hooks, floats, hunting gadgets, vestiges of cribs, sty, or pen, and even some ancient literature, render valuable help.

The animal species identified under the respective sites are shown in the appended table (Table 1). The summary of animal species recorded from the series of excavations may be grouped according to their natural habitat (ecological) preferences as follows:

Aquatic (freshwater) – *Chiti kankra* (potamon crab), *Mystus* sp. (arh fish), *Rita* sp. (rita fish), *Catla catla* (katla fish), *Chitra indica* (Asiatic soft-shelled turtle), *Trionyx gangeticus* (Ganga soft-shelled turtle), *Lissemys punctata punctata* (spotted flap shell turtle), *Batagur baska* (batagur), and *Gavialis gageticus* (gharial).

Aquatic (marine) – *Turbinella pyrum* (chank shell).

Deciduous (Sal) Forest living – *Gallus gallus murghi* (jungle fowl), *Columba* sp. (pigeon), *Canis lupus* (wolf), *Canis aurius indicus* (jackal), *Felis chaus* (jungle cat), *Cervus duvauceli* (swamp deer), *Cervus univolour* (sambar), *Axis axis* (spotted deer), *Axis procinus* (hog deer), *Muntiacaus muntjak* (barking deer), *Sus scrofa cristatus* (wild boar), *Bos gaurus* (Indian bison), *Bubalus bubalis* (buffalo), and *Panthera pardus* (leopard).

Scrub Jungle with grassland living – *Boselephus tragocamelus* (nilgai).

Domestic Species (Maintained by settlers) – *Equus caballus* (horse), *Bos indicus* (cattle), *Bubalus bubalis* (buffalo), *Capra hircus aegagrus* (goat), *Ovis orientalis vignei* (sheep), *Elephas maximus* (elephant), *Cammellus dromedarius* (camel), and *Canis familiaris* (dog).

Fossorial domestic pest – *Rattus rattus* (rat).

2. Discussion

Both physiologically and lithostratigraphically, all eight sites yielding animal remains fall under the same region (see the map), characterized by having a medley of detritus laterite with an admixture of alluvial soil over an Archaean bedrock. The entire area, as is now, was predominantly encompassed by hot, humid tropical environments. The border zone of this conglomerate of Chalcolithic settlements, as opined by Mukherjee, S.C. (1992), "was limited to Mayurakshmi river in the North, the Rupnarayan river in the South. The Kangsabati river in the West and Bhagirathi river

Table 1 Sites in the Said area, Explored and excavated during the Last Three and Half Decades

SITE	SPECIES RECOGNISED
Bahiri Birbhum 23°38'56"N 87°46'20"E Ferro-Chalcolithic 900 BC–610 BC	*Canis familiaris, Cervus dvauceli, Axis axis, Sus scrofa, Bos gaurus, Bos indicus, Bubalus bubalis.*
Baneswardanga Bardhaman 23°20'N 88°65'E Chalcolithic Around 1000 BC	*Lamellidense* sp. *Mystus* sp. *Chitra indica, Batagur baska, Gallus* sp., *panthera pardus, Cervus duvauceli, Axis axis, Sus scrofa cristatus.*
Bharatpur Bardhaman 23°28'N 87°20'E Chalcolithic Around 1450 BC	*Trionyx gangeticus, Gallus gallus murghi, Canis familiaris, Equus caballus, Cervus duvauceli, Axis axis, Muntiacus muntjak, Sus scrofa cristatus, Bos indicus, Bos namadicus, Bubalus bubalis, Capra hircus aegagrus, Ovis orientalis vignei, Boselaphus tragocamelus, Camellus dromedarius.*
Hatikra Birbhum 23°49'N 87°95'E Ferro-Chalcolithic 1200 BC–700 BC	*Chitra indica, Sus scrofa cristatus, Bos indicus, Bubalus bubalis, Capra hiracus aegagrus.*
Kotasur Birbhum 22°55'N 87°45'E Chalcolithic 1st Cent. BC–2nd Cent. AD	*Equus* sp., *Sus cristatus, Bos indicus, Bubalus bubalis, Elephas maximus.*
Mahisdal Birbhum 23°14'N 87°E Ferro-Chalcolithic 1,380 BC–855 BC–Period I 690 BC–Period II	*Canis lupus, Felis chaus, Cervus univolor, Axis axis, Sus scrofa cristatus, Bos indicus, Capra hircus aegagrus*
Mangolkot Bardhaman 23°32'14"N 87°52'20"E Chalcolithic 1,200–600 BC period I Chalco 600–300 BC Period II Mauryan-Sunga 300 BC1 Period III Kushan 1 OOBC–300 AD Period IV Gupta 300AD–600 AD Period V	*Turbinella pyrum, Mystus., Labeo* sp., *Chirta indica, Lissemys puctata punctata, Batagur baska, Gallus* sp., *Columba* sp., *Cervus duvauceli, Axis procinus, Sus scrofa, Bps* sp., *Bubalus bubalis, Rattus rattus.*
Pandu Rajar Dhibi Bardhaman 23°34'N 87°43'E Chalcolithic - Early historic Around 1,180 BC–800 BC	*Potamonid crab, Mystus* sp., *Rita* sp., *Labeo rohita, Catla catla, Lissemys punctata punctata, Gavialis gangeticus, Callus gallus murghi, Canis aureus indicus, Cervus duvauceli, Axis corcinus, Sus scrofa cristatus Bos indicus, Bubalis, Capra hircus aegagrus, Rattus rattus.*

in the East." The people living in the area during 1,500 BC to 300 BC very likely had some superficial racial akinness from the demographic point of view. The human skeletal remains (although very meager) unearthed from burials, especially from Pandu Rajar Dhibi, studied by anthropologists like Gupta and Pal (1970) brought out salient characteristics of these people. Their analysis unveiled that some of the buried people from Pandu Rajar Dhibi appeared to be long-headed, compared to other pre-existing neighboring pristine people in and around the valley, e.g., Santhal (a proto-australoid race) and Mundari-speaking people. On the other hand, it indicates a positive cultural migration there around 3,500 BP. The newcomer (precursor of Hinduism) whose akin-ness may be found in some of the present day Bengali groups there, like Uttor Rarhi Kayasthas, might have introduced some religious practices in the area. The occurrence of some pieces of "pala," a bangle made of lacca (produced by *Laccifer indica*) used to be worn by married Hindu women, from 2m beneath the surface layer of a trial trench at Mangolkot (undated), retrieved and identified by the author indicates adaptation of Hindu customs there in early historic time. It was already learned from the study of semi-fossilized stored food gains recovered from some of the sites, that they used to cultivate the paddy. Later, through sustained research, it also became evident that the people became adept in metallurgy (Chakraborti, 1993-1994; Chatterjee, 1993). So, it is reasonable to believe that after acquiring some metallic hunting gears, they became ruthless hunters and used to slay "games" from the forests and reverine grasslands for flesh or proteins diet, in an enhanced rate.

Some of the species unearthed from the Chalcolithic sites are still found with declined population in a few heavily shrunk habitats elsewhere in West Bengal. In context to the occurrence of *Bos namadicus*, an extinct Siwalik cattle, it would not be improper to say that after the 4th (last) glaciation, when the life of many large (Siwalik) mammals began to be exterminated, some species managed to escape the death and struggled to survive moving to not far, yet uncertain niches.

Remains of two species assumed to be used as domesticated animals and might had been utilized in transport or labour in the area were the Horse (*Equus caballus*) and camel (*Camellus dromedarius*). They were certainly imported in the area by the merchants in the later periods. That the horse might had been introduced by way of import through the maritime traders in Bengal in early historic times had been substantiated by unearthed seals from Chandraketugarh and related literary documents, as evinced by Chakraborty (1992). Similarly, the camel also arrived in this region very occasionally through the traders of northwest Asian countries. All those testify that trades and exchanges began very likely with the Aryan or Indo-Iranian people during the period (1,450 BC).

Regardless, the skeletal remains (also some bone tools) of the abovementioned animals unveiled by their occurrence that the entire region was very fertile, abounded with forests and affluent rivers. The people used to hunt wild boar and deer from the neighbouring forests. They also used to capture fishes and turtle from the rivers and water bodies within vicinity. All the eight sites show very close affinities or resemblance in respect of environments, animal life and animal husbandry as practiced by the inhabitants during the Chalcolithic period, very similar to one as reported earlier on the Pandu Rajar Dhibi (Ghosh and Saha, 1992). It may be be assumed that the ancient people who dwelt phase-wise in the Rarh area had in their possession dwarf breeds of goat (*Capra hircus*) and sheep (*Ovis orientalis*), introduced by the western nomads. But the pig and fowl, which are part and parcel even in the life of present-day aboriginal peoples like the Santhal and Munda, were very likely made domesticated from the indigenous wild stocks *Sus scrofa cristatus* and *Gallus gallus murghi* during the Late Neolithic or Early Agricultural phase. The author noticed that some of the young piglings, borne by the domestic sow in the tribal huts there, have whitish horizontal stripes on their body coat – strong evidence of their descent from wild stock. Similarly, when some of the pigs went feral in neighboring jungles, they began to regain some of the ancestral characteristics: canines grew stronger and longer, the nuchal crest developed very prominently, and the hairs on their back turned coarser and longer. Similarly, the domestic fowls in their possession, externally in the color and pattern of plumage and also in ethology and habit, show great akinness to the neighboring (though depleted) *Gallus gallus murghi*.

The occurrence of chank shell, *Turbinella pyrum*, from Mangolkot, proves that its use as an object for ritual performances (sacred to the Hindus) began there in late prehistoric times. The people had to procure the sea coast dwelling (benthic) mollusk from the traders. Wherever from the people came in the sites for settlement. They certainly became lured and happy with the nature's bountiful resources – plenty of game animals, fishes and turtles of the river and enormous fresh water. In one article, entitled "Mesolithic settlements in the Ganga plain" Pal (1994) opined "the pressure of a growing population and scarcity of food and water in the Vindhyan region brought by a dry climate in the terminal Pleistocene / Early Holocene period possibly compelled the Stone-Age inhabitants to migrate to the Ganga Plains after crossing the Ganga and Yamuna." It appears that with primitive technologies, initially our ancestors were capable to kill only few of the wild beasts. But shortly thereafter, they too followed the skill and technique, with newcomers adopted there for mitigating their gastronomic need. In their endeavour, they never bothered with the future consequence that might bring an irreparable damage to the nature. I dare to say even today most of us, if not all the mankind are indifferent to the imminent disaster that would befall us due to our mishandling of different vital components of the nature, amid which we are actually helpless puppet (cause behind global warming; outbreak of deadly deceases like AIDS and Cancer).

The huge remains of both dietary bones and fashioned out tines of hog deer, *Axis procinus*, from Pandu Rajar Dhibi and Baneswardanga demonstrate that the stags were especially targeted for their antlers in addition to their flesh. Similarly, it is not very improbable to guess that the cocks of the jungle fowl, *Gallus gallus murghi*, were also a preferred item for the hunters' choice of prey, for their colorful plumage in addition to flesh. The stags amidst the herd and dominating male cock amidst the harem (their ratios always much less) rarely escaped the lured eyes of the hunters and fell easy prey. Consequently, the herds and harems of those ground foraging species turned to be "all female groups" sooner and very likely, even if they escaped from the hunters aim, their natural reproduction cycle was disrupted for good, leading to decimation or extinction of the particular species. It is also assumed that during the monsoonal deluge when most of the beasts and ground feeding birds used to be stranded marooned in the comparatively higher patches, the hunters availed the full opportunity to kill or capture them. The reduction of the above species populations, in the wild, impacted on the natural growth of the Sal (*Shorea robusta*) and other trees, which caused the thinning out of the forests in vicinity.

3. Summary

It is surmised that some of the early settlers from the Vindhya mountainous region established themselves in the zone of colloquial "RARH" (a Bengali term, meaning red/reddish soil) during the Ferro-Chalcolithic periods (1,450 BC to 200 AD), despite possessing a number of livestock and having knowledge of nominal agriculture, were very much inclined to a game hunting and snaring economy for their livelihood for two reasons: First, prey or game animals were plentiful; and second, the people were better equipped than their earlier neighbors. Most of the exploited animals, some of which had been exterminated, were the denizens of that patch of deciduous forest and riverine grasslands. It appeared to be a fact that while hunting, the hunters preferred to target the "stags" for a twofold purpose – obtaining flesh and antlers (**Fig. 4**). The latter item was likely used for making points and fabricating lithic tools. It should be borne in mind that although they knew primary metallurgy, the procurement of proper ore materials in the zone was very difficult. There were both herbivorous and carnivorous beasts in the jungles, besides the presence of omnivorous pigs. Probably the hunters used to avoid

Fig. 4 A declining population of Hog Deer. *Axis Porcinus*

Fig. 5 Common Edible fresh water carp *Catla catla*, that used to grow magnum and breed in the torrential rivers of RARH region.

Fig. 6 The Gharial, once was a common occurrence, now vanished from the region

confronting fierce animals like the tigers and bears. The animals there were nature's helpers for maintaining a delicate equilibrium in the area which could had been termed as a "microcosm," itself. The magnificent size of some fishes – namely carps and catfishe – as estimated from their vertebral indices (**Fig. 5-7**) show that the affluent rivers were very congenial for their breeding and growth: 1,620 skeletal

Fig. 7 The Red Jungle Fowl ancestral species of numerous domesticated breeds foreseeing the "DOOMES DAY".

Fig. 8 Once was mighty, now reduced, yet the AJOY flows with depleted fauna.

remains, mostly dietary in nature, including some bone tools unearthed from the zone, have been meticulously examined. Some of the dietary remains possess sharp cut marks, indicating that these were chopped or butchered by metallic knives or daggers. A total number of 39 species of animals, 12 aquatic and 27 terrestrial, have been identified. Among the terrestrial forms, except the enigmatic extinct *Bos namadicus*, eight were of domesticated animals. Animals like gharials (*Gavialis gangeticus*) and turtles, which used to harbor in the water bodies for living, but which were exclusively dependent on the land (shore and bank) for breeding, disappeared quickly from the zone. The fate of land animals like nilgai (*Boselaphus tragocamelus*), hog deer (*Axis porcinus*), and samber (*Cervus unicolour*) followed suit. The extermination was expedited by hunting pressure and human population growth. With the disappearance of the species of deer and gallinaceous birds, the sal (*Shorea robusta*) forests also dwindled. All of this resulted in the loss of humidity in the atmosphere, less annual rainfall, greater soil infertility, and weakened affluency of the rivers; aggravated, on the other hand, by increasing average temperature, the denuding of humus-rich subsoils, and the deoxidization of water in water bodies (**Fig. 8**).

Acknowledgment

The author would like to express his gratitude to late Professor Asok Dutta, who passed away untimely and suddenly on July 31, 2012. He would also like to express his gratitude to Professor Yung-jo Lee, Gao, Peng Fei, Dr. Y. I. Mingjie, and the Organizing Committee for their invitation to the prestigious International Symposium in Commemoration of the 90th Anniversary of the Discovery of Shuidonggou, the 6th Annual Meeting of Asian Paleolithic Association, The 18th Symposium of Suyanggae and Her Neighbours. He is especially thankful to Dr. Yung-jo Lee for inspiring me to contribute a suitable article for the proceedings. He also thanks Mr. Parthasarathi Das for meticulously going through the MSS and some appropriate betterment. For accessing over research materials and relevant documents, he is indebted to the Directorate of Archaeology, West Bengal, and to the Director of The Zoological Survey of India.

References

Banerjee, S., 1981. Animal remains from Bharatpur (Dist. Burdwan, W.B.). *Rec. zool. Surv. India.* 79, 193-201.

Banerjee, S., ROY, S.K. and Talukder, B., 1991. Prehistoric fauna excavated from Hatikra District, Birbhum, West Bengal, India. *Rec. zool. Surv. India.* 90(1-4), 105-109.

Chakraborty, D.K., 1993-94. A note on the use of metal in Ancient Bengal. *Pratna Samiksha* Vol. 2 & 3, 155-158.

Chakraborty, R., 1992. Maritime trade in horses in early Historic Bengal: A'seal from Chandraketugarh. *Pratna Samiksha* Vol. 1, 155-160.

Chatterjee, P.K., 1993-94. Bahiri: A proto-historic manufacturing centre in West Bengal. *Pratna Samiksha* Vol. 2 & 3, 158-169.

Ghosh, M., Saha, K.D., Roy, S.K. and Talukder, B., 1992. A note on the domestic mammalian remains from Chalcolithic Kotasur, district Birbhum, West Bengal. *Rec. Zool. Surv. India.* Vol. 92, 5-8.

Ghosh, M. & Saha, U., 1992. Animal remains and bone tools from Pandu Rajar Dhibi. *Pratna Samiksha* Vol. 1, 89-100.

Ghosh, M., 1992. A brief report on the animal remains from Mangolkot. *Pratna Samiksha* Vol. 1, 123.

Ghosh, M., 1993-94. Animal remains from Baneswardanga and its affinities to other Chalcolithic sites in the district of Bardhaman, West Bengal. *Pratna Samiksha* Vol. 2 & 3, 144-154.

Ghosh, M., Saha, K.D. & Banerjee, S., 1993. Animal remains excavated from Bahiri, District Birbhum, West Bengal, India *Rec. Zool. Surv. India* Vol. 90, 111-115.

Gupta, P. & Pal, A., 1970. Human skeletal materials excavated at Pandu Rajar Dhibi. *Bulletin. Anthropological Survey of India* XIX, Nos. 3 & 4, Calcutta, 127-202.

Mukherjee, S.C., 1992. Archaeological activities in West Bengal: 1960-90. *Pratna Samiksha* Vol. 1, 1-26.

Pal, J.N., 1994. Mesolithic settlements in the Ganga plains. *Man and Environment* Vol. 19, Pune, 91-101.

Chapter 7.
Papers on Museums

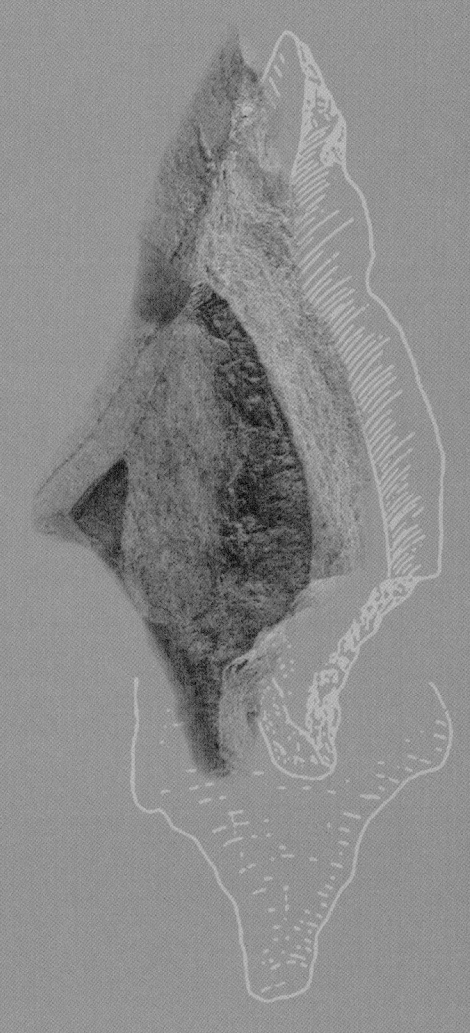

The Suyanggae and Gawaji Rice Museums from the European Perspective of Public Archeology

Marcel BARTCZAK[1], Lucyna DOMAŃSKA[1], Yung-jo LEE[2], Jong-yoon WOO[2]

[1] Institute of Archaeology, University of Lodz, Poland ; marcel.bartczak@uni.lodz.pl
[2] Institute of Korean Prehistory (IKP), Korea

ABSTRACT

The article discusses research on archaeological reserves, museums, and open-air museums, focusing on two prominent cultural sites in Korea. The first is the Suyanggae archaeological complex, a significant site for Korean Prehistory, discovered during dam construction in 1980. Excavations revealed it was a seasonal flint workshop during the Upper Paleolithic period. The Suyanggae Museum, established in 2006, combines research, conservation, education, and community awareness to protect and promote cultural heritage. The second is the Gawaji Rice Museum, showcasing Neolithic rice crops discovered in 1991 in Goyang City. Opened in 2001 and modernized in 2014, the museum combines modern exhibits with educational programs for children and local residents. Both museums align with ICOMOS guidelines, emphasizing protection, education, and the interpretation of archaeological heritage. These institutions set high standards for presenting the Stone Age despite the challenge of limited visible architectural remains.

국문초록

본 논문은 고고학 보호구역, 박물관, 야외박물관을 대상으로 한 연구결과에 관한 것으로 유물을 전시할 뿐 아니라 보존 보호하기 위해 만들어진 한국의 2개 주요 문화유적에 초점을 두었다. 수양개선사유물전시관은 문화유산 관련 연구, 보존, 대중화, 교육시설로 활용되고 있으며, 특히 지방 국가문화유산에 대한 의식고양을 통해 문화유산 보호와 보존의 중요성을 부각시키고 있다. 가와지 볍씨박물관은 고양시 젊은 계층의 교육, 시민 대상의 흥미있는 활동을 주로 실시하고 있다. 박물관 직원은 청소년을 대상으로 고고학과 식물재배 관련 주제로 교육활동을 실시하고, 고양시민을 위해 월 단위로 고양의 역사와 문화를 주제로 한 인문학 강좌를 실시하고 있다. 수양개선사유물전시관과 가와지볍씨박물관은 석기시대와 문화유산에 관한 높은 수준의 문화유산 보호, 교육, 지식 확산의 장으로 활용됨으로써 구미 선진국의 박물관과 같이 인류의 고대역사를 엄격한 과학적 기준으로 전시하는 현대적 교육센터이자 연구중심 기관으로 여겨진다.

Keywords : Gawaji Rice Museum, Suyanggae Museum, public archaeology, Goyang, Danyang

1. Introduction

In May 2019, thanks to the kindness of Professor Lee Yung-Jo, Professor Woo Jong-Woon and other authorities of the Institute of Korean Prehistory, Polish delegation members, i.e., Professor Lucyna Domańska and Marcel Bartczak could carry out research in Korea during a ten-day research trip. They traveled around Korea to collect information about dissemination methods of the results of archaeological research in Korea and to study processes of their presentation to the public. For the purpose of the presented article, all the authors discussed the results of their work on public archeology in Korea.

The polish delegation members have learned a lot about making the results of Korean archaeological research public. They have watched and studied how cultural institutions in Korea deal with the growing needs of tourists. They have learned that museums offer a lot of attractions and interesting forms of education to people.

The polish representatives have visited many great prehistoric archeological sites and museums: famous Jeongokri site, Wolpyeong site in the Boseong River Valley, Sorori site, Gochang Dolmen site, the Chungbuk National University Museum, the Chosun University Museum, Project "Culport" workshop at the University of Mokpo and many others.

All of these represented innovative patents and ways to promote and educate about archaeology, and to preserve archaeological heritage, which is so important in today's rapidly changing world. However, in this article we would like to focus in particular on two museums: the Suyanggae Museum and the Gawaji Rice Museum.

2. Suyanggae Museum

The archaeological complex of Suyanggae is one of the most important sites for Korean Prehistory. It is located at Aegok-ri, Jeokseong-meyon, Danyang County, Chungbuk Province, by the South Han River (Domańska, 2016; Lee et al., 2014; Lee et al., 2013; Lee, 2007). This archaeological site complex was discovered in 1980 when exploring the area where the Chungju Dam was to be built. Construction of the dam began in 1978 and ended in 1985 (Lee et al., 2015a). The dam was built in response to the need for regional development but its construction threatened Korea's valuable cultural heritage.

The site complex has been explored by archaeologists from the Chungbuk National University Museum, and later by researchers from the Institute of Korean Prehistory (Lee, 2007; Lee, Woo, 2008; Lee et al., 2015a). Both research teams were led by Professor Lee Yung-Jo.

The Suyanggae complex consists of open sites. Over a

Fig. 1 The Suyanggae Museum; photo by M. Bartczak

Fig. 2 The Suyanggae Museum; photo by M. Bartczak

dozen excavation campaigns have been carried out so far, and this site is among the most notable archaeological sites in East Asia. Moreover, the site was designated as National Historic Relic No. 398 (Lee, 2007; Lee, Woo, 2008; Lee et al., 2015a). Excavation works included localities 1, 2, 3 and 6. Only locality 2 shows remains of a settlement from the beginning of our era (Lee et al., 2014). The other sites are mainly flint workshops from the Upper Paleolithic, where the total sum of flint implements is over 100,000. The first works took place at locality 1 in 1983-1985. Immediately after the work was complete, the site was flooded when the Chungju Dam was built. About thirty years later the same fate befell locality 6, located 3.5km from locality 1. Excavations there were undertaken in 2013, in connection with the construction of another dam on the South Han River. In this place, apart from flint tools and products, fragments of Paleolithic portable art and one pebble stone with engraved lines were found (Suh et al., 2015; Lee et al., 2015b). However, the most important fact is that the Suyanggae complex was primarily a large flint workshop, used seasonally during the Paleolithic period (Lee, 2007; Lee, Woo, 2008; Lee et al., 2015a). These findings undoubtedly testify to the high development of representatives of the Suyanggae culture and the importance of this site for the world science.

Thanks to the field works performed by the Chungbuk National University, the Suyanggae Paleolithic complex

Fig. 3 Remains of open archaeological excavations in Suyanggae; photo by M. Bartczak

Fig. 5 Entrance hall of Suyanggae Museum; photo by M. Bartczak

Fig. 4 Sculptures depicting hunters and gatherers in Suyanggae; photo by M. Bartczak

Fig.6 Archeology lesson for children; photo by M. Bartczak

was saved from destruction by flooding. Another goal of the researchers of this site, was to protect the artifacts obtained during the excavation works. For this purpose, in 2006 the Suyanggae Museum was built (**Fig.1, 2**). The entire archaeological reserve – the Museum building and the extensive surrounding area, is a showcase of this area. The Suyanggae Museum is not only a research base and conservation base, but also serves as a popularizing and teaching facility.

The building of the Museum, towering over the meandering Southern Han River, along with the surrounding area, with an open archaeological excavation pit and sculptures depicting hunters and gatherers captured during their daily activities show a substitute for possible activities once performed by hunters-gatherers (**Fig. 3** ; **4**). This is very important for tourists to perceive this place as very important for local and the world's prehistory. The whole composition is also intended to raise awareness among local communities about the need to protect such places and their importance for the preservation of the National Cultural Heritage (Bartczak, 2019).

Inside the Museum, the most important artifacts obtained during the excavations have been carefully displayed: e.g., animal bones implements or flint and stone tools. The excavations and models showing the individual localities stratigraphies are reconstructed. For better perception of the place, many "themed scenes" from the lives of former hunters and gatherers were reconstructed and presented using multimedia devices inside the Museum. Furthermore, numerous exhibitions were also devoted to these prehistoric times. Each section is described in detail in Korean and English, thanks to which a tourist (even without a guide), will get to know history of this place thoroughly. The main theme of the Museum exposition is the Stone Age, especially the Paleolithic period, shown from a local perspective. However, education focuses on the entire fascinating prehistory of Korea and the world of the Stone Age (**Fig. 5**).

The Museum also conducts numerous activities aimed at popularizing knowledge about this important site. Archeology lessons organized for children from nearby schools are very substantive and interesting at the same time. Children do not get bored and after the lecture many right questions are asked (**Fig. 6**).

The Suyanggae archaeological reserve shows importance

Fig. 7 Suyanggae site area; photo by M. Bartczak

Fig. 8 Surroundings of Suyanggae site complex; photo by M. Bartczak

Fig. 9 The Gawaji Rice Museum; photo by Yung-Jo Lee

Fig. 10 Interior of the Gawaji Rice Museum; photo by M. Bartczak

of the excavation site. Although there are no visible traces of the Stone Age human activity on the surface, the entire reserve is built to make visitors aware of the prehistoric times. It is a kind of a "window into the past". In addition, the area is protected because the still existing, unexplored archaeological substance is waiting for the next generation of researchers (Fig. 7).

The beautiful landscape is also a great asset. It makes it even more encouraging to visit the "Suyanggae" (which means "shores overgrown with weeping willow"), just as it did encourage the Stone Age hunter-gatherers in the past (Fig. 8). In one sentence: it is an archaeological reserve showing how to properly care for an archaeological site and how to use its potential to popularize archeology and knowledge about the Stone Age hunter-gatherers and their daily activities Another place that we would like to describe is the Gawaji Rice Museum.

3. Gawaji Rice Museum

In 1991 at the archaeological "Gawaji" site located in Daehwadong, Ilsanseo-gu, Goyang City, Gyeonggi Province, Korea, the ancient rice crops were found. The site was investigated by the Department of Archaeology and Art History, Chungbuk National University. The oldest rice grains found along with pottery and chipped stone tools are related to the Neolithic period and dated back to 5,020 BP (Lee et al., 2016). The ancient rice variety discovered was named "Goyang Gawaji Rice" (Lee, 2017). Years of study of the Gawaji archaeological site and laboratory works on "Goyang Gawaji Rice" led to the results which indicate that the initial, fully purposeful large-scale rice cultivation in Korean Peninsula is related to the Neolithic period (Lee et al., 2016).

In 2001, ten years after the first excavations at the Gawaji site, in the city of Goyang, one of the buildings was converted into a museum, where artifacts from the site were stored. Re-examination of rice grains in connection with the scientific (academic) event related to establishing the origin of rice in the Korean Peninsula was a milestone for the Gawaji Rice Museum and exhibits. This event took place in Goyang City in 2013 and had an international character (Lee, 2017).

Firstly, a scientific discussion encouraged local authorities to renovate the Gawaji Rice Museum building. The Museum was modernized and reopened on March 19, 2014 (Fig. 9).

Secondly, the conference initiated a series of scientific debates on the Neolithic agriculture in the world. In the following years, not only representatives from China, Korea and Japan but also scientists from the United States, Canada, Malaysia, Denmark, Poland, Russia, Ecuador and many other countries were invited. The above mentioned events have

Fig. 11 Models of archaeologists working on the Gawaji site; photo by M. Bartczak

Fig. 12 Ancient rice grains; photo by M. Bartczak

Fig. 13 An exhibition presenting contemporary and Neolithic agricultural works; photo by M. Bartczak

Fig. 14 Artificial figures of the Joseon dynasty farmers; photo by M. Bartczak

had a huge impact on the development of the Gawaji Rice Museum.

The new interior of the museum makes a great impression. The walls are decorated with panels presenting the most important information about the excavation and the history of the discovery (**Fig. 10**). Behind the exhibition shafts one can see historical photos, reconstructed models of archaeologists working on the Gawaji site (**Fig. 11**) and of course excavated artifacts: pottery, flint and stone tools, and most importantly – ancient rice grains (**Fig. 12**).

In addition, the exhibitions show the entire history of rice cultivation, not only in Korea but throughout the Far East. Substantially prepared information about today and ancient farming fits very well into the prepared exhibition of photos of contemporary agricultural works and artificial figures of the Neolithic farmers at work (**Fig. 13**). The reconstructed interiors of the Joseon dynasty huts and barns, showing the Stone Age people during their daily work, are also impressive (**Fig. 14**).

The activity of the museum focuses not only on scientific research and organisation of scientific meetings, but also on the education of the youngest and popularizing activities among the citizens of the Goyang city. For example, the museum staff conduct lessons for children on topics related to archeology, but also with focus on cultivation and growing plants (**Fig. 15 ; 16**).

A special educational lecture was held for the "Goyang Citizens University" students. More than 300 students participated in four sessions on the origins and cultivation of rice. Monthly humanities lectures entitled "Goyang history and culture" organised for the Goyang residents, play an important popularizing role. The lectures are conducted by eminent scholars and well-known officials, and the topics discussed during the meetings range from archeology, through museology, heritage protection, to the cultivation of plants and rice. (Lee, 2017). The above activities show how important a role the Gawaji Rice Museum plays in the lives of the inhabitants of Goyang City.

Fig. 15 Cultivation and growing plants lesson; photo by M. Bartczak

Fig. 16 Cultivation and growing plants lesson; photo by M. Bartczak

4. Conclusions

The cultural facilities described above comprehensively fit into the scheme of a modern and innovative way of showing the past (e.g. Grima, 2017; Kobyliński, 2020; Paardekooper, 2012; Pawleta 2016). In our opinion, the first of the components of the role model scheme for a museum institution and archaeological reserve assumes a good interpretation and presentation of an archaeological site. A visitor must not only gather knowledge, but also experience the past by interacting with the artifacts discovered in the place visited in order to understand the entire context – this is one of the postulates of the ICOMOS Charter for the Interpretation and Presentation of Cultural Heritage sites (Quebec, 2008).

Therefore, it is important to combine a strictly scientific

Fig. 17 Professor Yung-jo LEE and Polish delegation: Professor Lucyna Domańska and Marcel Bartczak, at Gawaji Rice Museum; photo by Gawaji Rice Museum crew.

Fig. 18 Professor Yung-jo LEE and Polish delegation: Professor Lucyna Domańska and Marcel Bartczak, at Gawaji Rice Museum; photo by Gawaji Rice Museum crew.

institution with a modern teaching center, promoting the results of research on the most ancient human history and presenting them in an accessible manner. Moreover, as with Suyanggae, experience of the place itself and its landscape is an important element. As in the case of leading European open-air museums, Suyanggae Museum is embedded in the beautiful landscape without disturbing its values, and at the same time it manifests importance of this place and protects the entire complex of sites *in situ*, which is one of the main assumptions of the ICOMOS Charter for the Protection and Management of the Archaeological Heritage (Lausanne,

1990). In addition, the museum institution, through its presence, shows importance and orders care for unexplored archaeological substance, at the same time location of its attractions–whether it is a building or a theme park of artificial figures–does not harm potential archaeological sites, as the attractions are built on already explored sites. Such a model of conduct is also very important in the conventions of archaeological reserves in Europe and in the world (Kobyliński, 2020). Protection and preservation of archaeological sites *in situ* was also postulated in a ICOMOS document known as The Declaration of San Antonio (San Antonio, 1996).

This is a very difficult task, especially for museums representing prehistoric times, known only from archaeological research. In our opinion, a good interpretation and presentation of the Stone Age sites is one of the most difficult museum undertakings due to invisibility of architectural objects or monumental structures. Both Suyanggae Museum and Gawaji Rice Museum fulfill this task in an excellent way. Moreover, we believe that both the described museums are very attractive and understandable in their function for tourists and have a large educational impact on the local community. Without a doubt, these are outstanding institutions of the third decade of the 21st century.

Reference

Bartczak, M., 2019. Stone Age Archaeological Sites in the Landscape. Monumentalisation of Sites on the South Korea Example. Acta Universitatis Lodziensis. *Folia Archaeologica* 34. https://doi.org/10.18778/0208-6034.34.12

Domańska, L., 2016. Kompleks Suyanggae–dlaczego tak ważny?. in: Domańska, L., Marciniak-Kajzer, A., Andrzejewski, A., Rzepecki S. eds., *Archaeologia et Pomerania*, Lodz, 339-345.

Grima, R., 2017. Presenting archaeological sites to the public, in: Moshenska, G. ed., *Key Concept in Public Archaeology*, UCL Press, 73-92, https://doi.org/10.2307/j.ctt1vxm8r7.10

ICOMOS. 2008. *Charter for the Interpretation and Presentation of Cultural Heritage sites* – Quebec: .https://www.icomos.org/quebec2008/charters/interpretation/pdf/GA16_Charter_Interpretation_20081004_FR+EN.pdf

ICOMOS. The Declaration of San Antonio, 1996. https://www.icomos.org/en/179-articles-en-francais/ressources/charters-and-standards/188-the-declaration-of-san-antonio

ICOMOS. 1990. *Charter for the Protection and Management of the Archaeological Heritage*–Lausanne. https://www.icomos.org/charters/arch_e.pdf

Kobyliński, Z., 2020. Zarządzanie Dziedzictwem Kulturowym – wprowadzenie do problematyki, Warsaw: UKSW Press.

Lee, Y.J., 2007. Suyanggae: Why So Important?. in: Drozdov, N., Lee, Y.J. eds., *The XIIth International Symposium Suyanggae and Her Neighbours, Prehistoric migrations in Eurasia and America*, Krasnoyarsk, 7-23.

Lee, Y.J., Woo J.Y., 2008. Suyanggae: Why So Important (II). in: Lee, Y.J., Ambiru, M., Shimada, K., Otani, K. eds., *The 13th International Symposium for Commemoration of the 25th Anniversary of Suyanggae Excavation: Suyanggae and Her Neighbours* in Kyushu, Miyazaki Prefecture, 37-53.

Lee, Y.J., Woo J.Y., Lee, S.W., 2013. Suyanggae: Why So Important (VI)–with New Findings from Loc.III. in: Gao, X., Drozdov, N., Domańska, L., Woo, J.Y. eds., *Commemoration Int'l Symp. for the 90th Anniversary of Shuidonggou Discovery and the 18th Suyanggae and Her Neighbours for 50 Years of Prof. Yungjo LEE's Paleolithic Study: SHUIDONGGOU and SUYANGGAE*, Chungbuk, 124-127.

Lee, Y. J., Woo, J.Y., Lee, S.W, An, J.H., 2014. SUYANGGAE: Why So Important(VII)? - with the newly excavated Loc.VI, Suyanggae Site. in: Domańska, L., Lee, Y.J., Woo, J.Y. eds., *The 19th International Symposium Suyanggae and Her Neighbours in Poland, Lodz and Suyanggae*, Lodz, 191-197.

Lee, Y.J., Woo, J.Y., Lee, S.W., 2015a. Suyanggae: why so important(IX)?: 30 Years of the Suyanggae Complex. in: Lee, Y.J., Woo J.Y., Lee S.W., Lee, K.W. eds., *The 20th(2) International Symposium for Celebration of the 30th Anniversary of the 1st Site Excavations: SUYANGGAE and Her Neighbours* in Korea, Chungbuk, 247-262.

Lee, K.W., Lee, Y.J., Woo J.Y., Lee, S.W, Ahn, J.H., 2015b. Engraved stones found at Suyanggae Locality VI: signs of modern human behavior. in: Lee, Y.J., Woo J.Y., Lee S.W., Lee, K.W. eds., *The 20th(2) International Symposium for Celebration of the 30th Anniversary of the 1st Site Excavations: SUYANGGAE and Her Neighbours* in Korea, Chungbuk, 299-312.

Lee, Y.J., Woo, J.Y., Lee, K.W. 2016. Seed in History of 5020 years, Goyang Gawai Rice. in: Lee, Y.J., Park, T.S. eds., *International Symposium on the Prehistoric Cultivation in the World – with the focus on Goyang Gawaji Rice, 5020 years old*. Goyang Gawaji Rice Museum Research report No. 3, Goyang, 143-162.

Lee, Y.J., 2017. Present and future of Gawaji rice museum of Goyang city. (In: Lee, Y.J., Park, T.S. eds., *Goyang Gawaji Rice on Excavation, Research and Museum*) Goyang Gawaji Rice Museum Research report No. 4, Goyang, 153-185.

Paardekooper, R., 2012. Archaeological open-air museums across Europe. Their 125 years history and a debate on their future. in: Gancarski, J. eds., *Skanseny archeologiczne i archeologia eksperymentalna*, Krosno, 13-34.

Pawleta, M., 2016. Przeszłość we współczesności. *Studium metodologiczne archeologicznie kreowanej przeszłości w przestrzeni społecznej*, Poznań: UAM Press.

Suh, H.S., Lee Y.J., Woo, J.Y., Lee, S.W., Park, J.M., Ahn, J.H., Lee, K.W., Joo, Y.S., Choi, W.H., Yang, H.J., 2015. Measurement of Dimension and its Related Measurands of the Pebble Stone with Engraved Lines Excavated from Loc.VI of SUYANGGAE Site, Korea. in: Lee, Y.J., Woo J.Y., Lee S.W., Lee, K.W. eds., *The 20th(2) International Symposium for Celebration of the 30th Anniversary of the 1st Site Excavations: SUYANGGAE and Her Neighbours* in Korea, Chungbuk, 283-297.

A study on the interpretation and presentation of the prehistoric culture and ecological environment at the Suyanggae Prehistory Museum

Jong-ho CHOE [1], Yung-jo LEE [2]

[1] Director Gernal, Gyohak Museology Research Institute, Korea ; jhchoe58@hanmail.net
[2] Institute of Korean Prehistory (IKP), Korea

ABSTRACT

In order to recognize the value as a composed heritage of the prehistoric culture and ecological environment of Suyanggae site, to share the meaning of the community, and to clarify the academic and technological importance of the academic and technological importance, this article attempts to suggest the improvement of interpretation and presentation of prehistoric culture and ecological environment in the Suyangae Prehistory Museum on the basis of the paleolithic survey methodology and the "ICOMOS Charter for the Interpretation and Presentation of Cultural Heritage Sites" (ICOMOS 2008). After the team of Chungbuk National University Museum(CBNUM) first visited the Suyanggae site for the purpose of the submerged area survey of the Chungju Dam in 1980, CBNUM excavated Locs. 1, 2, and 3 of Suyanggae site from the first excavation in 1983 to the 8th excavation in 2001, and the Institute of Korean Prehistory (IKP) excavated Locs. 1, 3 and 6 of the Suyanage site from 2015. The Suyanggae site was designated Historic Site No. 398 in 1997, showing the essence of Paleolithic culture of the Upper Paleolithic in Northeast Asia around 20,000 years ago. In commemoration of this, the Suyanggae Prehistory Museum was established in 2006, on the basis of the survey results of the 13th excavation in 2015, museum activities are being carried out by exhibiting on mainly paleolithic artifacts and additionally paleolithic environment factors excavated from the cultural layers of the Middle Paleolithic Age to the Proto Three Kingdoms Period. In the future, a measure for the best interpretation and presentation of prehistoric culture and ecological environment in the Suyangae Prehistory Museum should be holistically and systematically applied to the paleolithic survey methodology validated at the International Symposium of "Suyanggae and Her Neighbours" including current ongoing research results, and the principles of ICOMOS Charter 2008.

국문초록

단양 수양개 유적은 1980년 충북대학교 박물관팀(박물관장 이융조)이 충주댐 수몰지역 조사로 처음 찾은 후, 1983년부터 2001년까지(1차-8차) 1·2·3지구를 발굴하였고, (재)한국선사문화연구원(이사장 이융조)이 2008년부터 2015년까지(9차-13차) 1·3·6지구를 발굴하였다. 이 유적은 2만 년 전후의 동북아시아 후기구석기시대 석기문화의 정수를 보여주는 유적으로서 1997년 사적(제398호)으로 지정되었다. 이를 기념하여 2006년 단양군은 수양개선사유물전시관을 건립하였다. 2015년 제13차 발굴까지 단양 수양개 유적의 조사연구 성과를 기반으로 수양개유물전시관은 중기구석기시대부터 원삼국시대까지 문화층에서 출토된 선사 유물과 고환경을 해석하고 표출하는 선사문화박물관 활동을 펼치고 있다. 수양개선사유물전시관의 선사 문화 및 생태환경 해석과 표출을 위한 최선의 방안은 단양 수양개 유적과 관련된 현재 진행형 연구성과뿐 아니라, 국제회의 "수양개와 그 이웃들(Suyanggae and Her Neighbors)" 등에서 검증된 구석기시대 조사연구 방법론과 〈문화 유적지 해석과 표출을 위한 이코모스 헌장〉(2008)의 원칙을 규범으로 선사 문화 및 생태환경을 해석하고 표출할 수 있도록 해야 한다.

Keywords : Chungbuk National University Museum (CBNUM), ICOMOS Charter 2008, "Suyanggae and Her Neighbours", Suyanggae Prehistory Museum, Institute of Korean Prehistory (IKP)

1. Introduction

In order to appraise the value as a composed heritage of the prehistoric culture and ecological environment of Suyanggae site, to share the meaning in the community, and to recognize the academic and technological importance in the world's academic field, this article attempts to suggest the improvement of interpretation and presentation of prehistoric culture and ecological environment in the Suyanggae Prehistory Museum on the basis of the paleolithic survey methodology and the ICOMOS Charter (ICOMOS, 2008).

After the team of CBNUM first visited the Suyanggae site for the purpose of the Submerged Area Survey of the Chungju Dam in 1980, CBNUM excavated Locs. 1, 2, and 3 of Suyanggae site from the 1st excavation in 1983 to 8th excavation in 2001, and the Institute of Korean Prehistory excavated in the Locs. 1 and 3 and 6 of Suyanggae site from the years of 2008 to 2015 (Lee, 2020) (Fig. 1).

The Suyanggae site was designated as the Historic Site No. 398 in 1997, showing the essence of Paleolithic Culture of the Upper Paleolithic period in Northeast Asia around 20,000 years ago ie. 20ka (Lee, 2020). In commemoration of this, the Suyanggae Prehistory Museum was established in 2006 on the basis of the survey results of the 13th excavation in 2015, museum activities are being carried out by exhibiting on mainly paleolithic artifacts and additionally paleolithic environment factors excavated from the cultural layers of the Middle Paleolithic Age to the Proto Three Kingdoms Period (Danyang-gun, 2020).

In the future, a measure for the best interpretation and presentation of prehistoric culture and ecological environment in the Suyanggae Prehistory Museum should be holistically and systematically applied to the paleolithic survey methodology validated at the International Symposia of "Suyanggae and Her Neighbours" including current ongoing research results, and the principles of ICOMOS Charter 2008 (Choe, 2021).

Fig. 1 Suyanggae Site Loc. 1, excavated 1983~'85 years.

2. Current Situation Analysis on the Interpretation and Presentation of Prehistoric Culture and Suyanggae site

There are tasks to be solved in order to comprehend the formation and nature of Suyanggae site. "First, it is necessary to make study of the connection of sedimentary layers between the Paleolithic sites of Suyanggae Locs. 1 and 3, and the formation period of the sites. This is because Loc. 1 is located above Terrace 2 (132m above sea level), and Loc. 3 is found above Terrace 3(156m above sea level). In addition, it is a matter of period of hand axes identified during the survey of the surface of the Suyanggae Loc. 3. This hand axe is from the age earlier than the Upper Paleolithic relics identified in Suyanggae Loc. 3, suggesting the possibility of distribution from the Lower to the Middle Paleolithic cultural layers after the formation of Terrace 3 and before the formation of Terrace 2. The Suyanggae site is a place where Terrace 2 and Terrace 3 are distributed together, and it is highly likely that people from the Lower and to the Upper Paleolithic periods lived (Kim et al., 2020).

Suyanggae site is located 132m above sea level on the riverside of the upper Namhan River. It is surrounded by high and low mountains, and the river flows to the southeast of the site. The rocks that constitute this site are the Bansongtong division of the Daedong supergroup, which is accompanied by sandstone and shale, and the large limestone division of the Joseon supergroup, and then alluvial layers are stacked in the fourth system; especially, limestone areas are well developed (Lee and Kang, 1996).

Investigations so far have confirmed that five cultural layers form a stratum from the Middle Paleolithic to the Bronze Age. About one-twentieth of the site or 85m² were excavated, and the patterned earthenware layer (IIIe) formed on the slope in terrace of the river, the Paleolithic cultural layer (IVa, IVb) and the Bronze Age cultural layer were revealed (Lee, 2013).

"In the comb-patterned pottery layer (IIIe) as a fine sand layer, stone axes and comb-patterned pottery pieces were found. Considering the grinding technique of chipped stone hand axe and the pattern form of comb-pattern pottery, it is thought to be a layer developed in the Middle or Upper Neolithic period. In this Neolithic cultural layer, relics with clear cultural characteristics such as comb-pattern pottery, chipped stone axe, arrowhead, net weight, etc. were excavated. In addition, in the Bronze Age cultural layer, the bottom of the polished stone adze, plane blade, and plain pottery were excavated, and the classification of the layers was clearly confirmed" (Lee, 2013).

"Mud-cracks phenomenon appears in the Paleolithic cultural layer (IVa, IVb) as yellow-brown soil layers (10YR4/4~5/6). This corresponds to the interglacial period with a warm climate, such as the habitation site of Upper Paleolithic in Seokjang-ni and the Cheongju Saemgol sites. The culture developed on this cultural layer was found to have been formed at different periods based on the state and nature of the excavated relics. As for the materials for the relics, quartz, shale, siliceous shale, and rhyolite were used a lot in both the upper and lower layers, and quartz, siliceous rock, obsidian, etc. were used little by little" (Lee, 2013).

"The upper (IVa) cultural layer of the Paleolithic period is the Upper Paleolithic cultural layer which is divided into two layers. The lower layer corresponds to the Lower and Middle Paleolithic period, and the upper layer is interpreted as a late cultural layer of the Upper Paleolithic period. The material of the relic is shale, which was found to have been quarried from Sanjegol away 1.5km from the site, and made tools. Among the relics, the hand axe is similar in shape and method to those excavated in France and Algeria, drawing great interest. Further, many of the hand knife excavated for the first time in Korea, chopping-tools, various types of tanged point, round end-scraper, and scraper were excavated. Especially, there are a number of flaking tools in a relics layer of the typical Upper Paleolithic period such as scraper, end-scraper, burin, point, micro-blade core in the boat shape and micro-blade etc. made by elaborately giving indirect percussion and retouch" (Lee, 2013).

"In addition, a large number of obsidian are presented as data on the origin issue and related trade and movement. The scraper in the shape of carene with the trimmed surface among small micro-blade cores, which is ahead of the Japanese Yubetsu technique, is compared to the relics layer of end scraper and scraper and the relics of habitation site in Seokjang-ni. The small micro-blade core and traditional stone tools in the shape of care·ne newly present the diffusion problem of this method in Korea and Northeast Asia such as Siberia, North China, Mongolia, and Japan" (Lee, 2013).

"The Middle Paleolithic cultural layer of the bottom layer (V) developed on a pebble layer mainly composed of sandstone, quartzite, and shale. The stone knapping technology is a direct or hurling technique using an anvil, which is applied with secondary retouch, and the stone tool is generally heavy and large, so there are few signs of retouch" (Lee, 2013).

"In the lower cultural layer (V) contains relics with a strong tradition of the Middle Paleolithic period, and materials for restoring of stone knapping technology such as anvil, hammer, core, and flake were excavated. In addition, various stone knapping technology are shown, and there are few multi-purpose stone tools, but many simple tools with only one function. The hand axe which made the inside and outside of the coil-type blade with cross-cutting, the biface hand axe which made the S-shaped warped blade, and the multi-rung round core which made of the plank gemstone of quartz shale applied for turning punch technique, show the characteristics of the Acheulean traditional Mousterian culture. Prism-shaped and similar Levallois core, and a pair of flakes were excavated" (Lee, 2013).

"The Suyanggae site is largely regarded as the Upper Paleolithic and Middle Paleolithic period, and as sunny relics of the riverside, such as Seokjang-ni, Jeongok-ni, Myeong-o-ri, and Changnae sites, have been presented the data on restoring stone knapping technology and broadly understanding the Paleolithic culture including the connection and diffusion of culture. In addition, there is a high possibility that a habitat site will be found on the basis of concerning the excavation of a great amount of charcoal. The relics excavated here include a hand axe, a point, and tang, which especially a hand axe is mostly similar to Acheulian Mousterian form" (Lee, 2013).

The above cultural layer is a typical Upper Paleolithic relic that can be compared to the habitat site of Seokjang-ri and Changnae sites, and the below cultural layer is a relic with a Middle Paleolithic tradition that is placed in from the Middle to Upper Paleolithic period.

"This site is an important relic for mutual comparative research on the Paleolithic culture developed in the central region, such as nearby Jeommal Yonggul, Sangsi Rock Shelter, Dodam Geumgul, Myeong-o-ri, and Changnae sites and understanding the Paleolithic culture of North East Aisa. The micro-blade cores and obsidian tools excavated from the cultural layer of the Upper Paleolithic period are critical data for clarifying the path of cultural diffusion through comparative research with nearby Chinese and Japanese sites" (Lee, 2013).

The survey and research results described in Danyang Suyanggae site by Yung-jo Lee and Sujin Kong are concentrated on the current status evaluation of prehistoric culture interpretation, and there is no current status evaluation of ecological environment interpretation and presentation of research results (Lee and Kong, 2003).

3. Proposed Improvement of Interpretation and Presentation of Prehistoric Culture and Ecological Environment of the Suyanggae Prehistory Museum

In order to compare and verify the principles of "The ICOMOS Charter for the Interpretation and Presentation of Cultural Heritage Sites", it is necessary to seriously examine Yung-jo Lee "My Prospect and Retrospect for the 40th Anniversary of Suyanggae site", he mentioned "One of the pillars of the study of Suyanggae should prepare a revised program to analyze the relics of Suyanggae Loc. 1(Lee, 2020). As the fastest way, referring to data from Chungbuk National University Museum, which selects and displays representative relics of Loc. 1, could be one of the ways. And don't forget to think about establishing a plan and examination to compare and examine the unique cultural patterns in Loc. 3 and the third and fourth cultural layers in Loc. 6. It is expected to be a good criterion for the chronology and character regulations of the entire Paleolithic culture of Suyanggae if you closely compare the fact that Loc. 3 is a small number of stone blade core and micro-blade core while utilizing shale as the principal gemstone. (**Fig. 2**)

As expected, the basis of Paleolithic research is to cross-check a good model in Suyanggae on the accurate analysis and interpretation of stone tools and they suggested a methodology for interpretation and presentation of Suyanggae's entire Paleolithic culture for comparative analysis and cross-examination (Lee and Kong, 2006).

In addition, Yung-jo Lee said, "While all Locs. 1, 2 and 6 excavated so far have been completely submerged and disappeared into Chungju Dam, this Loc. 3 is the only excavated site fully preserved. If so, of course, it is necessary to make good use of the phenomenon of the excavated ruins so that many domestic and foreign visitors to the museum can display the fact on-site using the latest exhibition method. Therefore, if it is displayed on the site along with the many relics excavated and studied so far, and its characteristics are well correlated with other relics, it will be no inferior to any other historical museum in foreign countries. In order to do so, it is necessary to expand and designate this area, named Loc. 3, and devise measures to preserve it at the national level," he said (Lee and Kong, 2006).

Concerning the current situation analysis of the Ecological Environment Interpretation and Presentation of Suyanggae site, suggested the application of theory and methodology based on Geology and Natural Environment in the Period of Korean Quarternary (Han, 1997), Flora and Fauna (Park, 1997), and Fossil of Human Bone (Kwon, 1997), And also important researches those are Identification of Charcoals Excavated at the Late Paleolithic site of Suyanggae (Park, et al., 2003) and A Study on Natural Environment of Upper Pleistocene in Korea Focused on the Pollen Analysis of Suyanggae and Changnae sites (Park, 2005) faithfully and sincerely suggested the current situation analysis on the interpretation of ecological environment of Suyanggae site. But merely suggested the current situation analysis on the Presentation of Ecological Environment of Suyanggae site, especially current status evaluation on the above presentation is regrettably few.

As of 2020, after a cross examination of Interpretation and Presentation of Prehistoric Culture and Ecological Environment of Suyanggae site based on the contents of the lobby introduction of the Suyanggae Prehistory Museum, it is necessary to suggest ways to interpret and present through the contents of the new exhibition hall lobby, the pre-cultural and ecological environment analysis and expression method of the Suyanggae Exhibition Hall, and the contents of the 3rd Exhibition Hall. Suyanggae site is a place that shows the essence of lithic culture in the Upper Paleolithic period in Korea and has the Paleolithic artifacts appearing in Northeast Asia around 20,000 years ago(Choe, 2021).

In order to implement interpretation and presentation for the 4th geology and ecological environment of the Suyanggae site based on the above research and analysis, workers at the Suyanggae Prehistory Museum should systematically reproduce, restore, experience, learn, and

Fig. 2 Suyanggae Site Loc. 3, excavated 2000-2011 years

Fig. 3 Suyanggae Prehistory Museum

exchange prehistoric culture and ecological environment by ICT-based digital media such as augmented reality, mixed reality, and realistic reality in exhibition rooms. (Fig. 3)

4. Conclusion

In conclusion, it is strongly recommended to interpret and present the principles of the Charter of ICOMOS for the Interpretation and Presentation Cultural Heritage sites based on the research results of the prehistoric cultural and ecological environment survey of Suyanggae site. In the future, the best way to interpret and present the prehistoric culture and ecological environment of the Suyanggae Prehistory Museum should be systematically applied to the Paleolithic research methodology verified at the International Symposia of "Suyanggae and Her Neighbors" (1996-2022).

References

Choe, J.H., 2021. A Study on the Interpretation and Presentation of the Prehistoric Culture and Ecological Environment at the Suyanggae Prehistory Museum. *Bakmulkwanhakbo* 40, 81; 84. (in Korean)

Danyang-gun. 2020. A Ring Prehistory Connecting with History: Suyanggae Prehistory Museum, Danyang-gun: *Suyanggae Prehistory Museum* 3. (in Korean)

Kim, J.Y. et al., 2020, Site-forming Process of the Suyanggae Loc. I, Loc. II, and Loc. VI Based on Morpho-sedimentary and -stratigraphic Context, Suyanggae Paelolithic Culture. *Report on the Excavation of Suyanggae Site (Loc. I and VI), Danyang.* (in Korean)

Kwon, Y.G., 1997. Fossil of Human Bone: Paleolithic Culture. *Korean History* 2, 73-83. (in Korean)

Lee, Y.J., 2013. Suyanggae Site. *Dictionary of Korean Archaeology*, Daejeon: National Research Institute of Cultural Heritage, 196-197. (in Korean)

Lee, Y.J., 2020. My Prospect and Retrospect for 40th Anniversary of Suyanggae Site. *Bakmulkwanhakbo* 39, 51; 52. (in Korean)

Lee, Y.J. and Kang, S.B., 1996. Danyang Suyanggae Site. *Encyclopedia of Korean Culture*, Seongnam City: Academy of Korean Studies. (in Korean) https://encykorea.aks.ac.kr

Lee, Y.J. and Kong, S.J., 2003. The Paleolithic culture and its age of the Suyanggae Paleolithic Site, Locality III. *The 2nd International Seminar for Commemorating the Chongokni Paleolithic Site: Geological Formation of the Chongokni Paleolithic Site and Paleolithic Archaeology in East Asia*, Ansan City: Hanyang University Research Center for Cultural Heritage, 33-41.

Lee Y.J, Kong S.J., 2006. Le Site Paléolithique de Suyanggae, Corée. *L'anthropologie* 110, France: Elsevier, 223-240. (in French)

Han, C.G., 1997. Geology and Natural Environment in the Period of Korean Quarternary Paleolithic Culture. *Korean History* 2, 40-53. (in Korean)

Park, Y.C., 1997. Flora and Fauna: Paleolithic Culture. *Korean History* 2, 54-72. (in Korean)

Park, W.G, Kim, Y.J., Lee, Y.J., 2003. Identification of Charcoals Excavated at the Late Paleolithic Site of Suyanggae. Lee, Y.J. and KIM, W.S. eds., *The 8th International Symposium for 20th Anniversary of Suyanggae First Excavation Suyanggae and Her Neighbours*, 49-61.

Park, M.S., 2005. A Study on Natural Environment of Upper Pleistocene in Korea Focused on the Pollen Analysis of Suyanggae and Changnae Sites. *Chungbuksahak* 15, 5-33. (in Korean)

ICOMOS. 2008. *ICOMOS Charter for the Interpretation and Presentation of Cultural Heritage Sites*. http://icip.icomos.org/ENG/groups_charter.html

National museums and national identity in South Korea

Yoon Ok Rosa PARK

Part-time lecturer in Dong Yang University, Korea ; park0851@hanmail.net

ABSTRACT

This paper explores national identity in national museums, which present the history and culture of Korea. As a "newly independent" country, Korea has a cultural identity that has witnessed a radical change in social, economic, political, and cultural frameworks following a painful colonial experience. In new nations, their histories and cultures, disturbed and distorted by imperial forces, have led them to ground their national identity in their ethnic roots, attempting to assert a sense of continuity. Yet, it must always be questioned whether national museums express the cultural identity of a nation, and whether they always reflect the current state of the nation and the lives of ordinary people. They may serve to provide a sense of belonging and security at national level, but may not always reflect what their people really want to see and know. Rarely do they reflect the diversity of people living in any one country. This is especially true in the contemporary world, where postmodernity and migration have increasingly led to both cultural diversity and acculturation.

국문초록

본 논문은 한국의 역사와 문화를 전시하는 국립박물관(역사박물관 포함)의 민족적 독자성을 분석하였다. 신생 독립국가로서 한국의 문화적 주체는 식민지 고통 경험 이후 사회, 경제, 정치, 문화 체제의 급격한 변화를 체험해 왔다. 새로운 한국에서는 제국주의 세력에 의해 교란되고 왜곡된 역사와 문화로 인해서 한민족의 기초를 민족의 뿌리에서 찾아 문화의 연속성을 주장하려고 시도했다. 한편 국립박물관이란 국가문화적 주체성을 잘 대변하고 있는지, 국가의 현재 위상과 서민의 삶을 항상 잘 반영하고 있는지에 대해 늘 문제제기를 해야 한다고 본다. 국립박물관은 국가 차원에서 소속감과 안전을 제공하는 데 도움이 될 수 있지만, 국민이 실제로 보고 알고 싶어하는 것이 무엇인지 항상 반영하는 것은 아니다. 국립박물관이 한 국가 안에 살고 있는 다양한 사람들의 삶을 반영하는 경우는 거의 없다. 특히 후기 현대사회의 문화적 다양성과 이주에 의한 문화변용이 증가하는 오늘날 세계에서 삶의 반영은 더욱 어렵다. 이러한 문화 다양성과 이주민에 의한 문화변용 아래 평화롭고 공생 공영하는 공동체 내에서 민족의 정체성을 공유하기 위해서는 민주화와 포괄적 평등이 주요한 선결 문제이다.

Keywords : national museums, contemporary history, national identity, colonial past, cultural diversity

1. Introduction

South Korea,[1] as a former colony with a turbulent history, falls under the category of a "new" emerging nation. The national liberation and emergence of the new Korea nation in 1945, after 36 years of Japanese rule, provided an impetus to a range of initiatives related to the preservation of the national past and its consolidation around core notions of national identity and cultural and historical heritage. National museums have made systematic attempts to cast off the Japanese legacy and to develop a modern national profile rooted in ancient, medieval, modern, and national revival periods. This paper explores national museums in South Korea, showing how they contribute to the construction of national identity through collections and display of objects of interest and through historical narratives.

The power of the heritage collected and presented by national museums allows them to make claims to be unsurpassable institutions in contemporary society, articulating and representing national values and cultures. Through national museums and their collections, new nations express their yearning for a golden and legitimate past and strive to balance the needs for continuity with increasing diversity and differences in present circumstances. In this contemporary society, defining national identity is a complex issue with multiple aspects, such as ethnicity, occupations, gender roles, sexuality, and age groups (Woodward, 1997) as well as historical traumas, divisions, conflicts, and tensions in the case of new nations. South Korea is going through this phenomenon, especially in terms of ethnicity, owing to increasing numbers of foreign workers as well as immigrant wives and their children since the end of the last century.

Korea cannot argue to be a single-race nation any more in the 21st century. Korean national identity has been firmly attached to the idea of one people as a nation, and thus national museums have been part of the notion of a brotherhood society. Koreans were vigorously imbued with the idea of homogeneous ethnicity until the foreign population flocked in for jobs and the chance to have an economically better life. Before the Korean Wave began in the late 1990s, for example, Korea was known merely for the Korean War or the 1988 Olympic Games. Now, this is considered to be quite different because of Korean entertainment and popular culture, such as pop music, TV dramas, and movies, spreading worldwide. In a time of globalization, culture may have become much more "transnational" through advanced communication media and international transactional systems. Any issue or event that occurs in a particular place is no longer confined within it: It instantly becomes global news and everyone's concern, be it politics, economics, or social issues.

Museums around the world have undertaken much good work in developing work practices and collections that respond to people's demand to know more about their history, national identity and their place in the world. Many of them still maintain elements of this purpose and, even if patriotism is not their main objective, they are still perceived as the caretakers of cultural treasures that hold the memory of the nation's glorious past. The construction of new museum buildings in the last decade in Korea show that national museums of archaeology and arts have been launching major projects instead of a national history museum, which opened in the end of 2012. In this study, the issues of identity will be investigated by analyzing two museums, the National Museum of Korea and the National Museum of Korea Contemporary History. These are the main agents in the museological presentation and mediation of Korean history with respect to explaining the history of a relatively new nation.

2. Nation-making of Korea

The Korean Peninsula has been subjected to external influences from ancient times and developed a sense of "us" – one nation, one people. In the meantime, Korea has witnessed an enormous change in almost every aspect of life during the first half of the 20th century through the Japanese occupation followed by the Korea War (1950-1953). Undergoing this period of turbulence, the links between the past and the present have also been threatened, marking a new era in modern history of Korea. In general, newly emerged nations have tended to mimic western lifestyles which are valued as goals to be attained in order to be "modern," and have thus focused on economic development by means of industrialization. This imitation may have had several side effects, especially in terms of morality, values, and identity. Korea has also pursued industrial development at the expense of its traditional culture, although its revival is observed in the process of globalization, adapting the form of the Korean Wave (*Hallyu*) – the revival of Korean traditional and contemporary cultures, like Korean cuisine, K-pop, and TV drams since the 1990s across Asia and beyond.

It has been suggested that the blind imitation of the West and the uncritical westernization that is ubiquitous in newly independent nations has caused a more severe dependence on western models of development in independence processes (e.g., Esposito, 1992; Guibernau, 1996). At the same time, revolutions and wars have been followed by the struggle for independence as well as for national formation.

---

1) Henceforth, Korea primarily indicates South Korea in this paper.

Civil wars have also been epidemic after independence as different ethnic-based groups or political parties within a nation have sought power. Thanks to the fact that individuals belong to the same ethnicity, however, it has been relatively easy to gather national power in difficult times, although there are some fractions between different regions because of their traditional lives in Korea. During IMF in 1997, for instance, people voluntarily took out gold from their closets and gathered them to pay national debts. The "Red Devils" of football fans in red shirts amazed the world by gathering in the City Hall Square to support the Korean national team during 2002 World Cup.

Revolutions have often been the driving force for the wars that have afflicted undeveloped countries. With this operation, single-party governments or military dictatorships have been endemic through the non-western world, causing internal partitions (Smith, 1983). In revolutions, it is common that the military takes a central position in the political life of the nation (Shils, 1962).[2] Korea could be regarded as a model of this role of military power and influence. In particular, the military governments (1960-1992) concentrated on the expansion of the middle class layer which was the axis of economic development, as the country strove for westernisation and modernisation.

Furthermore, the Cold War is effectively still ongoing given the division of Korea between China (or Russia) in the North and America in the South. With the help of the military, dictatorial governments (until 1992) and the rule of imperialism continued with foreign assistance, either/both through economic aid (until 1999) and/or through military bases. Consequently, the struggle against imperialistic domination took the pattern of a struggle against a dictatorial government and its social basis. Unfortunately, this pattern does not appear to have changed in South Korea even after the demise of the military government. As a result of the Korean partition into North and South, Korea itself still lingers as a victim of the Cold War as a result of the policy of division and domination of one half of Korea since 1953.

1992 was a turning point, with the beginnings of civil government and democracy in South Korea. The South Korean people today consider democratization and national reunification inseparable and claim national autonomy together with democratization and social justice (e.g., Ito, 1992). In this case, national identity could be forged with reunification as a whole. As Geertz (1973) demonstrated, the slogan of reunification is one people, one language, one nation from many, and collective harmony. Nationalism in Korea has come to mean the desire and the demand for freedom from all kinds of restraints.

In the new nations, along with established institutions in order to maintain national sovereignty within their borders, the unity of common experience to tradition, culture, national character or even human race, results in the foundation of a new identity (Geertz, 1973). Here may be one dilemma for Korea, whether to focus on restoring a traditional cultural identity or on building up a new identity which could be very different from the former one. Culture changes all the time; Korean culture underwent a dramatic shift throughout the twentieth century towards modernisation and westernisation. Some traditions may be kept in a genuine mode, while others have turned into a new version or have vanished altogether. Any community, regardless of its size from a nation to a village, is not immune to change, neither are individuals. That is, people's perceptions about culture might have changed, followed by their cultural identities. Now, as Korean culture accommodates diverse sub-cultures, it is hardly workable to describe its cultural identity in single terms; it is multilayered and fragmented. For this reason the issue of cultural identity is less likely to decide whether to adopt old or new, but more likely to be concerned with how to rewrite cultural identity through the process of gathering, selecting and arranging its potential elements.

Moreover, a sense of Korean identity in ethnic terms varies according to the growing number of foreign workers and immigrant wives and their children. The existence of notions of otherness and ethnic complexity are clearly more universal. Refugees from North Korea have steadily increased to as many as 27,518 (as of 2014),[3] coupled with hundreds of thousands of migrant wives from nearby countries, such as China, Thailand, the Philippines, and even some Islamic countries, like Bangladesh. It is obvious that those North Korean defectors and children from international marriages suffer from the matter of their identities. It is crucial for them to shape and redefine a sense of belonging and identity.

3. Museums and national identity

The museum world attempts to present cultural identity at national, regional and local levels. Museums have long served to accommodate objects of national significance, reflecting cultural heritage, and therefore helping to create a national identity. Museums have often fulfilled national ambitions to safeguard cultural heritage and to educate the public. In this way, the collections have been seen as relics of national history and proof of a legitimate unbroken continuity of the nation from ancient times (Avgouli, 1994).

---

2) See Johnson, (1962) for more about the role of the military.

3) The Ministry of Unification. http://www.unikorea.go.kr/content.do?cmsid=1518 (accessed on 10 February 2015).

National identity is developed and viewed as representative of the cultural identity of an individual as well as any community within a national boundary. Thus, very often, local and regional identities are enmeshed in it, composing a whole picture of a nation. It is commonly agreed that national museums have played a role in forging national identity as a collective expression of a people within a national boundary, despite the different functions of these museums in different states. Consequently, although any museum within a national border may speak for the nation in one way or the other, "national" museums are especially designated not only to enhance national life, but also to promote national glory and pride both to nationals and to visitors.

The establishment of national museums is related to nationalisation of major collections as well as the nationalization of image-making (Ames, 1992). They are characterized by collections of national importance, relating to historic events such as wars, struggles, and political disorder. These were transformed into symbols and displayed as images with a full meaning for the living. Thus, national museums were part of the search for, and discovery of, patriotic identity (Morales-Moreno, 1994). Museums, with nation building as a central part of its mission, can maintain the continuity of nation through the historical continuity of the institution. They are well suited to display key elements of the nation and its heritage.

Although museums in the world function in different circumstances, it appears that national museums have similar goals in the pursuit of representing a nation as an independent state in the global community. They can be used in a political manner to assert and promote national sovereignty, sometimes concentrating on preserving their traditional national culture. In other words, national museums appear to act as 'ambassadors', promoting the nation to the world, in Macmillan's words (1999). As such, they play a strong role for culture in political and economic development.[4] They are, as an essential and central part of the nation's cultural wealth, also large tourist attractions: They are an economic asset of significant importance, attracting tourist revenues. Today, as tourism has become a global phenomenon, museums are required to develop an international as well as national reputation, generating revenue from overseas tourists.

Most national museums in new nations seek to redeem the historical past by identification and assertion of traditional culture and customs before foreign impositions. It is common to demonstrate their national identities in terms of ethnic identity, which is rooted in a common language, mythic history, shared culture or the same ancestry. Their identities have thus been considerably formed on the basis of the experience of traditional cultural heritage in a national community. Korean cultural identity has witnessed a radical change in social, economic, political and cultural frameworks following a painful colonial experience. This has been enough to drive current Korean identity into chaos. In addition, the territorial division of North and South by political ideology has led to the huge gap in national unity and difficulty in accomplishing a coherent national identity.

4. The National Museum of Korea

While earlier museums of modern concepts appeared at the beginning of the twentieth century in Korea, it was not until the mid-twentieth century that 'national museums' were established when Korea gained independence in 1945. In a way, to understand the National Museum of Korea (henceforth National Museum) is to understand the complexity of modern Korea as museums reflect the society they belong to. The history of the National Museum runs parallel with Korean modern history – Japanese occupation followed by the Korean War, causing evacuations and frequent moves until it settled in the present location. For a brief history, an institution called "a museum" first appeared in 1908 under the title of the Imperial Household Museum (Lee Dynasty Museum). As Lee is the surname of the royal family, the Lee Dynasty was downgraded from the Joseon Dynasty by the Japanese aggression. The museum was built inside a royal palace of Changdeokgung. In 1915, the Japanese Government General Museum was established in Seoul, followed by some local museums that were built mainly in the old capitals, such as Kyeongju, Kongju, Puyo, Pyeongyang, and Kyesung during the colonial period. The National Museum displayed artifacts acquired from excavations, thereby acting as the headquarters of Korean archaeology. This tradition continues to the present day. Upon liberation in 1945 when Japan was defeated in the Second World War, the Japanese Government General Museum was renamed as the National Museum of Korea, and the local museums were absorbed as branches. The collections inherited from the colonial era have been succeeded as the nucleus, together with the collections of the Imperial Household Museum.

Breaking out in 1950, the Korean War caused great damage to the museum and its collection. Only 20,000 items were safely moved to Busan to avoid destruction. When returning to Seoul, the museum moved several places until a new building (Fig. 1) was completed in 2005 to respond to Korean people's aspiration to restore national history and spirit, conserve destroyed and damaged cultural heritage. This implies that they opened their eyes on the importance of

---

4) See Kaplan (1994), especially in the African and Asian context.

Fig. 1 The National Museum of Korea. Source: the homepage of the National Museum of Korea

Fig. 2 The Japanese General Government Building. Source: The Initiative of Yongsan Museum Complex (The National Museum of Korea, 2009, *The Initiative of Yongsan Museum Complex*, The 100th anniversary of Korean Museums)

national cultural heritage which was neglected by economy-first policies. After independence and the war, national museums were largely ignored by the government faced with harsh economic conditions. Even after economic development in 1980s and 1990s, the National Museum never had its own building, and its history remained an unfinished project. Using the Japanese General Government Building as the National Museum (**Fig. 2**) portrays a colonial mindset that seems eager to prioritize an economic logic. Currently, the National Museum has as many as 12 branches in every region, which focus on archaeological and arts objects. The National Museum displays relics and artifacts throughout six permanent exhibition galleries, such as the Prehistory and Ancient History Gallery, the Medieval and Early Modern History Gallery, the Donation Gallery, the Calligraphy and Painting Gallery, the Asian Art Gallery, and the Sculpture and Crafts Gallery.

The National Museum needed to adapt to new realities of national independence and political, economic and cultural transition. These complex environments evoke questions of national history and heritage. This indicates a number of side effects produced by the focus on the economic development. One of them is to redefine and reshape of a sense of national identity which could have been neglected during the first actions of "new nations" to assert their autonomy. One is to set up national museums since they often house national collections to glorify their history and culture. The history of national museums in Korea is deeply marked by its political history, where the country is on the periphery of all the political and cultural power centres.

Located in the capital cities, national museums tend to occupy a very important place in the cultural life of the society. It is possible for a newly founded nation to get back to its roots, to assert its own cultural identity, and to present itself on the international scene. In the case of Korea, however, the very building of Japanese Government-General of Korea as the symbol of oppression and ethnic-cleansing power became the National Museum (1986-1996) for a representative role for the cultural heritage and national values of Korea in all political and cultural terms. It was an ashamed point of pride, which directly or indirectly represented the uncleansed Japanese legacy which remained in many aspects of the Korean society. Borrowing the Japanese word, the term of "museum" in the Korean language is divided into two – one is for "museums" (博物館) and the other for art galleries (美術館), bringing on two definitions for museums and art galleries in the museums and art museums promotion law.

A major step in reshaping the museum after 1945 was adherence to the Japanese model and principles of dialectics and historical materialism, which were to emphasize the linear and logical historical development of culture. Somehow, it is understandable, since national museums are rooted in the colonial past. Yet, it seems that the development of national museums has followed a route similar to Japan, and Japanese museums are still a benchmark in various aspects. In terms of exhibition practices, attention has been given to reconstructing the usage and functions of the museum objects in society, in chronological order even though this practice is inevitable to some extent in archaeology museums.

The interest in the archaeological heritage found in the South Korean territory, the reassertion of medieval state glory through remnants of the Middle Ages, and the pride with the rich artistic heritage are the cornerstones through which the nation portrayed itself as having deep roots in the past and bearing a unique cultural specificity. Archaeology, the discipline that brings a nation closer to its distant roots, is used to support claims on the land. The expansion of the collection has been possible mainly through excavations throughout the country, and donations sent the museum with national values as part of the history of Korea. The emphasis placed on archaeology (majority of the national museums in regions) is justified within the discourse of Korea of 5,000-year-old country. The primary focus of attention at the time of nation-building was the archaeological excavations at the ancient capitals of three kingdoms. Major attention was paid to conservation and safeguarding of the national cultural heritage in a legitimate manner that all archaeological objects found under the surface would belong to the nation.

It is argued that "The museum played a significant role in restoring the damaged nation's cultural pride and correcting the false historical images of Korea."[5] Yet, the museum does not seem to be responsible for representing national history, which maintains the continuity of a nation from ancient to the present day in spite of the significance of nation building after the independence. The presentation of the national history ends in the Joseon Dynasty. The National Museum does not explicitly deal with Korean history, but it does overtly deal with Korean culture and art by, for example, displaying national treasures, including Pensive Bodhisattva (Korean National Treasure No. 78 or No. 83), Goryeo Celadon Openwork Burner (No. 95), and Gold Crown from Silla (No. 191) with the Calligraphy and Painting Gallery, and the Sculpture and Crafts Gallery. Certainly, the museum has evolved to become a world-class national museum, exploring national cultural heritage based on a more scientific study and a number of exchange exhibition programs with museums in other countries.

5. The National Museum of Korean contemporary history

The establishment of new museums may provide a more complete representation of a nation at different times and at a different pace. The National Museum of Korean Contemporary History (henceforth History Museum) was created in December 2012 (Fig. 3). Converted from a government office building (the Ministry of Culture, Sports and Tourism), the history museum is located in the very heart of the capital, Seoul. The museum presents Korea's growth, democratic movement, and the advancement of Korea in the global era in four galleries: Prelude to the Republic of Korea (1876-1945), Foundation of the Republic of Korea (1945-1960), Development of the Republic of Korea (1961-1987), and Modernization and Korea's Vision of Future (1988-present). The main message would be how Korea was able to transform itself from one of the poorest into one of the fastest developing countries in the world in just sixty years. This seems to be a miracle with a number of drawbacks underneath.

This museum is the first national history museum which focuses on presenting the history of South Korea from

---

5) See the National Museum of Korea homepage. http://www.museum.go.kr/site/homepage/menu/viewMenu?menuid=002005002003 (accessed on 12 January 2015)

Fig. 3 The National Museum of Korean Contemporary History. Source: the museum brochure

the end of nineteenth century to today in the context of the general Korean history. Korea has a troubled modern history as it opened its door to the outside world amid the growing influence of imperialism from the late 19th to early 20th century, falling into Japanese imperialism. Shortly after its independence, it suffered the Korean War that claimed 4 million lives. The museum is indicative of policies in representing national history in several respects – the outlined attention to economic development and the Korean Wave as an catalyst for globalization and cultural diversity in representing national history.

The museum would be a space of national history and a part of political struggle to define the nationals. History in national museums may inevitably become the focus of the central government although they have recently evolved and been resourceful in anticipating how to support a range of views about the past and even the present. The legacy of the past through museums can be made available to a larger audience and they are an important force in the formation of collective identities. Alissandra Cummins (2012), chairperson of the Executive Board of UNESCO mentioned, "*It is imperative that the museum seeks out and provides access to varying interpretations of the events in contemporary history shaping the national narrative,*" in a keynote speech at the symposium to mark the opening of the History Museum. Contemporary history is a recent past which is still in living memory and closely connected to the present day. In accordance, the museum can arouse a more lively interest in the complex texture of storytelling and first-person witness to history using oral history. On the other hand, it is often difficult to decide how to interpret contemporary history since the people involved in recent events are still alive and their views of history is very subjective. This is why it is difficult to reach a consensus on how contemporary history is viewed and explained to future generations because of controversy over the interpretation of modern history.

Certain memories seem to have deliberately vanished in the history museum to promote a more soft approach towards history. The memories of the colonial past form a significant part in the fabric of contemporary Korean society, although they are felt as difficult, shameful, and perhaps even unspeakable. Unlike other difficult and challenging histories, the most evident examples here are the issues of pro-Japanese personalities and comfort women (girls who were forced into sexual slavery by the Imperial Japanese Army). These are still under negotiation inwardly as well as outwardly. Museums are often considered neutral spaces in which past events are objectively interpreted and presented. Their political function is often overlooked in forgetting or suppressing other events like shameful stories. When it comes with the raison d'etat, it is not easy to confront them and seems more likely to elide in amnesia. These issues are still under the influence of the current political ideology and social climate, hence causing controversy and even diplomatic disputes.

Yet it is important to understand the colonial past and, more to the point, the context how it happened not to repeat the same history. The colonial past has been rendered largely invisible and unspeakable within museum contexts. In the History Museum, it is hardly observed in detail how ordinary people suffered from brutality and cruelty committed during the Japanese imperialism. For example, the history about comfort women and people who were conscripted and forced to do hard labour or drafted into the military by the Japanese colonial government are presented in images with subtitles and the text panel (Fig. 4, 5). Their "stories" are not heard. The displays stress independence movements and patriots, which is the most important element for shaping and reconstructing a sense of nationhood and national pride. Nonetheless, the issue of comfort women is of significance, which is not just a personal matter but an national/international one. Now, only 54 are alive and they will be all gone in 10 or 20 years' time. Apart from the Korean

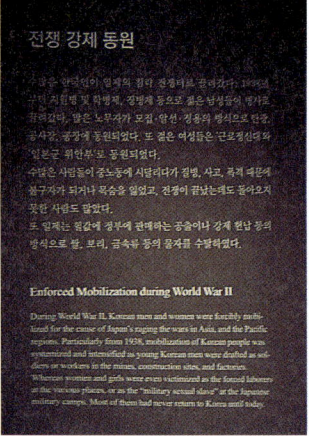

Fig. 5 Enforced mobilization during World War II. Source: photographed in the museum

diaspora (*Koreytsy*) living in the former Soviet Union,[6] more than 60,000 people who were taken to Sakhalin to work in mines could not come back until 1992 since it was vested after the WWII. Also, numerous young people were conscripted to mines in Hashima Island in Japan (Fig. 6). Those people were neglected long enough to be forgotten in people's minds until 1990. It might not be too much to say that the economic development has been achieved at the expense of the negligence. In such circumstances, Japan tried to make the island of blood and tears of the colonists listed in the World Heritage as the Modern Industrial Heritage Sites in 2008. It cannot be said that the site possesses outstanding universal value since it contributed to Japan's rapid industrialization on the slave labor of those oppressed by colonialism. The (hi)stories about those who were suffered and tortured during the national crisis should be told, recorded, documented, presented and taught in the History Museum. Sadly, this issue will not be explored at full length in this paper.

It may have been felt too early to talk about cultural diversity, a multicultural society in terms of ethnicity in the museum although a number of cultural activities have been tried to

Fig. 6 Hashima Island. Source: Wikipedia (Hashima Island, http://en.wikipedia.org/wiki/Hashima_Island (accessed on 10 December 2014))

6) Many of their ancestors emigrated to the Russian Far East, escaping from Japanese oppression during the early twentieth century. They and their offspring went through a tremendous suffering from deportation as stateless people. At the moment, approximately half a million *Koreytsy* reside in the post-Soviet states, primarily in Central Asia.

Fig. 4 Sexual slavery by the Japanese Military. Source: photographed in the museum

gratify the multicultural policies in many museums, mainly focusing on multicultural families formed by international marriages. According to the level of ethnic diversity in 2003 by James Fearon, South Korea was ranked 158 out of 159 countries.[7] Surely, it seems too far to go although the rank may have been higher now. Currently, the slogan of a racially homogeneous nation is not heard in the Korean society any more. Instead, the term 'multicultural' is often voiced through media, which usually implies international marriage families. In light of the growing diversity of Korean values, younger generations are more likely to be ignorant of the national history and people, whereas older ones are sensitive to the country's past. Colonialism, war, national division, and foreign workers and emigrants by international marriages are all part of the complicated mix in the contemporary Korean society. It can be said that Korean people may have had a kind of xenophobia with few opportunities to see foreigners in their daily life except the US Forces until 1990s. This xenophobia could be demonstrated in discrimination and exclusive attitudes against strangers without much understanding about otherness and other cultures. In this circumstance, museums can play a very important role in making it easier for the public to engage with and explore such issues personally as well collectively. Besides, they bring people together, providing a space where a diverse range of people can interact. This would lay the foundation for fostering a sense of equality and diversity and promoting shared values.

6. Conclusion

The National Museum focuses on the glorious past through the representation of national culture and arts, while the History Museum brushes over the colonial past with text and some objects, boasting how economic prosperity has achieved as fast as it is today. These two national museums appear reluctant to mention the shameful days: It is not easy to deal with such sensitive and emotional issues. Unlike written history, museums are places where history is told and experienced through permanent and temporary exhibitions, educational programs, and events. They enable the public to learn and experience the history with objects, archives, oral history and audio and video interpretive materials. Through exhibitions covering themes such as an embarrassing past and cultural diversity, museums seek to portray the contemporary state of society. Now, museums should give a voice back to those who were silenced or ignored, which is the contemporary practice of museums – the realization of democracy. This would be the mission of the History Museum for the near future, employing a few stories or oral history of the forgotten to bring the history back to life.

Apparently, it has been rather easy for the museums in Korea to interpret and present national identity due to the ethnic homogeneity until the second half of the twentieth century. Based on a united group tied in blood, however, the idea of a nation and a people is outdated, being replaced by the concept of a community and citizenship. There seems to be a decline in traditional identity – for example, a decline in ethnic identity in the Korean society. For this reason, defining national identity seems to be getting difficult in a time of cultural diversity. In this regard, it must always be questioned whether national museums express the cultural identity of a nation and whether they always reflect the current state of the nation and the lives of ordinary people. They may serve to provide a sense of belonging and security at national level, but may not always reflect what their people really want to see and know. Rarely do they reflect the diversity of people living in any one country. This is especially true in the contemporary world, where postmodernity and migration have increasingly led to both cultural diversity and acculturation. In time of multiculturalism, it seems democratization is not a big issue anymore, but the ideal of equality. It is undeniable that Korea is a multicultural society in terms of ethnicity, and thereby the equality issue is an urgent problem to be solved. As the Department of Culture, Media and Sport (DCMS) in Britain claims, "Museums can provide a tolerant space where difficult contemporary issues can be explored in safety and in the spirit of debate" (2005). The national museums explored in this paper could serve as a platform to discuss how people live together harmoniously. It is imperative that they should define and develop a shared identity in a democratic and inclusive process.

References

Ames, M.M., 1992. *Cannibal Tours and Glass Boxes: the anthropology of museums*, Vancouver: UBC Press.

Avgouli, M., 1994. The first Greek museums and national identity. in F.E.S. Kaplan ed. *Museums and the Making of 'Ourselves': The role of objects in National identity*, London and New York: Leicester University Press, 246-265.

Cummins, A., 2012. Repositioning of History. *2012 Inter-*

---

7) James Fearon. 2003. Ethnic and Cultural Diversity by Country. *Journal of Economic Growth* 8, 196-222. http://en.wikipedia.org/wiki/List_of_countries_ranked_by_ethnic_and_cultural_diversity_level (accessed on 27 January 2015).

national Symposium of the National Museum of Korean Contemporary History, 43-53.

DCMS. 2005. *Understanding the future: museums and 21ˢᵗ centurylife–Asummaryofresponses.* http://webarchive.nationalarchives.gov.uk/+/http:/www.culture.gov.uk/images/publications/understanding_the_future_responses.pdf (accessed on 20 December 2014)

Esposito, J.L., 1992. *The Islamic Threat: myth or reality?*, Oxford: Oxford University Press.

Fearon J., 2003. Ethnic and Cultural Diversity by Country. *Journal of Economic Growth* 8, 196-222. http://en.wikipedia.org/wiki/List_of_countries_ranked_by_ethnic_and_cultural_diversity_level (accessed on 27 January 2015)

Geertz, C., 1973. *The Interpretation of Cultures: selected essays*, London: Fontana Press.

Guibernau, M., 1996. *Nationalisms: The nation-state and nationalism in the twentieth century*, Cambridge, MA: Polity Press.

Hashima Island. http://en.wikipedia.org/wiki/Hashima_Island(accessed on 10 December 2014)

Ito, N., 1992. National question, nationalism and democracy in Asia. *History of European Ideas* 15(4-6), 773-777.

Johnson, J.J. ed., 1962. *The Role of the Military in Underdeveloped Countries*, Princeton, New Jersey: Princeton University Press.

Kaplan, F.E.S. ed., 1994. *Museums and the Making of 'Ourselves': The role of objects in National identity*, London and New York: Leicester University Press.

Macmillan, F., 1999. Communicating national identity. *Museums and Cultural Identity*. Presentation at the 5th Heritage Convention, 22-24 September, Edinburgh.

Morales-Moreno, L.G., 1994. History and patriotism in the national museum in Mexico. in F.E.S. Kaplan ed., *Museums and the Making of 'Ourselves': The role of objects in National identity*, London and New York: Leicester University Press, 171-191.

Shils, E., 1962. The military in the political development of the new states. in J.J. Johnson ed., *The Role of the Military in Underdeveloped Countries*, Princeton, New Jersey: Princeton University Press, 7-67.

Smith, A.D., 1983. *State and Nation in the Third World: the western state and African nationalism*, Brighton: Wheatsheaf Books.

The Ministry of Unification. http://www.unikorea.go.kr/content.do?cmsid=1518

The National Museum of Korea. 2009. *The Initiative of Yongsan Museum Complex, The 100th anniversary of Korean Museums.*

The National Museum of Korea homepage. http://www.museum.go.kr/site/homepage/menu/viewMenu?menuid=002005002003(accessed on 12 January 2015)

Woodward, K., 1997. Introduction. in K. Woodward ed., *Identity and Difference*, London: Sage in association with the Open University, 1-6.

The construction process and significance of Jeongok Prehistory Museum

Hanyong LEE

Director, Jeongok Prehistory museum, Korea ; mr1544@hanmail.net

ABSTRACT

Since the early spring of 1979, the area of Jeongok-ri, Yeoncheon-gun, had begun excavations to find handaxes, which afterward made a headline of a world-class discovery of Acheulean-type handaxes. Four consecutive academic excavations were conducted until 1983, and a huge number of stone tools, including handaxes, were found, establishing Jeongok-ri site as an important site where Acheulean handaxes were discovered, eventually designating Jeongok-ri as Historic Site No. 268 (770,000m² area). In the fall of 1993, when the initial Jeongok-ri Historical Museum, "old Jeongok-ri Relics Hall," was opened, a small festival was held as an event to commemorate its opening. The Paleolithic Festival, which began with the discovery and excavation of the Jeongok-ri site, is an important key activity of Jeongok Paleolithic Museum, which opened as a modern building in 2011. The festival, which started with 200 people, already marked its 31th anniversary in 2024, and has become Korea's representative cultural festival, visited by hundreds of thousands of people every time. Jeongok Prehistory Museum is a historical museum built on the site where the ruins are located both to preserve and utilize the Paleolithic ruins of Jeongok-ri. The most important point in the development of the Jeongok Prehistory Museum is an educational program, with both a prehistoric camp (for 2 days and 1 night) and a museum visit (Knock knock. Hello). Jeongok Prehistory Museum is operated by an educational instructor and is characterized by step-by-step programs, such as first-stage pre-learning, second-stage main learning, and third-stage post-learning. Finally, Jeongok Prehistory Museum will continue to make efforts to become a meaningful space for exhibition and to develop an educational program that will recognize the importance of humans and the environment.

국문초록

전곡선사박물관은 동아시아 최초로 아슐리안 주먹도끼가 발견되어 세계 구석기 연구의 역사를 다시 쓰게 만든 경기도 연천군 전곡리 구석기 유적에 건립된 유적박물관이다. 전곡리 유적의 항구적인 보존과 활용을 위해 2005년 박물관 건립을 추진하기 시작하여 2011년 4월 25일 개관하였다. 이 박물관의 건립에는 전곡리 구석기 축제를 통해 쌓인 대중의 관심과 성원이 큰 힘이 되었다. 전곡리 구석기 유적에 대한 홍보와 주민들의 인식 개선을 위해 1993년 전곡구석기유적관이라는 간판을 내걸고 문을 연 작은 전시관의 개관 기념행사로 시작된 전곡리 구석기 축제는 우리나라 대중고고학과 유적 체험학습의 본격적인 문을 열었다. 전곡리 구석기 유적 현장에서 펼쳐진 문화유산을 통한 지역사회와의 끊임없는 소통 노력은 전곡선사박물관으로 결실을 맺었고, 이는 우리나라의 대표적인 문화유산 보존운동의 결실임과 동시에 세계적인 모범사례의 하나라고 할 수 있다. 유적발굴 현장에 세워진 유적박물관으로서 유적 보존을 위한 기본적 사명을 충실히 함은 물론 생동감 있는 유적박물관으로 자리매김하기 위해 다양한 체험전시와 체험교육에 크게 노력하고 있다.

Keywords : Paleolithic, Jeongok-ri, Prehistoric site, Acheulean handaxe, Festival Public archaeology, museum, utilization, preservation, education

1. Construction process of the Jeongok Prehistory Museum

Greg Bowen, who worked for the US 2nd Infantry Division in Dongducheon in the late summer of 1978, was taking a walk along the Hantan River with his Korean girlfriend (Sangmi Bowen, who later married Greg Bowen). Now, few people play in the water due to the poor water quality, but in the 1980s, the Hantangang River was a famous summer resort with as many people as Haeundae, the location of a very famous beach resort.

Bowen was looking back at a hill a little away from the Hantan River, motivated by his curiosity of studying archaeology. Some strange-looking pieces of stone stood out to him. Bowen, who had come to Korea after studying archaeology at Arizona State University for two years, intuitively recognized the strange stones as handaxes. Finally, he found four more handaxes and sent them to Professor Kim Won-ryong, the Director of the Seoul National University Museum. Professor Kim Won-ryong, who understood the importance of stone axes, and Professor Jeong Yeong-hwa (former professor at Yeungnam University), who majored in the Paleolithic Age in France at the time, immediately toured the site and collected several more stone axes. Eventually, these stone axes turned out to be Acheulean handaxes, which had never been found in East Asia until then. It was the start of an amazing discovery to which the world paid attention.

The Acheulean handaxe is a representative artifact of the Early Paleolithic era. It is called an "Acheulean" handaxe because it was first found in the Saint-acheule region of France. The Acheulean handaxe, which looks like a water drop or almond fruit, is a stone tool that has been removed on both sides, indicating new advances in Paleolithic stone tool making. It was not found in the east, or East Asia, from India, until 1978. This was the Paleolithic culture dualism of Professor Harlem Movius, a famous American archaeologist.

The Acheulean handaxe is a artifact of more advanced technology. Therefore, even if it was not expressed directly, it could be suspected that it was a theory based on the so-called Western supremacy that Asia has already lagged behind the West since the Paleolithic era. Archaeology is a thorough evidentiary study. Until then, no Acheulean handaxe had been found in Asia, so Asian Paleolithic researchers could not oppose Professor Movius' theory. However, the world's Paleolithic culture dualism, which had been accepted as an established theory at the time, lost its persuasive power due to Acheulean type handaxes found along the Hantan River in Jeongok-ri, Yeoncheon-gun, Korea at the eastern end of Asia. Several Acheulean type handaxes discovered in Jeongok-ri site along the Hantan River basin in 1978 are the starting point of the Jeongok Prehistory Museum today.

Since the early spring of 1979, the area of Jeongok-ri, Yeoncheon-gun, had been crowded with many outsiders. A full-fledged excavation began to find a handaxes that made headlines as a world-class discovery. Yeoncheon is still a relatively backward border area – but at that time, it was a small town near the DMZ line, where few outsiders visited. The entrance to the Hantan River Bridge is 38 lines, so it was North Korean territory during the Korean War. Professors, college students, and journalists from Seoul were crowded in this place, so it was a good attraction to see for local people.

At that time, when the handaxes were discovered in the excavation, President Park Chung-hee even gave an incentive to the excavation team through Minister of Culture and Education Kim Sung-jin. With this incentive, the excavation team's on-site office could be built, which would play an important role in the construction history of the Jeongok Prehistory Museum. In any case, there was such a great excavation that even the president himself expressed interest – but as usual, public interest easily dissipated. Four academic excavations were conducted until 1983, and a huge number of stone tools, including handaxes, were recovered, establishing it as an important site where Acheulean handaxes were discovered, dated to about 300,000 years ago, and designating the 770,000m² area of Jeongok-ri as Historic Site No. 268, but there were no more action (Fig. 1). It was just that, filled with the resentment of those who had their private land taken away as cultural assets. On the surface, the interest around Jeongok-ri site cooled down and returned to the ordinary rural village, but the academic interest centered on Jeongok-ri was especially great for foreign scholars. However, from the early 1990s

Fig. 1 Landscape of Jeongok-ri site and Jeongok Prehistory Museum

that a new wind began to blow in places where wasteland full of all kinds of weeds and could not be easily visited, because of near Korea boarder, DMZ.

In 1979, when college students who were visiting the excavation site returned to Korea as Paleolithic researchers after studying in the United States, Jeongok-ri also faced a new turning point. As Professor Bae Kidong, who was first director of the Jeongok Prehistory Museum, was appointed to the Department of Culture and Anthropology at Hanyang University, the excavation and investigation of the remains of Jeongok-ri resumed. In the winter of 1986, there was an emergency investigation conducted by Professor Bae Kidong (then an international student at Berkeley University in the United States), but in 1992, a new excavation survey was launched in Jeongok-ri in about 10 years. The news that a new excavation began at the Jeongok-ri ruins attracted a lot of attention from domestic and foreign Paleolithic academia, and domestic and foreign scholars visited the excavation site of the Jeongok-ri ruins frequently. However, the Jeongok-ri ruins of the time were a wasteland and a national historical site where the world-renowned Acheulian fist ax was found, so I felt sorry for the guests who came looking too shabby. Efforts to promote the importance of the Jeongok-ri ruins began from this time. First of all, in 1979, the excavation site office built with Geumilbong Peak sent by President Park Chung-hee began to be repaired and turned into a small historical museum. It was a simple museum decorated by repairing half of the 10-pyeong building, but it was widely introduced to the media at the time, so is it not the first historical museum in Korea? I even think about that. In the fall of 1993, when the Jeongok-ri Historical Museum was opened, a small festival was held as an event to commemorate its opening. When I think about it now, about 200 people gathered to make stone tools and experience pig slaughter, I think it was also one of the first mass archaeology programs in Korea. The Paleolithic Festival, which began with the discovery and excavation of the Jeongok-ri site, is important key of built Jeongok Paleolithic Museum, which opened in 2011. The festival, which started with 200 people, already marks its 30th anniversary in 2023, and has become Korea's representative cultural festival visited by hundreds of thousands of people every time. The Jeongok-ri Relics Museum, which was started by renovating a shabby warehouse, was transformed into an ultra-modern Jeongok Prehistory Museum. It can be said to be a world-class best practice in the preservation and utilization of heritage (Fig. 1).

2. Symbolism of architecture of Jeongok Prehistory Museum

Jeongok Prehistory Museum is attracting a lot of attention for its unique and beautiful architectural beauty. In 2012, it received the Excellence Award in the Public Sector at the Korea Architecture Awards; and in 2013, it was named the Best 7 Architecture of the Year, so it is recognized for its architectural beauty. The Jeongok Prehistory Museum is the work of X-TU, France, which was elected through an international contest. It is evaluated as a work designed by exquisitely utilizing the topography without damaging the landscape of the ruins.

However, some visitors to the Jeongok Prehistoriy Museum have some doubts about the ultra-modern museum building, perhaps because of the image of the Paleolithic era. This is because Paleolithic and ultra-modern buildings do not seem to be related at first glance. However, everyone agrees to the explanation that such an ultra modernized building was built to make the museum building, for display the handaxes, the most advanced technology of the Paleolithic by use of the best technology of modern architecture. Curved museum buildings require very difficult technology not only to design but also to construct them, and it is no exaggeration to say that they are one of the most difficult building in the world among recently built museum buildings (Fig. 2).

The Jeongok Prehistory Museum is located at the southeastern end of the Paleolithic site in Jeongok-ri, which is designated and protected as Historic Site No. 268. In the process of building the museum, the related construction project was carried out only after thorough excavation and investigation to confirm the existence of the relics. Most of the questions about the construction of a state-of-the-art museum in Jeongok, which is only a short distance from the armistice line, are solved by explaining that the Jeongok-ri ruins are world-class Paleolithic ruins and a valuable cultural heritage for mankind.

Fig. 2 View of snow-covered Jeongok Prehistory Museum

In the part that if you excavate the back yard of the museum even today, you will find a fist ax, everyone understands why such a great museum was built here at Jeongok-ri ruins. Jeongok Prehistory Museum is a historical museum built on the site where the ruins are located to preserve and utilize the Paleolithic ruins of Jeongok-ri, so it is somewhat different in nature from general museums built in the city center. The exterior of the Jeongok Prehistory Museum has the same structure as a bridge connecting the basalt cliff, which symbolizes the role of connecting the past and the future. It has the same appearance as a time space shuttle that travels in time, making you feel like you are traveling in time to think about the Paleolithic era, the present, and the future. The interior of the exhibition hall is composed of cave-like images that were residential spaces for people in the Paleolithic era, and all exhibits are exposed to open spaces. It is not treated with a glass wall in between, but is displayed so that visitors can feel as if they are inside a huge exhibition hall, allowing them to feel the unique exhibition atmosphere of the Jeongok Prehistory Museum. The architect describes the theme of the construction of the Jeongok Prehistory Museum as the "door leading to the prehistoric era," and one interesting thing is that this area was a small road connected to Jeongok-eup according to the early topographic map of the Jeongok. It seems that the architect did not know about this fact when he designed it, but it is an interesting coincidence anyway.

One important point in the architecture of the Jeongok Prehistory Museum is that the architectural design and exhibition design of the museum were simultaneously designed and designed by a team. Since most museum buildings were built first and exhibition designs were designed roughly according to the building, it can be said that it had a significant impact on the museum construction project in Korea in that it dramatically improved the completeness of museum architecture and exhibition.

Fig. 3 Visiting Museum-ötzi (educational aspect)

3. Educational programs of Jeongok Prehistory Museum

As explained above, Jeongok Prehistory Museum is a museum built on the site of historical sites. Various educational programs are operated to improve the satisfaction of visitors to this place far from the city center, and as many as 50,000 people participate in various educational programs annually, it can be said that it is doing well in terms of utilizing the ruins.

The most important points in the development of the Jeongok Prehistory Museum education program can be summarized into three main categories. The first is how faithfully the museum's founding ideology is reflected. The educational goal of "understanding human evolution and Paleolithic culture" is clearly presented in the founding ideology of the Jeongok Prehistory Museum, which is "realization of universal values of mankind through the evolution of mankind and the understanding of Paleolithic culture." Therefore, the educational programs of the Jeongok Prehistory Museum are developed and operated with these two directions.

Second, it is the composition of an educational program that can appropriately utilize the exhibition contents of the museum. The difference between museum education and cultural lectures at the cultural center is that it is planned and operated based on the exhibition of the museum. The Jeongok Prehistory Museum's educational program also develops and operates an educational program that shows the characteristics of the Jeongok Prehistory Museum by properly utilizing major exhibits represented by paleolithic handaxes and auxiliary exhibition cases such as Ötzi, the Iceman that can attract ordinary visitors (**Fig. 3**).

Third, the development and operation of educational programs that can function as a local cultural center are mentioned. Yeoncheon has relatively weaker cultural enjoyment conditions than other regions. The Jeongok Prehistory Museum is the only provincial cultural institution in northern Gyeonggi Province and is obliged to develop and distribute various cultural contents that can be used by local residents. Based on this, various social education programs such as multicultural education, career-interrupted women's education, and senior citizens' programs are also

Fig. 4 Stone tool marking demonstration of open-air experience field

Fig. 5 Prehistoric Camp for two days and one night

being developed and operated (Fig. 4).

4. Representative educational programs of Jeongok Prehistory Museum

The Jeongok Prehistory Museum operates various educational programs for various target groups, including organizations, regulars, children and families, teenagers, and school connections. There are about 20 educational programs currently in operation, and among them, I would like to introduce the representative educational programs of the Jeongok Prehistory Museum.

4.1. Prehistoric camp for two days and one night

The one-night, two-day prehistoric camp is one of the representative educational programs of the Jeongok Prehistory Museum, which has been implemented since the museum opened in 2011 (Fig. 4, 5). In just one or two years, more and more places have run one-night and two-day museum camps, and the Jeongok Prehistory Museum's one-night and two-day program has probably had a lot of influence. In fact, the Provincial Museum of Art operated by the Gyeonggi Cultural Foundation has been operating a two-day museum camp since 2013 by benchmarking the prehistoric camp of the Jeongok Prehistory Museum. When planning a one-night and two-day camp at the Jeongok Prehistory Museum, what I kept in mind was to establish a differentiated educational program as a new museum and to allow those who were alienated from the camping boom that began to be popular at that time to experience camping at a low cost. Due to the special experience of spending a night at the museum while participating in almost all educational programs at the Jeongok Prehistory Museum for one night and two days, and the economical camping without the need for expensive camping equipment, the two-day prehistoric camp is so popular that reservations is very difficult. In particular, it is understood that the satisfaction of participants is very high because the interior of the museum is opened in rainy and winter. I think that the museum, which is lonely because no one is looking for it, has already forgotten the meaning of its existence itself. In this regard, the Jeongok Prehistory Museum's rather bold (?) one-night and two-day camp has many implications even if it does not recall the epigram that "the most active use is the most active preservation."

Fig. 6 Handaxe from the Jeongok-ri site   **Fig. 7** Handaxe from the Jeongok-ri site

4.2. Knock knock. Hello, this is Jeongok Prehistory Museum – Visiting the museum

Yeoncheon-gun, Gyeonggi-do, where the Jeongok Prehistory Museum is located, is the least populated area in Gyeonggi-do with a population of about 45,000. The population within a 30km radius is also slightly more than 300,000, which is a very disadvantageous place to operate the museum. It is about two hours away from downtown Seoul, and it is a place that can be accessed only by passing through unfamiliar places such as Dongducheon, Munsan, and Jeokseong, which have a strong image of US military bases. To overcome this vulnerability, the Jeongok Prehistory Museum has been operating a visiting museum program since the beginning of its opening. The commonly visited museum program is operated by converting a large bus into an exhibition hall, carrying artifacts, but the visiting museum program of Jeongok Prehistory Museum is operated by an educational instructor visiting the site with the museum's educational program. It is characterized by step-by-step programs such as first-stage pre-learning, second-stage main learning, and third-stage post-learning. Since educational instructors who visit schools in the pre-learning stage play a role in promoting visits in addition to classes, it often leads to second-stage main learning. In this study, students who took classes in pre-learning visit the museum in person and experience what they studied in pre-learning vividly. The third stage of follow-up learning is an in-depth and final learning process conducted by teachers themselves by lending educational Kyobo materials prepared by the museum to schools. It is receiving a lot of attention because it rents skull kits related to human evolution that are lacking in front-line sites. In particular, the museum visit program related to the second-stage main learning provides bus rental fees through various support projects, and the competition rate is quite high. As one of the visiting museum classes, a theme integration program that lasts for one semester for second graders of Sadong Elementary School in Dongducheon was also operated. In addition, Dongducheon Boyoung Girls' Middle School students conducted a science convergence education program for about a year through handaxe research program and won the first prize at the World Youth Science Competition. The fact that museums and front-line schools collaborated with each other to plan and operate educational programs that utilize museums shows the future of museum education.

5. Closing remark

The Jeongok Prehistory Museum, which was built on the basis of the decades-old excavation and research achievements of Jeongok-ri Prehistoric site and the popular archaeological program called the Jeongok-ri paleolithic Festival, is now a 12-year-old museum. Although it can still be said to be a new museum, various efforts are being made to create the epitome of a new historical museum.

In addition to fulfilling the basic mission for the preservation of the ruins, the role of the museum as an educational institution in modern society, where lifelong education is a hot topic, is not forgotten. The reality is that many important relics are still neglected in Korea. When recalling this reality, it can be said that the construction process and activities of the Jeongok Prehistory Museum have great implications.

There is a saying, "Know the past, look at the present, and know the future." Through the great journey of human evolution for millions of years, the Jeongok Prehistory Museum will continue to make efforts to become a meaningful space for exhibition and education that will recognize the importance of me, us, and the environment.

Appendix

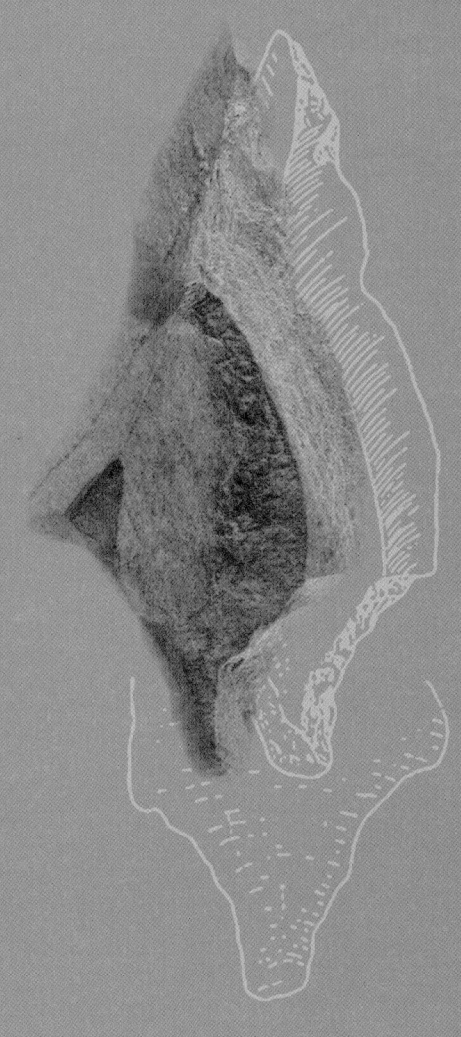

About the Contributors

prof. Emeritus **Kidong BAE**

- Hanyang Univ., Korea
- bkd5374@gmail.com

Jingjing BIE

- Key Laboratory of Vertebrate Evolution and Human Origins of Chinese Academy of Sciences, China
- bie_jj@163.com

Prof. **Wenting XIA**

- School of History and Administration, Yunnan Normal Univ., China
- xiawenting628@163.com

prof. **Shejiang WANG**

- Key Laboratory of Vertebrate Evolution and Human Origins of Chinese Academy of Sciences, China
- wangshejing@ivpp.ac.cn

Prof. **Guangmao XIE**

- School of History and Cultural Heritage, Xiamen Univ., China
- gmxie92@sina.com

Qiang LIN

- Guangxi Institute of Cultural Relic Protection and Archaeology, China
- linkg@163.com

Yan WU

- China Three Gorges Museum, China
- wuyan320@163.com

Kazuharu TAKEHANA

- Institute of Human Paleontology in France, JAPAN
- kazu-f19@sea.ncv.ne.jp

Prof. Emeritus **Kazuto MATSUFUJI**

- Doshisha Univ., Japan
- kuehiko2018@gmail.com

President **Yung-jo LEE**

- Institute of Korean Prehistory (IKP), Korea
- leeyj@ikp.re.kr

Assistant Prof. **Kaoru OTANI**

- Tokyo Metropolitan Univ., Japan
- kaoru_31@naver.com

Prof. Emeritus **Marcel OTTE**

- Liège Univ., Belgium
- marcel.otte@uliege.be

Prof. **Xing GAO**

- Institute of Vertebrate Paleontology and Paleoanthropology (IKP), China
- gaoxing@ivpp.ac.cn

Prof. **Mirosław MASOJĆ**

- Laboratory for Non-European Archaeology, Institute of Archaeology, Univ. of Wroclaw, Poland
- miroslaw.masojc@uwr.edu.pl

Prof. **Changzhu JIN**

- Institute of Vertebrate Paleontology and Paleoanthropology (IVPP), China
- jinchangzhu@ivpp.ac.cn

Prof. **Heon-jong LEE**

- Mokpo National Uni., Korea
- ruslee@mokpo.ac.kr

Curator **Sang-seok LEE**

- Jeonam Province, Korea
- lss629@korea.kr

Senior Researcher **Byeong-il YUN**

- Institute of Korean Prehistory (IKP), Korea
- mercury0323@hanmail.net

Prof. Emeritus **Gi-kil LEE**

- Chosun Univ., Korea
- kklee@chosun.ac.kr

Prof. Emeritus **Hiroyuki SATO**

- Tokyo Univ., Japan
- hsato@l.u-tokyo.ac.jp

Prof. Youping WANG

- School of Archaeology and Museology, Peking Univ., China
- ypwang@pku.edu.cn

Prof. Emeritus N.I. DROZDOV

- International Innovation Univ., Siberian Federal Univ., Russia
- kfurao@mail.ru

Prof. D.N. DROZDOV

- Siberian Federal Univ., Russia
- drozdov4765@gmail.com

Prof. V.I. MAKULOV

- Saint-Petersburg State Budgetary Professional Educational Institution "Polytechnic College of Urban Economy", Russia

Prof. Emeritus Jiří SVOBODA

- Academy of Science of the Czech Republic, Czech
- j.svo@volny.czj

Honorary researcher Ju-yong KIM

- Korea Institute of Geoscience and Mineral Resources (KIGAM), Korea
- kjy@kigam.sci.kr

Director Jong-yoon WOO

- Institute of Korean Prehistory (IKP), Korea
- woo10@hanmail.net

Honorary researcher Ho-seong SUH

- Korea Research Institute of Standards and Science, Korea
- hssuh0326@naver.com

Assistant Direct Seong-won LEE

- Institute of Korean Prehistory (IKP), Korea
- arch152@hanmail.net

Director Keun-chang OH

- Quaternary and Paleoenvironmental Research (QPR), Korea
- ock1027@daum.net

Department Director Eunjeong KIM

- RADPION Inc., Korea
- ejkim@radpion.com

Director Kaoru AKOSHIMA

- Tohoku History Museum, Japan
- akoshima-ka927@pref.miyagi.ig.jp

Assistant Prof. Hyewon HONG

- Okayama Univ. of Science, Japan
- h2w99s@gmail.com

Assistant Prof. Jungchul LEE

- Hallym Univ. Doheon Academy, Korea
- Jungchulle@hallym.ac.kr

Prof. Emeritus Sun-joo PARK

- Chungbuk National Univ., Korea
- sjpark@cbnu.ac.kr

Former Director Mokhtar SAIDIN

- Centre For Global Archaeological Research, Univ. Sains Malaysia
- mokhtarsaidin@gmail.com

Prof. V. A. GRISHCHENKO

- Museum of Archaeology, Sakhalin State Univ., Russia
- v.grishchenko@mail.ru

Prof. Retired Kimura HIDEAKI

- Sapporo Uni., Japan
- hkimura6408@gmail.com

Prof. A. A. VASILEVSKI

- Chair of Russian and World History, Sakhalin State Univ., Russia
- vasilevski@bk.ru

Prof. Ole GRØN

- Institute of Geophysics and Natural Resource Management (IGN) Univ. of Copenhagen, Denmark
- olegron111@gmail.com

Prof. **Torunn KLOKKERNES**

- Museum of Cultural History, Univ. of Oslo, Denmark
- torunn.klokkernes@gmail.com

Prof. **Lucyna DOMAŃSKA**

- Institute of Archaeology, Univ. of Lodz, Poland
- lucyna.domanska@uni.lodz.pl

Prof. **Marcin Wąs**

- Institute of Archaeology, Univ. of Gdańsk, Poland
- was.marcin@wp.pl

Prof. **Marcel KORNFELD**

- University of Wyoming, USA
- Anpro1@uwyo.edu

Prof. Emeritus **Mary Lou LARSON**

- University of Wyoming, USA (Deceased)

Prof. Emeritus **Michael JOCHIM**

- Department of Anthropology, Univ. of California, USA
- mjochim@ucsb.edu

Center chief **KyeongJa KIM**

- Korea Institute of Geoscience and Mineral Resources (KIGAM), Korea
- kjkim@kigam.re.kr

Prof. **Shengxiang TANG**

- China National Rice Research Institute, China
- sxtang93@163.com

Prof. **Jiarong YUAN**

- Hunan Institute of Archaeology of China, China
- Yjrhsh@163.com

Prof. **Seweryn RZEPECKI**

- Institute of Archaeology, Univ. of Gdańsk, Poland
- rzepecki@ug.edu.pl

Prof. **Pei-Lin YU**

- Boise State Univ. Minpaku/National Museum of Ethnology, Taiwan
- pei-linyu@boisestate.edu

Senior Researcher **Kiryong KIM**

- Mirae Institute of Cultural Heritage, Korea
- kiryong76@gmail.com

Prof. Emeritus **Bong Won KANG**

- Gyeongju Univ., Korea
- bongwonkang@naver.com

Prof. **E.G. DEVLET**

- Institute of Archaeology, Russian Academy of Sciences, Russia

Prof. **E.Y. GIRYA**

- Institute of History of Material Culture of the Russian Academy of Sciences, Russia

Manomay GHOSH

- Ret'd In-Charge Prehistoric Zoology, Zoological Survey of India, India
- ghoshmanomay@yahoo.com

Prof. **Marcel BARTCZAK**

- Institute of Archaeology, Univ. of Lodz, Poland
- marcel.bartczak@uni.lodz.pl

Director Gernal **Jong-ho CHOE**

- Gyohak Museology Research Institute, Korea
- jhchoe58@hanmail.net

PhD. **Yoon Ok Rosa PARK**

- Part-time Lecturer in Dong Yang Univ., Korea
- park0851@hanmail.net

Director **Hanyong LEE**

- Jeongok Prehistory Museum, Korea
- mr1544@hanmail.net

Yuan WANG
- Institute of Vertebrate Paleontology and Paleoanthropology (IVPP), China
- xiowangyuan@ivpp.ac.cn

Prof. Yue FENG
- School of Archaeology and Museology, Pecking Univ., China
- fegyuearchaedogy@pku.edu.cn

Prof. Emeritus Hisao KUMAI
- Osaka City Univ., Japan
- hkumai@sakai.zaq.ne.jp

Wenhui LIU
- National Museum of China, China
- wenhuiliu89@126.com

Wanfa GU
- Zhengzhou Municipal Institute of Relics and Archaeology, China

International Symposium: SUYANGGAE and Her Neighbours (1–25th)

The 1st International Symposium: SUYANGGAE and Her Neighbours

Host and Supervisers : Danyang Regional Culture Association (Korea) / Chungbuk Nat'l University Museum (Korea)

Sponsors : Danyang Regional Culture Association

Duration : 1996. 10. 25–28.

Place : Suyanggae Site Museum Hall (Danyang)

Organizers : Jae-ho KIM and Yung-jo LEE

Editors : Yung-jo LEE and Jong-yoon WOO

Contents

001 Upper Paleolithic Culture with the Focus of the Microblade-core in Suyanggae Site, Korea / *Yung-jo LEE, Jong-yoon WOO and Yong-hyun YOON* [Korea]

019 Microblade Industry of the Upper Paleolithic Monument of Middle Siberia / *Nikolay I. DROZDOV and Evgeny V. ARTEMYEV* [Russia]

025 New Paleolithic Sites in Primorye within Context of Microblade Tradition of East Asia / *Nina A. KONONENKO* [Russia]

043 The Upper Palaeolithic and Related Parallel (Later Stone Age) Industries in Africa: a General Survey / *Fidelis T. MASAO* [Tanzania]

057 Some Problems of Xianrendong Cave Culture in Haicheng, China / *Yucai GU* [China]

The 2nd International Symposium: SUYANGGAE and Her Neighbours

Host and Supervisers : Danyang Regional Culture Association (Korea) / Chungbuk Nat'l University Museum (Korea)

Sponsors : Danyang Regional Culture Association / Chungbuk Nat'l University Museum

Duration : 1997. 9. 21–30.

Place : Danyang Tourist Hotel(Danyang) / Chungbuk Nat'l University Museum(Cheongju)

Organizers : Jae-ho KIM and Yung-jo LEE

Editors : Yung-jo LEE and Jae-don LEE

Contents

001 Stone Industry and Formation Process of the Kumpari Paleolithic Site, Paju, Central Korea / *Kidong BAE* [Korea]

023 Excavation of Panxian Dadong, a Cave Site of South China / *Weiwen HUANG and Yamei HOU* [China]

037 Obsidian · People · Technology / *Hideaki KIMURA* [Japan]

057 Some Problems of Cultural Contacts in the Late Pleistocene ~ Early Holocene of Eastern Asia / *Nina A. KONONENKO* [Russia]

075 SUYANGGAE–Cultural Complex and Prospects– / *Yung-jo LEE and Jong-yoon WOO* [Korea]

109 A Cultural Exchange between Kyushu Island and the Korean Peninsula in the Upper Paleolithic Age / *Kazuto MATSUFUJI* [Japan]

127 Investigation of the Relationship between the Suyanggae Site and the Japanese Archipelago–from the Knife-shaped Stone Culture to the Late Microlithic Culture– / *Akira ORIKASA* [Japan]

139 On the Age of the Second Terrace Deposits Developed at Pyongsan-ri Paleolithic Site / *Chang-gyun HAN* [Korea]

157 Paleolithic Culture of Baume Bonne Cave(Quinson, Alpes-de-Haute-Provence, France)–with Special Reference to the Lithic Industry from the Middle Pleistocene to Early Late Pleistocene Periode– / *Mi-young Hong* [Korea]

187 The Fossil Bat of Turupong Cave Site at Chongwon, Korea: Systematics and Ecology / *Yung-jo LEE and Changzhu JIN* [Korea]

197 A Few Questions on the Study of Jiniushan Man / *Yucai GU* [China]

213 The Variousness of Upper Paleolithic Tool Making Tradition in Korea / *Heonjong LEE* [Korea]

231 Evolution of Paleoeconomy of the Amur Region Population from Upper Paleolithic to Neolithic / *Anatoly P. DEREVIANKO and Pavel V. VOLKOV* [Russia]

241 The Mousterian to Upper Paleolithic Transition through the Example of the Altai Cave and Open Air Site / *Anatoly P. DEREVIANKO and Anatoly N. ZENIN* [Russia]

The 3rd International Symposium for the Celebration of Chinese Academician Jia Lanpo's 90th Birthday :
SUYANGGAE and Her Neighbours

Host and Supervisers : Institute of Vertebrate Paleontology and Paleoanthropology(IVPP, CAS, China) / Chungbuk Nat'l University Museum (Korea)

Duration : 1998. 11. 24–28.

Place : Seminar Hall (IVPP, CAS, Beijing)

Organizers and Editors : Qinqi XU and Yung-jo LEE

Contents

001 An Outstanding Scientist, for the Celebration of Chinese Academician Jia Lanpo's 90th Birthday / *Yuzhang JIA and Chaorong LI* [China]

018 Recent Studies of Suyanggae Site, Tanyang, Korea / *Yung-jo LEE and Jong-yoon WOO* [Korea]

035 Paleolithic Stone Industries in Loess / *Tungsheng LIU* [China]

046 Adaptive Process and Pattern of Early Paleolithic Stone Industries in East Asia / *Kidong BAE* [Korea]

055 Pleistocene Faunal Remains from Saekul · Chonyokul at Turupong Cave Complex with Special Emphasis on the Large Mammalian Fossils / *Sun-joo PARK and Yung-jo LEE* [Korea]

071 Preliminary Notes of Third Excavation at Wodang-li Paleolithic Site, Yeoncheon, Kyeongki Province, Korea / *Mouchang CHOI* [Korea]

088 Distribution Pattern and Relative Age of Upper Paleolithic Sites, Korea / *Ju-yong KIM* [Korea]

098 Chronology of Upper Paleolithic in Korean Peninsula / *Heonjong LEE* [Korea]

110 The Current Situation and the Prospect of Korean Mesolithic Study / *Gi-Kil LEE* [Korea]

122 Early Blade Techniques in Northeast Asia / *Kazuto MATSUFUGI* [Japan]

129 A Tentative Discussion on the Paleolithic Archeology in Guizhou Province / *Senshui ZHANG* [China]

152 Evidence for Early Pleistocene Man in China / *Yanxian LI* [China]

166 The Theory and Practice of the Paleolithic Typology / *Chun CHEN* [China]

174 The Dental Evidence to Support the Continuity Evolution of Humans in China / *Wu LIU* [China]

189 Evolutionary Events and the Spring of the Great Year / *Qinqi XU* [China]

200 The Mammalian Fauna from the Yunzian Man Site / *Hongxiang JI* [China]

208 Discussion on the Biostratigraphy of Nanxiong Basin / *Jie YE* [China]

217 Biometrial Analysis of the Fossils of *Equus hemionus* in the Loufangzi Fauna from Hauanxian, Gansu / *Tao DENG and Xiangxu XUE* [China]

226 The Stratigraphic Position of *Hexaprotodom* sp. from Xialolngtan, Kaiyuan, Yun-nan Province / *Wei DONG* [China]

The 4th International Symposium: SUYANGGAE and Her Neighbours

Host and Supervisers : Danyang County Office (Korea) / Danyang Regional Culture Association (Korea) / Korean Association for Ancient Studies (Korea)

Duration : 1999.11.7–13.

Place : Danyang Tourist Hotel (Danyang) / Chungbuk Nat'l University Museum (Cheongju)

Organizers and Editors : Yung-jo LEE and Jong-yoon WOO

Contents

001 Suyanggae Tanged-tools in Korea : a Technical and Typological Analysis / *Yung-jo LEE, Jong-yoon WOO and Sujin KONG* [Korea]

037 On the Temporal Change of Korean Paleolithic Industry / *Seonbok YI* [Korea]

051 The Beginning of the Upper Paleolithic in Kyusyu Island / *Masanobu TACHIBANA* [Japan]

065 50 Years of Paleolithic Research in Japan / *Masao AMBIRU* [Japan]

081 New Development and Basic Framework of Paleolithic Archaeology in China / *Senhui ZHANG* [China]

109 Some Problems of the Early Paleolithic Culture of China / *Yanxian LI* [China]

The 5th International Symposium for the Celebration of Chairman KIM Jae-ho's 60th Birthday Anniversary:
SUYANGGAE and Her Neighbours

Host and Supervisers : Danyang County Office (Korea) / Danyang Regional Culture Association (Korea) / The Korean Paleolithic Society (Korea)

Sponsors : Korean Association for Ancient Studies/ The Korean Paleolithic Society/ The Hoseo Archaeological Society / Jbnews / Dongyang Daily News / New Danyang Regional Development Association/ Chungcheong Daily News

Duration : 2000. 12. 7–13.

Place : Danyang Tourist Hotel (Danyang) / Chungbuk Nat'l University Museum (Cheongju)

Organizers and Editors : Yung-jo LEE and Jong-yoon WOO

Contents

001 New Palaeolithic Data for the Lithic Assemblage from Locality I of the Suyanggae Site, Korea / *Yung-jo LEE, Jong-yoon WOO and Sujin KONG* [Korea]

029 The 3rd and 4th Excavations of Wondang-ri Paleolithic Site in Yeoncheon / *Mou-chang CHOI* [Korea]

041 Early Paleolithic in Kurtak Archaeological Area, Russia / *Nikolay I. DROZDOV, Evgeny V. ARTEMYEV, V.P. CHEKHA and Dennis N. DROZDOV* [Russia]

065 The Paleolithic Site of Hahwagye-ri, Hongchon County / *Bok-Kyu CHOI* [Korea]

091 A Study of Middle Paleolithic in Chonnam Province/ *Heonjong LEE* [Korea]

115 Wolpyong Site: A Typical Late Upper Palaeolithic Site in Northeast Asia / *Gi-Kil LEE* [Korea]

137 Formational Processes of Paleolithic Sites and Reconstruction of Hominid Behavior / *Kidong BAE* [Korea]

157 New Paleontological Approach on the Kunang Palaeolithic Cave Site, Korea / *Yung-jo LEE and Tae-sop CHO* [Korea]

189 The Early Pleistocene Deposits and their Mammalian Fauna from Renzidong Cave, Fanchang, Anhui Province, China / *Changzhu JIN, Longting ZHENG, Wei DONG, Jinyi LIU, Quiqi XU, Ligang HAN, Jiajian ZHENG, Guangbiao WEI and Fazhi WANG* [China]

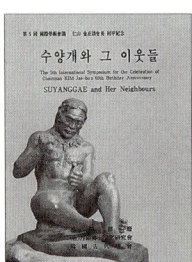

The 6th International Symposium : SUYANGGAE and Her Neighbours

Host and Supervisers : Danyang County (Korea) /Danyang Regional Culture Association (Korea) / Chungbuk Nat'l University Museum (Korea)

Sponsors : Korean Association for Ancient Studies / The Korean Paleolithic Society/ The Hoseo Archaeological Society

Duration : 2001. 12. 9–15.

Place : Danyang Tourist Hotel (Danyang), Chungbuk Nat'l University Museum (Cheongju)

Organizers : Yung-jo LEE and Jong-yoon WOO

Editors : Yung-jo LEE and Seung-won LEE

Contents

001 End-scrapers from Locality I of the Suyanggae Site, Danyang, Korea / *Yung-jo LEE, Jong-yoon WOO and Sujin KONG* [Korea]

031 Two Major Waves of the Early Human Population Migration into Asia / *Anatoly P. DEREVIANKO* [Russia]

061 Viewing Sites at Different Scales: an Example from the Paleolithic of Central Euro / *Michael JOCHIM* [USA]

071 Changes in the Blade Technology on the Territory of Northern Poland in the Period 10,000 ~ 5,000 BP / *Lucyna DOMAŃSKA* [Poland]

085 Points Fabricated from Flakes in Japan and their Context / *Masao AMBIRU* [Japan]

095 The Knife Blade Noticed the Bottom(Hakuhen-Sencoki) of the Kyushu Point Culture / *Yasuhiro KIZAKI* [Japan]

141 A Short Critical Review of Understandings of Ground Wedges at Paleolithic Sites in Korea / *Kidong BAE* [Korea]

153 A Brief Report on Jang-heung-ri Site, Jinju, Kyoungsang South Province, Korea / *Young-Chul PARK* [Korea]

161 Recent Reseaches of Upper Palaeolithic from Honam Area, Korea / *Heonjong LEE* [Korea]

The 7th International Symposium: SUYANGGAE and Her Neighbours

Host and Supervisers: Danyang County Office(Korea) / Danyang Regional Culture Association (Korea) / Chungbuk Nat'l University Museum (Korea)

Sponsors: Korean Association for Ancient Studies/ The Korean Paleolithic Society / The Hoseo Archaeological Society

Duration: 2002. 7. 14–21.

Place: Danyang Tourist Hotel (Danyang) / Chungbuk Nat'l University Museum (Cheongju)

Organizers and Editors: Yung-jo LEE and Jong-yoon WOO

Contents

- 035 Palaeolithic Culture of the Locality III, Suyanggae Site, Korea / *Yung-jo LEE, Jong-yoon WOO, Tea-sop CHO and Sujin KONG* [Korea]
- 051 Mammalian Evolutionary Events in China / *Qinqi XU* [China]
- 073 Out of Asia / *Marcel OTTE* [Belgium]
- 085 Two Types of the Handaxe in Hantan and Imjin River's Area / *Mou-chang CHOI* [Korea]
- 095 New age Determination of the First Hominid Presence at the Chongokni Site and Problems – New Tephra Evidence from E55 S20-IV Pit / *Kidong BAE* [Korea]
- 115 Upper Pleistocene Archaeology and the Middle Palaeolithic in Northeast Asia : A Review / *Seonbok YI* [Korea]
- 125 New Discovery of Outcrops of so-called "Aso Obsidian" / *Hiroki OBATA* [Japan]
- 137 The Late Palaeolithic of East Asia : An Overview / *Fumiko IKAWA-SMITH* [Canada]
- 149 Approach to the Stone Age in the Japanese Archipelago from the Standpoint of Obsidian Archaeology / *Masao AMBIRU* [Japan]
- 171 The Latest Palaeolithic in North China and Its Problems / *Zhan-yang LI and Shu-guang QIN* [China]
- 187 Man and Landscape in Past: Ustinovka Palaeolithic Complex, Russian Far East / *Nina KONONENKO* [Russia]
- 195 Le Paléolithique Supérieur en France / *Marie PERPÉRE* [France]
- 205 On the Raw-material and Lithic Variation from the Jungnae-ri Site, Korea / *Gi-Kil LEE* [Korea]
- 227 Geology of Palaeolithic of Derbinian Archaeological Region (NE Eastern Sayan) / *Stanislav A. LAUKHIN* [Russia]
- 233 Quaternary Geology and Environment of Gunanang Cave in Danyang Area, Korea / *Ju-yong KIM, Dong-Yoon YANG and Yung-jo LEE* [Korea]
- 253 Cranial Changes of the Upper Pleistocene and Mesolithic Hominids in Korea with Special Reference to Yonggok and Mandal Skulls / *Sun-joo PARK* [Korea]
- 267 On the *Oryza sativa* and Peat Layers from the Paleolithic Sorori Site in Cheongwon, Korea / *Yung-jo LEE and Jong-yoon WOO* [Korea]

The 8th International Symposium for 20th Anniversary of Suyanggae First Excavation :
SUYANGGAE and Her Neighbours

Host and Supervisers : Korea Research Foundation (KRF-2002-072-AM1023) (Korea) / Institute for Jungwon Culture (Korea) / Chungbuk Nat'l. University (Korea)

Sponsors : The 5th World Archaeological Congress Organization (WAC-5)

Duration : 2003. 6. 21–26.

Place : Catholic University of America, Washington D.C. (USA)

Organizers : Yung-jo LEE and Jong-yoon WOO

Editors : Yung-jo LEE and Woo-sung KIM

Contents

021　The Suyanggae Lithic Assemblage : with a Focus on the Microblade Industry and Tanged Tools / *Yung-jo LEE and Sujin KONG* [Korea]

037　Quaternary Geology and Environment of Suyanggae Site on Korea / *Ju-yong KIM, Yung-jo LEE, Dong-yoon YANG and Jong-gwon YUM* [Korea]

049　Identification of Charcoals Excavated at the Late Palaeolithic Site of Suyanggae / *Won-kyu PARK, Yo-jung KIM and Yung-jo LEE* [Korea]

063　The Site of Suyanggae and the Northeast Asian Palaeolithic in Light of European Palaeolithic Studies / *Michael JOCHIM* [USA]

077　Behavior and Subsistence of the Paleolithic Occupants of Kunang Cave in Korea / *Yung-jo LEE, Tae-sop CHO and Jong-yoon WOO* [Korea]

089　The Oldest Sorori Rice 15,000BP : Its Findings and Significance / *Yung-jo LEE and Jong-yoon WOO* [Korea]

099　Dating a Peat Layer of Sorori, the Paleolithic Site / *Jong-chan KIM and Yung-jo LEE* [Korea]

109　Late Palaeolithic History in the Japanese Archipelago from the Standpoint of Obsidian Archaeology / *Masao AMBIRU* [Japan]

121　The Dynamics of the Peopling of the Southern Part of the Russian Far East During the Late Pleistocene / *Nina A. KONONENKO* [Russia]

137　COMMENTARY / *Robert E. ACKERMAN* [USA]

The 9th International Symposium : SUYANGGAE and Her Neighbours
KOREA and JAPAN

Host and Supervisers : Meiji University Museum (Japan) / Archaeology Lab. of Meiji University (Japan) / Chungbuk Nat'l University Museum (Korea)

Duration : 2004. 5. 14–18.

Place : Meiji University (Tokyo, Japan)

Organizers and Editors : Yung-jo LEE and Masao AMBIRU

Contents

153 Middle Palaeolithic Correlates in Eastern and Southern Africa and Hominid Symbolic Behaviour : a Survey of the Industries and Related Hominid Remains / *Fidelis T. MASAO* [Tanzania]

159 The End of the Ice Epoch and the Adaptation to the Holocene Environment on the Polish Lowland / *Lucyna DOMAŃSKA* [Poland]

164 Investigating Ecological Models of the End of the Pleistocene: New Research on the Late Palaeolithic of Southern Germany / *Michael JOCHIM* [USA]

168 Geomorphic Distribution and Site Stratigraphical Formation of Suyanggae Archaeological Site in Korea / *Ju-yong KIM, Yung-jo LEE and Dong-yoon YANG* [Korea]

173 Suyanggae Tanged Points : a Comparative Approach on Korean Tanged Points–its Technical and Typological Characteristics– / *Yung-jo LEE and Sujin KONG* [Korea]

183 The Oldest Paleolithic Stone Tools of the Japanese Archipelago: Exploring the Possibilities of the Middle Paleolithic / *Hiroyuki SATO* [Japan]

193 Appearance of Knife-shaped Stone Tool Culture / *Masanobu TACHIBANA* [Japan]

203 Hakuhen-sentoki and the Neighbours–People with Stemmed Points Crossed over the Tsushima Channel– / *Kazuto MATSUFUJI* [Japan]

209 Propagation of Microlithic Culture / *Yasuhiro KIZAKI* [Japan]

217 The Late Paleolithic and Regional Characteristics of the Japanese Archipelago–East and West of the Kanto Plain / *Masao AMBIRU* [Japan]

222 Formation of Regional Defferentiation of the Upper Paleolithic Culture in the Far Eastern Asia / *Hiroki OBATA* [Japan]

The 10th International Symposium: SUYANGGAE and Her Neighbours

Host and Supervisers : Danyang County (Korea) / Institute of Korean Prehistory (IKP, Korea) / Chungbuk Nat'l University Museum (Korea) / Danyang Regional Culture Association (Korea)

Sponsors : Korean Association for Ancient Studies / The Korean Paleolithic Society / The Hoseo Archaeological Society

Duration : 2005. 11. 6–13.

Place : Daemyung Condo (Danyang) / Chungbuk Nat'l University (Cheongju)

Organizers : Yung-jo LEE and Jong-yoon WOO

Editors : Yung-jo LEE, Jae-ho KIM and Jong-yoon WOO

Contents

029 A Decade of "Suyanggae and Her Neighbours" International Symposium / *Yung-jo LEE, Jong-yoon WOO and Sujin KONG* [Korea]

043 A Research on Geomorphic and Stratigraphic Settings of Suyanggae Site on Danyang County, KOREA / *Ju-yong KIM and Yung-jo LEE* [Korea]

057 The Colonization of Lakeshores at the End of the Pleistocene in Central Europe / *Michael JOCHIM* [USA]

071 Chrono-Stratigraphic Frameworks and Raw Material Procurement System in the Upper Paleolithic of Japanese Islands / *Akira ONO* [Japan]

087 Traces of Oldowan Hominid Land Use during the Lowermost Bed II Landscape Succession in the Paleo-Olduvai Basin, Tanzania / *Fidelis T. MASAO* [Tanzania]

115 On the Chronological Context of 'Pic' from Jangsan-ri site, Kyounggi Province, Korea / *Young-chul PARK* [Korea]

127 A Significance of the Sizume Industry and the Beginning of the Upper Paleolithic Culture in the Kyushu Region / *Yasuhiro KIZAKI* [Japan]

145 The Emergence of Modern Human: biological and cultural process / *Hyeong-woo LEE* [Korea]

157 Reconstruction of Vegetation and Paleoclimate from the Charcoals Excavated at the Paleolithic Sites in Jungwon Region of Korea / *Won-kyu PARK, Yo-jung KIM and Yung-jo LEE* [Korea]

169 Shuidonggou Reinvestigated / *Xing GAO* [China]

177 New Data on the Formation of the Basalt Plain in the Imjin River Basin / *Seonbok YI* [Korea]

189 Paleoenvironmental Significance of Soricid Fossils from the Renzidong Cave, Anhui Province, China / *Changzhu JIN* [China]

197 Geoarcheology of Paleolithic Site Ust 'Izul' 1 (The South of Middle Siberia) / *Nikolay I. DROZDOV, S.A. LAUKHIN, E.V. AKIMOVA, I.V. STASYUK, A.F. SANKO* [Russia]

227 Dąbrouwa Biskupia Site 71–New Data for Evidence of the Early Holocene Specialized Camps from Poland– / *Lucyna DOMAŃSKA* [Poland]

247 Paleolithic Studies in the Japanese Archipelago and Obsidian Archaeology / *Masao AMBIRU* [Japan]

259 Gunanggul Cave Site in Danyang–Focused on New Dating Results / *Yung-jo LEE and Tae-sop CHO* [Korea]

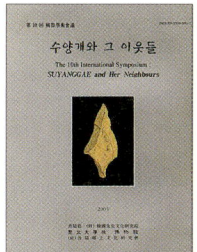

The 11th International Symposium : SUYANGGAE and Her Neighbours

Host and Supervisers : Łódź University (Poland) / Institute of Korean Prehistory (Korea) / Institute of Archaeology (Łódź University) / Chungbuk Nat'l University Museum (Korea)

Duration : 2006. 9. 17–24.

Place : Łódź University (Łódź, Poland)

Organizers and Editors : Lucyna DOMAŃSKA and Yung-jo LEE

Contents

Session Ⅰ. THE STONE AGE OF ASIA

021 Suyanggae Paleolithic Site: Characteristics and Meaning in Korean Paleolithic Culture / *Yung-jo LEE and Sujin KONG* [Korea]

031 The Burnt Stone Tools on Lim Jin River Terrace / *Mouchang CHOI* [Korea]

043 Paleolithic Cave Sites in South Korea. Paleoenvironment with the Faunal Observation / *Tae-sop CHO* [Korea]

057 Transition from the Middle to Upper Paleolithic in Korea. Based on the Recent Research of Youngsan River Region / *Heonjong LEE* [Korea]

073 Understanding the Palaeolithic Artefacts from Jeonbuk Province, Korea / *Hyeong Woo LEE, Chang Seung LEE and Eun Young SONG* [Korea]

081 New Insights from the Sinbuk Upper Paleolithic Site in Southwestern Korea Looking for Paleolithic Network in East Asia / *Gi-Kil LEE* [Korea]

085 Changes in Pointed-Tool Tradition in the Japanese Islands from the Late Pleistocene through Holocene / *Hiroyuki SHIRAISHI* [Japan]

093 Surface Modification as a Sign of Tool Curation and Life History. A new Application of Use-Wear Analysis to Paleolithic and Jomon Lithic Artifacts / *Shoh YAMADA* [Japan]

103 Microblade Industry in the Late Paleolithic: Microblade Cores of Middle Siberia as an Object of the Study / *Nikolay I. DROZDOV and Evgeny V. ARTEMYEV* [Russia]

123 The Stone Age of the Turanian Lowland. A Problem of Settlement Discontinuity / *Mukhiddnin KHUDZHANAZAROV and Karol SZYMCZAK* [Uzbekistan]

139 Le site paléolithique de Kharukhyn, Mongolie centrale (Bulgan Aimac) / *V. SITLIVYK, SOBCZYK, A. ZIĘBA, T. KALICKI, C.D. TSEVEENDORI, B. GUNCHINSUREN and Ya. TSERENDAGVA* [Belgium]

Session Ⅱ. MISCELANEA

171 The Oldwan at the DK Site Olduvai Gorge Revisited: A Conservation Exercise / *Fidelis T. MASAO* [Tanzania]

189 Palaeolithic of the Upper Nubia from the Nile IVth Charact Perspective / *Marcin WĄS* [Poland]

207 The Cultural Development and Contacts on Bornholm during the Late Paleolithic and Mesolithic–Some Preliminary Results and Hypotheses / *Claudio CASATI and Lasse SORENSEN* [Poland]

239 Zawołocze. Stone and Bronze Age Settlement in the Łęczyńsko-Włodawski Lakeland (Lublin Province) / *Tomasz BORON* [Poland]

268 Results of Excavations on the Area of Future A2 Motorway / *Lucyna DOMAŃSKA and Seweryn RZEPECKI* [Poland]

The 12th International Symposium : SUYANGGAE and Her Neighbours
Prehistoric Migrations in Eurasia and America

Host and Supervisers : Krasnoyarsk State Pedagogical University (KSPU, Russia) / Institute of Korean Prehistory (IKP, Korea)

Duration : 2007. 8. 7–15.

Place : Krasnoyarsk State Pedagogical University and Kurtak (Krasnoyarsk, Russia)

Organizers and Editors : Nikolay I. DROZDOV and Yung-jo LEE

Contents

- 008 SUYANGGAE: Why So Important ? / *Yung-jo LEE* [Korea]
- 025 The Jeongjang-ri Paleolithic Site, Geochang, Korea / *Heonjong LEE, Ho-pil YUN and Dae-hoon JANG* [Korea]
- 036 Strategy of Raw Material Exploitation and Organization of Lithic Technology: a Comparative Example of Central Korea / *Kyong-woo LEE* [Korea]
- 037 Characteristics of Wonpyoung Osong II-4 site, Chungbuk, Korea / *Dae-won SEO* [Korea]
- 038 A Study of Lithic Assemblage from the Yong-bang Paleolithic Site, Cheong-won, Korea / *Yung-jo LEE and Guean-hee CHONG* [Korea]
- 039 A Behavioral Model for Human Evolution in Pleistocene, China / *Xing GAO* [China]
- 040 A New Discovery in the Zhijidong Cave Site / *Youping WANG* [China]
- 041 Mammalian Fauna from the Lingjing Paleolithic Site in Xuchang, Henan Province / *Zhanyang LI and Wei DONG* [China]
- 055 Large Migrations of East Asia from the Viewpoint of Chinese History Evolution / *Mingjie SUO* [China]
- 056 Mesolithic Pencil-Shaped Cores and the Problem of Contacts with the Areas Situated to the East of Poland / *Lucyna DOMAŃSKA* [Poland]
- 062 Microlithic Projectiles Designs of the Middle–Late Epipalaeolithic in the Southern Levant (Tested by Archery Experiments) / *Alla YAROSHEVICH, Daniel KAUFMAN, Dmitri NUZHNYY, Ofer BAR-YOSEFS and Mina WEINSTEIN-EVRON* [Israel]
- 076 The Abrasion Phenomenon in Levantine Caves / *Abraham RONEN, D. ADLER, G. LENGYEL and J. SAREL* [Israel]
- 089 New Archeological Data of West Mongolia / *Nikolay I. DROZDOV, Evgeny V. ARTEMYEV, A. ZAIKA, V. MAKULOV, V.P. CHEKHA, M. GANDBOLD and Ts. DASHTSEREN* [Russia]
- 110 Malacofauna of Berezhekov Lacality in Kurtak Archeological Area / *A.F. SANKO* [Belarus]
- 114 Pre-Clovis Settlement of Small Beringia Western Part / *Nikolay I. DROZDOV, Stanislav A. LAUKHIN and V. MAKULOV* [Russia]
- 117 Geological Situation of Kymyneikei Site in the North of Chukotka Peninsula / *Stanislav A. LAUKHIN and Nikolay I. DROZDOV* [Russia]
- 135 Methodical Approaches to the Problem of Archeological Migrations / *Yu.P. KHOLYUSHKIN* [Russia]
- 137 Gerasimova I Locality of Paleolithic Culture ("Pereselenchesky Punkt I") on the Territory of Constructing "Zarechny" Residential Complex in Irkutsk City / *S. KOGAY, E. LIPNINA, German I. MEDVEDEV, D. LOKHOV, K. MAKSIMENKO, V. NOVOSELTSEVA, L. ORLOVA, E. OSCHEPKOVA, A. POPOV, E. ROGOVSKY and F. KHENZYKHENOVA* [Russia]
- 152 Listvenka Fauna(Primary Presentation)/ *N. OVODOV, S. VASILYEV, N. MARTYNOVICH and A. GULYAEV* [Russia]
- 157 Functional Planigraphic Analysis of Holocene Dwellings in the Far East / *P.V. VOLKOV* [Russia]
- 161 New Data of Studenoye-1 Site Study (on the Problem of Age of Cultural Layers) / *I.I. RAZGILDEEVA, S.A. RESHETOVA and V.B. POPOV* [Russia]
- 175 Equus Ex Gr. Germanicus-Gallicus as the Main Object of Paleolithic Man Hunting on the Territory of Derbino Archeological Area / *A.N. MOTUZKO and I. A. ORESHNIKOV* [Belarus]
- 180 Masterov Klyuch Site and Technological Aspects of Grounding Zabaykalye Middle Stage of Upper Paleolithic / *M.N. MESHCHERIN* [Russia]
- 190 Early Sartan Industry of Micro Blades in the End of Late Paleolithic on the Territory of the Middle Yenisei / *E. V. AKIMOVA* [Russia]
- 203 Relief and Ancient Man / *V.P. CHEKHA* [Russia]

206 Anthoropomorphs in Petroglyphic Art of Eurasian Paleolithic / *A. L. ZAIKA* [Russia]

209 Small Plate Industry» Site Disposition Regularities in Krasnoyarsk Reservoir Area (Tarachikhskaya Archeological Culture) / *I. V. STASYUK* [Russia]

The 13th International Symposium for the 25th Anniversary of Suyanggae Excavation :
SUYANGGAE and Her Neighbours in Kyushu

Host and Supervisers : The ad hoc Committee for the 13th SUYANGGAE Int'l Symp. in Kyushu(Japan) / Institute of Korean Prehistory (IKP, Korea) / Saitobaru Archaeological Museum of Miyazaki Prefecture (Japan)

Duration : 2008. 12. 5–10.

Place : Saitobaru Archaeological Museum of Miyazaki Prefecture (Miyajaki, Japan)

Organizers : Masanobu TACHIBANA, Masao AMBIRU and Yung-jo LEE

Editors : Yung-jo LEE, Masao AMBIRU, Kazutaka SHIMADA and Kaoru OTANI

Contents

Session Ⅰ. The Paleaolithic Archaeology from World Wide

037 SUYANGGAE : Why So Important (Ⅱ) / *Yung-jo LEE and Jong-yoon WOO* [Korea]

055 A Landscape in Stone: Using Lithic Analysis to Investigate Settlement Organization / *Marcel JOCHIM* [USA]

063 Hell Gap: Paleoindians and Their Distant Neighbours / *Marcel KORNFELD* [USA]

073 The Nature of Middle Pleistocene Handaxe from China and its Implications for East-West Paleolithic Cultural Variation / *Xing GAO* [China]

079 New Achievements of Houjiayao Site in the Nihewan Basin, China / *Fei XIE* [China]

083 The Evolution of Paleolithic Human Fire–use Mode: New Research Materials of Human Fire–use in SHUIDONGGOU Site / *Huimin WANG* [China]

091 A Preliminary Study of the Lithic Assemblage Excavated Xujiayao (Houjiayao) Site in 1977, Nihewan Basin, China / *Ning MA and Xing GAO* [China]

097 From Paleolithic Hunters to Megalith Builders: a Preliminary Characteristics of the Results of Archaeological Excavations

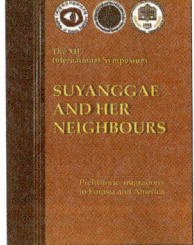

at the Site of Jastrzębiec 4 from Western Poland / *Lucyna DOMAŃSKA, Seweryn RZEPECKI and Marcin WĄS* [Poland]

107 The Main Problems of Initial Settlement of Middle Siberia: the Contemporary Condition of the Problem / *Nikolay I. DROZDOV and Evgeny V. ARTEMYEV* [Russia]

121 The Problems of Studying Late Paleolith of Middle Siberia at Present-Day Stage (on issue talking) / *Evgeny V. ARTEMYEV and Nikolay I. DROZDOV* [Russia]

141 Acheulian Culture and Animal Fossil Vertebrates from Gandheswari River Valley: a Study on Settlement Perspectives / *Asok DATTA* [India]

155 Terminal Acheulean or a Middlle Stone Age (Middle Palaeolithic) Variant? Archaeological Assemblages Discovered from Kabanga, Northwestern Tanzania / *Fidelis T. MASAO* [Tanzania]

Session II. Trends and Issues on Studies of the Palaeolithic Culture in Korea and Japan

161 Japanese Paleolithic Culture and the Korean Peninsula / *Masao AMBIRU* [Japan]

171 Development and Chronology of the Upper Paleolithic Industries in the Korean Peninsula / *Kidong BAE* [Korea]

181 The Current State of Studies on the Early Late Paleolithic Period in Kyushu / *Hiroaki KAMADA* [Japan]

189 The Great Eruptions of Aira Caldera and the Palaeolithic People / *Satoshi FUJIKI* [Japan]

201 Unewara: Southern Front of the Microblade Industry in the Japanese Archipelago / *Shigeru MATSUMOTO* [Japan]

205 Bulletin of George C. Frison Institute of Archaeology and Anthropology at the University of Wyoming, No 20, March 2009 / *Marcel KORNFELD* [USA]

209 The Memorable of the 13th Suyanggae Symposium in Miyazaki, Japan / *Ning MA and Xing GAO* [China]

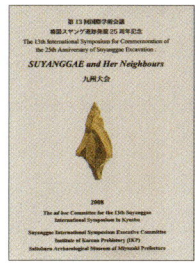

The 14th International Symposium for the Commemoration of the 80th Anniversary of the Discovery of the First Skull of Peking Man :
PEKING MAN and SUYANGGAE

Host and Supervisers : Institute of Vertebrate Paleontology and Paleoanthropology (IVPP, China) / Institute of Korean Prehistory (IKP, Korea) / Suyanggae Int'l. Symposuim Executive Committee (SISEC)

Sponsors : Kookmin Bank (Korea)

Duration : 2009. 10. 19–23.

Place : Xiyuan Hotel and IVPP (Beijing, China)

Organizers and Editors : Xing GAO and Yung-jo LEE

Contents

Session I. Chairpersons: Nikolay DROZDOV and Michael JOCHIM

003 Suyanggae : Why so Important (III) – with Focus on Handaxe / *Yung-jo LEE and Jong-yoon WOO* [Korea]

012 On Some Theoretical Approaches to Paleolithic Research in China / *Xing GAO* [China]

024 A Report of Investigation and Excavation at Shuiluo and Qingshui River Valley in Gansu Province in 2009 / *Feng LI, Fu-you CHEN, Xing GAO, De-cheng LIU, Hui WANG and Dong-ju ZHANG* [China]

036 Mid-Pleistocene Bifacial Tools at Fengshudao Site in West Bose Basin, South China / *Wei WANG* [China]

038 Understanding Environment and Cultural Adaptation in Acheulian , West-Bengal / *Asok DATTA* [India]

Session II. Chairpersons: Hyeong-woo LEE and Masao AMBIRU

055 Between Acheulian and Mousterian in the Levant: Recent Discoveries from Qesem Cave, Israel / *Ran BARKAI and Avi GOPHER* [Israel]

071 The Research Progress on *Gigantopithecus* Faunas and Modern Human Evolution from Chongzuo, Guangxi, South China / *Changzhu JIN, Wu LIU, Yuan WANG and Ying Qi ZHANG* [China]

079 Archaeological Excavation on the Paleolithic Lingjing Site in Xuchang, Henan/ *Zhanyang LI* [China]

088 New Handaxes from the Jangnamgyo Site and Implication to the Handaxe Tradition of the Hantan-Imjin River Basin, Korea / *Kidong BAE, Chulmin LEE and Semi CHUNG* [Korea]

097 Long Evolution Processes in Palaeolithic China / *Marcel OTTE* [Belgium]

Session Ⅲ. Chairpersons: Lucyna DOMAŃSKA and Wei WANG

115 Setting and Ways of the Most Ancient Migrations, Middle Siberia / *Nikolay I. DROZDOV* [Russia]

126 Specialized Household Complexes in Late Paleolithic of Middle Siberia / *Evgeny V. ARTEMYEV* [Russia]

129 Preliminary Report on the Excavations of Dosan Site Southwestern Korea / *Gi-Kil LEE* [Korea]

138 The Paleolithic Cultural Corridor around the Sea of Japan and Obsidian Road / *Masao AMBIRU* [Japan]

152 Preliminary Study on Stone Artifacts from Dadong Site in Helong City, Jilin Province / *Quan-jia CHEN, Hai-long ZHAO, Qi FANG and You-qian LI* [China]

Session Ⅳ. Chairpersons: Yung-jo LEE and Changzhu JIN

157 Environmental Change and the European Palaeolithic / *Michael JOCHIM* [USA]

170 An Early North American use of a Rockshelter: Two Moon, Bighorn Range, Wyoming / *Marcel KORNFELD and Mary Lou LARSON* [USA]

182 Acculturation or Co-operation? Two Models of Contracts between the Mesolithic Hunters and Neolithic Farmers / *Lucyna DOMAŃSKA and Seweryn RZEPECKI* [Poland]

191 The Early PPS Man from China / *Hyeong-woo LEE* [Korea]

The 15th International Symposium:
SUYANGGAE and Her Neighbours

Host and Supervisers : Danyang County Office (Korea) / Institute of Korean Prehistory (IKP, Korea)

Sponsors : The Dong-a Ilbo/ Kookmin Bank (Korea)

Duration : 2010. 5. 21–28.

Place : Danyang, Gyeongju, Cheongju and Seoul (Korea)

Organizers and Editors : Yung-jo LEE and Jong-yoon WOO

Contents

Session Ⅰ. New approach of the Paleolithic Studies

041 About the Opportunities of Paleolithic Man Latitudinal Migration along the North Fringe of Northern Asia / *Nikolay I. DROZDOV and Stanislav A. LAUKHIN* [Russia]

063 Geomorphic and Sediment Formation of Suyanggae Prehistory Site in Danyang County, Korea / *Yung-jo LEE, Ju-yong KIM and Jong-yoon WOO* [Korea]

073 The Evolution and History of the Mediterranean Cultural Landscape of Mount Carmel, Israel / *Avraham RONEN and Zev NAVEH* [Israel]

089 Faunal Evolution and Dispersal in Island SE Asia: establishing the hominin context / *Fachroel AZIZ* [Indonesia]

099 Lithic Use-wear Analysis: Method and Theory Now and Then / *Kaoru AKOSHIMA* [Japan]

117 Recent developments in radiocarbon dating and the origin of the Japanese Upper Paleolithic / *Shoh YAMADA* [Japan]

131 Indian Rock Art Paintings : a case study at Hazaribagh, Eastern India / *Asok DATTA* [India]

Session Ⅱ. The Research Result in the Old World

145 New Investigations at Peking Man Site / *Xing GAO* [China]

159 Handaxe Component in the Korean Peninsula / *Kidong BAE and Chulmin LEE* [Korea]

179 A New Discovery of Handaxes from the Chongokni Site, Korea / *Yongwook YOO* [Korea]

185 One of the Oldest Paleolithic sites in Japan, Tategahana Site in Lake Nojiri, Central Japan / *Hisao KUMAI and Nojiriko Excavation Research Group* [Japan]

197 Preliminary Consideration of Complexity of Culture Lines of Upper Paleolithic in Korea / *Heonjong LEE* [Korea]

209 Stemmed Points and her Culture / *Muneaki SHIMIZU* [Japan]

221 New Discoveries and Research of Paleolithic Sites in Yanbian Area/ *Quan-jia CHEN, Hai-long ZHAO, Qi FANG and Chun-xue WANG* [China]

241 Mesolithic Hunting Rituals – a Case from Northern Poland / *Lucyna DOMAŃSKA* [Poland]

Session Ⅲ. Section for the Young Archaeologists

253 The Research Progress on *Gigantopithecus* fauna from Chongzuo, Guangxi, South China / *Changzhu JIN, Yingqi ZHANG and Yuan WANG* [China]

257 The Beginning of the Upper Paleolithic in the Japanese Archipelago/ *Masao AMBIRU and Yoshiaki OTSUKA* [Japan]

267 A Study on Stone Quarry Sites in Japan, with Special Reference to the Procurement Methods/ *Masao AMBIRU and Shigeo IIDA* [Japan]

275 SUYANGGAE : Why So Important (Ⅳ)–with Obsidian Sutudies– / *Yung-jo LEE and Kaoru OTANI* [Korea]

The 16th International Symposium : SUYANGGAE and Her Neighbours in Nihewan
NIHEWAN and SUYANGGAE

Host and Supervisers : Yangyuan County Government, Hebei Province / Institute of Vertebrate Paleontology and Paleoanthropology CAS (China) / Institute of Korean Prehistory (IKP, Korea)

Sponsors : Hebei Provincial Institute of Archaeology and Cultural Relics (China) / Kookmin Bank (Korea) / Asian Paleolithic Association (APA)

Duration : 2011. 8. 14–21.

Place : Yangyuan Hotel (Yangyuan, China)

Organizers : Yung-jo LEE, Fei XIE and Xing GAO

Editors : Yung-jo LEE, Xing GAO and Fei XIE

Contents

Session Ⅰ. Chairpersons : Nikolay I. DROZDOV and Changzhu JIN

003 A Prospect of the Dawn of the Civilization on the Nihewan Basin / *Fei XIE* [China]

006 The Relationship between Strata Containing Hominin Remains and Chronology / *Qi WEI* [China]

016 The Xujiayao Site in Nihewan Basin, North China/ *Charong LI and Hao LI* [China]

027 Preliminary Study on the Age of the Disappearance of the Datong Lake and the Appearance of the Sanggan River based on OSL and ^{14}C data in the Nihewan Basin, China / *Yorinao SHITAOKA, Masatoshi SAGAWA, Tsuneto NAGATOMO, Qi WEI, CAO Mingming and Hu PING* [Japan]

Session Ⅱ. Chairpersons : Lucyna DOMAŃSKA and WEI QI

041 The Hearth Remains and Associated Findings From Shuidonggou, a Late Paleolithic Site in Northwest China / *Xing GAO and Ying GUAN* [China]

047 A Review of Early Pleistocene *Gigantopithecus* Fauna from South China / *Changzhu JIN, Yingqi ZHANG, Yuang WANG, Min ZHU and Yaling YAN* [China]

052 Pleistocene Cave Investigation in Southwest Guangxi, South China / *Wei WANG, Chaolin HUANG, Shaowen XIE and Dawei LI* [China]

053 The Revision of the Middle Pleistocene "Crocutoid" Hyaena from Durubong Cave Site in Korea / *Sunjoo PARK and Yung-jo LEE* [Korea]

059 Long Evolution Processes in East Asian Prehistory / *Marcel OTTE* [Belgium]

Session III. Chairpersons : Fei XIE and Hiroyuki SATO

075 Comparing the Earliest Stone tools from Africa, Europe, China and India: Implications for the timing of "Out of Africa !" / *Shella MISHRA* [India]

083 The Cognitive Abilities of the Earliest Inhabitants of the Southern Levant / *Avraham RONEN* [Israel]

096 Early Humans in the So'a Basin, Flores: Research and Prospects / *Fachroel AZIZ, Gert D. Van Den BERGH, Adam BRUMM, Iwan KURNIAWAN, Erick SETIABUDI and Michael MORWOOD* [Indonesia]

097 Paleolithic Open Sites in Lenggong Valley, Perak, Malaysia / *Mohd Mokhtar SAIDIN* [Malaysia]

108 Acheulian Culture in India: An Overview / *Asok DATTA and Arundhuti DATTA* [India]

123 The Polesie Site: from Neanderthal Man to the Motorway Builders / *Lucyna DOMAŃSKA, Seweryn RZEPECKI and Marcin WĄS* [Poland]

131 Retrospect for the 7-year Expedition on the Xuchang Man Site at Litgjing, Henan Province, China / *Zhanyang LI* [China]

Session IV. Chairpersons : Avraham RONEN and Sunjoo PARK

149 New Paleolithic Data from the Angara River / *Dennis N. DROZDOV and Nikolay I. DROZDOV* [Russia]

154 A Study of Regional Characteristics of the Upper Paleolithic Hunting Tool and its Migration in East Asia Pacific Region / *Heonjong LEE* [Korea]

160 Original Characteristics of Modern Human Behavior on Japanese Early Upper Paleolithic: Edge-Ground Axe, Circular Settlement and Trap Pit Hunting / *Hiruki SATO* [Japan]

173 Site Structure and Human Behavior at the Araya Site, Northeastern Japan / *Kaoru AKOSHIMA and Yoshitaka KANOMATA* [Japan]

193 Stone-Tool Manufacturing Site on the High Volcanic Mountain, Central Japan / *Hisao KUMAI* [Japan]

203 New Results and Major Progress of Stone Atrifacts (Obsidian) from Upper Paleolithic Sites in Eastern of Jilin Province / *Quanjia CHEN and Chun-xue WANG* [China]

Session V. Chairpersons : Hisao KUMAI and Youping WANG

219 Paleoindian Life in the High Rocky Mountains of North America / *Marcel KORNFELD* [USA]

230 Paleolithic-Neolithic Transition in Central Plain: A Case Study of Lijiagou Site in Henan, China / *Youping WANG* [China]

239 Characteristics of Distribution of Flint Raw Materials in the Late Mesolithic Communities in the Polish Lowland / *Piotr LUCZAK* [Poland]

247 Kitchen–Midden Sites (shell mounds) of Andaman and Nicobar Islands: A Case Study on Subsistence Behaviour of the Hunter-Gatherers of South Andaman / *Asok DATTA and Manomay GHOSH* [India]

263 Rock Art and Origins of Cattle-Breeding in Mongolia / *D. TSEVEENDORJ* [Mongolia]

274 Suyanggae, Why so Important (IV)–with Geoarcheological Implication of SUYANGGAE Loc. III / *Ju-yong KIM, Yung-jo LEE and Jong-yoon WOO* [Korea]

The 17th International Symposium: SUYANGGAE and Her Neighbours in KURTAK
KURTAK and SUYANGGAE

Host and Supervisers: Krasnoyarsk State Pedagogical University (KSPU, Russia) / Institute of Korean Prehistory (IKP, Korea)

Sponsors: Asian Paleolithic Association (APA) / Kookmin Bank (Korea)

Duration: 2012. 7. 4–13.

Place: Krasnoyarsk State Pedagogical University (KSPU) and Kurtak (Russia)

Organizers and Editors: Nikolay I. DROZDOV, Yung-jo LEE and Jong-yoon WOO

Contents

Session Ⅰ. Chairpersons: German I. MEDVEDEV and Araham RONEN

035 SUYANGGAE: Why So Important (Ⅴ) – with the New Tanged Points from Songam-ni, Korea / *Yung-jo LEE and Jong-yoon WOO* [Korea]

040 Paleogeographic and Paleoecological Common Factors of Evolution of Human Communities of Palaeolithic (on the Examples of the Yenisei River Basin) / *Nikolay I. DROZDOV, V.P. CHEKHA and V.I. MACULOV* [Russia]

046 Original Spirituality Lessons from Human Prehistory / *Marcel OTTE* [Belgium]

051 Lithic Tools from the Sangiran World Heritage Site, Java, Indonesia / *Harry Truman SIMANJUNTAK* [Indonesia]

052 A Metric and Geometric Morphometric Analysis of Hominin Fossils Maba, Southern China / *Christopher BAE* [USA]

053 New Discovered Acheulian Sites in the Qinling Mountains, Central China / *Shejiang WANG* [China]

054 Acheulian Culture of Gabdheswari River Valley: An Ecological Perspective / *Asok DATTA and Manomay GHOSH* [India]

055 Stone Industry and Chronology of the Mansuri Site, Korea / *Kiryong KIM and Kidong BAE* [Korea]

059 Neanderthal and Early Modern Human Habitations in the Galilee and Mount Carmel, Israel / *Avraham RONEN* [Israel]

060 Middle Palaeolithic Archeo-sequences from Southwestern France: Where do We Stand a Quarter Century After François Bordes? / *Jacques JAUBERT* [France]

075 The Heavy Tools in Hanshui River Valley, China / *Charong LI and Hao LI* [China]

Session Ⅱ. Chairpersons: Evgeny V. ARTEMYEV and Lucyna DOMAŃSKA

079 The Early Upper Paleolithic in North Mongolia: with Special Reference to Specimen Discovered at Bayangol 1 Site / *Toshiaki TSURUMARU, Y. OTSUKA, S. IIDA, B. TSOGTBAATAR, Masao AMBIRU, J. TAKAKURA, F. KHENZYKHENOVA, T. SATO, N. SCHEPINA* [Japan]

085 Stone Tool Caching Behavior in NE Japan at the End of the Pleistocene and its Implications / *Kaoru AKOSHIMA and Yoshitaka KANOMATA* [Japan]

088 New Result and Major Progress of Upper Paleolithic Sites in Benxi Area of Jilin Provinc, China / *Quanjia CHEN, Chun-xue WANG, Xia LI, Xiaoyang WANG, Jing SHI and Haibo WEI* [China]

091 Colonization of Late Pleistocene Siberia: Upper Paleolithic Siberia before and after the LGM / *Kelly E. GRAF* [USA]

093 Hell Gap Ⅲ and its Significance / *Marcel KORNFELD, Nicolas NAUDINOT and Mary Lou LARSON* [USA]

097 Perspectives on the Erdaoliang Late Paleolithic Site, China / *Fei XIE* [China]

099 Microlithic Technology and Raw Materials Use from Suyanggae Site, Korea / *Yung-jo LEE and Kaoru OTANI* [Korea]

104 Data Analysis of Paleolithic Sites in China / *Xin XU and Xing GAO* [China]

Session Ⅲ. Chairpersons: V.P CHEKHA and Sun-joo PARK

107 The Pomeranian Flint – How to Exploit it? Examples from Different Stages of the Prehistory / *Lucyna DOMAŃSKA* [Poland]

111 Geological Requirement for the Neolithic Camping Site on the Case of Volcanic Area, Japan / *Hisao KUMAI* [Japan]

112 New Discovery of *Gigantopithecus blacki* Fauna from Shuangtan Cave, Chongzuo, Guangxi, South China / *Changzhu JIN* [China]

113 The Middle-Upper Pleistocene Ursid's Fossils from Cheonyo Cave of Durubong Cave Complex in Korea / *Sun-joo PARK and Yung-jo LEE* [Korea]

116 The Middle to Late Pleistocene *Macaque* Fossils from Central Korea / *Yung-jo LEE and Masanaru TAKAI* [Korea]

120 OSL Dating of Imjin-Hantan Basin Sediments and Relevant Paleolithic Sites, Korea / *Yorinao SHITAOKA and Tsuneto NAGATOMO* [Japan]

123 Geoarcheology and Palynology of the Upper Paleolithic at the Gunang Cave Korea / *Ju-yong KIM, Yung-jo LEE, Jong-yoon WOO, Chang-gyun HAN and Sergei KRIVONOGOV* [Korea]

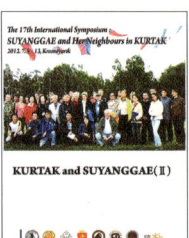

Commemoration International Symposium for the 90th Anniversary of Shuidonggou Discovery and the 18th Suyanggae and Her Neighbours for 50 Years of Prof. Yung-jo LEE's Paleolithic Study
SHUIDONGGOU and SUYANGGAE

Host and Supervisers : Institute of Archaeology of the Ningxia Hui Autonomous Region / Museum of the Ningxia Hui Autonomous Region / Institute of Vertebrate Paleontology and Paleoanthropology CAS(China) / Institute of Korean Prehistory (IKP, Korea)

Sponsors : The Shuidonggou Museum/ Kookmin Bank (Korea)

Duration : 2013. 6. 25–7. 1.

Place : Yinchuan Hotel (Hebei, China)

Organizers and Editors : Xing GAO, Nikolay I. DROZDOV, Lucyna DOMAŃSKA and Jong-yoon WOO

Contents

Session Ⅰ. Shuidonggou and Her Neighbours
(Chairperson : Nikolay I. DROZDOV)

025 General Introduction of SDG12 Cultural Transition Era of the Last Stage of late Pleistocene In the Northwest of China Cultural Phenomenon of SHUIDONGGOU Locality 12 / *Huimin WANG* [China]

034 New Cognition of the Xujiayao FM in Nihewan Basin / *Fagang WANG and Fei XIE* [China]

036 The Qiantie Cave Paleolithic Site of Changjiang County in Hainan Province / *Chaorong LI and Hao LI* [China]

038 A Study on the Small Flake Assemblage from Bailiandong Cave Site in Guangxi, South China / *Guangmao XIE* [China]

040 Source Provenance of Obsidian Artifacts from the Paleolithic Period Site of Dadong, Helong City, Jilin Province / *Wugan LUO* [China]

Session Ⅱ. Introduction to the Upper Paleolithic
(Chairperson : Guangmao XIE)

043 Palaeolithic Periodization in Central Siberia / *Nikolay I. DROZDOV* [Russia]

047 Patterns of Human Evolution in Northeast Asia / *Sang-hee LEE* [USA]

052 East to West("*Ex Oriente lux*") in Europe or West to East in Northern Asia? a Geographic Perspective on the Middle and Early Upper Palaeolithic to Late Palaeolithic / *Jacques JAUBERT* [France]

Session Ⅲ. After the Upper Paleolithic
(Chairperson : Kidong BAE)

055 Geological Requirement for the Paleolithic Site on the Volcanic Area / *Hisao KUMAI* [Japan]

060 FIRE and ICE: Paleoclimatic History of Last Canyon Cave / *Marcel KORNFELD, Thomas MINCKLEY, Judson FINLEY, Mackenzie CORY, Erik LIGHTNER, Mark CLEMENTZ and Mary Lou LARSON* [USA]

064 Late Palaeolithic in Southeast Asia: Evidence from Malaysia / *Mohd Mokhtar SAIDIN* [Malaysia]

068 Stone Age of Podkamennaya Tunguska River Valley / *V. I. MAKULOV* [Russia]

070 Neolithic Flint Harvesting Tools from Poland / *Lucyna DOMAŃSKA* [Poland]

073 Exploitation Beyond Subsistence of Faunal Resources at "RARH"(western West Bengal, India)by the New Settlers during Ferro-Chalcolithic Period / *Manomay GHOSH* [India]

Session Ⅳ. Young Archaeologists Session
(Chairperson : Marcel KORNFELD)

079 Kamenny Log as the Oldest Site in Central Siberia / *Dennis Nikolay I. DROZDOV* [Russia]

083 Geological Contexts and Age-estimation of Large Tools Component of Lower-Middle Paleolithic Sites in the Keum River Basin, South Korea / *Kiryong KIM and Kidong BAE* [Korea]

087 The Characteristics of Hand-axe in Late Pleistocene, Kore / *Hyeyeon LEE and Heonjong LEE* [Korea]

092 Afontovskaya Culture of Late Paleolith in Central Siberia / *Qiankun QUAN* [Russia]

095 Comparative Study with the Tanged Points from Suayngga Loc. Ⅰ and Nosan-ri Loc. Ⅱ, Korea / *Yung-jo LEE* [Korea], *Kaoru OTANI and Byeongil YOON*

Session Ⅴ : Suyanggae and Her Neighbours
(Chairperson : Lucyna DOMAŃSKA)

101 Expansion of Micro-Blade Technology into the Korean Peninsula : a Hypothetical Explanation / *Kidong BAE* [Korea]

105 New Records on Chronology and Lithic Industry of MIS 4~MIS from the Dosan Paleolithic Site in Southwestern Korea / *Gi-kil LEE* [Korea]

109 The Study of Blade Tool Culture of Korea / *Heonjong LEE and Sangseok LEE* [Korea]

115 Geomorphic and Sedimentary Process of Upper Pleistocene Sequences Illustrated in Sorori Site and its Surroundings along the Miho River, Korea / *Ju-yong KIM, Yung-jo LEE and Jong-yoon WOO* [Korea]

120 The Ancient Sorori Rice and its Evolution of Korean Rice Culture / *Kyeongja KIM and Yung-jo LEE* [Korea]

124 Suyanggae : Why So Important (Ⅳ)–with New Findings from Loc. Ⅲ – / *Yung-jo LEE, Jong-yoon WOO and Seung-won LEE* [Korea]

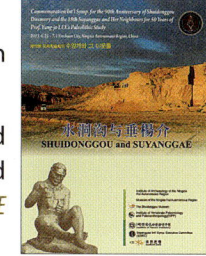

The 19th International Symposium SUYANGGAE and Her Neighbours in Poland:
ŁÓDŹ and SUYANGGAE

Host and Supervisers : Institute of Archaeology, University of Lodz (Poland) / Institute of Korean Prehistory (IKP, Korea)

Sponsors : Archaeological Museum in Gdansk (Poland)/ Kookmin Bank (Korea)

Duration : 2014. 6. 22–7. 1.

Place : University of Łódź (Łódź, Poland)

Organizers and Editors : Lucyna DOMAŃSKA, Yung-jo LEE and Jong-yoon WOO

Contents

Session I. Key-note Presentation
(Chairpersons : Jan Michal BURDUKIEWICZ and Marcel KORNFELD)

025 The Pioneer Modern Human Colonization of Europe: Demographic, Social and Ecological Perspectives / *Paul MELLARS* [England]

027 Middle Palaeolithic Flint Quarries–an Alternative Interpretation / *Avraham RONEN* [Israel]

035 Pre-clovis Settlement of Small Beringia Western Part / *Nikolay I. DROZDOV, Dennis N. DROZDOV, Stanislav A. LAUKHIN and V.I.MAKULOV* [Russia]

045 Ceramization of the Mesolithic / *Stefan Karol KOZŁOWSKI* [Poland]

053 Excavations at the Late Palaeolithic of Kappel, Southern Germany / *Micheal JOCHIM* [USA]

061 Development of Microlithic Industries in the Korean Peninsula / *Kidong BAE* [Korea]

Session II. Lodz and Her Neighbours
(Chairpersons : Avraham RONEN and Gi-kil LEE)

069 A Dynamic Technological Analysis Polish approach to Lithic Assemblages / *Jan Michal BURDUKIEWICZ* [Poland]

075 The Neanderthals from the caves–Two Decades of Excavation in Polish Jura / *Mikołaj URBANOWSKI* [Poland]

077 A multi-Faceted approach to the Jerzmanowice points from Nietoperzowa Cave, Southern Poland / *Andrzej WIŚNIEWSKI, Małgorzata KOT and Witold GRUŻDŹ* [Poland]

083 Advances in the Palaeolithic from Sudan(Fourth Cataract, Bayuda Desert, Eastern Desert) / *Mirosław MASOJĆ and Henryk PANER* [Poland]

089 10 Years After. New Results of Research on an Early Mesolithic Site at Krzyż / *Jacek KABACIŃSKI* [Poland]

093 Hunting-gathering Communities on the Kashubian Shoreland : the Early Settlement of East Pomerania, Poland / *Marcin WĄS* [Poland]

095 "Domestication" of the Tążyna Valley from the Perspective of the Flint Assemblages / *Lucyna DOMAŃSKA* [Poland]

097 Stone Age Apart from Lithics? / *Ole GRØN* [Denmark]

Session III. Young Archaeologist Session
(Chairpersons : Ole GRØN and Mohd Mokhtar SAIDIN)

103 The Characteristics and Changes of Blade Tool Techniques in Korea / *Heonjong LEE and Sangseok LEE* [Korea]

113 Newly Found Paleolithic Site in Southwestern Region of Korean Peninsula: Suncheon Bokdari Shingi Site / *Hyeyeon LEE and Heonjong LEE* [Korea]

121 The Lithic Assemblages and Chronology of Nosan-ni Paleolithic Site, Cheongju City, Korea / *Yung-jo LEE, Byeongil YOON and Kaoru OTANI* [Korea]

131 The Use of Flint in the Vicinity of the Outcrops by the Final Paleolithic and Mesolithic Societies–a Case Study of the Orońsko I Site, Southern Poland / *Mgr Katarzyna KERNEDER-GUBAŁA* [Poland]

Session IV. Suyanggae and Her Neighbours
(Chairpersons : Stefan Karol KOZLOWSKI and Nikolay I. DROZDOV)

141 A Paleoindian Red Ochre Quarry in Southeast Wyoming / *Marcel KORNFELD, George FRISON, Dennis STANFORD, George ZEIMENS and Danny WALKER* [USA]

147 About the Lower Paleolithic of Sakhalin, The Sennaya-1 Site / *Alexander A. VASILEVSKI* [Russia]

157 Prehistoric Culture Sequence in Lenggong, Malaysia: its

Contribution to the World Prehistory / *Mohd Mokhtar SAIDIN* [Malaysia]

165 Use-wear Analysis of Axes: a Review / *Shoh YAMADA* [Japan]

173 The Features of Upper Paleolithic Industries in South Korea / *Gi-Kil LEE* [Korea]

179 Chronology and Sedimentary Stratigraphy of Sorori Site in the Miho River, Cheongju City, Korea / *Ju-yong KIM, Yung-jo LEE, Jong-yoon WOO, Seung-won LEE and Keun-chang OH* [Korea]

191 SUYANGGAE : Why So Important (Ⅶ)?–with the newly excavated Loc.Ⅵ, Suyanggae Site– / *Yung-jo LEE, Jong-yoon WOO, Seung-won LEE and Ju-hyun AN* [Korea]

The 20-1th International Symposium SUYANGGAE and Her Neighbours in Israel :
SUYANGGAE and HAIFA

Host and Supervisers : University of Haifa, The Zinman Institute of Archaeology (Israel) / Institute of Korean Prehistory (IKP, Korea)

Sponsors : Faculty of Humanities, University of Haifa (Israel) / Kookmin Bank (Korea)

Duration : 2015. 6. 21–28.

Place : Auditorium of Haifa University Tower, MAROM Hotel (Haifa, Israel)

Organizers and Editors : Abraham RONEN and Yung-jo LEE

Contents

010 Decoding Prehistoric Art and the Origins of Writing / *Emmanul Anati, Fradkin Anati* [Italy]

011 Technological Analysis of Biface in Korea / *Kidong Bae and Myoungshin Cho and Kiryong Kim* [Korea]

012 Qesem Cave / *Ran Barkai* [Israel]

013 First Agricultural Colonization of the Polish Lowland in Flint / *Lucyna DOMAŃSKA and Seweryn RZEPECKI* [Poland]

014 Levallois in Siberia(history and problems) / *Nikolay I. DROZDOV and Dennis N. DROZDOV* [Russia]

016 New Analysis on Fire-use Evidence from the Peking Man Site / *Xing GAO* [China]

017 Reconstructing the Transition to the Neolithic Existence, and the Contribution of Functional Analysis of Flint Blades–a Case Study from the Southern Levant / *Iris Groman-YAROSLAVSKI* [Israel]

018 Goals and Constraints of Palaeolithic Archaeology / *Michael Jochim* [USA]

019 GIS-Based Analysis and Spatial Lithic Distribution Pattern in the Early Middle Palaeolithic Site of Misliya Cave, Mount Carmel, Israel / *Reuven Kapul, Yossi Zaindner and Mina Weinstein-Evron* [Israel]

020 Quaternary Geology and Matrix-forming Process of Suyangae Upper Paleolithic Sites (LOC. 1 and LOC. 6) / *Juyong KIM, Yung-jo LEE and Jong-yoon WOO* [Korea]

021 Of Proboscidean Bone Tools and Paleoindians / *Marcel KORNFELD, Mary Lou LARSON and George C. FRISON* [USA]

022 Classification and Methods of Research of the Upper Paleolithic Phone Instruments / *Lbova LIUDMILA and Kozhevnikova DARYA* [Russia]

023 Wolpyeong Upper Palaeolithic Site, One of Important Evidence of Modern Human Behavior in Paleolithic Korea / *Gi-Kil LEE* [Korea]

024 Regional 'Coexistence Model' in Upper Paleolithic of Korea / *Heonjong LEE* [Korea]

025 Suyanggae : Why So Important (Ⅷ)?–Thinking about the Oldest Microblade at the Locality Ⅵ – / *Yung-jo LEE, Jong-yoon WOO, Seung-won LEE, Ju-hyun AHN and Kyong-woo LEE* [Korea]

026 From Adorned Nudity to a Dignitary's Wardrobe: Symbolic raiment of the Southern Levant 13.500-3,900 BC / *Janet LEVY* [Israel]

028 Modern Flint Knapper's Camp Site from Volcanic Areas of Bayuda Desert in Sudan / *Mirosław MASOJĆ and Henryk PANER* [Poland]

030 Burial patterns in Ecuador's Upper Amazon / *Myriam OCHOA* [Ecuador]

031 The Looting of Archaeological Patrimony in Ecuador / *Ernesto SALAZAR* [Ecuador]

032 New Insights from Renewed Analysis of the 100 Layears Sequence of Tabun Cave, Israel / *Ron SHIMELMITZ, Avraham RONEN, Steven, L. KUHN and Mina WEINSTEIN* [Israel]

033 Early Ritual Behavior of Bear Hunters of Beringia gani / *Alexander A. Vasilevski* [Russia]

035 What was a Way and Reason of Dwellings Evolution on the Russian Far East during the Neolithic Period? / *Pavel VOLKOV* [Russia]

036 Game Traditions and Ancient Ritual Wine drinking in the Culture of East Asian Peoples: Anthropological Aspects / *Elena VOYTISHEK* [Russia]

037 New Archaeological Surveys and Excavations in the Hanzhong Bain, China / *Shejiang WANG, Huayu LU, Xuefeng SUN, Luda XING, Hongyan ZHANG, Haixin ZHUO, Wenchao ZHANG and Qingyao YU* [China]

040 A Preliminary Study on the Stone Artifacts of Shizilukou Paleolithic Locality in Luonan Basin, Central China / *Luda XING, Shejiang WANG, Gaike ZHANG, Tuo LIU, Xuefeng SUN, Huayu LU, Qingyao YU and Xiaobing ZHANG* [China]

042 Early Epipaleolithic Engraved Objects from Ein Qashish South, Jezreel Valley, Israel / *Alla YAROSHEVICH* [Israel]

043 The Natufian is still a "Revolution": Intensification and Sedentism in the Natufian Sequence of el-Wad Terrace, Mt. Carmel / *Le Reuven Yeshurun* [Israel]

044 Paleolithic Assemblage and Site Formation Process of Huaishuping Site in Luonan Basin, Central China / *Qingyao YU , ShejiangWANG, Huayu LU, Chen SHEN, Fuyou CHEN, Feng LI, Wenchao ZHANG, Luda XING and Xiaobing ZHANG* [China]

038 The Characteristic of Stone Assemblages from Tonghyeon -ri Paleolithic Site in Korea / *Jong-yoon WOO, Seung-won LEE and Byeongil YUN* [Korea]

045 Nesher Ramla Karst Depression, Israel: A New Evidence for Middle Paleolithic Adaptations during MIS 6 and 5 / *Yossi ZAIDNER, David E. FRIESEM, Amos FRUMKIN, Leore GROSMAN, Naomi PORAT, Ruth SHACHACK-GROSS, Alexander TSATSKIN, Reuven YESHURUN, Lior WEISSBROD, Laura CENTI, Marion PREVOST, Maayan SHEMER and Oz VARONER* [Israel]

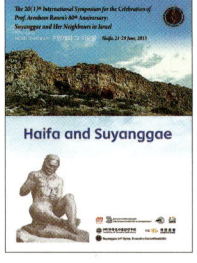

The 20-2ᵗʰ International Symposium for Celebration of the 30ᵗʰ Anniversary of the 1ˢᵗ Suyanggae Site Excavation : SUYANGGAE and Her Neighbours in Korea

Host Supervisers : Jbnews, Chungbuk Nat'l University Museum (CBNUM, Korea) / Institute of Korean Prehistory (IKP, Korea) / Suyanggae Int'l. Symposuim Executive Committee (SISEC, Korea)

Sponsor : Kookmin Bank (Korea) / Asian Paleolithic Association (APA)

Duration : 2015. 11. 1–8.

Place : Chungbuk Nat'l University (Cheongju), Danyang Tourist Hotel (Danyang, Korea)

Organizers : Yung-jo LEE and Jong-yoon WOO

Editors : Yung-jo LEE, Jong-yoon WOO, Seung-won LEE and Kyong-Woo LEE

Contents

Session Ⅰ. Key-note Presentation
(Chairperson : Ju-yong KIM)

023 Paleolithic Archaeology and Social Sustainability: Research, Festival and Preservation of the Chongokni Paleolithic Site in Korea / *Kidong BAE* [Korea]

039 Beyond Stone: Contributions of Bone and Antler Technology to Stone Age Archaeology / *Michael JOCHIM* [USA]

049 Astroarchaeology of Siberia / *Nikolay I. DROZDOV* [Russia]

057 Peopling of the Japanese Archipelago: An Evolving Scenario Viewed from Abroad / *Fumiko IKAWA-SMITH* [Canada]

069 Panxian Dadong and the Chinese Levallois / *Weiwen HUANG, Marcel OTTE, Yue HU and Yamei HOU* [China]

Session Ⅱ. Neighbours in Europe
(Chairperson : Sun-joo PARK)

095 The Late Neolithic Flint Production in the Tążyna river valley. New Evidence / *Lucyna DOMAŃSKA* [Poland]

105 The Sakhalin-Hokkaido-Kuriles' contincent to ocean contact zone and the problem of time of Human exploration of the islands between Amur-Hokkaido and Kamchatka (Based on the Radiocarbon Chronology of Sites on the Sakhalin, Hokkaido and Kuril Islands) / *A.A. VASILEVSKI* [Russia]

111 Submerged Stone Age – Access to a New Resource / *Ole GRØN* [Denmark]

121 Complex of Late-Paleolith Monuments on Afontova Mountain in Krasnoyarsk and New Results of Studying Afontova Culture / *Dennis N. DROZDOV* [Russia]

133 Paleolithic in Asia in the Light of the international series of the conferences "Suyanggae and Her Neighbours" / *Marcel BARTCZAK* [Poland]

Session Ⅲ. Neighbours in New Continent
(Chairperson : Lucyna DOMAŃSKA)

143 Hell Gap Revisited / *Marcel KORNFELD and Mary Lou Larson* [USA]

151 Early Lithic Industries of Preclumbian Ecuador / *Ernesto SALAZAR* [Ecuador]

161 Lowland Ecuador: An Archaeological Perspective / *Myriam OCHOA* [Ecuador]

Session Ⅳ. Neighbours in Asia
(Chairperson : Hiroyuki SATO

171 Research on Paleolithic Sites in Benxi Area, Liaoning Province / *Quanjia CHEN, Chen-chen WAN, Xiao-yang WANG and Xia LI* [China]

179 Lithic Assemblage from the Yuzui Paleolithic Site of the Lower Paleolithic in the Dangjiangkou Region, China / *Chunxue WANG, Dong WEI, Jing WU and Yalin LIU* [China]

195 A New *Gigantopithecus* Fauna from the Early Pleistocene Juyuan Cave in Boyue Mountain, Guangxi, South China / *Changzhu JIN and Yuan WANG* [China]

203 New Evidence of Human Occupation in the East before 1.8 Ma / *Qi WEI, Shu-wen PEI, Zhen-xiu JIA, Zhen-qing CHI, Yong WANG and Geoffrey POPE* [China]

205 A New Advance of the Early Palaeolithic Study in Japan / *Kazuto MATSUFUJI, Atsushi UEMINE, Kyoichi KIKUCHI and Yasuyuki SUGIHARA* [Japan]

211 Invisible Hearths and Restoring Human Behavior : High Resolution Archaeological Analysis at Yoshiizawa Site of Northern Japan / *Daigo NATSUKI and Hiroyuki SATO* [Japan]

219 Recent Researches on Early Human Arrivals into the Japanese Archipelago / *Kaoru AKOSHIMA* [Japan]

229 Experimental Study on the Blade Tool Techniques of the Upper Paleolithic in Korea / *Heonjong LEE and Sangseok LEE* [Korea]

235 The Prehistoric Whaling during the Neolithic Period in South Korea / *Sang-mog LEE* [Korea]

Session Ⅴ. Inside Suyanggae
(Chairperson : Kazuto MATSUFUJI)

247 Suyanggae, Why so Important (Ⅸ)? : 30 Years of the Suyanggae Complex, Korea / *Yung-jo LEE, Jong-yoon WOO and Seung-won LEE* [Korea]

263 Morpho-sedimentary Environment and Chronological Implications of Cultural Layers in Suyanggae Site(Loc. Ⅵ), Danyang County in Korea / *Ju-yong KIM, Yung-jo LEE, Jong-yoon WOO and Keunchang OH* [Korea]

271 Comparison of Cultural Layers with Radiocarbon Dates among Archeological Sites: the Suyanggae Sites and Gunang-gul Cave, Danyang, South Korea / *Kyeong Ja KIM, Yung-jo LEE and Jong-yoon WOO* [Korea]

283 Measurement of Dimension and its Related Measurands of the Pebble Stone with Engraved Lines Excavated from Loc. Ⅵ of SUYANGGAE Site, Korea / *Ho-Suhng SUH, Yung-jo LEE Jong-yoon WOO, Seung-won LEE, Ju-hyun AHN, Kyong-Woo LEE, Yeon-Sung JOO, Won-Ho CHOI and Hong-Jin YANG* [Korea]

299 Engraving stones found at Suyanggae Locality Ⅵ: Signs of Modern Human Behavior/ *Kyong-woo LEE, Yung-jo LEE, Jong-yoon Woo, Seung-won LEE, and Joo-hyun AHN* [Korea]

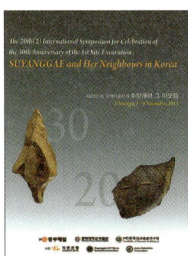

The 21st Suyanggae and Her Neighbours International Symposium :
Suyanggae and Hell Gap–Pleistocene-Holocene Archaeology from the Cape of Good Hope to Tierra del Fuego–

Host and Supervisers : College of Arts and Sciences, University of Wyoming Paleoindian Research Lab,. University of Wyoming (USA) / Institute of Korean Prehistory (IKP, Korea)

Sponsors : Kookmin Bank (Korea) / Anthropology Dept., Int'l Programs Office (University of Wyoming, USA) / Terry and Jim Wilson Vee Bar Ranch (Thermopolis USA) / Deer Creek Heights Ranch, Fresno (California USA) / Mike Toft, Sterling (Colorado USA)

Duration : 2016. 7. 26–8. 3.

Place : Anthropology Dept., Wyoming State University (USA)

Organizers and Editors : Marcel KORNFELD, Mary Lou LARSON, Yung-jo LEE, Jong-yoon WOO and Mackenzie CORY

Contents

Session Ⅰ. Keynote Addresses: Archaeology and Archaeological Problems from Bay of Biscay to Sea of Okhotsk (Chairperson : Jiří A. SVOBODA)

094 Peopling of the New World, as Seen from the Japanese Archipelago / *Fumiko IKAWA-SMITH* [Canada]

020 Post-depositional Processes and Explanation of Hominin Activities at Paleolithic Sites in Korea / *Kidong BAE* [Korea]

053 The Powars Ⅱ Site: Red Ocher, Tool Stone, Early and Late Paleoindian Procurement Activities on the High Plains of North America / *George C. FRISON* [USA]

039 Change and Continuity Traditions of Flint Processing from the Perspective of the Tążyna River Basin in Kuyavia, Poland / *Lucyna DOMAŃSKA* [Polana]

107 Palaeolithic and Mesolithic Colonization of the European High Alps / *Michael JOCHIM* [USA]

Session II. Neighbours from Cape of Good Hope to the Caucuses (Chairperson : Hiroyuki SATO)

076 People of the Desert, Dunes, and Deltas: Landscape Archaeology in the Interior of Southern Africa / *Robert K. HITCHCOCK and James I. EBERT* [USA]

206 Middle Stone Age in the Horn of Africa: Research Along Tributaries of the Blue Nile, Northwest Ethiopia / *Lawrence TODD, John KAPPELMAN, Neil TABOR, Marvin KAY, and Mulugeta FESEHA* [USA]

157 The Akhziv Tsunami(?) Deposit / *Avraham RONEN and Yamada SHOH* [Israel]

Session III. Neighbours from North Sea to South China Sea (Chairperson : Ju-Yong KIM)

029 Comparison of Tanged Points from Korean and Polish Areas–on the Basis of Two Distant Stone Age Sites / *Marcel BARTCZAK* [Poland]

193 Hunting strategies in Late Pleistocene Landscapes. Case of the Middle Danube Basin / *Jiří A. SVOBODA* [Czech]

229 Epigraphic Memorial Stele Mehyangbi («Incense Burial») as an Archaeological and Cultural Heritage of Medieval Korea / *Elena VOYTISHEK and Anna SHMAKOVA* [Russia]

245 Recent Discovery of Paleolithic Sites in Bubing Basin, South China / *Wei WANG* [China]

236 Human Behavioral Adaptation on Jinsitai Cave Site, Northern China / *Chun-xue WANG, Xiao-kun WANG, Quan-jia CHEN, Zhuo-wei TANG and Jian WEI* [China]

300 Microblade-based Societies: A New Perspective on Roles of the Microblade Technology in Northern China after the Last Glacial Maximum / *Meng ZHENG* [USA]

253 A Study on the Neolithic Chipped Stone Tools from Lingnan (South China) / *Guangmao XIE and Qiang LIN* [China]

287 Panxian Dadong Cave: Levallois Technology in Southern China (Poster) / *Weiwen HUANG, Marcel OTTE, Yue HU and Ya-mei HOU* [China]

Session IV. Neighbours from South China Sea to Bering Strait (Chairperson : Brigid GRUND)

116 Landscape and Soil-Sedimentary Matrix-Forming Processes of Sorori Paleolithic Site in the Miho River Since MIS 5, Korean Peninsula / *Ju-Yong KIM, Yung-jo LEE, Jong-yun WOO, Seungwon LEE, and Keun Chang OH* [Korea]

144 Suyanggae, Why so Important (X)? with the focus on Tanged-points from Cultural Layer 4 at SYG-6 / *Seung-won LEE, Yung-jo LEE, Jong-yoon WOO, Joo-hyun AHN and Kyong-woo LEE* [Korea]

170 Pleistocene to Holocene Archaeology in the Japanese Archipelago: An Overview / *Hiroyuki SATO* [Japan]

263 The First Floating Farmers: Tempo and Mode of the Neolithic Transition in Taiwan / *Pei-Lin YU* [Taiwan]

277 Stone Artifacts Analysis from Re-deposited Sediments in Seochon Paleolithic sites, Cheongju, Korea / *Byeongil YUN, Hyeongil JANG and Jong-yoon WOO* [Korea]

215 Chronology, Periodization, and the Main Features, of Sony Culture (Early Middle Neolithic Sakhalin Island) / *Alexander A. VASILEVSKI and V.A. GRISCHENKO* [Russia]

Session V. Neighbours from Bering Strait to Tierra del Fuego (Chairperson : Pei-Lin YU)

182 Useful Companions: Domestic Dog Use on the Northern Great Plains / *Rachael Lea SHIMEK* [USA]

130 Hell Gap Zooarchaeology: A Time to Reconsider / *Marcel KORNFELD and Mary Lou LARSON* [USA]

038 From Home to Hearth: Expanding on a Model of Tipi Transformation / *Mackenzie CORY* [USA]

057 Behavioral Ecology, Technology, and the Organization of Labor: How a Shift from Spear Thrower to Self-Bow Exacerbates Social Disparities / *Brigid GRUND* [USA]

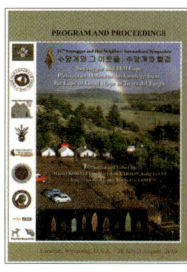

The 22nd SUYANGGAE International Symposium In Sakhalin : "The Initial Human Exploration of the Continental and Insular Parts of the Eurasia"
SUYANGGAE and OGONKI

Host and Supervisers : Governor and Government of the Sakhalin Region (Russia) /Sakhalin State University (Russia) / Institute of Korean Prehistory (IKP, Korea)

Sponsor : Kookmin Bank (Korea) / Institute of Archaeology and Ethnography, SB RAS

Duration : 2017. 7. 5–12.

Place : Sakhalin State University (Sakhalin, Russia)

Organizers : Alexander A. VASILEVSKI and Yung-jo LEE

Editors : Alexander A. VASILEVSKI, V. GRISHCHENKO, Yung-jo LEE and Jong-yoon WOO

Contents

Prenary Session

006 Suyanggae, Why So Important(XI)? Newly Excavated Tanged-points Form Suyanggae Locality 1 / *Seung-won LEE, Yung-jo LEE, Jong-yoon WOO, Ju-hyun AHN, Kyong-woo LEE* [Korea]

010 On the Specific Signs of Intentional Processing on Siliceous Rocks of the Old Stone Age Site Sennaya 1(Southern Sakhalin) / *A.A. VASILEVSKI, Y.Y. GIRYA* [Russia]

016 The Overall Study of the Most Ancient *Homo sapiens* from Kostenki XIV / *S.V. BASILYEV, S.B. BORTUSKAYA* [Russia]

018 Dating Chongok and Dating Paleolithic Industries in the Hantan-Imjin Rover Basin, Korea / *kidong BAE* [Korea]

019 At the edge : Acheulean Expansion in the Middle Europe / *Jiří A. SVOBODA* [Czech]

020 The Analysis of Tanged-points on the Suyanggae Site / *Eunjeong KIM* [Korea]

Session 1. From Lower to Upper Paleolithic
(Chairpersons : Kidong BAE, Nikolay I. DROZDOV and Jiří A. SVOBODA)

021 Assemblages of Small Flake Implements from South China and Southeast Asia / *Guangmao XIE, Qiang LIN, Yan WU and Dawei LI* [China]

023 Cultural Dynamic of Emergence and Diffusion of *Homo sapiens* in Korea / *Heonjong LEE, Sang Seok LEE and Donghyuk Son* [Korea]

026 Morphological Diversity and Functional Differentiation of Tanged-point / *Eunjeong KIM* [Korea]

027 Stratigraphy, Chronology and Paleovegetation of the Paleo-lithic Sites in the Keum-Miho River Basin(KMRB) in Korea / *Ju-Yong KIM, Yung-jo LEE, Jong-yoon WOO, Seung-won LEE, Sangheon Yi and Keun-Chang OH* [Korea]

031 Tolbor 21 site : A New Paleolithic Squence from Northern Mongolia / *Rybin E., Khatsenovich A., Zwyns N., Gunchinsuren B.* [Russia]

032 New Stratigraphic Division of IUP-EUP Assemblages of the Kara-Bom Site (Russian Altai) according to the Results of Spatial Analysis and Refitting Studies / *Natalya E. BELOUSOVA and Evgeny P. RYBIN* [Russia]

039 Osteological Evidence of Human Activity in the Ostantesvaya Cave (Central Sakhalin, Russia) / *Kirillova I.V.* [Russia]

041 Microblade Technologies in Final Pleistocene–Early Holocene Complexes, Northern Mongolia : Orign and Spreading / *Tabarev A.V.* [Russia]

048 Comparative Study on Microblade Industry of Northeast Asia / *Kaoru OTANI, Yung-jo LEE* [Japan]

049 Influence of Paleoclimate on the Structural Organization of Ancient Sites / *Razgildeeva I. I., Reshetova S. A.* [Russia]

Session 2. From Upper Paleolithic to Neolithic(Part I)
(Chairpersons : Kaoru AKOASHIMA, Evgeny P. RYBIN, Guangmao WIE, Gao Xin and E.Y. GIRYA)

052 Toward the Standardized Identification of Lithic Use-wear, for Universal East Asian Criteria/ *Kaoru AKOSHIMA and Hyewon HONG* [Japan]

060 The Open-air Site of Ushbulak-1(East Kazakhstan): a New Initial Upper / *A. A. ANOIKIN* [Russia]

064　Palaeolithic Stone Tools Workshop in Lenggong Valley, Perak, Malaysia / *Mohd Mokhtar SAIDIN* [Malaysia]

070　Northeast Asian Microlithic Industries Seen from Suyanggae Typology / *Kaoru OTANI and Yung-jo LEE* [Japan]

073　Paleolithic of Northern Angara Region / *D.N. DROZDOV* [Russia]

074　Study of Microblade Industry in Siberian, Korean and North China and its Cultural Relations with Contiguous Territories / *N.I. DROZDOV, D.N. DROZDOV, Donghyuk SON, Qianun QUAN* [Russia]

075　The Site Ushki-V(Kamchatka) and its Place in the Periodization of the Archaeological Cultures of the Northern Far East of Russia / *Irina PONKRATOVA* [Russia]

078　Coexistence of the Terminal Upper Paleolithic Culture and the Incipient Jomon Culture in Hokkaido / *Natsuki DAIGO* [Japan]

Session 3. From Upper Paleolithic to Neolithic(Part Ⅱ)
(Chairpersons : Lucyna DOMAŃSKA and Grishchenko VYACHESLAV)

081　Development of Obsidian Source and Distribution of Obsidian during Upper Paleolithic Age: Obsidian from Hokkaido Disperse into Sakhalin and Honsyu / *Hideyaki KIMURA, E.L.LAVROV(late) and Alexander A. VASILEVSKI* [Japan]

083　Blade Arrowheads Culture of Northen-east Asia Islands World (Sakhalin, Kuril Islands, Hokkaido)–the View from XXI Century / *Grishchenko VYACHESLAV and M. FUKUDA* [Russia]

086　Radiocarbon Dating and Analyzing Food Habits Using Charred Remains on Pottery from the Early Neolithic Sites in Northeast Asia / *Dai Kunikita* [Japan]

088　Neolithic Flint Mine in Krzemionki as an Example of the Popularization Method of the Archaeological Site / *Marcel BARTCZAK* [Poland]

090　Wang Ningsheng's Contribution to China's Ethno-archaeology / *Ningsheng WANG, Lingyuan KONG, Yujie LI* [China]

097　Chiroptera Remains First Discovered in China's Urban Archaeology and Research / *Xianzhu WU* [China]

106　The Formation Process of the Paleolithic Sites in the Imjin-Hantan River Basin: Artifact Concentration and Diffusion in the Upper Sediments of Basalt Bedrock / *Kiryong KIM* [Korea]

107　Reduction Sequences in the Microblade Assemblage of the Ishikari Low Land, Hokkaido / *Fumito AKAI* [Japan]

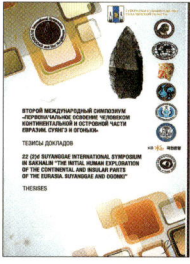

The 23rd Suyanggae International Symposium. in Malaysia for the Memory of Late Chairman Jae-ho KIM :
SUYANGGAE & LENGGONG : PREHISTORY ADAPTATION

Host and Supervisers : Centre for Global Archaeological Research (Malaysia) / University Sains Malaysia (Malaysia) / Institute of Korean Prehistory (IKP, Korea)

Sponsor : University Sains Malaysia (Malaysia)/ Kookmin Bank (Korea)

Duration : 2018. 7. 1–7.

Place : University Sains Malaysia (Penang, Malaysia)

Organizers and Editors : Mohd Mokhtar SAIDIN, Yung-jo LEE, Jong-yoon WOO and Shaiful SHAHIDAN

Contents

SESSION I. SISEC PRESENTATION
(Chairperson : Prof. Hsiao-chun HUNG)

041 Launching of a new Journal to establish long-lasing academy / *Yung-jo LEE and Kyong-woo LEE* [Korea]

033 Early Paleolithic of Yenisey, Siberia / *Nikolay I. DROZDOV and Dennis N. DROZDOV* [Russia]

033 Łącko site 6, Pakość commune, Poland : Symptoms of Ritual Behaviours on the Site / *Lucyna DOMAŃSKA and Seweryn RZEPECKI* [Poland]

035 Evidence for the Earliest Human Occupation of the High-altitude Tibetan Plateau / *Xig GAO, Xiaoling ZHANG and Shejiang WANG* [China]

039 Observing the Small in Palaeoindian Archaeology / *Marcel KORNFELD and Mary Lou LARSON* [USA]

040 Reconsideration of IUP Concept in Asian Continent / *Heonjong LEE* [Korea]

037 Site-forming Process of the Suyanggae Paleolithic LOC. 1, 3 and 6 in Danyang County, South Korea / *Ju-yong KIM, Yung-jo LEE, Jong-yoon WOO, Seung-won LEE and Keun-Chang OH* [Korea]

049 Three Paleolithic Cultures in the Japanese Archipelago / *Hiroyuki SATO* [Japan]

SESSION II. SUYANGGAE & NEIGHBOURS IN KOREA
(Chairperson: Prof. Xing GAO)

042 Overview of Suyanggae Locality 6 : Changing lithic Assemblage by Cultural Layers / *Kyong-woo LEE, Seung-won LEE, Kaoru OTANI, Jong-yoon WOO and Yung-jo LEE* [Korea]

032 Preliminary Report on the Chisel-typed Tool from Suyanggae-6(SYG-6), Korea–In Focus on SYG(VI) / *Dong Hyuk CHOI, Heongjong LEE, Jong-yoon WOO, Seung-won LEE, Ju-hyun AHN and Yung-jo LEE* [Korea]

036 Use-wear Analysis of the Tanged-points from Suyanggae Site, Locality 6, and its Implications / *Hyewon HONG, Kaoru AKOSHIMA, Jong-yoon WOO and Yung-jo LEE* [Korea]

038 Geological Age and Site Formation Process of Mansuri Paleolithic Site in Cheongju, Korea / *Kiryong KIM, Kidong BAE, Kazuto MATSUFUJI and Yung-jo LEE* [Korea]

046 The Mansuri Palaeolithic site and the Loess-paleosol Chronology / *Kazuya NAKAGAWA, Yung-jo LEE, Kidong BAE and Kazuto MATSUFUJI* [Japan]

SESSION III. NEIGHBOURS IN JAPAN
(Chairperson : Prof. Marcel KORNFELD)

034 Early Holocene Human Adaptations in the Northern Boundary of Temperate Environment (Russian Far East and Japanese Archipelago) / *Masahiro FUKUDA* [Japan]

047 Different Spatial Activity in the Late Glacial Microblade Site: A Case Study Based on the Yoshiizawa Site of Northern Japan / *Daigo NATSUKI and Hiroyuki SATO* [Japan]

047 Regional Diversity of Middle/ Upper Palaeolithic transition in South Asia / *Atsushi NOGUCHI* [Japan]

054 Demography, Territoriality and Inter-group Relationships : Perspectives on Japanese Palaeolithic Studies / *Shoh YAMADA* [Japan]

SESSION IV. NEIGHBOURS IN LENGGONG
(Chairperson : Prof. Jiří SVOBODA)

048 Open Site Adaptation in Lenggong, Malaysisa / *Mohd Mokhtar SAIDIN* [Malaysia]

036 Late Pleistocence-Holocene Cave Occupation of Lenggong

Valley, Malaysia / *Hsiao Mei GOH, Mohd Mokhtar SAIDIN, Saiful SHAHIDAN and Darren CURNOE* [Malaysia]

048 Integration of Geophysical Methods in Finding Bukit Bunuh Subsurface Structure for Impact Crater Evidences / *Rosil SAAD, Nordiana MOHD MUSTAZA, N,A.Ismail and Mohd Mokhtar SAIDIN* [Malaysia]

030 Metroite Impact Rocks in Bukit Bunuh, Lenggong, Perak, Malaysia : Evidence of Raw Materials in Lithic Industry and its Association with Higher Polymorph Minerals / *Nurazlin ABDULLAH, Nor Khairunnisa TALIB and Mohd Mokhtar SAIDIN* [Malaysia]

030 Used Wear Exploration : Typology and Functions of Palaeolithic Flake Tools in Bukit Bunuh, Lenggong, Perak, Malaysia / *Siti Khairani ABDUL JALIL, Jeffrey ABDULLAH and Mohd Mokhtar SAIDIN* [Malaysia]

SESSION Ⅴ. NEIGHBOURS IN CHINA
(Chairperson: Prof. Lucyna DOMAŃSKA)

037 From Forest Caves to Coastal Settlements: Maritime Adaptation, Population Formation, and Cultural Transition along the South China Sea / *Hsiao-chun HUNG* [Australia]

039 A Study on Dashuitian Site / *Lingyuan KONG and Yujie LI* [China]

051 Paleolithic Research of Suifen River Basin Discovered in 2017 / *WEI TIENXU* [China]

053 The Newly Discovered Stones Artefacts from FenglinSite, Jilin Province/ *Wanbo LI* [China]

054 Human Behavior in the Last Glacial Period: Evidence from Zhongshan Cave Site in Bubing Basin, South China / *Wei WANG* [China]

055 Recent Discovery of Late Pleistocene Modern Human Evidence in South China / *Yanyan YAO, Wei LIAD and Wei WANG* [China]

SESSION Ⅵ. NEIGHBOURS IN CZECH REP. and RUSSIA
(Chairperson : Prof. Gi-kil LEE)

050 Dolni Véstonice I: A Classic Paleolithic Site Revisited / *Jiří SVOBODA, Martin NOVAK, Sandra SAZELOVA, Šárka HLADILOVA and Petr ŠKRDLA* [Czech]

040 Pigment Compositions in Upper Palaeolithic Cultures of Southern Siberia / *Liudmila LBOVA* [Russia]

052 Technological Stages of the Prehistory Art's Production in the Late Paleolithic of Southern Siberia (Mal'ta Site) / *Pavel VOLKOV and Liudmila LBOVA* [Russia]

SESSION Ⅶ. NEIGHBOURS IN AFRICA & SEA
(Chairperson : Prof. Hiroyuki SATO)

044 Acheulean in the North-Eastern Africa / *Mirosław MASOJC and Ju-yong KIM* [Poland]

031 Choppers, Sumatraliths and Others: Evolution of the Late Pleistocene Heavy-duty Tools in Tham Lod Rockshelter, Area 2, Pang Mapha District, North-western Thailand / *Thanon CHIKTAMENT, Claire GAILLARD and Rasmi SHOOCONGDEJ* [France]

053 Subsistence Strategies and Adaptation to a Changing Environment during Late Pleistocene and Early Holocene in Mindoro, Philippines / *Rebekka VOLMER, Rebecca Maria FERRERAS, Kristine LIM and Alfred PAWLIK* [Philippines]

052 The Use of Mineral Materials in Vietnamese Hoabinhan Context / *Nguyen VIET* [Vietnam]

The 24th SUYANGGAE International Symposium for Commemoration of the 90th Anniversary of the First Skull's Discovery of PEKING MAN and Late Prof. Abraham RONEN
ZHOUKOUDIAN and SUYANGGAE

Host and Supervisers : Institute of Vertebrate Paleontology and Paleoanthropology (IVPP CAS, China) / Institute of Korean Prehistory (IKP, Korea)

Sponsor : Kookmin Bank (Korea)/ IVPP CAS (China) / Suyanggae Int'l. Symp. Executive Committee (SISEC, Korea)

Duration : 2019. 12. 1-8.

Place : Xiyuan Hotel and IVPP (Beijing, China)

Organizers and Editors : Xing GAO, Yung-jo LEE, Jong-yoon WOO and Heonjong LEE

Contents

Session Ⅰ. Key-note Presentation
(Chairperson : Xing GAO and Hiroyuki SATO)

024 Research on Modern Human Origins in China: Achievements and Challenges / *Xing GAO* [China]

026 Geomorphological Processes and Chronological Pattern of Paleolithic Sites in HIRB, Korea / *Kidong BAE and Kiryong KIM* [Korea]

028 Middle Pleistocene Small-dimensional Industries in the Center of Europe: Realationships to Asia / *Jiří SVOBODA* [Czech]

030 Middle Palaeolithic Flint Materials from Central Poland–Case Study of the Site Polesie 1, Lodz voivodship / *Lucyna DOMAŃSKA, Seweryn RZEPECKI and Marcin WĄS* [Poland]

032 Pleistocene Environment in Malaysia Based on Geo-archaeological Research / *Mohd Mokhtar SAIDIN* [Malaysia]

Session Ⅱ. Neighbours in Eurasia
(Chairperson : Ju-yong KIM and Zhanyang LI)

035 New Progress and Prospect of Lingjing Xuchang Hominid Site / *Zhanyang LI* [China]

037 The New Discoveries in North China and Related Questions / *Yuping WANG and Yue FENG* [China]

038 The Earliest Modern Human in South China?–A Review and Prospect– / *Wei WANG* [China]

041 A New Archaeological Evidence of Musashidai Site and its Implications for the Study of the Early Upper Paleolithic in the Japanese Archipelago / *Noriyoshi ODA and Hiroyuki SATO* [Japan]

043 Shatekiyama (Hirosato)-type Artefacts in the Late Stage of the Upper Paleolithic of the Sakhalin-Hokkaido-Kuriles' Paleo Peninsula / *Hideaki KIMURA, Evgeny Y. GIRYA, Vyacheslav A. GRISHCHENKO and Alexander A.VASILEVSKI* [Japan]

046 A Study of the Quartz Lithic Industries in Paleolithic Eurasia / *Kazuharu TAKEHANA* [Japan]

048 Palaeolithic Collections Dated by Tektites in Vietnam : Some Questions ! / *Nguyen VIET* [Vietnam]

049 The Deep and Old Submerged Stone Age Sites–How can we find them and what can they tell us?– / *Ole GRØN, Lars Ole BOLDREEL, Rostand TAYONG, Philippe BLONDEL, Bo MADSEN, Deborah CVIKEL, Ehud GALILI and Antonio DELL'ANNO* [Denmark]

Session Ⅲ. Suyanggae and Neighbours in Asia
(Chairperson : Lucyna DOMAŃSKA and Yuping WANG)

052 SUYANGGAE, Why So Important (ⅩⅢ)?–with the Focus on Characteristics of the CL 4 at SYG 6– / *Kaoru OTANI, Kyong-woo LEE, Jong-yoon WOO, Seung-won LEE and Yung-jo LEE* [Japan]

055 Late Paleolithic Site–forming Process and Chronology with an Emphasis on Suyanggae Open Site and

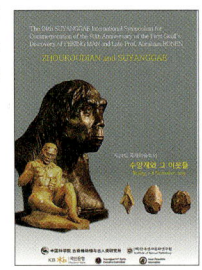

Gunang Cave Site in Danyang County, Korea / *Ju-yong KIM, Yung-jo LEE, Jong-yoon WOO, Kyung-ja KIM and Sunjoo PARK* [Korea]

058 Function of Tanged Points from the Suyanggae Site, Locality 6, and its Implications for Emergence of Modern Human Behavior / *Kaoru AKOSHIMA, Jong-yoon WOO, Hyewon HONG, Kaoru OTANI, Seung-won LEE and Yung-jo LEE* [Japan]

060 Techno-typology and Function of Chisel Typed Tool from the CL 2 at SYG 6 / *Dong Hyuk CHOI, Heonjong LEE, Jong-yoon WOO, Seung-won LEE and Yung-jo LEE* [Korea]

063 Migrations of *Homo sapiens* to the Korean Peninsula in UP / *Heonjong LEE and Seongkwen PARK* [Korea]

066 Jeongok Prehistory Museum : Miracle of Hantan River / *Hanyong LEE* [Korea]

The 25th SUYANGGAE International Symposium for the Commemoration of Prof. Yung-jo LEE's 80th Birthday

The 25th Suyanggae Int'l Symposium for the commemoration of Prof. Yung-Jo Lee's 60th Anniversary of Paleolithic Studies
JEONGOK and SUYANGGAE

Host and Supervisers : Jeongok Prehistory Museum / Institute of Korean Prehistory (IKP, Korea)

Sponsor : Kookmin Bank (Korea) / Institute of Korean Prehistory (IKP, Korea) / Suyanggae Int'l. Symp. Executive Committee (SISEC, Korea)

Duration : 2022. 9. 22.

Place : Institute of Korean Prehistory (IKP, Korea)

Organizers and Editors : Kidong BAE and Jong-yoon WOO

Contents

Suyanggae Research and its Internationalization / *Yung-jo LEE* [Korea]

Suyanggae Academic Awards (2008–2022)

1st (2008.12.6.)
Rector **N. I. DROZDOV**
(Krasnoyarsk Univ.)
Russia

2nd (2009.10.20.)
Prof. **Masao AMBIRU**
(Meiji Univ.)
Japan

3rd (2010.5.22.)
Prof. **L. DOMAŃSKA**
(Lodz Univ.)
Poland

4th (2011.8.15.)
Prof. **Xing GAO**
(IVPP, CAS)
China

5th (2012.7.6.)
Prof. **Changzhu JIN**
(IVPP, CAS)
China

6th (2013.6.26.)
Prof. **M. JOCHIM**
(Univ. of California, SB)
USA

7th (2014.6.25.)
Prof. **Heon-jong LEE**
(Mokpo Nat'l Univ.)
Korea

8th (2015.6.22.)
Prof. **A. RONEN**
(Haifa Univ.)
Israel

9th (2015.11.2.)
Prof. **Kidong BAE**
(Hanyang Univ.)
Korea

10th (2016.11.2.)
Prof. **M. KORNFELD**
(Univ. of Wyoming)
USA

11th (2017.11.2.)
Dr. **Ju-yong KIM**
(KIGAM)
Korea

12th (2018.11.2.)
Prof. **Hiroyuki SATO**
(Univ. of Tokyo)
Japan

13th (2019.12.4.)
Prof. **M. SAIDIN**
(Univ. Sains Malaysia)
Malaysia

14th (2022.9.22.)
Jong-yoon WOO
(Director, IKP)
Korea

SUYANGGAE International Symposium Executive Committee (SISEC)

- **CANADA**:
  Fumiko IKAWA-SMITH (Porfessor Em., McGill Univ.)

- **CHINA**:
  Xing GAO, Chang-zhu JIN, Shejiang WANG (Professor, Institute of Vertebrate Paleontology and Paleoanthropology (IVPP), CAS),
  Fei XIE (Director, Hebei Provincial Bureau),
  Youping WANG (Professor, Peking University)

- **CZECH Republic**:
  Jiri SVOBODA (Professor, Masaryk University)

- **DENMARK**:
  Ole GRØN (Professor, University of Copenhagen)

- **JAPAN**:
  Masao AMBIRU (Professor, Meiji University),
  Hiroyuki SATO (Professor, University of Tokyo),
  Kaoru AKOSHIMA (Professor, Dohoku University)

- **KOREA**:
  Yung-jo LEE (President and Professor Em. IKP),
  Kidong BAE (Professor, Hanyang University),
  Jong-yoon WOO (Director, Institute of Korean Prehistory (IKP)),
  Heonjong LEE (Professor, Mokpo National University),
  Gi-kil LEE (Professor, Joseon University),
  Ju-yong KIM (Honorary Researcher, Korea Institute of Geoscience and Mineral Resources (KIGAM))

- **MALAYSIA**:
  Mokthar SAIDIN (Professor and Director, Universiti Sains Malaysia)

- **POLAND**:
  Lucyna DOMAŃSKA (Professor, Institute of Archeology, Łodz University)

- **RUSSIA**:
  Nikolay I. DROZDOV (Director of Siberian Institute, International Innovative University),
  Anatoly P. DEREVIANKO (Director and Academician, The Institute of Archaeology and Ethnography, RAS SB),
  Alexander VASILEVSKI (Professor, Sakhalin State University)

- **U.S.A.**:
  Michael JOCHIM (Professor, University of California, SB),
  Marcel KORNFELD (Professor, University of Wyoming),
  Ted GOEBEL (Professor, Texas A&M University)

- **Chairman**: Yung-jo LEE (Korea)

- **Prime Vice Chairman**: Nikolay I. DROZDOV (Russia)

- **Vice Chairman**: Lucyna DOMAŃSKA (Poland), Xing GAO (China), Michael JOCHIM (USA), Kidong BAE (Korea), Hiroyuki SATO (Japan), Mokthar SAIDIN (Malaysia)

- **General Secretary**: Jong-yoon WOO (Korea)

Institute of Korean Prehistory (IKP) Overview

Establishment

The Institute of Korean Prehistory (IKP) was founded on April 15, 2005, by Professor Yung-jo LEE to advance research on Korea's prehistoric cultures, with a particular emphasis on Paleolithic studies. In 2025, the institute will celebrate its 20th anniversary, having grown into a leading research center specializing in Korean Paleolithic archaeology.

Objectives

Conduct and promote archaeological research on Korea's prehistoric cultural heritage.
Establish the historical legitimacy of Korean national culture.
Enhance global recognition of Korean prehistory within the field of world archaeology.
Protect, preserve, and popularize Korea's cultural heritage.

Leadership and Roles

President & Director:
Prof. Yung-jo LEE (April 2005 – December 2010)
President:
Prof. Yung-jo LEE (December 2010 – present, until April 2025)
Leads the institute's academic research initiatives, including international symposiums and collaborations with domestic and global research institutions.

Director:
Jong-yoon WOO (December 2010 – present, until April 2025)
Oversees the institute's overall operations.

Organizational Structure and Functions

Board of Directors:
Reviews and approves projects, budgets, and financial reports.
Research Department:
Conducts academic research and archaeological investigations.
Artifact Management Department:
Handles artifact restoration, preservation, and documentation.
Administrative Office:
Manages personnel and general administration.

International Academic Symposiums

"Suyanggae and Her Neighbours" International Symposium (2007–2022, 14 sessions)
Cheongju Sorori Rice Symposium (2003, 2015)
Goyang Gawaji Rice Symposium (2013, 2016)

Suyanggae Academic Award

Established in 2008 to promote and expand the Suyanggae International Symposium, this award honors scholars who have made significant contributions to Paleolithic studies, particularly regarding Suyanggae and Korean Paleolithic research. To date, 14 scholars from 8 countries (Russia, Japan, China, Korea, Poland, USA, Israel, and Malaysia) have received the Suyanggae Academic Award.

Academic Research and Excavations

205 archaeological excavations conducted.
169 research reports published.
5 academic monographs published.
3 special exhibition.

Major Paleolithic Excavation Projects

The Institute of Korean Prehistory (IKP) has conducted extensive excavations at 31 Paleolithic sites across Korea, spanning the whole Paleolithic periods. Notable sites include:

Mansuo-ri Paleolithic site, Cheongju City, Chungbuk Province (Excavation in 2005–2007)

Dogok-ri Paleolithic site, Yangpyeong County, Gyeonggi Province (Excavation in 2005–2006)

Bokdae-dong Paleolithic site, Cheongju City, Chungbuk Province (Excavation in 2006–2007)

Nosan-ri Paleolithic site, Cheongju City, Chungbuk Province (Excavation in 2005, 2008–2009)

Gunang Cave Paleolithic site, Danyang County, Chungbuk Province (Excavation in 2007–2013)

Unjeong Paleolithic site, Paju City, Cyeonggi Pronvince (Excavation in 2007–2010)

Suyanggae Paleolithic site, Danyang County, Chungbuk Province (Excavation in 2008, 2011–2015)

Gaejeong-ri Paleolithic site, Anseong City, Chungnam Province (Excavation in 2008–2009)

Usin-ri Paleolithic site, Cheonan City, Chungnam Province (Excavation in 2009)

Oebalsan-dong Paleolithic site, Seoul Metropolis (Excavation in 2012)

Tonghyeon-ri Paleolithic site, Yeoncheon County, Gyeonggi Province (Excavation in 2012–2013)

Sangga-ri Paleolithic site, Boeun County, Chungbuk Province (Excavation in 2013)

Seochon-dong Paleolithic site, Cheungju City, Chungbuk Province (Excavation in 2014)

Woojin-ri Paleolithic site, Boeun County, Chungbuk Province (Excavation in 2014–2015)

Bongsan-ri Jeomchon Paleolithic site, Cheungju City, Chungbuk Province (Excavation in 2016–2018)

Sintanjin-dong Paleolithic site, Daejeon City (Excavation in 2018)

Sagok-ri Paleolithic site, Jeungpyeong County, Chungbuk Province (Excavation in 2019)

Songjeol-dong Paleolithic site, Cheongju City, Chungbuk Province (Excavation in 2015, 2023)

Through these various Paleolithic excavations, the IKP has established itself as Korea's leading research institute in Paleolithic studies, making significant contributions to the understanding of national heritage.

Symbol of the Institute of Korean Prehistory

The IKP's emblem (CI) symbolizes Paleolithic culture, incorporating elements of Paleolithic caves and handaxes as cultural motifs. The dark brown circle represents the earth, which preserves cultural heritage. The white crescent shape symbolizes Gunang Cave in Danyang. The center represents the handaxe excavated from Suyanggae Site I in Danyang. The design as a whole conveys an insightful vision of prehistoric culture, reflecting a profound understanding of the ancient past.

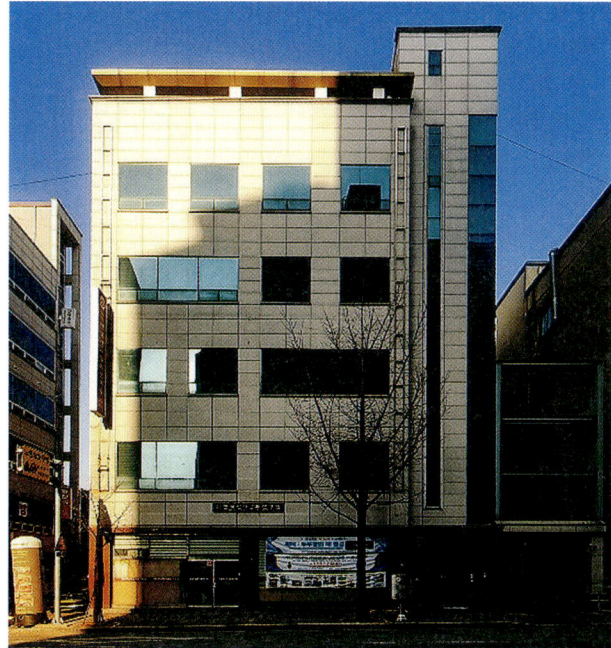

Index

I

Abakan River 161, 163, 164, 166
Acheulean 21, 22, 29, 30, 33, 34, 38, 41, 42, 44, 46, 48, 52, 59, 61, 65, 72, 88, 97, 98, 99, 100, 405, 417, 418
Acheulean handaxe 21, 29, 417, 418
Acheulean industry 33, 34, 38
Acheulean type handaxe 418
Africa 44, 46, 48, 81, 82, 84, 87, 88, 89, 92, 93, 97, 98, 99, 100, 101, 158, 257
agriculture 157, 160, 329, 330, 331, 332, 333, 335, 336, 337, 338, 339, 376, 385, 389, 398
Al / Be dating 28
Allee Effects Model 351, 353
America 88, 109, 147, 150, 293, 294, 295, 410
Amsa-dong site 364, 365, 366, 367, 369
AMS dating 252, 255, 257, 272, 298, 354
An Khe 45, 46, 47, 48
An Khe Museum 46
Archaeological Heritage 395, 396, 400, 412
Archanthropians 81, 83, 84
Assimilation Model 88
Australopithecines 81, 82

Bangudae petroglyphs 371, 372, 373, 374, 375, 376, 377
bifacial industry 41, 42, 48
blade 59, 63, 64, 65, 67, 73, 87, 88, 89, 91, 92, 93, 121, 122, 125, 126, 127, 129, 136, 144, 149, 150, 157, 158, 159, 160, 166, 170, 175, 178, 179, 180, 181, 182, 185, 186, 187, 188, 189, 190, 191, 193, 194, 196, 197, 198, 199, 200, 201, 202, 205, 206, 209, 210, 212, 213, 223, 226, 227, 230, 231, 235, 241, 242, 245, 247, 248, 268, 276, 286, 287, 288, 305, 306, 320, 343, 344, 345, 346, 348, 353, 377, 404, 405, 406
blade-microblade technology 159
blade technology 89, 91, 126, 129, 157, 158, 159, 160, 188, 190, 193, 197, 198, 199, 286
blade tool industry 121, 122, 125
blank 52, 57, 59, 63, 64, 65, 67, 68, 69, 70, 72, 73, 89, 90, 135, 157, 161, 162, 163, 164, 190, 191, 193, 204, 205, 206, 207, 208, 209, 210, 211, 213, 214, 215, 226, 227, 230, 231, 235, 271, 305
blank of standardization 204
Bolshoy Manok 161
bone tool 87, 89, 91, 92, 93, 238, 247, 248, 254, 322, 323, 325, 353, 354, 386, 388, 390
Bose industry 42, 44, 45, 46, 47

burin 122, 129, 134, 136, 188, 192, 205, 233, 241, 242, 244, 286, 288, 306, 405

camp site complex 152
cave human fossils 252
Central China 22, 33, 88, 90, 150, 157, 158, 159, 160, 325, 336, 338
Changguang site 355
Cheongju Sorori rice 311
China 22, 28, 29, 33, 34, 41, 42, 48, 52, 53, 55, 59, 65, 83, 87, 88, 89, 90, 91, 92, 93, 105, 106, 107, 109, 110, 111, 112, 150, 156, 157, 158, 159, 160, 167, 170, 257, 311, 313, 314, 315, 322, 323, 324, 325, 326, 327, 330, 331, 332, 333, 335, 336, 337, 338, 339, 351, 352, 354, 355, 359, 398, 405, 410
Chongoknian 21, 22, 30
Chongokni site 21, 23, 25, 27, 28, 29, 30
Chongok Prehistory Museum 22
chopper 27, 29, 36, 43, 44, 45, 46, 48, 59, 60, 61, 63, 64, 65, 67, 70, 72, 127, 128, 134, 241, 242, 254, 312, 353
cleaver 22, 23, 26, 28, 29, 43, 45, 46, 48, 52, 57, 99, 100, 134, 181
colonial past 408, 412, 414, 415
consciousness 76, 85, 247
contemporary history 409, 413
continuity of cultural tradition 131, 140
continuity with hybridization 87, 88, 93
core-and-flake technology 33, 38, 157, 159, 160
cortical fan 78, 82
cultivated rice 313, 314, 316, 323, 324, 325, 326, 327, 329, 331, 332, 333, 335, 336, 337, 338, 339
cultural comparison 41
cultural diversity 21, 30, 307, 408, 413, 414, 415
cultural exchange 34, 42, 89, 131, 136, 137, 141, 159, 277
cultural interaction 90, 274, 275, 277, 279
cultural traditions 160, 275
cultural variation 274
cultural variety 121
Czech 168

Denmark 276, 398
denticulate 45, 46, 61, 63, 64, 65, 69, 72, 127, 134, 135, 220, 221, 222, 223, 228, 229, 231, 233, 234, 235, 236, 241, 242
dispersals 89, 90, 91, 93, 357
dolicocephalic 385

double-platform 36

Early Holocene 42, 144, 268, 269, 270, 285, 293, 367, 388
Early Mesolithic 284, 285, 286, 289, 304, 306
Early Upper Paleolithic (EUP) 93, 121, 126, 128, 139, 149, 175, 179, 181, 185, 189, 194, 197, 199, 202, 236, 252, 256, 257, 320
Eastern Sahara 97, 98, 100, 101
ecological environment 247, 403, 404, 405, 406, 407
edge conditio 204
edge management 204
end-scraper 45, 46, 69, 89, 122, 127, 134, 135, 136, 166, 175, 178, 181, 188, 189, 198, 199, 204, 205, 206, 207, 208, 209, 210, 211, 212, 213, 214, 215, 241, 242, 343, 346, 349, 405
environmental fluctuation 144, 145, 146
ethnoarchaeology 167, 168, 279
Eurasia 48, 87, 90, 91, 93, 108, 109, 110, 137, 150, 167, 168, 170, 269

face-engrave sculpture 196, 199
F. Borde 68
feedback mechanism 76
Ferro-Chalcolithic 385, 386, 387, 389
Festival Public archaeology 417
flint knapping 276, 343
flooding 175, 176, 177, 178, 179, 180, 181, 187, 239, 241, 284, 285, 318, 365, 367, 368, 369, 397
fluvial–slope processes 175
fluvial terrace 175, 177, 178, 179, 181, 182, 187, 239, 316, 317, 319, 364
Fluvial wetland 316

Gawaji Rice 313, 395, 398
Gawaji Rice Museum 395, 396, 398, 399, 401
geosols 176, 177, 178, 179, 180, 181, 182, 316, 318, 319, 320
Germany 303, 304
Geum Cave site 243, 246
Geum River 53, 126, 127, 129
Graham Clark 29
ground water spring 152
Gunang Cave site 182, 238, 239, 243, 244, 245, 248, 256, 257

handaxes 21, 22, 23, 26, 27, 28, 29, 30, 41, 42, 43, 44, 45, 46, 47, 48, 99, 101, 126, 127, 128, 129, 134, 177, 178, 181, 247, 261, 417, 418, 419, 420
Han River 187, 338, 364, 365, 366, 367, 369, 396, 397
Hantan-Imjin River Basin (HIRB) 21, 22, 23, 26, 27, 28, 29, 30, 42
Hantan River 23
Hanzhong Basin 33, 34, 35, 37, 38, 42
hearths 89, 127, 134, 139, 274, 275, 278, 295, 353, 377
heavy-duty tool 27, 45, 46, 127, 134, 135, 136, 198, 242
Hell Gap site 292, 293, 294, 295, 297, 298, 299
Hemudu site 314, 323, 335, 336
Henry de Lumley 52, 66, 67, 68
Hoabinhian culture 261
Holocene 42, 92, 144, 146, 147, 149, 150, 245, 267, 268, 269, 270, 271, 272, 284, 285, 317, 339, 352, 355, 367, 388
hominin presence 97, 98
Homo erectus 30, 34, 55, 81, 97, 98, 99, 100, 101, 111
Homo sapiens 84, 87, 92, 93, 97, 98, 99, 100, 101, 175, 217, 252, 253, 254, 256, 270
Honam Paleolithic research 131
Human behavioral ecology 351, 352
human ecosystem 144, 145, 148
human evolution 22, 81, 88, 90, 93, 94, 420, 422
Hungsu Cave 252, 253, 254
hunter-gatherer 93, 144, 160, 272, 274, 275, 276, 278, 294, 295, 297, 303, 307, 351, 352, 353, 354, 355, 356, 357, 358, 359, 360, 398
hunting camp 132, 286, 306

ICOMOS 395, 400, 401, 403, 404, 406
Ideal Despotic Distribution 351, 353, 356, 357
Ideal Free Distribution 303, 304, 306, 353, 356
incipient Neolithic 268, 269, 272, 353, 355, 356, 357
India 68, 170, 335
indica 311, 313, 314, 323, 324, 325, 331, 334, 387
indica-japonica differentiation 322
indica rice 311, 314, 323, 325
Initial Upper Paleolithic (IUP) 89, 91

Janislawice culture 284
Japan 139, 144, 145, 146, 147, 235, 257, 314, 352, 398, 411, 414
Japanese Archipelago 53, 131, 136, 137, 141, 144, 145, 146, 147, 149, 150, 236, 268
japonica 311, 312, 313, 314, 322, 323, 324, 325, 326, 329, 331,

334
japonica rice 311, 314, 323
Jeongok Prehistory Museum 417, 419, 420, 421, 422
Jeongok-ri (Chongokni) 21, 22, 23, 25, 27, 28, 29, 30, 417, 418, 419, 420, 422
Jeongok-ri site 417, 418, 422
Jinlingsi site 34, 35
Jinshuihekou site 34, 35, 36
Jinyuan Cave 104, 105, 106, 107, 108, 110, 111, 112, 113, 114
Jinyuan Lower fauna 107, 108, 109, 110, 114
Jinyuan Upper fauna 104, 107, 110, 111
Jomon sites 141, 152, 314

Khakasko-Minusinsk basin 163
Khakassia 161, 162, 166
knapped lithics 274, 275, 276, 278, 279
Korea 21, 22, 23, 73, 113, 121, 122, 131, 134, 136, 138, 139, 141, 176, 197, 218, 235, 245, 248, 253, 254, 256, 262, 312, 313, 314, 315, 374, 375, 396, 397, 398, 399, 405, 406, 408, 409, 410, 411, 412, 413, 415, 418, 419, 420
Krasny Kamen town 161
Kuril Island 145, 268, 269, 270, 271, 272

labor-economic 28
l'Arago site 52, 56, 57
Last Glacial Maximum 146, 152, 159, 178, 316, 317, 333, 339
late *Homo sapiens* 252, 253
Late Mesolithic 284, 285, 287, 289
Late Middle Paleolithic 126, 128, 129
Late Neolithic 343, 349, 385, 388
Late Paleolithic 28, 91, 92, 129, 152, 161, 163, 164, 166, 175, 184, 200, 202, 238, 241, 242, 243, 245, 247, 248, 256, 276, 327, 333, 334, 339, 406
Late Pleistocene 34, 89, 91, 92, 93, 97, 98, 101, 105, 144, 145, 146, 147, 152, 153, 157, 159, 246, 247, 253, 255, 256, 261, 263, 268, 269, 272, 293
laterite 42, 45, 47, 385, 387
leaf-shaped point 134, 140, 199
Leroi-Gourhan 76, 81, 82, 84, 85
Levallois technique 29
line-engraved cobblestone 175, 180
lithic 21, 181, 182, 185, 187, 188, 189, 190, 193, 194, 205, 217, 218, 219, 235, 242, 245, 247, 248, 275, 276, 277, 278, 279, 305, 353, 354, 355, 389, 406

lithic analysis 190, 205, 284
lithic assemblages 23, 33, 34, 37, 89, 101, 135, 136, 139, 149, 185, 194, 205
lithic dimension 276, 277
lithic industries 21, 52, 57, 59, 60, 61, 63, 64, 65, 66, 67, 68, 69, 70, 72, 73, 87, 88, 90, 91, 93, 149
lithic reduction pattern 185
lithic technology 28, 29, 34, 37, 88, 89, 91, 92, 159, 194, 247
lithic workshops 134, 139, 241, 245
Long-range contacts 343
Lower Paleolithic 45, 48, 61, 68, 72
Luotuo Hill 104, 105, 106, 107, 111, 112, 114
Luotuoshan fauna 104, 106, 107, 108, 114
Lyudouliang site 34, 35, 36, 37

Maglemosian site 284, 285
Malaysia 42, 48, 261, 264, 313, 398
Mansuri Paleolithic site 67, 68, 70, 73
Matkechik site 161
Mesolithic 274, 275, 276, 277, 278, 284, 285, 286, 289, 303, 304, 306, 388
microblade core 158, 160, 178, 180, 181, 185, 186, 187, 193, 196, 197, 198, 199, 200, 201, 202, 241, 242, 245
microblades 127, 129, 160, 175, 178, 181, 187, 189, 193, 194, 196, 197, 199, 200, 201, 202, 241, 242, 245, 286, 320
microcosm 385, 389
Middle Paleolithic 52, 61, 65, 72, 73, 91, 98, 122, 126, 128, 129, 140, 141, 166, 241, 403, 404, 405
Middle Pleistocene 21, 22, 28, 34, 35, 37, 38, 41, 42, 45, 47, 48, 55, 63, 66, 67, 68, 72, 88, 97, 98, 99, 100, 101, 110, 112, 113, 114, 153
Middle Stone Age (MSA) 97, 98, 101, 290
Middle-Upper Paleolithic transition 121
Middle Yenisei River basin 380
mind tools 76
Mode 2A 21, 29, 30
Mode 2B 21, 29, 30
Modern Human 34, 81, 84, 87, 88, 89, 90, 91, 92, 93, 98, 139, 141, 156, 157, 158, 159, 168, 181, 185, 194, 217, 236, 257, 269
modern human migration 131
modern human origins 87, 88, 89, 93, 257
Mongolia 29, 91, 93, 111, 405
Mousterian 52, 61, 63, 65, 72, 91, 405

Movius Line 21, 30, 42
multi-platform 36
Multiregional Evolution 88, 93, 158

national identity 408, 409, 410, 411, 412, 415
National Museum 355, 365, 367, 408, 409, 411, 412, 413, 415
Neanderthal 81, 83, 84, 85, 87, 88, 91, 93, 141, 168
Neolithic 42, 126, 129, 136, 140, 150, 155, 156, 157, 159, 160, 261, 265, 267, 268, 269, 271, 272, 274, 275, 278, 313, 323, 325, 326, 327, 336, 349, 351, 352, 353, 355, 356, 357, 358, 359, 360, 365, 367, 368, 369, 371, 372, 374, 376, 377, 378, 388, 395, 398, 399, 404
Neolithic culture 150, 267, 268, 355, 365
Neolithic site 364
Nihewan Basin 53, 55, 107, 108, 110
non-blade technique 63, 64, 65, 67, 73
North America 109, 147, 275, 292, 294, 295
Northeast Asia 87, 104, 113, 114, 121, 122, 126, 129, 147, 150, 239, 245, 247, 248, 267, 268, 269, 271, 403, 404, 405, 406
Northern Circum Japan Sea Area 144, 145
Nosan-ri site 127, 128

oldest ancient rice 311, 312
Old Fluvial Deposits 316, 317, 318
organic material 265, 274, 275, 276, 277, 278, 279
Oryza rufipogon 329, 331, 332, 333, 334, 335, 336, 337, 338
O. sativa 319, 322, 323, 325, 327
OSL 28, 53, 89, 100, 101, 127, 157, 175, 179, 182, 189, 198, 242, 262, 265, 298
oval-shaped handaxe 26, 30

Palaeolithic 41, 42, 45, 47, 92, 197, 198, 201, 202, 235, 268, 277, 303, 304, 305, 306, 307
Paleanthropians 81, 83, 84, 85
Paleoindian chronology 292, 293
Paleoindian lifeways 292, 294, 295
Paleolithic archaeology 25, 28, 30, 88, 138, 156, 157, 168
Paleolithic-Neolithic transition 156, 157, 159, 160
pebble tool 55, 60, 63, 67, 69, 70, 87, 91, 93, 121, 122, 125, 126, 127, 128, 129, 150, 185, 261
persistence 93, 167, 352
petroglyphs 371, 372, 373, 374, 375, 376, 377, 380, 381, 382, 383

pick 26, 36, 37, 38, 43, 44, 45, 46, 47, 48, 70, 127, 128, 134, 135, 244, 382, 383
Pleistocene 21, 22, 28, 33, 34, 35, 37, 38, 41, 42, 45, 47, 48, 55, 63, 66, 67, 68, 72, 87, 88, 89, 90, 91, 92, 93, 97, 98, 99, 100, 101, 388, 406
Plio-Pleistocene 104, 106
pointed bifacial stone tool 261
Poland 284, 285, 289, 344, 398
polished bone tools 87, 91, 92
Post-Maglemosian 284, 285, 289
Pre-ceramic 353, 354, 358, 360
Prehistoric Culture 278, 279, 403, 404, 405, 406, 407
presentation 396, 400, 403, 406, 407, 409, 413, 415
proto-australoid 385, 388
public archaeology 395, 417

quarry site 152, 154, 155

radiocarbon age 178, 180, 181, 256, 312, 314, 316, 318
raw materials 25, 28, 38, 43, 44, 45, 46, 47, 57, 59, 60, 67, 68, 69, 70, 89, 90, 94, 101, 126, 127, 128, 129, 134, 137, 138, 157, 159, 160, 163, 185, 188, 190, 193, 194, 205, 209, 210, 213, 218, 219, 235, 241, 247, 248, 271, 275, 286, 305, 343, 344, 345, 349, 353
raw materials utilization 185
rice agriculture origin 329, 335
rice culture 311, 312, 313, 314, 315
rice origination 322
rice remain 323, 324, 326
rock art 371, 372, 373, 374, 378, 382
Russia 45, 110, 162, 168, 247, 268, 272, 381, 398, 410, 414

sand blowouts 161
Sangsi rock shelter 252, 253, 256, 257
scraper 36, 43, 45, 46, 61, 63, 64, 65, 67, 69, 72, 89, 122, 126, 127, 128, 129, 134, 135, 136, 161, 164, 165, 166, 175, 178, 179, 180, 181, 185, 187, 188, 189, 192, 193, 198, 199, 204, 205, 206, 207, 208, 209, 210, 211, 212, 213, 214, 215, 241, 242, 244, 263, 288, 312, 343, 346, 349, 405
settlement 101, 146, 150, 158, 159, 161, 162, 166, 268, 270, 271, 272, 277, 279, 285, 299, 303, 304, 305, 306, 307, 314, 315, 333, 334, 343, 355, 358, 360, 364, 365, 367, 369, 386, 388, 396
settlement patterns 158, 159, 303, 304, 307

Shalabolino rock-art 380, 381
Shiao site 326
Shuidonggou (SDG) site 89, 91, 92
single-platform 36
site formation 187, 247, 248, 292, 369
site formation process 22, 364
small blades 185, 190, 194, 201
soil wedge 127, 128, 176, 178, 241, 242, 243, 316, 318
South China 93
Southeast Asia 30, 41, 42, 47, 48, 261, 265, 352, 353
Southern China 37, 42, 47, 48, 68, 87, 89, 352
Stone Age 92, 97, 98, 101, 271, 274, 275, 276, 278, 290, 395, 397, 398, 399
stone bowl 188, 199
stone discs 167, 168, 169, 170
Sudan 97, 98, 99, 100, 101
Suyanggae and Her Neighbors 98, 403, 407
Suyanggae Family 307
Suyanggae Loc. 1 175, 177
Suyanggae Loc. 3 175, 179
Suyanggae Loc. 6 175, 180
Suyanggae Prehistory Museum 239, 241, 403, 404, 406, 407
Suyanggae site 175, 176, 177, 181, 185, 186, 187, 197, 198, 199, 200, 201, 202, 204, 205, 213, 215, 217, 218, 236, 238, 239, 240, 245, 247, 248, 256, 403, 404, 405, 406, 407
symbolism 167, 168, 419

Taiwan 145, 315, 323, 336, 351, 352, 353, 354, 355, 356, 357, 359, 360
tanged point 122, 126, 127, 129, 132, 134, 137, 139, 178, 180, 181, 182, 196, 197, 198, 199, 201, 202, 205, 217, 218, 219, 220, 221, 222, 224, 225, 226, 227, 228, 229, 231, 232, 233, 234, 235, 236, 241, 242, 256, 405
techno-typological analysis 52, 65
Terminal Paleolithic 267, 268
Tingkayu point 263, 264, 265

Tingkayu site 261, 262, 263, 264, 265
trace analyses 380
traceology 217
travelling expenses fees 161
typical Acheulean 21, 52

Ulsan 371, 372, 375, 377, 378
Upper Paleolithic(UP) 28, 61, 69, 73, 89, 91, 121, 122, 125, 126, 127, 134, 135, 136, 137, 139, 140, 141, 144, 145, 146, 147, 149, 157, 158, 160, 167, 175, 181, 185, 186, 187, 189, 190, 194, 196, 197, 199, 205, 213, 215, 253, 256, 257, 268, 269, 270, 271, 272, 317, 319, 320, 395, 396, 403, 404, 405, 406
use-wear analysis 217, 218, 236
Ust-Sos 161, 162, 163
utilization 36, 185, 188, 190, 193, 194, 200, 227, 230, 234, 248, 376, 419

Vietnam 41, 42, 45
Volhynian flint 343, 344, 348

Wanghai fauna 104, 106, 110, 112, 113, 114
Wilkostowo 343, 344, 346, 348
Wolpyeong site 132, 134, 135, 136, 140, 396

Xuchang 55, 93
Xuchang Man 55

Yatsugatake Volcanic Area 152, 154, 155
Young Fluvial Deposits 316, 317, 318
Yuchanyan ancient rice 329, 331, 332, 334
Yuchanyan site 314, 325, 329, 330, 331, 332, 333, 334, 337

Zhijidong Cave 156, 157
Zhoukoudian 57, 59, 63, 65, 90, 91, 92, 93, 105, 109, 110, 113, 114
Zhoukoudian Upper Cave 90, 93

International Members of Editorial Committee

• Chairman

Kidong BAE	Professor Emeritus, Hanyang University, Former Director General, National Museum of Korea, Korea

• Members

Ju-yong KIM	Korea Institute of Geoscience and Mineral Resources (KIGAM), Korea
Jong-yoon WOO	Director, Institute of Korean Prehistory (IKP), Korea
N. I. DROZDOV	Professor, International Innovation University, Siberian Federal University, Russia
L. DOMAŃSKA	Professor, Institute of Archaeology, University of Lodz, Poland
M. AMBIRU	Professor Emeritus, Meiji University, Japan
Xing GAO	Professor, Institute of Vertebrate Paleontology and Paleoanthropology, Chinese Academy of Sciences, China
Hanyong LEE	Director, Jeongok Prehistory Museum, Korea
Seo-weon KIM	Chairman, Suyanaggae Preservation Association, Korea
Heon-jong LEE	Professor, Mokpo National University, Korea
Gi-kil LEE	Professor Emeritus, Chosun University, Korea
Hyeong-woo LEE	Professor, Jeonbuk National University, Korea
Seung-won LEE	Assistant Director, Institute of Korean Prehistory (IKP), Korea

• Standing Advisor

Yung-jo LEE	President, Institute of Korean Prehistory (IKP), Chairman, Suyanggae Int'l Symposium Executive Committee, Korea